D0076015

JOHANNES BRAHMS

Life and Letters

For Ralph
with the very best
of wishes — one of
the few people who
knew this book when
it was still a gleam
in my eye!

Styra

april 18, 1998

& Terry

JOHANNES BRAHMS

ঌয়ৈ

Life and Letters

ঌয়ৈ

Selected and Annotated by
STYRA AVINS

Translations by
JOSEF EISINGER and STYRA AVINS

Oxford   New York
OXFORD UNIVERSITY PRESS
1997

Oxford University Press, Great Clarendon Street, Oxford OX2 6DP

Oxford New York

Athens Auckland Bangkok Bogota Bombay
Buenos Aires Calcutta Cape Town Dar es Salaam
Delhi Florence Hong Kong Istanbul Karachi
Kuala Lumpur Madras Madrid Melbourne
Mexico City Nairobi Paris Singapore
Taipei Tokyo Toronto Warsaw
and associated companies in
Berlin Ibadan

Oxford is a trade mark of Oxford University Press

Published in the United States
by Oxford University Press Inc., New York

© Styra Avins 1997
Translations © Styra Avins and Josef Eisinger 1997

All rights reserved. No part of this publication may be reproduced,
stored in a retrieval system, or transmitted, in any form or by any means,
without the prior permission in writing of Oxford University Press.
Within the UK, exceptions are allowed in respect of any fair dealing for the
purpose of research or private study, or criticism or review, as permitted
under the Copyright, Designs and Patents Act, 1988, or in the case of
reprographic reproduction in accordance with the terms of the licences
issued by the Copyright Licensing Agency. Enquiries concerning
reproduction outside these terms and in other countries should be
sent to the Rights Department, Oxford University Press,
at the address above

This book is sold subject to the condition that it shall not, by way
of trade or otherwise, be lent, re-sold, hired out or otherwise circulated
without the publisher's prior consent in any form of binding or cover
other than that in which it is published and without a similar condition
including this condition being imposed on the subsequent purchaser

British Library Cataloguing in Publication Data
Data available

Library of Congress Cataloging in Publication Data
Brahms, Johannes, 1833–1897.
[Correspondence. English. Selections]
Johannes Brahms: his life and letters / selected and annotated by
Styra Avins; translations by Josef Eisinger and Styra Avins.
p. cm.
Includes bibliographical references and index.
1. Brahms, Johannes, 1833–1897—Correspondence. 2. Composers—
Germany—Correspondence. I. Avins, Styra. II. Title.
ML410.B8A4 1997 780'.92—dc21 [B] 92–5417
ISBN 0-19-816234-0

1 3 5 7 9 10 8 6 4 2

Typeset by Hope Services (Abingdon) Ltd.
Printed in Great Britain
on acid-free paper by
Biddles Ltd
Guildford & King's Lynn

To pianist, conductor, and teacher Fritz Jahoda,
especially, and to the thousands of musicians like him who
were driven from career and country in a dark moment of history.
In their unwilling flight they brought their treasure of music
to an entire generation of young musicians on the
other side of the Atlantic.

Preface and Acknowledgements

❧

TEN years ago I discovered, to my amazement, that there was no general collection of the letters of Johannes Brahms in English. I was then the cellist of a piano trio specializing in nineteenth-century music, and we had hit on what we thought was the fine idea of reading the letters of the composers to the audience as a way of casting a fresh perspective on the music. All went well until we came to Brahms, and found that even those collections of letters which had once been translated—to Billroth, the Schumanns, the von Herzogenbergs—were no longer in print, and that a general collection had never been attempted. This book is a result of that finding.

It is probably a good thing that, much like a prospective new mother, I had very little idea of what I was letting myself in for. The decision to create the very book I was seeking changed my life, leading me on a long search for Brahms's letters in their original German in books and journals, libraries and private collections, and to the formidable body of literature which had to be read in order to annotate the letters. On the other hand, like a *fortunate* new mother, I had a lot of help. Two essential works had recently been completed: Margit McCorkle's *Brahms Verzeichnis*, and Thomas Quigley's annotated bibliography of the Brahms literature up to 1982. My work would have been impossibly difficult without theirs, and my list of acknowledgements has to begin with them.

In addition, Lesley Wyle gave me crucial aid in getting this project under way. Fritz Jahoda put his great store of musical knowledge and good will at my disposal. Nancy Reich extended encouragement and good advice along the way. By chance a number of friends were strategically placed, and they, as well as colleagues, went to the trouble of obtaining material which was hard for me to find, or of pointing me in the right direction: in Austria, Ilana Eisinger; in Canada, Eric Koch; in the Czech Rebublic, Otokar Jelenić; in England, Penelope Paul, Professor Cyril Erlich, Jennifer Glynn, and Jerrold Northrup Moore; in Poland, Professor Jan Cygan; in Germany, Professor Peter Brix, and George Striker; in Switzerland, Ulrich and Annelies Wehrli; in the United States, Professor Carol Avins, William Mims, Dorothy Reichenberger, Charles Shook, and Eva Vogel. Dr Richard Müller-Dombois, of Detmold, was exceptionally generous at short notice. When I appeared on his doorstep he invited me in and simply gave me the material I had come to see.

A number of private individuals made unpublished material available to me: Mr and Mrs Patrick Hedley-Dent, Marie Kuhn-Oser, Dorothy Reichenberger, Albi Rosenthal, Jocelyne Tait, and several who prefer to remain anonymous. Mrs Kuhn-Oser also made her long memory, family archive, and substantial photograph collection available to me, for which I am deeply grateful.

I was particularly fortunate in finding a group of people who were able and willing to transcribe innumerable unpublished letters of Brahms into the Roman alphabet: Lore and Martin Ostwald, Gabriele and Henry M. Hoenigswald, and Hilde Cohn. I shall never forget my occasional participation in their jolly round-table transcription-fests. Additional thanks go to Professor Ostwald for clearing up the mysteries of Greek.

My thanks to Heikki Väänänen for preparing a number of the photographs for publication. For reading parts of the manuscript, and for helpful suggestions, thanks to Jayn Rosenfeld, Jerrold Seigel, and Walter and Harriet Michel.

The directors and librarians of many institutions were kind and helpful to me. In particular, Melva Peterson of the City College Music Library, who had faith in this project before she had any reason to; the Austrian Cultural Institute in New York, its director, Dr Wolfgang Waldner and his staff, who opened many doors for me in Vienna; the Brahms-Institut Lübeck and the founder directors, Kurt and Renate Hofmann, who have been helpful to me throughout and who allowed me free run of their unique collection for several days; the Loeb Library at Harvard and its then chief librarian, Michael Ochs; and Elizabeth Auman and others at the Music Division of the Library of Congress, who treated me to treasures with infallible courtesy and a minimum of red tape. To the librarians in Dresden, Leipzig, and Zwickau, Germany, who received us before the Wall had come down, I am especially grateful. I am also very grateful to Dorothée Melchert and the Lippische Landesbibliothek, Detmold; Gustav Abel, Director of the Brahms-Haus Museum in Baden-Baden; Bruce Livingston and the inter-library loan staff at Drew University; Dr Stephen Lehman, at the University of Pennsylvania Library; Dr Hans Rudolf Schneider, Dichtermuseum Liestal, Switzerland; Dr Bernhard Stockmann of the Staats- und Universitätsbibliothek Hamburg, and his successor, Dr Jürgen Neubacher; Frau Christine Griem of the Museum für Hamburgische Geschichte; and Mag. Herwig Würtz and Dr Walter Obermaier of the Wiener Stadt- und Landesbibliothek. I had not suspected, beforehand, that so many people could be so ready to go out of their way for someone they hardly knew.

A number of Brahms scholars have been most kind, offering assistance and advice: George Bozarth, Alfred Clayton, Walter Frisch, Michael Struck, and above all, David Brodbeck, who read the entire manuscript with care and kept me on my toes. I should also like to thank my copy-editor, Mary Worthington, for her expertise, co-operation, and patience.

My husband, Josef Eisinger, did a very large share of translating, and assisted in more ways than I could possibly enumerate, leaving me with a debt of gratitude which I probably cannot repay.

It is a pleasure to thank Bruce and Carol Phillips for extending their friendly hospitality to me in Oxford on more than one occasion.

I cannot fail to salute my children, Alison and Simon, for accepting their mother's sudden obsession gracefully, and for flourishing better than ever without her close attention.

Last, but not at all least, I must thank my friends and Brahms enthusiasts, Bob and Roann Green, for keeping my household intact on my many trips away.

S.A.

'Cleehill', New Jersey
March 1997

Contents

List of Illustrations

(between pp. 420 and 421)

❦

List of Music Examples

✻

Additional Notes

✻

Additional notes, longer and more discursive than the footnotes, are found starting on p. 746. They are indicated by an asterisk and a note in the margin.

Abbreviations

❧

BB	Hans von Bülow, *Briefe und Schriften*, ed. Marie von Bülow, 8 vols. (Leipzig, 1895–1908)
Bil–B	Otto Gottlieb-Billroth (ed.), *Billroth und Brahms in Briefwechsel* (Berlin, 1935)
BW	*Johannes Brahms Briefwechsel*, 16 vols., published by the Deutsche Brahms Gesellschaft (Berlin, 1912–22); vols. xvii and xviii by Schneider Verlag (Tutzing, 1991, 1993)
Familie	Kurt Stephenson, *Johannes Brahms in seiner Familie* (Hamburg, 1973)
GdMf	Gesellschaft der Musikfreunde, Vienna
Hb BA	Staats- und Universitätsbibliothek Hamburg Carl von Ossietzky (Brahms-Archiv)
Hil	*Aus Ferdinand Hillers Briefwechsel*, ed. Reinhold Sietz, 7 vols. (Cologne, 1958–70)
JJ	*Briefe von und an Joseph Joachim*, ed. Johannes Joachim and Andreas Moser, 3 vols. (Berlin, 1911–13)
Kal	Max Kalbeck, *Johannes Brahms*, 4 vols. (Berlin, 1908–21)
Litz	Berthold Litzmann, *Clara Schumann, ein Künstlerleben*, 3 vols. (Leipzig, 1920)
May	Florence May, *The Life of Johannes Brahms*, 2 vols., 2nd rev. edn. (London [1984])
McC	Margit L. McCorkle, *Johannes Brahms: Thematisch-Bibliographisches Werkverzeichnis* (Munich, 1984)
Reich	Nancy B. Reich, *Clara Schumann: The Artist and the Woman* (London, 1985)
SBB	*Clara Schumann–Johannes Brahms: Briefe aus den Jahren 1853–1896*, ed. Berthold Litzmann, 2 vols. (Leipzig, 1927)
WSb	Wiener Stadt- und Landesbibliothek
ZfM	*Zeitschrift für Musikwissenschaft*

Note on the Translation

OF the many criteria which a valid translation must satisfy, accuracy is surely the most important. But in the case of letters, the translation should go well beyond: it should also capture the personality, sentiment, mood, and linguistic style of the writer and should do so—without wearying the reader.

With this in mind, we approached the challenge of translating Brahms's letters into English with justifiable trepidation, for compared to letters *from* his correspondents, most of Brahms's are terse and usually written in haste, in the language and cadence of everyday speech, with a modest vocabulary and virtually devoid of literary aspiration.

His language, nevertheless, has its own rewards. Like his music, there is no padding. The letters are generally clear and articulate, except when the writer intended to obfuscate. Elegance is a distant second to content and to economy of expression. Occasionally this results in an almost telegraphic style, a reflection of his avowed and oft-stated aversion to letter-writing. To save time, he structures his sentences in ways that let one verb serve two separate clauses, and he employs punctuation sparingly, contrary to German usage but very akin to contemporary English custom.

We have tried to retain these linguistic quirks in our translations. When faced with a choice of ways to represent a word or phrase in German, we have usually chosen the simpler, everyday expression. We have used slang only in the very rare instances where Brahms himself used it. To preserve the flow of Brahms's thoughts, we have largely kept the German style of run-on sentences replete with their clauses, although occasionally we have inserted commas or semicolons with a view to clarifying the meaning. Translating his puns, spoonerisms, and nonsense rhymes into English presented a more serious challenge, which we accepted as best we could. Slips of the pen have been corrected and words left out due to haste have been supplied by the editor, and appear in square brackets. The occasionally unfathomable sentence can usually be deciphered with reference to a letter by his correspondent, or by understanding the circumstances surrounding the letter. These passages have been identified in footnotes.

Where they occur in the letters (but not in commentary or notes), Brahms's nineteenth-century spellings of place-names have been retained, apart from cities which have English names. We have retained the German 'sharp s' (ß) under the same circumstances.

Finally, a comment about the unadorned style of so many of these letters, and our attempt to retain their flavour. We felt it was imperative that Brahms's letters reach the English-speaking reader in his own words, to the greatest extent possible;

it did not seem fitting that we should try to guess, except when absolutely necessary, what he would have written had English been his native tongue. No doubt some will feel our translations betray too much of their German heritage, but we share the sentiments of Johan Huizinga, who recognized the problem in his introduction to the German translation of his landmark history of the Middle Ages. Reminding his readers that a translation in the strict sense of the word was an impossibility, he asked, 'Why should we be so eager to obliterate fearfully the traces of what is foreign in that which is of foreign origin?' Spitta once remarked, of Brahms's use of folk material, 'It never occurred to him to alter the verse, to substitute elegant phraseology for rough, strange, or even tasteless expressions.' It occurred to us often, but we resisted, ultimately for the same reason: to preserve the voice of the man who penned these letters.

JOSEF EISINGER
STYRA AVINS

Chronology

1830	Marriage of Johann Jakob Brahms to Christiane Nissen, 9 June in Hamburg.
1831	Sister Elise born 11 February in Hamburg.
1833	Johannes Brahms born 7 May in Hamburg.
1835	Brother Fritz born 26 March in Hamburg.
1839	Elementary school education begins.
1840	Begins piano studies with O. F. W. Cossel.
1841	Moves to Dammtorwall (until 1851).
1843	First public performance as pianist. Begins studies with Marxsen.
1844	Begins middle school education (graduates in 1847).
1847	Starts to earn money giving piano lessons, playing at private soirées, *Schänken*, theatres.
1848	First solo piano concert, in Hamburg.
1849	Second solo piano concert, in Hamburg, with stellar review. Works as arranger for August Cranz Verlag under pseudonym.
1853	Concert tour with Eduard Reményi to Celle, Lüneburg, leads to meeting with Joachim, Liszt, and the Schumanns. Seven works are accepted for publication by Leipzig publishers.
1854	R. Schumann attempts suicide (February), Brahms rushes to Düsseldorf from Hanover, remains on and off until October 1856.
1855	Resumes performing career, playing with orchestra for the first time.
1856	Death of Schumann (July). Brahms returns to Hamburg (October).
1857–9	Spends three months each year as piano teacher and choral conductor at the Court of Lippe-Detmold. First and Second Serenades.
1858	Spends summer in Göttingen, meets and falls in love with Agathe von Siebold.
1859	Performance and failure of First Piano Concerto in Leipzig; break with Agathe (both in January). Founds Frauenchor in spring, his inspiration for many choral compositions.
1860–2	Attempts to make career in Hamburg. Teaches piano, continues Frauenchor. Composes the Handel Variations, First and Second Piano Quartets, First String Sextet.
1862	(September–December) First trip to Vienna, gives successful concerts. Shock at being turned down for conducting post in Hamburg. Piano Quintet.

1863	Appointed director of the Vienna Singakademie, a post he keeps for one year.

1864 Plays for Wagner in a villa outside Vienna. Meets Hermann Levi.

1865 Death of mother after severe domestic difficulties and breakup of family. Finances at low point. Work on *German Requiem*. Successful Swiss tour establishes reputation there. Brahms moves between Karlsruhe, Baden-Baden, Winterthur, and Vienna. Undertakes first tour as piano virtuoso.

1866 Remarriage of father.

1867 Second rejection by Hamburg Philharmonic. Summer walking tour with father in Austrian Alps.

1868 First major performance of *German Requiem* (April, in Bremen). Composes fifth movement of Requiem (June, in Hamburg). Prepares Hungarian Dances, Lullaby for publication. Financial difficulties end. Summer walking tour with father in Switzerland.

1869 *Liebeslieder Waltzes*, Alto Rhapsody.

1870 Attends First production of *Das Rheingold, Walküre*, in Munich. Outbreak of Franco-Prussian War.

1871 First performances of *Triumphlied, Schicksalslied*. In December, moves to permanent home in the Karlsgasse.

1872 Assumes directorship of choral association and orchestra of the Gesellschaft der Musikfreunde. Death of father, 11 February.

1873 Summer in Tutzing. Completes String Quartets Nos. 1 and 2, Haydn Variations. Benefit concert for Schumann memorial in Bonn leads to difficulties with Joachim. Awarded Bavarian Order of Maximilian for Science and Art.

1874 First concert in Leipzig since failure of First Piano Concerto. Reestablishes friendship with Elizabet and Heinrich von Herzogenberg. Summers in Rüshlikon, Switzerland. Meets Widmann, Hegar, Gottfried Keller. *New Liebeslieder Waltzes*.

1875 Resigns from Gesellschaft post in April. Summers near Heidelberg, finishes Third Piano Quartet, Op. 60. Serious rift and last visit with Levi.

1876 Tempted by, then turns down offer of Schumann's old post in Düsseldorf. Turns down honorary doctorate from Cambridge University. Holiday on the island of Rügen with George Henschel. Completes First Symphony, Third String Quartet.

1877 Large output of songs, Opp. 69–72. First summer at Pörtschach. Second Symphony, Motets.

1878 First visit to Italy, with Billroth. Second summer at Pörtschach. Violin Concerto.

1879   Third summer at Pörtschach. First Violin Sonata, two Rhapsodies for Piano. Tours Romania with Joachim. Awarded Honorary Doctorate by University of Breslau.

1880   Attends unveiling of Schumann memorial in Bonn. First summer in Ischl. Composes Academic Festival and Tragic Overtures. Concerned over the Joachims' marital problems.

1881   Second Italian voyage. Complete break with Joachim over divorce suit against Amalia. Summer in Pressbaum near Vienna. *Nänie*, Second Piano Concerto. Friendship with von Bülow. First visit to Meiningen to test piano concerto with orchestra leads to friendship with Georg II and Freifrau Helene.

1882   Summer in Ischl. Piano Trio in C major, String Quintet in F major, *Gesang der Parzen*. Third Italian voyage.

1883   Summers in Wiesbaden, socializing daily with von Beckeraths. Meets Hermine Spies. Third Symphony. Begins reconciliation process with Joachim.

1884   Turns down offer to direct Gürzenich concerts and Cologne Conservatory. Fourth Italian voyage. Summer in Mürzzuschlag (Carinthia). Begins Fourth Symphony.

1885   Joins in founding Vienna's Tonkünstlerverein. Completes Fourth Symphony in Mürzzuschlag. Joins von Bülow and Meiningen Orchestra on tour with symphony. Rift with Bülow.

1886   Death of brother Fritz. Named Honorary President of Tonkünstlerverein. First of three summers near Thun, on the lake. Second Cello Sonata, Second Violin Sonata (and third sonata, published later). Third Piano Trio. Establishes warm friendship with Widmann and his family.

1887   Fifth Italian voyage, second summer at Thun. Double Concerto, full reconciliation with Joachim. *Zigeunerlieder*.

1888   Sixth Italian voyage, with Widmann. Third summer at Thun. Completes Third Violin Sonata. Bitter political disagreement with Widmann.

1889   Awarded honorary citizenship of Hamburg. *Fest- und Gedenksprüche* and Motets. Awarded Order of Leopold by Emperor Franz Josef. Revises Piano Trio, Op. 8.

1890   Seventh Italian voyage, with Widmann. Summers in Ischl from now until death. Second String Quintet.

1891   'Retires' from composing, writes will. Inspired by Mühlfeld in Meiningen, composes Clarinet Trio and Quintet. Friendship with Adolf Menzel.

1892   Death of Elizabet von Herzogenberg and his sister Elise. Starts work on last piano works, Opp. 116–19.

1893   Death of Hermine Spies at age of 36. Eighth Italian voyage, with Widmann, F. Hegar, Robert Freund, in avoidance of sixtieth birthday festivities in Vienna.

1894   Publication of last collection of folk-songs, *49 Deutsche Volkslieder.* Deaths of Billroth, Spitta, and von Bülow in quick succession. Max Klinger's *Brahms-Fantasy.* Ischl summer produces both clarinet sonatas.

1895   Awarded Austrian Order for Art and Science. Meiningen Music Festival celebrates his music.

1896   *Four Serious Songs.* Death of Clara, 20 May. His own terminal illness apparent by summer.

1897   Last public appearance on 7 March. Death on 3 April, state funeral on 6 April.

Introduction

✤

'No one will learn anything about me from *my* letters', Brahms once told friends.[1] I hope the readers of this volume will disagree.

Brahms wrote letters not because he enjoyed the opportunity to distil his inner thought on paper, but because there were no telephones, and he had a wide-flung circle of friends and colleagues. Nevertheless and in spite of himself, almost everything of a personal nature known about him with any authenticity comes directly from those letters.

One does not reap information from his letters, however; one merely gleans it. Except in youthful letters, he was sparing with words, especially about himself. Nor did he ever grant interviews or answer questionnaires; when his first biographer, working during his lifetime and with his knowledge, asked for personal information, Brahms replied he had no records with him, and could not help—and when the book appeared, virtually all the information about Brahms the man was incorrect. There is no reason to think he was any more forthcoming to the friend who eventually wrote his biography in eight volumes, Max Kalbeck, even though there are hints that Brahms knew Kalbeck intended to be his Boswell. All the more reason, then, to look to his letters for authentic information, free from the overlay of interpretation by others.

That point of view has guided me in selecting the letters included here. My first priority was for those letters which have something specific to say about his music, or about music in general, but such letters are relatively rare. Next, I sought above all those which illuminate Brahms the person, both inward and outward. I chose letters which allow the reader to follow the outward path of Brahms's life and career, and which shed light, using Brahms's own words, on the many aspects of his life which have seemed enigmatic to his biographers—his relationship to his work, to friends, to women, to his colleagues, to his rivals, to his family, to Clara Schumann, to life at large. With few exceptions the full letters are given on the assumption that small talk is also instructive.

But be forewarned that Brahms's letters will not provide a straightforward answer to those who want to know who he was. Montaigne said it exactly: 'Nothing is harder for me than to believe in men's consistency, nothing easier than to believe in their inconsistency. He who would judge them in detail and distinctly, bit by bit, would more often hit upon the truth.'[2] It is my hope that these letters will make it

---

[1] R. Heuberger, *Erinnerungen an Johannes Brahms: Tagebuchnotizen aus den Jahren 1875 bis 1897*, 2nd edn. (Tutzing, 1976), 23.

[2] 'Of the Inconsistency of Our Actions', *The Complete Essays of Montaigne*, trans. Donald M. Frame (Stanford, Calif., 1965), 239–40.

possible to do just that, by letting us know Brahms in ungeneralized detail, as the tender, rough, erudite, intelligent, irascible, sarcastic, kind, clear-headed, tactful, tactless, funny, generous, idealistic, shrewd, romantic, cynical, enthusiastic, pessimistic, ruthless, sentimental, expressive, uncommunicative, conventional, spiritual, and free-thinking man that he was; and that we will learn to take him that way, 'intact and unsolved' (ibid.). But however inconsistent, Brahms was not one of the wind-blown mortals described by Montaigne. Characteristic threads run straight as an arrow through his life: his will to shape his life at every step towards the single goal of composing music; and his utter integrity and inability to be false. It is on these accounts that his friends not only forgave his faults, but cherished the man. And as I think these letters will show, far from being the isolated, lonely man he sometimes said he was, Brahms was in constant touch with a host of devoted friends.

Not all of them are well represented here. Inevitably, many of those nearest to him during the last third of his life were close at hand in Vienna: Theodor Billroth, Ignaz Brüll and his brother Edward, Anton Door, Julius Epstein, Bertha and Arthur Faber, Maria and Robert Fellinger, Eduard Hanslick, Max Kalbeck, Victor von Miller zu Aichholtz, and the various members of the Wittgenstein family. Indeed, they took the place of family, fed him on Sundays, celebrated with him at Christmas, arranged his household, tended him in his last illness, and, at the end, buried him. By virtue of their very proximity, Brahms's correspondence with them consists in little more than what would today be the subject-matter for a brief telephone call. The exception is Theodor Billroth, the brilliant surgeon and highly gifted musician whose need to assimilate each of Brahms's new compositions fitted in with Brahms's own need to hear intelligent and sympathetic remarks about his music, and with whom, therefore, a long and instructive correspondence was carried on.

Apart from letters to his many friends, casual or close, which make up the bulk of the correspondence, we have a large body of the letters he wrote to his publishers, his family, and his professional colleagues.

Brahms wrote more than 800 letters to his publisher Fritz Simrock alone; only a small fraction could be included in this volume. The reader will also find letters to other publishers when they throw light on his career or frame of mind. The letters to the Swiss publisher Rieter-Biedermann have a particularly friendly flavour, as Rieter had the acumen and generosity to support Brahms when he was abandoned by Breitkopf & Härtel, his first publisher, and while he was financially most pressed.

Letters to his family comprise another important body of information about the composer and his life, and yield some of the most unexpected pictures of the composer, as well as a wealth of detail regarding everyday life.

Another substantial collection of letters includes those written to colleagues, conductors, concert agents, and piano manufacturers, some of whom were also friends.

Not surprisingly, the most gripping of Brahms's letters are those he wrote to Clara Schumann and Joseph Joachim during the first decade of his public career. In them he was in turmoil and most vulnerable, and in them his writing was still quite uninhibited; and since he stands there revealed more than in any other letters or at any other period of his life, those letters are included in some disproportion. From that point of view, it is a great pity that Brahms destroyed the letters he had written to his parents during this same period, after they came back into his hands in the 1880s.

For those of us who find his music touches us long after the man himself is gone, it is of no small interest to enter into the world and the developing mind of the person who wrote that music, and in his letters the facts of his life, as well as his unusual character, come to life more directly than in a biography.

But while it is an act of homage to present these letters of Johannes Brahms to the English-speaking public, it is also an act of disobedience. Without question, this most reticent of men would have been incensed. In defending myself, I take comfort in the fact that Brahms himself read and possessed the letters of many great musical and literary figures—Schumann, Mendelssohn, Goethe, and Schiller, among them—and went so far as to own a number of them in autograph. And he was quick to agree that the facts of the lives of great men were of utility and interest to later generations, and should be written down.

'That was them, this is me,' one can hear him growl. Given his fundamental modesty, and his ever-present awareness of his own musical shortcomings, he could not have acknowledged that he himself would join such exalted company.

In some regard, too, a book of letters is bound to give the wrong impression of this complex man, since many first-hand reports describe Brahms's capacity for lengthy silence or monosyllabic conversation. The trait accompanied him all his life. That particular image of Brahms will be obliterated by this collection of fluent outpourings from his pen. But the fact is, he could be talkative, high-spirited, and witty in company, and often was; and he loved to engage in serious conversation with those whose intellect he respected. At least three friends wrote down the contents of their conversations with him each day, proof enough that his spoken word could be every bit as engaging as the written, when he was so inclined.[3]

With rare exceptions, Brahms's letters are not pieces of polished writing. 'I don't write letters, I answer them,' he told Ottilie Ebner. He meant he was not a stylist, or a producer of literature; one cannot revel in his letters as one does in some of his correspondents—notably Elizabet von Herzogenberg, Hermann Levi, Theodor

---

[3] Those who recorded their conversations with him are Richard Heuberger, George Henschel, and, although he does not admit to it, Max Kalbeck, who noted incidents and conversations with Brahms over the course of many years. To this can be added the diary of Laura Beckerath, and occasional letters home written by her husband, Rudolf von Beckerath, as he accompanied Brahms on holiday; or Julius Otto Grimm to his wife Pine Gur, under similar circumstances.

Billroth, Theodor Engelmann, and Julius Allgeyer—yet every sentence he wrote rings true and straight from the heart, unencrusted with custom or art.

For the editor and translator, who necessarily must spend years with Brahms the person, his letters provide unending pleasure bordering on inspiration; that the man who wrote such music was also a human being of such quality is a stroke of the greatest good fortune for the likes of us, and a source of deep satisfaction to all who have experienced this close contact.

PART I

※5%※

Prelude

1833–1852

※ Introduction ※

When Johannes Brahms was born, on the seventh of May 1833, in Hamburg, there was never a doubt in the minds of his parents but that he would become a musician. He was named after his father, Johann Jakob (and mother Johanna and grandfather Johann!), and it was expected that, like him, he would learn to play as many instruments as necessary to earn a living performing in dance bands, theatre orchestras, military bands, and symphony orchestras.

Johann Jakob Brahms, in fact, had a passion for music, played the flute, horn, violin, viola, cello, and double bass, and as a youth ran away from his home in Heide, Holstein, three times before convincing his parents to let him study music. When his five-year apprenticeship to Heide's town musician was completed he left Holstein, at that time under Danish control, and moved to the Free Hanseatic City of Hamburg. He was 19. Four years later he received the right of citizenship of the city of Hamburg, and played the horn in one of the city's Citizens' Militia bands (a position he held until he was in his sixties). To find other work was not easy, so he taught himself to play the double bass when he saw that good players were in demand. For decades he was on call as substitute player and then as a regular in the six-man band that performed daily at the Alster Pavilion, Hamburg's fashionable meeting-place. He could play the violin, viola, bass, flute, or horn, as needed. In the Hamburg Philharmonic he was an extra, primarily playing the double bass but occasionally called upon to play the flute; in 1864, thanks to his son's connections, he was hired as a permanent member of the orchestra.[1]

Johann Jakob proudly proclaimed the birth of this first son in the local newspaper, an unusual step at the time and something he had not done when a daughter was born, two years earlier;[2] and as soon as it was feasible, he set about the child's musical education himself. Johannes showed exceptional talent, but by the time he

---

[1] For the best sketch of the parents and siblings of Brahms, see Kurt Stephenson, *Johannes Brahms in seiner Familie*, henceforth *Familie* (Hamburg 1973), 10–25.

[2] Max Kalbeck, *Johannes Brahms*, 4th edn. (Berlin, 1921), i. 13. Henceforth Kal.

was 7 he was asking to learn to play the piano—an instrument the father neither played nor saw as profiting his son's future. Nevertheless, Johann Jakob was persuaded to find a piano teacher. The choice was fortunate; Otto Friedrich Willibald Cossel was a local teacher of high reputation, whose kindness, dedication, and excellent pedagogy gave Johannes tools that would serve him well for the rest of his life. Cossel taught him to the end of his eleventh year, giving him a foundation in touch, technique, and musicianship which he never forgot, nurturing his talent with Bach and the best classical composers, allowing him to practise in his own home, and rescuing him from the importunings of a would-be impresario who hoped to send the little virtuoso on tour in America; then he arranged to have him taught by Eduard Marxsen, Hamburg's leading pedagogue, and the man who had been his own teacher.

In the mean time, Johannes was attending school. The notion that Brahms came from a poverty-stricken home and had no formal education is widespread but entirely unfounded. The parents themselves were descended from modest, simply educated, self-respecting families. Poverty was no more part of their heritage than of Johannes's. Although money was always a nagging issue in the Brahms household, the record unearthed by recent scholarship shows mother and father regularly scraping together the rent, moving house frequently in an effort to find more suitable living quarters, and educating both Johannes and his younger brother Fritz Brahms (born in 1835) in the best schools and by the best music teachers they could afford. There was food on the table—even special foods for birthday celebrations and holidays. The family lived among the respectable working poor, a category which included people who are today classed as professionals: among his neighbours were a number of musicians, including his piano teacher. The Cossels, in fact, moved into a flat vacated by the Brahms family, an unlikely event if the dwelling had been the dismal slum biographers have presumed.

It is important to make this point, for many authors, borrowing from each other, have told the same unsubstantiated stories of the poverty of the young Brahms, and how, as a child, he was sometimes pulled out of bed at night to play the piano in disreputable bars, or sailors' dives or brothels. There is no evidence whatsoever to back up these stories, much as they appeal to the romantic imagination.

Brahms's mother was a religious and intelligent woman, devoted to her three children. She loved Johannes with a warmth and understanding reflected in many of her letters to him, and in his own later letters to family and friends. If the father was less sophisticated, and more modest in his ambition for his sons, he nevertheless devoted much hard-earned money to their upbringing. It defies plausibility that, having expended so much effort and money on educating their children, these parents would then require them to work in sailors' saloons and brothels that were dangerous and unsavoury. Recent scholarship supports this view. Modern researchers have sifted through much primary documentary evidence on the subject and paint a substantially different picture from that of the most widely quoted biography of Brahms, by a contemporary of Brahms's named Max Kalbeck. One distinguished historian writes: 'Even if Brahms himself speaks of having "played the piano at night in bars", it is out of the question that these were disreputable saloons. Kalbeck's remark [. . . the biographer expresses deep emotion at the picture of the innocent, blond-haired, blue-eyed youth playing in the worst possible company] is nowhere verified by him [Kalbeck], and is simply false.'[3]

Not only is there no evidence that Brahms played in low-class dives of the sailors' quarter (which was in the outlying area of St Pauli, while Brahms lived in the city near the Alster Pavilion), there is also no evidence, only perpetuated rumour, that Brahms played anywhere at all before he was 14 years old. In preparing her Brahms biography, the first to appear in England and, like Kalbeck's, written soon after his death, Florence May had the sensible idea of interviewing people who had known him. Christian Otterer was a violist who lived a few doors away from the Brahms family on the Dammtorwall and worked for years with Johann Jakob both at the Alster Pavilion and in the Hamburg Philharmonic. He had even participated in Johannes's first concert, a private subscription concert held when the composer was a 10-year-old, given in order to raise money for furthering the education of the exceptional little boy. Otterer told her: 'With the best will I cannot recollect that Johannes played, as a young child, in *Lokals* [drinking establishments]. I was daily with his father at the time, and must have known if it had been the case. Jakob was a quiet and respectable man, and kept Hannes closely to his studies, and as much as possible withdrawn from notice.'[4]

---

[3] Kurt Hofmann, *Johannes Brahms und Hamburg*, 2nd rev. edn. (Reinbek, 1986), 12. Among many recent scholars, the names of two Hamburgers stand out in particular: Kurt Hofmann and Kurt Stephenson. Their research makes use of Hamburg City documents and hitherto inaccessible family letters. These men's indefatigable researches into primary sources has put the record of Brahms's early life on a sound footing for the first time. Especially informative is the work cited here, and Kurt Stephenson's *Johannes Brahms in seiner Familie*.

Max Kalbeck's 2,000-page biography (the eight sizeable 'half-volumes' are nevertheless listed as a four-volume work) appeared within a decade of Brahms's death. Kalbeck was active as an essayist and music critic in Vienna, and knew Brahms personally during the last twenty years of the composer's life. That fact, along with the length, scope, and detail of the biography, has lent the work an air of authority which it does not in every instance deserve. The men were not intimate friends, and nothing suggests that Brahms confided in him. On the contrary, there is not a single piece of interesting correspondence between them, and they never addressed each other in the familiar 'Du' form. Kalbeck's research for the early part of Brahms's life was superficial at best; much of his information about Brahms's family is dismissive and incorrect. Nevertheless, Kalbeck's biography has served as the source of the 'facts' of Brahms's early life for almost every subsequent biographer, the answer to why the same mistakes appear in volume after volume. The present author is not the only one to express caution about Kalbeck: see Michael Musgrave, 'Brahms and Kalbeck: A Misunderstood Relationship?', in Susan Antonicek and Otto Biba (eds.), *Brahms-Kongress Wien 1983* (Tutzing, 1988), 397–404. But no disrespect is meant. Whatever its flaws, Kalbeck's eight volumes are still essential reading for every Brahms student.

[4] Florence May, *The Life of Johannes Brahms*, 2 vols., 2nd edn. (London [1948]), 71, henceforth May. Brahms's *father*, on the other hand, did play in low-class sailors' dives when he was first struggling to make a living. It was in moving out of the dockside area of St Pauli that he rented a room with the sisters Nissen, and so found himself a wife.

It is a curious set of circumstances that has allowed so much misinformation about Brahms to develop and stay in circulation for so long, resulting in part from the fact that the early German biographies of Brahms were all written by thoroughly middle-class men who had no realistic notion of working-class life, nor the setting in which it was lived. They confused lack of money with lack of morals, and would have entered Brahms's old neighbourhood, the *Gängeviertel*, with serious misgivings. Having arrived there at the turn of the twentieth century, they would have got the wrong impression, in any case. A fascinating and illuminating picture of that working-class quarter can be found in *Rund um die Gängeviertel Hamburg 1889–1930*;[5] but a word of caution is in order because the Brahms family left the *Gängeviertel* in 1841, just as it was in the process of becoming the intensely crowded slum it had become by the time *all* the early Brahms biographies were written. His biographers received no help from Brahms himself, who rarely spoke and never wrote about his early life. That Florence May obtained the most accurate picture was to little avail; as a woman and a foreigner, scant attention was paid to her work—Kalbeck himself refers to her book with condescension. And many important facts of Brahms's early family life were only revealed when the burst of new scholarship in the 1970s and 1980s made them available.[6]

Although the poverty of Brahms's youth has been exaggerated, money was continually in short supply in the Brahms household despite the fact that by the 1840s, Johann Jakob was earning more money than many a tradesman, and Brahms's mother, Johanna Christiane, née Nissen, was a highly skilled seamstress and a steady wage earner. There is no doubt that Brahms started to work at the age of 14, after his schooling was completed. The *Lokals* Brahms played in were establishments known as *Schänken*, simple restaurants where food, drink, and entertainment were offered to respectable people—respectable, but of the poorer classes. He played in the evenings and on Sundays, and earned 5 Marks for an afternoon's piano-playing in the countryside—not a bad salary when compared to a printer's weekly wage of under 10 Marks.[7]

---

[5] Walter Uka (ed.) (Berlin, 1986). The name means *The District of Narrow Alleys*.   [6] See n. 3.

[7] Rent for the little house on the Dammtorwall, which the Brahms family moved to when Johannes was 8 and where they stayed until he was 18, was at first 250 Marks, and then 300 Marks per year. School fees came to 60–80 Marks per year per child. Added to that were costs for music lessons and instruments and printed music; at his father's insistence Johannes studied the cello, and to that end Johann Jakob bought an instrument for 300 Marks. These expenses are all in addition to the general cost of feeding and clothing a family. By contrast, the entire yearly wage of a sailor, in 1847, was about 314 Marks; a farm foreman earned 110 Marks, a baker 156 Marks, a lithographer 780 Marks. Exact figures are available for the year 1837 at the Rammelsberg Mine (silver and lead) in the Harz Mountains, where wages ranged between 5 Marks down to 1 Mark 16 Silver Groschen per week. Five out of 180 men received the maximum of 5 Marks per week, but the largest number of workers took home salaries of half that or less. Carl Koch, *Der Rammelsberg* (Goslar, 1837, repr. Hornburg 1987), 19–23. Figures for Brahms are from Hofmann, *Johannes Brahms und Hamburg*, 24. The wage figures are quoted there from Antje Kraus, *Die Unterschichten Hamburgs in der ersten Hälfte des 19. Jahrhunderts* (Stuttgart, 1965).

The financial shortfall in the Brahms household was directly related to Johann Jakob, a restless soul with a particular bent for spending whatever was earned. The income of a freelance musician was uncertain, and to augment it Johann Jakob had all sorts of schemes—raising rabbits, then chickens, then doves in the back yard—all of which cost money to implement, and all of which failed. The family moved seven times in twenty-two years, not always in accord with Christiane's wishes, and in her view Johann Jakob bought furniture they did not need, musical instruments they could ill afford, and lottery tickets which did not win—often with money which she had worked for and saved with great effort.

The relationship between Brahms's parents was strained for other reasons. They had met shortly after Johann Jakob, barely 24, had acquired Hamburg citizenship. To do so the ambitious young man was required to join the Hamburg Militia, buy his own uniform and weapon, find two senior senators who would come with him in person to vouch for his character and means at the City Hall, and pay a sum of money which would have been sufficient to clothe a family of four for a year.[8] In keeping with his new middle-class status, he had moved from the sailors' quarter in St Pauli to the more respectable district of Neustadt. His new landlady and her unmarried sister ran a little shop which sold sewing goods: '*Geschwister Nissen—Holländische Waren*' was the sign on the door. Fräulein Christiane Nissen was 41 years old, of slight build, somewhat sickly, and lame. The record shows that her ancestors were aldermen, pastors, and teachers in Holstein, but she herself was brought up in Hamburg in much reduced circumstances and understood only too well how to live economically. Every description by those who actually knew her remarks upon her modesty, goodness, and fine understanding, and perhaps these are the traits that endeared her to Johann Jakob; but he cannot have thought much into the future when he asked for her hand—something he did within one week of becoming her lodger. This very oddly matched pair was married a few weeks later, a precipitous beginning to a long and increasingly trying union. In addition to the enormous difference in age, there was a considerable disparity in character. Christiane's last letter to Johannes, written two or three days before her death, describes how temperamentally unsuited mother and father were, and what difficulties she continually faced (Letter 191). Nevertheless, the new family started off astonishingly well, as three healthy children were born within five years.

Johannes was born in No. 24 Specksgange, an old, five-storey, half-timbered tenement house.[9] Scarcely eight months later, the family moved to a larger and

8 F. Georg Buck, *Handbuch der Hamburgischen Verfassung und Verwaltung* (Hamburg, 1828), and Georg-Wilhelm Röpke, *Zwischen Alster und Wandsee* (Hamburg, 1983).

9 Later renumbered as No. 60 Speckstrasse, and eventually graced by a plaque commemorating his birth. See Plate 1. The house was vividly described in its turn-of-the-century condition by Florence May, i. 55. Max Kalbeck incorrectly placed the Brahms family in the tiny Speckgasse flat for three years, or until after the birth of the third child. Every biography since has accepted his mistake. Hit by bombs in the Second World War, the site is now marked by a small monument—and as of this writing is a neglected and shabby spot, threatened by nearby construction.

rather more costly flat.[10] In 1841, with two more moves behind them, they moved into a little house at 29 Dammtorwall, a ten-minute walk from the Alster Pavilion, and there they stayed for the next ten years (see Plate 2).[11]

At 6 Johannes was enrolled in an elementary school nearby, and when he turned 11, he entered a well-known secondary school run by Johann Hoffmann for 'boys of the general middle-class'. He graduated, diploma and all, in the spring of 1847, just before his fourteenth birthday. By that time he was an accomplished pianist, and had mightily impressed at least two of the teachers in his school, one of whom asked the boy to give him piano lessons.[12]

1

Johannes Brahms to his Piano Teacher, Otto Friedrich Willibald Cossel

Hamburg, 1 January [18]42

Beloved Teacher!

Once again a year has passed, and I am reminded how far you have brought me in music in the year gone by. How many thanks do I owe you for that! True, I must also consider that at times I did not follow your wishes, in that I did not practise as I should have. I promise you, however, in this year to comply with your wishes with diligence and attentiveness. While wishing you much happiness for the new year, I remain

Your obedient student
J. Brahms

2

Johannes Brahms to his Parents[13]

Hamburg, Christmas Eve 1846

Dear Parents!

Today when the Christmas festival renews itself, this festival so joyful for every person, I feel myself permeated with the spirit of thankfulness,

---

[10] Hofmann, *Johannes Brahms und Hamburg*, 70.

[11] The houses on the Dammtorwall have been replaced by a large office block, but the street is still there; the Pavilion was destroyed in the Second World War and rebuilt on the same spot. It is still a fashionable meeting-place, where one can enjoy refreshments and live music.

[12] Which he did, gratis, at 8 a.m. For an eyewitness account of the school, of Brahms's first concert, and of the piano lessons he gave to his teacher, see Robert Meisner, 'Aus Brahms's Schulzeit', *Brahms-Studien*, 2 (Hamburg, 1977), 85–94.

[13] In what must have been a school exercise, Brahms sent his parents two versions of this letter, one in German and one in French. The French version is written on a large folio, the first page printed with sweeping Baroque arabesques around the margins. It contains a number of mistakes,

directed towards the Deity, as well as towards you, beloved parents. When I count all the good deeds and cares you have continuously heaped upon me[!], I do feel that I am still too weak to thank you sufficiently, but at least I will strive always to conduct myself so as to earn your love and to provide the joy of your old age.

Accept here my felicitations and the passionate wishes which I send to the Eternal one to extend your life to the greatest old age. To allow you always to enjoy good health, to grant you every good thing that you yourselves might wish.

With these sentiments I remain for all my life
your thankful son
Johannes Brahms

These letters, the first one written when he was 9, the next written at the age of 13 as he was almost ready to leave school, are the earliest known of the thousands of letters that were to come from Brahms's pen. The exquisitely even and careful handwriting of his youth is in the greatest possible contrast to the scrawl of later years. It is also a powerful witness to the fact that his early education was taken seriously (see Plate 3).

Brahms's formal education began in 1839, at the elementary school run by Heinrich Voss. Among other subjects, he was taught arithmetic, French, and Latin. Brahms retained a reading knowledge of French, and some of the English he learned in middle school. Florence May says he could read and understand it a little, but she never heard him attempt to speak English, and his accent in French was atrocious.[14] In a letter by one of Brahms's most knowledgeable Hamburg friends (Theodor Avé-Lallement to Hermann Levi, October 1873), Voss's establishment was described as 'a good middle-class school'.[15] Its headmaster was called a quiet and humane man by one who knew him well.[16] Herr Voss was later appointed director of St Petri Church School and for years also taught night classes at a teacher-training school for women, making it difficult to understand the suggestion, found in Kalbeck and as a result in other biographies, that the schools Brahms attended were of a very inferior sort.

lacking many required diacritical marks, and in several places letters begun in German Gothic script have then been carefully transformed into the unfamiliar Roman alphabet in use throughout most of Europe. It is the work of a dutiful, rather than a brilliant schoolboy. The letter as quoted in Kal² iv. 533–4, is a corrected version, with Brahms's errors washed clean. I am grateful to the Linderman Library, Lehigh University, for allowing me to see a copy of the French version while it was still in their possession.

[14] May, i. 7, 68–9.

[15] The letter is in the possession of the Library of Congress, Whittall Collection. It is quoted briefly in Kal⁴, i. 16.

[16] See Robert Meisner, 'Aus Brahms' Schulzeit', Brahms-Studien, 2 (1977) 89 ff. for this and details of the school curriculum, faculty, and students at Johann Hoffmann's middle school described below.

The curriculum in Johann Hoffmann's middle school included history, Latin, mathematics, natural sciences, singing, drawing, French and English, gymnastics, music, and diction (the last three subjects taught by the same person). Many of the teaching staff went on to distinction in their own fields. Brahms's classmates there were the sons of physicians, high city officials, merchants, and owners of large businesses.

In later life Brahms had occasion to recommend the school to others, and when Johann Hoffmann celebrated his Jubilee, Brahms sent him his photo and contributed money in the name of his brother Fritz as well as of himself.[17]

[17] *Familie*, 234, letter to Karoline Brahms, 23 Feb. 1878.

PART II

One Fateful Year
1853

Introduction

By the age of 19, Brahms was a virtuoso pianist, an aspiring and prolific composer, earning a bit of money in various unsatisfactory ways, and virtually unknown. If his musical horizons were broad, his professional prospects were exceedingly limited. He had never been far from Hamburg, and in Hamburg he could hope for little. His good fortune there was limited to having found two gifted and conscientious teachers: after Cossel, Brahms studied with Eduard Marxsen, who fostered not only Brahms's pianistic, but also his intellectual development.

Marxsen instructed him in theory and composition according to the principles he himself had studied in Vienna twenty years previously, and taught both Johannes and his brother Fritz without accepting a penny. For years he remained an adviser to the Brahms family.

But Marxsen was unable to extricate Johannes from the obscurity and artistic isolation to which his life had led him after leaving school; for whatever reason, he had no influence over Hamburg's musical establishment. Brahms gave poorly paid piano lessons; he played dance music late into the night in *Schänken* or provided music behind the scenes in theatres; he arranged marches and dances for outdoor orchestras. Composing was merely the luxury of his spare time, not an activity which found approval or a sympathetic ear at home.

There had been two major attempts to break out of this isolation: at 15 Brahms had given a début recital, followed by another concert seven months later; and in 1850 he had sent a selection of his compositions to Schumann's hotel when that famous composer was in Hamburg on tour.

Neither effort bore fruit. The concerts were received well enough but produced virtually no results, and Schumann returned the package of manuscripts unopened. It is interesting to speculate—so far it is nothing but—whether Brahms's inability to penetrate Hamburg's musical establishment was due to his lower middle-class background. Given the good concert notices and the fact that his teacher was the most esteemed pedagogue in Hamburg, it is difficult to understand what prevented the development of Brahms's career in his native city unless it were for some entirely extraneous consideration such as class. This is not the only point in Brahms's career at which one is forced to ask such a question.

In fact, his talents were *not* entirely unnoticed.[1] Occasionally he was hired to make piano arrangements of current popular music for the leading local publishers (conscious of their limited musical worth, the teenage boy used a pseudonym).[2] Sometimes he performed as soloist and supporting participant in other people's concert programmes,[3] and sometimes he was asked to accompany musical soirées at fine houses. One such occasion has given rise to the misguided story, often quoted, that Brahms was hauled out of bed to play dance music down at the harbour for a pittance—'Twee Daler un duhn'. The occasion was in fact a private evening of music in the house a wealthy Hamburg businessman, and the two thalers offered in Platt-Deutsch by the messenger was half the weekly wage of many a working man.[4]

Another occasion proved more fateful; the violinist of that evening was a flamboyant Hungarian on his way to America, fleeing the police in the wake of the revolution of 1848. His name was Eduard Reményi, he had studied violin in Vienna at the same time and with the same teacher as Joseph Joachim, and he became the means of Brahms's escape from anonymity.

Reményi was a flamboyant character, a type apparently at the far end of the spectrum from Brahms; but his theatrics seem not to have bothered the young pianist. For his part, the violinist was so impressed by the quiet youth that they played together on a casual basis quite frequently, until a tightening police net sent Reményi and other refugees scurrying out of Germany. He reappeared in the spring of 1853, by which time Brahms had already spent five years struggling to emerge into the world, grubbing out a living playing entertainment and background music, and giving lessons.[5]

By now, too, Johann Jakob Brahms was getting impatient. No longer willing to be responsible for feeding the entire family, and never happy with Johannes's bent for composition, he asked the help of some of his own friends in arranging a small

---

[1] In the *Hamburger Correspondent* of 2 May 1849, Brahms received a glowing and perceptive review of the concert he had presented on 14 April at the Jenisches Haus. The review acknowledged the exceptional talent of the 15-year-old as a pianist *and* composer. See additional note (p. 746) for the complete text.

[2] J. V. Widmann, *Erinnerungen an Johannes Brahms* (Berlin, 1898, repr. Zurich, 1980), 94 ff.

[3] Five such concerts can be documented in the years 1849–50. Joachim Thalmann, *Untersuchungen zum Frühwerk von Johannes Brahms* (Kassel, 1989), 83 ff.

[4] Hofmann, *Brahms und Hamburg*, 13.

[5] From *Dwight's Journal of Music*, Boston, 20 Nov. 1852, p. 51: 'The following, though from rather an old paper . . . may perhaps be interesting. "A violinist, named Remenyi, a Hungarian by birth, is exciting in Paris much attention. He was a friend and constant companion of Görgey, with him in all his campaigns, and was in the habit of exciting his countrymen by playing national melodies, and of chasing the clouds from the brow of the General by his tones. After Görgey, however, at the head of 40,000 brave troupes, surrendered to the Russians, the artist tore himself from his former friend and now wanders homeless through the world with no friend but his violin." '

concert tour through northern Germany for Brahms and Reményi, with Brahms definitely the accompanist.

The proposed tour was very short and included no important cities, but Reményi planned it so that they would visit his old student friend Joachim, who was, after all, a fellow Hungarian Jew. Even better, Joachim was already the most famous young violinist in Europe, and although only 22 years old, held the post of Concertmaster and Assistant Kapellmeister at the Court of Hanover, under King George. He was also a great favourite of Franz Liszt, with unrestricted access to the composer and his influential circle of disciples and friends, a circumstance which would allow Joachim to be exceedingly helpful to Reményi if he so chose. That he did so choose is due not to Reményi, but to Brahms. We have Joachim's own account of the effect that Brahms made upon him when he and Reményi walked, unannounced, into his rooms in Hanover.[6]

Struck by Brahms's rare abilities as a pianist, by his powerful music, and by his unusual personality, Joachim acted on Brahms's behalf without hesitation and began a friendship which lasted until the composer's death forty-four years later.

The news Brahms sent home was the cause of great joy. His mother wrote:

> . . . when we received your letter from Hanover, that was such an agreeable surprise and was so moving that none of us could read it. And when we came to the end we said: that fortunate Johannes, and we fortunate parents! . . . Only now, dear Johannes, is your life really beginning. Now you will reap what you have sown here with toil and diligence. Your hour has struck, thanks to a benign Providence. It sent you an angel who led you out of this darkness into the world where there are people who know enough to treasure you and all you have learnt.

Joachim was able to restore the young men's supply of money by arranging a concert before King George and his Court, and he sent a letter to Liszt which assured Brahms an enthusiastic welcome at Liszt's opulent villa at Weimar: and now, it was Reményi who was accompanying Brahms.[7]

But Joachim's best offer of help was for Brahms alone. He correctly foresaw trouble in the alliance between the theatrical Hungarian and the shy, idealistic, and silent North German, and urged Brahms to come to him should a rupture take place. The break came soon enough.

---

[6] Translated in full by May, i. 108. For Joachim's original speech, see: 'Festrede zur Enthüllung des Brahmsdenkmales in Meiningen', *Allgemeine Musikzeitung* (Berlin, 1899), no. 42.

[7] William Mason, *Memories of a Musical Life* (New York, 1901), 127 ff.

3
Brahms to Joseph Joachim

[Weimar, 29 June 1853]

Honoured Herr Joachim!

Did I not bear the name *Kreisler*, I would now have the weightiest of reasons to lose courage, to curse my love of art and my enthusiasm, and to withdraw as a hermit (scribe?) into the solitude (of an office) and lose myself in silent contemplation (of the documents to be copied).

Yes, dear fellow, such weighty reasons that my forced good humour is already giving out, and I must relate to you the bitter truth as sombrely as I perceive it.

Reményi is moving on from Weimar without me, it is his will; my behaviour towards him could not have given him the slightest cause, although it was more I who had to put up with his moods every day. I really did not need another such bitter experience, in this regard I already had sufficient material for a poet and composer.

It must have been the meanest and most trivial reasons that caused R. to take me with him from Hamburg, just as misunderstanding or overhastiness now drives him to leave me, [but] I cannot give the thing such a good name; I could explain everything to you in greater detail, but it is too disagreeable for me to write much about it.

Without any results to show I cannot return to Hamburg, where otherwise my c–g sharp-tuned heart would feel most comfortable just now; I must see at least 2 or 3 of my works published so that I can look my parents in the face with good cheer.[8]

Dr Liszt promised to mention me in a letter to Härtel, so that I may already hope for that. But you, dearest Herr Joachim, I would like urgently to beg to fulfil if possible the hope which you gave me in Göttingen of introducing me to the life of an artist.

Do write to me *as soon as is at all possible* whether, as would *please me indescribably*, you are still in G. these days, and if I can visit you there and talk things over with you, or if you are leaving very soon; in that case, I would

---

[8] 'Ich kann nicht ohne jedes Resultat nach Hamburg zurück, wo mir doch jetzt am wohlsten wäre mit meinem in c-gis gestimmten Herzen . . .' But the passage makes more sense if it reads '. . . mit meinem *in c-ges* gestimmten Herzen . . .', c–g flat being the very discordant tritone. Although the letter as published both in *Briefe von und an Joseph Joachim*, ed. Moser and Joachim (Berlin, 1911), i. 52 (hence forth *JJ*) and in *BW* v. 3, gives the *c-gis* reading, I cannot but wonder if Moser did not misread Brahms's handwriting here.

like to ask you kindly to write me a few friendly words and to send recommendations to publishers. I am perhaps immodest, but my situation and my low spirits compel me to ask you for really favourable and urgent recommendations (if possible to several publishers), so that I can have the hope of seeing a few things published soon.

Although I cannot hope ever to repay your kindness, be assured that you have not shown it to an ingrate.

Awaiting a truly quick answer or, if possible, an invitation to Göttingen,

I remain

Your faithful

Jos Brahms

Kreisler jun.

Address: Frau Weisse
     Karlsplatz, f.29
     (Weimar)

The Kreisler mentioned at the beginning of this letter refers to Kapellmeister Johannes Kreisler, the intense, sometimes wild musician invented by the poet, musician, and novelist E. T. A. Hoffmann. Along with a literary tom-cat, he is the hero of Hoffmann's comic novel *The Life and Opinions of Kater Murr*, as well as of two collections of short stories known as *Kreisleriana*, which also formed the literary basis for Schumann's set of piano pieces of the same name, Op. 16. Brahms identified powerfully with Kapellmeister Kreisler, so much so that he adopted the name of *Johannes Kreisler Jun.*, and used it until he was about 30 years old, even signing letters and putting that name to his compositions; and he named his youthful collection of literary quotations *Young Kreisler's Little Treasure Chest.*[9]

Joachim responded to Brahms's call for help with an immediate invitation to spend the summer with him in Göttingen. His parents, however, were dismayed. From his mother on 10 July:

> Dear Johannes, your letter astonished us greatly, although I have thought much about it in silence and concluded from your letter in Hanover that Reményi had become envious of you . . . but such an early parting of the ways we had not expected.

Her worry intensified when she learned that Joachim had taken Johannes under his protection, and she wrote again on 23 July:

> You have not written clearly enough about your circumstances. For example: you don't need any money! Even if you have lodgings and food and

[9] *Des jungen Kreislers Schatzkästlein*, ed. Carl Krebs (Berlin, 1909). E. T. A. Hoffmann, *Lebensansichten des Katers Murr* (Frankfurt am Main, 1967). In English, *The Life and Opinions of Kater Murr*, trans. Leonard Kent and Elizabeth Knight (Chicago, 1969).

> drink, you must also have clothes, your footwear will come apart, and
> above all, how can one live in a foreign land without money! If you have to
> ask Herr Joachim for every little thing you will be too beholden to him . . .
> you know people too little, and trust them too much . . . Herr Marxsen has
> told Father what it is you wanted in Göttingen and Hanover . . .

Indeed, much more than money was on Brahms's mind. His letter to Joachim
reveals that he was determined to return home as a composer, not a pianist, and that
his parents still needed to be convinced. Apparently Marxsen understood, and
explained to his parents that Brahms was searching for the opportunity to compose
undisturbed. His mother suggested, in that case, that he come home—but Brahms's
plea to Joachim was correct: without any results to show for his tour he could not
return to Hamburg, and as if to confirm it, his sister added a postscript, undoubtedly prompted by their father. It read:

> Even if Herr Marxsen or Herr Cranz[10] writes to you that it would be better
> if you came back to Hamburg, we think it more useful that you seek your
> fortune abroad, although we would like to have you in our midst . . .

Once again, Joachim lent his help.

4
Joseph Joachim to the Parents of Johannes Brahms

Göttingen, 25 July 1853

Allow me, though I am unknown to you, to address you and say how endlessly fortunate I feel myself to be in the company of your Johannes; for to
whom can one speak of the joy your son has provided better than to his parents! With your Johannes, a new, unhoped-for stimulus has been given me
in my journey as an artist; to strive with him towards a common goal is for
me a fresh impetus along the toilsome path we musicians follow in life. His
purity, his precocious independence, the unusual richness of his heart and
intellect is expressed as sympathetically in his music as his entire being will
bring joy to those who encounter his spirit.

How marvellous it will be once his full artistic power is plainly presented
in a work for all to see. And given his keen desire for perfection, nothing else
is possible.

---

[10] The Hamburg music publisher August Cranz, who occasionally gave Johannes work, and to
whose son, Alwin, Brahms gave piano lessons by the year 1850.

That I cherish the wish to have him by my side so long as it does not conflict with his duties towards himself, you will find understandable, because I believe that it must also be congenial for Johannes to live undisturbed in Göttingen, where he most surely has, in the person of Music Director Wehner[11] and my humble self, people who will gladly follow the unusual qualities of his life and art.

How happy it would make me to be able to render my dear friend Johannes a real service, sometime, for that my friendship is at his disposal goes without saying. I can only wish that our new-found bond enjoy the blessing of your approval.

Respectfully,
Joseph Joachim

The letter was irresistible. His mother responded:

> Dear, good Johannes, how immensely happy we are about you, that you are so happy and content in your association with such a marvellous man as Herr Joachim. You have surely earned it, my angel. We hear from Cranz that you already have work. But I beg you not to work as much at night as you are already accustomed to do . . .[12]

And Johann Jakob answered Joachim directly (assuredly with someone's help—probably Marxsen's, for his own writing style was exceedingly unpolished):

5
Johann Jakob Brahms to Joseph Joachim

Hamburg, 1 August 1853

Honoured Sir!

The kind lines you directed to me have gladdened me greatly. What can provide greater joy to a father's heart than your pronouncement regarding my Johannes's talent and his hard-won ability, as well as about the purity of his youthful disposition, which we pray heaven preserve for all time!—That he has had the good fortune to become acquainted with you, the so very famous artist, and that in consequence a bond of cordial friendship has been sealed between you and Johannes—for of that your and my son's latest letter

---

[11] Arnold Wehner, at that time music director in Göttingen. He took a lively and fatherly interest in the young composer, and is mentioned frequently by Joachim and Brahms during this period.

[12] End of July. Family letters quoted here are from *Familie*, 44 ff.

assures me—I hold to be an especially favourable dispensation of heaven, and I allow myself to look to the future with happy hopes and confidence.

With my sincerest thanks to you for your communication,
I commend myself to you
most faithfully,
Jakob Brahms

Then the new and faithful friend arranged financial matters as well, resupplying Brahms with money by means of a joint concert.[13] With pockets now full, family concerns resolved for the time being, and armed with Joachim's letters of introduction—including one to Robert Schumann—Brahms realized a precious dream; he set off on a walking tour down the valley of the 'divine' Rhine.

6

Johannes Brahms to Joseph Joachim

Mehlemerau, 10 Sept[ember] 1853

Very dear friend,

For several days now I've been visiting the Deichmann family in Mehlem and am overjoyed by the news that after the Carlsruhe Music Festival you and Herr Wehner will probably be coming to spend a few days here. I can't recommend a stay in this heavenly place warmly enough—you will treasure it all. From the first moment, everyone in the house will be kind and dear to you from then on. Herr and Frau D. are the most splendid of people and their children indescribably lovable.

When I arrived here after a marvellous Rhine journey (which I definitely hope to describe to you in person), I was in no mood to go through what I thought would be a stiff, formal visit, and found myself dreading it.

But by the next morning it was already impossible to consider going; and by now it is that much the more painful to think of parting.

How many acquaintances I've already found here, including Herr Wüllner, Breuer and Hartman, Fräulein Schloss, etc; Early on, I also got to meet the delightful gentlemen Wasielewski and Reimers, fortunately, they come to visit often so you will surely encounter them too.

I'm awfully sorry that there was no letter from me to greet you when you arrived in Hanover; When it comes to writing letters, my good intentions and strong will are of no use, I just can't bear it.

Hr. Deichmann requests that I ask you to send me a brief message as to

[13] May, i. 117.

whether and when you will be coming, for I cannot doubt but that you will come. I am certain that you will have an excellent time here and will find yourself wishing you could stay for a long time.

Farewell, dearest friend, and, should time and patience permit, give me the joy of a long letter and the promise to come here.

Yours,

Johannes

(The address here: c/o Frau Commerzienrätin Deichmann, Mehlem near Bad Godesberg.)

Forgive me for leaving both adjoining pages blank, but can't abide this dam——d letter-writing any more.

The Deichmanns were a wealthy family with a serious interest in the arts. Their house outside Bonn was a meeting-point for many musicians, especially devotees of Schumann's music. Brahms met people, both here and at other stops along the way, with whom he would remain in contact for most of his life, and whose names appear in many subsequent letters: Franz Wüllner, an important champion of his orchestral works; Carl Reineke, later conductor of the Gewandhaus Concerts at Leipzig; Albert Dietrich, lifelong friend whom Brahms first encountered at Schumann's house; Wilhelm von Wasielewski, music director at Bonn, member of the orchestra in Düsseldorf during Schumann's tenure and author of the first Schumann biography. Christian Reimers is the Hamburg-born cellist for whom Schumann wrote his Cello Concerto (Op. 129). He and Brahms saw each other and played together with some frequency over the next few years.

The Deichmanns must have been as delighted with Brahms as he with them, for they organized a further outing for him and their three sons.

7

Johannes Brahms to Joseph Joachim

[On the Rhine Steamer, Postmarked
Niederlahnstein, 22 September] 1853

Very dear friend,

Just think, I'm still roving around in the glorious valleys of the Rhine. Frau Deichmann had the happy thought that her 3 sons, who are spending their vacation in Mehlem, might still like to take a trip to the Valley of the Ahr and Lake Laach, then she had the even better one of choosing me as their guide and gave me permission to go as far as 30 thaler and my fancy would take me. So we have already visited the Valley of the Ahr, the most beautiful one on the Rhine, and Lake Laach, and here we are on a ship which is taking us to Coblenz, from where we still intend to visit the Lahn Valley. I'm writing this letter in the cabin, which is my excuse for the bad handwriting. Before my departure from Mehlem I had the pleasure of getting your letter; I was very much afraid that my hurried letter would be answered by a similar one, so it was with double the joy that I read your kind words.

A letter from my parents arrived at the same time as yours, and in it was enclosed this letter from Herr Marxsen which I am sending on to you as it is really directed at you. Please send it back to me with your next letter.

I wonder if you would subscribe to Herr Marxsen's judgement? I think so. Through your new, splendid overtures too broad a view has been opened, a new, too beautiful world revealed for you still to hang on to the overused one. I don't know if my opinion might not change, I really don't know the Hamlet overture well enough.[14]

Your letter has given me an immense desire to go to Carlsruhe;[15] but I suppose it's better to forgo this great pleasure for the time being or postpone it just until Hanover.

I have had so many sublime, heavenly pleasures that it would be self-indulgent of me to revel in them even longer.

I'm thinking of going from the meadows of Mehlem to Leipzig, to do every possible thing so as to get lots of work and spend the winter in Hanover working quietly and diligently. I dread the thought of this Leipzig!! There is much too harsh a difference between the mountains of the Rhine and the business offices of Leipzig.

I'm very curious whether you are playing your concerto in Carlsruhe—it would make my absence that much more painful. Write to me anyway, in your next letter.[16]

Farewell, best of luck, and have a good time at the Carlsruhe Music Festival.

Yours, Johannes

21 Sept. (I suppose my desk excuses the messy letter.)

His delight comes through again in a letter to the Bailiff Blume, an official of the village of Winsen-an-der-Luhe and one of the music-loving people who underwrote

---

[14] Marxsen's letter, written at Brahms's urging, was a critique of Joachim's works: overtures to *Demetrius, Hamlet,* and *Henry IV*. The *Hamlet* overture was finished in March 1853, and was highly regarded by Liszt, Schumann, and Brahms. It was performed during his lifetime, but not printed until after his death. *Henry IV* was still in progress.

[15] Joachim was on his way to Karlsruhe to take part in a music festival with Liszt and Hans von Bülow. Beethoven's Ninth Symphony was to be performed, and Brahms had never heard it.

[16] Violin Concerto, Op. 3, by Joachim.

his tour with Reményi. Blume, in his seventies at the time, had taken an especially kind interest in the young composer.

8

Johannes Brahms to Amtsvogt [Bailiff] Blume[17]

[Early September 1853]

Cherished Herr Bailiff,

Permit me to extend to you and to your wife my most heartfelt good wishes for the happy festivity you are celebrating this month.

The high esteem and love in which I have always held you may excuse my bothering you with these lines of mine from so far away, perchance even at the incorrect time, it's just that I only know you are celebrating your golden wedding anniversary in the middle of this month.

May God long preserve you in good health, so that I may often again spend such joyous hours at your house as before.

If you still take some interest in my fate, you may be pleased to learn that I have experienced as heavenly a summer as never before.

After spending gloriously inspiring weeks together with Joachim in Göttingen, I have now been roaming to my heart's desire along the divine Rhine for the past 5 weeks.

I hope to be able to spend this winter in Hanover so as to live with Joachim, who is equally noble as man and artist. While asking you to commend me most fervently to your wife and daughter, I beg you to convey my warmest greetings to your son, as well as his wife and children, to the cherished Uncle Giesemann, and all other acquaintances there.

With my best greetings,

your

Joh. Brahms

In the Lahn valley
Sept. 1853

Brahms kept in close contact with his family by letter. His mother, who wrote to him weekly (it is surely she who reminded Johannes to write a letter to the Amtsvogt), was not entirely happy about his Rhine trip. She had never left the vicinity of Hamburg, and had no clear idea of what mountains were like. She sent him the following anxious letter:

[17] In a foreign hand, at the top of the letter: *answered 25 July 1854, Schadowsplatz No. 16 in Düsseldorf, Music Teacher Br[ahms]*.

9

Christiane Brahms to Johannes Brahms

[Hamburg,] 3 and 4 Sept[ember] 1853

That's a marvellous trip you are taking, but sometimes very dangerous. I beg you, think how easily you can fall off walking over such rough rocks! I shudder when I think of it . . . Your heart is certainly strong, but one can overdo it with too much mountain climbing . . . Today Fritz took both your recent letters to Herr Marxsen, who is very happy about you and who sends his very best greetings. Many tears of joy are shed over you, my angel.

I want to remind you to buy a winter coat in good time so that you don't catch cold. If you lack money, be straightforward about it and write to us . . . I never forget you when I say my evening prayers, and when I get up at 6 in the morning my first thought is of you. I beg you, write to us again very soon, tell us what we can send you and when. . . .

Brahms did go to Leipzig, but not until November. In the mean time, his stay at the Deichmann house had given him his first opportunity to study an abundance of Schumann scores. What was revealed to him finally surmounted his antipathy, born of the incident three years before when Schumann had returned unopened the package of his teenage compositions. Now Brahms was overwhelmed to discover the degree to which his musical and literary ideals corresponded with those of the great composer.

Deichmann, Wasiliewski, and above all Joachim, had been pressing him to present himself to Schumann in Düsseldorf. Finally Brahms felt ready.

Schumann's diary entry of 1 October reads: 'Visit from Brahms, a genius.' From that point on, things moved very fast. During the next few days Brahms played, for Robert and Clara Schumann and various of their friends, those of his compositions which he felt were worthy. In the next two weeks Schumann wrote to Breitkopf & Härtel to prepare for the publication of a number of these works, and two weeks later he sent an essay to the *Neue Zeitschrift für Musik* which would project Brahms like an exploding missile into public view.

10

Johannes Brahms to Joseph Joachim

Düsseldorf, [beginning of October] 1853[18]

Beloved friend!

You have received a letter from the Schumanns, in which they also write about my presence here.

I surely don't need long to tell you how infinitely happy their reception, friendly beyond all expectation, made me.

Their praise has made me so happy and resolute that I can't wait for the time when I can finally quietly turn to working and creating. Out of pure joy over Schumann's approval, I promised them, in fact, to stay here until you come and take me with you to Hanover.

What shall I write to you about Schumann, shall I break out in hosannas over his genius and character, or shall I lament that once again people are committing the great sin of misjudging a good man and divine artist so much, and of honouring him so little.

And I myself, how long did I commit this sin. Only since leaving Hamburg and especially during my stay in Mehlem, did I learn to know and honour Schumann's works. I should like to beg his forgiveness.

Frankly, I have little desire to go to Leipzig (as Hr. Wehner advises me urgently in every letter). I am afraid of those enormous business offices, and also now believe I make better use of my time by continuing to study than by seeking to arrange my things as practically as possible.

I was as happy as a child to find my countrywoman Louise Japha here.[19]

It would be heavenly if you could come along to the Mehlemer meadow during one of your visits to Düsseldorf. You can't imagine how well I liked it there; you will like everything there, too.

If possible, do write to me when you are coming, *how long you are staying*, and if you have any time, write to me from Carlsruhe, especially about *your concerto*. I am longing for you as if it were years since we had met, also have so many, endlessly many fine things to tell you.

Your
Johannes

Düsseldorf
Sept. 53
NB. Many greetings *to Herr Wehner*, if you write to him!

---

[18] Brahms's own date at the letter's end is September, but Schumann's diary marked Brahms's arrival on 1 October. Very likely Brahms did not keep careful track of the date during his journey. At all events, this letter must have been written almost immediately after their first meeting.

[19] One of the few voices of encouragement from Brahms's childhood. Seven years older than he, she was a pianist and composer, studying at this time with the Schumanns. See May, i. 90–2.

11
Johannes Brahms to Joseph Joachim

[Düsseldorf] 17 October 1853

Dear Joseph,

Dr Schumann is promoting my interests at Breitkopf & Härtel with such seriousness and urgency that I'm beginning to feel dizzy. He thinks perhaps I ought to send off the first works within six days.

For the sake of variety, he proposes the following order of publication:

Op. 1 Fantasy in D minor for Piano, Violin, and Cello (Largo and Allegro)
Op. 2 Lieder
Op. 3 Scherzo in E flat minor
Op. 4 Sonata in C major [for Piano]
Op. 5 Sonata in A minor for Piano and Violin
Op. 6 Songs

Do write to me plainly with your candid opinion. I hardly know how to get a grip on myself.

I wonder if the Trio (I assume you remember it) is worth publishing? Only from Opus 4 is it entirely to my taste. Schumann, however, believes one should start out with the weaker works. In that he is right—either begin with them, *or drop them completely* and strive not to fail hereafter.

If I could start with the C major Sonata!

The F sharp minor and the B minor Quartet, says Dr S, can follow any other works and hold their own.

I would like to send you the Trio as soon as it's copied; it goes without saying that I've remedied a few weaknesses.

Do give me the pleasure of a few lines soon.

Your Johannes

In greatest haste!

One of the characteristics of Brahms's entire career as a composer is his stringent, even ruthlessly self-critical faculty. He composed far more than he published—of some twenty string quartets, only three reached the public—and rather than allow his rejected works to survive in manuscript, he burnt them. His judgements were cool-headed and unsentimental. Nowhere is this more clearly seen than at the very start of his career, where he questioned even Schumann's judgement as to the choice and order of publication of his first works.

In a show of independence and internal strength that must be considered unusual for a 20-year-old in Brahms's position, the order of publication eventually settled upon was his own, backed up by Joachim's moral support. The work Schumann suggested for Op. 4 became, indeed, Brahms's Op. 1, the first work which was 'entirely to his taste'. The Trio Fantasy disappeared forever, the violin and piano sonata was lost (the violin part found much later, but not published). Brahms offered four works to Breitkopf & Härtel, and they accepted: Op. 1, Piano Sonata in C major; Op. 2, Piano Sonata in F sharp minor; Op. 3, *Six Songs*; Op. 4, Scherzo in E flat minor for Piano. Another Leipzig publisher, Bartolf Senff, took his Piano Sonata in F minor as Op. 5, and a second set of Songs as Op. 6.

12

Johannes Brahms to Breitkopf & Härtel

Papensteig 4 (near the Egidien Gate)
Hanover, 8 November 1853

Most Esteemed Sir:

I take the liberty herewith of sending you a number of my compositions, together with a request that you look through them and then most kindly inform me if I may experience the fulfilment of my hopes that they be published by your house.

More than my own audacity, it is the desire of artistic friends with whom I have shared my manuscripts that has brought me to the point of offering them to the public.

May I ask you, distinguished sir, to pardon these few lines if their contents should be unwelcome.

With deep respect and appreciation,

Johs Brahms

Schumann's intention was to find not only a publisher for Brahms's music, but a public as well. To that end, he wrote the essay 'Neue Bahnen' (New Paths), for the *Neue Zeitschrift für Musik* of 28 October 1853, in which he proclaimed Brahms as the long-awaited genius who would express most ideally the musical trends of the time and do so not in gradual stages, but all at once, as one 'sprung fully armed like Minerva from the head of Kronion'.[20] Then he sent the article to Johann Jakob in Hamburg, along with a letter that would encourage the father to regard his son above all as a composer. Brahms must have been overwhelmed with conflicting feelings, for it was almost three weeks before he replied.

---

[20] See May, i. 131–2 for a complete translation, or Malcolm MacDonald, *Brahms* (New York, 1990), 18, for a long excerpt.

13

Robert Schumann to Johann Jakob Brahms

Düsseldorf, 15 November 1853

Honoured Sir!

We have come to value your son Johannes very highly; his musical genius has given us hours rich in joy. In order to ease his first entry into the world, I have expressed publicly what I think of him. I am sending you these pages and believe that they will bring some small joy to a fatherly heart.

So may you look to the future of this darling of the Muses with confidence, and be forever assured of my deepest interest in his good fortune!

Your devoted
R. Schumann

14

Johannes Brahms to Robert Schumann

Hanover, 16 November 1853

Revered Master,

You have made me so immensely happy that I cannot even try to thank you in words. God grant that my works soon give evidence of how much your affection and kindness have elated and inspired me. The praise that you openly bestowed upon me will arouse such extraordinary expectations of my achievements by the public that I don't know how I can begin to fulfil them even somewhat. Above all else it induces in me the greatest caution in the choice of which pieces to publish. I am thinking of not publishing any of my trios, and of choosing for Opus 1 and 2 the sonatas in C major and F sharp minor, for Opus 3 songs, and as Opus 4 the Scherzo in E flat minor. You will find it natural that I strive with all my might to disgrace you as little as possible.

I delayed writing to you for so long because I have sent the above four works to Breitkopf and I wanted to wait for their response so I could inform you right away of the result of your recommendation. But from your last letter to Joachim we already learn of this, so I have only to write to you now that I am taking your advice and going to Leipzig sometime in the next few days (probably tomorrow).

Furthermore, I want to tell you that I have written out my F minor sonata and changed the Finale considerably. I have also improved the violin sonata. In addition, I must say a thousand thanks to you for the lovely picture of yourself that you sent me, as well as for the letter you wrote to my father. With that you have made several good people immensely happy, and for life

Your

Brahms

Schumann's insistence that Brahms go to Leipzig was based on his conviction that Brahms must promote his music in person. He had written to Joachim:[21] 'Share the enclosed letter [from Breitkopf & Härtel] with Johannes. He must go to Leipzig. Prevail upon him! Otherwise, they will mangle his work; he must perform it there himself. This seems to me very important.' Brahms went. Thanks to connections made through Schumann, Dietrich, and Joachim, he was dropped into the centre of musical activity without further ado.

15

Johannes Brahms to Albert Dietrich

Leipzig, [after 17] Nov[ember] 1853

Dearest Dietrich,

You have arranged a friendly reception for me here in Leipzig far beyond what I deserve, and I am capable of being so ill bred as to spare you my letters completely.

Don't think too ill of me, letters flow from my pen with great difficulty. I have been in Leipzig since Thursday evening, but have spent only one night in a hotel. Our worthy and kind friend von Sahr would not permit it for longer than that. He is sacrificing himself here for me.

The Härtels have received me with unending friendliness, as have Moscheles and David. If our Master is still in Düsseldorf, do say this to him, and tell him how highly I esteem him, how much I like him, and how gladly I would be grateful.[!]

Would Frau Schumann take it unkindly if I dedicated the F sharp minor Sonata to her? Do write to me about it.

Be well, dear one, and now and then remember

Your Johannes

---

21 *JJ* i. 103, letter of 11 Nov. 1853.

16

Johannes Brahms to Joseph Joachim

To His Most Highly Esteemed Personage Herr Joseph Joachim,
Renowned Royal Concertmaster in Hanover.

[Leipzig], Sunday [20 November 1853]

Your Worship the Concertmaster will [probably] already have learned from the New-Yorker Herald [that I] have been received here with much love and joy, [that] I lodge with Heinrich von Sahr, and that my [indisposition], which the Cincinnati Weekly describes as a [serious illness], is improving daily.

So that Your Worship nevertheless be not discomforted by imprecise press reports in America and European newspapers, I am hereby writing a few further details.

I have decided, after all, to dedicate my first things; do write me your candid opinion as to whether it would be better to drop the idea. One shouldn't be too concerned about what people think. I thought I would dedicate the Sonata in C to my best friend, His Grace the Concertmaster; the F sharp minor Sonata to Frau Schumann; the Op. 3 Songs to the Countess Bettina.[22]

But it really doesn't look right to set such names upon one's earliest works. I will probably drop the idea after all.

Herr Senff has asked me to give him as many [of my works] as I wish. I think I'll give him the F minor Sonata [and the] songs, don't you think? So I would like to *implore* you [once more] to look through the sonata with a sharp eye. In any case I have to make changes, particularly to the Finale.

I am now acquainted with Herr Härtel 1 and 2, Wenzel, Senff, *Wieck*, Sahr, David, Moscheles, etc.[23]

I like Wenzel more than all the others—he has such a fine-looking head and splendid brow.

Yesterday evening I was at Härtels and played the C major Sonata and E flat minor Scherzo. A lady sang some of the songs. They are indeed wonderful people, so sincere and warm.

---

[22] Bettina von Arnim, an important figure in German Romantic literature, friend of Beethoven and Goethe.

[23] Ernst Wenzel was the premier piano pedagogue at the Leipzig Conservatory, Bartolf Senff an important music publisher and editor of *Signale für die Musikalische Welt*, Friedrich Wieck the father of Clara Schumann (hence the special treatment of his name), Ferdinand David the concertmaster of the Gewandhaus Orchestra, and Ignaz Moscheles one of the four or five greatest pianists of the time.

For the sake of politeness, I visited Herr David without waiting for your letter.

At this spot I was interrupted by Herr David, who came here in order to play the [sonata] with me. He played it wonderfully [at sight] in spite of the bad handwriting. [I played] the C major Sonata [words missing]

[the original of this letter is missing a section at the fold of the page. Words in brackets are the suggestion of subsequent editors. In spite of what is missing, the gist is clear: David came to see the young Brahms and played one of his pieces (probably the now lost sonata). Brahms played the C major Sonata for him again, and David offered his comments. Brahms was also invited for an evening with Moscheles.]

I am getting advice [from all] sides (from David, as well) that I should play at a Quartet soirée. Surely that is pointless? Even if artists make allowances for my deficiencies as a performer, the public is not so good-natured.

Many greetings from Sahr and all the others. They are waiting for you without fail and with great longing.

Do write to me when you can (right away, in fact), especially about the dedications.

Your Johannes

17
Johannes Brahms to Robert Schumann

[Hanover] 29 November 1853

Mynheer Domine!

Forgive this playful form of address by one who has been made so infinitely glad and happy because of you. I have only the best and most beautiful things to tell you.

I owe to your warm recommendation a reception in Leipzig that was friendly beyond all expectation and especially beyond all deserving. Härtels declared themselves ready with great pleasure to print my first efforts. They are these: Op. 1, Sonata in C major; Op. 2, Sonata in F sharp minor; Op. 3, songs; Op. 4, Scherzo in E flat minor.

To Herr Senff I gave for publication: Op. 5, Sonata in A minor for violin and piano; Op. 6, six songs.

May I set your wife's name at the head of my second work? I hardly dare, and yet I should like so much to give you a small token of my reverence and gratitude.

I will probably receive copies of my first things even before Christmas. With what feelings will I then see my parents again, after scarcely a year's absence. I cannot describe what happens to my heart when I think of it.

May you never regret what you did for me, may I become really worthy of you.

> Your
> Joh. Brahms

Brahms returned to Hanover for a week, prompting Joachim to write to Schumann on 29 November: 'I could tell you more about Brahms, who returned here weighted down with laurel leaves and a mint of money by the Leipzigers; but you will prefer that he tell you about his experiences there himself.'[24] Then Brahms went to Leipzig once more in order to make final arrangements for publication.

18
Johannes Brahms to Joseph Joachim

[Leipzig] Wednesday, 7 Dec[cember] 1853

Dearest Joseph!

First and foremost, today I heard Schubert's C major Symphony in the rehearsal for tomorrow's concert.

Few things have so enchanted me—I would like to write you of nothing else. The playing, though, did not satisfy me quite as I had expected. I found the tempi consistently on the over-fast side, the trombones and trumpets too loud, the horns thoroughly bad. In the Genoveva Overture, the horn players were unable to deal with the theme.[25] If you do the C major Symphony at the first Hanover concert, you can schedule it for the 1st of January, for my part—I'll definitely come.

Now on to the order of the day.

On Thursday evening I went straight from the train station to Helbig's; you should have seen the surprise.[26] Senff, Wenzel, and Sahr were there. Liszt had come to the Berlioz concert with all his disciples (also Reményi)—he did himself a great deal of harm. The exaggerated applause of the Weimar clique provoked some determined opposition. I'm really worried about his own concert on Monday. In spite of the violent distaste of some of the Leipzigers

---

[24] *JJ* i. 110. [25] The overture to Schumann's four-act opera of the same name, Op. 81.
[26] A famous Leipzig restaurant.

(Sahr, etc.) my first call on Friday was to Liszt. I was accorded a very friendly reception. By Reményi, too. I was careful to avoid any thoughts and recollections of the past. Reményi has changed a good deal, and to his disadvantage. Liszt also visited me with Cornelius etc. Friday I was at David's, also Liszt, Berlioz, etc. On Sunday evening at Brendel's,[27] notwithstanding the awful faces the Leipzigers made. Pohl, Berlioz, etc. were there, and before I forget, Schloenbach,[28] Giesecke, and all the literary nobility (or nobodies?) of Leipzig. Berlioz praised me with such exceeding and heartfelt warmth that the others meekly repeated his words. He was just as friendly last night at Moscheles. I have to be very grateful to him. Liszt is coming back on Monday (to Berlioz's greatest disadvantage).

Dietrich wrote a similar letter to Sahr as he had written to us. A personality such as *Helena Berg* must necessarily arouse more serious emotions than a *Berthe* etc.[29] I would hope that it's more than a mere exercise in loving (dallying) which makes him write such serious letters.

I suppose you have already had an answer from Härtel? They told me they've already been expecting the 3 things for a year![30] So I know their answer. I took care of your letter to H. Salomon.[31] I called on the Seeburg lady on Saturday evening.

Tomorrow I'm getting the proofs of my C major Sonata, and on Monday those of the songs. Since Senff doesn't publish violin music, he will wait till I've revised my F minor Sonata. You have no idea how much I'm looking forward to Christmas, have you ever experienced such a joyous and splendid holiday as I this year?

With what gratitude my parents and I will be thinking of you, to whose friendship I owe everything.

Gladden me soon again with a letter, and forgive my interminably long and disjointed letter, I must write it and send it off so hurriedly that it leaves me no time for reflection.

Your Johannes

[27] Franz Brendel, at that time editor of the *Neue Zeitschrift für Musik*, and therefore favourably inclined to Franz Liszt and his disciples, to the dismay of the conservative musicians in Leipzig.

[28] Arnold Schloenbach and Giesecke wrote for the *Neue Zeitschrift*. Schloenbach's account of the gathering appears in May, i. 145.

[29] Helena Berg was a singer, in whom Dietrich had a romantic interest for a time. Whether *Berthe* can be identified as the like-named housekeeper for the Schumanns at that time cannot be determined.

[30] Probably Joachim's Violin Concerto No. 1, the *Hamlet* overture, and the paraphrases for violin on the name Gisela. See *JJ* i. 115–16.

[31] Hedwig Salomon, daughter of a wealthy banker, much involved in the artistic life of Leipzig, later the wife of the composer H. von Holstein. 'The Seeberg lady' of the next sentence refers to her sister.

Brahms was not exaggerating Hector Berlioz's praise. Berlioz wrote to Joachim from Leipzig: 'Brams [*sic*] is having much success here. He impressed me strongly the other day at Brindel's [*sic*], with his Scherzo and his Adagio. I thank you for having introduced me to this bold, shy youth, who has taken it into his head to write new music. He will suffer much.'[32]

19
Johannes Brahms to Robert Schumann

Hamburg, December 1853

Revered friend!

I take the liberty of sending you herewith your first foster children (who owe their world citizenship to you), very apprehensive as to whether they will still enjoy the same indulgence and affection from you as before.

To me they look much too ordinary and timid in their new form, indeed almost philistine. I still cannot get used to seeing these innocent nature-children in such proper clothing.[33]

I am looking forward enormously to seeing you in Hanover and being able to tell you that my parents and I owe to your and Joachim's immense kindness the most blessed time of our lives.

I was overjoyed to see my parents and teacher again and am having a blissful time in their midst.

Please give to your wife and children my warmest greetings from Your
Johannes Brahms

20
Johannes Brahms to Joseph Joachim

Hamburg, December 1853

Beloved friend,

With your kind letter you gave me great joy, I hardly believed I would get another one.

Do you not have my last one which I wrote to you from Leipzig? In it I wrote my address.

---

[32] Letter of 9 Dec. 1853. *Correspondence générale*, ed. Pierre Citron (Paris, 1983), iv, no. 1664.

[33] Opp. 1 and 3, published by Breitkopf & Härtel in December 1853. He was, of course, referring to the sensation of seeing his works in print for the first time.

I am thinking of coming to Hanover on January 3rd, that's why I'm not sending you the first sonata (C) and the first volume of songs, and also not telling you all the beautiful and new things I have experienced.

We are as blissful as if we were in Heaven, my parents, my teachers, and I.

I hope you spent the holiday as beautifully, as splendidly. I am very curious where you spent the holiday; were you not at the Arnims?

How we longed for you to be here to share our joy.

See you soon,

Your

Johannes

21

Johannes Brahms to Barthold Senff [34]

Hamburg, the 26th December [18]53

Honoured Herr Senff!

Receive herewith the promised 'Sonata' at last. I have washed it quite clean so that it can now allow itself to be seen in public. Would you please excuse that it took so long. I ask you to send the proofs to me in Hanover. I am remaining here until the 3rd of January; should it be possible for them to be here in Hamburg by that day, I would stay here a few days longer for that reason (ditto the honorarium of 10 Friedrichsdor).

I beg you kindly to give the enclosed volume from *Marks* [35] to the Honourable Sir *Wenzel* with best greetings from me.

N.B. I have already sealed the 'Sonata' and do not want to delay any longer; I therefore request that you have the following little verse set at the head of the *first* Andante, in parenthesis and in *small* print. It may be necessary or convenient for comprehension of the Andante:

('Der Abend dämmert, das Mondlicht
    scheint,
Da sind zwei Herzen in Liebe vereint
Und halten sich selig umfangen.')

Sternau [36]

---

[34] Publisher of the Op. 6 songs, as well as the Op. 5 Sonata referred to here.

[35] Quite possibly his own 'Souvenir de la Russie', a set of six fantasies on Russian and gypsy melodies, arranged for four hands, and published some time before 1852 under his pseudonym, G.W. Marks. See McC 689–91.

[36] 'Evening draws nigh, the moonlight gleams, | As two hearts are united in love | And blissfully embrace each other' (Sternau).

N.B. Over the first Andante, there are two in the 'Sonata'. A thousand greetings to *Jahr* and as many thanks for his beautiful present; it pleased me deliciously.

I would like to ask *Jahr* to tell Härtels, when convenient, how long I am remaining here; the other day they asked me to write to tell them, and I have so little time.

With the best greetings,
Your Johs Brahms

PART III

❧❧❧

Turmoil and Apprenticeship
1854–1858

❧ **Introduction** ❧

When Johannes Brahms returned to Hamburg, in December 1853, he came home to a changed city. Doors which had long been closed to him now stood open; Schumann's public pronouncement had done its work. Prominent musicians, who had taken only passing note of his prodigious talent and then allowed him to slide back out of sight 'to create in quiet obscurity', in Schumann's words, were eager now to welcome him into their homes and on their concert programmes. The names Theodor Avé-Lallement, Georg Otten, Carl Grädener, the music publisher August Cranz, and Friedrich Grund, the conservative, ageing, conductor of the Hamburg Philharmonic, appear frequently in Brahms's letters to Joachim and Clara Schumann during the next few years. Robert Schumann's was not the only beneficial influence; Clara's approval undoubtedly played a part, too, for these are the same men who had been her avowed admirers and supporters since the days of her concert appearances in Hamburg 1840, shortly before her marriage to Robert.*

Additional Note p. 747

Theodor Avé-Lallement befriended Brahms almost immediately upon his return to Hamburg. A pianist and a teacher of piano and voice, he had co-founded the Hamburg Philharmonic,[1] on whose Board of Directors he served for decades. He owned a large library of early music which Brahms much admired; among other things, it included many manuscripts by C. P. E. Bach, who had spent the last years of his career as music director for the city of Hamburg, and who lay buried in the crypt of the church where Brahms was baptized. Brahms was allowed free access to Avé's collection, indeed, even invited to keep any duplicates he found. Avé furthered the young composer's interest in early music, at one point presenting him with a valuable eighteenth-century edition of Gluck's opera *Alceste*. Perhaps equally important, he gave the thin young man a warm coat, the likes of which Brahms had never known.[2]

---

[1] Theodor Avé-Lallement, *Rückerinnerungen eines alten Musikanten* (Hamburg, 1878), 13.
[2] *SBB* i. 164, letter of 11 Dec. 1855.

Georg Dietrich Otten was a well-to-do, well-educated musician, an admirer of the Schumann school, energetically involved in Hamburg's musical life. It is likely that he had noticed Brahms earlier on, recommending him as the piano teacher for the son of a friend in 1851.[3] Brahms was soon a frequent guest in his house. In 1857, in an effort to provide Hamburgers with a forum for contemporary music that would contrast with the less adventurous concerts of the Hamburg Philharmonic, Otten founded the Hamburg Musikverein. Through Brahms, he tried and sometimes succeeded in persuading Joachim and Clara Schumann to appear as his soloists,[4] and he extended an invitation to Brahms to perform with his orchestra when Brahms needed a hand in restarting his pianistic career (see Letters 62 and 64, September and October 1855).

Carl Georg Peter Grädener also befriended Brahms upon his return in 1853. Cellist, choral director, composer, piano and theory teacher, he was a close personal friend for the next six years, and a faithful friend to the family for much longer than that. He founded a Bach Institute in Hamburg, and apart from Brahms was the only person in all of Hamburg to subscribe to the Bach Gesellschaft's complete edition of Bach's works. Grädener was a passionate writer on musical topics, and a person of uncompromising ideals. He wrote a powerful defence of Brahms's Piano Concerto No. 1 (Op. 15) after a slighting review of it had appeared in Leipzig's influential journal *Signale*, soon after the première in January 1859.[5]

In spite of the considerable difference in age, Brahms was soon on 'Du' terms with both Grädener and Avé, even giving Grädener advice on how to deal with publishers;[6] and they, along with Otten, were consistently ready to help his career during the next six years.

❧ 1854 ❧

Brahms's immediate future looked as though it would be a continuation of the inspiring Autumn he had just lived through. With the end of the holiday season, he returned to Hanover in January to stay with Joachim and devote himself to composing. He put the finishing touches on his third piano sonata and started on new work. He was in high spirits.

[3] Walter Hübbe, *Brahms in Hamburg* (Hamburg, 1902), 4.
[4] For a concise account of his relationship to Brahms see Kurt Stephenson, *Johannes Brahms und Georg Dietrich Otten* (Hamburg, 1972).
[5] See Kal, i. 280, 351–2.
[6] Letter 88.

22
Johannes Brahms to Barthold Senff

Hanover, 8 January [18]54

Esteemed Herr *Senff*!

Deeply wistful I take up my pen in order to inform you that I am, unfortunately, not in Leipzig, but am trampling the pavements of Hanover.†
Incidentally, i. e. to what is actually the main point, I beg you very humbly to send the proofs of the F minor 'Sonata', once they are ready for it, to me here in Hanover to my own address: Papenstieg 4 in front of the Egidien Gate, Hanover.

Furthermore I am coming—no, I am not coming, but I ask you to be so kind as to send me a photographic print of my photographic portrait, of which several offshoots have already been put out into the world.—

And then I would like to burden you with yet one more request—I hardly dare to express it—if you need not go even one step out of your way for it—etc. etc. etc.—: i.e. if it is possible, could you do me the favour of sending me the *Reimer* caricatures of the Leipzig Gewandhaus Orchestra, that is, they are available at *Blau and Compagny*, printed.

The expense for both things I ask you to subtract from my honorarium which, for the time being, you are holding for me in petto.[7]

† Trampling pavements. Note: that means I, Brahms, lodge protest against Hanoverian pavements: According to my innermost conviction there are no pavements here, but only slush and muck, both of which are so arranged that one gets wet feet 5 times a day.

And finally, pardon me! Greetings to all!!!

Jean de Krösel le jeune.[8]

J. O. Grimm

Secretarius and *Plenipotentiarius* of the *divino Giovanni Brahmino-Kröselino juniore.*

L. S.[9] The *L. S.* is the glowing hot wax into which the Russky impresses his seal as attestation of the soul's harmony—Amen—.

[7] In petto: 'confidentially'. The phrase is Brahms's.
[8] Or Johannes Kreisler Junior. See p. 13.
[9] *In loco sigillis*, 'in place of a seal'.

The mad-cap ending of the letter (from 'Greetings to all') is written by Julius Otto Grimm. Brahms met the Latvian-born music student in November 1853, in Leipzig, where he was studying composition and conducting at the Conservatory. They quickly became fast friends, a relationship which continued virtually untroubled throughout their lives. Grimm held a position in Göttingen for a few years, then settled for the rest of his life as Director of Music for the city of Münster. He too spent a part of 1854 in Hanover and was there, visiting Brahms and Joachim, in time to greet Robert and Clara Schumann as they stopped off for a visit on their way home after a successful trip to Holland. It was the last time Brahms and his new friends would all be together; but unaware of the tragedy about to unfold, Brahms wrote joyfully to Clara after they left, enclosing copies of his freshly printed Opuses 2 and 4, and announcing Op. 5. The Sonata in F sharp minor, Op. 2, was dedicated to her.

23
Brahms to Clara Schumann

Hanover, 10 February 1854

Honoured Lady!

I have just received the enclosed new things from Leipzig, I hasten to send them to you.

I have dared to put your name at the head of the sonata. May you not find this as immodest as I now do, I hardly dare to send it to you.

At the same time as these things I received the proofs of the F minor Sonata from Senff; I expect to see it ready soon.

How desolate and empty Hanover looks now that you have left us. How I long for spring to arrive, which I hope will bring us all together again on the Rhine.

I would hope that you regard the F sharp minor Sonata as benignly and with as much love as the first, and remain favourably disposed towards me in spite of the immodest dedication.

Joachim, Grimm and I say a thousand greetings to you and your husband.

> Your devoted
> Joh. Brahms

The 27th of February 1854 was the most devastating day of Brahms's life: Robert Schumann threw himself into the Rhine in an attempt at suicide. His derangement interrupted a period of enormous creative momentum in the young composer's life.

Since leaving home in April 1853, Brahms had reworked two large piano sonatas and composed a third, reworked songs, a violin sonata, two piano trios, other piano music, and a quartet. In all, he had prepared seven works for publication and was just putting the finishing touches on his Piano Trio in B major, Op. 8, when the thunderbolt struck. Enough momentum was left for him to complete and publish two more works—the *Variations on a Theme by Robert Schumann*, Op. 9, and the Ballades for Piano, Op. 10. But after that there was silence for almost six years.[10] The disruption of his new-found world, whose joys he had tasted for a scant four months, shook him profoundly off track and pushed him in a most unexpected direction: he tried in some measure to take Schumann's place and to do his utmost to keep the Schumann household together, and his own new life intact.

His immediate reaction was to rush from Hanover to Düsseldorf, to Clara Schumann's side. With the support of Grimm, Dietrich, and Joachim, he offered what help he could. There were six small Schumann children to be cared for, Clara was pregnant with the seventh, and arrangements had to be made for Robert's physical safety (he would soon be taken to an asylum in Endenich, on the outskirts of Bonn).

His mother wrote:

> [5 March 1854]
> We received a very sad and distracted letter from you. We are immensely sorry that Schumann is so ill. You did the right thing in travelling there immediately, you owe much to those kind people. The dear Lord will see to it that the good man soon recovers . . . You, poor youngster, are in a very sad position; we are sending you 25 Marks today. Just write to us if you need more . . . We were already looking forward very much to being together on 7 May [Brahms's birthday], but now you have taken all hope away.

The letters from home changed their tune as Brahms remained in Düsseldorf throughout the spring and summer and his parents worried that he had no money and no prospects of earning any.

From his mother on 15 June:

> As to what concerns you, dear Johannes, things must get better soon. You cannot be in debt, that won't do. Herr Marxsen . . . has expressed his views on this at length and very seriously [. . . Even though] Schumann had paved the way for you so nicely, you would still have had to do more. You cannot live just by composing, even the greatest masters could not do that. You too, we hope, would have undertaken something if Schumann had not become ill. For the moment, you have done right to go there. But to stay

---

[10] Although published in February 1856, the Ballades were written in the summer of 1854. And although Brahms never stopped composing, his next publication did not appear until 1860.

there? That way you loose much time and money . . . Whether you pay
attention to it or not, only the person who has money is respected . . . then
is he free and independent, has no need to bow to anyone, can clothe himself according to his station. The artist is dependent entirely on the great
and wealthy, art is luxury. The working class can do without it, must do
without it. So the artist must seek friends among the rich. Oh, one doesn't
get through the world so easily and proudly, one has to put up with a lot
and bow and scrape . . . Do write us your correct address.[11]

But Brahms could not leave. Even apart from the debatable question of romance,
there is no doubt that in the Schumanns' cultured and artistic home, where high literature and art were a normal part of everyday life, the youth had found an atmosphere sorely missing from his previous life. Despite outward appearances, and the
worry felt by family and friends, the time spent in Düsseldorf contributed to an
extremely fruitful period of his life.

This is the time during which Brahms undertook to teach himself a great deal
more about counterpoint than he already knew, by means of a correspondence with
Joachim. Equally important, it is during this period that Brahms found the opportunity to make detailed studies of early music. He championed Scarlatti and made
copies of music by Palestrina, Handel, and Schütz. His interest was sharpened by circumstance: after Schumann's breakdown, Brahms was asked by Clara to reorganize
the Master's library in preparation for her move to Berlin. Now he had a chance to
study and copy the early music he found there. Moreover, the libraries of Otten, Avé,
and then of the Duchy of Detmold, were open to him.

Brahms became known as something of an authority. His début as musicologist
and editor occurred in 1859, during this period of apparent silence following
Schumann's breakdown, but his interest in early music remained for life. Philipp
Spitta and Gustav Nottebohm, two of the century's greatest musicologists and music
historians, became his friends in the next decade, and he himself was occasionally
consulted on matters of musical authentication. In the course of his life he served on
the editorial board of a number of publishing ventures concerned with bringing out
complete editions, and he participated in editing the complete works of G. F.
Handel, Chopin, Mozart, Schumann, Schubert, and the keyboard music of François
Couperin (with the musicologist Friedrich Chrysander). When Nottebohm died,
Breitkopf & Härtel even suggested that Brahms might replace him as editor-in-chief
of the revised Complete Bach Edition, an offer he turned down.[12]

For three of these 'silent' years he held a part-time appointment as piano
teacher to several members of the royal family at the Court of Detmold, a tiny Duchy
in northern Germany. His duties there also included conducting the court choir, and

---

[11] *Familie*, 56.
[12] Breitkopf & Härtel to Brahms, 7 Nov. 1882 (*BW* xiv. 342–3). See Letter 421.

performing at the piano. The pay was sufficient to leave him free the rest of the year to follow his other interests.

This is also the period during which Brahms founded and directed his Hamburg Ladies' Choir, a group which gave him great pleasure and provided the impetus for innumerable folk-song arrangements, many of which were published later.

If Brahms did not publish in the years between 1856 and 1860, he was nevertheless composing. Much of his effort went into the writing of his First Piano Concerto (Op. 15), which started life as a sonata for two pianos and underwent many agonizing revisions, lost to us now except through his correspondence with his friends to whom he showed the various versions. But the Piano Concerto by no means used up all his creative energy—this apparent dry spell was, in fact, extraordinarily productive. The two orchestral Serenades, Op. 11 and 16, the stark *Begräbnisgesang*, Op. 13, the String Sextet, Op. 18, his first published collection of folk-song arrangements (*Volks-Kinderlieder*, WoO 31), two movements of the Third Piano Quartet, Op. 60, both sets of Piano Variations in Op. 21, over a dozen songs, and the first movement of the First Symphony are just some of the many works conceived, sketched, or finished during this formative period of his life.[13]

In one other way these years set the tone of the rest of his life; this was the period of the only passionate, romantic involvements of his life, and both of them were unfulfilled. The first was with Clara Schumann—or perhaps it is more correct to say, *directed at* Clara Schumann, for there is no unambiguous evidence to tell us what she felt in return.

The second was with Agathe von Siebold, the 23-year-old daughter of a university professor at Göttingen and a voice student of Julius Otto Grimm, who was by then directing a women's choir and teaching music in Göttingen. Brahms and Agathe met in the summer of 1858, while Brahms was visiting Grimm and his bride. His passionate attachment to Clara was then over, but not his deep devotion. His romance with Agathe, who fell deeply in love with him, was conducted in part under the jealous eye of Clara. It led to a clandestine betrothal and exchange of rings, but ended abruptly in January 1859, when Brahms's friends, Grimm, in particular, pressured him for the sake of Agathe's honour to make his intentions public—this in the very same month that his First Piano Concerto, finished at last, was hissed from the Gewandhaus in Leipzig. The pain of the concerto's failure, Brahms's firm determination at that time not to be bound to a full-time position,[14] and Clara's highstrung behaviour, conspired to keep him from committing himself. Indeed, Clara's actions reveal a very confused state of mind. She had packed her bags and children and hurried away from Göttingen after seeing Brahms put his arm around Agathe

---

[13] A thorough listing appears in Renate and Kurt Hofmann, *Johannes Brahms Zeittafel zu Leben und Werk* (Tutzing, 1983), 23–45.

[14] Letters 107, 108 in this volume.

one afternoon—and later that autumn, she wrote to a friend that she had had a most dreadful summer holiday, although she gave no details; but in later years she was to say that if only he had married Agathe, Brahms would have been as marvellous a man as he was a composer. For many years after, Brahms would comment to one friend or other that he would like to marry,[15] and for the rest of his life he had more or less important flirtations; but he never again came so close to taking a wife.

It is tempting and probably not wrong to think that one may learn something about the young Johannes Brahms by forming a more complete acquaintance with *Johannes Kreisler*, the fictional Kapellmeister with whom Brahms felt such affinity.[16] Hoffmann's memorable character is an idealistic, romantic youth, who recognizes 'that yearning derived from a higher life [which] endures forever because it is never fulfilled'. He is woundingly sarcastic, ironic of tone, exceedingly reluctant to talk about personal matters or of his youth. He is the victim of overpowering restlessness when beset, as happens at the most unexpected moments, by thoughts of the barrenness and vanity of life. He says, 'There is only one angel of light that has power over this evil demon. It is the spirit of music, which often lifts me victoriously out of myself and before whose mighty voice all the sorrows of mortal afflictions are silent.' Indeed, music is for him the loftiest possible pursuit, but its practice is a source of anguish, since it brings him constantly into contact with Philistines who have only a shallow and frivolous understanding of his sublime art.[17]

Although Brahms was thoroughly familiar with *Kreisler's* ideals even in his teens, Kapellmeister Kreisler and E. T. A. Hoffmann remained literary favourites throughout his life; and as that life went on, as he encountered the benign influence of the Schumann home and then the sympathy and interest of Clara Schumann (analagous to the *Rätin* Benson in Hoffmann's novel, an appealing and sympathetic widow in her mid-thirties);[18] as he accepted a position as court musician in Detmold, a Duchy almost as tiny as the fictional Sieghartsweiler which Kapellmeister Kreisler inhabits; as he imagined himself in love with Julie Schumann and was distressed at her marriage to Count Radicati (the Rätin has a lovely, young, and musical daughter Julia, who is quite partial to Kreisler but who prepares to marry a nobleman), there must have been many moments when the relationship between himself and Hoffmann's hero seemed uncanny.

The best available portrait of Brahms, in the period immediately following Schumann's breakdown, comes from a letter Julius Otto Grimm wrote to Joachim soon after Grimm and Brahms had arrived in Düsseldorf to offer aid to Clara. Tragedy or no, the high spirits of two talented young men burst out in many directions. There are several references to Brahms as his *alter ego Johannes Kreisler*

---

[15] See e.g. Albert Dietrich, *Erinnerungen an Johannes Brahms*, (Leipzig, 1898), 39.

[16] See Letter 3 and commentary.

[17] *Lebensansichten des Katers Murr*, 83. In English trans. *The Life and Opinions of Kater Murr*. See esp. 62–4.

[18] *Rätin* is the title of a court councillor's wife.

(*Phantasiestücke in Callots Manier* is the name of one of E. T. A. Hoffmann's collections of short stories in which Kreisler appears), and he is affectionately referred to by yet another pet name, 'Krössel'. It is clear that his concentration, energy, and creative ability were still in high gear.

24
Julius Otto Grimm to Joseph Joachim

Düsseldorf, [9] April [1854][19]

Dear Joachim!

Would you believe that I am almost ashamed to appear before your eyes with this epistle?—On the other hand it isn't surprising that I blush, as I set off to thank you for your kind words after a lapse of almost a month, for I really don't understand how it happened,—have actually started to write you several times, but could never get past the beginning, and can nevertheless provide no excuse.—

Nor can I report any cheering news about what is closest to our hearts,— to begin with, immediately after receiving your letter I went to Dr Hasenclever, but failed decisively to interest him in your magnetism suggestion.[20] The news from Endenich was and is not encouraging—always the same—Schumann is calmer than at first,—except for a few weaker attacks which occur from time to time; Frau Schumann is as crushed as in the beginning;—often, when she speaks of him, or after playing some of his things, she breaks into sobs. The only good thing is that she is now not importuned as frequently by personal or written expressions of sympathy.

---

[19] The printed date in *BW* v (9 Mar. 1854) must be wrong. Schumann attempted suicide on 27 February; he was taken to Endenich on 4 March. Grimm had been in Hanover before rushing to Düsseldorf; the printed date allows for no month to have elapsed in answering a letter. Moreover, Clara could not have received all those consolation calls in five days, nor could Brahms have found and decorated an apartment in such a short time, to say nothing of composing three movements of the eventual Op. 15. And not even Brahms would enjoy lying in the moonlight on a hill along the Rhine in early March. Further confirmation is in Joachim's correspondence: Brahms to Joachim, 1 April: 'A few days ago we went to Cologne for Beeth 9th', and Julius Grimm to Joachim: 'Last week we heard 9th in Cologne'. Clara's diary states expressly that Grimm and Brahms went to Cologne on 28 March to hear the Ninth Symphony (Litz, ii. 310). And Brahms's 'second letter' about his sister carries the date 7 April.

[20] As a treatment for Schumann's illness. Hasenclever was not only the Schumanns' family doctor, he was their friend and an enthusiastic music lover, eventually serving as director of music in Koblenz. The German Romantic movement was deeply attracted to Anton Mesmer and other occult and pseudo-scientific practices; Wasielewsky describes with dismay his visit to Robert Schumann in the autumn of 1853 during which the composer displayed intense interest in 'table-tipping'. *Life of Robert Schumann* (Boston, 1871; repr. Detroit, 1975), 181–2.

We, i. e. Kreisler and I, have spent many wonderful hours with her; she shared many manuscripts with us, among them the most divine: *Faust*—she at the piano, playing from the piano score, we following the full score with eye, ear, and soul.—All three of us have longed for you often and strenuously and do so still, and beg you to appear soon. Your plan to remain in Hanover has our most decided disapproval—*O do come, and soon!*———

My dear cousin has informed me faithfully about you and all the music you have made and made known (Berlioz, Wehner, etc.)—and it is very kind of you not to desert the *Hanoverian thirsting-for-refinement*.[21]

The third chapter of this letter might well be taken up by Kreisler. He has commissioned me to ask you, in case you couldn't decipher either of his letters, to send them back so that he can copy them or have them neatly transcribed, in order to convey them to you once more;—for the content is important to him,—especially that of the second letter,—regarding his sister and her coming here.—I assume that the hieroglyphics are not as terrible as my cousin wrote; but Brahms has grown anxious because he has not yet had an answer from you. Br[ahms]—Kr[eisler]—is here just now and says he wants to render his smearacles into common written speech. Through illegibility, smearacles can often become miracles, which they otherwise are not.[22]—Last week the two of us were along the Rhine, i. e. in Cologne, Bonn, Mehlem, Drachenfels, etc. etc., drank Rhine wine and were altogether . . . I only wish you would come, and we could duplicate such a Scherzo as a Trio, in fact bigger and better.—Kreisler is the most wondrously magnificent man. No sooner has he delighted us with his Trio, than he has already finished three movements of a sonata for two pianos,[23] which seem to me even more heavenly. Apropos! He asks you to send him, as soon as possible, his arrangement of your Hamlet Overture;[24] he wants to look it through, change it where necessary, and mainly, to play it with Frau Schumann.

Oh God, I'm scribbling so dreadfully that you can hardly—but Krössel is pestering me and wants to go up the Grafenberg, where we want to lie in the woods by the light of the moon. He is chock-full of crazy notions—as the Artist-Genius of Düsseldorf, he has painted his apartment full of the most beautiful frescoes in the manner of Callot, i.e. all kinds of grotesque visages

[21] Grimm's cousin Wagemann is mentioned in several letters of this period. Apparently not much went on in the city of Hanover; Joachim's next letter to Brahms refers to it as 'the Capital of Boredom'.

[22] 'Schmirakel' in the original. Here Grimm uses this schoolboy term, derived from 'schmieren', to *scrawl*. It rhymes, of course, with *Mirakel*.

[23] Grimm uses the word *Flügel* rather than *Klavier* or *Pianoforte*, i.e. a grand piano.

[24] Joachim's Op. 4, for orchestra. Brahms's arrangement for piano duet was never published.

and Madonna faces—so that he may have worthy thoughts while doing his daily business.[25] But now, fare well. More and better next time. Your

J. Grimm.

Only do come soon—Chatting is better than writing.—Kreisler sends greetings. Of necessity you will have to play Brahms's Trio. Frau Schumann is yearning to make music with you.

But Joachim was not able to come for an extended visit just then. He was in the midst of his own personal crisis, something which seems never to have occurred either to Brahms or to Clara.

25
Johannes Brahms to Joseph Joachim

Düsseldorf, 1 April 1854

Dearest Gegenwärtler,

What confusing letters you write, without rhyme or reason—'to stay in Hanover for the summer, and come here for 2 weeks'—just what does this all mean?

Every day Frau Schumann asks if you haven't written something more definite about your coming, and we can't possibly repeat such—empty phrases—to her, since she is expecting you with such certainty and longing at the beginning of April—and secretly, as we all are, for the whole summer. Your letters could make us nervous if we didn't see from the address how you like to tease.

If you come soon, you'll probably see W. Bargiel here; his mother promised to send him shortly.[26]

I beg you, come soon and for a long time; I don't want to think that you considered what you wrote in your letters.

I was quite unprepared for what you write about the reception of your overture.[27] I had dreamed of terrific acclaim, curtain calls, and in short order, the journey (of the overture) throughout Germany.

[25] The scatalogical implications are the same in German and English. Jacques Callot was a French engraver and etcher of the 17th c. who specialized in the painting of grotesques—creatures created from man and beast. To take figures from ordinary life and transform them in the glow of one's inner understanding, 'as if in weird and wonderful apparel' (E. T. A. Hoffmann) was to work 'in the manner of Callot'.

[26] Woldemar Bargiel, Clara Schumann's half-brother.

[27] The overture was performed in Leipzig in March 1854, with Joachim conducting the Gewandhaus Orchestra. It received an ice-cold reception by the public. See Andreas Moser, *Joseph Joachim* (Berlin, 1898), 137.

One must not aspire to higher, purer feelings than those of the public—you can see from *me* how one may gain applause merely by dreaming its dreams and setting them to music.

Lonely soars the eagle, but crows gather in flocks; God grant that my wings grow mightily, and that I may yet one day belong to the other species.[28]

A few days ago the 9th Symphony was given in a concert in Cologne. I went there with Grimm, and heard it for the first time.

They say the achievement, especially of the choir, was outstanding (this according to several ear-witnesses—I have no opinion about it).

The following day we travelled to Bonn and went with Wasielewski and Reimers to Endenich, to the house where Schumann is now staying.

He is still very calm, gets upset only rarely and mildly, and sleeps a lot even during the day, which pleases the doctor because otherwise he would *be made* to sleep. He has lucid moments, in which he relates which mountains he's been on, and that he picked flowers in Düsseldorf, and which he would like; (he did recently pick some for himself). If he is thinking of such things, it is quite impossible that he would not also think of his wife. But then, didn't he always keep most of his thoughts to himself?

Grimm and I also went to the Godesberg and Drachenfels, the Mehlem Meadowlands, and Königswinter in the most beautiful spring weather.[29]

I've been reading about the most amazing experiments, and have also tried some of them with Reimers and Grimm. We saw such incomprehensible things that we blanched.

People were made to move according to the will of others, pencils writing down our most secret thoughts, and more such. I'm most eager to know what impression such magical matters make on you.[30]

Reimers is here now; I suppose we will have to play my Trio once more for Frau Schumann. I still want to change a few things in it, but I won't send it to you until you first write us more precisely and definitely about your coming. Do excuse my bad handwriting but it is late and my thoughts are too restless. Repenting sufficiently for the 'Kälbermarkt', are you? In any event, I can do no better than this.[31]

---

[28] This is an exact quote of entry no. 393 in Brahms's *Schatzkästlein des Jungen Kreislers*: 'Der Aar steigt einsam, doch das Volk der Krähen schart sich.' The *Schatzkästlein* was a handwritten collection of the young Brahms's favourite aphorisms and writings gathered from his voluminous readings.

[29] Castles, town, and surroundings of a noted resort area on the Rhine, near Bonn.

[30] See Letter 24, n. 20.

[31] An obscure reference. German towns frequently have squares with names such as the 'Calves Market'. Presumably this remark refers to a place where Brahms and Joachim shared an adventure.

Do write again very soon—you give us such great pleasure with your letters.

Your
Johannes

Very many greetings, of course, from everyone!

The appellation 'Gegenwärtler', 'Man of the Present', indicated the distance he and Joachim placed between themselves and the 'Musicians of the Future', as Franz Liszt called himself and his followers. Nevertheless, Liszt still looked upon Joachim with great affection, and with his circle of composers in Weimar continued to take a friendly interest in Brahms's progress.[32]

On 11 June 1854, Clara Schumann gave birth to her eighth and last child, Felix. A few days later, Brahms sent her a manuscript of his *Variations on a Theme by Schumann*, entitling them *Little Variations on a Theme by Him Dedicated to Her*. Clara thanked him, in the only one of her letters to him from this period which has survived. The work became his *Variations on a Theme by Schumann*, Op. 9.

26

Clara Schumann to Johannes Brahms

Sunday, 18 June 1854

Dear, esteemed Herr Brahms,

You have given me deep joy with your tender attention. What I felt when I read your dedication I cannot say, yet you knew it already, inasmuch as you wrote it, and so accept my written thanks, the sincerest, which I hope to give you soon in person. I read through the Variations, but reading music affects my head so greatly, nowadays, that I couldn't get to know them as thoroughly as I would have wished; but I hope to hear them very soon, played by you. Genuine Brahms they are, serious and humorous, that I know. On Tuesday I expect to get out of bed and if you were to visit me in the afternoon around 4, you would make me very happy.

The news of my beloved Robert was tolerable today, he has been calm, aside from a small insignificant disturbance. Oh, how all this is so very little for a loving heart that so longs to hope!—Very hard are the days that I now live through! when I look at the dear little one, and think of the dear father who is suffering far from all who love him, and who is not even aware of his

---

[32] See the letters from Liszt to Joachim, 23 Mar. 1854, in *JJ* i. 178–9, and Joachim to Brahms, *BW* v, 21 May 1854.

existence, then I feel as though my heart would break from sorrow and pain. But I distress you, and that is not what I wanted—so accept the friendliest morning greeting from

your

Clara Schumann

27

Johannes Brahms to Joseph Joachim

Düsseldorf, 19 June 1854

Most beloved friend,

Surely you have taken my long silence throughly amiss? You yourself are at fault. In your last letter from Hanover, it says you would write us more details about Liszt's arrival there; that letter I first wanted to steal from you and then of course to copy it. (Money!) Later Herr Preußer told us about L[iszt] and Herr Wagemann, about your departure, etc. etc.[33]

Since I can't write you anything new about the Schumanns now, I will keep almost silent about it and say only that I am seeing Frau Schumann tomorrow (Tuesday) since she will already be up and about, and—that she has decided upon the base plan of taking Julchen to Berlin, after a complete recovery (about six weeks) and of visiting with you for two weeks. I begrudge you that, I really do![34]

I want to tell you a little more about the precious patient, at the risk of repeating old news.

Herr Schumann once asked the doctor if it were not Dr Hasenclever and two other people who had brought him to Bonn; another time, whether any-one had sent him collars from D[üsseldorf], otherwise would the doctor now write for them, he now wishes to wear them. (He hasn't ever thought about this for a quarter of a year.)

Once he also asked in which direction Godesberg lay, and said that he had spent a summer there!

Are those not marvellous signs of a returning memory?

Now I still have to go on quite a lot about myself to you. My Trio and a

---

[33] The Preussers were part of the Schumann circle in Leipzig (Schumann dedicated the *Waldszenen* to the daughter of the house). The rest of this somewhat enigmatic paragraph refers, in part, to the previous letter from Joachim, which contains the suggestion that he and Brahms give a few concerts, possibly in Hamburg, in order to resupply Brahms with money. 'Why else would we have learned to play our instruments passably well?' (Joachim to Brahms, 21 May 1854).

[34] Julie, the Schumann's third daughter. Clara brought the sickly child to her own mother, who lived in Berlin.

volume of songs are being published by Härtel (12 and 8 L[ouis] d'or). Since I had to pay Grimm over 20 thalers, I would quite like to let you wait a little longer (if you can!), so that I'm not immediately without money again.

I would like to publish the enclosed things and therefore beg you as urgently as I can to look them through and write me your *most candid* opinion of them. I have so many doubts about their worth or lack thereof that I could come to no decision without knowing your definite verdict.

I would mainly like to ask you to write me a definite *Yes* or *No*, or *your misgivings*, for each piece and for each variation. I thought of publishing the things with the following title:

Leaves from the Diary of a Musician
Published by the Young Kreisler

1st Volume: Four Pieces for Pianoforte (Minuet or ? in A flat minor, Scherzino or ? in B minor, Piece in D minor, and *In Memory of M. B.* in B minor.[35]

2nd Volume. Variations, etc.

What do you think of it? The things should bear the anonymous title not so as to license them to be worse than my earlier ones, but for the sake of the joke and because they are occasional pieces.[36]

I am also unclear about the sequence of pieces and the individual titles in the first volume. Might the Variations be all too small and insignificant? Actually one doesn't need more such childish stuff. I wish I could give my D minor Sonata a long rest. I have often played the first three movements with Frau Schumann. (Improved.) Actually, not even two pianos are sufficient for me. I would also have liked to hold back the Trio, since I would certainly have made changes in it later.

I am in such a confused and indecisive mood that I can [not] ask you urgently enough for a really definite reply. Don't avoid an adverse one, for it can only be useful to me.

In conclusion:

[35] Mendelssohn-Bartholdy.

[36] Throughout his life Brahms declined invitations to write occasional pieces, music composed for a particular occasion. He made only two exceptions—a wedding cantata written somewhat reluctantly at the behest of his Swiss friend, the poet Gottfried Keller (published posthumously, WoO 16), and the perfectly delightful *Tafellied, Dank der Damen*, Op. 93*b*, which he composed as a gift for his friends in the Krefeld Singing Society on the occasion of their Jubilee. In thinking about his Op. 9, Brahms may have considered the Variations to be in that category because he wrote them specifically with Robert and Clara Schumann in mind. In fact, Brahms never published the other pieces mentioned in the letter, although the 'etc.' may refer to the two Sarabandes published posthumously (WoO 5).

Commend me as best you can to Frau and Fräulein von Arnim, also to the Herren Grimm[37] and Bargiel, whom I long for.

Wouldn't you all prefer to come here, instead of robbing us of Frau Schumann.

(((I believe I admire and honour her no more highly than I love and am in love with her. I often have to restrain myself forcibly just from quietly embracing her and even—: I don't know, it seems to me so natural, as though she could not take it at all amiss.

I think I can't love a young girl at all any more, at least I have entirely forgotten them; after all, they merely promise the Heaven which Clara shows us unlocked.)))[38]

I don't in the least want to make apologies for my request, although it is very considerable and probably also disagreeable; if you possibly can, do indulge me in this.

Fare you very well and keep me in your affection, as I very much do you.

Your

Johannes

Many thanks for your Opus 5![39]

By now, Brahms's preoccupation with the Schumann family and his attachment to Clara had become the most powerful force in his life, developing into a passion that was at times an obsession. Any hint of improvement in Robert's condition was seen in the most optimistic light, cause for intense rejoicing. When Schumann picked a bouquet of flowers 'you know for whom', as he said to his nurse-attendant, Brahms relayed the news to Clara as though Schumann's recovery were well under way.

His creative work still centred on the two-piano sonata which, by the time of his letter of 27 July to Joachim, had been transformed into the beginnings of a symphony.

---

[37] Hermann Grimm, no relation to Julius Otto Grimm, but Joachim's successful rival for the hand of Gisela von Arnim.

[38] The portion between triple parentheses (Brahms's marking) is deleted from *BW* v, and is restored here from the autograph.

[39] *Three Pieces for Violin and Piano*, dedicated to Gisela von Arnim. They were in the keys of Gis (G sharp), E, and La (A).

28
Johannes Brahms to Joseph Joachim

Düsseldorf, 27 July 1854

Dear friend,

I am very grateful to Frau Schumann for leaving it to me to convey to you the latest, joyous news from Endenich.

Yesterday evening Fräulein Hartmann returned from Bonn. At the ship [landing], where all of us, including Frau Schumann, awaited her, she presented Frau Schumann with a bouquet of flowers from her husband.[40]

This time, encouraged by Fräulein Reumont,[41] he had consciously chosen some preciously wonderful roses and carnations; (the last time he didn't know whom he was picking them for). Fräulein Reumont again asked him, where to and to whom: Oh, of course you know that! was his answer. So he had not forgotten the last consignment.

You know, he asked recently whom the flowers in his room came from. He was told, and will always be told unless he asks explicitly whether they came from his wife, that they came from Fräulein Reumont.

Fräulein Hartmann saw him taking a walk in the garden. (All in all she is to be envied for many things!) He was led to Fräulein Reumont's window by the doctor with whom Herr Schumann was talking; Fräulein Hartmann was standing behind a curtain. Fräulein Reumont addressed him and bid him pick flowers. He looked very well, better than Fräulein Hartmann had ever seen him. His gait was firm and rather quick, the flower-beds he inspected through his lorgnette, he spoke and greeted in a friendly way.

As he walked he waved his handkerchief back and forth as he always did when in a cheerful mood.

Fräulein Hartmann would have liked very much to open her dear mouth and chat a bit, which is how I would have felt.

Do share this with W. Bargiel, his mother, etc. Frau Schumann will not write about this since I'm doing so. Frau Schumann left all of you sooner than you expected, but naturally it was good; after the beautiful letter from Endenich I was expecting her daily.

We stayed longer than usual with her that evening.

The following morning, when I was with her, she was dancing around the room for joy. I have never before seen her so cheerful, happy, and calm.

---

[40] Matilde Hartmann, a singer from the Schumann circle in Düsseldorf. She was one of several godparents to the new-born Felix Schumann.
[41] An attendant at Endenich.

She told me about your new viola pieces; can't you send them some time?[42] How happy you would make us all, and me epecially; anyhow, you write nothing at all about your work! Your *Heinrich Overture* is finished, but I've known that for a long time; what else have you got under your pen? I ask you to please write explicitly about it some time.

How goes it with the glorification of the nation I'm descended from?[43]

Naturally I would keep your letter to myself.

Concerning my score, you have probably thought to yourself, and I have also entreated Frau Schumann to tell you that whatever good can be found in it I owe to *Grimm*, who stands by me with the best of advice. The shortcomings and defects, which probably are not too well hidden, were either overlooked by Grimm, or remain because of my stubbornness.[44]

I also want to tell you that originally I mainly wanted only the low D to be heard, and therefore have the F–B flat so weak in the clarinet and bassoon. Actually I was always pleased that everything is so compressed and short, don't know however, whether it is right, especially for orchestra? At the ending, it sometimes seems to me that it just ends, and sometimes, that the coda should only now begin!

Can you encourage me to the other movements? I seem brashly impertinent to myself.

From the heart your

Johannes.

Many greetings to Bargiel, Grimm, von Arnims!!

Clara, accompanied by three women friends, went to Ostend for a rest cure in August. Brahms, at her suggestion, went to the Black Forest. He intended to make a walking tour with his friend Julius Otto Grimm, made his way to Heidelberg, and got as far as Ulm. But overcome with restlessness and longing, he soon returned to Düsseldorf to await Clara's return.[45]

---

[42] *Hebrew Melodies*, Op. 9, and *Variations on an Original Theme*, Op. 10, for viola and piano.

[43] Possibly a reference to Joachim's letter of 27 June, in which he enthusiastically likened the Op. 9 Variations to Beethoven.

[44] The eventual Op. 15, which at this time was cast as a symphony. Brahms was in the habit of showing his orchestrations to Grimm, who, with his conservatory training, was better schooled in orchestration.

[45] Grimm described the situation in a letter to their mutual friend Albert Dietrich. 'A homesickness beyond my comprehension obliged him to turn back, in Ulm, although he had wanted to go to the Alps . . .' Albert Dietrich, *Erinnerungen an Johannes Brahms* (Leipzig, 1898), 21.

29
Johannes Brahms to Clara Schumann

Esslingen, 15 August 1854

Esteemed Lady,

On this whole trip, so far, I have not been as completely and happily carefree as one ought to be on a walking tour, and as I usually am.

At any moment I could turn back and would not be tempted again to leave Düsseldorf this summer.

Being together and making music with you in such an alive and inspiring way, hearing news of your beloved husband, ah, how can I dispense with that even for a short time; one ought not roam when one is as firmly attached to a place as I now am to Düsseldorf.

I want to tell you about my trip: I arrived in Heidelberg late on Saturday; about the magnificent castle ruins I would rather have a really long talk with you.

I searched for the house where your husband lived as a student. Because of Sunday observances the shops were closed, so I had to be content with guesses.

By noon I was already gone from Heidelberg, so as to be out into the world as soon as possible and lose my sense of longing.

I went on foot along the Neckar as far as Heilbronn and saw much that is wonderful, for instance the Schwalbennest, Hornberg, etc. I also had the finest weather until today, when it rained hard.

In Heilbronn I had to surmount great conflicts; I wanted to get to Ulm and beyond quickly, and wanted to turn back.

I often quarrel with myself, that is, Kreisler and Brahms quarrel with one another.

But usually each has his decided opinion and fights it out. This time, however, both were quite confused, neither knew what he wanted, it was most comical to observe it. Anyway, tears almost came to my eyes.

Now I've moved on, all the way to Esslingen by railway, and write to you while some bit of Eichendorff is let loose: dark midnight, slumbering fountains murmuring, confused voices, and deep melancholy of the heart.[46]

---

[46] Joseph, Freiherr von Eichendorff (1788–1857), one of the great Romantic poets and novelist, much read by Brahms as a youth. His nature poems were so widely known that they became part of the German folk culture. His works provided the text for many songs by Schumann and Mendelssohn, including the entire *Liederkreis*, Op. 39, of Schumann.

Often I have to put down my pen because I'm overwhelmed by the thought: I could simply turn back and let the forests and castles be where they are!

For your sake, however, I hope that I will see you again in 3 weeks and no sooner; I have heard many bad things about too short a stay at the seaside, I very much hope that your friends keep you firmly there for at least 3 weeks.

I also want to tell you that Herr Grimm is travelling with me; after I explained to him the state of our *joint* monetary resources and the approximate costs of the trip he came to a decision quickly. He is first paying a visit in Schlangenbad — to very dear friends, then he'll catch up with me.[47]

I will only be able to take care of this letter in Ulm, since the train leaves very early.

I am greatly looking forward to your letter.

After the 20th I expect to be back in Heidelberg. If you could write to me there (General Delivery) approximately when you would be back in Düsseldorf?

I suppose I am very immodest, but perhaps there is something really important to write, perhaps I won't find a letter in Ulm?

Please greet the Fräuleins Reichmann, Leser, and Jungé very sincerely for me, and be very, very well yourself.

(For the 12th, 13th and 14th I sent you 1000 greetings.)[48]

> your
> Johannes Brahms

30
Johannes Brahms to Clara Schumann

Ulm, 16 August 1854

Esteemed Lady,

I can't stand it any longer, I'm turning back today.

I arrived here this morning, I wanted to wait till 9 o'clock in the evening for a letter from you, then travel to Tübingen, but it just doesn't work out.

---

[47] They never did rendezvous.

[48] 12 August was Clara's name-day, 13 August the name day of Aurora. Robert and Clara Schumann celebrated 14 August, St Eusebius Day, as the anniversary of their betrothal. And in a letter written by 'Eusebius' to 'Chiara' (or Robert S. to Clara Wieck), one can find the following passage: 'Don't forget to look occasionally at the calendar on August 13, where an Aurora has bound your name to mine.' *Gesammelte Schriften über Musik und Musiker von Robert Schumann*, ed. F. Gustav Jansen, 4th edn. (Leipzig, 1891), i. 162.

The last post came at 4 o'clock, I left my Düsseldorf address and am going back. I wouldn't have cheered up during the entire trip; the names Tübingen, Lichtenstein, Schaffhausen, which otherwise would have filled me with shivers of delight, leave me cold, so colourless and dry does everything seem to me.

I am going to go home and make music and read alone, until you arrive and I can do it with you.

If you want to make me most happy, then let me find a letter in Düsseldorf, but do stay in Ostende, at least 3 weeks!

Perhaps Grimm was also unable to get further than Schlangenbad, and I will find him in Düsseldorf.

I will be better able to look over your friend's splendid homeland some other time, when I can more calmly be far from you and your dear husband.

If the great longing which I have felt in these days has an effect on my playing, etc., I really ought soon to be able to work magic with it.

Fräulein Leser is in Ostende, isn't she? I am quite certain, and hope that this will make your stay in Ostende much more agreeable![49]

Be well and come back to Düsseldorf healthy and as cheerful as you can be.

Your
Johannes Brahms

Please greet Frl. Reichman, Leser, and Jungé heartily.

I am writing in the waiting-room of the railway station, may this excuse a little my hasty, confused writing.

A thousand greetings!

Brahms wrote another letter in that same station, to his kindly benefactor from the village of Winsen-an-der-Luhe. The Amtsvogt must have cut an understanding figure, for the youth makes no attempt to hide his powerful devotion to Clara.

---

[49] Clara's neighbour in Düsseldorf. She was an important friend and support for many years, and is referred to frequently. As she was blind, her companion and aide was a Frl. Jungé. Henriette Reichmann was a travelling companion and friend.

31
Johannes Brahms to Amtsvogt [Bailiff] Blume

Ulm, 16 August 1854
answered 3 September 1854[50]

Esteemed Sir,

You must surely think that your treasured letter didn't give me the slightest pleasure, since I let you wait so long for a reply? Alas, it has been so unsettled recently that I was obliged to postpone it day after day. On the 10th Frau Schumann went to Ostende with a friend, on account of her health, and after much coaxing I decided to take a trip through Swabia during that time.

I didn't know how powerful my attachment to the Schumanns was, how I lived through them. Everything seemed desolate and empty to me, each day I wanted to turn back and had to travel by rail in order very quickly to get really far away and forget about turning back. It was no use, I got as far as Ulm, partly on foot, partly by rail, I'm turning back promptly and would rather await Frau Schu. in Düsseldorf than wander about in such darkness.

When one has found human beings as divinely beautiful as Rob. and Cl. Sch., one ought cling to them and not desert them, ought to be edified and inspired by them.

As to dear Sch. he is doing better all the time, as you have gathered from my letters to my parents. One could chatter on about his condition.

I find him[51] described best in several works of E. T. A. Hoffmann (Rath Krespel, Serapion, or even the magnificent Kreisler, etc.). Unfortunately, he took leave of his body too soon.

If you want to give me great pleasure, you'll have a letter waiting for me in Düsseldorf, is that much too immodest?

I will also write to you from there and, in fact, more sensibly; I am writing this letter in the waiting-room of the railway station which is why it has probably become very confused.

A thousand warm greetings to your dear Uncle Giesemann, I'll write to him, too, from Dsf; warmest greetings also to your wife and daughter.

Retain your affection for

your

Johannes Brahms.

On the way back to Düsseldorf, Brahms stopped off in Endenich.

---

[50] In a different hand.

[51] Or 'I find it', referring to Schumann's condition. The German language is ambiguous here. It is presumably Hoffmann who took leave of his body too soon?

32
Johannes Brahms to Clara Schumann

Düsseldorf, 21 August 1854

Revered Lady,

Two treasured letters I have received from you, a thousand thanks for them; through your letters you can make me forget for a little while that you are far away.

Words flow from my pen so laboriously that even my conversation may be more interesting. I would gladly write to you just in music, but what I have to write today, music cannot say.

I almost shrink from writing to you that I too have seen your beloved husband; it seems to me—hard—that we who stand so infinitely farther from him, we see him, rather than you; I begrudge myself that when I think of *you*.

On the 19th I was in Bonn, with Reimers I went to Endenich; we spoke to the doctor, and I was ecstatic when he let me hope that I could see Herr Sch[umann].

It was about 4 in the afternoon. Herr Sch. was having coffee and then came into the garden (the weather was fine).

Your dear husband has not changed in the least, he has only gained a little weight. His glance is friendly and bright, his movements are the very same as before, he kept one hand continuously near his mouth, he smoked by drawing in little puffs, as always; his gait and his greeting were freer and firmer, which is only natural, since no grand thoughts, no *Faust* occupies him. The doctor addressed him; unfortunately I could not hear him speak, but his smile, and apparently his speech, were just as before.

Then Herr Sch. inspected the flowers and went deeper into the garden, towards the beautiful distant view; I saw him disappear, gloriously set aglow by the evening sun.

I cannot describe to you my feelings in this hour; I trembled violently and it took all my strength not to call out, to rush to him. I could not wish you to be in my place, you would not have endured it; I scarcely could.

I want to relate to you a few other things that the doctor and Frl. Reumont told me. Your husband pointed out to Frl. R. all the songs in the Scherer songbook which he had composed in the past. Among other things he said that the song 'Du bist wie eine Blume' had been *his first*! That is indeed so.[52] In Fräulein R's room he recognized the beautiful head of

---

[52] From *Myrthen*, Op. 25, a song cycle with special significance for the Schumanns, as it was Robert's wedding present to Clara. But it was neither his first set of songs, nor is *Du bist wie eine*

Raphael which hangs in your room, and he told her *that he owned it in Düsseldorf.* Also Herr Sch. pointed out, in a book of portraits of famous men, all those he knew: Schiller, Goethe, Copernicus, etc. Then he pointed out the poets whom he knew personally, [and], pointing to Goethe said with a smile, 'Him, unfortunately, I did not know.'

Surely that is the genuine Schumann?

In just that regard I want to make a plea to you, revered Lady, which I would wish you not to misunderstand: be very careful with your letters to the doctors at Endenich!

The gentlemen believed they saw, especially in your last letter, that you were hoping too confidently for an *early* recovery, they thought Herr Grimm must have written to you too enthusiastically.[53]

I would like to counsel you, even though it is so very immodest of me: Not to display as much hope in your letters *as I hope you have*!

But hope, as I do, more and more firmly, for the complete, if slow, recovery of the cherished man.

These medical gentlemen do not know either of you; did I not also believe, before I knew you, that such people and such a marriage could only exist in the imagination of the finest of men.

The doctor does not know what you suffer, he can only judge you by your letters, and if these are over-enthusiastic, he takes you to be the same.

My head was spinning with everything that I wanted to say, tell, and ask the doctor; when I looked into his cold face, I could not get a word past my lips.

I would have preferred to tell you this in person, so that I could do it more cautiously and to substantiate it with more reasons, but I hope you will convince yourself of the necessity, and will realize that the doctors in their letters will be guided *somewhat* by yours, *somewhat.*

If they find these to be too full of hope, they will believe they must write more coldly.

I also must not withhold from you that your husband has had auditory hallucinations these last days.

Their recurrence from time to time won't be enough to unsettle you too much, will they?

I have had no letter from Joachim so far, nor from Wehner about the Variations, but a letter from Dietrich, he writes to me that he has completed

Blume the first song in the set. Was Brahms so eager to see signs of improvement in Schumann's condition that he concurred in this odd error?

[53] On 13 August, Julius Otto Grimm visited Endenich and saw Schumann. Shortly after, he sent a detailed description of his visit to Clara, included in Litz, 326 ff.

a largish work. His life is very lonely! In the summer in L[eipzig], that I believe, but in the winter!

Yesterday Grimm was with his friend Budkowski in Cologne, so you will receive his letter from there.

I was in your house and moved Frl. Bertha deeply with my account of Bonn.[54]

You have found a treasure in that girl, such are rare.

Wasielewski has gone to a spa in Thuringia and to Weimar to visit Liszt; he hasn't written to you about this?

I am a thoroughly bad musician after all!

Just think, at a concert in Düsseldorf this winter, I only wanted to hear your husband's symphony, I fled from a Beethoven overture and other pieces, what should I hear in them? I said; and I also said in Cologne that there wasn't much to Mozart, I could write such piano sonatas any day! At least that is what F.H. said of me in Mehlem.[55]

That gentleman also has his own notion of an artistic career; he is of the opinion one need [only] wait 5 years to find there will be no more talk of me.

I applaud such immortality!

Do forbid me to write, I chatter on far too long and tediously!

I wanted to visit Fräulein Hartmann, but she is staying with her brother-in-law, and I first always have to overcome a reluctance to go to strangers, but I'll do it.

May we hope to see you again in 2 weeks? We are looking forward to that with infinite pleasure.

To Frl. Leser and Jungé my friendliest greetings.

When you write to Frl. Reichmann, I would like to ask you to give her, too, my sincerest greetings.

---

[54] Housekeeper in the Schumann household.

[55] Probably a reference to the composer and conductor Ferdinand Hiller. Brahms's name surfaces in his diary for the first time on 4 November, 1853, as he read Schumann's article about Brahms. Shortly thereafter, a friend played 'the sonata by Brahms' for him at his house, but he did not get to meet the young composer until April 1855, at the house of Clara Schumann. The Düsseldorf Music Festival in 1856 gave him the opportunity of being with Brahms in the good-natured company of a group of musicians and poets, and from then on they were friends. Hiller's diary for 28 May notes that 'Brahms spent the better part of the morning at my house, played me sonatas for piano and violin by Em. Bach that are in his possession'. If the reference in this letter is really to Hiller, it is all the more amusing, as Hiller became not only an early admirer of Brahms the composer, but tried on many occasions to further his career, even offering Brahms a job at the Cologne Conservatory during that period of five years within which Hiller had predicted 'there would be no more talk of him'. But of that, more later. Quotes here are from Reinhold Sietz, *Aus Ferdinand Hillers Briefwechsel*, (Cologne, 1958), i. 129 ff., henceforth *Hil.*

Be well, and come back with your strength greatly restored.
With a thousand greetings
your faithfully devoted
Johannes Brahms

Excuse the shameful handwriting, but I cannot govern my hand when it writes words. Notes I draw better.

Don't get annoyed, but I must add yet another sheet of paper! As often as I have read your letters, I still forgot to answer a few things in them. [!]

Whether I have ever seen the ocean? No.

But I had to struggle with myself not to follow after you. The journey to Ostende and life in a watering-place is too expensive for me to have ventured it; at the time of your departure I couldn't overcome my reluctance; I only wish I had done so, now it's no longer possible.

That the people there, as you write, don't deserve the splendid panorama, that I believe! They also don't deserve that you both, Robert and Clara, *exist at all*, I shudder to think that I may live to see how people continue to *gush* over you—two such utterly poetical natures.

I could wish that the populace would forget you, so that you remain all the more sacred for the better sort.

You laughed over Mademoiselle Meikel? Did you also weep with emotion for Serapion? (at the beginning of the first volume, introduction). I couldn't read it aloud to you; in Krespel too, there is something which now and again will move you deeply, as it did me.[56]

With Kreisler Senior you must also get properly acquainted. (in *Kater Murr*, etc.).

On the significant days:
Clara, Aurora, Eusebius
I had the most glorious, sunniest weather. Do I need to tell you whether I was thinking of you both?[57]

You enquire about it! Only to be able to mention those days, I suppose?

I must pack up this letter quickly so that you can do something in Ostende other than read my letters.

Do keep thinking well of me!
Your
Johannes B.

---

[56] Mademoiselle M. is a character from a the novella *Fermate*, by E. T. A. Hoffmann. Many of Hoffmann's stories were published in a set of four volumes called *Die Serapionsbrüder*, published between 1819 and 1821. The story of Krespel forms the basis of the third episode in Offenbach's opera, *The Tales of Hoffmann*.

[57] See Letter 29, n. 48.

I still have to number the pages, so that you find your way; how I do make you dread my letters!

33
Johannes Brahms to Clara Schumann

Düsseldorf, 27 August 1854

Most esteemed Lady,

I cannot help repeating to you some passages from your last dear letter:

'I can well imagine that people who do not know me may consider me over-enthusiastic,—':

'the thought came to me, whether you (*that is, I*) in the end also consider me as such?'

I suppose that was not meant very seriously, isn't that right, dear Madame Director? That you are now giving a concert in Ostende did not surprise me in the least, I expected it with certainty but I thought of it with anxiety; it must have been a difficult day for you. For that day I would have liked to lend you my respect for the public (in other words, my flippant opinion of them).

I believe that you enter the concert-hall like a priestess to the altar? And so should it be, of course. I do not know this sensation in myself, since I only know the public from a distance, its closeness I shy away from.

I am very eager to know what you played? I hope you weren't too much affected by certain C sharp minor etudes?[58]

It is not my fault; I have been vainly recommending Heller's Promenades and other dawdlings to you long enough.[59]

I have received a letter from Härtels; because they heard about your trip to Ostende, they wrote to me; they are accepting my Variations,[60] but add the comment that I *should not set my honorarium too high* as the success of my things is not yet assured, etc.

Business people surely know no delicacy in money matters. On the one hand, one is reluctant to have to write more than three words about money and honoraria, and [yet] people like Härtels are able to write so crudely. But 10 louis d'or I must have, anyway!

Just imagine, Herr Wehner has still not written to me, nor sent the Variations. I suppose I must make up my mind to write to him.

[58] A reference to Schumann's *Études Symphoniques*, Op. 13?

[59] Stephen Heller, a Hungarian-born composer primarily of piano music, living at the time in Paris. Among his best compositions is a set of pieces called *Promenades d'un solitaire*.

[60] *On a Theme by Schumann*, Op. 9.

From Joachim I also have had no letter yet, I'll have to overcome my reluctance for writing and actually initiate the correspondence.

I have *replenished* my library of books. I bought Aeschylus's 7 tragedies and a volume of Plutarchs *Lives*. Soon I won't know what else there is to buy.

I have Shakespeare's and Schumann's complete works, Goethe's poems, Hoffmann's *Fantasiestücke* and still more!

When I [receive] my next 10 louis d'or, I will again have a hard struggle to stay away from book shops.

You, as poetess, will not be particularly astonished by a miracle that may be seen here. Our friend Grimm who, as you know, has for a long time been raving about momentous matters, is *now acquiring beautiful dark blue eyes!*

It is supposedly possible that by occupying oneself too much with such things and thinking too much about them, [one] acquires them oneself.

Psychic influence, magnetic affinity, etc.!

Grimm is now also composing songs, hot, fervent ones! All in E major 4/4, joyously excited, after Walther von der Vogelweide, among others.

I too gaze ever more deeply into a pair of wondrously beautiful eyes, they gaze at me now from out of the *Davidsbündlertänze* and the *Kreisleriana*.

Almost the whole day I sit in Bilkerstraße 1032 on the 2nd floor, and I have also assailed your cabinet; I must search through everything![61]

I thoroughly enjoyed your brother's Op. 1 and 4, which I knew less about until now. I am particularly fond of nos. 1 and 2 in the first, and nos. 2 and 5 in the fourth work. What fine first works, and what rapid progress, right up to the last work dedicated to you!

I found a wondrous Rhapsodie (Op. 13) by Norbert Burgmüller, deeply moving, and also among his songs I found some splendid ones.[62]

You will enjoy getting to know these things, if they are unknown to you.

I was at Frl. Hartmann's twice. The second time she sang me some songs by Schäffer, and by me. It seems to me that the conception of the ones by Sch. is too grand and profound for her, I myself have always experienced them more deeply; mine she sang very beautifully, fervently and warmly; I was quite enchanted.

Becker left this morning for Leipzig, Freiberg, etc. He asks me to give you his most heartfelt greetings.[63]

---

[61] This was the Schumann's address in Düsseldorf, but Brahms did not have his own room in the Schumann flat until they moved to Poststrasse, in 1855.

[62] 1810–36. Son of a founder of the Music Festival of the Lower Rhein, his short life was lived in Düsseldorf. Most of his works are for piano.

[63] Rupert Becker, principal violinist in Düsseldorf. Like the cellist Reimers, he was a frequent musical guest in the Schumann household.

A rapturous article about Liszt's Sonata appeared in the N[eue] Z[eitschrift] f[ür] M[usik], evoked, as I believe, by magnetic experiments.

Fantasies about the polar star have appeared by the dozen already, in case you're interested.

I want to close, otherwise I will end up copying all the latest Düsseldorf newspapers for you, just so I can keep on writing to you.[64]

In your next letter I suppose you will delight us with the news of *approximately* when you are thinking of coming back?

Will it still be long?

I long boundlessly to see you again, most precious lady, do not let us wait longer *than necessary.*

Many greetings to Frl. Leser and Jungé.

With the greatest possible esteem

Your

Johannes Brahms

In spite of the emotional turmoil—or because of it—Brahms continued work on his symphony.

34
Johannes Brahms to Joseph Joachim

Düsseldorf, 12 September 1854

My beloved friend,

Once again I've delayed writing for so long that I fear you'll find this letter only on your return from Vienna.

Do forgive me, and see how little you've missed.

I have nothing more to write to you than that I've received your letter with the overtures, and thank you from the bottom of my heart. (Actually, that's all I ever have to write to you.) As usual, you've viewed my symphony movement through rose-coloured spectacles—I definitely want to change and improve it; there's still a great deal lacking in the composition, and I don't even understand as much of the orchestration as appears in the movement, since the best of it I owe to Grimm.

You gave us *great* joy by sending the overtures[65]—I find the one to Heinrich uplifting, Grimm the one to Demetrius. I cannot comprehend how

---

[64] Brahms's mother used to copy the Hamburg newspapers for him when she ran out of news of her own.

[65] The reference is to Joachim's compositions.

you can take interest in my things, in little variations and sonatelles like mine! I see you ever vividly before me as you are when I play your things, deeply moved, highly uplifted, as though you were just creating them.

You don't write that I should send them back to you right away, and I am therefore holding on to them either until we see each other or until you write. Of our dear Robert I can write nothing new. His condition has stayed pretty much the same, he gets out for walks to the Godesberg, etc. No doubt you heard, while you were still in Berlin, that I saw him? If not, let me tell you about it soon in person—Grimm also saw him. Frau Schumann was in Ostende for four weeks and returned in good health. She plays again with her former strength, but yet more intensely, *even more like you.* Yesterday she played my F minor Sonata for me just as I had conceived it, but more nobly, with a more serene enthusiasm, and on top of that cleanly and with purity, and with the most gorgeous tone in the strongest passages—all kinds of small advantages she has over me.

Tomorrow, the 13th, is her birthday; I have fulfilled a longstanding wish of hers and arranged the Schumann Quintet for 4 hands. To keep her from suspecting anything, I secretly removed the manuscript from her cabinet while she was away in Ostende. I immersed myself ever deeper into it as if into a pair of dark blue eyes (for that's how it seems to me). That is also why I couldn't write this letter until now.

I've added another set of two to my Variations—through one of them *Clara speaks!*[66]

Härtels have offered to print them. My dear friend, as long as Frau Schumann is here I will not and just *can*not leave, but in early October Grimm and I will be in Hanover; I'll probably continue right on to Hamburg—I want to see my parents, and since I would have to go there during this winter in any case, I'd just as soon do it immediately. (And I will probably see Frau Schumann there.)

Surely, God willing, we will be together from New Year's on.

I feel a vast longing to see you and to live with you; I think the constant excitement here will not prove good for me, I'll be in need of recovery.

Right from the start, we should make music regularly in Hanover. I hope I am better at it now—I also have more repertory in my head.

As to money, I'm not doing especially well, can't think yet of returning the fifty thaler to you.

---

[66] Op. 9. A theme of Clara's is imbedded in Variation X. For more on this theme and its tangle of references to Robert Schumann and even to Clara's father, Friedrich Wieck, see Nancy B. Reich, *Clara Schumann: The Artist and the Woman* (London, 1985), 233 ff., henceforth Reich.

I bought myself the works of Shakespeare and Aeschylus, Faust, a volume of Plutarch, etc.! That's what happens whenever I have a few thaler.

I had fun making this little joke: the Scherzo from the Quintet has been

	Piano	
arranged for		alone.
	Frau Schumann	

She laughs about this sort of thing.[67]

I actually wanted to learn to play the flute, so I could accompany her this winter, but she finds the Kuhlau sonatas dull. You're coming through Düsseldorf on your way to Vienna, aren't you? We all *very much* wish and hope so!

Grimm will also be in Hanover for the winter. And I—of course—since you wish to put up with me.

My letter turned out longer than I had thought, and ghastly, worthless twaddle at that.

If at all possible, do make the detour via Düsseldorf. Please write that you are coming!

With warm greetings from Frau Schumann and Grimm, the very warmest

from

your Johannes

In the Autumn of 1854, Clara Schumann embarked on the job of supporting her family by giving concerts. Brahms, Joachim and Grimm were determined to help her in whatever way they could, Joachim by arranging concerts and performing with her whenever possible, Grimm and Brahms by accompanying her either in deed or letter.

His mother wrote (4 October 1854):

You are quite right to consider it your duty to stay on there; it is your most sacred duty, and even if it were not, what gladdens the heart more than when I am of use and serve my fellow man, to the extent my strength allows. That man is only half alive who lives merely for himself and not for others. I am alone this evening, but cannot amuse myself any better than by chatting with you.[68] . . . Father has had Schumann's picture framed and

[67] The work was first published in 1983, in Breitkopf & Härtel's volume of piano music, *Brahms und seine Freunde* (B & H Edn. 8303).

[68] Frau Brahms makes a clever pun here, using the same verb, *sich unterhalten*, in both of its meanings (to converse and to amuse oneself) while only writing the word once. Johannes came by his love of puns honestly (*Familie*, 57–8). On the recommendation of Johannes, Fritz Brahms had recently been appointed to his first post, as piano teacher to the children of Count Hohenthal. He was living in Schloss Dölkau.

has hung it over the piano . . . If I were you, do you know what I would do? When Frau Schumann goes to Leipzig, I would accompany her and at the same time visit the Count's family and my brother. Oh, how glad Fritz would be to see you!

Brahms did not comply with his mother's wishes. Instead, he and Grimm accompanied Clara on the first leg of her tour, from Düsseldorf to Hanover, where Joachim had scheduled her first concert. Then Brahms went home to Hamburg, only to find that the life he had lived among the Schumanns and their circle had made it difficult for him to accept the circumstances of his home life. Although he reassured Clara by writing, 'It's so splendid to be with my parents again! I'd like to be able to keep my mother with me always',[69] there was much in Hamburg that irritated him. He looked forward to Clara's arrival in Hamburg for some concerts, and spent his time searching out a suitable piano for her.

35
Johannes Brahms to Clara Schumann

Hamburg, 21 October 1854

Most revered lady,

May you have cause only this once to complain about my slowness in letter-writing, and doubtless you will excuse it just this time the more easily?

I only left Hanover at Thursday noon; we spent a few more fine days there, J[oachim] and Gr[imm] lying on the sofa at dusk, and I playing in the next room.

On the trip to Hamburg I was thinking more about you than about my parents especially just as I was entering H.[amburg], because you had to play for the second time just then. I found my father already at the bus. The songs had been sent by Härtel to me from Düsseldorf to H.[amburg], which is why my parents were expecting me with certainty. I found them to be well, along with my sister, and they wish to commend themselves to you most lovingly.

I was delighted by your dear letter, which had already come by early Friday morning; it was the most splendid welcome to H[amburg].

My teachers I also found well; I made each one guess who might have come and both guessed 'Our Johannes!'

I really pleased Herr Marxsen with my Ballades; I also had to play the Variations for him.

---

[69] *SBB* i. 27, dated 'End of October 1854'.

How indescribably your letter reassured me! Now I am no longer worried about you at all, but how terrible that you had to wait so long for news about the dear one.

From now until Christmas time will soon pass, then we'll stay together again in Düsseldorf? Or are you touring once more? but that we don't yet know.

Nevertheless I dream a lot about the winter, how we will both spend it alone, or wonderfully and in joy with your beloved husband.

How happily would I experience my apotheosis in your concert; it really does me too much honour.[70] When I look at you as you play, my things seem sanctified to me.

I was at Herr Avé Lallemand's house. He reveres you and your husband endlessly.

He philosophized such a dreadful lot about music and musicians; in particular Wagner had given him much occasion, just now.

You know that I thoroughly dislike discussing musicians and their 'tendencies', 'to analyse'. He fancied that through an exact study of Wagner's writings and music he had arrived at a firm judgement of him, but with every word that I interjected between his discourses I could get him to reverse himself.

Herr Avé invited me for an evening (with Herr Grädener), but he did not say, as you would, 'let's make some pretty music' but rather: 'then we'll have a *thoroughgoing* discussion about music'. I probably won't be able to stand it for long, and will interrupt with some C sharp, F minor, or F sharp minor chords.

I also went round regarding the grand piano but believe I can recommend that you have one sent by Klemms. Rechets[?] has one (but nothing special), but would not give it out to the hotel! There are Erards here, of course, but one can never be certain that they won't be sold, also if the action isn't too heavy for you.

Heins and Baumgardten, whom I mentioned to you, *unfortunately* have no grand piano, but once again I was enchanted by the marvellous tone of their square instrument. I always feel that I have never [before] found such a singing tone.[71]

My former acquaintances have become even more repugnant to me, I do not comprehend my former life.

---

[70] At her concert in Leipzig on 23 October, Clara played the Andante and Scherzo from his Sonata in F minor, Op. 5, marking the first time his music was played in public. This was merely the first of the countless times she aided his career.

[71] An instrument of this type is now on display in the Brahms Museum in Hamburg.

Since experiencing that wonderful summer with you, it would be impossible for me to remain here. Forgive the expression 'wonderful'! It was indeed a wonderful summer for me, despite its great seriousness; I shall never forget it. The winter will perhaps be infinitely more beautiful, at the very least it will have to be *as good*.

Farewell, greatly revered lady, and think kindly of

your

Johannes Brahms

My parents greet you with all their heart.

I noticed with pleasure the small seal (J.) on your letter.

Brahms wrote copiously to Clara, not only during this tour, but for the next two years as well. For a time he was writing to her at least once a day, thereby leaving us a treasury of letters which overflow with emotion and the details of his existence. The greatest portion of what we know about him during this and earlier periods of his life comes from what he wrote to Clara. (He sent long and detailed letters to his family, too, but unfortunately they fell into his hands when his sister died in 1892, and he fed them to the fire.)

His letters were a necessity for both of them. Clara told her diary they were 'her only joy'. She too wrote frequently, although her replies have perished. 'I have often written to him, which always cheers me up, for of course I cannot write to Robert of the things which occupy my mind; his spirit does not accompany me, when I go into a concert it does not feel to me as if he were wishing me success—then I am dreadfully melancholy, and the one thing that lifts me, that always strengthens me, when my courage threatens to fail, is that He, Johannes, the dearest, most faithful friend, thinks of me and accompanies me with his good wishes.'[72]

The letters which still exist are only a portion of what he wrote. As early as 1856, Brahms expressed the wish that he and Clara return their letters to each other and destroy them. Clara demurred, and Brahms did not press her. But eventually, in 1886, he had his way.[73]

Brahms wrote his letters ostensibly to keep Clara company during her long absences from home, but for posterity their great value lies in the opportunity they afforded him of venting his intense emotions and exposing the force of his passion as never before or again. In that regard, despite the thousands of other letters he later wrote, his early letters to Clara are unique.

---

[72] Quotes are from Litz, ii. 352.   [73] See Part VII, Letters 462 and 469, and p. 649 n. 13.

36
Johannes Brahms to Clara Schumann

Hamburg, 24 October 1854

Revered Lady,

What are you thinking of me? You are only now receiving my 2nd letter, in Weimar you did not find any waiting for you,—each day I thought I must write to you, and now I can scarcely get to it.

You probably think that I am so elated, so thoroughly torn out of my 'phlegma' that I do not have the tranquillity to write?

Not so. I can no longer find myself in my former life; I can no longer dwell four people in two rooms. In the past I would lie at the bottom, as a solid pedal-point, or float high above, and let everything pass me by; now I always tag along, I cannot detach myself and go my own way. I have become so accustomed to being alone that I have to ask my parents, etc., to leave me alone when I want to write to you.

I received my treasures only yesterday (Monday). Amid loud shouts of glee I extracted one piece of the coffee machine after another,[74] everything intact except for a *funnel*.

Now I feel more at home, since I am sitting amongst my beloved books and music; and now I am also wondering what you might bring with you; I'm only missing *a few* volumes of the complete works of Fl. and E.; which ones might they be?[75]

I have always found it unjust that you give me so many presents, even now. But each book, each volume that I have from you is doubly dear to me, is sacred to me, and you should see how tenderly I handle these books! I wish that I could have everything that I buy, or that I am given, first pass through your hands.

I play your husband's things for my teacher a lot; he said that I had never played anything as beautifully as the *Symphonic Études*! That I had been quite consumed by it; oh, now I would like to play them for you, your praise makes me so happy.

I have now seen just about all of my old acquaintances again; goodness, how unassuming I used to be, every conceited pup, I thought, was cleverer than I; I often shuddered with horror when I saw them again, it seemed to me as though they were firmly stuck in mud and that I had gone really far away from them.

---

[74] A gift from Clara.   [75] Schumann's *Florestan und Eusebius*, writings on music.

Ah, how I long to be away from here, to Düsseldorf; write to me *above all* whether you are really thinking of going to Holland after Christmas, and *for how long*!

I will come to you again and stay as long as you are alone; once the two of you are reunited as one, I will stay all the more.

What news have you of the beloved man?

You won't allow yourself to be made too sad by a less than joyful letter? You must hope *only* with gladness and gratitude! I dream and think only about the glorious time when I can live with both of you, I am living out this whole period as though I were travelling a road to the most splendid land.

I see from your letter that Hoffmann had its effect, you have two 'selfs'. You had already written as much from Ostende. I thought I would send you Hoffmann's *Fantasiestücke*, because I found a second, better copy here in the house.

I gave that one to my brother for Christmas in '53, he left it here in the summer; I suppose he doesn't understand them yet.[76]

How did you find Dietrich in Leipzig, changed? I suppose you'll tell me about him in Hbg. Do you by any chance have a programme of your Leipzig concert? Could you send it to me? it is very precious to me.[77] Will I get a letter from you from Weimar? I'm quite worried about you there. I suppose Joachim went there? Lucky fellow! Greet him for me then, that most faithful of friends.

I suppose you are glad that you took Fräulein Schönerstedt with you? Would you please greet her too.

Be very well, I'll write again soon if this will give you the least bit of pleasure.

With all my love and devotion,

your

Johannes Brahms

(You will commend me to Herr Liszt? Please!)

Clara added richly to Brahms's library during the 1850s. Among her gifts were the tragedies and dramas of Shakespeare, poems of Ossian, the complete works of Jean Paul, *The Thousand and One Nights*, and Dante's *Divine Comedy*.[78]

[76] *Fantasiestücke in Callots Manier*, by E. T. A. Hoffmann. Several months after this letter was written, Brahms's mother scolded Johannes roundly for taking back the books he had given his brother. 'He left them at home because he had enough to read, while working for the Count . . . You have a vast library, you could have left both little books for him . . .' *Familie*, 60, letter of 14 Feb. 1855.

[77] Because the programme included the first public performance of his music. See n. 70.

[78] For a more complete list, see George Bozarth, 'Brahms's Lieder Inventory of 1859–60 and other Documents of his Life and Work', *Fontes Artis Musicae* (1983), 98–117.

In the middle of November she came to Hamburg to perform with the Philharmonic, visited the parents of Brahms, was introduced to his treasured tin soldiers,[79] and wondered how it was possible that he had been able to develop under such conditions. She also came to the interesting conclusion that Eduard Marxsen did not understand his famous pupil.

Upon leaving the city, she wrote in her diary: 'It made me sad to part from this woman whose son has become so dear to my heart; I thought to myself, Who knows how long the good woman may live—perhaps I have been ordained to be mother to him in her place.'

Soon after, she, Joachim, Brahms, and Carl Grädener all met in Hanover, where Clara had a brief rest before going on to Berlin. To console Brahms for the long separation coming up, she agreed to use the 'Du' form in addressing him, a form reserved for close friends, family members, and people one loves. He was the only man outside her family whom she ever so addressed.[80] She wrote in her diary, 'He had begged me to do so in Hamburg, and I could not refuse, for indeed I love him as a son, so tenderly.'

37
Johannes Brahms to Clara Schumann

Hamburg, 25 November 1854

Dearest friend,

How lovingly the intimate 'Du' gazes back at me! A thousand thanks for it, I cannot read and look at it enough; if I could but *hear* it. Seldom have I so missed that *word* as much as in reading your last letter.

Your commission to Heins (not Heinz! After all, Prince Heinz must have something in front of his name!) has been promptly carried out, on the very first day, he is agreeable to everything. Your instrument will remain here until you write, it will only be exchanged if he makes a quite extraordinary one, that suits you, doesn't it?

Incidentally, you can depend with unshakeable confidence on Heins as a workman. I spoke to Herr Avé, he will soon send you a package (with documentation, I believe) with what came from England. The tuner has been paid, the bill is enclosed; the Committee has to pay 5 sgr [Silver Groschen], Avé will attend to it, 1 thaler will be deducted for postage, etc. etc.——

---

[79] His favourite toys, which he was long in outgrowing. The visit is described in Litz, iii. 352 ff., her diary quoted p. 355.

[80] Personal communication from Nancy B. Reich, author of *Clara Schumann*. It is also possible that for a brief period Clara was also on 'Du' terms with the composer Theodor Kirchner.

Our journey from Hanover was very sad indeed; I never could screw up my imagination high enough to mistake Grädener for you. We crossed the Elbe by ferry boat, Frau Gr[ädener] was quite marvellous, so cheerful and calm. Yesterday a concert took place here, several, actually.

Ballin

Hildebrand—Romberg

Gurlitt

Degenhardt

genuine Pepita in the Stadttheater

false Pepita—Thalia Theatre

at Romberg's, Frl. L[ouise] Japha played: Polonaise by Jul. Schäffer and her own F sharp minor Presto.

I was at Grädener's, where I played Grimm's B minor Scherzo and both volumes of pieces by Bargiel.

If only Bargiel could have seen us, our love for him would certainly have made him genuinely happy.

Avé had to credit him with more than just talent.

Do give him the friendliest greetings from me. I wish we could have him among us for one summer, he would cheer up soon enough.

Grädener has composed a study in the style of Bach (for 5 voices and Orchestra or Organ), which he has presented to his Academy[81] as [genuine] Bach, and also plans to perform in public using Bach's name. Yesterday we played it for Avé as a duet; naturally, the great Bach expert said nothing.

One ought to stand in awe of such a name, in solemn awe, and not misuse it; I even said so to Gr[ädener].

I, too, like to mystify with names, but Kullak, or at most Mendelssohn, must put up with it.

Ferd[inand] von Roda is performing an Oratorio: *The Sinner*! He has quite a selection to choose from, from Cain to Brahms!

My parents and sister talk constantly about you, Mother always refers to you as an angel! I am supposed to give you 1000 thanks for the beautiful hours you have devoted to us.

Oh, if I could thank you for the many wonderful hours I had because of you!

You write to me that your concerts will be finished by the 15th; will you be going to Düsseldorf immediately? Do write to me about it, so that I can start looking forward to it sooner.

I now await news from your dear husband quite calmly, it can only be better, and soon, the best.

---

[81] Grädener directed his own Singing Academy in Hamburg.

I have thought about whether it would not be best if you first spoke to each other for example at the Deichmanns, and perhaps stayed there for some time?

What do you think about that?

A reunion in Endenich would surely be very sad, that is, the idea of the kind of a house you are in might sadden you; in Düsseldorf it is impossible.[82]

The Deichmanns own a house in Godesberg which is totally unoccupied, they would surely be enormously pleased if they could make that first period more agreeable for you.

Do write your thoughts about this to me, it really is something to consider. Godesberg is only $1/2$ an hour from Endenich.

Farewell, dearest lady, and continue to think well of me.

Greet Bargiel, etc. etc.

Your
Johannes.

I still have to tell you this priceless joke—

Yesterday, when Grädener's boys returned from Romberg's concert, we asked them what Frl. Japha had played? 'Frl. Japha?—*she* didn't play, a certain Madam Schäffer [did]!' How a mere child can be malicious!

NB. I would like to send the arranged quintet to Härtel, do write to me if you made use of our little trick regarding the print copy; if not, don't do so anymore, for I'm already getting travel funds for the 15th! Do you find 6 Louis for the arrangement too much?

In any case, do write again very soon, specifically as follows: Lieber Johannes, Du——

Your most faithful friend
J.B.

Some of the composers and musicians mentioned in this letter are names still known today. Theodor Kullak (1818–82) was a composer of piano music, and a renowned piano pedagogue whose exercises are still in use. Cornelius Gurlitt (1820–1901) lived and worked in Hamburg, and wrote almost nothing but piano music. Many of his pleasant, small pieces are played today by students. The Romberg mentioned here is probably Cyprian, nephew of the famous cellist and composer Bernhard Romberg, and the only one of the Hamburg family of musicians still living there at that time. Louise Japha was Brahms's childhood friend. Other names are sunk in oblivion. Julius Schaeffer was a composer and editor of the works of Bach and Handel, in lush nineteenth-century style; he is mockingly linked here to Louise

---

[82] i.e. their reunion in the Asylum itself would be too upsetting; and in Düsseldorf, presumably, there would be too much commotion and not enough privacy.

Japha by one of Grädener's boys. Ferdinand von Roda was the founder of the Hamburg Bach Society, with the stated purpose of presenting the most complete performances of Bach's works possible. His methods did not quite live up to his mission, and he earned Brahms's eternal scorn by mixing bits and pieces of various works and calling the resulting pot-pourri a Bach Cantata.[83]

38
Johannes Brahms to Clara Schumann

Hamburg, 30 November
after the 6 ß = closing
i. e. after 11 o'clock

'Read it and then burn it immediately, I beg you.'

Well, the dear Frau Mama can ask a long time, it won't happen! The *per expr.* really frightened me.[84]

What you so sternly remind me of, while making nasty cracks at the whole male species, I had not forgotten, yet I can't, let's wait until I get to Düsseldorf. You won't take it amiss of me till then?

The conditions which you attached to the 'Du' I have long since been agreed to in my mind.

I have no secrets from you. In my thoughts I confide everything to you, isn't it the same as if I did it in words?

Beware of trickery, I shall gladly answer everything in your letter and will tug you this way and that a great deal.

In what you write about the Deichmanns you are correct, but not when you write that I considered you too calm. Neither in Hanover nor anywhere else. On the contrary, almost too much C minor 3/4.[85]

Whether I would like to accompany you to Bonn, I suppose you did not write as a question.

I prefer tomorrow to the day after tomorrow.

Mendelssohn and Kullak I did not lump together! I pull people's leg with names like K., etc, when I am annoyed. M's name I do not use in the presence of bad people, and only when I'm particularly proud of a piece.

You really shouldn't credit me with so little judgement and so little love for innately sincere music (and not only for such!). Who knows whether you or I have greater love for *his works*! In Lübeck you liked less of the A major symphony than did I,[86] of course you have heard M.'s works infinitely more

---

[83] Kal, i. 279 ff.   [84] By express mail.
[85] *SBB* i. 40 reads 'E flat minor'. Our version follows the autograph.   [86] The 'Italian', Op. 90.

often, and it would really be quite unbecoming for me to want to be as spoiled as my dear Frau Mama.

Since you left, I have not been to any pub; so you may rest quite assured about it, my craving is not nearly as great as you think.

. . . I took care of your letter to Otten this very evening. You have given him much joy; how happy and delighted you have made me with your so amiable letter!

Why can't I too show you properly how greatly I love and revere you.—

Today was the rehearsal for Beethoven's *Meeresstille*[87] and 9th Symphony.

The 9th went dreadfully. Grund literally *wrestled* with it. No tempo right, and shaky all the time.

Where it says *rit.* for half a measure he held back for 6 measures.

7 tenors were at today's rehearsal and there are only 2 (today and tomorrow) for chorus and orchestra together. It should have started at a quarter past 2 and towards 3 o'clock 2 horn players were still missing, etc.

The sopranos sing in 6/8:

And on account of this old, dried-up philistine who has been killing all musical life in Hamburg for 20 years, young, energetic people such as Otten and Grädener can do nothing, must spend their time giving lessons, and can make absolutely no effect in public.

Farewell for today, next to me there is so much loud talking that writing is becoming too difficult for me. Once more, a thousand thanks for your last letter, I was particularly pleased that not half the letter was completed, as you had written in the one before the last, but only 1/11! May those difficult letters become very easy for you, how much of that can you bear?

Your Johannes.

Unexpectedly, and while Clara was still away on tour, Schumann wrote to Brahms, who answered promptly.

[87] Op. 112.

39
Johannes Brahms to Robert Schumann

Hamburg, 2 December 1854

Most beloved friend,

How can I convey to you my joy over your cherished letter! So often you
have made me happy before, when you thought of me so tenderly in the letters to your wife, and now a letter belongs to me exclusively! It is the first one
that I have from you, and it is so infinitely precious to me.

Unfortunately I received it in Hamburg, where I had gone to visit my
parents; I would much rather have received it from the hand of your wife.

I imagine I will go back to Düsseldorf in a few days; I long to be there.

The extravagant praise which you consider my Variations to merit fills
me with joyful courage.

Since this spring I have been diligently studying your work; how pleased
was I to hear your praise for this, too!

This year I have been in Düsseldorf since springtime; I will never forget it;
I learned to revere and love you and your magnificent wife ever more highly.

Never before have I looked as joyfully and confidently to the future,
believed as firmly in a splendid future, as now.

How I wish it were near and nearer, that lovely hour when you are
restored to us entirely.

Then I shall be unable to forsake you again, I will try ever more to gain
your precious friendship.

Farewell, and think of me with love.

With deepest reverence, your
Johannes Brahms

My parents and your friends here think of you with the greatest reverence
and love. My parents, Herr Marxsen, Otten, and Avé ask me especially to
greet you most warmly.

40
Johannes Brahms to Clara Schumann

Hamburg, 8 December 1854

Dear Frau Schumann,

It gives me a very uncomfortable feeling not to know at all where you are
and where you will get a letter.

You probably found none in Breslau and are furious with me and 'do not expect that from me again'.

I don't believe that.

Right now, although I've just written to your husband, I would like to do so again straightaway, as if I could now write a great deal—and yet, should it perhaps come to that again, so would my 'pounding heart'.

I want to write to your dear husband about last summer; I could tell him about it for hours without causing him the least pain or making him feel dejected.

I wanted to write only about you, with what unbelievable grace and grandeur you bore your pain; that would awaken his yearning, his joyful, ardent yearning to belong entirely to you once again.

If I were able to write that to him, I wouldn't have to describe the future, wouldn't need to tell him of my most beautiful dreams for it.

It seems to me that I could make the best portrait of you.

If only I could send it to him!

Yesterday I had enormous pleasure, I played some of my things to Herr Otten. He already had the Variation[s and the] F minor Sonata at home and he pressed my hand very warmly. After that I played him the first movements of the sonatas; the first of the C major, the Variations, and 2 Ballades. Oh, he was really happy and his warm praise made me happy too; it came so straight from the heart.

If people only knew how much one loves to hear such praise, if only they didn't always suppose that a musician 'of the future' likes, or at least doesn't mind being misjudged and misunderstood.[88]

If through my music I stir or inspire others, then I myself am stirred and inspired, more and more, [but] when others remain unmoved, or listen so superficially, then the fire in me is immediately cooled.

The day before yesterday I visited Frau Petersen.[89]

Herr Avé accompanied me; Grädener needed to recuperate (the preceding few evenings had indeed been quite strenuous).

There was company present, but nice, congenial company. Only one lady infuriated me terribly, she was intent on a very audible task, sewing some sort of silken fabric.

---

[88] It is fascinating that Brahms here identifies himself with the 'Musicians of the Future', Franz Liszt's circle of composers, with whose philosophy of music he and Joachim were to make such a public and painful break six years later.

[89] The pianist Annette Petersen, who had once travelled to Dresden to study Schumann's music with Clara.

While I was listening (a concerto of Mozart with quintet of strings) and sitting in the next room, she sat just in front of my eyes and I kept seeing her hand rising and falling as she sewed.

When I played, I again saw that—white hand, and kept hearing the rustling of the fabric, and I kept imagining, now all the ladies are rising to leave, and it was merely the seamstress.

If it should happen that I have to write to your dear husband soon again, don't be alarmed by my audacious lies if I write to him that I have seen you again.

After all, I do see you often, as good as in person; e.g. at the trill in the final passages of the Andante of the C major Symphony,[90] at the pedal-points of great fugues, when you suddenly appear to me as St Cecaelia!

How impatiently I always await a letter from you, even as I wish you were relieved of writing; I cannot help it.

When I have no letter for 3 days, I always suppose you are ill.

But do write *a little*, as little as you like, only often; but I beg you most particularly to make use of the railway carriage for long letters.

With a fervent greeting
Your
Johannes

From parents and sister the finest and most cordial [greetings].

41

Robert Schumann to Johannes Brahms

Endenich, 15 December 1854

Dear friend,

Could I but come to all of you at Christmas!

In the mean time, I have received from my wonderful wife your picture, your familiar one, and I know its place in my room very well—below the mirror. I keep being edified by your Variations; many of them I would like to hear [played] by you and my Clara; I have not mastered them completely, especially the 2nd one, the 4th not in tempo, nor the 5th one; but the 8th (and the slower one) and the 9th—A reminiscence about which Clara has written me, is probably on page 14, where is it from? from a song?—and the 12th—oh, could I but hear [it played] by you! Clara has also sent me the

---

[90] The intensely romantic slow movement of Schumann's Second Symphony, Op. 61. St Cecilia is the patron saint of music.

poem by Rückert [dedicated] to us; the original; I am sorry about that, although it gave me great pleasure, for she had removed it from the album. She also wrote to me about Ballades by you; what work of yours has appeared during our separation? Not the Scherzo? Surely. How it would please me to get to know some of your new ones. Write to me again soon, dear Johannes, and also about our friends; that the ones in Hamburg remembered me pleased me greatly.

Could I but see again the city that I saw some time after the fire.—Now you will probably be in Düsseldorf again, since Hanover we have not seen each other. Those were happy times, indeed.

I am very pleased about my girls, Marie, Elise, Julie, and their considerable talents. Do you hear them sometimes?

Farewell, you faithful friend; talk about me and keep on writing.

> Your
> > deeply devoted
> > Robert Schumann

42
Johannes Brahms to Clara Schumann

Hamburg, 15 December 1854

Dearest friend,

I have just written the first chord of the Ballades, but my sister's pen is no good for writing music and my own I can't find, so I will write a few words to you.

I really ought to write to Bargiel and Joachim, but I think I may get enough time for two letters.

In my last letter I forgot to write about something that is making me very uneasy.

Your husband reads newspapers a lot, is that not very risky? Be sure to ask the doctor to check the paper carefully beforehand, to see if it has anything about you.

Almost every number of the illustrated paper has something about your travels.

How eager I am to find out what you think of my idea for Christmas. Actually, I probably haven't said anything; oh, who knows what to advise!

I wish the doctor would hire me as warder and nurse for Christmas; if that worked, I believe the worst would be over. I would write to you daily about him, and would tell him about you all day long.

What do you think, will you present him with more than the portrait, as I wrote, and some especially beautiful flowers?[91]

For if you are thinking of sending him the Ballades (or also the other), you probably should first enquire of the doctor whether Herr Sch. may use the piano on Christmas Eve, otherwise it may be better to present the music to him later.

Joachim and Bargiel and Brahms would have to gather their new things together! What do you think about that?[92]

I must write you something else that distresses me greatly, I am not bringing you a single new note of music! I just couldn't.

How little peace and quiet I have been allowed. Today Herr Marxsen, or with him somewhere or other, then Avé, Otten, or whatever their names are. If for once I am free, I must be in the same room with four others, someone always running in and out. Then I think so much (or all the time) of you and how I would like to be with you, that I am thoroughly out of sorts; I cannot stand it much longer. Early on Monday I shall probably go to Hanover. On Sunday morning at 9 I have to rehearse my Trio at Otten's, perform it at 2.30; how many violinists have already cancelled, how much trouble and how little I feel like doing it.

Today we are expecting my brother back from Leipzig. I am truly looking forward to seeing him; how might the association with Countesses have changed him?

Till now I have been writing while 5 in the same room held a very lively conversation about my new coat. Now I have managed to get rid of them, but once again they take me for a sullen, coarse lout; they ran off with the whole coffee set; my cup sits quite forlornly by me.

The next time I won't leave Düsseldorf when you forsake me! How gladly would I have written you a really lovely sonata, rather than all this twaddle. You have also undoubtedly often thought, 'What has Johannes produced for me?'

I must tell you something else about yesterday. We were at the v. Linds, and played both violin sonatas of your husband, the first movement of the B flat major Sonata of Schubert, *Études Symphoniques*, and *Carnaval*.

A fine programme, don't you think?

[91] The drawing of Brahms, done in the autumn of 1853 by the French artist J. J. Bonaventure Laurens, who was visiting the Schumanns in Düsseldorf at the time. See Plate 11.

[92] Brahms was hoping to give Schumann an assortment of new works by Joachim, Bargiel, and himself: presumably his Op. 9 Variations in addition to the Ballades; and Joachim's *Gis-e-la* violin pieces, Op. 5, the *Hebrew Melodies*, Op. 9, perhaps a score to one of his Overtures. He suggested Bargiel bring along his Violin Fantasy. See *BW* v, letter of 16 Dec. 1854.

I played the violin sonatas with the same alternating feeling with which I had decided to play them.

Singer played them really very well, but like a student in comparison to Joachim.

But playing like that, one hears from no one else!

Yesterday and today I had to sacrifice myself for Singer again; he happens to be here, I am the only one who has time to idle away because he does not make good use of his time teaching tricks to dilettantes.[93]

Tomorrow my brother will be here, on Sunday my Trio will be trotted out—oh, if only I were with my dear Grimm on Monday!

How I long to sit with him for a good long evening, if only in the railway pub, to be able to talk again heart to heart purely and simply about you alone.

People here are incapable of doing this; right away the conversation always turns to the girl students, and when the next musical evening will take place.

I have written you a dreadful letter, I recognize that. I will copy a second one for you from 1001 Nights. It describes my condition most clearly, although that writer was a prince, and I a composer.

So then, after Johannes quite sensibly says good night, the Brahmin arises laboriously from his couch, takes paper and kalane [stylus?] in hand, and writes: (in answer to your last letter).

'In the name of God the Merciful and All Holy*[94]—Thy letter has arrived, oh Mistress, and has poured balsam on a soul tortured with longing and desire, and healed a heart torn and ailing. Thy weary slave (how beautiful!) has understood all the gracious words of its contents and by thine head, o my Mistress! I am in that condition which the poet describes:—

'The heart is heavy and affliction gains, and sleepless the eye and weary the body, patience is scant, but the separation long-lasting, reason is confused and the heart is perplexed.' (Ah!)—Although lamentation does not extinguish the flames of grief, it brings relief to one deranged by desire and suffering from separation.

'Would to God it were permitted me today, instead of sending this letter, to repeat to thee in person that I am dying of love for thee. Tears prevent me from saying more. Fare thee well.—

Kamaralsaman Ibn Brah'

[93] A nice example of Brahmsian obscurity. Edmund Singer, leader of Liszt's orchestra in Weimar, was in Hamburg to give a few concerts (Schumann's Violin Fantasy and Joachim's First Violin Concerto). Another person might have used his spare time to earn extra money by giving lessons to local amateurs, but Singer presumably considered that occupation a waste of time, preferring to play sonatas with Brahms.

[94] Brahms notes: it goes without saying that the word must be taken here in its 'better' meaning.

When Ibn Brah had done with the letter composed with sighs and tears, he brought it to the Prussian Postal Service, cast it into the letter box and said: 'I entreat thee, bring this letter to my beloved Mistress, and greet her for me.'

J. B.

By writing here in the guise of the Prince, Brahms found a way to use the 'Du' form, even though he did not yet have Clara's permission. He knew very well the potential his name had as a means of inserting himself into this story. His friends referred to themselves as *Brahminianer*; and in this letter, the Brahmin is himself.

Since he wrote both to Clara and to Joachim that the story of Prince Kamar-ez-zemán 'described his own condition exactly', it is worth knowing that the story is about a prince who is wasting away for love of a distant and unattainable princess. *The 'Efreet's Beauty Contest, the Prince Kamar-ez-zemán and the Princess Budoor*, occupies nights 222–38 of the *Tales*, and tells the story of young Prince Kamar-ez-zemán, who, much to his father's dismay and grief, is so uninterested in women that he refuses even look at them. But by means of magic, he is transported to China in his sleep and shown a glimpse of the extraordinarily beautiful Princess Budoor. Immediately falling so violently in love that he cannot imagine life without her, he is prevented by complex circumstances from marrying her. For several years he hovers near death, refusing to eat or go about his normal life. Presumably Brahms was not sorry that the story has a happy ending.[95]

Brahms's need to gather again with people who knew the Schumanns now became urgent; he was impatient to leave Hamburg, find his new friends, and with them to adore, rhapsodize, rave, enthuse, and daydream over Clara—all included in one word, *schwärmen*. 'I can't hold out any longer. I have to be able to *schwärm* over you properly, for once, with Grimm', he wrote to Clara, and at the same time to Grimm:

43
Johannes Brahms to Julius Otto Grimm

[Hamburg, 17 or 18 December 1854][96]

Beloved friend,

Tomorrow (Monday) 2.30 I leave Hamburg, evening 9.45 I'm—[in] Hanover.

So try to be at the railway with Wagemann!

[95] *The Arabian Nights' Entertainments*, trans. Edward William Lane (New York, 1927), 315 ff.

[96] Dated with reference to Brahms's letter to Clara of 16 Dec. (*SBB* i. 59, letter 30): 'Tuesday write to me in Hanover. I'm travelling on Monday with the second train.' His letter to her on 20 December was sent from Hanover.

Do you want to? I have a powerful longing to be able once more to rhapsodize from the bottom of my heart.

In the worst case I could leave Tuesday morning at 7, then I will arrive in
H. about 2 o'clock and have coffee there. Don't let me arrive in H. alone! It
has been long enough since I've seen any Schumannians. I suppose we (I)
can sleep at Henke's? Greetings to Wagemann and best greetings to yourself
from your Johannes

Presumably Henke, Grimm's amiable landlord, put Brahms up. From there he went
on to Düsseldorf, to spend Christmas with the Schumann family.

❧ 1855 ❧

Brahms spent the winter of 1855 in Düsseldorf. By now he had become an integral
part of the Schumann household, keeping the household accounts, teaching the
older boys to read, taking care of some of Clara's correspondence, and keeping in
touch with Schumann, who seemed to be improving. In the first part of January he
went to Endenich; it was an unsettling visit, which he described in his letter to
Joachim (Letter 45), but during it Schumann promised to dedicate one of his last
compositions to Brahms. Brahms himself was having great difficulty composing. He
hardly turned out any music all year apart from making a start on a piano quartet
which would appear in print twenty years later as his third, Op. 60 in C minor.

In mid-January Clara and a travel companion set off for a concert tour to
Holland. Brahms accompanied them as far as Emmerich, intending to return to
Düsseldorf. But he changed his mind suddenly, and the next day followed them
to Rotterdam. One week later he was back home.

44

Johannes Brahms to Clara Schumann

Düsseldorf, 24 January 1855

Deeply loved friend,

How quickly one is parted!

Only yesterday at noon we were standing together, and now so far.

You are probably preparing for tomorrow's concert and already thinking
about tomorrow's trip and exertion; I, a man, sit idly by, and am allowed and
able only to think of you. Oh, if only I could work for you, if we could trade
places, how gladly I would do it. How well our short time together has taught
me what you must endure, I doubt I could do it in your place.

I found your dear portrait here and immediately appropriated it; I am very happy about it. Never before has a picture seemed so alive to me. When I gaze at it for a while, you positively step out of it, I believe I could give you my hand: And everything about it so familiar, the dress, the rings, the bracelet.

Your loved ones are all well, Bertha and the children were really happy. I received the letter from Emmerich and could convince myself quite easily it was new.

Now I am again sitting in my room, before me your medallion [and] the potted camellias with one bloom and many buds from your Robert's room. Everything just as snug and cosy and lovely as ever, only in your study and in the piano room it was too lonely for me. I suppose I won't go to wake you at about 3 o'clock, it's too very empty in that room.

Now I already regret having followed after you; if I hadn't done so I could do it now and at this moment I would much prefer that.

I'm enclosing a selection of 3 letters for you from M. B. I'm afraid my letter won't reach you in Amsterdam any more, I only arrived in Düsseldorf in the afternoon. The mail coach was late in Emmerich, and 3 gentlemen and I had to take a special postal coach as far as Oberhausen and leave from there at 2.

I am already worrying about you making this trip, if only things had got that far already! But now they are even worse.

I arrived here in good health; on the way and here too, *even to this very moment*, have thought only of you. I see you quite distinctly in your room, since I now know how you live while you travel.

I will close, my dearest friend; more soon. This is only intended as a greeting from home from

your
Johannes.

Joachim was eager for news of Brahms's visit to Robert Schumann.[1]

---

[1] According to Clara's diary, the visit took place on 11 January. Kalbeck's account of the visit (ii⁴. 200–5) confuses events of January and February. He had access to Joachim's letters, but not to Clara's, nor to Litzmann's biography of her.

45
Johannes Brahms to Joseph Joachim

[25 January 1855][2]

My beloved Joseph,

At last I am writing to you; if you would only remind me occasionally as forcefully as today, then I would get around to it.

Frau Schumann left for Holland more than a week ago; you are not the only one who is surprised; I followed after her the next morning, I could not do otherwise. The day before yesterday I returned from Rotterdam, where I left her quite well. We spoke about you daily, you probably know that. She cannot write to you with certainty about the Berlin trip yet, with the engagements in Holland still not definite.

I am sending the full scores back to you; they have been copied for Schumann, very beautifully. For Grimm from Frl. Hartmann there are 1 *Tl.* 10 *Sgr.* (*which I will place in one of the scores*). I'll write to him shortly and thank him for the Scherzos,[3] in the mean time give him my best thanks.

How dear to me are all the works which came into being this winter, as well as my Variations and Ballades; they remind me so much of twilight hours at Clara's.

I don't suppose I can tell you more about my visit to Schumann than his wife has done. For the first 5–10 minutes he spoke with horrifying haste and anxiety of what the voices, or else the doctors, had whispered to him, he confused the two. I didn't understand very much, he spoke with his hand held in front [of his mouth], and rapidly.

I spoke a lot about your splendid Heinrich Overture to him. He did not, however, request to see the score, as I had thought. He must want to avoid all strain and agitation.

Give the piano-and-singing-teacher Grimm best greetings from his more diligent colleague.

For I *am giving* lessons, to a little miss and to Frl. Wittgenstein[4] (Ah, AAAhhh!). Cramer études, scales, etc.

The trip to Rotterdam has cost me my last thaler; now I'm going to make a *great* collection of thalers so that I can send them to my dearest friends (you know them).

[2] Brahms returned from Rotterdam on 23 January, a date documented by his correspondence to Clara. Moser's dating in *BW* v is in error by one day.

[3] Grimm's latest compositions.

[4] One of Joachim's cousins, then living in Düsseldorf. She was related to the Viennese Wittgensteins.

NB. Since my visit to Endenich, no letter has come either from him or from the doctor. How sad for the wife. It has become quite late. Be greeted most warmly, I think of you always with the greatest affection.

Your Johannes.

Won't you send me the Variations in E soon?

One result of Brahms's visit to Robert Schumann is the older composer's dedication of the *Concert-Allegro and Introduction for Piano and Orchestra*, Op. 134, to his young friend.

46
Johannes Brahms to Robert Schumann

Düsseldorf, 30 January 1855

Dear revered friend,

I must say thanks to you myself for the great joy you give me with the dedication of your magnificent concert-piece. How delighted I am to see my name in print in this way! Most especially because like Joachim, a concerto now belongs to me. We often discussed both and which might be our favourite—we could not settle it.[5]

With bliss I still recall the brief hours which I was allowed to spend with you, they were so beautiful—but vanished all too quickly. I cannot tell your wife enough about it; it makes me doubly happy that you received me so joyously and kindly and that you still recall the hour with so much love.

And so will we see you again more and more often and joyfully, until we have you back again.

As you wished, I have brought the catalogue (the chronological list of works) to your copyist (Fuchs).

The letter from Jenny Lind, I imagine, you will want in the original. It must be the handwriting you want, for the contents I hardly need to copy out for you.

We are enclosing the new piece by Bargiel, which may bring you great pleasure, as it did us; there is indeed considerable progress from Op. 8 to Op. 9. Both are dedicated to your wife; I would like to do the same always, only I would want to alternate the names Joachim and Clara Schumann until I had the courage to set down your name; that probably won't happen to me so soon.

---

[5] Joachim's' concerto is the *Fantasy for Violin and Orchestra*, Op. 131, written in the autumn of 1853 and published in 1854 with a dedication to the violinist.

Now farewell, cherished man, and think now and then with love of your
Johannes.

Do you remember that as early as last winter you encouraged me to [write]
an overture to 'Romeo'? In any case, this past summer I tried my hand at a
symphony, even orchestrated the first movement and composed the second
and third. (In D minor 6/4 *langsam*.)[6]

47
Johannes Brahms to Clara Schumann

Düsseldorf, 3 February 1855

Ever lovely, lofty Lady,
 Whatever did I write that was so terrible that I deserve such a depressing
letter as your last one? As far as I remember, I wrote only briefly, but not, I
thought, inconsiderately.
 I do wish you would never be angry with me because of my writing, my
dear Frau Clara, how often have I told you that I so rarely succeed in setting
down my thoughts on paper straight from the heart.
 This happens to me exactly as with composing, you know how seldom I
write; I can think and feel for a long time without succeeding in hitting upon
the right tone; however warm I may be, it just doesn't overflow, my heart.
 So I often sit before the sheet of letter paper and would like to write to
you truly consolingly, truly beautifully—I have never yet succeeded in that,
for I cannot manage letters as I can notes.
 How tender your previous letter was! As for 'embracing', it's a good long
way from Amsterdam to Düsseldorf. It is quite innocent and most seemly.
 There was a concert here on Thursday; it was filled to overflowing
because Helene Berg was singing.
 Sch[umann's] *Abschiedslied* ('Es ist bestimmt in Gottes Rat') was performed; at the end a Swedish yodelling song repeatedly caused the greatest
furore. I don't much care for yodelling after Beethoven, Mozart, Handel,
Bach, Schumann, Mendelssohn, etc.
 But Helene is really a remarkably decent and noble yodeller, she achieves
whatever is possible in yodelling, one can actually stand her yodelling better
than the croaking and jubilation that follows it (the chorus of the dear public), which I however did not hear, for I didn't have a free ticket.
 Now I must write to you about more important matters. I have written
nothing to your dear husband about your tour, etc. Indeed, you might have

---

[6] A preliminary version of the Piano Concerto, Op. 15.

known that I would not do that without your explicit permission and without first sending you the letter—you enquire about it as if you had thought differently. I wrote only about the dedication, so loving, about my visit, and Bargiel's Op. 9.

By the way, I am now sorry after all not to have gone to Bonn, but from your letters I believed you thought about it as I did, that one must be careful not to pester the doctors, etc.—also, that the comment of your Robert was not as significant as I too had thought, at first. I wanted to go to Endenich only to obtain news for you sooner, that things were better again, I hadn't hoped for any more.

The copying of the *Concertstück* is finished, also the catalogue, as your husband wanted it, so when you write to him will *you send me the letter? I'll then enclose the catalogue* and forward them together to Endenich.

I have spoken with Klems.—Ah, already *on my very first day here*, now you can show me whether or not you hold my forgetfulness against me! He can do nothing about it; he wrote a memorandum concerning this, but the customs agent would not sign it—he reminds you, by the way, that he had asked you to have the grand piano *stamped* by Dutch customs authorities, did you do that? That's the way it was done last year, otherwise the gentlemen in Rotterdam would have to certify that it is the same grand piano in order for you to get back the money deposited.

I still have to write to you about the flat. I suppose Fräulein Leser has written to you that Herr Aschenberg will hear nothing of quarterly notice; now I was thinking, you might be able to rent out the two upstairs rooms and thereby take in more than 100 thaler a year. For I do think you are making the greatest, almost too great a sacrifice if you give up the flat, I can hardly imagine it, really. I have therefore spoken with Herr Allgeyer, he would take the one room, I or Herr Buthowsky the other. They are, after all, tolerable tenants.[7]

So do write to me what you think about this; the children would also have to sleep downstairs in their room.

Regarding England, I think you were right to agree, sad as I am at the thought of knowing you to be so far away. You don't know how indispensable your nearness is for me, you don't begin to know it. But I will remain in Düsseldorf, then you can be a little easier about leaving, knowing a faithful friend to be so near to your husband.

The camellias are blooming marvellously. We have pressed one for you. They are back in Robert's room.

---

[7] A pun. *Erträglich* means tolerable, but also profitable.

Just imagine, once I had addressed a letter to you to Antwerp, by chance Bertha brought it there and back to me. A thousand thanks for the many dear letters which I receive from you, you make me very happy with them. Be greeted most warmly by your

Johannes

I now know how to make canons in all kinds of artistic forms, now I am eager to see how I'll get on with fugues.

If I open your letters, they can nevertheless easily remain secret! I do it only because it is normally forbidden and also because it's cheaper.

48
Johannes Brahms to Julius Otto Grimm

Düsseldorf, January [*recte*: 20 February] 1855[8]

My dear Julius,
    You probably know the reason I haven't written at all? I wanted to be able to include Frau Sch[umann]'s greetings and thanks for the Scherzos! You believe that and are not angry with me? She arrived here on Saturday and wanted to surprise us and really did surprise us—me in bed. Well, now it's very fine here—in spite of Miss Leser, etc. I practised and did my writing in Herr Schu[mann]'s room the whole time, I was upstairs only at night. I was also in Rotterdam; I think I wrote that to Joachim—there is nothing there worth describing except the woman, whom you know.
    I often wished that you, or better still, both of you were here; with Frau Clara away I am utterly alone here. You know Allgeyer and B[uthowsky], being with them is not like being with you. Do write to me once in a while. You know that I think of my distant friends often and with pleasure, even if I don't write very often.
    I am going to write to Joachim shortly, simply on account of his overtures; I often feel quite powerfully impelled to write to him. How those overtures stick in my head! Do remind him that he should write to Frau Sch. She wrote to him twice from Holland, also sent a letter from her husband. He should write whether he intends to go to Berlin in a week, or later on. Prod him. She too is going to England at the beginning of April.

---

[8] The date, in Brahms's hand, is incorrect. The letter was written after Clara returned from tour (10 Feb.). Brahms must have allowed the letter to sit on his desk until Clara left for her next tour (19 Feb.), since the enclosed letter from Breitkopf & Härtel is dated 20 Feb.

I am sending along your Children's Scherzo; will you return the copy, it isn't yours.[9] What are you working on?

Send me something once in a while, also ask Joachim about sending me the D Minor sonata movement by movement; each one by itself has enough to it.[10]

When I have the Ballades printed, which I have so far done nothing about, I would like to dedicate them to an '1854-er'; may I do that?

Frau Schumann sends greetings, Buthowsky begs for a letter! Allgeyer *col primo*, Brahms *col secondo, tutti unisono!*

Greetings, and a letter, please. Excuse the shameful handwriting, but Frau Schumann is sitting downstairs and either she or I—one of us is longing for the other. Farewell

Your Johannes

P.S. Many greetings to Wagemann, Henkes, etc.

P.P.S. Should Joachim be away, unseal Frau Schumann's letters and return *his* (Robert's).

For Julius Otto Grimm my first Nikodemus Letter![11]

To Herr Johannes Brahms in Düsseldorf

Leipzig, 20 February 1855

Most honoured Sir!

We were unable to reply before now to your worthy offering of the four-hand arrangement of the Quintet by Schumann, because it seemed to us very desirable first to get to know this arrangement in a practical way; but the occasion to hear it was not so easily found. A few days ago, Herr Dietrich, along with another local musician, had the kindness to play it for us and we will delay in answering you no longer. Unfortunately indeed, hearing and seeing the performance forced us to the conviction that the work cannot be published in this form, and so on. Two experienced players with a substantial interest in Schumann's music found so many insurmountable obstacles and difficulties that we must presume that the public everywhere will be intimidated, and quite generally we do not understand how a performance could result unless those who know how to overcome the greatest difficulties devote special and extended study to it. But such an arrangement cannot possibly be intended for this purpose, therefore permit us to say frankly that we consider the goal mistaken because it is unat-

---

[9] A children's piece for piano four hands. Grimm was trying to put together a volume of pieces for children.

[10] Apparently a work by Joachim, never published.

[11] Nikodemus came to Jesus at night because he had neither the courage nor the conviction to declare his support openly. Brahms and his friends gave his name to rejection letters from publishers.

tainable, and hence must forgo publication. We return the manuscript to you herewith, and remain respectfully,

your humble
Breitkopf & Härtel

[For Clara]

Dear friend, I had already sealed the letter when this arrived and I just had to send it along. To tell the truth, I had so dearly hoped for the 6 louis d'or and *above all* to honour our cherished Schumann, but there's nothing to be done with 'old wives and publishers'. Should I convert it to an edition for children—I don't fancy doing that. Nor do I now want to send off the quartet.[12] Commending myself to you with greatest esteem,

Johannes

Please return this letter to me! My first Nikodemus.

It is in keeping with Brahms's character that he announced his intention to dedicate the Ballades, Op. 10, to Grimm so casually and enigmatically, burying the request in other news. Grimm was thrilled. 'You surprised me so blissfully that my thanks are much greater than I can say. At first I couldn't believe that what I was reading about your Ballades was really true,—and had to read it again: but then, are there any other "1854-ers" apart from you and me?'[13] Brahms was paying homage here to the friend who, like him, had given a part of his life to help the Schumann family try to come to grips with the catastrophe of that year.

49
Johannes Brahms to Joseph Joachim

[16 February 1855]

My dear Joseph,

Your letter to Frau Clara has arrived and has given great pleasure. It came with one from Schumann; she still had tears in her eyes as she was already laughing heartily over your jokes, e.g. the caricature of Friedländer.[14]

There are a few things I have to reply to. Frau Schumann is coming to Hanover on Monday with the first train. It would please her greatly if she could play for the King as early as Monday evening, particularly on account of the recommendation to England.[15] However, if she could play only on

---

[12] Most likely the early version of the Piano Quartet, Op. 60.
[13] *BW* iv. 22.   [14] A friend of Clara's in Berlin.
[15] Clara was hoping the King of Hanover would give her a letter of introduction to the English Court.

Tuesday evening, she would stay in Hanover for the day. Would you perhaps take the necessary steps? She is bringing along her husband's beautiful letter for you.

My dear chap, what shall I write, or say to you later on about the wonderful Variations?[16] What more indeed, than that they are exactly as I had imagined them, as your overtures gave promise.

The same thing happens to me with your works as with Beethoven. When I was getting to know a new symphony or overture, I was completely absorbed by it for a long time. All else was merely an arabesque around the grand picture. So it is with your works. So it was with the Hamlet Heinrich and Demetrius Overtures, so now with the superb new piece.

How often I had the urge to write to you when I had looked at a work [of yours] with ever greater astonishment, yet I could not, nor do I know what more to say than that I admire and love it all more and more. My total, warm attachment did not really develop until I had looked at them in amazement for a long time.

The Variations are perhaps not quite so much your own as the Overtures.

But possibly nobody has yet wielded Beethoven's pen with such power.

The *Hebraic Melodies*,[17] however, are totally Joachim, wonderfully affecting. Let me show you particular places (I mean specially beautiful ones) the next time we're together again.

I ask you, look at the mighty *crescendo* from your Op. 1 to now.

Where will that lead?

Beyond all seven heavens, indeed! I wish you knew even the half of how your things satisfy me, and with what love and high hopes I think of you.

With the best of greetings,

Your

Johannes

Can't you send me the first movement of the promised piano sonata when it is finished?

As compensation for the Viola Variations and Songs which Frau Schumann is bringing back to Hanover.

There can be no doubt that Joachim's creative talent was fundamental to Brahms's fervent friendship with him. From the very start, Brahms looked upon him as the

---

[16] *Variations on an Original Theme for Viola and Piano*, Op. 10. Joachim had just sent them to Düsseldorf for Brahms and Clara to see.

[17] *Hebrew Melodies* for Viola and Piano, Op. 9.

soulmate with whom he would share the trials, tribulations, and triumphs of creation. As years went on, however, and Joachim's life took a very different tack, Brahms had less and less reason to write such a letter. Joachim turned his energies to conducting, performing, and earning money. He founded and directed the Royal Conservatory of Music in Berlin; and after his marriage, he virtually abandoned composing altogether, knowing better than most what dedication it required. Brahms never quite forgave him—that is, he never entirely rid himself of the feeling that Joachim should have been composing rather than wasting his life on other things, nor did he reconcile himself to losing the creative companionship of the one person he considered to have the greatest talent of anyone he knew. The cooling off of his friendship with Joachim in the next decades has to be seen in this light, quite apart from other more specific causes. In 1855, however, disillusionment was a long way off.

Now Joachim turned to Brahms, who had just reorganized Schumann's library, to reclaim the copy of the Beethoven Violin Concerto he had once sent Schumann as a gift.[18] Brahms's reply gives us a fleeting glimpse of himself as a teenager in Hamburg, powerfully affected by that concerto, Beethoven's Fifth Symphony, and Mozart's *Don Giovanni*.

50
Johannes Brahms to Joseph Joachim

Düsseldorf [*c.*22 February 1855]

Dearest Joseph,

Herewith the concerto you wanted, if only I could hear it!

Again and again the concerto reminds me of our first encounter, of which you, of course, know nothing.

You were playing in Hamburg, it must be many years ago; I was surely your most rapt listener. It was at a time when I was still subject to chaotic infatuations, and I didn't mind at all taking you for Beethoven. So the concerto I always held to be your own.

Like me, you undoubtedly enjoy recalling single most *powerful* impressions, such as the C minor symphony, this concerto, and Don Juan.

Think of me when you play it, and wish some sounds my way; I sit here quite alone in the evenings and think of all of you a great deal.

Be very warmly greeted

by your

Johannes

---

[18] Moser, *Joseph Joachim*, 115 and *JJ* i. 59.

Ask Grimm to send me news of his position, does he have it already? Greet him and Wagemann and Nicola.

Clara returned home from her Dutch tour in mid-February, and was off again ten days later for a tour which led her to Berlin and Joachim. On impulse, Brahms paid Schumann another visit.

51
Johannes Brahms to Clara Schumann

Düsseldorf, 23 & 24 February 1855

My most beloved friend,

Just as I thought, this evening I have so much of what is most beautiful to relate to you that I don't know where to begin.

I was with your beloved husband from 2 to 6; if only you could see my delighted face, you would know more than after [reading] my letter.

He received me as warmly and as cheerily as the *first time*, only without the ensuing agitation that time. Then he immediately showed me your last letter and told me how much and how splendidly you had surprised him. We spoke for a long time about your travels. I told him I had seen you in Hamburg, Hanover, Lübeck, and even in Rotterdam. He then asked specifically, whether while in Holland you had stayed in the *same rooms* as last winter? I told him why you had mostly avoided this, which he found natural. He was very pleased with the beautiful Bach, Beethoven, and Schumann programmes.[19]

Then I fetched your picture for him. Oh, if you could have seen how deeply moved he was, how he almost had tears in his eyes and how he held it ever closer and finally said, 'Oh, how long I have wished for this.' As he set it down, his hands were trembling intensely.

He kept looking at it and stood up often to examine it again more closely.

He was delighted with the inkstand. Also with the cigars; he claimed he hadn't received any since Joachim's.

What probably happened is that he left some of them lying around and (as he also told me), he does not want to demand anything of the doctors. (He even told me specially, 'Clara has surely sent me some often, but I am not getting them.')

---

[19] Clara was one of the first performers to play programmes consisting entirely of serious music.

Then he invited me to walk into the garden with him. But what we talked about, well, I cannot possibly remember it all! I believe you'd find it difficult to think of anything that didn't come up. Very casually, I also asked him if he weren't composing something? That's how I learned he had written fugues, but I was not to hear them because they're not in shape.

He spoke of you *much and often.* How you play 'wonderfully' and 'just sublimely', e.g. the canons, especially the ones in A flat and B minor, the sketches *Des Abends* and *Traumeswirren,* 'which one could never hear [played] like that', etc. etc. He asked after all the children and laughed heartily about Felix's first tooth. He asked specifically about Frl. Bertha, Frl. Leser, Jungé, and Schönerstedt, Joachim (and how!), Hasenclever, etc. etc. Later he also asked about Bürgerm[eister] Hamers, Nielo, Massenbach, etc, whether they are still in Düsseldorf![20]

With great interest did he hear of Grimm's appointment, Becker, etc.[21]

He talked to me a lot about your trips, about the Siebengebirge and Switzerland and Heidelberg, spoke also about the Countess Abegg.

He looked over my C major Sonata with me and pointed out a number of details.

I asked him to give me a greeting (written) to take along to you and asked him whether he wouldn't like to write to you more often?

'Oh gladly every day, always, always, if only I had paper.' And he really had none. He just doesn't want to ask anything of the doctors but they give him nothing at all if he doesn't.

Thereupon I had paper brought; its large size displeased him greatly, and my method of making it smaller may not have pleased him either. He sat down repeatedly with the friendliest look on his face and intended to write. But he maintained he was too agitated, he would write tomorrow.

I only hope that tomorrow doesn't mean as long a wait as usual.

Your husband used a pencil to write in my pocket diary what he wanted me to get for him.

A cravat; his usual one is in poor condition, and the one he wore 'was altogether too grandiose'!

The *Signale;* I shall look through this year's numbers and send them to

---

[20] Dr Hasenclever was a member of the Düsseldorf Singverein committee, as was Nielo. Massenbach was District Governor. In 1852 they had protected Schumann when there was burgeoning discontent at his deportment as Düsseldorf's music director. For more details, see Litz, ii. 243. Countess Pauline D'Abegg, mentioned in the next paragraph, was the dedicatee of Schumann's *Variations,* Op. 1.

[21] Grimm had every expectation of being named music director in Göttingen. In the end, the appointment fell through. Rupert Becker was a violinist. See p. 60, n. 63.

him (a selection), then I'll write to Senff that Herr Sch. wishes to read the *Signale*.

We also spoke about the *Neue Zeitschrift für Musik*, and what a lot of wheeling and dealing and gossip that was.[22]

Die Gesänge der Frühe.[23] He told me several times that Arnold shouldn't wait for his corrections; whereupon I told him he had got them long ago.

But he declared *very forcefully* that Arnold couldn't have received them, because he had asked a very long time ago that they be dispatched, so that they would have appeared [in print] long ago. The doctors weren't dispatching anything.

We argued back and forth for a long time, I couldn't quite convince him.

Then at my request he wrote the title:

Concertpiece for Pianoforte and Orchestra,

Op. 134

dedicated to Johannes Brahms

by Robert[24]

Should I send Senff the score, etc., with title now?

Then he asked me whether there weren't 20 volumes of compositions upstairs in the bookcase, he supposed there would be no more room for the 21st volume; if there were, there would be plenty of material, the Bach sonatas, the cello and violin concertos, fughettos, etc.[25]

I offered to see to it, which he thought was very kind, but he wouldn't hear of 'sending it to him', smiling, as if to say that it would please him greatly all the same!

Shall we take care of that upon your return?

---

[22] Schumann and some friends had founded the *Neue Zeitschrift für Musik* in 1834. It was now under the editorship of Franz Brendel, a follower of Liszt and devotee of the 'Music of the Future'. *Die Signale für die musikalische Welt* was an important music journal, published by the Leipzig music publisher Bartolf Senff. It featured reviews, reports of new music, artists' doings, their concerts and tours, and was widely read.

[23] Composed shortly before Schumann's breakdown, *An Diotima, Gesänge der Frühe*, Op. 133, Five Pieces for Pianoforte, was 'dedicated to the great poetess Bettina' (Bettina von Arnim) and published in Elberfeld, December 1855, by Arnold.

[24] See Letter 45. Clara had already performed it in the Hague on 30 November 1853.

[25] He was referring to his complete works, contained in twenty volumes. Schumann provided piano accompaniments to the Bach solo violin sonatas, published without opus by Breitkopf & Härtel. Joachim performed the D minor Chaconne with Schumann's piano part on at least one occasion, the memorial concert for Schumann in Hamburg, on 22 November 1856, with Brahms at the piano (Kal, i. 287.) The other works referred to are: Concerto for Cello and Orchestra, Op. 129; *Fantasy for Violin and Orchestra*, Op. 131, written for Joseph Joachim; *Seven Pieces in Fughetta Form for Pianoforte*, Op. 126. The Overture to Julius Caesar, mentioned later, is likewise a late work, Op. 128.

I told him you were in Berlin with J[oachim], which pleased him. He was also glad to hear about the B flat major Symphony on Monday, and J.'s Variations.[26]

Of Joachim he spoke with an enthusiasm he normally reserves only for speaking of you. He spoke a lot about the Music Festival, how wonderfully J. played even in the rehearsal. That no one had ever had any idea the violin could produce such a tone.[27]

And then we even did some 4-hand playing! He invited me to do the Caesar Overture. But he didn't want to take the upper part. 'I am the bass.' We did not keep strictly together, but then how long hasn't he played duets.

You (or you and he) used to play it faster, he said. He also had high praise for the arrangement.

(Of the Quintet I told him nothing, of course.)[28]

The grand piano was badly out of tune, I have arranged for it to be tuned.

When I said goodbye to him he insisted on accompanying me to the railway station.

Under the pretext of fetching my coat, I asked the doctor downstairs whether this was all right with him. To my greatest joy, it was.

(I spoke no further [with the doctor], before that I hadn't even seen him.)

The warder always walked either behind or beside us (A few paces away).

I thought it wonderful that the heavy door, which is always bolted and locked, was opened wide as we left.

I had to take the programmes away with me, he claimed to know every number and [that] after all, they belong in your collection.[29]

He wanted to give my Ballades back to me, and was delighted that they were intended for him.

(I keep recalling all kinds of things, I must backtrack a little; he was so delighted that I had corrected and completed his catalogue with so much care, also that I had copied out 'The Bell'.[30]

---

[26] *Variations for Viola and Piano*, Op. 10. Joachim had recently sent his new composition to Düsseldorf for Clara and Brahms to see. The Symphony is presumable Schumann's First, Op. 38.

[27] The Festival of the Lower Rhine of 15–17 May 1853, the last Schumann participated in. It was here that Schumann and Joachim met for the first time, and recognized in each other artists with similar aims. Joachim performed the Beethoven Violin Concerto, a work he played incomparably and which he made his own during his sixty-year career. See Moser, *Joseph Joachim*, 112 ff.

[28] That Brahms had arranged the Piano Quintet, Op. 44, for piano duet, but Breitkopf & Härtel had declined to publish it. See Letter 48.

[29] Programmes of the concerts in Berlin. Clara was now keeping Robert informed of her performances.

[30] A poem Robert had written in 1844, while accompanying Clara on her tour to Moscow. It was not a happy time for him. See Reich, 118 ff., and Litz, ii. 74.

He enjoyed my Hungarian hat, as he had enjoyed my cap before, etc.)

Imagine my joy as I now tramped a long way and merrily with him, the precious man. I didn't look at my watch, and replied to his questions that I still had time, and so we went to the cathedral, to the Beethoven Monument, and then I brought him back to the road.

He used my eye spectacles often because he had forgotten his lorgnette.

Incidentally, Herr Sch. walks very happily at the well-known Brahmsian pace, which you can seldom put up with!

On the way he also asked me whether his Clara takes daily walks? I answered (though not quite truthfully) that when you were in Düsseldorf or anywhere with me, I took you for walks every day, you didn't like to go alone. 'That I do believe, we always used to walk together,' said your Robert, quite wistfully.[31]

We spoke a lot about his books and music, and he was happy as a king that I knew every single item and its place so precisely. We bantered with each other a lot about this, because first he had to think hard to recall specific books and then I had to, as well.

I left him at Endenich Way; he embraced and kissed me tenderly; at our parting he sent greetings only to you. Previously he had often done that, [had] also sent many greetings to Joachim, Bargiel, Fräulein Leser, Bertha, Jungé, Schönerstedt, Dr Hasenclever.

On the way [back] I was as if intoxicated, at times, so happy; you can probably imagine how much I wished you in Düsseldorf.

Your letter was a real joy to me; I felt I could touch your hand.

I could not write you anything sad, except that occasionally he urgently longs to be away from there; he spoke more softly and less distinctly at those times, for he fears the doctors; but he said nothing that was confused, unclear.

He also spoke about it being a year in March since he had come to Endenich, it seemed to him that everything had already been quite green then, he had had beautiful weather, the most beautiful blue sky.

Alas, I can only write you quite simply and drily what we spoke about together; I cannot describe the other, lovelier things, his beautiful, tranquil eyes, his warmth when he spoke of you, his joy at the picture. Just imagine it all as beautifully as you possibly can.

I don't suppose you will have any questions after such an exhaustive report? How I wish I had written more briefly but really beautifully.

---

[31] A daily walk had been part of Clara's routine from the time she was a very small child, a custom she followed faithfully during her marriage. See Reich, 37. The walk Schumann took with Brahms, from the asylum in Endenich to the railway station in Bonn, is several miles each way.

But I wanted to write quickly and, if possible, everything.

So be greeted most warmly by your Robert and by me, be content to accept my good intentions, you know how much I would like to bring you greater joy.

In heartfelt love and veneration

Your Johannes

Warmest greetings to dear Joachim.

52
Johannes Brahms to Robert Schumann

[Düsseldorf, 2 March] 1855

Dear, esteemed friend,

I am sending you herewith the things you wanted: a cravat and *Die Signale*. I must be held answerable for the first; since your wife is in Berlin it was for me to decide. I hope, at least, it is right and not too high?

I am sending along copies of the *Signale* from last year; some issues are missing, we probably didn't pay enough attention to it. From now on you will have them regularly.

I can already give you the firmest assurance, now, that Herr Arnold has received your proofs for the *Gesänge der Frühe*. That he has hesitated so long to publish is probably for another reason.

[I wonder] whether our long walk agreed with you? I do believe so. With what rapture I think back to that beautiful day, seldom have I been so overjoyed! Indeed, I have calmed and cheered up your dear wife with my rapturous letter.

All your friends here have commissioned me to send you their many greetings. I will particularly mention those of your children and Fräulein Bertha.

May all go well for you, and may you sometimes remember with love

your

Johannes

53
Johannes Brahms to Clara Schumann

Düsseldorf on the Rhine
In the year of redemption—1855
(In the year of the misfortune of the
birth of Friedr[rich] Wilh[elm] IV—61)
On the day of—Kunigund
The 3rd of the 3rd month = March
On the day a full moon was
promised us for the evening.[32]

Beloved Frau Clara,

Rarely have you given me as much pleasure with your letter as today. From earliest morning on I have been thinking of you so intensely that I had to put away my book, because you were so distinctly sitting beside. How happy you made me!

Yesterday I wrote to your husband and sent him the cravat and the *Signale*.

Yesterday, from the tower of the Academy, I saw the Rhine. The far bank is flooded far and wide. In Düsseldorf, the streets along the Rhine are under water too, one moves about in boats. Performances are impossible in the theatre, since the parterre etc. is flooded. Now, if the singers would sing, kiss, and murder in rowing boats and gondolas, and the audience had to move around the parterre in little boats, then I would go.

The stony guest would then have to arrive in a boat and instead of drawing Don Juan down under, he would have to toss him into the water.

Yesterday I was again at Frl. Leser's, Frl. Schönerstedt played the C sharp Etudes, and afterwards, I some of the Night Pieces, Album, etc.[33]

Just imagine, last night Ludwig slept in my bed! I brought him to bed and showed him your picture so that he might have pleasant dreams. I don't really sleep much, mostly I lie awake dreaming; the little one awoke very early and so we had a lot of fun together.

An awful lot of notes are now swirling around in my head and also on paper, if I only had more peace and quiet! But everything remains a beginning, I complete nothing.

---

[32] A curiously political comment by the young Brahms. Friedrich Wilhelm IV (1795–1861) was King of Prussia (and 61 years old at the time of this letter). The extreme conservatism of his early reign helped trigger the Revolution of 1848, but he opposed Bismarck's desire to suppress the civil war by military force. He presided over a period of social unrest and a demand for German unity, which he opposed.

[33] Schumann's *Nachtstücke für das Piano*, Op. 23, and either the *Album für die Jugend*, Op. 8, or the *Albumblätter*, Op. 124, or perhaps the last pieces of Op. 99, originally known as *Album*.

But I have begun all kinds of things.

Don't worry about my 'taking a trip to Hamburg'; I have a continual foreboding which drives me on, you know what it is.

But if I heard even one word that it might be inconvenient for you, I can never go on with it.

About the boys I can write you nothing but the best, they are becoming, so it seems to me, ever livelier and stronger. I have custody of a large bag of sweets from Frl. Hartmann and they have to work hard to earn each one. They also have to wrestle with each other.

Whoever pins the other down 3 times gets something, but then they may scuffle 30 times before one of them succeeds.

The two girls have invited themselves to our table for next Sunday; mainly on account of the potato salad which they have done without for a long time!

A letter has again arrived from England. Oh, if only that unfortunate tour were not to be, when I think of what you are suffering already, how will you be able to stand it!

I have no words to strengthen and encourage you, only to dissuade you.—But you really must consider whether you wouldn't like to take Frl. Bertha with you, if I remained here that would work quite well. We must certainly discuss that.

So, Joachim is going to play his Variations in public for once, in a little *soirée*? Then do make sure to send me the programme!

I have nothing more, as a matter of fact, had absolutely nothing to write other than a thousand greetings to you and to Joachim and just as many thanks for every letter. Frl. Bertha also bids me to give you the tenderest greeting—indeed, I even dare to breathe a very soft kiss onto your beautiful hand!

Be then greeted most exquisitely by your
Johannes.

Brahms's parents were more worried about him than ever; to all appearances, he had derailed a most promising career. Any parent of a talented youth who has apparently lost his sense of direction will recognize the tone of anguish and anger in this letter from his mother. It was probably written at the urgings of his father, and perhaps of Marxsen, as well.

54

Christiane Brahms to Johannes Brahms

[Hamburg, 20 March 1855]

... I suppose it is good that you are giving lessons, at least it is something. But you have always found it odious and it doesn't bring in much, I mean for you, who is capable of more. Frau Schumann also gives lessons, but nevertheless prefers to give concerts. You think the income (from the concerts) is not substantial. But then she would not do it, turning her family and household over to strangers and travelling around the world without a husband ... But since she earns a great deal, she considers it to be her duty to do so. I only wish we knew how to earn something here. On the 1st of April the theatre will be closed, then 40 musicians will be without bread. They have been told to plan on 6 months[34] ... How quickly the months will go by until Fritz has to draw lots [in the military draft lottery], then he may become a soldier. A surrogate now costs 12, even 15,000 Marks here. Where should that come from? You will say: borrow it. We won't begin with that, because we could never repay it and you know that your mother cannot rest if she owes even 50 Marks ... But someone whom God has endowed with so many gifts does wrong to sit back as placidly as you do ... What must Frau Schumann be thinking of you, as you sit back calmly while she accepts her life turning sour and you, a young, healthy man can just sit back ... Wouldn't it be better for you to bestir yourself a little more in the outside world rather than allow yourself to be towed along by others of your sort?

I write you all this reluctantly, you know that perfectly well; nor had I ever thought that I would have to. But since no one else writes but I, and you are not at home with us, I simply have to. We and all those who love you recognize that you are on the wrong track, and will amount to absolutely nothing, this way. Write to your old mother again very soon! Who knows how long ...

Clara's visit to Hamburg, in the next month, helped to alleviate his parents' concern. She accepted an invitation to stay in the Brahms flat (she and Johannes were in Hamburg to hear Otten's performance of *Manfred*), thereby getting her first look at Brahms in his home environment. Clara was quite taken with his mother, but wrote in her diary: 'How it pains me to see Johannes understood least of all by his own family! Mother and sister have some inkling of his extraordinary talents, but father and brother not even that.'[35]

Seen in this light, there is a sense of desperation in Brahms's next letter to Joachim.

[34] In fact, the Hamburg City Theatre did not close.   [35] Litz, ii. 372.

55

Johannes Brahms to Joseph Joachim

[Düsseldorf, 26 March 1855]

My beloved Joseph,

Won't you write me something more definite about your arrival, soon? It's probably more important to me, is closer to my heart than yours! Frau Schumann told me again that you had spoken of 'no small excursions, two months'. There are two rooms to let here in a garden apartment, do commission me to rent them for six months from April 12th! Do you want to live utterly alone, to spend the long summer in—Hanover? don't you ever ask after us? Last summer I remained silent, because you were in Berlin, but this time!

Are you angry with me that I spent so much of the winter in Hamburg? You probably know that it wouldn't take much for me to find myself sitting here for the summer, too, I didn't reflect and consider enough, you don't know the agony—.

How dearly I would have liked to hear the wonderful, the 'wonder-splendiferous' C major triad!

But it did not work out.

Included are two letters from the cherished Schumann, which will please you. We are now sending him the Heinrich Overture, which will fire him up.

Dear fellow, now I definitely expect a letter very soon and you immediately afterwards. Don't deny me that happiness, unless you can find better elsewhere than in Hanover. Every day I wait with greater anguish.

I had hoped to see you by the beginning of April! Won't it come to pass?

In most heartfelt love,

Your Johannes.

A thousand greetings from Frau Clara.

Be sure to return Schumann's letters right away! Otherwise we'll have Fischer issue a warning one of these days![36] Herr Schumann asks for the Paganini Variations; we can't find them; you won't forget to send the manuscript which you have? Many thousand greetings from Frau Clara.

---

[36] A conductor of the court orchestra in Hanover.

A one-word letter soon arrived from Joachim. 'Rent!', it said, and he settled in Düsseldorf for the next few months. He, Clara, and Brahms played a great deal of music together, and when Clara was away Brahms day-dreamed about her, spent time with his friends—primarily Joachim and Julius Allgeyer—read, gave a few lessons, tried to compose, and worried he had lost the ability to do so.

Brahms celebrated his twenty-second birthday in Düsseldorf. Schumann's gift was the manuscript of his Overture *The Bride of Messina*, Op. 100, with an inscription addressing the young man in the intimate 'Du'. From Joachim came a collection of his favourite tin soldiers, called *Bücklinge* (no relation to a type of smoked herring of the same name!). Clara's diary noted that this was her first happy day since Robert's hospitalization.

56
Johannes Brahms to Julius Otto Grimm

Düsseldorf, 8 May 1855

Accept my warmest thanks for kindly remembering, you made me really happy with that. If only you'd been here to see how splendidly mysteriously the large white cake came snowing in! I guessed all along it came from an infatuated Miss D.P., today I learned in a roundabout way through Langenberg how it had come. If only you had been here and had spent the glorious, jolly day with us. In the morning, among many beautiful flowers, the picture of my mother and sister, like enough to kiss. Then a photograph of the beloved Schumann (after the daguerreotype, but incomparably more beautiful), then books: Dante and Ariosto! In the afternoon around 3 o'clock Joachim, and with him a large shipment of *Bücklinge* (some soldiers) etc. with lovely letters from H[am]bg! Rarely was I so merry and glad of heart as yesterday.—Lots of music-making now, and wonderfully! Bach, Beethoven, Schumann, so that one can't get enough. Just think, our revered master remembered me and sent me the manuscript of *The Bride of Messina* with the most affectionate inscription. (Du!). Frau Clara will add a word, also sends along some things pertaining to him. Now very hearty greetings to you, dear friend, write to us often, we'll definitely do the same, Frau Clara too will stick to this. We think of you often, especially while making music, drinking, reading, and out walking, and what else do we do, anyway?

Affectionately your Johannes Brahms.

57
Johannes Brahms to Julius Otto Grimm

Heidelberg, July [18]55

Dear friend,

Unfortunately you are absolutely right when you complain about my long silence; don't be angry with me! If I could do as I wish, I would write to you every 3 days, but it just doesn't work out!—In *Summa Summarum* I will tell you about us all. First about the principal person. There, unfortunately, things don't look good; three months ago Frau Cl[ara] received the last letter (in Hamburg); the last lines were those of 7 May, addressed to me!

Since then he has suffered continuously from aural hallucinations, weakness, etc. The doctors maintain nevertheless that there is no set-back, and blame it on the sultry summer weather. At the request of the doctors, Frau Cl. has recently sent him another brief letter. Should anything better occur, I will write to you about it (for you alone).—I received your letter the day before yesterday here in Heidelberg; the three of us took off 2 weeks ago. Joachim bought himself a knapsack and wanted to go to the Tyrol, but also had a suitcase with him. Frau Clara, Bertha, and I travelled to Ems, where Cl. gave a concert with Jenny Lind (earned masses of money!)[37] In the mean time I went on walking tours to Braubach, etc. But afterwards—! we three marched forth from Koblenz with no more baggage than fitted comfortably into my knapsack, along the entire length of the Rhine to Mainz; we hiked stoutly through Stolzenfels, Marburg, Rheinfels and -stein, Oberwesel, Johannisberg, Bacharach, the Sauer and Schweizer valleys, the Niederwald, etc., etc. Then on to Frankfurt (with suitcases) and then to Heidelberg. There we have explored everything with delight: castle, Wolkenkur, Kaiserstuhl, Wolfsbrunnen, and even the Schwalbennest near Neckarsteinach.[38]—Those were delicious days; I would never have thought I could be so blissful on a journey with two ladies. Now sadly, sadly, Frau Cl. has gone to Baden-Baden. I feel quite lonely and sad here. I just don't know what to do. I must close as I must still write to Frau Cl. Hearty greetings to you from her too, no doubt she will write to you herself. Write to me again *soon*!

Your Johannes.

---

[37] The concert was a humiliation. See p. 765.
[38] Places of interest in and around Heidelberg. It requires a sturdy pair of legs to reach the Schwalbennest.

58
Johannes Brahms to Clara Schumann

[Düsseldorf] Sunday, 12 August 1855

My beloved friend,

All day now I've been practising and reading diligently and have thought all the while of you, but now I also want to tell you about it, at leisure. I think of you constantly, not for a long time have I thought of anyone so fondly and so incessantly; since early this morning I have been hoping for a letter from you in the evening which would say very lovely things from Hamburg; I long for it.

My swollen mouth has got fatter. This morning I kept a fig in my mouth constantly and wrapped up with wool, but since by noon it was still more swollen, I left it off out of spite; it's just too much of a bother to prowl around so bandaged up.

Frl. v. Meysenbug has written me a letter, thickly over-sugared, that I have become her greatly revered genius and Master![39]

What a notion people form just as soon as a young person writes something special! How many a youth wishes for eagles' wings for himself and even fancies he has them, then gets buried in his books and music, is immediately stuck in the dust and forgets to fly. Luckily I'm not afraid this will happen to me frequently, but it often makes me sad that I no longer know at all how one composes, how one creates.

I wish this time were soon past, and I were more free and more courageous; I am almost sickened with longing for a new, fresh sound.

Just think, sometimes I believe quite firmly that I shall get very sick and then become twice as healthy!

Then again sometimes that I had been very sickly and am now recovering.

How unhappy would I be if by some chance I did not have you! From you I keep learning that one cannot extract strength for living (= strength to live and create) from books, but only from one's own soul. One must not turn one's senses inward, but outward.

You must always remain with me as my good angel, then I shall surely become whatever it is I should and can.

---

[39] Laura von Meysenbug, from the Duchy of Detmold. She first became Brahms's student at Clara's suggestion; Brahms subsequently taught her for several years, and she helped smooth the way for him in Detmold.

I'm not going to reread my prattle, excuse it, and let yourself be warmly embraced by your

Johannes.

The children are all well, Bertha very melancholy and my new pupil, so far, an ox.

En route to a rest cure in Kiel Clara travelled through Hamburg, stopping for a night at the Brahms house. In the city she found an edition of Plutarch, which she knew Brahms coveted. But it was expensive.

59
Johannes Brahms to Clara Schumann

Tuesday, 14 August 1855

My dear friend,

What ever shall I do with the Plutarch? I can't find it in my heart to send him back, as I had in fact heroically resolved. I have never been able to read other than individual biographies by Pl., was never able to get him complete. Also the edition I told you about belongs to an 'inexpensive edition of classic authors' and so is not likely to be as complete as this one, certainly won't have as many explanatory notes.

How I look forward to your bringing him with you. Plutarch's descriptions of lives have a strange power over me. And then I'll have him complete by the same translator. What you write me about Coriolanus doesn't surprise me; sometimes (when one reads it for the first few times) one wishes he were different, gentler, more human. If you read it more often, this vanishes, and in such a powerful hero you accept his roughness and hardness, if, in the appropriate situation he is therefore really hard, as in the election by the people.[40]

But his betrayal is not the end! I keep forgetting the impression made by the scene with his mother and his death, that elevates everything.

By the way, I have to tell you that Shakespeare studied Plutarch very thoroughly. In Coriolanus, Caesar, etc, whole speeches are taken from Pl., in Coriolanus especially, the plot follows him exactly. (The sequence of scenes.)

Beethoven also greatly enjoyed reading Plutarch, and in his music one often pictures such a hero approaching. Many thanks for all the kind things you write me. This morning I got the letter from Kiel.

---

[40] Act II, scene iii of Shakespeare's play.

I'm sorry that the sea is not wider there, but I can do so little about that! If only I were there. I would like just to follow you. In the end, we might just as well have stayed in Rüdesheim?

Fräulein von Meysenbug is taking lessons from me. Probably 2 P[iano]f[orte]—and 1 theory at 1 Rth—that makes 3 thaler a week!

The little boy 2 at 20 Sgr makes 40 Sgr.

N. and Wollenhaupt[41] at 1 Rth. = 2 Rth.

[Fräulein] Arnold—1 Rth = 1 Rth.

I'm getting to be a rich man.

Now I can pay all my debts and on top of that give this one a Schiller, that one the complete works of Goethe. Besides that the money from the Ballades, about which I'll write soon, and the money from Whistling!

This evening I'm at Fräulein Leser's, who by the way is not going to visit her friend in the monastery now, but next month, and sends greetings.

Bertha is in ecstasies, almost too much so. The children are very well and well behaved. It's a peculiar thing with these ecstasies. I'm making old observations anew. It changes people so much, often to their disadvantage. When they catch love so unhappily, then consider it to be the main event, the reason the world exists, I just can't bear it.

A girl like that takes everyone into her confidence, not by what she says, but she fiddles about so and dramatizes everything so loudly that anyone within 10 paces notices it.

Incidentally, I think it will swell to even greater heights, I don't trust the officers.

My swelling is now completely gone. Yesterday I was furious and went outside in the cold; it was alarmed by this defiance and lost patience.[42]

Now I would give you, just for my sister, a very light, tender kiss. For you however, a right hearty one, as you are accustomed to from

Your

Johannes

Bertha, Fräulein Leser, etc. greet you.

A letter from Cologne is enclosed.

From Fräulein Sabinie there is a letter in which she talks nonsense about being unable to compose and unable to let it go, I suppose that one can stay here.

Brahms's projected weekly income of 6 thaler 40 groschen was not inconsiderable. Moreover, Breitkopf & Härtel paid 8 louis d'or for the Ballades, Op. 10, but that

---

[41] Woolly-head: most likely a nickname.

[42] In his youth Brahms occasionally suffered from boils.

was the last money Brahms would earn from his compositions for a long time. By way of comparison, Brahms's mother was delighted when Fritz Brahms was appointed as music teacher in a teachers' training school at a salary of 125 thaler per year,[43] and Schumann's hospital costs were 700 thaler per year.

60
Johannes Brahms to Clara Schumann

Monday, 20 August 1855

Dear Clara,

What a beautiful long letter I received this morning! A thousand thanks for that.

The lovely flowers also give me great pleasure; the ones from Hamburg, incidentally, are equally beautiful, have I not written that? Your letter found me still in bed (7:30), which only shows you that I don't get up early, but in fact quite late. At night I never can seem to find my way to bed, in spite of having firmly resolved to sleep more regularly. I only get home at 10, after supper, which I enjoy eating out with J[oachim] and sometimes Allgeyer. So, then I read with your picture before me, and am pleased that I am alone, alternate between gazing at you and talking to you, or read. Well then time passes quickly, and in between I play with the bell pull which, to my delight, is within reach.

How I spend my life apart from that is hard to recount because it's too irregular. I play, read, write, or talk to you in your room or mine. Then come the lessons, then Joachim or Allgeyer in between. This morning Fräulein von Meysenbug is starting theory. Because I have written myself out, indeed, because I have already become old, composing isn't going well, but none the less I have written something for you, for your birthday or for your return.

You can guess until then.

We walk to the Stockkämpchen and to the other side [of the Rhine] every day; yesterday (the three of us) bought ourselves lots of plums and pears on the way to the Stockkämpchen; there we ate clabbered milk and smoked. J. the whole cigar, that made him very ill, very! After that it was absolutely necessary to drink some bouillon.

N. B. In Bach's Allemande I find the tied A♭ is right:

---

43 *Familie*, 62.

The A♭ in the bass is correct:

because it continues stepwise in that line A♭, B♭, C, D.

Also the E♭

because E natural would be impossible.

The first-mentioned A♭ I find particularly beautiful.

About the embellishments I am very particular. But slovenly editions often force one to follow one's own taste.

And I take

Longer mordants (〰) I often consider as trilled notes, I don't take the little notes before the beat, as I do with the simple ones (〰 〰).

Altogether in Bach I don't render mordents and trills as embellishments, not *leggiero* (or only if it is particularly fitting), but I think one should use them to emphasize the embellished note, as must have been necessary with the old weak pianos. Yesterday after writing I just had to play my C major Sonata; how long I hadn't done that!

It gave me real pleasure, I didn't know the Finale.

Now I will look for all the things you asked for and pack and send them to you this afternoon, my warmest greetings go with them.

How I enjoyed your letter today; it tells me so much and so beautifully how you are living.

The children are well and well-behaved.

Bertha wrote to you yesterday.

Everyone greets you, myself most of all as your
most faithful
Johannes

Brahms's comments concerning the Partita in B flat (BWV 825) are especially note-worthy because they give a clear indication of his concept of harmony. In referring to the stepwise line of Ab, Bb, C, D, (which occurs in the third and second measures from the end of the Allemande) his ear has picked out the harmonic motion in a manner more akin to the musical thought of a later generation than to the classical views of harmony which Brahms would have been brought up on. Even his method of notation, showing Clara the notes her ears should focus on, harkens forward to the structural hearing practices of a later time.

On 6 August the Schumann household moved to a new flat. This time, Brahms moved with them, acquiring his own 'charmingly cosy room'.[44]

61

Johannes Brahms to Clara Schumann

Düsseldorf, Friday, 24 August 1855

Dear Clara,

One thing I can state about this night; I shall never forget it as long as I live. Everything turned out well, I can tell you about it from the beginning. We came back from Frl. Leser at about 11 o'clock, it was very sultry, as it had been all day. The moon was shining, the weather was splendid. Only yester-day I had had my bed turned round, and lay with my head towards the win-dow. I continued to read for a very long time, however at about 2 o'clock I awoke with a start, there was the most dreadful thunderstorm.

It looked as if the whole city were aflame, accompanied by the most dreadful thunder claps. A hail storm smashed my window, wind howled throughout the whole house. With horror I moved to the dark corner of my bed and thought it must be an earthquake, or the end of the world. Then came a thunderclap as if the earth were splitting apart. Bertha came scream-ing into my room and begged me to come, they were dying of fright. By chance Gretchen was sleeping downstairs, the two were screaming and slid-ing around on their knees and believed that the Judgement Day had come. Both boys [Ludwig, Ferdinand] were also sliding about the room. So I took them onto my lap and made them close their eyes. Felix was sleeping soundly, and Eugenie was calm.

I simply cannot describe to you how overwhelming the weather was. After an hour it calmed down, I made a light and we inspected the windows and closed their shutters, broken glass from many of them was already on the ground. I went back to bed, naturally I couldn't sleep; out of my two

---

[44] At No. 135 Poststrasse (Litz, ii. 361).

windows I could just see the two thunderstorms, blazing clouds hung there from which lightning bolts shot out in all directions. The thunder rolled continuously. It did not take long, and another hailstorm and lightning as powerful as the first arrived. I jumped out of bed, this time closed all the doors, which rattled continuously from the blasts. Then I struck a light and went into the nursery again. Hailstones were falling as though the windows were being pounded with cudgels. Shards of glass fell into the room continuously, water was standing everywhere.

For a good hour the immense fury continued again; never could one imagine such weather even in one's mind. Other storms are like child's play in comparison. Gradually, towards morning, it let up. 35 panes of glass are smashed to bits; those facing the Schwanenmarkt were more protected. In my room, all those facing the Poststrasse are shattered, the shards reached as far as the bed. What I was feeling I cannot even describe, I will never forget it. The whole night I thought of you, terrified that you might encounter this away from home.

Next time any kind of thunderstorm occurs again I'll go downstairs into the kitchen with everyone. In any case, have great confidence in my composure, which comes over me at the right time the moment I see others like Bertha.

I shall be very careful; the whole time I thought only of the children and kept them under my eye. One couldn't get out of the door. For me at least, it was impossible.

Towards morning, heavy clouds were still passing overhead. But it is more stifling today than yesterday.

In the morning it became more and more peaceful. Then came your dear, dear letter, and *everything* was bright again.

In the whole town hardly a pane of glass remained intact on the windward side. None in the barracks on the Rhine. Over 700 windows in different houses are smashed in.

This muggy air is terribly tiring, add to that no sleep at all and agitation such as I had never experienced, I cannot write to you as much as I should like.

Tomorrow I shall write you more; I cannot any more just now. Don't be cross with me for yesterday's letter. You too should see in everything the logic of my love for you, as I should with yours.

Will you do that? Remain good to me, perhaps one day I shall deserve it better and more.

With heartiest greetings

Your

Johannes

When Clara Schumann stopped off in Hamburg to spend a day and night with the Brahms family, she had a long talk with Johannes's mother. Although no record of the conversation exists, it is safe to say that an understanding was reached: Brahms's parents recognized once and for all his need to spend time composing, and stopped sending him reproachful letters; and Clara agreed to help him resurrect his abandoned career as a pianist and therby earn substantial money. During the next months he performed in Danzig, Bremen, Hamburg, Leipzig, Kiel, Altona, Göttingen, and Cologne, playing the works of Beethoven (including the Concertos No. 4 and 5), Bach, Robert Schumann, Clara Schumann, Schubert, and his own Trio, Op. 8. By Christmas he was able to send money home for the Christmas goose, and in June, 50 thaler for his father's fiftieth birthday.[45] The first Hamburger to offer him a concert appearance was Georg Otten.

62
Johannes Brahms to Georg Dietrich Otten

Düsseldorf, September 1855

Esteemed Herr Otten,

For longer than I had wished, you have been waiting for an answer from me, but I trust you will excuse me and understand that it is no small step for me suddenly to make my appearance as a pianist. I have resolved to play more often this winter and so I gladly accept your kind and estimable offer, it is the first I have received, and it cost me some effort to overcome my trepidation; a certain sensation (almost describable as fear) is difficult to banish.

I am really looking forward to such fine concerts as you promise, if only I could hear them all! In Hamburg there certainly is a need to give yourself and others such pleasure more often.

Unfortunately, I can't tell you anything definite about Joachim, he does not yet know where he will spend this winter and how far a concert would oblige him to travel, otherwise he is favourably inclined; it would be best if you wrote to him yourself later.

He would not be able to commit himself earlier than mid-October.

To begin with, I would like to have a free choice between the first two concerts; in mid-November I am thinking of being in Danzig; as soon as I can definitely decide and commit myself, I shall write to you.

---

[45] Kurt and Renate Hofmann, *Johannes Brahms Zeittafel zu Leben und Werk* (Tutzing, 1983), 28–32, and *Familie*, 65.

That I cannot relinquish an honorarium, much as I would like to, you will surely understand; but it is the need for money which obliges me to tour. I leave it to your discretion.

I hope to be able to write you something definite soon, and will be very diligent so that I can make your fine concert still finer, if possible.

With sincerest greetings,

Your

Johannes Brahms

To your esteemed wife and your children my greetings; Frau Schumann also sends her best greetings.

His anxiety at resuming his performing career persisted, pushing him to write another letter long overdue, this time to Julius Grimm. Although Grimm's position as University Music Director in Göttingen had fallen through, he had settled there anyway, teaching the piano and voice and directing a woman's chorus. Now he was betrothed to Phillipine Ritmüller, daughter of Göttingen's well-known piano manufacturer. In the long run, Grimm provided Brahms with his happiest view of domesticity, offering a cheerful hearth where he was welcome for decades to come; in the short run, Grimm's connections in Göttingen were to prove important for Brahms both musically and personally.

63

Johannes Brahms to Julius Otto Grimm

D[üsse]ldorf, Sept[ember] [18]55

My dear friend,

Finally I am getting around to sending you my warmest congratulations; in my mind I sent them to you every day, you surely believe that without my writing it! I am in a quite peculiar state of mind just now, which does not easily allow me to write.

I intend to play in public this winter and notice with horror that my aversion to playing for people has got quite out of hand. How will it go. At times I am seriously frightened. I do now practise a lot, also I have quite a lot of lessons to give; forgive me that for so long, because of this, I put off writing to you to express to you my deep interest and pleasure in your good fortune. Also, greet your bride and her parents most warmly from me. Congratulating them on getting such a husband and son-in-law is easy!

Now I must write to you about some other matters. To begin with: that Frau Schumann would like to play a recital in Göttingen towards the end of October (between the 25th and the 28th) if it can be arranged easily. Will you write about that? Then I would like to enquire whether it wouldn't be possible for me to play (for a small fee or none at all) in one of the Hille concerts?[46] I have *never* before played with an orchestra and I am supposed to do so on 22 November in Hamburg; I fear it won't go well unless I try it beforehand with a smaller orchestra, etc. etc. Or, even better, if you give concerts with orchestra, how I would love that; but I would want it particularly in the middle of November or earlier.

You must not speak of a 'Trial Performance' and 'No Fee' to Hille, but rather, present it as something practical for him, instead.

I beg you, write to me about it soon, and also [tell] me specifically about your good fortune.

Be greeted most warmly by your

Johannes

64
Johannes Brahms to Georg Dietrich Otten

Düsseldorf, 5 October 1855

Dear Herr Otten,

So then, } on

the 24th of November I am coming!

} for

I should like to play the E flat Concerto by Beethoven, and if you wish a 2nd number, the Chromatic Fantasy and Fugue by Bach.

In any event I should like to begin with the Concerto. Let me say right out that I still cannot come to terms with the programme. Could you not save up the Ninth and perform it some time later in its entirety? Will you close with the Adagio? or will you change the order of the two movements?

The other music does not fit properly at all, after it. The A major, F, and B flat major symphonies [of Beethoven] or those of Schubert have none of them been heard in Hamburg for a long time. Don't you always prefer a complete work?

---

[46] Hille was university music director and unlike Grimm, had orchestral forces at his disposal.

However, if the programme remains as it is, the E flat Concerto probably likely have to [follow], then the scene by Gluck, then the Chromatic Fantasy (i. e. if you wish it), then the closing overture.

For my fee I [~~must~~] want to suggest 10 or 8 louis d'ors to you. But I beg you not to speak about it, because elsewhere I must demand more. In Bremen, for example, I am receiving 12 ld'ors, must also, as you can imagine, keep to the best possible price. Nevertheless I gladly leave to your discretion the deduction of 2 louis d'ors, if there is no other way. All in all, do whatever you want.

You must not promise yourself good success, I am very concerned about that. My self-consciousness in performance has all too much got the upper hand, perhaps I will fail a few times, perhaps even in your concert!

I am playing in Bremen on the 20th of November; from Hamburg I am going to Danzig, where I intend to give a concert with Joachim. Just at the time of your concert he is in Berlin for [his own] concerts, it is therefore impossible for him to come.

I am writing in a hurry, therefore excuse the horrible handwriting.

With my most sincere greetings to you and your entire family,

from your
Johannes Brahms

Frau Schumann sends greetings!

Brahms's clumsiness in the matter of his fee is striking. He never did learn to inflate his reputation, but he was not one to undervalue his worth, either. ('I don't give a fig for medals,' he said much later, 'but I want them, anyway.')[47]

Once more, his musical integrity is on display just where a more diplomatic view of life might have made him cautious; the youngster, starting his career, does not hesitate to express his reservations about the programme to the conductor who is taking a chance on him. In the event, Otten took Brahms's point and postponed Beethoven's Ninth for a complete performance at another time. And Brahms received his 10 gold louis.

Although he tried, Grimm was unable to put together an orchestra in time to allow his friend the luxury of a trial run. Brahms's first appearance with orchestra therefore took place in Bremen, on 20 November. He played two works by Beethoven: the Emperor Concerto, Op. 73, and the solo Fantasy in G minor, Op. 77. By the time he got to Hamburg, he was ready.

---

[47] Reported by Albert Gutmann, *Aus dem Wiener Musikleben*, i (Vienna, 1914), 32.

65
Johannes Brahms to Clara Schumann

Sunday, 25th of November 1855

Dear Clara,

Your letter of yesterday reached me too late, I could not write to Berlin any more, but in any case you must have got my letter on Saturday?

How dear and lovely is the one from you, I have it lying in front of me and don't want to answer it at all, I would rather copy it out. Your reason for leaving Berlin is really dismal, it constrained my conduct, too, on the second occasion.[48]

But first I want to tell you that everything came off well yesterday; in the second rehearsal as well.

I had considerable applause, really enthusiastic for Hamburg.

My playing was very deliberately fiery, it went incomparably better than in Bremen.

I'll write out the programme for you:

1. Symphony by Mendelssohn, in A Minor ~~in which I was greatly delighted by the Scherzo, but bored by the Andante. I liked the first movement very much, the last one less so.~~

2. Aria by Mozart, sung by Frau Guhrau, with orchestra.

To my delight she was accompanied by two basset horns, which had been sought out with considerable effort.

I find that no instrument so moulds itself to the human voice as does the basset horn, whose sound is almost half-way between the cello (bassoon) and the clarinet.

Otten is always inclined to slow down too much, which also marred this aria. It was wonderfully beautiful. Then came a suite by Bach for orchestra (3 trumpets), from which the overture, an aria, the Gavotte, and the Gigue were performed. That was the most splendid piece, how it sounds! or how much better it could and should sound! That is something I cannot describe to you, I want to play through the score with you. Then came the E flat major Concerto, it went with great vigour.

Fr. Guhrau sang the *Veilchen* and a song by Marschner, I accompanied her and also coached her, so that I could do it again sometime later at

---

[48] Clara and Joachim were leaving Berlin for Leipzig to avoid the general commotion over the arrival of Franz Liszt. The incident, including a vague reference to Brahms's conduct upon his return to Berlin from Danzig, is explained—but not sufficiently to understand what actually happened—in Litz, ii. 392.

Chiarina's. Then I played the Canon in B flat minor by Robert and at the urgent request of Otten and Avé, the March by Schubert. Both had the same, quite considerable applause.[49]

The *Euryanthe* overture closed.

The *Carnaval* would have been too long, which is why I had to omit it. That I would like to play, sometime.

Oddly, I liked Frau Guhrau better than before. She has changed decidedly in many regards, and in addition there is the sympathy for her really sad fate.

She told me touchingly of her being together with you, then of her brief marriage; wherever she now turns her gaze, it is desolate.

She sang really beautifully in the concert, especially the Veilchen.

How pleased I was about the concert in Berlin! And about the H[einrich] overture etc. In the first rehearsal Otten also played the Faust overture by Wagner, which I definitely disliked, I advised him strongly to consider whether he is certain he wants to have the honour of the first performance in Hamburg.

You recall, we talked about it once, whether in Bach one should play a *Nachschlag* to end a trill.[50] I told you it runs too much counter to my sentiment. Now I want to copy a chapter from my Ph[ilip] Em[anuel] Bach for you that must convince you, since he is certainly the best teacher particularly of his father's works.

Chapter 2, 3rd section, § 13.[51]

'The trill over a note which is somewhat prolonged, whether ascending or descending, must always have a *Nachschlag*.

If the trilled note is followed by a leap, the *Nachschlag* is also employed.

Etc. also with dotted notes etc. A trill without notes that follow, e.g. at the *end* or at a *fermata*, etc. always has a *Nachschlag*.

§ 14. Dotted notes that are followed by a short ascent are also accorded trills *with* a *Nachschlag*.'

Further on: 'that the *Nachschlag* must be just as rapid as the trill'.

In general, we must give the Bach a thorough reading together!

I enclose the receipt and Senff's bill for you. I'd like it if you could take

---

[49] *Das Veilchen* (The Violet), K. 456, is possibly Mozart's most popular song. The Schumann canon is without opus, *An Alexis*.

[50] An *afternote*. The German word is commonly used in English, and refers to the standard way of terminating a trill with a turn.

[51] Our translation, which follows Brahms's letter exactly, differs considerably in language, but not in meaning, from the English translation of C. P. E. Bach's *Essay on the True Art of Playing Keyboard Instruments*, trans. and ed. by William J. Mitchell (New York, 1949). The relevant pages are 103–4.

care of it when convenient! I am sending the money for Senff—next time, I have no single thalers.

Now be well, my most precious Clara, I kiss you affectionately—oh, how I wish I could!

Incidentally, Frl. v. Meysenbug wrote a very enthusiastic letter to me, I ought to come [to Detmold]; now do advise me what to do, I probably must go soon so that we can be in D[üsseldorf] or *Minden* at the same time. I suppose you're definitely not coming to Hamburg?

A thousand greetings from everybody and above all from me, your
Johannes.

I bought a sonata for 2 pianos (written) by W. Friedemann Bach, which is surely quite rare, and some other things!!!

Brahms remained in Hamburg until the end of December. He joined in the musical activities organized by Otten, Grädener, and Avé-Lallement, and kept in touch with Clara, who was on tour.

66
Johannes Brahms to Clara Schumann

Hamburg, Monday 10 December 1855

Beloved Clara,

A right friendly good morning is what this letter is meant to say to you, I would like it better if it could have wished you a good night after your difficult journey. Today I won't forget you for a second, in my mind's eye I constantly see you sitting by the train window looking out glumly. You won't weep too much today?

You should have seen me yesterday, so furious and in the end desperate!

We played trios at Otten's, first Jaëll played Rubinstein's G minor, which is just like his other things. Now insignificant, now obnoxious, now and then imaginative.

Then I played your husband's 3rd, which provoked tremendous jubilation, unlike Rubinstein's, despite Jaëll's brilliant playing and all sorts of effects. Then J. played Chopin's C minor Scherzo and I Bach's F.[52]

Then J. and I ate at Grädener's, the travelling wine salesman was becoming more and more unbearable to me.

[52] Rubinstein Trio in G minor, Op. 15 No. 2, and Schumann's Third Trio in G minor, Op. 110. 'Bach's F' probably refers to the Toccata in F minor, which had been published in the Bach Gesellschaft volume for 1853. It became one of Brahms's reliable show pieces.

Then he tortured G.'s things on G.'s little piano, then Liszt's, until every-one's hair stood on end.

Now artists and the public had already told him very bad things about Rubinstein, but he now fell upon L[iszt?].

My head was quite confused, I sat down quite earnestly and played in B and B♭ at the same time, all of us were altogether giddy except for Jaëll. All day I longed to be able to sit alone at home for just an hour. It cost a great deal of effort, but how happy I was for once to sit at home before 10. Entirely dissolved in silent bliss. Now I've told everyone that I'm leaving tomorrow, don't believe I'll do it though, but for once I want to have peace and quiet the whole day, and I'll let Jaëll travel to Hanover today. In the concert on Saturday he played *very* well, he plays with notable bravura, but garbage! I went outside during *his* solo and the Tannhäuser, but came back in just as he began to play again, upon request, a dreadful Italian melody with variations.

It isn't right for me to chatter to you about such stuff, but I do it with the blissful emotion of having survived.

Please write to me only *here*!

A thousand hearty greetings, my Clara!

Your

Johannes

The 'travelling wine salesman' was Alfred Jaëll, a brilliant pianist who is referred to here and in other letters in a variety of uncomplimentary ways. Joachim described him as shallow and mercurial, but Jaëll was invited to Hanover quite frequently, nevertheless.[53]

In this letter Brahms used the familiar form for the first time, signing his name 'Dein Johannes', but reverting in the next letters to formal usage. There were other tentative explorations of this nature, until Clara requested the change herself in a letter of May 1856.

---

[53] *BW* v. 205.

❧ 1856 ❧

As 1856 began, Brahms's most pressing need remained the recapture of his creative vigour. Still entangled with the symphony, still brewing the quartet mentioned in correspondence of 1855 (the eventual Op. 60), Brahms was struggling. But whatever he suffered, as inspiration drained away, he alluded to his fears only briefly—and only to Clara. Given to action rather than to despair, he resolutely immersed himself in a systematic study of counterpoint in the hope of rekindling his musical inventiveness.

For help, he called again upon the friend and confidant whose musical intellect and creativity he trusted most, Joseph Joachim. He proposed that they exchange counterpoint exercises, a suggestion earnestly carried out first over a period of five months, and then sporadically for the next few years.

In those five months his efforts began to bear fruit, albeit of a very different variety from his earlier music: Fugue for Organ in A flat minor, part of a Mass in canonic form, vocal canons, Prelude and Fugue for Organ in A minor, one, possibly two sets of piano variations (Op. 21 Nos. 1 and 2), the *Geistliches Lied*, Op. 30.[1] More significantly for the works posterity knows him by, he was making progress on his piano quartet, and above all his symphony now took final shape as a piano concerto.

In other regards, life in Düsseldorf was by now running a familiar course. Brahms was at home keeping an eye on the Schumann children:

> Ferdinand is being too lazy, Ludwig too stubborn, Felix even more stubborn, Genchen [Eugenie] merely too hot-tempered, but they are all very sweet and nice. Yesterday Ferd. got a good many smacks on his bottom because he wouldn't read.

Another vivid glimpse of that period comes from Eugenie Schumann:

> I still see, as if in a picture, a flock of children in the corridor of a house in Düsseldorf; they are looking up in astonishment at the stair landing. There a young man with long blond hair is performing the most hair-raising gymnastics, swinging right and left, forward and back; finally he stands on his hands, stretches his legs high in the air and leaps with one motion down into the crowd of admiring children. We young Schumanns were the children, the young man was Johannes Brahms.[2]

Brahms was also making occasional visits to Robert Schumann, even spending some time searching out a better institution for him. Clara was mostly away on tour.

---

[1] The works for organ were published without opus number, WoO 8 and 9. See Letter 77.

[2] *Erinnerungen* (Stuttgart, 1925), 13–14. Gymnastics were part of Brahms's programme at middle school. He kept up his skills into his late twenties. The previous excerpt is from a letter to Clara of 26 Feb. 1856.

In April she travelled to England for the first time and in May, during the course of Brahms's correspondence with her, he began to address her in the familiar 'Du' form. During his visit to Endenich in April it became clear to all that Schumann would not recover. The end came in July, in August Brahms, Clara, and a few of her children went to Switzerland for a month, and on 21 October Brahms moved back to his parents' home in Hamburg. Told in bare outline this way, the sequence of events is rather abrupt. While letters fill in some details, they heighten, rather than remove the mystery; the striking change in tone from Brahms's letter to Clara of 31 May (the last one before Schumann's death) and 22 October (the first one to reach her after Brahms's return to Hamburg) is the surest evidence that something momentous, but known only to themselves, occurred in between.

67
Johannes Brahms to Clara Schumann

[12 February 1856]

It always depresses me a little that I am still not a proper musician, but I have the talent for it, more, probably, than is usual in young people nowadays. It gets driven out of one. Boys should be allowed to make jolly music, only nothing maudlin; the serious comes soon enough by itself. But how happy is the man who, like Mozart and others, arrives at a pub in the evening and writes new music. Creating is simply his life, but he does what he wants. What a man.

This letter fragment was lost by the time the Schumann–Brahms correspondence was compiled. Litzmann, who saw the original, notes that Brahms crushed his pen forcefully at the end of the letter.

Brahms returned to Düsseldorf after stopping in Hanover and Göttingen, where he gave a soirée with Joachim. His first concern was to report to Clara on her children.

68
Johannes Brahms to Clara Schumann

[Düsseldorf] Friday, 22 February 1856

My dear Clara,

So now at last I am sitting in my little room again, with my afternoon coffee. I have looked everything over first, so as to be able to write to you about everything. My letter from Göttingen reached Bertha today, when I was already here. The two boys I saw first; they greeted me with regular shrieks of joy. Bertha came from the attic, she was almost startled. The children all look splendid, healthy and happy. And now they know how to read and count! Songs they sing by the dozen, Bertha is taking care of that nicely. Then I inspected my library and had to rearrange it anew, because there has again been considerable growth.

As to money, I have aproximately 200 rt [Reichstaler], I was forced to keep the 96 from Göttingen. J[oachim] didn't want any of it.

Then I visited Frl. Leser. Agnes was there, of course. So far everyone cheerful and well.

When the girls pass through here I am going to give them the World History I wanted to give them for Christmas.

Today I ate with the children, I take great pleasure in them; now I am doubly glad that I didn't bring anything for them, when they are so agreeable it gives one a really good feeling. In my opinion children *cannot help* but disregard a homecoming on account of the gifts that are brought, etc. etc. Absolutely!

In Hanover, on the last evening, I received one more letter from you, dear Clara, J. too, that really pleased me.

I did tell J. about your earnings, after all.

I think to myself how beautiful it would be if we both made really vigorous strides and became capable, great musicians. Each of us places the other above himself, what is more natural but that we should squabble with each other, as long as we squabble only with each other. But I can't help assigning a lot of blame to J's brooding and so often mistrustful character.

Indeed, for me there is simply no other true born musician among the younger generation. In saying so I am not considering individual works, the whole person must be musical, must breathe music.—What might J. yet achieve? I often see myself as forgotten and lost when I think of him grown to maturity. That he should feel the same about me I do not understand, and yet it is often evident to me.

In answer to your letter, two small points:

1. J. positively did not mean you wanted to convince him to go to Vienna for your sake, but for him the *only* reason for going would have been to be helpful to you.

2. I was always completely unable to ask you very calmly whether you were going directly from Vienna to England. I must have thought it was because time was all too short.

Do you not know Ferdinand Schubert in Vienna? You have never written to me about him. Haven't you even looked at the complete Schubert and the works that were left unpublished? His brother has supposedly arranged everything in one room.[3]

How pleased I was that you played some Schubert.

One must do it, be it only for the sake of the beloved name, even if nothing is suitable for playing (in public). If I were a moderately respected pianist, and one who commands respect, I would have played a sonata in public long ago (the one in G, for example).[4] It cannot help but enchant people if it is beautifully played.

The evening after the concert in G[öttingen] we were all at Dirikle (?).[5] I most reluctantly, for I have a veritable dread of all cliquish ways. J. naturally played the [Mendelssohn] Concerto, during which the woman cried a lot. All rooms are hung full of pictures and sculptures of the brother. Even a drawing of him dying was hung there, and it was her brother, after all. I would have kept it in my most secret drawer. Of their children there are pictures at every age. Their art objects are everything to them.

I am truly fond of people who don't consider everything they do all too important.

I played the Chromatic Fantasy, 'which Felix also liked to play so much' and the [Wanderer] Fantasy by Schubert which she did not know and also did not seem to interest her all too much.

Grimm and Pinchen[6] really are a well-matched pair. One cannot help being delighted by them even when they kiss each other so excessively. I couldn't do that in the presence of others, especially with 8 workmen in the room.

Grimm showed us a pretty little canon for Pinne that he had composed for his 'joy and delight.'

How pleased I am about all the good fortune that is accompanying you on this trip, as it surely will on your English one, too.

On the other hand, I was deeply shocked at your father's proposal. I won't be able to relax until he leaves you again. Just be sure to commit yourself to nothing other than to a collaboration in Prague, for instance. I'm afraid that you are facing some unpleasant hours. But I am again delighted by your beautiful sentiments which I suspect will also guide you correctly.[7]

[3] i.e. Schubert's unpublished music, carefully kept in a room of his brother's house.

[4] Op. 78.

[5] Gustav Peter Lejeune Dirichlet (1805–59), one of the greatest of German mathematicians, at this time professor of mathematics at Göttingen. Rebecka Mendelssohn (1811–58), Felix's younger sister, was his wife.

[6] Phillipine, Grimm's wife, also called 'Pinne', and 'Pine Gur'.

[7] Probably refers to Friedrich Wieck's request that Clara include her half-sister, the pianist Marie Wieck, on her concert programmes, and even tour with her. Private communication from Nancy B. Reich.

I have forgotten until now to include the letter from the doctor. Incidentally, my opinion of water-cure establishments remains the same.

Whether Herr Schumann has a liking for it or not really shouldn't be a consideration.

People who have taken water cures and all that goes with them, a lot of exercise in the fresh air, etc., they continue this way of life, it *must* become second nature for them. What assurances for the future are provided by a cure in this establishment, or, for example, by a cure through magnetism? And that is just what this cure does, and after all, nothing is more essential for our invalid.[8]

Here it is very, very lonely without you, it is you I seek and think of everywhere. If you would only come soon, but I don't want to entreat you too much just now, this journey is as tolerable for you as any can be, and in that I take pleasure.

Now I will conclude at last, so that the letter can go on its way today.

Thousands and thousands of greetings from

Your

Johannes

69
Johannes Brahms to Joseph Joachim

[Düsseldorf, 26 February 1856]

My dearest friend,

Thank you for your friendly lines with the two enclosures.

The passport I discovered in Minden, and have badly missed the other thing here.

I should remind you that tomorrow (2 o'clock?) the children will be coming through Hanover; we will load them up here with bread and butter and oranges, so you should do the same with coffee. But especially I want to remind you, and beg you to carry out at last what we've so often discussed. Namely, to exchange contrapuntal exercises.—About every 2 weeks each one sends, with the other returning them a week later with possible comments and his own exercise, and continuing this exchange for a good long time until both of us have become oh so very clever.[9]

---

[8] Slightly obscure, but Brahms seems to imply that the cure in Endenich cannot have the same long-term benefits as a change in Schumann's way of life would provide. The 'magnetism' mentioned here referred to animal magnetism, as developed by the Austrian physician A. F. Mesmer, quack or proto-psychiatrist, depending on one's point of view.

[9] Brahms uses the sarcastic word *gescheut*, intead of *gescheit*, clever, as given in *BW* v. 123.

For why shouldn't we, quite reasonable and serious-minded people that we are, be able to teach ourselves better and more enjoyably than some ph[ilistine] could do it?

But to begin with, don't answer this at all (and especially not in words).

Send me your first exercises in 2 weeks. Should I send you the Marpurg? I own it.[10]

I'm hoping for and really looking forward to your first parcel. Let it become serious! It would be really fine, good and useful. I think it's beautiful.

Most warmly your
Johannes.

70

Johannes Brahms to Joseph Joachim

[Düsseldorf, *c.* 24 March 1856]

Dear Joseph,

I should come to Hanover and play in public again? Why, here it's already the most beautiful springtime! I believe that when you come home from your tour, you too probably won't be in the mood this year, and will be glad that I had already written to you about it of my own accord. In any event, wouldn't it be more sensible if we gave two soirées next autumn? After all, people are undoubtedly glad that the concert season is over, and H[anover] is just a small place. Have you already announced it? Probably not so far in advance? If it could be postponed it would really be nicer.

Frau Schumann is leaving on the 7th or 8th, moreover, so I wouldn't want to leave on a trip 2 days before then. Do think it over.

I'm sending along 2 little pieces as the beginning of our joint studies.

If you still feel like going on with the business I would like to tell you of a few conditions that I find useful.

Every Sunday, work must go back or forth. E.g. one Sunday you send the work, on the next I send it back together with my own, etc.

But whoever misses the day, i.e. sends nothing, must send one thaler instead, which the other can use to buy books!!! One is excused only if instead of the exercise, one sends a composition, received with greater pleasure, I dare say.

---

[10] Simon Sechter's 1843 edition of Marpurg's 18th-c. *Abhandlung von der Fuge*, which Brahms had just received from Clara in January.

Do you want to join in this? Then send me back the pieces together with other things next Sunday, or perhaps because of the tour, a week after that.

Double counterpoint, canons, fugues, preludes, whatever.

Regards to my parents, Grädener, Otten etc.

Frau Schumann sends best regards.

Your
Johannes

N.B.

I'm sending the music to Hanover, because otherwise a waxed-linen [waterproof] wrapping would be required.

Don't take it amiss about the concerts in Han[over]. But don't you also find the autumn more suitable? How do you like it in Hamburg? Did you visit Grädener, and didn't you like his house?

In the spring, Brahms took on the responsibility of travelling to Kenneberg to look for alternative medical care for Robert Schumann.

71

Johannes Brahms to Joseph Joachim

Düsseldorf, 25 April 1856

My dear, good friend,

Don't be cross that I must be reminded so often to write. Procrastination, that cursed thing, is entirely to blame.

When I returned from my trip I was at first quite dejected that I still hadn't received any work from you.

But now something arrives every day, and I will be royally pleased if this keeps up for a long time. On Sunday I'll send off everything and I will try to include more critical comments than you!

My trip turned out differently from what I had expected.

I stayed in Bonn for a few days, because Richarz, whom, by the way, I learn to appreciate more each time, granted me several lengthy and thorough conversations. Afterwards I saw Schumann. How he had changed!

He welcomed me joyfully and warmly as always, but I shuddered in horror—for I understood not one word he said. We sat down, but I became more and more distressed, I had tears in my eyes, he spoke constantly, but I understood nothing. I looked again at his reading matter. It was an atlas, and he was occupied with making excerpts, childish ones, of course. Towns, rivers etc., whose names begin with Aab, Ab, Aba etc., gathering together the many St Juans etc. He showed me a whole lot of paper completely covered with such writing.

On the other hand, everything was most carefully recorded, the country, river, e.g. the location of the city, with longitude and latitude provided.

He also had a penny magazine there which gave him much pleasure, the *Kölnische Zeitung* and Richter's picture magazine, in which he seems to have read the *Old Cock on the Tower*, for he smiled when I pointed to it.

He spoke almost continuously, often, to be sure, he merely blabbered, roughly like *bababa—dadada*. In his lengthy questions I made out the proper names Marie, Frl. Julia, Berlin, Vienna, England, not much more.

He, too, understood me with difficulty, probably only very little.

The result of the conversations with Richarz is, in brief, that he has only now come to a definite opinion about the illness, its development, and its likely outcome.

Last year's apparent improvement meant absolutely nothing and had not provided him with that insight. He now says that Schumann's brain is definitely affected (not a softening of the brain) and that all medical help is therefore useless, which are the same words the doctor in Kenneberg had used when I asked him (vaguely, without mentioning Schumann). In the most favourable case (according to Richarz) Schumann will remain in his present state of considerable aphasia; in 1, 2 months probably only nursing care will be required, and so it is up *to us* to give *very* careful thought to what should happen.

We need to see Schumann more frequently and accordingly consider and decide whether Frau Schumann could take care of him, something that others will also have to evaluate.

Whether his speech will improve with time, or rather will become more intelligible to us, whether his participation will increase, etc., all that will have to be observed.

I went to K[enneberg] partly because of Frau Schumann and partly because I hoped to find a really reasonable homeopath. But I took a distinct dislike to the resident doctor; the establishment apparently caters mainly for people loaded with money who wish to spend the remainder of their life with ruined health but cheerfully, and to extend it by healthier living; then there are always a great many young wealthy persons who have destroyed themselves by *onanism*.

Dear fellow, I hardly need to ask you to be *extremely* careful towards Frau Schumann in this business. By no means write her *any facta*, but rather try to divert her in other ways, something she is now in great need of.

I will write to you on Sunday anyway, also ask you what else you particularly want to know. Best greetings to Grimm.

In warmest friendship

Your

Johannes.

(Yesterday J[aëll], who came from Cologne to visit me, spoiled my entire day!) Shocking shithead.

Many thanks for Grimm's translation, which gives me great pleasure. The epilogue, too, is beautiful.

(F A E is easily solved with GIS E LA in a canon).

There is no doubt that by now, Dr Richarz, the director of the asylum in Endenich, knew that Schumann was suffering from the final stage of cerebral neurosyphilis. For reasons of his own, he arranged to withhold his findings from the rest of the world. Only in 1994 were the notes he kept made public.* Brahms's description of his visit to Robert Schumann, and his talk with the doctor, is echoed more laconically by Dr Richarz's own account of the visit, noted in his recently published records: '[Schumann] Had visit yesterday from Herr Brahms, was pleased, almost entirely incomprehensible. [Brahms] found him very changed for the worse since his last visit one year ago. During the visit a few words understandable.' Additional Note p. 747

Joachim was still toying with his motto, *frei aber einsam*, and the name of his erstwhile sweetheart, Gisela von Arnim *Gis (G sharp) E La*, although by now she was betrothed to his friend Hermann Grimm, the art historian and essayist, who had recently translated the essays of Ralph Waldo Emerson.

F A E and *Gis E La* form two sets of letters which, in music notation, are the exact inversion of each other, thereby allowing the possibility of a canon in inversion:

72
Johannes Brahms to Joseph Joachim

Düsseldorf, Sunday, 27 April 1856

Dear man,

Here are your things back, along with some of mine. I don't know how to deal with your fugue themes. No sort of stretto is conceivable for any of them. It might even be difficult to find a naturally flowing invertible counterpoint for them.

But send me some more and consider what to do with them, write strettos with them etc.

How the 'circle canon' in your last letter comes by its name, I do not understand. It ends reasonably in A major and can, of course, also be played in B major.[11] Only the coda permits the entry, and that is not enough.

I have rewritten the same theme for you as a circular canon; I find that only now is it really one, don't you agree?

In the *F A E* canon some empty spots are apparent to me. Octaves such as at # # do not bother me. There the bass note of the chord is doubled, but the B at ‡, the one[s] at † †.

But the F major canon is beautiful. Even if played as a solo voice with the harmony, the melody gives pleasure and the imitation makes it even more beautiful. In the 3rd measure before the end shouldn't the B♭ and the B♮ change places? To me that sounded beautiful.

At the beginning of the Fugue in A for Quartet you had a beautiful sound wafting in your ear. For our excercises this theme is *in itself* not practical, but you must realize it anyway.

I am now sending along my previous canons to you again; Apart from their skill, is it good music? Does the artistry make it more beautiful and more worthwhile? Does anything strike you? I don't know a thing!

I am also enclosing some small canons. I particularly want to ask for your opinion about the four-part circle canon. I want it played slowly and with feeling.

I also enclose a work which seems difficult to me and which I beg you, or assign to you, to complete.[12] The canonic imitations (rather free) over the c[antus] f[irmus].

Some intervals are still missing. They don't really sound good, but do try it, it's difficult.

---

[11] *BW* v. 133 reads 'F major'. A check of the autograph shows Brahms wrote *B* major.
[12] It was the subject of Bach's *Art of the Fugue*.

Later on, if you feel like it, let's treat the theme more beautifully and more freely together.

I await your next letter with longing. Also write to me properly about my things.

Save all the sheets of music you have sent me. I will too; then after a long time perhaps we'll look at them together and see splendid progress, I hope.

Be greeted most heartily and do not let me wait in vain. Something must be here again by Monday.

Your
Johannes

For my C minor canon I have string instruments in mind, whose sound sustains; on the piano they sound poorly.

I have such a bad quill, forgive the scrawl!

Greetings to Grimm, Sahr.

Some of the exercises mentioned in this letter are among Joachim's papers, preserved in the Staats- und Universitätsbibliothek Hamburg Carl von Ossietzky, so that it is possible to see what Brahms was referring to.[13]

Ex. 1 Circle canon study by Joachim, sent to Brahms *c.*24 April 1856 (realization by David Brodbeck)

[13] The exercises are transcribed and discussed in detail by David Brodbeck, 'The Brahms–Joachim Counterpoint Exchange; or Robert, Clara, and the "best harmony between Joseph and Johannes" ', David Brodbeck (ed.), *Brahms Studies* (Lincoln, Nebr., 1994). My profound thanks to Professor Brodbeck for making his essay, expertise, and musical examples available to me here.

Ex. 1 *continued*

Ex. 2 Brahms; circle canon after a subject of Joachim, from letter 27 April 1856 (realization by David Brodbeck)

Ex. 3 Joseph Joachim; canonic study on F-A-E, returned in Brahms's letter of 27 April with his markings (Letter 72)

Ex. 3 *continued*

Zum   Schluß

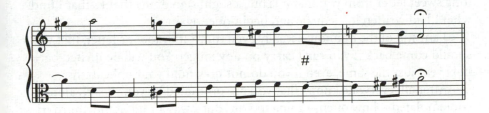

On the 7th of May, Brahms turned 23.

73
Christiane Brahms to Johannes Brahms

7 May 1856

. . . I am all alone . . . would like to chat with you a while. This morning I woke up at exactly the hour at which you first saw the light of day, 23 years ago. Half an hour later I had you in my arms, at my breast . . . and now you are so far away from me! It is surely hard that one cannot always remain together . . . Dear Johannes, if it were only in our power to do something for dear Schumann! I beg you, do not take it too much to heart. It doesn't help him and you are harmed by it.

On the occasion of his birthday, Brahms sent Clara his new Prelude and Fugue in A minor for Organ, one of the works which resulted from his contrapuntal exchanges with Joachim.[14]

Brahms was now regularly practising the organ, but had other matters on his mind, as well. To judge from this letter, Clara suggested to him that he address her in the familiar form—a big step for her, who until then had never conversed

---

[14] WoO 9. Litz. ii. 412; and *BW* v. 143–50. The autograph, with Brahms's inscription to Clara, is at the Library of Congress.

familiarly with any man outside her family. Brahms referred to her suggestion as though she had capitulated to a surprise attack, and then hesitated to comply.

74
Johannes Brahms to Clara Schumann

Evening of 24 May, 1856

Beloved Clara,

I had written you a letter this afternoon; now there comes along such a long sweet letter from you that it is but a slight sign of my thanks that I find what I had written inadequate and begin once again.

I am still of the opinion, actually even more after today's letter, that you should come back if you can't carry on any longer. You will be invited back next year just the same, even if you do not now fulfil your obligations.

After all, everyone knows that you are prompted by your health alone. I contemplated—how often—going to you. But I was afraid of the impropriety of it. Simply everything gets into the newspapers. Since I don't consider your premature departure from England to be as consequential as you now do, it was that much harder for me to make up my mind.

I consider it quite certain that you can go ahead and cancel everything on account of your poor health, and next year you will be received just as cordially.

How I would love to come! But would it do? If Bargiel went, people couldn't say anything, but it is just too conspicuous if I, who have no business there, come over.

I have even considered that I could be a passable virtuoso on the organ by next year, then we would travel together, and I would shelve my piano playing so that I could always tour with you [*Dir*].

Strange, for I am not a particularly sensitive person, altogether without nerves and empathy, and [yet] today something urged me mightily and incessantly to write to you about last testaments, which incidentally are often on my mind. I have always wanted to write mine, [but] my divine laziness prevents it, no matter how sombre my mood is.

For you it is quite proper to have provided for all eventualities, but for God's sake, always be sure to do this sort of thing as calmly as possible; simply because of all possible eventualities, but without specifically thinking of dismal ones, or even worse, being apprehensive about them. Just as one leans on the bannister of a staircase, for safety, but without thinking fearfully of falling.

I would like you to place a note on my letters that, next to you, they belong *only* and *immediately* to me, just as I have always intended to do with yours and will do right away.

But I keep thinking you have come to realize that you can come home sooner. You must. In any case it is also better, isn't it, to have to regain some of their regard next year rather than to be unable to make any use of the respect of the English because you are sick.

'I really don't want to take any notice just now of my recent sudden rout.'[15]

That is, concerning the 'Du'. I considered that I really did not want to make use of your [*Dein*] momentary kindness and affection, it may not please you [*Dir*] later. For that reason, I shall keep on writing 'Sie'. This siege and conquest business, I suppose, has some connection to the unanswered question? Or not?

Unfortunately I haven't received the glasses yet.[16]

I'm looking forward to it and await it with longing.

The organs in concert-halls are very convenient for us possibly next year; but beautiful in any case.

That you [*Sie*] occasionally tear up pages distresses me *greatly* because I wish I would receive more and more of them, even sad ones. I don't expect jolly ones, anyway. Into the suitcase for Stockhausen I'm putting a cherished volume of music which you must play from often in the evening, especially my favourites.

I wish you would always fasten your letters together so prettily for me, and I also wish it were always necessary.

The revision of my fugue I'm sending primarily because of the lovely paper (from Joachim). But it's horrible to have to write so small.

A thousand greetings, dear Clara, love me well, as I do you [*Dich*]

Your [*Dein*]

Johannes

Clara did not cancel the rest of her tour, but remained in England until July.

No letter from the month of June 1856 survived, so that the following letter is not only the first one written entirely in the 'Du' form, it is also the last letter from the period prior to Schumann's death. Brahms was in fine spirits, having just returned to Düsseldorf after attending the Festival of the Lower Rhine in Cologne, where he met and found himself appreciated by several prominent artists. There was

---

[15] A quote from Brahms's previous letter, 16 May.

[16] Clara had obtained lenses for a lorgnette for Brahms, who was very near-sighted. See the next letter.

Klaus Groth, the poet who wrote in Plattdeutsch (Low German) and whose volume *Quickborn* was one of Brahms's favourites. Groth came from Heide in Holstein, the very village of Brahms's ancestors and of his father's youth, and the friendship formed here lasted for life. Also in attendance were Ferdinand Hiller, the founder of the Cologne Conservatory and one of the most prominent musicians in Germany, a man who became his friend and supporter and remained so until his death in 1885; Otto Jahn, the archaeology professor and Mozart biographer; Karl Reinthaler, who exerted himself well beyond the normal call of duty, twelve years later, to conduct the first performance of Brahms's Requiem; the composer Theodor Kirchner, who remained a lifelong friend; and Julius Stockhausen, the greatest lieder singer of the time, a man who would cross paths with Brahms frequently in the next decades. In what was the first of many collaborations, Stockhausen invited Brahms to join him in local concerts immediately after the festival. Brahms played a number of substantial works (and music of Schubert and Clara Schumann); and he accompanied three of Schubert's *Schöne Müllerin* and other songs by Schumann, Mozart, Méhul, Boïeldieu, and his friend Albert Dietrich.

Schumann's birthday, on 8 June, was drawing near—his last one. Brahms and Clara were planning their gifts to him: from Clara a writing set (the 'writing thing' Brahms referred to), and from Brahms an atlas of the world, which Schumann had been wanting for some time.

It also seems clear from this letter that Clara invited Brahms to meet her in Antwerp on her arrival back on the Continent, so that they could travel to Ostend where he could get his first view of the sea. A surprising moment in this letter is yet another description of himself as a 'Musician of the Future' (as once before, in Letter 40), an association which became more and more odious to him, and a title from which he dissociated himself so publicly, four years later.

75
Johannes Brahms to Clara Schumann

Düsseldorf, 31 May, 8 in the evening [1856][17]

My beloved Clara,

I wish I could write to you as tenderly as I love you, and give you as much kindness and goodness as I wish for you. You are so infinitely dear to me that I can't begin to tell you. I constantly want to call you darling and all kinds of other things, without becoming tired of adoring you. If this goes on, I will eventually have to keep you under glass, or save money to have you gilded.

If only I could always live with you and my parents in the same city! How often I wish for that.

---

[17] The correct date is 30 May, as the Cologne concert was on 29 May.

I quite forgot to enclose the programme the other day, so then today. By yesterday noon just 15 tickets had been sold in Cologne, and in the evening it was also not well attended. That's Cologne!

But he sang the *Müller* songs [*Die schöne Müllerin*] magnificently! I have never had such delight from Lieder singing as I did yesterday evening. Only the eternal rustling was annoying. How deeply the songs engross one; and so much is experienced.

You should really have them sung for you as an entity, not individually, but—also don't forget to read the poems thoroughly ahead of time so you can experience it as a whole.

This is now my chief amusement, to cause a big commotion at bedtime and have a jolly rowdy time. That's something I've retained since childhood. I like to sleep in company. For instance yesterday with S[tockhausen], Jahn, and Dietrich; I take a royal pleasure in all that fooling around and don't get tired at all.

Yesterday St[ockhausen] gave me a lighter like the one I gave you for your trip; when I opened it I noticed gold inside; I gave it back to him and ran off, because I definitely had not wanted money. Now, after his departure today, I found it in my cigar case.

5 Friedrichsdor. Now I must confess that actually I am—greedy for money and sometimes like to get a lot of it, but it is awkward for me nevertheless. Do try to find out whether he can afford it, otherwise I don't want to keep it. Don't worry if it's not possible for you to send the writing thing here for the 8th of June. Just this morning in Cologne I bought your Robert the *biggest* atlas. 83 gigantic maps, beautifully bound and new. At the second-hand bookshop, amazingly, I didn't buy a single book for myself. So then I'll take the world atlas with me.

But if your writing set does arrive, I beg you to let me give him the atlas!

But only if it's all right with you and if you don't want to give a lot of presents.

I actually think the 2 atlases are sufficient, it might excite him too much. That by way of consolation, in case your present doesn't arrive.

The huge atlas is magnificent!

From your brother I found the enclosed letter waiting, with the writing folder.

From you I found a dear letter waiting.

NB. The doctors told me nothing new about Robert, only that some time ago he wished for the largest atlas.

Now for your letter.

I will come to Ostend and we'll have a good look at the ocean together; I wish we wouldn't stay long in Antwerp, rather go to the Rhine soon.[18]

I beg you, [more] about the wild animals and the beautiful organ.

I had a Klems along with me in C[ologne] and Bonn. In the *Kölner Zeitung* I was given really high praise.

And something else that's funny. Yesterday evening we were together in Cologne for a long time; Hiller, Reinthaler [*sic*], and then Bischof came late. Before I was even introduced to him, he lunged at me, gave my hand a tremendous squeeze and paid me the greatest compliments.[19]

That I didn't expect at all, for I have never visited him, and my status as 'musician of the future' makes him his natural enemy, after all.

A cello concerto by Haydn I don't know.

Polyphony means many-voicedness. And many-voicedness [*Vielstimmigkeit*] must now be distinguished very carefully from a whole handful of notes [*Vollgriffigkeit*].

Such a Bachian sea of notes can hardly be compared with others, can it?

N.B. I would surely forget my head if it got just a little bit wobbly! Today at noon I also found the lorgnette waiting! And the lenses fit, but exactly, and the l[orgnette] is beautiful and I already have it around my neck and have used it to look at you, and thank you a thousand times.

I'm delighted at the splendid growth of your library. The quartets! What's the meaning of Joh. [?] Clara [?] Be sure to explain that to me![20] But write soon and warmly and kindly. Your letters are like kisses to me. My parents' birthdays are in the next few days. I've sent them 50 thaler, with the urgent request that they spend them, and one thaler for punch and cake.

I wish I could be there.

And also here.

And also have my Clara here.

Heartily I greet you.

Your
Johannes.

---

[18] They were planning a vacation on the Rhine with Brahms's sister Elise accompanying them as mother's helper. That trip never materialized.

[19] Ludwig Friedrich Christian Bischoff (Brahms mis-spelled his name), was the founder of one of the most conservative music journals of the time, the *Rheinische Musikzeitung* (later the *Niederrheinische Musikzeitung*), in Cologne. He also wrote music criticism for Cologne's daily newspaper, the *Kölnische Zeitung*. His devotion to Haydn, Mozart, and Beethoven made it difficult for him to appreciate Schumann, let alone Liszt and the New German School.

[20] Litzmann, who worked from the autographs in editing these letters for publication in 1927, noted that this part of the letter was partially illegible.

The words *Vielstimmigkeit* and *Vollgriffigkeit* were used to distinguish between music in which each musical line is an independent voice which can make musical sense by itself; and music in which many notes could be grasped by the fingers at one time, without regard for an independent musical line.[21] Most likely the terms implied a silent, scornful reference to the bombastic style of piano writing by composers such as Thalberg, Moscheles, and Liszt.

Perhaps Clara's question about the Haydn Cello Concerto was prompted by her knowledge that Brahms had studied the cello for a few years as a young boy.[22]

Brahms delivered the atlas to Schumann on his birthday, but found his speech incomprehensible. This time, Schumann showed little interest in his visitor, instead setting to work immediately making alphabetical lists of place-names.[23]

Whatever else preoccupied him at this time, Brahms was still seriously carrying on his counterpoint exchange with Joachim and was hard at work. He had recently sent sections of his *Missa canonica*. Now, at last, an envelope thick with work arrived from his friend.

76
Johannes Brahms to Joseph Joachim

[Düsseldorf, June 1856]

Your letter made me quite excited with joy, my dear Joseph. I had to run outdoors, because I didn't want to jump for joy in the room.

It makes me extremely happy that you like the fugues so much, you are absolutely right in everything that you faulted, and it will all be revised when you see them again. Incidentally, there is a ♮ missing here. But I can hardly imagine that you would have played a C sharp. You probably find the following measure difficult:

---

[21] I am indebted to Fritz Jahoda for the definitions of these uncommon terms, as well as for the assurance that Brahms did not invent them.

[22] Styra Avins, 'Brahms the Cellist', *Newsletter of the Violoncello Society*, May and November (1992), 1–4, 5–6.

[23] From Dr Richarz's account of the visit: 'Was greeted yesterday on his birthday by Herr Brahms: showed himself annoyed, sullen, spoke of poison as chocolates were served, conversed hardly at all, busied himself with his atlas [. . .]' 'Robert Schumanns letzte Lebensjahre', 23.

I did notice the fifths at the end of the A flat minor, but at the time I found them appropriate. I shall see.

I wish I could also excuse the smaller number of exercises the way you do, and wish that I had better things buzzing around in my head. But I work little, on nothing else or more than what you see. Most of the time I am in the most miserable mood, and then such a letter from you is delectable medicine.

Your two canons in D minor (Bach) are the best of all the ones we have made on it. But the theme really does not suit it at all, unless one treats it more freely (more broadly). That is why I have to admire several of the melodic passages.

In the Variations I also like the canon very much. But I particularly like the 1st var., the 2nd, the 4th, and the last. This last one is splendid!

In the 3rd, I cannot find enough connection to the theme, nor in the March, either.

Sometimes I reflect on variation form and think that variations should be treated with greater strictness and purity.

The old composers strictly maintained the bass line of the theme, their true theme, throughout.

In Beethoven the melody, harmony, and rhythm is varied so beautifully.

But sometimes I find that later composers (like the two of us!) do more rooting about (I don't know how to express it) in the theme. We timidly stick to the melody, but we don't treat it freely and really create *nothing new from it*, but merely encumber it. But the melody, as a result, is quite unrecognizable.

Not even I understand this the way I've written it here, but look at your 3rd, the March, and the one following it. In that latter one I find it also to be so. That the notes of the melody are there is quite appropriate. But of course in D major we hear them on different degrees of the scale. And only with our eyes can we find them!

The Kyrie I'm sending you is merely a study. The other pieces belong to a (forthcoming) Mass in C major for 5 voices. The Agnus Dei follows after the F major Benedictus which you know.

Before the Sanctus the Amen of the Credo is in C major. Perhaps I'll also include 2 innocent canonic melodies.

I keep thinking of the beautiful 6/8 Presto variation and then play it for myself. Write out the Variations in proper order sometime and dedicate them to us pianists.

I have a feeling that I haven't yet thanked you for the magnificent fine? I enjoyed it very much, but would nevertheless much prefer to see your work and letters regularly instead of fines.[24]

Doesn't a Mass modulate too much if the Sanctus and Osanna are in A flat, the Benedictus in F, the Agnus goes from f to a minor, and the entire mass is in C major?

Write to me again really, really soon, and enclose a lot of things.

From the heart your

Johannes

A recent acquaintance was the jurist Adolf Schubring, whose lively and erudite interest in music made him a well-known music critic. With him Brahms was able to discuss his works, and even some aspects of his life, in a straightforward manner untroubled by the tensions which marked his almost familial ties to Joachim and Clara Schumann. Schubring's interest in Brahms's music showed itself a many ways, not the least surprising of which was his request that Brahms stand as godfather to a new-born son, even though at the time Schubring and Brahms had not yet met.

77
Johannes Brahms to Adolf Schubring

Düsseldorf, July 1856

Dear, esteemed Sir,

Honestly ashamed and repenting my negligence, indeed, my misconduct, I send herewith the required replies to your kind second letter. The music is one of the replies and at the same time my signature, for I really don't want to put my name to it. You will surely discover the name in it and will act in accordance with the letter, namely: return [them] to me with thoroughgoing reviews; I must request, however, as soon as possible, as I have no copy of the fugues and must practise them.[25]

---

[24] Joachim missed a deadline, and had to send money instead, as agreed to by the terms of the exchange. Brahms's copy of *Altdänische Heldenlieder, Balladen und Märchen* [Heroic Songs, Ballads and Fairy Tales of Ancient Denmark] bears the inscription, in his own hand, 'Joh. Brahms, May 1856 (from J. Joachim as fine)'. Karl Geiringer, *Brahms: His Life and Work*, 3rd edn. (New York, 1982), 48 n.

[25] Brahms clearly sent him his two organ works written that spring: the Fugue in A flat minor, WoO 8, and the Prelude and Fugue in A minor, WoO 9; the letters of Brahms's name were encoded in the first one. Those which can be converted to musical notes are capitalized: joHAnnEs BrAHmS, if S='Es', the German way of denoting E flat; H=our B; and B=our B flat. Both fugues were eventually published in the *Allgemeine Musikalische Zeitung* in 1864. It is difficult to validate Kalbeck's suggestion that Schubring's name is also encoded. The little-known works are discussed in David Brodbeck's 'The Brahms–Joachim Counterpoint Exchange', in Brodbeck (ed.), *Brahms Studies* (Lincoln, Nebr., 1994). Schubring's remarks about the Scherzo, Op. 4, were presumably the

The second reply is: that I, unnamed being, was born on the 7th of May in Hamburg, sired some 9 months earlier by a musician of the same place. That person and his wife, my much-loved mother, are splendid people whose copious love I can never repay.

Thereafter I was baptized, memorized the catechism according to Luther, also read the Bible diligently, and have thereby become worthy of being listed in the Dessau church register as godfather of the little Schubring. That you have also deemed me worthy in other respects, for that I thank you very much.

Do commend me to your wife, and to little Johannes give a hearty kiss. I look forward to the time when he can study Marpurg and Mattheson with me.[26] I would gladly send you more (there's not much here), for your letters give me great pleasure.

Right off, I deem your comments about my Scherzo to be correct (based on the tone and style of what you write). I don't have it sufficiently in my head to be able to do so note for note.

In spite of all that, I look forward with pleasure to your appraisal of the two fugues.

But there is one thing I must ask of you once and for all, namely that you will in no way keep anything of my manuscripts, for they are unfinished and require correction, and also that you will not let them out of your house.

I greet you warmly and ask you to remain well disposed towards me,

> Your
>> sincerely
>>> penitent one.

In late July, news came that Schumann was dying. Brahms accompanied Clara to Endenich, now that she was finally permitted to see her husband.

78
Johannes Brahms to Joseph Joachim

Bonn, 28 July 1856

Frau Schumann writes this to you just in case you wanted to see him for the last time. But I will add that you might want to think it over, it is very, very

same as those later printed in the *Neue Zeitschrift für Music*, 18 April 1862, in which he comments on a similarity between that work and Chopin's Op. 31.

[26] Authors of two of the most widely respected 18th-c. treatises on theory and practice of music: Friedrich Wilhelm Marpurg's *Abhandlung von der Fuge*, and Johann Mattheson's *Der vollkommene Capellmeister*. No musician was well schooled without them.

wrenching and pitiful. Schumann is very wasted, there is no question of his talking or being conscious.

But he *did* know his wife, embraced her and smiled.

For the past 6–8 days he has taken in nothing but a little fruit jelly. I don't know what more to write, cannot.

We are staying at the Deutsches Haus in Bonn.

your Johannes

Dietrich sends greetings. I will telegraph.

79

Clara Schumann to Joseph Joachim

Bonn, 28 July 1856

Dear Joachim,

Just a few words! I have been here since yesterday with Johannes—we are staying at the Deutsches Haus, but spend the day in Endenich.

I saw him yesterday—let me be silent about my suffering, but I did receive a few tender glances—those I will take with me throughout my entire life! Once he even embraced me, he recognized me! Ask God for a gentle end for him—it can not last much longer, as Richarz says. I will not leave him any more! Ah, Joachim, what pain, what suffering to see him again in this way! But that glance—not for all the world would I miss it any more. We are just on our way there again!

Think of him and
of your
Clara Schumann.

Johannes sends greetings.

80

Johannes Brahms to Julius Otto Grimm

Heidelberg, September 1856

My dear Julius,

What must you be thinking of me for not answering at all? Don't be angry! You ought to have been so clever and [kindhearted] as to write to Frau Clara as well, then you would not have had to wait.

Instead of apologizing, etc., I prefer to give you some news of that period.

I was with Schumann on his birthday (June 8th). I found him changed, strangely and suddenly, compared to the last time. Then Frau Clara came from England. Along with her arrival, even worse news from Endenich. A week before his death (Wednesday) we received a telegraphic message. I only read it, it said something like, 'If you want to see your husband while he is still alive, hurry here immediately. His appearance, to be sure, is horrifying.'

We went. He had had an attack, which the doctors thought would be followed immediately by death. (I don't know the term, a lung-spasm?) I went to him, saw him, however, just as he was in convulsions and greatly agitated, so that I too, like the doctors, dissuaded Frau Schumann from going to him, and persuaded her to go home.

Schumann just lay there, took nothing more than wine and jelly from a spoon. But Frau Clara's suffering during those days was so great that on Saturday I *had* to suggest that we go there once more to see him.

Now and forever we thank God that it happened, for it is absolutely essential for her peace of mind. She was able still to see him on Sunday, Monday, and Tuesday morning. That afternoon at about four he died.

Surely I will never again experience anything as moving as the reunion of Robert and Clara.

At first he lay for a long time with eyes closed, and she knelt before him, more calmly than one would believe possible. But after a while he recognized her, and also on the next day.

Once he plainly desired to embrace her, flung one arm wide around her.

Of course he had been unable to speak for some time already. One could understand (or perhaps imagine one did) only disconnected words. Even that must have made her happy. He often refused the wine that was offered him, but from her finger he sometimes sucked it up eagerly, at such length and so passionately that one knew with certainty that he recognized the finger.

Tuesday noon Joachim [came] from Heidelberg; that delayed us somewhat in Bonn, otherwise we would have arrived before his passing; as it was, we came half an hour afterwards. It was for me as for you as you read it; we should have breathed easier because he was released, and we couldn't believe it.

He had passed away very gently, so that it was scarcely noticed. His body looked peaceful, then; how comforting it all was. A wife could not have stood it any longer.

Thursday evening they buried him. I led the way, carrying the funeral wreath, Joachim and Dietrich came with us, members of a choral society carried the coffin, there was wind music and singing.

The city had arranged a beautiful site for the occasion *well beforehand*, planted with five plane-trees. Another comfort to Frau Clara was the Institution itself. All the bad rumours about it which had come to her (from Bettina, for example) were discredited.[27] I wish I could write everything to you as I would like, but it can't be done. In any case, if I write the raw material to you, you can imagine, just as well as read, how sad, how fine, how deeply moving this death was. We (Joachim, Clara, and I) have organized the papers Schumann left behind (and that is simply everything that he wrote!). Being in touch with him in this way, one learns to love and honour the man more deeply with each day.

I will be steeping myself in it much and often.

Be well, excuse the hurried scrawl. But I cannot find the calm for a calm letter here. We're now in Heidelberg, after spending a few weeks on the Vierwaldstätter Lake.

If you write to Frau Schumann and me, do so to Düsseldorf; we're going back soon.

However, we're here for another week still!!

Next time more, and calmer. Greet your dear wife. And don't be angry with me.

Affectionately your
J. Brahms

[*In Clara Schumann's hand*]: Notwithstanding——I greet you and all of you sincerely.

Frau Cl. is as well as one can expect, not as one could wish. I forgot that you would ask after her.

Brahms left Düsseldorf for Hamburg on 21 October, to return to his parents' house. The pretext for his abrupt departure was an invitation to perform Beethoven's Fourth Piano Concerto (with his own cadenza) at one of Georg Otten's concerts. But clearly other forces were at work. Although he wrote to Clara immediately upon arriving in Hamburg, the tone of his letter is in striking contrast to his previous ones.

[27] Bettina von Arnim visited Robert Schumann during the summer of 1855 and informed Clara, in imposing language and vivid detail, that Endenich and its doctor were unequipped to treat him. Her letter led a very anxious Clara to ask Brahms to search out other possible facilities. Litz, ii. 375–7, and Reich, 146.

81

Johannes Brahms to Joseph Joachim

[Düsseldorf] Sunday, [19 October 1856]

It has suddenly come about that I must play at Otten's on Saturday.

So now I will be coming through Hanover on Tuesday (at coffee time, around 2) but unfortunately cannot stop over. The first time that I travel *through* Hanover!

I shall see you anyway, won't I, dear Joseph?

That hour in which I can talk with you is important to me, I hope it will again set in motion many a written get-together. How I miss that! You put me off from one letter to the next, it's always the next one that's supposed to bring more and the important.

Some order will have to be re-established.

So don't pass up that hour on Tuesday, I *must* unfortunately go right on. Frau Clara greets you heartily, as does your

J. B.

I have to thank you for Beethoven and Friedemann Bach; how much pleasure they both gave me, and yet they vexed me, each time I thought I was getting a new instalment of our studies.

Frau Clara is enclosing a bill upon my urgent admonishment, she didn't want to come out with it.

82

Johannes Brahms to Clara Schumann

Hamburg, Wednesday, 22 October 1856

Once again the first greeting from afar, my dear Clara, and each time I write it to you with more love and reverence, if only you could really sense it and be glad of it.

I have found everyone here as well as wished for.

The coach arrived earlier than usual, and so Fritz, Father, and I ran back and forth past each other.

We spoke of you a great deal, they all love you so much.

They spoke of almost nothing but you and—Dr Krüger.

In Hanover I saw Joachim. It was a good, worthwhile hour. If only it would bear fruit! How useful it would be for us both if he were more independent of his moods, etc. By the way, he's planning to write to you, Grimm, and to Allgeyer in Rome.

But the trip from Hanover to Hbg. is dreadfully boring, and I thought about you a great deal, how many days of travel you have like this, and worse.

Otten was here early this morning and also brought me a letter which had been returned to him from Gersau, in which he wrote *very* heartfelt words about Robert's death. In this we had therefore done him an injustice.

Joachim has given much thought to a symphony, but was in a more discouraged and wobbly mood than usual. He is not playing in Leipzig, hence probably [illegible]. Wehner wants to perform the Peri.

Otten's programme is:

Manfred

G major Concerto

and Overture to the Abenceragen.[28]

I will think of you a great deal, my Clara, I must. I only hope you will retain your good health. One cannot wish you anything else.

All conceivable good things will come to you by themselves and those that are bad and sad, no wish can change.

In 14 days we'll see each other, and will have some happy days for ourselves!

There seems to be no emergency about the piano; I'll take care of it this morning. Tomorrow afternoon at 2 I may rehearse.

Do fare well, and be sure to think of me with much love.

Write to me how your trip went, and whether you saw the ruins in bright sunshine.[29]

Greetings also to your travelling companion.

Were you at the Leser's, yesterday evening?

Be greeted a thousandfold.

Utterly yours,

Johannes

Everyone sends greetings.

The Hamburg Philharmonic's concert to honour the memory of Robert Schumann took place on 22 November. Both Joachim and Brahms took part, performing two of the *Fantasiestücke*, Op. 73, in the arrangement for violin and piano, the Chaconne

---

[28] To Cherubini's opera of 1813.

[29] Clara, accompanied by Frl. Jungé, was off on a concert tour to Frankfurt, Karlsruhe, and Heidelberg. The ruins probably refer to the Castle in Heidelberg, which glows a strikingly rich red colour in the westerly sun.

from Bach's solo violin suite in D minor with Schumann's piano accompaniment, and the Piano Concerto in A minor, Op. 54, with Brahms as soloist. For Brahms, it was also a chance to have his friend with him in Hamburg for a few days.

83
Johannes Brahms to Joseph Joachim

[Hamburg, 18 November 1855]

The concert is on Saturday, dear Joseph. It would be best if you could leave Hanover at noon on Thursday and rehearse on Friday afternoon at 2 o'clock. Perhaps on Saturday morning as well, with Grund 2 rehearsals are probably necessary. It is more pleasant after all if you arrive here in good time in the evening, than at 5 in the morning, for example. Write to me, at least, if you come at some time other than Thursday evening, so I can expect you.

But now I'm hoping to have you here for a few days at least, dear friend, hoping to see new things of yours and to show you something. Avé and Grädener are also looking forward to a pleasant music- (and oyster-) evening.

What do you think, do you want to sleep at our house? In the end, it's more pleasant than sleeping alone in a hotel. Just write me a line.

I'll have to play the A minor Concerto after all, the members of the Philharmonic are afraid of the New.

Grädener has a new Trio which I'm supposed to try out for the first time tomorrow. That, as well as my Quartet, we would like to try out with you.[30]

Man, make yourself free for a week, you may well like it here for 8 days, let's make merry and kill time enjoyably.

From Avé, Grädener, my parents, brother, and sister, I'm supposed to give you heartiest greetings.

Do write to me right away when you are coming and if you want to stay with me or prefer to stay by yourself.

Your Johannes

NB. There can be no rehearsal on Saturday morning! You have to rehearse on Friday afternoon at 2 o'clock.

In all the many volumes of correspondence to and from Brahms, nothing quite approaches the letters he and Joachim exchanged over his First Piano Concerto (there are more than twenty of them). For one thing, the confusion and helplessness

---

[30] The eventual Op. 60, which Brahms was still experimenting with. The 'New' was Brahms's piano concerto.

he displays in his letters is in enormous contrast to the intensity and power of the music itself. For another, Joachim's answers, lengthy, detailed, thoughtful, and skilled, are extraordinary testimonials to his own talent, and to the awe and admiration he felt for his friend.

Many of Joachim's suggestions, carefully noted by him in pencil on the working score, have been preserved to the present day. They give some idea of the scope of his participation in the concerto's creation (one letter even includes a guide to his pencil marks).[31]

84
Johannes Brahms to Joseph Joachim

[Hamburg, c.25 November 1856]

Dear Jussuf,[32]

Here then the first movement of the concerto, which, in haste, I have made simpler and easier. You know how it would please me no end if you looked at it very carefully (if it's at all worth the trouble) and let me know every one of your thoughts and reservations, even the smallest.

I'm expecting the Quartet back any day now and am eager to hear what you think of it.

You have made those few days so lovely for us that I'll long remember them.[33]

One more thing: I just can't forgo the e sharp (pizzic.) in the Quartet, though the way it sounded on Sunday (they were also playing e and f sharp at the same time) is not how it sounds in my inner ear. I believe the long cadence toward g sharp, the calm and the subsequent development, create the effect that I desire and create room for the E sharp. However, one cannot philosophize about such notes; rules cannot defend them, but a good ear like yours can condemn them. Farewell, write to me soon, and send the overture, too.

In a rush,
Johannes

Once again, the soundness of Brahms's musical instincts proved itself early on. The pizzicatos under discussion belong to an early version of the C minor Piano Quartet,

---

[31] *BW* v, July 1857, 188–91.

[32] Joachim's nickname, by virtue of the fez he often wore when smoking his strong Turkish cigarettes.

[33] Referring to the visit of 22 November, during which the Piano Quartet, Op. 60, was first tried out.

Op. 60, at that time in C sharp minor. Brahms accepted Joachim's suggestion to change the key to one kinder to stringed instruments, but he would not give up the disputed pizzicatos. By the time of publication, the E sharp had become an E pizzicato, heard first from the viola, at measures 28–9, and then again from the violin, measures 29–30 (and in the recapitulation, measures 224–6). Donald Tovey has beautifully described this extraordinary moment of the Quartet in his *Essays in Musical Analysis, Chamber Music*,[34] and calls these pizzicato E's 'the greatest dramatic factor in the whole movement'.

Brahms continued to wrestle with his concerto. He let Joachim know that in Hamburg he was having difficulty finding the necessary peace and quiet, but then neglected to answer his friend's letters. Joachim returned the concerto with his comments.

85

Johannes Brahms to Joseph Joachim

[Hamburg, c.11 December 1856]

Dear Joseph,

What must you be thinking of me for not writing at all? Perhaps simply the truth. You gave me something to think about, and I could never come to terms with it. Every day I wanted to set off to see you; it never happened chiefly because of my parents, who have me so rarely and so briefly, also so that Frau Schumann finds at least one friend here right away.

So I'm sending you the Finale to be rid of it at last.

Will it satisfy you? I doubt that very much.

The ending was actually becoming good, but now it doesn't seem so to me.

A thousand thanks for looking over the first movement so kindly and carefully.

I have learned a great deal from your excellent comments. As an artist I really can wish for nothing but more talent, so that I could learn more from such a friend.

Be well, dear fellow, I think we're coming on Monday. In January I definitely must have a longer stay with you.

I really long for that.

Scold and cross out in the movement as you see fit.

Greetings from everyone here in the house.

Affectionately your

Johannes

---

[34] (London, 1944), 205 ff.

Clara was on her way through Hamburg and Hanover to Düsseldorf, in time to spend Christmas with Brahms and some of her children. After the holiday, Brahms stayed on to continue work on his concerto, while Clara was on tour once again.

❧ 1857 ❧

86
Johannes Brahms to Joseph Joachim

[Düsseldorf, beginning of January 1857]

Dear Friend,

I have already waited so long in vain for your Overture as well as my Rondo.[1] When shall I finally get them both?

Surely you are not shy about making big—and very big—cuts in the Rondo? I'm very well aware that these are necessary.

Send it to me soon—both things!

I'm enclosing a copy of the first movement for a second—and very rigorous—revision. As well as the Variations, about which I should like to have a clear statement from you. Frau Schumann doesn't care for the Finale in b flat minor (the key! not the movement).

Strangely enough, however, an Adagio is coming with it. If only I could finally take pleasure in a successful adagio! Do write to me about it very decisively. If it pleases you at all show it to our dear friend—otherwise, not.

On pages 18 and 19 I cannot find a role for the orchestra, nor really on 16 and 17.

The small change on page 19, 2nd [system?] is more to my liking, but reminds me of Wagner?

Do send me the Rondo and the Overture very soon; and the Adagio too, if you don't like it—otherwise: show it first and send it later.

Dear Joseph, I'm so happy to be able to send you my things—it gives me a feeling of double security. If only we could begin our counterpoint studies again!

Without further ado, I want to recommend a book to you: *Personal Protection—from the English—by Dr Laurentius in Leipzig.*

You yourself will sense whether you (not your body!) are in need of it.

I believe that our parents and teachers should early on show us such a book or [take us around] a hospital. Escapades of any kind need not harm a

---

[1] The last movement of the piano concerto.

person, but thinking or ruminating about such things can give one a bad time and can also, I think, harm one's body and temperament. Such books (point of view) can restore our former cheerful frame of mind, so that one doesn't have to wrestle with thoughts of being a frivolous playboy or a philistine—one is aware of these notions.

I seem to have sounded off about some very confusing stuff—but knowing you, you'll understand what I mean. You know that there are times one would be glad to have a readable anatomical museum.

Now, Adieu dearest friend, write and send soon; a thousand thanks, in advance, for cuts etc—

In the best of friendship,

Your

Johannes

Greetings to Frau Clara when she comes; perhaps the Adagio can be a friendly greeting to her, I'm eager for that.

Regarding the Variations, I would dearly like to know if they're actually printable.

The Concerto parts etc. for Frau Schumann are enclosed.

The 'dear friend' was Clara Schumann, the Adagio referred to is the sublime slow movement of the Piano Concerto (the 'gentle portrait' Brahms told Clara he was painting of her).[2] Brahms was also sending along his *Variations On an Hungarian Theme*, Op. 21 No. 2, a work which did not actually appear in print until early in 1862.

Although the counterpoint exchange was momentarily in abeyance, Brahms could still count on Joachim for help with his compositions, and in personal matters Joachim, who was only two years older, was the friend he could confide in.

The book by Laurentius (which Joachim was unable to find, in spite of Brahms's urging), was about sexual anatomy, disease, and behaviour. Published in Leipzig as *Der Persönliche Schutz*, by 1855 it had gone into its 17th German edition. The text included both the most up-to-date knowledge of venereal disease, and copious misinformation about sexual behaviour; but at least it dealt frankly and openly with a subject that has rarely been so treated even today. It was illustrated with detailed and excellent anatomical drawings, and proffered the reasonable advice to stay away from quacks and self-medication. The author urged moderation verging on abstinence in matters sexual, and gave the impression that it was possible to be sensible about sexual activity. Perhaps this is what appealed to the young Brahms, for it is otherwise hardly a comforting book.[3]

[2] *SBB* 197 ff., 30 Dec. 1856.
[3] The original English title reads: *Self-Preservation, a Medical Treatise on the Debilities and*

87
Johannes Brahms to Joseph Joachim

[Düsseldorf, 22 April 1857]

My dear Joseph,

Here comes the Rondo for the 2nd time. I'm asking for the same as last time, your very *exacting* appraisal. Some of it has been completely changed for the better, I hope, some of it is merely different.

It's the ending that I mainly hope to have improved; it was too fleeting and didn't produce the effect that it wanted.

One place has remained as it was with a mark on its forehead. Does it definitely have to go?[4]

In the first movement I think I have improved one of the weak passages; with the first one I wasn't so successful, so I left it, perhaps for now.

I am enclosing both first movements once again,[5] perhaps you'll tell me of some other things I can improve.

On pp. 18 and 19 in the Adagio, wouldn't it be better for the winds to take over the melody? Where the melody comes for the 2nd time wouldn't it also be better to have eighth-note motion? Hiller always insisted on this at every little quiet spot, but here perhaps it's better?[6]

In the Finale there are some places where the orchestration is still very naked, I am still much too ignorant in this and really don't know how to help myself.

I have also landed in some confusion with the horns, I suppose. Must they be low B flat horns and can't one make more use of them again, perhaps at the end as D horns?

I suppose we had better do away with the piccolo, it has only 8 notes in the first movement after all?

So, dear friend, send it back to me as soon as you can, for I'd like to be able to breathe freely soon again, and I might still have to work on it.

Diseases of the Generative Organs Resulting from Solitary Habits, Youthful Excess, or Infection, by Samuel La'Mert. A 20th edition was printed in London, 1846. Brahms would have read the German translation, *Der Persönliche Schutz, Aertzlicher Rathgeber bei allen Krankheiten der Geschlechtstheile, die in Folge heimlicher Jugendsünden und übermäßigen Genüssen in der geschlechtlichen Liebe und durch Ansteckung entstehen*, in the Enlarged and Improved Edition (Leipzig, 1855). It included 'Practical Remarks about Premature Impotence, Female Sterility, and their Cures'. The German author is given as Laurentius, Hohe Strasse No. 26, Leipzig.

[4] Reference to the sign on Cain's forehead after he slew Abel, indicating his wickedness?

[5] Probably of Op. 15, and of the eventual Op. 60.

[6] Brahms must have studied Ferdinand Hiller's works closely, but there is no evidence that he studied *with* him.

I say a thousand thanks to you in advance for this and all your help with this work. Without you I wouldn't have done it.

Frau Schumann is leaving tomorrow evening for England. I would probably shed tears if I had to go to the land of fog now that all the trees are splendidly green.

She greets you affectionately, as do I.

Utterly your
Johannes

Through his network of friends, Brahms stayed in touch with events in Hamburg. Grädener was 45 years old when Brahms sent him this letter, addressing him in the 'Du' form, and advising him on how to proceed with publishing his instrumental version of Schumann's *Zigeunerleben for Chorus with Piano*, Op. 29.

88

Johannes Brahms to Carl Georg Peter Grädener

[Düsseldorf, early part of 1857][7]

Dear friend,

Please be content with this very brief answer to your kind letter. I am somewhat plagued by a toothache and hardly in the mood to write letters. But I mustn't keep you waiting.

Publishers are miserable curs!

Another of the deep insights yet unknown to the Ancients and which in vain I seek in Plutarch. Of knowledge and learning there is no end!

But *do not, absolutely not*, send your things without an honorarium. In the worst possible case, all Härtels would have to do, to erect a friendly monument to Schumann, is to utilize the profit they made on the song arrangement, since after all, it is a token of esteem and friendship.

Anyway there is no need for *me* to jabber on, my sensibilities are decidedly opposed to that. Yours is the least agreeable portion of the whole venture. You know that nothing is less appreciated than making arrangements etc. Anyone who might conceivably also have done it has the right to find fault with it, and one really makes use of that too much here.

Then I must still tell you that the aforesaid *Zigeunerleben* was performed in Barmen *this winter* (recently) in an orchestration by Reinecke.

I suppose that's all right?

---

[7] Dated by reference to Otten's performance of Reinthaler's oratorio *Jephta* on 25 March 1857, as listed in J. Sittard, *Geschichte des Musik- und Concertwesens in Hamburg* (Leipzig, 1890), 210.

It is too obvious that a printing could only be to Härtels' advantage. The song is very popular and this mode of performing it is very pleasing and spirited. Incidentally, the Elberfelders have already placed an order in advance. Here and in Cologne, for instance, it was bought right away.

Write them a *thick* letter, but one that is also pointed (but I think they won't take it anyway).

Although I had expected a lot from Otten, nevertheless it goes beyond my comprehension that he is performing *Jephta*. Makes no difference whether he had heard it or had simply groped blindly for something new, one is done with him regardless!

You would [give] me a great deal of pleasure if you'd tell me more about this business. Gossip about what Otten might have said about it, if he was patronizing when he introduced it etc. Maybe you could dictate it to one of your two fifth- or sixth-graders.

Frau Sch[umann] sends warm greetings to everyone and decidedly offers you the same advice as I.

My warmest greetings to your wife and children, Also Avé with family.

With my best greetings,

your Johs. Brahms.

For the fourth time in his relatively young life, Brahms became a godfather, this time to the Grimms' first-born. In all, he would accept this honour at least fifteen times, with increasing bemusement. Along with his answer, he sent a collection of movements from his *Missa canonica* for Grimm's comment.

89
Johannes Brahms to Julius Otto Grimm

Düsseldorf, 8 May [18]57

Dear friend,

I'm exceedingly delighted that you want to give my name to your boy; Do also call him Johannes, I beg you! I am as fond of you as of anyone, and wherever I can, I want to merit it as far as the boy is concerned. I'm only sorry that you were so impractical as to announce the baptism to me three days beforehand, otherwise I might well have been able to arrange to come; but since I must go to Detmold very soon, it is unfortunately impossible. I think I'll not go to Hamburg until winter-time and will seriously consider whether I couldn't come to Göttingen in the mean time. Give my best greetings to your wife and the Ritmüllers. I'll be with you in spirit on Sunday and wishing you all the best.

I ask you to greet Joachim most warmly and to convey my best thanks for his dear letter and yesterday's fine enclosures.

That he is by and large satisfied with the concerto, for the time being, makes me quite happy.

By the way, I'm asking him not to keep it any longer than necessary, because I would like to extract a piano part and send it to Frau Schumann. As a matter of fact, I have to write to him myself. Is there finally a prospect of reaching a contrapuntal rapport?! Frau Schumann doesn't write the best of things from England. Now they're even in mourning there.[8]

Yesterday I was happy as a king, Frau Sch. had the piano reduction of the *Sängers Fluch* sent to me, from which I noticed that the work [is] dedicated to me! Schumann had written several times from Endenich that this was his intention, but not in my dreams had I expected it would happen.

Frau Sch.'s address in London is 32 Dorset Place, Dorset Square, NW.

What can be done with the impossible alto part in my sacred things? I had got myself so enmeshed in my passion for low alto, without considering that they aren't around any more.

I don't want to continue with the Mass until I'm clear about it. (Possibly a string quartet with it?) Farewell, my warmest greetings to your family and to Joachim, and on Sunday and many other times too, think of

your

Johannes.

His friend gave him expert and detailed advice, commenting particularly on the impracticality of Brahms's writing for alto. Brahms was slow to learn his lesson, for three years later Grimm was still chiding him gently for writing such low parts: 'My girls long for notes which confine themselves to the five lines and four spaces of the staff.' (7 May 1860). Twenty-one years later, reworkings of the Benedictus and Agnus Dei found their way into the motet *Warum ist das Licht gegeben dem Mühseligen*, Op. 74 No. 1.

When Brahms left Düsseldorf, in October 1856, his intent was to return home. But the move back to Hamburg was not entirely successful; his parents' house was simply too small. He urged them to find one where he could have his own room, and after seven weeks went back to Düsseldorf to compose. His mother wrote:

(28 December 1856) Just finish up all your work, so that you are not grumpy here. When you are here, we want you to be just as merry as always.

(14 February 1857) We are very happy that you are coming back to us again and want to stay with us. You are most heartily welcome by all, but you

---

[8] Because of a death in the royal family.

must bring money with you, that is, as much as you need, and what ever
you don't bring you can earn; there will be plenty of opportunity for that,
don't worry, and we'll soon see about another flat. If nothing else, we'll rent
a studio for you, and afterwards a suitable flat for us all ...

In fact, Brahms remained away from Hamburg for almost a year and meanwhile
made the decision to accept his first real appointment, as musician at the Court of
Count Leopold III zur Lippe in Detmold.

In area, the Duchy of Detmold rivalled Sieghartsweiler, that diminutive land
where Johannes Kreisler, Meister Abraham, and his tom-cat Murr fought so many
battles against the Philistines. At the time of Brahms's appointment—which he
gained as the result of a week-long piano-playing marathon during which he performed the favourite music at Court (Beethoven's Piano Sonata, Op. 27 No 1, and
Fourth Piano Concerto, and Schubert's 'Trout' Quintet)—no railway yet led to
Detmold, and paper money was still unknown. Tucked away at the edge of the great
Teutoburger Forest, scene of the dramatic slaughter of three Roman legions at a crucial moment in ancient German history, the little principality was reached by horse-
drawn coach and belonged to another century.

The reigning Prince was enormously enthusiastic about music, the reigning
Princess an accomplished pianist. Brahms's official duties, which lasted from
October to the end of December, consisted in giving piano lessons to the Princess,
playing at Court, and conducting the amateur choral society, 'larded with royal
highnesses',[9] which met weekly at the castle by invitation of the Prince. He had many
private students—not only Laura von Meysenbug, the daughter of the Hofrat,
whom he was already teaching in Düsseldorf, but many lady pianists at court; since
his principal student was the Princess Friederike, prudence and etiquette suggested
that the others study with him as well, whether or not they had talent or desire. He
charged high fees so as to discourage such students, but this solution only succeeded
in earning him more money than he had expected. Occasionally he received permission to conduct the orchestra, although the regular court conductor, one
Kapellmeister August Kiel, viewed Brahms's arrival with considerable mistrust.

Brahms's adventures in the tiny Duchy have been vividly described by the two
people there he knew best: Carl, Freiherr von Meysenbug, the teenage nephew and
grandson of two musical Detmolders; and the violinist Karl Bargheer, the concertmaster of the orchestra, who had already met Brahms while he was a student of
Joachim. The three young men struck up a lively friendship and were frequently
together.[10]

[9] Brahms to Bertha Porubsky; see Letter 120.
[10] Willy Schramm, *Johannes Brahms in Detmold*, 2nd edn. (Hagen, 1983), esp. pp. 21–34. Also
Carl von Meysenbug, 'Aus Johannes Brahms' Jugendtagen', *Neues Wiener Tagblatt* (3 and 4 Apr.
1902), and Hermann von Meysenbug, *Neues Wiener Tagblatt* (9 May 1901).

Occasionally, Brahms's letters from Detmold complain of boredom and isolation, but the memoirs by Bargheer and von Meysenbug describe some of the most droll and uninhibited incidents of Brahms's life, and it seems clear that all in all he found companionship and good cheer. 'We are pleased that you feel so happy there,' his mother wrote on 5 October. He was well fed, well housed, and well located. He was learning the craft of conducting and orchestration, learning new repertory, performing regularly, and taking the opportunity to become intimately familiar with some Bach cantatas. He made use of the Ducal library and read voraciously. Moreover, he earned, in the course of three months, ample money to last him the entire year and leave him free to compose the rest of the time.

The three seasons he spent there brought forth both Serenades, the Sextet, Op. 18, many solo songs and choral works, three collections of folk-songs, and the completed piano concerto.

Ultimately the constraints of life at Court were felt to be too burdensome, but by the time Brahms left Detmold for good, he was ready for the second phase of his career; the years of turmoil were behind him.

90
Johannes Brahms to Clara Schumann

Detmold, early Sunday morning, 11 October 1857

My Clara,

How pleasantly you surprised me yesterday evening! I had just come home an hour before my *Singverein*; there I found your package. First the wonderful letter, which had such delightful girth, and then the magnificent present!

It doesn't seem at all right to me that you spent so much money for it, but that aside, it naturally gave me the greatest pleasure.

It is so enchantingly tasteful, as well as practical, and awakens such lovely intimations of letters fashioned just like the one enclosed. A thousand thanks. For your letter I give even more thanks.

Your written words read as though your eyes looked out from them and smiled at me.

Dear Clara, you must seriously strive and take care that your sombre mood doesn't exceed all bounds and persist endlessly.

Life is precious; such a frame of mind ravages the body severely.

Do not persuade yourself that life is of little worth to you. That's not true, that's true for very few people.

If you give yourself over completely to such a mood, you won't even enjoy happier times, as you could. The more you endeavour and accustom yourself to passing sombre periods with more equanimity and calmness, the more will you enjoy the happier time which always follows. Why else has man received that heavenly gift, Hope?

And it isn't even necessary for you to hope anxiously, you know that agreeable months will follow these, as they follow every disagreeable period.

Don't take this lightly, it's very serious.

Body and soul are damaged by such lingering of a dark mood, which one must more *thoroughly* subdue, or prevent from arising.

It is as if one expected to feed one's body on the unhealthiest dishes and then take consolation in going on a milk cure for the summer. The body might recover somewhat for a while, but it is damaged and quickly goes to ruin.

Such unhealthy food for the soul as unremitting depression ruins body and soul as does the worst pestilence.

You must seriously transform yourself, my dearest Clara. Every morning resolve anew, quite seriously and simply, to be that day and for all time more even-tempered (more harmonious) and more cheerful. Passions are not an inherent attribute of mankind. They are always exceptions or excesses.

The person in whom they exceed normal bounds must consider himself an invalid, and must take care of his life and his health with medicine.

Calm in joy and calm in pain and sorrow is the beautiful, true human being. Passions must soon fade away, or they must be driven off.

Consider yourself an invalid, dear Clara, as someone seriously ill, and take care of yourself, not anxiously, but calmly and ceaselessly. Do forgive me this chatter, but I don't write well, I haven't learned to organize my thoughts and to express them. Only do think this through seriously and act accordingly, then everything will get better, and you'll feel increasingly happy, and all those who belong to you will be even happier.

The Mozart concerto went rather well, the other day. They played the *Ruy Blas* Overture beforehand, and afterwards the C minor Symphony by Spohr.

Yesterday I had the *Singverein*. As I rehearse, I feel as if I had already done it for 25 years.

My voice is gaining a not insignificant benefit from the loud speaking. I make use of this advantage as I do of every one I can seize.

My voice—it is becoming majestic. When the chorus sings *forte*, I exercise it and roar in the midst, actually just for my sake, and for practice. We also took up the *Zigeunerleben*, and it will certainly go splendidly before long.

What child's play such things are compared to old church music. And my *Salve Regine* is still easy, as these things go. This piece you would like very much.[11]

I cannot tell you much about Rovetta, except that he lived in about 1640. The people like both pieces very much and take great pains over them. The *Zigeunerleben* is charming and sounds wonderful.

Yesterday morning, along with Bargheer, I had to accompany the Prince in his singing. I don't exactly wish for this to happen often.

I shall look through the Requiem most carefully as soon as I can and send it back, if possible with the Quintet.[12]

My thanks for the music you sent.

The gloves are excellent! Again, thank you.

As to how to organize your music, that's not easily done in writing. At all events, the scores must be together in one cabinet. Händel all together, Bach next to it, and of course complete on 1 or 2 shelves, the big one, the Peters', and all other editions all together. The operas written by Kuntsch, Don Juan, Fidelio, Gluck, and next to them similar scores, such as Marcello, Sachini, Cherubini, Rameau, etc. etc.

Then modern operas, such as Mangold, Hiller, Wagner, together. And finally, perhaps in the same bookcase, all the complete quartets and symphonies and full scores together with the remaining smaller ones. Among the latter, for example, I have Scottish Songs by Beethoven, Crucifuxus by Lotti.[13]

As far as I know, your husband had nothing significant by Vogler. His most famous works I was unable to get to know, not even with the best of intentions.

In particular, there is a Requiem, published by Schott in full score. I don't know whether we would grow rhapsodic over it, but it is said to be important.

I cannot agree with you about the article by Debrois.

What he writes about me (as the dear principal character), I found reasonable beyond all expectations, except for some downright stupidities, as

---

[11] *Salve Regina* by Giovanni Rovetta, *c.*1595–1668. Clara had written fine works for a cappella chorus herself, which may be the basis for Brahms's observation. The *Zigeunerleben for Chorus with Piano*, mentioned next, are Schumann's, performed by Brahms some time in November in the instrumental version by Grädener (see *BW* iv, 80).

[12] Probably referring to Schumann's Piano Quintet, Op. 44, and his Requiem, which Clara was trying to decide whether to publish (the eventual Op. 148).

[13] Johann Gottfried Kuntsch, Schumann's old piano and counterpoint teacher in Zwickau (?–1854). Georg Joseph Vogler (1749–1814), much decorated prelate, composer, educator, and conductor of the last quarter of the 18th, and first decade of the 19th c. Antonio Lotti (*c.*1667–1740), Venetian composer who worked in Hanover and Dresden.

when e.g. he is of the opinion that the B minor variation was not intentionally written to imitate the corresponding piece in your husband's work!
Something that is surely clear as day. N.B. The said piece is the one following the F sharp minor theme, therefore everything is quite simple. About
Joachim, that's just pure rubbish. All in all, the bad thing is that in some
places, Debrois exposes such dilletantish weak spots that the Leipzigers can
give him a terrible thrashing. But whoever wishes to write against this Liszt
clique *must spread gossip.*

For these people maintain themselves by gossiping, and by having the
meanest and most convoluted personalities; one has to expose them if one
wants to stir up their nest.

The most blockheaded thing is that little Debrois insists on his vision of
the pinnacle of the completed cathedral of music.

Who can ever say that something which has no end has now reached its
end? Small-minded people have always wanted to place a full stop after every
genius. After Mozart, if we want to stick to the last-but-one.

About [Robert] Franz, I can find nothing that Debrois has overstated. I
suppose you took the passages cited from the *N[eue] Z[eitschrift] f[ür]
M[usik]* to be his opinion?

Anyway I find it tiresome to write about this kind of thing. If I could do
more than mumble in my beard, it wouldn't be so tiresome to me.

But these petty scribblers are nothing more than people who like tussle,
they merely get in the way a little.

In art, only a creating genius can convince.

Be sure not to buy the Hogarth. Beautiful copper engravings, after all,
are the main thing. And the continuation is very problematical. By now it is
too late to want to explain Hogarth, we'll probably always have to be satisfied with Lichtenberg's beginning.

Perhaps one day I'll find the prints cheaply and in fine condition, then
I'll buy them.

Just describe your flat to me soon, I can still be surprised as always.

By the way, day in and day out I think of the pleasure with which I'll be
going to Hamburg for the New Year!

How I then rejoice inwardly!

Warm greetings, my beloved Clara, and read once more *da capo* until the
Alternative.[14]

---

[14] Or rather, *Alternativo*; i.e. go back to the beginning of the letter and read until the first variation. Just where that begins, however, is a Brahmsian mystery—or is it where he discusses his
Variations, Op. 9?!

Remember me to Woldemar [Barghiel].
Your
Johannes.

Go for a walk and look attentively and lovingly through Woldemar's things.

This letter ranks among the most informative pieces of autobiography Brahms ever wrote. How to deal with passions—passions which needed to be irrevocably subdued? Brahms was by now an expert and took his own advice, perhaps for the remainder of his life, perhaps thereby drawing a line between himself and the true Romantic.

In another insight into his character, he informs us of a view of life which was borne out by his own daily routine: although a pervasive, long-range pessimism was a fundamental given in his life, in the short term one's daily life offered plenty to look forward to. Life was precious, there were very few people who had reason to regard it as worthless—and neither he nor Clara were among them.

Brahms's assertion that he made use of every advantage he could seize is a remark which applied to matters both large and small. In this instance, he was using the choral rehearsals to exercise his voice in an attempt to lower its unusually high pitch, an attempt which succeeded but which is also the probable cause of his rasping voice.

The reference to Debrois is of particular interest, because it allows us the supposition that when he composed, the musical allusions Brahms made to other composers were quite conscious. Karl Debrois van Bruyk, working in Vienna, had just written the first friendly appraisal of Brahms to appear in print since Schumann's paean, 'Neue Bahnen' (in the *Wiener Zeitung* of 25 September 1857). Oddly, in discussing Brahms's *Variations on a Theme by Schumann*, Op. 9, Debrois apparently thought that Brahms was unaware of the connection between his set of variations and Schumann's own *Bunte Blätter*, Op. 99. If one takes a quick look at Schumann's piece No. 5, it appears identical with the 9th variation of Brahms's set; and although the similarities are merely superficial, it is absolutely clear that Brahms was paying homage to Schumann here. Even the key relationships are maintained: Brahms's 9th variation, in B minor just as Schumann's No. 5, follows an exact statement of Schumann's original theme, in the correct key of F sharp minor—an unmistakable clue, as Brahms pointed out to Clara.

And in this letter, we get another chance to glimpse a non-musical interest already well developed in the young Brahms. Not only widely read in literature and poetry, Brahms had a keen interest in the graphic arts, with strong opinions to match. Both interests stayed with him lifelong. How one would like to know what was on Brahms's mind as he advised Clara to stay away from those Hogarth prints! Brahms may have become acquainted with the prints in Göttingen, where there is a large collection in the University library, thanks to the scientist and philosopher Georg Christian Lichtenberg (1742–99). Lichtenberg's commentary on Hogarth's series of engravings, *High Life, Marriage à la Mode*, is still the classic in the field. It is probable that Clara had expressed interest in buying an edition with somone else's commentary.[15]

The unusual length of this letter to Clara undoubtedly reflects the isolation Brahms felt in Detmold. He called on his other best friend for news:

91
Johannes Brahms to Joseph Joachim

Detmold, 5 December 1857

Dearest Joseph,

I am extremely uneasy that it will now soon be 3 months that I've been here and that I hear and see nothing of you. Make up for it, some time, I do so herewith, and had I had anything to send you that was worth reading, I would have done it long ago.

Send me your concerto or whatever, so it will feel as though I myself had been industrious.[16]

The pleasures of Their Serene Highnesses leave me no time to think of myself. In fact I am pleased when they make serious demands on me, and I benefit from many things that I had greatly lacked until now.

How little practical knowledge I have! The chorus rehearsals have shown me great weaknesses, they will not be useless to me. My things are certainly written in an excessively impractical way!

I have rehearsed numerous things and fortunately, right from the first hour, with sufficient audacity.

Salve Regina by Rovetta, songs by Schumann, Mozart, Praetorius, etc. Now we are doing the Messiah, and for my enjoyment I am experimenting with folk-songs!

I am rehearsing triple concertos by Bach, I have already played 2 by Mozart, etc.

Now I have practised the Triple Concerto by Beethoven with Bargheer and a cellist,[17] and so I beg you to lend me the orchestra parts, if possible.

---

[15] The prints, with Lichtenberg's commentary, were recently reissued with remarks by Arthur S. Wensiger and W. B. Coley, by Wesleyan University Press (Middletown, Conn., 1970).

[16] The *Hungarian Concerto*, Op. 11.

[17] Julius Schmidt. In spite of the nickname 'Sleepy-head', which he earned by falling asleep once at a rehearsal, his head resting peacefully on his cello, Schmidt played not only the Triple Concerto and Brahms's Trio, Op. 8, but other demanding music as well. He was accorded the title of Kammermusicus in recognition of his fine chamber music performances. See Schramm, *Johannes Brahms in Detmold*, 26, 34, n. 19. For a more complete list of repertory he played with Brahms, see pp. 6–8 and 31.

You did play it last winter in Hanover. Kiel has lent his out and forgets to attend to it.

I would have liked to play it on Friday, could I get it right away?

It's most agreeable for me to have Bargheer here, as you can imagine. Otherwise there is a complete desert of musical friends here, with the exception of a few ladies.

I won't say a lot about what is pleasant and not so pleasant here.

Indeed, I even refrain from talking about it to myself; it is better so.

But I live very comfortably here (in the room where you stayed) and with Kiel I get along somewhat better than not at all.

You probably are not getting many replies from Frau Schumann?

She fell ill in Munich, unfortunately, so that she has already been confined to her room for 10–12 days, and only wishes she could get going again shortly.

As a result, the poor woman must spend the holidays in Switzerland and after that, once more to Munich, Augsburg, etc.

This is rather sad.

I have with me another new trio by Woldemar Bargiel, which I don't want to send back to him at all. I find it most disagreeable.

Dear friend, do write to me at long last, I have truly yearned for it for a long time. Can't you include anything new? Something contrapuntal? Greetings to Grimm, whom you must occasionally see in your house.

How are things in Hanover? It's really just as if I had emigrated. As if I had already rusted into a Detmold Capellmeister!

Don't let's make over-long pauses in our correspondence. It pains me.

With all love

Your

Johannes

Bargheer sends best greetings. If possible, do send the orchestra parts for the Triple Concerto by return mail.

Brahms was indeed living very well in Detmold. He was housed in the centre of town, directly before the gates of the palace grounds. In Detmold's best inn, Zur Stadt Frankfurt, meals and wine were included (Plate 16).

༖ 1858 ༖

As the new year began, Clara and Joachim had every reason to express to each other their satisfaction that Brahms was well established in his new position. From Hanover Joachim wrote to Clara on 3 January 1858: 'Johannes came by . . . He was in good spirits, and I think we can congratulate ourselves with the thought that Johannes, with his competence and good sense, has made a good start at providing an untroubled subsistence for himself in Detmold.' And Joachim exulted over yet another revision of the Piano Concerto in D minor, saying that by now it was almost too rich. 'But that is a benevolent reproach! How much my every hope of experiencing the new and beautiful in music rests with my dear friend.' In the next months he proved his friendship repeatedly, as he sought to gain a hearing for the concerto.

Joachim was not the only friend eager to help. Julius Otto Grimm offered to perform the concerto in Göttingen, if Johannes would play. Brahms answered:

92

Johannes Brahms to Julius Otto Grimm

[Hamburg, beginning of February 1858]

Dear friend,

Of my concerto there exists no reasonable score, let alone any parts! Your letter was such a forceful reminder that I instantly set myself to copying, to ensure having at least one rehearsal in Hanover.

I would be sorely tempted to loaf around at your place, but I have various fissures in my fingers (from the cold or the heat of the stove) and so I don't know when I dare start practising; not now, anyway.[1]

I'd be glad to play my concerto if you take on the burden of rehearsing it, but in less than a month it's quite unthinkable!

Frau Schumann travels incessantly from here to there, from Swabia to Switzerland and back again. So far she is doing well, also, as I hear, quite handsomely with her earnings. My parents etc. send you very warm greetings, it would give them great pleasure if you would really come there in the spring (with Wife Most Dear)! Let's have a letter one of these days that cheerily tells me about yourself. I myself am doing curiously well, I had a very good time in Detmold and also profited in a number of ways. Among other things, money for the whole year. I hope it will be the same next year.

Joachim just won't return the first movement of my concerto, although I asked him for it. If you see him, do remind him.

[1] A recurring problem throughout Brahms's life.

If the concert comes off well, why don't you arrange for an engagement with you next year!

Fare you well. Greet your wife, little Johannes, and your parents-in-law with all my heart. Do please write me a long and leisurely letter, some time. I can only think that you are forgetting me completely.

I am with all my heart

Your Johannes.

Joachim returned the concerto movement shortly.

93

Joseph Joachim to Johannes Brahms

[Beginning of February 1858]

My dear, dear friend,

Here, finally, is your piece back—it is completely revised, and I would like to hope that the orchestrated sections please you. If that is not the case, then take in hand a solid chunk of eraser, which cannot be lacking in Hamburg, that proud city of yours which dominates the sea and islands! But man, I beg you, for God's sake, let the copyist get at your Concerto, at last: when shall I finally hear it? Do you have any prospects for trying it out in Hamburg? If not, let's stay with my suggestion of the Hanover Orchestra. I am now on tolerable terms with the musicians and bandsmen of this region of the Leine, and the gentlemen will do us the favour of giving it a proper playing in a rehearsal. Your composition requires a very good orchestra; it would be a pity if you allowed your first joy over it to be soured by mediocre players ... I restrain myself from any further comments so as not to delay the copying again ...

I just want to add my warmest greetings to those whom you love, and with whom you live. Adieu!

Your

J. J.

94
Johannes Brahms to Joseph Joachim

[Hamburg], Friday, [26 February 1858]

Dearest Friend,

Well, within a few days all the parts will have been copied out, I would just like to wait for a piano part and then come to you.

I would be in Hanover by about the end of next week. Above all else I look forward to seeing and talking with you. Is it possible to arrange a rehearsal? Must that be set well in advance or only days in advance?

What's the situation with a piano? Can I possibly find a usable one in Hanover, at Kuhn's? Otherwise, would Ritmüller be willing to make the sacrifice?

I must write to you about something else, do think it over.

I am supposed to play the concerto on March 25th with Otten. I cannot say that I do it willingly, I am afraid and the dreadfully indifferent public here is not appealing.

Besides, Ney is also singing, the Lurley finale etc. And finally, Otten tells me that he has invited you, as well.

I don't find this sensible; it means really overwhelming the audience.

You can hardly play another big concerto and—no trivia, either.

On the other hand, I would have wished very much that you were here for the concerto. What do you think about it! Please write about it and do as you think, it's not clear to me.

I keep thinking that it won't happen that I play my concerto, I have so little courage and inclination. I am distressed that I am firmly engaged, but particularly if you do *not* come and play! It is accursed.

Your Schubert Duo is back with me, and will not be performed!

Grund finds the instrumentation very beautiful but the composition he does not like at all! It is boring and without any melody!

In the first rehearsal the musicians, especially Lindenau, the gallant concertmaster of the orchestra, confirmed this verdict and thus it won't be played!

Would you be so good as to drop me a few lines as to what you make of the Otten business. Shall I perhaps wait with my rehearsal in Hanover until Frau Clara comes and can also play it? Only that will take too long.

Let me hear something from you and then soon, *auf Wiedersehen.*

Warmly your
Johannes

My people send many greetings.

'Joachim's' Schubert Duo is the the the *Grand Duo*, the Sonata in C Major for Piano Four Hands, Op. posth. 140 (D 812). In Schumann's judgement, it was a symphony waiting to be orchestrated, a challenge Joachim took up in 1855. There was a first performance in Hanover, and Joachim had hoped for a performance in Hamburg.[2]

Brahms was outraged that Joachim's orchestration was not to be performed, while the works of such lesser composers as Louis Spohr, his student Jean Joseph Bott, and Henry Litolff could find their way onto Grund's programmes with ease. The performance of Brahms's concerto under Otten did not take place, either, for reasons set out in Letter 96. Another year would go by before it was heard in Hamburg, in a concert of the Philharmonic Orchestra, with Joachim and Julius Stockhausen as his co-performers. His letter to Clara confirms his scorn for Hamburg's musical life, as well as his doubts about himself.

95
Johannes Brahms to Clara Schumann

Hamburg, Wednesday, 24 February 1858

Clara, love of my heart,

I must not wait until there is something to reply to, your ailing arm and the frantic pace of concerts, which has probably already begun again, must teach me patience.

To cheer you up I wanted to tell you a little musical tale from here. The Schubert Duo is back with me, and will not be performed. Grund told me that he didn't like the work at all for piano, but the orchestration was beautiful. The work boring and *unmelodious*.

They recently rehearsed it once and after Lindenau, the concertmaster of the orchestra, and the others, confirmed that judgement, they put the work aside.

No melodies in it!

Is boring!

Otten's concert was not beautiful.

The Schubert symphony was rushed madly, the Overture to the Bride from Messina even worse. A very boring concerto by Spohr and an even worse one by Bott himself also brought no relief.

The singer went on.

To finish, the Robespierre Overture.[3]

The score was lying open on the desk. Otten takes a look at it, picks it up, raises it, shuts the book and hands it to Böie, who looks at him with aston-

---

[2] See Moser, *Joseph Joachim*, 161, Litz, iii. 32, and Kal, i.[4] 326.
[3] By Henry Litolff (1818–91). At this time he was frequently in Hamburg.

ishment. Then Otten stretches out his wings and—he has in his head all the fine discourses which his magic wand now coaxes from the orchestra.

I haven't seen Otten again, but must make the decision to go out there one of these days, although on the other hand he might well decided to say a word of thanks to me for playing in his miserable, scruffy soirée.

The Apel woman has now received her picture and has shown it to me. I find it peculiar. The facial features are hers, but it looks so different from her that I wouldn't have taken it to be her portrait.

Whatever flesh can be seen seems well painted. But although I haven't seen her as naked as this, I maintain that those are not *her* arms, etc; instead, those of the picture appear somewhat imposing, like those of a lady, whereas in that state she surely looks more like a plump, brash, middle-class girl. Or else I am totally deluded.

Never be surprised, dear Clara, that I do not write about my work. I do not like to and cannot.

I do believe that all of you, especially you, always perceive me as being different from what I am. I am never, or only very rarely, even moderately content with myself. Indeed, never comfortable, rather alternately of good cheer or in a dark mood. But I have so little taste and inclination for lamenting to others about my lack of genius and skill that without trying, I always present a different appearance. Add to this that the pleasure that I occasionally give to others and, for example, even to you, makes me so happy, that it is quite perceptible and everyone concludes it is on my account alone that I'm so exhilarated and confident of victory. Oh that one were not capable of looking inside oneself and of knowing how much Godliness one has within! . . .

Write to me how your arm is. Know too that for several weeks now I've had a bad finger which, because of failure to apply ointment and my untameable playing, I intend to retain for a long time yet.

It is, as a matter of fact, a fissure, probably worked over jointly by frost and heat.

Farewell, beloved creature, write to me and about you, very, very much about you.

Your
Johannes

Everyone sends greetings.

96
Johannes Brahms to Joseph Joachim

[Hamburg], Monday [1 March 1858]

Dear Friend,

My concerto also will not be performed here.

The only usable grand piano, which belongs to Herr Cranz, has been denied me. It's true that Aloys Schmitt,[4] Jaëll etc. have played it, but just now he is calling a halt.

Glad as I am on the one hand not to have to play my concerto, especially before our most unresponsive audience, the reason does annoy me, because—it is so typically Hamburgian.

I had precisely the same experience with your Duo, which will be better off in my bookcase than under Grund's hands and before our audiences.

Should I come? Or is your Rostock trip coming off soon; that I'd like to wait for here, and if you could then spend a few days here that would be splendid.

Altogether it's really one and the same to me when I come to Hanover and when I rehearse.

Therefore write candidly. My anxiety is likely to hold me back.

I hear so seldom from you, and about what you're doing nothing at all any more. I long for that continually. Can't you send something, which I would then bring back with me?

Yours from the heart,
Johannes

Once again, Joachim to the rescue. He wrote back:

> As to your concerto, it will be either in one of the rehearsals for the next concert or for the last . . . Hear it we *must*, this winter. [If Frau Schumann can come,] how splendid it would be if all three of us together could hear it with orchestra for the first time.

In the event, the King allowed Joachim an extra rehearsal with orchestra for the sole purpose of trying out the new concerto. The run-through took place on 30 March, with Clara Schumann in attendance.

---

[4] Pianist, just then appointed court conductor in Schwerin.

97
Johannes Brahms to Joseph Joachim

[Hamburg, 9 March 1858]

Dear Joseph,

I am waiting with the rehearsal until Frau Clara can come along. Since I am not playing the concerto here it is all the same when I rehearse.

I have let Otten know through my brother of your *acceptance*, but since then the concert has been postponed, I believe to the 23rd, and so he will probably have written to you.

As I told you I don't see him, and it seems it will remain that way.

It's too long and drawn out to write you how this came about. But the fault is not mine, rather in his boundless vanity etc.

I assisted him at a private performance of his academy, in disregard and neglect of my artistic self-esteem, with a performance of the Fantasy with Chorus—without orchestra. He said not a word of thanks to me, nor now even a word of regret that he is unable to do my concerto. And then he depicts the crisis in the most insufferable manner and expects none the less that I will continue my patient visits, in spite of him never approaching me.[5]

It is boring for me to write about it, the whole thing is really too dull.

Everybody is looking forward greatly to seeing you here, including Herr Marxsen, whose feelings towards me are as friendly and warm as ever.

In the end *I* may not be here at all. I am thinking of going to Berlin and from there to you, and so I must unfortunately miss you here, of all places. I would so much like to roam around Hamburg with you one day.

In our house they are overjoyed at seeing you again, you are venerated here like a household god.

Warmest greetings from me and my family.

Remember me to Frau Medem, don't let yourself be seduced by the bosom of her dress, she herself has none.

Utterly yours.
Johannes

Have you read how they put you down in the new Zeitschrift? From out of Dresden.

I've said it all along!
You're done for!

---

[5] i.e. never coming to Brahms's house.

98
Clara Schumann to Woldemar Bargiel

Hanover, 30 March 1858

Dear Woldemar,

I think you must be pleased to hear that the rehearsal came off splendidly today; although there was time only to play through the concerto once, it went almost without a stumble, and even ignited some of the musicians. Had you heard it, everything would appear quite clear to you today. Almost everything sounds so beautiful, much of it even more beautiful than Johannes himself thought or hoped for. The whole thing is wonderous, so rich, deeply felt, and such unity withal. Johannes was blissful, and for pure joy played the last movement prestissimo. We took a walk, then, it was as though the Heavens wanted to endow the day with a special brilliance. Johannes enjoyed it in full measure; I wish you could have seen his blissful happiness . . .

'Now it would really be very nice if you could decide quickly and come here,' Julius Grimm wrote from Göttingen in June, extending an invitation to Brahms to spend the entire summer with him.[6] Clara was planning to spend the month of August there on holiday. With five of her children, she would stay with the Grimms. During that period, Johannes could find inexpensive rooms nearby and take his meals with them all.

Even at the risk of offending Clara, Brahms hesitated.[7] Dissatisfied with what he had accomplished during the spring, he was out of sorts, and only reluctantly accepted Grimm's enthusiastic and generous invitation to visit the small university town. But then as now, Göttingen was a lovely place at the edge of the mysterious Harz mountains, and by agreeing to come, Brahms entered into the most romantic and lyric months of his life. In beautiful summer weather, under the approving eyes of two of the people he felt most comfortable with and under the jealous and discomforted eyes of Clara Schumann, he fell in love with Agathe von Siebold, the 23-year-old daughter of a professor of medicine at the University. She was Grimm's voice and music student, and the best friend of Pine Gur (Phillipine), Grimm's wife.

---

[6] *BW* iv. 61 ff.   [7] See Clara's letter to Brahms, dated Wiesbaden, 1 July 1858. Litz, iii. 40.

99
Johannes Brahms to Julius Otto Grimm

[Hamburg, July 1858]

Dear friend,

Sincere thanks for your kindness, I shall certainly yet savour it appropriately this summer. I rack my brains over it quite a bit. I wish I could just rush out of the door. But in view of my immense indolence I don't see why I should reward and entertain myself with such fine free time.

Consideration towards my parents also holds me back.

But for how long, all this?

Bargiel planned to pass through here on his way to Göttingen, I shall write to him, then let the summer begin when it will (so far, I haven't got into the spirit).

Just imagine, Sahr surprised me recently. He was on his way to a spa in Holstein and stayed here for a day and a half.

Also, he is thinking of going home by way of Göttingen. You'll be pleased to see how he has changed (at least in some ways) and has made himself more human. He is actually very pleasant.

Here everything is fine, except for the familiar troubles of my female household gods.[8]

When is Joachim likely to come from England? Is he going to Scotland? Is he coming to Göttingen? I always regret the time he fritters away like that. The only person who knows how to make poetry, and he wears himself out in England.[9]

I'm looking forward with pleasure to you and all of you who will make my summer so beautiful.

When shall I leave here? I would like to have more details from Bargiel, for I'm getting somewhat impatient. The arrangements for food and lodging suit me fine, of course. My warm greetings to your wife, your young one, and your old ones.

From my parents, the best to you.

Ditto from your
Johannes

[8] Mother, who had trouble walking, and sister, suffering from migraine headaches since childhood.
[9] See commentary between Letters 49 and 50.

Brahms stayed in Göttingen from the end of July until the end of September. He made music with his friends, hiked with them to the local hills (the Hardenberg and the Plesse), played games of tag, loafed about, and acted as people do when they are in love; he left only when he could no longer delay taking up his duties in Detmold. Only one person was missing from the 'Congress' of friends, as he called it.

100
Johannes Brahms to Joseph Joachim

[*c.*23 September 1858][10]

Most beloved friend,
    Do come here!
    I'm remaining until the 28–29th. Can't you arrange it so that you can simply stay here until then? Our joy at your coming will keep you in the best of spirits.
    I would have come to Hanover in any case, but you leave us the lovely choice, so come! Come!
    Starting this evening we are expecting you hourly.
                    From the heart,
                        Johannes
In haste.

101
Julius Otto Grimm to Joseph Joachim

Göttingen, Thursday, 23 September [1858]

Dear Joachim!
    We all yearn for you most urgently, Johannes, Pine, Gathe, little Hans, and I, and it is really less complicated for you to come here; so leave your house-moving to Rabe[11] and come! As quickly as possible, moreover, for Johannes is only staying until Tuesday. Pine Gur will make a room and bed ready for you; we can't even conceive that you stay at home, and have been on the look-out for you all summer in vain. There would still be a few exquisite days left for loafing around on the Hardenberg or the Plesse, and here at home it's wonderful. Little Hans chatters and runs around and is full of nonsense, and Johannes has composed marvellous songs, which Gathe

---

[10] The date is based on the similar letter from Grimm to Joachim, given next.
[11] Joachim's manservant.

sings for us, and we are all of one opinion that it's a magnificent time—you and you alone are missing, so come! All send warmest greetings,

Your

Julius Grimm

These joyous expressions were followed, after his departure, by a series of letters Brahms wrote to the Grimms from Detmold. Since they were meant for Agathe, as well, they would seem to be the closest he came to writing her love letters, unless one counts the songs she inspired him to send her.* In his letters he makes frequent allusion to his *Kleeblatt*, his 'clover leaf'. It was his way of referring to the close-knit association of the Grimms and Agathe. Occasionally he included himself, and spoke of a four-leaf clover.

Additional Note p. 748

Decades later, Frau Dr Agathe Schütte née von Siebold wrote a short memoir for her children.[12]

> I think I may say that from that time until the present, a golden light has been cast on my life, and that even now, in my late old age, something of the radiance of that unforgettable time has remained. I loved Johannes Brahms very much, and for a short time, he loved me.

For Clara Schumann, that summer had an entirely different feel. Later that autumn she wrote to an old friend:

> Don't take my silence to heart, I really couldn't, for I spent a bad summer, and even in September, when I was on a visit to Fräulein Leser in Düsseldorf, I spent four weeks there so miserably nervous that I couldn't do anything.[13]

Although Brahms had been reluctant to take a summer holiday because he was dissatisfied with his work, his sojourn in Göttingen plainly provided the stimulus he needed to create again; subsequent letters are full of the mention of new music. Soon after Brahms returned to Detmold, a parcel of his latest compositions arrived back in Göttingen, where they had been written, with a request for comments. Among them were movements from the Serenade, Op. 11, and his song 'Die Liebende schreibt', Op. 47 No. 5, a setting of the sonnet by Goethe.[14] It seems a safe guess that the text of the sonnet was understood as a message to Agathe. Julius Otto Grimm answered, in a clever allusion to Agathe, the sonnet, and the song:

---

[12] *Allerlei aus meinem Leben.* Excerpts from it are found in Hans Küntzel, *Brahms in Göttingen* (Göttingen, 1985), 91–8.

[13] Letter to Emilie List, 18 Nov. 1858. Litz, iii. 48, and Eugen Wendler (ed.), '*Das Band der ewigen Liebe*', *Briefwechsel mit Emilie und Elise List* (Stuttgart, 1996), 215.

[14] But not published for another ten years.

102
Julius Otto Grimm to Johannes Brahms[15]

[Göttingen, mid-October 1858]

Dear Johannes,

Your Writing Beloved has so many exquisite emotions that she needs must find her love most warmly requited, particularly as, with tears dried, and murmuring of the woes of love, she begs ever more fervently for a sign.—

I would want to make several comments to you if you were here; I cannot do it in writing without appearing wooden and pedantic to myself; but it was really curious that at first sight, the lines of the sonnet offered me no real musical satisfaction. But you must know all that better than I—the more I read through it, or hear Gathe sing it, the more engrossed I become, for it is marvellously conceived and one is compelled to feel its warmth.—Send soon what you are withholding from me, I'm impatient—and always write something to go with it. There is something curious about a letter, and it makes no sense to discuss writing—but a tender page does provide such heartfelt joy—all three of us thank you for it . . .

Last Thursday the young Meysenbug dropped in on our evening—but did not bother us; we like him, all the more so because he can talk to us about Detmold.

Next Sunday my singing society starts up,—I'm looking forward to the cantate *Ich hatte viel Bekümmernis*,—and am making quite a few plans for January or February.—

   For if you should come, two concerts will have to be launched,—one of them in the church, if possible, specifically the choral cantata . . . Then you play the organ.—The second would have the following programme (I'll take care of good winds, the Bargheers, Herner, Bach must also come). (We're also getting a beautiful tenor.)

1. Serenade by Joh. Brahms (under the direction of the composer) (That way you'll have time to rehearse it properly, and the chaps from the Harz don't blow at all badly.)—

2. Any lovely vocal piece for Bertha.

3. Concerto in C Minor by Mozart, played by Joh. Brahms.

4. Act III of Armide by Gluck or Scenes from Iphigenie or both. I'm looking forward to it like a child . . .

---

[15] For the complete letter, see *BW* iv, no. 42.

Dear Bertha complains that she has nothing from you and claims you had promised the Falkenstein to her, which I know nothing about, Gathe won't give it up, of course. Gathe is immensely diligent and is growing *really* more musical; more and more often I have the feeling that she is gradually beginning to know to what purpose she opens her mouth.—And all three of us are playing wonderfully!—. . .

Grimm's letters from Göttingen provide a richly detailed picture of the encouraging, friendly, and closely-knit milieu waiting there for Brahms: Bargheer, the friend from Detmold and concertmaster of the ducal orchestra, at this time married to one of the women from Grimm's Women's Chorus; Karl von Meysenbug, Brahms's other Detmold comrade, and now a university student in Göttingen and frequent visitor to the Grimm household; Friedemann Bach, a young, highly regarded violin student of Joachim (and a descendant of J. S.); Bertha Wagner, a student of Grimm and member of his Women's Chorus, to whom Brahms evidently promised 'Das Lied vom Herrn von Falkenstein' (published as Op. 43 No. 4) She later married Bargheer, after the death of his first wife. Leading the group of admirers were Agathe, and Grimm himself—with cheerful wife and baby named Johannes—whose friendship for Brahms was almost limitless. The 'good winds' he was able to procure came from the little lead and silver-mining town of Clausthal, deep in the Harz mountains, a goodly way from Göttingen even by modern automobile. The Clausthalers have a long tradition of wind-band music to this day, and provided a ready supply of players for concerts in Göttingen.

Brahms answered:

103
Johannes Brahms to Julius Otto Grimm

Thursday Ev(ening) [Detmold, late October 1858]

Many thanks for your lovely letter. Well, here is something for the time being, so that I shall soon get another one. The remaining movements of this Serenade are still too much in disarray, also there are other things that are keeping me busy. What will it sound like? Should I keep writing? Don't think of yourself as wooden and pedantic again because that doesn't do me any good. Also, construct your sentences as precisely as possible, sometimes I don't know whether you are referring to my song or to the writer in love, etc.

Pour les dames I am including a few songs, so that the best ones in your house also receive something. For you, furthermore, 33 popular variations which I took away today from a lady, who seemed to let them lie around uselessly, in order to present them to a musician. You don't have them? The

Triple Concerto in C I don't want, but would like both duos. However, it's not essential.[16]

I would have liked to hear more about the young Meysenbug. I have heard here that he got along well with Anne M. and I consider myself asinine that I did not immediately think of this combination right away.

About January! I still have not written to Leipzig. If and when I go there, concerts in Göttingen would suit me just fine. But—no organ playing. Why such experiments? You already have a perfectly good organist, and I can't find my way around either the pedals or the stops. Moreover, no piano-playing. I don't have the least desire to play in public. However, I would like to suggest Bargheer as soloist. He has a great desire to play outside Detmold, for once, and he plays really well. How would that be? Write to me about it. I hope that the rest, particularly *Armide* or *Iphigenie*, will take place.

For your dear Bertha I will be sure to write down some songs, in any case.

Forgive me, most beautiful ladies, who may be reading along in this letter and who would like to be a little entertained, for discussing business for so long with your Husband and Fatherly Friend. But it had to be, and unfortunately now the paper is at an end and bedtime long past.

But I can start another sheet of paper to report that unfortunately, I know of nothing for you. Now we'll start a game of *Höllenspiel*, to sustain the urge to write.[17] Why can't I send you ladies a Serenade. You write much more agreeably than your H. and F. Fr. and unfortunately, much more rarely.[18] V. Meysenbug feels a great inclination for Aunt Gur and has written quite delightedly about *all the* black eyes and dark hair he has seen in Göttingen (but only to his mother!). Your H. and F. Fr. should restrain the young man from associating with you, for I know he has a very amorous disposition. From Frau Schumann I hear, as usual, that she is doing quite well. She played in Aachen, Elberfeld, Düsseldorf, Crefeld, and Cologne. Now she's on her way to Berlin and is probably going from there to Vienna soon. Forgive this abominable handwriting, most beautiful ladies, but I am not switching on a better one for your H. and F. Fr. and now I'm in the swing of it.

[16] Probably the Diabelli Variations of Beethoven, and Mozart's Triple Concerto for Three Pianos, K.242.

[17] According to the violinist Richard Barth, who edited these letters in 1906 and was able to question Agathe von Siebold Schütte, still living in Göttingen, this was a game of forfeits which Brahms played with his 'clover-leaf'.

[18] The 'Husband and Fatherly Friend' appears more and more frequently in the remainder of this letter.

To Gur's parents I send my warmest greetings. I hope you have always delivered them of your own accord?! I had Frau Donop play for me on one of Papa's pianos.[19] It has an excellent sound, and I caress it as if it could feel.

Affectionately,

Your J. Br.

N.B. Your H. and F. Fr. has to write with lightning speed about my Serenade, and you too must write, or the devil take you all!

For Agathe, I must still enclose a reply! I greet you, dear ladies, and to your H. and F. Fr., I tender a pair of donkeys' ears.

104

Johannes Brahms to Julius Otto Grimm

Friday, [Detmold, late October or early November 1858]*   Additional Note p. 748

Now evening has come at last, or rather night has fallen. I am alone and undisturbed and can write to you, dearest cloverleaf.—

There won't be much news.—

With me everything peters out into dashes—

Here again is something to review.

I must have the Bridal Song back, right away! Ise must get on to it on Sunday and send it back the next day. Without delay, please.[20]

And then about the *Serenade* and with critiques. Lengthy and precise ones. I'll forget about philistinism. I don't give a hoot if none of the new pieces appeals to him one bit. In that case I shall turn to the ladies, they don't ask for scores. A few songs, in place of letters for which I have no time, are also on their way.

It's now turning cold and I'll not spare the Prince's woodlands, but go for walks anyway, something you've all probably given up entirely.

News from Göttingen I can only get by having it told to me, delivered regularly by Herr v. Meysenbug.

[19] Frau *von* Donop was the wife of the Royal Gamekeeper, a person Brahms evidently did not much care for; in his indifference to persons of rank he has something in common with Beethoven. The von Donops were one of the most influential families in the rich little Duchy. To this day, the elaborate fountain in the small town square bears a donors' plaque with their name. Brahms must have made a comment to Joachim about him and Kiel, the Kapellmeister; Joachim advised him *einen Esel zu bohren*, to make the sign of donkeys's ears at him, an ancient and unflattering gesture that still arouses hostility when used today. Brahms reported he carried out Joachim's message, with 'unlooked-for' results (*BW* v, 5 Oct. 1858). Brahms uses the expression once again to Grimm, in a good-natured way, at the end of this letter.

[20] Grimm's pet name was Isegrimm, no doubt after the wolf Isegrim in Goethe's play *Reineke Fuchs* (*Reynard the Fox*). See n. 23 re. the Bridal Song.

I shall not write for a couple of weeks. You people owe me a reply and this (the music, too) is yet again a letter.

Greet Agathe for me. I enclose a few songs for her, that—one of them—well, and with it, I wished, well—in brief, very politely for me.[21]

And don't be embarrassed, Ise, to grumble about my things.

A cheerful person must be forgiven much.

We cloverleaf four, I do adore. But not so much our letter-writing. Those long rests, those scant notes!

By Tuesday or Wednesday I hope to have my music back.

A thousand goodnights
and yet again.

Your melancholy
Johannes.

105
Johannes Brahms to Julius Otto Grimm

Monday morning [Detmold, early November 1858][22]

Many thanks, dear friends, for the lovely letters and especially for the extensive critiques of my things. I only wish that the review didn't tootle and pipe as pleasantly as the compositions are supposed to do. Those few comments which have a different sound are, simply said, correct, and I ought to be ashamed that they were necessary. But I was too hurried and too distracted when I wrote and sent them. The Bridal Song is shamefully ordinary and weak, that poem could be composed exquisitely.[23]

But this is an injustice! Here a miserable composer sits sadly alone in his chamber and fools himself into achieving things which are none of his business, and there a reviewer sits himself down between two beautiful women—I cannot bear painting any more of the picture.

I recently performed the Bach cantata with instruments. Now I am studying another one (*Ich hatte viel Bekümmernis*).

---

[21] 'Ich lege ein paar Lieder für sie ein, die—einer—na, und ich wünscht dabei, na,—kurz, recht höflich für mich.' One cannot translate this halting embarrassment without guessing. What is certain is that Brahms couldn't bring himself to write what he meant.

Additional
Note p. 748
[22] Dated from the publication of the *Volks-Kinderlieder*, WoO 31, which appeared in print in November 1858.* Brahms was paid the goodly sum of 6 Friedrichdors. The *Volks-Kinderlieder with Piano Accompaniment, Dedicated to the Children of Robert and Clara Schumann*, were the first of a number of collections of folk-music published by Brahms, and reflect a lifelong involvement with German folk-song.

[23] The forerunner of 'Von ewiger Liebe', Op. 43 No. 1. See McC 679.

Half my tenure is over, thank God, the Princess has at times already told me so, with sighs.

She is the only one whom I enquire after, and who also enquires after me, with the exception of Bargheer. Your studies of the thorough-bass do appear to me to be somewhat meagre, dearest ladies! It seems that Ise must stuff the rules down your throats like pills.

You ought to consider that it only works the other way round. One only learns what one drags out of the teacher. At least, whatever I know I acquired by asking and demanding.

You could write to me what you are up to sometime, can you already harmonize chorales or compose waltzes?

Now dear married couple, permit me to drop behind a little with Agathe and to dawdle. That lovely old custom must not be abandoned.

Kiss Hans from me.

Warmly

Your

Johannes.

[. . .]

(Here I ask for God's blessing)

Finally, I beg your pardon for the miserable pen, I am now taking a good one.

Morning has turned into evening, and it is too late to frank the letter.

The Children's Songs arrived today and next time something needs to be sent, I'll enclose a volume.

Autumn 1858 marks the first time Brahms was able to put into practice his growing knowledge of Bach's music by conducting some of the cantatas. Aware of his lack of practical experience, he turned yet again to his more experienced friend, Joseph Joachim, not only for the music but for advice on how to double the chorus with instruments. Joachim answered in a letter filled with detailed advice.[24] Brahms was so pleased with the performance of Cantata No. 4, *Christ lag in Todesbanden*, that he embarked on the study of Cantata No. 21, once more asking for Joachim's help.

---

[24] *BW* v. 214 ff., dated 'mid-October 1858'.

106
Johannes Brahms to Joseph Joachim

[Detmold, 26 November 1858]

Dearest friend,

I am writing again and as usual, have only thanks and a request.

I thank you for the first Bach cantata and ask you for a second one.

I have now done the E minor several times with instruments, to my great pleasure. Naturally, everything already sounded [fine] and certain things, e.g. the horn in the 'wunderlichen Krieg' quite superb. Rehearsals and performances were even tolerable to my singers, because I am being permitted to rehearse a second one. I'm taking the first in Vol. V, I, *Ich hatte viel Bekümmernis*. Although I have well understood and considered your advice for the first one I still don't know how to begin here. My chorus is very weak, if at all possible I wouldn't like to let them sing without support. My pianist is of little use.

If you have the inclination and time and would like to write to me about this cantata in as much detail as about the previous one, you will make me exceedingly happy!

Mozart concertos I am not playing, but I coach the Princess in them and conduct them. Not that I thought I do it better than Kiel; but it's really more agreeable to see the Princess play with gusto than to play myself and see a bored person on the podium.

If by chance you hear from Grimm that he knows new things of mine, don't suppose that I might just as well have sent them to you.

I don't have the heart to do it! If I were satisfied with a piece you would be the first I would give it to; but I prefer to let it pass through several stages and hope that it improves before I let you look it over. How goes it with my Serenade, can't I get to see it again some time? Have you heard it? It probably sounded bad?

I have now written to David that I'll be glad to play there in January. After that beautiful rehearsal in Hanover my head was full of everything I wanted to improve in the Concerto, now I don't know anything any more. Don't a number of things in the orchestration have to be changed, even before the great performance?[25]

I suppose your concerts are under way? Your compositions, too?

---

[25] Ferdinand David, concertmaster of the Gewandhaus Orchestra, who invited Brahms to play the concerto in Leipzig.

Be greeted most warmly and write to me as soon as possible.
Your Johannes

Many have suggested that Brahms broke off his relationship with Agathe because he was financially unable to marry. Brahms himself is perhaps the chief author of this notion, having told the writer Josef Viktor Widmann and the singer George Henschel that he never married because at the time he most wished to, he was not in a position to do so. Although this explanation has been cited by almost every one of Brahms's biographers, one need not accept it at face value, for in the course of his life Brahms found many excuses for not marrying; long after, in opposing his sister's union to a much older man, he claimed in exasperation, that he had refrained from marrying on her account. (Letter 224).[26]

In regard to Agathe von Siebold, the documentary record shows that had he wanted it, Brahms had the foundation of a steady career waiting for him just at the very moment he was most in love with her; had he been more unequivocally involved, there is no question but that he could have had his bride.

The available job was with the Cologne Conservatory. Ferdinand Hiller, the Conservatory's director, offered Brahms that position in the summer of 1858 with the consent of Robert Schnitzler, President of the Board. In a letter to Hiller, Schnitzler wrote (Cologne, 3 August 1858):[27]

> Regarding my view about quickly finding a teacher to replace Frank, I am, for lack of a better suggestion, in agreement with the opinion which you had once expressed, that we should give it a try with Brahms. He is some-one who will draw the interest of a large, not inestimable faction over to us, and is said to be too good a musician, and at the same time, too accom-plished a person to drive us into the arms of the eccentric singlemindedness of a faction . . . He would be capable of teaching as well as anyone, and at the same time our circle of local musicians would acquire an aspiring, and in all respects interesting talent, who will present us, perhaps even in the first year, with not too trivial or too learned a symphony.

Hiller's offer to Brahms concluded that he could easily earn 400 thaler a year from his duties at the Conservatory (teaching score-reading, piano, and ensemble classes for two hours daily), and performing in public. And he would be living in a large town, not a tiny Ducal village.

Brahms replied:

[26] Widmann, *Erinnerungen*, 48. Sir George Henschel, *Personal Recollections of Johannes Brahms* (Boston, 1907), 48 (also cited in the German version he gave to Kalbeck, *Johannes Brahms*, iii³. 86). In any case, Widmann's account has been widely misinterpreted, since he reports that it was not lack of money which frightened Brahms off marriage, but lack of outward success, and the pity his putative wife might have felt for him.

[27] *Aus Ferdinand Hillers Briefwechsel*, ed. Reinhold Sietz (Cologne, 1958–66), i. 130–1 (henceforth *Hil*).

107

Johannes Brahms to Ferdinand Hiller

Göttingen, August [18]58

Esteemed Herr Capellmeister!

Nothing nicer could have come to me from the Rhine than your letter, which shows me that you still regard me with the same kindness with which you have already honoured and delighted me in Cologne. My sincerest thanks for it.

It is difficult for me to write that I probably cannot accept your invitation. For this winter, as for last winter, I am engaged in Detmold, and am involved in discussions regarding the extension of this engagement.

All further contemplation is unnecessary, since I could not come to Cologne this winter in any case, otherwise I would have to consider seriously what to give up, the stimulating intercourse here, or the work with chorus and orchestra there.

Whether this letter is a question mark or a No, I would be glad to learn from you.

Once again, however, my best thanks for the great joy you have given me with your letter.

I beg you to remember me to your wife.

> With particular high regard,
> Your most devoted Joh. Brahms

Hiller tried once more, so that the first thing Brahms did upon his arrival in Detmold was to decline in less ambiguous terms.

108

Johannes Brahms to Ferdinand Hiller

Detmold, 1 October 1858

Most esteemed Herr Capellmeister,

As much as I regretted it, it was impossible to maintain as lively an exchange of messages between Cologne, Detmold, and Göttingen as I had intended. My head was too agreeably and completely taken up with work and pleasure. Will you forgive me for that?

Now that I am here my first act is to write to you. I must decline your offer. When I consider my position here, I do see much that is pleasant, and much that I would have to forgo in Cologne. What is decisive for me is the great amount of free time (the whole summer is mine), and the stimulating occupations.

I desist from further consideration of this matter almost reluctantly, for there is something (one person) that lures me powerfully to Cologne. But it must be. I again say my best thanks to you for your offer.

I beg you to commend me to your wife.

With the greatest respect and esteem,

your devoted

Johs. Brahms.

As a matter of fact Brahms could have managed to support a wife even more easily on his Detmold salary, had he been so inclined—his friend Bargheer did, and on less money than Brahms was earning. According to court records, Brahms was paid 566 Reichsthaler 20 Silbergroschen for his three-month appointment, in addition to room and board. By contrast, the *yearly* salary at Court was: court conductor, 650 thaler; solo cellist, 336 thaler; solo flute 312 thaler; solo horn 300 thaler; average musician, 220 thaler. In addition, Brahms gave high-priced lessons every day, and so was earning more money than most of his colleagues—all this for only three months of work.[28] Whatever his reason for not marrying Agathe, lack of money was not it. Which accords with Agathe's recollection: 'I love you, I must see you again, but I cannot be bound!', says the lover in her autobiographical story.

But as of yet that decision had not been made; at year's end Brahms was in love, and looking forward to returning to Göttingen for the New Year holiday.

109

Johannes Brahms to Julius Otto Grimm

Thursday morning [Detmold, after Christmas 1858]

Dear friend,

So then, the day after tomorrow, God willing. I leave here early in the morning, will be in Hanover at 2 o'clock. There I'll have to see how I can kill three hours. From 5 to 8 I'll be on my way to Göttingen.

I shall see you at the railway station? All of you? It would be serious if the two women were telling lies once more and again.

I'm not bringing any *Baumkuchen* with me.[29] The Prince sent me a great big one, but Meysenbug paid it daily visits and gave it much loving attention. From the Princess I have received nothing less than the *great edition of Bach*

---

[28] Schramm, *Brahms in Detmold*, 28, 51.
[29] A traditional German Christmas cake, baked in the shape of a standing tree trunk.

for Christmas. But why am I prattling on like this, I must still be asleep. The day after tomorrow off I go. I am somewhat pleased.

I thank you for the sausages, ditto Bargheer.

I couldn't get into writing.

Saturday you will all be better able to see how happy I am to see you again.

A scoundrel, whoever doesn't come!

Johannes Brahms

PART IV

࿎

In Hamburg Again

1859–1862

ஐ Introduction ஐ

When Brahms accepted the position at Detmold, his primary residence shifted back to Hamburg once again.[1] He lived first with his parents and then in the nearby suburb of Hamm, when his need for privacy and space prevailed.

His return marks the start of one of the liveliest and most varied periods of his life, despite an oft-quoted description of the time as one of 'withdrawal and study', a phrase that implies he was readying himself for the move to Vienna.[2] On the contrary, Brahms was vigorously involved in the musical and social life of Hamburg, working hard to lay the foundation for what he hoped would be a lifelong career in his native city. His music was performed in important concerts—thanks, usually, to Joachim, Clara Schumann, and the singer Julius Stockhausen, who all came to Hamburg chiefly to promote his works—and he himself was engaged as soloist with the Hamburg Philharmonic and in concerts organized by Georg Otten and Carl Grädener. When a leading violinist died suddenly, his *Begräbnisgesang*, Op. 13, was included in the memorial concert.

At the same time, Brahms was expanding his knowledge of early music, thanks to unlimited access to the collection of eighteenth-century music owned by his friend, mentor, and champion, Theodor Avé-Lallement, and he began his career as editor of early music with the publication of two sonatas by Bach sons Friedemann and Carl Philip Emmanuel (Letter 114).

He socialized companionably with Grädener—showing up with him once at a party as a mechanical doll, and falling off the piano bench when Grädener failed to

---

[1] A lively and detailed account of Brahms's life at this time is given by Walter Hübbe, *Brahms in Hamburg* (Hamburg, 1902). See esp. pp. 33–5 for the details mentioned here.

[2] By his friend Albert Dietrich, in the *Erinnerungen*, p. 28, written decades later. But Dietrich, preoccupied at that time with the birth of his first two children, his wife's dangerous illness, his move from Bonn to Oldenburg to escape the bureaucrats who were interfering with his duties as city music director, and his own impending nervous breakdown, was not in the best position to assess Brahms's activities.

wind him up in time—and was most frequently to be found in the company of Avé-Lallement, in whose home he was now a very frequent guest. Avé, it will be remembered, was on the Board of Directors of the Hamburg Philharmonic.

He used this time to augment a formal education which had ended at the age of 14. His library continued to grow, and his entry into the home of J. G. Hallier opened the way to new activities. Brahms participated regularly in Hallier's discussion group, during which he showed himself to be something of a radical free-thinker, a position he defended vehemently within the circle of 'artists and artistically inclined people' who gathered weekly at the hospitable and well-to-do home.

He attended the lectures in art history which Hallier presented, studied Latin with Hallier's learned son, and arranged to be tutored in history by a professor at the academic Gymnasium.[3] He even took up gymnastics again.

The rest of the time he gave piano lessons to a number of talented young women, and composed. Although the list of music published during this time is relatively modest, the list of music conceived, worked on, or finished is long and varied, and includes some of the works he is best known for.[4]

But without a doubt, his greatest pleasure and satisfaction derived from the small chorus he conducted, his beloved Hamburg Women's Chorus (the Frauenchor), a group of about forty enthusiastic young women in a group initially assembled by one of his piano pupils. They met at least once a week, at the home of one of the founders; a smaller group of a dozen singers met for additional rehearsals, and there was even a solo quartet drawn from the best singers. Brahms went to great lengths to arrange and compose for them, and they performed with him in private.[5]

His preoccupation with a women's chorus was not as quaint as it might seem now. Choruses were potent vehicles for social intercourse, which had been severely restricted in many places after the uprisings of 1848. The *Liedertafel*, or choral society, was a conscious and clever way round a general ban on gatherings, and were very popular throughout German lands. Apart from the personal pleasure he derived, his connection to the Frauenchor held the possibility of aiding his career: the wives and daughters of his colleagues sang in the chorus, and among the other participants were quite a few who regarded him with fervour, girls who were willing to defend his

---

[3] The secondary school preparatory to an advanced degree.

[4] See Hofmann, *Johannes Brahms und Hamburg*, 56–9. For a good discussion of the music, see MacDonald, *Brahms*, ch. 4.

[5] Sophie Drinker, in *Brahms and his Women's Choruses* (Merion, Pa. 1952), gives a full account of the founding of the chorus and of its activities. Mrs Drinker quotes excerpts from diaries kept by several of the members of the Frauenchor. Walter Hübbe's account in *Brahms in Hamburg* (1903) is engrossing and factually correct, despite the efforts of Max Kalbeck to dismiss it. Some of Kalbeck's dissatisfaction arises from the fact that his information regarding the founding of the Frauenchor differed from Hübbe's, but subsequent research indicates that Kalbeck's informant was not in fact aware of all the details; diary entries by Friedchen Wagner, quoted by Sophie Drinker, confirm Hübbe's account.

character against the charge of arrogance, and who would go from shop to shop asking for his music in the hope of developing a market for it.

From the diary of Franziska Meier, member of the Hamburg Frauenchor, describing the rehearsal of 29 August 1859:[6]

> After our poor director [Brahms] had worked so hard to beat these new things into us, he was besieged . . . to play something for us! He has the reputation of being unaccommodating, proud, arrogant, and disagreeable. O, how can one wrong a person like that? . . . I found him unusually accommodating. Indeed, he played 12 Etudes for us. One could hardly believe it— 12 Etudes! [Schumann, *Symphonic Études*.]

One girl, in particular, caught his attention; Bertha Porubsky, daughter of the pastor to the Protestant community in Vienna. She was in Hamburg for the year, and in 1859 her aunt, Auguste Brandt, acted as chaperone to the Frauenchor, in which capacity she had occasion to invite Brahms to her home and provide him with the good cooking he loved so well. Brahms and Bertha were sufficiently taken with each other to engage in a lively correspondence through the medium of Aunt Auguste (Letters 119–23 in this volume), who warned Bertha not to aim too high by quoting a Goethe text Brahms had already set to music:

> One does not crave to own the stars,
> But loves their glorious light.[7]

Arriving in Vienna, a year or so later, Brahms's slightly guilty conscience was much relieved to discover that Bertha was about to marry a well-to-do industrialist. Bertha and her husband, Arthur Faber, remained in his closest circle of friends for the rest of his life. Their right to an enduring footnote in history was assured upon the birth of their second son: the famous Lullaby was written for him, and includes in the piano accompaniment one of the Austrian folk-songs Bertha had taught Brahms in Hamburg (see Letter 222). The tradition of women's choral singing lived on in Bertha's Viennese home for decades, in a chorus conducted by Eusebius Mandyczwesky.

This second Hamburg period is marked by a number of other milestones: the failure of his Piano Concerto at its first performance; his irrevocable break with Agathe von Siebold; his gradually growing reputation as composer and conductor; the only polemical act of his life, participation in a public protest against the music of Franz Liszt; and his decision to explore Vienna, in preparation for what Brahms hoped would be his recall to Hamburg to assume an important post there.

Two of these major events occurred within the month of January 1859: the very notable failure of his Piano Concerto at its première in Leipzig, on 27 January, and Brahms's rupture with Agathe. Of the two events, the concerto fiasco is documented by letters, while for a contemporary account of his break with Agathe, there is only

---

[6] Drinker, *Brahms and his Women's Choruses*. The diary is quoted on pp. 30–1, the shopping expedition on p. 40.

[7] *Trost in Tränen*, Op. 48 No. 5. Drinker, 46.

In Memoriam J.B., the autobiographical story she wrote for her children after Brahms's death. It contains a paraphrase or quote—one doesn't know which, although the style is not like anything else he wrote—from the letter Brahms wrote to Agathe after Grimm took it upon himself to tell Brahms that he must not return to Göttingen without declaring his intentions towards Agathe. 'The answer came: I love you! I must see you again! But bound I cannot be! Write to me whether I am to come again, to fold you in my arms, to kiss you, to say that I love you!' According to Agathe, duty and honour forbad her to see Brahms again, as she informed him by letter. Not only has all the relevant correspondence vanished, if it ever existed, but the correspondence between Grimm and Brahms ceased altogether for a year, as the Grimms tried to comfort a devastated Agathe, and showed obvious displeasure with Johannes.[8]

Even if one grants that the icy reception given the Piano Concerto was a severe blow, his disappointment cannot be taken seriously as the real reason he turned his back so entirely and abruptly on the only woman he was ever engaged to. In her fictional autobiography, Agathe explained it simply: 'His love was not strong and deep as hers.' Brahms's reasons may have looked more complicated, but essentially she was correct. Nevertheless, traces of regret lingered long in Brahms, as some of his music, song texts, comments, and subsequent letters to Julius Otto Grimm show, and one is justified in surmising that the self-inflicted loss of Agathe left its mark.[9]

No surmises, however, are needed to recognize that the pain of his concerto's failure cut very deep.

ॐ 1859 ॐ

110

Johannes Brahms to Joseph Joachim

[Leipzig] Friday morning [28 January 1859]

Dearest friend,

Still utterly intoxicated by the edifying delights presented to my eyes and ears in beholding and conversing with the sages of our music city in the course of the past several days, I force this sharp and hard steel pen of Sahr's[10] to

---

[8] Agathe's story is reproduced in Küntzel, *Brahms in Göttingen*, 99–105. There is a fascinating aside to Brahms's rupture with Agathe. Only once in his life did Brahms set a dramatic text to music. His oratorio, *Rinaldo*, tells of the efforts of a young Crusader to break free from the love spell of the enchantress Armide, and to return to duty—a popular theme, set in verse by Tasso and Goethe, and to music by Handel, Haydn, and Gluck, among others. On two occasions that Brahms knew of, Agathe sang the role of Armide in Gluck's opera, once before and once after her entanglement with him, and both times under Grimm's direction.

[9] Letter 133 in this volume, and above all his letter from summer 1864, *BW* iv. 111–12.

[10] Heinrich von Sahr.

describe to you how it came about and was happily brought to completion, that my concerto here has been a brilliant and decisive—flop.

First of all, it really went very well, I played significantly better than in Hanover, the orchestra outstandingly.

The first rehearsal roused no emotions whatever among the musicians or the listeners.

But for the 2nd rehearsal, no listener showed up and not one musician moved a face-muscle.

In the evening, the *Elisa Overture* by Cherubini was performed, then an *Ave Maria* by the same, sung lifelessly; and so I hoped that Pfund's drumroll would come at the right time.[11] The first movement and the 2nd were listened to without any kind of emotion. At the end, three hands attempted to fall slowly one into another, whereupon, however, a quite distinct hissing from all sides forbade such demonstrations.

There is nothing further to write about this event, for nobody has said the smallest word to me about the work! Excepting David, who was very friendly and took an exceptional interest in it and took some pains over it.[12]

Neither Rietz, nor Wenzel, Senff, Dreyschock, Grützmacher, Röntgen, made even the most irrelevant comment.

I asked Sahr for some specifics this morning, and enjoyed his candour.

This flop, by the way, has made absolutely no impression on me, and the slightly distasteful and sombre mood following it faded when I heard a C major Symphony by Haydn and the Ruins of Athens. In spite of it all, the concerto will be well liked some day when I have improved its anatomy, and a second one will certainly sound different.

I believe this is the best thing that can happen to one; it forces one to collect one's thoughts appropriately and raises one's courage. I am plainly experimenting and still groping.

But the hissing was surely too much? Your letter, which I received last night in the pub, was very comforting, and I was not irritated with Herrmann etc., who were cheerfully drinking with me and said not a word about the concerto etc.

Frau Schumann is still in Vienna, as I found out here; she is someone I would have liked to have here! Concerning Enzio you probably have an answer. Greetings have been and will be taken care of.

The faces here appeared pathetically sombre when I came from Hanover and was accustomed to seeing yours. Monday I am going to Hamburg.

---

[11] The dramatic opening of the Concerto, Op. 15. Pfund was the famed timpanist of the Gewandhaus Orchestra.

[12] Ferdinand David, concertmaster of the Gewandhaus Orchestra.

Sunday there is some interesting church music here, and in the evening
Faust, at Frau Frege's.[13]

Please send Hanover newspapers to me in Hamburg!

I'll write again from there. Be warmly remembered, dearest fellow! Greet
Zillinger etc. etc.

Your Johannes.
(Hurriedly)

As to the concert in Hamburg, just as you prefer.
Hohe Fuhlentwiete 74 in Hamburg

The concerto received only one encouraging review, from Schumann's old journal,
the 'progressive' *Neue Zeitschrift für Musik*. But by the other critics, it was savaged.
The failure of this one concert checked Brahms's career in Leipzig for many years to
come; not until the 1870s did any of his music find approbation there, and the concerto itself was not heard again until December 1874, when Clara played it at a
Gewandhaus concert. The people named in this letter were among the leading musicians in town, many of them the very same who had welcomed Brahms so enthusiastically six years earlier.

Joachim, who never lost faith in the work, prevailed upon Avé-Lallement, who
in turn persuaded the Hamburg Philharmonic to place the concerto and its composer on their programme for 24 March. The orchestra committee went so far as to
engage Joachim and Julius Stockhausen for the same concert, thereby setting the
stage for Brahms's most successful appearance yet.

In the meanwhile, Brahms owed a letter of thanks to the Princess Friederike for
her splendid Christmas present of all volumes of the complete Bach Edition then in
print.[14]

[13] Probably Schumann's. The singer, Lydia Frege, was Clara Schumann's old friend. She often
arranged private performances of important works at her house.

[14] 1851–7 inclusive. Karl Bargheer's unpublished 'Erinnerungen' (Lippische Landesbibliothek,
11) differs specifically in this respect from May's account, i. 252, which gives the years 1851–5: of some
importance to those who want to know what of Bach's music Brahms knew at this time in his life.

111
Johannes Brahms to Woman Courtier, Detmold [Laura von Meysenbug][15]

[Hamburg, 22 March 1859]

Much esteemed, gracious Fräulein,

Before all else, I beg you to express to her Serene Highness the Princess Friederike my most humble thanks for her dispatch of the new Bach works.

How often will this present remind me in the most beautiful manner of her Serene Highness's kindness. You know how much I love this godly man, and can imagine that his music (so dreaded by you) often resounds about me.

I am delighted that Her Serene Highness is carrying on with her music-making so diligently, and only wish I could in some way take part and provide encouragement.

In the Trio which you cite, the simplest thing, of course, is for the left hand (which is resting, in any case) to assist the poor right hand. For such predicaments one is indebted to the wicked excesses of composers!

The day after tomorrow I am playing my piano concerto here, and a few days later, will perform another of my works in a concert of my own. Joachim and Stockhausen, who are coming for it, will provide a veritable music feast.

In spite of the most disparate judgements which my works are experiencing, I am quite pleased with my first orchestral attempts, and I confidently hope they will gain friendly listeners in Detmold, as well.

And may I venture to hope, above all, for fruits that will ripen later and swell in beauty.

I beg you to commend me most kindly to Their Most Serene Highnesses, and remain

with particular esteem,
your devoted
Joh. Brahms

Although much of the enthusiasm aroused by the concerts mentioned here was due to the participation of both Joachim and Julius Stockhausen, Brahms received his share of the credit and felt he had cause to rejoice.

[15] Although no one is named in the salutation, Brahms is clearly familiar with the recipient, who is obviously one of his pupils and who approaches Bach with a certain apprehension (Brahms had once written to Clara that he was going to make Frl. von M. fear Bach). Another letter from Brahms to Laura von Meysenbug is preserved in the archive of the Lippische Landesbibliothek, Detmold; written several months later, it displays the same mix of formality and friendliness.

112
Johannes Brahms and Joseph Joachim to Clara Schumann

Hamburg, the 26th of March 1859
Saturday morning

That I am only able to write to you about our concerts here is very painful for me, dear Clara.

I am unfortunately so unwell that I can enjoy only the smallest part of the pleasure. A badly swollen cheek (and neck) is causing me serious anguish.

Thursday evening came off well and fine. That Joachim and Stockhausen were recalled goes without saying, but it happened to me too, and today we are already reading the highly commendatory review of my work by [Stephen] Heller.

The concert was enormously well attended. Hundreds of people were unable to get tickets. Joachim rehearsed my concerto marvellously well and played it brilliantly. I don't know what more I should write, it was all just as one might have wished.

The gentlemen of the Committee, e. g., were greatly delighted with the concerto. The rehearsals were very well attended.

In short, the Leipzig reviews have done no damage.

Hans von Bronsart came over from Hanover. A pleasant man and my only regret is that I can feel no sympathy for his compositions.

Very soon now there is a rehearsal of my Serenade. We are using quite a substantial number of violins.

Monday we are giving our concert, and presumably a good one.

Joachim is staying with me. Stockhausen at Avé's. I would be beside myself with merriment if my cheek didn't make me so exasperated.

I must take great care that a fever or the like doesn't develop.

I will close and soon write more, and more exhaustively. I'll also send on reviews! Write soon. It is, God knows, an injustice that for the third time, you are getting reports in writing of what you really should have witnessed.

Warmly
your Johannes.

Dear friend!

I add a greeting to Johannes's lines, in order also to give you a visible indication of how much we would have liked to have you here as a third member in the music confederacy and how often we think of you. Johannes's concerto went really well, the musicians, as well as audiences were decidedly for it—donkey ears opposed to all new events exist everywhere of course; I can only say that I have had the most decided pleasure in having come here. I must be off right away to the rehearsal of the Serenade; I am also conducting on Monday. I am going back on Tuesday, and will report from Hanover about our soirée with the charming Stockhausen, and I am going to answer *your last*, very kind letter properly.

For today, with warmest greetings,
J. J.

The three artists presented their own concert four days later, performing songs of Schumann and Schubert, arias from the *Messiah* (from the original score, according to the programme), the 'Devil's Trill' Sonata of Tartini, and the Serenade, Op. 11, 'for small orchestra', by Brahms.[16]

113

Johannes Brahms to Clara Schumann

Hamburg, Tuesday, 29 March 1859

Dearest Clara,

How dismal that I must write and keep on writing to you! The Serenade was performed yesterday before almost 1,200 people, and you were not among them, and you did not share the joy, and I had to contemplate you far away and alone. Unfortunately it did not go very well, the winds, particularly horn and flute, were weak, the latter, indeed, bad.

The rehearsals were always crowded with people, and it was already well liked here.

Yesterday's concert was extremely effective, it seems.

The work-out with the hands persisted until I came down and out in front.

Our concert must have been the best-attended one that ever took place here.

Usually, as in the last Philharmonic concert, only 900 tickets are issued.

We'll probably earn quite well too.

I enclose the programme. After every piece there was shouting, you wouldn't have recognized the Hamburgers at all.

Stockhausen is giving a recital in Leipzig in the beginning of May (and if

---

[16] The programme is given in *SBB* i. 253, the event is mentioned in Hübbe, *Brahms in Hamburg*, 25. The final version of the Serenade, for large orchestra, was completed in December of the same year. *BW* v. 254, and Letter 125 in this volume.

possible, with you). He wants to do my Serenade if some uncertainties are settled there.

I am glad to do that and look forward to it, and will myself come and force myself on you, so that you will finally have to listen to something.

If you were to be there, I would be as happy as a king, otherwise it is pretty much all the same to me. I would like to ask you not to send your letters always by registered mail. It often causes the postman a lot of running around, and what's the use of it, anyway?

Early this morning Avé and I brought both those lovely musicians to Harburg. What a great deal of trouble Joachim took over my things! For this occasion I would just have wished him some better musicians, but in the future, I hope and wish that the works will be better. And indeed they will. The way I feel, it is no small step ahead, to hear one's own music sound out so loudly.

I will remember Joachim's stay here for a long time and with real emotion.

Now adieu, dear Clara, be content, and enquire whenever you miss anything in my reports.

Everyone sends warm greetings,
as does your
Johannes.

That spring, Brahms made his début as musicologist and editor. If very little attention is currently given to this aspect of his career, outside scholarly publications, Brahms's participation in the preparation of the critical editions of the works of Schubert, Schumann, Mozart, Chopin, and Couperin constituted a major part of his musical activity throughout his life. Brahms was so highly regarded as a careful and erudite editor that Breitkopf & Härtel asked him to oversee the remaining revision of the complete edition of Bach works still in progress when Gustav Nottebohm, its chief editor, died suddenly—a request he declined.[17] But he made his début with works he himself had unearthed in Hamburg: two Sonatas for Violin by Carl Philipp Emanuel Bach, and one Sonata for Two Klaviers by Wilhelm Friedemann Bach.

[17] *BW* xiv. 342 ff.

114
Johannes Brahms to Melchior Rieter-Biedermann

Hamburg, Hohe Fuhlentwiete 74 [2 April 1859]

Dear Sir:

Here come some sonatas by the younger Bachs.

I consider them well worth printing (or possibly reprinting?). Ask others as well and decide to do whatever you wish.

I cannot vouch that these sonatas are authentic, beyond the fact that they sound so to me, and the old manuscripts from which the copies were made are from Ph. Em. Bach's estate. Mr Avé-Lallemant, who lives here and owns a whole lot [of manuscripts] could write and tell you the particulars.

Nor can I vouch for the accuracy of the copies.

The autographs of these sonatas might possibly be in the Berlin Library. Perhaps you will get someone to compare them? I have noticed nothing questionable, apart from a few small details in the sonata by Friedemann Bach.

In my opinion, only the parts for this Sonata for Two Keyboards need to be printed. The Sonata is listed in Gerber:[18] I found my old copy at a second-hand dealer's.

I should add that the name of the other [Bach] is Carlo Filippo Emanuele.

Would you please let me know, when convenient, whether you wish to keep the sonatas or return them to me.

I look forward to seeing new works by Kirchner and ask you kindly to send them to me.[19]

> With best regards, I remain,
> Yours faithfully,
> Johs Brahms

Then in June the women's chorus was formed, called by its members the Hamburg Frauenchor, or simply the Frauenchor. Conducting and arranging music for the group occupied Brahms for most of the summer, but he was also finding himself more and more irritated with Liszt's music and the school of composition it represented.

[18] Ernst Ludwig Gerber, *Biographical Dictionary*, 1791–2.
[19] The composer Theodor Kirchner, friend of Schumann and important early Brahms enthusiast. At this time he was working in Switzerland.

115
Johannes Brahms to Joseph Joachim

[Hamburg, 7] Aug[ust 18]59

Beloved Friend,

In the end, I can't keep from writing you a few words.

If I had only just done so long ago, instead of forever fretting uselessly about the distant and alluring England.

Before all else I would like to find out if it is indeed true that you are going to Ireland in September and October?

With your permission, I would consider that appalling.

I suppose it's foolish of me to ruminate over whether you are squandering your time uselessly there or finding relaxation by playing concerts. But less foolish, if I turn quite mawkish at the thought that I, poor fellow, will be unable to see you during the winter, and, if the English passion persists, never more during the summer.

Regarding the first, the joke will probably be on me if you've been really diligent and I horribly lazy, and you in the meanwhile will be able to tell me all the beautiful and inspiring things you've seen and heard and I—can but listen in amazement.

I have not been further from Hamburg than my feet will carry me. A small singing society (only ladies) holds me, otherwise I would surely be on the Rhine or in some beautiful forest.

Ah, and if you were anywhere within reach, the choral society would have ceased! Apart from that, absolutely nothing is happening here.

The Weimar people continue to make their noise. Weitzmann[20] has now proved that starting with the first century after Christ, all geniuses were unrecognized, forgets however that from Hucbald till Bach and beyond all Esteemed Reformers were recognized as the good or best musicians and composers, and that only 'peculiarities' or some such came under attack. Now, since no one has ever termed Liszt a fairly good composer, a few items require further explanation.

Those compositions are becoming more and more dreadful, e.g. *Dante!* I wish certain matters did not decidedly stand in the way of being able to deal with those people but it just cannot be done, or am I really a Philistine?

My fingers often itch to start a fight, to write some anti-Liszts. But I!

---

[20] Karl Friedrich Weitzmann (1808–80), 'a learned and excellent writer on musical subjects' [*Groves²*]. Among his works is a volume of 1,800 preludes and modulations, and a *History of Seventh Chords.*

Who can't even write his dearest friend a greeting because he lacks material, and whatever else his laziness talks him into.

But it would be wonderful if you were to be sitting in Germany this summer, were composing beautifully, and in the mean time were to knock these people dead with a few flying pages of manuscript, and I sat by you enjoying it and helping to write music.

At times I can only imagine that you might want to get married! You can see how distorted my view of your life in England probably is.

I greet you warmly, and write me at least a few words to say whether you are really not returning before winter!

In most faithful love
Your Johannes.

(Hohe Fuhlentwiete 74)

The Frauenchor rehearsed not only music which arose out of Brahms's experience with Grimm's chorus and with his own at Detmold, but new music written especially for them. In a letter to Clara Schumann, he described writing Psalm 13, Op. 27.

116

Johannes Brahms to Clara Schumann

Hamburg, Sunday afternoon,
on Goethe's birthday
28th of August 1859

Your dear letter reached me early yesterday, beloved Clara, but first I had to give a lesson and then to Bergedorf. I had promised long ago to pay a visit there to von Tinde (I believe you know his wife).

Now my first concern is to write to you.

Tomorrow my girls are rehearsing a Psalm by me which I composed for them. I wrote it exactly one week ago, on Sunday evening, and was quite elated till after midnight.

It is the 13th, in case you want to look at the text sometime. Since it is with organ accompaniment, we are going to sing it once again in the church, this and my *Ave Maria*.[21]

But your return trip comes too late, otherwise it would be wonderful if you could listen to Psalm 13, perhaps on the 13th of September![22] But also

---

[21] The Psalm, published in 1864 as Op. 27. The *Ave Maria*, Op. 12, published in 1860, dates from September 1858.

[22] Clara's birthday.

later in the month, if you wish it, I could arrange it. 40 girls I now have in abundance!

It really isn't right that you have not taken good care of yourself. Now winter is coming, and you ought to have built up fresh strength! Let the practising be, at least for now, and don't convince yourself that it is so dreadfully necessary.

I am sending along the letters of the boys. There is nothing more I can say about this, I could offer no better advice and I see and understand too little of such things.

My main reservation, as I said, is that the boys could become more arrogant, indifferent, if they constantly see new, unfamiliar faces.[23]

The letters do not seem important to me, the one by Ludwig is certainly pretty bad for a 12-year-old boy. The one from Ferdinand is no different from any youngster who writes without giving it a thought and is looking forward to getting it over with soon.

I would like to ask you for Joachim's address, I wrote to him, but have heard nothing in return.

My Serenade I cannot send, the last movement must to the mint once more to be recast.[24]

NB. Don't take it amiss if I don't talk to Avé and Gr[ädener] about the boys. Avé is a Pietist,[25] and Grädener would say nothing new.

Silcher must be quite a dear old man and definitely in the right place with the students in Tübingen. But his book is unbelievably wretched.[26]

By the way, it occurred to me that in Berlin you have Schneider's *Treatise on Harmony*, also Mara, *General Musicianship*, Lobe, and several others. Therefore I would rather not send anything; after all, a bookcase should not become a haystack.

I have to play quite a lot, e.g. for my 40 girls. At Avé's they always have to have the last sonatas of Beethoven.

You would give me great pleasure, dear Clara, if in Heidelberg you could select some—but only a few—stereoscopic views of Heidelberg, or perhaps of towns along the lower Rhine; but here I go, asking for something.

---

[23] Clara was considering moving her sons Ludwig and Ferdinand from Jena to Bonn, where they would be cared for in pension. It was yet another upheaval in their lives, something Brahms's judgement warned him against. It is not only his musical instincts which were sound. The boys, however, were moved. In any case, Ludwig was already showing signs of the mental deterioration which led to his commitment in an institution some years later.

[24] Op. 16, in A major. [25] A follower of the German mystic P. J. Spenger.

[26] A second edition of the *Harmonie und Kompositionslehre* of Friedrich Silcher (1789–1860) appeared in 1859.

The idea of still getting to the Rhine for a few days is buzzing around in my head, but I am afraid that at the end of my stay here, a lot will pile up that will have to be dealt with.[27] But I am looking forward immensely to Detmold, i.e. at least to your guest appearance.

I feel it ever more keenly and firmly and it makes me ever more happy, that you are my friend, it is necessary for me to presume that, and you will come to feel it and believe it anew.

Write soon, and not again that you were unwell, and certainly not reflections again on the brevity of time and that one therefore cannot write letters.

Later in Detmold I will also tell you about the most beautiful girl in my [choral] society and all kinds of items that I won't turn to dust by writing of them.

Addio, dearest Clara, think well of me and be firmly convinced that you have no more faithful, better friend than I.

Your
Johannes.

Brahms described his last concert and leave-taking from the Women's Choir. It was a scene that made a lasting impression on some of the girls in the Frauenchor, as well.[28]

117

Johannes Brahms to Clara Schumann

Detmold, early Friday morning, 30 September 1859

Dearest Clara,

The first quiet hour belongs to you.

I have just finished unpacking after moving to a better room, where I hope to remain, and so your little letter was the first that was forwarded to me.

Before all else, I have to write of my charming Hamburg ladies' choir.

O my dear girls, where are you!

I won't even turn around to look, when they are here singing the lovely pieces for me that I had written for you, all 40 of you will stand before me and in my mind I will see and hear you. I tell you, the ladies' choir is one of my most endearing memories, and just imagine for yourself its lovely funnel

---

[27] Clara was spending time near Bonn. Brahms did not join her, but went directly from Hamburg to Detmold.

[28] Drinker, *Brahms and his Women's Choruses*, 40–3.

shape: First the large one, then a small one for which I arranged 3 part folk-songs and rehearsed with them, and then one that is even smaller and that only sang my one-part songs for me, and presented me with red ribbons.[29]

On Monday in church! That was a touching farewell! Everything was sung twice over, the audience really had cause to be delighted with such a concert.

When I got home that afternoon a small carton was waiting for me. Charmingly hidden underneath some flowers I found a silver writing object 'In memory of the summer of '59, from the Frauenchor'!

Actually I have already become something of a cult object here in Hamburg; but I don't think that can do any harm. At least I'm writing with increasing zest, and it rings inside me as if with time something heavenly will have to emerge. Next year you must take part in this joyous business! You'll enjoy it a lot and, in a manner of speaking, I believe you will positively leap into beastly winter.[30]

It would suit me and please me if Hiller were to perform something by me. But I am not sending parts for the Committee to examine, but gladly send the full score to Hiller for that purpose.[31]

Recommend the Concerto to him, First Serenade, then the *Ave Maria* and Psalm 13 for women's chorus with small orchestra (both pieces) and the *Begräbnisgesang* with all wind instruments (mixed chorus). Here we'll begin with the last three pieces. In the *Ave Maria* my girls were fantastic, if you would just not smile at them with condescension!

I have by now inspected everything, and actually have enough [infor-mation]. If only you would come! Incidentally should you have serious qualms about compromising yourself, I can think of nothing else but to let the whole matter rest and forget about it, for I couldn't possibly suggest other arrangements at this time. By the way, nobody here really imagines that you are coming for the sake of the small fee, but I flattered myself (or still flatter myself) that you are coming to hear my *opera*. Do write to me which dates you could manage, so that I can make arrangements for you to hear as much as possible . . .

[29] Brahms's oblique way of telling Clara about Bertha Porubsky. At least one of the songs she sang for him was the Austrian folk-song which stayed with him for a long time, and which turned up in the accompaniment of the Lullaby he wrote for the birth of her second son nine years later. See Letter 222. See also Letter 119, tied with a ribbon.

[30] i.e. she will be put in such a good mood she will face the beastly winter concert season with eagerness.

[31] Once again Ferdinand Hiller, head of the Gürzenach Concerts and the Conservatory in Cologne, was willing to promote Brahms.

I greet you a thousand times and beg you to consider this a rather sensible letter, in spite of the possibly impermissible rapture for 40 girls.

Also greet Frau and Fräuleins Deichmann, fare very well.

Take care of yourself and don't wear yourself out completely with Hiller's music.

Yours entirely,
Johannes.

Brahms treasured the silver ink-well that had been hidden among the flowers—it was still among his possessions after his death.[32] He thanked Friedchen Wagner, who was not only his best piano student in Hamburg but was also the originator of the Frauenchor.

118

Johannes Brahms to Friedchen Wagner

Detmold, [end of September] 1859

Esteemed Fräulein,

Nothing nicer than to be so pleasantly obliged to write a letter as I am now.

I think constantly of my delightful surprise when I set eyes on the writing implement charmingly concealed under flowers, the memento of the Frauenchor.

I have deserved it so little that I would be ashamed, did I not hope to write much more music for you, and really, more beautiful tones will resound about me when I see the lovely and beautiful gift on my writing table. Will you express my warmest greetings and thanks to all whom you can reach.

Seldom has a more agreeable pleasure come to me, and altogether our gatherings will be one of my fondest and most delightful memories.

But not, I hope, for years to come!

With best greetings to you and yours.

Your
sincerely devoted
Johs. Brahms

Although his letter of thanks went to Friedchen Wagner, Brahms had good reason to believe that the impetus for the gift lay elsewhere, and he sent a less formal but

---

[32] To be more exact, his sister Elise kept it for him. He asked for it after her death in 1892.

even more heartfelt thank you letter to Auguste Brandt and her niece, Bertha Porubsky. His letters to Bertha, the envelopes addressed to Aunt Brandt out of propriety, provide the best picture we have of Brahms in Detmold.

119
Johannes Brahms to Auguste Brandt and Bertha Porubsky

Detmold, on the 9th of October 1859

Most revered, dear friends,

A splendid Sunday morning!

I think of the day with relish.

But first I want to chat a little with you, then it's off into the forest and not back before late in the evening.

I wish you had seen my delighted face when I found your letters and read them. The first lovely handwriting was already familiar, I had indeed looked upon it that last evening in Hamburg, and how often, since then. And then the daintily beribboned one! Many thanks! Such letters are dear guests for me, for sadly, there are few faces here that I would wish to see often.

It felt strange when I beheld the wooded heights once more and walked into the magnificent forest.

I have not seen nature this beautiful for a year. Much has changed since then. Yet I was completely happy. I only thought music.

I am in love with music, I love music, I think of nothing but, and of other things only when they make music more beautiful for me. Take note, I am composing love songs again, not to A–Z, but to music.

If it continues like this I may evaporate into a chord and float off into the air.

That last evening in Hamburg was a very great joy for me. I thought I knew where the handwriting and flowers had come from, but for various reasons I wrote to Fräulein Wagner.

Ah, I like to work for such a reward, I would want and wish there were no other honoraria.

Fräulein Bertha should console herself—Herr Grädener has spoken without thinking much. Otherwise, he would have considered that if Frl. Bertha marched on until she was the equal of the best amateur in Hamburg, she would still not see more of the cathedral of music, yes, even if she took the gigantic step to Grädener's or to my wisdom, she would not notice that she had become any cleverer.

What matters is the How, and not the How Much.

It is often distressing, particularly also among amateurs, to see them chase after the 'how much'. The only thing that is exhilarating in art is to see someone in full enjoyment of his power and learning.

I am very delighted about the acquired piano, now if only I could try it out sometime!

I have unwittingly written to you both and indeed have prattled on a lot, as I notice. I wonder if I shall soon have to write an answer again? Otherwise, I'll dispatch a heap of questions!

Remember me kindly.

I greet you most heartily.

Your

Johs. Brahms.

120

Johannes Brahms to Auguste Brandt and Bertha Porubsky

Detmold, the 25th of October 1859
Tuesday

Revered Lady,

With your dear letters which speak to me so warmly, you give me great pleasure.

Grädener wrote to me too, even if things have not been so wonderful, it was not all that bad.

He is inviting me to his first concert. I am delighted as a king about the yet-to-be-requested vacation and the few days in Hamburg.

I learn with pleasure that the women's chorus still exists as a small republic. Should I send some songs? Cheerful, lively little songs? If you wish it, I would keep you supplied faithfully.

Who then, has joined the alto section? My guess is Frl. Gabain, but I really wish a few more would join. And the new Viennese girl, is she by any chance the famous pianist Marianne? In the end, a 'certain grizzled one' [Grädener] might then come to the house too?

For to whom could ladies' hands be better entrusted?

He won't take them to bowling alleys, and he doesn't compose sonatas which might break them.[33]

Spohr is dead! He may well be the last one who still belonged to a more beautiful era of art than the one we are now suffering through. In those days

---

[33] Alluding to his own physically demanding sonatas, which many women considered too strenuous to play.

one could eagerly keep a look out every week for what new and even more beautiful work had come from this or that person.

Now it is different. In a month of Sundays I see hardly one volume of music that pleases me, but on the other hand many that even make me physically ill.

Possibly at no other time has an art form been maltreated as badly as our dear music nowadays.

I hope better things are quietly maturing, otherwise, in the history of art, our era will look like a trash heap.

You are reading a lot of Shakespeare? That is marvellous. In him one has everything and everyone all in one, while all the others together don't add up to a Shakespeare.

You may often find me in the forest, and occasionally you may well find me in your company.

Often when I have to go to the castle in the evening, I hardly have time to change my clothes.[34]

The other day, therefore, I conducted my choral society, which is larded with nobility, without a necktie. Fortunately I had no occasion to be embarrassed and aggravated, for I noticed it only when I went to bed.

This is the fourth letter today, and what's more, it will introduce a twin. If I could only read a new one, instead of writing another one!

Writing just doesn't work well, but I really know how to read and enjoy a letter!

But why do you make a secret of our ongoing exchange of letters? If someone should ask me, which is not at all impossible, I could hardly repudiate it?

Incidentally, 'Dear Herr Johannes' would please me much better than 'Dear Herr Brahms', which is not a lovely salutation.

Moreover, I send warm greetings, and I am often and intensely on the look-out for a double letter.

Wholly yours,
Johannes Brahms.

Grädener's concert of 2 December, which opened his Academy, and which Brahms was so pleased to take part in, involved him as soloist in Schumann's Piano

---

[34] Not surprising. The Teutobuerger Forest stretches over some 80 km. on hills about 300 m. higher than the surrounding countryside. From castle to forest edge is about 6 km.; the path to the top of the highest local hill, one of Brahms's favourite walks, rises sharply through perhaps another kilometre of deep oak and beech woods. But Brahms's hotel faced the entrance to the castle park; once home, he did not have far to go to get to work (see Plate 16).

Concerto, and as conductor of his *Ave Maria*, Op. 12, and *Begräbnisgesang*, Op. 13. That required a rearrangement of his obligations to Otten, with whom he was now on frigid terms. The following letter therefore displays the opposite oddity from early letters to Clara: it is written with starch formality—and in the 'Du' form.

121
Johannes Brahms to Georg Otten

[October or November 1859]

Dear Otten,

I regret not to have informed you sooner that I have turned my *Begräbnisgesang* over to Herr Grädener for performance!

It would have required more vanity than I possess to infer from your speech and finally from your letter that you had a special affection for the work and were contemplating its performance with some certainty.

Therefore I could not possibly consider myself obliged to save this work for you, since naturally, what matters to me above all else is to hear it and let it be heard.

I hope all the more you are not annoyed with me for this, since the piece may well deserve a repeat performance before a fairly new audience, and indeed because other works of mine could replace it, if you so wish.

Sincere greetings to you and yours,

your Johs Brahms.

122
Johannes Brahms to Auguste Brandt and Bertha Porubsky

Detmold, Sunday, 20 November 1859

You see, most revered one, such is the demand on my time that your lovely letter finds me at home on this beautiful Sunday.

I am really kept extremely busy, unfortunately not in the way I want, but as others want.

But your letters of 1 November are also before me, so the postal clerk has prophesied poorly. But surely I must have written in the mean time?

At least I want to hope so for the sake of my good manners.

You must have a curious conception about my vacation. It is a question of coming and going!

But for two or three days, anyway, I will be beyond the borders of Lippe, and can stretch my limbs.

Whether I see a piano other than my concert grand is very questionable.

In any case, you will easily be able to round out your conversational material until the New Year.

I had company. Avé and Joachim devised the most agreeable days for me. Now I am back pulling the old cart.

With regard to our clandestine correspondence, I must agree with your aunt after all.

Since St Peter did not go to hell for disowning a certain person, I shall probably also be forgiven, if I should disown you on occasion.

It hardly requires letters to start people gossiping.

Strangely enough, good girls appear to have their eyes fixed so unwaveringly on their careers that they all too quickly sniff out the scent of someone wishing to give a helping hand to one of them.

This is very silly and intolerable. But since people can hardly conceive of creatures male and female writing quite harmless letters to each other, it is probably better if the songs stay behind and are presented sometime to the Frauenchor *in corpore*.

I have to close, although it feels as though I had hardly begun.

I scarcely find any time to prepare my fingers a little for Hamburg, and that is really very necessary.

Next time I'll write more. Dare I hope to hear from you soon?

Sincerely devoted
Your
Johannes Brahms.

123

Johannes Brahms to Auguste Brandt and Bertha Porubsky[35]

Detmold, 2 January 1860

Your kind words helped my Christmas tree illuminate my room so beautifully that I would consider myself ungrateful if I waited with my thanks until I see you.

I was not shamed by your kindness, because no one could have had better intentions to write than I.

---

[35] This is the last surviving letter to Fräulein Bertha Porubsky via her Aunt Brandt, although throughout his life Brahms occasionally wrote to her as *Frau* Bertha Porubsky Faber, and she was among his intimate circle of friends in Vienna. Contact between the families was maintained for a long time. Brahms urged Clara to board Julie Schumann with Aunt Brandt, and Bertha's brother lodged with Brahms's father and stepmother in Hamburg for a year. Brahms saw some of the Brandts when he came to Hamburg in 1889, to receive his honorary citizenship.

Such heavy demands are made on my time, however, that I could not. It is now night, as I write you these hasty lines.

I shall leave here within the next few days and will be in Hamburg shortly.

There I'll also hear 'O Strassburg' and 'Wach auf, mein Hort'!, which I am greatly looking forward to.[36] *

Additional Note p. 749

It is like bathing, as if one were being anointed with precious oil.

I am also hoping to catch the 10 measures of Soprano solo.

But now, I wish you would use your imagination to continue reading the blank paper a while longer, while I go to bed.

Do read the friendliest words, I send them in my thoughts.

In Hamburg, I will make up in conversation for what I must now deny myself.

Farewell, and remain kindly disposed towards me.

Sincerely devoted
Johannes Brahms

Judging from his letters, Brahms recaptured some of his old confidence during this autumn of 1859. He had new compositions ready, and was anxious to get them performed. Although Clara's proposed trip to Detmold fell through and she did not give in to Brahms's pleadings to be in Hamburg for the performance of his latest works, she responded with enthusiasm and a letter which displayed great insight into his *Ave Maria*, Op. 12, and Psalm 13, Op. 27. She offered to show them and the Serenade to Ferdinand Hiller, whom she was about to visit in Cologne.[37]

124

Johannes Brahms to Clara Schumann

Detmold, Wednesday, 9 November 1859

Beloved Clara,

Your letter gave me the greatest pleasure yesterday! I won't comment on it, otherwise you will consider me vain and will suppose that I like to hear flatteries. But I am indeed having great fun with my things. I really do believe dear Clara, that I am growing!

You will also be able to understand 'how one sings praise to the Lord that He does so well, so well for one'. Has He not done so very well for me!

How wonderful to be creating with restored power.

---

[36] Two of the many German folk-songs Brahms collected and sang with his Frauenchor.
[37] Litz, iii. 65.

How wonderful that you and others participate in it.

I think wistfully of the Magnificent One who used to do so with such fervour, such intensity.

Frau Schrödter has sent me a beautiful album-leaf for you.[38] I will dispatch it very soon, I don't want to do so without including some music:

The complete 2nd Serenade, which has now been copied but which I don't need here, at least the 1st movement of a septet for string instruments, and the choral songs. First I'll have to torment my guest with it (Avé), who is coming on Friday.[39]

I am sending my 1st Serenade to Hiller, I would be exceedingly pleased if he would perform it. A mere rehearsal would naturally be less useful to me. They are also, with pleasure, at Dietrich's disposal. I have no greater wish than that my things be performed, that would give me life (in addition to what I now have). Should they perhaps fancy it in Honnef, that would be fine with me.—The *Ave Maria* and the 1[3th] Psalm are also at the disposal of anyone who will have the parts copied out (but which would not be his property)!

By New Year I shall probably ask for the return of the 1st Serenade, it's scheduled in Hamburg. It would therefore have to be given in Cologne and Bonn before then. In that case I would be glad to come.

When convenient dear Clara, I beg you to order the Great Mass in D by Beethoven for me (the full score, from Schott in Mainz). I would like to present it to my teacher, Herr Marxsen, for Christmas.

I completely forgot that I also haven't thanked you for your previous letter and for what you sent.

The pictures are lovely, I just want to pay for part of them. In any case, I request the bill for the music.

I'm very glad that you agree to all I have done here in that business. I say not one word about you now.

If you play in Bremen at the end of November, is it by any chance possible that you will be in the audience on December 2nd (Friday) in Hamburg?[40]

I too will be there only for a few days, and since we'll mostly be out on the street, we could both manage quite well at my parents'. Or if you have Marie with you, she or I can stay at Avé's.

---

[38] Wilhelmine Schrödter-Devrient (1804–60), was a friend of the Schumanns. She was one of the most famous singers in Germany, the prima donna of the Dresden Opera for twenty-five years.

[39] The septet was very likely an early version of the string Sextet, Op. 18, the choral pieces most of Op. 22, *Seven Marienlieder*.

[40] To hear him perform in Grädener's Academy concert.

Soon (Sunday or Monday) I will send and write. Don't be frugal with the paper, I enjoy every one of your flattering words.

Warmly your
Johannes.

Greetings to Miss Leser, Jungé, Woldemar, Hiller, Dietrich, etc. Incidentally, it is always very distressing for me to hear such bad news about Nettchen. Be sure to write to me again how it goes.

125

Johannes Brahms to Joseph Joachim

[Detmold, 8 December 1859][41]

My dear Joseph,

Your note has just arrived, and if I let the soup get cold, I still have time to answer.

You can let Frau Schumann tell you how and why I cannot, unfortunately, get free here at Court. Actually, she also doesn't really know what's happening, except that they are all lily-livered, etc.

But I could so easily spend Sunday and Monday with you in Hanover if only they weren't so petty here.

I beg you to send me, along with the Serenade, half or maybe even an entire quire of manuscript paper, wide format with 16 (or 14) staves and about a quarter of a quire of narrow paper with 20–24 staves.

I am forced to be dreadfully tormented here with impractical music paper. And there is no one here willing to draw it specially.[42] Be so kind, but soon. I'm really waiting for it.

If only I could decide to go to Hanover on Saturday night! I have no commitments until Tuesday but I fear they will consider it as leave and expect me to stay longer after New Year.

I need the paper to convert the first Serenade into a symphony, at long last. I realize that this work is a sort of hybrid creature, neither this nor that.

I had such beautiful, grand ideas for my first symphony, and now!—

Bargheer is arriving, adieu. A thousand greetings, dearest man; to Frau Schumann my most heartfelt ones. I await everything anxiously and will be very grateful to you if it doesn't take long.

Altogether yours.
Johannes.

[41] Incorrectly dated as 1858 in *BW* v. My thanks to David Brodbeck for pointing this out.

[42] With a special five-pronged pen known as a Rastral. A quire consists of 24 sheets.

Although the very affectionate friendship between Grimm and Brahms would last for their entire lives, it was sorely strained in the aftermath of Brahms's break with Agathe. After almost a year of silence, they made contact again, aided by Joachim's gentle intercession.

126

Johannes Brahms to Julius Otto Grimm

[Hamburg] Dec[ember] [18]59

Dear Grimm,

Every day I was reminded to send you the promised things, have daily thought with joy, indeed, that I may still regard you as my cherished friend.

I had planned to tidy up a number of things in what I now send just as it is. I couldn't get to it. I was occupied by other matters. Moreover, my free hours are unfortunately so very few.

Otherwise I would like to write you a number of things about which my mouth was closed at our last meeting.

My heartiest greeting to all who wish it.

I should like the things back as soon as possible, and according to the old, cherished practice, let me also hear what you think of it.

Your

Johannes

In a rush!

⟡ 1860 ⟡

The year 1860 marked a distinct turn in the life of Johannes Brahms. Far more confident, now, he was eager to see the fruits of the past six years in print; and with the publication of six opuses (nine works were ready), his career as a composer was firmly, permanently back on track.

When January came and Brahms left Detmold, his attention turned to preparing for publication both Serenades, several choral works, two sets of songs, and of course the Piano Concerto, all compositions which had been in existence for at least a year. He was also ready to publish a brand new work, *Four Songs* for Women's Chorus, Two Horns and Harp, Op. 17.[1]

---

[1] The six works which found publishers—Serenade in D for full orchestra, Op. 11; *Ave Maria*, Op. 12; *Begräbnisgesang*, Op. 13; *Songs and Romances* for Solo voice with Piano, Op. 14; Piano Concerto in D Minor, Op. 15; Serenade in A, Op. 16—were all more or less in print by the end of the year (i.e. the score but not the parts for Op. 11, and parts but not the score for Op. 15). Equally

Brahms toyed with the idea of giving up his women's chorus, but was persuaded otherwise, and instead wrote up his *Avertimento*, a humorous set of rules of conduct in mock-legalese, in order to regularize rehearsal sessions. The chorus met at night, sang and serenaded in the moonlight whenever possible, went on excursions and picnics, and left behind a number of memoirs which describe a glorious time.[2]

In the same year, Brahms finally gave in to his itching fingers and, with Joachim, organized as many composers and writers on music as he could to sign and publish a declaration of protest against Liszt and his 'Musicians of the Future', who claimed to have cornered the market on all forward-thinking composers of the day. Brahms honestly considered Liszt's music to be a threat to the integrity of the art, but his letters to Joachim state unequivocally that he was taking aim *only* at Liszt and his school. Neither Wagner nor Berlioz were included, and he specifically wanted the wording of the protest to make that clear. Although Brahms and Joachim gathered promises for signatures of twenty musicians or so, a provisional form of the Declaration brought by Joachim to Leipzig was leaked to the press. The protest appeared in print in Berlin with only four signatories: Joachim, his Hanoverian colleague Berhard Scholz, J. O. Grimm, and Brahms himself.

In this form it was a decided dud, and is an exercise in politics which Brahms never experimented with again.

After his third season in Detmold, the first thing Brahms did was to catch up on his sleep. His letter to Clara sets the tone for his activities and concerns during this period.

127
Johannes Brahms to Clara Schumann

Hamburg, Friday, the 27th January 1860

I will now report on everything that has been happening here, dear Clara.

The most interesting and best item came from you people in Hanover.[3]

In any case, you will be back from Holland before it will be the Serenade's turn in Hanover, but it would be disgraceful if you were to miss it! Here I have made erasures and corrections in the parts of the 2nd

ready but slower to find a publisher were the *Four Songs* for Women's Chorus, 2 Horns and Harp, Op. 17, *Five Poems* for Solo Voice with Piano, Op. 19, and *Three Duets* for Soprano and Alto, Op. 20. The Sextet for Strings in B flat, Op. 18 was also finished in 1860, but not offered for publication until the next year, and the *Psalm 13*, Op. 27, finished in September 1859, was not published until 1864.

  [2] See Drinker, *Brahms and his Women's Choruses*, 49 ff. (translation of the *Avertimento* on pp. 53–5) and Hübbe, *Brahms in Hamburg*, 26 ff. Fuller-Maitland's biography, *Brahms* (London, 1911), also includes the *Avertimento* in English and German (pp. 17–22).

  [3] The news of a command performance of the Serenade, Op. 11, in its final revised version, for full orchestra. See Brahms to Joachim, 24 Jan. 1860, *BW* v. 257.

Serenade, its turn will come on February 10th. Is that just when you will be on your return trip? Otherwise, it would be splendid if you attended.[4] As I said, I really have slept my fill here, in the true sense of the word. I don't know, I really was rather exceedingly bored in Detmold, felt awfully tired and worn out, am now gradually getting some life back. Can you comprehend this? I really had a lot to do there, boring and monotonous it was, and when I was alone, I always had to tear myself forcibly out of my lassitude.

The Romances for Women's Chorus by your husband are really very popular here.[5]

3 choral groups have already sung excerpts from them in their performances!

I must get going and let a dozen ladies sing for me. They sang my new German folk-songs for me, which they had worked hard to learn.

Now we get together in a very friendly manner one evening a week, and I expect that the beautiful folk-songs will entertain me quite pleasantly.

I believe I'll really learn something, since I will have to consider and hear the songs with care and in earnest. I want to truly absorb them. It is not enough to sing them once enthusiastically and with appropriate feeling.

Songs are sailing such an erroneous course nowadays that one cannot impress the ideal too sharply on oneself. And that's what folk-song is for me.

Yesterday, Otten became the first to put works by Liszt in a respectable concert. *Loreley*, a song, and *Lenore* by Bürger, with a melodramatic accompaniment.[6] I was terribly annoyed. I expect that he will yet do a Symphonic Poem this winter.

The plague will continue to spread and will certainly lengthen and ruin the donkey ears of the public and of youthful composers.[7]

The 2nd Symphony of Robert was performed really badly.

The things were here waiting for me, thank you very much for the trouble. I will sell your music sometime. But not Berger[?], I suppose? On the other hand I see much that's useless (Hiller songs) in your cabinet.

I have 505 th. here excluding what is expected from the King.

Be good enough to keep my small debts or deduct them from the interest, *if that doesn't cause you too much trouble.*

---

    [4] Brahms played Schumann's Piano Concerto with the Hamburg Philharmonic, and conducted his Serenade No. 2 in A major, Op. 16.
    [5] Two volumes, *Romanzen für Frauenstimmen mit willkürlicher Begleitung des Piano-forte*, Opp. 69 and 92, composed in 1849.
    [6] *Loreley* was probably performed in the version with orchestra accompaniment. The poem *Leonore* is declaimed with piano accompaniment.
    [7] The length of the donkey's ear was an indication of its stupidity (a dubious genetic linkage).

I would like nothing better than to perform something with you in the audience. But the 1st Serenade.[8]

See to it that it will be *after* the concert in Hanover, in which it will be performed. I have promised the first performance to Joachim, and I therefore want to, and have to, rehearse and hear it there first. With a strange orchestra, it's risky.[9]

It all depends very much now on the benevolence of my copyists.

Here everyone is well and of good cheer, they send their greetings.

Be sure to write to me if you can come here on about the 10th of February (Friday). Then I would practise twice as happily and well.

Give my regards to Miss Leser, Jungé! etc. etc. Travel happily, acquire and retain a cheerful state of mind, and think with pleasure of your friend who loves you dearly.

Your
Johannes.

Brahms and Joachim set out to attack 'the plague' in earnest, scouring the ranks of their musical colleagues, friends, and acquaintances for potential signatories of their Declaration of Protest, and taking great care over its wording. Although some composers and critics agreed to sign, many more were disinclined, either out of prudence, timidity, or conviction.* Brahms's wistful comment that it wouldn't work as a quartet—with four signatures, in other words—was prophetic.

Additional
note p. 749

128

Johannes Brahms to Joseph Joachim

[Hamburg, 10 March 1860]

Dearest friend,

Received the printer's proof with pleasure. Now on with it. Mainly I'm awaiting Grädeneresque responses. If I could only count on Gade and Bargiel, then it seems to me it would be all right.

Jul. Schäffer and Franz I am still hoping for. I hardly suppose it would work as a quartet?

Grädener's line of reasoning is useless, unrealistic. We can't permit ourselves to get involved in evidentiary proceedings for we cannot reply *in corpore*, must therefore watch out for any sentence that could be answered in

---

[8] i.e. rather than the second.

[9] The entire paragraph refers to the revised version of Op. 11, the form in which it is now played. Its première was on 3 March in Hanover, with Joachim conducting.

the form of a question. Furthermore, should we wish to cite some basic rules of music as having been disregarded by them, they could *certainly* prove that each of these rules is contained in their statute book. Without going into details, that wouldn't work in any case. Examples would be required, so that an entire volume of music would have to be appended.

Worse still, every one is supposed to be invited to have his say! Presumably that would then be scrutinized, etc. etc.

In all his livelong day nothing will come of that.

I forgot to ask you in Hanover to lend me your score of my Concerto. Could you send it to me when convenient? I'm supposed to play it with Otten.

I really yearn to have your Concerto. Couldn't you send me the old copy, even if only the first 2 movements?

In Bremen they want to coerce you for the 27th. But Grädener's concert is on the 30th. Will that work? NB: The Dresden Composers' Society is requesting my 2nd Serenade (for the time being, through Klemm). Can you not tell me what kind of a man the Society's Music Director is (from whom I'm first awaiting a letter), and whether one can entrust the work to him?

In the 2nd sentence of the Declaration I don't particularly like the 'it' instead of 'as', may I change it back when copying it out for the newspapers? I also miss the 'long ago' after 'Music of the Future' and it makes the sentence less explicit for me. Have we not, haplessly, let it to come to pass 'long ago'.

If possible, let me have both D Minor scores.

In heartfelt love

Your

Johannes

129

Johannes Brahms to Joseph Joachim

[Hamburg, 19 March 1860]

Dear Jussuf,

Since the affair is progressing at such a very leisurely pace there is still time to remind you that you might want to send our protest to Bagge and Debrois v. Bruyk in Vienna for their signatures.

That is presumably in order. Besides, they seem decent and most of all, they will have to deal with it. Apart from them, I intend to favour only Bischoff with it. To my knowledge, the Berlin newspapers are so colourless that it is unnecessary, and we may as well also bypass the *Signale*.[10] I would be very much for that.

We haven't thought of Karl Müller in Münster, and I believe he has even composed, a *Tasso*, no less!

I have received a Yes from Dietrich, Bargiel, Wüllner, Bruch, and Kirchner. Grädener is also with us. Do you know nothing of our *heroes*? Do send to Vienna. As an editor, Bagge may wish to stay away, but in that case we must honour the species in Debrois.

I am going to come to a quick decision and write to Härtels. To offer the Concerto or Serenade. I must be rid of the things at long last, before the summer. Quite definitely.

Unfortunately I expect a No and fear that will be detrimental to me, e.g. with other publishers.

Do send your Concerto *immediately* after the Saturday [concert], which I probably won't come to after all.

Also mine with it, as I already requested. Grimm may come along! I am looking forward enormously to your work.

Best greetings.
Your Johannes.

130

Johannes Brahms to Clara Schumann

Hamburg, Monday morning, the 2nd of April 1860

I must write to tell you about a splendid week, dear Clara; I wish you had been part of it, or would come the next time and see how lovely it can be here.

Friday was Grädener's 2nd concert. Genoveva Overture, an overture by Handel, Cantata by Bach, a sacred work by Em. Bach, etc., and Joachim's Concerto! What joy this concerto will give you when you hear it again. It has become magnificent. The first movement in particular, with such a full measure of beauty and so calmly, intimately warm that it is a joy. Without anything much in it actually being different, the previous year's reading seems nevertheless like a rather wild sketch compared to this beautifully formed work of art.

You simply would have to have heard it, I shall not describe it.

---

[10] *Signale für die musikalische Welt*, an important music journal published in Leipzig. See Letters 51 and 52.

Incidentally, it is so crystal clear and leaves such an agreeable impression that it is bound to please the public everywhere, and here as well.

I had to show my talent as conductor. I haven't seen it since Detmold, and he got out of the coach and went immediately to the rehearsal. I conducted it, to my quite exceptional pleasure.

Each evening was spent in merriment, but Saturday's was especially delightful. That was accomplished by my girls, whom I assembled in honour of Joachim or, actually, in their honour.

I had in fact intended to give the whole thing up and had set this Tuesday as the last evening. Now it was really delightful. I had told Joachim about a girl who wore a black dress; when we arrived, they were all in black! In spite of their joy over Joachim, they meant to mourn the end of our evenings. Is that not sweet? Unfortunately, a harp was not to be found. Two bad hornists played along. Joachim found the greatest enjoyment in the affair and I had to promise him not to put *Fine* to it.[11]

But then, it is really quite delightful. The girls are so charmingly lively and enthusiastic, without ever being sweet or sentimental. On the way home (an hour away) it rained, unfortunately. Otherwise glorious singing and serenades are presented along the way.

For my girls will actually parade into a garden without embarrassment and awaken people after midnight with their singing. Every day we wished you here. And now I keep thinking that you must come the next time. That could be very nice indeed, for the 19th of April. That is when I play my concerto with Otten, and the girls we can have at any time. They will surely give you enormous pleasure, and also you don't yet know Ossian, Shakespeare, etc. with harp and horns.

If you can get around to writing letters before May, don't forget to write to me whether you can arrange to be here for 19th of April. No greater joy could come to me.

Yesterday afternoon we took Joachim to Harburg. Tomorrow evening we shall probably finally have a harp to go with the horns.

If only you were present one of these days!

My Serenade I also sent to Vienna a few weeks or months ago. I suppose it has arrived?[12]

At times I too have derived pleasure from the quaint fabrications of newspapers. If you want to hear more from Hamburg, try to let that be known.

---

[11] They read through the *Four Songs for Women's Chorus, Two Horns, and Harp*, Op. 17.

[12] At Clara's suggestion. She had interested two Viennese conductors in the work. Clara to Brahms, 3 Mar. 1860, *SBB* i. 300–1.

But I would grumble terribly, if I were to find out in May that you don't want to come for the 19th of April.

With deepest love
Your Johannes.

Grädener's concert was the occasion of the first public performance of Joachim's Hungarian Concerto.[13] Brahms's pride in his own abilities as a conductor is patent (apparently he conducted the dress rehearsal of the violin concerto), lending credence to the notion that in the long run he had his eye on the directorship of the Hamburg Philharmonic. The concert with Otten took place shortly after; his piano concerto was the disaster Brahms feared it would be, given Otten's meagre musicianship, and it marked the last time the two men worked together.[14] Clara could not arrange to be there and was, in fact, getting ready to go to England, much to Brahms's distress. When her plans fell through he importuned her to come to Hamburg for a visit, urging a brief trial visit with a view to spending the summer there.

131

Johannes Brahms to Clara Schumann

Hamburg, 26 April 1860

Dear Clara,

This very moment I received your letter and am overjoyed that nothing will come of that dam..d journey.

Strange to say, I just couldn't get it out of my head that you were leaving yesterday, as I thought, and that I had not even gone to Berlin, indeed could not go.

So now I beg you in all seriousness and as affectionately, urgently as possible, do come here for the summer. I can, after all, do various things to make the time agreeable for you, quite possible that Joachim will also be coming. Have no fear, when I write I'll work as hard as possible, you will surely find any number of other pleasant diversions which without your noticing or wanting to will occupy you at odd times.

Shall I relate to you, dear Clara, that now and for ever more I have the greatest love for you and for him who has left you? How gladly would I prove this to you.

I assure you, you have enough childlike spirit to take pleasure in my

---

[13] 30 March. See *BW* iv. 92, Brahms to Grimm.   [14] See Letter 133.

Frauenchor (at least at one of the pleasurable meetings).[15] It will stay in existence and you will feel very comfortable and quite blissful.

Imagine, I have now been talking for an hour to convince you to come here on Sunday or Monday (or even better, Saturday). Then you'll look over everything, the chorus meets on Monday evening, and since the best alto is forsaking us after that, you must hear it then. Then we'll run around and consider where you might live.

Dear Clara, I have such a uselessly large amount of money, let me pay for the trial journey.

Perhaps you can even simply stay here, and your children can come after you and you can let Frl. Werner take care of affairs in Berlin.[16]

Maybe Marie could just come along with you.

Dearest, make an earnest effort to travel here as soon as tomorrow, it's a small trip, after all, what need is there for lengthy deliberation? But you must definitely share in the pleasure of Monday so that you get a taste of the most important aspects, just now the moon is full, and just now we are in a particularly agreeable house ($^1/_2$ hour out of town).[17]

My duets too, you can hear only on that day (for the time being), because of the departure of the good alto.[18]

Today is Thursday, I beseech you, dear Clara, to leave on Saturday morning or Friday evening.

The Düsseldorf music festival is useless in the extreme, and if you want to go there, I shall go with you and we'll make a tour (perhaps with J.) into the Ahr Valley and then, if you like, come back here.

But without fail come now for a few days to look around and try it out.

I would be very glad to get under way right now and be with you early tomorrow, but I have faith in you, dear Clara, and believe staunchly that you will decide to travel on Friday evening or Saturday morning. Send me a telegram, and I will come part of the way to meet you. Give me this proof of your love and I will return it a thousandfold.

Be here on Saturday, I beg you, because on Sunday afternoon or evening I must pay a visit to some nice girls outside town. If you are here on Saturday you could come and walk out there with me for a while on Sunday, and get to know some agreeable people.

[15] An exceedingly obscure sentence in the original, even for Brahms; ungrammatical, almost like a stream of consciousness, and untranslatable without some degree of guesswork. The 'pleasurable meetings' are literally 'periodic diversions'. We have taken some liberty here.

[16] Governess and housekeeper for Clara in Berlin.

[17] Belonging to the Hallier family. Clara eventually stayed with them on some of her Hamburg tours.

[18] Op. 20, for Soprano and Alto.

I would like to start again from the beginning, such genuine anxiety do I have that you might consider for too long. But what is this little trip to you, which may after all present you with the prospect of a more or less pleasant summer.

Therefore come in any case, I would be heartbroken not to see you on Saturday.

The warmest [greetings] from my people.

Your

Johannes

If you come with Marie, you will be my guest at the hotel.

Do grant me a telegraphic answer immediately, I am waiting with such great longing.

V. S.

I have nothing to do all day, and also no work planned that preoccupies me. Naturally you can stay with me or with Marie in a very agreeable hotel, where you will find the pleasant lady who admires you deeply, and me at any time of day you please.

You will see, I really know my way around Hamburg, I am only now getting to know it properly. You won't get to see a single note of music from me the whole summer if on Monday you don't listen to some quite charming new Minnelieder.

I intend to show you as much love as you require and can ask for.

Tomorrow morning I am getting a telegraphic message, and you the day after, aren't I?

As Clara replied, she could not resist such a request. She came first for a few days and then returned for several weeks in time to surprise Brahms on the morning of his birthday. Clara's diary notes that in Hamburg, Brahms was occasionally in a bad mood but that on the whole she had a good time. There were charming moments involving the Women's Choir, including the excursion to Blankenese often cited in biographies, where Brahms conducted the group of singers from his perch on the branch of a tree. He kept his promise to go with Clara and Joachim to the 37th Music Festival of the Lower Rhine in Düsseldorf, and then on to the valley of the Ahr, joined now by Stockhausen and Bargiel.[19]

As always, Brahms continued to work.

---

[19] Litz, iii. 77–8. See also Drinker, *Brahms and his Women's Choruses*, 58–9.

132
Johannes Brahms to Joseph Joachim

[Hamburg, *c.*5 May 1860]

My dearest friend,

Because there are all sorts of things to say, this letter is being sent out ahead of the real one, which will shortly have to accompany my exercises again.

Your chorales are hereby returned, adorned with a heap of crosses.

Mainly they indicate six-four chords and chords lacking the third.

$^6_4$ and even $^6_3$ I don't care for in chorales. Used simply throughout, they sound tired and eccentric, and even when they come at the good part of the measure and are effective I check to see if they fit in. There are exceptions to both rules, as is demonstrated by the second part of *Wie schön leucht' uns*, your No. 1; there I would let them stand.

The third, in my view, must also not be consistently omitted. Rarely also the 5th of the diminished 7 chord, as it often signifies the 7th of the 9 chord (in which the bass note is missing.)

Purely as an afterthought to my chorales, I'm enclosing what I have. Next time I shall do it properly.

I ask for appropriate annotation with crosses. It would give me the greatest pleasure if we really got rolling with our exercises.

These days I have been arranging my 2nd Serenade for 4 hands. Don't laugh! It has put me in a really euphoric mood. Rarely have I written music with such relish, the sounds permeated me so lovingly and gently that I was cheerful through and through. But I can honestly add that my sense of elation was not heightened by the thought of myself as the creator. But it was ridiculous just the same.

For the *Entführung*, my warmest thanks. But I am sorry, after all, you could have had the complete Mozart with the *Zauberflöte*?[20]

---

[20] Apparently Brahms suggested Mozart's *Abduction from the Seraglio* as a gift for Joachim, not knowing that he already owned it but not the *Magic Flute*. Joachim gave his extra copy to Brahms.

Frau Schumann is probably coming here tomorrow, to stay for 2 weeks. Do write to me where you are, sometime.

I have little inclination to go to Düsseldorf, except to hear your concerto and if I cannot catch hold of you any other way.

I don't suppose you want to come here? You will of course be offered nothing but space to lie down and to walk about, which can be found anywhere. I don't know whether and how long I shall remain here. NB: If *you* don't come.

Our *Declaration* has been signed by our friends from the Rhine, Kirchner, von Perfall, Reinecke, E. Naumann.[21]

Meinardus also, although he hopes it won't come to pass and that a journal may be established instead. G. Schumann and Krigar have signed, therefore perhaps their friends in Berlin may now come limping along.

Flügel, Schäffer are not doing it; their 'because' is not of interest. From Volkmann I have had no answer (but is he in Vienna?). Bagge and Bruyck naturally consider their signatures to be useless.

I'm sending along two letters from Lührss. I request they be definitely returned to me, so that the 'document file' remains together for the time being. I see no sense in them.

With our refutation no one can have Wagner in mind. In any case one must show the same concern for Berlioz and Franz. Only Liszt can be finished off as we are doing. With Lührss, who really comes down hard on the entire essay, it would all dissolve into vapour, just there the wording is directed against all of them.

etc. etc.[22]

Raff, Litolff, Laub, Rubinstein are impossible for this reason or that. You see it all as clearly as I. Do we want to keep on trying?

Funny, I had written to Lührss that with 'Liszt and his students, or whatever' not enough is said, for Weitzmann, Raff, Lassen etc. are not that!

Laub! We can also ask Bülow to participate.

What does Scholz, to whom I ask you to give my greetings, say to that?

Should the two of us [go it] alone? or with Bargiel, Kirchner and a few others?

Apropos!! If you go to Leipzig, don't forget me, and try to find out something definite as to whether I can offer Härtel a Serenade etc. I'll wait before writing?

Additional
Note p. 749

[21] See Additional Note p. 749.

[22] He was typically too impatient to write what he thought, particularly when he felt certain his correspondent knew what he meant in any case.

Excuse the long twaddle, it would be better to be together. Couldn't that be? In Hamburg or elsewhere?

Write very soon and if possible order lodgings, then you or we together can go on an outing.

Utterly yours.

Johannes.

133

Johannes Brahms to Julius Otto Grimm

[Hamburg] 6 May [18]60

My dear friend,

It is probably my fault that I haven't heard from you for so long. I wish that our appetite for writing were not in such a bad state. At least I would like to hear more often from you and yours.

I continue to sit here, in the end for the whole summer again, however am constantly yearning to get away but can't get a proper grip on anything. I don't want to reassemble my Frauenchor all the time, I mean to get away to the Rhine, or somewhere, soon. Frau Schumann is coming here tomorrow, probably for two weeks. Therefore I should like to ask you to send me my Frauenchor pieces after all, I should like to have them sung for her. If you get them off right away, I could certainly have them by Wednesday.

Evenings, a small circle of girls always sings at my place, really pleasant and cheerful. German folk-songs, and whatever I happen to write.

If you are not making use of the Sanctus, include it. I assume you have it, I do not find it among my things.[23] The Otten concert was dreadful, a good thing that you didn't come for it. My concerto fared very badly and an Italian singer made one blush with shame to listen, and worse, to have participated.

Our 'Declaration' contra Liszt will probably run aground on the misgivings, etc. of the most honorable composers. Not even 20 names can be collected. Can't you come here sometime during the summer? Do write to me about really everything when you send the music.

What is Hans up to?[24]

I suppose Bargheer is again coming to your house?

And you don't need the music any more, do you?

---

[23] The Sanctus is from Brahms's *Missa Canonica*, and survived only in Grimm's copy. Long thought to be lost, it came to light again in 1981, and in 1984 was published together with the Benedictus and Agnus Dei as WoO 18 (Doblinger Editions, Vienna).

[24] His godchild Johannes Grimm.

Be sure also to write and tell me your misgivings and opinions concerning composition and vocal writing. I would like to enquire about all kinds of things in Göttingen, but I do think you will write to me very nicely. I am glad to hear about everything, important and unimportant, and for a moment I would like to have the sensation of being there.

Greet your wife and your child (or children?).

More the next time, don't let's lose touch.

Letters and music may aid one's thoughts; mine go often enough to all of you.

Think kindly of

your
Johannes.

Some time during the summer Brahms decided to give up his post in Detmold. He had agreed to return provided he could conduct the orchestra with some regularity, but officials at Court, unwilling to offend the ageing and faithful Kapellmeister Kiel, could offer Brahms only the compromise of conducting whenever choral works were performed. Unhappy with this solution, he resigned, sending a letter of which a fragment has survived.[25]

134
Johannes Brahms to [Hofmarschall von Meysenbug]

Hamburg, Summer 1860

After repeated consideration, I must now, after all, request you most respectfully to express to his Serene Highness, the Prince, my regrets that I shall be unable to come to Detmold this winter. To the reasons motivating me to this action, of which I have already had the honour to inform you, must now be added that I will be greatly occupied with the publication of my works, with revising the proofs of some and preparing others for the engraver, and on that account alone, therefore, I must decide to remain here for the winter. To her Serene Highness, the Princess Friederike, I beg you to express my particular regrets that I shall not, as usual, be able to take pleasure in her progress in playing, as well as in her deep interest in music.

Over the course of the summer, Brahms corresponded with Breitkopf & Härtel in his most civil and deferential manner, hoping they would publish his latest works.

[25] The letter came into the hands of Karl von Meysenbug, whose father was the official charged with hiring Brahms.

He was rudely disappointed. The firm agreed to take his First Serenade but turned down the vocal works and the piano concerto, citing in their letter the very unfavourable reception of the Concerto at its Leipzig première in 1859.

135
Johannes Brahms to Breitkopf & Härtel

[Hamburg] 13 August 1860

My dear Sirs!

I have just received your worthy letter and my manuscripts.

I am sorry that you have so little confidence in my 'Concerto'.

But I would not have believed that the effect of the same could be so profoundly terrifying. You do not dignify the other works that were sent along with a single word; I had sent you those which, according to my judgement, were my best and most serviceable pieces but had left the selection to you.

Unfortunately, I did not discover from your letter whether I may expect an engraved full score of my 'Serenade'.

I had not stipulated this, now almost to my regret, but I understand that it is your rule not to let an orchestral work appear without a full score. I would be greatly obliged if you would belatedly drop me a line about it.

I found the most recent *Bach* volume waiting for me here and take the liberty of enclosing herewith my subscription for the coming year.

With special regards,

faithfully,

Johs Brahms

Brahms did not wait even twenty-four before deciding what to do next. He sent the entire lot of rejected music to the Swiss publisher Melchior Rieter-Biedermann, whom he knew through Clara. Rieter took a chance on Opp. 12, 13, 14, and 15, and in the process, the cordial relationship between the two men developed into a genuine friendship. In subsequent years, Brahms was a frequent and welcomed guest in the Rieter household, and at one time Clara alerted Brahms to the fact that the rather beautiful daughter of the house, Ida, would look upon him favourably as a suitor.

Rieter did not lose by his willingness to take a chance on the young composer; among many other of Brahms's works, he was the publisher of the Piano Quintet, Op. 34, and the *German Requiem*, Op. 45.

136
Johannes Brahms to Melchior Rieter-Biedermann

Hamburg, 13 August 60

Esteemed Sir!

In accordance with my promise, I herewith offer you some of my new works for publication.

What matters to me above all else is to receive a quick and decisive answer, so that the works can appear before winter, regardless.

Therefore I am enclosing the same herewith so that you may see the extent of them, etc., and so that in case of a favourable outcome, you are able to have the engraving begun right away.

Apart from these, *Härtel* and *Simrock* are bringing out some other things. To you I offer the following:

'Piano Concerto' in D Minor, for which I request 10 Friedrichsdor as honorarium.

'Ave Maria' for women's chorus etc. ditto 10 Friedrichsdor. A full score would of course be advantageous (not costly), but not urgently required. The organ part to be printed separately.

'Begräbnisgesang' for mixed chorus etc. ditto 10 Friedrichsdor.

Here a printed full score is essential.

'Songs and Romances' 12 Friedrichsdor.

I want especially to publish the last 3 items at the beginning of winter.

They are the most practical things that I can offer you, the 'Lieder', for a start, my best.

In any case, I request a reply at your earliest convenience. Should my offer be agreeable to you, the requisite parts are at your immediate disposal. If one or the other work does not appeal to you, I beg that it be returned to me as soon as possible. In any case I hope to hear from you quite soon, and remain with particular high esteem,

Your devoted
Johs Brahms

Hamburg, Hohe Fuhlentwiete 74

Brahms was now making an organized effort to augment his education, attending lectures in history and art, taking lessons in Latin and French, and pursuing an old hobby, gymnastics.

137
Johannes Brahms to Joseph Joachim

[Hamburg, 13 September 1860]

Precious friend,

Your delightful greeting from Heidelberg is still lying on my table; I am really a scoundrel not to be moved to write even by that. But when I am not writing notes and sending music, it always seems so useless to me to take up my pen.

Here nothing happens other than that my girls sing; this very evening, and we are going across the Alster for it.

If you were only with us, you would have fun and even you wouldn't be against hearing the jolly and wistful little folk-songs.

Here Grädener has got music into a mess. He has created utterly unreasonable confusion.

It's too long-winded and boring to write about his completely ruined Academy, which he abandoned, but retained.

I'm doing gymnastics diligently and am now starting Latin. You absolutely ought to do the first, too!

Bargheer is really not sensible. Now, with his bride coming here, he wants to do the same for a couple of days; what's the use of that? And what's the use of keeping at the Philharmonic committee until they engage him? If he had just stayed around for even a short while during the summer, he might have realized how well and comfortably he can stay and live here.

Is there no news? so that I feel even more ashamed than just when I look at my bare music paper?

You know that Härtels have sent back my Concerto with objections, and at the same time returned other things without a word (possibly out of kindness). I went one step further and incidentally, by the way, mentioned my Harp Songs. Now they write: 'That they hoped the harp would be replaced by piano, also *only if* the horns were not obligatory, etc.', they wished to know more about the length and honorarium, and then, if circumstances etc. permit it etc. and then perhaps.'

All too grotesquely cautious.

Have you finally sent off your Concerto? Be sure to do it, so that we have it and can enjoy it more often.

Now I wish that music would soon be travelling from Hanover to Hamburg and the other way around.

Greet Grimm, when you see him,
                        and be good to
                        Your
                            Johannes.

One more work received its final form in 1860. Although the Serenade No. 2 in A major, Op.16, has no dedication, Brahms sent it to Joachim as a Christmas present, commenting that it was to him that the work owed its genial character. And he thanked him for the score to Mozart's *Idomeneo* which Joachim had sent him.

138
Johannes Brahms to Joseph Joachim

[Hamburg, end of] Dec[ember 18]60

You have made me so happy with your beautiful present, dearest Jussuf, that I cannot let my thanks get so old [as to wait] until you come. Therefore I send herewith my warmest, and at the same time a new publication number from the same firm. Look upon the piece with some affection, best friend, after all, it both belongs to and sounds very much of you. In the final analysis, when music has such a friendly sound, where does that come from if not from those few people of whom one is as fond as I am of you.

But I shall not go along to Vienna, as much as I am tempted. Perhaps I shall spend the whole of next winter there. Now I am flat broke, money etc. etc.

Will you stay with me, when you come? My room is quite comfortable now, since all the walls hang full of pictures and all their faces have a cheery expression all the time. Also write when you are coming, so one doesn't miss even a few hours of you.

Well, more soon in person and once again warmest thanks.
                        Your
                            Johannes

Heute Dienstag den 15 Januar, Abends 7 Uhr,
im grossen Wörmer'schen Saale:

CONCERT

von Frau *Clara Schumann*,

unter gütiger Mitwirkung eines **Damen - Chors** und der Herren
Joseph Joachim, Johannes Brahms und
***Nicolaus Schaller*.**

Programm.

1. **Sonate** für Pianoforte und Geige Op. 47, von *Beethoven*, vorgetragen von Frau **Clara Schumann** und Herrn **Joseph Joachim**.

2. **Lieder** für Frauenchor mit Begleitung einer Harfe und zweier Hörner, von *Johannes Brahms*.
   a) „Es tönt ein voller Harfenklang", von *Fr. Ruperti*.
   b) „Komm herbei, komm herbei, Tod", von *Shakespeare*.
   c) Der Gärtner, von *Eichendorff*.

3. **Symphonische Etuden**, Op. 13, von *Robert Schumann*, vorgetragen von Frau **C. Schumann**.

4. **Andante** und **Variationen** für zwei Claviere von *Robert Schumann*, vorgetragen von Frau **C. Schumann** und Herrn **J. Brahms**.

5. **Barcarole** und **Scherzo** für Violine von *Spohr*, gespielt von Herrn **J. Joachim**.

6. **Lieder** für Frauenchor von *J. Brahms*;
   a) Minnelied von *Voss*.
   b) Der Bräutigam, von *Eichendorff*.
   c) Gesang aus Fingal, von *Ossian*, (mit Harfe und Hörnern.)

7. **Notturno** von *Chopin* und **Gavotte** von *Bach*, gespielt von Frau **Clara Schumann**.

Druck von J. J. S. Wörner jun.

Fig. 1 Announcement of a concert featuring Clara Schumann, Joseph Joachim, and Johannes Brahms on the same programme. Hamburg, 15 January 1861

❧ 1861 ❧

In outward appearance 1861 was not a remarkable year, apart from the fact that Brahms finally made the decision to live in the suburb of Hamm, away from his parents. That summer, in the house of Frau Dr Elisabeth Rösing, the aunt of Frauenchor members Betty and Marie Volkers, he rented a large room surrounded by a large garden; and here he created some of the works he is still best known for—the Piano Quartets in G Minor and A major (Opp. 25 and 26), and the *Variations and Fugue on a Theme by Handel* (Op. 24).

He gave a number of concerts in Hamburg: some with the assistance of his famous friends, who went out of their way to help him, and some with his Frauenchor. He appeared as piano soloist with the Hamburg Philharmonic, conducted that orchestra once with Joachim as soloist and again in a performance of his Second Serenade. He was living the life of an up-and-coming musician of Hamburg, but making no move to seek outside engagements except in the surrounding cities. And at last he found publishers for his piano concerto and other works which had long been finished.

139
Johannes Brahms to Melchior Rieter-Biedermann[1]

2 January 1860 [*recte*: 1861]

Most honoured Sir,

I send herewith the certificate of ownership and the revised proof sheets of my Concerto. It would probably be good if I could have another revision of the same thing, for, as you see, there are still quite a lot of mistakes in it and it is therefore doubly easy to overlook others. You will now inspect the engraving with a more expert eye than I.

For me the difference between the large and small notes is often not distinct enough. In the first movement, in particular, where I have expressly marked specific places (pp. 7, 10, 13 and the following ones).

If it seems so to you too, and if it is possible to change something, I presume you will do the rest.

Should I get another revision, I will attend to it very quickly, as I have also attended to this and the previous one.

I suppose I may soon expect my copies of the other things?

[1] This previously unpublished letter makes it clear that Brahms had to wait until early 1861 to see Opp. 12–15 in print; the date '2 January' explains why Brahms mistakenly wrote '1860' at the head of his letter in clear, bold numbers.

I should like to ask you to grant me 6 copies of the score and 3 of the piano score (6 of the songs), but on the other hand not to send *any* orchestral or choral parts.

In spite of all the treble clefs, I am looking forward to the works.[2]

I wish you a good new year a[nd] am, with sincere greetings

Your faithful

Johs Brahms

I forgot to transmit my thanks for the second money draft.

Brahms studied music constantly, and urged Clara, too, to widen her repertory. During an engagement in Detmold, she had the opportunity to hear two of Mozart's piano concertos for the first time.[3]

140
Johannes Brahms to Clara Schumann

Hamburg, Sunday morning, the 7th of February 1861

Your dear letter gave me great joy, best Clara, as did the enraptured words about the Mozart concertos. Indeed I knew very well that you would find them quite something to celebrate, and that's why I was annoyed that in the end you might leave Detmold without that.

How gladly I would have been there, one simply cannot experience greater joy than to have these concertos come to life. The mere reading of it is just no substitute. As if drawn from a genuine Fountain of Youth.

But unfortunately, one is actually alone in savouring the delight. The very same public that continually harks back to Mozart and derides modern formlessness relishes only the latter and is untouched by the former.

By all means keep the G major Concerto (if you have mine), I don't need it.[4]

Should you ever play one in public, choose the one in C minor. It is the most effective one and, after all, is still new to you.

Yesterday at Frau Petersen's, I played the G minor quartet by Mozart, also the Quartet by your Robert, among others.

---

[2] Referring to his *Begräbnisgesang* (see McC 41–2). In preparing the score, Rieter was unwilling to indulge Brahms's fondness for the old vocal 'C' clefs—for which a good many singers were undoubtedly grateful. Later, as Brahms grew more successful, he was able to have his way at least in the full scores.

[3] Litz, iii. 94.

[4] K. 453. The other works mentioned here: Mozart's C minor Concerto, K. 491; the Piano Quartet, K. 478; and Schumann's Piano Quartet in E flat major, Op. 47.

You will have gained some idea of how beguiling a post at this little Court is. One can really make a lot of music for oneself, but unfortunately one can't keep the fun inside forever, and so after a while one is disgusted by the faces. Indeed one could turn into a misanthrope!

Nature's beauties can be enjoyed on one's own, but when making music in a concert-hall and in front of people, one doesn't want to be alone then, too.

The Hanoverian honorarium would give me much pleasure if I knew that the passage—for services yet to be performed—were dictated merely by a certain prudence. Apart from that there's really not so much to it.[5]

If only you would write to me that you do indeed have the firm intention not to work more than you have need for, which means not to give *more* concerts than you need in order to manage. Have you given up England, then?

Surely you have enough money, it is much more practical and better for you to safeguard your health and your whole beautiful self.

This evening, i.e. right away, for the clock has in the mean time struck 7, I shall be with Bargheer at Avé's. Greet Marie warmly, and all the others, as though their names were written here.

Do write really soon, and think of me kindly.

Your

Johannes.

Clara accepted Brahms's advice regarding Mozart piano concertos, taking the C minor work into her repertory and performing it that next autumn in Leipzig and Hanover—but Brahms's personal remarks infuriated her and were the occasion of their first serious tiff.[6] She was, however, glad to have his advice (and Joachim's) in deciding which of Schumann's unpublished works to allow into print. Under discussion were the Mass for Four-Part Chorus with Orchestra and Requiem for Chorus and Orchestra, both composed in Düsseldorf, 1852.[7] Brahms, who was never an enthusiast of the metronome, gave Clara some interesting advice on this matter as well, a bit of practical wisdom from a 28-year-old musician.

---

[5] Clara had received the considerable sum of 100 louis d'or from the King of Hanover, with a note saying that the money was for performances dating from 1859, as well as for those that were to come. 'What do you make of that? What are my obligations, now? Have I been done a favour or not?' she asked Brahms.

[6] See Reich, 205.   [7] They were eventually published as Op. Posth. 147 and 148.

141
Johannes Brahms to Clara Schumann

Hamburg, Thursday, 25 April 1861

Dearest Clara,

Requiem and Mass from you and Rieter have reached me. Now that I have them here, there are still a few things I must ask you about. Since you are in Berlin anyway, do check if the vocal parts at least are available, as I believe. For the Mass, probably the orchestral parts as well, for of course it was done in Düsseldorf. Then you could simply send these to Cologne— unless perhaps you want to ask Stern beforehand—for Cologne is not the most agreeable place for it, in spite of Hiller. Then one of the piano scores could well be sent there right away, it is replaceable, if necessary, could how- ever also be copied first, if you wish.[8]

About the proposed metronomization we have already once spoken at length. So you want to do it even so?

I consider it impossible as well as unnecessary; just as I also believe less in Schumann's faulty metronome than in the uncertainty of making a decision.[9]

Worse yet, to provide metronome markings to some dozens of works now, as you wish, does not seem possible to me.

In any case, you will naturally set the work aside for at least a year and scrutinize it from time to time. Then you will mark them with fresh num- bers each time and finally will have the best selection. Consider carefully, too, that one cannot arrange performances of choral and orchestra works for oneself just for this purpose—and on the piano, because of the lighter sound, everything is played decidedly livelier, faster, also is more forgiving in tempo.

I advise you to stay clear of it, for intelligent people will pay little atten- tion to your painstaking labour and will not use it.

---

[8] Julius Stern, founder and director in Berlin of the Stern'scher Gesangverein, an organization known for its high level of choral performances: Stern gave Mendelssohn's *Elijah* its première. In the event, the Mass was performed later that summer by Franz Wüllner, a performance which dis- pelled any doubt Clara might have had about publishing it. Litz, iii. 107. See also Brahms to Wüllner, *BW* xv. 40–1. In all likelihood that letter is incorrectly dated and should be placed in Hamburg, [June] 1861, in keeping with this letter to Clara.

[9] 'Ich halte es sowohl unmöglich als unnötig; wie ich auch weniger an Schumanns falsches Metronom glaube, als an die Unsicherheit der Bestimmung.' There was some talk that Schumann's imperfect metronome markings were the result of a faulty metronome. Brahms was clearly not convinced. He didn't trust the way Schumann or anyone else came to make his decision, and was dubious about the whole process.

Until Tuesday evening I had actually hoped for you; you would have heard quite a lot here these days. The Cherubini Requiem, really beautiful.

Now I impart to you in a very low voice that on Sunday evening Stockhausen is repeating the *Schöne Müllerin* (a real delight), and that I'm rehearsing my 2nd Serenade on Monday at 2 o'clock. On Tuesday we have a concert together, in which the *entire Dichterliebe* will be sung by Stockhausen!!!

Now then, since I'm giving the concert with him, but really neither need nor desire the income, I'd like nothing better than for it go to lodge my dearest lady friend for a few days in Hamburg, that would be quite splendid.

I even believe I could possibly drum up my *Grabgesang* and would be pleased to have it played just for you. Still in regard to the metronome markings, I note that, by and large, I have the complete works of R. Schumann and would gladly give you a hand with the work. In any case, it is better done in company.

Stockhausen sings marvellously, and I beg you to consider that he will sing the complete *Müller* Lieder on Saturday, and on Tuesday the entire *Dichterliebe*, and will sing both very beautifully.

2nd Serenade, *Grabgesang* and new canons and wonderful old things by my Frauenchor as well. The new flat in Berlin can surely wait a little longer.[10]

Julie has written me a charming little letter.

I must close.

However, you missed the most magnificent event of last Tuesday, a cantata by Bach, where with the first note one felt oneself transported to heavenly heights. In any case you ought to come, when beckoned from Hamburg. Will you do it this once?

But the time! Where does mine go in the midst of this turmoil!

Warm greetings from me, to the little ones too, and the big Marie and Frl. Werner, also artists, when you see them, Radecke, Lührsz.

Utterly yours,
Johannes

It occurs to me that it is my birthday in a week. How lovely it would be if you were here then; during that time we could write a heap of numbers ($\rho = 56$) into your Robert's works![11]

---

[10] Clara had moved again, and needed to settle in. Litz, iii. 102.

[11] The Greek letter 'rho'. How did Brahms come to use this symbol? In the numbering system used in classical Greek, letters stand for numbers, and $\rho = 100$. There is no indication that this information was in common usage, but he assumed Clara would understand the principle. See also Letter 38, and the use Brahms made of the letter β (Beta), and its value of 2.

This concert by Brahms and Stockhausen was a historic event, the first complete performance of Schumann's *Dichterliebe*.[12]

More works were ready for publication.

142

Johannes Brahms to J. P. Simrock

[Hamm near Hamburg,] July 1861

Most honoured Sir and friend,

Forgive me for failing to answer your esteemed letter for quite some time.

As a consequence I do not feel the need to start my letter with an 'if' or a 'but' but can do so right away as follows:

Should your lovely publishing house wish to accept some of my works once more, I am able to send:

Op. 18, a sextet for strings, which you have presumably heard last winter in Leipzig. This one, together with a good 4-hand arrangement by myself, comes to 16 Friedrichdors.[13]

Furthermore, perhaps a volume of songs and a volume of duets for soprano and alto with piano, each one at 10 Friedrichdors.

True, there are only 3 duets, but I just don't want to include any others and I envisage earning 10 Fr. for them. They must also be published individually, and I believe they will be bought. However, should you not entirely trust my gift of prophesy, I would also accept 8 Fr. Accordingly I request your kind reply as to whether these 3 *opera* would suit you.

Herr Dietrich visited me recently and on that occasion, Herr Cranz took on a trio and a cello sonata by him.[14]

I was, as usual, delighted with his great talent and skill and I was surprised that one had not done more on the Rhine to hold on to him. I should think it would be easy to hold on to someone there.

---

[12] Some time before, in Vienna, Stockhausen gave the first complete *Schöne Müllerin*. Stockhausen's practice of performing complete song cycles in recital set the precedent for future Lieder singers—a great number of whom were his pupils.

[13] 'You arranged it to be wonderfully playable and to sound well,' Joachim wrote to Brahms in a letter (15 Oct. 1861), and commented that even he and Bernhard Scholz could play it with relative fluency.

[14] August Cranz was the Hamburg publisher whom Brahms had known since childhood. Quite likely Brahms was already able to use his influence to help his friend Albert Dietrich, who had recently left his position as city music director in Bonn and moved to Oldenburg, in order to escape interference from the eleven members of the city council, referred to later in the letter.

Indeed, 11 concert directors, as you write, are bad business for a music director.

Should you so desire, more works are gladly at your disposal, e.g. variations for piano, motets, and songs for chorus, some of which you may possibly have heard at Frau Dr Frege's.

My address at the moment is Hamburg, Ham, Schwarze Straße, at Frau Dr Roesing's.

With sincere greetings,
your devoted,
Johs. Brahms.

143
Johannes Brahms to J. P. Simrock

[Hamm nr. Hamburg,] July 1861

Honoured Friend,

Enclosed the pieces discussed and promised. I think you will be satisfied with my precision. All misgivings, which exhibit themselves twice as powerfully at this moment of decision, I chase off and dispatch.

In general I request, should that be necessary, that no repeats (or verses in songs) be engraved unless they are written out in the manuscript; or at the least, to ask me.

Whether you want a full score of the sextet I leave entirely to you, but please let me know because I am asked repeatedly and indeed ask it myself.

This not essential, since the 4-hand arrangement replaces it to some extent. I am sending my own score to you, with a view to correcting the proofs, but request its return after that. NB.

For the time being, I request one set of parts of the sextet in due course, but of the arrangement and the remaining things, the customary 6.

I include 2 volumes of variations which are not very difficult, not nearly as difficult as previous pieces by me. You may not want to make that judgement from the poor manuscript. I have had them played several times by lady students, and found that they are exceedingly playable, even by amateurs.[15]

I would want 16 Friedrichdors for both volumes, and in the event that the work does not suit you, you'll surely have the kindness to return them very soon.

---

[15] Brahms either had very talented students, or was an exceptionally good teacher, or had a powerful imagination.

You probably send complimentary copies to editors of music journals? Herr Bagge, for instance, has expressed the wish that I encourage my esteemed publishers to do so. For us composers this is naturally very desirable, and I would think that the interest of the publisher must demand it as well.

You will undoubtedly have proofs of the work sent to me?

And so may everything arrive in the best of shape and meet with the best of approval.

With sincere greetings,

Your honestly devoted

Johs. Brahms

Simrock accepted the Variations for Piano, Op. 21 No. 1 and 2, along with the Sextet in B flat, Op. 18, *Five Poems*, Op. 19, and *Three Duets* for Soprano and Alto, Op. 20. A score for the Sextet was printed in addition to the four-hand arrangement, perhaps thanks to the keen interest of Fritz Simrock, son of the publisher. The young Simrock was already an enthusiast of Brahms's music, a point of view which eventually made him a rich man.

The other works referred to in the previous letter had to wait a few years before being published.[16]

Feeling somewhat isolated and in need of musical stimulation, Brahms reported to Joachim on his latest compositions.

144

Johannes Brahms to Joseph Joachim

On Sunday evening [September 1861]

My best friend,

I live only half a life since I live it so completely without you.

Not enough that I don't see you, I haven't even seen your handwriting for a year and a day.

I can't bear that any longer.

You must write me a letter, I would also like to see the music which I hear has been written.[17]

---

[16] Op. 29, *Two Motets* for 5-part mixed chorus a capella (Breitkopf & Härtel, 1864); the choral songs are probably *Twelve Songs and Romances* for Women's chorus a capella, Op. 44 (Rieter-Biedermann, 1866).

[17] Joachim's Violin Concerto in G major, occasionally performed by him but not published for several decades. Moser, *Joseph Joachim*, 164.

If I had anything I could trust to really please you, I'd enclose it immediately, but naturally you might also have an assortment of things.

Which one should make a start? My Sextet I sent off to Simrock long ago, reluctantly and with a pounding heart. Even now I have the most troubling concern at not having sent it to you beforehand, as I had intended. I thought you'd be loathe to see my things. Would you have had anything to remind me about? There's still time when the proofs are revised.

I'm looking forward eagerly to seeing new music from you, be it ever so little. I now live very cosily (at the moment of course I miss having the stove, and therefore sneeze several dozen times a day), also I'm stuck fast to various threads (none pink-coloured), otherwise I would be off and away. But this winter I'm definitely off.

Grädeners's plan to go to Vienna reached a dead end today. He'll have to get used to us again, and put up with us. That will require several more glasses of *grog*. I am really sorry on his account.

Otten is doing the great Mass to which (the performance, I mean) I hope you won't come, as talk around here has it. Be sure not to; for it will be dreadful.[18]

Dearest friend, can't we start a course of study again? To send one another contrapuntal things regularly, waltzes, variations, and any other stuff there is to do that might be useful?

Indeed it's also particularly good for my temperament, which otherwise gets nothing done because of my indolence and day-dreaming.

But mostly so that I'd have to hear from you, I cannot do without that.

My warmest greetings. They shouldn't be so long in coming, again.

Your Johannes.

Ham, Schwarze Straße, at Fr. Dr Rösing's, Hamburg

I am including a few things after all, which I request back in a week, however; if possible let me have a word even before that, then another one later on.

What the 'dreamy and indolent' Johannes sent Joachim was a portion of the summer's output: the Piano Quartets in G minor and A major, Opps. 25 and 26. Joachim was deeply impressed with these latest works. He told Brahms he hoped to hear them before saying more, feeling sure that with time, he would get used to the passages he had not quite digested. Since Clara Schumann was just then passing through Hanover, Joachim wondered if he might give her the quartets to take with her.

[18] Probably the *Missa Solemnis* of Beethoven, which has a violin solo in the Benedictus, and which was revered by Joachim and Brahms.

145
Johannes Brahms to Joseph Joachim

[Hamm near Hamburg, 3 October 1861]

Dear friend,

I do request my quartets sent here.

Your letter is much too kind, I kept on shaking my head over it. Just let me have a few NBs and don't wait to hear it and certainly not 'to get used to it'.

You will probably have seen, with a few sighs, that my Sextet is already in print. It's true, if I had waited longer it might perhaps have become better, but waiting also has its detrimental aspects.

So now I shall send my Marienlieder to Rieter, and while at one time it gave me pleasure to hear them, now I look at them as upon a blank sheet of paper, don't want to send them off, couldn't do otherwise with them, in brief, I wish I were rid of them.[19]

Whether I am likely to get music from you? That would be wonderful.

When returning it I'll again enclose something.

Frau Schumann will probably give concerts again here and in Altona. Should we invite you to take part, or rather not?

I can't frank the letter here in Hamm and am not coming to town today; excuse that and also excuse the opening of this letter being upside down.

I don't suppose you would still be game now to go hiking in the Harz for a week? That lovely autumn haze beckons.

Frau Schumann won't come for 2 weeks, and it would really be splendid.

Well then, more soon, dear fellow.

Your Johannes.

The indolent Brahms had also made a start on a number of important works which would be finished over the course of the next few years, had prepared the *Seven Marienlieder* for Mixed a Capella Choir, Op. 22, for publication, and finished the *Variations on a Theme by Handel* for Piano, Op. 24, which he wrote with Clara in mind. He was anxious to arrange performances of his new works in Hamburg, and especially insistent that Clara be involved—at his expense.

---

[19] *Seven Marienlieder* for Mixed Chorus, Op. 22.

146
Johannes Brahms to Clara Schumann

Ham near Hamburg, Friday morning, the 11th October 1861

Dearest and best Clara,

Your letter has just reached me and I can tell you that it does not sit well with me at all. My hasty letter-writing and bashful way of glossing over money matters is much to blame, of course. Therefore I will try today to employ a measure of clarity in order to put an end to the matter.

In everything which concerns me, you have been and you will be as if I am yours entirely, and in everything which concerns you, I am not permitted to be anything to you.

Had I no money, I would stay with you, had I a house, wouldn't you also live with me? However, I do now have this purse full of useless money, which out of sheer annoyance I shall soon cut to pieces (government bonds), simply because it is of no use to me where it might be, for once, namely, e.g., here.

I assure you, I shall be horribly annoyed if you and Julie will not be my guests here.

If you don't do it, I shall throw my money out of the window in 4 weeks, what use is all that trash to me, anyway?

But now I also want to set forth much gentler reasons.

As the first: I would make my landlady here utterly blissful if I relinquished my room to you for the duration, I never mentioned anything about it for I wouldn't want to obligate you to an unknown person in any way.[20]

In that case I would have taken other lodgings and in this way paid for you, for I pay absurdly little here and must consider it a real kindness of Frau Dr Rösing that she takes any money at all for the cheerfully relinquished room.

2. Now, following your awful letter, I would go and visit you in Berlin straightaway, were it not for two imminent concerts of Grädener's to which I have agreed.

But if you don't now come instantly, I will be there within the next few days and will on no account stay with you but instead will rent horrendously expensive quarters for myself and travel here to each of the Grädener concerts by first class and each day will bring you the most expensive present, simply in order to annoy you and to prove to you how dear I hold my money, since it is of so much use to me with you. After that you'll readily agree that

[20] Frau Dr Elisabeth Rösing, Betty and Marie Volker's aunt, the cultivated and sympathetic owner of the house where Brahms rented a large room. He dedicated his Piano Quartet, Op. 26, to her in gratitude.

I would have got off 10 times more cheaply with two guests here.

3. it is pleasanter here than in Berlin, but that makes no difference to me because there is much I can hear in Berlin, and by squandering a sufficient amount I can have plenty of fun.

4. I have written variations for your birthday which you still haven't heard yet, and which you should have prepared for your concerts long ago.

6. [!] I intend to rehearse my Quartets here and won't lift a finger if you don't come.

7. it would be dastardly of you if immediately upon receipt of this, you did not write me a confirmation for the 200 tlr. received, and squander them here.

8. otherwise I'll travel to Berlin tomorrow and squander everything.

9. *da capo.*

10. Hanover and Oldenburg is the least of what I promise myself of this reunion, for I want to be able to have a look at you at leisure and then at the end, go on a little trip with you.

And indeed, you must be here on Sunday, Sunday morning. For on Monday you may *possibly* miss me, and if you come on Sunday we'll be together in Sachsenwald, etc, you'll like it.

Good Lord, I think Tuesday is a Grädener concert, in short, we must have the Sunday first, otherwise the story has no beginning.

But the only thing I know for sure is that there will be trouble if on Sunday I don't play my little variations for you, here or in Berlin.

Shameful, Bargiel snapped them up in September already, and you, whose name is on the title-page, pay no attention to them at all.

So, in short, do you want my money? Or do I toss it away so that you see it glitter.

But in all friendship, I am coming to Berlin most amicably, must merely ask how it is with Grädener and then will come here with you, and to Hanover and Oldenburg.

Your concerts here, and I am thinking of 2 here and 1 in Altona, will come off well, you'll see, it's not that bad. You'll surely earn enough.

At any rate you must write a line or telegraph this very minute, for otherwise I'll bundle myself off to the railway.

Are you always able to read my crow's scratches? If not, order me to write more slowly. So then, in the firm expectation that for once you will be good as an angel and take my money, there awaits for 2 more days

Your

faithful

Johannes

By way of a post script, I repeat that I really can come to Berlin, but if you then go to Dresden or Leipzig, that does no good. Can't you postpone the concerts and give concerts here at that time? with regard to the Philharmonic, it's no problem to give an additional concert. There really are more possibilities here than elsewhere.

In short, think it over and decide quickly, and be an angel in any case.

You would do better to telegraph, since I can't know when the Grädener rehearsals will keep me from home; then I'll take care of making things pleasant.

If you came on Monday, it would be just as good as Sunday, of course.

In the aftermath of this letter, Clara, with daughter Julie, spent almost a month in Hamburg and gave first performances of the Piano Quartet in G minor and of the *Variations on a Theme by Handel*, the manuscript of which (but not the published version) bore the dedication 'für eine liebe Freundin'. [21]

❧ 1862 ☙

In spite of the best efforts of his champions and close friends, Brahms's Hamburg career was proceeding only modestly. True, he had some local engagements in the surrounding areas. His old friend Dietrich had recently moved to Oldenburg which, like Detmold, was a small, independent Duchy with a music-loving Archduke. The charming little opera-house built at that time is still in use.

147
Johannes Brahms to Albert Dietrich[1]

Hanover, [January] 1862

Dear Friend,

I've been here for some time now and received your letter only by way of Hamburg.

Tomorrow I'm going back and I just want to write a few words in all haste.

[21] The Quartet was premièred on 16 November, the Variations on 7 December. Clara wrote to her eldest daughter, Marie: 'Johannes has written marvellous things, and Variations which have quite enchanted me, full of genius, and closing with a fugue.' There are several descriptions of this visit: see Litz, iii. 110–11; Hübbe, *Brahms in Hamburg*, 42–4; May, i. 290–1; Kal, i. 463–4.

[1] Details of this and other letters to Dietrich are given in Appendix D. It should be noted here that Dietrich was not always able to date his letters correctly, and that the letters published in his memoir are often shortened and imperfectly transcribed.

I am much drawn to visiting you and to getting to know some [people] whose names I have heard in such a friendly way for some time now, otherwise I would say No.

I'm coming and will see how much loafing about I can permit myself by then.

What shall I play? Beethoven or Mozart? C minor, A major or G major? Advise!

And for the 2nd, Schumann, Bach, or may I also venture new Variations by me?

My Serenade you will conduct, of course. We have played my quartets a good deal, here; I'm bringing them with me and would be delighted if they sounded pleasantly to you and to others.

I shall probably speak with Seppe in Hamburg.[2] Apropos an honorarium: I must have something like 15 Louis, but would like to have it arranged beforehand that, should I happen to play at Court, this would be paid separately! You will find this concern understandable. The matter of an honorarium is the concern of the Office of the Director, why should I donate money to it that I really need, *pro sec[undo]*: my time is precious to me and I let myself be lured to concerts with reluctance, but if so, then the *other*, also.

Write to me to Hamburg, Ham, Schwarze Straße, Dr Rösing.

More soon, and excuse the rush.

Warmly your
Johannes.

Greet the wife.
a[nd] M.J.K.[3]

148

Johannes Brahms to Albert Dietrich

[Hamm near Hamburg, March 1862]

Dear Friend,

If I can arrange it, I'll leave here on Monday evening and travel to you by hackney coach, by way of Bremen. Is that in fact the practical way? And will

---

² 'Seppe' is one of several standard nicknames for Joseph, so presumably this refers to Joachim.
³ Max Hermann Karl, here referred to as M[ax] J[ohannes] K[arl]: Dietrich's first child, and one of Brahms's godchildren. But the Dietrichs omitted 'Johannes', when they named the boy; Brahms often called him by his entire name, thereby teasing his parents about their negligence. Their next child, Clara, he usually called by the elaborate name of Thusnelda Maria Theresia. When Dietrich published the letter in his Memoir, he wrote the initials *M u. C* in this place, presumably standing for the initials of both of his children, for reasons of his own.

I then arrive in time for the Tuesday rehearsal? What is the connection to Oldenburg like? Does one simply transfer to another coach?

So, I shall play the G major Concerto by Beethoven. Do you have parts? I may own them or can manage to get them if that is not possible. With regard to the second number there's plenty of time, my memory permits me a great deal and the fingers will keep up well enough.

I suppose that Seppe will come to the concert. However I shall have to return promptly, for I promised young Auer I would play in his concert which is coming up soon.[4]

My Second Serenade was recently performed in Neu York [sic]. As far as I know, the first performance anywhere since the things were printed!

Here in Ham it is very beautiful, and if I don't look out of the window at the bare trees I can believe it is summer, so merrily does the sunlight dance about inside the room.

Do write a line to me regarding the journey and Tuesday.

Greet your wife and the little ones.

Affectionately,

Your

Johannes.

Brahms's published works did not always have the kind of success his publishers wished for.

149
Johannes Brahms to Breitkopf & Härtel

[Hamm near Hamburg 25 March '62]

Most esteemed gentlemenn!

Since I am in the process of publishing a new work which is particularly dear to me, I do not want to neglect to offer it to you for publication.

They are 24 Variations and Fugue on a Theme by Händel (op. 22 and price 15 Friedrichdors).[5] Perhaps you have become acquainted with them through a performance of Frau Dr Schumann.

---

[4] The violinist Leopold Auer (1845–1930) was a student of Joachim, who took a lively interest in his career and is undoubtedly the person responsible for securing Brahms's participation in this concert. Auer went on to a career as one of the most important violin teachers in modern times, first in Europe, and then in America. His students included Mischa Elman, Ephram Zimbalist, and Jascha Heifetz.

[5] The opus number was changed later.

I would take the liberty of sending you enquiries of this kind more frequently, were it not that modest reticence in a youthful composer is natural, in view of the splendid, fine activity of your firm, and that doubly so with me who, moreover, harbours the fear that you may have all too little confidence in my talent.

Should I be mistaken in this, and should it by chance be suitable and agreeable to you, and were I now and then simply to notify you of works ready to be printed, that would naturally give me particular pleasure.

I request that you kindly address your answer:

Ham (near Hamburg),

Schwarze Straße at Frau Dr Rösing's.

However, for the lexicon which you intend to publish I request that you use, in case you desire a more precise address, my usual one in Hamburg, Fuhlentwiete 74.

Looking forward to your kind answer, I remain with particular respect,

Your devoted

Johs Brahms

Breitkopf & Härtel expressed themselves happy to hear from Brahms, greatly interested in and willing to consider all offerings, but unable to hide the disappointing sales of his works so far. They bemoaned the recent state of music publishing, and wondered how many engraved plates the Variations would require. After seeing the manuscript they returned it with regrets; Brahms was asking far too much money, they would have to sell 1,000 copies just to recover their costs, and '—we mean you no harm in saying so—but of that there is no chance'.

Brahms was anxious to see his Variations in print at the same time as the group of works being published by Simrock,[6] fearing that otherwise they would 'go out into the world rather lonely', as he wrote to Breitkopf. And he was quite determined that only Breitkopf, the premier German music publisher, should publish this piece of which, in a manner most uncharacteristic for him, he was so proud.

150
Johannes Brahms to Breitkopf & Härtel

[Ham near Hamburg, 14 April 1862]

Most esteemed gentlemen:

Once again I take the liberty of writing to you regarding my 'Variations'. I would not so quickly like to relinquish my wish to see this, my favourite

---

[6] The Harp Songs, Sextet in B flat, *Five Poems, Seven Marienlieder*, Opp. 17, 18, 19, 22.

work, published by you. Therefore, if it is primarily the high honorarium that prevents you from taking on the work, I will be pleased to let you have it for 12 Friedrichsdors or, in case this also seems altogether too high, for 10 Friedrichdors.

I hope very much you do not conclude that I chose the initial honorarium quite arbitrarily.

I consider this work to be much better than my earlier ones, and also more practical and therefore easier to distribute, so that with this in mind, I judged the honorarium I requested to be quite appropriate.

In my copy of the *Beethoven* Sonata, particular attention should be paid to a *piu moto* which there indicates the correct place, even if only by a series of dashes, while in the new Original Edition it appears very decidedly and disagreeably in the wrong place.[7]

Looking forward to your kind reply

with the greatest esteem,

faithfully

Johs Brahms

Breitkopf agreed to Brahms's lowest bid, and paid him 10 Friedrichsdors.

151

Johannes Brahms to Melchior Rieter-Biedermann

[Hamburg, 28 May 1862]

Dear Sir!

Your esteemed letter of the 6th did not reach me until the 25th, in spite of 'Urgent' on it; I suspect it must have come by way of a local music dealer.

I just cannot consider a 4-hand arrangement of my 'Concerto' practical. It would be enormously difficult to play no matter how much one wished to water down the content, yet would sound incomprehensible and unclear.

I must definitely presume that Mr *Köhler* had an arrangement for 2 pianos in mind, and there of course, I must readily admit that it would have been very practical if I had originally published it in such a way that one could play the orchestra accompaniment on a 2nd piano, always, to be sure, with the assistance of the soloist; and that is why, unfortunately, it is not so easy to make up for the missed opportunity.

Perhaps sometime one might publish the Adagio by itself in this

---

[7] Op. 110. In possession of a copy with corrections in Beethoven's hand, Brahms had offered it to Breitkopf for use in preparing their complete edition.

manner, and should the work receive some recognition, you will know whether you could risk publishing it in its entirety in such an edition.

I have just now received another letter from you and learn, to my pleasure, that the Reverend *Oser* is not offended, and furthermore, that you like my 'Sextet' and indeed, that I shall be parading at the grand Exhibition.[8]

Concerning the 4-hand arrangement, I can think of no better advice than just to let it be.

A *Beethoven* Concerto also could not be arranged for 4-hands; otherwise we would have had one long ago.[9]

With the warmest greetings

Your devoted

Johs Brahms

Your last letter was written in Winterthur and sent from Leipzig! I don't quite know whither the answer.

For some time and for various reasons Brahms had been planning to visit Vienna.

For one thing, Clara had long urged him to give concerts in a city where she herself had had great success. She was quite convinced that Hamburg was no place for Johannes to make his career. Joachim, too, was in favour of a Viennese visit, and on two occasions he and Brahms had even made tentative plans to give joint concerts there. Eduard Marxsen had studied there, Carl Grädener had just settled there. Bertha Porubsky had returned home there, her charms presumably not entirely forgotten, and a newer attraction now beckoned—Luise Meyer-Dustmann, chamber singer at Court and prima donna at the Court Opera in Vienna (Plate 20).

Brahms met her at the 38th Festival of the Lower Rhine, June 1862, and appears to have been powerfully impressed by her voice and her capabilities, to say the very least. Hard information is lacking, but Kalbeck, without ever being specific, alludes quite plainly to a liaison between them during Brahms's early years in Vienna, and informs us that Frau Dustmann was the only person ever known to get away with addressing him as 'Hansi'. In the course of time, she would introduce a number of his songs to the world. She would also create the role of *Isolde* for the first Viennese performance of *Tristan*, thereby winning Wagner's appreciation of her 'soulful voice and complete mastery of her role'.[10]

---

[8] His music was exhibited in London.

[9] Brahms was in error here, as a four-hand arrangement of Beethoven's Fourth Piano Concerto had been published in 1856. In any event, he changed his mind a few years later when he needed money. See Letter 177.

[10] R. W. Gutman *Richard Wagner: The Man, his Mind, and his Music* (New York, 1990). There is probably more to this story than we know. For example, Dustmann spent a holiday in Tutzing at the time Brahms was there in 1872, and then in Pörtschach during the summer of 1878, when Brahms was there—long before either location was a famous watering place. Brahms looked out for her interests on several known occasions, writing to Bernhard Scholz to hire her in Breslau

There is no evidence that Brahms's journey to Vienna was conceived as anything other than a short visit. Regardless of what Clara thought of the suitability of making his career in Hamburg, Brahms seems to have had every intention of doing just that. As he set out, he had reason to believe he would soon be appointed to the post of associate conductor of the Hamburg Sing-Akademie, the choral society which was sister to the Hamburg Philharmonic; and there are many reasons to suppose that he had hopes—albeit silent ones—that the appointment would eventually lead to the position of music director of both organizations. Their ageing director was retiring at last, and Brahms's hopes were based on the the fact that Avé-Lallement, his influential friend and champion, who sat on the both committees, had him in mind for the Sing-Akademie, once Wilhelm Grund was gone.

It was therefore an untroubled, adventurous Brahms who left for Vienna.

152
Johannes Brahms to Albert Dietrich

[Beginning of September, 1862]

Dear friend,

Your letter was doubly welcome, since I had heard about the peacock story, greatly enlarged, by way of Cohnitz-Apel-Bartels. I did not even want to ask you about it for I had feared something much worse than had in fact occurred.[11]

So, on Monday I'm off *to Vienna*! I am looking forward to it like a child. How long I'll stay, I don't know, of course, we'll see what happens and hope to see each other sometime during the winter.

The Symphony is not yet ready, unlike a string quintet (2 V-cellos) in F minor, which I would really like to send you and get you to write about it to me, but I suppose I had better just take it with me.

In due course.

Enclosed are my Handel Variations; the *Marienlieder* are not here yet.

The title-page for your Trio is still not finished.

I enclose the trio by Meinardus. I would like to ask Franz about it, but I find the fellow too repulsive, I can't do it.[12] Give my greetings to the Oldenburg Meinardus, in fact to all the friends there.

when it was obvious her voice was past its prime and she needed help to find engagements. There are occasional mentions of him visiting her flat in the 1870s and 1880s, and she was on the list of those who received complimentary copies of his music from Simrock. Whatever the nature of their friendship, it lasted a long time.

[11] One would like to know more about this peacock. But Dietrich is surely the only person who could have shed the necessary light, and in his Memoir he suppressed this paragraph and the one dealing with Bargiel, below.   [12] The composers Robert Franz and Ludwig Meinardus.

I am enclosing Bargiel's letter. Indeed that's the same condition, what can be done about it? A letter is surely the most useless thing in the world (a reply is not!). I could only recommend physical exercises and a few other things to him, but he wouldn't do them anyway. This will continue for a little while and then off into the institution. Should one write to his mother?[13]

I beg you not to leave me utterly without letters. You could occasionally write through Haslinger, or Wessely and Büsing.[14]

How should Jos. Salwizki's [?] name and title be written on a title-page?

Meanwhile, dear Albert, the warmest farewell to you and your wife.

Your
Johannes.

A substantial part of the first movement of Brahms's First Symphony was already in existence in the summer of 1862, when Brahms was on holiday with Dietrich and Clara Schumann; both friends saw the manuscript. They and his publisher would have another fourteen years to wait before the work was complete, but in the mean time the news aroused considerable interest. This letter also contains the first mention of the eventual Piano Quintet, Op. 34, in its first incarnation as a work for two violins, viola, and two cellos.

Although Brahms was kept very busy in Vienna, he missed his friends.

153
Johannes Brahms to Julius Otto Grimm

[Vienna, November 1862]

Dear Friend,

On the very day of my departure from Hbg. for here your letter with the picture arrived and just at that moment pleased me twice as much. Only now do I find the time to send you a hurried, but warm greeting (and since I can find no paper, I have to tear off the excess page from another letter).

Yes, so it goes! I have settled in, I live here ten paces from the Prater, and can drink my wine where Beethoven drank his. It is also quite jolly and pretty here, so that it really couldn't be any better. Of course, to wander about in the Black Forest with a wife as you do is not only jollier, but more beautiful, too.

---

[13] Woldemar Bargiel, half-brother to Clara Schumann, was apparently suffering from what one would now call a nervous breakdown—from which he recovered. To Brahms, the symptoms seemed no different from Schumann's illness. When Brahms wondered about telling his mother, he was speaking of Clara's mother. Brahms was shaken to find Dietrich himself suffering a breakdown not long after. He too recovered.

[14] Music shops in Vienna.

I wanted to mention, in all haste, that you cannot have the quartets you wanted as I have to send them off to Simrock next week.

On the other hand I will shortly have the printed *Marienlieder* sent to you and hope you will have them sung for you. I don't know whether you have the recently printed variations, duets (3 volumes), songs, but I don't have them here. But I do promise you the 4-hand Variations which I am sending to Rieter shortly.[15]

Meanwhile, I must be satisfied with sending you this hurried greeting, but hope that you are not too lazy to write, I'm not, for I miss my friends too much. Your picture gave me great pleasure; unfortunately I don't have a better one of myself as thanks.

Greet your wife for me, the little ones, Bargheer, and whatever else may wish to be greeted.

Jägerzeile, Novaragasse 39, II, 2.

That's where I beg you to address something very soon

to your friend

Johannes Br.

Joachim wrote from England, intrigued by rumours of a symphony.

You would give me genuine proof of your unchanged attitude if you were to let me know something of your symphony; Frau Schumann recently wrote to me about the 1st movement. . . . You were right to warn me about going to London (for the summer). However many attractions the city may have, it holds true for concerts that if you give the devil a hair, he'll soon have your hide (if you want to earn money). I have all I can do to believe again in nature and genuine art, or at least to overcome a certain disgust at playing here and there, after my concert-hall experiences.[16]

154

Johannes Brahms to Joseph Joachim

[Vienna, end of September 1862]

Dear Joseph,

Well, whoever really wants to make money is surely owned by the devil, hide and hair. I know of nothing further at all to ask or say about that. That

[15] *Variations for Piano four-hands on a Theme by Robert Schumann*, Op. 23. It appeared in print in April, 1863. The other works mentioned in this letter are *Marienlieder*, Op. 22, for mixed a capella chorus, *Three Duets*, Op. 20, *Variations on an Original Theme* for Piano, Op. 21 No. 1, No. 2 *On a Hungarian Theme*, and the Piano Quartets, Opp. 25 and 26.

[16] 19 September, *BW* v.

one can with some effort overcome a certain revulsion to Certain Matters I cannot comprehend, I could never manage that with regard to all sorts of things.

I have been in Vienna for almost 2 weeks and so your letter reached me too late to still have allowed me to reply to England. A speedy reply was meanwhile not so essential, since for the time being you may put a ? after 'Sym. by J. B.'. On the other hand, I do want to send you something, to which you can add whatever comments you like.[17]

As evidence of unchanged attitude, which is never necessary, you may gather from this that the enclosed quintet has no wish whatsoever to go out into the world before you haven't seen it. [sic].

But naturally I do hope that you have time these days to look at it so that I have it back as soon as possible and know what you think of it.

Should you actually have the wish to make it ring out, I ask you to have it copied at my expense. Only, I really beg you urgently to speed it up in that case too, so that I can have it back soon and hear of its effect.

In that case, I would also have to ask you to make appropriate corrections to the bowings and double stops and whatever you want. Naturally, whatever you do suits me.

Here I sit somewhat homesick for Hamburg after all. If the powers that be would only provide a person with a little more musical activity there so one didn't lie about quite so lazily, hear nothing sensible, and have absolutely nothing sensible to do, then I wouldn't leave to go elsewhere to do my ears, at least, some good.

I couldn't resist starting a collection of visiting cards and ask you for your photograph (à la Vienna). I saw very beautiful ones from England; do you have any of those?

My address is; Jägerzeile, Novaragasse 29, 2nd stairway, 2nd floor. Let me hear a word from you really soon, and give greetings to Scholz, your quartet, and other friends from

your

Johannes

Additional
Note p. 750 Brahms was uncomfortable with Joachim's frequent need for reassurance about their friendship, something he confided to his friend Gustav Wendt many years later.[18] *

In any case, Brahms's letter was ill-fated. He replied to Hanover, but since Joachim remained in England for much longer than intended, neither the letter nor

---

[17] i.e. the quintet he mentioned to Dietrich.

[18] In Thun, Switzerland, where both men were on holiday. Gustav Wendt, *Lebenserinnerungen eines Schulmanns* (Berlin, 1909), 157.

the manuscript of the Quintet reached Joachim, whose mail was not being forwarded in spite of repeated requests to his servant and to his colleague. Brahms had
no way of knowing any of this; far away in Vienna, trying to make a good impression by presenting his best new compositions, he knew only that there was no word
from Joachim and no news of his latest creation. He lost his temper.

155

Johannes Brahms to Joseph Joachim

[Vienna, mid-October? 1862]

Dear Friend,

It must now be four weeks since I sent you a quintet, so I think it's time
for me to enquire what has happened to it.

I thought even at that time that you would be very busy in Hanover and
would demand peace and quiet above all, I would therefore not have sent it
to you if you hadn't written to ask about the symphony.

Therefore don't feel in the least embarrassed, but simply have Rabe[19]
wrap it up and bring it to the post office. In the mean time, I would like very
much to try it out here and all the while will be looking forward to hearing
you play it, some day.

In Hellmesberger's 1st quartet [concert] I am playing mine in G minor
(the choice was made by the members).

Also, everyone is urging that I give a concert of my own, besides; in the
long run, this may really happen.

In about a week Tofte will be coming to you, he had stayed here for some
time and is presenting a soirée tonight.

Your brother thinks you might come here after Christmas? Will you? At
that time I really had planned to be in Hamburg again, but 'that is, after all,
a very special occasion'.

Now I beg you for a word and, as soon as possible, for the quintet.

My address:

Leopoldstadt, Novaragasse 39, 2nd Stairway, 2nd Floor.

I asked you for your photograph; isn't there one of your Quartet in the
form of a visiting card? That I would really like to ask for again.

Warmly

Your

Johannes.

---

[19] Joachim's manservant.

156
Johannes Brahms to Joseph Joachim

Vienna, [31 October 1862]

Only in the most exasperated mood can I sit down to write once again for my Quintet.

I request and demand it most earnestly and you might consider that I am entitled to feel more resentful than others whose manuscripts are lying around at your place.

I am thoroughly fed up and only wish the matter were at an end to the extent that I had my music back, so that I could begin to chew the cud of irritating emotions of these past days.

If only I could assume you were in England! But I suppose eventually I shall have to ask Scholz to write to me where you are.

That mouth and arm does not reach to Hanover—you'd be in for it! My fingers are much too impatient for calm letter-writing, they would rather punch the pen into the paper.

In the future your time will be safe from my demands upon it.

Etc.

J. B.

Joachim received none of the things Brahms had sent until 4 November, at which time the Quintet arrived by itself, unaccompanied by any of the urgent letters; Joachim was still unaware, therefore, of just how badly Brahms wanted his work back. 'In case you need the Quintet in Vienna,' Joachim wrote, 'write, or send a telegram.' He was deeply impressed with the Quintet, thought it not advisable to let Hellmesberger play it, and asked to keep it long enough to have it copied. He requested news 'not only heroic, but personal', wanted to know about Bertha Porubsky, his Figdor family relations,[20] and the impact Brahms had made on Viennese girls.

In the mean time, Brahms had no inkling that Joachim had still not received his letters.

---

[20] One of whom had married a Wittgenstein, thus providing Joachim with an extensive set of well-connected relatives.

157
Johannes Brahms to Joseph Joachim

[Vienna, 7 November 1862]

In all haste—that I have received your letter and that I really do want my Quintet back, as you could have gathered from my letters, incidentally. I hope that now, at least, there is no more long-winded business to interfere. But I suppose that a performance during my concert has become impossible in any case, since the piece is difficult and I would have had to rehearse it at leisure. In the mean time, I would now really definitely like to hope that I'll have it in the next few days.

In short: that B[ertha] P[orubsky] is engaged to a wealthy young man.

When I first saw her here, I found her very pale and sickly, and my conscience felt considerably better soon after when I received the relevant card with a few words.

I became acquainted with the Figdors, if you can call it that, because apart from colleagues I seldom become better acquainted with people.

You are right about Hellmesberger, and here music of a more excited character is more popular just now (probably partly through Wagner); my Sextet leaves them cool, in contrast my Concerto pleases greatly, my A major Quartet did little, the G minor on the other hand etc.

I have no time.

Incidentally you might enclose a photograph with the Quintet if that is actually dispatched.

Your J. B.

If my letters appear as angry as they were meant to, console yourself with the thought that in my mind I wanted to write even more angrily, and indeed I will guard against being exasperated again by your unreliability. Which I hope will be found to be quite understandable.

No more than a few days can have gone by before Brahms's next letter; but given the usual efficiency of mail at that time, Brahms again put the darkest possible construction on the fact that he was still without his Quintet.

158
Johannes Brahms to Joseph Joachim

[Vienna] another Friday, [14 November 1862]

In my mind I see another 4 weeks gone by and me without a letter from you, or Quintet.

As agreeable as is the feeling I usually have in knowing that my things are with you, I cannot rid myself now of the most unpleasant thoughts, not knowing for such a long time whether it has received a glance. I feel as though I call out into a soundless void where I had expected a friendly echo.

I therefore request most urgently that you take a moment of your time to tell Rabe my address and to give him the Quintet to pack up and attend to.

Very soon it will already be scarcely possible to request a rehearsal from people, since every day there is more to do for the concerts.

I'll write again the day after tomorrow, for the sake of simplicity however only an envelope, which may remind you through the 4 groschen you'll have to pay

of your
J. Br.

159
Johannes Brahms to Joseph Joachim

[Vienna, *c*.16 November 1862]

I who desire and demand my Quintet.
J. B.
Vienna, Jägerzeile, Novaragasse 39, II, 2.

By now Joachim had received Brahms's increasingly rancorous letters.

160
Joseph Joachim to Johannes Brahms

London, 8 November [1862]
40 Pall Mall

My dear Johannes,

I cannot be surprised that you were greatly astonished and aggravated about your Quintet's failure to arrive. You are not used to this kind of thing from me, and would never have had the opportunity of having such an experience, were it not for the most extraordianry circumstances.

Immediately after I learned from Hanover that a manuscript of yours was there, I sent Scholz the *urgent* request to send the music to London forthwith. He wrote to me in response that it would arrive shortly—but only after admonishing three times did it come into my hands, just a week ago! The fault was not mine. *Your three admonitory letters have only just arrived from Hanover:* For what reason I also do not know, because I had left strict instructions to forward all letters immediately. One can indeed depend on no one but oneself. I am profoundly sorry, truly from all my heart, that I have thwarted any wish you had for a performance; wouldn't it be disagreeable to me even with respect to anyone else.—However, since the Viennese know neither your Sextet, nor other things that would be more accessible *to them* than your Quintet (not to me, to whom it appeals extraordinarily), the consequences of not seeing your work again until the present mailing may in the end not be so serious. *I am pleased that Hellmesberger is playing your things as a favour.* Don't be a tea-kettle, and don't take it for sentimentality born of resigned magnanimity. I wish I could play with you myself.

. . . If your path passes my way during [the 6 months I must remain in Hanover], perhaps you will forget your rancour and the phrases of your most recent letter-writing style so inimcal to friendship.

I who ask your pardon sincerely, and who forward your Quintet to you.

J. J.

Joachim was more hurt than he let on. He mentioned the matter to Clara, who answered him with her own tale of mistreatment over the same piece,[21] and in his next letter to Brahms he wrote:

[London, mid-November 1862]
I had no photographs to hand. I must also say that I could hardly have brought myself to send you one. As long as you do not consider your last

---

[21] *JJ* ii. 268.

letter superfluous, you could scarcely care much about me. But perhaps my explanation, which must have reached you only lately, will satisfy you, and it would please me, would please me with all my heart, to hear this from you.

If Brahms replied, the letter has not survived. Joachim sent Brahms a Christmas greeting nevertheless, and by then the tantrum was over.

161
Johannes Brahms to Joseph Joachim

[Vienna, 29 December 1862]

Nothing dearer could have come to me for Christmas than your greetings, dear Joseph. I had already taken up my pen several times to fetch them forth, and I could not have done without them much longer.

I hope you have long since thrown my useless letters into the fire and have forgotten my equally useless agitation.

And so, first of all, my warmest thanks. I suppose it best just to send along the thing that brought me so much aggravation and yet so little joy. If I had superfluous money, or if I could earn some up there, I would rather come along myself, times are lean here now. Only I just can't travel back and forth and after all I do want to stay here for a while.

Frau Schumann will probably call for your advice about a certain matter. For I am publishing a set of variations on a theme by Schumann, which he wrote during his illness.[22]

So it simply seems appropriate to me to add the comment:
'composed on the . . . .th February 1854.'

Frau Schumann is not in favour, and naturally I want to contradict her feelings only gently. This secretiveness seems rather less tender to me, however, particularly since the theme really sounds like a wistful, softly spoken word of farewell and the variations do not stray too far from this idea.

I only fear that Frau Schumann has something against the Variations, perhaps I should not have had them published. The theme is not particularly suited for variations and they are just not at all important.[23]

---

[22] *Variations on a Theme by Robert Schumann* for piano duet, Op. 23, dedicated to Julie Schumann.

[23] Thirty year later, as editor of the Supplemental Volume of the *Complete Works of Schumann* published by Breitkopf & Härtel, Brahms included this theme as the last work in the volume. The music, to which Schumann himself wrote a set of piano variations, was 'composed' shortly after Schumann was hospitalized in Endenich; the variations are the last music Schumann wrote. Although he had used the same melody for the slow movement of his Violin Concerto, he

Wagner is here, and I shall probably be called a *Wagnerian*: primarily, of course, because of the opposition to which any reasonable person is provoked in face of the frivolous manner in which musicians here speak against him.

Also, I socialize particularly with Cornelius and Tausig—who by no means wish to be or to have been *devotées of Liszt*, and who, what's more, can doubtless accomplish more with their little finger than all the other musicians with their whole head and all of their fingers.[24]

It is quite good here but still I shall probably go back to Hamburg.

But if I go north you will probably do the same and unfortunately, probably remain in England for longer, or forever?

Give my warmest greetings to Scholz, to your quartet, among others, and don't let me do entirely without you, I cannot let go of you.

Your

Johannes.

In mid-November, Brahms received a letter from Avé-Lallement which altered the course of his life. Rather than the expected invitation to work with the Sing-Akademie, it was a letter telling him that the committee had decided to offer Julius Stockhausen the position as director *both* of the Philharmonic and the Sing-Akademie. Brahms reacted with passionate bitterness. It was a blow he never forgot, never forgave, and in some personal sense, never overcame.

---

apparently forgot this fact and believed the theme had been heaven-sent by Schubert. Clara was not opposed to the publication of Brahms's set of variations. On the contrary, she wrote to him on 3 November 1862: 'It never occurred to me that you would not publish them, I was only uneasy about the theme, but find it simple enough if you merely say: Variations on a Theme by R. Sch. No date, nothing further, people don't need to know . . . How can you think that I would have it on my conscience to withhold from the world such a work of yours!—So, on with it, and I can only approve of the dedication to Julie.' Schumann's own set of variations, posthumously known as the *Geister-variationen*, were published in 1939 by Karl Geiringer. For an edition with commentary see Walter Beck, *Robert Schumann und seine Geister-variationen* (Tutzing, 1992).

[24] Wagner was in town with three concerts scheduled at the Theater an der Wien. The pianists and composers Peter Cornelius and Carl Tausig were both students of Franz Liszt. Brahms soon became fast friends with Tausig, who was a tremendous pianist; the Paganini Études were written as a friendly challenge to his technique. Tausig taught Brahms many things, including a taste for cognac, expensive cigars, and Schopenhauer. Brahms later had a falling-out with Cornelius in part, at least, over a disputed Wagner manuscript. See Letter 198.

162
Johannes Brahms to Clara Schumann

Vienna, 18 November 1862

Dear Clara,

I feel the need to share the enclosed letter with you.

For me it is a much sadder event than you may think or perhaps find conceivable. As I am above all a rather old-fashioned person, it is also true that I am not cosmopolitan, but instead, am attached to my native city as to a mother. Now you must know that by autumn, the Sing-Akademie was seriously considering taking on a second director. There was only talk then of Deppe and myself.*

Additional
Note p. 750

Just before my departure for here, I was asked *privatim* whether I was interested.[25] Now this hostile friend comes along and pushes me away—forever, I suppose.

How seldom does someone like us find a fixed abode, how I would have liked to find it in my native city. Now, here, where so much beauty delights me, I nevertheless feel and would always feel that I am a stranger and can find no peace.

You have certainly learned of this matter already and also perhaps thought of me in connection with it, but it probably didn't occur to you that it would cause me such great pain; still, it only required the smallest hint for you to see how much I have lost.

If I could not hope here, then where? Where may I and can I! You have experienced it with your husband and know generally that they would most like to set us loose and have us fly about all alone in empty space. And yet, one wants to have ties and a livelihood that makes a life into a life, and one is afraid of loneliness. Activity in lively union with others and lively social relations, family happiness—what human being doesn't feel the longing for that?

Furthermore, be amused with the honey-sweet way in which my friendly enemy hands me my poison to drink. On the one hand talking of the blossoming future which awaits me and on the other, already forgetting this, happily looking forward to a future without me.

I am also writing a few lines to my parents, meant for you too. The contents of this letter, indeed its very existence *just* between us, especially not for Avé, Stockhausen, and my parents.

Warmly, your Johs.

[25] '. . . frug man privatim bei mir an', which can mean either 'I was asked indirectly' or 'I was asked in private'.

Clara answered Brahms's distress call immediately, having just performed with the offending orchestra. She had even hesitated to go on with her performance, after hearing the news from Avé.

[written from Hamburg, Friday evening, 21 November 1862]:

. . . You know how deeply I am affected by anything that concerns you and you can imagine how painfully I was moved by your letter. Until now, I had never taken the affair seriously, for Avé has so often spoken of plans, with no thought of executing them, but now I feel with you all the anguish, the very same that I suffered for years with my Robert. The day before yesterday Avé received me with the news as soon as I arrived, we sat together until late into the night, I told him my heartfelt opinion, that I simply would not have thought it possible for him to take such a step, that it was a disgrace etc.—he responded with all kinds of reasons, for instance, that to begin with some basic issues had to be worked out, which is not the business of your sort of musician. That is what Stockhausen should do and then you should join in, and indeed Stockhausen also speaks with firm confidence that you two could work together beautifully. How this would turn out I do not know—the business doesn't quite make sense to me. Well, who knows! But to which artist was it ever given to be able to establish hearth and home in his native city? That's precisely what is always so sad! But you are still so young, dear Johannes, you will find a fixed abode, and 'if one takes a loving wife, every town is heaven enough'. That is what my husband said so tenderly in his little poems, and surely you will find the joy of a family and a home!—everything! That you still feel a stranger in Vienna I can understand, but that will surely dwindle somewhat in the course of a longer stay and eventually many things will even bind you there. I hope only for the best for you, it does happen so often in life that what seemed so harsh, leads to good fortune later on. . . .

At the very time of this powerful rebuff from his home town, Brahms was in the midst of giving two Viennese concerts which were so successful that they laid the foundation for the rest of his career. In the first one, he participated in a concert given by the prominent Viennese violinist, Joseph Hellmesberger, playing the piano part in his Quartet in G minor, Op. 25. That was on 16 November, just before the arrival of the unwelcome news from Hamburg. Then on 29 November, he gave his own soirée, performing the Piano Quartet in A major, Op. 26, his Handel Variations, and works of Bach and Schumann. The hall for this concert was rented and paid for by the pianist Julius Epstein, a local musician who had immediately understood Brahms's talent and had set about to help him, sending him students and insisting he present his talents to the public.

However wounded Brahms may have been over the news from Hamburg, he was in no way crushed by the event, but instead rose to the occasion to give the best performance of his life. It is a very strange turn of history that the greatest disappointment of his life coincided with his greatest success as composer and pianist up to that point; he won acclaim in Vienna just as the doors in Hamburg closed behind him.

163
Johannes Brahms to Christiane and Johann Jakob Brahms

Vienna, 30 November 1862

Dear Parents,

Yesterday brought me great joy; my concert went quite splendidly, much better than I had hoped.

After my Quartet had been very cordially received, people were exceptionally pleased with me as a pianist. Every number received the richest applause; I believe there was real enthusiasm in the hall.

I could now go on giving fine concerts, but it's not what I want to do; for it would take up so much of my time that I wouldn't get to much else. I seem to have covered the costs of this concert; apart from that the hall, of course, was filled with free tickets.

I played as freely as if I'd been at home with friends—but of course this audience stimulates a person very differently from ours.

You should see how attentive they are and hear and see their applause!

Incidentally, I should make clear that Herr Bagge is apparently the only one to write so negatively about my Quartet [Op. 25]—the rest of the papers praised me highly that time.

I feel wonderful about having given this concert.

I imagine you are now rid of your guests, so perhaps you'll find a minute to write to me?

Share this letter with Herr Marxsen, and also tell him that Bösendorfer could not send a piano before New Year, since they're in use for concerts. Should I now look around for another one for him, I await his *ordre*.

Grädener fared very badly in his concert, as far as audience and reviews are concerned. The papers gave him an awful going-over. I believe my Serenades are going to be performed next Sunday.

I really wanted to do some of my vocal things in my concert, which cost me a terrible lot of running around and other unpleasantness, one of the main reasons I want peace and quiet at last.

CONCERT

des

Johannes Brahms,

Samstag den 29. November 1862,

Abends halb 8 Uhr,

im Saale der Gesellschaft der Musikfreunde.

Programm:

1. **Johannes Brahms,** Piano-Quartett, (A-dur) 1. Satz:
   Allegro, 2. Satz: Adagio, 3. Satz: Scherzo, 4. Satz:
   Allegro, vorgetragen von den Herren **Hellmesberger, Dobyhal, Röver** und dem **Concertgeber**.

2. **Joh. Seb. Bach,** Toccata (F-dur) vorgetragen vom
   Concertgeber.

3. **Gesang.**

4. **Johannes Brahms,** Variationen und Fuge über ein
   Thema von Händel, vorgetragen vom **Concertgeber**.

5. **Gesang.**

6. **Robert Schumann,** Fantasie, Op. 17, (in 3 Sätzen,
   C-dur) vorgetragen vom **Concertgeber**.

Obengenannte Mitwirkende haben aus Gefälligkeit für den
Concertgeber ihre Parten bereitwillig übernommen.

Die Claviere sind aus der Fabrik Bösendorfer.

Cercle-Sitze zu 3 fl.
**Parterre-Sperrsitze zu 2 fl. Gallerie-Sperrsitze zu
1 fl. 50 kr. Eintrittskarten zu 1 fl.**
sind in den k. k. Hof-Musikalienhandlungen der Herren HASLINGER
und SPINA, in der Musikalienhandlung des Herrn G. LEWY, und am
Tage des Concertes an der Kasse zu haben.

Fig. 2 Concert announcement of Brahms's first solo appearance in Vienna, 29 November 1962 (see Letter 163).

Wednesday you all had egg nog together? Do write to me about that and everything else.[26]

The local publishers, specifically Spina and Lewy, have been pressuring me for material since the Quartet, but, since publishers are among the things I particularly like better in Northern Germany, I'd rather forgo for the time being the couple of extra louis d'ors they might pay.

Does Avé visit you often, and did he have anything special to tell about Stockhausen?

What's happening with the Girls' Quartet photograph, am I not getting it?

And, NB: every time I write I forget to ask: if Fritz is now completely back to good health? And is he hard at work? He should plunge into his studies so that he can give trio soirées in Hamburg next winter, I'll be glad to give him a lot of help. But he's got to practise hard and get an overview of music.

Do write soon, and send love to

your

Johannes

Warmest greetings to Herr Marxsen and don't forget about Bösendorfer.

The whole family congratulated him. From his mother:[27]

> The sheets of paper [i.e. newspaper clippings] you sent us have given us endless joy. It is the best Christmas present for us all. But now also with one blow all hope is gone that you are coming for Christmas.

To which his sister added:

> I am making copies of everything, really a great deal [of work], but with what admiration I do it . . .

Then a letter from his brother:

> Dear Brother, I am sure I don't need to tell you the specifics of how royally I rejoice in your splendid reception by the Viennese. Surprising for us Hamburgers is that they were so friendly and obliging, and one would have suspected more hostility on the part of the critics.

Many are the speculations as to why Brahms was passed over as director of Hamburg's leading musical organizations in favour of Julius Stockhausen. It is true that Brahms did not openly express a wish to be named music director of the orches-

---

[26] Clara and her daughter Marie were in Hamburg, sampling Frau Brahms's famous egg nog. Brahms was also curious to know whether news of Stockhausen and the Philharmonic had reached his parents.

[27] This and the following letter from his brother: *Familie*, 92–3.

tra, but Joachim's letter to Avé, two months later, plainly demonstrates that Brahms had indeed been considered for that position as well as for the Sing-Akademie, and that he was looking for a career as a conductor.[28] Given his inexperience with orchestral conducting, the answer to why he was passed over would be obvious but for the fact that Stockhausen had an equally limited background in the field. And surely Brahms would have been eminently suited to conduct the Sing-Akademie.

Perhaps the simplest explanation is the best one—that the committee found it would be more efficient to have one person fill both posts, and that Julius Stockhausen, renowned singer and thoroughly well-trained musician, fluent in English, French, and German, urbane and at ease in society, was an obvious choice. Equally in his favour, Stockhausen was known to champion public concerts and low prices for 'the People' and had some experience in accomplishing that end, as he had recently given a song recital in Cologne for an audience of more than 2,000 enthusiastic listeners. He believed firmly that one must present only the highest quality art even to the masses.

In contrast, Brahms had something of a reputation to overcome, both as a person—'unaccommodating, proud, arrogant, and disagreeable'—and as a free-thinker, having made no secret of his unorthodox religious views.[29]

Class differences may well have played a part, even if unspoken. It is not an unreasonable surmise that the Committee had misgivings about Brahms's background. (For his part, Brahms's father never trusted Avé, as later letters between father and son reveal. In reality, Avé was nothing but helpful in his relations with the family, and it is unlikely that Jakob Brahms had any basis for his misgivings other than his own class prejudices.)

According to Stockhausen's diaries, the Philharmonic Orchestra did not make him a firm offer until 21 November, and Stockhausen wrote: 'Answer postponed'.[30] Brahms's anguished letter to Clara is dated 18 November; the committee had already decided against Johannes before offering the job to Stockhausen, and would not have offered it to him even had Stockhausen turned it down. Perhaps Brahms was never really in the running, despite Avé's interest in him.

Stockhausen, whose admiration for Brahms was sincere, expressed uneasiness about the whole affair in his diary and letters.

---

[28] See *JJ* ii. 274. In fact, Joachim's remark, that given a choice between Brahms and Stockhausen he couldn't understand how the committee had chosen Stockhausen, is quite explicit. And since the final straw that pushed Brahms to resign from Detmold was the failure there to allow him to conduct the orchestra regularly, it seems clear that in his own mind, he envisaged his future as a conductor. See also Letter 130.

[29] From Franzisca Meier's diary. Drinker, *Brahms and his Women's Choruses*, 30–1. For Brahms's religious and political views see Hübbe, *Brahms in Hamburg*, 33.

[30] Julia Wirth, *Julius Stockhausen, Der Sänger des Deutschen Liedes* (Frankfurt am Main, 1927), 233.

164
Julius Stockhausen to Johannes Brahms

Hamburg, 27 November 1862[31]

Dear friend,

I feel compelled to write you from your home town which perhaps will become mine as well. How this will all take shape I can't foresee as yet; but what I can say with certainty is that I would find it very painful if you did not stay in Hamburg. Frau Schumann speaks of it as though you might not return! No doubt it's very beautiful in Vienna, but home is even more beautiful & I think a collaboration here would be very exhilarating, splendid, & instructive for me. Just consider! Grund is being pensioned off, retaining his present salary. I'm supposed to conduct the six concerts, but I am also supposed to sing, & when I sing somebody has to be around to help out, after all. Opportunities you shall have aplenty to get lots of practice becoming profficient in conducting and then—if you like it, I'll go my way & find me another position. M[usic] D[irectors] die just like other people and must be replaced everywhere. For example, who is to conduct Faust or Walpurgisnacht when I sing? Should they put a baton back into old Grund's hand for works he might rehearse in his own fashion? Do think it over! It would be wonderful. I'll gladly take on the roughest parts and rehearse the work, if the many preliminary rehearsals become burdensome for you! There's not much money to be made in this in any case; but we'll surely raise money with private concerts! For that's also a necessity of life! It's dreadful how that metal slips through the fingers!

Did you think of us a lot recently? Be with us in spirit on December 4th, in Leipzig for Faust,[32] & see to it that you're back home at the end of February. I'll be rehearsing Schumann's work for 6 weeks in Hanover and Joachim will probably conduct. I'll be with him from January 15th to March 1st. On the 6th of March I'm supposed to conduct the 2nd Orchestral Evening and have made my selection: Symphony in E flat major Mozart, fragment from Prometheus. Beeth.—Schubert C Major Symphony—

Your letter of July 22nd I have had with me the whole time so as not to forget about the picture! I send it to you herewith. It was made by a delightful girl: Josephine Backofen in Darmstadt. Does she have eyes! Black as coal and so faithful (ostensibly), for none of them are, and I now recognize, *some-*

---

[31] Stockhausen accepted the post in Hamburg on the same date.

[32] The first complete performance of Schumann's *Scenes from Goethe's Faust*, at the Gewandhaus. Stockhausen sang it again later in Hanover, under Joachim's direction.

what late, that we chaps are indeed very different from this *weak* gender! But enough! You're on territory that's somewhat dangerous and can have all kinds of experiences! I wish I could visit you in Vienna from December 5th to January 15th. I'm going to write to Spina about the Schöne Müllerin & Winterreise. Maybe something can be arranged.[33]

And finally, ♡ felt greetings to you from your singer,

J.S.

And from his diary: [Hamburg] 28 November [1862] '. . . visited Brahms. My heart shrank as I set foot on the first stair! He isn't there! This intelligent, vigorous character has left his homeland. He is in Vienna.—Will Brahms come back?—'

Stockhausen took on the music directorshop on a provisional basis, agreeing to conduct the Hamburg Philharmonic for six concerts, or one season's worth. He wrote to Clara [7 March 1863]:

How it came about that I found an orchestra in Germany and have become a conductor is still a puzzle, a dream to me, and I owe my happiness most of all to you, dear friend; therefore my speediest and warmest thanks. If you had not come to Guebwiller,[34] if you had not played there with our wretched orchestra, then recommended me as someone who had the [necessary] equipment, I would perhaps not be concert director in Hamburg . . . One has heard as good as nothing from Brahms for three weeks; in the end, he will show up unexpectedly for the big national holiday on 18 March.[35] That's what his parents think! I don't believe that he takes it so seriously. I cannot foresee how everything will work out; but something will happen, certainly: we are getting Paris pitch this winter, and with it, better wind instruments . . .

and then again from Hanover [11 May 1863]:

I saw Johannes three days ago, in Hamburg. He seems depressed, is short with Avé; one would think he was piqued that the Committee didn't think of him to conduct the concerts. The affair concerns me, and threatens to spoil all my happiness. Yet early on Brahms himself told me he wouldn't be the right man to wrestle with people in order to transform the orchestra, but that the right person could accomplish something with those musicians. And now he seems to be wounded! How much music we could make together, how well and how profitably, give full-scale concerts and chamber music matinées either with or without vocalists, and perform his

[33] Complete performances of the song cycles, still a novelty at that time.
[34] Town in Alsace, where he was living and working.
[35] Fiftieth anniversary of the expulsion of French troops in Hamburg by the arrival of the Russian Colonel von Tettenborn, 18 March 1813. The date is celebrated as a civic holiday by the Free City of Hamburg.

compositions really beautifully; for until now the orchestra has only played his Serenades indifferently; I was witness to it! What do you think about it? Dear Frau Schumann! has Brahms all of a sudden acquired talent as a conductor? Earlier on he didn't have any, and the musicians allowed themselves remarks, etc. More details another time. Are you coming to Düsseldorf? I'll be there on the 21st of May.

It is not likely that Brahms ever knew Stockhausen's true opinion of his capabilities as a conductor, nor of the role Clara Schumann had played in Stockhausen's appointment to the Hamburg Philharmonic.

That Stockhausen was genuinely distressed at Brahms's permanent departure from Hamburg is plain to see from his letters; to Avé-Lallemant (1 Sept. 1863):

I didn't want to believe that Brahms was gone, till I learned he was in Baden at Frau Schumann's house on his way through to Vienna. Now he's gone, really gone, and that pains me very much. In every respect, nothing worse could have happened to me! In the end, after all, he is our single most important man in Hamburg, and to lose him is hard.

Joachim, who worked with Stockhausen and knew him well, and whose judgement of his character must therefore be taken seriously, was blunt with Avé (31 January 1863):

... What can I say to *your Committee's* plan for Stockhausen, now, after the fact. You know I hold Stock's talent for singing in the highest esteem, and he is probably the best musician among singers; but my limited musical understanding cannot fathom how, in the choice between him and Johannes as head of a concert institution, one can decide for the former. Specifically as a *human being* on whom one can rely, I have the most particular regard for Johannes's gifts and strength of mind! There is nothing he could not grasp and conquer with his seriousness of purpose. You know that just as well as I do—and if all of you in the Committee and Orchestra had approached him with love and in confidence (as you, as his friend, *always* did in private) instead of with condescension and misgivings, that would have eliminated the harshness in his nature; instead of which, his patriotism towards Hamburg (which is touching and almost childlike) has to make him ever more bitter at seeing himself set aside (for someone of much less talent and character). If I am to avoid becoming sad, I dare not think of how his own compatriots have passed up the chance to make him more contented and gentler, and the accomplishments of his genius more accessible. I should like to give the Committee a moral thrashing (and a corporal one as well!) for having left you and your intentions in the lurch. The history of art will not forget the wrong done to Johannes.[36]

---

[36] *JJ* ii. 274–5. Quotes from Stockhausen's letters and diaries: Wirth, *Julius Stockhausen*, 236, 241, 247, 251.

Whatever his feelings towards Hamburg's musical establishment, Brahms did not allow his relations with Stockhausen to become embittered. For his part, Stockhausen made amends as best he could. Very early in his tenure as music director of the Philharmonic, Brahms's father was given permanent status in the double-bass section; and in January 1864, Stockhausen agreed to join Brahms's rather less brilliant brother, Fritz, in his début piano recital in Hamburg, lending him his beautiful Erard piano, and ensuring the concert's success.

But Brahms found it difficult to forgive Avé, in spite of any real evidence of perfidy. In Avé's defence, correspondence shows that both Clara and Joachim felt no conflict of loyalty in remaining friendly with him, and Avé tried hard to remain a friend to Brahms. He stayed in touch with the family, could be counted on in need, provided mother and sister with a steady supply of concert tickets, continued to act as adviser and sometime banker, and indeed it is Avé, a few years later, who helped bury his mother and later still informed Brahms of his father's grave condition and impending death.[37] Although Brahms relied on him in these ways and even showed him certain courtesies, for him the friendship was essentially over. It was supplanted by the many new ones waiting for him in Vienna.

[37] Telegram in the Brahms Archive of the Staats- und Universitätsbibliothek, Hamburg.

PART V

❧❧❧

In Vienna, Sometimes

1863–1870

❧ **1863** ❧

That Brahms stayed in Vienna through winter and spring is due to circumstance rather than plan. His family probably had some inkling of the hopes that had been dashed in Hamburg—his sister's letters, in particular, sometimes allude to what life would have been like 'if . . .'—but Brahms kept his hopes of an appointment to Grund's old job a secret to all but a very few people. As far as his acquaintances knew, the decision not to come home was simply due to the success of his exploratory trip to Vienna, a rather striking success in fact, gained in remarkably short order in a city where music held a place of honour far greater than in his own. With introductions from Clara and the excellent connections of his old Viennese friend Bertha Porubsky, he had quickly made contact with the most important musicians of the city, and within two months of arrival had appeared in two concerts which established his reputation securely.

No one was less surprised than Clara, who told Joachim that Johannes was extremely pleased with Vienna, 'which was only to be expected', and that he would stay there for the entire winter. She must also have been relieved that he had finally made a move, for she was convinced that Hamburg was useless to his career.[1]

But something other than success kept Brahms in Vienna. He now foresaw no musical future for himself in Hamburg: and indeed, at just this time he wrote the vocal quartet 'Heimat' (Op. 64 No. 1), one of his most passionate works, pervaded with the sense of loss of place.[2] Brahms did not make an appearance in Hamburg until the next May, barely in time for his birthday.

Letters from this period describe his utter delight at being in Vienna, his occasional distress, his homesickness, but above all his ability, well honed by now, to get on with life, to compose, to get his works published and performed, to focus on the

---

[1] Letters to Joseph Joachim, 10 Nov. 1862 and 2 Jan. 1860 (*JJ* ii. 67, 258).

[2] There is more evidence that the work was written in response to his 'loss' of Hamburg. Many years later he gave a handwritten copy of it to Toni Petersen, daughter of the Mayor of Hamburg who conferred honorary citizenship on him.

essential kernel of his existence. And to make the best of his circumstances, as he had once written to Clara: in this case, to pursue his devotion to Schubert's works.

Brahms's enthusiasm for Schubert, already well developed before he ever set foot in Vienna, would now be given free rein. He tracked down manuscripts, copied some of them in his own hand, acquired them where possible, did his best to see that Schubert's works were published, and anonymously edited a substantial number of them for publication.[3]

Brahms still had fence-mending to do with regard to Joachim, but his friend had other things on his mind. He was in the midst of rearranging the terms of his employment at the Hanoverian Court—and he was in love. Joachim had written briefly to Brahms at the end of January, saying the letter was just 'an ice-breaker; I'll write soon again more explicitly, also about the Quintet'. There is no doubt, though, that his shock at the rudeness of Brahms's recent letters to him had not entirely worn off. Apparently Brahms understood it was now up to him to make amends.

165
Johannes Brahms to Joseph Joachim

[Vienna, 12 February 1863]

Dear friend,

Till now, unfortunately, nothing has followed your 'ice-breaker', so for the time being my thanks for it. Such machinery isn't necessary, either, I shouldn't think! The most beautiful spring weather, and all waters are flowing freely.

Where I'll be this summer? It is probably somewhat childish to let myself be tempted and quite seriously consider, and even conclude, that it would be grand to spend it together.

Moreover, I don't know what will happen. I'll be a fool and abandon the Prater and the mountains at the most beautiful time of year and go to Mother. In these things I am very old-fashioned.

I wish I could travel back and forth. In that case I would go to Hamburg and to Hanover now, and when May comes, off to wherever it is at its most beautiful.

But I must be content if my purse can hold out in one locality, either here or in Hamburg. It cannot stand strenuous activity.

My A Major Quartet is with me for proof-reading just now. Both of them will soon be published by Simrock.

I am so often told about a new Hungarian concerto, but never about the

---

[3] See McC 737–40 and 751–2 for a full list.

right one![4] If by chance there were a movement to be looked over, I would request the pleasure of doing so. Laub is coming here again to present six quartets. He is really a first-rate violinist. What keeps him from being able to delight me is what he lacks as a person, to such a degree that one doesn't even demand or expect it. On the other hand, though, it's the same with Hellmesberger and ultimately with everyone.

If you write to me again be sure to let me know how long you are definitely staying in Hanover and what your plans might be.

You can go ahead and write me dozens of them. I suppose that Hamburg wouldn't suit you at all for the summer?

Raff is arriving shortly. He is the composer of the prizewinning symphony 'To the Fatherland'.[5] Nobody knows the name of the second prizewinner.

Since Tausig and Cornelius themselves tell me that Liszt is *probably* going to enter a monastery there must be something to it, and it seems to me that this is the right and virtually inevitable ending to the remarkable life of this man.

Here I go again, starting to ask for a visiting card! Isn't there one of your quartet? Actually Scholz owes me a picture. Warmest greetings to Scholz and the quartet, and do let the words flow. To hear something about my Quintet would certainly be very appreciated and valuable to me.

Yours affectionately.
Johannes.

Novaragasse 39, II, 2
Leopoldstadt.

Joachim's letter, when it arrived, contained startling news: he was engaged to be married to Amalie Schneeweiss (Snow-white), a young singer at the Court Opera in Hanover, possessed of a magnificent alto voice.

---

[4] Joachim was then working on his G Major Concerto, a work not published for another twenty years, and then only after substantial revision.

[5] Joseph Joachim Raff. The prize was offered by the Gesellschaft der Musikfreunde, in Vienna. Raff was an admirer of Liszt and the New German School.

166
Johannes Brahms to Joseph Joachim

[Vienna, 24] February 1863

You fortunate fellow!

What more can I write than a few more such exclamations at best! My good wishes would sound almost too ceremonious and solemn were I to write about them.

No one will feel your good fortune more than I, and particularly now, for your letter blew in when I was in a mood to be deeply moved.

For here I cannot stop thinking whether it is preferable, since I protect myself better against other dreams, to enjoy and experience everything here except for one thing, or go home, have the one thing, simply be at home, and give up all else.[6]

Then in the midst of this you come along and quite boldly simply pluck for yourself the ripest and most beautiful Apples of Paradise!

What better can I wish you than that it may all become as beautiful and good as it clearly is good and beautiful and desirable. Beyond that, what comes into view is the lovely snow-white inside of the apple and the beautiful young apple trees, and more apples producing more apple trees, etc. *ad infinitum.*

So may it go according to my most deeply felt wishes and I look forward to the time when I can crouch over a cradle in your house, as I already have in the house of many another faithless friend, and upon seeing the dear laughing baby face, forget to begin my contemplations.

Give my warmest greetings to your bride!

The name has a fairy-tale sound, and at first I didn't know whether you were telling me your pet name for her or her real name.

So then, I have one more reason to go northwards and home. Otherwise when shall I see you in your happiness? My best greetings to you and hold

dear your

Johannes.

[6] It is very curious that on some level Brahms's vision of life was so provincial that he couldn't imagine family life except in Hamburg. In various forms, this comment is occasionally repeated during his life, although obviously he knew dozens of people who married away from their home towns—including Joachim!

167
Johannes Brahms to Joseph Joachim

[Vienna, 13 April 1863]

Jo - sef,   lie - ber   Jo - sef mein,   hilf mir   wie-gen mein Kind-lein klein.

[Jo - sef,   dear - est   Jo - sef mine,   help me   rock_   my child so fine.]

One of these days I'm going to send you a wonderful old Catholic song for use at home, a more beautiful lullaby you won't dig up![7]

Sincere thanks for your letter, but from a bridegroom and very busy musician I really expect so little more than *a single* word that I am especially grateful for each additional one that I receive.

If I had received the above-mentioned letter and its news a little sooner I could have joined in relishing all kinds of things. Just now it came to me too suddenly. Yesterday and the day before I was still busy with concerts, etc.

It appears that the position of chorus master of the Singakademie here is being offered to me.

I'm asking nothing about it and fear the moment an official approach may soon oblige me to think about it seriously anyway.

I can live here pleasurably and well without holding a position, in Hamburg, without one, I wouldn't be allowed to stroll about in boredom. And I'm fool enough to regret that I had the same experience as the King of Greece, and that our pious friend, who was forever sighing that for him I was the most important thing in Hamburg, shut the door behind me as soon as I had turned my back to go on a little jaunt.[8]

So, now I do request that you do send my quintet here after all, to *Wessely & Büssing, Kohlmarkt.*

If I can get to it at all I would really prefer to hear it without excessive roughness, if possible. Therefore please, the MS. MS. MS. MS.[9]

---

[7] 'Resonet in Laudibus', later published for Alto and Viola as Op. 91 No. 2. By the time the work was in print, many years later, Joachim and Amalie had separated, so that this work, so obviously intended for two of his dearest friends, lacks what would have been the obvious dedication.

[8] In 1862, while on a short trip away from Athens, the King of Greece discovered that he had been overthrown. The putative perfidious friend is Theodor Avé-Lallement.

[9] The Quintet had been back in Joachim's hands since the end of January. In his previous letter to Brahms, Joachim promised to send it the moment Brahms asked for it, but urged him not to have it performed without some revision, commenting that even for him there were passages in it of great roughness, and adding that he knew what he was talking about as he had played it twice. At this point, the work was still a string quintet with two cellos.

I was offered the complete works of Schubert by Spina, partly already selected those I am missing, and can complete from Hamburg.

I'm bringing you a beautiful picture of Sch[ubert] which is not for sale anywhere.

I am being interrupted, and so farewell for today; however, do send [the quintet] very soon, for I am thinking of travelling to Mother any day.

Affectionately,

Johannes.

Brahms was in the delicate position of trying to maintain good relations with his German and Swiss publishers while building friendly contacts with those in Vienna. C. A. Spina was therefore the publisher of Psalm 13, Op. 27, and the Vocal Duets, Op. 28, but Rieter was to have many more of his works before their relationship dwindled. Brahms's search for Schubert manuscripts led him to begin the work of interesting publishers in issuing unknown works of Schubert. The first publisher he turned to was his Swiss friend and supporter.

168

Johannes Brahms to Melchior Rieter-Biedermann

[Vienna, 18 February, 1863]

My dear Herr Rieter!

My best thanks for your kind letter, which gave me great pleasure. You estimate my talent so highly and tell me so many fine things that I am really quite embarrassed and prefer—for the moment—to remain silent. In any case, I will try to bring honour to your publishing house with one of my next works.

For the time being, however, I suppose I must leave at least a few things for Herr *Spina* here, who has already vainly expressed a wish for the 'Quartets' [Opp. 25 and 26]. There is a wonderful thing here, that publishers are able to provide *Schubert* manuscripts as a garnish, of all things, which is of course very enticing for the likes of me.

Quite generally, I owe my most beautiful hours here to unpublished works of *Schubert*, of which I have quite a number of manuscripts at home. However, as delectable and enjoyable as the study of these is, equally sad is almost everything else connected with them. So, for example, I have many things here in manuscript form which belong to *Spina* or *Schneider*[10] and of

---

[10] Schubert's nephew, Dr of Law Eduard Schneider.

which nothing exists but the manuscript, not a single copy! And Spina no more keeps the things in a fireproof safe than I do.

Recently a whole pile of unpublished things were offered for sale at an unbelievably low price, but fortunately they were acquired by the *Gesellschaft der Musikfreunde*. How many things are scattered here and there in the possession of private persons who either guard their treasure like dragons or allow them to vanish without a care.

The enclosed proof arrived on the same day as your esteemed letter. The honorarium arrived some time ago, please excuse me for not notifying you.

Finally I would like to ask you to send me your photograph by way of a visiting card and if possible, also one of friend *Kirchner*, whom I ask you to greet warmly.

Should you also engage in this modern hobby, as I do, my picture is naturally at your disposal.

I would be deeply obliged if you would give me that pleasure by doing so.

With friendly greetings,

Your deeply devoted
Johs Brahms

Brahms's frequent mention of photographic visiting cards reflects his interest in a rapidly advancing new technology. He continued to collect photographs of friends and of works of art throughout his life.

On his way to Vienna, in September 1862, Brahms had stopped off in Dessau to meet for the first time and to stay for a few days with Adolf Schubring. In the previous spring Schubring had published a comprehensive series of articles discussing all of Brahms's music then in print. Coming from one who had paid careful attention to Brahms's work from its earliest publication, the essays made a deep impression on Brahms, all the more so because they contained astute and unequivocal criticisms along with embarrassing praise which compared him to Goethe.[11] ('I read your essays about my works . . . with great joy, greater shame', Brahms wrote to Schubring in April 1862.) Now that Brahms was settled in Vienna for the time being, he renewed contact with Schubring.

---

[11] Opp 1–18, in five issues of the *Neue Zeitschrift für Musik*, vol. 56 nos. 12–16, starting with 21 Mar. 1862. It is worth noting that when Brahms reworked his Trio, Op. 8, thirty years after its first appearance, the new version addressed many of the points Schubring had faulted in his essay.

169
Johannes Brahms to Adolf Schubring

[Vienna, 26] March 1863

Greatly esteemed friend,

Now this will really and truly become a letter, and I would be downright annoyed if you yourself have not sometimes been so over its long failure to appear.[12]

Well, against all expectations, I have spent the entire winter here, very distracted but quite delighted and cheerful, and I can only regret above all that I did not know Vienna sooner. The gay city, the beautiful surroundings, the sympathetic, lively public, how stimulating all that is for the artist!

For us, especially, the sacred memory of the great musicians, whose life and work here one is reminded of every day. That's particularly true of Schubert, of whom one has the sensation that he is still alive! One keeps meeting new people who speak of him as a close acquaintance,[13] and one keeps seeing new works of whose existence one knew nothing and which are so untouched that one could brush the sand from them. The *Lazarus* manuscript really tempts me to do so. I have that one with me, along with how many others, and it looks as if it had been written yesterday. By the way, tomorrow (40 years after its creation) the work will be performed for the first time.[14]

In a somewhat old-fashioned manner I am suffering from homesickness, and so I shall probably leave here during the loveliest spring weather and go to my old mother.

Therefore no stop-overs will be possible along the way, as much as I would have liked to visit you once again on the return trip. Let us get together occasionally by letter in any case, and so I remind you that I can always receive letters at the Hamburg address: Hohe Fuhlentwiete 74.

I already told you in Dessau how and why it gave me particular pleasure

---

[12] A fine Brahmsian sentence: i.e. Brahms would be annoyed if he thought Schubring *hadn't* become cross with him for being so tardy in answering his letter.

[13] Moritz von Schwind was one. Dr Josef Hauer, the father of his new friend, the singer Ottilie Hauer, was another. Hauer had been the boyhood companion of Franz Schubert, and like him, a *Sängerknabe*. Hauer had manuscripts of Schubert and Beethoven at home, and Brahms took enormous pleasure in visiting the doctor and hearing him tell of former times, a circumstance which undoubtedly enhanced Ottilie's appeal.

[14] On 27 March 1863. The work, unfinished, is a religious drama in three parts for orchestra, soloists, and mixed chorus. Brahms discovered the manuscript in Spina's music shop, and copied out parts of Act I. Kal, ii. 78 ff., and McC 737–8.

to have met you personally, and also how I think back with pleasure on the congenial days in your home.

Perhaps you might come to Hamburg this summer? That could be most welcome to me—if I were also there. Well, perhaps I'll hear something about it.[15]

I must be off to the 'Lazarus' rehearsal, and ask in closing that you also write a few lines and enclose your picture and that of little Johannes (as a visiting card).[16] My address for at least another 4 weeks is: *Vienna, Leopoldstadt, Czerningasse 7, IV*, Stairway 43.

Even though this may not constitute a letter, a kind friend can at least take it as a warm greeting, which is what I ask of you.

Greet your family and any others who kindly remember me. How about a rendezvous in Hamburg this summer?

Warmly your

Johs. Brahms.

Schubring responded to this letter with the suggestion that Brahms address him in the 'Du' form, a suggestion Brahms joyfully accepted.

Brahms repeated his enthusiasm for *Lazarus* to other close friends.

170

Johannes Brahms to Albert Dietrich

Vienna, April 1863

Dearest Friend,

In vain have I awaited your Trio and your picture for all this time.[17]

I'll probably stay here till the first of May; do send me the picture of you and your wife!

And do write me a few words of how you and everyone imaginable is getting on. If you still have me in mind for the Trio, it would now be better to send it at your convenience to Hamburg, where tender feelings for my parents will soon draw me.

Please be sure to write to me how long you are remaining in Oldenburg, maybe I'll make a side trip from Hamburg to see you!

I suppose you are going to the Music Festival in Düsseldorf?

---

[15] Brahms may have been considering going to Baden-Baden, where Clara had just bought a house.

[16] His godson, Max Johannes Schubring. See Letter 75.

[17] Dietrich's Piano Trio, Op. 9 or Op. 14, published in 1862 by August Cranz.

It occurs to me that I can send you my *Marienlieder* and the 4-hand Variations, which recently arrived.[18] And I enclose with them some pieces from an Easter Cantata by Schubert which I copied out for myself from the manuscript, also the complete text, which I ask you *to be sure* to take good care of so that I get it back. Those are not some outstanding sections from *Lazarus*. Not at all; quite arbitrarily I copied only the beginning and the end of the first part.

The music is like that all the way through, even Simon's Aria! Oh, if only I could send you all of it, you would be enchanted by such loveliness!

You can keep it pretty much until I go to Hamburg, then I'll request it back together with the text and your Trio.

If you plan to copy it, it should naturally be *for you*. Although there is absolutely no fuss made over Schubert manuscripts, and I am not in the slightest bit committed to secrecy, in the long run, after all, it's Spina's property.

Write a few lines soon.

With warm greetings to you and your wife and any other friends,

your Johannes

I enclose a Quintet after all, also to be kept until I come to Hamburg.

NB, I would urgently like to ask you for your photograph, for here there are no people who could make it possible to forget one's old friends, even if one were so inclined.

171
Johannes Brahms to Melchior Rieter-Biedermann

[Hamburg, 15 May 1863]

Dear Herr Rieter!

I didn't have any photographs available at the time, and so my thanks for yours and the obligatory rejoinder is a little late. I was still in Vienna when I received the '4-Handed Variations' and was greatly pleased by its beautiful appearance. Fortunately, others too were pleased, with both the inside and out.

Concerning *Schubert* and a possible association of that lovely name with yours, I have often spoken to owners of *Schubert* manuscripts.

In the contract which *Spina* signed with *Ferdinand Schubert*, however, there is the clause that he owns the publication right for all works of

---

[18] Rieter-Biedermann issued the *Variations on a Theme by Robert Schumann for Piano four-hands*, Op. 23, in April 1863.

Schubert, those that are now in his possession and those that may turn up, anytime and anywhere!

But this cannot be sustained in court, say the experts, and smile at *Spina* himself and the unenforcability of the contract. However, ownership of the manuscript alone also does not confer a right of publication? And so you must first of all decide for yourself to what extent you will take *Spina* into account.

The son of Schubert's sister is a Doctor of Law *Eduard Schneider*, Vienna, Josefstadt, Schlösselgasse 2. He owns a great many manuscripts (6 symphonies etc.) and is greatly inclined to correspond with you. Apparently he has not received a letter from you, for he did not mention that to me. (I forgot to ask.) I have often spoken to him about you, and if you feel like it, just write to him. He is very agreeable and very musical and has the most unselfish interest in the matter.

Another Doctor of Law, *Endres*, has a dozen charming dances, for example, that he would make available for publication without fuss (but perhaps for a small honorarium). From your side, only *Spina* needs to be considered there. This indeed being the main concern generally. I consider it quite useless to approach him. He takes it to be a kind of honour to be *Schubert*'s publisher, does in fact take on everything and sticks it in his cupboard along with all his other things.

But it is now understood, dear sir, that I am telling you all this in strict confidence. Should you proceed in this matter, I will perhaps hear about it. I am most interested in it.

A revised edition based on the first edition of the 'Müllerlieder', for example, would surely be a practical and useful enterprise. For almost every song has subsequently been more or less disfigured. Maybe you could prepare something like this for 1867?

Meanwhile my warmest greetings. I am staying here for the time being (Fuhlentwiete 74).

With friendly commendations to Herr Kirchner and to you

Your very devoted

Johs Brahms

To my delight, Hermann *Levi* was here for a few days.

Brahms's mention of Hermann Levi introduces that enormously talented musician and conductor. Aged 24 at the time, he had come from Rotterdam specifically to visit Brahms, whose music had already made a deep impression on him. Their friendship blossomed the next year, after Levi accepted the post as Court Opera Conductor in Karlsruhe.

Additional
Note p. 751

Schubert would have been 70 years old in 1867. Brahms eventually acquired the Twelve Dances mentioned above himself, and published them anonymously through C. A. Spina in 1864.[19] * While Rieter-Biedermann did not follow most of the suggestions Brahms gave him regarding Schubert, he did publish two first editions with Brahms as the anonymous editor: the piano score of Schubert's Mass in E flat major, D. 950 (in 1865), and the *Drei Klavierstücke*, D. 946 (in 1868). It is also due to Brahms's persistence that the *Quartetsatz* in C minor was published (D. 703, by Bartolf Senff, Leipzig, in 1870). Brahms owned the manuscript of that work, and held it in high esteem; once again he edited the work anonymously.

In spite of occasional comments to Dietrich and others that he had made no friends in Vienna who could take the place of his old ones, Brahms had in fact rapidly met people who not only were kindly disposed towards him, but who went to unusual lengths to further his career. The pianist Julius Epstein rented the hall for his successful début concert of November 1862, the professor and eminent music critic Eduard Hanslick invited him to illustrate the prestigious public lecture series on music he gave in January 1863; Otto Dessoff, the young conductor of the Philharmonic concerts, hired Brahms to perform with the orchestra in March and programmed his A major Serenade, and the jurist-musician Josef Gänsbacher was the driving force behind Brahms's selection as the new director of the Singakademie. For the rumours Brahms hinted at in his letter to Joachim (Letter 167) were true; that spring, he was offered the post of choral director of the Wiener Singakademie. The appointment went a long way towards removing the sting of his rejection in Hamburg, although he might have been startled to learn that the Committee had selected him by a margin of just one vote.

However much he dithered before accepting the position, once he had made the decision he thanked his friends and immediately set about getting help in planning his programme for the coming year. Inevitably, the prospect of a job in Vienna caused some anxiety.

172
Johannes Brahms to Committee of the Vienna Singakademie

[30 May 1863]

Most honoured gentlemen!

That your choice as conductor of the Wiener Singakademie could have fallen to me is a mark of confidence that surprises as much as it honours me, and which I cherish gratefully. And so I would like first of all to express my lively pleasure at the proposal presented to me, and how greatly I am

---

[19] *Twelve Ländler*, Op. 171 [D. 790].

inclined, indeed how much I desire that I may earn the trust you have placed in me by means of my work on behalf of the Akademie. I now hope to learn, and that partly through your kindness, some details about the Akademie and about the activities expected of me, and I very much hope that will make the offer appear ever more acceptable to me. That I should be pondering at all whether to accept your esteemed invitation you will find understandable, since a position of this kind will certainly effect far-reaching changes in my present way of living. I therefore take the liberty to set out for you some matters which I ask you kindly to give me information about. Above all I should like to know quite generally for how long, and to what extent I am obligated to the Akademie. According to the statutes the rehearsals last until August, but in reality that is probably not the case? Will a vice-chorus director be retained as heretofore, and will I therefore be able to travel for one or several weeks, if I so desire, and leave the rehearsals to him in the mean time?

Then I should like to know, what is the number of *singing* members of the Akademie at this time, and that according to the voices (soprano, alto, tenor, bass); furthermore, how well the *men* were represented during, say, the normal rehearsals last winter. This is related to the question of whether, between now and the start of the season, care will be taken to attract new members, and who is taking over their audition and admission. I should like it very much if, through your kindness, I could survey the activities of the Akademie until now, perhaps by sending the programmes, so that I see what was accomplished and hence what is to be accomplished. If it were possible to obtain the same from Herbeck's singing society that would of course be extraordinarily to my liking.[20] (Because of new works to be selected, if for no other reason.) Finally, I also speak, reluctantly, about the matter of money. However, when I consider that my position at the Akademie will keep me in many ways from looking around for it elsewhere, it does have to be considered. Perhaps it would be simplest if I were to ask you to determine the supplementary income of the former chorus master, which I also heard about from you, in a way that the total amount would constitute an adequate fixed salary for me. But I fear I take far too much advantage of your patience. It's just that it is a very special decision to give up one's freedom for the first time. However, whatever comes from Vienna sounds all the more beautiful to a musician, and whatever beckons there, entices all the more powerfully. Would you therefore, I implore, very kindly excuse my long-windedness.

With the greatest esteem
your most devoted
Johannes Brahms.

[20] The rival, and much better-funded chorus.

173
Johannes Brahms to Josef Gänsbacher

[Hamburg, 30 May 1863]

Dear friend,

I could certainly not have sent my letter off to the committee without writing you a coda of the same. Now I must send everything to you and ask you kindly to take care of it. For I live two hours from here in Blankenese, have written [the letter] here today, but have left the committee's letter, and with it the address, out there. I very much hope you are sufficiently part of the committee that you will join in reading my letter and my wishes, and perhaps also in replying. I have not named any definite sum, for I found the one offered (420 fl.) too low. I should surely be able to reckon on at least 600 fl.[21] Furthermore, I am earnestly counting on being able to see the previous programmes of the Akademie, and would like to know which particular pieces were new. Bach's Christmas Oratorio has presumably been performed by you (in Vienna)?

Perhaps it might not be useless if, aside from the usual rehearsals, the men's and women's choruses were alternately assembled separately each week. On these evenings one would naturally sing mainly works for men's or women's voices and only when necessary, say for a concert, would works for mixed chorus be rehearsed. Perhaps this might succeed in attracting the men to some extent, and could compensate them for the regular rehearsals and at the same time serve the Akademie well.[22]

Does the Academy still have much in its library that has not been used? What, for instance? perhaps substantial collections of older sacred things— Proske?[23] Quite generally I hope with confidence that I may continue to enjoy your kindness and that you will find a quarter of an hour now and then to write to me. The correspondence is a little slow, just because I do live far away and come to town or request forwarding at irregular intervals.

Don't be embarrassed to let my 30 fl. simply remain there or to send them back. In my mind I had pocketed them. Dr Enderes would in any case

[21] In her letter of 3 November 1862, Clara informed Brahms that 5 gulden (or florins) = 2 thaler 15 silbergroschen; (or, 1 gulden = 0.50 thaler). Brahms took an enormous cut in income when he accepted the post in Vienna, in comparison to what he had earned in Detmold: 300 thaler for the *year*, rather than something over 500 thaler, plus what he earned by giving private lessons at Court, for a mere three months in Detmold.

[22] Did Brahms think it was a trial for the men to have to rehearse with the women? It certainly sounds that way.

[23] *Musica Divina*, an important and celebrated collection of religious music collected by Karl Proske (1794–1861), and published in 'cheap, accurate and legible' volumes (Groves²).

be unable to transfer actual publication *rights*, and after all I'm only paying for the manuscript, and one would certainly have to catch Spina in a good mood, were he to shell out for it.

Greet Dr Schneider, Hanslick warmly, and all those who kindly remember me.

With best greetings,

Your

Johs. Brahms

[Post scriptum (on the envelope)]:
To the—to a—
To an estimable—to an honoured
To a most honourable—from—from—to——
I really don't know whether polite formalities belongs on the outside as well?—the inside I have furnished with as many as possible. May the envelope therefore not be incorporated in the file, and kindly be excused.

Josef Gänsbacher's many-sided friendship for Brahms included help in acquiring Schubert manuscripts for him, in this case (unsuccessfully) from Hofrat Dr Enderes; it is to Gänsbacher that Brahms dedicated his Cello Sonata in E minor, Op. 38.[24]

The letter to the very influential music critic, Eduard Hanslick, indicates how quickly, after Brahms's arrival in Vienna, these two men became friends. Although Hanslick often lacked the sort of understanding for Brahms's music possessed by many of his other friends, their personal affinity ran extremely deep, and by the time of this letter they were already on 'Du' terms, even if Brahms still exhibits a certain stiffness here.

---

[24] It is not obvious to me that Kalbeck is correct in considering the dedication of the cello sonata to be payment for the manuscript of Schubert's 'Wanderer', which Gänsbacher obtained for him. (Kal, ii. 72 ff.) Brahms had a far more important reason to be grateful to him, namely, his appointment as music director to the Singakademie. Although Gänsbacher had many talents and was eventually appointed to the voice faculty of the Vienna Conservatory, he was not the most accomplished of cellists, and was the butt of a Brahmsian growl: as he played through the Sonata with the composer—this work in which it is notoriously difficult for the cello to be heard above the piano if the pianist is not considerate—he complained that he could not hear himself. Brahms answered him with 'You're a lucky fellow'. Reported in Alfred von Ehrmann, *Johannes Brahms* (Leipzig, 1933), 192 n. 2.

174
Johannes Brahms to Eduard Hanslick

[Hamburg, Summer 1863]

My dear friend,

You will be wondering why a most delighted and grateful response does not come more quickly than the friendly letters you and so many others sent me. But I feel like one praised undeservedly and would prefer to crawl into a hole for a while. When I received the telegram (through Flatz, who always has to start the ball rolling!)[25] I decidedly wanted to be content with an invitation that does me such honour, and to tempt the Gods no further.

But now I much more decidedly want to accept and to come. And since for me there are no issues except whether I have the courage to say 'Yes', it will simply happen. Had I had declined, my reasons would have been foreign to the Academy and to you Viennese in general.

I must still express my great thanks for your outstanding book about *Beauty in Music*, to which I owe most delectable hours, enlightenment, yes, a kind of tranquillity. Each page invites one to build on what was said before, to attempt the most beautiful development sections, and since in this, as you do say, the theme is the main thing, the pleasure owed to you is doubled. But for one who understands his craft there is work to do everywhere in our art and science, and I wish that we may soon be as handsomely enlightened about other matters.[26]

For today, with warmest greetings and thanks

     Your

     Joh. Br.

175
Johannes Brahms to Albert Dietrich

Hamburg, July 1863

Dear Albert,

I hope that this and the enclosed will still reach you in Oldenburg, and that it was arranged to have it follow you to lovelier lands, on the Rhine or the sea. I would wish that the sea may not be all too essential.

---

[25] Franz Flatz, another enthusiastic supporter of Brahms within the Singakademie.

[26] *Vom Musikalisch-Schönen* (Leipzig, 1854). Brahms first read this book shortly after its publication, when he received it as a gift from Clara Schumann. He was not impressed at that time.

The Quartet I took with me from Hanover, and I promised to bring or send it to you. But now I can't get myself to further shorten the brief time my parents have with me.[27]

For I have indeed accepted the position as chorus director in Vienna and so must be there by some time in August.

Now I would like very much to ask you to tell me a little about matters relating to that. Straight off, for I actually don't know what to ask, and yet feel enormously timid about testing my talent for this undertaking in Vienna, of all places.

Perhaps you could recommend a really practical Oratorio by Handel, with which a novice can make his début with some confidence. Specifically, how did you manage with Bach's Christmas Oratorio? That I would surely like to take on. Did you perform it in its entirety? In two evenings? Only some sections? The first two seem practical, upon quick inspection.

All in all, if you, as venerable and highly learned court conductor, can counsel or suggest, I beg you to.

NB. *Alexander's Feast* by Handel[28] and the *Christmas Oratorio* are particularly on my mind and I would be glad to hear anything at all regarding instrumentation, and so on.

NB. If by any chance you should have arranged the latter with or without organ and could let me have it to look through and for study, I would like that best of all! Even if it is only in scattered pages and isolated sections, just so I might appreciate the principle and the ways and means in general.

Sometime at the beginning of August or the end of July I would very much like to visit Frau Schumann in Baden-Baden. So I ask if you too have similar intentions; then I would wish twice as much to make it possible.

Write to here.

And should we pause for too long in our correspondence, maybe until September, address [letters] to Büsing or Spina in Vienna.

But I hope to hear from you shortly.

Couldn't Düsternbrook near Kiel be of use to you? That would of course correspond to my fondest wish!

Warm greetings from my folks.

Your Johannes.

---

[27] Most likely one of the piano quartets.
[28] 1736; vol. xii in the complete edition by Chrysander.

❧ 1864 ❧

By January Brahms had discovered that he was not entirely suited for the job of leading a musical organization.

176
Johannes Brahms to Adolf Schubring

[Vienna, 17 January 1864]

My dear friend,

Inasmuch as I resolve to dispatch these pages to you, it must be apparent to an initiate that I have long cast my thoughts abroad and desired to
send a greeting.[1]

And in fact it will be nothing more than the friendliest greeting, saved
up for a long time.

When your last refreshing article arrived, so soul-stirring to read, I was
instructed to transmit without fail this greeting to you from me and from
Gustav Nottebohm, who with his seriousness, his extensive knowledge and
quiet diligence, reminds me most gratifyingly of north-German musicians
and friends.

At the time you were probably thoroughly bored by his articles about
Beethoven studies, but had probably also considered that a serious invest-
igation of a serious subject doesn't exactly look amusing.

I like Vienna and everything in it just as much as last year. There is much
about my post that is pleasant, the dubious and unpleasant I knew about
beforehand and must merely endure what I had resolved to bear.

While in any other city one might well hope to have some outside occupation, in Vienna one lives better without such. The many interesting
people, the library, the Burgtheater, the galleries, all that offers plenty to do
and to enjoy outside one's room.

Your kind letter from September is before me. The Italian prize I naturally did not bother with; I did want to attend to the Aachen prize, but I let it
go as well, and so there will be absolutely no help for my empty pocket from
that quarter.

I am literally looking forward to heading north in the spring and fantasize with pleasure about how I want to surprise many a friend as delightfully
as you [surprised] me last year.

[1] '. . . cast my thoughts abroad'. From Goethe, *Die Liebende schreibt.*

Will you allow us soon again to read such fresh and lively essays with such lovely Schumannesque supplements as the last time? I forgot to tell you, the last time, that Nottebohm and I thought it most splendid, and that we enjoyed it enormously.

I hope that sometime this summer we'll see each other once, or more often and possibly even somewhat longer than has always been the case until now.

I hope the family is well and please give them my best greetings. And may you too be greeted, dear friend who understands so well how to live in music.

Your

Johannes Brahms.

Brahms's friendship with the jurist and music critic Adolf Schubring had been strengthened by a surprise visit Schubring paid him in Hamburg, the previous summer. Now Schubring had just written an essay about Robert Schumann which included a 'supplement' in the form of two previous unpublished letters by the composer.[2]

Gustav Nottebohm is another friend quickly acquired in Vienna, his friendship for Brahms an exception, in the musicologist's eccentric life. His innovative studies of the Beethoven sketchbooks were just then under way; Brahms followed that work with keen interest, and brought Nottebohm's *Beethoveniana* essays to the attention of Rieter-Biedermann, the eventual publisher.

The composer must have been particularly short of money, those first years in Vienna. The Singakademie position paid very little, and there were only a few pupils. One good opportunity to acquire a substantial amount of money had come and gone; a prize of 400 thaler for a large work for men's chorus and orchestra, offered by a choral society called the Aachen Liedertafel. Brahms had hoped to enter his cantata *Rinaldo*, but missed the 1 October deadline (apparently he wasn't satisfied with the final chorus, and the work did not take final shape until 1868).[3] By 1865 he would make the decision to overcome his distaste of performing and use his ten fingers to give concerts; but in the mean time, he was driven to a kind of work which even he had not foreseen.

---

[2] *Neue Zeitschrift für Musik*, 4 Dec. 1863.
[3] See Brahms's letter to Franz Wüllner, 1 Oct. 1863 (*BW* xv. 41–2).

177
Johannes Brahms to Melchior Rieter-Biedermann

[Vienna, 11 February 1864]

Most esteemed friend,

To my own and perhaps also to your surprise, I am sending off to you today a 4-hand arrangement of my 'Concerto'.

In the course of the work I thought only of you and I believe that I may be permitted to boast of how practical and indeed easily playable the arrangement turned out to be.

Once more, however, I have this request: that you do not mention my name as the arranger!

After all, it is just a lot of scribbling, and it does not look right if the Master himself creates out of his own work as ungainly a monstrosity as a 4-hand Concerto is bound to be!

Furthermore, too often I had your interest in mind rather than mine, and arranged it for Playing and not (as is very much the fashion these days), for Reading.

Incidentally, you will see for example that my 'Sextet' and 2nd 'Serenade' are published by *Simrock* without my name and that both works are being played with enjoyment.

I would like lots of money for it! Especially because I have the greatest need for it. But I leave this entirely to you and when convenient, I request an answer that jingles according to your pleasure.

Do recommend to the engraver and the proof-reader that they have the printed piano part at hand, and for myself I request a printer's proof not on individual sheets, but such that I can use it for playing. Please, don't forget.

With regard to *Schubert*, nothing will come of it! The other day I asked *Spina* about the waltzes, and he requested them most insistently for himself, talks about a Complete Edition and what not—which, coming from his mouth, means little, unfortunately.

In any case now that he is aware of it, it is impossible to circumvent him.[4]

Wüllner's Variations are giving much pleasure to many others besides me and I hope that people will remember the work and the name. You will

---

[4] Brahms's efforts to procure for Rieter-Biedermann Schubert's opera *Fierrabras* and twelve waltzes 'which had the loveliest faces' came to naught.

no doubt have noticed that *Kirchner* is heard and played with pleasure, hereabouts?[5]

For now, warmest greetings and best wishes for your good health
Your devoted
Johs Brahms

178
Johannes Brahms to Melchior Rieter-Biedermann

[Vienna, 18 February 1864]

Dear Sir,

In a great hurry, my thanks for your lines. However I do not have a letter from you from Feb. 2nd, and *Gotthard* is also unaware of one!

As I said, I beg you do your calculations as you see fit; when I requested, in the most advantageous way for me, that was because my purse has really eked out a most miserable existence for some time, which I also beg to offer as excuse for the following frankness.

You ask about the 'folk-songs'. You have probably heard that some of them were performed in 2 concerts here, and as a matter of fact with great success. Now *Spina* is pressing me hard for them, and I do not wish to conceal that this gentleman quite generally pays substantially more than I can obtain out in the Reich or in your Republic, as I discovered with respect to two trifles which were published by him.[6]

I do not have to discuss why I nevertheless etc. I do not haggle about my things.

But the above-mentioned state of my finances has me considering that the 'folk-songs' are just the very opportunity for alleviating it, and so I ask whether you have great confidence in their success.

For the time being, I was considering collecting 10 of them together and providing them for 4-part mixed chorus and at the same time, for a single voice with piano. Thus, 2 volumes for chorus, solo voice *ad libitum*.

But now I am contemplating up to 30, 32 Friedrichsdors, and ask if that seems conceivable to you.

As yet I have given little thought to the number of songs, what kind of an edition, also what commitment I have towards *Härtels*, in short all sorts of things, and ask you to consider this merely as a very preliminary enquiry.

[5] Franz Wüllner, composer and conductor, was a friend from the time they had met at the Deichmann home in Melhem, in the autumn of 1853. The piece referred to here is his *26 Variations on an Old German Folk-Song*, Op. 11.

[6] The Psalm 13, Op. 27, and *Four Duets* for Alto and Baritone, Op. 28.

In view of the popularity which the songs have enjoyed here, I cannot neglect to give some thought to my own advantage.

Should you wish to take note of this very casual enquiry and intimation, I request that you write to me about it. Initially the songs, almost without exception, will appear with accompaniment. A continuation is always possible.

I beg you not to take this amiss, and to make do with these hurried words.

NB. A draft drawn on Leipzig might be troublesome for me and I request that the 'concerto honorarium' be transmitted to me either in thaler or through *Gotthard*.[7]

You write about 'variations', presumably that refers to a letter of the 2nd?

Warm regards,

your

Johs Brahms

Rieter came to Brahms's financial rescue munificently, paying him the enormous sum of 40 Friedrichsd'or for the songs, with an advance of 40 thaler.[8] The pieces were published as *Fourteen German Folk-Songs for Mixed Chorus* (no arrangement for solo voice ever appeared). Brahms performed five of these songs with the Singakademie during his one season as their director, and dedicated the whole set to them.

Rieter was now also ready to publish—anonymously—the edition of some sonatas by two Bach sons which Brahms had unearthed in Hamburg in the late 1850s (see Letter 114). Brahms's introduction of Heinrich von Herzogenberg to Rieter, incidental to the events here, was a portent of a future friendship which would be very precious to him, as Herzogenberg became the husband of Elizabet von Stockhausen, the highly gifted musician to whom Brahms was devoted.

179
Johannes Brahms to Melchior Rieter-Biedermann

[Vienna, 26 March 1864]

Dearest Herr Rieter,

I am shocked that I seem to have left your last esteemed letter unanswered. Unfortunately, I cannot claim that a letter of mine must have got lost, since I do not keep a record and I can indeed believe myself capable of

---

[7] For his piano four-hand version of the Piano Concerto, Op. 15.

[8] Somewhere between 320 and 400 thaler in all, which exceeded Brahms's Viennese salary for the year. An exact equivalent is difficult to calculate, but see Helmut Kahnt and Berndt Knorr, *Alte Masse, Münzen und Gewichte*, Bibliographisches Institut Mannheim/Wien (Zurich, 1987). Is it chance that this sum was about equal to the Aachen prize?

all sorts of things in this regard. Therefore I beg your pardon and thank you belatedly for the honorarium of 40 thaler, which arrived in good order. Also, regarding the 'folk-songs' it remains as agreed upon, to my great joy, and sometime soon I must collect together some appropriate and suitable ones. I hope very much that you did not take amiss or misinterpret my letter, which was intended solely in friendship! At worst I might have written all too hastily and vaguely or all too frankly, but *desired* nothing other than simply to tell you the situation and not to embarrass you in your decision-making. As indeed you may be assured quite generally of my sincere esteem and friendship for you, and you may believe me that it gives me real joy to be of service to you and to prove my affection.

'Variations on the Rakoczy-March' by me do not exist. Frau *Schumann* merely had it set for piano by me, a form in which it has however been published by various people and thus could no longer fill a long-felt need.

There is in these parts a young man, Herr *Heinrich Freiherr von Herzogenberg*, a student of the conductor *Otto Dessoff*, whose quite agreeable songs I have seen and who has a lively desire to see himself in print. Having the highest regard for your firm, which is self-evident, he has requested that I make enquiries of you. He lays no claim to an honorarium, I have however given him to understand that for one thing, *you* may well set conditions, and consequently it would be satisfactory to him to make the transaction acceptable by possibly committing himself to a number of copies or by some other way. Would you perhaps have the kindness to write me a word under what conditions you would accept an Op. 1.

I saw a considerable number of songs, of rather variable worth however, most of them easy to perform and some with a quite direct expressiveness. Some time soon I will inform myself more precisely and maybe I will hear from you whether you are at all inclined.

The Sonata for 2 pianos by *[Wilhelm] Fr[iedemann] Bach* I ask you to send to me; maybe I will even find a good copy at the court library.

I enclose a scrap of paper, which constitutes the preamble for the 2 violin sonatas [by C. P. E. Bach]; I thought it could find its place on the reverse side of the title-page.

With best regards,
your
Johs Brahms

Brahms sent a glimpse of his life in Vienna to Clara, who was now on tour in Russia. The picture he paints for her is rather different from the scene he described to Adolf Schubring! (Letter 176).

180
Johannes Brahms to Clara Schumann

Vienna, 4 April 1864

Dearest Clara,

My best thanks for your most informative letter, which unfortunately has to travel an ever greater distance to me. Even more depressing, of course, is that the prospect for the next one is getting to be ever further away and soon unimaginably far.

Still, this is only noticed by someone who leads a quiet life, as I do.

By now the first big concert has passed, and probably several others, and I hope they went most beautifully. That you also encountered such fine appreciation of your husband's work in Livonia[9] and Russia doesn't surprise me at all. By the age of 50 your husband would have been able to see how the beautiful sounds of his music rang in every heart.

Or would it be different if he were still living? Would people in their spirit of contradiction have waited until his death in any case? Here, no one is more popular, and this indeed in the finest sense.

I would be happy to hear a lot about Rubinstein; perhaps I think and expect so much better of the Man than one did of the Composer, for of the latter one can hardly expect great things any longer.[10]

This autumn he played a piano quartet here which became enormously famous, have you heard it? But then he writes so much that the quartet is probably already obsolete.

Unfortunately, I now must decide whether I want to keep the Akademie for next year. If only someone else could do it for me!

In our 3rd concert, the *Christmas Oratorio* (Parts 1, 2, 3, 4, 6) went indeed quite splendidly, I must say. I and the chorus, at least, enjoyed it. Faced with the local critics, a Bach work has a difficult time.

Hanslick must have suffered the torments of hell for a week, for the *St John's Passion* was performed by Herbeck 2 days later.

Unfortunately we have yet another concert on April 17th, and *unfortu-*

---

[9] Present-day Latvia. Riga, its capital, was home to a large German-speaking enclave. In the 19th c. Riga maintained a thriving musical life under several Leipzig musicians; Richard Wagner spent two seasons there as conductor of the opera (1837–9).

[10] Relations between Anton Rubinstein and Brahms had warmed up somewhat, after a rather sour beginning in the 1850s. In Baden-Baden during the summer just ended, Rubinstein had been very generous to Brahms, making his house and piano available when Brahms needed to practise. In the long run, however, the two men viewed their obligations to their art too differently to allow a friendship to prosper.

nately I had reasons to accept the Committee's suggestion to present only 'Brahms'!

The *Ave Maria, Marien-* and other choral Lieder, a motet, solo quartets, the String Sextet, and finally, with Carl Tausig, my sonata for 2 pianos.[11]

This last will surprise you the most, for you probably have a horrendous concept of Tausig. He is however a curious little fellow, and a quite exceptional pianist who, by the way, keeps transforming himself to his advantage as much as it is possible for any person to do.

Things by Rubinstein, Chopin, and of course principally Liszt, he often plays wonderfully. He had already asked me for the Sonata for his concerts, and so that will now happen.

Härtel is publishing several of the *Geistliche Chorlieder* and 3 solo quartets (*Wechsellied zum Tanze*). They are astonishingly agreeable and ask for whatever there is! Even before this they wrote to me of their own accord and asked for new things! My concerto for 4 hands will shortly be published by Rieter. Arranged to be very easy, but it may be dismal to play because the sound gets to be so uniform.[12]

Meanwhile my worst problem is the above-mentioned decision which has to be made. The Akademie has certainly given me quite a lot of pleasure, but for all that there is also plenty that is unpleasant along with it.

That people are musical, that they read at sight, and practise nicely, is all well and good, but life here is too hectic, in the short season neither a person nor an institute can survive that doesn't lurch along, but would prefer to exist quietly and seek enjoyment and enlightenment *within*. Here everyone is bent on excitement, on dancing from one concert and one surprise to another.

What also puts pecuniary and artistic matters in a dubious position is the absence of a really eminent and eminently artistic person at the top.

I could manage musical matters quite well and adequately, but things here being what they are I would need to possess an organizational talent which I lack.

There is not much I could tell you about my life apart from that. My real friends are the old friends; unfortunately, my heart can take pleasure in them

---

[11] Sonata for Two Pianos Op. 34*b*, the second version of the Piano Quintet (but not published in that form until December 1871). The entire programme is given in Renate and Kurt Hofmann, *Johannes Brahms Zeittafel zu Leben und Werk*, 64.

[12] i.e. the Piano Concerto arranged for four hands (see Letter 177). Although the solo piano part was published in 1861 and the orchestra parts probably in 1862, the full score was not published until 1874; so this four-hand arrangement was for many years the only way for the public to have access to the complete music. *Two Motets*, Op. 29, were published by Breitkopf & Härtel in July 1864, along with the *Geistliches Lied*, Op. 30, and the *Three Solo Quartets*, Op. 31.

more and more only in my imagination. There is no one here to replace any one of them.

—But that was taken amiss by my Viennese friends yesterday morning, and I was kept from writing any more from then on. They came one after the other, until I locked up shop and left with the last one.

Now this morning, I must confess, my next concert and the decision I have to make again occupy my head in a most uncomfortable manner.

If a person had money, he could surely make much better decisions and do whatever he likes to his heart's content! Without that, one is really always quite fettered. How dearly I would like, for example, to go to Hamburg soon (but first I want to inspect a few beautiful mountains here) and sit in my old room for a few evenings! However I am drawn just as much to Baden, when you come back. I will boldly try to discover just what kind of exertions Härtel's gold can stand!

My folk-songs arranged for chorus were extraordinarily well liked here and Spina was very greedy for them, but since Rieter is very insistent on them and the honorarium is immaterial to him, he is getting them.[13]

I have the Schubert song that you saw at my house last year waiting for you. I got it for you from a pretty girl with whom, God knows, I would have done a silly thing if luckily someone hadn't swiftly hooked her at Christmas.[14]

My family is well, only my love makes me fearful that my mother is getting really old, who knows how soon I will be fated to suffer the deepest grief.

Write to me very soon and a great deal about you and the children, whom I like so much to hear about, that they are well, and where they are.

With my warmest love
your Johannes.

I have just received a letter from Dietrich, I enclose it for you in case you may not have heard directly so soon. What can one say and hope for? One can hardly, without any further ado, join in the lovely Easter festivities. His handwriting looks strangely altered. You are of course also writing to him?

Albert Dietrich was in the throes of a nervous breakdown. He would recover completely, but gave both Clara and Brahms a scare as they relived some of the horror of Schumann's mental collapse.

---

[13] Clara was astonished and delighted at the small fortune Rieter paid for them.

[14] A reference to Ottilie Ebner née Hauer. Brahms came close to proposing marriage at a Christmas party in 1863—only to discover she had become engaged that very morning. See Ottilie von Balassa, *Die Brahmsfreundin Ottilie Ebner* (Vienna, 1933), 43 ff., and several letters in this volume.

Hanslick firmly believed music began with Mozart. He had little enthusiasm for the growing appreciation of J. S. Bach, and less than none for Brahms's interest in the music of Couperin and Scarlatti.

Now a letter came from Joachim: 'Man, in Vienna can one find dearer friends and better musicians? Do write a "No".' He too was concerned about Dietrich.

181

Johannes Brahms to Joseph Joachim

[Vienna, after 5 April 1864]

Dearest fellow,

It was very kind of you to send me Dietrich's letter; it's being returned here with my best thanks. I myself had already had a letter from him and now for a second time felt the same deep and most anguished sympathy for the good fortune he paints for us with such warmth.[15] For in reality, after these letters I sense no glimmer of hope for his well-being. The strangely altered handwriting, and of course far more, the manner in which he describes his present and particularly his former condition, only frightens me. Let us then hope and wish for the best!

Unfortunately, it seems to me much simpler for one to lose his sanity than to recapture it once he has lost it.

My best Jussuf, there are here no dearer friends and better musicians! Not even a single one of those whom I am constantly deprived of is being replaced for me! And so the decision to commit myself again for next year is difficult for me.

However many pleasures the Akademie affords me, there's nevertheless plenty to give one thought.

Don't be too greatly or unpleasantly surprised if you should shortly come across a 'Brahms' programme!

The Akademie must present a concert, and I simply had no choice but to accede to the committee's request. The concert is supposed to make money and has to be rehearsed within 2–3 weeks. Rather than prostitute myself as a mere *Capellmeister* and bore the public with a long succession of choruses, I prefer to take what comes as a composer; whoever attends knows full well what fun he is getting into.

I'll probably not come up north in the beginning of May, but I am drawn to Mother and other things.

I hear it's certain that you are going to England and then again to

---

[15] Ironically meant. Brahms was deeply disturbed over the misfortune of his friend.

Aachen, Hamburg, etc. Let me know, when you have a chance, how long you'll be in Hanover and whether you're going to England. I definitely want to arrange my trips accordingly.

Would I then still find you in the romantic tower apartment?

The Christmas Oratorio went very well and gave me great joy. That the 2nd concert fell somewhat short was hardly my fault, and even today (probably as the only one in the know) I have to admire my skill in programme-making etc. displayed thereby.

Meanwhile this sort of an Akademie and this sort of a directorship has its hooks and one has to learn to grab hold of them.

How I would have preferred to take Dietrich's place this winter!

For now, best greetings to you, the wife, the Scholzes, and all others.

I hope we'll see each other in the spring and that I will hear in the mean time!

Affectionately your
Johannes.

Brahms had reason to be sarcastic about his 'skill in programme-making'. Rather than try to appeal to his audience, his second concert had presented a programme of relentlessly sombre music, to the decided disadvantage of the till. In contrast, the all-Brahms concert must have been a success: by unanimous consent, Brahms was reappointed as director of the choral society. He resigned nevertheless, for reasons set forth here quite explicitly.

182

Johannes Brahms to Adolf Schubring

[Hamburg, 19 June 1864]

Dear friend,

So I bolted past you after all and came here! I might have known that the yearning for Mother wouldn't let me stop on the way.

Before anything else I'd like to ask now if you can't take a holiday for a few days at about this time and dawdle them away here. If so, I'd send you the Sonata for two pianos right away so that you can prepare yourself, and quite generally, Hamburg is pretty good for a few days.

But I have no intention of staying here longer than that. Would the good Themis really drop her scales straightaway if you were to set out forthwith and abandon her for a few days?[16]

---

[16] Greek goddess, personification of justice and righteousness.

It would be harder for me to get away. The brief time here—after that I plan to go to Baden and finally to accomplish a more complete removal to Vienna.

I have given up my post there! In spite of many joys which the chorus there provides, unfortunately it had to be.

The nature and circumstances of the Institute are such that I would be occupied less with musical than with other matters. [The Singakademie] would have to be helped out by means of concerts which taste more agreeable to the public, etc., I would have to pay too much heed to primadonnas, to a thousand things that are no concern of mine, and in Vienna one need not look for things to do, time flies by in the loveliest waltz tempo as it is.

I am pleased that you didn't hurry into accepting Schuberth's proposal. That man is such that one has cause to think twice when he makes a proposal.[17]

As far as my quartets are concerned, I wish you would use the opportunity to say a word about mutes. They come in wood and in metal, the latter dampen the sound far too much for passages in chamber music, as in mine, etc. etc.[18]

That it always gives me great pleasure when my things are so much to your liking, I need not mention. I hope you have fun with the Solo Quartets at Härtel's.[19]

I wish you could still incorporate in the aforementioned article a *Ricercata*, which I'm supposed to provide as a supplement to the Härtel journal. But unfortunately I don't know when. I haven't sent it off yet. If it arrives in time, I would like to ask you to be careful with an illustration of the themes and their inversion; maybe I'll write it out for you.[20]

But now—the main thing is, couldn't you come? Give me the pleasure.

My parents send their warmest greetings. And be greeted by me as well, together with your wife and little children.

Your

Johs. Brahms

Rather than the few nostalgic evenings at home in his old room Brahms was dreaming of, he returned to Hamburg to find his family in disastrous discord. His parents

---

[17] Julius Schuberth, of the publishing business of J. Schuberth & Co., Leipzig and New York. He was planning an edition of Schumann piano works.

[18] Each of the Piano Quartets, Opp. 25 and 26, call for mutes in one of the movements.

[19] The Vocal Quartets, Op. 31, were just about to be published by Breitkopf & Härtel (July 1864).

[20] *Ricercare*, 'a fugue of the closest and most learned description'. Probably the Fugue in A flat minor, WoO 8. Brahms was asked to contribute to the *Allgemeine Musikalische Zeitung*, Breitkopf & Härtel's house journal, where the fugue appeared that July.

had come to a bitter parting of the ways, his father insisting he could no longer live with an aged wife and the ailing daughter he viewed as a malingerer (she suffered from migraine headaches). The events leading to this crisis are impossible to sort out in detail, given the surviving facts. Certain it is, however, that Kalbeck's description is not even marginally accurate.[21] The current difficulty was nothing new. Life in the Brahms household had been troubled for a very long time, as witnessed by the details of the letter Christiane Brahms wrote to Johannes just before her death (Letter 191), and had now come to a terrible climax. By July, Johann Jakob had left his family and stopped supporting his 73-year-old wife, who was becoming blind. She too was forced to move. Brother Fritz and sister Elise never forgave their father; to Clara's astonishment, Brahms had some understanding for him, as indeed he did for all the parties involved, and he tried to reconcile his parents.[22] When that failed, he urged the family to remain on speaking terms (in vain), acted as go-between when that too failed, and did his utmost to provide money for mother, father, and sister. As a consequence, the next few years were the leanest ones of his life, as there were now separate households to pay for. His brother's role in these events is still unclear, but apparently the financial burden of helping his parents fell far more heavily on Johannes; the falling-out between the brothers seems to stem from this period.[23]

At the same time, the Sonata for Two Pianos was in the process of becoming a piano quintet, Göttingen and Agathe were on Brahms's mind again as the second String Sextet was taking shape, and he had to get away from Hamburg in order to compose. He made arrangements to visit with friends: Joachim, Grimm, and in Karlsruhe, his new friend Hermann Levi; then, as of old, he took refuge with Clara, who was now in Baden-Baden. From there he kept in touch.

183
Johannes Brahms to Julius Otto Grimm

[Hamburg, July 1864]

Dear Grimm,

I have the most decided need to hear about you—and would most prefer to hear it from you yourself. If, as I imagine, you are visiting now at the Georgia-Augusta, then dip pen into inkwell right away and let me know how things are in all those houses that one liked so much to visit. About that particular house and garden near the city gate write to me as well.—

---

[21] Kal, ii. 142 ff. [22] Clara to Brahms, 19 July 1864, *SBB* i. 458.

[23] A volume comprising the complete, unabridged correspondence within the family is now contemplated, and would probably clarify the picture. Private communication from Kurt Hofmann, Brahms-Institut, Lübeck.

But do it soon, I am leaving here in the next few days, and unfortunately the saddest aspect is not that I don't know which point of the compass I'll head for.

Is Joachim coming to Göttingen as well, after all? I only know that he is back from England.

Have you got my Pf-Quartet? Do you subscribe to the Härtels-Bagge paper, if not I will send you a supplement by me and will include mo- and quartets with it.[24] Give my warmest greetings to your wife, and just how many children have you, now?

How dearly I'd like to see you, so at least don't make me wait for a written letter.

That's always a poor substitute.

For the winter I'm probably going back to Vienna, although I have given up my post.

Be content with this brief greeting and consider that all those most friendly greetings I'm enclosing wouldn't fit on the blank pages attached hereto.

Affectionately,

Your

Johannes Br.

Hohe Fuhlentwiete 74.
Hamburg (in the summer 64)

Georgia Augusta is the name of the University in Göttingen; Brahms used it here to refer to the town. Six years after his romance with Agathe, he had not put her out of mind. The 'house and garden by the gate' was hers; she herself was in Ireland, working as a governess. Brahms incorporated Agathe's name into the first movement of his new string sextet, Op. 36 in G, where the letters A-G-A-[T]-H-E are woven into the second theme.[25]

---

[24] The *Ricercare*, Fugue in A Flat minor, WoO 8 (see n. 20), the Motets, Op. 29, for five voices a capella, and the Vocal Quartets with Piano, Op. 31.

[25] Measures 162 ff., violin and viola I, and subsequent material to the end of the exposition. In German usage B is denoted by the letter H. Even in the different key of the recapitulation, he manages to work in the same notes from measure 508, in a canonic cascade of Agathes.

184
Johannes Brahms to Joseph Joachim

[Baden-Baden, 29 August 1864]

Dear friend,

If it were worth the effort, I could tell you about the Carlsruhe festival, where I was driven by thirst of knowledge or—confounded curiosity. It was as ugly as one would imagine after what was previously encountered, but at the same time as feeble and boring as one wishes ugliness would always be. In fact, the chief rascals weren't there, and there were too few of the ones who unabashedly deal in *boom-boom divisi*. Reményi played abominably. Unbelievably impudent and ridiculous how he performs the Rakoczy March, the Huguenot Fantasy, etc. It was as contemptible *of* me as it was *for* me to listen to him mistreating your Concerto. I had to repent with a severe headache.

With the exception of a few silent musicians, who were driven out of their mind alternately by laughter or by anger, the public was well pleased by the business and throughout four days shouted relentlessly and demanded *da capos*.

But the whole affair was quite bearable in the company of Hermann Levi, the local musical director. That young man, in spite of all of the theatre-conductor routine, is so fresh and gazes so brightly onto the loveliest heights that it's truly a pleasure.

Allgeyer is merrily photographing everything in sight which might please his friend—he expects great things of the new art! I also have a picture (of me) for you.

Did you leave a letter from him unanswered some time ago? If so you might still give him the pleasure of writing a few lines; *His* reason for writing has now naturally disppeared.

If, as I hope, you are in possession of my F minor Sonata for two pianos, do let me have it without delay, Lichtenthal 14, through Frau Schumann. If you feel like it, do write a line at the same time whether the Sonata should in fact be printed???

I have been staying here for some time and since Frau Schumann will shortly be returning from Switzerland, I will probably stay here a while longer. How did you find Dietrich?

My warmest greetings to your wife and let me have the Sonata and also a letter.

Your
Johannes.

185
Johannes Brahms to Johann Jakob Brahms[26]

[Baden-Baden, August 1864]

Dearest Father,

just a few words—simply the plea to write me a few lines soon about how you are and how things stand in general. I suppose Fritz didn't take the flat again? Will you continue to live in your little room?

Do you go to Fuhlentwiete 74 more often? Write to me explicitly how everything is going.

About me there's not much to tell. After a few happy days that I spent with Joachim and Grimm, I came here and although Frau Schumann has gone to Switzerland, I am staying anyway, for I enjoy it quite a lot and there is nothing really to draw me anywhere. Really, I would have liked to spend the summer at home with you, only that if I wanted to create for myself any sort of mood for working, I was really obliged this time to go away and seek sometimes to feel less intensely what is never out of my mind.

Write and tell me if you also read my letters to the others—I hope so![27]

But in any case you must always write a few lines to me yourself, so I know where I stand.

I hope the first step was the worst and that things will now be getting more and more friendly.

And of you, I firmly believe that you will do whatever possible to make it so.

Address letters to: Baden-Baden, Lichtenthal 14, at Frau Schumann's.

I am staying elsewhere and in fact very charmingly, in a garden in Baden. Here one sees all kinds of people, the most beautiful surroundings, and so it is bearable.

Let me hear, and that clearly and distinctly. Don't save the money I gave you, it doesn't need to last until New Year.

And so with all love,

Your Johannes

[26] Of the letters Brahms sent home before the breakup of his family and subsequent death of his mother, very few survived. They were preserved by his sister, but when she died in 1892, they all came back to him—and fed his stove. Letters to his father written after the separation, on the other hand, were kept by his stepmother. When she died they passed to her son, Fritz Schnack, an ardent admirer of the stepbrother who had treated him with such generosity. Schnack carefully preserved every memento of Brahms in a collection of items which forms a basic element of the Brahms Archive at the Staat- und Universitätsbibliothek in Hamburg. Fortunately, Brahms saved the letters of his mother and sister *to himself.*

[27] To Elise and his mother.

186
Johannes Brahms to Johann Jakob Brahms

[Baden-Baden, beginning October 1864]

Dearest Father,

I really miss news from all of you, while at the same time I can hardly hope it might be encouraging.

I live so quietly and peacefully here that I like to imagine that you too are together and more content.

That mother and Elise have provided a room for me might please me a lot if I could suppose that you would use it a great deal! And I hope that will happen, after all, you could often take your after-dinner nap in the company of my books and from there it is not far to Fuchs.[28]

Don't skimp on money when it comes to mother, whether it lasts till New Year is not important and money puts a smile on many a face that would otherwise be glum. Do whatever is possible, even though your anger might occasionally rise up! Be helpful to them in moving and by no means allow yourself to be driven away; the time will come when we'll all be grateful to you for it!

I am probably leaving soon for Vienna, if you write immediately I'll still get your letter (Lichtenthal 14).

I shall write to Marxsen about the matter, you, once and for all, must pay no mind to what others think, just do more than is necessary, and your duty, to set everything on a good course.

Can you read my writing?

When are you moving and where to?

I am supposed to give you warmest greetings from Frau Schumann. She is coming to Hamburg before Christmas, do visit her then, you needn't say a word to her!

Where do you take your noon meal? Surely you still go there? Maybe you could settle a few of mother's expenses for me, for instance, just now for shipping the music to Vienna. Make a note of it and I will send it along on the next occasion.

---

[28] In August Elise had written: '... I have found quite a charming flat, comprising one room and a small sleeping chamber ... then in the rear, behind the garden there is a very cosy room for you when you are in Hamburg. [Since the room is empty], we can already bring your books there' (*Familie*, 101). Fuchs was the name of a famous dance parlour, where presumably Johann Jakob could find work.

Joachim has had a son, have you already heard? on the 12th of September.

Write to me soon and in great detail and explicitly. Most affectionately, your Johannes.

Johann Jakob complained bitterly at the thought that his son had spent jolly days with his friends while he himself was going through such difficulties. It looked to him, he wrote, as if Johannes were going out of his way to forget about the trouble at home.

187
Johannes Brahms to Johann Jakob Brahms

[Vienna, mid-October 1864]

Dearest Father,

Your last letter gave me much sorrow and pain. I beg you once and for all just to believe me that no son could ever love his father more dearly than I love you, and that no one could feel the sadness of our circumstances more keenly and more deeply than I now do, unfortunately.

When writing, it is hard to refrain from wishing and guessing, but I appreciate how easily that can be misunderstood.

Joy I do indeed feel when I experience beauty as an artist or as a human being. But you can well imagine that careless gaiety is not my mood when I must think of my dearest ones with sadness.

I wrote to you that you needn't say a word to Frau Schumann.

You might have considered, however: that she knows everything anyway, that you can speak for yourself, and that no one can speak better for you than I. Therefore discuss these things or not, and be assured that Frau Schumann thinks only the very best of you. But in any case, visit Frau Schumann, you see her at the rehearsals anyway.[29]

I hope you will write to me and will always at least mention the others even if nothing has happened, so I will know just that.

I have been in Vienna for several days now, and am doubly glad to have given up my post, for it would not have given me much pleasure this winter.

Before that, I was in Baden, in the company of several friends and mainly Frau Schumann; I did not forget any of you for a single day, but could often revive myself through friendship and music.

---

[29] At rehearsals of the Hamburg Philharmonic, in which Johann Jakob was now a permanent double-bass-player thanks to its conductor, Julius Stockhausen.

I am living at: Vienna, Singerstraße No. 7, Staircase 7, 4th floor.

Write to me really soon and also about your music-making.

Do you have the new pitch?[30] and are you beginning with the 9th Symphony?

Do you need money? or do you need any for the others? I asked you not to skimp on the ducats for them.

Do you see Fritz?

How are things with Herr Marxsen? Should I possibly write to him about these matters?

You can probably pass the enclosed letter on to Fritz if you don't go there yourself?

Can you read my handwriting? At least you can see that I'm trying!

Now write to me a great deal, and never suspect that I could ever be anything but the most tender son to you.

Do you have 2 rooms once again? and are you satisfied with the new flat?

I greet you most warmly,
your Johannes

But his father was not forthcoming with money for his wife and daughter, and when Clara visited the women later in December, she found them in a pitiable state, out of food and without money. She immediately handed over the 100 thaler Brahms had saved up for their future expenses, and wrote to him that she did not see how they could possibly carry on that way (5 December 1864).

In October, Brahms left the pleasant environment of Baden-Baden and his friends and returned to Vienna, where he intended to teach, compose, and pursue his interest in Schubert.

188

Johannes Brahms to Clara Schumann

Vienna, the 13 of October 1864

My dearest Clara,

I must make use of a quiet moment here at Nottebohm's to say a friendly word to you. I travelled in such contentment, my heart was so full of love and joy, that all the clouds vanished which for so long had hidden from it what is most worthy of love, and the heart just has to say a word at once!

[30] In 1858 the French government appointed a commission to standardize pitch, which had risen alarmingly from the classical A = 425 cycles per second [more or less] to as much as A = 457. The new 'Paris' pitch was set by French law at A = 425. Stockhausen introduced it to the Hamburg Philharmonic, where it meant that the orchestra would have to acquire new wind instruments.

I arrived here yesterday at noon and will do my utmost to be sitting in my own flat by tomorrow and will therefore permit myself no rest till then. I had to remain in Munich for 24 hours because, without having been tired or tipsy, I utterly failed to hear the departure announcement.

I saw Perfall, Schwind, v. Sahr and Jul. Jos. Maier, the Pinakothek and all kinds of things from the outside and only the Hofbräuhaus from the inside as well.[31]

The weather was so mild even at night that your blanket stayed in the portmanteau, and now too, it is still so mild that I imagine you are taking the most beautiful walks and thinking very cheerfully and very kindly of me while you do.

No letter from Härtel's was waiting for me, but neither, I hope, have you received the songs by now. Otherwise do send them to me right away, it no longer distresses me, and anyway I still have money.[32]

When I am sitting cosily at home the day after tomorrow, or even by tomorrow, I will also write cosily and sensibly, but for today be content with this greeting, because N. has a thousand Beethoveniana to show me and I must run soon, and at best I can still try to send a telegram while I pace up and down and am

sitting	sitzen
and sweating	und schwitzen
and glu–	and lei–
ing rhy–	men Rei–
mes to shab–	me schof–
by ver–	le Stroph–
ses; wro–	en; schrie–
te I let–	be ich Brie–
ters or rath–	fe o–
er mu–	der auch No–
sic, 'twould	ten, 's wär

[31] Karl von Perfall, one of the composers who agreed to sign the anti-Liszt Declaration. He later became Administrative Director of the Munich Court Opera. J. J. Maier was curator of the Munich State Library. Moritz von Schwind? If so, the intimate friend of Schubert. Heinrich von Sahr was an old acquaintance, who had put Brahms up in Leipzig during his first visits there in 1853. The Hofbräuhaus, then as now, was an enormous and very noisy beer hall.

[32] To Brahms's disgust, Härtel turned down the *Magelone Lieder*, Op.33, not only because they were too expensive, but because the piano accompaniment was too difficult. Brahms scornfully wrote to Clara he had not noticed that octaves harmed the 'Erlkönig', and he wondered which of the songs Selmar Bagge, by now a music critic in Leipzig and *not* a noted pianist, had been unable to read at sight (*SBB* i. 472).

likely be more	wohl mehr
worthy of thanks.	des Dankes wert.
So then:	Also:
In Oos	In Oos
I started off,	ging's los,
of moisture much	des Nassen viel
from eyes did fall,	dem Aug' entfiel
That Brahms,	der Brahms
he took	der nahm's
Handkerchief from pocket	Tuch aus der Tasch
and Levi quickly,	und Levi rasch
instantly,	sofort
these words	das Wort
his mouth did issue:	dem Mund entsandt':
Oh friend, these maidens	o Freund, kein Tand
so dear and fine	sind dir
no playthings are	und mir
for you	die Mägdelein
and me	so lieb und fein,
indeed—for sure	und gar—fürwahr
it's clear and true	's ist klar und wahr,
no item so rare	keine War' so rar
as such a woman	als solche Frau,
as we obser-	wie wir sie schau-
ved her;	eten;
oh, if	o wenn
we were now to feel shame	wir jetzt der Trän'
for these, our tears,	uns schämeten,
'twould be scandalous,	's wär skandalös,
truly even wicked!	recht eigentlich bös!
To Brahms	dem Brahms
it comes	dem kam's,
as it would come	als käm's
to him	wie dem's
who does no-	wohl kommt, der nicht-
thing but make poetry.	es tut als dicht't.
And beginning to trot with mounting	Und anhub beschleunigten Trab
speed	er

In three-eight time, he said—do read—	Im Dreiachtel-Takte wohl sprach er—dieses—lies es
Oh should your tears of pain	O würdet ihr Tränen des Schmerzes
turn into words and rhymes of love,	Zu Worten und Reimen der Liebe
Nary a heart unmoved would remain.	Kein Herz ungerühret doch bliebe.
But that's enough of the jest for now,	Und nun muß genug sein des Scherzes,
For it can't go on.	Denn es will nicht mehr.

Now I must really be off in a big rush, and regrettably have to leave the fourth verse as it stands, otherwise it might well have become quite a nice four-liner for a canon.

So dearest Clara, be well and joyful, joyful that love cannot be slain after all; my best greetings to the children and to Levi, if you lay eyes on him.

Affectionately your
Johannes.

Write by way of Spina or Wessely.

Oos was the nearest railway stop for Baden-Baden. Brahms's outrageous rhymes are impossible to translate, but we have tried to provide enough English equivalents so that the reader can enjoy the silliness in something like the way Brahms and Clara did.

High spirits also mark one of his earliest letters to Hermann Levi, the first por-tion of which, in stilted mock-archaic German, is given here in an English ap-proximation. Brahms and Levi struck up a friendship marked by wit, artistic collaboration of the highest order, and a sometimes painful competitiveness. By the time of this letter, they were on 'Du' terms. For Brahms the friendship with the young conductor could not have come at a better time, as he had just lost the bach-elor companionship of Joachim. Like Joachim, Levi was a Jew; unlike him, he never renounced his religion, and the little ditty Brahms composed suggests that religion was a topic of discussion between them as well Levi's co-religionist, Paul David, the assistant Kapellmeister and son of Ferdinand David. He is the one with the white trousers.

Clara, who formed a friendship with the young conductor at about the same time, informed Brahms that in Levi he had gained a firm friend.[33] The Elise men-tioned in this letter is Elise Schumann, Clara's daughter, who had just accepted a

---

[33] *SBB* i. 459, 15 Oct. 1864.

post in the household of Princess Anna von Hessen, in Karlsruhe. Levi took a protective, not a romantic interest in her.

The 'magnificent silent friend' is Julius Allgeyer, photographer and engraver, and third member of the 'gang'. The 'ambience' Brahms breathed, impregnated with rose of Saron, was apparently due to a particular Turkish tobacco, purchased from a particular pretty girl in Karlsruhe.

189

Johannes Brahms to Hermann Levi

[Vienna, December 1864][34]

Yr. Lordship,

I am in receipt of Yr. worthy letter of such-and-such date of the still current year and I hasten to counter with the following. I scarcely comprehend that this can already be a reply and I would modestly put off my writing, considering it too presumptuous of me to desire to attempt to recall myself so soon to Your Eminence's recollection, were it not that Yr. Eminence's most gracious letter represents an incontestable fact.

So may this, my aforementioned sentiment, be a token, *quasi* a *testimonium* of the unforgettable nature of the great amiability shown me by Yr. Eminence and his distinguished friends and how, in a manner of speaking, I continue to breathe the same ambience (mightily impregnated with the fragrance of roses of *Saron*).

And verily, the moon will not go through many more changes, and the white trousers will be changed even less often, before I again immerse myself totally [in that ambience] and gladden and refresh myself, as when:

> With his Capellmeister he'd go for a walk
> Dressed in trousers as white as chalk.
> While one in Jewishness himself did immerse,
> The other his little voice would rehearse.

All that, just as if it were happening today! How

> The splendid Balmung[35] at each performance he wielded,
> And though tender in years, his talents unshielded
> And a fine, secure position that yielded.
> I make no comment nor dip pen into ink,
> T'would hurt his feelings, I really do think.

---

[34] After Brahms's death, Levi dated his letters as best he could, and gave them to Kalbeck to use (see Kalbeck Convolut, Brahms-Institut, Lübeck).

[35] The name of Siegfried's sword, Wagner notwithstanding.

This will only rhyme with a drink, and that would make me too verbose. But about that magnificent silent friend I will make no verses, do greet him and all the others.

I suppose Rieter was with you. Is he giving you my things, as I have advised him for the sake of better sales?

All in all, I can now insist on a letter with a clear conscience, for I observe from my ever more swiftly moving hand that I myself am writing one, and I have an urgent need for answers to all my questions.

Are you taking care of Yr. good health? Are you dutifully drinking Yr. coffee, among other items? Are you entertaining Frl. Elise well? Are you going to treat yourself to a Frau Capellmeister? But this is hardly the place for that.

Are you still tormenting one another with your immortal creations, photographs and symphonies?

Just now I should actually have liked to have a sensible chat, but a young Viennese maiden is already waiting, wishing to learn the art of touching (the piano keys). I like it here indeed it suits me well here as I thought it would and as I told you this summer. I am here because I am nowhere else and if one is truly nowhere it is really very pretty here. But wherever one lives one participates in all facets of life and it is conceit to think that one can pick and choose what is to one's liking and that one can enjoy listening to a symphony if the flutes are well played.

And so I am greatly looking forward to Frau Schumann's arrival, and greatly to the opening of the Casino.[36] When does that happen, anyway? Oh, when shall I once more see ye sacks of flour, ye white trousers, ye forests and mountains!

My dear friend, write once in a while, give greetings to the whole gang and for yourself, the best greetings

from your

Johs. Brahms.

[36] In Baden-Baden. Brahms had to prove his age before being admitted to the gaming rooms.

❧ 1865 ❧

190
Johannes Brahms to Hermann Levi

Vienna, late January 1865[1]

Esteemed friend,

In a few days the opera *Fierrabras* by Franz Schubert will reach you. Regarding which, the following explanation. Rieter Biedermann will presumably take several major works by Schubert (masses, etc.) for publication, and so perhaps this opera as well.

Accordingly I would like to ask whether you and *Devrient* would have the piety and devotion to look at the opera with respect to theatrical performances.

Could one alter the text *without too much difficulty*, annotate cuts, etc. for a production? Would you wish to see it performed?

In any case, it will be extraordinarily interesting for you to see the work, and more, I hope that it will impress you and your director deeply. It would really be a pity if a performance were possible and the published score were not usable.

The whole business requires haste, write a word, at least.

As in any case you might have written a word long ago. If not for the kind Elise, I wouldn't know whether you're alive, that you have surrendered yourself to counterpoint, and other things.

If it were not so late at night I'd pour forth my grievances and read you the riot act. And there you all sit in your cosy little nest and to cap it all, you *too* are griping—?

If I had not rented my lodgings and if I were not awaiting Frau Clara, and if I were not such a decorous person who indulges in no extravagances, I would have gone to see the *Yburg* again long ago, and it shan't be long now.[2]

But enough, may my wrath and the Schubert Opera descend upon you. Write to me about the latter regarding *its suitability for performance and*

---

[1] Mis-dated in *BW* vii as February. The letter cannot have been written after 1 February, as Brahms was on his way to Hamburg, where his mother died on 2 February. Clara was to play in Vienna, but that too was postponed, due to an injury to her hand on 12 January.

[2] A castle ruin in the neighbourhood of Baden-Baden.

publication. My greetings to David, Hauser, Lessing, Schrödter, complete with wives, and to Allgeyer and yourself.[3]

Your

J. Brahms.

Levi looked into mounting the opera in Karlsruhe, but nothing came of it. His letter to Brahms remained unanswered—Christiane Brahms had suffered a stroke at the end of January, and died on 2 February, before Johannes could reach Hamburg. She had spent most of the week before writing a ten-page letter to her distant son. It is a gripping and disturbing document, powerfully written in her phonetic, unschooled spelling, essential to an understanding of the young Brahms but virtually suppressed until 1985.[4] In all likelihood, Brahms received the letter immediately before the news of his mother's death. When he speaks of his difficult youth, one cannot assume he is referring merely to his family's chronic shortage of money.

191

Christiane Brahms to Johannes Brahms

Friday afternoon 26 Jan. 65
[letter written 26–30 January]

Dear Johannes

Elise is at the dentist again—I am alone and want to try to write to you, you can't believe how hard it is becoming for me, the eyes weak, the hand unsteady, the content of the letters not as before. Christmas Eve was not as you thought. Father had long before been invited by acquaintances in Altona, & Aunt and I could neither of us go there on foot and so each of us the evening in her own flat. Fritz spent the evening with us, New Year's Eve

---

[3] Carl Friedrich Lessing and Adolf Schroedter were prominent painters, who, with their musical wives, were part of the Karlsruhe group of intellectuals and artists which included the classicist Gustav Wendt, later a close friend of Brahms. Josef Hauser was a highly regarded singer. See Ekkehard Schulz, 'Brahms' Karlsruher Freundes- und Bekanntenkreis', in Joachim Draheim *et al.* (eds.), *Brahms in Baden-Baden and Karlsruhe* (Karlsruhe, 1983).

[4] The letter, which is in the Archive of the Gesellschaft der Musikfreunde in Vienna, has a curious history. It must have been known to Kalbeck, and was certainly known to Geiringer and to Stephenson, who drew on the archive of family letters stored at the Gesellschaft when they wrote their books in 1933 and 1983 respectively. Stephenson even reproduced a small portion of the letter with the comment that the rest of it was not suitable for publication; Kalbeck and Geiringer simply suppressed it, for reasons known best to themselves. In Kalbeck's case, his attitude towards Brahms's mother can be estimated by his comment that her death occurred as a consequence of neglecting to take care of herself properly. The letter was rediscovered by the Brahms scholar Kurt Hofmann, who has included the complete letter in his book *Johannes Brahms und Hamburg*, (Reinbek, 1985). Our translation is based on that publication.

Christian had something to do, so the good Heinrich[5] stayed with his mother, Fritz was with friends and we two alone,[6] the 4th was Fritz's concert, which took place, probably you read it in the newspapers, it was pretty full, and also everything was well received, your Trio and everything else. The two Marscens,[7] whom I had not seen in a long time, were very friendly, congratulated me with the words, my children must give me great joy; when you write to us again, Please leave out the words laying something away, I always get annoyed about this because the thaler I gave Elise every month isn't worth talking about, she received no salary, doesn't a young woman need a few Marks once in a while? She would also like to give a little pleasure to her brothers, last Christmas you got the money purse that she had intended for Fritz,

I know full well it is Father's fault that you think such bad things, he tells everyone we don't know the value of money, He has never know[n] it, otherwise things would be better with us; Aunt and I, we grew up so simply, I was 13 years old when I went out to sew, evenings I came home with 6 S[hillings], my pleasure was to buy little things and to help my mother out, and in the evenings I often sewed until 12, and this for 6 years. Then I served 10 years as housemaid for honest gentlefolk, and then again I went out sewing for 8 years for those good people Helmer's and Neitler's, if they were stil alive, they would not allow that I should suffer so unjustly, then Aunt got married and I stayd with her, watched over the store and earned what I could by sewing.

Father rented a room in our house and that is how we met, after he had live[d] with us for only a week he wished me to be his wife, then he declared himself to Uncle who told me; I couldn't even imagine it because we were so different in age, Uncle brought it up several more times, so I took it to be my destiny, Father had been very friendly with a 17-year-old girl where he had lodged before, afterwards he often said he was glad that he hadn't taken her, later she married a tailor, she works as a hairdresser, Father often tells me that he had spoken to her, also when you wrote to us from Düsseldorf that we should rent a bigger flat she said at her house there was one that might be suitable for us, we looked it over but didn't like it, This summer after Father had already left us, this tailor came one afternoon, he had heard from his

---

[5] Christian Detmering, Caroline's brother-in-law, Brahms's uncle: Heinrich, his son and Brahms's cousin.

[6] i.e. his mother and sister Elise.

[7] Eduard Marxsen, piano teacher of both Fritz and Johannes Brahms, and his sister, who kept house for him.

wife that Father had told her he was divorced from his wife, the man was as if in despair and railed so fearfully against Father, he said it was certain that Father was carrying on with his wife, I tried what I could to talk him out of it, but he insisted that in the 8 years since we had come to look at their flat they lived very unhappily, for at that time Father had fallen in love with her again, she told him that herself, this discussion lasted a long time and upset us so that the next day Elise lay in bed, then they both came, she wanted to clear herself with me, that she had nothing to do with my husband, I said I didn't want to believe anything of the whole business, in any case it was all the same to me now, They had to try to reconcile again,

At the time we Married, Father earned little, rented us a cheap flat but it was too hot for him, after one year we moved [to] a 2nd, I had earned some beautiful linen with some sour, some difficult work, and still had 300 Marks which I surprised him with; when we had been together a short time, he got hold of it immediately gave notice, soon also gambled away 100 M in the Number lottery; you don't earn money so easily with a sewing needle. I never said anything to him about it, Bleicher had led him on to do it, and he was annoyed enough with himself; for 50 M he bought the instrument that you have always played on,[8] then his earnings improved, and he had to have a bigger flat, then he bought a Sopfa [sic] for 90 M and a table for 40 M, we lived there for 1½ years, then we moved to St Pauli because he earned more there, for me it was a great burden with 3 little children, the flat was in such disorder that the new sofa and table had to stay in the attic for 6 weeks, after 2 years we moved back into the city because he didn't want to play dance music any more, so we lived 1 year in the Scharmarckt, then to Ullricusstraße right next to Aunt; what a lot of money all that moving and fixing up of flats cost, he didn't want his acquaintances coming to us if it wasn't elegant enough, and what a lot of money did he spend on instruments

and all that sheet music, and in general he bought everything that he liked, and you both had to have music lessons in school, everything cost money, he

---

[8] From the fact that Brahms practised at his teacher's house and at various other locations in Hamburg, the assumption has been that Brahms had no piano at home, one more bit of evidence for the poverty of Brahms's youth. This letter is evidence, along with another from the 1880s by his old childhood friend Elise Denninghoff (née Giesemann), that there was indeed a piano in the Brahms household. That the young Johannes didn't practise much at home is far more likely to be due to the number of people living in the little house on the Dammtorwall, and the very poor sound-proofing of half-timbered buildings—a condition I had a chance to discover in 1990, when I stayed in a small half-timbered hotel just a few blocks away from where Brahms was born, and was able to hear much more than I wished of the details of other people's lives.

acquired more than we needed, the last 6 chairs 10 times I begged him to forget about them, since we have 17 chairs, but it was no use, so there never was
any money, I couldn't even get the necessary things for you children, then he
had the notion to start a shop like Aunt's, but we didn't have a Schilling to
our name so that didn't work; as Uncle died and Aunt sold the shop, she
offered [it to] us [for] 300 M, which was as much as nothing, and of course
Father had to put in from his earnings, he also wanted to be very helpful to
me because he had nothing to do the whole day long, but first he got himself
a dog to play with, then rabbits, the[n] chickens, for which he had a fence
built for 20 M, for which they took merchandise, you got an instrument for
300 M, for which they took merchandise, you got cello lessons, for which
they carried off so much merchandise I was left with 39 M, with what was I
supposed to do the buying again;⁹ now the garden was too damp for the
chickens, they were given up and stones were brought in, that didn't last
long, the chickens were got rid of, then came doves, a big dovecote, everything cost a lot of money and I had to work myself to the bone in the shop,
for me it was a bitter hard time, Fritz pleaded with me, he so wanted piano
lessons, I paid for them for many years from my shop, and also for the music;
then one time we wanted all of a sudden to go to America and quickly everything was sold, naturally at a loss, that wasn't my fault, I gave in to everything,¹⁰

it was very hard at home, my good Elise has stood faithfully by me for the
last 4 years then we moved to the Kurze Mühren¹¹ then your education lasted
far too long for Father, he was often ill-tempered and accused me of all kinds
of things, the both of us always sat there together evenings, you know, to me
it is as though it were happening now, I was probably rather quiet and you
said Ah, Mother, Father is always so peculiar, now you too, and then I had to
tell you, Father wants you to go out into the world, he doesn't want to take
care of you any longer, you were so upset and we both cried and went late to
bed, and Elise lay in bed and couldn't get air, so you fetched the doctor and
she got an emetic, it was the middle of the night; when you came back I had
made you a lovely cup of coffee, and once I had to write you an unplesent letter in Düsseldorf,¹² I always had a lot of battles with Father's unhappy
moods, and E[lise] has often heard it and shed many tears, how often has he
said The children will come to nothing, you'll see; no matter how much I
tried to change his mind it didn't help, I bore it all with patience and have
always rejoiced over my good children and thought, once all of you were self-

---

⁹ To restock the shop.   ¹⁰ The shop was given up in 1843.
¹¹ A street in Hamburg.   ¹² See Letter 53.

supporting, then he would be happy with me, and he would also regret that he didn't save his money better, last year he bought himself yet another horn for 100 M, which he uses maybe once in the year,

when I asked him early last year for some linens, which we absolutely needed, the first time in 34 years, he was so frightfully rude and said he had earned 1,800 M and spent nothing, so that I thought he had lost his mind, I never could have imagined, to demand money from me that he had spent in part so heedlessly, I also don't know how long ago it was since he earned that, he has always written down what he earned but never what he spent; that I could not keep quiet about it is true enough, but he became more and more offensive and a few days later had me served with a citation, how is it possible? a wife who certainly has always fulfilled her duties faithfully and has good sons and a fine daughter, something I have always rejoiced over, who just as I, always held everything together, it wasn't possible for me now to go before a judge with the husband, and if I had done it, things would be different now, it would be more peaceful, Fritz spoke with him and he withdrew the notice; so undeservedly as I now had to put up with all kinds of rudeness, I wanted to force myself as far as Possible, I believed it would pass, I did not want you to find out about it, ah, what a reunion was it, I also didn't say anything about it to you, and also don't know whether you know about it from Father or Fritz,

now everything is falling apart, first F went, whom I had so begged to stay with us, now he is gone too,[13] nothing but boredom have brought him to take that step, he had nothing to do all day but sit in the attic, horn to his mouth, and make himself miserable with silly notions instead of thinking of his good children and being glad; also he didn't need to sit in the attic and freeze, Fritz's room was warm, wen he gave lessons he could play there [but] probably it has been his intention for a long time to leave us for he has set money aside for himself for a long time already, never had spoken about it, I often thought, Now he is no longer such a spend-thrift, now he sees that money increases, but that he believed I was putting money aside for Elise never occurred to me, and I also don't know where I would have got it from; Elise has nothing but the 200 th that Heinrich has;

she had already saved up 100 [th] from the time she was a child and you and F once gave her 100 [th], now every one suspects that I haven't taken better care of my child, I could not turn to him about it, he would have said, I have

[13] Johann Jakob.

nothing, let Johannes and Fritz give her something, spoke with the two of you about Elise's future, then it was, don't worry, we won't abandon Elise, [but] we saw that last summer, if it hadn't been for me, the Father wouldn't have troubled about his child and the brothers about their sister, and slandered, to boot; naturally everyone suspects that Father, having left a wife whom he lived with for 34 years, has lost control, is ridiculous, he wants to know where his money has gone, but he can't say that to everyone, Old Stubbe says, just let him come to him, he'll tell him for sure where his money has gone; he was forever shopping, and others know that too, now he is starting to say all sorts of bad things about E[:] that she made too many demands that he couldn't fulfil them, that isn't true; two years ago F gave me 10 th for shirts for E and if she once in a while bought herself a good dress, it was from you two, F always gave her good Christmas presents, and every year you gave her something, from Father she didn't get a penny,

Then he would say She has drunk extracts of coffee and tea and had gone running after others, and when she didn't feel like working, she went to bed; Madam Plambeck visited us last week, E was still crying about it, she consoled her and said, The people who know us don't believe it, and we musn't care about strangers, poor E has such weak eyes from her headaches and so much crying doesn't make them better, many a time we are up half the night and then she does nothing but cry, but you will see that we can never again be together with such a man, towards Doctor Dammert he maligned so bitterly that he said Be quiet, I don't want to hear this, she is your flesh and blood, Fritz he called a parasite;

he gave me 12 s[hillings] to that I had to add my own for our Simple noon meal, in the evening simply bread and butter and tea, you [both] gave 1 M for the whole day, but I could not take more than 12 Silling—without breakfast, he was never satisfied, you two always added too little, especially F, of course you were always the Best one, for me all my children are equal because they are all good,

I have written something every day, it is 9 o'clock Tuesday evening. E is thinking [of going] to the dentist and wil take the letter along.

Father must have plenty of money now, he bought himself a bookcase [for] 19 M, a chest and mirror 20, a mantle clock 40, wolen [sic] table cloth, bed spread, I had given him one, which is enough, I gave him the big packing case that you brought back from Düsseldorf which I had made tight on the inside with paper, because I had kept linen in it, and his large books and then he has your hanging cupboard, so he doesn't need a clothes cupboard, none of it is our business, only he musn't say he has no money, and since for sure we don't speak much to each other directly, I am writing it to you so that I can die in peace, that my child has no misgivings about me, I close now with the hope that we have a better year before us. Be well and write us soon again,

many greetings from your Elise
and Mother

192
Johannes Brahms to Clara Schumann

[Hamburg] 6 February 1865. Early Monday morning

Dear Clara,

As you are getting this letter of mine from Hamburg, I can hardly seek to try to inform you gently and gradually of what has befallen us.

And so, may it at least be a consolation to you that God made the farewell from mother as gentle as posssible for us.

Elise is very well, thanks to the fact that she is constantly occupied; she doesn't have one minute to sit down and reflect, and as a result seems even quite collected.

I am concerned about her for later on, but thank God, she got through the trying first period well.

On Tuesday evening my mother returned from a concert in very good spirits, was still joking with Fritz from inside the coach. No sooner had the coach started than she complains that her tongue feels so heavy, and my sister sees with horror that her mouth was twisted sideways and her tongue swollen and protruding.

Knowing full well that Mother had suffered a stroke, Elise nevertheless has to console Mother and remain calm while Mother complains that her whole left side is so benumbed. At home, having been brought there with help, she thinks herself quite well and believes Elise's assurances that her chill would soon get better in bed. Her speech was barely intelligible. The doctor told Elise right away how grave her condition was.

In bed she was still able to recognize my sister most tenderly and to press her hand, then she closed her eyes and gently went to sleep. Perspiration, eventually the death rattle—on the following night at 2 o'clock she passed away.

At this point Fritz telegraphed me and I arrived here early Saturday morning. Her death I had of course surmised, although my brother had left the word unspoken.

Yesterday at 1 o'clock we buried her.

She was quite unchanged and looked as kind and gentle as in life.

Everything that can be consoling in the face of such a loss was done for us, particularly for my sister. The fellow residents of the house stood by her side in a really touching and devoted manner! So also her other friends, men and women.

After my last letter to you, I kept wanting to send another, because I was afraid you might consider me all too detached.

Look now, my sister feels her pain eased, and sighs almost gratefully when she thinks of a terrible misfortune that has just befallen one of her friends and of the cruel fate which awaits my mother's sister.

We hardly dare complain of the harshness of a fate that took a 76-year-old mother from us, we may only lament our loss quietly, and take pains that our sister does not feel it too harshly.

But I've become increasingly concerned about your hand, and I am really anxious to hear what the situation is following the removal of the bandage and the passage of some 3–4 weeks, now.[14]

I don't know exactly when I will go back again, I will probably be kept here for a day or two more.

My father is well, and it must have been good for that excellent man that I came.

Stockhausen and Avé were most compassionate and Avé and a great many young musicians escorted my mother on her last journey. Many were the flowers and wreaths that adorned her coffin, and in spite of the grim cold weather, music provided the last farewell.

Elise sends you her warmest greetings, today too, everything is going really very well, and I have absolutely no fears about her.

If you must take care of your hand later on, how would it be if in each of your concerts I played some ensemble pieces and then you [play] just a few solo things?

So then for today, farewell, the warmest greetings from all of us.

Your Johannes

Brahms's explicit narrative is filled out in moving detail by the eyewitnesses Florence May interviewed for her biography; they describe Brahms's attempt to reconcile his father with his dead mother, and his father with his sister. His attempts were only marginally effective.[15]

[14] Clara had fallen on her hand, and was unable to play for more than a month (Litz, iii. 172).
[15] May, ii. 363–4.

193
Johannes Brahms to Clara Schumann

Vienna, 20 February 1865

My dearest Clara,

With your dear and warm letter I felt your nearness in the way one can only wish to feel the nearness of a friend. It only reached me here, for I was in Hamburg scarcely a week, or not even that. There was nothing further that I could do or accomplish, and during the last afternoon I perceived only too clearly, unfortunately, that there can be no thought of attending to things or putting them in order. Elise becomes so passionate when the discussion then naturally turns to Father. Avé was present during the scene and understood only too profoundly and too clearly the sad rupture which the passage of time had gradually created. He stood valiantly by my side and above all had to advise me to leave, for after having taken that initiative, I could no longer console my sister by my presence.[16]

Time changes everything for better or for worse, no, not changes, but shapes and unfolds. And so, after this unhappy year, it will only be later on that I lose and miss my good and dear mother more and more. I do not want to write of how much consolation was actually an aspect of our loss, how it ended a relationship that could only have grown ever more troubled.

And for that I can only thank heaven, that it let mother become so old (76 years) and let her pass away so gently.

Elise will live together with the Cossels (my old piano teacher), where Frl. Garbe also lives. Naturally she can arrange everything as she likes, can take her time, and so forth. Fritz lives alone, also Father, who, I hope, can now look forward to a truly peaceful and fine old age.

Just how does it stand with your coming here? Unfortunately I am increasingly concerned about your hand, but if it is only so-so and is only good enough, say, for a beautiful *Lullaby*, you really should give concerts here. In that case we'll give them together! I have been assured that now is an opportune time here, and anyway you know that the public is most content when you play the easiest, best-known pieces. Absolutely! And I will see to the sing-song and also take care of the rest, and it seems very practical to me. I am already being badgered enough for not playing, it would really give me a special delight to fill out your programmes. So I beg of you, don't play any over-hasty pranks and don't cancel the concerts here!!!

---

[16] With this obscure sentence we can surmise that there was a serious argument between Brahms and his sister, with Brahms attempting to convince his sister to reconcile with their father.

I scolded myself in Hamburg on account of my impudence! When I visited Wackernagel and Lessing and heard that you had dragged all that stuff around with you![17]

Rieter is presumably going to publish a few Schubert things, so for instance 2 masses, etc. If only one could rely more on people here, Spina, for example, upon whom various things depend.

All in all, it is so that life here, that all of Vienna, is becoming ever more comfortable; but the people and even the artists, ever more obnoxious; the attitude they take towards the public and reviews, how they perform for them and depend on them, robs one of all desire to join with them as a colleague in this swindle.

I hardly dare to go to Frau Wagner on behalf of the lodgings. Reassure me soon that you are coming, and that you are coming soon.

Greetings to your secretary, Frl. Leser, etc. etc.

Your faithful Johannes.

His mother's death urged him on to a work he may well have been thinking about since Schumann's death: the writing of a Requiem with German text. Florence May, whose biography has the inestimable advantage of having been conceived and written while many of the principal players were still alive, is quite explicit. She writes: ' "We all think he wrote it in her memory, though he has never expressly said so," Clara Schumann told the author some years later.' Albert Dietrich remembered seeing the march which constitutes the second movement when it was the slow scherzo of the two-piano sonata-turned-symphony-turned-piano concerto, ten years earlier—a connection to the turmoil and anguish surrounding Robert Schumann's illness and death. Whatever the origins of the work, it is first mentioned in a fragment of a letter to Clara in the beginning of April, and again more explicitly in this letter to Clara:[18]

---

[17] Carl Friedrich Lessing. See n. 3. Philipp Wackerwagel, an historian, wrote several learned works on German church song.

[18] Brahms was perfectly aware, as he worked on the Requiem, that it was a work of importance; there are an unusual number of references to it in his correspondence at that time. For a thorough listing, see McC 170–1. Long after, Kalbeck made the interesting discovery that Schumann, too, had thought of the idea of a German-language requiem. In a newspaper article, he speculated that Brahms might have seen the title while looking through Schumann's *Project Book* (Kal, ii³. 252–3). Although Brahms was interested enough to draw Clara's attention to Kalbeck's essay, his subsequent letter to her does not support Kalbeck's supposition (22 Dec. 1888; *SBB* ii. 373).

194
Johannes Brahms to Clara Schumann

Vienna, Monday 24 April 1865

Dearest Clara,

It is all very annoying that you really are in England now, that the loveliest springtime has to manage without you, that I am still causing you useless vexation with sheet music, and whatnot!

So then, on Saturday or Sunday, the 29th or 30th, I will duly go directly to Carlsruhe and Baden. I would certainly appreciate it—since the music is hardly going to arrive in a few days—if it were addressed to Levi or to your Elise. For otherwise Gotthardt could sniff around to his pleasure in what must already have been opened at the post office. On the other hand—it's all the same in the end.

But write to me in Carlsruhe now, by way of Levi. If it is not too late, I would ask you not to show the choral piece to Joachim—it is in any case probably the weakest piece in the aforementioned German Requiem now. But since this may yet evaporate to nothing before you come to Baden, do read here the beautiful words with which it begins.

A chorus in F major without violins, but accompanied by harp and other beautiful things:

> Blessed are they that mourn,
> for they shall be comforted.
> They that sow in tears
> shall reap in joy.
>
> They go forth and weep,
> and bear precious seed
> and come joyfully
> bearing their sheaves.

I compiled the text for myself from the Bible.[19] The chorus I sent you is No. 4.

The 2nd one starts in C minor and in the tempo of a march.[20]

---

[19] Matthew 5: 4, and Psalms 126: 5 and 6. The next quotation is from I Peter 1: 24. The complete text was assembled from the Old and New Testaments.

[20] In B flat minor, in fact. Is this a misprint? A misreading? A change of plan? There are various theories: see McC 170, among others.

For all flesh is as grass
and all the glory of man
as the flower of grass.
The grass withereth
and the flower falleth away. etc.

You could appreciate such a German text as much as the customary Latin one, couldn't you?

I have high hopes for putting together a unity of sorts, and hope to retain courage and desire for once.

[. . .]

Yesterday I was in Schönbrunn and its beautiful palmhouses. Spring has already breathed a lovely green onto everything. Although I don't go out into the countryside, springtime has none the less made my life twice as distracted. The spring is magnificent here and the ladies make it even more beautiful, so that one often doesn't know where to turn one's eyes.

You'll soon hear from Carlsruhe or Baden. I'll probably ramble around again for a bit in Carlsruhe first, but then it's off to look for lodgings in Lichtenthal and to wait for you.

Very warmly,

your

Johannes

Greetings to Marie.

The lodgings he found were in a small cottage in the village of Lichtental, which even then was part of Baden-Baden. The house is now the Brahms-Haus Museum (Plate 25). In it he finished the second String Sextet, Op. 36, and the first Cello Sonata, Op. 38, wrote the Horn Trio, Op. 40, and must also have spent time on the *German Requiem*, a work which would keep him busy for the next year.

195

Johannes Brahms to Hermann Levi

[Lichtenthal bei Baden-Baden,] 7 May [1865]

Dear Levi,

I came, I saw—and straightaway took the first available lodging. And it is so truly the best available that you'll be delighted. It sits on a height, and I look out over all the mountains and lanes of Lichtenthal and Baden.

It is written: Lichtenthal 136, at Frau *Advokat Becker's*—and I hope one writes or sees it [written] very soon.

Although my visit in Carlsruhe is over, all the bother is not. It could well be that a large suitcase that wants to come to me will be shipped to your house, in which case I'd like to ask that you show it the way; and I request the same kindness on behalf of packages and letters.

Furthermore, I'm missing a *Gibus* and wonder if you could bring it or send it along some time.[21]

I read in the *Badeblatt* that the *Nachtwandlerin* is playing here on Wednesday? Well, then of course you'd come, and I hope that a Tuesday or Thursday could also be spared for Baden—particularly if it proved possible to include a visit to the Signale's most charming co-worker?[22]

But why murder the beautiful morning with scribbling letters since for sure the roads in both directions are passable again and will be travelled frequently all summer long I hope.

Greetings to Allgeyer and Miss Elise, if you're still keeping her there.

With best greetings,
Joh. Brahms

Because of Sunday, it's possible that the courteous fr[anko] may be missing [i.e. prepaid postage].

Brahms had no piano that summer, a circumstance which did not prevent him from working.

196

Johnnes Brahms to Hermann Levi

[Lichtenthal bei Baden-Baden, Summer 1865]

Dear Levi,

I believe you will find it worth the trouble of unpacking and repacking if I first send a piece of a Schubert *Mass* to you, instead of directly to *Rieter*.

However, I must now ask you to send it on as *quickly* as possible to *Winterthur* (unfranked), since the business has already been delayed for several days (because of *Allgeyer*).[23]

---

[21] A collapsible opera hat, worn by Brahms at a rakish angle, according to a charming eyewitness account of his first visit to the Duchy of Detmold in 1857 (by Karl von Meysenbug, *Neues Wiener Tagblatt*, 3 Apr. 1902).

[22] The journal *Signale für die musikalische Welt*. Whoever the charming co-worker was, it was not Clara Schumann, who was in London at this time.

[23] Allgeyer, a multi-talented artist, also played the piano (and once rebuilt a decrepit instrument when it was the only one he could lay his hands on).

I have made a piano reduction of the piece, which was missing, and since you have a piano at home you might look at it at the same time, [see] if it will do, apart from trifles that can be changed in proof.

Frau Schrödter wrote to me yesterday to ask for musical verses, and I suppose it's all right to impose on you to enclose a page for her?[24]

Aren't you coming to see the *Firestream*? Aren't we going to hear the *Dismal Isolde*?

Greet Frl. Elise and be heartily greeted yourself.

J. B.

The piano score for Schubert's Mass in E flat major (1828), anonymously prepared by Brahms, was published by Rieter-Biedermann later that year.

More plays on words—'the Firestream' is painter Anselm *Feuerbach*, whose name in German is literally 'fire brook'. *Triste* is the French word for *sad*—but also a German word for *dismal*.

To Schubring went another rare letter discussing, however fleetingly, his music old and new. The evident pride he takes in his detailed knowledge of Schubert's works is as striking as his pleasure over a manuscript he had discovered and seen into print—again, anonymously.[25]

197
Johannes Brahms to Adolf Schubring

[Lichtenthal bei Baden-Baden, 25 June 1865]

Dear friend,

I have been meaning to send you a greeting for such a long time, already, and now your last letter has followed me here from Vienna, so there'll be no more musing, but letter writing instead, as lengthy and as zealous as the beautiful summer morning will only permit.

First of all, I have been in Baden-Baden since the 1st of May (letters to Frau Schumann in Lichtenthal).

Should you find yourself in the south at some time, let yourself be lured here, not only would you delight me greatly but you yourself would also take delight in nature and in the people. Besides, I dearly wish Frau Schumann would get to know you personally—it would give you pleasure for the rest of

---

[24] Alwine Schroedter, wife of the painter Adolf. Brahms wrote out four canons for women's voices for her on a page which she then decorated with her famous flower motifs. (See Letter 190, n. 3 and Draheim, *Johannes Brahms in Baden-Baden und Karlsruhe*, 38–40, 44–5.)

[25] Brahms was the unnamed editor of Schubert's *Twelve Ländler*, published in Vienna, 1864, by Spina.*

Additional Note p. 751

your life. I am exasperated even before the event at the silly dolts who will blather books-full to us about these two. When in fact, they were such beautiful and excellent individuals that a solemn word ought to be spoken.[26]

For your critiques, my best thanks, I kindly ask you to do as much for others to follow, will also shortly give you bigger nuts to crack. There should also be something to break your fingers over.

And to show you that I take the thanks and the request seriously, I will respond step by step.

I don't have Eichendorff and the duets here, but I think I know for certain that the knight is down below passing the monastery in a boat at twilight, which is surely a situation for a single voice. Incidentally, one (I) seeks poems for several voices so zealously that a little nonsense may be excusable. 'Gang zum Liebchen' goes like a graceful, moderate waltz, I cannot describe it more closely.

The bass in No. 1 of the 'Kinderlieder' goes:

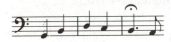

The three stars in one place of the *Album für die Jugend* denote the day of Mendelssohn's death, I thought that the date is given there.

Strange to say, of Op. 32 only Nos. 1 and 2 come readily to mind. I would not really want to term the extremely moderate Allegro in No. VI of the *Magalone* an *Allegretto*, but some adjective is missing, I suppose. More of this stuff is coming.

Something to do with Schubert is supposed to have escaped me! And I am supposed not to know the beautiful A minor waltz in the German Dances! But this new first part is interesting for just that reason. In the original, they are designated 'German Tempo'. [The word] *Ländler* is an invention of Spina's. Incidentally, I have more of this type by him and—actually quite a few, some of which I will presumably publish this summer, since they give such pleasure to friends.[27]

---

[26] A curious reference to the posthumous life of Robert and Clara Schumann.

[27] They were eventually published in May 1869 by Gotthard, in Vienna, under the title *20 Ländler for Pianoforte . . . [Posthumous]*, with Brahms once again the anonymous editor. Schubert's Op. 33 dances (D. 783) were published during his lifetime. Brahms possessed the original manuscript of another set of dances (D. 790), marked in Schubert's hand 'Deutsches Tempo, Mai 1823'. The two sets of dances, D. 783 and D. 790, have one piece in common: Brahms discovered that the first half of his No. 3, in the *Twelve Ländler* he edited for Spina, differed from the previously printed version. Apparently Schubring was not sure that Brahms was aware of the difference. Brahms's connection to the other *Ländler*, which he owned in manuscript (the 20 published in 1869), is detailed in David Brodbeck,

In the end I almost forgot to write to you about the Capellmeister position. It seems after all that that I can free myself of my involuntary vagabond's life. Dessau is not the only town to wink at me quietly.

But on the map the region is not to my liking, and the neighbourhoods of which you boast are not to my fancy.

But what is it like otherwise? Would one have to be called Capellmeister No. 2? Does one have to accept for the rest of one's life? Is there plenty to put on one's plate? Isn't the theatre perhaps as insufferable as your concerts certainly are not?

In any case, I am not at all indifferent to suggestions of this kind and beg you to write me more details soon, all the more so since a number of things are in fact drawing nearer. But your holidays are the most important thing for me. Couldn't you make arrangements to come here? The journey would be well worth it.

Forgive my awful scrawl, but unless I set my pen aquiver and let it take flight, I can't coerce it into letter-writing.

Are there no photographs in your household? I don't have a collection or an album, but do like to have my friends in facsimile.

Greetings to your family and a warm greeting to you yourself
from your
Johs. Brahms

Only now do I notice the uneven margins and ask to be excused.

Brahms was answering questions about some of his vocal music here,[28] and alluding to his latest: the *German Requiem*—'a big nut to crack'—and the Paganini Variations,—'something to break your fingers over', written as a challenge to his friend Carl Tausig.

Not long before, this same friend presented Brahms with a valuable additon to his manuscript collection: Wagner's autograph of the Paris version of the *Venusberg* music from Tannhäuser, which Tausig in turn had received as a gift, he thought, from Wagner himself.

When Cosima von Bülow moved in with Wagner, she apparently urged him to retrieve all the manuscripts he had given away, and went so far as to write the letters demanding their return herself. Brahms was not the only one so ordered to return

'Brahms's Edition of Schubert Ländler', in George Bozarth (ed.), *Brahms Studies*, 229–50 (Oxford: 1990).

[28] The vocal duet 'Die Nonne und der Ritter', Op. 28 No. 1, set to a poem by Eichendorff; the vocal solo quartet 'Gang zum Liebchen', Op.31 No. 3, which indeed *is* a waltz in its other version, No. 5 of the Waltzes for Piano Duet, Op. 39; 'Dornröschen' from the Children's Folk-Songs, WoO 31; No. 1 and 2 from his nine *Lieder und Gesänge*, Op. 32; and two of the *Magelone* songs from the second volume.

his manuscript; the Wesendoncks were asked for *Rheingold*, and Mathilde Wesendonck received a letter in Cosima's hand asking for the return of all of Wagner's literary manuscripts.[29] Brahms apparently did not reply to Cosima, and he certainly did not return the autograph. Wagner's young disciple Cornelius was then asked to try to retrieve it. For the eventual outcome one has to wait for the year 1875; but Brahms's—tardy—reply to Cornelius's letter was the final blow to their already shaky friendship, although it had been inaugurated by Cornelius with such enthusiasm only three years earlier in Vienna. Ironically, Cornelius was simply used as a middleman, and was under the impression that the manuscript had been given by Wagner to *him*![30]

198
Johannes Brahms to Peter Cornelius

[Lichtenthal bei Baden-Baden, after 6 September 1865]

Esteemed Herr Cornelius!

I positively have to rid myself of the awkward sense of having behaved in a quite irresponsibly unfriendly manner towards you. Better late than not at all, indeed, perhaps better a 'No' once again than nothing at all. And so, I sincerely ask your pardon and merely excuse myself just a little bit by noting that it had been made awkward for me to have to write to you, of all people, about this particular affair. You know in any case that in the matter of the Wagner manuscript, I have received apart from yours, several letters from Frau von Bülow. Now every one of these letters enumerates new reasons for handing it over in such a conspicuous manner that I finally formed the disagreeable impression that one simply wishes to get the manuscript *out* of my hands. Add to this the peculiarly delicate question that Tausig had made a *present* of it. I, in his place, would not tolerate yielding up a present in this manner. Most of the reasons for wanting the manuscript have probably become irrelevant, in the mean time; and so above all, I must beg you very earnestly and sincerely to consider these lines as having been received much earlier, and then to look upon them in an altogether friendly manner. Lastly, I send you my warm greetings and hope it is not begrudged me to keep the manuscript in peace, so that when we meet again, soon, I hope, you will show your usual friendly face.

Your J. Brahms.

[29] Erich H. Müller von Asow, *Johannes Brahms und Mathilde Wesendonck* (Vienna, 1943), 43.

[30] For further details about their relationship see Josef-Horst Lederer, 'Cornelius und Johannes Brahms', in *Peter Cornelius als Komponist, Dichter, Kritiker und Essayist*, ed. Federhofer and Oehl (Regensburg, 1977). Cornelius wrote to Tausig about the affair asking for clarification, saying 'Brahms has graciously declined to answer', and this is also where we find Cornelius saying that in any case, he thought Wagner had given him the manuscript.

By early September a series of new works were ready for publication. Brahms offered the String Sextet, Op. 36, and Cello Sonata in E minor, Op. 38, to P. J. Simrock, along with a variety of choral works.[31] When the offer was declined, he wrote to Breitkopf & Härtel, who declared themselves delighted to hear from him and accepted the sonata and sextet sight unseen. Brahms sent the sextet off immediately, especially keen to see it in print. Then on 29 September, Breitkopf wrote a letter in which they essentially reversed themselves. They agreed they were honour-bound to publish those works they had accepted, but were 'in a difficult position', as they wrote, and therefore 'had a difficult request to make': would Brahms withdraw the sextet from consideration. Without giving details, they hinted at an outside consultant, and hoped Brahms would not insist on his legal rights. Brahms seethed. Still rankling from their refusal to publish his *Magelone* songs in the previous year, he wrote:

199
Johannes Brahms to Breitkopf and Härtel

[Lichtenthal bei Baden-Baden, *c*.5 October 1865]

Most esteemed gentlemen,

As much as I dislike doing so, I nevertheless cannot refrain from replying to your last esteemed letter in some detail.

I must confess that I found it to be the most hurtful, yes the most insulting thing that has yet happened to me.

Even though my first preference would simply be to request the return of the manuscript, my self-respect and a necessary concern for my interests oblige me to communicate to you a few questions and misgivings and then leave the decision to you once more.

Should your letter have been prompted by a possible trial of the work, then I ask by what right you might have arranged this without my consent, if that was to be conclusive—but also—with what expectations—since you know as well as I how little sympathy my works meet with in Leipzig.

Which of my works, do you really think, would ever have come to your publishing house upon a recommendation from Leipzig?

If it was occasioned by the judgement of a single individual, that too I must protest against as an insult. Willing as I am to respect your business considerations, I want the judgement of musical matters entirely entrusted to and bestowed upon me.

Regarding other matters that bear particularly on such a first quick

---

[31] Opp. 41, 42, and 49.

judgement, I request that you read, in an earlier issue of *Wiener Zeitschrift für Musik*, the way my first Sextet was initially also dismissed in 10 lines. As singular proof of sharp eyes and attentive observation, one may also cite how in your paper (in the appraisal of the Solo Quartets), whether sneeringly or instructively I no longer recall, I was blamed for [parallel] octaves that are not there at all! Furthermore, I might remind you that the rejection of *Magalone* brought me the satisfaction, at least, of seeing your own magazine call them my best songs and of learning that Stockhausen, Hauser, and others sing them in Germany, Switzerland, and England.

Now I must however inform you of what I had out of delicacy concealed from you; namely, that the present publisher of these songs had at that time heard from a third person in Leipzig, and probably from the referee, that songs of mine were 'knocking about' there.

Mr Rieter has now approached me to let him have the Sextet. Since he knows and shares my devotion to your firm, he knew that it would be offered to you and I informed him right away of your acceptance of the work.

Of course, I could also offer the work to other publishers, but after what I have told you, you will comprehend that I would only do so with the greatest reluctance and I would feel mortified if perchance I had to read in the reply that the manuscript's journey to Leipzig were already known. Several people know about it from me, and you will not contradict me when I express the opinion [that others know of it] from Leipzig as well—in a less friendly sense.

Of course, it would offer me some kind of satisfaction if just now you were to publish some other works of mine. But this affair must appear curiously more benign to you than to me if you believe I wish to ship other works to Leipzig for a trial, or that I am keen to procure novel and rather unexpected experiences for myself once again.

In view of all this, I believe that my honour and my interests definitely demand that you keep the work. Since I now appeal to your sense of justice and honour, as well as to your cognizance of how inconclusive a first arbitrary judgement is, I expect the assurance that this work will be published without delay and in the same manner as the first Sextet, in full score, parts, and piano reduction.

However, should you be of a different opinion and decide—that the manner in which my work is being returned to me is not insulting, and that the present and future awareness of this affair, which would be confirmed by my reacceptance of the manuscript, could not damage my interests—then I leave it to you [whether] to send the Sextet back to me.

Finally may I request that this letter most definitely remain among our-selves,[32]

With complete esteem
Your very devoted
J. Brahms

Thursday

It was understandably difficult for me to dispatch the above letter to you and, instead of simply being able to request the return of work, perhaps to see it sent into the world in such an unfriendly way.

And so the letter remained here until today, and an enquiry about the Sextet which arrived today is doubly welcome.

After some reflection, I cannot conceal the foregoing from you; however, since the practical considerations have now faded, I leave all else to your judgement.

May I in any case request a prompt reply.

The above.

The newly-arrived enquiry was from P. J. Simrock, who had changed his mind and now wanted publication rights for both pieces. Breathing an uneasy sigh of relief, and with a letter which tried to soothe Brahms and justify themselves at the same time, Breitkopf sent the Sextet back. It was the last time they would have the oppor-tunity to turn down any of Brahms's music. Although in later years he co-operated with them on editorial undertakings in the complete editions of Chopin, Mozart, Schubert, and Schumann, he never sent them another note of his music, not even upon request.

The state of Brahms's finances finally forced him to do what he had been trained from childhood to do—give public concerts. He now arranged a 'Virtuoso tour' for himself, no doubt aided by having often watched and helped Clara arrange her own. For the next five years, concert fees were his major source of income, and they went a long way to solving his financial problems. The first place he thought of, naturally enough, was Hamburg. Stockhausen was willing, perhaps too much so. In the end, his Hamburg friends are the only ones who failed to find a way to invite him to play.

---

[32] On this point Breitkopf acquiesced. The correspondence was neither included in their 200th anniversary collection of the firm's correspondence (ed. Oskar von Hase, Leipzig, 1919), nor in the volume of letters to publishers comprising *BW* xiv., and were not published until 1933. See *Sources*.

200
Julius Stockhausen to Johannes Brahms

Hamburg, September 30th [1865]

Dear friend!

Avé and I have long argued back & forth about your enquiry to play here and finally decided not to put the *enquiry* before the committee for the time being. We find above all that as a composer you would not have sufficient freedom in a Philharmonic concert. Avé and your most obedient singer are of the opinion that when you appear again in Hamburg you must also be seen as a composer and conduct one of your works, & perhaps a vocal piece for chorus has to be performed & songs sung & you can't do all that in the subscription concert. In a word, if Johannes Brahms wants to play in his home town he ought to give a concert of his own and for example have his Serenade in D, Psalm, and songs performed. Now tell us when you were contemplating coming so I can rehearse the chorus in time, also hold a preliminary orchestra rehearsal. You would be doing me in particular a favour if you accept my suggestion. I had hoped the gentlemen [of the committee] would agree to my suggestion to present 10 subscription concerts; but they are too timid & are staying with six. I wouldn't want to pass up an opportunity like this to offer the public something authentic & to prove to our gentlemen that it's possible to entice the subscribers into the hall more than 6 times.

1st your Serenade, 3rd the Bach Triple Concerto, 2nd a chorus, 4th song [and] piano performance & a short symphony (A major by Mendelssohn or B flat major by Gade) would, I think, be a suitable programme, and I ask you to give me an answer very soon, so I may look forward to it if you are willing & take other steps if you are not. A chamber music soirée cannot very well be arranged this winter, at another time the local forces would certainly be at your disposal, but we don't have the personnel. Rose is in America, it's not known if he will return. [Emil] Hegar has been called to Rotterdam with a 1,000 gulden honorarium. *In face of that,* what can be done by the rich Hamburgers, God's gift to man!?—And one more thing: If, Franco-German that I am, I have been lacking, have been lacking in some way, don't be angry with me; I'll gladly pronounce another *mea culpa.* Basically no one means better than I & and I hope the intentions of Frau Schumann, Joachim & you are as good towards me. But it just cannot be & that is why I remain the wild Frenchman.

                              J. Stockhausen.

Wife *and son* send loud and warm greetings.

201
Johannes Brahms to Julius Stockhausen

[Lichtenthal bei Baden-Baden, October 1865]

I really owe you and Avé my warm thanks for discussing my possible coming to Hamburg so thoroughly and for taking such a lively interest in it.

There's only one thing you are forgetting,—that I won't even consider experimenting with a money purse that's perpetually suffering from consumption as it is. And giving concerts is the same as experimenting.

Concert with orchestra, however, is far more like an assassination of the above-mentioned purse.

I am unfortunately obliged to search laboriously through the *Hamb[urger] Nachrichten* if I want to learn anything new about my home town and Avé in particular might well have the time to keep a person better supplied with such.

How glad I would be to hear of Grädener above all! Give him my warmest greetings. I suppose he is doing well there in any case, and at the start the chilly bath in Hamburg rudeness will probably feel good after the lukewarm friendliness and politeness of the Viennese.[33]

Just what are you doing about a violin and cello? Is Böie not in favour of a closer affiliation between Prussian and Hamburgian hegemony in musical and military matters?[34]

I'm going to Switzerland before long, the weather is as delightful as if rain had been abolished and winter had become a myth.

Give my warmest greetings to your wife, also Grädener, and to whomever else you wish.

May I ask you to toss the enclosed letter into the letterbox? A quintet of sixty-seven pages is waiting to be corrected,[35] consequently, in some haste and all friendship,

your Joh. Brahms

Before leaving Baden-Baden, Brahms received an unexpected letter from his father, with the news that he was planning to remarry. Describing his present life as bleak and empty, Johann Jakob asked his son's blessings.

[33] Grädener had just moved back to Hamburg.

[34] A barbed reference to the fact that Prussia had just then taken over responsibility for Hamburg's military security, although the city nominally remained the Free and Hanseatic City of Hamburg, as it still does today. See Andreas Fahl, *Das Hamburger Bürgermilitär, 1814–1868* (Berlin, 1987).

[35] Op. 34 in its final form as a piano quintet.

202

Johannes Brahms to Johann Jakob Brahms

Baden-Baden [in Johann Jakob's hand: 21 October 1865]

Beloved Father,

When I opened your letter and found that it covered three pages, how I did anticipate with pounding heart the news that would prompt you to write so much? And so I was really also surprised, but most of all surprised that I had not expected it sooner!

Dearest Father, the thousand blessings and fervent wishes for your well-being that I always harbour accompany you here, as well. How I would like to be sitting with you now, to press your hand and to wish you as much good fortune as you deserve,—and that would be more than is needed for one lifespan.

This step is surely just another handsome tribute to you and says how well you have deserved the most contented family life.

But there is a troubling thought that I just cannot get rid of. If things were as they should be, and as you deserve with regard to ourselves, we would be living together happily and you would never have been allowed to discover that life can be barren and empty. You know why I couldn't very well remain in Hamburg, but if you had merely informed me of your intention, instead of the [accomplished] fact, I would have had to follow my heart and requite you and replace what you are deprived of.

But now that it has been decided, may God give it his richest blessings. Commend me to the mother-to-be and tell her that she could not have a more grateful son than I, if she makes my father happy. I suppose I don't know her, for you don't write her name. She is childless?

I am considering, and now of course far more seriously, coming to see you in December. But for now, write again and also even more explicitly, you can imagine, after all, how interested I am in every word, and how many things I would like to ask about.

Whether she be a compatriot, whether she has children, where she lives, how long you have already known her, etc.

I am sure you won't rush things too much—but how could I presume, and how can anyone offer to give advice to a man! You do know how weighty, how difficult the path is!

And yet, I cannot tell you how much I would have liked to be there and to have first met her and got to know her and taken pleasure in the choice. But now I can only consider your decision to be a natural and correct one, can only be very troubled that we children had let it come about, and after that, as one would expect, anxiously try to visualize your chosen one to myself.

I'm staying here for another week, after that write to me at: Carlsruhe, c/o Herr Capellmeister H. Levi. But frank the letter. I'm going to Switzerland soon, where I have concerts in Zurich and Basle, then in Carlsruhe, on the 12th of December in Cologne. Thereupon I will come, presumably with pounding heart, to Hamburg. So perhaps write here, still. You will wait as long as possible, won't you?

That shouldn't be a lot, of course.

And so many greetings to you.

With affectionate love
your son Johannes

Whatever you spend on my behalf (Bach), do please get Elise to repay you through Fritz.

Amidst all the speculation as to why Brahms never married, virtually no attention has been paid to the unhappy marriage he was continual witness to as he was growing up. His comment to his father here, 'You do know how . . . difficult the path is', is revealing; so is the fact that his brother, too, never married. This time, however, his father chose well for himself. Karoline Schnack, Brahms's future stepmother, was eighteen years younger than Johann Jakob. She came not from Hamburg but from the Holstein countryside; in other words, she was indeed Johann Jakob's compatriot. Aged 41 at the time, she was capable and self-sufficient, proved herself an excellent wife to Johann Jakob, and apparently a considerate stepmother: she eventually succeeded in gaining the trust even of Elise and Fritz Brahms. Johannes was soon devoted to her. His correspondence and support continued uninterrupted after the death of his father in 1872, until his own death twenty-five years later.[36]

The Bach mentioned here was the latest volume of the Complete Bach Edition, which Brahms had sent to Hamburg each year to join the rest of his library.

By now Brahms was on terms of friendship with so many working conductors that he was able to arrange his tour exclusively to cities where they held conducting positions.

---

[36] For an excellent sketch, see *Familie*, 35 ff.

203
Johannes Brahms to Albert Dietrich

[Basle, November 1865]

Dear friend,

Now I'm really under way, and there is every indication that I shall have to play for several audiences.

In Carlsruhe I did so with my concerto, and people had the surprising friendliness to be quite satisfied, to recall me, to praise, and what not.

Now I am at, and am writing you from, the *Riggenbachs* in Basle, where only last evening we spoke of you. I shall see Zurich, Mannheim, and Cologne on my big tour, and at Christmas or New Year, you in Oldenburg.

Think also about what music we might make together? Could we not risk my D minor Concerto at the orchestral concert? In Carlsruhe it certainly gave us some fun, and no annoyance to the audience, it seems.

For a quartet evening, I can recommend my Horn Trio with a good conscience, and your horn player would do me a very special favour if he would do as the one in Carlsruhe, practise the *Waldhorn* for a few weeks to be able to play it on that.[37]

I am also bringing with me new Magelone and other new songs.

In Oldenburg I'll have the most splendid free time for friendship and friendly music-making.

Greet your family and take care that my prospects in Oldenburg remain so favourable.

Very sincerely
your Johannes Br.

Brahms's tour also took him to Detmold, where Karl Bargheer was now in charge of the court orchestra.

---

[37] Brahms was very specific: the Waldhorn (natural horn), without valves, was softer, and would therefore impose the correct balance on the other instruments even in public performance. He knew what he was talking about; as a child, he had not only studied the cello for a few years, but the horn as well, apparently with his own father. Brahms was so insistent that he required his publisher to re-engrave the title-page to read *Trio für Pianoforte, Violine und Waldhorn oder Violoncello*, and made it clear that at a pinch, he preferred the cello to a valved horn (letter to Simrock, *BW* ix. 53, and Kal, ii. 182 ff. 186).

204
Johannes Brahms to Karl Bargheer

[Autumn 1865]

Dear Herr Bargheer!

In order finally to pay some long-promised visits, I will probably be on the road for part of the winter. And so my route takes me so close to Detmold in December that I cannot help wishing I might be permitted to make the short detour into the little land, so that I might reminisce in contentment over the fine and jolly times I spent there with you.

Of course I would gladly come to the Teutoburg Forest and to you without asking. But since other matters cannot possibly be overlooked, I would be very grateful to you if you would devote an errand and a letter to letting me know what the Princely [house] etc. might say and do about my coming.

In any case, I would have plenty of time to enjoy the pleasures of home and forest, and perhaps I shall once again see the Christmas lights burning in Detmold.

Would you then kindly take the trouble of enquiring in the right places, what in general and what in particular. I am ready and willing to play in theatre and court concerts, but you know (between us), that one likes to know for how much.

My address is, until the end of November, Rieter-Biedermann in Winterthur, then Capellmeister Levi in Carlsruhe, from the 10th to the 15th December, F. Hiller in Cologne.[38] I write in great hurry and distraction, would you kindly forgive this, greet your wife warmly, and in any case be sure to answer with a line

your
very devoted
Joh. Brahms.

In Cologne, Brahms played Beethoven's 'Emperor' Concerto and conducted his D Major Serenade. Neither was appreciated, and Hiller was roundly castigated in the press for having allowed a foreigner to take up so much of the programme! (An evening of his chamber music with Königslöw and Hiller was much better received.)[39]

---

[38] For Brahms–Hiller letters regarding these concerts, see *Hil*, ii. 70–2.

[39] Otto von Königslöw was concertmaster of the Gürzenich Concerts orchestra, and also led a quartet.

In Detmold, he revisited some of his old haunts, and with Bargheer was soon up to his old tricks; Brahms must have felt especially carefree in the little Duchy.[40]

He reported to Clara and to Joachim.

205
Johannes Brahms to Clara Schumann

Carlsruhe, the 3rd December 1865

As far as I know I have only written to you once from Switzerland? Or else more? Well, it was quite an unsettled time, dearest Clara, and you know how easy it is for me to let things slide. Now I've been here since yesterday, so this morning at Levi's I'll tell you in detail how well I have fared.

As a matter of fact, far beyond my expectations in every regard. Above all, what pleases me most is that I really have the talent to be a virtuoso. The only thing I am completely dependent on is the piano I have, if it is good I play with the greatest comfort and best of ease. The bigger the pieces, the better. I have twice played the Fantasy Op. 17 and twice the Paganini Variations, besides that, organ pieces (D minor), among others.[41] I have brought about 1,800 francs back with me!

How warmly people have received me you can see from the fact that after the first concert in Zurich, where I performed the D Major Serenade, several friends of music (particularly Dr Lübke, Prof. Billroth and Wesendonck) organized a private concert on Sunday morning so that they could also hear my Concerto and the A Major Serenade. They hired the orchestra, sent telegrams all over the place so that the parts, etc, would be certain to arrive, and anyone who took an interest in it was allowed to attend without further ado. So I first rehearsed the Concerto with the orchestra, and Kirchner conducted it for me, then to finish, the Serenade. The musicians were exceedingly devoted to me, so that the whole affair was most agreeable.

I had a beautiful Erard, the personal property of Hug, which also trekked to Winterthur along with Hug and a tuner, and in the end gave thanks for the honour, having cost nothing; Hüni, whom I needed for the orchestra, was just as obliging, in short, people have spoiled me throughly!

My Horn Trio here on Monday, Tuesday in Mannheim: A Minor Quartet by Schubert, Fantasy by Robert Schumann, and my A Major Quartet.

---

[40] Bargheer's memoir recounts some of the adventures (see Willi Schramm, *Brahms in Detmold* (Hagen, 1983), pp. 57 ff.).

[41] Op. 17 by Schumann; according to Florence May, the organ piece was the Chromatic Fantasy and Fugue by Bach.

On the 12th and 19th of December I play in Cologne and on the 20th in Detmold, where indeed I'll be staying over Christmas.

In Cologne I'm staying with the Königslöws, and in Detmold at Bargheer's (until the end of the year, at least).

I sent the parts to Damrosch from Zurich straight off, but since I didn't remember if a score was included, we sent another one off from here yesterday.[42]

Did you get my letter (about the concert in Basle) in Berlin? I don't understand the calendar, but the concert was on the 19th, after all, and you ask about it on the 28th! I had surely written straightaway to Berlin that I had earned 800 francs, etc. etc.??

I received your letter from Hamburg and the one at Rieter's, from Dresden, and thank you a thousand times. Where will you be for Christmas, in Munich, I suppose? If you were in Düsseldorf, I could actually come! Do write to Cologne! I'm there from the 6th to the 19th.

But now a very warm farewell, I have more letters to write, and even though I have written to you hurriedly, I think of you often enough in the loveliest Adagio-Tempo and very *con espressione*!

Utterly yours,
Johannes.

Levi sends greetings.

The Swiss concerts described here were particularly momentous. Two members of his audience were destined to become his closest friends: Theodor Billroth, then working in Zurich, and Josef Viktor Widmann, then in Winterthur. A third member of his audience, Mathilde Wesendonck, had hopes of becoming so, but more of that later. For the moment, the importance of these concerts lay in the financial and artistic success they provided then and promised thereafter.[43]

[42] Leopold Damrosch, conductor, composer, violinist, later active in America.

[43] Widmann has left his vivid impression of the 33-year-old Brahms: 'Brahms . . . immediately gave the impression of a powerful individuality, not only by means of his mighty piano-playing, which cannot be compared with even the greatest of merely brilliant virtuosity, but also through his personal appearance. It is true, the short square figure, the almost straw blond hair, the jutting lower lip which lent the beardless youth a slightly sarcastic expression, were conspicuous and hardly prepossessing peculiarities; but his entire aspect was permeated by strength. The broad lion-like chest, the herculean shoulders, the mighty head at times tossed back energetically when playing, the contemplative, beautiful brow glowing as if by an inner light, and the Germanic eyes framed in blond lashes and radiating a marvellously fiery glance, they all betrayed an artistic personality brimming to the very fingertips with genius. There was also a certain confidence of victory in his countenance, the glowing cheerfulness of a spirit happy in the execution of his art, and without turning my eyes from the young master who gripped the keys with such power, there came to mind Iphigenia's words on the Olympian gods . . .' from J. V. Widmann, *Erinnerungen an Johannes Brahms* (Berlin 1898), 17–18.

Brahms's report to Joachim contrasts with his comment to Dietrich, whom he told he could not overcome his dislike of the restless concert life.

206
Johannes Brahms to Joseph Joachim

[Detmold, *c.*20 December 1865]

Dearest friend,

Because I fervently hope that you'll be on the look-out for me on the 24th, but yet cannot admit that this will happen in vain, I accordingly send herewith my best greetings and report that I have to save the Christmas joy of seeing you both until later.

I'm playing here today and presumably still have my own concert here on the 28th. After that I must be off to Oldenburg, which will probably be the end of my merry virtuoso tour for this year.

I hear that you are playing your concerto in Hamburg on the 19th. I will hear it one way or the other, and am greatly looking forward to it.[44] But you're probably not staying in Hanover until then, otherwise I might be able to pick you up for the trip?

My little concert and business trip was more enjoyable in every respect than I could have expected and hasn't spoiled my appetite in the least!

But I'm just about to have a rehearsal for the concert, I'll undoubtedly be able to tell you stories soon enough, anyway.

So spend the lovely holiday merrily and drink to my health sometime.

Bargheer greets you warmly, and I do with all love.

Johannes.

⁂ 1866 ⁂

For the time being, Brahms had no fixed home. Stockhausen was harbouring his library—the Stockhausens had been a great help to the Brahms family during its ordeal of death and disintegration—and his father, brother, and sister were each living in separate quarters in various parts of Hamburg. For his part, Brahms spent most of 1866 in Karlsruhe, staying with Allgeyer and working on the Requiem; and then in Switzerland, first as a guest of Rieter-Biedermann, then in his own summer lodgings, just outside Zurich, and then on tour with Joachim. (Clara to Ferdinand Hiller: 'Brahms in Zurich, thank God.') During a six-week

---

[44] Probably his third concerto in G major, frequently performed by him at this period but not published for another twenty years.

interlude in Baden-Baden, he finished the Requiem. (Clara to Hiller, again: 'Brahms has finished a new work, which seems to me his most important to appear in a long time: it is "A German Requiem".')[1]

In March, his father remarried.

207

Johannes Brahms to Johann Jakob Brahms

[Karlsruhe, 21 March 1866]

Best of fathers,

My warmest wishes for tomorrow's festivities, and for the many days and years to follow. In my thoughts I will be with you all, and am not very happy that you get to see merely a few words from me, not me myself. But when one loves one another, as we do, dear Father, one can in fact sense the nearness of the other—be he miles away.

I must come to the aid of my new mother however, and therefore enclose a picture with the friendliest possible expression. It is just a visiting card, incidentally, I had actually hoped that you would hang a large picture of myself in your room. But the sun required for making it failed to shine lately, and so it will arrive in the near future, begs for a spot on the wall, and that you look upon it occasionally in a really friendly way.

You're staying at home, or going to Schwarzenbeck, or where?[2]

How long are you staying where you are, then? Write the new address to me in good time.[3]

So be greeted a thousand times and think of me once in a while, as I shall be thinking of you all with all my love.

Your faithful son Johannes

Allgeyer sent the promised portrait photo of Brahms directly to Johann Jakob several weeks later. Preserved for posterity by his stepbrother Fritz Schnack, it is one of the outstanding Brahms portraits (Plate 21).

---

[1] Excluding the fifth movement, written two years later. Clara's letters are from 14 July and 25 September (*Hil*, ii. 78, 79).

[2] A resort town near the Saxon Forest.

[3] The frequency with which Johann Jakob moved is remarkable. But this next move, to Valentinskamp, was his last.

208
Johannes Brahms to Julius Allgeyer

[*c.*10 May 1866]

Dearest Allgeyer,

I have just received such a rapturous letter from my father that I am joy itself, through and through, and simply have to write you a line with his and my warmest thanks. My father is so unused to writing that he is unlikely to make up his mind to answer you, in spite of all the enthusiasm. I hope you won't take that amiss, and if you would see how his letter to me beams with delight and bids me to thank you, you too would be greatly cheered.

For a proper Swiss tour, I seem to have selected a truly unsuitable season, I notice. Although I also can't extend my stay here now, I do want to see the mountains of ice from an ever nearer nearness, nevertheless. Aside from that, one does forget everything over a political lead article. And unfortunately, whether they now fight for 30 or for 7 years, the fight is as little on behalf of mankind as in those days when they fought for 30 and 7 years.

I expect we'll see each other again at Whitsuntide. Once more, my warmest thanks for your trouble and give my greetings at home, in the Nassauer Hof,[4] and wherever else you wish.

Your Joh. Br.

Brahms's ardent admiration for Chancellor Otto Bismarck is well known. Far less so is his antipathy to Bismarck during the Prussian–Austrian war, which was in progress at the time of this letter. Brahms was so disgusted with current politics that he spent increasingly more time in Switzerland, and for the time being preferred to have his music published there. '30 and 7' refers to the Thirty Years War (1618–48) and the Seven Years War (1756–63), brutal events much fresher in people's minds then than now.

Before leaving for the Swiss mountains, he wrote another letter.

---

[4] An hotel and restaurant in Karlsruhe. It served Jewish cooking, apparently much enjoyed by Brahms, who ate there frequently with Levi and their friends. Brahms's patronage was considered a great honour by the family, providing the necessary encouragement for the daughter of the establishment to study the piano. She went on to become a well-regarded pianist—information passed on to me by Dr Henry Isaacs, her grandson, now living in Princeton, NJ.

209
Johannes Brahms to Eduard Hanslick

[Karlsruhe, April 1866][5]

[Dear friend],

Just as I was writing the title of the four-hand Waltzes, which will appear before long, your name came to me as if by itself. I don't know, I thought of Vienna, of the pretty girls you play duets with, of you yourself—the connoisseur of such things, the good friend, and whatnot. In short, I feel the need to dedicate it to you. If it's all right with you to leave it that way, I thank you most obediently, but if for any reason you don't want the thing, just say the word and the engraver's order will be countermanded. They are two volumes of little, innocent waltzes in Schubertian form—if you don't want them and prefer your name on a proper work of four movements, 'command, I shall obey'. In the next few days I am going to Switzerland. Shall I complain to you that I wasn't in Vienna this winter? My arrival next year will say it more clearly. In all sorts of hurry and in old friendship,

your

Joh. Br.

210
Johannes Brahms to Frau Rieter-Biedermann

[Zurich, August 1866]

Dear Frau Rieter!

For quite some time I've been thinking, with my usual decisiveness, of leaving tomorrow.

Since it probably won't come to that tomorrow morning either, I would like to ask you please to let me know how things are with you. From Herr *Rieter* I have heard nothing at all directly. I thought this horrible weather might drive him home, and in that case I would so like to meet once again in the *Schanzengarten* to say Hello and Farewell and Thank You.

This most of all; for each morning, with the deepest gratitude, I appreciate with what kindness and motherly concern you have made sure that I should feel—if not more comfortable in my own skin—extraordinarily more comfortable in my linen, and I no longer always have to spend a long time searching for the correct hole into which to convey my limbs.

---

[5] Hanslick's date 'August 1866' must be wrong, as Brahms was already in Switzerland by then.

I think I may still want to go to Baden for a short time, then think I actually want to go to Vienna; there is, certainly, nothing that either keeps or
lures me, thank God and sad to say, absolutely nothing! Whether it is possible to wait out the weather for a little tour?

In brief, at all events, I would really like to know if your *husband* is going
to stay on the Rigi for a still indefinite time, and how his health is.

To your esteemed *son* I beg you to say that no proofs of the 'choruses'
have come yet. It should bear the opus number 44, and above all I urgently
request that on the title-page the 'with *discretionary* pianoforte accompaniment' be changed. I don't know if the title-page is already finished, but *that
word* has to go.

'12 Songs and Romances
for Women's Chorus *a capella*'
(with piano accompaniment *ad libitum*)

Or something like that!⁶

With warm greetings, and 'till further word from you,
your very devoted
Joh. Brahms

Brahms's very cordial friendship with Rieter extended to other members of the family, and on several occasions, in the company of Rieter's daughter Ida, he and his
publisher made walking trips in the Alps. Frau Rieter, a good-hearted woman who
took up many a social cause, was the butt of more than one good-natured comment
from Brahms. The *Schanzengarten* was the name of the Rieter home in Winterthur.

211
Johannes Brahms to Hermann Levi

[Lichtenthal bei Baden-Baden, August 1866]⁷

Dear friend,

This time *I* take the liberty of replying in telegram style, although for so
much kindness a large sheet of paper would be more fitting. For book and
letter and errand my best thanks. If I didn't think we would see each other
again very soon I would quite simply set aside an hour to write to you. As
things stand, forgive me if I wait until I can ask you in person not to react

---

⁶ Published in October 1866. These songs were written earlier for the Hamburg Frauenchor.
Brahms had tried for several years to interest publishers in them.

⁷ Undated in *BW* vii; but as Brahms notes he has just come back from Zurich and expects to see
Levi soon, he must have been in Baden-Baden and it must have been August.

bitterly to what I said with such sincere good intentions, and just let it sink in nicely and well and kindly. Otherwise I shall be only too correct in often voicing my doubts about trying to bend a person, and that silence is all too often the best policy.

Be sure to write to me how things are progressing with your brother. Where two people ought to and want to be together, I have few fears.[8]

What seems so problematic to you, 'to dedicate oneself totally', is not at all so to me.

However—I simply can't, forgive me. I have just arrived from Zurich, and so much stuff has piled up I must not. On the other hand I will gladly chat on about it even in writing and will do so as soon as I possibly can.

Kirchner sends greetings and is the same as ever. *Ditto Rieter.*

Be of good cheer, be reasonable, allow your wings to grow back, there are 7 heavens (the Composers' Heaven you won't get into)—keep flying ever more to the left and become a partisan.

With all my heart
Your
J. B.

One of the sources of tension in this complex friendship was the fact that both men had ambitions as composers and conductors, both had a strong sense of their own capabilities—and both had a desire to be on top. Levi had notable talent as a composer, but agonized over his sense of insufficiency. Nevertheless, he and Brahms once set the same poem to music, and Levi's version stands up so well in a comparison with Brahms's that the latter even borrowed from it.[9] But he was unable to encourage Levi the composer, and in this instance we can assume that he had spoken tactlessly, even heartlessly. Levi wrote that he felt as though his wings had lost all their feathers. Brahms's answer was meant to reassure him, and for the time being the wounds were healed.

---

[8] A reference to Levi's brother, Wilhelm Lindeck, who became a Catholic in order to marry, thereby distressing their father, who was not only a rabbi himself, but descended from a long line of distinguished rabbis culminating in his father, the Chief Rabbi of Hessen.

[9] *Dämmerung senkte sich von oben*, Op. 59 No. 1, from Goethe's *Chinesisch-deutsche Jahres- und Tageszeiten* (*Chinese-German Hours and Seasons*, 1830). See references in Brahms's correspondence with Allgeyer and Levi in early 1869 (Letter 231). Levi's version is in the Toscanini Archive at the New York Public Library at Lincoln Center.

✝ 1867 ✝

Once more the post of music director in Hamburg was vacant. Once more, Brahms was overlooked; this time the personal nature of the rebuff was unmistakable. His father understood, as Brahms casually asked who the new conductor was going to be.

212
Johannes Brahms to Johann Jakob Brahms

[Vienna, 19 March 1867]

Dearest Father,

I send you this weighty letter in the very highest of spirits and ask you—to convey 100 thaler to Elise through Aunt Detmering, and to use the other 100 thaler for your own pleasure. And how happy it would make me if you would use them only for really useless, jolly things! But in any event, spend them; write and tell me how quickly they disappear!

The day before yesterday, Sunday the 17th, I had a concert here (my first) and had exceptionally good success. Before that, I was in Graz and Klagenfurt with just as much pleasure; besides that, I saw magnificent regions in the most beautiful weather and was suitably delighted. My piano-playing has made quite an impression here and I am surely not regressing.[1]

Please greet Herr Marxsen for me and tell him about that in the mean time, I'll write to him soon—but convey this greeting in the mean time. Tell him that my waltzes are appearing for 2 and 4 hands, were recently played in the Redoutensaal on two pianos, and have also paid me passably well.[2]

I'll write to Herr Marxsen when I have some things to send. Unfortunately I don't have newspapers and programmes here now.

How are things going with all of you in Hamburg and above all, with you at home? Do you know who might be coming as conductor, and above all, are you in really good spirits and happy at all times? Write to me precisely how you all are, also what you are earning!

Things are fine with me and my concert gave me a lot of fun. I hadn't played here for so long that the people didn't know at all what to expect, and meanwhile everything went famously that evening.

---

[1] See May, ii. 387, for details of the concerts and the rave reviews. Brahms must have been in good form at this time, as his piano-playing also received outstanding reviews in Budapest.

[2] Op. 39, published in two versions (1866 and 1867) by Rieter-Biedermann. 20 Friedrichsdors for the four-hand, 20 Napoleon d'ors for the two-hand version. Stephenson calculates a total of 1,000 Marks (there were 3 Marks to the thaler). (*Familie*, 127, n. 34).

And you must write straightaway so that I know you've received the 200 thaler.

I wish, however, that Elise would leave the money with Heinrich [Detmering, their cousin] and come to get only what she needs.

Be greeted most warmly, all of you, and hold dear

Your Johannes

(Postgasse 6) Are you now a member in the Zoological Garden? If not, join today with Mother, I beg you urgently.

Johann Jakob's thanks contains his first written acknowledgement that his son's destiny was as a composer, not a performer. 'I am only sorry that the situation is not reversed and that I am not in a position to provide you with the tranquillity needed for creating, as befits your talent . . .' He slipped in the answer to Brahms's question as casually as it had been asked: 'The last Philharmonic concert was conducted by someone or other from Leipzig by the name of Julius von Bernuth.' And he wondered what Brahms would do with his books now that Stockhausen was leaving. Brahms replied that he intended to stay in Vienna: 'Presumably I'll even ask you to take care of sending me my books, soon. That will be no easy job for you! But I have no one else I can ask to do it, and as I do want to feel more at home here, the books surely belong to that, and here.'

'So Vienna will be your sanctuary,' his father wrote, 'I can't hold it against you.'[3]

Although in fact it was several more years before Brahms moved his books and considered himself at home there, he wanted his father to get to know the great city. His letter of invitation bears the stamp of an astute traveller.

[3] Quotations are from letters of March and May 1867, *Familie*, 128–9. To us, endowed as we are with hindsight, there can be no doubt that *musically* Brahms was far better off in Vienna, that in Hamburg he would have had an endless struggle to achieve the standards he demanded. Amy Fay's vivid book, *Music Study in Germany* (Chicago, 1880, repr. New York, 1965, 335 ff.) provides an innocent's view of the dismal state of music in Hamburg in the 1870s under Bernuth's leadership. In fairness to Bernuth, it is not clear that the fault was with him. The Hamburg Philharmonic was the last orchestra in Germany to put its players under contract—in other words, to become a cohesive, professional orchestra—and that not until the 1880s. Hans von Bülow and Gustav Mahler conducted in Hamburg for years without producing an orchestra of the first rank. The violin virtuoso Richard Barth, who conducted the Philharmonic from 1894 to 1904, has left a memoir which recounts the difficulties involved in making music with the orchestra—difficulties more closely related to the attitude of the Board of Directors than to the abilities of the musicians. See Kurt Hofmann, *Johannes Brahms in den Erinnerungen von Richard Barth* (Hamburg, 1979), 56 ff.

213
Johannes Brahms to Johann Jakob Brahms

[Vienna, 23 July 1867]

Beloved Father,

Well, you're probably returning from Heide tomorrow, and, I hope, are in as good spirits as I could wish for, in such good spirits—that you will right away do what I ask of you.

You have now been to see beloved old things,[4] now see something new: come to Vienna! Don't think it over for long, consider only that at your age travel becomes more difficult and less enjoyable with each year; and that this year, with each passing week, summer is getting hotter and Vienna not getting any more comfortable. For a friend thought Vienna by itself might well be of more interest to you than the entire Rhine, I do realize he is right, and beg you urgently to visit me here and to go on little tours with me starting from here.[5] It goes without saying that the trip will cost you nothing, nor any loss of [playing] time, and that we'll arrange everything in a way that won't tax you.

Now you absolutely must not contradict, nor think it over, but if possible get started this very evening.

I hope for that with such certainty that I will now merely write out how you must travel!

You make arrangements so that you can stay away for 2 to 3 weeks, and must also plan for a somewhat longer time. Then you see to it that you have, or can get, about 40 thaler—I have no Prussian bills at home and it is Sunday.

Now you get a ticket direct to Vienna by way of Berlin, Dresden, Prague. The ticket must be valid for 5–8 days. Be sure of both things!

Costs about 30 thaler second class all the way. There are only two trains. You can of course travel through in one go—in about 32 hours. That works only if you have rainy, cool weather! Otherwise you couldn't stand it. But since the ticket is good for a week, you can also stop over for a day or half a day in each city, and look around it. But if so, go first of all to a good hotel and make use of porters and [public] servants for hire as guides. If you continue on right away in Berlin you must take a hackney to the other station.

---

[4] It was Johann Jakob's first visit back to the town of his birth, where he still had relatives. Brahms himself was never taken there as a child—never knew his grandparents, uncles, aunts, and cousins on his father's side—nor did he visit there in later life. The Brahms family house in Heide has recently been restored, however, and is now a museum.

[5] Initially Brahms had suggested they tour the Rhine Valley together.

A policeman hands out the voucher at the exit. Before you travel the night through, as is practical in the heat, drink a glass of grog so you sleep well. But take along very little, for example no scruffy things for the trip! No cigars, nothing new, nothing that is taxable. You'll find every conceivable thing here with me. Don't let that make your journey uncomfortable.

Here now the two trains and Fritz [Schnack, his stepbrother] can explain to you how you can make a stop-over wherever you like, and wait for the next train.

Hamburg		10.30 at night	Or	7.30 in the morning
Berlin	arr.	5.20 in the morning	—	3.57 afternoon
	dep.	6.45	—	7.00 evening
				(3 hours rest)
Dresden	arr.	11.40 noon	—	11.30 at night
	dep.	12.45	—	1.03 at night
Bodenbach	arr.	2.20 afternoon	—	2.30 at night
	dep.	3.10	—	3.05 at night

Here luggage is examined and passports inspected. So have nothing on you except the passport.

Prague	arr.	7.00 evening	or	5.50 in the morning
	dep.	7.24	—	6.09

(If you take this train, you can rest for the day and continue on at 7 in the evening).

Vienna		7.56 in the morning	or	3.12 afternoon

All this Fritz must make very clear to you and write it down plainly so that to some extent you are always informed. Ask the conductor frequently, too.

When you get on try to get a corner seat and between Dresden and Prague sit on the left side for the sake of the view (Saxon Switzerland). How much I'd prefer to fetch you, but that would really be very complicated. I would also like to say that Mother should come along, but that too would be relatively all too complicated, expensive and whatnot.

So don't even stop to think it over. Should you happen to be taking along your last or other people's money, we'll send it to Mother from here straight-away.

Right now the summer is still splendid, with every week the green becomes greyer from dust.

By coming right away you'll give me the greatest pleasure I could hope for.

So, first of all: ticket that is valid for 5–8 days, getting off and staying over, or else continuing on, whichever is more agreeable to you, *very* little luggage.

Have you a summer overcoat? Tails are not at all necessary, no scruffy clothes. Attend to the luggage in Bodenbach, *nowhere else.*

NB.: You can always send a telegram from the railway [station]! Vienna, Postgasse 6, it's quite reasonable.

And should you by some chance not find me at the station, that's where you go and enquire in the house downstairs, at the concierge. Just write to tell me when you are *leaving*, then I'll be sure to be on the look-out.

I enclose 5 gulden, valid from Bodenbach on, but other currencies are also accepted.

I have all the cash here.

Also, don't forget at all times to eat well whenever there is time, have breakfast, etc.

I beg you, dearest father, give a farewell kiss to Mother right away and add one from me. Get under way, you will *have a great, great deal of pleasure* and will give me the very greatest.

I wait impatiently for you simply to report your departure to me.

Your Johannes

His father came. As Brahms corresponded with Joachim to arrange another concert tour for 1867 (they first toured together in the autumn of 1866), his father's visit was still fresh in mind.

214
Johannes Brahms to Joseph Joachim

[Vienna, 22 August 1867]

Dear Joseph,

Your brother is just leaving me, and although I have neither said 'really' nor 'on my honour' to it, I am already sitting down and scribbling letters.[6]

It's splendid that you're indeed serious and want to come; it would of course be fine if your wife came too, but I expect there are more important things than singing songs.

---

[6] *Buchstaben,* letters of the alphabet. With his scribbling of letters, Brahms probably meant he was already drafting possible programmes. Many examples of programme suggestions in Brahms's and Joachim's hand have survived. The opening of this letter is a paraphrase of an old joke, based on an ancient Greek conundrum: 'If I say "really!", you don't have to believe me; but if I say "On my honour!", you can believe "really".'

Well, I think it would be best to take the hall for three quartet evenings to begin with, if you want to give Hellmesberger that pleasure, two or three concerts in the Redoutensaal, and I also think that we could play some music together for the Viennese on at least two more evenings.

There are three courtesies which I suppose you will have to fulfil, to the Philharmonic orchestra, to Herbeck, and to the Concordia; in my opinion you shouldn't do so before the end of December and shouldn't agree to it too quickly; but in any case you understand that sort of thing better than I.[7]

As a result of my father's visit and a little trip we took together, my spirits revived more splendidly than they had in a long time.

My father's delight at all the new things he saw was only the least part of my pleasure. And until then he had never seen a mountain, never looked down from a mountain, so you may imagine his astonishment was no small matter; nor was it by any means unimportant to him that he saw the Emperor here with the Pasha, and in Salzburg the Emperor together with Napoleon.

Now I sit here once again and will also remain here peacefully, but my soul is none the less refreshed as the body after a bath: of this my good father has no notion how much good he has done me; I almost travelled back with him to Hamburg, then I would also have seen your garden, which I greet fondly in the mean time, along with all who walk about in it.

Warmly your
Johs. Br.

Brahms helped arrange a very successful tour with Joachim. His approach was unusual, to say the least, as he arranged for his second visit to Budapest. His contact there was Johann Nepomuk Dunkl, 'first and eldest student of Franz Liszt',[8] and partner in Budapest's leading music shop and publishing house. Dunkl and Brahms had met in Vienna when Brahms first arrived, and judging from this letter, got along quite well.

---

[7] The Concordia was Vienna's most prestigious press club, comprised in the main of the city's liberal journalists. It played an important role in Vienna's social life, organizing many evening functions for its members, including a concert series; to appear there by invitation was a significant honour. For a description of the kind of glittering reception Concordia could mount, see Carl Dolmetsch, *Our Famous Guest, Mark Twain in Vienna* (Athens, Ga., 1992), 41 ff.

[8] Norbert Dunkel [*sic*] in *Die Musik*, Brahms Number, 25/8 (May 1933), 612.

215
Johannes Brahms to Johann Nepomuk Dunkl

[Late summer or early autumn, Vienna 1867]

Esteemed Herr Dunkl,

Give the devil a—etc.

Here I go calling upon your kindness once again, am consequently writing as briefly, as confusedly as possible, and beg that you reply to me as fully, clearly, and kindly as possible. Joachim is coming here in the middle of November and we both want to give concerts here, in Prague, Brno, etc. It goes without saying that Pesth is not least on our mind, and that's why I need only to paint a large question mark to cause you, if you have retained your accustomed kindness, to have a great deal to write and to do.

According to my inexact, rather amateurish perusal of the calendar, we could try for Pesth on the 3rd of December, and if more is desired, again on the 9th and 12th (on the 7th and 14th, here). The two of us always manage alone very well, once we get to sit in the concert-hall. But till then! That isn't as easy as tinkling and scraping.

What do you think? What do you say? What do you write, what do you do? Do you want to adopt the poor waifs?

An advance payment of 10 fl[orins] (one of us comes from afar) would also not be scorned.

In short

?

?

'Give a sign' Göthe

X, 5, IV, 317   ?

'Command, I shall obey'

Mozart XXII, 56

'I place my hopes in thee'

J. Sirach 51, 57

Greetings to woman and man, believers and heathens.

Postgasse 6

J. Brahms.

Brahms and Joachim gave two performances in Budapest. In one of them, Brahms tried out his Hungarian Dances as an encore; Norbert Dunkl ruefully relates that his father turned down the chance to publish them at the time—and how rich Simrock became, in his place.

'Hold on to the accompanying "Requiem" until I write to you,' Brahms wrote to Dietrich, just before setting off with his father. 'Don't let it out of your hands. And . . . tell me in all seriousness what you make of it.'

Brahms was anxious to get the work off his hands and into performance, and told Dietrich he would look very favourably on a performance by the conductor Karl Reinthaler in Bremen. Dietrich, who had permission to send the manuscript to Joachim, took the liberty of sending the work on to his friend Reinthaler, instead.

216

Johannes Brahms to Karl Reinthaler

[Vienna, *c.*2 October 1867]

Most esteemed Sir:

I have just now learned from Joachim that you are in possession of my 'German Requiem'. May I request that you let me have the same *without fail and without delay*. I have long and impatiently expected it back from Dietrich or Joachim, and it is only because of my slothful writing habits that I discovered only today that I must request it from you.

I cannot fail to mention that it is somewhat embarrassing for me to know my work is with you. It still displays such serious traces of haste and hurried writing that it can only present itself to good musicians whom I can at the same time regard as indulgent friends. Would you kindly take note of this after the fact and use it to excuse a great many things in the mean time. None the less, it would now give me great pleasure if you would tell me your honest opinion of the work, in brief or at length.

It is possible that I shall have a performance here very shortly, and I therefore repeat my request for the immediate dispatch of the manuscript, so that I might duly look it over and work on it.

I ask that it be addressed to Herr Spina's music shop.

With particular esteem

your devoted

Johs Brahms.

'I have probably kept your treasure at home longer than circumstances justified,' Reinthaler wrote back, and expressed his interest in performing the work in Bremen Cathedral on the next Good Friday. But in his respectful and detailed reply he worried that the Requiem, at that time still without solo sections, would overtax any chorus and perhaps any audience, too, by its length and difficulty. He also found Brahms's text puzzling. 'For Christian sensibility the central point about which all else turns is missing—namely, redemption through the death of our Lord,' he wrote, and hoped that Brahms would follow the text of the last movement, *'Blessed are the dead which die in the Lord <u>from henceforth</u>'*, with an additional, more obviously Christian movement. Brahms replied:

217
Johannes Brahms to Karl Reinthaler

Vienna [*c*.9 October 1867]

Esteemed Sir.

I very much wish I could reply to your esteemed letter easily. Letter-writing, however, is so little my strong point that this time, too, I shall have to console myself with the possibility of meeting you in person and then chatting to our heart's content.

However, I do have the need to tell you what a great pleasure you gave me by the sincere interest with which you read my work. I appreciate it twice as much since I saw the work again with some horror and did some energetic housekeeping with my pen. Concerning the music, I have answered *so* much more than you, indulgently enough, had asked and said.

As far as the text is concerned, I will confess that I would very gladly omit the 'German' as well, and simply put 'of Mankind', also quite deliberately and consciously do without passages such as John Ch. 3 Verse 16.[9] On the other hand, however, I did accept many a thing because I am musician, because I was making use of it, because I cannot challenge or strike out the text of my revered bards, not even a 'from henceforth'.[10]

But—I'll stop without having said all I have to say, and want to mention just one more matter which would not only please me, but would also be

---

[9] 'For God so loved the world, he gave his only begotten Son, that whosoever believeth in him should not perish, but have everlasting life.'

[10] i.e. that he was making use of that passage in the Bible. This portion of Brahms's letter has been translated many times, always, in our opinion, incorrectly, so that Brahms is made to say, 'because I am a musician, because I needed it [. . .]'. The problem is the similarity between the past tense and the past participle of the words *brauchen*, to need, and *gebrauchen*, to use. The German reads: 'habe ich nun wohl manches genommen, weil ich Musiker bin, weil ich es gebrauchte, weil ich meinen ehrwürdigen Dichtern auch ein "von nun an" nicht abdisputieren oder streichen kann.' The phrase 'weil ich es gebrauchte', means *because I was making use of it*, and *gebrauchte* is the first person past of *gebrauchen*, to use. The past participle of *brauchen*, to need, on the other hand, is *gebraucht*, without the 'e'. Had Brahms intended to say he *needed* that 'from henceforth', his German would have read: '. . . weil ich es gebraucht hatte'. We know of no example in Brahms's letters where *brauchen* and *gebrauchen* are used interchangeably. For a nice example of the two words used side by side, see *BB* vii. 327: '—Dieser schwer gefaßte . . . Erhebungsentschluß Chrysander's zeigt an, *daß er das Geld brau= und gebrauchen konnte*.' (This difficult decision over his laudation . . . shows *that he needs and could use the money* [emphasis added].)

important to me. That is a performance in Bremen Cathedral, which you mention.

I will, for various reasons, perform the first half here (on Dec. 1) and will most likely not have the opportunity to hear it in its entirety. Should you be seriously interested in a performance in your city, I should be greatly obliged to you. To some extent, of course, the financial aspect would also have to be considered; perhaps I could play in one of the subscription concerts, or perhaps also present a concert of my own? In short, I will eagerly look out for a possible further letter from you and will be delighted if the business materializes. Specifically, from the end of January on, I am completely free, and nothing prevents me from staying as long as I please in your city and its surroundings.

In hopes, therefore, of hearing from you at some point concerning this,
with exceeding high regard,
your devoted
J. Brahms.

(Vienna, Postgasse 6)

218
Johannes Brahms to Karl Reinthaler

[Vienna, end of December 1867]

Most esteemed Sir.

Allow me to reply hurriedly and briefly to parts of your kind letter.

I am certainly not thinking of leaving Vienna and moving to Bremen or to anywhere else. If I can get away at all in the near future, I mean to roam about in Northern Germany *in general* up until your performance, that is for ¼ year. I will make the overnight trip between the two free cities entirely according to whether it is necessary or convenient. To Oldenburg and wherever else I plan to go in any case.[11]

[11] The 'two free cities' were the Hanseatic Republics of Bremen and Hamburg. Brahms did in fact perform throughout northern Germany, accompanying Stockhausen in Hamburg, Kiel, Copenhagen, Berlin, and Dresden, earning a substantial amount of money. Stockhausen's letters from this period provide an unvarnished view of Brahms's piano-playing. To his wife Clara, from Copenhagen, 22 March: 'Brahms accompanied the French aria even worse than in Hamburg, but that didn't bother him,—only me.' To Clara Schumann, on the same day: 'Today Brahms is practising the Schumann concerto like mad, which means he is learning it by heart; for you know that with him, it is rarely a case of real practising. He is surely our greatest musician; I have not yet encountered such an organism, allied with his knowledge, but a piano player he will never be; any kind of practising bores him so much that he only—plays' (Julia Wirth Stockhausen, *Julius Stockhausen* (Frankfurt am Main, 1927), 310).

I enclosed the score for the last three movements with the parts I sent you, because the parts (viola and all winds) still have to be copied from it. I suppose you had best have that happen as soon as possible!

Unfortunately, I have only my poorly written score and bad piano vocal score. But I will see today still, if I can't send them to you in a reasonably usable state.

The most important element of the performance is simply: to be able to rehearse as much and as often as I want. *Just between us*: It is quite all right by me to earn a heap of money,—but—again just between us—also quite all right by me if I can have extra rehearsals only at my own expense. In particular, I should find it desirable if we could use [a] double quartet in the later rehearsals.[12]

But I hope I can soon pack my suitcase and will then most likely travel first of all by way of Bremen to Hamburg. We could then easily discuss whatever is necessary and I, wretched composer in such urgent need of a protector as I am,—could thank you very cordially.

Hoping to chat with you soon,

your very devoted

J. Brahms.

❦ 1868 ❦

Reinthaler's doctrinal misgivings were shared by other members of the clergy in Bremen, and it was therefore decided that the performance of the Requiem would have to include text concerning redemption through Christ even if that meant inserting another work into the programme. Midway through the Requiem, then, Joseph Joachim played some violin pieces, and Amalia Joachim sang Handel's 'I Know that My Redeemer Liveth', starting a tradition which persisted in Bremen for many years.

From Clara's diary:

> Good Friday, the 10th. Performance of the Requiem, along with Frau Joachim singing an aria from the Messiah, accompanied by her husband on the violin, more beautifully than I have ever heard her. This Requiem has moved me as no other . . . I kept thinking, as I saw Johannes standing there so with baton in hand, 'should he once take magic wand in hand and work with chorus and orchestra'—which today came true . . .[1] After the

[12] i.e. a double set of violins I and II, viola, cello, and double bass at the chorus rehearsals, a request he repeated in March.

[1] A paraphrase from Schumann's *Neue Bahnen*, his 1853 article about Brahms which so precipitously launched Brahms's career (see p. 23).

performance there was a supper in the Ratskeller, where everyone was jubilant . . . a mass of friends were gathered, Stockhausen, Bruch, Dietrichs, Grimms, Rieter . . . but remarkably, apart from a few women from the chorus [four members of the old Frauenchor, who came to sing in the performance], no one from Hamburg . . . , only Johannes's father.

Reinthaler held a speech about Johannes that so moved me that (unfortunately!!!) I broke into tears. I thought of Robert, what joy he would have felt had he been alive.

One hundred friends were gathered there, to witness and celebrate the event which brought Brahms decisive and international fame at last.[2] Brahms's association with Reinthaler led to a lifelong friendship with him and his family, and by the time Brahms thanked Reinthaler for his efforts, they were already on 'Du' terms.

219
Johannes Brahms to Karl Reinthaler

[Hamburg, *c.*23 April 1868]

Most esteemed friend,

Well, I ought to have made the most wonderful speech to you long ago, on a much larger piece of paper than this. Inexcusable, that I did not do it, for whatever I now write, it will merely seem like a receipt, I suppose.

But no, you surely know as well as I that I take care of just the lesser portion when I say that the letter and enclosure from the Board of Directors surprised me most pleasantly.

Indeed, both of us also know very well what joys I am grateful to you for. In all sorts of ways—hospitality not being the least—you gave me a few days which will remain unforgettable for me. That sounds banal! But 'I love you' also sounds banal, and who the devil stops to make up variations when he wants to say a thing like that.

So I am really travelling with the Bremen mailcoach on Sunday evening? Otherwise, I imagine you would have written; and my table of joy has been so well laden that it cannot fail to include dessert.

But I must clink glasses once more. Do please deliver the enclosed letter—but to whom?

[2] In the audience was at least one man who had come from England for the purpose. Florence May has described the event in detail. May, ii. 407–10. Eye-witnesses to the event include: Dietrich, *Erinnerungen an Johannes Brahms* (Leipzig, 1898), 61–5; Kurt Hofmann (ed.), *Johannes Brahms in den Erinnerungen von Richard Barth*, 15–16. Clara's observation regarding the lack of Hamburgers was accurate in spirit; the absence of Hamburg's music establishemt is notable, but the father of one of the Volker girls (from the Frauenchor) attentively accompanied Johann Jakob to and from Bremen. Marxsen was unable to attend because of illness.

I'm doubly glad to be coming to Bremen; writing is an altogether rotten business, and especially when one has many and very affectionate things to say.

Greet your wife beautiful, and your children small, and be yourself greeted warmly and with warm gratitude by

your

Joh. Brahms

The Requiem had its second performance in Bremen a few days later, with Reinthaler conducting. Brahms was among the listeners—the 'dessert' he referred to. The letter Brahms enclosed was his gracious thank you to the Committee of the Choral Society, in which he praised the singers for the 'diligence and love with which they sang my Requiem', and expressed his appreciation of Reinthaler's extraordinary skill.[3] One more movement was composed, shortly after, and for the whole work Brahms asked for and received a fee that was about five times larger than for any work he had sold before (excluding the small fortune Rieter had paid him for the choral Folk-Songs). The Requiem therefore marked a watershed for his bank account as well as for his fame; financial difficulties ended at last as subsequent fees rose substantially.

220

Johannes Brahms to Melchior Rieter-Biedermann

[Hamburg, 24 May 1868]

Dear Herr Rieter,

I take up a new pen to write to you that I am sending the 'Requiem'. It is, in all seriousness, also a sacrifice to friendship; for my part, I would prefer to let it lie.

I am sending the parts well corrected. The full score and the piano vocal score from Cologne, where I'm going for Whitsuntide, perhaps will also see you?[4]

A 7th number has now been added, No. 5, soprano solo with some 16 measures of chorus. I will, in any case, send this only later, since first I must have it copied and look for a place where for money and kind words I can have it performed for me.

Therefore I note that in my score it is 17, and in the piano score, 6 pages in length; you can make preparations accordingly.

[3] *BW* iii. 18.

[4] The Music Festival of the Lower Rhine always took place on the Whitsun weekend. The year 1868 was the festival's Golden Jubilee.

Should the C clef for soprano, alto, and tenor be retained in the piano score? i.e. may it be? could it be? I would like it. In my opinion, the text must be printed *at the head* of the full score and of the piano score, and that precisely according to the enclosed text—in stanzas!!

The trombones can often be placed on a single stave, occasionally must occupy 2.

In any case, devote a letter some time to letting me know your thoughts regarding the engraving.

And finally, I should like an honorarium of 100 Napoleons; But before this can even approximately be considered an honororium, I should like to ask you for a further 10 Napoleons as a small contribution to my expenses. No. 5 will easily cost me that much and you can easily calculate how many expenses I have had apart from this, since I needed 3 piano vocal scores, 12 sets of quartet [string] parts, 200 vocal parts. It's true that I could now sell these in Vienna and Bremen; but I suppose neither of us would want that. I'm not even counting the boots I wore out walking in Winterthur and Baden trying to find the notorious pedal-point.[5]

What seems most practical in this work, I suppose, is that each movement can definitely be performed individually. At the repeat performance in Bremen we were in doubt for a long time—in the end it was done in its entirety.

NB. I could just accept 10 Napoleons simply for the new movement, which I hope will make a whole of the work even more than before.

Frau *Schumann* asks me to write to you that she does not want to publish the 'Symphonic Etudes'. This [is] her decided opinion; her grounds are not mine.[6]

Lastly, I wish you a great deal of enjoyment with the new publication; for my part, I have done my level best.

Warm greetings to the entire population of the *Schanzengarten*.[7]

---

[5] A nice little bit of commercial blackmail, here. 'The notorious pedal-point', those 36 measures at the end of the third movement, which evolve over a sustained low D, gave Brahms a lot of trouble. Although most of the movement was probably composed in Karlsruhe, it seems that the working-out of this famous passage took place in Winterthur, in the course of the early morning walks that were his custom.

[6] In Schumann's papers, Brahms discovered five Études not included when the *Symphonic Études*, Op. 13, were first published. Clara objected to Brahms's wish to publish them now. They were later published by Simrock in 1873 with her reluctant consent, and then included in the Supplemental Volume (XIII) edited by Brahms in 1893 for Breitkopf's complete Schumann Edition. For more on this, see Linda Correll Roesner, 'Brahms's Editions of Schumann', in Bozarth (ed.), *Brahms Studies*, 252–82, and Letter 515 with preceding commentary.

[7] The name of the Rieter residence.

At Whitsuntide, c/o *Hiller's* or *Königslöw's*, otherwise, as usual, Anscharplatz 5.

Your

J. Brahms

There is still no organ part, and I am undecided whether it should also appear in the full score.

I should like to ask most particularly to send me honest-to-goodness Napoleons. A payment of honour must be in gold, not paper.

221

Johannes Brahms to Melchior Rieter-Biedermann

[Bonn, 13] June [18]68

Dear Herr Rieter,

This morning the orchestral score and piano reduction of the Requiem are going off to you. No. 5 is in its proper place; no rehearsals were possible just now in Oldenburg, Carlsruhe, among others, and so I don't want to hold matters up. In return, I request you make a rehearsal of this number possible before the publication of the work, i.e. produce full score, piano vocal score, orchestra and chorus parts for me as soon as you can, so that I can correct them in case that is necessary. 2 or 3 each for violin [strings] and chorus.

I beg you not to forget this and let me know as early as possible when I can receive the necessary material.

The chorus parts will naturally be engraved in treble clef.

In the full score, however, the C clef will remain throughout for soprano, alto, and tenor. That you won't object to.

I also wanted this for the piano vocal score. That is why I asked you, however!

With regard to the harp it must be noted that a minimum of two players are desirable and necessary.

Trombones can for the most part get along with one system, but also at times spread themselves out on 2 or 3 or 4.

A *Latin* text is thoroughly out of place in this work. You will understand this yourself if you think the matter over even a little bit. It can in no way whatsoever be sung in place of the *Latin* [Requiem Mass] in church. In Holland everything is sung in German. France is not under consideration. That leaves only England and an English text, which would do quite well, certainly, and in any case already fits of its own. *Joachim* will be glad to take care of that. In case you too wish it, turn to him. But I don't believe very much in the possibility of an English performance.

The organ part is lacking for the moment, but can be delivered at the time of the proofs and can even be delivered with pleasure afterwards.

For the moment I am living in Bonn for four weeks, Kessenicher Weg No. 6 at Frau *Endemann's*.

I draw attention again to the printed proofs for No. 5, to the C clefs in the full score without ? and C clefs in the piano vocal score with ?.

Warm greetings to you and everybody in the *Schanzengarten*

Your

J. Brahms

The organ part was not included, the orchestral score merely indicating where the organ does and does not play. The part itself was finally printed in 1871. It is clear from other correspondence that Brahms's chief interest was in bolstering the bass line.

Rieter made one more unsuccessful attempt to include a Latin translation of the text. Brahms was obdurate:

> ... but dearest Herr Rieter, why then is it called a 'German Requiem'? Who needs the Latin text, and where do you plan to get it from? For it cannot simply be translated at will, fits with difficulty under the same notes, etc. etc. The English, on the other hand, fits easily ...[8]

If the Requiem established Brahms's reputation as a great and serious composer, another work from that period brought him into every home in Europe and America, however musically modest. During the summer Brahms sent his Viennese friends Bertha and Arthur Faber a present upon the birth of their second son. The manuscript bore the title 'Lullaby, to Arthur and Bertha Faber, for cheery general-purpose use. July 1868'. With it went an explanatory letter:

222
Johannes Brahms to Arthur and Bertha Faber[9]

[Bonn] Aug[ust 18]68

Dear Herr Faber,

Your letter was far more necessary to me than you imagine. I wrote my last letter with deep anxiety—that I am compelled to the enclosed explains and says everything else.

[8] *BW* xiv. 156.
[9] The envelope is addressed to Bertha, the letter to Arthur, the song dedicated to both of them.

Frau Bertha will immediately see that I composed the cradle song yesterday specifically for your little one; she will also find it quite appropriate, as do I, that while she sings Hans to sleep, her husband sings to *her* and murmurs a love song.

By the way, Frau Bertha would do me a favour if at some point she could obtain for me the music and words of the said love song ('Du meinst wohl, Du glaubst wohl'). It buzzes in my ear only somewhat approximately. You, however, have to write new verses for it, fitting ones!

My song, on the other hand, is equally suitable for girls as well as boys, and you needn't order a new one each time!

I wish I could add that I am coming to Vienna sometime very soon, but unfortunately—I cannot yet see when and how that might take place. In the autumn I seem to be busy one way or another in Germany and Switzerland, and Vienna is much too far away to go there as the occasion arises. Maybe Stockhausen will be going there and that might provide me with a special occasion. Are you living and staying entirely in your town house the whole time, then?[10]

The fiftieth anniversary celebration here has been tiring for me, as I suppose the sharpshooters' meet was for you?[11]

Now you'll become Gotthardt's 'work of art', I suppose?

Do give my greetings to him and whomever else you see. That will have to be all for today, for the Festival guests are gradually departing and still not leaving me in peace.

Very warm greetings

from your

J. Brahms

Ten years earlier, when Bertha was 17 and a member of Brahms's Frauenchor in Hamburg, she had sung him a popular love song by Alexander Baumann, 'Du meinst wohl, Du glaubst wohl'. The tune remained with him. He used it as the counter-melody in the piano accompaniment of this lullaby, taking pleasure in the dual message thus conveyed by the song.

For years the Fabers constituted the nearest thing to family that Brahms had in Vienna; he spent many a Christmas Eve with them, Arthur was his banker and financial confidant, and when Brahms was away from Vienna but needed something sent

---

[10] The Fabers had a summer house in the mountains of what is now Slovenia.

[11] The fiftieth anniversary of the University of Bonn. Hiller was awarded an honorary doctorate, prompting Brahms to comment, '*that* was an honour one could really be pleased about, more so than a medal or knighthood' (Letter to Clara, *SBB* i. 589). A sharpshooters' meet (*Schützenfest*) is a country fair centred around shooting competitions, food, beer, and dancing.

to him or taken care of, it was to the Fabers he turned. In addition to the Lullaby, Brahms made Bertha gifts of several other song manuscripts.[12]

Another set of pieces was soon to make Brahms supremely popular—the Hungarian Dances. It is probably no coincidence that Brahms's most widely accessible works were prepared for publication just as he was himself most actively involved in performing before audiences; in addition to the Lullaby and Hungarian Dances, the *Liebeslieder Waltzes*, Op. 52, too, were written and published one year later, in 1869.

223
Johannes Brahms to a French Publisher (Probably J. Maho)

Vienna, Dec[ember 18]68

Esteemed Sir,

Some time ago you had the kindness to write to me regarding my compositions and their distribution in France.

I am now about to publish 'Hungarian Dances' in volumes of about the same size as my 'Waltzes', for 4 and 2 hands.

Our publishers, as I know, do not like to see us dealing with foreign publishers on our own, the doubled business of selling is also an inconvenience and I have no idea of the value of our things for France.

But since I would not like to let your kind offer go unheeded, I know of no other way of taking care of my interests than to ask your permission to enquire: approximately what honorarium would you have given me for something like the Op. 39 Waltzes or, parenthetically, (~~roughly~~) what would be agreeable to you for the volume of Hungarian Dances, to begin with, for 4 hands.

Will you kindly forgive me if asking this is perhaps unbusinesslike, perhaps even indiscreet. My address is: Vienna, Spina's Music Shop.

In any case I would like to ask you to let me have a reply by return post; should you be able to enlighten me as requested, that would of course please me greatly.

> With the highest regard,
> faithfully,
> Johs. Brahms

This letter, published here for the first time, is the only surviving evidence of Brahms's direct dealings with a French publisher. He seems to have abandoned the

---

[12] Some are presently in the Glinka Museum in Moscow. The Second World War undoubtedly played havoc with the Fabers's letters, and perhaps with other material as well.

idea soon enough, though. Shortly thereafter he offered the Hungarian Dances to Simrock. 'They are *genuine* children of the Pusta and Gypsies,' he wrote. 'Not begot by me, merely nourished by me on milk and bread.'[13]

For the past year or so, serious trouble had been developing between Brahms and Clara.[14] He had irritated Clara considerably in 1866, and was not in Baden at all for the summer of 1867. At the beginning of 1868 he wrote a letter to secure her presence in Bremen for the Requiem. But in it he touched again upon an old theme which had once before aroused her hostility—the idea that she retire from the concert platform and give up her unsettled life as a travelling virtuoso as soon as she was financially able to do so. Brahms seems really to have had no idea of the extent to which performing in public was crucial to Clara's spiritual well-being, even apart from any financial necessity. There is no doubt that the letter was well intentioned; but it was ill-timed, perhaps written just then because Brahms himself was on tour, and was reminded how much *he* disliked that kind of life. But for Clara it came just as her life was burdened with yet another round of tragic problems, and her need for both artistic fulfilment and money was especially great.

224
Johannes Brahms to Clara Schumann

[Hamburg, 2 February 1868]

Your letter from Brussels was just on its way to Vienna as I was travelling here, and so I had to do without it for a time.

If you could come and listen on Good Friday, that would be an unbelievable and great pleasure for me, that would be half the performance for me! And should it come off even a little as planned, you may well be astonished and pleased. But unfortunately I am not the kind of person who succeeds in attaining more than people give him good-naturedly of their own accord, and that is always very little.

And so I am also preparing for everything being rushed, too rushed and perfunctory, this time as in Vienna; only do come!!

That your Christmas holiday should be celebrated without Julie I would not have imagined. How sad for you, to know the poor girl (whom one really cannot think of without considerable enthusiasm) to be so far away and suffering, as well.

---

[13] *BW* ix. 61. See also Letter 235 in this volume.
[14] See Reich, 205–6, and May, ii. 418–25. While May's description of this period is perhaps psychologically unsophisticated, it has the merit of having been written by an intelligent observer who knew Clara Schumann, her daughters, and Brahms, personally.

And to look at Julie, one would suppose all sickness far away, in spite of her delicate nature. I always find myself having high hopes for certain periods of time. Well, Julie is fully grown up, of course, but in your place I would continue to harbour some consoling hope. Only I cannot converse with you very easily about it. Right now I am greatly tempted to get myself an unfurnished apartment in Vienna, that calls for making a decision!

What I wouldn't give to know if you are considering more or less moving there soon. I think there is much to be said for it and it seems to me that a suitable point in time for you will have been reached next year.

In spite of what you replied, I would still like you to consider that your unsettled existence must eventually come to an end.

There can be only *one* motive that counts, and that one counts for everyone and for me as well! Whether it is essential for you to earn money in this fashion. I think that nothing else must be considered either by you or by others. Including, how strong you feel, etc. You might ask yourself how much of it may be founded on illusion and habit. I will not tell this to you, because after all I don't hear you [play] in public, and also because I would decidedly not trust my judgement for many reasons.

In any case, I probably am and will remain the only one to speak to you about this at all, but I would like to ask you to keep the inevitable always in mind, and to let only the one motive count and determine your decisions. Let others in similar situations serve merely as examples for you, and don't put your faith in exceptions.

But I hope we'll talk again soon, and that you believe more firmly than ever that I couldn't harbour the smallest indifferent, unfriendly thought about you.

Frau Rösing in Ham is moving to Hanover now (May). Tell me then, what are we going to do with Robert's grand piano, which the good woman has taken care of for so long. I know, of course, not to let it stay here, space is money.

But in Baden you also don't have room for such a precious but bulky souvenir. Well, and even selling it here is also almost impossible, as I am told by Heins, and one hardly likes to contemplate it. Be sure to write to me about it and soon. If I were living here, I wouldn't even consider giving it away, but now I really have to make a decision—and you?[15]

Furthermore, if it's worth your trouble, I would like to tell you that I

---

[15] Robert Schumann's Graf grand piano, a gift from Clara Schumann to Brahms after Robert's hospitalization. When Frau Rösing moved, his parents kept it for a time until it was exhibited in Vienna at the International Exposition in 1873, after which Brahms gave it to the Gesellschaft der Musikfreunde. See Letter 282.

have outgrown my still perfectly good fur coat and actually have not used it for a long time. Could Ferdinand or Felix use it, *and* anyway where do these two live in Berlin, I'm thinking of going there some time, you know.

Finally, I'd like to know what honoraria your husband received, for example, for the Paradise and Peri, the Requiem or similar works. For I have no idea what to charge for my Requiem (*in- or ex-cluding arrangements for 2 and 4 hands*).

And now on to what as a good son and brother I should have begun with. I found everyone here well and in good spirits, am staying with father and so far I have a very comfortable feeling when I go strolling around. My sister promises to cause me considerable worry, still, for she has most unfortunate thoughts of marriage!

But I hope this goblet too shall pass, isn't it enough that I do not sip from that delectable goblet on her account.[16]

So let me hear from you very soon and let me hope that you will be among the listeners on April 10. And it certainly isn't merely for the sake of listening, seeing is equally important to me.

With all my love
your Johannes.

Clara was incensed, but held her peace. Despite misgivings and fatigue, she appeared in Bremen Cathedral just in time for the dress rehearsal of the Requiem. But in August, replying to a letter now lost, she took him severely to task for February's letter, displaying the resentment of a capable woman towards a man who does not hesitate to tell her, from afar, how to arrange her life. She also told him bluntly why he had been less than welcome in her home in Baden-Baden the previous summer: his continual moodiness had wounded not only her but her children, and she was no longer willing to expose them or herself. Brahms was shaken.

225

Johannes Brahms to Clara Schumann

[Switzerland, between 6 and 12] September 1868

I cannot get over it, dear Clara. I would have liked to reply to your letter, which certainly says many hard things, as innocently as possible, to neatly

---

[16] Of all the various excuses Brahms gave to himself and his friends for not marrying, this is surely the most astounding. Elise Brahms was not deterred by her brother's objections, and married her man. Christian Grund was a widowed watchmaker fourteen years older than she, with six children at home. Brahms added her new family to the list of people to whom he regularly sent large sums of money. *Familie*, 27 ff.

skirt the ruins of the temple of my friendship that may still be standing, not to disturb them—I cannot.

My much-quoted letter keeps running around in my head.

I only want to reply briefly that I understood very well what you wrote about your interest in my art.

But it seems impossible that you, too, have *not* sensed how gladly anyone would decline such interest with thanks. It is through my music that I speak.

It's just that a wretched musician such as I would like to cling to the belief that he is better than his music.

You write of my moodiness in Baden. Here again, there is no argument, everyone has his say and insists on being right. I, too, had reason to complain that I could not begin to gain a sympathetic hearing in your house, as was usual before. It always seemed to me that I first had to surmount other obstacles.

I cannot get my letter off my mind. I see it between us as a great wall. I keep wanting to butt up against it although I know it is in vain.

I have no hope of convincing you, *but* do read what now flows from my pen; later on, much later, it may make your thoughts about me softer and milder—and in any case you will have to reflect: He is the only one to infuriate me on that account.

Admittedly, there is one thing that makes this letter, as every other, hopeless for me: I have no patience for writing. You have always known this fault of mine, but don't I now have the right to expect the same or greater indulgence from you than before?

Apart from that, what have I done?

I said not a word to you questioning your artistry, I did not pass on to you any questioning words of others—I spoke a warning truth to you and asked you to consider it for yourself and to make use of it.

The 'What' is nobody's fault, for the 'How' a good friend can surely count on indulgence and forgiveness.

And perhaps I said that truth at the wrong time, perhaps in the wrong way.

I mean to have said one thing above all:

If your circumstances call for it, [consider that] I had not written, and so should not be given the slightest thought.[17]

That aside, I may be wrong in everything. Above all, in my view of the

---

[17] In other words, 'ignore the letter'.

matter. But I have often heard you discuss such things and heard you mention such names as Garcia, Rettig, on the other side, Fichtner, etc.[18]

Where you are concerned, I may err. But I myself certainly did not pass judgement or listen to others. I left the decision entirely to you although, it's true, not as much to your feelings and custom, as to the general experience of others.

I may have erred in the timing.

I should have written in the autumn instead of the spring—but even now I would also have trouble searching for the right moment for such an admonition. I might just as well have written 1878 instead of 1868—but my reminder ought in any case to have come earlier *than is necessary*, and so the mistake in timing does not seem all that important to me.

Where I am concerned I may have been mistaken. A good friend is gladly allowed to say things which are spurned when coming from one not so entitled.

Forgive this person for having told you too much of the truth. He really informed you of a perfectly ordinary universal truth, for use completely according to wish. He said no harsh words to you and specifically, did not have in his secret innermost mind the gossip of others, nor did he relate any to you. Whatever else there is to be forgiven, forgive it in the good friend, or what is still left of him. It is, after all, mainly an old fault—he is incapable of writing letters—nor can he write diplomatically, something you like to needle him about.

By the way, I do not expect an answer to this; as I have said, I struggled in vain to write of other matters; all this just needed to be said, but ends disconsolately, as it began.

Always and in any case
completely devoted to you
J.B.[19]

In time for Clara's birthday, Brahms sent an album leaf, enclosed in a decoratively painted box from Switzerland:

---

[18] Probably artists who knew—or didn't know—when to retire. Manuel Garcia (1775–1832) was an immensely successful singer, and one of the most important voice teachers of the 19th c., the father of Pauline Garcia-Viardot and Marie Malibran; I have not been able to identify the others.

[19] As a letter from 1859 demonstrates, Clara herself was not averse to telling a friend when it was time to retire, in a manner even more straightforward than Brahms's. When she became aware that her friend Wilhemine Schröder-Devrient, the great opera singer now well past her prime, was planning a concert tour, she wrote her a long letter to try to dissuade her from the undertaking—to no avail and to the considerable annoyance of the singer. When the woman died, in the next year, Clara wrote in her diary: 'I must consider it fortunate . . . for she had outlived herself and could not bear

226
Johannes Brahms to Clara Schumann

[Switzerland] 12 September 1868

Thus sounded the alphorn today:

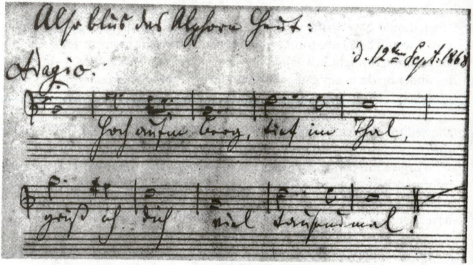

[High on the peak, deep in the vale, I greet thee many thousand times!]

Clara unburdened herself of one more explicit letter regarding Brahms's irritable behaviour, and then calmed down. Visibly relieved, Brahms accepted the justice of her point of view.[20]

227
Johannes Brahms to Clara Schumann

[Hamburg, after 15] October 1868

I would need a truly quiet hour, dearest Clara, to be able to express my thanks for your letter properly, from the bottom of my heart.

Since I could not find it, my thanks should at least come sprinting to you in my customary letter tempo.

So much—or everything—in your letter is true, I must say that ruefully, saddened; but I was greatly cheered and deeply moved when I realized how

it. May heaven spare me such a sorrow, how unspeakably unhappy I should be not to be able to carry on artistically with full strength.' Litz, iii. 49 ff., 70.

[20] *SBB* i. 597 (15 Oct. 1868). See also Reich, 205.

fine it is, as fine as only a good and angelic soul such as you could write. So be thanked a thousand times; should I believe more than before, or may I only hope that your kindness shall not again have to take the form of forbearance towards me!

There is a mad polyphony in life, and sometimes a good woman such as you can nevertheless bring off a splendidly tender resolution!

My suitcase has arrived and with it much that is dear to me. I must write to Allgeyer regarding other things.

I still know little about my winter.

On the 11th of November I have a concert here with Stockhausen, before that, in Kiel. If it can somehow be fitted in, I should like to come to Oldenburg and Bremen when you are there.

Here my Requiem will be produced at Eastertime, in Basle I don't know when, ditto in Vienna, and here (in Vienna) I should like to get them to take on Rinaldo.

It may well be all the same to me just when that will be published, in any case it wouldn't have been as worthwhile to sell it *before* the Requiem, now it will brings in 100 L[ouis]. Incidentally, it has been polished up very neatly and looks better with its big Finale.[21]

Did you find the Variations for 2 pianos and couldn't we play them in Vienna? I must go there in any case and would like to go in November. A symphony by Dietrich will be performed for you in Oldenburg. It would be better if you used a little more gentleness than frankness there!

Here everything is as usual, tomorrow it'll be the same at Friedchen Wagner's house.

Kirchner's wedding will have taken place on 15th October, according to what his betrothed wrote me a few days before that.

I am duly plagued by corrections and revisions, apart from that I am practising the piano . . .

Addio for today, I dearly hope to see you in Bremen, and am and remain at all times

totally your

Johannes.

The crisis dissolved in a round of joint concerts. Brahms and Clara appeared together in Bremen, Oldenburg, and Vienna, performing the Schumann *Andante and Variations for Two Pianos, Two Cellos, and Horn*, Op 46, mentioned in the above letter; Brahms's Hungarian Dances; and Waltzes, Op. 39.

---

[21] Apart from the last movement, *Rinaldo* was complete in 1863.

Brahms's relationship to Wagner is remarkably complicated, given that the two men hardly had anything directly to do with each other. Those two great figures weave about each other for a substantial part of the nineteenth century, however, and even touch fleetingly.

Although the men symbolized genuine and profound differences about the role of music in the arts, these philosophical differences cannot explain the contempt and nastiness with which Wagner spoke and wrote about Brahms.[22]

Wagner's antipathy has usually been explained by the part Brahms took in promoting and signing a public manifesto, specifically denying Liszt and his friends and followers (thereby implying Wagner) their role as the only valid composers of the day—'the Musicians of the Future'. But this cannot be correct.

For one thing, the Manifesto was published in 1860, but Wagner was still civil to Brahms for another few years. For another, Brahms's letters to Joachim make it absolutely clear that Wagner was not the intended butt of the protest;[23] subsequently two young adherents of Wagner who also knew and admired Brahms—Karl Tausig and Peter Cornelius—succeeded in convincing Wagner that the intent of the Manifesto was to take aim at Liszt and his tone poems, music which Wagner himself was not enthusiastic about. Tausig even obtained Brahms's co-operation, in 1862, in copying out parts for a Viennese performance of excerpts from the *Ring* and *Meistersinger*; and Wagner, who saw Brahms at that time, described him as 'modest and good-natured'.

Then in February 1864, years after the flap over the Brahms–Joachim Manifesto, Wagner invited Brahms to come and visit him for an evening in his borrowed villa in Penzing, outside Vienna. It was a festive evening, with a group of Wagner's disciples and friends an attendance. Brahms played some Bach, and then his own Handel Variations, Op.24. According to an eyewitness account, Wagner was in a fine mood, and 'with the most unaffected warmth, overwhelmed Brahms with appreciation of his work'.[24]

The two never met again. What happened, subsequent to February 1864, so to arouse Wagner's hostility to Brahms? To understand, it may be instructive to examine the relationship of both Wagner and Brahms to Mathilde Wesendonck.

During Brahms's first solo concert tour nine months later, in the autumn of 1865, he had occasion to meet Mathilde and Otto Wesendonck, wealthy patrons of the arts, as they joined with a few other Zurich music lovers in hiring a private orchestra so as to hear more of Brahms's music. Mathilde, as many know, is the woman who inspired not only Richard Wagner's Wesendonck Songs (they are set to

[22] The opposite was not true. Brahms himself never abused Wagner publicly, nor allowed his friends to do so in his hearing, something a number of his friends have attested to. See e.g. Klaus Groth, *Erinnerungen an Johannes Brahms* (Heide, 1933), 47, and many quotes recorded by Richard Heuberger in his *Erinnerungen*. On the contrary, he was deeply respectful and cognizant of Wagner's achievements, as one quickly discovers from reading his letters.

[23] See Letters 128–9 with commentary, and especially 132.

[24] From an account by Gustav Schönaich, the stepson Dr Josef Standhartner, friend of Wagner's and member of the Gesellschaft's Board of Directors. Both men were among the invited guests of the evening. Otto Biba, *Brahms in Wien* (Vienna, 1983), 34.

her poems), but the opera *Tristan and Isolde*; and Mathilde herself was Wagner's mistress during ten of the most productive years of his life. But in 1865 she seems not to have been disturbed by the philosophical differences which separated the two men in the practice of their music; she was as enthusiastic an admirer of Brahms as the other influential music lovers of Zurich had become since the time of the first performances of Brahms's music there two years earlier. For many years thereafter she made every effort to tempt Brahms to stay at the Villa Wesendonck, her luxurious mansion atop a hill outside the city.

In the course of those passionately lived years during which she and Wagner were lovers, Mathilde had persuaded her husband to build for Wagner and his wife Minna a garden villa on land next to the Wesendonck villa, and to remain his gracious patron all the while she was Wagner's mistress. This remarkable arrangement came to an abrupt end in 1858, but contact between Mathilde and Wagner did not stop entirely. On 23 November 1863, he came to the villa to see her again at a time, as it happens, when she had just heard the music of the young Johannes Brahms for the first time (10 November, a concert at which his D major Serenade was performed and very well received). Wagner came to press the Wesendoncks for a loan, but his request for money was gently turned down (M. W. to Wagner, 21 December 1863); and when he came to Zurich again one year later, the doors to the Wesendonck house were firmly shut.

There is no way to document whether or not Mathilde spoke to Wagner at that time about the young star on the horizon, but the following chronology is certain: in November 1863, Mathilde Wesendonck, along with the rest of Zurich's cultural élite, became an overt admirer of Brahms, both the man and the composer. Three months later Wagner asked Brahms to visit him. Sometime late in the following year, Wagner was denied entry to the Wesendonck household, while Mathilde was soon to invite Brahms to come and stay like 'a happy swallow' in the little house which had once been Wagner's sanctuary.[25] It probably will do no harm to an assessment of the situation to turn to a photograph of Brahms in 1866 (Plate 21).

The earliest surviving letter in the Brahms–Wesendonck correspondence is from Mathilde, dated 1867, in which she again urges Brahms to come and visit. Brahms's first known letter to her is dated 1868, but the tone and content of both letters (corroborated by passages in other correspondence) makes it clear that Brahms was already an honoured acquaintance and much-sought-after guest.[26] Wagner could no longer claim that privilege, and perhaps it is not so surprising after all, that in spite of such a very promising first meeting in 1864, Wagner never again met Brahms privately, and had nothing to say about him in public that was not offensive.

[25] Erich H. Müller von Asow, *Johannes Brahms und Mathilde Wesendonck, ein Briefwechsel* (Vienna, 1943), Letter of June 1867, 59–61. All other quotes and letters are from the same volume.

[26] Theodor Kirchner to Julius Stockhausen, Zurich, 10 May 1864: '. . . What are Brahms's plans for the summer? If he should come here, he is invited to stay with the Wesendoncks, completely undisturbed'; Julia Wirth, *Julius Stockhausen, der Sänger des deutschen Liedes*, 271. In 1866, Clara wrote to Brahms (8 July): 'I found it very shrewd of you not to take the Wesendoncks up on their invitation, that would have obliged you to these people in a way that would have fallen heavily enough on you.'

228

Johannes Brahms to Mathilde Wesendonck

Anscharplatz 5, Hamburg, [November] 1868

Most revered Madam,

I had a very curious, bitter-sweet feeling as I found the beautiful, slender tracings of your handwriting upon my return from Switzerland. I *was* recently in Zurich, twice, each time for half a day. Although there was much else I needed to do, I was hoping to visit you. [But] as Hegar told me you were not at home, unfortunately, it did not happen.

It now appears I can soon hope to make up for what I missed. As of now, your projected travels and mine show signs of cordial agreement. For one thing, I should be coming to Switzerland again in the winter, specifically to conduct my German Requiem in Basle. For the time being, I will be kept here doing proof-reading and other work which makes my hand and my pen so impatient that I earnestly beg your forgiveness for their discourteous haste.

I have a strong urge and desire to respond at length to the kind words of your letter, but—meanwhile—favour me with a copy of your GUDRUN, which shall then be read with the same love.[27] If only your path would lead you to this pretty Oyster-Republic![28] Because, you understand, for now I am held fast here. I beg you once more to excuse my hasty pen, and assure you of my greatest esteem and devotion.

Most faithfully yours,
Jhs Brahms

229

Mathilde Wesendonck to Johannes Brahms

[Zurich] 30 December 1868

These few words today will merely inform you, most honoured Sir, that your lines reached me in Dresden, and that for several days now we have been back on our tranquil Swiss hill. Novices that we are, Berlin held so many attractions for us that we wish to save Vienna for a later journey.—

As we enter the new year, permit me to put into words something which you should long since have known and probably already do—isn't it so? I

---

[27] A five-act play by Mathilde. Brahms was already looking for a suitable opera libretto, a fruitless search which went on for many more years. He kept the libretto she sent—it was found among his papers after he died.

[28] *Austern-Republik*, in German. A play on the the German name for Austria, *Oester-reich*.

would not wish to have lived in this century without at least having invited you most warmly, and with some urgency, to rest at our hearth. Having said this, I have done my part, and it now rests with you to do yours. 'Enough words have been exchanged, let us at last see deeds,'—and now I shall take my leave of you, expressing the wish that I may be able quite soon to greet you on Swiss soil at the performance of your work. Please let me know when I can come to Basle, as I should like to attend one or two of the rehearsals. Here in Zurich, the mixed choir's rehearsals of your Requiem are starting today for performance on Good Friday.

With best wishes for all good fortune, and my most sincere esteem,

Yours,

Mathilde Wesendonck

Your rooms are ready for you at any time.

Nothing came of Wesendonck's efforts to incorporate Brahms into her circle. A few years later she sent him an *Ode for the Ceremony of Cremation* in the hopes he would compose for it.

'I should like to arouse your interest in the fine old custom of cremation, which in every respect accords better with the views of the nineteenth century than the ugly, bad Semitic custom of burying the dead,' she to wrote him.

What the letter did arouse was astonishment and mirth in a wide circle of Brahms's friends, and it marks the end of their communications.

❦ 1869 ❦

In response to a call for help from a young, penniless, and determined Viennese singer studying in Hamburg with Julius Stockhausen, Brahms wrote:

230
Johannes Brahms to Rosa Girzick

[Vienna, January 1869]

Most esteemed Fräulein,

Fortunately, your letter and your picture do not look nearly as hopeless as you believe, and so your youthful spirit won't exactly be harmed by the little bit of anxiety and distress which it now must live through.

You want my advice then, to confuse yourself a little more? In that case, I advise you first of all not to pay too much attention to it, and to reach for it gingerly and only if there is nothing better around.

For a start, in your place I would definitely not even begin to give lessons. But to say something positive, in case your esteemed teacher does not attend to it and no engagements are to be found, I would travel to Berlin, to music director Julius Stern. Under this very competent and highly regarded gentleman you would learn the necessary roles and through his mediation would then undoubtedly find an appropriate position very easily. Herr Stern will certainly also be open to the suggestion that you begin to demonstrate your gratitude in Prussian currency only after having become a famous singer. Moreover, it should be easy to facilitate this temporary stay in Berlin, and should you still require a small portion of a banker I believe that one of my size and quality should suffice.

Are you discussing your affairs and possibly this plan with Stockhausen? Will he give you a letter to take with you? It is probably strange if I do this behind his back. Otherwise, you could turn to the publisher Fr. Simrock, Jägerstraße 18, with my greetings or my letter. He would be glad to introduce you to Stern, and together with his lovely wife, would surely take good care of you generally.

Finally, however, the best advice: remain pretty merry—or both.[1] Drive off your melancholy thoughts with Viennese waltzes, and very often with letter-writing. If you should see my sister, I ask you to greet her from me, and be yourself warmly greeted

by your devoted
J. Brahms.

Brahms was still without a home to call his own. His possessions were scattered in various places, so that letters to his father during the winter of 1868/9 are filled with requests to look in his cupboard and send scores and music to friends, colleagues, and publishers, and to be ready to receive various of his belongings as they arrived in trunks and suitcases.

231
Johannes Brahms to Julius Allgeyer

[Vienna,] Jan[uary 18]69

Dear friend,

Indeed, it seems to me I have unsuccessfully asserted once before: the attic of your house still shelters things that belong to me. Nevertheless I cannot help but propose this sentence once again, and definitely not as a

---

[1] The word play works equally well in German and English.

hypothesis. I therefore turn to you with the plea that you make ready for the journey straightaway, ascend to the above-mentioned attic, and survey the scene.

Also raise up on high dishes worn out by diverse usage and blankets full of dust, open boxes and crates and observe if they don't harbour books and linens. Should you, in addition, find boots and breezy summer things which cause a tear of emotion to appear in your eye on behalf of the friend who had worn such scruffy stuff—just toss the mouldy things onto your neighbour's roof.

But drag whatever is still usable downstairs, pack it up for me with great care and write Father's address on it: *Hamburg, Anscharplatz 5*. However, should you wish to contest the existence of these treasures, or, on the other hand, give pleasure by means of some written matter to the distant one: *Vienna, Gotthardt's Music Shop, Kohlmarkt*. Have the kindness also to add what had been laid out for boxes or expenses. Along with that write a great deal else, for in the midst of this carnival solitude one longs to hear from people and friends.

Can you pass on secret stuff about Levi's Chinese-German composi-tions?[2]

The pen is too awful, the ink is worthless, farewell. Greetings in the house, in town, in the theatre and wherever you wish.

Most of all, remain kind to

your Johs. Brahms

In Karlsruhe, Levi was rehearsing his chorus for a performance of the Requiem, which he hoped Brahms would conduct (he offered to play timpani himself, so as to avoid a repeat of the moment, in the first performance in Vienna, when the tim-panist's unbridled attack on his instrument drowned out chorus and orchestra dur-ing the great pedal-point of the third movement).[3] At the same time, he was interested in the recent discovery of a *Passion according to St Luke*, supposedly by Bach, and wanted Brahms's expert opinion regarding the work's authenticity. Brahms replied first to Allgeyer, then to Levi.

---

[2] For Clara Schumann's birthday in 1868, Levi set music to one of the poems from Goethe's cycle, *Chinesisch-deutsche Jahres- und Tageszeiten* (*Chinese-German Hours and Seasons*). See p. 344.

[3] Levi's letter (22 Feb. 1869, *BW* vii. 33 ff.) also beautifully describes the growing eagerness and devotion of the chorus members as the rehearsals progressed.

232
Johannes Brahms to Julius Allgeyer

27 February 1869

Dear Friend,

I still owe you my thanks, above all, for your kind—and very beautiful letter, above all. Now another one has come from Levi, and I'm caught in such a bustle of concerts that I can't cut a new quill, as I would like, and answer everything at leisure.

So then, first of all the most urgent items—and perhaps this will do for Levi at the same time.

Let me put your mind at ease about my things. I've been missing my Hölderlin all along, but as you mention the hymnal, which I have, the other must be hiding somewhere else.

From Frau Schumann I've only received one trunk so far. But enough.

I've looked at the *Lucas Passion* briefly and hurriedly. But more than that I don't want to do, either.

Now if, indeed, the authenticity of a *Bach* manuscript has been proved beyond all doubt, then by all means it should be printed.

That this Passion is such a one, no one can prove to me, and I would not lift a finger to see it appear under his name. Now as I write this, I realize that I did look at it quite well enough. Any given page in it suffices fully—so as not to think of *Bach*. Whom to assign it to is another question. However miserably they often write, I would not want to blacken the reputation of any of his predecessors and contemporaries—whose names we still know—by ascribing it to one of them.

Is his name on the title-page? If not, it seems to me that the handwriting alone proves nothing; for the *Bach* who is supposed to have composed this must have a different one from our man. But it's not a child's hand either, and the endlessly repeated defective voice leadings, poor declamation, and illogical modulations in the recits—all this says so clearly that *Bach* could never have written it; if by some coincidence an ass has the same handwriting, what of it.

Why *Levi* wants to mistreat his choir with it, however, I don't know.

But I *am* in fact writing to *Levi*! So now I can enjoy reading your letter after all, but *Levi* asks all sorts of other things.

I'm not going to Holland, but it would be curious to hear or conduct my *Requiem* in *Carlsruhe*, the only city where the latter is decidedly unnecessary and, N.B., the only one where listening will be a pleasure! And in *Basle*,

Hamburg, Cologne, Leipzig, I am cancelling, and will leave my defenceless work to its fate.

I read the article [about Feuerbach] in the Augs[burg] Allg[emeine] with great pleasure, and even guessed you as the writer. The only thing I missed is that softest layer of down (such as your new soprano has on her cheeks).

Stockhausen, like me, is staying at the Hotel Kronprinz next to the *Aspern Bridge.* Hiller, too, will be staying here in a few days.

Well, it really is an act of friendship to have written at such length. Kindly consider that the address is intended for two—and may both of you answer.

With warm greetings,
J. Brahms

His pleasure at hearing the Requiem in Karlsruhe would be due to the fact that Levi would conduct. Allgeyer hoped Brahms would attend so as to hear the work in the city where most of it had been written. Although Brahms could not attend the first performance there, he did conduct another performance later in May.

233
Johannes Brahms to Hermann Levi

[Vienna, March 1869]

Dear Levi,

I have 3 concerts this week, 4 in the next, and who knows how many other obstacles and things to do!

Procure my forgiveness, therefore, when I reply to the flattering and gratifying letter from your Concert Association committee through *you.*

I'd be extraordinarily pleased to come to Carlsruhe to hear or conduct the Requiem. It seems to me, from the letter, that your group has finished learning it. Stockhausen and I still have concerts for the immediate future, and other things also keep me.

In brief, I can only repeat that I will gladly do whatever possible to come, and ask you in any case to tell me when the performance is set for.

I'd particularly like to have Prof. Lübke in the audience—who has an article about Die Meistersinger in today's N[eue] Fr[eie] Presse.

I wrote to Allgeyer regarding the so-called Bach Passion, and can only repeat today that I find not a single measure in it that would fit into another Bach work—and conversely, in all of Bach I can find no measure that I could incorporate into this.

Regarding the physical evidence of the handwriting, I think that similarities [of handwriting] are likely to be shared by contemporaries—which surely change, however, in the life of an individual. Moreover, it is easy to demonstrate that the said Passion is by no child, and if *our* Bach should indeed have written it, it must have been when he was still wetting the bed. But I must stop.

Send my kindest regards to your Committee, for whose invitation I'm most grateful. If at all possible, I will come.

Regards to Allgeyer, and to whomever else you wish—and to yourself warm greetings from

Your

J. Brahms

Brahms based his assessment of the St Luke Passion purely on the music, and time has shown him to be correct. But the Bach scholar Philipp Spitta was convinced of its authenticity because the manuscript seemed to be in Bach's hand. As indeed it was—because he had made a copy of the work!

Karlsruhe was not the only city preparing to perform the Requiem; Ferdinand Hiller, in Cologne, carried through his plan to perform movements 1, 2, 4, and 6.[4] Brahms's comment regarding his instrumentation of the Requiem and other compositions deserves attention.

It is also apparent from this letter that Brahms was once again being offered a position at the Cologne Conservatory, an invitation he had first turned down in 1858.

234
Johannes Brahms to Ferdinand Hiller

Febr. 1869

Cherished friend,

It is hardly all that mysterious a force that newly attracts so many talented people to old Cologne, thereby obliging others to seek them out there. I wish I'd yielded to the above-mentioned magnet the first time—most assuredly! without considering that I might also be sought out and brought there.[5]

And indeed it is you alone who, this time too, compels me to consider your offer so seriously and uneasily.

---

[4] Max Bruch reported to Brahms on this performance. *BW* iii. 93.
[5] i.e., 'I wish I had accepted a job there the first time it was offered to me.'

The town (and its environs) are the worst adversaries. I'm a little spoilt by Hamburg, Vienna, and my involuntary freedom.

The salary as Cologne Piano Teacher I could, of course, earn far more easily in that noble business here or in Hamburg. Harmony or counterpoint teaching I would not like to take on. I consider myself in part not reckless and nimble enough, in part not sufficiently prepared and skilful in this material to deal with it in the manner customary, and probably also necessary, in 'music conservatories'.

And so my very lively desire to live in the same town with you is joined by the small crescendo: activity with the chorus.

But I don't want to go on jabbering to you, but will let the business turn over in my mind instead, and will now put an end to talking to you [about it].

You have chosen excellently with my Requiem—like an insurance company against failure! Of course I don't ever expect to hear *more* than one harp! But then I also write for *Waldhorns* and the most beautiful D flat trumpets without hope of hearing their sound. In fact, I'll also write for contrabassoon, indeed two of them, simply because I find that we should have them or else be deprived of a lovely bass—not merely for my D.[6]

Would you be kind enough to inform me of your articles? I am very greedy for this. Until now I have searched in vain in the Cologne [Zeitung] for anti Gervinus, but I don't get to see it regularly.[7]

I played your duet for 2 pianos only today, but on the other hand have not yet seen your highly regarded B minor variations for 4 hands.

I ask to be commended very particularly to your ladies and I greet you from the bottom of my heart,

your Johs. Brahms.

On 28 February my Rinaldo is being put on here, so that my coming for the 2nd of March is probably also impossible.

In the course of his life, Brahms wrote many condolence letters, remarkably direct and devoid of clichés. What follows is not quite one of them, but rather, one of the few which mixes sympathy with business. This breech of his usual practice was occasioned by the sudden possibility of the première of his cantata *Rinaldo* (it took place in Vienna on 28 February 1869, with Brahms conducting), of which the final chorus had been composed in the summer of 1868, five years after the rest of the work. Simrock *fils* was not offended, as he himself did not hesitate to include business

---

[6] i.e. the pedal-point in the third movement.

[7] *Groves*[2] describes Hiller's frequent contributions to that journal as 'a crowd of interesting articles, biographical, critical, and miscellaneous'.

matters along with descriptions of the sad events in Bonn surrounding the death of his father, the publisher P. J. Simrock.

235
Johannes Brahms to Fritz Simrock

Vienna, 2 January 1869

Dear Herr Simrock,

Of my sincere sympathy you may be sure, in this difficult time you are living through; I have often thought of you in Bonn, and how, alongside mother and sister, and presumably heavily burdened with other matters, your life could hardly have been enjoyable.

Now I want vehemently to indict and deplore my impractical nature very seriously. I have simply let the revision of *Rinaldo* slide because the *Viennese Men's Choral Society* cannot perform it.

Now the local *Academic Men's Choral Society* has heard about it and begged me urgently to let them have the work for February 28th. Consequently, I ask and request: can you have the necessary parts run off for us very quickly?

> 30 first tenors
> 45 2nd   "
> 50 first basses
> 40 2nd   "

Could we definitely have them in the course of this month? There is really very little to correct! Would you make the necessary arrangements and write to me *when* the parts are likely to be here?

Furthermore I enclose two volumes of Hungarian [dances]. Probably the most practical article that an impractical person such as I can deliver. The title reads:

> Hungarian Dances
> for Pianoforte Four Hands
> *arranged*
> by
> J. B.

At the same time it could be noted at the bottom:

'Edition for Piano 2 Hands.' Or a distinct title? [Nos.] 1–5 first, 6–10 second volume. It might be so arranged that a 3rd and 4th volume can be added to the title-page.

For the time being, I would like the volumes organized in this way, later on the 2-hand version, in particular, could be published individually.

As honorarium I would ask 40 Fr[iedrichsdors] for each volume and would not like to ask anything different for the 2-hand version. Every single one of these is now a practical concert piece. But if you wish [other volumes] after that, we could talk.

With regard to the honorarium I would like to comment that it applies to all countries. I have little desire to write a lot of letters, but do have very good offers, e.g. from Maho in Paris. Sales there, to England, Belgium, I gladly leave to you.[8]

If these sons of the Pusta appeal to you, I request copies of the *page proofs* for correction, when the time comes.

Copies do already exist, but the alterations etc., made it impossible to rehearse it properly.

I urgently request that sectional repeats *not* be engraved—only where indicated. The volumes will be bulky as it is. Incidentally, my address here is: *Hotel Kronprinz at the Aspern Bridge.*

In a great rush, with sincere greetings to Frau and Fräulein
Your
J. Brahms.

Brahms made no claims that the Hungarian Dances were his own (although some dances in the later volumes are), and consequently they were published as arrangements and without opus number.

How curious that the Hungarian Dances and *Rinaldo* are dealt with in the same breath. The dances are perhaps his most widely-known works, the cantata almost never performed.

But *Rinaldo* comes closer to opera than any other of Brahms's music. Written as it was in the 1860s by a sentient musical intelligence, it could not help but be influenced by Wagnerian developments. There is even a pliable leitmotiv to represent the enchantress *Armide*, although one has to listen attentively to catch the various appearances as they streak by. To Adolf Schubring, who enjoyed tracking such musical permutations, went a long and sometimes teasing letter.

---

[8] See Letter 223.

236
Johannes Brahms to Adolf Schubring

[Vienna, 16] February 1869

My dear friend,

So the loquaciousness of woman has its good side for once, it brings me a letter from you and even sets my pen in motion. How long and how often have I wanted to write you—before and after the Schumanniana No. 12.[9] Perhaps it didn't happen mainly because I'd like to chat with you, and I can't accomplish this by letter. Even at this moment I must make up my mind, late at night, at least to send you greetings and thanks right away, for in the wild concert season now approaching I really have no time to myself.

I wonder if you will hear my Requiem this Thursday in Leipzig! I really would have liked to go there and personally raise the child out of Leipzig's baptismal font. But I have to do the same here for *Rinaldo*, which the *Akademiker*, it seems, are going to sing very well and lustily.[10]

Lobe, volume IV, I don't know—but so far I've needed no learned outside scholarship to conclude that the available libretti are bad. And I waste a lot of time over this because I've craved an opera libretto long and ardently.[11]

Which ones, then, are my 'weird' song texts? Surely not my dear Hölty, for whose beautiful, warm words my music is simply not strong enough for my taste, otherwise you would see his verses more frequently in my work. Rieter is publishing another volume, in which—there is again a Hölty. But read it carefully and tell me if it and the entire person is not delightful.[12]

It's long past midnight now, serious writing is no longer possible, make do with what's there. Incidentally, I've now shipped my things from here to Hamburg, which means: I really don't live here, and soon Dessau won't be so far away any more, and it will be easier to see one another occasionally. Letters always reach me via Hamburg, of course!

Is it possible that you haven't yet discovered the political allusions in the Requiem? It starts right away with '*Gott erhalte*'—in the year 1866.

[9] Schubring's article about the *German Requiem*, published in the *Allgemeine Musikalische Zeitung* of Jan. 1869.

[10] The Viennese première was on 28 February 1869, in a concert by the Akademischer Gesangverein (Academic Choral Society). Leipzig was the site of the first complete performance of the Requiem, including the fifth movement for soprano solo, 'Ihr habt nun Traurigkeit'.

[11] Johann Christian Lobe, a prolific writer on music. The fourth volume of his recent *Textbook of Musical Composition* (1867) was devoted to Opera.

[12] Op. 43 No. 2, 'Die Mainacht', one of Brahms's most beautiful songs. He included two more in Op. 46, 'Die Schale der Vergessenheit', and 'An die Nachtigall', Nos. 3 and 4.

Greetings to your wife and the children, I sincerely hope that we are getting closer and will see each other again very soon.

With warm greetings

J. Brahms

In the morning:

I am ashamed of the slip of paper which so badly conveys thanks for the friendly conversation of your letter. I want to tell you, at least, that I have conversed with you extensively, sometimes *without* writing. All that has remained is the bad joke at the end, which you'll immediately have interpreted, quite correctly, as a dig at a particularly brilliant side of your talent.

When I read your latest article (I am silent about the joy which it, and everything you write, gave me), I smiled as I mused to myself: you have applied your theory of the development and transformation of motives only most timidly.

A few hurried and brief words about this. I dispute that the themes of the various sections in No. 3 *are meant* to have something in common with each other. (Except for the small motif ♩· 𝅘𝅥𝅮 ♩·) *Should this be so, however,* (I purposely summon nothing to my memory): I want no praise for it, but admit that when I work my ideas don't fly far enough, hence unintentionally often return with the same thing.

However, if I *want* to hold on to a single idea, it should be clearly recognizable in every transformation, augmentation, inversion. The other would be the worst kind of playing around and always a sign of the most barren invention. Unfortunately, the fugue in No. 6 is evidence that (for the sake of 'momentum'?) I am not exactly strict.

In 'Rinaldo' an amusing example of transformation jumps to mind. In the beginning Armide casts a delightful spell, and later on the same motif describes the destruction of the gardens and palaces.

Leaping arbitrarily to another topic: in a theme for variations, almost the only thing that *actually* has meaning for me is the bass. But that is sacred to me, it is the firm footing upon which I then build my tales. What I do with the melody is merely playing around, or ingenious—playing around. I recall with horror:[13]

---

[13] The first three notes of the *Variations on a Hungarian Theme*, Op. 21 No. 2, and two chromatic alterations used in the variations.

When I vary the melody, I can hardly do more than be clever or charming, or lend depth to a beautiful thought, albeit with genuine feeling. On top of a given bass, I truly invent the new, I invent new melodies for it, I create.

(Instead of reading, you really must try seriously to take your ideas for a stroll.)

Just take a look at Bach's G major variations,[14] the Passacaglia, etc. (The chorale variations are a special case.) You find that G major theme also in Handel (also in Muffat). Furthermore, look at the trail which the Art of Variations makes, look at melody variation in Herz and better ones of that period.[15]

Then examine Beethoven's, and if you like, mine.

I think you will find *your* variations only in Schumann (and thoughtless imitators). But couldn't we differentiate between variations and fantasies upon a melody, a motif? (See: *Études.. ?..*),[16] Fantasy variations. But, unfortunately, there are reasons I cannot be over-strict even towards myself.

There are also reasons for me to stop. Forgive the hasty scrawl.

Send me your photograph, and one of Johannes Schubring.

Be warmly greeted,

J. B.

If you'll be in Leipzig on Thursday, do write to me! Do you by any chance still have Schuberth's American newspaper (for my father)?[17]

The 'particularly brilliant side' of Schubring's talent was his ability to discover underlying motivic unity in Brahms's music and the transformations Brahms worked upon his material. But as Brahms was quick to point out in his long postscript, he was just pulling Schubring's leg, and it is mere chance that the opening of the Requiem (cellos, third measure) conforms exactly to the beginning notes of the Austrian national anthem with its opening line of 'Gott erhalte, Gott beschütze'.[18]

---

[14] The *Goldberg Variations*, BWV 988.

[15] Heinrich Herz, 1806–80. Viennese born, he made a highly successful career in Paris, and wrote 'an immense number of variations' (*Groves*[3]).

[16] *Études Symphoniques*, of Schumann. Brahms apparently did not want to write out the name.

[17] The *Musik Zeitung*, a journal of the music publisher J. F. G. Schuberth in New York City, begun in 1867.

[18]

In 1923 Austria's anthem would become Germany's national anthem as well (with entirely different words), only to become a tune despised by a large portion of the world because of the events of the 1930s and 1940s.

His reference to 1866 concerns Austria's decisive defeat by Prussia at the Battle of Sadowa (Königsgrätz) in Bohemia, marking the first time that Habsburg military might was overcome by another German-speaking nation: a requiem for the centuries of Habsburg supremacy?

In *Rinaldo*, however, there really are several examples of thematic connection and transformation. The motive which represents the enchantress Armide is altered rhythmically and melodically at several points in the Cantata, in a meaningful interplay with the text. [19]

By now admiration for the music of Brahms was spreading from a small party of enthusiasts to a much wider circle. When Philipp Spitta, the Bach biographer and great musicologist of the nineteenth century, became familiar with the Requiem, he wrote Brahms a modest, almost apologetic but deeply felt letter, claiming that he was one of many who had become a better person through having made the acquaintance of that music.[20] It was the beginning of a mutually respectful correspondence which lasted, with a nine-year break, until Spitta's sudden death in 1894. Brahms was hardly impervious to such praise, but uncomfortable nevertheless, and he answered with a letter characteristic for its ambiguity and half-thoughts.

[19] Armide's siren call not only appears at the beginning of the piece, but permeates the first part of the cantata (mm. 1–281). A few examples:

In its plainest form it appears again at the Allegro con fuoco (mm. 981 ff.) as the island paradise is destroyed. Perhaps Brahms was pulling Schubring's leg here too, when he pointed out that the motif appears at these two places, because the music throughout the entire work is based on rhythmic permutations and fragments of the motif, not only the first three hundred or so measures but also at measures 616 ff., 981–1055, and the phrase starting in 1088, with its long extention of the phrase and the characteristic feminine ending.

[20] Max Bruch was another; he took the trouble of going to Bremen for the first performance, and dedicated his first symphony to Brahms as a sign of his great admiration.

237
Johannes Brahms to Philipp Spitta

[Vienna,] Jan[uary 18]69

Most honoured Sir!

As I do not want to have my debt to you on my mind any longer, I want to tell you at long last what genuine and sincere pleasure your warm, sympathetic letter has given me.

Many a thing could excuse me for being in general, and this time in particular, a slow and bad correspondent—I prefer to express the wish: of hearing from you more often should any of my music instil enough interest in you. Should this be the case with the new (Simrock) songs, for example, that would please me very much. As I know that Herr Rieter's publishing house proceeds into the world very slowly, I am sending you herewith the quasi-final volume of that collection.

I cannot help wishing your first letter—(a polite way of putting it)— many an addition.

I believe I am not mistaken in concluding, from earlier pages of Rieter's Journal, that you have just now made a more thorough study of the Oratorio.[21]

In short, from him who says Yes so warmly and enthusiastically, one is also glad to hear the Perhaps, and also the No.

I write very hurriedly and beg you to look upon these lines only as a provisional, sincere greeting and expression of thanks.

With the greatest of respect,

very devotedly,

Joh. Brahms

Brahms refers here to Spitta's only letter to him so far as his first letter, and describes this characterization as an expression of politeness; a roundabout way of asking for more letters.

He sent Spitta the four songs of Op. 43, which had only appeared in the previous month, although they had been with Rieter since August—hence Brahms's comment about Rieter's slow pace. The new Simrock songs were his Op. 46–9, published in October.

When he wrote 'From him who says Yes . . .' he undoubtedly meant that he respected Spitta's opinion and judgement and would be interested in hearing not only his praise, but also his criticisms and reservations. Spitta took him at his word,

---

[21] 'The Oratorio as a Form of Art', in the *Allgemeine musikalische Zeitung* (1868), nos. 18–21.

and in the next year wrote of his doubts about the opening of *Rinaldo*, an opening which almost seems to be more the middle than the beginning of something. This led Brahms, most unusually, to write expressly about his musical intent.

238
Johannes Brahms to Philipp Spitta

[Vienna, late] Febr[uary 18]70

Honoured Sir,

While I thank you sincerely for your kind letter, and pocket its praise without scrutiny and without carping, I cannot fail to respond there where your praise becomes muted.

Somewhat dubious—but very human.

The beginning of *Rinaldo* appears to come as a surprise to people and to be ineffectual. You are the first one who, with an apology, seeks the basis for my concept. Since I do not normally open my mouth of my own accord to speak for my things, you are also the first one to whom I am making my thoughts known.

Well then, I believe that merely a brisk chorus [to open the cantata] would not be suitable, would not be sufficient. The composer has to be something of a Gropius,[22] and must definitely let us breathe the very special air which wafts over the island of the enchantress. Even the knights should feel a certain oppressive uneasiness and experience a gentle shudder as they sing

Here let the strong man prove himself![23]

Actually, I believed I was also conveying this to people at the performance by having a verse from Tasso printed before the text.

Maybe it's just playing around that the motive of the introduction also assists Armide in the destruction [scene].

A descriptive introduction, followed by a brisk chorus of knights who show themselves to be quite unmoved by the beautiful enchantress, didn't appeal to me for a variety of reasons.

---

[22] Karl Wilhelm Gropius (1793–1870), renowned Berlin set painter. He was one of the first painters to specialize in dioramas, so as to surround his viewers with a landscape.

[23] Measure 183. Brahms is quoting from the text of the Cantata, as well as his music.

I do remember very well, however, that I actually thought of none of this when I first took up the poem. I simply found myself on the island with the knights, and to this day still don't find that so silly.

Additional
Note p. 751 It goes without saying that I have now noticed, from the reaction, that my realization [of this idea] may well have misfired and bears all the blame.*

And here I should like to say briefly that your information regarding Bach was entirely new to me, and most agreeably surprising.[24]

I wish you all possible luck in your treasure-hunting; to wish us an early completion of the work would be egoistic, for the labour may be as far-reaching as it is fine and stimulating.

Nevertheless, I would be quite eager to know whether you might have a word to say about my remarks?

I saw with pleasure that you are writing about music (Bruch's Mass). But (just between us), don't you find Chrysander's journal more congenial?[25]

For now with best greetings,
Your very devoted
Johs. Brahms

Brahms was under no illusion about *Rinaldo*'s success.

239
Johannes Brahms to Fritz Simrock

[Vienna], March 1869

Dear Herr Simrock,

I continue to wait in vain for the parts for Rinaldo; as soon as they are brought I'll send everything to you.

---

[24] About Spitta's current project, the Bach biography that would become one of the great works of German musicology. Spitta's letter of 21 Feb. 1870 read: 'I don't know whether you might be interested in the news that for several years, now, I have been busy with the preparatory work for a Bach biography. If only I may succeed at long last in bringing about something that is not totally unworthy of the great Master. Here in Thuringia I am fairly close to the biographical sources, for the most part, and I have spared no effort to get to the bottom of them. As it happens, this bottom is most often found soon enough; it takes a much greater effort to discover the sources themselves. Some items very important to Bach's life have been flung almost to the ends of Europe, and it is half a miracle that they have been preserved and eventually found by me. I hope to be able to offer various new and interesting material (even with respect to the chronology of Bach's works) and will in any case try to work the collected material into a coherent picture with a broad historical foundation.'

[25] The musicologist Friedrich Chrysander, an old friend of Brahms, was at this time editor-in-chief of the *Allgemeine musikalische Zeitung*. Spitta had just written a review of Bruch's Mass in a rival, Wagner-friendly journal (the *Musikalisches Wochenblatt* (1870), nos. 8–10).

Since the performance, I have already had 2 concerts (with Stock-hausen), am also otherwise so much in demand that I cannot proof-read the parts yet again.

Some NBs which I beg you to retain and to pay heed to: [In] case I some-how catch hold of a metronome and the necessary time, I shall yet indicate them. Space can be left for that, can't it.[26]

The text will presumably be printed ahead of the music in the orchestral and piano scores? That being so, I wish to have the verse from Tasso added, as in the accompanying programme.[27] The chorus parts must still be proof-read with care. One change is also required in the final chorus. It is pasted over.

It still remains to insert *the study-letters* into the full score, chorus, and orchestra parts *according to the piano-vocal score!*

Also, the markings for the chorus parts ($<$ $>$ etc.) are correct in the piano score and those in the full score and the parts must be made to con-form.

The words: *Rec.* and *rit.* and *rall.* on pp. 21, 21, 37, and 42 in the full score go into all the orchestra parts.

The solo in the final chorus (G major) still has to be added to the solo part of Rinaldo. To be sung *ad libitum*. He sings 'to me' where the others sing 'to you'.[28] Finally, I request the return of my full score and hope it won't be copied just in time for the printing, and that it will be treated with some care.

But now you are undoubtedly longing to hear about the first perfor-mance, and I'll tell it quickly. Above all, I had a lot of fun and have no regrets. But then it was as good as I shall scarcely live to see again. Walter was enthu-siastic about his part and sang it exceptionally beautifully. The Chorus (300 young people) was excellent and the orchestra, after all, the regular Opera Orchestra here.[29]

Well, I suppose it is the audience and the reviews that are most import-ant to you—but there, as usual, there's not so much glory to report.

It is true, Rinaldo was not energetically hissed, as was my Requiem last

[26] He did so in April; the metronome indications printed in the first edition are his.

[27] Brahms wanted Simrock to print not only the text of Goethe's poem, but also the relevant verses from Tasso's *The Deliverance of Jerusalem*, which was basis for Goethe's Rinaldo. See Letter 238 to Philipp Spitta.*

Additional Note p. 751

[28] In the final chorus, 'Mir/dir begegnet das gesegnet Angefang'ne', there is a tenor solo 'as eas-ily overlooked in the score as it is missed during a performance' (Kalbeck's comment, *BW* ix. 67 n. 2). The score from the Complete Edition, however, calls not for solo, but small chorus, with Rinaldo singing along in unison; it is an effective moment in the work (mm. 218 ff.).

[29] i.e. exemplary.

year, but I can hardly speak of a success, either.[30] And this time the reviewers listened with score in hand and accordingly scribbled a lot of stuff. It is a commonplace experience that people always have specific expectations, and, just as surely, always get something quite different from us. So this time there were high hopes at least for a *crescendo* of the Requiem, and definitely for a lovely, excited and lecherous Venusberg menage at Armide's.

Etc. I cannot use the fact that I was recalled more than three times to think in terms of a success.

That, incidentally, is why I ask you to think the matter over some more! It is an extensive work, after all, and that it gave me and some enthusiasts pleasure isn't saying much. A few words about *Rinaldo* by Hofrat Billroth may appear in Rieter's journal.

Apropos, have you sent your songs for this or another journal to *Dr. Deiters*? He would certainly be glad to discuss them.[31]

Next week I'll be in Pesth, otherwise I am remaining here for the time being.

Friendly greetings to yourself and the ladies,
Your
J. Brahms

His unwillingness to capitalize on the obviously crowd-pleasing possibilities of a 'Venusberg menage' probably explains as well as anything why Brahms never wrote a real opera. His writing for the love-bewitched hero, while glorious in its way, is hardly guaranteed to appeal to a wide public, and the fact that Armide's alluring traits only appear at second hand in the anguished thoughts of Rinaldo, as he struggles to free himself of her, is reason enough to doubt a dramatic sense which could have appealed to a general public.

Brahms's possessions were still packed in trunks, wandering the rails in Germany. By now the realization that he would have to find a permanent residence away from his native city was evident to him; Brahms's sense of rejection in Hamburg is at its most explicit here.

---

[30] It is curious that so much is made of the hissing and so little of the enthusiasm which greeted even the flawed first performance of the Requiem. But Joachim, who was present with Brahms, reported to his wife in a letter written immediately after: 'The public listened attentively—a compact little group with devotion and enthusiasm; a few hissing rabble were unable to prevail, Brahms was loudly recalled and the applause kept on, although it took him five minutes to come from the hall up the steps into the orchestra' (*JJ* ii. 450).

[31] Signing himself 'th', the surgeon Theodor Billroth continued his earlier hobby of writing music reviews, this time for the *Allgemeine Musikzeitung*. Hermann Deiters was a regular contributor to that journal, and an early admirer of Brahms. See Letter 388.

240
Johannes Brahms to Johann Jakob Brahms

[Vienna, 30] April, 1869

Dearest father,

How long have I intended to write *tomorrow, definitely*, and each time I keep postponing it! Now, briefly, that the suitcase has arrived; my fur coat is already at the furrier's here.

I suppose Fritz [Schnack] will be leaving soon on his trip? I send my heartfelt good wishes.

Don't you both need money for the 1st of May?[32] Elise will probably let me know, only write to me precisely what you require, then I'll take care of it at the same time. Herr Rieter has written to me from Hamburg that you think that I would soon be in Switzerland, something I myself know nothing about so far.

But in truth, I probably won't be coming to Hamburg this summer, the journey is just too far and my piano player across the way would quickly drive me off. When I came here in the autumn, I didn't think I would stay for so long—but I have to conclude that we're really wasting rather a lot of money on my rooms at your house!

I always like to contemplate how I want to be at home with you—but, in the end, it actually doesn't work out. To gratify this favourite notion of mine, I have now spent the winter in a room at an inn. Books, music, I do without everything, and when I consider it sensibly I do realize that I'm not making use of them in Hamburg. I really must make the decision to live here; I must finally decide to pay my rent where I intend to live.

After all, I surely have no reason for wanting to settle down in Hamburg, and even if I visit you for a shorter or longer time, we can hardly keep two rooms for the whole year for that. How seriously I vacillated about going to Hamburg none the less, that is: to you alone, you can see most clearly from the way I've pestered you all winter with all those things.

Now I wish I hadn't done this, and now had a nice flat here instead and that you'd visit me here.

Even now, I'm dearly tempted to go to Hamburg all the time. But the music in the street and at the neighbours leave me no peace, and since it costs money for the one as much as for the other—after all, I can do without the view of the Kamp!?[33]

[32] For rent.
[33] The Valentinskamp, a public square in Hamburg at the corner of the Anscharplatz.

Besides that, and in the long run, what am I supposed to be doing in Hamburg? Apart from you, who is there whom I still want to see? Etc. You yourself know very well how in every respect there's nothing there for me.

In short, I finally realize that I must be somewhat at home somewhere, and so I've decided that for the next autumn I want to make myself a little more comfortable here in Vienna.

In the mean time, you could certainly rent the room where my piano is and keep all my things together in the middle room.

That I cause you so much trouble, so much commotion, that I spend such a lot of money needlessly, comes about only because it's so very difficult for me to decide to be not completely at home in my father's house. But what do you think about it? Doesn't it look like a useless, expensive duplicate household to you, too? Now, I'll probably have to leave here shortly—since I'm just staying at an inn, after all. Where to I don't yet know for certain, a performance in Carlsruhe is still uncertain. I'll write again soon, meanwhile write to me what you think about this and write also whether you and Elise need money.

Nothing has come from Carlsruhe?

> With deepest love,
> your Johannes

Many greetings to Marxsen, I always mean to write to him.

Johann Jakob's reply must have reassured his son:

> ... As I always say, Vienna is too important to exchange with Hamburg, where everyone has his eye on business, Vienna, where you find understanding and recognition to allow you to work and create. Of course it's understandable that you struggle with yourself to be able to live with us, it is, after all, your home town. It is also understandable how much it pains me that we can't be together. We always did think it would come to this ... I was at Herr Marxsen's, he also finds it natural and agrees with me completely.[34]

As Brahms told his father, a date for the Karlsruhe performance of the Requiem was not yet fixed, and in the mean time, Levi suddenly had reason to look about for another post. Brahms's advice shows him to have been an alert observer of the Viennese scene. The men he mentions were the major figures in Viennese musical life.[35] Levi did not take Brahms's advice to come to Vienna, but shortly thereafter was appointed to a major post in Munich.

[34] Johann Jakob to Johannes, *Familie*, 160.
[35] Dingelstedt was general manager of the Court Opera, Dessoff was a good friend of Brahms and the conductor of the Vienna Philharmonic. Herbeck took on the post of Court Opera

241
Johannes Brahms to Hermann Levi

April [18]69

Dear friend,

Be sure to keep me informed regarding the 3rd of May, I could come and would like to come. Even if it's a 'No' let me know as soon as possible.

First, in passing, that 'some girls from Carlsruhe' have sent me a laurel wreath (or 2 from C!); as far as I can recall, c/o Dessoff.

Well, your recent letter surprised me quite extraordinarily and I would most prefer to discuss the matter in person. I can only write hurriedly and briefly about a few things, but since I do know Vienna, I can answer any *question* that you have.

Above all I am of the decided opinion that you should come. (To be followed by all kinds of discouragements!)[36]

It is hardly likely that the 2,500 Fl. will be increased by the K.K. side. (Maybe, after all, to 3,000.)[37]

Dessoff gives a great many lessons, Herbeck, Hellmesberger etc. have to hold down a dozen positions in order to feed a family. You know how (badly) things stand at the opera, and salvation can hardly be expected from Dingelstedt. On the other hand there is splendid material here and it is possible to work.

The conductor for the Phil[harmonic] concerts is elected *each* year. Well D[essoff] is definitely and in every regard not the right man for this, the only enviable position in Vienna. There are special reasons why he is still beating time, [and] not one soul gives his blessings to it. The orchestra has really gone to pot because of him.

In short, you would have these concerts next year—what can be done with Dingelstedt and the opera, I don't know. Here too, indications are you would easily be Number One.

Whether they will award the title and a higher salary to one of the three, I don't know.

It seems quite important to me that there is only one choral society here (Herbeck). Anyone who knows how to organize could turn a second one not

conductor instead of Levi, and Hellmesberger was at this time director of the Conservatory, concertmaster of the Opera orchestra, and founder of the leading string quartet in Vienna. Their names occur frequently in the correspondence.

[36] This sentence was added as an afterthought, in the margin.
[37] Kaiserlich-Königlich, i.e the government.

only into a (modest) source of income for himself—but he would be the leader of the regiment, and it would be most desirable to present the whole music-making business here with a new face.

And it might well be delightful to reign here as Number One, for the audience here is really different from the one in Carlsruhe and one can do things with it.

One can heap praise on the audience here, but the child wants good discipline and its schoolmasters here (our worthy colleagues) exposed their utter wretchedness so conclusively on the occasion of the recent Liszt-fraud that I was ashamed.

I am shocked at my muddled writing, but I cannot begin again. Today I am playing the D minor Concert-Allegro by Schumann. Saturday I have the last concert with Stockhausen.

Then I'm free—only I cannot leave in just a day or two!

Nothing has arrived in Hamburg from Carlsruhe! What is going on with your mysterious mail! Greetings to Allgeyer. We now have 5 pictures by Feuerbach here. [I wish you] A blossoming, singing springtime, a glorious *Bianca Capella, Orpheus* etc.

My warmest respect to Devrient.[38]

Your J. Br.

Brahms spent the summer in Baden-Baden once more. The engagement and marriage of Julie Schumann to the Italian Count Radicati di Marmorito seems to have hit him hard, to Clara's astonishment (see p. 759). It is difficult to know what to make of the fantasy which could have allowed a man who had very little patience with illness to imagine himself in love with a woman in fact dying of consumption. At all events, that summer brought forth the *Liebeslieder Waltzes*, Op. 52, and 'their sequel', as Brahms sometimes called it, The Alto Rhapsody, Op. 53. None of which prevented a little flirtation with Anna de Dobjansky, a young, charmingly gullible Russian composer of piano music who was spending the summer in Baden-Baden.[39]

---

[38] Eduard Devrient, manager of the Court Opera in Karlsruhe at the time.

[39] Mlle. de Dobjansky, writing to Ferdinand Hiller [original in French] (21 August 1869): 'Since being in Baden (apart from some piano pieces), I have succeeded in writing three parts of a sonata, as for the finale, I don't know what to do with it; it is coming along, but with difficulty. Mme. Schumann, as well as Rosenhain, Brahms, all find that I have much talent as a composer. M. Brahms claims that, having good ideas, I do not work with enough care. He has said that if I wanted to sell him my compositions for a good price, he would work them in his fashion while keeping the ideas, but that afterwards, he would have them printed under his name. Admit that the proposition is flattering ...' (*Hil*, ii. 136). Her *Capriccieto et Nocturne*, Op. 2, published by Simrock, is 'composed and dedicated to Monsieur Johannes Brahms'.

242
Johannes Brahms to Fritz Simrock

[Lichtenthal bei Baden-Baden, 4 September 1869]

Dear Herr Simrock,

It does seem to me that in the printing of the new waltzes, some precautions are in order; I therefore sit down once again. Could we not simply pull two copies of the first or the first few pages once they are engraved, and have them sent to Berlin and Baden?!!

The score must be practical throughout, clear, and easy to read and play for both players.

The vocal parts definitely small! I consider the separation between the two sets of piano staves to be ample. A prominent brace { in front of every set all the way through, and perhaps, throughout, with I and II in front of it. Thus:

$$
\text{I} \left\{ \begin{array}{l} \text{[G cleff]} \\ \text{[G cleff]} \end{array} \right.
$$

$$
\text{II} \left\{ \begin{array}{l} \text{[F cleff]} \\ \text{[F cleff] through the whole score!} \end{array} \right.
$$

None the less, the printing should be as dense as possible, for the sake of the price. Couldn't you arrange to let us take a look at the first few pages? It would really be a shame if a rotten layout were required for practical reasons! The text, the whole well-mannered flirtation, is so nice. I therefore keep carefully to the contract here.

Do please prepare a reasonable bill for our Russian lady! For things are indeed such that the publishers in Paris (where she is going) would offer money immediately as soon as she plays them. But she doesn't want to wait.

But then, I too have a bill to present!

Something like this: A fresh modulation, per tonality, 3 pf.[40] (thus, from C–E flat by way of F–B flat   = 12 pf.)

A new bass for the melody   = 1½ sgr.

A rapturous ending, per 4 measures   = 5 sgr.

A middle section patched   = 2½ sgr.

Preparation of a completely new middle section   = 15 sgr.

One of these days we'll send you a stack of nocturnes and—will bill you indulgently.

---

[40] pf = pfennig; sgr = silbergroschen, old currency denominations.

The title: *Liebeslieder* is being forced on me here. They have very simple titles (as is also fitting), otherwise I would suggest that the word be veiled.

For today, addio.

Your

J. B.

Is it necessary to note here that a modulation from C to E flat by way of the intervening fifths, F and B flat, would be the most pedestrian modulation possible?

243
Johannes Brahms to Fritz Simrock

[Lichtenthal near Baden-Baden, 5 October 1869]

My esteemed friend,

The proofs arrived (yesterday) just in the nick of time; I have to take them with me today to Carlsruhe where the waltzes will be given in concert tomorrow and Frau Schumann will now be rid of the dread of reading from manuscript.[41]

I must admit that on this occasion, for the first time, I grinned at the sight of a work in print—of mine! Moreover, I gladly risk being called an ass if our *Liebeslieder* don't give a few people pleasure.

On p. 41 there is a serious misprint which may well cost two plates their life.[42] You misunderstood the supplement I sent later. This is where 4 measures *prima* and 4 *seconda* must go. Fortunately these very pages are printed very spaciously. But I beg you to be careful!

With the proofs I enclose a little novelty for which, in consideration of its excellence, I desire 40 Friedrichsdors. You can look it over, and perhaps the publisher in you will be enticed by the most exquisite score in existence.

'Postlude to the Composer's Lovesongs, Op. 52.'—The thing is called:

Rhapsody (Fragment from Goethe's *Harzreise im Winter*) for Alto, Men's Chorus, and Orchestra (or Pianoforte). It is the best prayer I have yet recited, and even if our esteemed altos will not be eager to sing it right away, there are plenty of people who have need of this kind of prayer. In any case, I would like to get it out speedily, and therefore announce it now and send along the score at once; the piano reduction follows.

---

[41] At an open rehearsal of the season's first subscription concert, under Hermann Levi's direction. Clara Schumann and Hermann Levi were the pianists, with local singers.

[42] Referring to the engraved plates. Often a minor mistake can be corrected on the plate by means of acid, but apparently not in this case.

Frl. Dobjansky commissions me to have the revisions of her things sent *to me*. Meanwhile she declines the 50 copies with thanks. For the time being, send her maybe 6. She is going to Paris (middle of October), letters would probably reach her through Flaxland.[43] To the uninitiated, your bill indeed seems thankfully reasonable, and so the Fräulein probably also intends to send more presently.

I envision being in Vienna around the 15th of October. Please *do not* send any vocal parts with my copies of Op. 52—in return I would like to be entitled to additional scores!

Best greetings.

I suppose the vocal parts are also coming?

Greetings to the ladies.

Your

Johs. Brahms.

This letter casually confirms what those close to Brahms knew at the time: that the text and music of the Alto Rhapsody was intensely significant to him. He was soon referring to himself ironically as the Outsider (after the opening words of the fragment from Goethe's poem: 'Who's that, standing off to one side?'—('Abseits, wer ist's?'), a view of himself which intensified with age (see Letter 277).

The Rhapsody, a fragment from *Journey through the Harz in Winter*, is often associated with the engagement and marriage of Julie Schumann, but it is worth noting that the Harz mountains, with their steep wooded hills, deep valleys, and rich treasure of fairy-tales and hidden mineral wealth, are outside Göttingen, and formed the backdrop to his romance with Agathe von Siebold.

244
Johannes Brahms to Hermann Deiters

September [18]69

Esteemed friend,

I sincerely wish you would look upon shipments of music as letters; then I would not have to reproach myself so very often. I had Simrock send the 'Rinaldo' score to you, and before long you will receive from the same a collection of waltzes for four hands and four voices. I believe that anyone who likes my music at all will see these with some gratification.

First of all I have a request. I remember having seen a volume of songs by Reichardt (possibly Zelter) at your house, which contained a stanza from

---

[43] A music dealer and publisher in Paris.

Goethe's Harzreise ('aber abseits, wer ist's?'). Could you lend me the volume for a short time?

I need hardly add that I have just composed it and would like to see the work of my predecessor. I call my piece (for alto solo, male chorus, and orchestra) 'Rhapsody', but believe I owe that title, also, to the esteemed speaker who preceded me.

I'll hear it shortly in Carlsruhe and even if I should not have this somewhat intimate music printed or performed, I shall inform you of it anyhow.

You will also shortly receive 3 volumes of 'Magelone'.[44]

To hear from you about this sort of thing, in private or through the journals, belongs to my most particular pleasures. Only I am probably too much inclined to keep the dissent and unfortunately also the thanks to myself.

I hope that your family is very well and I send warmest greetings to all of you.

Your devoted

Joh. Brahms.

That autumn, Brahms returned to Vienna, once more without a permanent place to live.

245
Johannes Brahms to Emil Streicher[45]

[Karlsruhe], Oct[ober 18]69

Honoured Sir,

I am planning to be in Vienna at the beginning of next week. Now although I don't know just yet which room I shall make myself comfortable in, I would like nevertheless to think that in any event—it will be in front of one of your beautiful grand pianos. Should you be of a mind not to wean me of this agreeable habit, I shall inform you of my arrival.

But if for any reason the matter should be inconvenient, I ask you definitely not to feel awkward about it. I will call on you in any case, also have high hopes of finding all of you very well.

In the mean time best greetings. Your very devoted

J. Brahms

---

[44] Op. 33, vols. 3–5. They were published by Rieter-Biedermann, and appeared in December 1869.

[45] Head of the Streicher piano firm in Vienna.

By 1869, money was no longer in short supply. Brahms's honoraria for 1868 were almost quadruple those of 1867, followed by a similar income in the next year. He took evident pleasure in sharing this bounty with his family, making arrangements for Avé-Lallement to act as his father's banker, since the elder Brahms refused to keep large sums of money in the house. Evidently Brahms maintained ties to his old friends, Grädener, Avé, and Marxsen and even relied on them occasionally, despite his sense of abandonment by his native city.

246
Johannes Brahms to Johann Jakob Brahms

[Vienna,] November 1869

Dearest Father,

You won't permit cash into the house!!! Well, just for that you'll now have to sign the enclosed receipt and give it to Herr Avé-Lallemant, after he has given you the 350 thaler.

Go there this very day, you'll take a liking to the money! I hadn't written you anything about it because I hadn't quite believed in it.

Then send 50 thaler to Elise right away, keep the rest with you, naturally take whatever you need.

In my pocket I already have 100 thaler that I've been meaning to send one of these days. In case you don't need it all at once, you can let 100 or 200 thaler earn interest. But in such a way that you can always have whatever you and Elise need right away. Sometime or other, you might write to me how it gradually disappears.

I am sending music for Herr Marxsen, whom I ask for a letter in return telling me how he likes it.

For you I'm sending a wonderful panorama that you need *not* have framed, however.

That house at the top is where we slept. Only it was a new one, a larger one. From St Wolfgang we drove by way of the Wolfgangsee to Mondsee. From there in a carriage along the lake, one fine day, and then we had a fine climb up the Schafberg.

We too stood in front of the building where the people are in the picture, and saw in the background—that is: below us, the pretty Mondsee and the Bengal fire.

I couldn't resist buying it for you and imagine you will enjoy looking at it.

Do send me a new permit when you can.

The letter to Grädener you can leave with Avé when you fetch the money.
Letter to Elise and 50 thaler sometime soon. To Marxsen best greetings.
Just be sure to have a fine old time with the money!!!
Warmest greetings to you both from
your Johannes

What kind of a celebration did you have on October 26?[46]

The panorama showed a scene from the holiday Brahms had spent with his father
in the summer of 1867. The Wolfgangsee and Mondsee are lakes in the Salzkam-
mergut region of the Austrian Alps, *Bengal fire* a kind of blue fireworks. The
Schafberg is a not inconsiderable mountain: Johann Jakob, telling Johannes how he
recounts his adventures to interested friends: 'I got to the very top, but I don't say
that I rode the last third of the way.'[47]

❧ 1870 ❧

Brahms wrote no opera, although he intensely wished to do so. The hunt for a suitable libretto went on for many years, and was one of two major concerns just at this
moment in Brahms's life—the other being his continued search for a suitable job.
But just what constituted suitability?

In the case of a job, his letters often mention the wish to work regularly not only
with an orchestra, but also with a chorus. Although both Hiller and Joachim had
tried, in 1869, to win him to their respective conservatories in Cologne and Berlin,
Brahms declined. Brahms was particularly sought as head of the *piano* faculty of the
Royal Conservatory of Music, just then being founded under Joachim's leadership,
and Hiller too would have given Brahms piano pupils. But if Brahms was going to
tie himself down, it would only be in order to have at his disposal large forces with
which to try out his compositions. To this end, Brahms even toyed with the notion
of taking on Max Bruch's job in Sonderhausen, a provincial city with a very small
population (Letter 253). At about the same time, in Vienna, the Gesellschaft der
Musikfreunde was beginning to show some interest in him. Johann von Herbeck,
their current director, was becoming restless; and as Brahms hinted in a letter to
Clara (Letter 249), he had long had his eye on on Herbeck's position. Nevertheless,
when the first approach was made, he showed the ambivalence so characteristic of
his attitude towards anything which could interfere with his freedom. In the end,
Brahms accepted the Viennese position the following year.

He was not similarly successful in finding a libretto. What was he looking for?
To judge from his comments about the libretti he turned down, he wanted a plaus-

[46] Karoline Brahms's forty-fifth birthday. The 'new permit' was a fresh passport.
[47] Johann Jakob to Johannes, 3 Sept. 1867.

ible work of literature, emphasis on *plausible*. The libretti he most admired, whose equivalent he would have most liked to find, were *The Marriage of Figaro* and *Fidelio*—one comic, one heroic. In later life he was also a great admirer of Bizet's *Carmen*, and gave the score as a present to many of his friends. Apart from their intrinsic musical value and the power of the plot to engage an audience, two of these operas also share *spoken dialogue* rather than through-composed music. Brahms's ideal opera would use music only when the spoken word was insufficient to express the emotions of the moment. Unfortunately for his operatic ambitions, however, he could not seem to find a text to match his ideal.[1]

Nevertheless, his friends were more than willing to search out, commission, or create a libretto for him, and the list of those who did so is considerable.*   Additional Note p. 752

Of his friends, it is Hermann Levi who was the most anxious for these efforts to bear fruit. Levi, already a renowned opera conductor, was keenly disappointed and somewhat hurt that his efforts were to no avail. The topic is integral to much of their correspondence over the next few years, and crops up occasionally in Brahms's other correspondence, particularly with Allgeyer. Whether Brahms had unrealistic literary standards, was uncertain of his ability to deal with drama—*Rinaldo* is not a roaring success—or was, in spite of denials, concerned that he could not compete with Wagner, we shall never know, although there has been plenty of speculation on this account.

But if an opera was an elusive goal, Brahms could at least enjoy the success of a vocal work of an entirely different nature. His *Liebeslieder Waltzes*, Op. 52, had been an immediate success, and Brahms was asked to make an arrangement for orchestra.

247
Johannes Brahms to Ernst Rudorff

Vienna, January [18]70 [postmark: 2.2.70]

Esteemed Herr Rudorff,

Your letter was for me mainly a somewhat embarrassing reminder that I still have not thanked you for the dedication of your 'Fantasy'.[2] I hereby do so from the bottom of my heart; I think I have previously expressed to you how greatly I appreciate and cherish this particular thoughtfulness.

I only have time for a few very hasty words now and don't want to keep you waiting.

---

[1] *Carmen* is often performed with sung dialogue, but in its original version all the dialogue was spoken and it was produced at the Opéra-Comique rather than at the Paris Opéra.

[2] Rudorff's Op. 14, for piano.

Of course I had learned through Frau Sch[umann] that you wanted my 'Waltzes', but I thought equally that you were aware of my approximate No. At the time you said nothing about *when* you would want the waltzes, and so I believed I could only say no.

But now the business is probably moving too quickly, and all I can do is show you my good intentions. So far, absolutely nothing has yet gone to the copyist! In fact, there were merely a few notions hanging about. [?]

When I now tell you that tomorrow I will send 9 pieces off to you nevertheless, you will not doubt that I have done my utmost.

I leave the things to your discretion. I doubt—that you will get the copying done, and that the performance with orchestra [will] appear so simple and unproblematical to you. Not to me, and since I am sending the 9 pieces off straightaway, I cannot even look them over.

I do not need to mention that the tempo is actually that of a Ländler: moderate. Particularly the livelier ones, moderate (C minor, A minor), please don't drag the more sentimental ones, (hop-tendrils).[3] I think the 9 pieces will serve for one concert number.

Solo—not chorus, in my opinion.

Should an occasional *piano* or *mf* still be necessary for the orchestra, please not to hesitate at all.

Mainly I ask—since I really only want to oblige and am in too great a rush—that you look at the material very carefully and think it over.

And so for today, once more my best thanks and sincere greetings

Your devoted

J. Brahms

The 'Overture' arrived today; my best thanks. But it was not allowed to interrupt my work today.[4]

Ernst Rudorff was at this time a young pianist and composer (eventually distinguished and influential), recently appointed to the faculty of Joachim's new conservatory in Berlin, where he occasionally conducted the orchestra in Joachim's stead. The orchestral version of the waltzes was performed at the conservatory in March.[5]

---

[3] See Liebeslieden Waltz No. 5. Hops (*genus humulus*) have long twining tendrils.

[4] Probably Rudorff's Op. 12, the Overture *Otto der Schütz*.

[5] The orchestral version was first published in 1938 by Peters, Leipzig. The waltzes are set for flute, oboe, clarinet, bassoon, horn, and the normal set of strings, and are in the following order: Op. 52, Nos. 1, 2, 4, 6, 5, Op. 65 No. 9, Op. 52 Nos. 11, 8, and 9. Op. 65 was not in print until 1875, but obviously a few of the waltzes from the later set were already completed. For further details see McC 220.

In February Brahms moved not to his own flat, but to an old hotel, Zur Goldspinnerin, a Gasthaus known to Beethoven, as well (Plate 26). What was then a suburb is now just on the far side of the Ringstrasse, at the corner of Ungargasse and Linke Bahngasse, in an interesting neighbourhood where even now some of the buildings date from long before Brahms's time. Brahms's hotel is gone, however, replaced by the larger Hotel Goldene Spinne—from which there is still a fine view of the Stadtpark and inner city.

248
Johannes Brahms to Johann Jakob Brahms

[Vienna, end of] February 1870

Dear Father,

Nothing lasts forever, not even beautiful bass and flute-playing. That's just the way it is, cannot be changed, and I hope that you will come to terms with it.

True, the pain in the foot and hand are nasty extras. But this may well be eased by a spa. You should seriously consider whether you might not go this summer to Rehme [in Westfalia] after all.

I have just moved to a new apartment and for the first time in Vienna, I have a really beautiful view. I live at the edge of a suburb and look out over the Stadtpark. Once I've reached a better understanding with the piano below me, I will begin to be thoroughly delighted.

Rubinstein spoke to me with great pleasure about Frl. Völkers, at whose house he had spent an evening. Give my best greetings to Völkers and Schradiek. When are they getting married?[6]

I am sending something to Herr Marxsen this very day. Do ask him sometime if I have sent him my 'Liebeslieder-Waltzes'. Otherwise I'll do it right away.

Are the 300 thaler from Grädener still nicely intact? How much do you still have? Just take good care of yourself and do whatever is necessary and beneficial. Writing, I hope, is not harmful.

I know nothing at all about Hamburg, because now I don't read the news reports either.

Warmest greetings
your Johannes

---

[6] Betty Völkers was a former member of the solo vocal quartet of the Hamburg Frauenchor. The name Henry Schradiek is known to thousands of violinists as the composer of obligatory Studies. The marriage did not take place.

The view was good, but his rooms were ice cold. This letter to Clara, a picturesque account of his life at that time, also contains one of the most frequently quoted passages in his correspondence, pertaining to his attitude towards writing music in general and an opera in particular.

249
Johannes Brahms to Clara Schumann

[Vienna, 28 March 1870]

Dear Clara,

The thanks for your dear letter should have come long ago. I have to laugh that even so your concern for a warm room has still not become superfluous. Actually, I have two large stoves, but my rooms face north and are hard to heat. The winter this year is so tenacious that the good Viennese are not accustomed to it. We have in the fullest measure everything that goes with winter. The snow has rarely been as deep—and concerts take place every day with a regularity I had never known before. The *Peri* performance was very mediocre throughout. The chorus and orchestra were very dubious and the soli, with the exception of Frau Dustmann and Fräulein Burenne, quite inadequate. Add to this the large hall (which I don't wish on that work) and the daylight, which together with the multicoloured walls and ceiling did not allow an appropriate mood to develop, at least not in me. Herbeck now has 4 more large orchestra concerts! But actually has had no success so far this winter. On this occasion of the *Peri*, and at other times, the smaller journals are actually audacious enough to blame and attack him. But meanwhile he still has the big ones in his pocket, and I don't really believe this will change so soon.

The *Meistersinger* was announced and cancelled 5 times. But now the repeat performances are causing just as much trouble. That in itself naturally keeps the public from generating enthusiasm, because a certain momentum is needed for that. I found the public much less sympathetic than I had ever expected. I do not wax rhapsodic—neither about this work nor about Wagner in general. But I listen to it as attentively as possible, that is, as often—as I can stand it. Of course it is tempting to chit-chat a great deal about it. But I am pleased that I'm not obliged to state everything explicitly and in a loud voice, etc., etc.

This much I do know: in everything else that I attempt, I step on the heels of forerunners who make me feel self-conscious, [but] Wagner would certainly not keep me from going at an opera with the greatest relish.

Incidentally, among my many wishes, this opera ranks even higher than, e.g. the position of music director.

Recently I was in Klosterneuburg, something which will happen more frequently with the coming of spring. It is one of the wealthiest religious foundations, and I wish you could see an operation like that sometime.

As to duties, the pious fathers have absolutely none when they are at home. There are, I believe, 60 of them, of whom about 20 are obliged—by their own choice, of course, to hold the richest livings around here (e.g. Hietzing with 5,000–6,000 fl[orins]), another 20 administer the enormous estates in Hungary, etc., and the rest stay at home engaged in the above-mentioned occupation. A proper monastery, Einsiedeln in Switzerland, for example, is certainly more interesting. Here the life of idleness and glut-tony—as the gentlemen will tell you quite frankly and cheerfully, soon allows them to cease thinking or doing anything at all. For variety they travel to Vienna, where they have a house; their priestly garb, however, they are per-mitted leave outside! NB! When they are tired they put it on again.[7]

But for our sort it's a lovely change. The monastery is beautifully situ-ated on the Danube, and the enormous rooms where one stays, the wine one drinks, the entire hospitality in general, is exemplary.—As soon as spring makes a bit more of an appearance, I also want to get out [more], I really know very little of Austria.

One thing you should also resolve to do: to go to Oberammergau for the Passion festival. Maybe when you're finished in Carlsbad (or where?). You know that these plays are only repeated every 10 years. As far as I know, you haven't seen them—but have surely heard them talked about, often with great enthusiasm.

There are no personal matters that come to mind. This evening I'm at Anna Franz's![8]

The Osers are spending all their time in Baden, you know that the child is dying.

O what a miracle, piano sketches and an Adagio by Kirchner have appeared. Not yet received by me.

For today, farewell, may everything be well with you generally and may your hand be better. Greet Marie and stay fond of

your
Johannes.

---

[7] If this sounds suggestively scurrilous, it would not be unique in the annals of Viennese history.

[8] One of the Wittgenstein sisters, as is Frau Oser of the next sentence.

Never hesitant to poke fun at himself, Brahms sent Reinthaler his Alto Rhapsody, and added some other interesting comments, including a glimpse into the kind of pleasure composing gave him.

250

Johannes Brahms to Karl Reinthaler

[Vienna, 26] Feb[ruary 18]70

Dear friend,

This writing paper has lain here several times, ready for you. But now sincere congratulations for your newest opus shall be written upon it. I suppose you worked at it with more appetite and love than on the '*Wüste*'? Which, incidentally, says nothing against the latter, but it must be gratifying to be able to express in more than one way one's urge to create and work, one's sense of form—one's loving heart—!⁹

Ah, poor outsider that I am! Have I already sent you my epilogue to the 'Liebeslieder'? What do you say to the stuff? To the one or the other?

The other day I was reminded of you (in a lonely room that isn't necessary, but here you wouldn't have come to mind of your own). I was leafing though Frau Dustmann's music and laughing over the dedications until I placed a volume on the stand and (indeed, perhaps for the first time) she had to sing it seriously.

To me there is always something serious about dedicating works of the intellect (although at the same time, I myself have rarely meant them seriously). Therefore the 'prima donna-ish' dedications of all of you are often incomprehensible to me. Or are there also some Neapolitan stories behind this?

I'm really curious about the Dietrich choral work. I, needless to say, as a man without a fixed position or a garden, can hardly comprehend how one can spend even three days setting a 'Plea for Rain' to music.¹⁰

If you will delight me by sending your 'Psalms', you might at the same time enclose my manuscripts, which have annoyed you for quite some time already, and which can now do so again to me. (Annoy me).

Sunday we had Bruch's symphony, today the first rehearsal of Rubinstein's 'Tower of Babel', tomorrow 'Meistersinger', then 'Paradise and

⁹ *In der Wüste*, Op. 26, was a very successful cantata based on Psalm 68. Many of Reinthaler's compositions were Psalm settings, not surprising considering his job and that he was an ordained cleric. The new work was either Op. 34 or 35.

¹⁰ 'Have you sold your *Hymn of Supplication* yet?' Brahms wrote to Dietrich. 'Reinthaler praises it highly.' Albert Dietrich, *Erinnerungen an Johannes Brahms*, 67.

the Peri'. How gladly would I dispense with each and every one (of these) and travel north. But it's a long way, after all, and I don't want to feed my envy by visiting conductor friends.

Be greeted most warmly, both of you, and write, and send.

Your

Johannes Brahms.

The schedule for this one week is a good example of the prodigious pace Brahms maintained in attending opera and concert productions. He was present at the first Viennese performance of Bruch's First Symphony, Op 28, dedicated to him (his letter to Bruch on the day after praises the excellence of the performance), and within the next few days he heard Anton Rubinstein's *Tower of Babel*, a Sacred Opera in One Act, Op. 80; Schumann's now neglected *Paradise and the Peri*, Op. 50; and, finally, the first Viennese performance of Wagner's *Meistersinger*.

Answering an invitation from his Hungarian impresario to visit Budapest, Brahms couldn't resist a pun on the man's name. *Dunkel* is the German word for *dark*.

251
Johannes Brahms to Johann Nepomuk Dunkl

[Vienna, sometime in February 1870][11]

Dear Dunkl!

What darkness (*Dunkel*) must prevail in the heart and mind of one who does not even say thank you for such a kind invitation! Why didn't I just up and leave on the next day, and why don't I go now instead of 'this scrap of paper'. Yes indeed, something always thwarts and keeps me—But come I shall! I have the serious intention of coming at last, with no other intent but to savour your beautiful Pesth.[12] I'm thinking of departing right after the Destruction of Babel, Paradise and Peri, and several Meistersingers—all of which must be consumed in the very near future. You, of course, will be responsible for providing gypsies, wine, dumplings, and much else—all I have is the desire and the time to enjoy it all.

But today I shall do nothing other than to ask you most warmly to forgive my bad manners and to send you my equally warm greetings, but even warmer ones to your wife. Apart from that, I ask you to offer my greetings to

[11] The letter as it was first published bears the incorrect date of Easter 1867. Brahms's reference to the opera performances firmly places it in 1870. See the previous letter.

[12] A pun in the original, with the word *Absicht* meaning both intent and purpose.

all the womenfolk, and if there is no further demand among them, to all the menfolk.

In the mean time, as usual,

your hurried and very devoted
Johannes Brahms.

From Hamburg came the news his father had fallen seriously ill.

252

Johannes Brahms to Karoline Brahms

[Vienna, 28 May 1870]

Dear Mother,

First of all, I want to explain my slow response. Your letter was held up because the stamp had fallen off during its journey.

I received it today and hasten above all to thank you for having written me and, as it seems to me, written as explicitly and truthfully as I had hoped.

You can imagine how your letter had alarmed me at first. Now it seems to me that for the time being I can calm down a little.

But I ask you urgently not to try to reassure me in your letters, but always to write me the truth clearly and precisely.

Since for the time being, apart from my most sincere and warmest good wishes, I probably can do nothing but provide money, I ask you furthermore always to be clear and straightforward in that regard as well.

In case of illness, it is of course the best and also the cheapest thing to do whatever one can to cure it. Don't even think of saving money, that will only cause the illness to drag on and become more expensive.

I do hope and urgently request that you write to me again right away, and tell me how things are and what you need. I don't have any money at home but I can obtain it right away, whatever and whenever you want. Christian [Detmering] or Herr Völkers will surely also give you some if there is a greater rush.

Also with regard to the spa, don't ask what it costs. You will probably go along on the trip, for the main thing in getting well is a cheerful mood, and that only you can provide for Father.

Why don't you also get advice from Herr Völkers, regarding the journey, etc.

In any case, write as soon as possible and the plain truth—and, I hope, very encouragingly.

My best wishes and greetings to both of you.

Johannes

As the offer to become Artistic Director of the Gesellschaft der Musikfreunde gained in likelihood, Brahms turned skittish of the pitfalls of a job in Vienna. Rather astonishingly, he turned to Max Bruch, with whom he was then on reasonably friendly terms.

253

Johannes Brahms to Max Bruch

[Vienna, c.11 June 1870]

Dear Bruch,

Only a few words in haste with the request to answer soon—as briefly or as conveniently detailed as you wish.

I hear or have read that you have given up your position and for now wish to remain in Berlin. That I want a position for myself, i.e. a job, goes without saying. Would you write me a few words about it as clearly and frankly as possible, among other things, whether there is a choral group in S[onderhausen], about the countryside, the relations with princely personages, holiday leave, duties, honorarium—whatever comes to mind.

That I am not particularly eager for S[onderhausen] you can imagine; it is by no means a place in which to remain, and my years do remind me of that.

Between ourselves, I can tell you in fact that I am being considered here (in place of Herbeck). But this position has so much that is highly questionable that I actually wished people here would spare themselves the official offer and me the difficult deliberation.

For your friendly letter and the ample shipment my best thanks, in the mean time; I hope you will be in the mood to write soon, but today I will only enquire and greet you sincerely.

I hope this letter finds you still in Berlin.

Sincerely

Your

J. Brahms

(Gotthard's Music Shop)

With a population of 6,000, Sonderhausen was a deep backwater in Thuringia. Bruch, who was just leaving his job there as Court Conductor, answered immediately and explicitly, saying, among other things, that one could survive the summers through good orchestral music, attractive surroundings, and the constant, inspiring dealings with Spitta (who taught at the Gymnasium there); but that the place was monotonous and oppressive in winter.

'Curious,' he wrote, 'you yearn for constraints to all your freedom, and I for freedom from all my constraints!'

Brahms gave up the idea of Sonderhausen, turning now to Levi for advice. He wrote to Allgeyer to obtain Levi's address, and discovered that in the mean time Allgeyer had produced his own version of the story of *Norma*, for Brahms's eventual use as a libretto.

254
Johannes Brahms to Julius Allgeyer

[Vienna, probably June 1870]

Dear Allgeyer!

I'm just picking up a scrap of paper to ask you please to give me *Levi's* address by return mail. I'm going to Munich on the 14th and 17th,[13] 24th to Oberammergau and then—to be honest, I don't know, but I imagine to Carlsruhe. Dear, good fellow, how your *Norma* poem moved me. As though I had read the most beautiful tragedy. Now I don't know if it doesn't contain a touch of that—but there was surely something else as well that so melted my heart.

From *Levi* you will now already know that it would be senseless for one of our kind to want to compete with even bad Italian or French operas. He will also have told you that in *Bellini's* N[orma] there are some really quite extraordinary and beautiful things.

Well, as I said before, I look forward to having a few hours for chatting.

I ask for a brief response, here until about the 11th, then until the 24th through *Baron Perfall*.

I'm looking forward to the new paintings of *Feuerbach's*—as I am to those few people for whom I can yearn.

Affectionately your Joh. Br.

---

[13] To hear *Rheingold* and *Walküre*, in a semi-Ring festival conducted by Franz Wüllner. Saint-Saëns, Liszt, and Joachim also attended.

255
Johannes Brahms to Hermann Levi

[Vienna, July 1870]

Dear friend,

I am likely to be in the greatest need of you and your advice in the near future.

Wouldn't you like to let me know where you'll be roaming about, in Iceland, Italy, or where?

My most pressing questions then thirsting for answers will concern Herbeck's succession which—as was meanwhile decided—will apparently be offered to me within the next few days.

I mustn't get started on talking about it now because otherwise it's difficult to stop and so far I've taken good care not to brood about it.

But should it come to an offer, I want to be able to inform you and ask you about it.

From the 12th to about the 20th of July I'll be in Munich and should be coming back to Munich on the 24th, after the Passion play is over.

Where to after that I don't know, but I'll probably be drawn instinctively to Carlsruhe and Baden.

I still ought to thank you for your very kind letter. I am truly pleased that you are accepting the Munich post after all.

I firmly believe you're in Carlsruhe? Then I'll probably come to Baden for August and September—much as I fear the heat and the collective company.

For today then only this *preludium* to further requests—but how dearly do I wish it would remain a *preludium*!

Warm greetings,
J. Brahms.

So write through Perfall!

Levi's answer was probably not what Brahms was hoping for, although without question it eloquently voiced some of the very doubts Brahms himself had. A portion of it is presented here because in the editor's opinion, it reflects on the rivalry present in their relationship, and has a bearing on the eventual dissolution of their friendship; in spite of a great deal of justice in what Levi wrote, it is difficult to avoid the impression that he was not enthusiastic at the thought of Brahms as the music director of such an important organization, and impossible to imagine that Brahms didn't bristle at the mention of posts in Oldenburg or Münster as being more suitable for him—positions which happened to be filled at the time by two men far less talented than he, although they also happened to be two of his best friends (Julius Grimm and Albert Dietrich). Clara, on the other hand, when she learned that Brahms was being considered for the highly prestigious post in Vienna, offered him her unreserved enthusiasm and expressed complete faith in his abilities.

256
Hermann Levi to Johannes Brahms [fragment]

Westerland-Sylt, 14 July 1870

Revered friend,

. . . With respect to your candidacy for the throne, my humble opinion, for what it's worth, is that you should do as Prince Leopold did.[14] I simply cannot see you giving up the kind of concentration you have had now, dissipating and using up your powers for so problematic a goal, quite generally to know you to be at the service of the *moment*, for we are surely entitled to expect from you different deeds, in other realms . . . To dedicate more than your leisure time to anything other than writing down music would—again in my humble estimation—be wrong. That you have the capability to conduct like no other, I saw—with impartial eyes—in Carlsruhe. But you are not the man to take on and carry through to victory the struggle with the thousands of little unpleasantnesses which unfailingly attend every public position. You would, I fear, be quickly defeated by them, and would then be compelled to retreat, embittered and hurt, and seek refuge within yourself. These are my thoughts with regard to the question of whether or not you should accept a conducting position *at all*. If I think specifically of Vienna, I am amazed that you should even give the matter serious consideration. In Vienna you are now honoured and loved, have a large group of admirers there, but that is, after all—only one faction. It would be quite different if you were carried by your nation, as was Mendelssohn, for example—if, in other words, you were made this offer—in itself of course a most gratifying one—as the natural expression, as an extension of an already existing popular sentiment, and if it were generally understood as such. But we are not that far along yet——not so long as your adherents are considered to be biased and—not so long as Wagner confuses the best of minds and alters the standard by which we judge the essence of our art. You can live in a great city only either as a free and silent man who may, at his pleasure, step into the public arena, but definitely not dependent upon it, or—as one who rules 'par la

[14] He had recently declined an offer to ascend to the Spanish throne.

volonté de la nation'.[15] If a position were being offered to you in Oldenburg or Münster, where the individual can shape the circumstances—and not the other way around; where, even though in a small sphere, you can do as you please while also having a passable orchestra constantly available; where the public is not already spoiled by some 'operator' like Herbeck, with his bare-back circus stunts—and where a hundred envious detractors were not instantly carping at your heels; then I would reconsider right away whether to counsel you against acceptance. But here, I say without hesitation; *don't do it!!* Bleib' von Se!![16] . . . I sympathize completely with your longing to have a real home, to be tied to an activity not dependent upon momentary mood and inspiration . . . but, above and beyond all this looms the duty to hold out and not shift the centre of gravity of your life to terrain which, after all, can be crowned with success only by the drudges of art, not its masters!—This youth's words of wisdom make no claim to novelty; it suffices that they help to recall words of your own. And with this, farewell. My thanks to you for having thought of me.

Yours in loyal affection,
Hermann Levi

In July the long-threatened war between France and Prussia broke out. Brahms followed events with keen interest, although they frustrated his long-laid plans to go to Oberammergau for the Passion Play. He went instead to Salzburg to visit Joachim.

Brahms's antipathy for France probably started with the first-hand stories he heard from his mother about the siege and occupation of Hamburg under Napoleon's troops, one of the bitterest moments in Hamburg's history. The Franco-Prussian war revealed the ardent German patriot in him; Brahms developed a deep admiration for Chancellor Otto Bismarck, owned and read Bismarck's speeches, and for the remainder of his life kept the Iron Chancellor's picture hanging on his wall, crowned with a laurel wreath.

He was looking forward with intense anticipation to being in Germany in time for victory celebrations and was proud to discover his Requiem was being performed to honour the war dead.

---

[15] 'By the will of the people.'   [16] 'Keep away from them!!' in Berlin dialect.

257
Johannes Brahms to Johann Jakob Brahms

Salzburg, 5 August 1870

Dear Father,

I was in Munich and had intended to go to Baden, and in the autumn also to Hamburg—but the war intervened, my suitcase didn't come after me, nor I onward.

I've now been staying on in Salzburg and wait eagerly for the French to get a good thrashing. I hear that there are also many soldiers in Hamburg and that all people who pay more than 300 Marks in rent have soldiers billetted on them. So be sure to let me know right away how you two are.

If you need money, as one may very well suppose, just write; I can arrange it through Faber, in spite of war.

I was offered the directorship of the Gesellschaft concerts in Vienna. I still doubt, however, that I will accept this particular position. You can imagine that I have my sound reasons.

You probably know that Fritz is coming to Hamburg in the very near future. Elise found out about it only by chance. Is it that he now wants to remain in Hamburg? I would be glad to come, only for the time being that won't be possible.[17]

Today, the first news of victory arrived (from the 4th).

Might you up there also have lived through a few things? I dearly wish I could be in Germany now. Here one is so on the outside, but it concerns one nevertheless. Even though one can't join in the shooting, one wants to see compatriot soldiers and be at home when victory is proclaimed.

What does the Elbe look like?

Is it fortified and have precautions been taken against French ships?

Well, you're hardly going to write me that much! So just write about what concerns you, and whether mother has recovered from the exertions of the trip, and if you have already quite forgotten your illness.

Salzburg, *poste restante*, (Austria).

Affectionate greetings, also to Fritz when he comes.

Your Johannes

I think of you very, very often here! Joachim is also here.

---

[17] Fritz Brahms was returning after several traumatic years spent in Venezuela.

258
Johannes Brahms to Melchior Rieter-Biedermann

Vienna, 15 October [18]70

Dear Herr Rieter,

Travelling and writing has almost ground to a halt this year. I was doubly sorry that by one thing or another I was prevented from joining the jubilation in Germany, but I do hope to see the returning conquerors.

Today above all, a very serious urgent request. Simrock played the same trick on me as you and recently sent me an arranged 'quartet' [Op. 25] with my fair name as the arranger. By my speedy protest, I will now probably keep someone or other from puzzling over this, my noble occupation—but now it's your turn! I urgently request (and insistently, since I have constantly reminded you about it), that you delete my name as arranger for 4 hands as quickly as possible from the 'Concerto' [Op. 15] and the 'Requiem'.

Scrap the title-pages now in stock and I will gladly pay the cost of the new ones. I cannot look at the 'Requiem' without becoming annoyed.

That you do not grasp how ludicrous this regurgitation of one's own works is! Indeed I have never done it because I relished it, but only so that I myself would earn the thaler and because arrangements by others would be sent to me in any case and would make much more work. That I do the work well is demonstrated by the 'Sextet', 'Serenades', and what has appeared without revealing the regurgitation.

Do give me the pleasure of notifying me immediately that the steps required to redress that ugly business have been taken!

Up till now I have tried in vain to get hold of my 'Quintet' (for 2 pianos), but I'm hoping to have it soon.

For I really wish you would publish this piece as 'Sonata for Two Pianos', instead. At the bottom of the title-page, based on the 'Quintet' Op.?

I think this way it will be played with pleasure, whereas a 4-handed arrangement would certainly become exceedingly awkward, unplayable, and murky. Naturally only *one* score would be printed, so that two *identical* copies are required for playing together, as for example for the 9th Symphony, arranged by Liszt.

In your newspaper you have published 'Beethoveniana', by Nottebohm. Are you aware that N. has some extremely thorough and significant works on Beethoven ready? As far as I know there are 3 works in particular. One on Seyfried's studies of Beethoven and their spuriousness, a very substantial one about *Beethoven's* studies with *Haydn* and *Albrechtsberger*, and finally, a collection of smaller things (such as those in the newspaper) that should actually appear in book form. A very friendly relationship to *Härtels* has now become so strained for him (as for everyone) that he hasn't offered the things to them yet. Would you feel like it? I am not a scholar; I ought not attach my recommendation to Nottebohm's works, but you may be assured that they are the products of immense diligence and that they are of the greatest interest to artist, expert, and connoisseur. That in addition he unflaggingly employs luminous brevity and good German style you can see in his 'Beethoven's Sketchbook', for example. In my opinion you should not let the things escape, and quite generally you should 'hook up' with *Nottebohm*, also for new editions of old works (*Härtel's Scarlatti* was edited by him).

I have taken the liberty of picking up my 'Songs' at Gotthard's at my own cost (or my own indebtedness).

Like yourself, several others have asked me about Gotthard. I am naturally reluctant to give an answer, since I am not, after all, precisely acquainted with his circumstances. He married a girl from a moneyed (merchant's) family; he himself probably had nothing. A certain consul Renkin has given him the necessary money. In this way he means to provide for his growing son, who is very devoted to music.

Gotthard prints a dubiously large amount and poor stuff. I don't trust any businessman in Vienna—and so what I reported would be as confused as possible.

But with all this chit-chat, don't forget my request at the beginning!!!

I beg you to greet Frau and Fräulein most sincerely and remain, evermore faithful and ready to help,

your

J. Brahms

Brahms never acknowledged his exemplary piano arrangements in public. He was in fact the unnamed arranger of the Sextet in B flat, Op. 18, and the piano four-hands version of the two Serenades, Op. 11 and 16, mentioned in this letter. The piano duet version of the string quartets is also his, and is still in print.

Taking Brahms's advice, Rieter 'hooked up' with Nottebohm and published the *Beethoveniana* (1872), *Beethovens Studien* (1873), and *Zweite Beethoenviana* (1887, posth.).

In November, the first of many performances of the Requiem to honour the war dead was performed in Cologne, by a young protégé of Ferdinand Hiller named Friedrich Gernsheim. At the composer's request, he sent the programme from Cologne, and now was on his way to Vienna to appear as pianist with the Philharmonic. Brahms offered his help, sounding very much at home.

259

Johannes Brahms to Friedrich Gernsheim

[Vienna, December 1870]

Dear Herr Gernsheim.

Just in a rush and briefly, my thanks and the advice you asked for. Whatever you do, don't go to any hotel in the centre of town! I can recommend the *Kronprinz* [Crown Prince] near the Aspern Bridge to you. Two winters ago I stayed there myself and the same year, and as satisfied as I, Hiller Stockhausen, Deppe and others.

The horse-drawn railway passes in front of the hotel and you can reach the concert-hall, Dessoff, the Opera, and such like, without walking 10 steps. I suppose it is safer if I reserve a room for you?

What's the situation with a piano? That too I could take care of for you if I knew whether you are familiar with Streicher or Bösendorfer and have a preference. Frau Schumann, Hiller, and my worthless self play Streichers.

It is not excessively good manners when I tell you I will be glad to meet you at the railway station. One looks forward here with great pleasure to someone from the Reich!

In any case, do let me hear from you again and I will reserve a room for you and be your first (and very knowledgeable) guide.

Best greetings to Hiller, the Königslöws, etc.

your
J. Brahms.

(*Bruch stayed privately*)

260

Johannes Brahms to Friedrich Gernsheim

[Vienna, December 1870]

Dear Hr. G.

In case you don't find me at the railway, I should like to remind you that you are staying at the *Kronprinz* near the Aspern Bridge, Leopoldstadt—otherwise the coachman will take you to some Bastard-prince or other, so demand the real thing; in any case, with him you will then find me.

Your hurried
J. Brahms

PART VI

❧❦❧

At Home in Vienna

1871–1876

❧ Introduction ❧

In every way, the year 1871 was a turning-point. By the end of it, Brahms had a permanent address and a permanent job. After almost two decades spent lodging in temporary quarters or staying with friends and family in Germany or Switzerland, Brahms found himself a flat in the Karlsgasse, Vienna-Wieden IV, and never moved again.

He lived within walking distance of the building which housed the Gesellschaft der Musikfreunde, of which he was now the music director elect. Although his new flat was modest, his new position was not; as the conductor of the Gesellschaft music forces, he had one of the most desirable jobs in Europe. For the next three years he also had what he had so often expressed a wish for—steady interaction with orchestra and chorus.[1]

It is no surprise that these years led directly to the orchestral masterpieces which are the foundation of Brahms's present popularity. Perfectionism, rather than timidity, is the more likely reason he refrained from producing his first symphony until the age of 43; he was unwilling to publish for orchestra until he had worked with one himself. Brahms's entire creative life follows a pattern of writing almost exclusively for musical combinations he is personally familiar with: solo piano and strings with piano for a start (as a child, he heard his father play the violin and read chamber music at home); choral music—for women's voices, at first, followed by full chorus after his job with the *Wiener Singakademie*; music featuring the cello or horn, both of which instruments he had played as a child. His large output of solo

---

[1] The orchestral association of the Gesellschaft der Musikfreunde was made up entirely of amateur musicians, but for concerts the orchestra was enhanced by professors from the Conservatory, and by the time of Brahms's tenure, with musicians from the Opera orchestra. The choral association was another branch of the organization, of which Brahms was also the director. The Gesellschaft's orchestral association acquired its first professional director (Karl Heissler) only in the late 1860s. Rubinstein followed in 1871, then Brahms, as the Gesellschaft made its move to take a place among the first rank of European orchestras. The orchestra was distinct from the Vienna Philharmonic, which was comprised entirely of professionals.

songs might be considered the exception; but it is demonstrable that Brahms was in close contact with singers from the very earliest stages of his career and undoubtedly accompanied them on the concert platform even in his teens. And now, under the stimulus of his work with the Gesellschaft orchestra, the flow of orchestral music began: the *Variations on a Theme by Haydn*, four symphonies, two overtures, two solo concertos (the difficulty his earler piano concerto caused him was directly related to his lack of experience with orchestra at that time), and finally, the Double Concerto, his last orchestral work.

In another substantial change to his life, Brahms's bonds with Hamburg loosened suddenly. Early in 1872 his father died. His connections there were now to a brother with whom he did not get on very well, a sister who was a source of some tribulation to him, an aunt, uncle, and some cousins, and his stepmother and her son, to whom he behaved with notable generosity. If he did not altogether lose sight of his former colleagues, friends, and benefactors there, he kept track of them only marginally, and did not set foot in Hamburg again until 1876. The focus of his artistic life was Vienna, and his personal life consisted of a web of friendships which stretched over the German-speaking lands of Europe, but excluded his native city.

Once Brahms settled into a predictable rhythm in Vienna, very little about his outward life changed from then on (particularly after 1875, when he relinquished his conducting position), and the interior traits so characteristic of the man were firmly set. Up to this point, the life and career of the man Johannes Brahms could be described by a series of events: he had grown up in a poor family which was attentive but rife with tension, gone out into the world utterly unknown at 19 and returned home famous and published at 20, had made connections to two people who would henceforth be central to his life, and had fallen traumatically in love with one of them; he took his first job, attempted to build a career in Hamburg, made lasting friendships, fell in and out of love again, experienced ambition, failure, and humiliation, experimented with Vienna, and discovered within himself an unyielding artistic incorruptibility and independence. Notable and tangible, these events come alive by following his letters chronologically.

But after 1872, Brahms's personal history is virtually an account of the works of art which come from his pen one after the other. The man and the artist have merged. For the most part, now, it is a matter of convenience to organize his letters by date.

In these later letters some of the contradictions which puzzled his friends then and display his complexity to us now are on display: he is the man who relishes daily living, but is the deepest pessimist about life. He is the kindest and most generous of friends, and wounds almost all those closest to him. He is the most gregarious of men, but requires to be alone. Frequently enticed by the idea of a regular position, orderly and predictable in his personal routine, he is deeply reluctant to commit himself to a steady job.

1. Schlütershof im Speckgang 24, the birthplace of Johannes Brahms. The family moved away eight months later, before the area became a slum. Photo by the Hamburg photographer R. Dührkoop, 1897

The real Brahms house, at Dammtorwall o. 29, Neustadt/Nord, where the Brahms mily lived from 1841 to 1853. Photograph c.1920

3. Letter from the 9-year-old Johannes Brahms to his piano teacher, Otto Cossel, 1 January 1842. The beautifully trained hand is evidence of careful schooling (Letter 1)

4. Elise Brahms, *c.*1860

5. Fritz Brahms, *c.*1870

6. Johann Jakob Brahms in 1838, unsigned oil-painting. The existence of this portrait, painted when Johannes was 5 years old, is one of the many reasons to doubt stories of the family's poverty

7. Christiane Brahms, *c.*1860

8. Eduard Reményi (*left*) and Brahms, photographed in Altona (Hamburg), early spring 1853, just before their joint concert tour

9. Brahms at 20, photographed in autumn 1853, during his first trip to Leipzig

10. Robert Schumann, autumn 1853, at home in Düsseldorf, pencil sketch by J. B. Laurens. The artist called Clara's attention to his enlarged pupils, an indication of serious illness

. Brahms, autumn 1853 at the Schumann house in üsseldorf, pencil sketch by B. Laurens, made during e period of Brahms's first t there. Schumann had the awing during most of his stay in Endenich

12. Brahms, in Düsseldorf, to
Robert Schumann, in Endenich, March 1855
(Letter 52)

. View of the asylum and garden in
denich, where Schumann spent his
last years. Brahms, Joachim, and
Grimm visited him here

14. Clara Schumann, 1859, pencil
sketch by Eduard Bendemann

15. The ducal theatre in Detmold, 1866. Both Brahms and Clara Schumann performed here on several occasions. The theatre was later destroyed by fire

16. The ducal palace in Detmold, winter 1850, as seen through the main gate from the hotel which housed Brahms during his three seasons there. His practice room was at the top of the tower of the palace

17. Agathe von Siebold, some time after her engagement was broken off. Recovery was neither quick nor easy

18. Brahms in Detmold, late 1858, or in Göttingen, January 9, at the time of his engagement to Agathe von Siebold. He is wearing her ring

19. The composer of the Piano Quintet, Op. 34: Brahms in 1862, during or just before his first visit to Vienna

20. Luise Dustmann, prima donna at the Court Opera in Vienna, shown here in 1860 as 'Donna Anna'. Brahms met the first Viennese *Isolde* during the summer of 1862. Lithograph by Kriehuber

21. Brahms, Karlsruhe, April 1866, photographed by Julius Allgeyer. The photograph was a gift from Brahms to his father, upon his remarriage

22. Hermann Levi, in a pencil sketch by Franz von Lenbach. The artist used it as a stu for his paintings of John the Baptist, and of Jesus

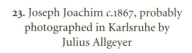

23. Joseph Joachim *c*.1867, probably photographed in Karlsruhe by Julius Allgeyer

24. Julie Schumann after her marriage to Count Radicati di Marmorito. This photo was a gift of Clara Schumann to her friend, Josefine Oser

Baden-Lichtental
Brahms-Haus.

25. Brahms's summer residence in Lichtenthal/Baden-Baden, seen in a late nineteenth-century photo. It now houses the Brahms-Haus Museum. The composer spent part or all of eight summers in Lichtenthal, most of them in the two attic rooms of this house. The First Symphony was completed here

26. Hotel Zur Goldspinnerin, Ungargasse No. 2, Vienna. Brahms spent the winter of 1870 here. From his windows he had his first good view of Vienna, across the Stadtpark to the Stefansdom, Vienna's famous cathedral. There is still a hotel at this site, now called Hotel Goldene Spinne

27. Brahms in 1868, photographed in Bremen at the time of the first major performance of the *German Requiem*

28. Amalie Joachim. The singer, wife of Joseph Joachim, premièred many Brahms songs and took part in his first concert as director of the Gesellschaft der Musikfreunde

29. Brahms (*seated*) and oseph Joachim, Klagenfurt, in 1867

30. Brahms in Vienna, 1869. Photograph by Adele, Wien

31. George Henschel. The Breslau-born singer, conductor, and pianist was a great favourite with Brahms

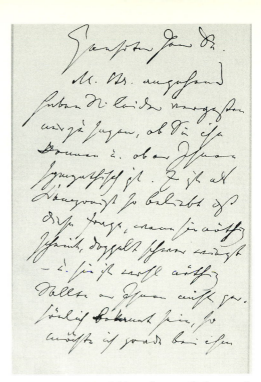

32. Brahms to Dr Adolf Kaufmann, Chairman of the Orchestra Committee in Breslau [1882], mentioning Max Bruch and George Henschel (Letter 418). The handwriting is characteristic of his mature years

33. The *Elizabethbrücke* (Vienna IV) with the *Musikverein* building (*left*) on the far side of the river Wien, and the Karlskirche (*right*). From 1871 Brahms lived close by the church and would have traversed the bridge every day on his way to the inner city. Chromolithograph from a water-colour by Franz Alt

34. Brahms in Vienna, 1875. By now he had relinquished his post with the Gesellschaft. This may be his last portrait without a beard. Photo by Fritz Luckhardt

35. The contralto Hermine Spies (*right*) with her sister Minna

36. Brahms *c.*1884

37. Brahms's music room as it looked for the last decade of his life. The piano is a 7-foot Streicher. Above the couch: the Sistine Madonna; to its right, a relief of Bismarck (the gift of Georg II of Meiningen) draped with one of Brahms's laurel wreaths, and a bust of Beethoven. An electrified lamp hangs over the table

38. Clara Schumann in 1889, pencil sketch by Richard Scholz

39. Alice Barbi and Brahms, 1892, in an amateu snapshot taken on the Ringstrasse, Vienna, in fro of the Hotel Imperial

40. Brahms *c.*1889. The famous 'triplex' was taken by O. Brasch, court photographer in Berlin

41. Palais Wittgenstein, stairway to the music room

42. Richard Mühlfeld, the clarinettist who inspired Brahms's works for the instrument. The musical quotation is from the opening of the slow movement of the Clarinet Quintet

43. The music room of the Palais Wittgenstein, Alleegasse 4, Vienna. The Clarinet Quintet had its first hearing in this room, which was decorated with panels by Gustav Klimt, and sculptures by Max Klinger; for scale, note two grand pianos ranged left. Brahms was a frequent guest here, his chair placed near the door so that he could come and go discretely. The house was destroyed during the Second World War

44. Adolf von Menzel, *Figure Studies*, c.1874–5. The renowned illustrator was one of Brahms's favourite artists and friends. Carpenter's pencil, 38 x 26 cm

45. With Adele Strauss, third wife of Johann Jr., in Ischl

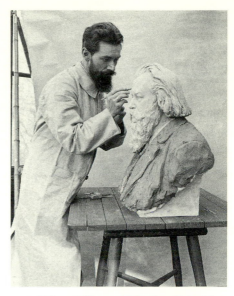

46. Charcoal drawing by Paul Wittgenstein (uncle of the pianist by the same name), sketched in 1894, during a soirée at the Wittgenstein palace

47. Robert Fellinger, Richard and Maria's son, at work on the bust of Brahms made shortly after the composer's death

49. Brahms in the courtyard of the home of Richard and Maria Fellinger. Vienna, May 1893. The photo is by Maria, shown here in the size of the original negative

. The Fellinger family did not easily come to terms with ᴫrahms's death. This group portrait of Maria, Richard, ˌnd their son, with the life-size bust of Brahms, is only ˌe example. At Christmas 1897, the bust was placed on its own table, decorated for the holiday

50. From a series of pencil sketches by Willi von Beckerath, made over a number of years: this one *c.*189

As always, it is rare to learn something of his music directly from his correspondence; instead, one discovers attitudes towards specifics—pianos, metronomes, tempi, programming.[2]

By reading between the lines of his letters we can follow, too, the steady rise to fame which eventually leads Clara to write in her diary, 'Brahms is celebrating such triumphs everywhere as has rarely been experienced by a living composer.'[3] The outer drama of his life, markedly restrained despite his growing fame and wealth, is found by following the threads which connect him to his friends, either to hold, strengthen, disintegrate, or snap.

And there are new friends: the musicologist and great Bach scholar, Philipp Spitta; the biochemist, Theodor Engelmann and his charming wife Emma, a pianist of the first rank, who nevertheless withdraws from the concert world to marry Engelmann and raise four children. In 1874 Brahms becomes reacquainted with the composer Heinrich von Herzogenberg and his enchanting wife, Brahms's former piano student, Elizabet von Stockhausen. Other new friends are the pianist and first superstar of the conducting world, Hans von Bülow; the Swiss journalist and playwright, Josef Viktor Widmann; the poet from his ancestral home in Heide, Klaus Groth; and a number of people whose friendship he cherishes, although he either does not see them often—the von der Leyens, the von Beckeraths, the poet and playwright Paul Heyse—or sees them so frequently in Vienna that he scarcely has need to write to them: the various Wittgensteins, Fellingers, Fabers, Müller zu Aichholz, Hanslick, and his bachelor cronies.

Ottilie Ebner, an old friend from early days in Vienna, will become someone he can write to and visit with unabashed companionability. His friendship with the surgeon Theodor Billroth is now at its warmest, a centre-piece of his social life. The friendship with Hermann Levi will not survive the decade, but on the contrary, that with Levi's reluctant rival, Franz Wüllner, will intensify and last for life. The connection with Joachim will falter and recover a number of times before it ruptures altogether—and is then firmly, soberly secured once and for all. His relationship with Clara is now on a very different footing from the early days, but some things have not changed: he still can write more expansively to her than to any other person, and she often still gets to see his manuscripts before anyone else, and always before they are published. The bond between them will survive some very serious threats.

That, essentially, is the plot of the rest of this volume.

---

[2] Distaste for all-Brahms programmes, for one. To a young Dutch enthusiast planning an all-Brahms extravaganza lasting at least five hours, Brahms sent a brief postcard saying 'Appealing—but appalling' [schön-aber schrecklich]. And talked him out of it.

[3] In 1882. Litz, iii. 424.

❧ 1871 ❧

Brahms's response to Bismarck's success in defeating France and creating a unified Germany was the *Triumphlied*, Op. 55, a work in four movements for eight-part chorus and orchestra. Now possibly his least-known work, it was quickly incorporated into the repertory at the time, and began its life alongside the Requiem in yet another Good Friday performance in Bremen Cathedral.[4]

261
Johannes Brahms to Karl Reinthaler

[Vienna, end of February 18]71

My dear friend.

I have a truly irresistible yearning for Germany. Although just now it is less feasible than ever for me (for financial reasons), each reason for making the trip looks ever more weighty to me. I had already heard from Frau Schumann about your Good Friday. It seems to me: I'm coming.

What is most likely to prevent me is the foolishness of *once again* conducting the 'Requiem' there. Now then, I would much prefer to listen, and that way it would be manageable.

In order further to eliminate foolishness from this affair, I send you today the first chorus of a 'Triumphlied'. Do your best so that we can do the chorus as the last number!!! In any case, have the voices written out immediately, meanwhile I'll write out the orchestra. The chorus is merely strenuous, aside from that still needs rehearsing, of course. But naturally, nothing further should be expected from the chorus! I imagine the Wilt can sing 'I Know that My Redeemer Liveth', and the rest of the time you can play away at the organ![5]

---

[4] Malcolm MacDonald is surely correct in stating that 'no valid *musical* reasons [for its obscurity] exist; the work's neglect seems to be a historical accident . . . The *Triumphlied* is now grossly undervalued, because grossly under-performed. [. . . the] work carries to extremes certain aspects of the composer's genius, and is yet unlike anything else in his *oeuvre*' (*Brahms*, 207). Two world wars, each ending in a defeated Germany, have made the nationalistic sentiments of the text unpalatable to her erstwhile opponents, and embarrassing even to Germans, although the text is biblical rather than militaristic.

[5] Marie Wilt (1833–91) was one of Vienna's leading dramatic sopranos. Brahms to Reinthaler, 21 Feb.: 'Frau Wilt has been pestering me for the longest time to arrange for her to perform in your beautiful cathedral! . . . I think she will do it for nothing! or for 10 (Friedrichsd'or).' Ecclesiastical policy of Bremen Cathedral required an addition to Brahms's Requiem text, hence the Handel aria (see p. 355).

I have talked the Wilt out of an honorarium, and now she merely mumbles about maybe a present (jewellery), which is probably readily obtainable for up to 10 Frdr.

Your concert series is probably over—otherwise, however, I would find it agreeable if I could get an honorarium for, say, my piano concerto!

If only you had written to me sooner! I might really have made better use of the carnival season. As it is, I had to overcome incredible reluctance to write down the enclosed chorus—one of my political commentaries about this year! You will find the remainder of the text in chapter 19.[6]

In any case, let me know right away, whether—that—it is possible to sing the chorus (maybe instead of the Handel Halleluja).

Warmest greetings! How dearly I do wish: *auf Wiedersehen*!

> Your
> Joh. Br.

To achieve the effect he wanted, Brahms needed the 'the strongest possible cast', as he wrote to Reinthaler a few weeks later, and asked his old friend Dietrich for help.

262
Johannes Brahms to Albert Dietrich

[Vienna, March 1871][7]

Dear friend!

This note is no more than a finger rapping on the door. For I am about to enter, and must be prepared for an irritated expression on your face.

Forgive me, it's just that when it comes to letter-writing I am even lazier than in writing music—what that means you will learn with horror!

I will shortly be coming to Germany, I am almost afraid. We on the outside have become accustomed to merely rejoicing over what is happening; to all of you, the gravity and horror of this fine and noble time has become dreadfully evident, and you may well have a somewhat solemn air.

In any event, we shall surely see each other in Bremen. I suppose you know that I sent the opening chorus of a *Triumphlied* to Reinthaler. He complains about his weak choir. Couldn't you come up with some volunteers from Oldenburg who would join in singing the 8-part *forte*?

It's not difficult, only *forte*.

---

[6] Revelation 19: 1–2, 5–7, 11, 15–16. The words to the first chorus: 'Alleluia! Salvation and glory and honour, and power unto the Lord our God, for true and righteous are his judgements'.

[7] Dated incorrectly in Dietrich's memoirs, if the dates of Brahms's letters to Reinthaler are correct.

Dear fellow, don't be angry when I come, greet the wife, your children, and all human beings in your town very warmly from
your
Joh. Brahms.

While preparing for the performance, Brahms was Reinthaler's guest.

263
Johannes Brahms to Karl Reinthaler

[Lichtenthal bei Baden-Baden, 21 May 1871]

Dear friend.

I am enormously pleased to have this occasion of sending you, both of you, the warmest greetings. Without a specific occasion it just won't work; I could only—with tenderest affection welling within—charge the clouds and the winds with it, not the paper.

So then: I must have forgotten the proofs of some things by Couperin at your house. Piano music, octavo format, French titles; you'll know it easily by that. First and last pages missing. Do look for it carefully; it should be in your room, for at one time I had intended to play the things for you, something you can now hurriedly do yourself.

So I have to request that you send me this Couperin, and with it the delayed laundry could also come along!

I have already inspected many a house to see if it is worthy of harbouring you. It seems to me there are quite a few of them. But write to me in any case before you consider coming.

On Wednesday we will have 'Medea' by Cherubini here, from the Carlsruhe Opera. However, we're not languishing here—even after such choice treats.[8]

But enough for today; my best greetings to you both and do include two long letters with the Couperin and the laundry.
Affectionately your
Joh. Br.

Brahms was editing Books I and II of Couperin's *Pièces de Clavecin* for the series *Denkmäler der Tonkunst* (Monuments of Musical Art), whose general editor was the

---

[8] *Medea* was translated, edited, and conducted by Hermann Levi. Brahms treasured the work. From his letter to Levi about the forthcoming performance (*BW* vii. 82): 'We'll never be done with jabbering about Tristan, and this splendid work we accept quietly, take so completely for granted.'

composer's old friend, Friedrich Chrysander. The volume appeared in December of the same year.

After an absence of several years, the singer Ottilie Ebner moved back to Vienna, a return Brahms greeted with pleasure. Following the death of her eldest child, she gave up music for almost a year. In an effort to 'lead her slowly back to music', Brahms came to play for her almost daily, referring to his visits as 'piano lessons'.[9] The easy friendship which developed, revealed in the many letters they exchanged over the years, gives lie to the notion that Brahms's relations with women were inevitably condescending or difficult.

They corresponded during Brahms's spring concert tour, and Ottilie accepted the invitation to come with her husband to spend some of her holiday in Baden-Baden.

264
Johannes Brahms to Ottilie Ebner

[Hamburg,] May [18]71

My dear friend!

When it comes to writing, even to you, I am not as prompt as with visits, known as piano lessons.

Don't wear a peevish expression on your face, but one as merry as mine when a letter from you arrives. The lovely billfold couldn't make me any merrier, at best only its contents, at which your busy fingers should kindly not take umbrage. I thank you from my heart for everything, it was lovely, and if there hadn't been such a lot of turmoil on the trip I would have said it sooner. But I cannot pass through any town without being plagued by concerts and such like. As now, in a great hurry, in Bremen, Oldenburg, and Carlsruhe. Now I have been sitting in my long familiar room for two days, and am hoping that they will definitely be disturbed by you!

Don't change your fine plan, and savour it very thoughtfully and fully. The Rhine has nothing to offer to the hasty traveller, I suppose one really ought to live there in order to discover how beautiful it is. I am certainly not being an egoist when I advise you to be sure to linger in Oberwesel and Gerashausen, for example, to climb bravely up to the ruined castles, to do a lot of walking, to travel into the valleys and up the mountains and by boat. Finally, reserve two days for Heidelberg and a big finale with a ⌒ for
Baden-Baden

[9] From her daughter's biographical memoir, Ottilie von Balassa, *Die Brahmsfreundin Ottilie Ebner* (Vienna, 1933).

You should stay here in Lichtenthal at The Bear.[10] And I suppose you will advise me in time to rent. You will be staying in closest proximity to Frau Schumann and to me, and your husband won't have far to walk and by the most beautiful route—to the casino and other glories. Frau Schumann is not yet here, but should come soon.

Now give my very best greetings to your lovely valley including all of its inhabitants, and let me hear when you will be starting off—and occasionally before that![11]

And once again, my best thanks for the letter and billfold.

Your affectionately devoted

Joh. Br.

Lichtenthal 145 near
Baden-Baden, Grand Duchy of Baden.

Appended to a letter from Clara Schumann to Ottilie:

265
Johannes Brahms to Ottilie Ebner

Baden, the 20th of June 1871

I may already have lost what scant reputation I had as a 'kind and obliging person'. Each and every day you will be subtracting [from it]! But that shall end this very day, I am going home immediately to take up paper so as to repeat to you how exceedingly I am your devoted

J. Brahms.

The resurgence of interest in the music of Franz Josef Haydn owes something to Brahms and Joachim, who shared a devotion to his string quartets and enthusiasm for the Hungarian elements in his music. An inveterate browser in libraries, Brahms came upon two works which particularly pleased him. One was the *Chorale St Antoni*, as orchestrated by Haydn; the use Brahms made of it requires no comment. The other work was an Andante from a symphony which he liked so much he made an extra copy of it for Joachim.[12] The barbed comment here regarding unending melodies refers to a notion long current that Wagner invented this melodic style.

---

[10] Brahms's favourite hotel, placed at the edge of the lush park which runs the length of the little Oos River as it flows through the town. The Bear is still in operation (1994).

[11] The Oed, north-west of Vienna. Ottilie's father was the only doctor in the sparsely populated valley where she grew up.

[12] Sinfonie in B, Hob I: 16. The manuscript is described by McCorkle (McC 743).

266
Johannes Brahms to Joseph Joachim

[Baden-Baden?], Oct[ober 18]71

Dear friend,

For the time being and until I hear from you here, the sight of [the] Hungarian [pieces] gives me so much pleasure that I would really like to give you a little too. For that, I know nothing better than to copy out *an Andante by Haydn for you and your chorus of violins*. Frau Schumann can take it along for you. To me this little piece seems a paragon of beauty, and I know of no better example of the newly invented 'unending melody'. I have copied it from a poor copy—faithfully, except for the most pointless mistakes.

I really hope you too will rave about it, and that I'll get to hear it from your students when I come to Berlin in the course of the winter.

That your wife will sing my Rhapsody pleases and interests me greatly; I only fear the Hanseatics will not think likewise, and that it won't make them merry!

However, dear chap, there'll be no letter-writing! I intend to come to Berlin this winter and make a proper stay of it; after all, I can hardly sing to the Bohemian Ministers in Vienna a song I have written acclaiming Bismarck; so that will in any case steer me to Germany, and then I'll hear music where you are, as well.

For today, warm greetings, also to your wife and the children.

Yours utterly,

J. Brahms

A north German living in Austria, Brahms was obviously mindful of the ongoing struggle for dominance between Prussia and the Habsburg Monarchy. Not for the first time does his correspondence hark back to the events of 1866. The Bohemian-Austrian Ministers in Vienna would not yet have forgotten them either—when Bismarck's Prussian army invaded Bohemia and mauled the Austrian army at the battle of Sadowa (Königsgrätz).[13]

The Alto Rhapsody became the centre-piece of Amalie Joachim's repertory, and she its quintessential interpreter. This letter may mark the first time she sang the role.

Another work for chorus and orchestra was now finished, the *Schicksalslied*, Op. 54, having occupied Brahms for a few years. The first performance took place in Karlsruhe under Levi's direction.

[13] See Letter 236 to Schubring, and Brahms to Allgeyer, Letter 208.

267
Johannes Brahms to Karl Reinthaler

[Vienna, *c.*24] Oct[ober 18]71

My dear friend.

How long and how often have I wanted to write to you! Now I would have the time and the urge, but now this spiky steel nib aggravates me too much, and so let me just respond to a few things.

I had a chorus 200 strong for the 'Rhapsody' here! 24 would be somewhat too few for me, the more the better if they sing *pp*, so then, 48 if at all possible!

The 'Schicksalslied' is being printed and in the last Adagio the chorus is silent. It is merely—a silly idea or what have you, but there's nothing to be done. I was feeling so low that I had written something for the chorus into it; but it really doesn't work at all. It may be a sort of failed experiment, but this kind of pasting over would result in nonsense. As we have discussed often enough: I do say something that the poet does not say, and it would of course be better if what is missing had been the main point—but now, etc.

But should you perform it, work above all on this postlude. The flute must play with great passion and a multitude of violins must sound beautiful. In Carlsruhe the thing made a remarkable impression. With respect to the 'Halleluja', I am considering Cologne. The means in Carlsruhe are somewhat modest (in number), I don't want to misuse the Hanseatics on the Weser, and those on the Elbe don't ask after me.[14]

I have been in Vienna for three days now and am living at II (suburb Leopoldstadt = II), Hotel Kronprinz.

I'm glad you enjoyed the spiritual visit. Poor man! In a nest like that he constantly plans how one must take a wife without fail and at all costs, and once he's on the outside, he turns delicate and waits for the naked little boy who is apparently expected to shoot off two arrows.[15]

But for today my best, warm greeting, also to the wife and children—don't give up letter-writing; I too will get better.

Your

Joh. Br.

---

[14] The Weser runs through Bremen, the Elbe through Hamburg. Both cities were once members of the old Hanseatic League.

[15] We shall not get to discover more about the man's troubled love life, suffered by a Pastor Kolatschek, who delivered a misunderstood sermon and came to see Brahms about it. See *BW* iii. 97.

It is a rare moment in this composer's correspondence when one finds specific comments not only regarding his musical intentions—even if veiled and truncated, as here—but also as to performance directions. The 'experiment' refers to his treatment of Hölderlin's text, which begins by describing scenes of bliss in Elysium as experienced by the Gods, and continues with an abrupt shift to scenes of the grim reality of human life on earth. Brahms was not willing to end on that depressing note ('I do say something the poet doesn't say'), and added the lush, enigmatic Postlude. He first experimented with the idea of bringing in the chorus in an obligato role, as the final Adagio returns to the opening music, but then accepted Levi's suggestion to recapitulate the music of the first part without any chorus at all.[16]

From the Gesellschaft der Musikfreunde, Brahms finally had an offer he could not refuse. In October he informed Levi that he had definitely accepted. 'I know of no way of getting out of it, because whatever I say they arrange according to my wishes. I shall have at least 32 members of the Opera Orchestra for concerts; in general, every possible thing.' In fact, the final negotiations dragged on for months, but in the end his contract promised him 2,000 gulden per year, with another 1,000 guaranteed for extra concerts; programme and artists to be chosen only by him, no work to be performed without his consent.[17]

268

Johannes Brahms to Dr Franz Egger, President of the Board of Directors of the Gesellschaft der Musikfreunde

[December 1871]

Most esteemed Herr Doktor.

While I am generally in complete agreement with the contents of your distinguished letter of Nov. 27th, these lines were none the less delayed, for which I very much beg to be excused.

I meant to inform you of a few reservations that are on my mind; in the end they did not seem important enough and will probably be settled sometime in a conversation with gentlemen from among you.

For the present I will therefore regard it as sufficient to express the hope

[16] The piece is one of the very few for which Brahms's sketches are available; his choral 'experiment' is in the Library of Congress (MS Music 1178), along with the full autograph. The usual method of making significant changes in a manuscript was to paste over the old version.

[17] Letter to Levi: *BW* vii. 84–5.

and my pleasure: of being able to devote my powers to your Institute next year.

> With particular high esteem
>
> your very devoted
>
> Joh. Brahms

Now it was time to find a permanent home.

269
Johannes Brahms to Johann Jakob Brahms

[Vienna,] 31 December 1871

Dear Father,

Many thanks for you dear letter and the picture which turned out very well. Thank God, one cannot tell from it that you've endured so much. Just go on taking a great many walks and soon you will have forgotten all about it.

I think I'll enclose a note for you today to the establishment where you've already picked up money sometimes. And since you have to pay the doctor for the useful cat's pelt, I'll send 150 thaler right away. If anything's left, have a really good time!

Always be sure to write when you have such special expenses.

I have now finally found a flat which I like very much; very near to the *Carlskirche*, which you must have a picture of. You could now do me a favour if you would send me the suitcase I packed in Hamburg, last time.

Ship it as freight and address it to Gotthard, music shop.

If it's *not full*, I would be very pleased if you would pack some of my *candlesticks* into it. If it's still not full, add a few books or ash trays or something like that (from 1), maybe Schiller or Goethe, if you find it.

When you've received the money, write me a line and with it, a letter. My address is:

Vienna IV, Carlsgasse 4.

What is Herr Marxsen doing, have you been out to see him?

Soon I'll send you music that you might bring him, since you often go for walks. Otherwise of course I could send it directly, but I imagine you might have a chat with him sometime.

Dr Gehring has indeed got me the *Kölnische Zeitung* and I'll send to you soon.[18]

---

[18] Franz Gehring wrote music criticism for that newspaper, and was soon to take a post in Vienna.

Now be very well, both of you; today, as the new year begins, I'll first of all think very much of you both, and drink to your health.

In devoted love

your Johannes

⅍ 1872 ⅏

Brahms's duties with the Gesellschaft der Musikfreunde did not begin until the autumn, so finding an opera libretto still remained a major concern. It is not for lack of trying that the devoted Levi failed to come up with one which met with his approval. He even contacted a prominent ecclesiastic to work on a biblical story. *Sulamith* was the dubious result.

Tact quickly gave way to sarcasm.

270
Johannes Brahms to Hermann Levi

[Vienna, January 1872]

Dear friend,

I have certain qualms about beginning this letter. So let's speak of something else! For instance, tell Allgeyer that he has given me the greatest pleasure with the Feuerbachs! They are almost a necessity for me, for I don't like playing dead composers all the time, and accordingly he is the best or the only one.

Then I could also remark that I understand violins to refer to the complete quartet and that I really wish the copyist had more time.[1] It's going very slowly and I wish he would copy the score as well (but quickly) and that I would get it soon. For all I care, one movement at a time.

Now I'll really take the easy way out and ask you—mainly because the text is not really ready—to explain its merits to me.

After your letter, I naturally thought of the bible immediately, of the Book of Kings, 'the Maccabees', Saul, and whatever other dramatic material from it came to mind. The title was therefore naturally a great surprise and disappointment to me. There has been a lot of experimentation with those poor love songs; there is even an opera about it already! You probably approached it without prejudice, but did the drama really seem immediately plausible to you? or were you perhaps taken by it just because of the new

---

[1] To copy the string parts of the *Triumphlied*.

translation, became interested in that and possibly even in more recent studies as well, which may make the drama viable when taken literally?

I don't know what I am still missing of the 1st act, but as of now I still feel that after all one cannot make a symphony out of a duet for two flutes.

That the characters speak in biblical phrases whenever possible, couldn't that also be the allure of novelty for you, of seeking and finding? I know about that and just now, for instance, I have an oratorium text here which is made up entirely of authentic quotations. Does it seem to you, for example, that the scene between Salome and Sulamith in the 1st act can be composed and staged? N.B. for living persons and in our worldly theatre?

Well, I am aware of your opinion of me and of opera texts for me, and while I also hope that that you won't take the 'cancellation' as being too stinging, well—I nevertheless feel uncomfortable and wish that tomorrow I might see it your way and call myself a fool.

But once more I must emphasize very firmly that I'm lacking the entire 3rd act, and since in any case it is peculiar to wish to force a drama into a love poem, and it is equally extraordinary to have our women singers defend themselves by means of biblical quotations when hard pressed by a king—you might well devote a letter to this!

Furthermore, I am long since in a great rush. I hope you will write anyway, but also about Salome! The missing 3rd act is really critical. For today the best greetings, also to Allgeyer and whoever else wants them.

Affectionately your
Joh. Brahms.

Levi was crestfallen, and named all their Karlsruhe friends who supported him in his high opinion of the libretto. He told Brahms to send back the two acts, and ended:

> . . . this is a matter of inclination, and affairs of the heart are not debatable.—I have taken special note of your words: 'Well, I am aware of your opinion of me (?) and of opera texts for me' . . . and you'll not be troubled in the future. May this still-born child of sorrow be buried. God give it eternal rest—possibly even a joyous resurrection . . .[2]

Whatever else occupied him, Brahms composed songs. Frequently there was an outside stimulus: in this case, the return of Ottilie Ebner to Vienna and the possibility of trying out the sixteen songs in Opp. 57 and 58 with her.[3]

His penchant for using translations of folk poetry caused occasional problems: in the following letter, Brahms is impressed with refinements made by the poet Paul

---

[2] *BW* vii. 95, letter of 15 Jan. 1872.

[3] She owned the autographs of some of these undated songs, and although some or all may have been composed earlier, she sang them with Brahms at this time.

Heyse to the text of his Calabrian songs, 'Die Spröde' and 'Blindekuh'.[4] Just at this time his Lullaby was about to be republished, and Simrock desperately wanted a second stanza. Levi and Allgeyer were charged with coming up with something suitable.

Characteristically, the sensitive issue of the opera libretto, still a lively concern, is buried towards the end of the letter.

271
Johannes Brahms to Hermann Levi

[Vienna, after 15 January 1872]

Dear friend,

Heyse has done his work so splendidly that I am really annoyed not to have waited for it. I don't know now if he wants to be named with respect to it, and I don't want to decide among the different versions—I therefore ask you to please take the trouble to send the text for the tigress to Rieter right away.[5] 'Blindekuh' seems less important to me, and the 3rd stanza I *don't* want changed. I hope to visit Heyse at long last on my trip to you, and apart from thanking him for this delightful and kind bagatelle, I will naturally also talk about other things with him.

Should you be sitting around with Allgeyer for a little while or on some other occasion, reflecting: softened by 'the falling drops' of drops of water,[6] you might just straighten out the following, for which I am being pressed very hard: *Stanza 2.*

> Good evening and good night,
> Angels keep you in sight,
> in your dreams they'll show thee
> the Christchild's own tree.
> *In paradise, high up there,*
> *softly sleep without care.*

---

[4] Op. 58 No. 3, and 1. Using Heyse's suggestions, Brahms and Levi both worked on reshaping the text to 'Die Spröde'; it is most instructive to see the use to which Brahms put Heyse's lines, combining several versions of the poem to suit his needs. The Heyse–Levi–Brahms text was used for the second and subsequent printings. See Robert Münster, 'Brahms und Paul Heyse: Eine Künstlerfreundschaft', *Brahms-Studien*, vii (1987), 51–76.

[5] 'Die Spröde'.

[6] i.e. of *water*, as opposed to alcohol, which would have been the more likely drops to 'soften' Allgeyer and Levi , had they been sitting around anywhere—with Brahms as the third in the party, they had sat many an evening in taverns over a bottle of something. But the allusion is to the text of 'Die Spröde', however, in which drops of water soften a stone.

The last two lines must be changed and naturally can have only one meaning.

> Softly sleep without care,
> dream of paradise fair.

Brrr—! Should something come to you, you could also immediately send that to Simrock, who even has 2nd verses from Berlin poets, by now.

This aside, I was greatly cheered by your sister getting better all the time! It must be a singular emotion for you, indeed it almost makes me shudder when I contemplate this turning back so close to the great gate.

In response to my criticism of the opera text I might very well have anticipated—some snide comments. All the same, it really is not fitting. Your opinion of me etc. is now that there is no way to satisfy me. And in that regard, first of all, I don't consider that the text in question can be used as proof. Do take a serious look at it now (I have sent it with *Uthal*).[7]

If the first scene between the King and Sulima is not to be performed as a pious nativity play acted by marionettes—very different words are needed. But to expound on this in writing—that I cannot manage. If you really maintain your point of view, do write a word to explain, a more attentive reader you cannot find.

My *Schicksalslied* came off very badly here on Sunday. Rubinstein is simply a mediocre conductor, and did not offer to let me conduct, consequently I let the thing run its course. I will therefore reconsider Düsseldorf and the *Triumphlied* once more![8]

Let me hear from you and if possible be a good friend and take care of getting the two texts in print as quickly as you can.

I live in Vienna IV, Carlsgasse 4. *But packages to be addressed to Gotthart, please.*

Forgive the haste, the scribble and the never-ending commissions. Greet Allgeyer and others and warmest greetings to yourself

from your

Joh. Brahms.

I have had no news from Mannheim?![9]

---

[7] *Uthal*, by Méhul (1763–1817), an opera which had long interested Brahms, perhaps because, like his Serenade in A major, Op. 16, it dispenses with violins and relies instead on violas. The score was in the library at Karlsruhe.

[8] See Letter 276 n. 16. In April, speaking of his doubts about letting Rubinstein conduct his *Triumphlied*, he wrote to Levi: '[Rubinstein] is a *very* mediocre conductor and unforgivably rough and irresponsible' (*BW* vii. 112).

[9] Referring to Levi's brother, the banker Wilhelm Lindeck. See Letters 341–4.

In February, Johann Jakob Brahms died of cancer of the liver, the same disease, at about the same age, to which his son would succumb twenty-five years later.

272
Johannes Brahms to Ottilie Ebner

[Hamburg, early February 1872]

Esteemed friend!

In a few words I do want to let you know how I found things here, and above all: that I am very glad I came.

My father is very weak; fortunately, however, suffers no pain but lies continually in a light slumber. But he listens willingly as soon as spoken to, and also likes to join cheerfully in chatting a little.

I was therefore able to tell him about you and about many other friends and we also discussed how very beneficial Carlsbad would be for the summer.

In any case I am a great comfort to him, to say nothing of my second mother, who otherwise goes ever so sadly from one sickroom to the other.[10]

I hardly know at all when I can think about the journey back, but you will certainly find out as soon as I can tell.

Incidentally, my father is only 66 years old. Death would really be arriving too soon, his life has been hard, you know, nothing but struggle and toil. What a happy old age he has—tasted; he deserves to live it out.

But enough for today. Greet your husband and our friends and be yourself warmly greeted by your

J. Brahms.

273
Johannes Brahms to Julius Stockhausen

[Hamburg,] 16 February 1872

Dear friend,

I have wanted to write and thank you for the pleasure and surprise of your dedication for a long time.

Now I do so at a particularly sombre moment, which probably represents the end of a phase in my lonely life.

---

[10] Her son was also very ill, but recovered.

I've been here in Hamburg for two weeks and on Sunday I lost my father. A cancer of the liver caused him not all too much suffering, fortunately, but took him from us. You know my love for my father and know what deep sorrow his loss is to me. You also know my weakness for my home territory and can imagine with what peculiar feelings I walk this time through streets which I probably shan't see again for a long time.

I saw your house, too, the windows without curtains, without flowers, it did not look comfortably inviting, as formerly.

But now, my thanks again for your songs. That I consider a dedication to be a beautiful present under any circumstance you can see from my title-pages, which rarely carry one! I don't want to praise them right off; for I have a bad reputation for that and am always being misunderstood. But with songs by you, one does always hear them in spirit as sung by you—and then one succumbs!

Gotthard can be well pleased with the material, and you needn't be all too polite in requesting the requisite specimen copies. You'd have to become an annoyingly prolific composer before interest in Stockhausen songs were to cease. Meanwhile a French Romance in B major suggests the next instalment to me.[11]

I return to Vienna this very day, therefore forgive the pen for running on so. Between Easter and Whitsun I'll probably be in Carlsruhe, and you as well, perhaps?

Your wife will presumably read this letter first and then send it to England. So I greet you both most warmly by these means, and hope we will indeed hear from one another occasionally.

Warmly your

Johs. Brahms.

The belated thanks were for a group of songs. In an enthusiastic letter, the singer Julius Stockhausen had informed Brahms he was venturing to dedicate the set to him even though his exacting colleague had once said, upon being shown one of his early works, 'Let's see how it's done by someone who hasn't learned how to do it.'[12]

---

[11] An unpublished composition which Stockhausen once showed to Brahms while they were touring together.

[12] Wirth, *Julius Stockhausen*, 35. Letter of 28 Dec. 1871.

274
Johannes Brahms to Karoline Brahms

[Vienna,] 4 March 1872

My dear Mother,

Several times, already, I have had paper lying in front of me to write to you. Then I would think of you most affectionately and would think further and further back to the past—but it wouldn't take shape on paper, and nothing consoling at all. Nor can I really attempt to console you now, I know too well what we have lost and how lonely your life has become. But I hope you perceive very tenderly and twice as much the love of others, of your son, your admirable sister and her children, and ultimately, my love, which belongs to you entirely.

Here I have found so many expressions of sympathy that you would have been pleased to see how much Father was appreciated by everyone who knew him.

I have not ordered a headstone and since I don't really know when I will be coming to Hamburg, just do whatever you wish and pick one, possibly with your sister.

What kind of an inscription do you have in mind? Just name and date?

I'm glad that the business at the notary's is settled. Fritz, who gave his share to you, is undoubtedly Fr. Brahms? Would you then have to pay only 200 Mark for Elise? So you see that the business ended very well. For the time being, therefore, don't cash in any certficates.

We can still think it over, after all.

When does the American bond come due?

I want to send you 100 thaler today still (maybe a transmittance). You can give Elise her share from this in the mean time. May I also ask you to write to me in good time when and how much money I should send you? Just simply the amount that you need. But to that I will naturally add, apart from what you yourself require, the funeral costs, the doctor, the headstone, Elise's 200 Marks etc, etc. I would be very pleased and very grateful to you if you would not find it awkward simply to write down the figure. Even with the best of intentions, I cannot know what expenses there are in such exceptional circumstances.

I hope Fritz [S.] will soon give you the pleasure of having himself transported to Pinneberg. It is true, the house will become even lonelier, but that way you can look forward to his recuperation and in the spring you too will go over there. Although you now probably feel sad in the woods, the fine air will do you good anyhow, and will ease a little what only time, it is true, can heal.

See whether you can find out anything about Schumann's letter to Father and about what Klaus Groth had written.

The things are not likely to be in Pinneberg?

Now be greeted from the bottom of my heart, and just as you surely believe that I loved my father, so believe now that I will be yours in faithful and grateful love, always and at all times.

Your Johannes

Warm greetings and best wishes to Fritz [S.]

These were no empty words. In the years ahead, Brahms wrote dozens of letters and sent thousands of thaler to Karoline, kept her informed at all times of his whereabouts, and stayed in touch as lovingly and dutifully as if it were she who had given him life. But for the next four years he avoided Hamburg.

Schumann's letter was the one sent to Johann Jakob with a copy of *Neue Bahnen* (see Letter 13). In 1868 Klaus Groth wrote a memoir of his youth in Heide for Johann Jakob; the younger Brahms read it so attentively he could correspond with Groth about it as late as 1896, but unlike the letter, that memoir was never found.[13]

Gustav Nottebohm's researches on Beethoven were a continuing source of interest, and Rudorff had access to the great library in Berlin.

275

Johannes Brahms to Ernst Rudorff

[Postmark: Wieden in Vienna, 20] March [18]72

Dear Herr Rudorff.

Herr Nottebohm is working on a splendid work about Beethoven's studies. Some day it is going to give you great pleasure; pardon if today it causes you a small inconvenience.

With regard to the enclosed requests, I know of no better or more reliable address for him than you.

For the time being, Herr Nottebohm naturally wishes only to learn if and what is available. Should something look more important to him, the request to arrange for a copy of such will follow.

We both owe you the best of thanks should you take the trouble.

[13] See Volquart Pauls, *Briefe der Freundschaft* (Heide, 1956), 54, 141, 144 ff.

You can use Gotthardt's music shop as address for both of us.
With sincere greetings,

yours in devoted friendliness,

J. Brahms.

276

Johannes Brahms to Clara Schumann

Vienna, Easter Monday, April 1872

My beloved Clara,

Holidays I always spend all alone, quite by myself, with a few dear ones up in my room, and very quietly—given that my own people are dead or far away. How happy I am, therefore, when I have the blissful sensation of love utterly filling a human breast. I am of course dependent on the world outside; the turmoil in which one lives—I don't laugh at it, I don't join in the lies—but it is as if the best part of one could lock itself up, leaving merely half the person walking away in a dream.

How fortunate you are, or should I say, how beautiful, how good, how right. In my view you wear your heart as a much more secure possession—we have to hide it at every moment. You look at everything with such warmth, such lovely calm—so truly from within yourself, and calmly also give everyone his due. All this sounds so stupid and indeed, I can't express it, can at best speak even more stupidly of lilies and angels—and then allude to you and your nature.

But to come down to earth, which is where my pen belongs: the other day I read the first page of your letter, and absolutely did not know where my head had been at. For I hadn't given a single thought to Stuttgart, nor did it occur to me! But by chance a letter from Lübke had arrived at the same time, and then I noticed from your envelope what wanderings the letter had made.[14] By the way, I'm told the Requiem went very well there and produced earnings, for once. Likewise in Munich, and from Breslau Scholz writes to me very enthusiastically about R[equiem] and *Schicksalslied*.

All winter long I have been doing counterpoint exercises very assiduously! What for? To be better able to disparage my pretty things—for that it wasn't necessary. To become a university professor—also not. To learn to

---

[14] There must be a letter missing here. Clara was in London at this time, and it is impossible to know what the sentence refers to. Lübke was an eminent art historian who lived in Stuttgart, and whose writings Brahms admired.

write music better—that too I'm not hoping for. But still it's somewhat tragic when in the end, one gets to be cleverer than is useful.[15]

You really have no idea, it seems to me, nor can you have any concept of, and interest in the confusion that reigns here (I am not speaking or thinking of Wagner.)[16]

It gave me great joy that Felix brought you so much [joy]![17]

Regarding the Serenade, just have what you think recorded in the green book, more than that I also don't know. I suppose its first performance was in Hanover, probably under J[oachim]. What you remember, however, is our private, very first one, for which Grimm, Bargiel, and I wrote out the parts and musicians from the Harz camped in Rittmüller's house.[18]

I hope we'll savour the greening and blossoming in Baden together. But I hear nothing of whether you and Joachim have in fact accepted for Carlsruhe!

I greet you straight from my heart. And also greet Marie, Joachim and your friendly hosts.

> Wholly your
> Johannes.

The hope expressed of seeing his friends in Karlsruhe referred to a forthcoming performance of the complete *Triumphlied*, conducted by Levi. With the conductor's impending move to Munich, the event became his farewell concert, a gala send-off which included Clara and Stockhausen among the performers. To his deep regret, Theodor Billroth could not attend. Instead, he sent a silver goblet bearing the inscription: 'To the Master of German musical art, Johannes Brahms, in remembrance of the fifth of June 1872'.

[15] Perhaps the exercises were not so useless after all. Soon to come were the *Variations on a Theme by Haydn*, Op. 56, which contain some of the most miraculous counterpoint Brahms ever wrote (see e.g. Var. VIII).

[16] He was thinking of the thorny relations between himself and Rubinstein, who had offered to conduct his *Triumphlied* at the Festival of the Lower Rhine. His capacity to do so effectively was much doubted by Brahms, as Rubinstein had conducted a mediocre performance of the *Schicksalslied* in Vienna. The events led to a complete and permanent break between the two men (see Kal, ii³. 290 ff.). Interestingly, Brahms was carrying out Clara's fervent advice when he alienated Rubinstein by making it known that he wanted to conduct the *Triumphlied* himself. See her letter to Brahms from Basle, 1 Jan. 1872.

[17] He had passed his examinations.

[18] Serenade No. 1 in D major. There was a private reading in Göttingen, in the summer of 1858, before the first public performance by Joachim in Hanover. See Letter 102.

277
Johannes Brahms to Theodor Billroth

Lichtenthal bei Baden-Baden, [9 June 1872]

Dear friend,

No attempt to write and thank you satisfies me. It would have to turn into an account of the emotions with which I held the postal notice in my hand, for instance, or how Frau Schumann's noble face beamed, or how we sat together at Levi's and spoke quite solemnly about men of your kind. Doing the exceptional comes so naturally to you that you do not realize the effect, and would be surprised by it.

The goblet was filled how many times, on that night and afterwards—whenever I held it in my hand I could only think most warmly of you. One cannot accompany thanks by trumpets and timpani, on the contrary, the warmer they are, the softer they get; therefore simply believe that you could not have surprised, touched, or delighted me and my friends more than you did.

In retrospect I must greatly deplore that you did not hear the concert. You could hardly have heard a more elegant or beautiful one. I don't suppose that I have ever so completely had the impression that everyone was doing far more than his duty. Everybody sang or played as if everything depended on him alone, as must indeed be the case if something magnificent is to result. But this time, it was almost comical to see and to hear. And so, although it is intended for more sizeable forces, I am unlikely ever to hear my song with greater pleasure. The people really did as our soldiers in France, where one thousand at their posts also accomplished as much as otherwise a hundred thousand. The piece confronted one with such wonderful boldness and vitality, I was hardly surprised that it ignited such a storm—but a second performance I will carefully skirt around.

But now, my dear friend, I will close, for I am tempted to start up again about the chalice. I wish I had had as good an idea for the Triumphlied, it contains none as good.

Be greeted right from the bottom of my heart, your
Johannes Brahms.

Brahms began his duties with the Gesellschaft der Musikfreunde in the autumn of 1872. During the next three years, he would programme first performances of works by Beethoven, Schubert, and Mozart, and of Bach cantatas. Scores of letters to performers and conductors—among them Hiller, Wüllner, Levi, and Joachim, attest to the demands of his job and the seriousness with which he took it on.[19]

[19] Details of these and many other Brahms concerts are found in Hofmann, *Zeittafel*.

The first concerts took place in November and December. For these pro-grammes, he turned to his friends Joseph and Amalie Joachim both for help and to right a wrong from long ago: more than ten years after the piece had been spurned in Hamburg, Brahms opened his career as a conductor with Joachim's masterful orchestration of Schubert's Grand Duo, the Sonata C major, Op. posth. 140 (D. 812). It was a graceful nod of thanks to a faithful friend.[20] Amalie sang, and Brahms showed what he could do with a chorus.

278

Johannes Brahms to Joseph Joachim

[Vienna, 6] October 1872

Dear friend,

You know that I want to do *your Schubert* Symphony in our 1st concert.

Now it appears that the score which I borrowed from Spina really had paid a visit the engraver's.[21] The bookbinder can probably be of no further help, since no two pages have stayed together. My score is in Hamburg, and so I ask and beg whether you can't lend me one? Furthermore, I would be really pleased if you could perhaps lend *a few* parts to go along with it. We are missing something like 3 first, 3 second violins, 2 violas, and 2 basses. But that merely parenthetically—in case you don't have any, we will of course have them copied. And now comes another enquiry, and the most agreeable. Wouldn't your wife like to sing an aria in our 2nd concert on 8 December?

I need hardly describe at length how greatly I desire her acceptance—beyond that, however, I can't brag loftily about the sacrifices we are willing to make for it, unfortunately. Let me know how kind and undemanding your wife can be under these circumstances![22]

Unfortunately I will be unable to manage Saul at that time. I have a con-cert with the following programme:

1. Organ concerto by Handel (probably the D Minor).
2. Double Chorus by Mozart (D major with violin and organ).
3. Aria (Bach, Gluck, Beethoven? Handel?)
4. Prelude and Fugue for organ by Bach.
5. *Triumphlied* by me.

Now let me hear a word as to whether I may look forward to the 3rd number?

---

[20] See Letters 94–5.   [21] i.e. was ruined during its use as an engraver's model.
[22] Her 'fee' was a men's choir, so that she could perform the Alto Rhapsody.

The business with the dedication did indeed come off perfectly easily and simply, I'm most grateful to you for it!

Finally, my best greeting to large and small; I look forward eagerly to a favourable reply.

With all my heart

your

Johs. Brahms.

IV, Carlsgasse 4.

Amalie offered to sing 'Divinités du Styx' from Gluck's *Alceste*, with tenor and chorus, which she customarily sang one tone lower than the original.

279

Johannes Brahms to Joseph Joachim

[Vienna, 22] October 1872

My dear friend,

Your things were just now brought to me and I hasten to respond with the essentials. It goes without saying that I will do whatever possible by telegraphing and writing to arrange the concerts in all of Austria in such a way that will enable your wife to sing with us on the 8th. There is such a deluge of concerts here that it's impossible to switch even one of the [Clara] Schumann–[Amalie] Joachim concerts, much less ours.

I'll take care of the Schubert score this very day. Your idea of restoring the dedication is so simple, right, and beautiful that at most one can be annoyed at having had to be told. But do you really still call the work a Duo? I doubt that the title '*Grand Duo*' is Schubert's. Did you by any chance check the manuscript at Frau Schumann's? But in any case, it ceases to be a Duo when it's for 50 voices.

Isn't its title then Symphony by Schubert, adapted from the Duo, Op.[1]40, orchestrated, or however and whatever else?!

The scenes from Alceste suit me and are welcome as they are, but nevertheless I can't refrain from asking once again if we shouldn't try to connect them? In my opinion it ought to make an outstanding piece for concerts and music festivals. If somewhere or other the baritone and the chorus is in fact lacking, the orchestra can simply skip over the passages in question. The connection is so uncomplicated in spite of the transposition—I would have no qualms about that either. I assume you have the French score and will take the trouble to look it up.

The beginning is just too imposing; how does this convey one to the scene swiftly and make the action evident.

Now I would begin at p. 71 and not be bashful:

On p. 81 I would continue:

And, finally, on p. 84 I would quite calmly state:

If you have no objections in principle to joining things together this way, your wife could sing with the same orchestral parts in the future, either without or with the priest and chorus, according to circumstances.

Do take another look at it from this point of view and if it seems worth the trouble to you, write a word *without delay* so I can take care of chorus and orchestra.

In case your wife would prefer to sing her usual scenes, I would again like to request an early word saying whether she has the parts or if we can borrow them from somewhere along the Elbe or the Rhine.[23]

But now I must be off, to see what more has to be inflicted on the inhabitants of Pesth and Graz, so that we won't come up short.

Very warm greetings!

Your

Johannes.

[23] The parts were in Hanover, on the river *Leine.*

Brahms's suggestions were accepted enthusiastically, his supposition regarding Schubert was correct: the piano duet bore the title 'Sonata C Major', and was only given the name 'Grand Duo' by the original publisher, Diabelli, who presented the autograph to Clara. Joachim's transcription, originally made at Robert Schumann's urging and now re-engraved, included Clara's dedication of long ago. It read: 'Frau Schumann dedicates this edition of the Schubert Duo Op. 140 (*dedié à Mademoiselle Clara Wieck*) to Joseph Joachim.'

With the dissolution of his circle of friends in Karlsruhe—Levi *and* Allgeyer were now in Munich—Brahms left behind a loyal following, especially among a lively group of women who had come to know him while singing in performances of the Requiem, *Triumphlied*, and *Schicksalslied*. Particularly devoted was the writer Anna Ettlinger, who had gone to the trouble of producing an opera libretto for him (*Melusine*). In some people's minds they were linked romantically—but apparently not in Brahms's. The amusing aspect of this letter is that it was written by five different hands.

280
Anna Ettlinger et al. *to Johannes Brahms*

Dear Herr Brahms!
    Levi has let us know we should send you the enclosed picture, which was taken at the Carlsruhe Fair. We don't know how you will take it. Should it give you pleasure, there are to be seen
    1) one Miss Schwarz
    2) two Miss von Poetzes
    3) three Miss Ettlingers

If it gives you none, it's someone else.
[Here are] Some of your Carlsruhe admirers.
Many of them aren't here, or they would also be in the picture. On the whole it is very lonely here, and it would be very,—**very**—*very*—*very*—**very** nice of you if you felt like convincing yourself of this soon.

Anna Ettlinger
Johanna Schwarz
Rudolphine Ettlinger
Emma Ettlinger
Linele Poetz
Elise v. Poetz presently in Munich
Carlsruhe, the 19th of November 1872

Nostalgic for former days in Karlsruhe, Brahms wrote to Levi even in September: 'You, after all, will spend Christmas in the usual circle, but whether and when I shall again see the Princely Seat and the nice people in it!?'

281

Johannes Brahms to Hermann Levi

[Vienna,] 23 Dec[ember 18]72

Dear friend,

I simply must be there with you in Carlsruhe—but of course merely in affectionate thoughts and by way of this hasty greeting, for which, however, in festive solemnity, I had *almost* cut a fresh pen nib.

I have [a] rehearsal any minute and no time, absolutely no time to travel to M[unich]. On the 30th, Dessoff has the Ninth, for which I am supplying the chorus, on the 5th of January we have the *Sängers Fluch* and *Walpurgis-nacht* once again,[24] so no chance. You can see from this how much our chorus has to accomplish and that I can take no holiday, appoint no substitute. For April, May, and later I can make plans, although I have agreed to the *Triumphlied* for the first concert of the International Exposition in May.

So don't read the Bayard too slowly but let me read, soon.

California is certainly not an enticing region for making music—better the Caucasus, Spain under the Arabs, which are truly tempting for an operatic visitation.

I don't know *Euphorion*, but believe that the destruction of S. takes place in it—so now my fear of the Great Opera has settled on *E[uphorion]* and Bayard! Heyse has already worked on Gozzi, after all, wouldn't he like to take a chance on a fairy-tale?[25]

Do write again regarding the 2nd Jonathan and what sort of demands he might make—whether *under* 200 fl[orins] (in Austrian currency).[26]

But all this is really only written because I would like to anticipate being mentioned in the circles where the cheerful Christmas lights are shining for

---

[24] Schumann, Op. 139, and Mendelssohn, Op. 60.

[25] More talk of opera librettos. Paul Heyse sketched *Ritter Bayard* specifically for Brahms. Apparently a story about the Gold Rush in California was also available, but Brahms was more inclined to a fairy-tale and in a previous letter refers to Gozzi's *König Hirsch* and *Love for Three Oranges* as interesting him particularly (*BW* vii. 128).

[26] The 'first Jonathan' was Gustav Walter, an eminent Viennese tenor (who sang the first *Rinaldo*, very much to Brahms's liking). Apparently he was not available to sing the solo in Handel's *Saul*, which was programmed for the coming March. Levi had suggested a young singer from Munich, to which Brahms had answered, 'Unknown outsiders we don't readily allow to come—unless they come very cheap' (*BW* vii. 127).

you. Therefore give my affectionate greetings to your sister [and] the 6 ladies who will presumably again form an artistic grouping, just as they did in the market stall.—Two of them are unfortunately so vain that they even try to embellish their eyes with a lead pencil. Oh vanity, thy name is Anna![27]

But now I'm eager to find out how many ladies will have time for me today and am off to the rehearsal.

With best greetings

your

Johs. Brahms.

❧ **1873** ☙

282

Johannes Brahms to Karoline Brahms

[23 February 1873]

Dear Mother,

I have heard nothing from you for such a long time—write again sometime, and in great detail, greater than I can for I am truly living in tremendous turmoil.

This time I had *not* written to Avé concerning the Philharmonic concert rehearsals, just remind me next autumn and you will certainly be able to attend them.

My old grand piano will be called for shortly! And you'll laugh: It's going to the International Exposition!! For, you see, it had been Schumann's, and others, of Mozart, Beethoven etc. are also there.

When they come to fetch it, they will probably show you a paper from Senator Jahns or Matthies from Altona.

So far I am doing very well and I have become very fat! Seriously. Up to now I can also be well satisfied with my position and cannot complain. But I would like to hear good things about you and Fritz [Schnack] and at the same time write also if you don't need money. Where do you have it from, anyway?

Now if you should sometime feel like rummaging among my books, you could do me a favour. I'll write a few things down here that I'd like to have; I would be really pleased if you could find them, or some of them, and would pack them in a box or some other way, and send them to me.

---

[27] Anna Ettlinger. See the previous letter.

But it is not absolutely essential, only if you can look for them and attend to it at your leisure.

All these things are among those marked with No. 1!

The Bible. *Quickborn* by Klaus Groth (there are 2 copies). Reuter (things in *Platt-Deutsch* [Low German]—if you find some of them). The works of Goethe, 6 large volumes, dark blue. Joh. Müller, General History, 3 volumes, rather old. Folk-songs by Kretzschmer and Zuccalmaglio, 2 books of music, normal book format, one of them well bound, one old. Just don't spend long looking for the last items, but the rest you will perhaps find more quickly.

You can see that unfortunately I'm not expecting to come to Hamburg so soon, else I could more easily look for them and others. However, I just don't know if it will be possible this summer. I yearn for Hamburg perpetually and I pass my favourite, albeit melancholy, hours sitting alone in the evening and reminiscing.

If you should send the books, address them to the music shop Gotthardt, Vienna, *Am Graben*. Letters as usual.

Now give my greetings to Fritz the Pinnebergian, write soon, ask for money, lots of money, live in health and happiness and think well of

your Johannes.

Tension was never far from the surface in Brahms's dealings with Clara Schumann and Joseph Joachim. Now a particularly sensitive occasion was about to cause general misunderstanding: a music festival in Bonn to raise money for a memorial to Robert Schumann.

Joachim was to conduct; Brahms was asked to write a piece specifically for the occasion but declined, eventually agreeing to a performance of his Requiem, instead. The organizers of the event did not respond to Brahms's letter; Joachim, always made nervous by any hesitation from Brahms, over-reacted to his laconic letters, joined by Clara who had her own backlog of grievances against him (although she was sympathetic to his position and wanted the Requiem on the programme). And Brahms, typically, could not be bothered to stay informed of what was going on and ended by being surprised and embittered that his Requiem was not to be performed after all. At the time, he was busy with the Op. 51 string quartets, the Haydn Variations, and some of the Op. 59 songs. For a while he was ready to give up the idea of attending the festival altogether.

It took Levi to patch things up, writing to Joachim that it pained him to see the three people who had been united in a powerful common experience all those years ago, now separated by petty differences. He asked Clara and Joachim to take Brahms as he was: that either he had been worth their friendship all these years, or they were mistaken all these years, but that Brahms himself had not changed and he would not be the one to make the first move.[1] In the end, the friends were reconciled, Brahms appeared in Bonn, and then spent several peaceful days with Clara in Baden-Baden where he showed her the summer's harvest.

283
Johannes Brahms to Friedrich Heimsoeth

[Vienna] Jan[uary 18]73

Most esteemed Sir,

I must not delay my reply to your worthy letter any longer and must decide to admit to you that I see no possibility of participating in your celebration in the desired spirit.

My reasons are so profoundly my concern alone that I would like to state beforehand or in passing: I know or can find absolutely no appropriate text. Should a poem such as Hölderlin's 'Schicksalslied' come my way, I don't know to what length it would entice me, in spite of my reservations. Having a text prepared especially for this occasion I do not consider possible, and it seems to me that your letter echoes the same opinion.

In the event that you were unable to help me in this, I could of course remain silent about my true reason—which I can probably not clarify briefly. But I just cannot get it through my head: why should I speak up, when the speaker should be he who speaks my language better [than I]? Or, if you like, why should anyone speak out at all, other than the one whose memory you are celebrating.

I suppose that when Joachim told me, during the summer, of your intention to perform my 'Requiem' on that occasion, I had the same scruples. At that time, I could keep them to myself, since it wasn't my business. But if I were now to write a piece expressly for that day, the same qualms would return more powerfully, be my business, and deter me.

I suppose I may be permitted to leave everything else unsaid. *The memory of Schumann is holy to me.* The noble, pure artist ever endures as my ideal and I will probably never be allowed to love a better person—and will also, I hope, never witness the progress of such a dreadful fate from such ghastly proximity—nor have to share so in enduring it.

How seriously I weighed your request, you have naturally taken as self-evident. Now I should like to know if you may perhaps find me right, in

---

[1] *JJ* iii. 115–16. See pp. 102–25 for a series of letters about this affair to and from Clara Schumann, Levi, and Brahms.

essence. What would most easily make me receptive to the opposite view, of course, is a text which could let me forget my scruples.

With great esteem, your very devoted

Johs Brahms.

284

Johannes Brahms to Joseph Joachim

[Vienna,] 3 April 1873

Dear friend,

Your letter just arrived and I sit down immediately.

I have never had much respect for committees, this winter I was able to study that species more minutely and must now acknowledge that your committee in Bonn is an outstanding specimen.

They do not contradict, but unless you are very obstinate they have their own way by means of lies and delays.

I have turned down the proposal to write a new piece for that occasion. I believe myself to have written to Heimsoeth at the beginning of January—since then I have heard *not one word*!

It is clear to me that in the question of the programme, the management thinks differently from you; but when on March 17th Wasielewski still writes about pending discussions with me, they are asserting their will in a less than honest fashion.

I might indeed even have looked for a reply from Heimsoeth, for although I had quite definitely declined, I still had hoped to listen politely to his opinion and possibly his approval of my point of view, my reasons.

This is precisely the way that my management dealt with the exhibition concerts just now—for which however I have no contractual obligations, therefore can simply decline the whole business.[2]

Why you should wish to perform my Requiem there—although—but I just cannot express my reasons for opposing it—so let it pass.

Why I should not like to deliver a special prologue, I hardly need tell you—but telling it to the committee would be in vain, which is why I emphasized above all that I know of absolutely no appropriate text.

Herr Ad. Behrens from London wrote to me recently in a very friendly manner, and sent me a rare book at the same time. Unfortunately I can not discover his address from his letter so as to thank him.

---

[2] The International Exposition, Vienna 1873.

Will you not take it on to tell him how greatly I was overjoyed by this token (etc.) and am indebted to him.

Your wife has unfortunately left us in the lurch for Saul!

On the other hand, keeping her word could have become even more dangerous for me! For we had to postpone our concert and your wife could not have come then anyhow!

I can be well satisfied with my winter and with my position, and above all, Bach's Easter Cantata gave me great pleasure recently.

Therefore, be careful in dealing with your committee and according to circumstance be rude, at any rate obstinate; by that method I have managed to get through the winter quite well.

Affectionate greetings!

Your J. Br.

285

Johannes Brahms to Joseph Joachim

[Vienna, end of April 1873]

Dear friend,

I have just come from Graz and am going to go to Munich this very day, therefore, just very hurriedly, a word or two. Wasielewski's last suggestion seems to me the best, and I would leave it at that.[3] The chorus will be greatly stressed, it's true; it's not clear to me how all this is supposed to be accomplished.

With regard to my possibly conducting the Requiem, I really don't quite know what to say. I can see no reason why I should not conduct it—but absolutely none why you shouldn't. Moreover, after removing this there would really be too little left for you, the actual director of the festival.

Here the decision is perhaps best left to the committee, in that it either wants you to conduct or, since I am cautious in my dealings with committees, fails to reach agreement with me. As I said, I don't actually know what to say, and should you be driven by some sentiment, act accordingly.

Maybe it would be better to omit the Variations for Two Pianos, *in case* I don't conduct?

Letters would probably reach me best through Levi, Munich; I don't know where the wind will blow me.

Very warm greetings also to your wife and so forth.

Your

Johannes.

[3] That Wasielewski conduct Schumann's *Peri*, and Joachim or Brahms conduct the Requiem.

On the occasion of the monument's unveiling, seven years later, Brahms was better able to voice his reservations about participating. At that time he wrote to Clara, 'To me it's an all too peculiar idea that a great musician should have his praises sung by a lesser one.'[4] But for the present, his inability to speak his mind led to a very serious misunderstanding.

286
Johannes Brahms to Joseph Joachim

[Munich-Tutzing, end of] June 1873

Dear Joachim,

From the newspapers I learn that my Requiem will not be performed in Bonn; I was even less pleased, however, to hear that you allude to a letter from me as the motivation.

I am supposed to have written diplomatically and supposedly it was unclear whether the performance would be to my liking.

If my letter was indeed the cause, I would of course have been pleased if you had simply written that to me or had devoted a second question to it, for I believe to have answered succinctly the one that was put to me. Otherwise, a good deal could all too easily be ascribed to a person who doesn't like to answer and argue. I am supposed to have written diplomatically? True, I did *remain silent* although there was much on my mind—about the whole affair itself. But not diplomatically, rather, simply according to my lazy writing habits. Here indeed it is urgent to make a clean breast of everything; to hold high the memory of the splendid person and artist in face of many reservations—and misinterpretations, to let the manner in which it is conducted provide a clear justification for the celebration.

But for that I write too hurriedly and with too little enthusiasm even about the most essential points. And I am therefore also unlikely ever to have written a diplomatic letter.

Nevertheless I believe that I have my wits sufficiently about me to know *what* I write, and that is reason enough why it would be very annoying to me if that letter said anything other than what I believe to have written. I also think that it would hardly have required the special insight of a friend to give it the correct reading. The matter itself, after all, had been discussed between us long ago; in your letter you merely asked which one of us should conduct and I simply said: that anything you wished and decided would be all right with me. I told you then that quite generally, another name seemed desir-

---

[4] *SBB* ii. 175–6, June 1879.

able, indeed necessary, to me. As leader of the festival, I would perhaps have closed it with Cherubini's Requiem, or something. After all, a performance of this kind is, for a living person, undoubtedly and under all circumstances an honour. But, indeed, an honour to which one's attitude would be rather silence, or even reluctance, out of a sense of most genuine modesty. Well, I certainly don't know if you think me capable of such modesty. In any case, modesty can easily look foolish, and prefers to remain silent—the way, indeed, I had [remained silent] towards you. But in this case: If you were to consider the situation and how it relates particularly to me, you would know how much and how profoundly a piece like the Requiem is altogether Schumann's. And how, in the secret recesses of my mind, it therefore had to seem quite self-evident to me that it would indeed be sung to him.

In any case it would have become difficult for me to comment further on this as well—in case that was expected. Now I also feel truly remote from the other participants—but in other matters one separates the artist and the person assiduously and energetically? This time a heavy stone falls once again upon the better half by far—but my long-windedness is not going to help him get down! [5]

I mustn't go on writing.—Let me confess and do believe this: I had actually intended to write to you very cheerfully that I had never believed in a performance because the committee did not wish it and—'the esteemed director be a polite gentleman'. I would be sorry if you took that amiss, but I prefer to think this is the case and do believe it.

That my letter now has a different ring, is that due to a growing melancholy, or merely the aversion to writing? But in any case,—if my last letter was not sufficient proof, this one surely is—that I am no letter writer. Be it long or short, I believe sincerely that even with the best of intentions, one can extract from it little that is good—but one can effortlessly read into it much that is otherwise.

Do not do so, deal gingerly with it. In spite of all the confusion, this [letter] was actually intended to provoke a warmly reassuring reply. Since I can scarcely hope for that, I close without a question mark.

Your J. Brahms.

[5] i.e. bring Schumann back to life?

287
Joseph Joachim to Johannes Brahms

[Berlin] 7th July 1873

Dear Brahms!

You write that I allude to a letter from you as the motivation for having at the last minute abandoned the idea, originally warmly embraced by me, of performing *your* Requiem for the Schumann celebration. But as my reason I have *expressly* stated that after careful attention to the Schumann works which are to be performed, it seemed to me impossible to crowd into a span of two rehearsals and two performance days so much that needs learning; and that I would rather forgo my pet idea than to let the performance suffer from it. *Nobody* will have read *a different* word from me, and apart from my wife only one other, a very intimate friend of ours,[6] heard me say that your letter, your whole manner, unfortunately, gives me the impression that you did not truly support the matter with heart and soul, and might in the end prefer not to have your name tied to it. Well, a person cannot always resist his impressions! But let us be quite open: I sensed quite generally, in recent years, that whenever we got together you were unable to recapture your former tone towards me, one which, I will gladly admit, you even made several very polite attempts to rediscover. There could be ten different reasons for this and I am very far from saying that it might not also be partly my fault. Indeed, have I not surely disappointed many expectations you entertained for my development, have I not seemed to you in many ways more indolent than you would have liked, was I not also needlessly more sparing in tokens of my assuredly genuine affection—God! what accusations can an honest man not make against himself![7] What then was more natural than for me to imagine that although you flinch from saying so, you perceived our old connection, which precisely with respect to the Schumanns, filled me with great warmth, as a vexation rather than as something desirable. You require so much energy for your work that I understand when you do not always consider it worth while to make your feelings explicit to others, preferring to let things run their course as they will. But on this occasion in particular, I seemed to feel duty bound not to deceive myself, and so vanished the enthusiasm with which I had at first thought I could satisfy you,

---

[6] Either Clara Schumann or Hermann Levi.

[7] Joachim was correct here with regard to Brahms's earlier expectations for his development. See Brahms's letter to Joachim, 16 Feb. 1855 (49) and the comments which follow, and his letter to Grimm, July 1858 (99).

in spite of many difficulties with the work. You asked for an answer soothing
to the soul; I wonder if this is one? It would give me real grief, but nevertheless I should almost consider it a consolation, if you were sorry that now
your work will not sound out at the celebration.

With great esteem, your faithful

Joseph J.

288

Johannes Brahms to Joseph Joachim [postcard]

[Tutzing, 20 July 1873]

Dear Joachim. The letter was of course the most I could have expected.
Perhaps a quiet moment will turn up in Bonn—I just wanted to say a word
beforehand.

As ever,

and as ever in a hurry,

your

J. Brahms.

In the midst of this drama, Brahms was preparing to spend the summer near his
friends in Munich, choosing the village of Tutzing on the Starnberger See, in the
foothills of the German Alps. It proved a fruitful choice, both socially and musically.
He fraternized with people who became influential enthusiasts of his art, and completed the Op. 59 songs, the Haydn Variations in both versions, and both string
quartets in Op. 51.

289

Johannes Brahms to Theodor Billroth[8]

Tutzing, Bavaria [July 1873]

Dear friend!

I am about to publish my string quartets—not the first, but for the first
time.

It is not merely the affectionate thought of you and your friendship that
prompts me to put your name at the head of the first one; I just like to think

---

[8] Billroth and Brahms must have agreed to address each other in the familiar 'Du' form shortly
before parting for the summer holiday. This is the first letter written in that form.

of you, and with such special *plaisir*, as violin and 'sextet-player'.[9] You would doubtless accept a volume of enormously difficult piano variations more kindly and would find it more befitting your attainments? There's no help for it, you just have to put up with the dedication even with the droll little ulterior motive.

I wouldn't have gone to the expense of two letters for this, but you have so many titles that I don't know which ones—to leave off. One who is unaccustomed to wearing them handles the stuff with greater caution!—Would you kindly provide me with the necessary modulation?

Quartet
for 2 Viol . . . .

. . . .
. . . .

by
J. B.

Actually, I really ought not disclose to you that the quartet in question derives from the famous C minor, for now when of an evening you think about it and fantasize in it, you will all too readily over-fantasize, and thereafter—you will like the second one better. My address is Tutzing on the Starnberger See. (Actually, Carlsbad may well be a better address?) With warm greetings to you and your wife,

Your
Joh. Brahms

Billroth was aware of the distinction this dedication would confer. In 1890 he predicted—correctly—to his friend and fellow physician and scientist, T. W. Engelmann, the dedicatee of the third quartet Op. 67, 'I'm afraid these dedications will keep our names known longer than our best work.'[10]

This letter, in any event, contains many riddles. Why shouldn't someone prefer the second one? Is 'the famous C minor' an earlier quartet of his? Or perhaps a reference to the still unfinished First Symphony, which Billroth had already seen? Or to the work of another composer? Why might Carlsbad, a famous medicinal spa, have been a better address? The comment is probably a self-deprecatory joke; one cannot possibly take seriously Kalbeck's suggestion that Brahms had an inkling of ill health to come, 25 years later, and of his eventual sojourn in Carlsbad. Brahms was then in the prime of life and virtually never ill.

---

[9] Referring to soirées in Billroth's house and to an incident highly embarrassing to Billroth: while still in Zurich in the 1860s, Billroth became so nervous at the prospect of playing the viola in the Sextet in B flat that someone else had to take his place. Billroth was a better pianist than violist.

[10] *Bil–B* 201 n. 4.

290
Johannes Brahms to Simrock

[Tutzing,] 27 August 1873

Dear Simrock,

... Something like half an hour later I passed through Bonn, for together with Hiller, I had fortunately missed the first train. Today I am finally here and find everything quite lovely—except for pen and ink!

I left the 2 quartets in Munich yesterday, in order to hear them again one of these days. When I send them to you I would like to reserve for myself the sales for France and Belgium. England, Morocco, and other robber-nations will be left to you.

But are a thousand thaler for 2 scruffy quartets not too much for you? I would like to enclose letters in order to make the demand plausible. Arrangements for four hands I would supply at 30 Friedrichsdors a piece. I have not said the final word to my French publisher, but I suppose I should include his honorarium? You can write whatever you like to me, for I didn't use your letter from Baden as collateral.[11] It was however very enjoyable in Baden and people asked after you, at the 'Bear'. And every evening, as a certain somebody passed a certain window, he whistled

and longing swelled his breast, and sighs sounded in the still of the night, and he begs to send his greetings as your devoted

certain somebody

J. Brahms.

The quotation from the mandolin accompaniment to the Serenade in Mozart's *Don Giovanni* was Brahms's affectionate greeting to Clara Simrock. Whatever letters of recommendation he was referring to here, one arrived a week later from an acquaintance who had just heard the quartets performed at Levi's house: 'To me, yesterday, it was as though I witnessed the baptism of two children who are destined to become famous men.'[12]

To Joachim went a veiled apology for not having dedicated these, his first published string quartets, to the man who was not only his oldest friend but the most consummate quartet-player in Germany.

---

[11] To secure a loan.   [12] Rochus Freiherr von Liliencron (*BW* ix. 146 n. 1).

291
Johannes Brahms to Joseph Joachim

[Vienna, mid-October 1873]

Dear Joachim,

I have just heard from Simrock that on Saturday you are playing my A minor Quartet—in just two words I'd like to say how especially that pleases me. Actually, I didn't mean either of the two for your violin, but waiting for something better eventually seemed useless—you must also have thought something of the sort?

The quartet will never before have pleased me as well as when I think of you on Saturday and listen in my thoughts.

Warmest greeting, to your wife and others too.

Utterly your

Johannes

The International Exposition of 1873 drew Brahms's friends to Vienna from all over. The Haydn Variations were premièred on 2 November, Brahms conducting Dessoff's Philharmonic Orchestra from the manuscript.

292
Johannes Brahms to Hermann Levi

[Vienna,] Oct[ober 18]73

Dear friend,

Your memory must be deceiving you. I believe to have said that I would be glad to use *Manfred* as the occasion for inviting Bernays to Vienna, but that in Lewinsky we had a splendid narrator who has also recited *Manfred* several times and that I can therefore invite no one else.[13]

I hope very much that you are coming at month's end, Allgeyer too! I hope you'll then also listen in on a rehearsal of the Variations—otherwise I'm a far too lonely listener and critic.

You could do me a great favour by smuggling in as much tobacco as possible. Stuff your pockets with Strassburg packets, I beg you, it's very easy and not dangerous, to me a good deed for the whole winter.[14]

---

[13] An old acquaintance, Michael Bernays, had just been called to the University of Munich as Extraordinary Professor of Literature.

[14] There are many similar requests in Brahms's correspondence, made to a variety of friends.

Schieber (or Hieber) was here. He has not seen Stephan yet, but seems to be studying diligently day and night.[15]

My warmest greetings to you and forgive me that this does not bother to look like a letter.

About the International Exposition I've probably already provided an account, and to some extent you're both prepared for what awaits you.

Best greetings to everyone conceivable.

Your

Johannes.

293

Johannes Brahms to Hermann Levi, [in pencil]

[Vienna, end of October 1873]

In case you are free this evening: you will find Lachner, Nottebohm, me, at Gause's, Johannesgasse (beer hall). Until about 8–8.30, I'll be at home.

J. Br.

Gause's Beer Hall was the setting for Brahms's *Stammtisch*, the table regularly set aside for him and his mostly bachelor friends. They called their *Stammtisch* 'The Cynic's Bench', and met to drink, talk, tease, and poke fun at each other. Gustav Nottebohm, Eduard Hanslick, the exceedingly witty and well known satirist Daniel Spitzer, and the music critic Ludwig Speidel were some of the regulars. Not all guests enjoyed the rampant sarcasm.[16]

࣭࣭ **1874** ࣭࣭

Late in December 1873, Brahms was awarded the Order of Maximilian for Science and Art by King Ludwig of Bavaria (the other recipient that year was Richard Wagner). The honour was the more surprising as Brahms's music was virtually ignored in Munich at that time; but friends were at work—Franz Lachner and Paul Heyse had come to know Brahms well during his summer in Tutzing, and their influence carried the day. Levi proved indefatigable at guiding the newly acclaimed composer through the required formalities. The result is probably the stiffest letter Brahms ever wrote—yet even here the artist says more than mere formality demanded.[1]

---

[15] The Cathedral of St Stephen, a prime tourist attraction of Vienna, affectionately referred to as a person.

[16] See Kal, ii³. 423 ff.

[1] Twelve years later Levi would coach Bruckner, too, on the correct manner of writing to King

294
Johannes Brahms to Ludwig II, King of Bavaria

Almighty King, Most Gracious King and Lord!

Your Majesty has had the noble grace to favour the undersigned, your most humble and obedient servant, by most graciously bestowing your Order of Maximilian. While I beg that Your Majesty deign to accept my thanks for this so great and happy distinction, as humble as they are deeply felt, I feel keenly how much words fail me in giving adequate expression to these thanks. Just as to the artist in his earlier youth no goal seemed too high, too difficult to attain, so now for the more mature adult does the time not come easily when he believes he has reached the goal, merited the prize. Only the certain knowledge that by further and earnest striving I will not become less worthy of the Order, do I permit myself to dare to wear the esteemed badge, and to express to Your Majesty my most humble and deeply felt thanks.

I remain Your Majesty's most humble and obedient servant,

Johannes Brahms

Vienna, the 10th of January 1874

To his stepmother, he was more relaxed as he answered her query: 'It's true, I did receive a notable medal, which is worn large as life on one's chest and is by no means one of the worst.'[2]

Brahms had received the first volume of Spitta's Bach biography just before leaving for Tutzing. It provided his summer reading. Now, with evident pride, Brahms sent the Bach scholar programmes from two of his recent concerts, at which he had performed some of Bach's most demanding choral works: *Christ lag in Todesbanden* (BWV 4) was a first performance in Vienna. A few months later he had presented an a capella performance of the choral 'Es ist genug', and the massive *Nun ist das Heil und die Kraft* (BWV 50), a fugue for double chorus, orchestra, and organ.[3]

Brahms repeated the last named work as the Gesellschaft's contribution to the grand concert organized to honour Liszt's farewell from the Viennese concert stage. Undoubtedly he thought that with such exalted music he was paying Liszt a very

Ludwig when thanking him for accepting the dedication of his Seventh Symphony, advising him to fill his letter with ' "Your most humble servant, and Your most gracious Lord", since he sets great store by such formalities' (letter of 26 Apr. 1885).

  [2] 16 Feb. 1874 (*Familie*, 212).

  [3] An a capella performance was surely a *tour de force*. The final chorus of Cantata BWV 60 ('O Ewigkeit, du Donnerwort') is tonally so ambiguous that Alban Berg easily incorporated it into his violin concerto; and the double chorus is long and arduous.

great tribute, but not everyone agreed and there was grumbling that he could find the choir nothing more agreeable and less lengthy to sing than the 'horrible' double fugue.[4]

Spitta, naturally, was not among the grumblers; he considered the 'gigantic work, with its crushing weight and its savage cry of triumph . . . an imperishable memorial to German art.'[5] Much taken with the passacaglia of the Haydn Variations, he now announced his intention to send Brahms two unknown Ciaconnas and a Passacaglia by Buxtehude. The composer was delighted.

295
Johannes Brahms to Philipp Spitta[6]

Vienna, [before 11] Jan[uary] 1874

Most Honoured Sir!

Just in a rush and briefly I would like to thank you wholeheartedly for your letter, which gave me great pleasure.

In thinking about your friendly intention, I would like to inform you that I found here and have already copied Buxtehude's D minor Passacaglia.

Naturally, I am all the more grateful for further news about such treasures.

You got hold of my quartets faster than I could have had them sent to you through Simrock. That is what he wrote to me when I placed the order.

I thought of you warmly recently, and wished you here as a listener.

It is true that in Germany, Vienna is spoken of with a certain shrug of the shoulders. But do you think major performances of such Bach works as on the enclosed programmes are easy to do?

I can't help but think of Reinthaler in Bremen, who tried several times in vain to get through the easy *Ich hatte viel Bekümmernis*.[7]

My chorus sings the things with enthusiasm, and in concerts that is the main thing for the public and critics. So naturally I will have nothing further to do with discussions in the *Allgem[eine] Musik[alische] Zeitung*.

Regarding the reputation of that gentleman (Prof. Weiß), you can learn about him from reviews in earlier issues of that journal. Indeed, his

---

[4] The concert took place on 11 January 1874. Liszt's name was printed on the programme in large letters, with all other participants, including Brahms and the choral society of the Gesellschaft, listed in small print. See Kal, iii. 19.

[5] *J. S. Bach* (Leipzig, 1873, 1880), ii. 562.

[6] Incorrectly dated in *BW* xvi. This letter, No. 15 in the collection, must have been written before 11 January (the date of the Liszt concert), and should follow No. 12. The rest of the published sequence is correct.

[7] BWV 21. Brahms had performed it in Detmold during his appointment there.

suggestion to sing the double fugue *lower* and to alternate with piano is sufficient evidence.

My chorus sings the fugue a capella and as gladly and easily as a Mendelssohn psalm.

I'm prattling with you about useless stuff, contrary to my usual practice.

Perhaps that is because we sang that chorus again yesterday evening. We are performing it on Sunday for the 2nd time (in the Liszt Concert).

If only you could be there: it is a splendid thing! I don't know if Nottebohm has carried out his intention to write to you. He is most delighted with your book, calls it simply the best biography written about a musician.

Finally, excuse the hurriedly written mess and accept the best greetings of your

very devoted

J. Brahms

The Professor Weiss who earned Brahms's contempt wrote a review faulting Bach's very conception in crafting the entire cantata *Christ lag in Todesbanden* out of the material of the chorale. Weiss wrote, '[the] strange property of the work was more evident to the score reader than to the listener'. The work lacked sensuous beauty, he continued, and he called it gloomy, strict and dry, more oppressive than exalted, and artfully complex. He claimed his right, as a genuine admirer of Bach, to speak his mind, grudgingly praised Brahms's performance of it, then went on to nitpick.[8] Undeterred by comments like this, Brahms had gone on to make the public aware of the even more severe double fugue. Now he was interested in making Buxtehude's Passacaglia known to the world: on his own he had discovered a copy of one of the very pieces Spitta was having copied for him. There is only one known source— a book formerly in possession of Andreas Bach, one of Johann Sebastian's nephews.[9]

---

[8] *Allgemeine Musikalische Zeitung*, No. 16, 16 April 1873, 252–3.

[9] Both Chaconnes and the Passacaglia came from this source, which Spitta must have had. The chaconnes were later catalogued as Bux WV 159 and 160, the Passacaglia in D minor as Bux WV 161. The terms are confusing; Brahms uses chaconne and passacaglia interchangeably, while Spitta does not. Both forms make use of an ostinato, a motive repeated incessantly throughout the music: in Spitta's definition, the motive of a Passacaglia provides the bass line, in a chaconne it is allowed to move to upper voices. The Finale of the Haydn Variations is a chaconne, because from mm. 426–45 the motive moves through the oboe, flute, and horn. In this case, the key makes clear which piece Brahms had in hand.

296
Johannes Brahms to Philipp Spitta

[Vienna, *c*.19] January 1874

Dear Sir,

Allow me a hurried question; when I get to know such beautiful things as the D minor Chaconne by Buxtehude, I can hardly resist letting a publisher know about them, quite simply on the basis of giving pleasure to more [people].

But as to this piece (with which I wanted favour Rieter), I would like to ask you beforehand whether for any reason whatsoever you have anything against publication (either of this one or an occasional other).

In the most favourable case: [I wonder] whether you have a particularly reliable version. Mine came to me with Joh. Andr. Bach's organ book (1754) by way of Michaelis from Nottebohm; it is not entirely trustworthy.

I will add that this is definitely not a business proposition for me; also, that my name will not appear; you can therefore say a simple yes or no without embarrassment.

Wouldn't you like to do this soon, as I have to go to Leipzig in a week and might put the piece in my suitcase.

Nottebohm is particularly curious about the Suites by Böhm; he assumes you got to know more and better ones than he in Leipzig.

Perhaps the package you kindly promised will answer this? Of course, whatever you send goes back, if you wish.

In haste, with my best greetings,

your very devoted

J. Brahms

It is an interesting comment on the spate of editions of Baroque music then pouring forth that Spitta opposed publication of the Passacaglia separately, fearing the piece would disappear in the flood of new works appearing daily. It was later included in Buxtehude's *Collected Works for Organ*, published in two volumes by Breitkopf & Härtel (1875–6) and edited by Spitta alone. Spitta suggested they might work together to publish practical editions of the cantatas of Bach (Brahms's participation would help sell copies, he wrote) an idea which bore fruit several years later.

The Georg Böhm mentioned here (1661–1733) was an organist and composer active in Lüneburg, where Bach spent important years of his youth. Spitta considered four of Böhm's keyboard suites to have been of importance to Bach. He answered Brahms's enquiry by placing the manuscripts at Nottebohm's disposal, a nice reminder that 'networking' is not a new concept.

Leipzig, first the scene of Brahms's astonishing early success, then of his most painful failure, was now ready to receive him again after a long period of neglect bordering on disdain. Brahms was invited to play and conduct an all-Brahms programme at the Gewandhaus. His answer went to the conductor.

297
Johannes Brahms to Carl Reinecke

[Vienna, beginning] Jan[uary 18]74

Esteemed friend,

I suppose I may direct this reply to you, as well. Given the haste in which I write, it suits me to be able to write without any fuss to a friendly colleague. As you see, fate makes rapid strides. Now the 'Quartet' and 'Rinaldo' and one Yes leads to the next. How often have I forsworn playing in public! Either not at all or all the time. Here, where I am after all known and was prompted often enough, I do not play, and now I am supposed to do so in your town. On the other hand, it seems to me childish to refuse.

My chamber music is played often enough in Leipzig, isn't it? I don't wish to resort to your method of aiding it: I suppose I am secretly too vain about my playing. Therefore go ahead, as far as I am concerned you may put a piano performance on the list. I'll practise.

Nor do I want to turn down the 'Rinaldo', but I am afraid to look at it. It seems to me a fairly useless piece and people in Leipzig will comprehend less and less why I came.

Forgive me for all this chatter and the long-windedness. I am something of a hermit and inept in my outside dealings. Commend me to your fellow directors and tell them that I am grateful for their invitation and—resigned to my fate.

With my best greetings,

your
J. Brahms.

As a matter of fact Brahms's chamber music was hardly ever played in Leipzig. But as a consequence of the Gewandhaus invitation, three concerts of his music were scheduled in the course of the week. Brahms played his *Variations on a Theme by Handel*, the *Liebeslieder Waltzes* with Reinecke, and appeared in Leipzig's first hearing of the Piano Quartet in G minor. He conducted *Rinaldo*, the Alto Rhapsody, the Haydn Variations, and three Hungarian Dances in his own orchestration (the only ones he ever sanctioned). Clara made the trip to Leipzig especially for the occasion, and Brahms renewed his connection with Heinrich and Elizabet von Herzogenberg, the start of one of the most important friendships of his life.[10]

Honours came from all sides, now. If Brahms once had reason to fret that the director of the Music Festival of the Lower Rhine had not invited him to conduct his *Triumphlied* himself (Letter 276 n. 16) Hiller made up for that offence by extending a very warm invitation to the current year's Festival. Brahms was quick to answer.

298
Johannes Brahms to Ferdinand Hiller

January 1874

Dear and cherished friend,

If paper could speak as easily and plainly as one's face, this letter would be smiling at you most pleasantly. I value a performance at your festival as highly as a very special 'Maximilian' and I'm as much embarrassed by it as I am perhaps secretly delighted by the award.

Luckily, jolliness is always in good supply—or don't you incidentally find it very jolly that I should be performimg my Triumphlied at three music festivals this summer? In May with you, June in Basle, July in Zurich. Besides that, I am strongly urged to perform it here in April, which I'm naturally resisting with all my might.

Naturally, I request that my piece precede your Oratorium.[11] There might be less need for a lot of words here than—to gratify my pleasure and my thanks a little.

We're now reading your Mendelssohn book with the greatest enjoyment here. The most dissimilar people here are united in praise and admiration of you and your hero.[12]

Our Liszt week was most interesting. I had been somewhat apprehensive about it and now am delighted above all at how dignified and good his behaviour was throughout. That's also the way he played—therefore not quite to the satisfaction of one 25th of the people; all in all, that's also the reason enthusiasm did not really build. As you know, people are used to

[10] For Clara's spirited description of the events, see her long letter to Hermann Levi in Kal, iii³. 8–9, and Litz, iii. 310–11. On Brahms's relationship to Leipzig see Johannes Forner, *Johannes Brahms in Leipzig* (Leipzig, 1987). The Hungarian Dance arrangements were for Nos. 1, 3, and 10, orchestrated by him in self-defence, as he told Levi, as arrangements were 'raining down on all sides'. (*BW* vii. 162).

[11] In answer to Hiller's request for the order of the programme.

[12] Hiller's latest book, *Mendelssohn: Letters and Recollections*, based on their childhood friendship and with many letters from Mendelssohn to Hiller. The English translation, prepared with Hiller's co-operation shortly after, makes fascinating reading in its own right.

exceptional entertainment from Liszt. We have him here quite often and so I'm really pleased that at last, grey hair and all, he presented an image which does not make a complete caricature of the magnificent person. You must now be feeling very content, and I wish I could invite myself to join you for coffee, sometime.

I am actually travelling to Leipzig soon, but the route is no longer by way of Prague and moreover I am in such a great rush—as in writing letters!

I beg you to excuse this rush, to give my best greetings to your daughter and to commend me to her.[13]

Sincerely devoted, your

J. Brahms.

In a woe-filled letter, Clara revealed her latest trial: Felix had just been diagnosed with tuberculosis. From Munich, where Levi had arranged a pair of concerts for him, Brahms replied:

299
Johannes Brahms to Clara Schumann

Vienna, 19 March 1874

Dear Clara,

It is unutterably difficult for me to express in even a few words with what heartfelt sympathy and anxious concern I think of you. Since I last saw Felix—with what melancholy I constantly think of you. I feel your sorrow and pain far too deeply to attempt to give it words. My own pain, too, I am thoroughly used to keeping entirely to myself and deep within me.

My feelings for you go far deeper, are far more loving; no thought goes out to you but that it envelops you totally and is conscious of all your sorrows. But I can only await in silence how far this new trial will take you. God grant that the greatest pain of all is not again in store for you, for one human lifespan you have borne enough.

I cannot attempt to console you; in your efforts to bear up, you will long since have tried on your own anything I could suggest. May you succeed in this as in the past—whatever may be in store for you.

From ever so many [people] I am to convey the most affectionate thoughts. Let this earnest love also be some consolation to you—I love you more than myself or anyone or anything on earth. But of course one can only share your suffering, one cannot relieve you of even the smallest portion!

---

[13] The letter found Hiller in Prague, where his daughter was making her stage début.

I hardly need to tell you about Munich, everything was probably just as you might have imagined it. The performances very good, the public very friendly, and all of us, beside the musicians, particularly Heyse and Bernays, happily and often together. Wüllner and Lachner also always with us.[14]

That you (and I, too) are not at the Conservatory is certainly a great bit of luck.

The stories are far from pleasant, and since they are unfortunately based on serious causes, the prospects are not promising.

And now that 'fraudulent' performance of Christ with an outside conductor, conservatory, and Stockhausen! You might dictate something about that to Marie sometime.[15]

Unfortunately we have masses of music during Holy Week. Apart from the Sing-Akademie and the Men's Choral Society: the *Messiah* and another concert in the opera, and I, *Salomo*.[16]

I cannot ever abide the thought of 'too much music'!

Many people are travelling to Italy; among our acquaintances for example, Billroth, Hanslick, Dr Ebner, etc.

Frau Ebner is very well and the little one (who is horrendously big) is too.

I now send my most affectionate greetings to yours, and let me hear from you as soon as you can.

I think of you most tenderly.

Your Johannes.

That summer, after two months of travel and concerts, Brahms found another lakeside dwelling, this time in the Swiss village of Rüschlikon, near Zurich. Songs, vocal quartets, and the *New Liebeslieder Waltzes* were among the summer's yield.[17] There were new friends (a trio of Swiss artists; playwright Josef Viktor Widmann, poet and novelist Gottfried Keller, and the conductor and violinist Friedrich Hegar) and as was his custom, Brahms invited old friends as summer visitors.

[14] The poet Paul Heyse, one of the first Nobel Laureates in literature, and Professor Michael Bernays, Professor of Literature and long acquainted with Brahms. For an account of the concerts, see Kal, iii. 21 ff.

[15] Both Brahms and Clara had declined invitations to join the faculty of Joachim's Hochschule several years earlier, and now felt justified by one of Joachim's irrational episodes having to do with anxiety over Stockhausen's participation in a performance at the rival Stern's Conservatory. *Christus* was a recent oratorio by Friedrich Kiel, professor of composition at the Conservatory, but until 1870 on Stern's faculty. Clara's arm was ailing at this time, requiring that she dictate her letters to her daughter.

[16] By Handel. Brahms performed a fragment of the oratorio.

[17] Opp. 61, 65, much of Op. 63, some of Op. 64. He was also at work on the First Symphony, and the Piano Quartet, Op. 60.

300
Johannes Brahms to Ottilie Ebner

Rüschlikon on Lake Zurich, June 1874

Greatly esteemed dear friend!

Your kind letter saw quite a few cities and people before it found me; I suppose by rights this note should now describe the journey? But I prefer imagining myself in your quiet valley or looking out of the window at the lake and mountains to thinking back to all that turmoil. This is surely ungrateful of me, for everyone sincerely meant well by me everywhere. I too would take the greatest pleasure in it [the trip] if I could still watch my father being delighted at how his son is being spoiled. Now I am staying very prettily on the lake, and indeed I secured the *very* windows in the *very* house that I had picked out as the most desirable, from the steamer. I have a certain amount of skill and much luck with dwellings.[18]

Before that I spent 4 weeks in Bonn; with me you would have enjoyed the Rhine festival a lot more than that time alone. And while the Gürzenich [in Cologne] is a lovely concert-hall, the Münster in Basle is that and more, and the cloister next to it is wonderful to walk in, and through it one looks down on the beautiful Rhine. Actually I was very cheerful the whole time and enjoyed everything enormously. The good wine, the beautiful—landscapes, and whatever else is of the best. I suppose your husband has had enough of all that for one year, unfortunately, so you probably won't be travelling to Switzerland? In Zurich there is another music festival!

I am less worried about Franz[19] than about the condition of your father. He is probably staying at your house, and I suppose everyone's gentle feelings allow him to bear his suffering so patiently.

It would be really friendly if sometime you would sit down at your writing desk again. You wouldn't believe what pleasure it is to read a letter from you, one senses its contentment.

My best greetings to your father, mother, husband, sister, and to whomever else you wish. With the warmest devotion, your

Johs. Brahms.

Among the nine songs of Op. 63 are three set to texts of Klaus Groth.

---

[18] His technique was simple: he would go to the local barber and strike up a conversation, thereby discovering what was for rent in the neighbourhood.
[19] Her brother.

301
Johannes Brahms to Klaus Groth

[Vienna,] September [18]74

Dear friend,

I should have written a letter so long ago that I cannot possibly make up for it today—and also cannot possibly offer any excuses for myself! I just want to pose a small question.

In a forthcoming volume of my songs there will appear your poems:

'How cosy was that little hamlet'
'Oh would I knew the way back'
'As a boy, I saw the flowers bloom'

(p. 35, 36, 37 in your High German poems). Now I would like to ask if perhaps a collective title, or a heading for each one comes to your mind?

I am unfortunately not satisfied with my composition of the pretty 2nd one! I want to reserve the possibility of setting it to music again and better, one of these days; meanwhile and till then this will have to suffice—I should like to keep the 3 together.

I also wish to thank you most warmly for your last kind letter. Feuerbach has not painted me yet—I am in even greater dread of that than of writing paper![20]

I do have pictures of you, and naturally you won't find yours among the 'jumble', I have other shelves as well!

Were it not for the wrapping, I would send you a big picture of myself at once, I'll resolve to do it soon.

But I do want to request your 3 boys together![21]

Now be greeted from the bottom of my heart and best greetings also to Dr Thomsen, Uncle Köster.[22]

Entirely yours,
J. Brahms.

IV, Carlsgasse 4.

[20] Anselm Feuerbach's plan to paint Brahms's portrait faltered in November 1873. 'I wasn't angry with Brahms for a second, but for the time being his canvas has been put aside,' he wrote to his mother.* Additional Note p. 753

[21] Groth, visiting Brahms's home during the International Exposition in the previous year, noticed a table full of photographs. Now he wrote, 'My wife thinks that you would enjoy owning a picture of our three fine boys . . . Naturally I didn't tell her how many pictures of beautiful ladies I saw in a jumble on your table. Therefore I hardly dare ask if you have a picture of my wife and me.' Then he asked the composer for a copy of the large photograph which he had seen in a music shop in Budapest.

[22] Groth's friends in Hamburg, avid admirers of Brahms's music.

302
Klaus Groth to Johannes Brahms

Kiel, 27 September 1874

Dear friend!

In vain have I tortured my brain for two days, trying to find suitable titles or something appropriate. If the title isn't both short and pregnant, one is always better off using the opening words. 'Heimweh' and 'Longing' and their synonyms are too over-used, two-part headings such as 'Child's Happiness, Man's Yearning', sound and taste too sophisticated. Were you to write

'From the Paradise of Childhood'

it would be fine with me; should you find something suitable for all three songs together or for each one separately on your own, go ahead and use whatever titles you like: Most important, after all, are the words underneath, and even more important for me, your music (for I am not attached to my own words). . . .

Brahms's solution was simple. He named the songs 'Heimweh' I, II, and III. In doing so, he attached the notion of unattainable longing, in this case for irretrievable childhood, to all the three songs. Brahms's dissatisfaction with 'the second one' is not shared by many: 'Heimweh' II, 'O wüßt' ich doch den Weg zurück' (Op. 63 No. 8) became one of his best-loved songs.

In planning his concerts, Brahms frequently programmed music by contemporary composers of the classical-romantic school such as Albert Dietrich, Josef Rheinberger, Carl Goldmark, and Robert Volkmann. Volkmann's cello concerto interested him—Schumann's concerto was seldom played and Dvořák's had not yet been written, so Volkmann's substantial work was something of a novelty.[23] A composer's concern for the integrity of his music speaks out here.

303
Johannes Brahms to Robert Volkmann

[Vienna,] Nov[ember 18]74

Most honoured Sir,

On the 28th of February we will have the pleasure of hearing your concerto for violoncello in a Gesellschaft concert. And now, in spite of all their

---

[23] Three editions of the work were still available in the early 1960s.

enthusiasm for the work, our esteemed cellists persistently speak of 'cuts' that are supposed to be absolutely necessary.

I have before me a score in which Herr Popper's cuts are indicated.[24] I now permit myself to enquire whether you might possibly be in agreement with *these* cuts?! Whether you wish to indicate others (cuts and cadenzas)— or want the work performed as it was printed.

My virtuoso, the young, very talented Herr Hummer, will undoubtedly follow your wishes, as will I. May I request you very urgently to say a word regarding this as soon as possible?

Excuse the haste in which I write, with the best greetings
from
your very devoted
J.Brahms

IV, Carlsgasse 4.

Volkmann replied: '*Popper's* cuts save *one minute* or *a minute and a half* at most, and aren't worth the trouble of *crippling* the performance.' He was delighted with the possibility of a complete performance (which, however, did not materialize).

ঙ্গ 1875 ১৯

There would be only three more concerts under Brahms's leadership. Viennese intrigue and Brahms's unwillingness to compromise on the quality and style of music he programmed led to the inevitable: an old rival, Johann Franz von Herbeck, saw the opportunity to take back his former position. Brahms resigned. But amidst the manœuvring, there was still a complete performance of Bach's St Matthew Passion to prepare. The following letter is a powerful reminder that Brahms grew up in the household of a working musician. With obvious conviction and a minimum of punctuation, he dashed it off and sent it despite several ink smudges.

---

[24] David Popper (1846–1913), leading cellist and pedagogue. His technical studies are still the foundation of cello technique. Reinhold Hummer was the cellist of the Rosé Quartet.

304
Johannes Brahms to the Directors of the
Gesellschaft der Musikfreunde

[19 March 1875]

Honoured Sirs,

I take the liberty of informing you hurriedly and briefly of the following matter and of commending it to your kind attention.

For the performance of the Passion on Shrove Tuesday I had originally scheduled 3 full rehearsals with orchestra for Friday, Saturday, and Monday.

Because of the participation of the Singverein in today's Artists' Evening the second rehearsal has become impossible. (Mainly in consideration of the ladies taking part.) It follows, naturally, that both remaining rehearsals are of unseemly length. Instead of the customary 3 rehearsals of scant 2 hours each, this time we have 2 rehearsals of a good 3 hours.

This and related matters were openly discussed by the orchestra at yesterday's rehearsal, and I could not help but declare that for my part, it had not entered my mind to lay claim unduly to the gentlemen's time and effort and—thereby hoping to save a rehearsal (and the money for it) at the same time. Therefore I did not fail belatedly to submit to the gentlemen the simple mathematical equation, that 2×3 is as good as 3×2—i.e. that under these circumstances I am holding 2 rehearsals and consider myself obliged to pay for 3.

I expect I hardly need to indicate the particulars: that the Passion requires such extensive rehearsals; that I relinquished today's rehearsal most reluctantly; that I cannot offer the gentlemen some arbitrary small compensation, but can only concur that they have earned their customary wages and have merely accomplished it in a different way; that, for various reasons, I do not wish to shorten Monday's rehearsal and possibly rehearse individual sections early on Tuesday morning etc. etc.

To me the whole matter seems quite simple and, I hope, equally so to the other esteemed gentlemen of the Committee. Should this not be the case, I most urgently request that the gentlemen of the orchestra definitely be compensated as usual for 3 rehearsals, since I will very gladly accept personal responsibility in any case.

Finally, I ask you to excuse the haste and hurry of this communication.

With extreme respect
Your very faithful
J. Brahms

305
Johannes Brahms to Hermann Levi

[Early? April 1875]

Dear friend,

Of couse it can all be said in one word: *Herbeck*! Nothing has happened, but the prospects are not pleasing and so I prefer to go. I do not wish either to quarrel with him nor wait until he has got rid of me.

To relate details in writing is too long-winded and boring for me.

But perhaps it could be done in person, I don't know where my path will lead. My table is covered with *Italian* travel books, although I'm thinking of leaving that till autumn.

Meanwhile best greetings, to Allgeyer and to many another.

Your hasty
J. Br.

By May he was settled for the summer in a village near Heidelberg. *En route* he visited Levi; what occurred can only be guessed at by Levi's subsequent letter.

306
Hermann Levi to Johannes Brahms

[late April or early May 1875]

. . . This time I had a severe hangover from our being together, was in fact not prepared for your sudden departure; precisely on the following morning, for which I had freed myself of all obligations, I had intended to bring up a number of things. Your comments on the first day had also pained me deeply. I don't wish to hark back to it again, but there is one thing I would like you to reflect on: that I have in fact dedicated my life to a specific goal, which I must cherish. I take pains to discharge my profession fully and completely. But that can only come about on condition that I enter into it with a fullness of heart. I would consider it a misfortune if I confronted as stranger and foe the material which, as an opera director, I am expected to replicate and represent. One who is staunchly self-reliant, like you, or who, like Allgeyer, need not deal with the external world and can avoid everything which is disagreeable to his nature, is free to go his way, untouched by his own time—and to rise above it. For me there was initially the satisfaction which the conductor derives from having overcome the technical difficulties, then the genuine interest of a theatre person, and finally the need to give an accounting of this interest to myself, and to defend it against those who differ. To my mind this has nothing at all to do with 'transformations'; it is instead a natural progression, and anyone who, for instance, saw me recently after the *Schicksalslied*, would consider it unthinkable that anything that I ever truly loved could pale for me as a result of more recent impressions. The fact that I shy away from any conceivable association with the future gang, and am thoroughly hated by it, might also give you cause to ponder whether I had actually deserved—your really cruel words.

I have not often plagued you with my own affairs since we have known each other, and would also like to leave it at that today, after this brief *oratio pro domo*.[1] Should you need someone to jump into a great deep on your behalf, turn to me. And besides, it's absolutely no business of yours that I hold you dear.

In unalterable loyalty and devotion
your
Hermann Levi.

This time the breach between the friends was irreparable. Although civil contact was maintained for at least another five years,[2] and although for a while Levi imagined their friendship was back on the old footing, Brahms visited Levi no more, and was less and less forthcoming regarding performances of his music. Many have connected the broken friendship to Levi's growing regard for the music of Richard Wagner; indeed, this is the obvious conclusion from the content of Levi's letter. It is not an explanation which stands up to scrutiny, however, for Franz Wüllner, who conducted the premières of *Rheingold* and *Walküre*, and who never ceased to put Wagner and then Bruckner on his programmes despite Brahms's disapproval, remained a friend for life.

Eugenie Schumann reports that Brahms's stated reason for cooling off his friendship was that Levi had sacked his butler for stealing cigars. Brahms's attitude: Levi should not have left expensive cigars where a poor man could be tempted.[3] While this can hardly be taken seriously as a reason for wrecking a close friendship, it probably tells us that Brahms was increasingly bothered by certain aspects of Levi's character. And one example is plainly visible in the correspondence—Levi's rivalry with Franz Wüllner.

[1] A speech for use within the household.

[2] In 1880 the men were in touch over the Complete Schumann Edition.

[3] Eugenie Schumann, *Erinnerungen* (Stuttgart, 1925), 188. For those who wish to read Eugenie's own words, a caution: this episode, and all other references to Levi and other Jewish friends of the Schumann family are expunged from the German language reprint, which appeared in 1942 under the National Socialists. It is included in the English translation, however (see bibliography), as well as in the original edition.

When Levi came to Munich in 1871, it was on the basis of an agreement which promised him much that was contractually due to Wüllner, already working there as chief conductor at the Court Opera. Levi, it must be stressed, had no warning of the snake-pit he was coming to. He had been lied to and misled by the man who hired him (Baron Richard von Perfall, manager of the Court Opera), and arrived in Munich to find a very unpleasant situation awaiting both himself and Wüllner—but in the end it was Wüllner who found it intolerable and was driven to leave Munich. Levi fought tenaciously for supremacy, and stayed on as the man who came out on top. Brahms was privy to the thoughts of both men, since Wüllner was an old acquaintance from the heady days of the autumn of 1853. Levi's letters to Brahms are full of comments which denigrate Wüllner's abilities in comparison to his own, and ask for reassurances by Brahms. In contrast, Wüllner's letters to Brahms express dismay at the situation, but never fault Levi as a musician. As early as 1873, Brahms chose to help strengthen Wüllner's position by allowing him, rather than Levi, to give the Munich première of the Haydn Variations. The balancing act between his two friends went on for years, causing pain to Levi whenever Wüllner was preferred.

There is no questions that Levi was the more inspired conductor; nevertheless, Brahms had a long-standing loyalty to Wüllner, a serious, capable, hardworking, dedicated, and thoroughly straightforward character. From the time of the First Symphony performance in 1876, they were on 'Du' terms with each other.

On the occasion of that performance Brahms congratulated himself for having brought Wüllner and Levi 'splendidly together again', but it was a superficial reconciliation.[4] Not coincidentally, Brahms's letters to Levi virtually ceased just as Wüllner felt compelled to give up on Munich and accept a vexatious position in Dresden.[5]

Blaming the rift on Levi's devotion to Wagner's music makes even less sense in the light of the fact that Levi and *Clara* remained on good terms for decades after, and Clara was far more opposed to Wagner's music than Brahms ever was; had Levi really given up his interest in Brahms's music, she would certainly have turned away from him on ideological grounds.

If Levi's interest in Wagner's music was not the true basis for the dissolution of their friendship, it seems to have been an excuse that everyone could live with, masking the more painful, genuine reasons for the breakup, whatever they were.[6]

[4] Brahms to Dessoff, *BW* xiv. 151.

[5] In 1877. The one available letter from Brahms to Levi in 1878 denies Levi a performance of the Second Symphony and declines to help him out with parts to Handel's *Saul*. If not definably rude, it is utterly unhelpful; and based on this editor's experience with a large number of Brahms's autographs, it is written in his most careless handwriting, virtually illegible. The autograph is in the Library of Congress, Whittall Collection.

[6] In a weird symmetry, Wagner blamed his problems with Nietzsche on Brahms's music! See Robert Gutman, *Richard Wagner: The Man, His Mind, and His Music*, (New York, 1990), 354. Levi was a complex character in his own right. For a fascinating view of the great conductor see Peter Gay's *Freud, Jews, and other Germans*, which has a chapter on Levi and the 'self-hatred' he suffered

Ten years after the matter had first been broached, Brahms was again asked to relinquish possession of Wagner's autograph of the Paris version of the Venusberg Scene from *Tannhäuser*, a manuscript he had received from Carl Tausig who had it from Peter Cornelius. Both Tausig and Cornelius were now dead; this time it was Wagner himself who wrote.

307
Richard Wagner to Johannes Brahms

Most esteemed Herr Brahms!

I request that you send me my manuscript of the second scene of Tannhäuser, revised by me, which I require for a newly revised edition of the score. Although it has been reported to me that, by virtue of a gift from Peter Cornelius, you make claims of ownership of this manuscript, I believe that I need pay no heed to that report, since Cornelius, with whom I had merely left the manuscript, but to whom I had certainly not given it, could not possibly have disposed of it to a third person, something he has most vehemently assured me he had never done.

Presumably it is quite unnecessary for me to remind you of these circumstances, and no further discussion will be needed to induce you to return, willingly and amiably, this manuscript which you can only value as a curiosity, while for my son it might endure as a treasured memento.

With the greatest high esteeem, your most devoted
Richard Wagner.

Bayreuth, 6 June 1875.

308
Johannes Brahms to Richard Wagner

June 1875

Most highly esteemed Sir,

While stating right away that I will return the manuscript in question 'willingly and amiably', I must nevertheless permit myself to add a few words.

Your worthy spouse already approached me several years ago concerning the return of that manuscript; at that time, so many different things were

from—a trait he shared with many German Jews. This is presumably what allowed him to put up with the anti-Semitic abuse he endured at the hands of Cosima and Richard Wagner. Unlike most other prominent Jewish musicians of the time, however, he never renounced his religion.

supposed to induce me to it that in the end I could sense only the one thing: Ownership of your autograph was simply to be begrudged me. Unfortunately I would be doing violence to the import of your letter were I to understand anything different from it, and then as now, I would certainly have preferred to make the sacrifice in response to a simple request from you.

For your son, after all, the ownership of this scene—as compared to the great sum of your works—can hardly be as valuable as to me, who without actually being a collector, nevertheless likes to keep autographs that I treasure. 'Curiosities' I do not collect.

I do not wish to continue the disputes regarding our late friends, and the claim to ownership which I consider I owe to them. It might indeed have been preferable and easier for them simply to confess to me that they might have been too rash.

I almost believe it to be an obligation to myself to respond in greater detail to your letter and, belatedly, to that of your spouse—but I would probably have to be concerned about unavoidable misinterpretations, for, if you will permit me, the proverb about eating cherries could hardly be applied more appropriately than to someone like me vis-à-vis you. But you may possibly find it quite agreeable if I can no longer regard myself as having presented a gift to you. In that case, I say that since you are robbing my autograph collection of a treasure, it would please me greatly if my library were to be enriched by one more of your works, perhaps the Meistersinger.

I don't suppose that I can expect you to change your mind, and so I am writing to Vienna this very day to have the folder containing your m[anuscript] sent to me. I very urgently request that you kindly notify me in a few words of its arrival.

With exceptional high regard and esteem,
your very devoted
Joh. Brahms.

Ziegelhausen
near Heidelberg.

Brahms was alluding to the saying: *Mit grossen Herren ist nicht gut Kirschen essen.* 'It's not a good idea to eat cherries with great men',—or, 'Don't tangle with powerful people'.

309
Richard Wagner to Johannes Brahms

Most esteemed Herr Brahms!

I thank you very much for the manuscript just returned, which, although it does not distinguish itself by external beauty, having been very badly defaced while being copied in Paris, is nevertheless of value to me because it is more complete than the copy furnished at that time with a large cut by Cornelius.

I regret that instead of the Meistersinger score you requested (which, in spite of repeated back deliveries from Schott, has again run out), I can offer you nothing better than a copy of the Rheingold score; this I am sending to you today without awaiting your concurrence, because it has the distinction of being the showpiece once proudly displayed by Schott at the Vienna International Exposition. On occasion the charge has been made against me that my musical things were stage decorations: Rheingold will have to suffer mightily from that allegation. On the other hand, it might perhaps not be uninteresting to perceive, in following the subsequent scores of the Ring of the Nibelung, how I managed to construct all kinds of musical thematic material upon the stage set which is here established. In that sense, it could be that perhaps Rheingold, in particular, might be accorded your kind attention.

Greetings with the highest esteem
from your very devoted and indebted
Richard Wagner.

Bayreuth, 26 June 1875

What Wagner sent was the gold-stamped, leather bound, special first edition of *Rheingold*, exhibited by the publishing house of Schott at the Viennese International Exposition of 1873. On a page at the front of the volume Wagner wrote, 'To Herr Johannes Brahms as a well-conditioned substitute for an ugly manuscript. Bayreuth 27 June 1875. Richard Wagner.'

310
Johannes Brahms to Richard Wagner

June 1875

Most esteemed Sir,

The parcel you sent has given me such exceptional pleasure that I cannot fail to tell you this briefly, and say how deeply grateful I am for the splendid present which I owe to your kindness. Indeed, I give the best and most appropriate thanks daily to the work itself—it does not lie here without being utilized. Maybe this section is not, at first, such a great inducement to the thorough study which your entire great work demands; this Rheingold did pass through your hands in a very special way, however, and so let the Walkyre [*sic*] radiate her beauty brightly, so as to outshine its accidental advantage. But pardon this sort of comment! The more likely cause is that we do scant justice to one section, [and] that we are compelled to look beyond it at the whole. With this work by itself, we happily make do for some time to come.

After all, we have the truly inspiring, but strange delight—like Romans unearthing a gigantic statue—of watching your whole work emerge piecemeal and come to life. Your ungrateful task of watching our astonishment and gainsaying can of course only be ameliorated by a secure feeling in your breast, and the ever more general and growing respect which is generated by your magnificent work.

I repeat my best thanks and am,
with the greatest deference and high esteem
your
very devoted
Johs. Brahms.

These four letters represent the entirety of the correspondence between Brahms and Wagner, but there is another amusing letter. In February 1878, apparently unwilling to obtain a Brahms work in the usual manner, and unable to find what he wanted in the town he had made his own, Wagner wrote from Bayreuth to an unnamed correspondent:

Dearest Friend!
I think you are connected with a music lending library? Would you be so kind as to procure for me Brahms's Symphony in orchestra and piano score for a short time on guarantee of the fees required? I'm not learning

anything any more of what happens in the world and here you can't get such a thing. . . .[7]

A great weight must have lifted off Brahms's shoulders when he gave up the Gesellschaft job. He was in high spirits all summer, displayed in the cheerful letters he wrote to many friends. He worked on the First Symphony, finished the C minor Piano Quartet (Op. 60), wrote his third string quartet (Op. 67), and a set of vocal duets (Op. 66); and he could not be induced to leave his very pleasant quarters.

Eugenie Schumann remembered visiting Brahms in his artist's atelier in Ziegelhausen: '. . . he occupied two or three beautiful simple peasant rooms with many windows and little furniture. There one could see how undemanding he was in the matter of conveniences, but when it came to light and airiness and room to move around in, he could be extravagant.'[8]

Declining a cordial invitation to hear students at the Music School in Munich perform his Requiem, Brahms took refuge in the lines of a little poem:[9]

311
Johannes Brahms to Franz Wüllner

Ziegelhausen near Heidelberg, July 1875

Dear friend,

This is how long it takes to bring off a No!

You know how much I admire your choral achievements, and to hear the Requiem done by these young people must be a joy. Your letter did indeed tempt me mightily to leave my pretty house here and to follow you to one of your lovely lakes. But, in the end—I suppose it's lethargy, I remain sitting here, but then I could still come, just for listening.

The journey, after all, is really very far for such composer's bliss? Once upon a time, a very reasonable man decided to go outside in order to see the R[hinoceros]—but no further than in front of his door?

So I'll probably continue to sit here, now and then also writing quite useless things—so as not to look a sombre symphony in the face.

I wish you the most wonderful summer and vacation days and greet you and your dear wife sincerely,

your

J. Brahms.

[7] Letter of 2 February 1878 (*The Letters of Richard Wagner*, ed. John N. Burk (New York 1950), 657). Wagner was undoubtedly looking for the First Symphony, published in October 1877 (the Second wasn't published until March 1878).

[8] Eugenie Schumann, *Erinnerungen*, 160. See also Kal, iii[3]. 55–6.

[9] 'Der arme Greis' [The Poor Old Man] by Christian Fürchtegott Gellert (1715–69).

312
Johannes Brahms to Ottilie Ebner

[Ziegelhausen near Heidelberg], August [18]75

My very dear friend!

I really would so like to know how you, and particularly your father, are. For that there is probably no better means than writing to you that I am quite well, and I could say the same of a multitude of other people, for I see new ones every day—only all too many! But you will be pleased to hear this of Frau Schumann, for example. She was here, on her way to Switzerland together with her daughters, and very jolly, cheerful and healthy.

Your acquaintances from Carlsruhe I also see quite often, and they reminisce with pleasure about their dear singer.

Frank often comes over, and you would really like his primadonna— who is probably more than that to him. I often speak with him about you and the *Oed*, which he's most enthusiastic about.

Is your esteemed father now well, as I hope? in that case, you really should look at a piece of the world again—I refer naturally to the piece upon which Ziegelhausen is situated! You could live comfortably here, with the people whom you had enjoyed staying with before. Heidelberg, Mannheim, Carlsruhe, everything is close by, and I think that getting out and looking around a bit can do no harm!

I suppose that I may interpret your not writing about your brother in a favourable way? I spoke to Frank about the affair. In case of an emergency he would of course gladly attend to it, although it is somewhat dubious none the less. In any case it would be better if it were not necessary.

Let me hear a little about how things look there, and don't judge my interest according to scraps of paper like this one! In warmest friendship, your devoted

Joh. Brahms.

Ernst Frank was a conducter in Mannheim, at the time, a friend of both Brahms and Ottilie from Vienna. Apparently he knew her family well enough to offer to put in a word with Ottilie's younger brother, who was spending too much money and slacking off at school. For a few years, Frank and Brahms saw a lot of each other.

313
Johannes Brahms to Ernst Frank

[Before 21 October 1875]

Dear Frank,

From   "   furt someone writes me

a   "   ed letter

saying that I have given you my agreement for January. Not I, but my
pocketbook approves of my making the trip to the Free and Imperial City!
But later!

Don't you and the Frankfurters have concerts in March or February, and
couldn't you fix it so that I am invited by you for both of them??

This morning after breakfast, an old letter fell into my hands on which I
found a notation of your name a[nd] 100 Reichsthaler. One moment
more—and never again would I have been able to read it! Gone and forgotten! I am writing to my *Banquier* immediately! Perhaps at the same hour and
in the same place you can still find a supplement to the Au[gs]b[urg]
Allgem[einer] Z[eitun]g, where there is supposed to be a special essay about
my Requiem.

For the rest, I greet you and anyone else in the greatest hurry and friendliness.

Your

J. Brahms

'Gone and forgotten', 'Versunken und vergessen', the last line of Ludwig Uhland's
'Des Sängers Fluch'—a poem every schoolboy knew from memory. Some time in
the future, while seated in the comparable part of his house, Max Reger would write
an angry letter to a music critic: 'I am sitting in the smallest room in my house. I
have your review before me. In a moment it will be behind me.'

Frank received his money through Levi's brother, the banker Wilhelm Lindeck.
But Brahms sometimes arranged for money through his publisher, too.

314
Johannes Brahms to Fritz Simrock

[Ziegelhausen, 21 August 1875]

Yr. Esteemed Highness's
widely renowned kindness and benevolence give me the courage to
approach you with a great entreaty. My situation is terrible, I face an

appalling future, the abyss yawns before me, I plunge into it—unless your rescuing hand hauls me back! I must now be off to the 'Eagle' with my last 100 Mark note—but with what apprehension will I be eating and even drinking. Too near do I see approaching the dinner-time when there will be nothing left even of this last one. In this desperate situation, might I be permitted to petition most devotedly Yr. Greatly Esteemed Highness for a loan of 100 thaler? I solemnly promise to pay the money back by the middle of September! A hostile fate compels me moreover, to take a pleasure trip one of these days, and the great heat forces me to drink more and more—help, save me! By the way, my greetings to your ladies, the composer there with you, etc.

Your

J. Br.

Two large pieces occupied Brahms that summer: the First Symphony, and the piano quartet first mentioned in letters to Joachim in 1855 and 1856. They both stemmed from the turbulent days of his youthful involvement with Clara and Robert Schumann. The symphony still required another year of gestation, but the quartet, provided with two new movements (Andante and Finale, movements three and four) received its finishing touches and was published as Op. 60.[10] Brahms announced it to Simrock, who was on holiday in the village of Bönigen, Switzerland (in the company of George Henschel and Julius Stockhausen). No other utterance comes as close as this letter to revealing the inner anguish of that early period. The 'man in the blue frock coat and yellow trousers' is Goethe's *Werther*, an impassioned young man who commits suicide because of his desperate and unrequited love for a married woman. All educated Germans knew Goethe's novel, so that Brahms's proposal for a cover illustration for his quartet would have been widely understood.

315

Johannes Brahms to Fritz Simrock

[Ziegelhausen, 12] August 1875

Dear S.

Actually I need and want to write to Henschel, but since one cannot write 2 letters to the same village, what follows here is for his benefit: that one

---

[10] The last two movements were largely written sometime in 1873–4, probably after his trip to Leipzig. It is tempting to speculate that the lush slow movement was inspired by the tender emotions undoubtedly aroused by his recent meeting with Elizabet von Herzogenberg. Whatever its genesis, the manuscript of that movement became a treasured gift from him to her shortly after its publication.

must not go to Rome before the end of September. It is the worst month on account of the Siroccos, etc., as I am told by Feuerbach who knows Rome very well. As a matter of fact, you told me that H. has a pocketful of other plans, so this news will allow him to cruise through his travel plans in even greater contentment! By the way, I know Bönigen, and if only the wife hadn't been with him, Stockhausen's girl students could have made one very content.[11] I have already sent the voice parts to Berlin and enclosed the arrangement for 4 hands, without voices.[12] I had a very fine rehearsal of the quartet and would have sent it to you the following day if I had known your address. The worst of it now is that Peters will gladly give me 1,000 thaler for a piece like this! It's not worth it—but what business of mine is that? I do not offer advice, and wash my hands. The piece does have one advantage. No matter how you mistrust my talent, *this one* can offer excuses for itself. Whether you consider me enfeebled by age or narrow-minded, or hold the opposite opinion, I am only now finally learning a few things—this quartet is half old, half new—the whole creature is therefore good for nothing! Furthermore, you might display a picture on the title-page. Namely a head—with a pistol pointing at it. Now you can form an idea of the music! I will send you my photograph for this purpose! You could also give it a blue frockcoat, yellow trousers, and riding boots, since you appear to like colour prints. Apropos, do have the book of songs from Rüdesheim sent to me! I mustn't send the quartet to you in Bönigen—it turns the most beautiful blue sky foggy. And I would not want to begrudge you and your singer-composer any conceivable pleasure.

Greetings to wife and young ladies from your

J. Brahms.

Brahms was still involved with Spitta's Bach Cantata project, and beginning to have doubts. However much he protested otherwise, over the years, this is one of several letters which illustrates Brahms's sound sense for the commercial aspects of publishing.

---

[11] Clara Stockhausen chaperoned the female students who followed her husband even on vacation.

[12] Of the *New Liebeslieder Waltzes*, Op. 65 and 65a.

316
Johannes Brahms to Philipp Spitta

[Vienna, 22 September 1875]

Esteemed Sir,

As a result of a letter from Herr Rieter, I allowed myself to be seduced last night into voicing all sorts of reservations about his new venture. Perhaps somewhat over hastily.

In any case, in order to prevent any misunderstanding, I want to express myself quite candidly—but just as hurriedly and hastily—to you as well.

Straight out, namely, I wonder whether it might not be advisable, in view of the Peters edition, to desist from our undertaking!

Mainly, of course for the simple reason that H[err] Rieter can in no way compete with Peters.

From what I know of the business situation, it seems to me quite certain that P. will sooner publish all of the cantatas before R. publishes one.

Even if, next season—if he hasn't already brought them all out, by then—P. has to wait for you to practise one cantata, he will still bring out this and twelve others faster than R. the one.

That is even more certain than—that P's arrangers will overtake us in the same way.

Now you are presumably saying that our undertaking, and especially our work, will differ from theirs in many ways.

Unfortunately, I must confess that here my thoughts do not carry me very far.

For whom should I make the piano score? for the intelligent amateur who has roughly my technique and who wants to have the most faithful possible likeness of the whole work presented to him?

Or should the piano reduction be used by the pianist who is supposed to accompany the chorus and keep it together, should as many members of the chorus as possible be able to practise and play it at home?

Now in Bach's works I consider piano reductions other than those simple enough to be serviceable for choral rehearsals as a most difficult, questionable undertaking.

For example, how do you visualize the piano setting of 'Liebster Gott' *quite generally*, and in this instance, how do you imagine the possible difference between the editions of P. and R.?[13]

---

[13] BWV Cantata No. 8, *Liebster Gott wann werd' ich sterben.*

Fidelio or *Figaro* can always be arranged for the better, and for the ever greater pleasure of the good amateur; but how I should deal, in that regard, with something like the first chorus in the *Matthew Passion* is less clear to me. Even so, the practical purpose mentioned above should also not be lost sight of altogether!?

I have already seen some of the Peters cantatas. It appears that practical musicians are working on them.

With us, the work will presumably be done with more devotion and enthusiasm. That would be rather pretty and praiseworthy. But honestly—if we stood on the outside and *needed* a piano reduction—and otherwise we wouldn't even look at one—we would take the most playable and cheapest one and recommend it out of consideration for the usually modest powers of the accompanist, the same as the organizations' cash-box and that of its members.

Had I more patience for writing, the organ part would deserve a lengthy word.

You will not believe what an effort it cost me to let you have mine for the printing. Then as now I lacked the patience to express myself, and I did not want to appear unfriendly.[14]

I firmly believe that one does this kind of thing only for use on a particular occasion. (Loans it out and so lets it get as far as it will.) But to offer it to the world as a finished thing and as something which one somehow connects with the notion of a thing deserving or requiring publication, that to me is a most repugnant thought.

Much could be said about this, but in the end I say the best: this note requires no reply. If you stick to your intentions I'll go along.

So as not merely to have said 'no': perhaps it mightn't be a bad idea to make a four-hand piano version of some of the cantatas. Many things

---

[14] His realization of the continuo for organ in the cantata *Christ lag in Todesbanden*. In the autumn of 1874, Spitta had informed Brahms of his intention to perform the complete Bach cantatas in authentic manner in Leipzig (this was the beginning of the Leipzig Bach-Verein, founded by Alfred Volkland, Philipp Spitta, Heinrich von Herzogenberg, and Franz von Holstein) and asked urgently if Brahms would send the realization of the organ part he had once made for a performance in Vienna. At that time Brahms complied, but 'not altogether willingly, for I believe each person makes that sort of thing for his own use, although not easily to another's satisfaction' (*BW* xvi. 64). Then, half a year later, Brahms made this organ realization available to Rieter-Biedermann for the piano-organ edition of Bach Church Cantatas undertaken by the Bach-Verein. Spitta was overjoyed, and asked Brahms to make the piano score as well, saying it was the will of Bach. In August, Brahms wrote a short postcard to Spitta from Ziegelhausen near Heidelberg, where he was spending the summer, saying he had thoughts and questions about their business, but not to hold things up. The next letter in the sequence of their correspondence is the one given here.

could be rendered quite nicely, and it could even be used for small house-performances.

Excuse this lengthy scribble—it was not done with pleasure!

In sincere veneration,

Your devoted

J. Brahms

Wien IV. Carlgasse 4

The first delivery of the Bach-Verein Editions arrived in the summer of 1876. Brahms showed them to George Henschel when they were vacationing together on the Isle of Rügen, commenting adversly on the piano settings: correct in their voice leadings, they were not practical to play. As Brahms remarked to Henschel, in such an undertaking playability is the most important consideration, and voice leadings be damned.[15]

Autumn and winter tours on behalf of his own music were a regular feature of Brahms's year. Bernhard Scholz, an old friend, was now music director in the Silesian university town of Breslau, where he regularly presented Brahms's music.[16] The composer agreed to a performance of his Piano Concerto, Op. 15, in the following March, and offered advice for a performance of the A Major Serenade, Op. 16, scheduled for December.

317
Johannes Brahms to Bernhard Scholz

[Vienna, 8 November 1875]

Dear Scholz,

So let's leave it at March 21st.

The 'Serenade' has just been newly revised, specifically, better marked. If Simrock should send you a copy one day, it's for me and is my copy. I therefore ask you to accept it on my behalf and to make use of it for your purposes.

A pity about that delicate piece!—In any case you will have to devote some effort to it with rehearsals, etc. I would play it for them beforehand when convenient (in case you trust your winds with it at all), so that the musicians become familiar with it. The Adagio, in particular, cannot really

---

[15] Henschel, *Personal Recollections*, 33–4.

[16] The city is in the part of Poland that was ceded by Germany after the Second World War, and has been renamed Wroclaw. Not a single German sign on street or building remains to remind visitors that this was a German city for hundreds of years, but the architecture of the centre of town, with its opera-house and old, once luxurious hotels, reveal its past.

be rehearsed—on account of the strain. In the Trio of the Minuet you can let *one violin* play the oboe solo!

Do have a look at it—when the piece goes really well, and it is actually not difficult—it seems to me that for a quarter of an hour one can easily forget the sombre question that occupies the three of us so much.

Frau Dustmann asks me to send you greetings and the message that, starting at the end of December, she will no longer belong to the opera, but on the other hand would very much like to sing in concerts and would particularly like to see Breslau again. Maybe you can say a word to me or to her herself (Vienna I, Parkring 20).

'New Liebeslieder' have already appeared.

Should you do the 'Serenade', do see to it that a goodly number of the 4-hand [arrangements] get to Breslau beforehand!

Best greetings to both of you,

your
J. B.

318
Johannes Brahms to Bernhard Scholz

[Vienna, 16 November 1875]

Dear friend.

It would be grand indeed if you would devote some effort to the 'Serenade', postpone the performance if possible, and make the musicians comfortable with the piece in frequent rehearsals. That seems to me to be the main point.

8 violas or even more, 6 violoncellos, 4 basses or something like that, seem appropriate to me. It really depends on how well they play. Indeed, the first movement and the Adagio are difficult to bring off really beautifully and well.

When I reached for the writing paper I secretly had a rather Wagnerian inclination to write very beautiful and long-winded things about my lovely opus! That can now be replaced by the warmest greetings, for my urge has long since evaporated.

'New Liebeslieder' have come out, and Simrock could send them 'for inspection'!

Affectionately,
your
J. B.

Implicit in his doubt as to whether Scholz's winds could be trusted is Brahms's recognition of the demands made particularly upon the flute, oboe, and clarinet. The Serenade, written without violins, gives to those instruments much of the responsibility usually assigned to the high strings. His concern for the wind players is an indication of how much technique has improved in the mean time: modern orchestral wind players have no particular problem with this piece, indeed love to play it just because their instruments are so prominent and are kept so busy. No doubt a mutiny would result were a conductor to substitute a violin for the solo oboe in the Minuet!

✷ 1876 ✷

In the spring, a serious letter came from Julius Allgeyer, still trying to restore the friendship between his best friends, Levi and Brahms. He had just heard Levi conduct the Alto Rhapsody.

319
Julius Allgeyer to Johannes Brahms

Munich, 11 March 1876

Dear Brahms!
    Yesterday I was so compellingly reminded of you that today I am cloaked in shame for not knowing just where I have to send my thanks and greetings. For half a year now I have received vague accounts of your external life solely through paltry newspaper articles or semi-accidental private contacts. But now, having been spoken to once more by your innermost language, uniquely your own, whose soulful depth and harmonious sound were first 'discerned by my ears' almost twenty-five years ago, [sounds] which have grown ever more familiar since, I feel compelled, after such a long pause, to hear in simple, plain German, how you are. It almost appears that one must seriously consider that you, 'outsider', want to push through the undergrowth alone. The rumour about it that reached me was all too well suited to clouding the conception which I have harboured until now of your bright, temperate nature, for me to lend it any weight. But perhaps you will grant me the fine privilege of allowing me, in disregard of everyone's prattle, to ask you straight out whether I must reckon with more than a passing mood of dejection. You will grant that I put this question to you prompted by an inner urge and without having been commissioned. If I knew how adequately to explain the events to myself and how to approve of them, I would

let it go at that. But as I understand them at this time, they appear to have been so badly muddled by persons not concerned that I might feel called upon to say it isn't good this way, and bad were it to remain so. For years it has been my special pleasure to observe the way your personal maturity kept stride with your artistic one, unlike my friend on the Danube who grows ever more lonely, and how, and with 'unclouded vision', you surveyed people and their condition from limpid heights. Allow me to retain the belief that your thinking is too grand and noble for you to turn without any compassion from a man for whom, throughout all the changes in his excitable nature and his exciting profession, you and your art have basically always provided, and will continue to provide, the highest meaning. He is now doubly in need of compassion; he conducted the Rhapsody under the sway of a telegram which threatened to call him, at any moment, to the death-bed of a person for whom he retains a devotion which at times calls for superhuman strength. If he could bring her a small token of your former sentiments towards him, it would be an act of charity for her and balm for him; and for me, a sincere wish come true.

As for me, you will have heard that circumstances have driven me onto the path which you had trepidations about, on my account. For the present, I perceive it to be the more honourable condition, time will tell if it is also the desirable one in other respects.[1]

With my sincerest greetings, your
J. Allgeyer.

Altheimereck, 11. III.1.

The Rhapsody was, in view of the profundity of the work, more effective than I had ever dared hope.

The lonely friend on the Danube was the artist Anselm Feuerbach, now living in Vienna. The man in need of compassion, of course, was Levi, whose betrothed was near death. Brahms's answer must have disappointed Allgeyer deeply.

---

[1] Allgeyer resigned his position and struck out on his own. Brahms's forebodings proved accurate, as Allgeyer's business failed; Allgeyer is one of the people whom Brahms eventually supported (anonymously) with a large gift of money.

320
Johannes Brahms to Julius Allgeyer

Vienna, 18 March 1876

Dearly loved friend,

I thank you from the bottom of my heart for your kind letter. If I could only let my pen walk about the paper as graciously as you, I would want to merit by my confidential chatter—a continuation of your letter-writing. But unfortunately, in my whole life I have not written a confidential letter, above all because I lack the patience.

At bottom, however, in response to what you enquire about so secretively and with such friendly concern, there is just nothing to say, other than that there is nothing at all to it, because absolutely nothing has changed in me and about me.

But on the other hand, the matter you mention so casually is complete news to me and makes me want to hear more. That your relationship to *Br* has already been dissolved and you—but now you'd have to write more or I'd have to see![2]

Your news about me, on the other hand, seems to sound as suspicious as it is incorrect. Since it probably has its source in my relationship to *Joachim*, *Feuerbach*, and *Levi*, I really want to repeat especially that also with respect to them nothing has changed in me—except for the manner of our intercourse on my part.

But that too, after all, is not a new experience, at most I practise it with greater determination. From *J(oachim)* I have learned nothing new in 20 years. I don't need to expound to you how one may have the most splendid opinion of our friends and nevertheless have reason to shun a more intimate, more confidential relationship. Whether I am too narrow-minded, too one-sided, whether I'd miss more by a Yes or a No—*that* you might sense and consider further by putting yourself in my place, I think.

In *Feuerbach*, so long and so profoundly unappreciated, and so greatly revered by me, I have cheerfully overlooked a great deal. But what is unbearable is his boundless indifference towards everything and everybody, as well

---

[2] Undoubtedly referring to the job Allgeyer left, working for someone whose name began with *Br*. In his transcription of the letter (p. 109 of the correspondence), Alfred Orel assumed this passage referred to Brahms himself. The passage, however, makes no sense if 'Brahms' is the missing name: rather, the friend is referring to Allgeyer's surprising news that he has left his job as photographic assistant—probably to the Munich photographer, Bruckmann. Brahms refers to himself in the next paragraph without coyness, another indication that 'Br' refers to someone other than himself.

as his excessively polite, intimate friendliness towards anyone at all who latches on to him and merely sits down with him. I see him almost every day and am, unfortunately, content with saluting him.

But it is difficult to write about human beings—*I* will not attempt it.

My warmest greetings to you then and do also consider that for you I have not only all conceivable love, but also some money. You are certainly not the only friend for whom it is available.

Incidentally, should you have heard something in particular and particularly incomprehensible about me, do write to me about it—I know of nothing. In any case, write to me about yourself and what concerns you; Nobody will listen with deeper interest

than your J. Brahms

In one specific regard, 1876 was a banner year: the First Symphony finally saw the light of day. Started at least fourteen years earlier while Brahms was still living in Hamburg, the symphony's completion somehow required a return to his native soil. Brahms filled his ears once again with Platt-Deutsch, spending a month on the island of Rügen in the North Sea (in the company of the singer George Henschel, who described the time in a delightful memoir[3]) and then returning to Hamburg for the first time since his father's death. 'I have the need to walk, stroll, saunter—whatever it's called—in Hamburg once again', he told Klaus Groth just before leaving Rügen.[4] Then he withdrew to Baden-Baden, and completed the work. The symphony was performed in quick succession in Karlsruhe, Mannheim, Munich (with Wüllner, not Levi), Vienna, Leipzig, Breslau, Cambridge, and London.

The year 1876 also marks the composer's last serious flirtation with a steady job—this time as Municipal Music Director for Düsseldorf, Robert Schumann's old position. The offer was an earnest one, coming from the highest officials of the province. Brahms was presented with a list of 2,000 signatures urging him to accept. He would have a three-year contract at 4,500 Marks per year, leadership of the orchestral and choral society concerts, and some ambiguously defined duties at an as yet non-existent music conservatory. Right from the beginning, Brahms was sceptical and cautious, for reasons old and new—fear of committing himself too firmly, dislike of official committees, and a reluctance to leave Vienna, which by now was home. There were serious problems. Schumann's replacement, Julius Tausch, hurriedly installed after the suicide attempt, was still on the podium after more than twenty years of 'temporary' work without a contract. Although there were many who faulted his musical abilities, sentiment was now strong that he was being treated unfairly. Parties sprang up in Düsseldorf for and against Tausch and Brahms,

---

[3] *Personal Recollections of Johannes Brahms* (Boston, 1907).

[4] Pauls, *Briefe einer Freundschaft*, 94. Brahms's references to walking are always an indication that he is composing.

with broadsides and newspaper articles playing their part. One can hardly imagine a less appealing scenario, and indeed Tausch's situation is the reason Brahms gave for backing out, in the end, writing '. . . it would never have entered my mind to push aside someone whom so many people, and rightfully so, believe they should retain.'[5]

There were other noteworthy events. Brahms composed his third and last string quartet, dedicating it to his other musical scientist friend, Theodor Wilhelm Engelmann; and thanks to Joachim's consistent efforts on behalf of his music in England, the University of Cambridge proposed to confer on him an honorary doctorate. Brahms turned the honour down, unwilling to appear in person in Cambridge as required, then looked around for a German university willing to confer the same honour.

321
Johannes Brahms to Joseph Joachim

[Vienna, 13 April 1876]

Dear Brother Doctor,

Best thanks for your dear letter; that little Dr has already caused me all kinds of excitement. For Macfarren's official letter says not a word about the reservations expressed by you and your friends.[6]

I am not exactly talkative, but although I refrained from telling Speidel and a gathering of others of my lovely adventure, I told Hanslick about it.

After receiving your letter I informed him of its contents etc. etc.

Nevertheless today I discovered, with alarm, a notice in the *Freie Presse*—but *fortunately*, of the report in a German newspaper of *your* Doctor title, taken from the 'English Athaeneum'!

So there's also no further need for me to explain or offer excuses, and I prefer to say what extraordinary pleasure the thing itself gives me. Let's hope that it remains without an unpleasant after-taste. For in that I'd have to include the trip and my Requiem. However, as I said, Macfarran writes nothing of the kind and invites me only in a P.S., very politely, to the Requiem. Naturally I responded only to that, keeping secret that I know better.

Incidentally, the Berlin Academy [of Arts] was also of the opinion that it wouldn't work without an account of my life. But it did work and with no fuss.[7] If not, however—you have this to add to your many other merits! Let's

---

[5] Letter to Carl Hermann Bitter, quoted in Kal, iii³. 130.

[6] That Brahms would have to appear in Cambridge in person on 18 May.

[7] Brahms was asked to provide a curriculum vitae when he was proposed for membership in the Academy. He declined, and was inducted anyway.

hope then that you'll find your wife well restored and that a pleasant spring-time in Berlin will now do the rest.

Give her my warmest greetings and also to Billroth, who travelled there a few days ago and whom you will presumably see.

Incidentally, if your innkeepers are the famous family of singers (and not on tour), you could have a great deal of enjoyment.

Frau Schumann wrote about my quintet and how beautiful it sounded. She wrote 'we'; I gather therefore that you played too?

Once again, warmest thanks and greetings

from your

Johannes Brahms.

322
Johannes Brahms to Theodor Wilhelm Engelmann

[Sassnitz, on the island of Rügen, 9 August 1876]

Most esteemed one,

Only hurriedly: I am travelling to Hamburg early tomorrow (Hotel Petersburg, Jungfernstieg). How long I will stay, what will happen next, I don't know, for I want to get my fill of strolling about and reminiscing. It's possible that I will be somewhere on the Rhine or in Baden in Sept., only do let me know of any developments.

Could you not, through your wife's connections, procure a small *Dr* for me? I cannot just keep saying to all parties and in public that I am not called Dr and that I will hardly become one this time, either!

The English pester me terribly. I must have the doctor's hat placed on my head in C[ambridge], that entails concerts and more of the same in London. But I have absolutely no desire to go to England. Absolutely not! It is dreadful how I am being plagued by this business, and by Englishmen generally.

I will probably publish a string quartet shortly and may need a physician in attendance (like the first). Now this 4tet resembles your wife a bit—very pretty—but ingenious! So then, what sort of title have you? Dr? Professor Th. W. E. It is no longer a question of a forceps delivery, but merely a matter of standing by. There is no violoncello solo in it, but a viola solo so tender that for its sake you may well change your instrument!

But I am in a hurry and must pack. The best greetings of your

J. Brahms.

Brahms's urge to be in Hamburg is apparent from a letter to his friend Ottilie, written upon the death of her father.

323
Johannes Brahms to Ottilie Ebner

[August 1876]

Dear friend!

Your message of bereavement followed me here. It was in this room that I suffered the same loss, albeit more unexpectedly and, unfortunately, much earlier. I think with the sincerest sympathy of you and particularly of your mother, who is suffering the hardest blow. I would like to hear how she is bearing her loss—presumably she scarcely perceives it as deliverance from heavy cares and great exertion, as yet.

I spent a lot of time on Rügen and truly relished the wonderful fresh sea air. Now I'll go walking here until I have had my fill so that I won't rhapsodize so pointlessly over my native city. Incidentally, if you are going to a seaside resort on the North or Baltic Sea, as planned, you must not miss making a thoroughly agreeable stop here. Hamburg is a most beautiful city and if you do a lot of walking or travelling around here, you will comprehend what I miss in Vienna.

My address is: Hamburg, Anscharplatz 1. Do let me know if you are carrying through with your plan and if I couldn't possibly serve as a guide here. But perhaps you've already gone somewhere or other and I can look forward to your return?

In that case I won't detain this note for even a minute! If you are in the lovely Oed just now, give my greetings all around and my warmest greetings to your mother and sister. In the hope of still seeing you away from and before Vienna? Your very devoted

J. Brahms.

324
Johannes Brahms to Ottilie Ebner

[October 1876]

Dear friend,

If a letter could consist of 3 words, you would have had one long ago; if you can kindly accept one of 3 sentences, I am now writing?!

I would so much have liked to express my sympathy in person—but I hope that by now everything is long past and you are enjoying the lovely autumn in all contentment. Furthermore I must tell you that I am now being urged to leave Vienna.

I am supposed to take over the post of Music Director in Düsseldorf. For the time being nothing has been decided, and I will come to Vienna in the middle of November (possibly only until the New Year). To add a cheerful 3rd sentence, I report that in the Gesellschaft concert on 17 December, I will perform a symphony. After all, you have hoped for this, on occasion, and now let's see if it will suit you in retrospect, as well!

So—that's all and along with it, warmest greetings.

The awful scratch marks are intentional!

But give my greetings to all those unfortunates who cannot read them and if possible, report really good news to me about you and all of yours. Your sincerely devoted

J. Brahms.

Lichtenthal near Baden-Baden,
and in the same room where you have also sung.

Simrock had been waiting a very long time for this symphony, virtually panting after it for years. The manner of informing his impatient publisher of both the symphony and his third string quartet comes under the heading of classic Brahms.

325

Johannes Brahms to Fritz Simrock

[Lichtenthal bei Baden-Baden, 24 October 1876]

Dear S.,

You and your dawdling are really hard to bear! The quartet still not printed, Schuster in Carlsruhe would have finished it long ago. It might help if I send the score herewith, *according to which the parts [which are] with Joachim will have to be corrected*, the changes being especially in the 2nd and 4th movements.

Quartet for Violin, etc., Dedicated to his Friend Professor Th. W. Engelmann in Utrecht, by J. B. with the next [opus] number. But I need the parts! When can I have a copy without the latest correction? As honorarium I request a mere 5,000 Rtlr. From this you will deduct 1,000 Rtlr. out of innate meanness; for keeping you waiting 500; for further keeping you waiting for the 4-hand piano reduction 500; for only 2 key signatures in B flat 250 Rtlr.; for cigars, tobacco, odekolonje[8] etc. 750 Rtlr.;

---

[8] *Sic.* Read aloud, the puzzle is solved.

because of mistakes in tallying and calculating another 1,000 will be lost, and 200 Rtlr. you had loaned to me, that leaves a remainder of 800 Rtlr. Should a bill for 24 shirts and 48 pocket handkerchiefs then come along: that leaves even less, from which small amount I request that you send *immediately* 50 Rtlr. to Frau Karoline Brahms in Hamburg, Anscharplatz 1. The rest, however, to be paid to me punctually in quarterly instalments of at least 10 Rtlr. Royal Hanoverian thaler-certificates I don't accept at face value, discounted at 2½ Sgr. Furthermore, I must also demand: Because the Adagio is so short 15 Rtlr.; for sending the autograph, 2½ Sgr. per movement = 10; for sketches of the tender movement at 2 fl. apiece, = = ?

Too bad that you're not a conductor, otherwise you could have a symphony. It will be [performed] in Carlsruhe on the 4th. I expect a reverential present from you and other publishers of my acquaintance for not importuning you with such things. With which thought I hope to fare well and I remain, always gladly at your service, punctual, etc., your

J. Br.

Brahms was paid 800 thaler for the quartet. The astonishing honorarium of 5,000 thaler (15,000 Marks), is in fact what Simrock paid him for the symphony. Of course, Brahms was ragging his publisher in several ways at once. *Schuster* was a small music dealer in Karlsruhe, and Hanover's currency had been worthless ever since the kingdom was annexed by Prussia in 1866.

Characteristically, Brahms was unwilling to publish the symphony until he had heard the work performed; characteristically, he could only hint to Dessoff of his desire.

326
Johannes Brahms to Otto Dessoff

[Lichtenthal bei Baden-Baden, *c.*11 October 1876]

Dear friend,

I don't know what I wrote you yesterday in my sleepy stupor since, arriving home tired, I found letters from Mannheim, Munich, and Vienna.

For it was always a secret, fond wish of mine to hear the thing for the first time in the small town which has a good friend, good conductor, and good orchestra.

But since you never said a word, and the thing also does not commend itself by its genial character—I therefore ask to be sure to get copies made with the swiftness of a little brown bug.

Sincerely,

your

J. Br.

Karlsruhe fitted the composer's description on all counts. There were many good friends still there from the days of his lengthy stays with Levi and Allgeyer. Otto Dessoff was both a good friend *and* good conductor (and overjoyed at Brahms's veiled request—like Brahms, he had been pushed out of his position in Vienna through intrigue, and had settled in a calmer but less prestigious post, Levi's old job in Karlsruhe). And there was the Court Orchestra, an experienced group which had already given world premières of other Brahms works. The distinction of presenting the première of this first symphony was an honour not lost on them.[9]

Joachim had wind of the new symphony, and even more to the point, of the new quartet. Brahms gladly granted him the first performance of Op. 67, which took place on 30 October in Berlin. The composer's comments regarding nuances and open strings are as rare for him as they are illuminating for us.

327

Johannes Brahms to Joseph Joachim

[Lichtenthal bei Baden-Baden, 18 October 1876]

Dear friend,

With the greatest of pleasure, naturally, and whether or not I can hear both concerts hangs by just one, or a few threads. But on 4 November I am having my symphony in Carlsruhe, hence rehearsals a few days before.

---

[9] Shortly after the première, Carl Will, the concertmaster of the court orchestra, wrote to Brahms: 'At our last gathering in the Crown Prince, on that evening after the concert, I was scheduled to make a long speech conveying the orchestra's gratitude for the confidence and honour you bestowed upon us by allowing us to be the first to perform your wonderful symphony; but as I saw the master of ceremonies, Herr Wendt himself, wrestling to find the right words to express his thoughts, and Herr Lachner, with a similar beginning, calling down your humorous reprimand upon his head, I gave up. I did not wish to suffer a similar fate, and so I reach you by letter to thank you, in the name of the court orchestra, for your personal efforts during the rehearsal of your work; and in particular, too, for the proof you gave us that contrary to superstition, the last word in symphonies shall not be spoken as long as there are people who, with requisite knowledge and ability, can delve into themselves and are thereby capable of speaking their own musical language. Continue, dear friend, to reveal your feelings and thoughts to us in your usual manner, and be assured that we shall greet with joy each new blossom you present to us.' The complete letter is reprinted in Draheim (ed.), *Johannes Brahms in Baden-Baden und Karlsruhe*, 175.

(Unfortunately this is not the beautiful 'At the *Wissower Klinken*' but an old, familiar one from the famous C minor.)[10]

You probably know that I'm supposed to become Music Director in Düsseldorf? It's an offer I don't want to accept—and to reject—too quickly, but I don't feel particularly comfortable with the idea.

While I now think back with much pleasure to how well you all made my quartet sound, I can't keep from mentioning that at this spot in the Scherzo:

it definitely does not say *scherzando*! It must not change its character there and I suppose I really ought to mark it: *poco a poco tempo primo* (perhaps at the 3rd measure).[11]

Forgive me, but you probably didn't think me capable of being so fastidious and of considering such niceties. I always seem very crass at least to myself, when I am precise or have others be so. But while I compose I have all kinds of delicacies in mind!

In Carlsruhe I had rather hoped for certain other listeners—but all in all it's probably just as well that I was alone in the little residence!

Best greetings to you and yours and several others.

J.B.

For now, do give Spitta my best thanks, I had the Buxtehude shipped to me here and greatly enjoy the man and the edition.[12]

This request is probably in vain: Would you, in the difficult passages, alter a few *notes* for me, particularly in the first movement? To me, fingerings are always just evidence that something is rotten in the violin scoring. But a few open strings here and there, they delight my eye and calm my spirit.

To Frank in Mannheim, while rehearsals were under way in Karlsruhe:

---

[10] i.e. not inspired by Rügen's spectacular north-east coast, with its steep and famous chalk formation near Sassnitz, (the *Wissower Klinken*), but rather, the symphony long known to Joachim. To Simrock, Brahms joked that his symphony had 'got hung up on the Wissower Cliff' (*BW* x. 13).

[11] Measures 57–8. The published score is marked *poco a poco in tempo* from measure 57 itself.

[12] See Letter 296.

328
Johannes Brahms to Ernst Frank [postcard]

[Lichtenthal bei Baden-Baden, 30 October 1876]

Be careful with the rehearsals, the symphony is long and difficult. I hope I don't need to give up much of the 2 rehearsals to you before the dress rehearsal?! Are you rehearsing *Manfred* in another, fourth? Otherwise, we won't get through it. Tomorrow I go back to Carlsruhe.

Best greetings,
J. Br.

Munich was his next destination. Normally happy to stay with friends while on tour, this time the difficulty between Levi and Wüllner intruded, and he stopped at a hotel.

329
Johannes Brahms to Franz Wüllner

[Lichtenthal bei Baden-Baden,] October 1876

Dear friend,

I suppose there isn't all that great a rush? On the 7th I have a concert in Mannheim, after that I can bring score and parts myself. For your kind invitation, my best and most sincere thanks. But for various reasons I would like to stay at a hotel and would like to know if the Maximilian can be recommended, apart from its practical, good location. After all, the Hotel Levi would still stand in the way of yours, and I don't know whether you have come to friendly terms with him—indeed, I don't even know if I can send greetings to him through you!?

But unfortunately, that's the way it is everywhere one goes.

Now what is your programme like? My symphony is long and made of C Minor. I assuredly would not want it at the end, would most prefer it in the middle, maybe after an overture and aria.

My address from November 1st is Carlsruhe, Dessoff; from the 5th, Mannheim, Frank.

Incidentally, I'm greatly looking forward to your orchestra and even more to you and yours, to whom I send greetings with all my heart.

Your
J. Br.

The clearest expression of Brahms's ambiguity about his invitation to Düsseldorf went to Billroth.

330
Johannes Brahms to Theodor Billroth

[17 October 1876]

Dear friend,

By now you will have learned through Faber that a call to Düsseldorf was bestowed on me. I had hoped for a position, an activity, for so long and so earnestly, that I must now put on a serious expression to consider it. I am loath to leave Vienna and have all kinds of objections to Düsseldorf in particular. The question of money is also involved and Stockhausen's and Frau Schumann's appointments at the Conservatory foundered on it (and little else). The attitude of the Ministry of Culture is, for the time being, very friendly, etc. In the event of a Yes I would have to go there by New Year.

There's a bright side to everything, you will perhaps be saying now. For through it I decided to come out with a symphony. I felt that I really ought to say goodbye to the Viennese by playing something worthwhile for them. Herbeck asked me to do so (I have no idea how one had occurred to him), and I find it actually quite agreeable to be able to play it for the Gesellschaft and my choristers—even as I muse somewhat wistfully about the men of the Philharmonic.[13]

Now, since a symphony by me is something of a rarity, it has already been widely telegraphed and written about.

I'll probably do it in Carlsruhe on the 4th of November, the 9th in Mannheim, the 15th in Munich, the 17th of December where you are.

I dislike writing too much, otherwise I would tell you in greater detail that in its form and manner, the invitation to Düsseldorf had to be most gratifying to me. The best men took the most sympathetic interest in it, and their letters were such that they had to silence any misgivings. My main reasons against it, on the other hand, are childish in nature and must remain unspoken. Maybe it's the good taverns in Vienna, the harsh, disagreeable Rhenish speech (particularly in Düsseldorf) and—and—while remaining a bachelor in Vienna is not an issue, in a small town, an old bachelor is a caricature. I no longer want to marry and—indeed, have reasons to fear the fair sex.

---

[13] The Gesellschaft orchestra was outclassed by the Vienna Philharmonic, comprised entirely of professionals.

In Carlsruhe for the symphony, I do hope to see Lübke. My belated best thanks for your kind letter to Rügen. I did, meanwhile, hear about you occasionally through others. Were I to do what is proper for my body, I should probably run into you sometime! Maybe in Carlsbad! But now, good night and forgive the scrawl, I just had the desire to send you greetings and now I ask you to also convey them to your wife and our friends.

Affectionately your
J. Brahms.

No one was more anxious for Brahms to accept the position as music director for the city of Düsseldorf than Ferdinand Hiller, who would have happily welcomed as his neighbour the prominent composer he had once predicted would fade from view within four years. Hiller not only lived nearby in Cologne, he was an experienced musical politician himself. He understood local conditions, and was someone with whom Brahms could discuss his misgivings.

331
Johannes Brahms to Ferdinand Hiller

[Karlsruhe, early November 1876]

Dear friend,

The last question is tricky; I have a powerful prejudice against women pianists and anxiously avoid listening to them. Nevertheless, I naturally know the Viennese women thoroughly—why else do we have ears? And so, unfortunately, I cannot highly recommend the one in question. Unfortunately, for she is a musical and clever woman. But as a pianist she has deteriorated alarmingly since her marriage. I don't want to be too positive in my judgement (that being so, I probably really ought to keep quiet) but nevertheless I don't think that I ought to advise it.[14]

Today I have [to deal with] a sharp steel nib in addition to my aversion to writing!

But just 'between you and me' I want to say that the Conservatory is merely a pretext for obtaining an advance from the Ministry of Culture. I am not even considering it and neither is anyone in Düsseldorf. I have been told in writing that there will be no question of it during the next 3 years.

But apart from that I have all kinds of objections to D[üsseldorf] and the situation there. All kinds of things which I cannot write about to them there,

---

[14] The question was whether to engage as pianist with the Gürzenich orchestra a woman who had been recommended to Hiller on the supposed advice of Brahms.

but which I would gladly discuss with you, to have them refuted by you or, as I fear, confirmed. Better twice the work than to have to battle with any kind of intrigue and what have you. After all, isn't that the *only* reason I gave up my position in Vienna, otherwise so dear to me.

If I were to come to D[üsseldorf] I would be glad to bring you the Symphony. Otherwise it's probably difficult since I have only a handwritten score and parts, and I can scarcely dispense with them.

To me it also seems heartening that the rehearsals here can be recommended![15]

Sincerely and hastily your
J. Brahms

Hiller tried to reassure Brahms that in Düsseldorf 'everyone belonging to the educated, influential circles desires your coming . . . And, that you have good friends in residence here, that within an hour you can be in old Cologne, is also worth something.'[16] But concern over Julius Tausch now reached the point—after twenty years of careless treatment—where the issue came up at a meeting of the Düsseldorf town councillors. Although seventeen councillors voted in favour of Brahms, seven were for Tausch. Between that and the murky conditions surrounding the non-existent Conservatory, Brahms had the excuse he needed to back out of the invitation.

332
Johannes Brahms to Ferdinand Hiller

[Vienna,] Dec[ember 18]76

Dear friend,

My ceremonial entry in January can't be celebrated yet—nor am I of a mind to undergo the crucifixion that is entailed! I would have written you about the entire affair in confidence long ago, but the main point to that would have been your confidential response, and I am most loath to request such a response from you who are so much busier and more industrious.

I am supposed to take up my post as of the 1st of April. Originally, the 1st of January. This postponement suits me, I might otherwise have been over-hasty and I am now discovering more and more that I will probably be doing something stupid if I do accept.

I suppose you know more about the whole affair, and in more detail, than I. Such as: that the Ministry of Culture is contributing to the salary on

---

[15] i.e. in Karlsruhe, with a co-operative orchestra. In Cologne Brahms usually had to do battle, although not with Hiller himself.

[16] Hil, iv. 19.

condition that I take over a Conservatory, if one should *perchance* be founded. I want no part of that; that this is not being considered in Düsseldorf I have in writing from the President of the Government, among others,—but not from the Chief Mayor and the Ministry! Add to that the business with Tausch, which I had a rough idea about and am even now learning certain things.

How unpleasant the situation could become if the Ministry were to make certain enquiries after 3 years or so, etc.! Dear friend, it seems entirely superfluous for me to go on chattering to you. If you could send me word right away I would be very grateful to you. It will probably fortify me in my decision? I don't need to tell you that I wish for just such work, chorus and orchestra, that I should so like to be sitting pretty in the midst of German cities, good musicians and friends! It's just quarrelling that I don't like!

But now to come to your question. I expect to be in Leipzig on the 18th of January, therefore could probably be in Cologne on the 23rd. But forgive me: do you pay well enough to make the long journey worthwhile, and if that's the case, won't you take it amiss if I do my symphony in Barmen (as I have often promised)? The symphony 3 times, that I wouldn't like—one needs a little variety. Meanwhile I'll enquire in Barmen.[17] Though I was about to write to D[üsseldorf] to decline, now I suppose I must still wait for a word from you.

With best greetings,
your
J. Brahms.

Vienna IV, Carlsgasse 4.

Brahms received an invitation from the Herzogenbergs to be their guest when he came to Leipzig for the Gewandhaus's performance of the new symphony, and was late in replying.

333

Johannes Brahms to Heinrich and Elizabet von Herzogenberg

[Vienna, 1] December 1876

Treasured friends,

I am really very sorry that I behaved like an ostrich and in such a clumsy and ill-mannered fashion. I thought that I should not impose on your kind-

---

[17] A relatively unimportant town near Düsseldorf, but one where good friends were very eager for the symphony.

ness,—but a 'No' just did not want to flow from my pen! Now I am profoundly embarrassed by this so friendly reminder!

But I shall arrive very, very early and won't leave again until Saturday!
Your wife continues to count on my having been educated and toughened in
Sassnitz and is seriously misinformed about conditions in Rügen! But
now—may all of us be spared from disaster. Three days before the concert I
start to sweat and to drink camomile tea, and after the fiasco—suicide
attempts in the Gewandhaus, etc. You shall see what an irritable composer is
capable of doing!

But forgive all this foolishness, I have written too many letters for today.
I thank you therefore most sincerely and ask that you write your house number to me on a postcard—just in case.

As hurried as he is devoted, your
J. Brahms.

Details of the January performance still had to be worked out.

334
Johannes Brahms to Karl Reinecke

[Vienna, December 1876]

Dear friend.

Best of thanks, and so as to put an end to the torture I ask you to pick up
a postcard at your convenience and to write to me how many violin parts,
etc. you require. I have more than enough and prefer not to lug them around
uselessly.

Now I'd like to give you the presumably very surprising news that my
symphony is long and not exactly charming. I would therefore really not like
to do it at the end, rather at the beginning, and even better: 1. overture, 2.
aria, 3. 'symphony', 4., 5., 6., etc. *ad lib.*

But Henschel will be sensible and will sing a lovely aria; and afterwards,
if the symphony was a flop, my most genial song!

Hurriedly,
your sincerely devoted
J. Brahms.

Brahms's '4th, 5th, 6th etc. *ad lib*' was not a joke. One of the reasons his music
failed for so long to gain an audience in Leipzig was the style of programming at
the Gewandhaus, which produced concerts of 'unbearable length' and placed the

première of Brahms's Second Symphony, for example, at the end of a long evening. In the present instance the programme read: Beethoven, *Coriolanus* Overture; three Brahms songs, sung by George Henschel; Schumann, Cello Concerto; then the new symphony; four more songs by Brahms; and to end, the Haydn Variations![18] Nevertheless, the symphony was far more of a success in Leipzig than at its performance in Vienna, where Brahms felt especially grateful for the sympathetic ears of his friends.

335
Johannes Brahms to Theodor Billroth

December 1876

Dearest friend,

I wish there were two words, for more just won't do to say quite clearly how grateful I am to you for these days which came to a close with your dinner yesterday noon.

I don't exactly want to say that my bit of composing is idle toil and trouble, just a continual aggravation that nothing better comes along—but you would not believe how glorious and heart warming it is to experience an interest such as yours; at that moment one does regard it as the best part of composing and everything connected with it. Only rarely is it given to one to experience the grace and perfection with which you know how to show it. After all, a lot went into it! From the piano-playing after the meal, which in this case was by no means the worst, right on up to your wife—for whom there was much enthusiasm in the *Kaffehaus* that evening!

But although I will now cease this stuttering, and in spite of saying nothing yesterday—I hope you do sense how truly you did me and all of us good. I thank you therefore most sincerely and only wish I might deserve such great joy many more times.

Utterly your
J. Brahms.

[18] Johannes Forner, *Johannes Brahms in Leipzig* (Leipzig, 1987), 74, 61.

PART VII

❧❧❧

Independence
1877–1890

❧ 1877 ❧

In some respects, 1877 is the year Brahms hit full stride. He came to terms with the freedom his financial independence allowed him, and was at the height of his creative powers. He began to travel to Italy, and to spend the better part of his summers in mountainous regions of great natural beauty. He still had almost half of his creative output before him.

From our present perspective, the year is most notable for the works he created during this first summer at Pörtschach, an Austrian village on the banks of the Wörthersee in the Styrian Alps. For his friends, however, the great event was a memorable party in Leipzig, with admirers coming from as far away as Holland to hear Brahms conduct his First Symphony with the Gewandhaus orchestra. Their days together were spent in an atmosphere of high spirits.

336
Johannes Brahms to Emma Engelmann

[Wieden-Vienna, 11 January 1877]

If, in the Thomaskirche on Sunday, you would just listen to the lovely little motets, and along with them to the sermon (on Mark 10: 14, 15, 16), I would escort you home with my most civil behaviour, for I am planning to come early on Sunday. I hear that you whistle the Handel Variations very beautifully? My greetings to the Professor but tell him nothing about church—3rd pillar on the left—red rose in the button hole—wear a smile!
Your very own.

Matters were still pending in Düsseldorf. His formal letter declining the appointment went directly to Carl Hermann Bitter, head of the provincial government.

337
Johannes Brahms to President Carl Hermann Bitter

January 1877

Highly esteemed Herr President,

Just as I had suspected, there really wasn't a quiet minute to be had during my trip. Although I have but little to say, I can only employ this, the hour of my return, to do so.

It was, however, most gratifying for me to learn in the course of my trip that a number of colleagues with whom I spoke definitely shared my view of the affair. I may thus be permitted to make reference to my previous letters. If I cannot be allowed to await a change with regard to matters of Tausch and the Conservatory, then my letter of refusal has already been written.

I cannot get past this ante-chamber. In your last letter you informed me of a few additional details.

Compared to my qualms in the matter of 'Tausch', it would appear coarse (Hamlet would say: it is coarse) were I to say that some of it is not very encouraging.

The limited local resources, primarily with regard to numbers; on the other hand the large hall, the inadequate number of rehearsals, etc.; instead of my going on about it, I prefer to say how much I regret that I must once again decline the offer. I should like to move to Germany, I should like to have steady work with chorus and orchestra and know of no city where most aspects are as congenial to me as Düsseldorf. If not for those two reservations which I cannot overcome, I would look over everything from close-up and could probably come to terms with the rest.

But as it is—it is not tidy—and although people much cleverer than I might maintain otherwise—one cannot go against one's innermost feelings. And these have spoken to me in the same way from the beginning and were only reinforced by everything that has happened.

Even the kind speeches of so many splendid gentlemen, they could make me do many things, soothe me in many regards, but in this matter alone they could not conquer my thoroughly reluctant feelings.

I am tired from the night journey and therefore beg you to excuse these hasty lines. I sincerely regret their content, and although additional words would not alter it, they would do greater justice to my feelings of gratitude towards you and the others.

With the greatest esteem,

your very devoted
J. Brahms

By April, Brahms had twenty-three songs ready to send around to his friends for their perusal. Most of them were composed or completed in March—a remarkable number for him, and it is tempting to connect this creative burst to his rediscovery of Elizabet von Herzogenberg, whose guest he was in Leipzig for the Symphony performance. She was certainly the first to see them, and only then did they go to Clara. There are many references to the songs in his correspondence during the rest of the year, leaving the distinct impression that Brahms was particularly pleased with them.[1]

338
Johannes Brahms to Clara Schumann

Vienna, 24 April 1877

Even if this letter should turn out to be a lengthy one, contrary to custom, it will nevertheless require just a quarter of an hour of your time! But in the next few days another one will arrive which would like to have a few relaxed hours devoted to it!

For I want to publish my songs, and I would really like it very much if you would first play through them sometime, and say a word to me about them. I would most prefer to be sitting beside you—but after Düsseldorf I really couldn't, and in Berlin it was also touch and go.

Simrock is waiting anxiously! If necessary—in case you are unable to enjoy so many confections at once—give him one opus at a time!

The songs are numbered.

Thus, Op. 69 from 1 to 9, and, if he behaves himself nicely, he'll get Op. 70 tomorrow.

But to me, write whether you like any of it—and if there are other things, perhaps, that you dislike intensely.

Particularly the latter, maybe I would listen attentively and thank you!

But don't straight away find something too crude, and if you dislike a poem, read it through a second time, for example, the 'Maiden's Curse'! [*Mädchenfluch*] which might startle you. Forgive me! It's just that I'm afraid of a scolding.

After the above-mentioned confections you can restore yourself with the enclosed Etude. I find it a lot of fun to practise, also difficult!?[2]

Also, do please ask Simrock not to send me any money. For I want to ask you if you wouldn't invest the money with the National (or whatever?) Bank there? In fact, the money which I now have with Levi's brother in Mannheim

---

[1] Opp. 69–72. They were all published by Simrock in the autumn.

[2] The *Presto after Bach* (from the Sonata for Violin Solo, BWV 1001), published in 1878 by Bartolf Senff. See *BW* xiv. 296.

I would also like to keep there in Berlin. Don't you think that's better? I won't tell you today what I am getting for the songs (and the symphony). It corresponds too wretchedly to their worth and is bound to predispose one unfavourably. But do take a guess!³

Meanwhile, I'm delighted that Felix is going to Zurich. For I too am seriously thinking about it and about my lodgings in Rüschlikon. You'll surely come too? There are actually many delightful places to stay in the vicinity, for instance, Bochren near Horgen (on the lake), etc.

And then, a few beautiful autumn weeks in Baden! But I must be off. I hope tomorrow's letter won't seem inordinately dismaying! If possible, write me *a brief word* for each one. You might simply indicate opus or number:

op. X.   5. bad
          6. shameful
          7. preposterous

Finest greetings,

your
Johannes.

It took Clara less than a week to look through all the songs.⁴ In her conscientious report she wrote, '*Mädchenfluch* is one of my favourites—the music is so lilting and interesting from beginning to end that I forget all about the hateful text.'

Joachim's third son was born on Brahms's forty-fourth birthday.

339

Johannes Brahms to Joseph Joachim

[Vienna, 13 May 1877]

My warmest best wishes, dear friend. The seventh of May certainly seems to me to be a particularly lovely day for greeting the world. Under the circumstances, it is no longer possible to wish for the very best thing—not to be born at all, as they say. So, may the new citizen of the world never think such thoughts, but enjoy the 7th of May and his life for many long years.

I am supposed to pass on masses of greetings from here to your wife. But I won't try to list them because I don't want to do even a single person the injustice of forgetting him. Therefore I'll express only my own, and that straight from the heart. This is a joyous spring for you!

My very best, your
Johs. Br.

³ See p. 521.   ⁴ *SBB* ii. 96 ff.

It was probably Bertha and Karl Kupelwieser who recommended the beauties of Pörtschach to Brahms, for in 1877, the village was anything but a well-known resort. They spent their own holidays there, but could hardly have known how much the world of music would owe to the three summers Brahms was resident.

Karl was the son of Schubert's friend Leopold Kupelwieser, and Bertha was a sculptor. She was also one of the several Wittgenstein sisters who sang in the women's chorus Brahms conducted when he first came to Vienna. Like many Wittgensteins then and later, she was devoted to Brahms, and took pleasure in doing little things to make his life easier.

Brahms spent his first Pörtschach summer right on the lake, in the caretaker's tower attached to the local castle. He ran into trouble with his piano.[5]

340
Johannes Brahms to Emil Streicher

[Pörtschach,] 13 May [18]77

Most esteemed Herr Streicher,

My very best thanks to you for having dispatched the piano so *promptly*, and I also thank you especially for having curbed your sense of honour by not doing a lot of checking and improving first! In return I shall also be candid and tell you that—I am by no means waiting for the piano, that it could by no means have been brought up the stairs to my rooms! Here, at Dr Kupelwieser's from Vienna, I found a baby grand that could just barely pass through the stairway—my grand now has to go to the doctor's Villa in return—where it will be well taken care of and where it will in any case have and give more pleasure.

For today, then, my warmest thanks once more, I shall inform you of the happy arrival.

With my best greetings, also to your spouse,
your very devoted
J. Brahms.

When Brahms's income rose considerably after publication of the *German Requiem*, he was faced with the chore, ungratifying to him, of having to look after his money. Levi's brother was the banker Wilhelm Lindeck, and as early as 1871 Levi had suggested Brahms might be relieved of the details of banking and investing his money, as well as making transfers to his family, through the services of his brother. By 1872

---

[5] He lived at Schloss Pörtschach, owned by Baron von Pausinger and his over-enthusiastically musical wife, Freifrau Fanny. To escape her unwanted attention, Brahms spent the next two summers in other accommodation.

Lindeck quite literally became Brahms's personal banker (see Letter 313), invested his money, clipped his coupons, sent money to his sister and stepmother, and regularly sent him a statement. In 1877, Brahms decided to transfer his financial assets to Simrock's care, a plan he carried out, not coincidentally, at the same time that the relationship to Levi chilled. But Brahms had no quarrel at all with Lindeck, and worried he would hurt his banker's feelings by dropping him altogether, a concern he expressed both to Clara and to Levi. His solution was to leave some investments with Lindeck.

'. . . I would be very grateful to your brother if he would hang on to position, title, and a small sum of money with all its irritations!', he wrote to Levi.[6] Not until 1882 did he transfer the remainder of his assets, at which time he thanked Lindeck repeatedly, sent him a signed photograph, and presented him with signed autograph of 'Feldeinsamkeit', Op. 86 No. 2. Brahms made the version for bass specifically for the banker, who had been a fine opera singer before his marriage.

The letters to Lindeck have a cheerful, breezy character to them, quite unlike his usual tone. It is clear that Brahms enjoyed having money, and that he was not quite as oblivious to the details of his financial holdings as one has been led to think from some of his other letters and public utterances.

The first letters to survive are from September 1872.

341
Johannes Brahms to Wilhelm Lindeck

[Vienna,] Sept[ember] [18]71 [*recte*:1872][7]

Dear Sir,

My Hamburg friend very much desires a statement that you received the money that was sent, while I, on the other hand, come to pester you with new things, but first this by way of a prelude.

Your brother will have told you that he encouraged and had to coax me rather insistently to cause you this aggravation. You know how kind-hearted he is, and also, somewhat absentminded and heedless.

I recall gleefully the curious face your sister made when I was once supposedly invited to dinner at her house! Well, that was easily remedied, but if

---

[6] *BW* vii. 191, summer 1877. It is a long, tired, and condescending-sounding letter, Brahms's last substantial letter to his old friend.

[7] This letter is identified and published here for the first time. It corresponds with the circumstance that in July 1872, Levi again encouraged Brahms to make use of the services of his brother (*BW* vii, Letter 59). Although Brahms miswrote the date as 'Sept. '71', it must read 'Sept. 72', and should follow Letter 1 in Michael Martin, *Johannes Brahms, Briefwechsel mit dem Mannheimer Bankprokuristen Wilhelm Lindeck* (Mannheim, 1983). Alexanderbad was Hermann Levi's favourite spa, and perhaps that of his brother, as well.

you are in a similar position, I must beg you very sincerely to excuse me for wasting your time so uselessly with my affairs.

I have already written to you that I was advised to consign my papers to the deposit bank here.

Although I have not yet noticed any greater convenience and have some reservations about having everything in one place, I would be glad to hear from you if this or that bank is sufficiently secure. For no matter how irksome property of this kind is for someone like me, it is nevertheless very necessary to hold on to it firmly.

If you would now have the kindness to buy some other safe paper (Prussian?) for me in place of the unsuitable ones, I would be most grateful to you.

But finally: I need money just now and would appreciate it greatly if you would retain about 100 g[ulden] of the money from that exchange and send it to me very soon.

Is it possible that this office business will pursue you even to Alexanderbad! In any case, I beg your pardon and say my best thanks!

Your
very devoted
J. Brahms

Vienna,
IV, Carlsgasse 4.

342

Johannes Brahms to Wilhelm Lindeck

[Pörtschach, end of June 1877]

Dear and Honoured Herr Lindeck,

Your brother will give you a lengthy lecture concerning me, one of these days—I am extremely grateful in advance to you and to him for all sorts of things. Today, however, I say this only briefly, [as] I have no time to thank you because, *naturally*, I have something to ask of you!

On 1 July you will be clipping coupons for me and on that occasion will, I hope, have more German money in hand than I. Well then, I would like to send 1,000 (thousand) Marks to 'Frau Elise Grund, Hamburg, St Georg, Hammer Landstraße No. 172.' However, you do not need to wait until the first [of the month], and I would like very much to have word that the money was sent. I am staying at Pörtschach am See in Carinthia, which is a most lovely place to stay, and at the gateway to what is most beautiful, [places] which I am still hoping to see.

If Francesca had been produced in your town, I might be sitting in Germany now, in Baden.[8]

I am continuing to indulge in warm water bathing (the lake is hardly ever below 19° C [66° F]) and in Austrian warmth, called *Gemütlichkeit*. But enough for today. Give my best greetings to your brother, to your house-mates, and to other mutual friends, as well.

from your sincerely & thankfully devoted

J. Brahms

Brahms took particular pleasure in swimming very early in the morning, when no bathing suit was necessary.[9] But only someone who had swum in the Baltic Sea could call that water warm! And 1,000 Marks was a lot of money to send to his sister, particularly when one considers that he once asked Lindeck for 150 Marks for his own vacation expenses (1 July 1876). The 'mille' for his sister was a request Brahms would repeat many many times, now of Lindeck, later of Simrock.

343

Johannes Brahms to Wilhelm Lindeck

[Pörtschach, before 17 September 1877]

Esteemed Hr. L.,

Save me. Help me, in other words send as soon as possible as much as possible!

Would you send at least 300 [gulden] (in Marks, if convenient) to Herr Arthur Faber, Wien I, Esslinggasse 5 . . .[10]

. . . and once again you are being robbed of your conductor! Your the-atre will utterly deteriorate this way, and Mannheim really does not deserve that.[11] I thought I might come to your part of the world in the autumn, to

---

[8] The opera *Francesca da Rimini*, by Hermann Goetz. In fact, Brahms was present at its first performance in Mannheim, on 30 Sept.

[9] Willi Reich, *Johannes Brahms in Documenten zu Leben und Werk* (Zurich, 1975), 130.

[10] Part of the letter is missing.

[11] A reference to his friend, the conductor Ernst Frank, who was forced at this time to resign his post in Mannheim. Frank's dismissal by Wagner's partisans is an unpleasant story, tainted by anti-Semitism (Frank was Jewish) and snide remarks about Brahms. The remarks have survived in let-ters between Emil Heckel (who engineered Frank's dismissal) and Richard Wagner, and give chilling insight into some of the musical politics of the day. See Martin, *Johannes Brahms, Briefwechsel mit Wilhelm Lindeck*, 22–3.

Baden, but Austria has a tight grip on me and so I'm still sitting in . . .
[Pörtschach].

344
Johannes Brahms to Wilhelm Lindeck

[Lichtenthal bei Baden-Baden, after 17 September 1877]

Dear Hr. Lindeck!

Didn't you receive my cry for help? For a man who has to take care of others must certainly not go travelling!

I, however, am thinking of going off on Monday, and if I don't receive a beautiful bank balance I'll have to touch every court conductor along the way for a loan. That is not so very promising, however. (I asked you to send 100 thalers to Elise Grund, Hamburg Hammer Landstraße 172.)

On Tuesday or Wednesday I'll be in Munich and hope to find your brother very well once more.

All the best,

your

J. Brahms

It is Joseph Joachim who brought Bach's D minor Chaconne for solo violin into the concert repertory (from the Partita, BWV 1004), and Brahms never tired of hearing it. He sent his version of it for piano left hand to Clara, by chance just as she had injured her right hand.

345
Johannes Brahms to Clara Schumann

Pörtschach, June 1877

Dear Clara,

I do believe that it's been a long time since I sent you anything as diverting as today—if your fingers can stand the pleasure! The Chaconne is for me one of the most wonderful, incomprehensible pieces of music. On a single staff, for a small instrument, the man writes a whole world of the deepest thoughts and the most powerful feelings. If I were to imagine how *I* might have made, conceived the piece, I know for certain that the overwhelming excitement and awe would have driven me mad. Now if the greatest violinist is not around, then the best enjoyment is probably just to let it sound in one's mind . . .

But the piece provokes one to become involved with it in all possible ways. After all, one doesn't always want to hear music merely ringing in thin air, Joachim is not often here, one tries it this way and that. But whatever I choose, orchestra or piano—my enjoyment is invariably spoilt.

In one way only, I find, can I devise for myself a greatly diminished but comparable and absolutely pure enjoyment of the work—when I play it with the left hand alone! At times the story of the egg of Columbus even comes to my mind![12] The similar difficulties, the type of technique, the arpeggios, they all combine—to make me feel like a violinist!

Do try it sometime, I wrote it out only for your sake! However: don't strain your hand unduly! It demands such a great deal of tone and power, so for the time being play it *mezza voce*. Also, make the fingerings practical and comfortable for yourself. If it's not too strenuous for you—which I believe to be the case, however—you are bound to have a lot of fun with it.

I suppose you have heard from Groth there?

My greetings to the beautiful Baltic Sea and to that dear secretary, and do give dictation to her again soon

for your

Johannes.

Wüllner's decision to leave Munich, where his position *vis-à-vis* Levi had become untenable, was now final. But Brahms was uneasy, based on his (correct) assessment of the even worse conditions which Wüllner would face in his new job in Dresden. In particular, he worried that his friend would have to deal with men whom he himself could not abide: Ernst Schuch, the court conductor there, and Julius von Platen, director of the Court Theatre.

346
Johannes Brahms to Franz Wüllner

[July 1877]

Dear friend,

I just want to tell you that all this time I have felt the most heartfelt need to write you a long letter, to chat with you at length about your situation.

But particularly by letter, it is as difficult as it is useless, I suppose. There's nothing new I can tell you, and ultimately every man knows for himself what he wants or has to do.

---

[12] Columbus is said to have solved the thorny problem of how to stand an egg on end by setting it down so firmly he crushed the bottom, thereby creating a stable base.

I may never have told you how I view your affairs and circumstances there, but I hope I don't need to. It is a fact—that I prefer to express myself to the other side, as I have indeed done often enough to Levi.

Nevertheless, I wish you would stay in M[unich]. If I were in your place, I would gladly give up a great deal of the theatre—if I were made Director of the Conservatory etc.

You have had serious, sorry experiences with friend and colleagues. But—Platen and Schuch are people with whom one cannot even have that!

From what I now hear, I suppose every word comes too late and the advice to be careful, indeed, suspicious under the new circumstances is probably also superfluous. And so, I just wish you all the best that one can wish a person. The main portion thereof you have at home, in Munich as well as in Dresden! Do let me know briefly if your departure is indeed quite decided?

With my warmest greetings to you and yours,

your J. Brahms.

Pörtschach am See, Carinthia.

Wüllner was much moved by Brahms's concern for his well-being, and responded to his friend's letter with a very congenial visit to Pörtschach a few weeks later.

In the leisure of the summer, Brahms also had time to advise Clara to produce a complete edition of the works of Robert Schumann, rather than agree to an English edition of the vocal and piano music. His efforts towards Breitkopf & Härtel on her behalf were astute and successful.

347
Johannes Brahms to Clara Schumann

Pörtschach, July 1877

Dearest Clara,

So once again, my best thanks for the very dear letter, I am greatly pleased that the Chaconne wasn't just a childish impulse, and gave you pleasure, and by all sorts of other things. I am very sorry about Groth, to say nothing of Marmorito. But have you been told of Heyse's continuing enormous misfortunes?[13]

---

[13] Groth's wife was mortally ill. Marmorito—Clara's son in law—had just lost his eldest son. Heyse was another of the many friends who lost young children. 'Above all don't marry,' was a comment Brahms once made to a friend on such an occasion.

I, on the other hand, have time for nothing.

I am long overdue with a letter to Härtel—and so I wanted to write to you about the business once again—but nothing will come of it. All I ask is that you write nothing definite, either to England, or to H. Keep everything vague and stay free!

For my part, I am sufficiently impudent and liberated to write this very day to H., approximately as follows. If you don't like it, you may upbraid me and write to them that *you have nothing to do with it* and [it] *doesn't suit you.*

—'I do not know how I can make any further comments about the Schumann affair, unless I do so very candidly—and possibly hurt your feelings.

The English intermezzo came about as a result of a simple offer. Frau Sch. has every reason to heed such a one. But I utterly fail to understand why you don't just as simply wipe it out of existence by also making an offer?

I, and many others with me, dearly wish that the two names R. and Cl. might be united in a German edition of the Sch. works. The reverence which is paid the _ _ _ pair can only increase for ever and evermore, and unite their names ever more intimately.[14] They were united as gloriously in life as in art, and in the one as in the other, that noble union should be hallowed by an external symbol.

There is no need for me to expound to a publisher how dearly everyone would want to own particularly the piano things and songs, in such an edition. That is an advantage and a most beautiful ornament unlike any you can obtain with any other work.[15]

The Englishman has offered 1,000 tlr. for the piano things alone, without laying claim to their sole ownership. If I were to add to this the songs and everything else, then 3,000 tlr. seems modest to me, to start with. In general, you do take risks with a venture like this; with *this one*, however, I dispute that you risk anything. No other publisher can acquire the ornament of those two united names. But the whole world will bestow ever more love and devotion on both together—something I don't wish to consider from a business point of view.

You know Frau Sch.'s delicacy in money matters, you are also aware of her circumstances which make those important for her. Should *you* now remain silent, like Frau Sch., however, it is impossible to forsee where the matter will end.

---

[14] In his almost identical letter to Breitkopf, Brahms replaced the dashes with the word 'heavenly'.

[15] Because Robert wrote the songs *to*, and piano music *for*, Clara.

Apart from you, there are perhaps 2 other German publishers that I would want to consider. *This* I must confess, however, that should the estimated proceeds for Frau Sch. seem even dubious—I would do everything to induce her to allow the proposed edition (especially the piano things and songs) appear in Paris, London, Petersburg, thereby setting a monument for the Germans such as they have richly deserved here and often enough with regard to their great men.

I will mention as an aside that for this venture, I put myself at your and Frau Sch.'s disposal, completely and without any reservations.

Frau Sch. knows nothing of this letter, but I will inform her this very day of the liberties I have taken concerning *you and her*. Now I sincerely beg both of you to *forgive me for any conceivable thing that might require it.*'

That, roughly, is what I will copy out straight away. It doesn't actually concern you—but don't rush into anything, and let me know by a word if you are angry—but if I had asked beforehand—there'd be no end to it.

But for today,
most affectionately,
your Joh.

Brahms kept his word. He sent virtually the identical letter to Breitkopf with wondrous effect, particularly for a man who often claimed he had no business sense. The publishing house sent a contrite, slightly apologetic answer to Brahms, and offered Clara a contract for 10,000 thaler for editing the complete works.

348
Johannes Brahms to Breitkopf & Härtel

[Pörtschach, 27] July 1877

Highly esteemed gentlemen,

With only the fewest words I tell you that your letter has brought me the greatest pleasure. I am about to go on a little excursion, but do not like to keep my thanks locked in my heart and am writing to Frau Schumann in the highest of spirits.

Even though my immodest letter might or could have been necessary, I will gladly also feel somewhat ashamed—or do whatever else is left in such a case to one who means well or writes badly.

For today, once more my best thanks!

Herr Iwan Knorr is here on a visit. I commend most earnestly what he will write to you, together with Herr Wüllner, who is also here.[16]

[16] See Letters 349 and 354.

I don't have time, since the railway is supposed to transport all 3 of us as well as this letter.

Your very devoted

J. Brahms

Clara had misgivings about her editorial abilities, and asked Brahms to promise he would edit the orchestral and choral works. He agreed; many of the final editorial decisions in the piano works, too, were left to him, and every proof sheet went through his hands. The project took more than ten years to complete, with Brahms supervising the work of several editors—Rudorff, Bargiel, and Dietrich among them. Only the last, supplemental volume bears his name. Ironically, but not surprisingly, the collaboration led eventually to some of his most difficult moments with Clara.[17]

349

Johannes Brahms to Clara Schumann

Pörtschach am See, August 1877

Dear Clara,

I don't believe that you need to give much thought to additional conditions. You can take the P.S. of Härtel's letter seriously; they will never contradict you if, when the case arises, you should have a wish.[18] But in this I too have no experience, after all! It's ridiculous, but I believe that without my letter, this fine business would not have come about!

Now I understand how serious your suggestion is concerning half of the honorarium—but, unfortunately, I have neither the inclination nor the patience to respond seriously and in detail.

Let it go until we have a chat sometime. You know, after all, that I am used to and have no problem picking up a few thousand Marks—but for the time being do accustom yourself a little to the idea that where my dealings with you and your husband are concerned—in a manner of speaking, and under certain circumstances, and so to speak, and quite generally—and then do some heavy thinking and don't insist on keeping all benevolence to yourself, but leave a wee bit to others.

But an absolutely essential condition is: that Härtels pay you the money *before* work on the edition begins. At least one half this year in which you

[17] On Brahms's contribution, see Linda Correll Roesner, 'Brahms's Editions of Schumann', in George Bozarth (ed.), *Brahms Studies* (Oxford, 1990), 251 ff.

[18] Their letter urged Clara to trust them with every doubt she might have along the way (Litz, iii. 360).

begin to work! The second half at this or that time. You must talk that over with an experienced man.

After all, *your work* could be finished before publication, and in any case you will forgo other earnings because of it!

If you were to do only the essential work on it, it would indeed be well paid—but the work you'll do will be much more than necessary, or is paid for with 10,000 tlr.!!!

As for the orchestral and choral things, right now I don't know that the editor will have much to do. Only the early piano things present difficulties, and specifically those which were published twice by your husband.

I recently accompanied Wüllner and Iwan Knorr (a young Russian who has written the most exquisite orchestral variations) on a walk and then went trekking in the Ampezzo Valley for two days—A more splendid walk one surely cannot take!

Our landscape, by the way, resembles that of the Starnberger See a little, except that we have higher mountains in the distance, the *Karawanken.* In today's picture, you see M[aria] W[örth] from the shore, our Pörtschach lies on the opposite side, to the *left.*[19]

How delighted you would have been in the Ampezzo Valley! Towering over everything, the mountains (dolomite rock with the most peculiar shapes and colours, so that one cannot get one's fill of them), the lakes, the flowers, the splendid road and what not.

Wüllner's visit gave me great pleasure—but I have no wish to start writing about his business.

I repeat my warmest best wishes for Elise, and to all of you my best greetings.

Once again, I remind you of the condition: the honorarium to be paid *as of now.*

You also need have no qualms about any possible bleak presentiments. After all, I am a collaborator, and your name on the title-page is in fact justified even before the work is completed.

Send word very soon to

your

Johannes.

Of course he declined her offer to split the honorarium. He picked up more than a few thousand Marks that summer—for the First Symphony and the songs Simrock paid over 25,000 Marks. But having sold his music to his various publishers, he gave up all further claim. In principle, Simrock or Breitkopf could hire any hack to make

[19] M.W. is an island town in the lake.

any kind of arrangement of any piece they owned. In practice, they tried not to stray too far from the wishes of Brahms, who was particularly fond of Theodor Kirchner's work. The latter was therefore commissioned by Breitkopf to make a four-hand arrangement of the Handel Variations, Op. 24.

350
Johannes Brahms to Theodor Kirchner

[Pörtschach, 10 August 1877]

Dear friend,

You can tell from the many scratch marks that I looked through your work with the deepest gratitude and delight.

Just do whatever you want with it all! Double it, cut it, ornament it—you'll see, it's going to turn into a pretty 4-hand piece. In Var. XIX the 1st part seems awkward to me? XXV, the accompaniment; playing the *Nachschlag* may be easier with 2 hands, almost. Sheet XI and earlier, the overlaying and crossing of hands seem very difficult to me? Finally, I am also having a heap of songs sent to you, as thanks for quite a few such delightful shipments. With it, my wishes for much enjoyment, if I may express the hope! Some may be nice for Kirchneresque piano pieces?[20] Once more, my best thanks and warmest greetings, also to your Maria.

Affectionately,
your
J. Brahms

Few composers can have had relationships with their publishers to rival those of Brahms. His publishers became his friends, or rather, he only did business with those who could be friends. Complete confidence on both sides was an essential element—and the reason Breitkopf was abandoned, years earlier. His publishers could count on Brahms's best under all circumstances; Brahms could rely on his publishers to go out of their way to comply with his requests and to deal with him in a straightforward manner.

However true this was of Rieter-Biedermann and Max Abraham (of Peters Editions), it was particularly a feature of his relationship to Simrock. The men became close friends, even to the point of exchanging 'Du's' towards the end of Brahms's life. Brahms could vent his anger and annoyance over some of Simrock's business practices and occasional vapidity, Simrock could nag for pieces he was anxious to publish. Simrock had infinite patience with Brahms's sarcasm, and knew how to defend himself. The men teased and joked, and understood each other's

[20] Kirchner published a number of arrangements of Brahms songs for solo piano.

peccadillos. Money was never a troubling issue between them—Brahms entrusted Simrock with the custody of his entire fortune, made him privy to the contents of his will, and to some of his most private thoughts. In turn, Simrock confided in Brahms; one of his letters is an urgent appeal to talk over some problems, and he calls Brahms the person he most trusts.[21]

A few letters from 1877 convey some idea of their friendship, starting with a letter from Simrock, addressing Brahms's reluctance to name his price for the songs and symphony.

351
Fritz Simrock to Johannes Brahms

[Berlin,] 12 April 1877

Dear Brahms,

Joachim I haven't seen yet, I arrived back early yesterday morning. But the symphony is in England, while Joachim has been here since March 31st. I do in fact find it injudicious, for all possible and impossible reasons, to leave the manuscript in the hands of strangers without further ado!! I hope that everything will soon be in your hands; I would really like to publish it at the beginning of September and will say again that it is not always easy to have fine engravers available. Could I at least count on it confidently by the beginning of June? For even if you really intend to make changes, you could surely estimate roughly how long—at the *very most*—it would take?—

Nothing seems more awkward to me—than having to make you an offer! I confess I just wouldn't know at all how to approach it, and it is surely more fitting that you leave things as they are and state your demands according to *your* view:—for in any case that would be the decisive one, and nothing more embarrassing could happen *to me* than to have a disagreement with you in such matters! Simply believe this, as I told you at the beginning of our relationship—and I can only keep on repeating it: no demand of yours is ever too high for me. From that point of view, I suggest therefore that you kindly retain the present *modus [operandi]*—and, for that matter, that you not cause me the pain of handing over your manuscripts to other publishers—be they now songs or anything else—it is simply that I am *personally* devoted to every note of yours.

On Lake Geneva it is again amazingly beautiful—but Sunday and Monday in Rüdesheim it was warmer, at least—and add to that those lovely children!!! I suppose Billroth has been there for quite a while already—at

---

[21] Stephenson, *Weg einer Freundschaft*, 207–8, July 1886.

least, he left here last week. *Please,* do send me the *address of Billroth and* that of Frau Faber—I would like to send them a thing or two.

Op. 65 and Op. 67 4 hnds you will have received? Today I am sending Op. 56 and Op. 60, 4hnds. Do you want more? Naturally, I will provide [them] to Frau Schumann and Fritz Brahms—do you have any other wishes?

Warm greetings from your F. Simrock

Does Frau Faber *play* the piano?[22]

Given his bent for variation, Brahms found innumerable ways to tease Simrock about his business practices.

352
Johannes Brahms to Fritz Simrock

[Pörtschach, 16 June 1877]

In the Finale of the symphony, would you arrange to have it set as *Allegro <u>non troppo</u>,* instead of *Allegro <u>moderato</u> ma con brio.*

The engravers haven't got that far yet, and so it won't be necessary to correct all the parts later on.

How are you otherwise and what are your plans for the summer? How are things at Joachim's? How would it be if you made editions of the *Lullaby* in minor, for naughty or sickly children? That would be one more possibility of increasing the number of editions![23]

All the best,
your
J. Br.

To honour the long-awaited First Symphony, Simrock had a specially bound edition of it sent to Brahms. It reached him at home.

---

[22] Indeed she did, having studied the piano in Hamburg with Carl Grädener.

[23] By 1877 there were arrangements for two, four, or six hands at the piano, Salon and other fantasies for piano, arrangements for one or more flutes or violins and piano, or for cello and piano. The arrangments for four-part male choir, zither and voice, harp, or orchestra, came after this letter was written. See McC 201–2, for the complete list.

353
Johannes Brahms to Fritz Simrock

[Vienna, 8 November 1877]

Dear S.

I don't know if you have sufficient imagination to be able to picture the pleasure which your kindness has given me, and how grateful I am to you! For it is hardly possible describe it—the emotion, in particular, is really hard to put into words! Really, just imagine quite seriously a delighted composer, and since you know me well enough to know that I am not exactly vain, you will know that for all it's splendour, I actually relish only your great kindness! I also regard it as the only blemish of the magnificent volume that name and number are already inscribed on it—otherwise, I would seek out what *belongs* in it. It is lying on the piano now and delights and astonishes everyone—I have to shield it from the gaze of young composers, otherwise you would be getting too many symphonies!

You know that you have to deliver 7 first, 7 second, 5 violas, cellos and basses and individual wind parts to the Gesellschaft der Musikfreunde, here. I suppose that Mannheim, Breslau, Munich are being heard from? The new symphony [Op. 73] is supposed to be done here on December 9th. I'm afraid, however, that the copyists won't permit that. After that it might be possible on the 30th. In any case I'm definitely going to Leipzig at the beginning of January—where presumably you will also be in the audience. In any case, it will be a complete flop, and people will declare that this time I took it easy. But my advice to you is to be careful! Be glad that you got away with the first one. By the way, there are a mass of symphonies, etc., lying about in my place, they are by persons applying for a State Stipend and the Beethoven stipend. You could acquire all of them—a bargain sale.

Give my warm greetings to Frau Joachim, I would so much like to hear my songs done by her! She really ought to give some concerts here with Frau Schumann, do tell her.

Concerning Herbeck, that is, his succession, one cannot say anything as yet. There is nothing to report, either from me or from Stockhausen. Naturally I don't think of or about such matters before I am hard pressed by them.[24]

Should you actually be tempted to acquire a second symphony for yourself, I suppose I need hardly ask you to think the matter over very amicably

---

[24] Herbeck died suddenly, leaving the Gesellschaft orchestra conductorless.

and without embarrassment—after listening to it. In general I am not at all sensitive, but towards you—that would be sinful indeed!

And now I am once again overcome by emotion and I'll go and feast my eyes and murmur my thanks to you!

Sincerely devoted,

J. Br.

Brahms sat on the committee charged with deciding which aspiring composers from the Austro-Hungarian Empire to support with central funds from Vienna. In this way Antonin Dvořák came to his attention, and found he had a benefactor.

354
Johannes Brahms to Fritz Simrock

[Vienna, December 1877]

Dear S.

In connection with the State Stipend, I have for several years now found pleasure in the things by Anton Dvořák (pronounced Dvorschak) from Prague. Well, this year he sent among other things, a volume of (10) duets for 2 sopranos with pianoforte, which strikes me as so very beautiful and *practical* for the publishing house. He appears to have had the volume printed at his own expense. The title and, unfortunately, the text as well, are only in Bohemian. I have urged him to send the songs to you! When you play them through you will be as pleased by them as I was and, as a publisher, you will be especially pleased by their piquancy. Now what has to be taken care of very intelligently is a very good translation! Some of the texts may already have been translated by Wenzig (who died recently). Otherwise, Dr Siegfried Kapper in Prague may be available for it. Dvořák has written all sorts of things. Operas (in Bohemian), symphonies, quartets, things for piano. He is in any case a very talented person. And poor, by the way! Please to take this into consideration! The duets will appeal to you and may become a 'good article'. The address is: Prague, Korntorgasse No. 10, II.[25]

I don't look at my symphonies very often, but I can hardly ever look at a volume of music without catching a mistake. (Unfortunately I don't make

[25] Simrock published them in 1879 as *Moravian Duets*, Op. 38, for Soprano and Alto. There are four collections of duets, some songs of which appear under several opus numbers, so that not all of the songs mentioned in this letter were published by Simrock at the same time. Safe to say that by 1878 Simrock had the Slavonic Dances for Piano Duet under his imprint, and by 1879, several collections of duets. Brahms's knowledgeability about translators of poetry from the non-German parts of the Empire stemmed from his own interest in folk literature. Joseph Wenzig and Siegfried Kapper were leading poets from Bohemia, whose translations Brahms had just used in his Op. 69.

good use of this talent.) Page 46, measure 2, Violin II must read ( ), 32nd instead of 16th (but it doesn't matter!). Tell me, would you please send the scores of my duets and sextets to Dessoff? All in payment for the beautiful *Robert le Diable*.[26]

If you were to send me as printed matter, and at your convenience, a volume of Mendelssohn, my fingers and my soul would raise no objections. For instance, volumes 2, 3, 4 of the piano music, 3 church music pieces Op. 23 and his Lindblad songs![27]

Yesterday we did the B flat major Sextet. On Sunday Walter will sing 4 of the new songs.

There is nothing doing in Munich this month. This forces me to give in for the 30th, I suppose, since in fact I would prefer to rehearse more than in Leipzig. From L. I'll probably have to go to Hamburg and Bremen (for the C Minor).

Incidentally, apart from Dvořák, I also have in stock a young Russian who has written some excellent variations for orchestra![28] But I'll bide my time, and more! But you know and will take into consideration that I do not recommend lightly, and will look over the jolly and refreshing Bohemian duets accordingly?

All the best,

your

J. Br.

By 1877, Brahms's relationship to the Herzogenbergs, particularly to Elizabet, was marked by a mutually high level of humour, ease, and obvious warmth.

As he was one of the editors working on the complete edition of Chopin underway at Breitkopf & Härtel (with Franz Liszt, Woldemar Bargiel, and Ernst Rudorff, among others), he wrote to Elizabet, hoping, on the advice of her former piano teacher, that she could help him: in Paris her father had once studied the piano with Chopin, giving rise to the supposition that he owned manuscripts and first editions with corrections in the composer's hand. Brahms was also planning to conduct his Second Symphony in Leipzig at the beginning of January. In his letter he used the simplified spelling, *Sinfonie*, and studiously refrained from inviting himself to stay with the Herzogenbergs, much to Elizabet's dismay.

[26] The opera by Giacomo Meyerbeer. An especially fine score was sent to Brahms by Dessoff, with the request that Brahms send some of his own scores in exchange (*BW* x. 53).

[27] Simrock was the German publisher of the eight volumes of *Songs Without Words* for piano, as well as the *Three Pieces of Church Music,* for Solo, Chorus and Organ.

[28] *Variations on a Ukranian Folk-Song*, Op. 7. Iwan Knorr, German-born and Russian-bred, visited Brahms in Pörtschach in July, a visit he described vividly to Max Kalbeck (Kal, iv. 152 ff.). Brahms took an immediate liking to him. Breitkopf, not Simrock, published the variations.

355
Johannes Brahms to Elizabet von Herzogenberg

[Vienna, 13 November 1877]

Most cherished friend,

When you behold my handwriting, you'll undoubtedly assume that I wanted to start 'making up to you' in plenty of time; possibly ask to be commended to Hauffe-Härtel or the Hauffe Hotel. But that is not so. True, I'm coming to Leipzig in the beginning of January, but I'll rely on my good luck—if necessary, even on the stars,—with which Baedeker designates so many houses in Leipzig.

But I have a request and furthermore ask for an answer, please. I am being pressed by Härtel to take an interest in a complete edition of Chopin.

And so I'd like to know whether your parents have manuscripts—or, what would be most important for me, examples [or proofs] of his things in which he had made corrections or notations!

Could one have such things sent to Vienna? Or could one perhaps look at them in Dresden or Leipzig?

If I were a respectable person, my letter would only now begin in earnest; were I of brazen character, I would be tempted to slip a bad joke on music paper into the envelope.[29]

I am neither and so I commend myself to you (all three of you) most warmly and ask for permission to be allowed to invite you personally and most devotedly to the performance of my latest *Sinfonie.*

Your wholly devoted
J. Brahms.

IV. Karlsgasse 4.

Elizabet immediately replied with an invitation to Brahms to stay with them (this time he spent eleven days as their guest). She chided Brahms for referring to a *Sinfonie* rather than a more elegant *Symphony*; and scolded him for not having started his letter by inviting himself to their house outright (Leipzig, 15 Nov. 1877):

Now tell me yourself if it wouldn't have been much nicer to begin thus:
'I'm arriving on the 1st of January, make sure that good coffee is at hand, this time provide fresh cream instead of boiled, since you finally did notice that I prefer it, also don't let me get so hungry again but give me a decent second breakfast the approximate dimensions of which were indicated to

---

[29] See Letter 356.

you by Emma Engelmann; if you attend to of all that properly I'll play the new symphony for you in the course of the first few days and won't wait until J. Stockhausen arrives' etc. etc.

She ended her letter by blaming herself for having been too modest to invite him sooner.

356
Johannes Brahms to Elizabet von Herzogenberg

[Vienna, 22 November 1877]

Most esteemed lady!

Modesty is the most impractical garment a person can wear. Are you just putting me on, or did you really not notice the bashful gall with which my letter stroked the beard, that lovely one on your husband's face? Nor do I need any instruction in world history, which you only distorted anyway. The virtuous storks return and deliver in December, not in January, etc.[30]

But the latest one really is no symphony, but merely a *Sinfonie*, and there is no need for me to play it for you beforehand. All you need do is sit down, place your little feet alternately on both pedals, and strike an F minor chord for a good while, alternately low and high, *ff* and *pp*—then you will gradually gain the most accurate picture of the 'latest'.

But I must really ask your forgiveness for doing nothing but contradict you! To make up for it, I'll report that Goldmark arrived here yesterday and will presumably also be in Leipzig in January, on account of his opera. Unfortunately the opera draws him away all the time—not only from his workshop in Gmunden, but also from here. I wish I had him here. He is a most delightful person, and not many like him can be found here.[31]

But this is the umpteenth letter of the morning! I cannot go on. If I stick it into its envelope anyway, it is only because it seems to me that you may really have misunderstood my previous one?

It was actually a begging letter. (Epstein's stories had led me to expect more of your Chopin!?)

For today, only the best greetings

from your very devoted

J. Brahms.

Several more letters were exchanged before the Leipzig visit.

[30] An allusion to the text of the song 'Alte Liebe', Op. 71 No. 1, which Elizabet seems to have misinterpreted.

[31] The composer Carl Goldmark and his opera *The Queen of Sheba*.

357
Johannes Brahms to Elizabet von Herzogenberg

[Vienna, 12 December 1877]

Dear revered friend,

There was the writing paper, all ready for you—along comes a letter from Limburger and invites me to play my Concerto in Leipzig on the 1st of January! I really don't know what I should do, and won't write you a letter right now, so I can think about it!![32]

You can imagine the respect your last letter instilled in me, how it impressed me with your insight! One could say that it reads like—one of Beethoven's sketchbooks. One sees dawning, emerging—just sketch in the rest for yourself.[33]

But can you also tolerate bad jokes? As a peace-offering I had planned to enclose the Andante from my third Piano Quartet, which I still had here and which you had liked, after all. Whether I had saved it out of vanity or tender feelings, I don't know. I'll bring it along.

Considering your perspicacity, I need not explain the enclosed bad joke, nor say that I am very much in favour of the reuse use of invented themes! The Veil of the Night should now find general acceptance, as also the boy's secret wish ('oh that the moon would hide behind the clouds! Would it were dark!'). How intelligently and intelligibly one can write nowadays (to those in the know).

But you can see, my thoughts are with Limburger! I'm supposed to do the F minor here on the 30th—then play the piano!?!?

With all my heart, your devoted

J. Br.

Brahms continued to refer to the mournful key of his new symphony ('F minor'), but the 'bad joke' was something else: the enclosed copy he had made of the vocal quartet, 'O schöne Nacht', Op. 92 No. 1. It made use of a theme by Heinrich von Herzogenberg but was set to an 'explicit' poem by Daumer. Since Elizabet had recently objected to Brahms's use of another suggestive text, primly reminding him that certain sentiments were only acceptable in folk-style,[34] Brahms left blank the space where the words 'The youth steals near to his beloved softly—softly—softly—'

---

[32] Paul Bernhard Limburger (1826–91) was a member of the Gewandhaus Board of Directors, and notably partial to Brahms's music in the otherwise cool Leipzig atmosphere.

[33] Brahms's remark in a previous letter was at first misunderstood by Elizabet; the light dawned as the letter progressed, giving rise to this comment.

[34] 'Willst du, daß ich gehe' Op. 74 No. 4, to a poem by Lemke.

should have been, and wrote across the score, 'Stop, dear Johannes, what are you doing! At best such things can only be spoken of in folk-style, unfortunately you've forgotten *again*! Only a peasant is allowed to ask if he may stay or should go—and alas you are no peasant! Don't offend that fair head with its glory of gold—have done, simply repeat'—and here the correct text begins again: 'O schöne Nacht'. It was a neat way of teasing and complimenting the golden-haired Elizabet at the same time.[35]

Brahms agreed to play his piano concerto in the Gewandhaus, nineteen years after its ignominious first performance there. It fared only slightly better this time.

358
Johannes Brahms to Heinrich von Herzogenberg

[Vienna, 13 December 1877]

Worthy friend,

I forgot to say yesterday that in case I do play in Leipzig, I would find it very agreeable to have to stay in a hotel for a few days. For I am embarrassed to practise in the house of friends, and that has to happen! So, if I should go through with the silly prank of saying Yes, I would ask you to engage a room and a *pianino* for me, at Hauffe's or wherever you wish.

Then, after your rooms become free, I will be too, and can make a ceremonial move through the streets into your house!

NB. Presumably I have a concert here on the 30th, will therefore arrive at the last moment. Are you on sufficiently good terms with Reinecke to discuss the concert grand with him? I'll be going directly to the rehearsal, and would really like to find the *very best* there?!

With my best greetings,

your most hurried

J. Br.

Elizabet dissuaded him from the hotel, promising food, solitude, and her piano: 'You only have few meagre hours to practise, and without proper supervision you are sure not to put them to proper use—but I'll make sure, sit you down at the piano and then leave, so you won't be "embarrassed. . .".'

---

[35] With this letter we have a glimpse into the composer's mind, as well, for the 'Veil of the Night' is his own alternative title for 'O schöne Nacht'. Neither 'the veil' nor the 'boy's secret wish', i.e. that the moon stay behind a cloud, is anywhere to be found in Daumer's poem, but is undoubtedly to be sought in Brahms's setting.

359
Johannes Brahms to Elizabet von Herzogenberg

[Vienna, 29 December 1877]

At this distance, it's impossible to discuss hotel, dessert, and grand piano. Hope, however, that you make no fuss and scorch none of them.

I am supposed to arrive on Monday at 12.45 and go immediately to the rehearsal; maybe your husband could enquire if I might not dispose of my things beforehand, and perhaps even be permitted to wash! But it's no use—
Ever your unwashed

J. Br.

Musicians *here* play my latest one with black crepe armbands, because it sounds so very mournful; it will also be printed with a black border.

Work on the complete Chopin Edition was a job Brahms took very seriously. His comments to Ernst Rudorff are in answer to a number of questions the editor of the Ballades had posed in his previous letter (Rudorff had just finished the revision of the G minor Ballade, Op. 23, and was working on the F major, Op. 38, with its section in A minor). This letter tells us how important proof-sheets are in preparing a critical edition of *Brahms's* music, for it highlights Brahms's belief that a composer was more likely to make last-minute changes to the proof-sheets rather than to the autograph.[36]

During the next decade, Brahms would repeat his wish that complete editions might be available to scholars and students in strategically located libraries, eliminating the urge to publish every scrap a composer wrote. (Regarding his own work, his solution was to burn everything he did not publish.)

360
Johannes Brahms to Ernst Rudorff

[Vienna, 1 November 1877]

Dear Herr Rudorff.

I send you my best thanks for your repeated enquiries, and do so all the more gravely since I must confess that my view of the thing itself, of our current work, is not exactly a very hopeful one; but what I find most consoling and encouraging is that we are tackling individual [works] and seeking to advance them, so we can—delude ourselves as to what was achieved or can be achieved.

---

[36] *BW* iii. 164, 21 Oct. 1877. See also this volume, Letter 355.

I don't need to point out to you that the manuscripts leave much to be desired, that they are not absolutely authoritative, that I do not wish someone else's insight and decisions introduced into the text itself etc.

But I swim against the stream at times. And so I want to confess that I am not exactly enthusiastic about the editions of Handel and Mozart.[37] I wish that instead of [publishing] this one—no, at least beforehand—it could be arranged for several large libraries to possess good copies of the complete works not just of those two, but of other masters as well. I wouldn't insist on cramming my room full of a goodly number of the works of Handel or Mozart if only I could locate them for use in the library, and along with them, the authentic, complete works for example of Haydn, among others.

But to *Chopin*. More important than anything we can do in the text, I find, is the information about it that we can provide in supplements, in a report on the revisions. I want to be as expansive in this, as modest in the other. It would be unfortunate if no such supplement were to appear (as in Beethoven's case).[38]

The revision of the the G minor Ballade was very much along my ideas; of course—I would want the few more important changes to be in that supplement—unless by chance they have appeared in Brandus, an edition I consider very important. (Don't you have a good friend in Paris who could keep a sharp look-out for any proof-sheets that might still be around?)[39]

In the A minor Ballade, although is incomprehensible to me, too, I would let it stand. Also this A, which corresponds somewhat to the subsequent . But the 3 fifths I endorse most decidedly!

In general, one probably has to make one's own decision in specific instances, particularly where accidentals and other minor points are concerned. More rigid guidelines would probably bother one person or another soon enough, [and] a group can only reach a very rough concensus on certain points, I suppose.

I hope very much that Bargiel agrees with us that we should not try to

[37] Which Breitkopf had under way at this time.

[38] Brahms disliked editions of music crowded with footnotes, preferring a supplemental volume of comments.

[39] Brandus, Dufour, & Co., publishers of the first editions of Chopin's works. Brahms's admiration of this edition did not blind him to the misprints he suspected they contained.

improve Chopin's spelling![40] It would be just a small step, then, to attack his sentences as well.

But forgive my chattering on so long—which may make it that much more confusing!

I would be glad to hear more about the 'Symphony'.[41] I wish it would look as good beside my other things as your last 'Variations' do beside your other works. But that, unfortunately, is not the case, it's merely a number, one more piece.

With my best greetings, your very devoted
J. Brahms.

❧ 1878 ❧

Performances of the Second Symphony in Leipzig, Dresden, and Amsterdam, gave Brahms the opportunity to visit some friends and to help out another.

The first stop was Holland, which offered many pleasures including the Engelmanns' new baby, and the zoo.

361
Johannes Brahms to Theodor Wilhelm Engelmann [postcard]

[Amsterdam, 3 February 1878]

Sunday morning is a rehearsal in the Hague, for Saturday evening I'm invited here. Tomorrow evening is a rehearsal. Today's was very good. The parents are very cheerful. I haven't seen the little one. It was sold for 10,000 florins. I mean the *Hippopotamus*. The parents are very cheerful? The little one will be shown off tomorrow? I mean, in the *Kramvisite*.[1] And I had so wanted to see the little one! Here and there. Oh, those cruel mothers and Dutchmen! If something comes from Leipzig, don't give it to the museum.[2]

Fine greetings. Your
J. Br.

Franz Wüllner, now settled in Dresden, requested Brahms's appearance at a benefit concert for widows and orphans on Ash Wednesday, and was delighted to learn from

---

[40] Musical spelling, that is: whether to write e sharp or f natural, for example.
[41] A performance of Brahms's First by the Berlin Conservatory students.

[1] In Holland, a ceremonial visit to the new mother.
[2] Julius Röntgen, the violinist and long-time friend of the Engelmanns who edited the German edition of these letters, says the item was 'a wonderful doll for the "Little Prince" '.

Brahms that Clara Schumann, a native of Dresden, might also perform. There were a few problems to overcome, however: a limited fee for Clara, and the programme itself—which comprised not only Brahms's Second Symphony and the Beethoven Choral Fantasy, but also Wagner's 'Fire Music' and 'Wotan's Farewell' from *Walküre*; there was serious discussion as to whether Clara would agree to take part in any programme which included Wagner's music. Brahms wrote to Wüllner, instructing him on how to handle Clara, and then to Clara, encouraging her to accept.

362
Johannes Brahms to Franz Wüllner

[Hamburg, January 1878]

Dear friend,

The honorarium question is no obstacle—it was the same last Ash Wednesday, after all. It's true, to our friend the programme will seem—dreadful. I suppose you'll have to try by clever and kind words to make it plausible to her. Explain the Before and the After to her, mumble something about the home town, about income—I think it'll work.

I would actually consider the Fantasy more beautiful and more suitable for the programme. Well, I suppose you'll let her decide. (I don't suppose you are bothered by the conditions concerning the subsequent purchase of the symphony?)[3]

Hurriedly and affectionately
your J. B.

363
Johannes Brahms to Clara Schumann

Amsterdam, Brock's Doelen Hotel, January 1878

Dearest Clara,

It's a crying shame that you didn't accept the engagement here! Everything is so relaxed and lovely here and the symphony will come off beautifully, the orchestra and all the others are being exceedingly cheerful about it.

On the 4th and the 8th (*Felix meritis*)[4] it will be here, on the 6th in the Haag.

I'm just extraordinarily fond of Holland and feel very comfortable there. I find Verhulst so congenial, he reminds me so much of your husband!

---

[3] The Symphony would be performed from manuscript, but the orchestra was obliged to buy the parts once they were in print.   [4] 'Good fortune well deserved'.

On the 4th he's doing the Overture-Scherzo and Finale.[5]

Well that won't exactly go wonderfully, but I have the greatest pleasure in seeing his enthusiasm in rehearsal, more than at a more correct performance.

It was ditto lovely in Utrecht. Garlands, honorary membership, and lovely photographs, besides. My new *Liebeslieder* were sung in exemplary fashion by a small chorus and were repeated by them 2 days later. At the Engelmanns' everything is very well and the little woman is probably coming here for the symphony.

I am really pleased that the Magic Fire Music doesn't deter you from going to Dresden. But write to me if you change your mind—since I'm only going *on your account*, will otherwise stay at home.[6]

In Utrecht we had the 1st Symphony, of course. It's true the forces are very modest (some Amsterdamers were added), but little Hol is so good at what he does, had studied the material superbly, so that one couldn't help but enjoy it.[7]

Incidentally your 'congenital good fortune' always steers you very well, as now too with respect to the festivities in Leipzig, as also with Dresden and the Magic [Fire Music], which I had expected would have a terrible effect on you.

I imagine that Joachim will have a great success in Berlin with the 9th, and I am greatly pleased for him even beforehand.

My arm would allow me to continue writing for a long time, but I lack the time. Be content for now with this greeting and, if possible, delight me with one, however brief. I am leaving on the 9th to go home. I long for it fervently. Knocking around is hard to bear in the long run.

The very best greetings from

your

Johannes.

Concern over Clara's reaction to Wagner's music had been unnecessary. She calmly wrote, 'The Fire Music doesn't frighten me—I don't need to listen to it.'

In January, Dvořák wrote to Brahms with profuse thanks for the latters's interest in his work, and asked permission to dedicate his D minor String Quartet, Op. 34, to him.[8]

---

[5] Schumann, Op. 52. The conductor Johannes Verhulst was an early and enthusiastic supporter of Schumann, and chiefly responsible for the latter's success in Holland.

[6] Not really. In the end, Clara could not go for reasons unrelated to Wagner; but Brahms kept his commitment to Wüllner.

[7] Richard Hol (1825–1904), Municipal Music Director in Utrecht.

[8] That letter is included in *Dvořák, Correspondence and Documents*, ed. Kuny *et al.* (Prague, 1987–9), i. 133–4.

364
Johannes Brahms to Antonin Dvořák

[Vienna, end of] March [18]78

Most esteemed Sir,

I regret most exceedingly that I was away on a trip during your stay here. All the more so since I cannot hope, on account of my great aversion to writing, that conversing by letter can be even the least substitute. And so I will simply tell you today that it gives me the greatest pleasure to occupy myself with your things, and that I would therefore give a lot to be able to chat with you about particulars. You write somewhat hastily. However, while adding the many missing sharps, flats, and naturals, you might also take a closer look at the notes themselves, sometime, at the voice leadings etc. Do please forgive me, it is very presumptuous of me to express such wishes to a man like you! I do indeed welcome them most gratefully just the way they are, and would consider the dedication of the quartet an honour bestowed upon me.

It would seem to me sensible if you would give me both quartets I know of at the same time. Should Herr Simrock not be receptive, I could try elsewhere? . . .

For today, again my best thanks for the information[9] and sincere greetings.

Your very devoted
J. Brahms

365
Johannes Brahms to Fritz Simrock

[Vienna, 3] April 1878

Dear S.

I am off to Italy within the next few days, together with Billroth and Goldmark. Presumably I'll hang myself or will get hung up in Pörtschach am See—if it gets too hot in Italy. I wouldn't even have written that much to you if I didn't have *Dvořák* on my mind. I don't know what further risks you want to take with the man. I also know nothing about business, and how larger things generate interest. I am also reluctant to recommend, since I have nothing but my eyes and ears and these are quite peculiar. Maybe you should let him send you 2 string quartets in D major and minor, in case you

---

[9] Regarding a performance of Brahms's Piano Concerto in Prague.

are at all considering anything further, and have them played for you.[10] Dvořák possesses the very best of what a musician must have, and it is also in these pieces. I myself am such a terrible philistine—I wouldn't publish even my own things for the love of it.

In short, I want to say no more than to recommend D. in general. For the rest, you do have your own ears and a business sense, which also plays a part, after all.

To both these I would also commend Karl Eschmann, who would like to have more piano things printed. Op. 68, etc. He will be known to you and doesn't need my recommendation, since you have noticed with envy Luckhardt's many editions.[11]

Apart from that, I wish you the good life and beg to send greetings!

Your
J. Br.

I still have to find time to answer Herr Keller's questions![12]

Simrock declined to take the quartets, and Brahms did find another publisher for 'his' D minor (Schlesinger), at the same time inspiring Joachim to perform Dvořák's String Sextet and Quartet. (Ten years later, Simrock published a revised version of the E major String Quartet, changing the opus number from 27 to 80).

Following his first trip to Italy, Brahms settled in Pörtschach again for the summer. He was relaxed, working on piano music, a violin concerto, and a violin sonata, and in the mood for a practical joke. He wrote to the Schumann daughters, who were in the midst of moving house from Berlin to Frankfurt.

366
Johannes Brahms to Eugenie and Marie Schumann

Pörtschach am See, Carinthia

May I permit myself a request, most esteemed friends, to carry out a joke together with me?

I possess a few pages of music manuscript which bear the name of your dear mother and apparently contain fragments of compositions from her earlier period! Now I'd like to excite your mother about them a little or a lot by enquiring if the things had been published, if she had others, whether she

---

[10] Brahms was mistaken here: one quartet was in E major.
[11] Johann Karl Eschmann (1826–82); Swiss pianist and pedagogue of importance.
[12] His copyist. Brahms's correspondence with Keller is found in *The Brahms–Keller Correspondence*, ed. G. Bozarth with W. Martin (Lincoln, Neb., 1996).

couldn't still recall the missing beginning here, the missing ending there, and if she could supply it.

To that purpose I think it would be neatest if you would permit me to send you the pages, and if perhaps you said or wrote that you had found them in the course of the move.

Of course, one hopes that your mother doesn't simply toss the pages aside all too contemptuously; if you should be going to Baden, you could help to raise the level of interest.

For today I only request you to tell me if this has in fact reached you, and where I may send the pages? After that of course, I hope to hear in considerable detail how the affair is proceeding and succeeding.

In the most affectionate esteem,
Your
J. Brahms

June 1878

As Clara had just arrived in the new house and the family was leaving for the entire summer on the very next day, Brahms's plan could not be carried out as envisaged.

'But perhaps you can send the manuscript to us in the autumn,' wrote Eugenie, quite willing to help, 'we still have lots of boxes of music to unpack, and would have the opportunity to make a fine discovery. If only Mama could be induced to fill in what's missing!' She reported her delight at recently hearing his Second Symphony in Düsseldorf, as well as her boredom at sitting through Gluck's *Orpheus*, and gave details of the family's summer plans.

Brahms was unwilling to wait. His next letter tracked Eugenie down on holiday with a friend (the 'other appendage' mentioned in the following letter).

367
Johannes Brahms to Eugenie Schumann

[Beginning of July 1878]

Dear Fräulein Eugenie.

There's nothing I can do about it, it can't wait until autumn, and if, as it appears, you are most disdainfully breaking off all diplomatic relations and retiring to the highest mountain range—I will try to find you and to smuggle into your hands this precious testimony of motherly diligence.

So please, do me the favour and send them to your mother. *If* you had indeed found them in Berlin, it would certainly be unfair to haul them around with you in the wilderness like this. Afterwards get her to write to you, and you will likewise write and tell me what sort of face your mother made.

Anyway, you might at least have written to me where you are summer-holidaying! After all, I plan to go on occasional walks in the Austrian mountains, and it would certainly be a shame if I were to walk right by you and your second and other appendages.

For your kind praise, my warmest thanks. Our kind hears this sort of thing with great pleasure and in return even allows an otherwise cherished colleague (in this case, Esquire Gluck) to be hauled over the coals a bit.

Since I must hope and do desire to be permitted to write more to you soon, for today I commend myself most warmly to you and your purported appendages

as your devoted
J. Brahms

Pörtschach am See, Carinthia

The elaborate hoax was on Eugenie, as well as Clara. The bits of music were Brahms's own, from his latest piano compositions, the *Eight Piano Pieces*, Op. 76, written in a copyist's hand on old manuscript paper which had Clara Wieck's name printed on it; the whole thing seems to have been his way of learning what Clara thought of the pieces before she knew what they were.

She, however, could not be fooled. 'That is not at all ordinary,' she told Marie who reported to Eugenie, 'but it isn't by me; it could be by Papa, likewise also by Brahms.—I'll have to ask him about it some time, he knows every scrap of paper we have.'[13]

The first indication Joachim had of something wonderful in the making was the arrival of two short letters in quick succession, discreet heralds of the Violin Concerto. They reached him at his summer villa near Salzburg.

368
Johannes Brahms to Joseph Joachim

[Pörtschach, 21 August 1878]

Dear friend,

I wish I knew how long you'll be there and would like to send you a number of violin passages! I need hardly express the request which goes with

---

[13] Eugenie Schumann, *Erinnerungen*, 162–5.

them, the only question being whether you're too deeply engrossed in Mozart and perhaps Joachim himself, to devote a bit of time to this![14]

With the best greetings all around

your

J. Br.

369
Johannes Brahms to Joseph Joachim

[Pörtschach, 22 August 1878]

Dear friend,

Now that I have written it out, I don't actually know what you can do with the part by itself!

Naturally, I was going to ask you to make corrections, thought you should have no excuse either way—neither respect for music that is too good, nor the excuse that the score isn't worth the trouble. Now I'll be satisfied if you say a word, and maybe write in a few: difficult, uncomfortable, impossible, etc.

The whole business has four movements; I wrote out the beginning of the last—so that the awkward passages are forbidden me straightaway!

It's really a shame that I don't live in Berchtesgaden. My best greetings to all of yours and we'll wait and see what happens next.

Affectionately

your J. Br.

From Joachim, in August, came an excited reply:

> To me it's a great, genuine joy that you're writing a violin concerto (in four movements, no less!). I have immediately looked through what you sent, and here and there you'll find a note and a comment regarding changes— without a score, of course, it can't really be relished. Most of it is manageable, some of it even very original, violinistically. But whether it can all be played comfortably in a hot concert-hall I cannot say, before I've played it straight through. Any chance that one might get together for a couple of days?[15]

[14] Joachim was at work on his own music, the *Variations for Violin and Orchestra* in E minor (without Opus number).

[15] Andreas Moser, Joachim's associate and colleague for many years, and the editor of *BW* v and vi, notes that this copy of the violin part of the first movement of the concerto remained in Joachim's possession until his death, and bore numerous comments in his own hand, most of which related to matters of violin technique. See McC 327, for an additional description.

370

Johannes Brahms to Joseph Joachim

[Pörtschach, end of August 1878]

Well, dear friend, none of this sounds at all hopeless, and along with my best thanks I'll tell you right off that nothing need keep me from travelling to Salzburg once again.

On the other hand, since it would be really nice if you saw this region sometime, I will tell you that the journey here is very pretty and not all that bad. If you leave early in the morning at 6 (by way of Liezen, Selzthal, etc.) you are in Klagenfurt at 8 o'clock in the evening—just in time to miss the train here! However, at the railway station there are one- and two-horse carriages which will bring you here in a brief hour, and if an evening were agreed upon, I'd agree to be in Klagenfurt too.

Perhaps Simrock would come along? In the jolly open-air coach, bad jokes waft quickly away.

You would give a quite enormous pleasure here to your women friends Franz and Kupelwieser, and with the latter you'd be staying *very* comfortably.[16]

But I'm prattling on as though I'd never said what I did at the beginning! Most important, say right away how long you'll actually be staying?

I have just returned from a hot and arduous hike and tell you all this in the greatest hurry so as to get to some beer.

Best greetings to big and small from your

J. Br.

The Hamburg Philharmonic Society was celebrating its fiftieth Jubilee. When Brahms neglected to reply to an invitation to conduct his new symphony, an urgent message went to Hanslick to discover whether Brahms was planning to attend. Brahms replied to Hanslick's question.

371

Johannes Brahms to Eduard Hanslick

[Pörtschach, September 1878]

[Dear friend,]

You have already preached to me in public once before; I wouldn't like it

---

[16] Anna Franz and Bertha Kupelwieser were not merely friends, but Joachim's cousins.

to happen a second time without it being my fault, and therefore I will tell you that if I don't appear at their music festival, the blame lies with the Hamburgers. I have no occasion to display politeness and gratitude; on the contrary, a certain rudeness would be fitting if I had the time and felt like spoiling my mood in that way. I also don't want to spoil yours with particulars, and therefore will only say that in spite of enquiries, there was not a word of an honorarium or any kind of compensation. In this way am I, poor composer, so dubiously estimated that I lose all rights to sit at the banquet table, possibly next to your wife! So this time I ask you to show some indulgence for my already tarnished reputation as a well-behaved man.

For the symphony, on the other hand, I do not ask indulgence—but I fear that if *Joachim* is not invited to conduct, as I wish, there will be a miserable performance. Well, festive dinners in Hamburg are good, the symphony is of a propitious length—during it you can dream of Vienna! I am thinking of going to Vienna very soon, but I have had an excellent time again in Pörtschach.

With warmest greetings to you and your wife,
J. Br.

Brahms reconsidered.

372
Johannes Brahms to Joseph Joachim [postcard]

Pörtschach, 21 September [1878]

Just to report briefly that we will see each other in Hamburg after all. Without actually lending credence to all sorts of misunderstandings and oversights, I really couldn't be so crude as to stay away, I suppose. And so I look forward to a happy reunion! Best greetings to everyone at home.

Your J. B.

Brahms conducted the Second Symphony himself, on an occasion where he was showered with flowers and praise.

A trip to Breslau followed on the heels of his journey to Hamburg. Again the Second Symphony was on the programme, and a string quintet by Scholz, dedicated to Brahms, was set for a second concert. By now Brahms was commanding a very high fee.

373
Johannes Brahms to Bernhard Scholz

[End of September 1878]

Dear friend,

True, the 600 M[arks] found their way onto paper somewhat by chance; let's keep it between you and me, so that others are not offended. Incidentally, if you should also take care of the meals at the 'White Eagle', that amount will soon become more nebulous!

I would like to request the quintet, and then it would be nice if Frl. Assmann were to sing another Scholz and some Br[ahms]—but—spare me from playing *solo*, I don't ever play or practise and always decline to play at all!

But worst of all: I'm arriving with a big beard! Prepare your wife for the grisly spectacle, for one suppressed so long cannot be beautiful.

I don't suppose my 'quintet' will be on the programme? Which of my other pieces, I don't give a hoot. Your

J. B.

Some commentators have given much meaning to this beard, but before embarking on deep psychological interpretations, it is worth noting that in growing his long, full beard, Brahms was now in step with almost every one of his male friends: Allgeyer, Billroth, Engelmann, Epstein, Feuerbach, Gänsbacher, Grimm, Hanslick, Herzogenberg, Joachim, Levi, Nottebohm, Reinthaler, Simrock, and Stockhausen. Among others.[17]

In November, Brahms was once more occupied by the Violin Concerto.

374
Johannes Brahms to Joseph Joachim

[Vienna, November 1878]

Dear friend,

Two things have greatly troubled me lately, one a Yes and one a No.

You see, it had been my intention to offer you my fingers for your concerts here, while on the other hand still keeping my violin concerto to myself. I have been utterly unable to make up my mind to do the first, and am consequently ashamed and annoyed at myself.

---

[17] For a convincing suggestion as to why these men all saw fit to grow beards, see Stephan Zweig, *The World of Yesterday* (Lincoln, Nebr., 1964), 33–4.

I have allowed my aversion to any concertizing to grow all too much, and have accustomed myself all too readily to playing only for myself. But it is a most dismal thought for me that you should be ranging through these regions while I stand by, entirely mute. Well, this could be alleviated only by my Concerto, with which we could make music here, in Pesth, or in Prague. If it were not for this trip of yours, I would certainly have let the Concerto sit for the time being, I consider it—however, etc. I have had one part copied out neatly and would like to send it to you, along with the score, so you can honestly say—if this is what one calls hospitality! The middle movements fell in battle—and, naturally, they were the best! But I'll have a poor Adagio written for it.

I suppose we'd better let the Leipzigers have the pleasure, we can still reconsider it here at the piano, after all.

I imagine you are back from Holland—did you not hold it terribly against me that I let Epstein play? I mean that quite seriously and will now go for a walk and make myself feel inadequate!

Most affectionately your
J.B.

It is unlikely that Brahms had much in common with his remaining family, even with his brother Fritz, a well-regarded piano teacher in Hamburg. Rather, his relationship to his family is marked by the satisfaction he took—for the most part at a distance—in seeing to it that their needs were well met, and that their lives, from his point of view, were in order.

375
Johannes Brahms to Karoline Brahms

[Vienna, 5 December 1878]

Dear Mother,

I'm sending you 150 Marks through Herr Simrock, but ask very urgently: let me know if that's enough!

You can have more at a moment's notice, I just don't have it with me here.

I don't get to read any Hamburg newspapers nowadays—but for me the most important is that all of you are well, and that they don't report, you'll just have to write that by yourselves. The storm here was quite terrible, it was even dangerous to walk about in it as I did.

Won't Fritz make up his mind sometime to move into your corner room? Do talk to him, I'd be glad to pay the rent to the extent that it's too expensive for him. I'd find that very nice and cosy. But I suppose you count on providing board to your lodgers and Fritz prefers to go to a tavern?

So say whether your cash box is healthy again! I don't know how much you earn with your rentals, but I imagine that it would be possible to arrange something with Fritz, I'd gladly contribute.

Best greetings to everyone from
your Johannes

❧ 1879 ☙

376
Johannes Brahms to Karoline Brahms

[Vienna, 26 February 1879]

Dear Mother,

I thank you very much for your letter and today say only hurriedly that I will definitely send you 50 thaler every quarter. Since I haven't sent anything yet this year, I'll have 100 thaler remitted to you immediately for January 1st and April 1st—because I have money coming in just at this time. Now if that should be too much for you, just say so! But also, if you want to have something extra or more!

I am very sorry about the Krügers, but I hope he'll recover quickly from the damage?[1]

Give them my best greetings; I suppose you are already making plans for the spring and for Pinneberg?

It would be nice if Fritz [Brahms] could write once in a while, why else does one keep sending!

But as usual I have no time and simply greet all of you with all my heart.
Your Johannes.

Work on the Violin Concerto continued well beyond the date of the first performance in Leipzig (1 January), and even beyond subsequent performances in Budapest, Vienna, and England. The year, however, started out on a very sad note: Felix Schumann died at the age of 25 of tuberculosis. He was Clara's youngest child and Brahms's godson, and the most gifted of the Schumann children.

---

[1] Relatives in Pinneberg whose house had burned down.

377
Johannes Brahms to Clara Schumann

[Vienna, second half of February 1879]

Beloved Clara,

It's true that with each of your last letters I might have anticipated the mournful news which your letter today brings.

But as I held this one in my hand, I was certain of its message, and opened it while holding you in my gaze with all my thoughts.

One might think that at such a moment one should feel liberated and delivered. I have not felt that yet.

Gathered within me are the memories of what was good in the past and the thoughts of the good things I had hoped for and expected.

At this moment I simply feel twice as deeply as before what times past had made me feel.

I suppose it is a good thing that I myself cannot be struck by fate many more times. I fear that I would take it hard and bear it badly. So I hope with all my heart that you will have in fullest measure everything that a human being either has within him or can acquire from without—to console you in your sorrow and help you bear this blow too, as so many a hard one before.

I would be particularly concerned about Eugenie, who clung to him so dearly—but it does calm me that you are together, that you endure together and are taking care of each other. I wish I were there; for, no matter how long I sat here with my paper writing—none the less I would feel easier and better were I sitting silently with you.

From my heart,
your Johannes.

Joachim was on his spring tour to England, where he gave the British public their first hearing of the Violin Concerto. By now he had it memorized and could report a decided success, but both performer and composer still felt the need for revisions.

378
Johannes Brahms to Joseph Joachim

[Vienna,] March 1879

Dear friend,

My best thanks for your news. That you are keeping the concerto somewhat longer is no calamity for the piece or the world.

But I am very eager [to see] how frequently and how energetically your handwriting shows up in score and part afterwards, whether I'll be 'convinced' or will have to ask still another—something I wouldn't like to do. In short, then, is the piece good, all in all, and practical enough to allow for printing?

I am planning to travel to Frankfurt, Cologne, etc. sometime soon. So it's better if you simply send the concerto to Frau Schumann (32 Mylius Str.). If you think of it: preferably score and parts separately, in two parcels! So that the unicum may not perish!

German newspapers say that you are about to exchange your position in Berlin for one in London. I hope they are lying, as usual; but unfortunately the opposite may indeed be quite possible?!

From my heart, your
J. Brahms.

Joachim made suggestions regarding orchestral texture and, in particular, bowings. Now he wanted the score and parts for a performance in Amsterdam.

379
Johannes Brahms to Joseph Joachim

[Vienna, middle of] May 1879

Dear Jussuff,

I had actually not asked for my part back at all, but had just written to Simrock that he could probably have the piano reduction, once you had scribbled enough into the [solo] part. If you know of other questionable things be sure to say so, and meanwhile accept my best thanks.

But by what right, since when, and upon whose authority do you violinists write the sign for *Portamento* ($\overbrace{\cdots}$.) where that is not what it signifies? At the octaves in the Rondo you indicate ($\frown$) and I would set martelé points ' '.[2] *Must* that be? Up to now I have not given in to the violinists, nor accepted their cursed slurs $\frown$. After all, why should $\frown$. mean something different for us than for Beethoven?

I'll have parts and score sent to Amsterdam straightaway; The reminder was necessary, however, for I didn't know the day. I have made no changes, so that there'll be no confusion; my pale ink will be annoyance enough for poor Verhulst!

---

[2] Brahms says, literally, 'pointed bow stroke marks', for which the term presently in use is *martelé*. What he wants are short, accented notes.

Once more, my best thanks!
With my warmest greetings to you and yours,
hurriedly your
J. Br.

NB. Take a look at the Serenade for Wind Instruments by Dvořák; I hope it gives you as much pleasure as it does to me. You wouldn't have thought him capable of such a good piece, and you can hardly gain a lovelier, more refreshing impression of a true, rich, and attractive creative talent. Do have it played for you; I should think it must be a delight for the wind-players![3]

It is very odd that Brahms was so open to Joachim's *musical* suggestions, but was so slow to acknowledge his authoritative advice regarding the conventions of string-writing. He stubbornly ignored the fact that bowings (articulations) for string instruments are indicated by the same shorthand which, for piano music, is used to indicate phrasing and touch (but see Letter 495, by which time he had learned his lesson). For string players, the curved slur line over dotted notes does *not* signify *portamento*, a long, almost legato motion from one note to the next, but rather, tells the musician to play a given number of separated notes on one bow stroke ⌒ i.e., one pass of the bow going in the same direction. Brahms's ˙ ˙ indicate heavy, short notes; Joachim was telling future performers that both heavy short notes should be played on one bow.

By the end of June the concerto was in publication; Brahms and Joachim worked on the proofs together.

380

Johannes Brahms to Joseph Joachim

[Pörtschach, 22 June 1879]

Dear friend,

I very much hope to read the proofs of the concerto with you in Salzburg, and for recreation we can then also play a little sonata! Do let me know how it looks as far as coming and staying is concerned! You'll find that I have taken proper notice of your twiddlings. But I couldn't get myself to change the following place according to your suggestion:[4]

---

[3] Op. 44, published that year by Simrock.
[4] Measure 337, first movement. The examples are based on the autograph of Brahms's letter and differ in some details from *BW* vi.

I don't want to do without the low and high beginning notes. The place doesn't seem forceful enough to you? Couldn't one omit notes or double them?

Or something like that? Also more notes:

You'll take care not to ask for a concerto again? It is something of an excuse that the concerto bears your name, so you are hardly answerable for the violin scoring.

Very warm greetings
to you and yours.

The recreational 'little sonata' was Brahms's Op. 78 in G major. He began it in the previous summer after visiting Felix Schumann in Palermo, where the youth had been sent in the vain hope that his health would improve. Felix had studied the violin seriously before his health failed, using Joachim's Guanarius violin. The slow movement of the sonata was written with Felix and his violin in mind, just before the young man's death.[5]

He sent the work to Clara apologetically, almost diffidently. In contrast, it was received with much emotion. Clara was particularly taken with the inclusion of the 'Regenlied', one of her favourite songs.[6] It appears in the last movement.

---

[5] According to a letter Brahms wrote to Clara, dated February 1879. It is not part of the Litzmann collection. See Michael Struck, 'Revisionsbedürftig: Zur gedruckten Korrespondenz von Johannes Brahms und Clara Schumann', *Die Musikforschung*, 41/3 (1988), 239–40.

[6] 'Regenlied'/'Nachklang', Op. 59 Nos. 3 and 4. There are two versions of the song.

381
Clara Schumann to Johannes Brahms

Düsseldorf, 10 July 1879

Dearest Johannes,

I must send you word to tell you how deeply affected I am by your sonata. I received it today and naturally I played through it right away and afterwards, out of joy, had a really good cry over it. After the first fine, enchanting movement, and the second, you can imagine my delight when in the third, I rediscovered *my* so ardently beloved melody with its delightful eighth-note rhythm! I say *my*, because I don't believe there is a *single* person who perceives this melody as joyously and as wistfully as I. After all that wonderful delight, then the last movement as well! My pen is poor, but my heart beats for you in emotion and gratitude, and in spirit I press your hand. I plan to be in Frankfurt on Sunday, then I can straightaway play it with H[eermann]. The two other pieces I must study first, I believe I'll get on with them as with most of the other piano pieces which (except the one in F sharp minor) I only gradually learned to cherish. I'm remaining in Frankfurt until the 19th or 20th, will write again from there.

I spent a day at the Grimms, very pleasant, if I had only had the sonata there!

Farewell, dear Johannes.

Your faithful
Clara.

The two new piano pieces were the Rhapsodies, Op. 79, which had arrived with Brahms's previous letter. 'The other piano pieces' mentioned by Clara are the eight from Op. 76.

In lovely, kind language which displays great devotion to Brahms, the composer and conductor Vincenz Lachner wrote two letters to Brahms, expressing his admiration and wonder at the Second Symphony, and displaying detailed understanding of the work which is so intricately woven out of such economical material. Nevertheless, Lachner raised objections to some of the most telling moments in the first movement: the mysterious-sounding drum roll at measure 32, and the threatening sound of trombones and tuba first heard in measures 33–43. His objection was to the intrusion of dark moments—trombones have a long association with death, in the language of the Lutheran Bible—in this otherwise glorious and sun-filled landscape. He also objected to the ending phrase, with its super-imposition of plagal and tonic, saying that not even a day-long discussion with Brahms could make his ears want to hear that (Brahms had invited him to Pörtschach for *eine Plauderstunde*—a pleasant little chat).

Brahms's answer to Lachner is simple and unyielding. What lies behind the reply is a native character far deeper and more complex than that of many of his friends. He could celebrate life's pleasures and yet contemplate the certainty of death—at the same time and without panic. Brahms alludes in the letter to his motet 'Warum', a dark work which quite bluntly questions the purpose of life. It was written during the same summer as the Second Symphony, in spite of or because of that same lovely view over the Wörthersee, with its monastery on the far shore, and it bears the next opus number. Brahms makes it clear to Lachner that in his understanding of the world, shadow is *never* far from light—something the meeting with his dying godson in sunny Palermo would have grimly reminded him.

382
Johannes Brahms to Vincenz Lachner[7]

[Pörtschach] Aug[ust] [18]79

Very dear friend,

My letter will scarcely tell you what great and genuine pleasure yours give me. They leave nothing to be desired but the continuation you promised. I will be silent about the excessive praise you heap on me, but it does one much good to learn that what has been created with love and diligence is lovingly and attentively regarded by another. Your incisive and perceptive words are the first of the kind that I have seen about that work, either in writing or in print. They deserve that I contemplate a reply, but that I cannot do; I can only contemplate a first movement![8]

Only because I know you are spending these days at your brother's shall at least a fleeting word of thanks reach you there.

I'll tell you just as fleetingly that I very much wanted and tried to manage without trombones in that first movement. (The E minor passage I would gladly have sacrificed, as I now offer to sacrifice it to you.) But that first entrance of the trombones, that belongs to me and so I cannot dispense with it nor with the trombones, either. Were I to defend that passage, I would have to be long-winded.

I would have to admit, moreover, that I am a deeply melancholy person, that black pinions constantly rustle over us, that in my works—possibly not entirely without intent—this symphony is followed by a small essay on the

---

[7] By kind permission of the Library of Congress, Whittall Collection. For both sides of the correspondence, see Reinhold Brinkman, 'Die "heitre Sinfonie" und der "schwer melancholische Mensch". Johannes Brahms antwortet Vincenz Lachner', *Archiv für Musikwissenschaft*, vol. 46, no. 4 (1989), 294–306.

[8] Or sentence. Pun intended.

great 'Why'. If you do not know it (motets) I will send it to you. It throws the necessary sharp shadows across the lighthearted symphony and perhaps explains those trombones and kettledrums.

But I also ask you not to take all this so very seriously or tragically, particularly that passage!

But that A in the G minor in the coda, that I would like to defend!

To me it is a sensuously beautiful sound, and I believe it comes about as logically as possible—quite of its own accord.

After this, dear friend, it will seem peculiar to you if I ask you to let me know most of all—what is *not* much to your liking. But, whether it is useful or whether I pay no heed to it in a particular passage, I will have heard the qualms, it will be of use and will apply some other time.

As to over-enthusiasm, that is something *you* need not be concerned about. In reading a letter, the face of the letter-writer appears of its own accord. In yours, life has chiselled beautiful, thoughtful lines, and that is also why one listens to what you say.

But now, finally, fare you well and be greeted along with your brother from the bottom of my heart.

I hope to hear more from you!

With complete devotion, your

J. Brahms.

That Brahms followed his own advice not to take himself too seriously is displayed in his correspondence with Simrock over the dedication of the two Motets, Op. 74. They are entitled 'Warum ist das Licht gegeben dem Mühseligen' (Why is the Light of Day Given to the Hard-pressed), and 'O Heiland, reiß die Himmel auf' (Oh Saviour, Fling Open the Heavens). Brahms offered to let his publisher announce them as

Motets

by

Joh. Br.

No. 1. *Warum?*

No. 2. *Oh!*

In September, Joachim and Brahms embarked on a joint tour to Transylvania (then part of Hungary, now in Romania). Settled centuries ago by German artisans from Saxony, the old Saxon German—archaic but intelligible—was still the native language of many inhabitants, making it easy for German speakers to travel there.

383
Johannes Brahms to Joseph Joachim

[Pörtschach, 5 September 1879]

Dear friend,

The best side of your travel companion is that in general he is always agreeable to everything!

Calamity, run thy course, he said this morning and with a calm spirit sent off a telegram.

I have just written to Kugel regarding the piano.[9]

You, on the other hand, could perhaps point out to him that our names are not to be ordered according to body size, age, or some other way, but simply according to the alphabet.

Indeed, the Siebenburg letter already shows that—in you he certainly has the better customer, hence puts you first. This is involuntarily noticed by one who quite generally, and by virtue of his elegant initial, likes to jostle himself ahead!![10]

Surely you're not playing my concerto to be considerate! In any case, take Bruch's first along too, it is truly well suited for piano accompaniment.

I'll try to dig up the required violin sonatas in Klagenfurt.[11] For the first two concerts in the first two towns you might put down as my solos:

    1. Brahms; (*a*) Variations, (*b*) Scherzo
    2. Schumann, from the Noveletten

---

    1. (*a*) Gluck, Gavotte; (*b*) Scarlatti, Caprices.
    2. Schubert, Andante, Scherzo and March

Should you need more, insert between any two numbers, *Bach*, Adagio, Gigue, Fugue; *Schumann*, from the Davidsbündler, or *Beethoven*, Sonata Op. 111, C minor. Or anything else; I don't know at all what sort of grand piano I'll get.

How are we travelling? Might you perhaps come here and then go to Pesth past Lake Balaton [Plattensee], or are you going by way of Vienna? Where are we off to first?

---

  [9] Their concert agent for this tour.
  [10] i.e. himself. Brahms often used stationery with an elaborately engraved monogram.
  [11] The nearest town of any size. Joachim programmed Beethoven's C minor, Op. 30 No. 2—the same sonata Brahms had played from memory with Reményi, twenty-five years before, and transposed up a semitone on the spur of the moment; and Schumann's Op. 121 in D minor. Violinists may be interested to know that, in planning the other concerts, he gave the timing of Brahms's Violin Concerto as 35 minutes.

Actually, I would like to say a confidential word to you, namely that I am happy to make the trip just for my pleasure, but will gladly let you pay for everything, etc. I can expand on that in the railway carriage, we'll have time enough there.

Meanwhile many warm greetings to all of yours.

Most hurriedly,

your J.B.

Joachim acquiesced in the order of their billing, but not entirely without resistance. 'Naturally I had already concluded on my own that we could only be announced as Brahms-Joachim;' he wrote, 'although in any case it will be read as

Jo   a chim - Brahms

The tour led the two old friends from one triumph to another. From the newspaper review in Temesvár (now Timesoara), 15 September 1879: 'The concert of 15 September 1879 produced a great commotion in the city. A great mass of people swarmed through the streets. The audience filled the concert-hall completely. The performance of both artists will long remain in memory [. . .] Brahms is the most talented composer of the day.'[12]

384
Johannes Brahms to Clara Schumann

[Vienna, end of] September 1879

Dear Clara,

Back since the day before yesterday, I had hoped to have written you already, now your letter arrives and I'll reply first to the business matters.

If only it weren't always the same! If only you wouldn't get excited about the same useless things each time!

For now, Härtels can print nothing other than what they themselves have at the publishing house! The things are really all in the very best of order and aren't giving us a bit of trouble. They should simply send what they have just printed! The metronome story is also an old one and I think you might finally put an end to it and let the matter run its course.—Or

---

[12] From a German summary of the Hungarian-language reviews, in Ludwig Koch, *Brahms-Bibliográfia* (Budapest, 1943), 21–2.

else—contradict me and assert that you can find the correct numbers or that you have them. I don't think we have the right to delete the old markings (even if wrong). Should you have better ones, they could be added in parentheses; I advise very strongly against attempting the work. The Schumann things that I have from you will only get here from Pörtschach with my piano, and that, strange to say, has still not appeared . . .

Just don't allow Härtels to unsettle you—that, too, I'm telling you for the 100th time. They are forever prodding and are themselves never in a rush, not even prompt.

I'm glad that the house in Baden is sold; to keep it as a souvenir is somewhat complicated and expensive, isn't it. I am even more pleased that both of you are doing better, I hope you are living very comfortably and quietly so that everything will get better and better. What's happening with Bonn? Are you going there in October?[13]

Our trip was truly nice and jolly. To travel in the loveliest weather through a strange, interesting, and often very beautiful country, to make a little music on the side and to let others sing and drink to you, I suppose that's fine for a few weeks, one can put up with it.

But there are too many letters sitting here, and mainly long-winded letters regarding concerts, otherwise I would give you some details.

I would be happy to make such concert tours more often! A concert every few days, so that one has time to get to know land and people. But today's virtuosi have need of too much money for that. There has to be a concert every day, one arrives an hour before and leaves an hour after the concert. For me, that would be the most disagreeable and despicable activity.[14] And our kind is so well off! Received by the Mayor and the Committee at the railway station, one is straightaway introduced to the best circles, and people don't know what goodness and kindness to shower on you.

Though someone else, Billroth, let's say, also often comes to Hungary and similar countries, he sees nothing but the Jew he has to operate on. We, on the other hand, can see and hear everything that's worth the trouble—only we mustn't be in too much of a hurry.[15]

---

[13] For the unveiling of the Schumann monument.

[14] That is exactly how Joachim often toured.

[15] Comments like this must have fallen from people's lips with great ease for such a casually snide remark to come from Brahms, because Brahms was no anti-Semite. Even the partial list of his Jewish friends is far too long for that: Ignaz Brüll, Otto Dessoff, Julius Epstein, Maria Fellinger, Ernst Frank, Carl Goldmark, Eduard Hanslick, George Henschel, Paul Heyse, Ferdinand Hiller, Joseph Joachim, Hermann Levi, Eusebius Mandyczewski, Daniel Spitzer, Carl Tausig. And when the overtly anti-Semitic Karl Lueger was elected vice-mayor of Vienna, Brahms was agitated, calling anti-Semitism 'madness' and predicting dire consequences in 1895. (See Heuberger, *Erinnerungen*, 82.)

We gave concerts in Arad, Temesvar, Kronstadt, Pressburg, Hermann-stadt, and Klausenburg.[16] It was interesting everywhere and I'll describe all sorts of things to you in person soon.

I am just informed that I'll get my piano tomorrow, and so the Schumann music as well. As I recall, however, there is nothing among it that Härtels may engrave and publish at this time! For the moment, you could only put some order into the already published songs or the quintet etc.!

For now my warmest greetings to you, more the next time.—Also best greetings to all of yours, Francks, etc.

from your Johannes.

With passing years, Hiller and Brahms became increasingly good friends; their letters have the sound of two people chatting in cheerful competition with each other. The following letter is part of an exchange about a performance of the Requiem Brahms was coming to Cologne to conduct. It is one of many which indicate that Brahms liked to use a large orchestra and chorus. The score of the Requiem calls for a doubling of harps, but Brahms was happy to have even more.

In the previous letter, Hiller congratulated Brahms on the great success of the Requiem performance at the Vienna Opera House, which he had heard about from a friend. Writing of his own latest activities, Hiller described how he gave a speech to ensure that no untimely applause would interrupt a performance of Mendelssohn's A minor Symphony (the 'Scottish'); and with an apology ('no harm meant')—presumably referring to the fact that Brahms's first and second symphonies were already before the public—Hiller called Mendelssohn's the most consummate symphony since Beethoven.

385

Johannes Brahms to Ferdinand Hiller

[Vienna,] Nov[ember 18]79

Well, dear friend, one does experience all sorts of things and recently I did too, not one, but two grand and good performances of the Requiem in the opera-house.

Actually it was going to be nothing but Brrr, but I was able to insist on the improved programme: Athalia Overture and Eroica Symphony, before and after.[17]

---

[16] In 1996: Arad, Timisoara, Brasov, Bratislava, Sibiu, and Cluj.

[17] A sort of pun: *Br* = Brahms, *Brrr* = the German equivalent of 'ugh!'. Hans Richter conducted the Vienna Philharmonic and the opera chorus, not the Gesellschaft forces.

But I gave no speeches, and if you should read in the newspapers that at the end, in front of the audience, I presented a wreath to the ladies,—you mustn't take that to be a photograph of your friend!

But afterwards I did dedicate a laurel wreath to the opera chorus (augmented for the performance), because it had done a particularly pretty job. You and Cologne came to mind especially often because of certain things. We had 4 harps—will I have even one with you? a piano is just too wretched! furthermore, the only thing really bad at the performance were the soloists. Since I didn't know of any gold among the singers of the 2nd rank, I took the first rank—that way I couldn't be faulted for making a bad choice, etc. Who sings with you? Dr Kraus is very good, Frl. Sartorius too?? or who else? the soprano could sing an additional aria, after all! Whether I was pleased with my work? In a case like this, let's say, I have to be careful to avoid taking another look at the music at home! Consequently, this time I was inordinately fresh and cheerful at the rehearsals and Capellmeister Richter and orchestra and chorus were, I believe, praised more loudly than the composer.

Mendelssohn's A minor Symphony the most 'consummate' since Beethoven; I would like to find that correct, but I suppose that the term is chosen judiciously and I don't know how to justify it with respect to Schubert's. I suppose we are faced with something like that in considering Beethoven beside Mozart. But before you say: no harm meant, you could go on to name quite a pretty string. What not to do, and how not to do it we probably learn best from our immediate predecessors; but we are also clever enough then to envy them for what they do. But now, no harm meant, we are the We for very young people! I attach hereto the loveliest greetings and if I should run into someone from the Concordia, I will, with your permission, convey very rude ones from you.[18]

All the best, your

J. Brahms

---

[18] In August the Concordia Club decided to honour Hiller with one of its ceremonial evenings (see Letter 214 n. 7), but no further word had been received by Hiller by the date of this letter. With Brahms's intercession, the omission was soon cleared up. Hiller commented that such confusion was possible only in Vienna (*Hil*, iv. 94 ff.).

ᷤ 1880 ᷤ

In response to the question whether the printed tempo indications in the *German Requiem* should be adhered to, a letter went to George Henschel, who was now living in England. Henschel asked the question on behalf of the English conductor Otto Goldschmidt (the husband of Jenny Lind).

386
Johannes Brahms to George Henschel

[Vienna,] Feb[ruary 18]80

Dear H:

Your letter reaches me just as I happen to be at home for a few days; a very rare occurrence this winter, worse luck!

Post festum my best congratulations upon the success of your concert, which must have been splendid indeed.[1]

The question in your letter received today is somewhat obscure, indistinct; I hardly know how I should answer Herr Goldschmidt's question. In my view, the metronome isn't worth much; at least, so far as I know, many a composer has withdrawn his metronome markings sooner or later. Those which are found in the Requiem are there because good friends talked me into them. For I myself have never believed that my blood and a mechanical instrument go well together. The so-called elastic tempo is not a new discovery, after all, and to it, as to many another, one should attach a 'con discrezione'.

Is that an answer? I know of none better; *what* I know, however, is that I indicate my tempi in the heading, *without* numbers, modestly but with the greatest care and clarity.

Commend me to Herr Goldschmidt and tell him, please, that in the forthcoming performance I regret only *one* thing, namely that No. 5 will not be sung by his wife. I wish I had heard that once from her!

In haste and with kindest greeting,

Yours,

[J. B.]

When the Schumann grave monument was ready for unveiling, there was once again a commemorative gathering in Bonn. By now Brahms had learned not to involve

---

[1] Henschel directed the first English performance of the *Triumphlied*.

himself too closely in those sorts of arrangements, but there were limits to what he would accept.

387
Johannes Brahms to Joseph Joachim

[Vienna, 5 April 1880]

Dear Joachim,

I had planned to spend tomorrow in Berlin, but it won't work out; accordingly I now have to make a very urgent request.

In Bonn everything is going contrary to my wishes and suggestions, good and clever as they are. But since I didn't make my participation conditional on it, I have to let everything run its course. In one matter, however, you can help.

I find it not nice and not appropriate that in the orchestral concert, my violin concerto is the only number which is not by Schumann.

I think that you should either play the Fantasy by Schumann *or else*: one should put on any solemn overture by anyone at all (e.g. op. 124 by Beethoven)[2] and furthermore you should be asked to play another number solo (e. g. Chaconne by Bach).

I need not go into details, you'll doubtlessly concede I'm right—it's simply a question of whether you'll intercede with a word, a very forceful one.

I consider it rather useless to write to Wasielewski; I believe he might not even mention it to the committee?! Maybe you know a better address?

I'll be passing through Berlin on Wednesday; if you have time, you might talk it over with Simrock and we could see each other at the railway station.

But I beg you from my heart, take this matter on, it's really not nice.

In a great rush, but with the warmest greetings,

your J. Brahms.

Is it pure coincidence that Brahms wrote his own and only solemn overture just a few months later?

Hermann Deiters, reviser of Otto Jahn's biography of Mozart and translator of Thayer's biography of Beethoven, took the plunge and became the first biographer of Brahms. Preparing what he called a biographical sketch to go along with a discussion of the composer's music, he did not get much help from his subject in spite of writing to inform him of the project; and when the book was published, most of the facts about Brahms's life were incorrect.

---

[2] *Consecration of the House.*

388
Johannes Brahms to Hermann Deiters

[Ischl, 8 August 1880]

Honoured friend,

At long last I must tell you that I was very pleased by your letter and thank you for it earnestly and warmly.

Must tell you—for I will offer no proof for it, and an answer I cannot provide!

I really know absolutely no dates or years concerning myself; but here, naturally, I also cannot try to look up old letters, etc. Having said that, I need hardly add that I dislike talking about myself, also dislike reading anything that concerns me personally.

I think it would be wonderful if every artist, great or small, would quite seriously provide a confidential chronicle—I don't have time for it, but it's a pity! But with regard to what La Mara, etc. profess to tell about me—I do not appreciate it and fail to see why it is told from time to time.[3]

— —But now I have practically jumped right into it—forgive me—but I won't start on a fresh sheet of paper.

I do understand, of course, that it is necessary for your purposes, but even with my best intentions I just cannot answer your specific questions.

Except: J.B., born 1834 in Altona on the 7th of March (*not* as often stated, 7th of May 33 in Hamburg), I read that often, to my amusement, and what is in the parentheses is correct.

My father has unfortunately died (*after* 1870, as evidence of my inability to answer)! I became Dr in Breslau (two or three years ago!).[4] Before that (several years), I was awarded the title in Cambridge. In such a case, because of Parliament, one must suffer through certain ceremonies there in person—I preferred to be impolite, and so it didn't come to pass.

The stories about the C and A minor Sonatas might be true for all I know. That doesn't require much youthful exuberance and I often perpetrated more potent stuff.[5]

---

[3] The writer Marie Lipsius (La Mara) published her *Musicalische Studienköpfe*, a collection of short biographies, in 1875. Brahms was not fond of the essay about him, which appeared in various other versions under her name.

[4] Barely one year before.

[5] The allusion is to the occasion when Brahms, on tour with Reményi and playing from memory, transposed Beethoven's Violin Sonata in C minor (Op. 30 No. 2) a semitone up to compensate for a piano tuned too low (May, i. 99–100). In a newspaper article about Brahms a decade later, Schubring related the same story, but with the Kreutzer Sonata. The violinist Karl Bargheer writes

But isn't *Ermen*keil what the pretty garden in Bonn is called? Couldn't it also have been Kley? But Ermenkeil or Kley, Detmold or Bückeburg—if I'm not telling you about something very beautiful or serious, it seems to me that my music is always a bit more interesting.[6]

But now, do forgive these highly confusing scribblings and let me just inform you that I am supposed to be in Breslau on January 4. Couldn't you possibly make yourself free for a few days at that time? That would be splendid; otherwise, I will consider a detour to Posen, but the former would be better.

With warm greetings to you and your wife,
your most devoted
J. Brahms.

Although one suspects Brahms was exaggerating the defects of his memory, he did have trouble remembering names. As Hanslick was about to visit Holland, the scene of so many enthusiastic receptions for Brahms, the composer struggled to provide his friend with introductions. His letter provides a good look at the pleasures he took in his Dutch tours.

389
Johannes Brahms to Eduard Hanslick

[Vienna, Spring 1880]

Dear friend,

I have a deplorably poor memory for persons and names. That is my least shortcoming, but the most highly perfected. How many friendly, dear people now appear more or less distinctly before my mind's eye. I feel deeply ashamed, uncouth, and ungrateful—I search for their names in vain.

Well, you'll only stay a short time in Amsterdam and the Hague and so I believe that my enclosed [visiting] cards will furnish you with everything you need in the most agreeable fashion.

If at all possible, don't fail to get to know *Verhulst* (M.[usic] Dr.[ector] in Amsterdam, lives in the Hague). Outstanding musician, friend of Mendelssohn and Schumann, highly original person, exceedingly kind, with childlike gentleness. He is bound to be of great interest to you—right up to

that no matter what he and Brahms performed for their ducal patrons in Detmold, he never knew which key Brahms was going to start in, a circumstance guaranteed to provide him with considerable excitement.

[6] Brahms and Deiters met in the hotel garden *Erme*keil in Bonn. Hotel Kley is similarly in Bonn, Bückeburg a town between Hanover and Detmold.

his songs which sometimes are, as they should be, a very attractive likeness of him. Go also to Scheveningen with him; while there, drink an 'advocate' with him and Herr Zilken, also go to the casino for a dinner or supper.[7]

For Amsterdam I recommend the following very good guides: Herr *Sillem* (bachelor, most amiable and cultivated) will be the best and most agreeable companion for you, from morning till evening and wheresoever you might be drawn to. N.B. Here and in The Hague, the magnificent art galleries and the many historical monuments are self-evident!

If you should stay in Amsterdam for a few relaxed days, Herr Sillem will also introduce you to homes and families where you are bound to feel as content as anywhere at all. If, for example, you could coax the name of the biggest coffee merchant out of him—without embarrassing me too greatly—do please ask parenthetically, as though I had talked about him and *you* were the forgetful one! It might be best to send the cards to Röntgen and de Lange, adding a note with your hotel and a time? In case Sillem isn't there, they could readily substitute for him as guide, *Röntgen* (of Dutch ancestry, born in Leipzig) was a very curious *Wunderkind* and has meanwhile become a very proficient, finely inspired musician. *De Lange* is one of the best Dutch musicians, cellist, fertile composer, critic, and pleasant person—as may happen now and then, after all. I suppose you probably will meet a few Dutchmen even in Brussels, for instance, *Nicolai* from The Hague, publisher of a 'Cecilia', for whom you naturally don't need a card, *Hol* from Utrecht who is probably the most capable young director and musician in The Hague. You won't be staying in Utrecht? Then I suppose you won't meet Professor *Engelmann* either; making the acquaintance of him and Herr Riemsdyk would be splendid for you, and in that event, I ask you to convey my greetings.

You can tell from my lengthy chatter how much your trip interests and engages me. It's a scandal that I can't go tossing names around. But I hope and believe that with the enclosed cards you'll get along and also get to people! I imagine that afterwards you will sing the praises of country and people.

With best greetings and wishes, your sincerely devoted
J. Brahms.

The Ballades and Romances, Op. 75, very nearly bore a dedication to Elizabet von Herzogenberg, but instead Brahms acknowledged a friendship of longer standing by setting Julius Allgeyer's name on the title-page.[8] He made amends, however. To her

---

[7] *Avocaat*, the potent Dutch eau-de-vie, still very much appreciated.

[8] Thereby acknowledging that it was Allgeyer who introduced Brahms to Herder's *Stimmen der Völker*, with its translation of the Scottish ballad 'Edward', set by him for the second time in this Opus.

went the dedication of the *Two Rhapsodies*, Op. 79. The letter reached her in Florence.

390
Johannes Brahms to Elizabet von Herzogenberg

[Vienna, 22 May 1880]

Most revered friend,

It is really not nice of you to go so far away without even leaving your address! As a result the best business deals can come to a complete halt and today—I have to speak of business.

If Herr Astor doesn't know how to attend to this letter, it's not my fault. For Herr Simrock is not concerned with my woes and will send a blank title-page into the world.[9]

You see, I want to publish the two piano pieces that you know.

Do you know of a better title than: 'Two Rhapsodies for the Pianoforte'?—a better dedication you cannot know. But do I have your permission to attach your dear and revered name to this trifle?

But how is that written? Elsa or Elisabet? 'Freifrau' or Baroness? Born or not? Make all kinds of allowances for this doltish youth, but send a word straightaway and that to Ischl, Salzburger Straße 51, where I am planning to travel tomorrow. At the same time I hope you will say a few other things, and specifically that you are very well and that that you are waxing rhapsodic in that wonderful city!

In the greatest hurry and with warmest greetings to you and Herr Heinz, your utterly devoted

J. Br.

Elizabet ended her delighted reply with: '. . . to answer your last question, you know of course that I am, and am called, your faithful Elizabet von Herzogenberg. You have always properly addressed me this way—what brings you to this idiotic question?'

In all, Brahms would spend ten summers in Ischl. This summer of 1880 was his first, made at the suggestion of Ignaz Brüll, with whom Brahms often played duets. The Brülls are among the Viennese families with whom Brahms felt particularly at home.[10] His other friend there was the conductor, Ernst Frank. In defiance of the excessive rain and cold, the summer produced some great music.

[9] Edmond Aster, Rieter-Biedermann's son-in-law, was now running the publishing business. He must have been forwarding the Herzogenberg mail.

[10] Brüll's biography by his sister, Hermine Schwarz, gives a good picture of their long friendship and frequent contact in Ischl: *Ignaz Brüll und sein Freundeskreis* (Vienna, 1922).

391
Johannes Brahms to Theodor Billroth

[Ischl, 1880]

Dear friend,

I probably take up writing paper most easily when I ask you to help me a little with composing.

Our dear old chap Hlawaczek (Lammgasse 12) likes to write at a leisurely pace; would you therefore please give him the enclosed beginnings so that he can start copying the parts out for me. *Afterwards*, I would quite like to have the score copied too, beginning with the C major. Is it really worth the trouble to keep taking walks with it?

To Ischl, on the other hand, I must give high praise, and since people threaten with just one thing, that half of Vienna gathers here, I can relax— I'm not opposed to the whole of it.

I live most comfortably at Salzburger Straße 51. For now, my only competitors here are Frank and Brüll, but now we simply compete in taking walks and loafing about—and in that I surpass all my colleagues!

I need hardly recommend Ischl to you and your family, you probably know it. Perhaps it's the climate that keeps you away; the air is very warm and soft and it rains a lot. On the other hand, the accommodation, the trails, and the taverns, too, are fine.

You really should consider or investigate it!

—Stop—and I close in serene awareness of this sheet being as useless as the others! But the new Hungarian things will come before long, and I think we'll have fun with them.

Greetings from the bottom of my heart and commend me warmly at home.

Utterly your
J. Brahms.

Please to keep the enclosures for yourself alone and also to instruct Hlawaczek accordingly!

The enclosed 'beginnings' were the first movements of the C major Trio, Op. 87, and a trio movement in E flat which was later destroyed by its critical author—although Billroth preferred it to the survivor. 'The Hungarians' were Joachim's arrangements for violin and piano (see Letter 395). The surgeon took Brahms's advice, eventually building a large villa right on the Wolfgangsee at St Gilgen.

Anyone who has read the eight volumes of Max Kalbeck's Brahms biography will enjoy finding that writer fittingly described in this letter (he is 'your Breslau Hanslick').

392
Johannes Brahms to Luise Scholz

[Vienna, 31] March [18]80

Dear Frau Scholz,

Since I don't know if your husband has already returned home, I'll tell you how deeply I sympathize with the loss that you have suffered. But a fine and peaceful departure it is, such a full and active life behind him, and such a substantial flock of children and grandchildren before him!

My greeting is a little late in coming—I had actually hoped to announce my coming along with it! For I have to go to Königsberg in mid-April, and the route from here is by way of Breslau. But unfortunately, I am (and naturally, always in great haste) in Schwerin beforehand, and in Hanover afterwards. No matter how I orient the map, Breslau is totally off the track! But I must be permitted to come next year and you must also be present at the doctoral banqueting and bowling party!

You undoubtedly subscribe to our new *Allgemeine Zeitung*, so you can continue to read your Breslau Hanslick? I only know that he writes very much and at great length, such length that one can hardly read it thoroughly and precisely. But I hope that he will soon write about his most recent and, as it seems, highly romantic adventures—that's rather more interesting and entices the reader![11]

But now, greetings straight from my heart to you, along with the entire big (big and small) family, and if you are kindly you won't begrudge a few words

to your very devoted
J. Brahms.

393
Johannes Brahms to Bernhard Scholz

[Ischl, about 19] August 1880

Dear friend,

So you are not too greatly embarrassed by your guest, I have written an 'Academic Festival Overture' for the 4th of January. I don't exactly like that

---

[11] The circumstances leading to his marriage.

title, does another come to mind? I do hope this will interest Kauffmann, therefore please let him know—through Fritzsch, as far as I'm concerned—so it will be smoother sailing![12]

I suppose I could have written *this much* on the renowned postcard, but another matter I must keep under wraps, since I don't know what guests are staying with you.

For at times I suspect that you may wish to please me with my 'Violin Concerto' on the 4th, and with your concertmaster. If that is so, I want to ask you not to do so. Joachim (and Rich. Barth) are, for various reasons, apparently not possible and I have no particular fondness for your H[immelstoss], as you may already have noticed. Am I perhaps doing him an injustice?

Now my best greetings to the wife and the big and little ones. I hope that where you are, too, summer is finally coming to its senses and that you are enjoying it a lot.

Most affectionately, your

J. Brahms.

No one has unearthed any letter Brahms might have directed to the University of Breslau as thanks for having granted him the Honorary Doctorate he so desired. The title was formally conferred by decree on 11 March 1879—Brahms was not present—and some time later he casually sent Bernhard Scholz a postcard asking the friend to convey his thanks to those responsible. Only now, one year later, did he indicate that his thanks would take a more tangible shape.

But although Brahms failed to send a letter of thanks to the University, he was not so insensitive as to appear in Breslau without a new piece in their honour, and during the summer Brahms composed what has become one of his best-known works.[13]

Scholz disliked the name, finding it pedantic. He suggested the overture be called *Viadrina*, the Latin name of the River Oder, which flows through Breslau; Brahms toyed with the name for a while, then gave it up. Scholz also seems to have hoped the local firm of Hainauer would gain the rights to publish the work.

[12] Kaufmann was founder and chairman of the Breslau Orchestral Association. Fritsch, in Leipzig, published the music newsletter *Musikalisches Wochenblatt*. He and Brahms were on friendly terms, although Fritsch leaned rather towards the Liszt-Wagner school.

[13] Eventually, in 1881, Brahms sent the University a score of the Academic Festival Overture, bound especially for them and including his handwritten dedication on an additional page (*BW* x. 177–8). I wish to thank Professor Jan Cygan of the University of Wrocław, for taking considerable pains to search the University Archives in 1994, and for enlisting the help of Professors Maciej Golab and Maria Zduniak, Polish scholars currently writing on Brahms's connection to the University of Breslau. They all confirm the complete absence of any material in Brahms's hand. The specially bound edition of the Academic Festival Overture disappeared during the Second World War.

394
Johannes Brahms to Bernhard Scholz

[Ischl, 17 September 1880]

Dear friend,

Unfortunately I won't be able to make Herr Hainauer unhappy, since in the meanwhile I am already having at least the violin parts engraved, and moreover, 2 overtures are involved. In fact you can add to the programme for the 6th [of January] a 'Dramatic' or 'Tragic' or 'Funereal Overture'. You see that this time again I am unable to find a title; can you help?

Viadrina doesn't sound beautiful and is an ever so unfamiliar name; I had to question long and hard before I found out about the beautiful blue Oder.

Best greetings. Your

J. B.

To other conductor friends he wrote of the overtures, 'The one laughs, the other cries'; but he never improved on his provisional titles. They entered his catalogue as the *Akademische Festoverture*, Op. 80, and the *Tragische Overture*, Op. 81, the second one written written directly after the first.

When Brahms was 14 years old and suffering dizzy spells from over-work and lack of sleep, and possibly even from poor nutrition, his father arranged a stay in the countryside for him with a family named Giesemann. Herr Giesemann was a businessman and a regular patron at the Alster Pavilion, and apparently Johann Jakob was on sufficiently friendly terms to ask such a favour.[14] With plenty of fresh air and food, the young Brahms recovered his health in the company of Giesemann's daughter, Elise, who was the same age and who shared his love of reading and music. The three summers he spent with her family left him with a rich supply of memories and a depth of gratitude (see Letter 31).

The two families remained on friendly terms for a long while, then gradually lost touch. Unexpectedly, a letter arrived from Elise, now Frau Denninghoff, and the mother of an aspiring singer.

---

[14] See May, i. 73 ff.

395
Johannes Brahms to Joseph Joachim

[Vienna, 20] October 1880

Dear friend,

I come to you with a request which I ask you very urgently to consider and to fulfil. It concerns one of your voice students: Frl. Agnes Denninghoff. I am indebted to the family of the girl (even to the grandparents!) for much love and friendship and I retain a memory of her grandfather as beautiful as any kept in human heart.

I have learned that it is not easy for D.'s parents to take care of their children as well as they do.

First of all, then, a question regarding this school year: whether it is possible to procure a stipend at your school and whether this is justified by her talent? If that is not the case, well then I would like to pay the tuition—naturally without her learning of it.

In that case, you might well say (as will indeed actually be the case), that aside from the official tuition-free places you have extraordinary funds and what not at your disposal. In short, you can certainly see my ardent, sincere wish to show my grateful love to that family and you'll send me word right away, won't you, that it is possible to do so in this manner.

I hope your school is again giving you much pleasure; couldn't you also send me some other good news? How dearly I wish for that![15]

What has happened with the Hungarians! I suppose you are discovering new audiences every day and everyone else must wait on their account![16]

Most warmly,
your Johannes.

Brahms paid the tuition. He picked up his relationship with Elise where it had left off twenty-five or thirty years before, addressing her by her first name and in the familiar form. Clara aside, there is no woman outside his family to whom he wrote in this fashion.

---

[15] A reference to Joachim's marital problems. See Letter 397.
[16] Joachim had just finished a violin and piano arrangement of some of the Hungarian Dances from Volumes III and IV. They were published later in the year.

396
Johannes Brahms to Elise Denninghoff neé Giesemann

[Vienna,] October [18]80

Dear Elise,

I have just written to Berlin and now I hasten to tell you what a great pleasure your letter gave me, as unexpected as it was extraordinary.

The memory of your parents' home is among the most precious I retain.

All the kindness and love shown me there, all the youthful ardour and happiness I enjoyed there lives on in my heart; and how often does the image of your good, dear father come to me, and the happy, grateful memory of you all!

To my delight, your letter tells me also about your family and that your revered mother is in fact still living happily in the circle of her grandchildren.

Well, I am truly sorry to have robbed you of a memento in the shape of that manuscript. One doesn't like to preserve the visible signs of one's youthful pranks (and early works belong to those). But I will surely be able to replace it for you, particularly since your Agnes sings, once I have discovered if she also sings Lieder and what her range is.[17]

For today, then, just this brief word of thanks, I do hope to hear more of you and yours. I hardly need to assure you explicitly what pleasure it will give me to demonstrate to you in some way the grateful memory I bear you.
With sincere greetings to you and yours
J. Brahms.

Karlsgasse 4.

Joachim's troubled marriage to the singer Amalie Joachim was not news to their friends. For all his exceptional artistic and humanitarian qualities, Joachim was also abnormally jealous, and now became convinced of his wife's infidelities with the publisher Fritz Simrock. With very few exceptions, observers and close friends agreed that Joachim was utterly unjustified in his suspicions of both parties. Brahms took the unusual step, for him, of writing a long and very explicit personal letter to Amalie. It was a potent character witness in her favour and specifically alluded to Joachim's unreasonable jealousies. Amalie used the letter in court, Joachim lost his

---

[17] Posterity would have been very interested in that manuscript. Elise Denninghoff reported it contained three youthful compositions Brahms had composed for the men's choral society he conducted, in the neighbouring town of Winsen an der Luhe, when he was about 15. Brahms now asked for its return, more than thirty years later, and destroyed it. His 'poor memory' worked quite well when it came to knowing the whereabouts of even his most obscure manuscripts.

divorce case, and Brahms lost his oldest friend. There was complete silence between the two men for several years.

Joachim first began to confide his fears to his 'dearest, oldest friend', in the summer of 1880, asking Brahms never to speak of him or his family to Simrock, and refusing even to open parcels of music the publisher sent him. Brahms prepared to visit his friend in Berchtesgaden.

397
Johannes Brahms to Joseph Joachim

[Ischl, 27 July 1880]

Dear friend,

I had some hope, although not much, that your letter would sound more reassuring and hopeful than is now the case. It has made me profoundly sad and comes to mind often and gloomily enough. So much there was that united you that one envisaged a long and happy life together. And now—! A tangible, serious cause is hard to imagine; nor is it likely to exist. I am unfortunately quick to take a gloomy view of this altogether; one thing is certain, that two people come apart more easily than back together again, just as it is easier to lose your mind than to get it back. And so, I don't want either to say or to ask much; I only want to wish with all my heart that through something unexpected—but no misfortune—the matter will take a turn for the good.

And now the dissonance of a friendship torn apart has been added, as well! I don't suppose that you could have much interest in my work or in yours now. But I am nevertheless sending the things to you *with my card*, which should expedite matters that much more and should suit you, since S[imrock] is not in Berlin.

If anything should occur that is news for me, you won't keep it from me, will you. Thoughts of you preoccupy me incessantly, word of improvement would be deliverance for me.

With warmest sentiments,
your
Johannes.

That December, Brahms accepted an invitation to visit the Joachims in Berlin. Ostensibly there to hear Joachim's students perform his Requiem and try out his two new overtures, he seems really to have come to see for himself how his friends were getting on. Uncharacteristically, he even stayed with them for several days. Shortly after the visit Amalie wrote to him; his reply was the long, deeply-felt letter she later used at her divorce trial, taking Brahms at his word that she might use his letter in any way she saw fit.[18]

398

Johannes Brahms to Amalie Joachim

[December 1880]

Dear Frau Joachim,

If you had any idea of how I longed to have a confidential and friendly talk with you, the other day in Berlin, and how I have yearned to write to you like this ever since, then you would also understand that your letter is a true blessing for me, and these lines a kind of deliverance.

Your situation has been known to me for as long as it has existed, and let me say first of all: Neither in word nor thought have I ever considered your husband to be right, nor, of course, could I ever have done so. Indeed, I have thought about you with sympathy during all this time, but since I was in your home, how utterly am I filled with sympathy now, how dearly would I like to do something.

But alas—I have no courage and confidence left and now I can only sense the relief of being allowed to say a friendly word to you. I don't believe that anyone can comprehend your circumstances as clearly and correctly as I. That may seem questionable to you, even though you know that my friendship is older than your marriage.

At all events, you may have noticed that, despite a 30-year friendship, despite all my love and admiration for Joachim, despite all the artistic interests that should have bound me to him, I am none the less very careful in my intercourse with him, that I rarely socialize with him for long and intimately, and that I wouldn't even think of wanting to live in the same town and join him in a common undertaking. And so I need hardly tell you that I knew, even before you, about that unhappy character trait with which Joachim tortures himself and others so irresponsibly. Friendship and love I want to breathe as simply and freely as the air. When I sense that lovely feeling in a complicated or artificial form I skirt it with diffidence, particularly when sustained and heightened by pathological, embarrassing agitation.

I abhor useless scenes evoked by someone's imagination. In friendship, too, a partial divorce is sad, but it is possible just the same. And with Joachim I rescued just a small portion [of our friendship] by exercising caution; without that, I would have been left with nothing long ago.

---

[18] Geiringer, *Brahms*, 144.

Dear friend, in view of this, I need hardly confirm that you are right in the particular instance you write about—as, for instance, at the rehearsal. As a result of Joachim's dismal fretting over everything over and over again, the simplest matter becomes so puffed up, so long-winded, that one doesn't know where to begin and how to deal with it. He will then twist and turn so obstinately in even the smallest of circles, just as he unfortunately does in that great circle of delusions and errors which may deprive him of all his happiness.

I simply want to tell you expressly and clearly, as I have already told Joachim countless times, that according to my understanding and in my opinion, he has done you and Simrock the greatest injustice and that I only wish he would desist from his mistaken and horrendous imaginings.

Your love may, however, be so great that it can forget all that has happened, while his forbearance and Simrock's good will may be so great that a tolerable relationship between the two men can be established. Should this happen, which is to be devoutly hoped for, Joachim would have to admit error on his part anyway, and therefore couldn't insist on you and Simrock atoning for it. Furthermore, I want to say:

My discretion in this matter is so great that I have not exchanged one word about it, for example, with Frau Schumann, my best friend. I say this because the other day, I discovered that the Herzogenbergs, who are staying at Spitta's, were completely informed about everything and these excellent people asked me about the matter. And so I couldn't refrain from expressing my opinion in detail and with reasons, and I also as much as asked them to convey my opinion to Spitta and to request that it be considered. On that occasion I discovered what a pack of lies is being spread about Simrock quite apart from our business. In short, I fear that gradually such a web of imaginings, inventions, hasty conclusions, has been fabricated, as well as lies and deceit, that I don't know how J. will rescue his life's happiness from it. I would gladly mistrust my insight. But irritated by my dissent, J. has gone to great lengths to convince me. And in the end, if he were right, if I were the only one of his friends who is mistaken—then everything would have been over long ago! It is bizarrely comical that he himself doesn't think of drawing the only correct conclusion, that he should call everything by its proper name. Either error, imagination or—! To me that has always been sufficient evidence that it is just his impassioned imagination playing a sinful and unforgivable game with the best and most sacred thing that fate has granted him.

You can see from this long letter how unsuccessfully I try to satisfy myself.

If you could only sense even a small portion of the affection (I am not ashamed of the emotion) with which I think of you and write to you, and if I could only hope for the same from him and could write to him in the same way! But it is difficult not to be bitter towards him and, unfortunately, one must expect that he will perceive what is well meant with bitterness and even as wrong.

And so, do believe me that you have a sincere, faithful friend in me. I am at your disposal in whatever manner and whenever you think I can be of use to you. You can, unfortunately, see that I have little hope of being able to do so.

Devoted to you

with all my heart,

J. Br.

Although Joachim failed in his attempt to divorce Amalie, they separated for life. Brahms kept his word to be of use to her should the need arise; many concert engagements came her way through his efforts, and judging from the mentions of her in his letters to Simrock over the years, he seems to have kept track of her where-abouts—unlike Clara Schumann and Elizabet von Herzogenberg, who virtually snubbed her from then on.

Brahms never set foot in England, but why he avoided the country where so many of his closest friends had so much success is hard to say. His reluctance surely had something to do with a dislike of formality, unease in situations he did not entirely control, and a genuine dislike of being lionized. He once assured George Henschel that he had nothing against Britain, that if he could go incognito, he would be glad to visit; and went so far as to tell Chrysander, the usual go-between in such matters, that he would accept an invitation.[19] One reason frequently offered to explain Brahms's reluctance is that he feared boat travel, a notion wholly repudiated by his willingness to travel by sea in Italy.

There were many attempts to entice Brahms to England; the Royal Philharmonic, in particular, invited him regularly, and this time hoped to rejuvenate their concert season by inviting him to conduct a series of concerts.

399

Johannes Brahms to the Directors of the Royal Philharmonic[20]

[Vienna,] 9 Dec[ember] 1880 Most Honoured Sirs,

I am just returning from a journey, and so as not keep you waiting any longer I send a few exceedingly hurried words in response to your letter and telegram.

---

[19] Chrysander to the Phil. Society, Jan. 1879. Philharmonic Minute Book, B.L. Loan 48/2/7.
[20] Previously unpublished. By kind permission of the British Library.

Unfortunately I cannot make up my mind to accept your kind invitation.

My inclination for concerts is extremely limited, and I have more to do with them than I like here and in Germany. Therefore the decision to travel further for further concerts is too difficult for me—even though it is my lively wish to see and hear for myself what my friends have so often and so highly praised.

Please believe in my liveliest gratitude for kindly offering me the opportunity!

With the highest esteem,
faithfully,
J. Brahms

The full story behind this invitation and the consequences of Brahms's answer bears telling. At the time, the Royal Philharmonic was conducted by William Cusins (later Sir William). The Directors of the Royal Philharmonic included Walter Macfarren and Charles Hallé (not yet Sir Charles), two leading British musicians, both of them disenchanted with Cusins. When the six-member Board of Directors voted 'that Herr Brahms be invited to conduct three of the concerts next season and Mr Cusins the other three' (November 1880), Macfarren proposed an amendment that would have appointed Brahms the conducter for the entire season. The amendment was seconded by Hallé, but lost 4–2, and the original provision carried. Several directors, Macfarren and Hallé among them, promptly resigned.

From the minutes, 4 Dec. 1880: '. . . It was ordered that a telegramme be sent to Dr Johannes Brahms requesting an answer to the letter of Nov. 30.' 21 December 1880: '. . . Letter read from Herr Johannes Brahms declining to accept the invitation whereupon it was resolved that Mr Cusins be the conductor for the season.'[21]

It is certain that Brahms never knew how much it had been hoped, in certain circles, that he would be the means of upgrading London's musical life.

---

[21] Minutes of the Royal Philharmonic Society Directors' Meetings July 1879–1883, British Library.

❧ 1881 ❧

Brahms's friend Friedrich Chrysander devoted his life to producing a complete edition of the works of George Frederick Handel, an undertaking which left him chronically short of money. To improve his friend's finances, Brahms suggested offering six of Handel's Italian duets for Soprano and Alto to the publisher of Peters Editions. Chrysander would prepare the translations and he would make the piano realization from the figured bass. Brahms called them 'the greatest and most beautiful' of all of Handel's duets and requested a large fee, to be divided equally between them. The publisher demurred, expressing the opinion that Brahms was too generous. In the end, a smaller amount was agreed upon, which Brahms insisted on sharing.[1]

400
Johannes Brahms to Max Abraham

[Vienna, 12 March] 1881

Most Honoured Doctor:

My best thanks for your friendly or business-like arguments[2] which I have every reason to respect. I also declare myself in agreement and ask to have the famous 'half' sent to Herr Chrysander (Bergdorf near Hamburg).

But now I must permit myself to add a few words, for you will hardly be surprised that I am nevertheless not exactly of your opinion.

My requests for fees are not determined by the worth that I attach to my work.

Through repeated offerings, I learn the approximate worth they must have for the businessman. These 'Duets' have cost me as much or more time and effort as any of my own works. Nevertheless, I judge my contribution to them to be scant; *Chrysander*, on the other hand, has quite literally presented them to the world. I must admit that only because of him did I get the idea for our undertaking at all.

We owe a lot to that capable and hard-working man; yet he gains nothing from it but ingratitude of every kind—as is of course customary among good Germans. Although the duets are not copyright, you will presumably be the sole publisher of these absolutely splendid things for a long time.

And so I considered it proper that the man to whom we owe the work, as well as the business, should in all fairness participate in the business, in

---

[1] Kal, iii. 268. See *BW* xiv. 314 ff. for Brahms's dealings with Peters. Abraham paid 1,000 Marks for the duets; Brahms originally asked for 1,500 each for himself and Chrysander.

[2] Echoing Abraham's previous letter in their correspondence.

case it is good. Instead of which, he has now obtained a paltry fee for an arduous translation which, by the way, he undertook out of devotion to the thing, and which could easily be done badly, but hardly better.

Certainly, once we have presented the 'Duets' to the public anybody can have them arranged and printed, also can pay the persons involved, as is fitting. In our case, and specifically with respect to *Chrysander*, allow me to retain my particular view.

Why I don't withdraw the work, in spite of this hope having been dashed, I really cannot say. It's a sort of lethargy, but also the conviction that you are acting with the best intentions, also probably aren't expecting business to be especially good.

But do tell me how you are planning to deal with the languages. The Italian must never be missing, of course; 2 editions are therefore probably necessary, German–Italian and English–Italian?

But for your trio of operas I offer my best congratulations. Without any doubt, the whole enterprise and the previously published works will gain enormously in attention, through further publication.[3]

The publication of the 'Weiße Dame', for instance, is still very little known. A growing number of musicians will definitely consider acquiring a good operatic library for themselves.

But for today, enough for now.

Forgive all this chatter.

Your very devoted

J. Brahms

The second of Brahms's eight Italian journeys took place in April. He was particularly taken with the imposing Greek ruins at Girgenti.

401

Johannes Brahms to Karoline Brahms

[Rome, 25] April 1881

Dear Mother,

I just want to send you greetings and report that my trip has been splendid and wonderful and that I am now slowly on my way home. For I have been further south, in Naples and Sicily!

---

[3] At Brahms's suggestion, Peters was about to publish Spohr's *Jessonda*, one of Brahms's favourite operas; and Marschner's *Hans Heiling*. The publisher had already brought out *Weisse Dame* by Boïeldieu.

You must see, must form an impression of that divine land through pictures and letters, for I cannot attempt to describe it. Where to begin? With the oranges and figs that grow there, or with one of the thousand things whose glow is so very different here from at home?

Do look among my books (perhaps sometime when Fritz comes by) for a volume: Seume, A Walk to Syracuse. It is well bound in 2 or 3 volumes, dark. I would like to ask you to send that to Vienna. Along with it do also write to me, kindly give my best greetings to Elise—I won't write specially to her for one really has no time here except for enjoyment.

Therefore—be content with this brief greeting and conclude from it that thinking affectionately of you is

your Johannes.

402

Johannes Brahms to Julius Otto and Philipine Grimm

[Vienna, 17 May 1881]

Dear friend,

I thank you very much for all kinds of friendly greetings and I ask you also to allow Frau Hedwig to participate in them, for now!

Then I'll just hurriedly tell the Westphalian that I visited Herr Dohrn in Naples twice, on my way to and from Sicily; that I dined with Herr and Frl. Schücking in Rome and we said many and good things about you all, that I was then the philistine fool and travelled home. Because that one shouldn't do unless one must. It was marvellous. In Sicily, particularly *Girgenti*, Taormina, and Palermo. Besides that, I was in Venice, Pisa, Florence, Siena, and Rome (and Naples). Accept my best wishes, too, for the start of the golden age of your marriage, and let me also know how the examination went and how it's going with Barth.

Most affectionately,

your J. Brahms.

Dear Frau Pine,

I add my very best greetings to you and if your Friend and Concertmaster should leave you, do write a word.[4] I should really like to live with you a little more than just in my mind.

Affectionately and hurriedly,

your J. B.

---

[4] An echo of the letters Brahms wrote to the Grimms and Agathe in the autumn of 1858. The reference in this case is to Richard Barth, the young violin virtuoso leading Grimm's orchestra and living in his home, as he was too young to live on his own.

Theodor Engelmann liked to discuss his work with Brahms, and sent him a number of his scientific papers, mostly concerning neuro-muscular investigations. His scientific work also included pioneering studies of bacterial photosynthesis, investigations which helped lay the foundations of that field. One of the papers Brahms received described an ingenious method of using bacteria to measure the generation of oxygen (O).[5] Brahms's light-hearted answer went to Frau Engelmann. He was apparently struggling somewhat with the Second Piano Concerto and *Nänie*, and also needed to explain why he did not dedicate his new piano concerto to her—she had joked she would leave her husband for such a thing.

403
Johannes Brahms to Emma Engelmann

[Pressbaum, 7 July 1881]

Dear friend,

I really ought to be writing to your worthy husband to thank him for the reports of some truly interesting investigations.

But for the present I prefer to write to you since, after a hasty reading, I am unfortunately in all too little agreement with him.

Unfortunately, right from the start I am opposed to this O-exhalation. If not for that little bit of O and Ah, what should sensitive people like us do, eh? I also can't stand it when people rage so against these swarming/swooning[6] bacteria and assorted womenfolk, one should gladly let them swoon or swarm a little. If one lets the gentlemen just keep on working all the time, it'll soon do harm to all of music—for what is this [music], after all, other than a big, beautiful O and Ah, eh?

But for me, everything is going awry. Here am I, gabbing where I ought to be working, I really shouldn't, and I am supposed to be producing music which I do not understand very well. That's the way my whole life is, transposed; including even the place where I endure it!

Just imagine, in Rome I ate large fava beans noon and night! In Mecklenburg I could do the same! But I, poor fellow, am obliged to sit

---

[5] 'New Methods for Detection of O_2 Evolution in Plant & Animal Organisms', *Pflügers Archiv für die Gesammte Physiologie*, 25 (1881), 285–92. Engelmann detected photosynthetic evolution of O_2 in a variety of plants and micro-organisms, using putrefying bacteria sensitive to O_2. I am indebted to Professor Martin Kamen, photobacteriologist, splendid violist, and Brahms enthusiast, for describing and summarizing the significance of Engelmann's career for me. See his paper, 'On Creativity of Eye and Ear: A Commentary on the Career of T. W. Engelmann', *Proceedings of the American Philosphical Society*, vol. 130, no. 1 (1986), 232–47.

[6] The German word 'schwärmen' means to 'swarm' and to 'swoon over'. Brahms's 'opposition' was probably due to the fact that the bacteria died when deprived of oxygen!

between the two fava-poles, among Phaeacians who do not appreciate them![7]

Other misfortunes I don't have to bear by myself, at least. Like Hiller, I have rashly written a beautiful, large piano concerto, without considering beforehand whether there might be a woman who would abandon her husband for its sake! So here I sit—the baby on my lap and no one to suckle and play it.

Ah, there is in it an extra Scherzo of such tenderness, of such sweet scent, of such O, to express it in a single letter! With this piece I also intended to show how the artist must forswear all passion so that he can swoon or swarm in the purest ether with the previously considered bacteria.

Elsewhere again, I intended to demonstrate how in an orchestra the kettledrum is useless and how, when it comes to singing, the piano replaces and surpasses it by far.[8] Ah, O, what in the world doesn't the man intend and reflect upon while composing, or the woman while playing the piano—but the rude rabble, the professors—

Suffice it that you have endured my ugly mood for 5 minutes.

It only remains to inform you that I am staying in Pressbaum near Vienna; and where will you be going, do sometime inform your most devoted or, I should say, most hurried

J. Brahms.

Hans von Bülow's admiration for Brahms's music first manifested itself soon after his appointment as music director in Hanover, shortly after his break with Wagner. Once he moved on to lead the court orchestra in the small Duchy of Meiningen, Bülow was free to give vent to his enthusiasm. He invited Brahms to rehearse new compositions with the Meiningen orchestra at leisure and without the pressure of a performance, exactly what Brahms needed before publishing a new work. There developed a genuine, if sometimes fragile friendship. The connection puzzled Brahms's friends, knowing as they did Bülow's neurotic, quarrelsome, and high-strung nature, and more than one friend asked directly about it. Hiller, in particular, had seen enough of Bülow to keep his distance. Brahms preferred to keep his own counsel.

---

[7] Brahms is playing with the word *Sau*, which means 'sow' and is a component of the word for 'fava bean' (Saubohnen) and 'oxygen' (Sauerstoff). The two poles referred are Mecklenburg (where Emma came from) and Rome. The Phaeacians were famous for appreciating good food, as well as for bringing Odysseus home at last, after they had rescued him when he was cast upon their shores, but they also gave their name to the Viennese, who were widely referred to as Phaeacian in their enjoyment of life.

[8] Probably a reference to the extraordinary passage which begins the Coda to the first movement, measure 332.

404
Johannes Brahms to Hans von Bülow

[July 1881]

Most esteemed Baron and revered colleague,

I must take a few words to tell you that I have lately given much thought to you and your kind suggestion to hold thorough rehearsals in Meiningen some time or other. The opportunity would [now] be at hand, but it's a piano concerto that would require these rehearsals! But added possibly to other modest reservations, I feel considerable reluctance to play that piece 'at sight' for you, of all people.

You know a little about my somewhat odd relationship to the piano and as a pianist, but you surely also know what respect I have for you!

I'm writing these lines so that this will not tempt me to preceed silently past your splendid offer into the next subscription concert. The matter would be quite simple if you would say that a piano concerto is contrary to our understanding and is of no interest to you!

My address is *Pressbaum* near *Vienna*.

With sincere high regard,

your devoted

J. Brahms.

405
Johannes Brahms to Ferdinand Hiller

[End of October 1881]

Most esteemed friend,

Indeed Hanslick and I are the ringleaders,[9] and indeed I did not want to send a telegram from Meiningen, of all places. But you and others probably aren't interpreting my 'Bülow-journeys' simply enough.

I was in Meiningen above all in order to be able to play and rehearse a new piano concerto in peace and without the discomfiting anticipation of a concert. That's something I can do nowhere else. Nowhere else would this have been considered strange, either, even if I had selected the biggest fool of a conductor.

Why then here and with regard to B[ülow], who is, certainly, a very peculiar, a very testy, but nevertheless an intelligent, serious, and competent

---

[9] They congratulated Hiller on his seventieth birthday.

man? You must also be able to imagine for yourself how outstandingly his people have been rehearsed; and so when someone like me comes along and makes music with them, so straight from the heart, I really don't know where he could do any better.

I assure you that this winter—if the music should chance to appear and people feel so pleased with themselves for having worked so hard and achieved so much—I'll think back often and longingly to those truly industrious people and their magnificent accomplishments.

But now I'll just close with my best greetings and wishes—we are already preparing the next festive day, they follow each other ever more closely now . . .

Joh. Brahms.

Hiller's doubts, however, were not frivolous. Bülow was a difficult character. One week after raving about Brahms's new piano concerto to their mutual friend, the concert agent Hermann Wolff, Bülow wrote to him again, now complaining bitterly about how much of his time Brahms had taken up. It is also true that in the mean time, von Bülow had been in bed for five days with one of his excruciating headaches; and there can be no doubt that his physical ailments contributed to his erratic actions.

The other composition of the summer was *Nänie*, Op. 82, a setting of Schiller's poem. The text ('Even Beauty must die') was meant to honour the memory of the painter Anselm Feuerbach, extraordinarily handsome in youth and creator of some of Brahms's favourite paintings, who died in Venice in 1880. Feuerbach's stepmother was an exceptional woman in her own right, a writer and philosopher, much honoured and admired by Brahms. He wrote to her once the piece was finished.

406
Johannes Brahms to Henriette Feuerbach

[August 1881]

Highly esteemed lady,

Permit me without any further preamble to present you with a request. I have recently composed the poem 'Nänie' by Schiller for chorus and orchestra. Very often, when the beautiful words went through my mind, I couldn't help thinking of you and your son and involuntarily I sensed the desire to dedicate my music to his memory. In order to make this tangible I take the liberty of asking if, in case I publish it, I may dedicate the piece to you.

It is possible that you do not wish this, indeed, that you may not exactly be glad to be reminded of me? For, among other things, you heard not a word from me at a time when you doubtless received many expressions of sympathy. And yet, there were probably few who thought of you more sincerely, and surely few who revered your wonderful son more earnestly than I. In case you retain a little of your goodwill towards me, and in case the thought of seeing the name of your son joined to mine in the indicated manner is not disagreeable to you, I ask for a word of consent.

With great esteem,

your devoted

Johs. Brahms

For a long time Brahms considered publishing some of his music through *Peters Editions*, in Leipzig. He was in sympathy with the goal of Max Abraham, its owner, of providing the public with inexpensive editions. But he found it very difficult to disregard his loyalty to Simrock, who was both anxious and upset at Brahms's intentions. In evident conflict with himself, Brahms backed away from his original intention of giving Abraham the new piano concerto. The self-deprecating sarcasm and almost black humour of this letter is very characteristic of a Brahms ill at ease.

407

Johannes Brahms to Max Abraham

Pressbaum, 23 September [18]81

Esteemed Herr Dr,

I had the fine intention of furnishing your stockroom with my music by the ton—in that I was going to offer you an enormously large Piano Concerto. But your colleague Herr Simrock is much too kindly disposed towards you. He absolutely insists on accepting the heavy cross himself and bearing it for you!

Well, I can do nothing about that other than offer you a very very small and delicate one in the mean time.

It is a little piece for chorus and orchestra: *Nenie*,[10] by *Schiller*, which—for the time being, I'd like to hear.

In such a case Herr Simrock always has the kindness to have violin[11] and vocal parts engraved. Whichever singing associations I rehearse with will naturally acquire the parts for themselves—before the actual publication, which then follows in quite leisurely order. But I don't know whether such a relaxed and deliberately slow pace suits you?

---

[10] Schiller's spelling. Brahms soon changed it, claiming it sounded 'too Berlinish'.
[11] i.e. the string parts.

As honorarium I thought of receiving 3,000 Marks. However, you won't be able to inspect the piece until it comes back from the copyist.

I understand you are taking on a collection of canons from *Stockhausen*?

In that case, I would like to ask you urgently to send me the manuscripts of the things that concern me, *before* engraving them! If only for the sake of comprehensibility, caution is needed here. Since I merely tried to be obliging with these trifles, it's quite natural that I hear not one word and have no idea where I'm at.[12]

There is no need for you to express to me your gratitude and joy with regard to the 'Concerto'. I really did have the malicious intention.—Would you now prefer to wait for the next more extensive work?

For the time being, my address is still: Pressbaum near Vienna.

With the greatest esteem,
your devoted
J. Brahms

408

Johannes Brahms to Fritz Simrock

[Pressbaum, 19] September 1881

L[ieber]. S[imrock].,

Yes indeed, you would actually have every right to scold me severely? For the longest time now have you been the most exemplary and best publisher, while I'm not obsequious with exemplary gratitude. It would come out very unclear if I were to try to explain to you my apparent desire to be occasionally independent, and as though occasionally contemplating the time when you will finally have had enough of my music. One thing only is clear; it must be apparent to you too, that it is this one thing which is the cause of all uneasiness, and that on this account, at least, you must never construe my behaviour as bad or false.

That one thing is the confounded relationship to money which, unfortunately, is still customary between musicians and publishers. Regarding that, we musicians are treated like children and incompetents, we don't in the least know for what and how payment is actually made, whether we are giving or getting, whether we rob or are being robbed. (I hasten to add that,

---

[12] Brahms agreed to prepare the final revisions of a group of vocal canons Stockhausen wrote for his School of Singing, published by C. F. Peters. He worried that the canons needed careful editing: 'It is not usual to sing and print canons, nowadays,' he explained in another letter. 'One has to be doubly careful to make them easy to handle and comprehensible' (*BW* xiv. 359). The canons did not actually appear in print until 1884.

as far as you are concerned, I'm only afraid of doing you an unjustice!) But you must understand that this is an uncomfortable feeling, *just precisely* when, as in my case, one has no complaints, but only doubts and fears.

After all, I have no idea if you are taking risks, if you have to count on the future and hence might seriously miscalculate. You will surely understand that this is not conducive to tranquillity. Why can't we musicians have the same relationship to publishers as do authors? After all, G. Freitag knows why and for what he gets money.[13] That being so, it wouldn't even occur to one to consider any publisher other than the one who has been his long-dependable friend? etc. I merely repeat that this doesn't cast even the slightest shadow on your wonderful character as publisher and also is not meant to be an attempt to make a change.

But it is wrong, in view of my popularity, that I was unable to insist on this change. However, I am too impractical, too lazy, too indecisive—and in view of my lamentable solo status, simply not personally interested—but it is wrong, all the same.

So then: You now have the concerto and I hope you will digest it well. My wish to give this particular morsel to Peters—if you reflect on the above— was very well meant. I am so reluctant to give him the Nänie that I probably won't do it.

As honorarium I was thinking of 9,000 Mk., the same as for the violin concerto, and if in retrospect that one doesn't seem like *sheer* folly to you, you could well risk it here too! But be honest about it, *we* must not be parted by money issues!

I now urgently request that you *not announce* the concerto yet, nor the Nänie, *in case* I give it to you, before I tell you that I *have given* P. some useless songs or what have you. But you must not complain about Dr A., he didn't remind me with a single word.

Soon I'll send you the violin parts, for the time being there is nothing else to engrave! One more word regarding the two-hand overtures which I'll enclose shortly; it is purely a business matter, you'll know if it is needed and wanted. K[eller] is a splendid man and does everything so diligently and properly that he cannot be faulted. But do I need to tell you that a two-hand arrangement by him reveals the philistine, and that it could be of no interest to a player with any sophistication? This sort of thing by Bülow or Kirchner (see: arrangements of Liszt) immediately has a very different feel. I wanted to make changes, but that's impossible, one can only write afresh.[14]

[13] The German writer Gustav Freytag, 1816–95.
[14] The solo piano version of his two overtures was made by Robert Keller, who worked for Simrock not only as a copyist but also as an arranger. Brahms was never enthusiastic about that side of his work.

So do whatever business requires—but don't make use of me to hurt the estimable Keller's feelings!

I left the crate unopened since I'd prefer to ship it to Vienna as is. I really can do nothing other than give you my warmest thanks for also lavishing such ornaments on my overtures—but if you'd just picture the pleasure it would have given [X], for instance, so to see his works, doesn't it occur to you that you are wasting your kindness on an unworthy when bestowing it on me?

Finally—could you, when convenient, purchase and send to me as printed matter: *J.V. Widmann:* Rector Müslin's Italian Journey. (Zürich, Schmid.)

I plan to start in Meiningen on 16 October! Namely, to practise diligently and rehearse the concerto under Bülow . . .

. . . Finally, *Addio* and warm greetings from
your
J. Br.

Brahms played a Streicher piano at home—a seven-foot instrument presented to him by the manufacturer. None the less, when he played in public his preference was not for Streichers or one of the other older pianos he had grown up with, but for the modern grand piano—even when it came to performing those of his early works which were written before technology brought the piano to its current state. In this, the documentary record is most informative.

409

Johannes Brahms to Julius Bernuth

[Leipzig, 30 December 1881]

Honoured Sir,

I shall definitely attempt to arrange it so that I am already at the rehearsal on the 3rd. May I ask you to reserve a room for me in the Hotel Petersburg for the evening of the 2nd (perhaps on the second floor)? Since I do have to trouble you about a grand piano, I ask if I will find a very good and *powerful* Bechstein (or American Steinway) waiting for me? And could I also impose upon your kindness to have an instrument brought to the room (A pianino will suffice!)? Further, and lastly, may I ask you to reserve a few tickets for me.

I should particularly like to spend the evening after the concert with you if we could be pleasantly among ourselves. I am not fond of larger gatherings and, quite seriously, also cannot bear them——!

and, quite seriously, also cannot bear them——!

Excuse the haste and the immodest requests.

Your very faithful

J. Brahms

I suppose you will let me know *when* the rehearsal on the 3rd takes place and will have the servant collect the music?

The occasion was a performance of his Second Piano Concerto, but he made a similar request for a performance of his First. This letter, published here for the first time, is not the only one in which Brahms mentions his preference for Bechsteins and American Steinways in the concert-hall. From the early 1880s, he made it plain to the conductors he worked with that he was unwilling to play on other pianos (while by contrast, to Schubring in 1873, he specifically recommended Streicher pianos for use *in the home*). Moreover, two first-hand accounts describe Brahms's great enthusiasm for American Steinways, and according to both accounts he exclaimed that they were the best pianos he had ever played. Brahms's affection for Steinways and Bechsteins was not a passing fad.* I have located no letters from his mature years in which he praises or requests any other manufacture of piano. Additional
Note p. 753

The importance of these comments about pianos lies in the fact that both the Bechstein and Steinway of the 1880s were essentially the modern grand piano, very near in tone, action, and volume to their modern counterparts.[15] Brahms would have understood the current interest in 'authentic instruments' when it suited his purposes; he himself preferred the sound of the natural horn, and leaned towards authentic practices as he understood them, in the performance of Bach and Handel. But he was cynical about a performance on authentic instruments which he attended in Italy,[16] and the desire to perform his piano music on early pianos, which he used simply out of necessity, would probably have astounded him and engendered a sarcastic comment. If he wrote with a quill pen and deplored the advent of the bicycle, it is also true that he was a man who welcomed photography, railways, electrification, phonograph recordings—and the full sound of a modern grand piano.

Brahms was also willing to experiment with new ideas for the placement of instruments in the orchestra. He answered a letter of George Henschel, the multi-talented singer who had been called to Boston to become the first conductor of the newly-founded Boston Symphony. Included with Henschel's letter had been a diagram of his experimental seating of the orchestra.

[15] On a personal note, I have played the 1888 American Steinway 'O' owned by Fritz Jahoda, and do not believe that any but the most experienced piano technician or performer could distinguish it from my 1927 'L', except for those qualities in which all pianos can differ from each other. The 1888 Steinway has the resonance and richness of sound of the 20th-c. instruments, as well as the characteristic feel of the Steinway keyboard.

[16] Josef Viktor Widmann, *Sizilien und andere Gegenden Italiens* (Frauenfeld, 1898), 130.

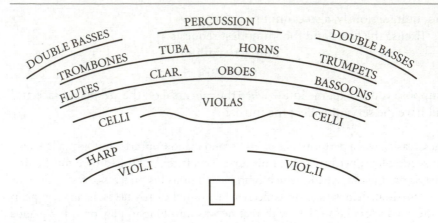

410
Johannes Brahms to George Henschel

[Vienna, mid-November 1881]

. . . Only with a hurried greeting can I answer your kind and chatty letter. I am always on the road, and under the circumstances less than ever inclined and able to write.

Just now I am coming from Budapesth and going—tomorrow—to Stuttgart, etc.

Your experiments in regard to the placing of an orchestra look very good and interesting. I should almost give preference to the first of the two draw-ings on account of the horns; the violas, however, seem to give trouble up to now?

By far the best feature in both arrangements, however, is the fact that no committee will be sitting in front of them. There is not a Capellmeister on the whole of our Continent who would not envy you that!

The *Nänie* is being published by Peters—better are duets by Handel issued by the same firm. Have you seen them?

Enough for today. A very hearty greeting; and thanks for every greeting from you which always gives great joy to
Your
[J. B.]

Among the families in whose homes Brahms felt comfortable, two generations of Wittgensteins rank at the top.

411

Johannes Brahms to Josefine Oser neé Wittgenstein in Mariabrunn

[Pressbaum, 5 August 1881]

Dear Frau Pr[ofessor],

I have just received a telegram *without a signature*, which invites me to dine tomorrow in Weidlingen. I addressed the answer (a No) to you, consequently beg you not to *marvel* if by chance you should not have invited me and some other *oversight* is at hand. I don't even know if you are back home already—only that you gave Frau Schumann an extraordinary pleasure by your visit, and even afterwards.

Meanwhile, best greetings, your J. Brahms

412

Johannes Brahms to Josefine Oser neé Wittgenstein

17 March 1881

Joachim and I have already agreed to meet together in a tavern—oh how disgraceful!—with Billroth.

Sincerest regrets,

J. B.

Brahm's connection with the family was one of long standing and came through Joseph Joachim. As a boy in Vienna, Joachim lived with his cousin, Fanny Figdor, who was central to the development of his career as a violinist. When she married Hermann Wittgenstein and moved to Leipzig, she took Joachim with her to continue his studies there. The Wittgenstein sons and daughters were as brothers and sisters to Joachim, and when Brahms first came to Vienna he was quickly introduced to the large family where music was the overriding cultural activity of the household. Even Karl, who became one of Austria's great industrialists, played the violin. (At the time of Brahms's arrival in Vienna, Karl had run away to New York and was giving violin lessons to support himself.) A number of the girls sang in the women's chorus Brahms conducted, and two of them, Anna and Bertha, became noted sculptors, as well. As the sons and daughters married and founded their own households, Brahms remained in contact, and was a regular dinner guest in virtually all of their homes. A note he wrote to himself as a reminder of his social obligations over a certain three-week period includes five Wittgenstein names.[17] There were wider

---

[17] Probably dating from the late 1880s. The card is in the collection of the Brahms-Institut, Lübeck.

connections, too: Josephine's sister-in-law, Betty Oser, was a pupil and sometime travelling companion of Clara Schumann and a friend of Marie Schumann.

In the last decades of the century, the palatial home of Karl Wittgenstein was a focal point of artistic life in Vienna, and music was the focal point of that home. The gorgeous music room, decorated with murals of Klimt and sculptures of Max Klinger, was often host to Brahms's chamber music in the 1890s, including a run-through of the Clarinet Quintet before its first Viennese performance (see Plate 43). Just inside the door of the room a chair was reserved for Brahms, who could in this way come and go during performances without disturbing other listeners.

> I remember that Brahms was once invited to our house for lunch, and that upon greeting the household, he tousled the hair of my nine-year-old sis-ter Gretl, whose head was covered with short curly locks. Upon my mother's comment, that this particular hair style had been chosen because her hair didn't seem to want to grow, Brahms opined in all seriousness that in such a situation, only champagne would help. Champagne was duly fetched from the cellar and Brahms ceremoniously poured a few drops on the child's head. I still think with pleasure, too, of how, some years later, Gretl and I awaited Brahms at the front door for a musical performance in our house, how he took each of us by the hand and how, proud and happy, we walked with him thus up the grand stairway to the Music Room. [Plate 41][18]

Of the sisters, Clara Wittgenstein, Josephine Oser, Bertha Kupelweiser, and Anna Franz are the most frequently mentioned, and there are many references by Clara and Brahms to Betty Oser. Nevertheless, there are only a few letters from Brahms to the family, who were too much a part of his Viennese circle, living in such close touch that letters were unnecessary. They communicated mostly via messages delivered in person, by visiting cards, and by means of the thrice-daily *Rohrpost*, Vienna's pneumatic postal system. But a few letters have survived:

413

Johannes Brahms to Theodor v. Brücke

[no date]

Honoured Herr Dr,

Herr Demuth keeps sending me very kind and lovely letters from Frau D—so as to have them circulated! Are you in agreement with me when I find

---

[18] Hermine Wittgenstein, 'Familienerinnerungen', Vienna (June 1944). Unpublished typescript. *Gretl* is Margarete, later married to Jerome Stoneborough and painted memorably, full-length, by Klimt. Obviously the champagne treatment was succeessful.

the continuation of these communications not quite proper, or at least, indelicate?

How often one has occasion to honour and rejoice over your brother-in-law Ludwig!

Yours faithfully

J. Brahms

The praise was directed at Louis Wittgenstein, who gained Brahms's approval by speaking out publicly in favour of the rights of indigent orphans and the elderly to receive aid from the city of Vienna, even if they were not native Viennese; and by buying fine old instruments for the members of a string quartet led by Brahms's protégée, Marie Soldat Roeger.[19]

❧ 1882 ❧

414
Johannes Brahms to Fritz Simrock

[Ischl, 25 June 1882]

D[ear] S[imrock],

Straightaway I'd better grant you complete exoneration with regard to your last accounting, indeed, I even volunteer my best thanks for the trouble you went through—what's the point of starting a lawsuit over those few zeros that didn't add up correctly?!

I suppose the song transpositions can wait until I finally get proof-sheets? It's an awful torture with the individual tattered proofs. In any case, what's holding up the songs?! Actually, I couldn't care less—but this indolence of publishers! And when they finally do arrive each volume will surely cost more than 50 thaler. My thanks for that on behalf of the conductor and composer in Berlin!

And finally, a question or request. I would very much like to acquire the score (not the piano reduction) of Bizet's Carmen. Are you on good terms with *Choudens* in Paris? Could you write to him, or can you tell me, what it would cost for me? It's not for a theatre, after all, but for my own very special enjoyment—for in fact I love it more than all of the things you publish, which isn't saying much and not enough. Perhaps Choudens could send it

---

[19] According to a note by daughter Lydia Oser, who attached it to the letter for the benefit of future generations of interested family members.

directly here? A few francs won't make a difference, after all, as long as the price is not extraordinarily Simrockish.[1]

Surely you have read Bülow's flatteries of you?[2] It's natural enough for you to worry about Hanslick's health, and sooner or later it would also be natural for you to be right. We, on the other hand, have already been concerned about him for a long time, and when he got married his friends thought that he wouldn't live another half year. But he became stronger and more sprightly than before!

But he is a good and well-meaning person and superbly talented *for his field*; that he is forever being pushed into another and then judged unfairly is not his fault. Let me hear about Carmen soon, or better still, let me see the score!

Perhaps sometime you will publish the songs of Bizet (*Vingt Melodies*) in German—?—?—! Next to your other song rubbish, it'll do fine.

All the best,

your

J.B.

Brahms was an early and potent German champion of the music of Georges Bizet; he considered *Carmen* one of the great contemporary operas. Eventually his library included eight volumes of the Frenchman's work. At the time of this letter Simrock was about to publish seventeen of Brahms's songs, divided into three sets: Opp. 84, 85, and 86, the manuscripts of which he had since April. (Other compositions of the summer were the Piano Trio in C major, Op. 87, and the String Quintet in F major, Op. 88. Speaking of the quintet: 'I tell you, you haven't had such a beautiful thing from me before, haven't published such a thing perhaps in the past ten years!!!'.[3])

Friendship bloomed rapidly with Hans von Bülow, who, unlike Hanslick, was every bit Brahms's intellectual equal, and a witty, polylingual, if hyper-active sophisticate. Bülow's punishing experience with Cosima Lizst did not deter him from remarriage, this time to the actress Marie Schanzer. Brahms sent his congratulations.

---

[1] Choudens was Bizet's publisher.

[2] Bülow, in praising a Norwegian publisher for furthering the cause of Norway's music, likened him in importance to Simrock.

[3] *BW* x. 216.

415
Johannes Brahms to Hans von Bülow

Ischl, [May 1882]

Esteemed friend,

I should have returned your congratulations for the 7th of May long ago in equal coin and with my thanks. But do I know where in the world you are, and do I know whether this time, for a change, the world speaks the truth? Gradually it seems so, and therefore I want to send you my best and heartfelt wishes. To make them sound convincing I should really give some sort of proof of their veracity and follow your example! But this just cannot be, for a person has his principles, and I have long since adopted one for this situation. Sad it is, however, that one does not know and believe early enough how fertile zeros are, and how a person, without intent or effort but unfortunately also without purpose, turns into a capitalist!

You are constituted with a far happier nature than I. You have fun with so many things and pursue so many earnestly—to both of which I bring along almost the opposite, however.

I have been in Ischl for about a week; since yesterday as a summer guest, for the day before yesterday we were still having a splendid snow storm. You will be preparing yourself for Aachen and can be proud of yourself for having managed to bring even to a music festival such a work of ill repute as the D minor Concerto.

If I should send you a few volumes of songs in the near future—or not—don't take it amiss. I don't yet know whether I should be embarrassed or whether I can consider the bridegroom capable of being gently befuddled.

But now commend me to your bride as best you can, hence show her a photo that is twenty years old and play for her no Sonata in F sharp minor but maybe an Intermezzo in A flat major—which, what's more, you play so incomparably.

Do greet friend Wüllner warmly, in Aachen. I hope that music and everything else there will do him good after his recent experience. I'm actually supposed to be at Lake Como, and fear that your much revered and beloved Lord and Lady will be unable to consider and grasp various things—and even take them amiss![4]

---

[4] The Duke of Meiningen and his wife. He had turned down their invitation to visit them on Lake Como. See Letter 417.

Forgive the long chit-chat. Now your bride can simply read the reverse side.

Utterly and warmly your devoted
J. Brahms

Why the reverse side? Because Brahms wrote this letter on Bülow's personal note paper, which had a line drawing of the pianist printed in the upper left-hand corner. Brahms turned the folded sheet over and used it upside down, so that the picture appears upside-down on the last side of the letter; and where he obtained the sheets is anyone's guess. He must have had a good supply—I have seen two more letters on Bülow's paper written in this fashion, and others are mentioned in some of the printed collections.

The veiled comments about his personal life—cryptic references to marriage, to fertile zeros (the thousands of thaler his works earned him), the regrets at having money and no one to spend it on, at not having believed earlier in life that he would one day have money, fit a familiar pattern. Brahms never lost the need to excuse himself for not having married.

A number of the summer's events are hinted at: Bülow was about to perform Brahms's Op. 15 with Wüllner, in a performance which fortunately met with great success, for just as Brahms feared, his old friend was having a rough time in Dresden. For his part, Brahms's songs Opp. 84, 85, and 86 had just appeared in July. His advice to Bülow on how to introduce himself (Brahms) to Marie contrasts the Piano Sonata Op. 2, a long and passionate and stormy piece, with the Intermezzo, Op. 76 No. 3, graceful and dreamy. Von Bülow had given the première of Op. 2 the previous February.

During the same summer, Brahms almost made up his mind to visit Bayreuth, but when Simrock was not free at the time Brahms suggested, the plan fell through.

416
Johannes Brahms to Fritz Simrock

[Ischl, 30 July 1882]

D[ear] S[imrock],

It's scandalous!

You want to make a pilgrimage to Bayreuth in September and every cultivated person knows that the hallowed festivalizing will be over by then. Among publishers, it's true, only Dr Strecker might know it. If you were a bit more than a publisher you might well have read and kept the Aesthetics, instead of charging my account with 10 or 20 M. for it![5] But you publishers

---

[5] Strecker was Wagner's publisher, owner of the firm of B. Schott & Sohn. Brahms owed Simrock money for the book *Aesthetics of Music from Kant to the Present*, by Heinrich Ehrlich, which he asked for at the beginning of July.

simply have no sense for anything other than your own junk! Well now, here are these songs, for which one has had to wait for months, and whose publication one has boasted about for months! I was ashamed; not because someone could have written such a thing, such nonsense a person can turn out all day long—but that someone should print such a thing and sell it for good money! Is there no state examination for publishers? So one will know if they can tell dung from salad and vegetables?

With the lovely picture of me, you surely mean the one by Bruckmann in Munich? Ordinarily I don't take an interest in my likeness, but that picture has thoroughly enraged me and I wanted to protest loudly against its sale. And it's the only one that is widely circulated. Couldn't you beg Hug[6] really urgently, in my name, to stop taking and selling that picture! Luckhardt in Vienna has good ones.

NB. You cannot publish the first volume of songs transposed as an entity, only perhaps certain individual ones. The other 2 volumes, of course, and I'll shortly indicate the key signatures. Could you please send the full score of the Concerto to Dietrich and Grimm—I cannot think of anyone else.

Should you really want to go to Bayreuth, I would *very much like* to go with you! And any time you wish, only I do believe it would be good to decide soon. I could do it any day beginning with the 6th—I would therefore be very grateful if you would promptly order 2 tickets and 2 lodgings and let me know the day. I have already had complimentary tickets twice and couldn't go! It seems I'm bound to part with the 30 Mk. Enclosed is some money, in case you don't have enough for the pilgrimage![7]

And so, with my best greetings to you and the Fräulein

your

J.B.

If Brahms's friendship with von Bülow developed quickly, so too his relationship with Bülow's employers, the Duke of Meiningen and his wife, Freifrau Helene von Heldburg (Ellen Franz, the actress). The following letter is from the early days of their acquaintance, and consequently rather stiff and awkward. His manner would soon soften in the warmth of their personal affection for him. In fact, Their Highnesses' letters exhibit extraordinary cordiality from the very first, a quality which continued undiminished until the composer's death.

Not only did the couple encourage Bülow's hospitality towards Brahms, they invited the composer to enjoy Meiningen's other great asset, the well-funded

---

[6] The major music distributor in Zurich. Simrock was on holiday in Switzerland with his daughter at this time.

[7] A joke.

repertory theatre, where Freifrau Helene had once been a leading actress. Over the years Brahms attended many performances of new theatre works, and among other people there he met Ibsen, whose plays were among those presented.

In the spring, they asked Brahms to spend May with them at the Villa Carlotta, their estate on an island in Lake Como. He declined, hence his comment above to von Bülow, and this letter, which also contains what is for him a remarkably explicit description of his manner of composing.

417
Johannes Brahms to Georg II, Duke of Meiningen

Gracious Duke,

I wish to express to Your Highness the wish, as devoted as it is fervent, that I might be permitted to dedicate to Your Highness a new work. It is a composition of the *Parzenlied* from Goethe's *Iphigenia* for which I request this distinction, and which, I dearly hope, may not be wholly unworthy of such favour. For myself, however, it would thereby become a symbol of the memories of so much benevolence and kindness which Y[our] H[ighness] has bestowed upon me, and of those fine, artistically most stimulating times I owe to Y. H.

In addition, I take the liberty of relating that I was at the Villa Carlotta in mid-September, a few hours after H. H. the Crown Prince had left the castle.

I thought back wistfully to the May that I had missed out on; could not complain, however, for I had spent the time in accustomed solitude, taking walks with thoughts of *Parzen* and other lovely creatures.

But I am so used to utter solitude that I require it, if going for walks is to imply more than moving one's feet.

Well, my question and humble request of today concerns one of the results of such walks.

How happy I would be if I could sometime perform it for Y. H., and my request of today would then not seem immodest. The *Parzenlied* will ring out very soon for me; by Dec. 10th in Basle, on the 18th in Zurich.

I need not tell Y. H. with what sympathy I think of the esteemed Bülow.

From afar one wants to enquire continually, but has to tell oneself that answers which necessarily sound similar over a long period cannot give satisfaction. But all the same, today I did request news from Herr Hilpert in hopes of finally hearing a more gratifying report.[8]

---

[8] Friedrich Hilpert (1841–96), one of the Meiningen musicians and cellist of the Florentine Quartet.

May I request Y.H. to kindly commend me to His wife when the occasion arises.

With the greatest deference and devotion

Your Highness's most humble servant,
Johannes Brahms.

Vienna,
23 Nov. 1882.

Max Bruch and Johannes Brahms were not friends, but they had a number of friends in common, and their paths often crossed. Now Bruch was being considered for the post as Director of the Breslau Orchestra, a position which Bernhard Scholz was vacating. The Chairman of the Orchestral Association asked Brahms for his advice. Bruch's 'personality and his knack for alienating people'[9] was well known to Brahms, if not from personal experience or conversation with mutual friends (Hiller, Reinthaler, and the von Beckeraths), then surely from comments by Simrock, who, as Bruch's publisher, received many a bitter and complaining letter from him.

In the following letter, newly discovered, Brahms exhibits considerable tact in the way be praises Bruch's musical abilities while delicately urging caution. Bruch got the job. There is no indication that he ever knew of Brahms's involvement and kind words. Rather, he maintained a somewhat sour, uncompromising attitude towards the man in whose shadow he always remained.

Brahms's comments about George Henschel reflect his admiration and warm friendship for the Breslau native.

418

Johannes Brahms to [Dr Adolf Kaufmann, Chairman of the Orchestra Committee in Breslau]

[Autumn 1882]

Esteemed Herr Doktor,

With regard to M[ax] Br[uch], you unfortunately forgot to tell me if you know him and if you find him congenial. He is so popular as composer that this question, should it seem necessary, is twice as important—and I suppose it is necessary. Should you be personally acquainted with him I wish, particularly in his case that you could have him with you as a guest. Perhaps he could conduct the *Odysseus* at Schäffer's?[10]

[9] Christopher Fifield, *Max Bruch: His Life and Works* (London, 1988), esp. 214.
[10] Julius Schaeffer, conductor of the Breslau Singakademie. The *Odysseus*, Op. 41, was Bruch's very popular secular oratorio, a work which Brahms himself had conducted at his last regular Gesellschaft concert.

Apart from that I could only congratulate you for gaining such a talented and accomplished artist and at the same time, such a highly regarded and popular composer.

Meanwhile, George Henschel came to mind. You surely know him and I hardly need to tell you that he is very talented (for all sorts of thing). As conductor, he has now gone through 2 years of rigorous schooling in Boston. That way you could bring back to Germany a very fine singer whom we sorely miss.

For these few hurried lines that say nothing, forgive

your

sincerely devoted

Joh. Brahms.

Gustav Nottebohm fell desperately ill while on holiday; several urgent appeals for help brought Brahms to Graz, which was as close to home as Nottebohm was able to travel.

419

Johannes Brahms to Gustav Nottebohm

October 1882

Dear Nottebohm,

This morning I packed my portmanteau to travel to Graz. Now, after having talked back and forth with Pohl, I merely send this letter. I do believe that I can say nothing more or different from what this letter can. I can only ask you very sincerely to talk over with your physician and possibly Dr Karajan or Hausegger what is best for your condition, then to do it without thinking of anything else—specifically not about the necessary money, *which is available without further ado.*

I would think that in the long run the hotel is uncomfortable. Would you like a good hospital there? Would you like to and could you come here? I think in that case, too, you should decide to go to the hospital. You know that we have very good friends there and you would be taken care of exceedingly well. Once you have recovered, I do think you should go south for the winter—or could you do that right away?

As I said, think it over and make your decision without troubling yourself about anything other than your health. In closing I say that I can come any day and will be glad to come, that I will be glad to carry out all of your commissions. I hope that you will just as gladly commission and make use of

your devoted
J. Brahms.

Brahms arrived a few days before his friend's death, stayed with him to the end and arranged the formalities after he died. He undertook to inform Nottebohm's closest friend.

420
Johannes Brahms to Robert Volkmann

[November 1882]

Most esteemed friend,

When I found your last visiting card on Nottebohm's desk, I resolved to write to you. I thought warmly about you. As I have always thought, you are after all the only person to whom Nottebohm was seriously and sincerely attached!

I shall try now, in response to your letter, to apprise you of a few things. Nottebohm had been in Salzburg for about 4 weeks and in Gleichenberg for 6–8. Then, on his way to Vienna, he got only as far as Graz and had to be carried up to the first floor of the 'Erzherzog Johann'; the last three days he was in hospital—always with the best of care. Upon being alerted by us, several distinguished gentlemen (Prof. Karajan, among them) took a friendly interest in him. I don't understand his doctor here, for his illness must have been growing worse for a long time; his one lung was entirely, the other largely, destroyed.

I found Nottebohm already seriously weakened. He was delighted to see me, but could only speak a little and was difficult to understand. (On the other hand he ate and drank a great deal and with pleasure.)

Apparently he did not suffer and he died very quietly and easily. The four local musical societies participated in his funeral. The death announcements were for the most part copied from Hanslick's notice, which appeared the very day after his death. Unfortunately I don't have a copy here. An essay by Carl Grün should appear shortly in the *Augsburger Allgem[eine] Zeitung*. Grün is from the same town and attended the same school, and his wife was Nottebohm's most assiduous student. Nottebohm made no arrangements regarding his estate; nor did he seem to have any thoughts of death—since he was still making plans for the winter and Italy!

He leaves behind only two sisters and children of his brothers, who are apparently entrusting his legacy to us. Herr Pohl will attend to what is necessary. The legacy, as far as I have seen up to now, is considerably less significant and interesting than you think.

But now forgive me for putting paper aside and accept heartfelt greetings from

your

devoted

J. Brahms.

Nottebohm's death left a monumental undertaking without its editor-in-chief, Breitkopf & Härtel's revision of the Complete Bach Edition. The publishing house asked Brahms if Nottebohm had been able to give any thought to the matter before he died. They also asked for Brahms's advice, expressing the hope he would agree to take Nottebohm's place.

421

Johannes Brahms to Breitkopf & Härtel

[9 November 1882]

Most honoured gentlemen,

Unfortunately I can report nothing further than that *Nottebohm* died painlessly and quietly. I tried in vain to obtain specific instructions or information from him. He was partly too weak to speak of serious matters at any length, partly also he apparently did not think he would have to die; at least, he gladly went along with the plan to go to Italy for the winter.

Indeed, he could have made significant contributions for the revision of the *Bach* edition. That you should now be thinking of me for this lofty artistic task is flattery that goes too far. I lack all sorts of the requisite knowledge. In this I can only take pleasure in the fine and earnest diligence of others while gratefully savouring it, and ponder to myself alone, with utmost modesty—any possible reservations.

Herr *Pohl* will tell you in greater detail about *Nottebohm's* bequest.

But in the mean time, I suppose we shall have to wait and see how the relatives decide these matters and whether they will even put various things at our disposal at all.

With my greatest esteem,

your devoted

J. Brahms

❧ 1883 ❧

The summer of 1883 was spent on the Rhine. Brahms appeared in Wiesbaden for a few days in May to visit his friends Laura and Rudolf von Beckerath, and ended by staying the summer. He lodged in a former painter's studio, a charming house standing in a large garden surrounded by old trees, commanding a view of all of Wiesbaden, the Rhine, and its valley. Here he settled down to write *his* Rhenish symphony (the Third, Op. 90) and for the entire summer spent almost every evening with the von Beckeraths.[1] Their friendship went back to Zurich, 1875, and ever since he had been the beneficiary of Beckerath's wine, enjoying gifts which arrived by the case. With Rudolf, an excellent amateur in possession of a Stradivarius, he read violin sonatas (mostly Beethoven and Friedrich Kiel, a local composer) and made good use of the Beckeraths's superb cellar.[2]

Towards the end of the summer Beckerath's heart disease forced him to bed, for a time.

422
Johannes Brahms to Laura von Beckerath

[September 1883]

How is he?
What is his pulse?
    "   " his colour?
    "   " the—etc.?
    "   has he eaten?
    "   "   " had to drink?
How much?
Has he read a sensible book?
Or just the newspaper?
Has he played the violin?
Beethoven, Kiel?
Or merely Br?
Is he wearing his handsome jacket?

[1] There are convincing arguments for finding a nod of recognition to Schumann's Third Symphony, Op. 97 (the 'Rhenish'), as well as to Wagner—who died earlier that year. See Robert Baily, 'Brahms's Third Symphony', in George Bozarth (ed.), *Brahms Studies* (Oxford 1990), 405–21; and David Brodbeck, 'Brahms, the Third Symphony, and the New German School', in Walter Frisch (ed.), *Brahms and his World* (Princeton, 1990), 65–78.

[2] For details of the delightful summer see Kurt Stephenson, *Johannes Brahms und die Familie von Beckerath* (Hamburg, 1979), 21 ff.

Or just the grey one?

Does he speak of Jäger, Schopenhauer, the migration of souls, of being buried alive?

Or does he make bad jokes?

Can he say 'bab' with the necessary energy?

Can he escalate that to 'pappe'?

A detailed response and compassionate report is requested.

It is needed, it would provide, as does the goodness of cream to coffee, tranquillity to the ailing spirit of your Br. . .

At summer's end a letter of thanks came from Vienna, hinting at a thirty-two-page letter (a phantom, of course), and of a new violin sonata—real, and probably stimulated by their months of sonata playing, particularly Beethoven's sonatas in A major, the Kreutzer, the Op. 12 No. 2, and Op. 30 No. 1.

423
Johannes Brahms to Rudolf von Beckerath

[Vienna, October 1883]

Dear Herr v. Beckerath,

I must beg your pardon for the 32 pages I wrote to your dear wife yesterday. I was more than a little shocked when I discovered while registering it at the post office, that the letter was a double, a twin—a monster! For that's how you'll regard it should you be sentenced to listening to it!

I hope you will consider that it is impossible to write briefly and nonchalantly if, as in my case, one has to thank for so much and such great kindness. How cordially I thought back on it during the beautiful journey here, for which I had ordered as my very own overcoat the most splendid weather; well—after all, I did describe it in verse that was unassuming but perhaps too enthusiastic! I discoursed at too great a length, but prettily perhaps, on how everything will linger safely and warmly in my heart.

And finally—will you believe it even though I use too many or too few words or bad jokes! But you really did cost Simrock and the world a violin sonata! Just about every Sunday I happily started on one, and in the evening, after you had immersed me so agreeably in one unsurpassable A Major or another, I naturally couldn't go on. But don't celebrate too soon, I'll write one for you yet, and since with violin sonatas the third person is the most important thing, I'll make sure that its page turns are beautiful and full of feeling!

This however, is only intended as a hasty greeting and to excuse the writer of the over-long letter yesterday, or may I call him a poet?

I suppose that I enclosed the 200.—yesterday?

But to the person named overleaf I request that you convey warmest greetings and to a few others as well, e.g. our daughter-in-law and her mother, Ruth and Kurt [v. B.] and Wolff v. Wurmb and—next time I'll write sensibly—but I am very cheerful and happy when thinking of you most affectionately.

your J. Brahms.

The 'person named overleaf' is Frau von Beckerath; the 'daughter-in-law' is the singer, Hermine Spies, whom Brahms met that summer through the Beckeraths, and who soon developed into his latest flame.

Another voice confirmed the summer's success.

424

Antonin Dvořák to Fritz Simrock

10 October 1883

Dear Friend S[imrock]!

To have allowed me to hear nothing at all from you for so long is so baffling to me that I'm making a start myself.

The first item is that I was recently in Vienna, where I spent very fine days with Dr Brahms, who had just come back from Wiesbaden. I have never yet seen him in such a cheerful mood. We were together every day, for dinner and in the evening, where we chatted about many things. His contact with me seems to have pleased him and I was really so enchanted by his kindness to me as an artist and person that I could love him! What a heart and soul there is inside that man!

You know, of course, how very reticent he is even to his dearest friends and musicians in regard to his work, but towards me he was not so. At my request to hear something of his new symphony, he was immediately forthcoming and played its first and last movements for me. I say without exaggerating that this work surpasses his first two symphonies; if not, perhaps, in grandeur and powerful conception—then certainly in—*beauty*.

There is a mood in it which one does not often find in Brahms! What magnificent melodies are there for the finding!

It is full of love, and it makes one's heart melt. Think of my words and when you hear the symphony you will say that I have heard well. But enough of that.

This work redounds to the glory of art, and congratulating you in advance is

Your

Ant. Dvořák

Permanent estrangement from Joseph Joachim seemed unthinkable. True, there were other violinists Brahms admired (in particular Joachim's former student, Richard Barth, filled the gap to some extent), but it was more than the sound of Joachim's violin that Brahms missed. He set about quite consciously to win back his friend, using the Third Symphony as a first step. His plan was to offer Joachim the first Berlin performance of the work for a concert at the Conservatory, with Joachim conducting, and shortly after to conduct the work himself at one of Wüllner's concerts.

The series of letters he wrote to Joachim and Wüllner in order to carry out his plan—once again he had to juggle the requirements of two friends—is a striking display of diplomacy and iron determination to attain his goal. Not even the number of letters he had to write elicited a complaint.

425

Johannes Brahms to Joseph Joachim

Vienna, 30 October [18]83

Dear Joachim,

It is a special small occasion which prompts me to write to you. But I had already felt the urge to do so for a long time, and it might have been good—right, in any case—had I yielded to it sooner.

In the sad business of your wife I could never take your side, I would always have to deplore most profoundly your course of action therein. That could not remain without having an influence on our relationship, nor did it for my part. That these sentiments had to be brought to light quite as brusquely as you have intimated, I fail to see and can also have but one basis, but one I felt duty-bound to speak out on at the time.[3]

It is, however, a letter from me to your wife.

Up until the date of that letter, I had not exchanged a single word about this matter with either your wife or with Simrock, had heard about it only from you throughout that long time.

---

[3] Brahms's perception of Joachim's unreasonably jealous nature.

If, as a result, my view of this matter gains in value for your wife's friends, then the discretion I exercised for so long may well lay claim to the respect of your friends.

Writing that letter is something I cannot repent. It was for me a solace, a liberation, to be able to tell your tormented wife—the same things I had told you often enough.

That my opinion became public, that my letter in fact was entered into the official record, upset me greatly at the time. I have no judgement in the matter, merely an opinion and that has no place before the judge. But what in the world wasn't submitted to him!

In short, if you can permit an acceptable relationship between us in spite of these events, which I regret but for which I cannot ask forgiveness—I should like to have extended my hand.

And so to today's occasion, although it seems so insignificant to me that I must force my pen. Last year I refused Wüllner my participation, this year I let myself be persuaded. (For the 28th of January, Berlin.) Wüllner saw a new symphony at my place last summer and I promised it to him on the condition that the performance not be announced as a première. For I wanted to offer it to you in Coblenz.[4] I would now like to do whatever I can to avert a misunderstanding, a misinterpretation, and tell you therefore that the symphony is at your disposal. It will be performed here on the 2nd of December and you can have the parts after that; the score even sooner, and I'd ask that you decide only after examining it.

This letter expects no reply and concerning the symphony, the briefest word will suffice for

your
J. Brahms.

Carlsgasse 4 Vienna

Joachim accepted the proffered hand and asked for the score as soon as possible, adding that he was particularly anxious to avoid giving rise to any difficulty between Brahms and Wüllner.

---

[4] Brahms attended the Festival of the Lower Rhine there in July, intending to attempt a reconciliation. Nothing came of it.

426
Johannes Brahms to Joseph Joachim

[Vienna, 12 November 1883]

Dear Joachim,

Your answer gave me the greatest joy, and I thank you for it from my heart. I am not hampered by Wüllner. He knows that I had the fervent wish for you to be the first to perform the symphony in the town where you live. That's why I had explicitly asked that his performance not be announced as a première of the piece (as indeed was not done?).

But now I have promised you more than I can deliver. I'll be glad enough if the parts are ready for the 2nd of December; I won't have a copy of the score before then. But on the 3rd it can all be dispatched to you, I think you can take a chance and schedule the performance.

The Symphony can surely be played at least once, and in the worst case, a repeat by W[üllner] will be impossible!

How many violins do you need? Here we have nine firsts, six seconds, six violas, five violoncellos, five basses (desks). But I can send more.

Incidentally, there is no rush for your performance for I don't plan to make use of the parts in December. I would nevertheless like to be able to keep them at my disposal as much as possible.

Once again, then, the most earnest, heartfelt thanks
of your
J. Brahms.

427
Johannes Brahms to Franz Wüllner

[November 1883]

Dear friend,

It has happened as I expected and you do know how much I hoped for it with all my heart: Joachim is going to perform my Symphony.

You know and understand that this is a very solemn joy for me—I need not explain all sorts of things to you.

But now I send a large ? ? ? Do you want to postpone the performance of the S[ymphony]? (Joachim will probably do it soon after the 2nd of December.)

Or should we cancel our arrangement?

Or do you want to wait for the first performance before deciding?

Whatever you do, don't feel embarrassed, you are above all a presenter of concerts, but for me concerts are most unimportant!

But let me have a word anyway, so I know if you are ranting or if you can enjoy my joy.

With warm greetings to you and yours

J. Brahms.

As Wüllner did not entirely understand Brahms's plan, he was dismayed for reasons having partly to do with concern about the similarity of programmes. He needed to be reassured that Brahms would not appear in Joachim's concert.

428
Johannes Brahms to Franz Wüllner

[Vienna, November 1883]

Dear friend,

Under no circumstances am I going to Berlin in December and to Joachim's concert.

But in this instance you mustn't accuse J[oachim], who wants to perform the Symphony only if I feel no obligations or awkwardness towards you. I had told him that it is at his disposal, but had hoped he would first examine it, which cannot happen before the concert here on the 2nd of December.

You know our peculiar, difficult relationship, which I dearly hope won't become too unpleasant. Think the matter over and justify it to yourself as a friend—then act as a presenter of concerts!

The former is really easy, with the latter may the holy Wolff help you![5]

Sincerely and hurriedly,

your

J. Br.

---

[5] Hermann Wolff, the Berlin concert impresario, apparently in charge of Wüllner's concert series.

429
Johannes Brahms to Franz Wüllner

[Vienna, 3 December 1883]

D[ear] fr[iend],

Only today did I hear from Joachim about you-know-what.

His invitation to conduct the Symphony and my Violin Concerto on the 4th of January I shall not accept—but I am sending him the Symphony!

I ask once again that you charge everything disagreeable regarding this matter to my account—but also cannot fail to tell you or make clear to you that I cannot act otherwise. You need no further explanation about this from me, for you know everything that can be put in words and will also understand and respect completely my sentiments and wishes.

It might however be a neat solution if Joachim were now to play the Violin Concerto at your concert?!

I remind you once again that you have no obligation towards me, that I am in fact expecting a cancellation from Wolff!

Only do forgive the skimpy letters, but where would it lead me if I wished to pursue this intricate business by letter. Nor do I need to say more explicitly how sorry I am that you find the matter more irksome.

The Viennese audience was very kind yesterday.

With warm greetings

your

J. Br.

430
Johannes Brahms to Joseph Joachim

[Vienna, 3 December 1883]

Dear Joachim,

To Wüllner I make the sacrifice of *not* accepting your invitation, but will send the Symphony in time. I have the advantage of course, that you'll study my piece superbly—but you have the small hall and I the large one.[6] I hate the one as much as I have a weak spot for the other.

If your audience is as kind as the Viennese yesterday, then W[üllner] need not feel embarrassed about the repetition![7]

[6] Joachim conducted the work at the Academy of Art.

[7] The première of the Third Symphony, under Hans Richter, was one of Brahms's greatest successes.

In any case it's all the same to me; it gives me the greatest, gravest pleasure that you are doing my piece and I hope for the lesser one, besides, that you might also like it!

By the 20th everything should be in your hands.

With my best greetings

your J. Br.

❦ϗ 1884 ϗ❦

Among the mutual friends who remained loyal to Joachim and therefore broke off with Brahms, in the aftermath of the divorce fiasco, were Philipp Spitta and Ernst Rudorff, both of whom were on the faculty of Joachim's conservatory. Joachim was not the only person to soften under the influence of the new symphony.

431

Ernst Rudorff to Johannes Brahms

Lichterfelde, 5 January 1884

Esteemed Herr Brahms,

Even yesterday, between the dress rehearsal and performance of your symphony, I experienced the liveliest desire to write to you. But a reluctance which you will probably understand held me back, and so I took refuge in expressing to Frau Schumann what I felt and thought. Now the performance is over, as well, and the feeling of having to say a word to you directly is too strong for me to wish to suppress it any longer. Yes, you have completely conquered me with your music; no first impression has affected me to such a degree for a long time! To my mind, the 'Symphony' belongs to those few exalted works which seize a person mercilessly, which thrust themselves on him with the first sound, not to release him with the last but to pursue him further and to make him feel that they had taken possession of him for all time. One even forgets admiration, which, after all, is otherwise a fine thing, and simply lets oneself be carried along on magnificent waves. By what means of enchantment you accomplish this, from the softest and sweetest to the stormiest fury, I hardly need to tell you. I hope you will read, between the lines, that at this moment I would like to accord you as much grateful enthusiasm as can be given to a person; then I will try to console myself that words are invariably inadequate, and seem particularly so to this writer.

Your
Ernst Rudorff.

432
Johannes Brahms to Ernst Rudorff

[Vienna, 7 January 1884]

Dear Herr Rudorff.

Accept my best thanks for your kind words, which gave me the deepest pleasure.

But I am even less likely to try being more explicit! Just read nicely between the lines and well beyond the card—and accept the cordial greetings

of your devoted
J. Brahms.

That performance of the symphony was only the beginning of a long process of reconciliation. Just before Wüllner's concert, Joachim wrote:[1] 'I should however tell you how deeply sorry I am not to hear your symphony under your direction tomorrow; for although I no longer have a claim on you as a person, I retain my love for the beauty you create.'

Almost two more years went by before their next contact. The reconciliation was eventually effected through the mediation of the Herzogenbergs, sealed by means of the Fourth Symphony and the Double Concerto.

Despite the sphinx-like quality of some of his letters, Brahms was capable of writing explicity. When asked about the tempo for the last movement of the Second String Quartet, Op. 51 No. 2, he sent Alwin von Beckerath (a violist and another highly musical—and very tall—member of that family) an informative discourse on metronome markings. Brahms wrote his letter on the blank page of yet another person's urgent request for advice about tempos (in that case a job was at stake) and sent both letters to 'Uncle' Alwin.

433
Johannes Brahms to Alwin von Beckerath

[January 1884]

Dear Uncle Alwin,

You can see, that comes up often!

But in your case, where your neck is not on the block, I can quite easily start you on a subscription for metronome markings. You pay me a tidy sum

[1] 27 Jan. 1884.

and each week I deliver to you—different numbers; for with normal people, they cannot remain valid for more than a week.

Incidentally, *you* are right, and the first violin *as well*!

In a decent quartet, the viola must be the retarding element—But you don't need my wisdom and I don't have any numbers.

So, please pass my very cordial greetings all around and here and there, my tender ones. I'm coming to Cologne for the 9th of February and hope I can then swing myself up into your arms!

Your

Johannes Brahms.

At the age of 71, Ferdinand Hiller retired from his post as director of the Gurzenich Concerts and head of the Conservatory in Cologne. His dearest wish was that Brahms should succeed him.[2] Brahms turned down a very handsome offer, sending his definitive rejection to Robert Schnitzler, Chairman of the Board of Directors of the concert committee. Twenty-two years after the Hamburg Philharmonic had passed him over, and now at the peak of fame and success, the bitterness of that event was still with him.

434

Johannes Brahms to Regierungsrat Robert Schnitzler

Vienna, 20 April 1884

Highly esteemed Councillor,

I thank you and all concerned from the botton of my heart for the great distinction which I deem your esteemed offer to be. Unfortunately, I must resolve to decline it. This answer is difficult for me, and I am only too tempted to put it off, from day to day.

I would like to make suggestions, however, express wishes and reservations, and yet it must be clear to me that I don't have any, that the answer has only to do with me alone.

Let me therefore say just briefly that unfortunately, I cannot believe that I am the appropriate person for that attractive and distinguished post.

I have been too long without a position of this kind, have become only too accustomed to a quite different style of life, so that I have on the one hand grown more indifferent to many things for which one in that position must have the liveliest interest; and on the other hand, have become unpractised and inept in things which should be dealt with routinely and with ease.

---

2 *Hil*, v. 72 ff.

How dearly I used to wish for such a post, which is not only desirable, indeed necessary for the creative artist, but which is also the only one which enables him as a person to lead the proper, correct existence. I have my native city Hamburg in mind, for instance, where on several occasions, during the period in which I believed I might be among those under consideration— my name did not even come up.

But forgive me! Anything beyond my simple answer can hardly be of interest to you, and with regard to you, I have only the need to express my sense of gratitude most warmly. That this should now have taken the form of airing a confidential chat, I must beg you to to forgive!

With exceedingly high regard,

your very devoted

J. Brahms.

Brahms did not leave Cologne entirely in the lurch. He suggested Franz Wüllner in his stead, a solution which pleased everyone.

Knowing of his interest in musical autographs, Hanslick sent Brahms two newly discovered works of Beethoven, *Cantata on the Death of the Emperor Joseph II*, and *Cantata on the Accession of Leopold II.*[3]

435

Johannes Brahms to Eduard Hanslick

[May 1884]

Dear friend,

You have gone off and left me a treasure without even having looked at it yourself. I certainly have to write a few words of thanks to give you a rough idea of the significance of the treasure. There can be no doubt that with this, the two cantatas that Beethoven wrote in Bonn on the occasion of the death of Joseph II and the coronation of Leopold II have been found. That is, two major works for chorus and orchestra from a period to which until now we could assign no composition of any significance. If it weren't for the historical date (February 1790), one would certainly guess at a later period—but of course only because we knew nothing from that time! But even without any name on the title-page one could guess at no other—it is all Beethoven through and through! The beautiful and noble emotion, the magnificence of feeling and fantasy, the power, even ferocity of expression,

---

[3] In 1790. The first-named was published by Breitkopf & Härtel in 1887, after a first performance in November 1884 with the Gesellschaft der Musikfreunde orchestra, at Brahms's suggestion.

moreover the voice-leading, declamation, and in [regard to] the last two [categories], all the characteristics that we can observe and ponder in his later works.

Of great interest, naturally, is the cantata for the death of *Joseph II*. For that, no 'occasional music' will do! Were we to celebrate that man today, still remembered and never replaced, we would go at it as fervently as Beethoven and everyone at that time.[4] For Beethoven it is not occasional music either, if one bears in mind that the artist never ceases to shape and strive artistically, and that this is probably more readily observable in the younger man than in the Master. With the very first choral lament it is utterly Him. Not a single note or word would make you doubt. There follows a remarkably spirited recitative: *Ein Ungeheuer, sein Name Fanatismus, stieg aus den Tiefen der Hölle. . .* ['A monster, Fanaticism by name, is risen from the depths of Hell. . .'] (It is crushed underfoot by Joseph in an aria.) I cannot help it, in this connection it is a particular satisfaction for me to think back to that time when—as the impassioned words confirm—the whole world realized what it had lost in Joseph. But the young Beethoven also knew the grandeur of what he had to say and he said it loudly, as is fitting, starting right with a powerful prelude. And now, with the words: 'Then mankind rose up into the light, etc.' the wonderful F major section from the Finale of 'Fidelio' rings out.[5] There, as here, with the moving, beautiful melody given to the oboe. (Admittedly it is not suited for voice, or only very laborously.) We have many examples of our Masters using the same idea a second time and in a different place. It gives me particular pleasure here. How deeply Beethoven must have felt that melody in the Cantata (and hence, the meaning of the words)—as deeply and beautifully as later, when he sang the noble song of the love of a woman—and also of a liberation—to its conclusion. Following further recitative in arias, the work concludes with a repetition of the first chorus; but I don't want to go on with my description; certainly not of the

[4] Joseph II, co-ruler from 1765 with his mother, Maria Theresa, and sole sovereign from 1780 to 1790, was a symbol of enlightenment and egalitarianism then and in Brahms's time and place of writing. He reformed the judicial code, abolished torture, limited the death penalty to cases of high treason, founded orphanages and hospitals, effected a modest land reform, promulgated an Edict of Toleration that emancipated the Jews (in 1781), and generally showed some willingness to use the wealth of the Empire to alleviate misery and promote progress. 'Few of his precipitate reforms survived him,' is the way one modern German historian puts it (W. H. Maehl, *Germany in Western Civilization* (Tuscaloosa, Ala., 1979), 257). Evidently Brahms and Beethoven would not have agreed with the adjective. Indeed, the fervour expressed in this letter comes closer to revealing Brahms's humanitarian leanings than any other, and must be taken into account when discussing his political views.

[5] Part IV in the Cantata, 'Exsurgunt, ad lucem'. Leonora sings the same music in the Finale to Act II, as she loosens Florestan's chains ('O Gott, welch ein Augenblick', mm. 169 ff.).

second cantata. What is mainly interesting here is the music alone and all the particulars that pertain to Beethoven.

But now, dear friend, in my mind I can already hear you ask when the cantatas will be performed and when printed? And there my joy ceases. Printing has now become so much the fashion, particularly the printing of things which don't warrant it at all. You know my old pet wish, that the so-called complete works of our masters should not be printed all too completely—not even their primary ones, but definitely not their secondary ones—and that, *but now really completely*, good copies should be incorporated into the major libraries. You know how zealously I always sought to get to know their unpublished works. But to possess *everything in print* even of some of the most popular Masters, that I do not wish. Nor can I find it right and proper for amateurs and young artists to be enticed to stuff their rooms and their brains to the brim with all 'Complete Works', and to confuse their judgement.

The honour of a Complete Edition has yet to be bestowed upon our *Haydn*. A truly complete edition of his works is in any case as impossible as it is impractical; on the other hand, how desirable a *hand-copied* collection of them might be, duplicated for public libraries. In contrast, how little is being done about new editions of various works whose study and dissemination seems desirable. Specifically, older vocal music of every kind. True, you'll say it's not used, either—but it should be, and will be, more and more, without any doubt. Even sacrifices might be in order here, and their chance of paying off would surely get better in every regard.

But these are far-ranging themes and I don't want to dream up any more variations on them for you; they are also too exclusively in minor, and I know very well that some in major are also possible and necessary.

But do come soon and share with me the quite unique sensation and pleasure of being the only person in the world who knows these first deeds of a hero.

Most affectionately,

your

Johannes Brahms.

For the fourth time, Brahms took his holiday in Italy. His companion this time was Rudolf von der Leyen, an excellent amateur pianist, and nephew of Alwin von Beckerath. When Freifrau Helene von Heldburg of Meiningen again invited Brahms enthusiastically to the Villa Carlotta on Lake Como, he brought Rudolf along. As usual, with summer came a jovial mood.

436
Johannes Brahms to Rudolf von der Leyen

[Cadenabbia, 23 May 1884]

Dear friend,

I hope you have not forgotten, or worse still, come to rue having made an appointment with me for Sunday! You must do that the less so as I am *not* travelling by way of Milano, but directly through the Gotthardt! Their Gracious Lordships have issued the friendliest and most cordial invitation to you and confidently count on your coming.

The usual dining hour is 2 o'clock, so that it's no great hardship to wait for the 2.30 boat.

But I hope that *as usual*, you will get up terribly early and will depart with accustomed energy *even* earlier!

But now! If you wish to be especially agreeable bring the arrangement of my Symphony with you and play it with me here!

You are not merely a 'victim to science', then, but of art as well![6] I would be happy to hear a 'Yes' in response, because the second piano is in the building next door and it is possible that the two might not be tuned alike. I request this very urgently and you can tell me at the same time whether or that you are coming with the first boat. I'll use that as a walking tour and pick you up at the next station.

I almost forgot: Their Lordships also request that you remain in the Villa Carlotta for the night—you can breakfast as late as you like!

Perhaps you will be so good as to telegraph a word, because I think you may possibly have gone to your sister in Genoa.

With best greetings,
> your
> Johannes Brahms.

(Dress coat is explicitly proscribed.)

Robert Schnitzler was also in the neighbourhood; Brahms's high spirits extended to him, too.

---

[6] Referring to an etching the two men had seen at an antiquariat, showing 'Victims to Science' burned at the stake.

437
Johannes Brahms to Regierungsrat Robert Schnitzler

Esteemed Councillor,

His Highness, the Duke, directs me to invite you and your wife most kindly to dinner at 8 o'clock.—Not bad—but now, I take the liberty of inviting you to the concert which will take place afterwards.

Programme: 3rd Symphony for two pianos

Virtuosi: Herr v. d. Leyen and I!

Well, that probably requires some thought, and I kindly request a nice wordlet. Tail coat, top hat and previous commitment His Highness specifically will not stand for—for my part, attendance in tail coat will cost 20 Lire.

I stopped by your place earlier, but found only the English church.

Very devoted,

your

J. Brahms.

The Duke turned pages for Brahms as did Freifrau Helene for Rudolf, during an evening which Rudolf described to his wife in rapturous detail.[7]

Brahms's ties to Hamburg were kept alive by his interest in Julius Spengel, the choral conductor whom he called the only musician in North Germany who knew how to elicit a good a capella performance from a choir; from now on, Brahms's choral compositions are intended for him. Brahms had *Six Songs and Romances* for Mixed Chorus a Capella, Op. 93*a* ready. The following letter also concerns the *Triumphlied*, and is clear evidence for the large choral and orchestral forces Brahms had in mind for some of his works.

438
Johannes Brahms to Julius Spengel

[Mürzzuschlag, 11 September 1884]

Dear Herr Spengel,

Herr Simrock has a volume of choral songs and I'll write to him to send you a copy of the score as soon as possible, so that you can see whether there is something suitable in it for you. Of the *Triumphlied* you will surely take only the first chorus! The piece quite simply calls for massed forces. A smaller chorus, however good, exhausts itself and the listener.—That

---

[7] Rudolf von der Leyen, *Johannes Brahms als Mensch und Freund* (Düsseldorf, 1905), 48 ff. This little book is a choice memoir.

reminds me: It seems to me that you economized on the orchestra last year?? That would very much spoil my pleasure and I'm hoping we'll have the utmost possible!—I look forward greatly to finding you in comfortable domesticity and send my best greetings to you and to her who must be obeyed!

Your devoted
J. Brahms.

Among the most prolific composers of the time was Joachim Raff. When he died, his widow asked von Bülow to help arrange for the posthumous publication of symphonic overtures to four Shakespeare plays—*The Tempest, Romeo and Juliet, Othello*, and *Macbeth*. Bülow turned to Brahms, whose answer gives us some slight idea of what it cost him to finish a composition.

439
Johannes Brahms to Hans von Bülow

[Mürzzuschlag, middle of October 1884]

Dear friend,

I'm returning to Vienna tomorrow, and before that and while packing I want to say a few words to you—but don't quite know what! Simrock is not at all receptive to things like yours. For the 100 Variations by Marxsen, for example, I paid cash.[8] Your case is as uncommonly sympathetic to me—as it is difficult!

As far as I know, S[imrock] has no works of Raff; the question as to whether he wanted or wants them seems quite superfluous. We can imagine approximately what he'll first ask or say. But especially as a present,—acceptance is impossible!

Although I'm trying to find an answer—my thoughts have been occupied more—with the composer himself! I am so greatly inclined to envy my prolific, swift-writing, quick-witted colleagues. I gladly assume that they write not on account of encyclopaedias, but out of the same need, for the same reasons, as I—the best, that is. How often someone will cheerfully write his *Fine*, which actually says: I'm finished with what I had on my mind! How long I can sometimes carry about with me the smallest finished trifle before reluctantly attaching that 'finished'!

Quite casually R[aff] writes four overtures to four of the most glorious tragedies. It seems an enviable thing to be able to find fulfilment so often, to

---

[8] In 1883, defraying the cost himself, Brahms had Simrock print Marxsen's *100 Variations* to celebrate his teacher's golden jubilee.

feel satisfied, liberated. Did R., in fact, have time for the hangover? He was intelligent enough for it! Or was he simply happy in the possession of his talent?

That we lesser ones rarely are—and to what great heights these 'lesser ones' aspire!

But now to Simrock! What should I do? Are you full of praise for the things? Include them enthusiastically in your programme? What do Raff's actual editors say?

Additional
Note p. 754   Next time more.—*

❧ 1885 ❧

Brahms and Bruckner were contemporaries in Vienna for over thirty years. Geography apart, however, they had little in common except the degree to which music was their essential reason for existence. What distinguished them from each other above all, and kept them in worlds which barely touched, was a philosophy of life and an aesthetic of music which differed in every possible regard. Moreover, their uneasy relationship was bound up with Viennese politics of that time, polarized as it was around the Liberal/Jewish vs. Conservative/Catholic factions, with Brahms feted by the former and Bruckner the latter.[1] But despite the efforts of their respective followers to denigrate the music of the other, and despite utterances such as the following letter, Brahms, unlike his friends, was not impervious to some of Bruckner's gifts and was always respectful to the man in person. In later years he directed at least one commission to Bruckner, obliged the new director of the Gesellschaft der Musikfreunde to perform his music (it would be the last time Bruckner heard one of his works), and was in sorrowful attendance at his funeral.

For the most part, there are only second-hand reports about what Brahms thought of Bruckner;[2] but shortly after Nikisch's performance of Bruckner's Seventh Symphony, Elizabet von Herzogenberg wrote to ask Brahms for his opinion. Ambiguously, he encouraged her opinion on one hand, but declined to provide her with any anti-Bruckner ammunition of his own. His curiosity must have been aroused, though, for he eventually added the score of the symphony to his private library.

---

[1] The atmosphere is fully described in Margaret Notley, 'Brahms as Liberal: Genre, Style, and Politics in Late Nineteenth-Century Vienna', *19th Century Music*, vol. 17, no. 2 (1993), 107–23. In addition to this very specific essay, see also Allan Janik and Stephen Toulman, *Wittgenstein's Vienna* (New York, 1973); Carl E. Schorsky, *Fin de Siècle Vienna*, and Carl Dolmetsch, '*Our Famous Guest*': *Mark Twain in Vienna* (Athens, Ga., 1992). Mark Twain was in Vienna soon after Brahms died and stayed for twenty months while his daughter studied the piano with Leschetizky. His experiences there throw much light on the political climate of Brahms's world.

[2] In Kal, iii. 409; and in Heuberger, *Erinnerungen*, whose apparently verbatim quotes of conversations with Brahms ring true whether on Bruckner or any other subject.

440
To Elizabet von Herzogenberg

[Vienna, 12 January 1885]

Most revered Lady,

I understand: You have allowed Bruckner's symphony to surge over you, and now when people lecture you about it, you don't trust your recollection and its impression on you.

You may safely do so, anyhow; your wonderfully delightful letter says clearly and distinctly all there is to say—or what one has said oneself, and wished one had said so well. You won't mind, will you, that Hanslick is also of the same opinion and read your letter with all due reverence and pleasure? Incidentally, a symphony and a quintet by Bruckner are in print. Try to get a look at them to steel your sentiments and judgement—me you definitely don't need.[3]

Everything has its limits. Bruckner lies beyond them, one cannot make head or tail of his things, one cannot even discuss them. Nor him as a person. He is a poor, deranged man whom the *Pfaffen* of St Florian have on their conscience. I don't know whether you have any idea what it means to have spent one's youth with the *Pfaffen*? I could tell such stories about that and about Bruckner——

Together with a philistine here, he takes care of the teaching of composition! Apart from that, the Wagnerians and other riff-raff present him as a ludicrous figure, that is, they play fast and loose with him when four-hand arrangements of his symphonies are played, etc.

Ah, such ugly things one shouldn't even discuss with you!

Highly vexed and deeply devoted and with warm greetings

your

J. Br.

Pfaffen is a mildly derogatory term for Catholic clerics. Bruckner spent his adolescence in the choir school at the magnificent Augustinian monastery of St Florian, near Linz. Until the performance attended by Elizabet, Bruckner's Symphonies had been rarely heard, and then usually in four-hand versions for piano, with cuts and changes urged upon Bruckner by self-appointed 'assistants'. Nikisch's performance in Leipzig was Bruckner's first public triumph. Brahms was well informed of Bruckner's travails, quite possibly through conversations with the young Gustav Mahler.

[3] Bruckner was now well into writing his Eighth Symphony, but very little of his work was in print.

Hans Richter directed a complete performance of Bach's Mass in B Minor. Although Catholic Vienna was not always attuned to the Lutheran Bach, this time there was a ready audience.

441
Johannes Brahms to Theodor Billroth

Vienna, 1 April 1885

Dear friend,

It really is a crying shame that you didn't hear the Mass yesterday evening.

You've never had such an impression of grandeur and nobility. Nor would one credit a human creation with the capacity to be so exalted and deeply moving.

Indeed, the performance was an immense joy in every regard.

I had some misgivings—but right from the start people fell ever so nicely into the trap, that is into the famous title 'High Mass'. It was sold out a week ahead; the whole world was studying the piano score; in short, the requisite enthusiasm was there. And now it burst and poured forth, and people dived in and never became sated, nor tired of diving in. The arias were just a respite, a sorely needed little cooling off. That donkey R. [a singer] was the only one to overdo this, the only blemish. For, anything else I might say are subtleties which I gladly keep to myself, when someone presents the thing to the outside world as well and brings it off as enthusiastically as Richter.

For the inexpressible feeling afterwards you would gladly have traded your entire Abbazia—which however I don't now want to keep you from enjoying any longer!

Best greetings to Hanslick; Every small courtesy I wish to show him comes to naught. I wanted to give him a pretty little brandy bottle to take along for the overnight trip, and what happens? he had already left early that morning.

I'm gazing Italy- and Rhine-wards—so will probably remain sitting in the middle.

But I did rent again in Mürzzuschlag.

With affectionate greetings,

your
J. Brahms.

La Mara was preparing a volume called *Musicians' Letters from the Past Five Centuries.*[4] Having obtained some by Brahms, she wrote for permission to use them. He was not amused.

442
Johannes Brahms to La Mara (Ida Marie Lipsius)

[Vienna, 27 May 1885]

Highly esteemed Fräulein,

I do indeed have the courage to ask you to leave the letters in question unprinted. I know and admit that I never write other than reluctantly, hurriedly, and hastily, but I feel ashamed when an example like yours is laid before my eyes.

It requires a kind of courage to write to a cultivated and well-meaning person, whom one has never met, as carelessly as I did in this instance.

But to consent to having such letters printed, expressly to say Yes to it— that would take something other than courage!

If you will permit me to state expressly here and now that no one could do me a worse turn than to have my letters printed—I will be pleased to make an exception for this particular one.

You may incorporate it in your book all the more readily because through it, your readers will learn that not you, but I, am to blame for a *manco* in this matter and—that I was careful to draw no conclusions from the contemplated inclusion of my letters, regarding the other contents or the merits of your book.

There exist, as I know not merely from 'Schiller and Goethe' but also from the most agreeable personal experience, plenty of people who write letters gladly and well.

But then there also exist those of my kind, and if the writers are otherwise deserving, their letters should be read and interpreted with indulgence and care.

A letter from Beethoven, for instance, I am happy to keep as a memento; I am appalled, however, when I consider all the meanings and explanations such a letter is supposed to hold!

It is the same with the posthumous works left by a composer.

How eagerly I have always traced their tracks, studied and often copied them. How in Haydn and Franz Schubert, for example, I treasured the countless superfluous proofs of their industry and genius.

---

[4] *Musikerbriefe aus fünf Jahrhunderten* (Leipzig, 1886).

I always had the wish that such precious and instructive treasures be copied for larger libraries, so as to be accessible to those seriously interested in them.—I will not elaborate with what different emotions I then see these beloved treasures in print—or even have to take care myself that this be done, at least, as correctly as possible!

Here, as there, quite incredible misunderstandings and misinterpretations occur, and whether such a publication is necessary, beneficial, or superfluous, and even harmful—I do not know!

Accepting the risk that you will consider the beginning of this epistle as idle hypocrisy,

I remain

with great esteem, your devoted

J. Brahms.

This letter was in fact included in La Mara's book, as the only sample by Brahms. The determination to keep his letters private had more to do with native reticence than with a moralistic aversion to reading other people's mail. He owned, read, and collected not only autographs of the letters of Goethe and Schiller, but of a great many others, including some from Mendelssohn, Schumann, Beethoven, Hölderlin, Schopenhauer, Cherubini, and E. T. A. Hoffmann. Towards the end of his life he even bowed to the inevitable and agreed in principle to the publication of his correspondence with Joachim. How seriously he took La Mara's invasion of his privacy, however, is reflected in his letter to Hanslick.

443
Johannes Brahms to Eduard Hanslick

[May 1885]

Dearest friend!

The enclosed two letters will make the situation clear to you. Impractical as always, I didn't wait for your card the other day but gave to Dr Fellinger, who was visiting me, a letter addressed to you, and the unsealed one to Lipsius,—with instructions to post the latter, in case he didn't come across you in Vienna! Frau Fellinger copied the letter, however. Consequently, I can send it to you after the fact and make my request. Do read it and tell me if it is in itself a folly, or if it contains such! I consider myself capable of anything in this regard—but I would also gladly keep my big mouth shut! I can quite readily write a different one belatedly, or make some changes in this one, and so: I ask for a word!

Best greetings to Simrock, and I'll probably write to him yesterday or tomorrow! But what the devil, when one is so plagued with letters from and to Fräulein Lipsius, the desire to write letters, slight in any case, surely goes out of the window.

And so do also forgive the peevish scrawl—but the business annoys me. My heartfelt greetings and may you live as well, gleefully, and happily, as you deserve.

Affectionately,

your J. Brahms.

In May, von Bülow sent a treasure to add to Brahms's collection of manuscripts: Berlioz's *Ballade sur la morte d'Orphelie*, Op. 18, which bore the date of 7 May 1842, Brahms's ninth birthday. Brahms reciprocated with his own treasure, a copy Beethoven made of a Palestrina Gloria.

444
Johannes Brahms to Hans von Bülow

[Vienna?, 7 May 1885]

Most gracious of all friends,

My best thanks for remembering me and May 7th so kindly. The pleasure of seeing your handwriting normally increases with the number of pages of the letter! But this time, though, and in such company, you can be sparing with the words! Since I am, without wanting to be, a collector of sorts, you've hit the bull's eye; I didn't have a single sheet by Berlioz. Incidentally, the date May 7th on this Ophelia stares at me quite peculiarly; no armour can protect a man against this kind of the most gentle sentiment.

But as compensation for that Unholy Frenchman, my classical enclosure will do quite nicely, don't you think? Beethoven, who copies a Gloria by Palestrina! So once again, my heartfelt thanks—I like to think that you are reading it in Meiningen while granting yourself some cosy peace and quiet.

[No Salutation]

Fritz Brahms's health deteriorated rapidly in the last year of his life, climaxing in behavioural disorders and a diagnosis of 'inflammation of the brain'. It is quite likely that he was suffering from tertiary syphillis. If Johannes sent the money Fritz needed, it is Karoline Brahms, the stepmother, who gave him the care he needed. Brahms's detachment is notable, and chilling.[5]

[5] Our present ignorance of the essential facts of the relationship between Johannes and Fritz Brahms precludes a sound understanding of the composer's attitude. The projected publication of the complete family letters should shed light on the brothers' estrangement; until then, the sketchy

445
Johannes Brahms to Karoline Brahms

[Postmark 13 August 1885]

Dear Mother,

My heartfelt thanks for so kindly taking care of Fritz.

I hope you won't lose patience—I know very well how much of it is needed! Whatever any of you do is of course fine as far as I am concerned, I only wish I could help you. But I wouldn't know how. It also seems quite pointless to me to want to write to him now and then.

You are supplied with money, I presume—also for the worst case? You could then advance it from the recent 1,000 Marks. But in any case, write to me what you have spent for him in general during all this time! In case Fritz should really pass away—I suppose it would be a blessing for him and peace for you—I wish, when it comes to it, that his music and books stay together for the time being until I have seen them. There will be very little and it might be best if you could ask Christian Detmering to allow it to stay in a box at your place.

Do of course give Fritz my greetings, as always, and my wishes for his well-being—though to be sure, he would have had to do more for it himself!

My affectionate greetings to you both and again many thanks.

Your Johannes.

The Fourth Symphony was finished that summer in Mürzzuschlag, a small Austrian town beyond the Semmering Pass in Styria. Brahms was more than usually diffident in announcing the work, and seems to have had no doubt that its austerity would leave even his friends dismayed. He was correct.

information we have is based only on sparse excerpts *from* the siblings to Johannes, and occasional clues in other correspondence. See e.g. Brahms to Simrock, *BW* x. 18 (Nov. 1876), in which Johannes asks his publisher to send 11 works to his brother, published between 1863 and 1873. 'I hardly need to say that these opus numbers hark back to a time during which I could unfortunately give my brother nothing. I think I may with much justification call myself "mediator", in my family, and most recently in Munich.' The latter remark refers to his efforts at that time to reconcile Levi and Wüllner, so that although Brahms writes to Simrock laconically, his use of the word 'mediator' is clear.

446
Johannes Brahms to Elizabet von Herzogenberg

[Mürzzuschlag, 29 August 1885]

Dear esteemed friend,

Well, it seems I miss out on one opportunity after another for a visit. The fault may lie with my lethargic dread of the many on the train one does not know, and of the ever-so-many in your vicinity one does know—who also expect a visit from me. Are you staying there a while longer and do you have peace and quiet again? If I were to send you a piece of a piece of mine, would you have time to look at it and say a word? Unfortunately, my pieces are generally more agreeable than I, and one finds less in them to correct?! But in these parts cherries don't get to be sweet and edible—so don't be embarrassed if the thing isn't to your taste. I am not at all eager to write a bad No. 4.

Incidentally, when is No. 1 coming?!!? Must one wait for the concert season like conductors?

Is Astor not yet finished? I have looked forward greatly and for a long time to taking a closer look at this No. 1.[6]

With my very warm greetings,

your

J. Brahms.

Talk of sour cherries does a disservice to the lovely area beyond the Semmering. To Georg II he gave a different slant to his doubts about the symphony. 'This time I fear I shall abuse Bülow's indulgence and the endurance of his copyists and musicians, all for the sake of a piece which, I'm afraid, will sound alarmingly—"unmarried".'

The symphony was rehearsed in Meiningen and then, in an unprecedented move, Bülow took the orchestra, Brahms, and the Fourth Symphony on a tour of Germany and Holland, lasting several weeks. Brahms conducted his new work in half of the concerts, using the rest of the time to visit friends. When he accepted an invitation to conduct his new symphony with the Frankfurt orchestra at one of their Museum Concerts, without first discussing it with Bülow (the Meiningen Orchestra was scheduled to appear again in that city shortly after), Bülow felt himself so ill-used that he resigned his post in Meiningen forthwith, to the astonishment and dismay of both Brahms and Georg II.[7]

[6] The firm of Rieter-Biedermann, now headed by his son-in-law Edmond Astor, was about to publish Heinrich von Herzogenberg's first symphony. The publisher was notoriously slow in bringing out editions.

[7] Bülow's assistant, the very young Richard Strauss, replaced him. For Bülow's side of the story

447
Johannes Brahms to Georg II, Duke of Meiningen

[Vienna, 30 November 1885]

Your Highness,
Most Gracious Duke,

I feel I must express to Your Highness my great joy over the tour now concluded, and how grateful I am to Y.H. for having once again shown me so much kindness. Unfortunately, the celebration of the very fine and happy tour was seriously clouded by a most unnecessary misunderstanding. Not just for me, but, what grieves me far more, for Herr v. Bülow. Without being pressed, I would not wish to take the liberty of reporting on this at greater length, brief and simple as my account and explanation would be; For I hope above all that Herr v. Bülow calmed down after brief reflection and that this momentary dissonance was thus resolved and silenced long ago.

But to that last evening in Wiesbaden I think back with the greatest of pleasure. After the quite outstanding playing of the orchestra, we remained in the company of the gentlemen for some time. Various matters combined to put us in a serious mood, but it was a fine, friendly seriousness, and I would have wished Your Highness had sensed how deeply our thoughts were also specifically with the esteemed Baroness. Unfortunately we were troubled, as I am even now, about the condition of your greatly revered wife. This casts a pall over the otherwise very congenial memories.

With the highest esteem,

most gratefully devoted to Your Highness,

J. Brahms.

Vienna
30 Nov. 1885

The Duke described von Bülow's resignation as 'an enormous loss for Meiningen and the orchestra', and asked for Brahms's own account of the misunderstanding. There is no hint of reproach in George II's letter. On the contrary, he writes with dismay that Brahms should have had such an unpleasant experience on *his* account.

Brahms replied with what is probably his most explicit letter regarding a personal misunderstanding, and it is most unlikely that he would have agreed to supply such details to anyone other than the Duke, whose wish carried a certain weight.

see *BB* vi. 386–401. Clearly there was more to the story than Brahms knew: Bülow's letters to his wife, while he was on tour, became more and more cranky with regard to Brahms even before the great *faux pas*, and in retrospect, some sort of explosion seems to have been inevitable.

448
Johannes Brahms to Georg II, Duke of Meiningen

[Vienna, after 9 December 1885]

Your Highness,
Most gracious Duke.

My thoughts are often enough in Meiningen, and I am happy that they can once again stroll undisturbed and untroubled into the castle. How rarely do they behold and take pleasure in as beautiful, dignified, and happy a human existence as is lived there. May it now, after such a grave interruption, be granted to Y.H. again, entirely and fully; surely that could delight no one more deeply than me.[8]

Your Highness's wish to hear more of my experience with Bülow embarrasses me more than I had thought. I realize that it is not possible to depict this insignificant and petty business in three words, and I am afraid of abusing Y.H.'s patience without making the matter clear. Nevertheless, I shall try. It had been arranged from the very beginning that B. would perform my Symphony *only* in his *first* concert in Frankfurt, because the Museum committee had invited me earlier to conduct it at their concert.

Well, the success [of the Symphony] seemed so slight to me that during the trip I intimated in passing that the committee would hardly protest, and that it would presumably not embarrass him too much, if he scheduled a repetition for his 2nd concert.

But in Crefeld,[9] letters and telegrams from the committee awaited me requesting the Symphony, *in case* B. did not repeat it.

I sent off a telegram right away, and only several days later did I write to Amsterdam in passing that I really had done 'something foolish', and had been unnecessarily inconsiderate towards those gentlemen.

B. thereupon changed the programme with no further ado and very graciously put into the programme: 'Out of consideration towards the honourable Committee' etc. I had certainly not expected that, otherwise I would have asked and requested it most innocently. Therefore I regarded it merely as exceptionally friendly and kind. But what a shock I had upon meeting him and discovering at last how B. had construed my letter. I was quite overcome at seeing him so anguished; as if he had lived through the most awful ordeal,

---

[8] Referring to the Baroness's recovery from a grave illness.
[9] Where Brahms had gone alone to visit his circle of friends there, the von Beckeraths and the von der Leyens.

had peered into the deepest abyss of a selfish human soul. 'He had lived through it once with Wagner, a second time, he could not.'[10]

And all for the sake of 'that foolishness', a slap in the face that I had dealt myself—(and how often am I in a position to deal myself one!—), and for the sake of a concert!

Bülow must surely know by now that I would *much rather* be considerate towards the least of his musicians than towards any committee, that the smallest rehearsal in the smallest hall in Meiningen is more important *to me personally* than any concert in Paris or London.

However—Your Highness cannot have become more irritated over my chatter than I am now myself. If only I had stayed with my first theme! My soul would now be comforted and warm.

And so I will let my thoughts stroll once again along the former path and hope with all my heart that Y.H. might take the arm of the Baroness and literally and cheerfully walk up to the cosy little house where that crowd of children have been deprived of their kind benefactress long enough![11] May I also ask to be most kindly commended to her. So too to H. H. Princess Marie, who has, I hope, praise for much else in Amsterdam than the famous physician.

With my great esteem, I sign myself,
deeply devoted to Your Highness,
Joh. Brahms.

Vienna
Dec. 1885

Towards von Bülow, Brahms made persistent attempts to smooth over the misunderstanding. A first letter went astray, followed by another early in the next year (Letter 454); but Bülow remained unforgiving for another year.

Apparently it was easy for Brahms to be churlish to his friends without noticing where his words would lead him. After tempting Wüllner with news of the Fourth Symphony, Brahms sent him the following tactless letter when the conductor expressed an interest in the new work for one of his concerts in Cologne.

---

[10] An extraordinary comparison. Wagner played a uniquely constructive and then destructive role in Bülow's life, on one hand convincing Bülow's father to allow the young man to become a musician and literally creating his career; then taking his wife and driving him to the brink of a nervous breakdown.

[11] The orphanage in Meiningen, founded by the Baroness. After the death of Georg II she spent the last years of her life living in the building along with the children.

449
Johannes Brahms to Franz Wüllner

[October 1885]

D[ear] fr[iend],

With regard to the Symphony, I can say nothing for now. But: the Bülow orchestra is coming to your neighbourhood in Nov. In case we feel at all comfortable with the S[ymphony], I can hardly deny B[ülow] a performance here and there!? I believe, however, that in Cologne and Frankfurt they might be laughing up their sleeve at this, as they reflect on his brilliant string quartet![12]

It therefore depends on the S[ymphony] whether you want to keep the 5th of Jan. in mind. Regarding that, forgive me for adding that I have exceedingly little interest in all these first performances and the whole modern chase after novelties.

Indeed, I know scarcely a friend whom I want to keep informed, from whom I long to hear.

What does count, above all, is the novelty and whether its stock happens to be high, as is Bruckner's today, for example. Forgive me, but that's the way it really is!

I'm planning to go to Meiningen on Thursday—I look forward to the calm rehearsals—perhaps Bülow will continue to calm down, too!!

Warm greetings to you and yours.

J. Br.

The mention of Bruckner was no accident; Wüllner was scheduled to perform his Seventh Symphony shortly. The duration and depth of Wüllner's friendship made it possible for him to take Brahms firmly to task, and defend his motives on both counts.

450
Franz Wüllner to Johannes Brahms [fragment]

[Cologne, 15 October 1885]

Dear friend,

. . . I understand completely that you should first try out your symphony in Meiningen. I also understand that Bülow should perform it, if that is your

---

[12] An allusion to the the small size of the Meiningen string section.

wish. But I do not understand your comment about the chase after novelties—at least not if it is supposed to refer to me and my wish to perform your Symphony. I would think that in the thirty-two years we have now known each other you might have realized well enough that I do not perform your works because I want to bring piquant novelties before the public, but because I love them and because it is a celebration for me to conduct them, or to hear them conducted by you . . . I understand still less how you come to mention Bruckner and yourself in one breath. Were it not you yourself who did so—I would not forgive anyone else. That does not preclude Bruckner's E major symphony from appearing on one of my programmes this winter. Even in May I had put it on my list of programme possibilities by virtue of the extremely good reports I received from musical acquaintances in Munich and Leipzig . . . In fact it has not lived up to my expectations, but still [. . . I found it] more interesting by far than a new symphony by Gernsheim, Cowen, Scharwenka, etc. In any case, I don't read or take *any* music journal, therefore don't know whether the Bruckner Symphony stock is high;—I hardly know how it could be, it has not even appeared yet . . .

But if, to my great sorrow, I can almost conclude, from your comment that you scarcely knew a friend to whom you wished to send news or from whom you wished to hear, that I have deceived myself with respect to my relationship to you up till now, let me tell you once again for my part that my convictions about you and your works can never become other than what they have always and ever been, and that I do not perform your works as novelties but as works of our Brahms, a new work of which it would be unjust to withhold longer than necessary from the musical world and that small portion of it which our public comprises. . . .

Most truly F. W.

Brahms retreated immediately.

451
Johannes Brahms to Franz Wüllner

[Meiningen, October 1885]

Dear friend,

You may very well be right in everything you write. But you are surely responding to more and other issues than to those I said. Given my aversion to writing, I ought to be very careful about starting in on a specific subject, I lack the patience to argue it to the end!

So don't read too much into it—there's nothing to be forgiven but the rush and haste.

Considering my limited sympathy for the concert business, it may well be that I'm too prickly and unkind when looking at anything connected with it. Where my own things are concerned I am anxious and suspicious, and with respect to you or Joachim, say, perhaps unjustly so when I worry that you may on occasion be thinking just of the novelty!

That it is my greatest artistic joy if you love and praise my things and keep performing them—well, that I surely need hardly say!?

But my feelings towards you and old mutual friends have never changed—the less so since they are also not being crowded out by new ones.

Again, everything rushed and in haste! So too the report that I have much pleasure from the rehearsals here and hope that you'll have some from the Symphony, later.

It's being done here on the 25th [of October] and the 1st of Nov; on the 3rd, in Frankfurt. Then I'll probably ramble along with the Meiningen people for awhile, whether I'll be able to stand it to Cologne, I don't know. So, you won't let your feelings be hurt by a performance there, will you! Whether it will embarrass you will depend on the not exactly pleasant piece.

Affectionate greetings to you and yours.

Your J. Br.

Brahms helped establish the Musician's Association in Vienna, the Tonkünstler-verein. Moritz Fürstenau had founded the first such organization in Dresden, 1854, a fact obviously known to Brahms.

452

Johannes Brahms to Moritz Fürstenau, in Dresden

Vienna [Autumn 1885]

Honoured Sir,

A serious attempt is being made here in Vienna to bring a proper Association of Musicians into existence.

I am unfortunately aware of how little I can advise and assist in this, but believe that I might be enabled to do so if I knew more about your Association.

Above all, would you be so kind as to allow me to obtain the statutes of your Association? Then, perhaps, whatever else about its history and effectiveness has been said—i.e. printed, and seems pertinent to you for my purpose?

Excuse the inconvenience and accept in advance the best thanks
of your
sincerely and greatly devoted
J. Brahms.

Vienna, Carlsgasse 4.

Establishing the Tonkünstlerverein was a serious matter to the composer who lived alone but who needed lively intercourse with friends. The nucleus of the organization was a group of Brahms's long-time Viennese colleagues and their wives, who had dined together regularly for years. The Association became an important focus of his social life and kept him in touch with young musicians, and innumerable anecdotes about him are set there. In 1886 he was elected Honorary President of the organization which commanded his loyalty until he died.

❧ 1886 ☙

Sometime in 1885, Simrock expressed his intention to commission the artist Max Klinger to provide etchings for the title-pages of Brahms's music. The artist and his work interested Brahms greatly, but he was dubious about the plan. In the event, he approved of Klinger's sketches for his songs, Op. 96 and 97, but as the composer bluntly told his publisher, he was very disappointed with the finished etchings when they appeared with the new songs in March 1886. To Klinger himself he was more tactful, leaving the door open for future cordiality which culminated in Klinger's epic series of etchings entitled the *Brahms-Fantasy*, and Brahms's dedication of the *Four Serious Songs* to him in 1896.

453
Johannes Brahms to Max Klinger [1]

[Vienna, March 1886]

Highly esteemed Sir,

I should have told you long ago how pleased I was with the thought of seeing your fantasies on the title-pages of my compositions. The whole style of your art—your rich and fantastic invention which is at the same time of such splendid earnestness, of such momentous depth, leading then to ever

---

[1] Compare the following letter with *BW* xi. 116, to Simrock.

further musings and imaginings—seems to me to be very appropriate for announcing music. (Of course, the beautiful curtain should also conceal only the most beautiful music!)

The individual sketches which Simrock showed me at the time interested and pleased me enormously—as does all of your work which has come my way. Specific ones, like the page for Feldeinsamkeit, or the just as curiously beautiful fantasy for the Cello Sonata, have never relinquished their hold on my memory.

Well, to my thanks for everything you give us, I could now simply add my specific thanks for the first printed title-pages of my new songs.

But that would be dishonest, and I regard you much too highly not to speak to you—as I would to myself.

Honestly, therefore: so far, I cannot take as much pleasure in these pages as I had expected on the basis of your sketches. It seems to me that I detect Simrock's—dubious—influence, namely his prodding.

I cannot possibly be mistaken; after all, I even saw the very first page among those sketches, and was it intended for 'Feldeinsamkeit'?

If I am right—how dearly I wish it could have appeared in that volume, instead of here, where it may remain ineffective because it is too enigmatic and unintelligible (if I may be the judge of that, since I believe I know it). But I suppose Simrock was impatient—the good publisher is allowed to have a very different concept of time and patience from us—however, his haste does not concern us!

But forgive my chatter. I am convinced that I will continue to look and enter ever more deeply into your pages and, as I already do in individual ones, will surely take ever greater pleasure in the whole.

If you knew how very dear to my heart other creations of yours are to me and what beautiful vistas your sketches have afforded me, I am sure you would gladly pardon these immodest lines of

> your
> greatly and sincerely devoted
> Joh. Brahms.

Before leaving Vienna for the summer, Brahms received a birthday telegram from a group of friends which included the signature of Hans von Bülow. This seemed like a good opportunity to repair the rift between them.

454
Johannes Brahms to Hans von Bülow

[Vienna?] 8 May 1885

Most revered one,

I learn from H. H. Princess Marie that you had not received a letter from me which I wrote immediately after we parted this winter. It was a detailed, very serious, and well-intentioned letter, with which I hoped to set aside a misunderstanding which lay more heavily on my heart than you might presume. I may be correct in assuming that your wife (to whom I had addressed it) withheld it in the hope of sparing you unpleasantness. In that case, I hope you can read it belatedly, for I cannot attempt to repeat its contents, at least for the time being. Its serious aspect would lead me too far afield—that is, you and my feelings for you, and I have got accustomed to taking you very seriously. But concerts and anything connected them just don't count as very serious matters with me, and it is difficult for me to recall, offhand, the concerts of last winter in any way other than with pleasure.

Let me assume therefore that that letter is still around, and simply permit me to append my sincerest thanks for the greeting with which you and the other gentlemen delighted and honoured me yesterday.

With unaltered sentiments,
J. Brahms.

Bülow was not ready to be reconciled. He acknowledged the letter stiffly, and refused Brahms's apology until January 1887, then resumed his devotion to Brahms as intensely as ever; for her part, Marie von Bülow crisply denied ever setting eyes on the old letter.

The Thunersee, a large lake at the edge of the Bernese Oberland in Switzerland, provides the backdrop for Brahms's summer activities for the next three years. He took the entire top floor of a farmhouse situated at the edge of the river Aar, in the village of Hofstetten, and cultivated his friendship with the writer Josef Viktor Widmann. Despite Brahms's comment to Wüllner that he had no new friends to replace old ones, his association with Widmann was one of the most satisfying of his life, of great value to both men for as long as they lived.

Widmann's long memoir (*Erinnerungen an Johannes Brahms*), presents Brahms as a dearly cherished guest, and from the letters Brahms wrote to Widmann and later to his eldest daughter, it is obvious that the composer was much at ease in the Swiss home. Widmann was of Viennese parentage, but grew up in a small Swiss town near Basle in a house which served as a place of political refuge in the turbulent aftermath of 1848. Widmann's father was himself once a refugee, a Catholic cleric who made the mistake of falling in love with a young woman in his church choir. Having fled with her to Moravia, where Widmann was born, he became a Protestant and found refuge as minister in the Swiss town of Liestal, providing an unusually cosmopolitan note to an otherwise utterly provincial spot. This exceptional background produced a man extremely congenial to Brahms. Every other Sunday he followed the Aar down-river to Bern and stayed until Tuesday, ate Frau Widmann's *Zwetschkenkuchen* (a buttery plum pastry also beloved in Vienna), offered her recipes, and even helped the daughters of the house to set the table, returned books borrowed from Widmann's library during the previous visit, selected a fresh supply, and took the train back to Hofstetten.

455
Johannes Brahms to Josef Viktor Widmann

I don't want to, I should not, I must not, I cannot, but I must! I have to check if the little one still hasn't returned. No matter how much you write, dear agreeable Tandem, there is never a mention of that pearl of the house, of the street, of the town, etc.[2]

Affectionately,

Your J. B.

This postcard is a telling introduction to the quality of friendship between Widmann and Brahms. The 'little jewel' was Johanna Widmann, the writer's youngest daughter. For years Brahms referred to her as his bride, so that Widmann became 'father of my Johanna'. Nevertheless, the men were never on 'Du' terms, something Brahms seems to have reserved for those he actually worked with.

As the son of a trained musician, Widmann was knowledgeable about music. His published writings include not only literary and political essays, but numerous concert reviews. Now he was thinking of publishing something on the vulgarity of brass bands and male choruses.

---

[2] The Swiss playwright Carl Spitteler, a close friend of Widmann's, used the pseudonym Tandem. Brahms's interest in his work stretched over many years; he is mentioned frequently in correspondence with Widmann.

456
Johannes Brahms to Josef Viktor Widmann

[Thun, 17 July 1886]

Dear friend,

The weather has belatedly proved me right and, unfortunately, seems to be doing so for some time yet. Meanwhile, Simrock was here and is now in Gurnigelbad. He is full of enthusiasm for Kandersteg, where he had been a long time ago. If a trip comes off, I'll send a telegram, which will at the same time ask you to reserve two little rooms for us.

I am all the more anxious to obtain Heyse's essay because I also profess to have an image—a very agreeable one—of the author in question.[3]

Your zeal against male singing and crass brass music, and your intention to give it expression remind me—of the temperance societies that solicit my sympathy now and then.

I don't have any—it is so easy to deprive the people of the brandy they so often need—I would support them eagerly if such a society had the intent and the power to provide a substitute, [or] of making wine, beer, coffee cheaper.

Well, similarly for the ordinary man, male choruses and the modern brass instrument are convenient; others need to be studied and got accustomed to more conscientiously and earlier. Among the so-called better classes, any appeal of an instrument other than the piano has as good as disappeared.

It would be most desirable and worth striving for to have parents let their children study other instruments, violins, violoncello, flute, clarinet, horn, etc. (that would immediately create more interest all around for all sorts of things).

In the public schools, more and *better things* could be done for singing, and boys could very well be handed a violin quite early on. I have seen that often in Austrian villages—singing Mass in Catholic churches is also not stupid! Sight-singing, reading in all cleffs, being on a first-name basis with fugues!

But forgive the twaddle! I mustn't get involved with such a far-reaching topic, since I have no patience for writing.

Affectionate greetings to all the ladies! Incidentally to you,

from your
J. Brahms.

---

[3] Widmann himself, included in Heyse's essay on treasures of new German literature.

The time in Thun produced some of Brahms's best work. From the first summer came the Cello Sonata in F, two violin sonatas, and the Piano Trio in C minor,[4] as well as two of his best-loved songs: 'Immer leiser' and 'Wie Melodien zieht es mir', from Op. 105.[5]

Brahms's latest flirtation was with the North German singer, Hermine Spies; on holiday in Switzerland, she was now set to visit Bern. It was easy to arouse Widmann's curiosity about the songs and the singer they were intended for (Widmann's 'crime' in the next letter). Brahms proposed a first performance in Widmann's music room, adding thanks for a shipment of new books, including Nietzsche's *Beyond Good and Evil*.

457
Johannes Brahms to Josef Viktor Widmann

[Thun, 23 September 1886]

Dear friend,

Let the punishment follow the crime close on its heels. I have accordingly induced the 'singer' (Frl. Spies, Hermione without the o) to break into your house upon returning from Lake Geneva next week, and to subject you, with my assistance, to rigorous torture by song.

You could now keep your door bolted and invite Professor Vetters and Professor Stern so as to reduce the pain by half.[6]

But that aside, you are really too kind! Of course, I immediately placed an Italian novel on top of the Nietzsche, so that I'll consider carefully whether to take a stroll under a blue or a grey sky!

Your new story has a very delightful and good-humoured beginning; I am only concerned that I won't be around to find out how you dispose of all the lovely people.[7]

If not sooner, I'll probably come with skewers and sticks on Wednesday afternoon.[8]

Affectionate greetings
from your
J. B.

[4] Opp. 99–101 and 108.

[5] Other works completed or begun in the same summer are the songs from Opp. 104, 105, and 107.

[6] Vetters was Widmann's son-in-law, Stern a friend.

[7] Widmann's story was serialized in the *Bund*, and would not be finished until after Brahms returned home.

[8] Pun on the name 'Spies': *Spiessen und Stangen* are torture implements.

This was not the first time he had offered songs to Hermine, whom he met during the summer of 1883, in Wiesbaden.

458
Johannes Brahms to Hermine Spies

[December 1884]

Dear and esteemed Fräulein,

If you receive some singable things by me in a few days, do believe me that I am not a little ashamed and annoyed at myself on their account.

So you will be too, and will think: What a truly tiresome person this composer is! That's what comes of having met a pretty and cheerful maiden from the Rhineland and hearing his things sung wonderfully and merrily by her! Off he goes and writes songs about 40 years and other silly stuff.

Even the best misinterpretation cannot turn it into anything like twenty years, and of what concern are forty to you!?

Etc., but maybe it'll turn out a little better, next time, and better suited to your so lovely misinterpretation.

Meanwhile, be indulgent towards the shipment and towards these lines. I am going to Hamburg today; from there I'll travel very cheerfully to Bremen, where, in hopes of seeing you, and of being scolded and sung to by you, I am

your affectionately devoted

J. Brahms.

In December of 1886, Maria Fellinger, a member of Brahms's closest Viennese circle, told Hermine she was convinced 'Brahms belonged to her', as she put it, and in Hamburg, Elise Brahms was already congratulating her brother. Prematurely, of course.[9]

Theodor Billroth often spoke of his fraternal relationship with Brahms, by which he must have meant the serious and confidential nature of their friendship. They shared a certain inner loneliness known only too well to Brahms, and seem also to have shared a touch of fashionable misogyny. Billroth, who was in a generally depressed state of mind at this time, wrote to Brahms about Hanslick's latest published articles, saying: 'Friend Hanslick's Letters from London are probably the weakest things he has written. Is it the perpetual presence of his wife, his age, the paucity of stimulating material?'[10]

[9] See Hermine's answer to Maria Fellinger in Minna Spies, *Hermine Spies: Ein Gedenkbuch für ihre Freunde* (Leipzig, 1905), 273–5.

[10] Hanslick's London Report, included later in his *Musical Sketchbook* (*Die moderne Oper*, part IV). For the English translation, see 'Letter from London', in *Hanslick's Music Criticisms*, trans. and ed. Henry Pleasants (New York, 1988), 246–74.

459
Johannes Brahms to Theodor Billroth

[Thun, 22 July 1886]

Dear friend,

Thank goodness the little book was sent off yesterday. For your hand-writing wouldn't have looked at me as amiably this morning, had I not had that slight sense of relief.

But now, my best thanks for having been kinder than I. I am so bothered with 'Answering' that I don't get to letter-writing; indeed, there are even more that I don't answer—but that costs even more in time and good humour.[11]

As best as I can, I gather from your letter that you are on better terms with the E minor Symphony, and that gives me great pleasure.

I suppose I gave Hanslick only a somewhat cursory reading (and have now loaned it out), because the material doesn't exactly interest me. But I had the impression that he has looked around diligently and attempted, with good success, to give as comprehensive and graphic a picture of the condi-tions in London as posssible. As a result, it may appear more sober than one is accustomed to from him—and a more serious and more thorough person, like Chrysander, for instance, shouldn't really be second-guessing him!

But now let me also tell you that I'm very glad to have come here. For me the decision was hard, but I simply wanted to go to Switzerland again. You have no conception of how beautiful and comfortable it is here in every respect. You can picture for yourself what's involved—delightful lodgings, lovely walks and rides, good taverns, pleasant people especially from Bern who see to excellent reading material, etc., etc.

It always sounds a bit melancholy when you write of feeling increasingly lonely. I have a sympathetic understanding for it, and wish you would be wary in time. I am the same way, after all—for I have long been and continue to be a terrible loner!

I hope my little book can still make you laugh, and hope you have the loveliest holiday in St Gilgen.

With affectionate greetings, utterly your
                                              J. Brahms.

---

[11] Brahms once told another friend (Ottilie Ebner) that he didn't *write* letters, but merely answered them. A fine distinction which, in his case, is often justified.

Brahms changed his mind about the London Letters. 'Hanslick's London articles grow on me,' he wrote to Billroth, 'one gets a grand, detailed picture of local conditions from them. They especially mean something to me since I definitely don't want to go there, and he now confirms the sort of opinion I always had.'[12]

❦ 1887 ❦

In all, Brahms's love of Italy took him there eight times. It is difficult to reconcile his reputation as a taciturn North German with the enthusiasm he displayed in a group of letters he wrote over a three-week period to Simrock, the novice who was about to accompany Brahms on his fifth trip. Brahms looked forward, as he said, to seeing Simrock's mouth hang open at the first sight of Venice.

460
Johannes Brahms to Fritz Simrock

[Vienna, 16 April 1887]

D[ear] S[imrock]

I suppose I can destroy the long letter from Gr[oth?] along with others? Or do you keep that sort of thing?[1]

So then, I am planning to leave here at 9.25 in the evening, to arrive in Innsbruck at 9.30 in the morning, and from there to proceed *with you* at 3 o'clock. Of course we must definitely stay in Verona for 2 nights, I suggest: Albergo Cola. We might do well to skip Vicenza. Better to see less, but with tranquillity, in comfort. Try your best to arrange it so that you are not over-constrained by the return trip. You have no conception of the riches you will look in on, much too hurriedly and cursorily. I suggest Verona 2–3 days, Venice at least 3 days; or Verona 2 days and Vicenza 1 day—ah, one doesn't know where to turn!

Your

J. B.

[12] *Bil-B*, 8 Aug. 1886.

[1] Regarding Groth's protégé, Gustav Jenner. See also Letters 468 and 471.

461
Johannes Brahms to Fritz Simrock

[Vienna, 17 April 1887]

D[ear] S[imrock],

Now I'm contradicting myself once again and hope that will be it. For I am in favour of Verona, after all. If you travel the nights through, you get to Venice at 5 in the morning—totally incapable of even enjoying your breakfast, let alone Venice. I am going by way of Salzburg and will meet or wait for you somewhere or other from Rosenheim on. We'll then sleep comfortably in Verona and start on our merry way bright and early. *Let it now remain at that.* I don't know about round trip tickets, and for the likes of us, who are absolutely free and unfettered, they are rarely suitable. This time, however, you could probably take what's indicated. Munich—Verona—Vicenza, Venice, Bologna, Florence, Pisa, Genoa, (Milano) Gotthard.

Wüllner might well claim that I did agree somewhat to the music festival. Pledged to it I am not, and I'll gladly look for a way out of the back door. Otherwise I'll play my Trio and conduct the *Triumphlied*, if necessary. When the new things appear, you will take care, won't you, that Frau Schumann and Ed. Marxsen receive a copy *right away*! In case you send [them] here to Hanslick *and Kalbeck*, you must also steer one Dömpke's way.[2] My best thanks for the newspapers. You're just like all the women: at the first 'However', the critic is an ass and a scoundrel.—So we'll see each other at noon on the 27th, and in Verona we'll sup Italian for the first time!

Your
J.B.

N.B. Are you travelling first class? It's all the same to me, I just don't want to pay for 1st class and then come to you in 2nd. But for the long journey and in general: I suppose you'll be in 1st class.

Most of the summer was spent in Thun again, with a brief interruption to attend the annual Music Festival of the Lower Rhine, which this time was held in Cologne and was conducted with unusual brilliance by Franz Wüllner. Even Brahms, who was reluctant to attend, reported with excitement afterwards. On the programme was the new Trio in C minor, Op. 101, along with the Violin Concerto and the *Triumphlied*. With summer leisure came time to reconsider the question of a return of letters he and Clara had written to each other. She had already broached the topic one year earlier.

[2] Opp. 99, 100, 101, all published in April 1887.

462
Johannes Brahms to Clara Schumann

Thun, May 1887

Dear Clara,

It's really cruel, the demands fate makes on you. As deeply as I sympathize with you: I don't want to visualize the particulars to myself clearly and explicitly, nor can I continue to speak of them to you. Apart from the blow that hits so hard and is so terrifying, the other equally sad matters also continue on their melancholy course, I suppose. Your beautiful nature won't allow you to become insensitive to any ray of sunshine life or art grants you, that for me is the only consolation.

But do say a word to the Sommerhoffs to convey my earnest sympathy.

Once again, in magnificent Italy, there was no one I thought of as much and as wistfully as you. How I wish that you might still have as much strength for this greatest of delights as you do for your art. I know of no one who would relish everything there, relish it utterly, as you would—if your body didn't dissent.

I was greatly favoured again by the most splendid, gentlest spring weather; our tour would have been too much for you, but if you had spent these lovely weeks in Florence, for instance—no greater joy could be bestowed on a human being!

Our route went through Verona, Vicenza, Venice, Bologna, Florence, Pisa, Milano, and through the Gotthard to here. Not one day that was not filled with the greatest beauty. Simrock and Kirchner were my companions. It was S.'s kind notion to allow Kirchner to see Italy. 20 years earlier and it might even have found fertile ground. Companions are congenial and almost necessary for me in I[taly]—even if they don't always exactly increase my enjoyment, or merely not disrupt it.[3]

I'm now enjoying a 2nd early spring here and feel very content. I don't like to think that I'm expected to attend the music festival in Cologne at the end of May, but I suppose I must keep my word to Wüllner. And the beautiful trip along the Rhine could even become a welcome thought—if you could feel somewhat the same way about a brief visit with you?!

Simrock has published a catalogue of my things. When I have it sent to you, I hardly think I'll need to tell you that I didn't instigate it; I argued against it for as long as I could, but I couldn't forbid it.

---

[3] *Sic.* The joint trip was not without its personal difficulties, but Brahms put the best face on it.

But I almost forgot: It is far more important that my letters are returned than yours! Those you can have at any time—and so could your children—a situation I do not foresee. My letters, on the other hand, have no return address once I am gone! I request most kindly therefore, send them to me, and if I ask that you send them soon it isn't because I'm in a hurry to take them to the bookbinder!

The news of Frank and Herzogenberg is dismal indeed. The former seems very serious, but with H., I suppose one can hope for the best—unfortunately I know of a very similar case here just now, where gradually all hope is ending![4]

But now, finally, with warm greetings,

your
Johannes.

The catalogue mentioned here was a complete listing of Brahms's works to that time, published by Simrock. Brahms was quite opposed to the idea for many reasons, among which was the fear that it seemed vain.[5]

Clara's latest family disaster was the death from diphtheria of a 4-year old granddaughter, and the continuing decline of her son Ferdinand. On his way to the Rhine Festival Brahms did stop off in Frankfurt to stay with her,[6] but he had another social call in mind as well.

463

Johannes Brahms to Laura and Rudolf von Beckerath

[Thun, 20 June 1887]

Dear friends,

I'll shortly be travelling, most unwillingly, to the Cologne festival and look forward (should they be granted to me) only to such things as your cellar and your violin, the wife pouring and the husband tuning. But naturally you, as usual, are in Italy with your grammar and neither know nor want to hear anything of our latest music history.

In the most favourable case—for me—I'll tell you anyway that I plan to be in Frankfurt, Mylius Straße 32, on Thursday or Friday, and have in mind to drink the cup of affliction in Cologne from Sunday on. This will be served

---

[4] Herzogenberg eventually recovered from his rheumatic illness, but Ernst Frank, whose conducting career had been very successful, now suffered a mental illness which sent him to an asylum, where he died two years later.

[5] See his letter to Simrock of 16 June 1885, *BW* xi. 98, among many others.

[6] For Clara's view of the chaos this visit occasioned, see Litz, iii. 490–1.

in the Gürzenich [Hall], better ones I'll get at Bahnhofstraße 4, at R. Schnitzler's.

Therefore, do tell me at one of those two addresses where in Italy you are and if the key to the cellar was taken along? I am driven by bitter necessity, for otherwise I'd have to rest up in beautiful cities like Mannheim, Crefeld, or Utrecht!

Most affectionate greetings from your
J. Brahms.

This self-invitation to Rüdesheim bore the hoped-for fruit: Brahms was subsequently able to announce the consumption of great quantities of the best wine.

The remainder of the summer was spent on the Thunersee, devoted to the creation of the Double Concerto, Op. 102. Three letters throw light on Brahms's sharply alternating needs for sociability and solitude.

In an almost illegibly turbulent scrawl, a postcard went to Elizabet von Herzogenberg. Unbeknownst to Brahms, the card reached her just as her husband's battle with a paralysing form of rheumatism intensified, a struggle which effectively removed them from circulation for years.

464
Johannes Brahms to Elizabet von Herzogenberg

[Thun, 14 July 1887]

I have the urgent need to hear from you and am writing a letter right away just to ensure I deserve it.

But is the address on the other side valid or is it already Liseley?[7]

A brief word in response is requested by
J. Brahms   Thun, in Switzerland

Brahms's need for solitude, as well as his ability to 'find enjoyment in life' were never better expressed than in the next letter.

465
Johannes Brahms to Freifrau von Heldberg

[Thun, 11 August 1887]

Most esteemed Baroness,

It is a specific motivation that prompts me to write to you. But I would like to begin with something I have wanted to say to you in strict confidence

---

[7] The Herzogenberg newly-built summer house near Salzburg.

for the longest time. For I believe that you must often consider me ungrateful and dishonest, and in a certain sense then you may also be right. That is the case when I am invited to enjoy your very great and beautiful kindness and benevolence towards me.

That I can enjoy these with the fullness of my heart, that you have seen and cannot doubt. But I decline so often and you do not understand the reason. Let me now acknowledge that in such a situation I am certainly not dishonest, but also not open; the honest, candid answer just won't come out because I dislike speaking of myself and my peculiarities. The confession is plain: I need absolute solitude, not only in order to accomplish what I am capable of, but also, quite generally, to think about my vocation. This is rooted in my temperament, but it may also be readily explained otherwise.

For we 'little folk' must realize early on what we are obliged, sadly, to do without.

Well, someone like me, who finds enjoyment in life and in art beyond himself, is only too much inclined to savour both—and to neglect other matters. That might even be the right and the smartest thing to do. But just now, with a new and major work sitting finished before me, I really do take some pleasure in it and have to say to myself: I would not have written it had I enjoyed life ever so splendidly on the Rhine and in Berchtesgaden.

And now, dear gracious lady, I ask you to set my chatter into verse for yourself if possible, and allow me to get to what I am supposed to be writing.

Joachim asks me, if at all possible, to direct the attention and benevolence of His Highness the Duke towards a young man from Meiningen. He is the 16-year-old Döll, of whom J[oachim] writes that, as he is far advanced for his age, he has a tuition-free place at the Berlin Conservatory and is his personal student. J[oachim]'s only regret is that the young man is somewhat lacking in intellectual breadth, simply because, apart from his music, he hasn't learned enough, etc. In short he would consider it fortunate if, through H.H.'s favour, it were possible to place the young man with a sensible, cultivated family. The parents are poor peasants (Christian Döll) in Rosa, near Wernshausen. Perhaps it might be possible for the youngster to be permitted to introduce himself to your Highnesses, to play for them? He would undoubtedly be at home during the vacation?[8]

---

[8] The request was granted. Döll finished his studies and eventually emigrated to the United States; he settled in Atlantic City, where he was last heard from in 1939.

May I request you kindly to commend me to H.H. the Duke and H.H. the Princess Marie and would you also excuse the contents of this epistle?

With great deference and devotion,

J. Brahms.

Thun in Switzerland.

Another self-invitation to the Widmanns, this time with a citation from the Book of Moses (43: 34).[9] Whether the 'B' stood for Benjamin or Brahms, the essential point lay in the rest of the passage!

466

Johannes Brahms to Josef Viktor Widmann

[Thun, September 1887]

Sunday the 11th.

'And food was served to them from his table. But to B. was given five times more than to the others! And they drank and became drunk with him.'

Thus it was, and thus is the custom in Josef's palace—to the delight of the

B.

On a postcard and in a stiff and formal manner, Brahms asked permission of Joachim to give him news 'of an artistic matter'. Joachim answered with equal formality, but could not hide his excitement at the possibility of a new piece.

467

Johannes Brahms to Joseph Joachim

[Thun, 24 July 1887]

Esteemed Joachim,

Your friendly greeting allows me to make my confession much more cheerfully than I had hoped!

But get set for a little shock! For I was of late unable to resist ideas of a concerto for *violin and violoncello*, however much I tried again and again to talk myself out of it.

---

[9] In the Revised Standard Bible: 'Portions were taken to them from Joseph's table, but Benjamin's portion was five times as much as any of theirs. So they drank and were merry with him.'

Now, I am indifferent to all sorts of things about the thing except for the question of your attitude to it.

Above all, however, I ask you in all sincerity and friendliness not to be in the least embarrassed. If you'll send me a postcard which simply says: 'I decline', I'll know enough and how to fill in the rest myself.

Otherwise, my questions begin: Do you want to see a sample of it? I am writing out the solo parts just now; would you and Hausmann take the trouble of looking them over with a view to their playability? Could you consider trying the piece somewhere, sometime, with Hausmann and with me at the piano, and eventually, perhaps, in some town or other with orchestra and us?

I ask for a word and I repeat, that I——Well, maybe you'll write the above-mentioned postcard anyway, once you have seen the sample!

I shall not say out loud and explicitly what I silently hope and desire.

But give my best greetings to Hausmann, and I am with deference, as of old,

your

J. B.

Clara called it 'The Reconciliation Concerto', something Brahms's letter confirms. To date, their contact had been via letters; now they would meet and speak face to face. The cellist Robert Hausmann took news of the concerto with him to a spa on the North Sea island of Sylt, where he found Hermine Spies and the poet Klaus Groth. Hausmann had already written to Brahms, 'I cannot begin to tell you of my unbounded joy when I heard from Joachim about the Violin–Violoncello Concerto . . .'[10]

Hermine Spies now wrote her own letter, describing jolly days buried in sand on the beach with Groth and Hausmann. Both men were tall; Groth was about 25 years her senior, but jokingly considered himself Brahms's rival for her attention. Brahms answered:

468

Johannes Brahms to Hermine Spies

[August 1887]

Dear and very esteemed, or esteemed and very dear Fräulein!

Eight pages I wrote to you yesterday, but I cannot send them off, they are a pure and unadulterated E flat minor chord, so sad, and by the way, replete with poisonous envy of cellists and poets, and how well off they are!

---

[10] Friedrich Bernhard Hausmann, 'Brahms und Hausmann', *Brahms-Studien*, 7 (1987), 29.

Sometime when you are lying in the sand with your lanky poet, you might tell him that he had recently sent songs to Simrock which I consider so pretty and talented that it would be a shame if they were published. (For they are, among other things and incidentally, quite unfinished and impractical.) I wish that the young man had a valiant teacher who would show him how this or that of his songs can be improved, if it is capable of being improved.[11]

You can see, my pen over-exerted itself yesterday with those eight pages!

Greetings to your slaves or friends, whose elongated shapes must surely be getting tiresome—a change is definitely needed there! And that might as well be provided by your poor, complaining

Outsider!

As far as I know, I shall be on the Rhine in mid-September, and I suppose your lanky cellist will also be coming? Would you please tell him that he must be sure to inform me if he leaves there before the 28th!

469
Johannes Brahms to Clara Schumann

Hofstetten, August 1887

Dear Clara,

You'll now have arrived at your cherished Berchtesgaden. Stronger, refreshed? This time that hardly seems necessary to me! Yes, I imagine you are taking a walk down your mountain every day to visit this friend or that.

We certainly have a peculiar way of dealing with our letters! I had always thought quietly about an exchange, but would never have uttered the word. Then I sent your letters, but didn't have the courage to look into them first and read in them—because I assumed that then I would be unable to send them. You're a foxy one, you bring the matter up, but send nothing, and read!

Oh well, I'll wait a while longer!

Herr Wendt is here and sends warm greetings. But you do indeed have a most delightful sister—let's swap!

I have now taken care of the French copyright business. That's what comes of having no family; whatever I make use of, also in quite considerable measure on behalf of others, I earn quite easily; and have no need at all to concern myself with sources of income.[12]

---

[11] Reference to early work of the composer Gustav Jenner, whom Groth was trying to help. See Letter 460.

[12] In a previous letter Clara reminded him to see that he received the royalties due him from French editions, as the amount of money was considerable.

The Herzogenbergs send best greetings, unfortunately he is not better at all and it seems to be the same case as the one I am witnessing here with an acquaintance; I told you about it.

Regarding myself, I can tell you something really droll. That is, I had the jolly idea of writing a concerto for violin *and cello*.

If it succeeds at all, we may well have some fun with it. You can probably imagine how one could show off in this situation,—but don't imagine too much! I had the same thought afterwards, but by then it was finished.

I really should have passed the idea on to someone who knows strings better than I (Joachim, unfortunately, has given up writing, of course). After all, it is quite different to write for instruments whose character and sound is only approximately in one's ear, which one hears only in the mind—instead of writing for an instrument one knows through and through as I know the piano, where I know precisely what I write and why I write this way or that. Well, we'll wait and see. Joachim and Hausmann are going to try it. J. says Cologne is the proper place, and I, Mannheim and Frankfurt!

Now my warmest greetings to you, and to Marie, Herzogenbergs, Franz, Frl. Wendt—however many acquaintances are still teeming about there—give my friendly greetings. Only the Frank house is empty, I suppose?

Entirely your
Johannes.

Brahms's insecurity with regard to writing for strings is curious, what with a violin concerto, two sonatas for cello, and three for violin already to his credit. No doubt his concern had more to do with the combined sonorities of violin and cello as solo instruments than with his knowledge of each instrument alone.

Clara now agreed to return his letters, although deeply reluctant. 'In giving [them] back I feel as though I were already taking leave of you!', she wrote, and at the last minute, apparently elicited his permission to keep those which were particularly dear to her.[13]

---

[13] The great quantity of letters he allowed her to keep demonstrates his implicit trust in the discretion of Clara and her daughters. Or does it? Kalbeck's account (iv². 50 ff., esp. 51 n. 1) is quite different, and hints at deception on Clara's part. Kalbeck may be correct; it is true that in Clara's published diary there is no mention of her request, nor of Brahms's acquiescence (entry for 16 Oct.), but only a description of Brahms's brief visit and the tearful handing over of his letters—and a footnote added by Litzmann to explain the letters which did survive. There is good reason to be suspicious. Nevertheless, Kalbeck's view is not based on any facts at his disposal, and one must take into account that in his biography of Brahms, he is generally highly unsympathetic to Clara. Kalbeck's treatment of this very matter is a good case in point. He writes, 'In the middle of August, or therefore after waiting in vain for a quarter of a year, he returned to the same topic [of the letter return].' But it is Clara who first asked for the return of *her* letters almost a year previously, and who therefore waited far longer than a quarter of a year before getting them back. *SBB* ii. 320, and Litz, iii. 489 ff., esp. 491 n.

How Viennese Brahms had become is evident from the pleasure he took at returning home, however briefly, before the series of Double Concerto performances.

470

Johannes Brahms to Josef Viktor Widmann

[Vienna, 11 October 1887]

Dearest friend,

You wouldn't believe how often and warmly I think of you, how often I have wished a large sheet of paper were lying there with me writing down each day what is happening here and asking how it might be going there.

If I tried to catch up now (I've only written 5 letters so far) an awful hodgepodge would result and I would probably forget the best part.

And so I just cannot describe any more, only briefly report, e.g. that it was enormously friendly and lovely in Baden and that I found my flat furnished most comfortably,[14] and that we take the most wonderful walks. Are you also having such continuously splendid weather? I eat outdoors noon and evening, the chestnut trees are blooming for the second time, a few are full of lush, mature blossoms.

Yesterday I was present when Billroth and his students saw each other again for the first time—that would be very lovely to describe, and equally so, how I had an evening visit from the authoress of 'Songs of a Mormon Woman'.

By the way, it has escaped you that these are to be taken allegorically and pertain to Vienna and the matrimonial circumstances of the more genteel folk!

The Hanslicks and Kalbecks think of you most tenderly! Your two composers are also here and now I would tell you all kinds of things if I didn't also have questions to ask!

So then, father of my Johanna, how is Argos doing, and wouldn't he take it as a tender greeting from me if you gave him a nice piece of meat sometime, instead of little breadballs?

Has Professor Vetter returned and did he bring a whole museum with him? And why did the accounts of his travels stop just when he had made the acquaintance of enough ladies to make them interesting?

---

[14] In the spring of 1887, Brahms's landlady died, leaving his future living arrangements at Karlsgasse 4 much in doubt. Maria Fellinger came to the rescue in a number of ways; by the time the summer was over, Brahms had the same address, but a new landlady, a larger flat, and better furnishings.

But if you and your wife are travelling to Germany, do let me know when and where to. I will probably go there several times this winter and it would be exceedingly nice and pleasant if we could meet somewhere or other.

You can't tell by this twaddle how many friendly and warm thoughts preceded it, but do believe it comes from your deeply devoted

J. Br.

Argos was Widmann's little dog, and had accompanied the writer on an outing to the Grindelwald icefield shortly before. The terrier disappeared, and as darkness fell, had to be left behind on the mountain. Four days later, on the very day Brahms was to leave for Vienna, a scratching at the door announced the miraculous return of the exhausted animal. It had somehow managed the very long, dangerous trip home. Brahms shared in the family's jubilation, and as a consequence of this letter the dog got his meat.[15]

The evening visit was by Sidonie Grünwald-Zerkowitz-Kolokotroni, author of a number of remarkable and unorthodox books and poems. She was particularly concerned with the condition of women in their relations with men, opposed to a double sexual standard, and for the women of Vienna championed Viennese, rather than Parisian fashions. One would like to know more about this visit to a man not always known for his patience with the fair sex. [16]

471

Johannes Brahms to Klaus Groth

[before 23 December 1887]

Dear friend,

I'm glad there is now another inducement which obliges me to write to you at last. But first I want to settle the old debt.

Simrock sent me your letter a while ago and I wanted to tell you in response that I would be glad to see your protégé, and after a few more congenial meetings, I might also have hopes of being useful to him. However— whenever I come to your neighbourhood it is for a few hectic days, and it's a long way to Vienna!

Young North German artists live here all the time; whether your friend is in a mood and position to do so, I don't know. I also don't know with

---

[15] Widmann, *Erinnerungen*, 79 ff. *Recollections*, 140–1.

[16] Her book, *Songs of a Mormon Woman* (*Lieder einer Mormorin*), quickly went into many editions. Its sequel, *Today's Gretchen* (*Gretchen von heute*), was an equally great success but was banned in Austria; in 1959 the ban was apparently still in effect. *Oesterrichisches Biographisches Lexikon 1815–1950*, vol. ii, ed. Hermann Böhlaus (Graz-Köln: 1959).

whom he has studied or is studying still? etc. In short, there is easily more to ask than to answer!

Now for the New, and, in fact, a request. Lately, a university lecturer, Herr Janssen, has been living in Kiel (I believe his field is English literature or history) (Holtenauerstraße 141). His wife is a daughter of my quite extraordinarily revered piano teacher, Otto Cossel. She is very musical and a keen pianist, but now, in her new circumstances, she greatly misses her former musical connections, etc. Would you do her the kindness of letting her meet you, and if auspicious, to arrange for her to meet Herr Stange and Herr Toeche or others, and now and then provide her with concert tickets? I am sure I have often talked to you about her father, for when I think of him I readily start to chat. He was quite a remarkable and exceptional person and teacher.

I learned of the death of our dear Marxsen only belatedly, upon returning from a trip.

I hope you are doing most splendidly, as usual, along with the three little ones?!

I dearly hope to see you in the course of the winter and will let you know beforehand, I'd very much like to spend a few relaxed days or weeks in our part of the world!

With my warmest greetings,

your

J. Brahms.

The Groth protégé was Gustav Jenner, a young man from Kiel. He would shortly become Brahms's only composition student.

It is entirely in keeping with Brahms's character that affection for his first piano teacher should show itself in concrete form even decades later.

Marxsen's death evoked a more expressive letter to the brother of his old teacher. Upon finding the death announcement waiting for him at home, he wrote: 'However much I told myself that each parting from the cherished man might be my last, [your announcement] was an unexpected shock nevertheless . . . I need not tell you what he was to me and what his memory will be for me'. Then he permitted himself one request—the return of his letters, all of which he destroyed.[17]

---

[17] Brahms to Leopold Marxsen, no date, HbBA 1962.942.

❧ 1888 ❧

472
Johannes Brahms to Josef Viktor Widmann

[Vienna, 7 January 1888]

Dearest friend,

Since then, I've been—all over the place! Ultimately, for Christmas, very happily to Meiningen, and for the New Year ditto to Leipzig. Your last letter toured with me and got more and more company!

But now at the very least, I really want to see a Sunday Bund again sometime, and that's why I am finally writing my thanks![1]

Apart from that, your letter would have to have come twenty years earlier.

Have I never spoken to you, father of my Johanna, of my fine principles? They include: Never again to attempt an opera or marriage. Otherwise, I believe I would immediately attempt two of them, operas that is, *König Hirsch* and *Das laute Geheimnis*.[2] Incidentally, I have a complete libretto of the latter, made for me some time ago by the same copper engraver Allgeyer who has just written the beautiful essays on Feuerbach.

My dear friend, if you have truly liberal ideas and principles, you can appreciate how much money I will save and have left over for an Italian journey—if I do not marry before the summer or buy myself a libretto for 1,000 F!

For that [amount], couldn't we both go together? I cannot manage well in Italy on my own, and a more agreeable companion than you I cannot imagine or hope for.

(The money for Thun has been taken care of, I suppose? Knechtenhofer was one of the two names of the shipping company.)

If it didn't all need to be written out, I would tell you all sorts of amusing things about my journeys, about Pesth, about Christmas at Court with beautiful music and the Maiden of Orleans and Ghosts by Ipsen[!] and what not![3]

How are Professor Vetter's ladies from Lappland?[4] Although I don't

---

[1] Widmann's newspaper, the *Bund*, published a Literary Supplement on Sundays.
[2] *King Stag* and *The Loud Secret*, both by Gozzi. See Letter 281.
[3] In Meiningen, where he met the playwright.
[4] The anthropologist was Widmann's son-in-law.

know them, give my greetings to them and all the other exquisite ladies and maidens whom I do know, and spin wonderful fantasies of Italian journeys for your

J. Br.

Simrock negotiated with Breitkopf & Härtel to buy all the works of Brahms for which they held publication rights, and informed Brahms by letter just before the deal was sealed. Now, asking for his sympathy, he hoped Brahms would agree to help him reach his goal of being the sole publisher of his work. Brahms's astonishment and mock anger undoubtedly had something to do with his disapproval of the high prices Simrock charged for his music, in contrast to Peters' inexpensive editions; he refused to pledge fealty to Simrock, but never seriously threatened their long and mutually advantageous relationship.

473
Johannes Brahms to Fritz Simrock

[Vienna, 30 March 1888]

My best S.

This is supposed to call for congratulations!??!? I, however, cannot think of a single word to say—because I don't understand a single word of it. And what I would like to say and ask seems to me too indelicate and presumptuous. It's not my fault if you overestimate me quite outrageously. My conduct and my words have certainly not contributed to it. But I can hardly attempt the opposite either, and prostrate myself abjectly before you.

I am supposed to view it with 'sympathy'! Oh God, yes; I am touched by your sympathy, but I consider it unreasonable beyond all measure for you to buy Härtel's things—I can *not* imagine for how much—which will have cost you about 100 l'dors and which in no time at all won't be worth a farthing. That I don't give new things to any others I don't need to promise, based on our past experience. My desire to do so, as I hope you do believe, is founded on very childish feelings, and murky ones, to boot.

You will just have to tolerate a little bit of empathy for Peters Editions. I am aware of everything that speaks against it—but nevertheless it has to give joy that buying scores or Liebeslieder, for instance, is made that much easier. It's simply a fact that there is a better public in the galleries than in the loges. . . .

But now to demonstrate my sympathy to you, or actually my compassion for your great sympathy, I literally and earnestly want to establish that from now on I receive no further honoraria; instead, as I suggested recently,

I will procure a credit balance each time, which I can draw upon in an emergency, and which is simply extinguished upon my death.

You know my circumstances (better than I) and know that I can live in comfort even without any further honoraria. That will I do, too, to the extent that my non-Wagnerian nature feels a need. After my death, however—I really should bequeath whatever is left to you so you can extricate yourself a little from the Härtel affair. Well, then, I congratulate you, but wash my hands with phenol and what not!

And so, with all my sympathy and with deep compassion, your affectionately devoted

J. B.

On April first! I wish it were an April fool's prank!

For a time Simrock and Peters actually talked of collaborating on a low-cost edition of Brahms's works, but when nothing came of that, Brahms gave Peters the publication rights to his vocal quartets, Op. 112, and the Canons for Women's Voices, Op. 113. Those works apart, Simrock published the rest of Brahms's output, and even offered Brahms the opportunity to revise the works newly acquired from Breitkopf, an offer which resulted in a second version of the Piano Trio, Op. 8, two years later.

As two volumes comprising 752 letters attest, Brahms was in touch with Clara Schumann all his life. At this time the concern between them was the unpublished score of the first version of Schumann's Fourth Symphony, Op. 120, a version Brahms preferred and spent some effort to gain approval for. In 1886 he sent it first to the Herzogenbergs, then to Joachim; now Clara had it.[5] He felt strongly about the superiority of the early version, and hoped to win her agreement for a trial performance at a Museum Concert in Frankfurt. In July Clara wrote that the local conductor did not share Brahms's high opinion, and the cost of copying the parts merely for the sake of curiosity would be too high. The conductor in question was one Carl Müller;[6] a comparison between the opinion of this routine musician with his own did not sit well with Brahms. But for the time being that portion of Clara's letter was overshadowed by the account of her latest predicament—the incurable illness of her son Ferdinand and the related need to raise and educate his five children. Brahms's concern for Clara, and his preoccupation with how to alleviate her financial worries without angering her, pushed the symphony out of mind.

<hr>

[5] See his very explicit letter to H. von Herzogenberg, *BW* ii. 127. In this form the symphony dates from 1841, but was reorchestrated in 1851 in order to meet the needs, Brahms was convinced, of the poor orchestra in Düsseldorf.

[6] 1818–94.

474
Johannes Brahms to Clara Schumann

Thun, 24 July 1888

Dear Clara,

The mere sight of your dear letter was enough to give me great pleasure; 'so much written in her own hand', I thought, the rheumatism must not be all too severe, we can be satisfied.

But I nevertheless put off replying to the dear letter. There was, in fact, something on my mind and in my thoughts that just wouldn't flow from my pen. But ultimately it cannot be helped, so gather up all your kindness and good feelings for me, listen, and then say a friendly Yes.

I take the deepest interest in everything affecting you, and so also in all the worries and troubles which are inescapable in a life as rich as yours—but which are bestowed on you in truly lavish measure.

Of the lesser ones, the money worries, I have no exaggerated apprehension and anxiety. But it annoys me that you should have those too—while I swim in money without noticing this at all and without deriving any pleasure from it. I cannot, don't want to, and will not live any other way; it would be useless to give more to my family than I now do, and where my heart demands it, I am able to help and do good to any degree without noticing it. After my death, however, I have no obligations or particular wishes.

In short, the situation is straightforward.

These days, however, I was again thinking through just how I could go about sending you a sum of money: As a rich friend of the arts, through an anonymous letter, as a belated contribution to the Schumann Fund, or some such. I can do nothing of that kind without drawing someone sufficiently into my confidence to enable him to advise me correctly.

On the other hand, if you consider me as good a person as I am, and if you hold me as dear as I want you to—then the second part of this business is also straightforward, and you simply permit me, for instance, without any further ado, to contribute with my very superfluous mammon to the expenses for your grandchildren this year with something like 10,000 M.

Simrock again has a whole stack of choruses, quartets, and songs. I notice nothing at all of the lovely honorarium, it wanders silently and uselessly into the *Reichsbank*.[7]

---

[7] For the songs and a capella choruses, Opp. 103–7. He received 6,000 Marks for Op. 103; the other payments were not recorded.

Just consider what great pleasure the things and the honorarium would give me if you were to say a nice, round 'Yes' to me.

But since there are 2 sides to everything I say, failing this, I shall resolve to commission Simrock to pay that amount to the Schumann Fund.

Next time, about the remainder of your dear letter; for the present merely that in regard to the Wieck affair, I am very much in favour of complete silence. I believe the book will be so bad that it won't actually see the light of day. I don't know what one would have to do to me to induce me to engage in a public controversy.[8]

Dear Frau Röntgen must have just died! Julius [Röntgen] was with me a short while ago, and then a telegram arrived that summoned him to Leipzig. As I said, more next time, and for today I just ask for a friendly postcard which merely says a cheerful Yes to your, in that case, very delighted

Johannes.

475
Johannes Brahms to Clara Schumann

July 1888

Dear Clara,

I anticipated your answer with some concern, and so to begin with, I was reassured and very grateful to you. You decline in such a *friendly* fashion that I suppose I must be satisfied with you; but unfortunately, not with me. I should have gone about it more cleverly and now I stand here, as before, with my pretty bunch of gillyflowers. Actually, since you take such a friendly view of the business, and since furthermore you must be afraid that I could do something stupid, you might go a step further and follow up with a kindly Yes!?!?

I always wanted to write to you more explicitly about the Symphony but I hope sometime I can prattle on to you about it, score in hand. I'll gladly let you keep it for the time being, but Wüllner was recently here and asked me earnestly to let him have a look at it. W. naturally has more insight and judgement than Müller. Unfortunately I don't like the Gürzenich for the performance specifically of that piece, and you are not likely to attend a rehearsal there, are you? But perhaps you could send the score to Wüllner sometime or other?

---

[8] Marie Wieck's book about their father, *Aus dem Kreise Wieck–Schumann*, included some letters of Clara to her father, used without her permission. Clara was furious, but took Brahms's advice. The book *was* published, but not until 1912 (by Zahn & Jaensch: Dresden; 2nd edn. 1914).

I hope you are very comfortable in Berchtesgaden. Two houses there you will always look at very wistfully![9]

I have heard nothing directly about the Herzogenbergs for a long time—but it's hardly likely to sound more encouraging. I hear they'll go to B.-Baden later on and you'll probably see them there; give them my warmest greetings then. I would be glad to write to them more often, but it's just too sad always to have to begin with the same enquiring minor chord. I have very little hope, however, and I am ever so sorry for both those excellent people.

I'll probably go to Vienna very soon. I would like to stop in Berchtesgaden for a few days on the way, but it depends on circumstances. Would you, in any case, let me know by postcard whether one could obtain lodgings where you are, at the Pension Moritz? I believe that Frau Franz has invited me to stay with her—but i don't know this for certain, and her house is probably very far from yours?

With my warmest greetings to you and the Fräuleins,
utterly your
Johannes.

476
Johannes Brahms to Clara Schumann

[Vienna, 3 October 1888]

Dear Clara,

Don't be angry if I come to you with a *da capo*. This summer you declined my intended remittance in *such a friendly manner* that I'll risk it anyway, now that we are both at home. Maybe I should have been able to approach the whole business more adroitly—but I still don't know just how.

If I didn't want to be identified with the remittance, somebody or other would have to write your address—etc., in short, would have to have some notion of the business. Therefore please acquiesce tomorrow, when I very devotedly lay 15 Thousand [Marks] (thanks to interest and interest on interest!) at your feet and I beg you sincerely just to write on a postcard that they are lying there—nothing else!

After all, I know and think with pleasure how conscientiously you are now working your way through the huge mountain of birthday letters, and how thoroughly your diligence melts it away daily!

Beside that, I often like to think of you now relishing the lovely autumn days and taking pleasure in your cosy home and lovely garden!

---

[9] Those of Ernst Frank, now in a mental hospital, and the Herzogenbergs.

I greet you all from the heart and ask you to be sure not to be angry and to take a right friendly view of the whole affair.

Utterly your
Johannes.

Brahms's 15,000 Marks eased Clara's concerns substantially. For a time several of the grandchildren lived with her in Frankfurt, and she did her best to plan for their education.[10]

The matter of Schumann's Fourth symphony was dropped for a year, after which Brahms asked Clara's permission to let Härtel publish it in an edition prepared by Wüllner; Clara did not respond to this part of his letter then or later, but when he quietly assisted in its publication two years later, Clara's fury almost severed their friendship once and for all.[11]

A more immediate rift in an important friendship arose from a serious disagreement with Widmann over the maiden speech of the new, inexperienced Kaiser, Wilhelm II. Widmann found it alarmingly brutal and said so in print.

477

Johannes Brahms to Josef Viktor Widmann

[Thun, 20 August 1888]

Dear friend,

Could you please get me the other works of Dr Kurz, particularly the third volume![12] Your friend can have them back soon, of course. I wish I had been in Bern yesterday, we would have chatted about something I am now tempted to let loose on a definitely very stupid sheet of paper! Hoping that he'll withstand the temptation is,

with warm greetings, your
J. B.

He did not withstand temptation. Later that day he sent one of his most often-quoted letters.

---

[10] For an account of this period as seen by her grandchildren and their descendants, see Dietz-Rüdiger Moser (ed.), *Clara Schumann: Mein liebes Julchen*, (Munich, 1990).

[11] See Letters 475, 489, 505–6 in this volume. See also *SBB* ii, letters 508–18, April–July 1888.

[12] Hermann Kurz, *Gesammelte Werke*, ed. Paul Heyse.

478
Johannes Brahms to Josef Viktor Widmann

[Thun, 20 August 1888]

Dear friend,

When I read the imperial speech, the other day, I quietly turned the page and wished that not every single word would have been spoken or reproduced exactly.

I regret your harsh comments about it. But that's the way everything coming out of Germany is criticized, although the Germans themselves lead the way in this. That is so in politics as in the arts. If the Bayreuth theatre were in France, it would not require anything as grand as Wagner's works to get you and Wendt and the whole world to make a pilgrimage there and to wax enthusiastic about something so ideally conceived and created. If a Gambetta or Garibaldi had spoken about Alsace as the young Kaiser now did, it would by and large sound something like this in the newspapers:

'These are not words, they are living flames which cannot be extinguished! These are weapons, which cannot be withstood! Return the Alsace; not mere justice, but fervour such as this demands and compells it.'

Even the N[orddeutsche] A[llgemeine] [Newspaper] doesn't dare fault these words. After all, they are not an edict of the state, nor were they spoken in public in front of a monument. A young man, not yet 30 years of age spoke them, a glass of wine in hand. The precise wording is not certain, only the sentiment, which is definitely backed by the whole nation. But the one and only word* that might distress us—that we did not hear being spoken and don't know the precise context; but it does not distort the plain sentiment of the sentence, it is merely that someone with finer sensibilities would wish the unconsidered, indeed unseemly, word out of existence. But it cannot possibly occur even to the N. A. to want to blow it out of proportion and fly into a temper about it. It reminds us of many a sharp word ascribed to the great Napoleon or the great Louis XIV. But when we consider these great and noble persons and their situations in Russia or the Palatinate, then these words have a different ring for us, and our thoughts and observations do not turn into criticism.

But if a poet were to portray these great, noble persons and heroes to us, he would have selected from among other words and deeds of theirs, or would describe their situation so insistently and movingly that those hard words would be appropriate![13]

[margin note, left: Additional Note p. 755]

---

[13] From a letter Brahms wrote to Clara in 1855 (Letter 59): 'What you write about Coriolanus

In any case, how much finer is this indestructible enthusiasm than the hypocritical manner in which certain other heroes spoke of battlefields, or the sanctimonious way in which they praised God's help!

Therefore return the Alsace, and while you're at it, Hanover and Hessen as well!

Yes, dear friend, that's the way it is. You confer respect and honour on the individual great person—but not on a lineage like the Hohenzollers with Fr[ederick] II and W[illiam] I? You have respect for every young man who, well prepared, strives towards a far-off goal—but not for a youthful new Emperor of the German people, who has surely prepared himself earnestly and with dignity for his high and difficult office, who may well still fulfil all kinds of hopes.

I don't wish to have greeted him at the beginning of his great and far-reaching reign as you, to have pictured him brashly without a trace of respect or sympathy—on the basis and with the evidence of a single fleeting and uncertain word.

In this matter you can convince me of nothing else. It might shame me somewhat if you could inform me of any tiny article in which you approved of any single word or deed of Bismarck or William I before its fulfilment!?

And the other way around with Gambetta, etc.!?

Apart from that, all the best from your

J. B.

The danger to their friendship is not obvious from Brahms's letters alone (Widmann destroyed his own); but according to Widmann, the incident imperilled their friendship and embittered their next few meetings, strained as they were by heated arguments over the wider question of Republican vs. Monarchical forms of government. Widmann was a champion of the Swiss Constitution and the rule of written law, while Brahms, a son of the Free and Hanseatic Republic of Hamburg, defended his devotion to the royal family of Hollenzollers. The irony did not escape their mutual friend, the Swiss novelist Gottfried Keller. Widmann described one of their subsequent meetings to his old friend, Henriette Feuerbach: 'He spoke harsh words to me such as I would not have borne from any other person. Outwardly we parted politely as friends. But I feel that a block of ice lies between us, which is his unimaginably chauvinistic German point of view.' And in his household diary, in a hand uncharacteristically small as if to minimize the whole affair, Widmann wrote:

doesn't surprise me; sometimes (when one reads it the first few times) one wishes he were different, gentler, more humane. If you read it more often, this vanishes, and in such a powerful hero you accept his roughness and hardness, if, in the appropriate situation he is therefore really hard, as in the election by the people.'

'Discussion with Brahms. Not pleasant.' Their friendship held, but it was a long time before they talked politics again.[14]

During this last summer in Thun, Brahms completed work on over twenty vocal works (Opp. 103–7), and the Violin Sonata in D minor, Op. 108. He sent the entire output to Elizabet von Herzogenberg, and received an enraptured review of the sonata.[15]

479
Johannes Brahms to Clara Schumann

Vienna, 2 November 1888

Dear Clara,

I sent the violin sonata I mentioned a short while ago to the Herzogenbergs, and received a friendly letter about it so much beyond my hopes that I keep wondering if you might like it too. I'll presume that you would care to see it, but if you also have time for it, write a word to the Herzogenbergs that they should send you the sonata right away. You might want to try it with Koning, or, since I hear that you are going to Berlin, even there with Joachim. The Herzogenbergs have a very legible copy and also the violin part.

Forgive me for not sending you the sonata first. But you won't believe my main reason!?

I never consider a new piece capable of appealing to someone. So also this time, and I am also still very doubtful that you will sign Frau Herzogenberg's letter! But if you do *not* like the sonata when you play it through, don't bother trying it with Joachim, but send it back to me.

I hope you have survived your festive days happily and joyfully, I thought about you a great deal.

Sincerest greetings all around

from your
Johannes.

---

[14] Josef Viktor Widmann, *Briefwechsel mit Henriette Feuerbach und Ricarda Huch*, ed. Charlotte von Dach (Zurich, 1965); letter of 8 Oct. 1888. The unpublished household book is part of the collection of the Dichtermuseum Liestal, Switzerland, and is quoted by kind permission. Widmann's discussion of the incident in his *Erinnerungen*, 81 ff., is considerably more thorough than the English translation (141 ff.).

[15] *BW* ii, letters 233 and 235, pp. 210, 215.

❧ 1889 ❧

Brahms was such a frequent visitor at Billroth's table that he did not hesitate to add his own friends to the guest list for a dinner the surgeon was giving for Joseph Joachim. Billroth had probably invited Julius Epstein and 'forgotten' Anton Door: both Door and Epstein were pianists on the faculty of the Conservatory, and for years, members of Brahms's circle of dining and walking companions. Richard von Perger was a young composer whom Brahms had reason to believe Joachim would want to meet.

480
Johannes Brahms to Theodor Billroth

[6 February 1889]

D[ear] fr[iend],

In view of the beautiful evening you are promising us, it is highly immodest to voice wishes and guidelines, to boot.

Forgive me therefore: when I declare that Door goes with Epstein as the cantor with the rabbi; and when I hope that you won't begrudge Herr von Perger an invitation—the more so since Joachim played a quartet of his in public in Berlin.

But in any event, I am greatly looking forward to the evening and greet you affectionately,

J. Br.

In May unexpected news reached Brahms in Ischl, where he would now spend the rest of his summers: he had been named Honorary Citizen of Hamburg, a distinction then shared by very few people, von Moltke and Bismarck having recently preceded him.

The immediate response was a telegram to Bürgermeister Petersen, then a letter to Hans von Bülow, who was in fact the driving force behind the nomination.

481
Johannes Brahms to Bürgermeister Dr Carl Petersen

Gratefully cherish your message as the finest honour and the greatest joy which can be bestowed on me by mankind.

482
Johannes Brahms to Hans von Bülow

[May 1889]

Cherished friend,

I have written the loveliest letters to the Bürgermeister these past days and dispatched the most wretched one today! You'll understand how, on such a completely unexpected and truly beautiful occasion, I pass all too easily from the hundredth to the thousandth topic—none of which has anything at all to do with the Burgermeister, so that what's left for him in the end is a plain zero.

I never expected it, even in my wildest dreams—but I don't dream of honours—and I also perceived it as something quite different, although— [for that] the main thing is missing! My good father should have lived to see it; his joy would have given me pleasure, and how!

I'll make every effort not to forget July 6th, but who keeps a calendar at hand or in the head as you do!

But now, (since I've composed so many letters to no avail), let me just simply pose a question which I cannot ask you enough to consider and treat with absolutely no embarrassment whatever. For I may have quite a suitable number for your music festival, if circumstances and conditions are not against it.

They are three short, hymn-like epigrams for 8-voice chorus a capella, which are almost intended for days of national celebration and commemoration, and in connection with which those days of Leipzig, Sedan and the Kaiser's coronation could even be mentioned expressly, as far as I am concerned. (But better not!)[1] Now that would all be fine and good in this particular situation—but you have to consider what speaks against it; the presumably very unsuitable hall, the unsuitable time [available] for rehearsing the chorus, the rest of the programme, etc. The pieces are not very difficult, I wouldn't mind if the wind section joined in; on the second day, for instance, the sound might be a nice change—only again the However d[a] c[apo].

Meanwhile it occurs to me that I could simply send the choruses along with this! That will happen herewith, and since I don't have a precise address I ask for a card telling me that letter and roll have arrived!

I ask once again, don't be embarrassed to give voice to all the 'Howevers'!

---

[1] Napoleon was decisively defeated at the Battle of Leipzig, in 1813. Napoleon III suffered the same fate at the Battle of Sedan, 1 Sept. 1870, when 82,000 French troops surrendered.

Boieldieu has not yet travelled after me, I thank you sincerely for him and for your kind letter. (Your friendly word about the sonata did give me reassurance of sorts.)[2]

But now I really want to go for a walk, and since it cannot be to the Neroberg, I ask you at least to give my best greetings to your wife and to Frau Cäcilia.

Affectionately, your
J. Brahms.

The three pieces for eight-part chorus were the *Fest- und Gedenksprüche*, Op. 109, 'Epigrams of Celebration and Commemoration'.

483
Johannes Brahms to Clara Schumann

[Vienna, end of June 1889]

Dear Clara,

For a long time I have greatly felt the need to know how you are after your Italian exertion, and what your summer plans look like. It was always my dearest wish to see you in Italy, and yet I am glad that I wasn't with you this time. It just wouldn't have satisfied me on your account, your years and strength do not allow you to 'immerse' yourself adequately. But you have probably got an inkling of how delightful it is to travel and stay there, if one doesn't have to conserve one's strength and save one's time.

That I have been made an honorary citizen in Hamburg you know, of course. Everything connected with it, incidentally, was as beautiful and enjoyable as the thing itself. My first thought in such a situation is my father, and the wish that he had lived to see it; fortunately, he didn't depart dissatisfied with me, even without this.

My second thought is for the letters such affairs cost and which spoil my mood and time more than necessary. Yesterday and today I received unexpected and unintelligible telegrams and a card from Vienna and Austria—I can sniff something like an Austrian decoration, but this time, all I can think of are the unavoidable thank-you letters! In the beginning of September I suppose I have to go to a music festival in Hamburg, in general and specifically because 3 short double choruses a capella by me are being performed.

---

[2] Boïeledieu's *La Dame blanche* was a favourite opera of Brahms's, recently republished by Peters. Bülow sent it for Brahms's birthday. The sonata was the Third for Violin, Op. 108, dedicated to Bülow.

'German Epigrams of Celebration or Commemoration', for festive days such as Sedan, etc. (wonderful words from the Bible).

But now, do let me hear from you occasionally, and also tell me how you found the Herzogenbergs. I was very pleased with the thought that you were in their company and Hildebrandt's in Florence.[3] But incomprehensible to me was their stay in that heat in Florence and then, for a change, Berchtesgaden! I send heartfelt greetings and request a quarter of an hour's worth of appetite for letter-writing for

your Johannes.

It is typical of Brahms that although he informed her of the very considerable honour he had received, that news is not the first item of his letter. Clara was pleased but puzzled. 'You are, of course, a citizen by right, are you not?' He was not. His next letter to Clara explains that he was merely the son of a citizen.[4]

To document his citizenship, Brahms was presented with a hand-decorated scroll. It was displayed in the Municipal Art Museum for four weeks, then delivered to Brahms back in Vienna by the artist himself.

484

Johannes Brahms to Bürgermeister Dr Carl Petersen

Vienna, October 1889

Your Magnificence,
Highly esteemed Herr Bürgermeister,

Through Herr Duyffcke I have finally come into possession of my most precious treasure and it gives me particular pleasure to be provided with an occasion to address a few words to you. Since my return from Hamburg I have felt the most lively desire to thank you, most esteemed Sir, and indeed to thank you quite personally, from the very bottom of my heart. As a result of having made your acquaintance and because of unforgettable hours in your home, inextinguishable images have entered my soul; they will accompany and enhance good thoughts of my native city. If I were writing music instead of words, I would here indicate: molto espressivo, teneramente, con intimissimo sentimento!

---

[3] The Herzogenbergs were visiting Elizabet's sister, who lived in Florence as the neighbour of the noted sculptor Adolf von Hildebrandt. For much more on the intricacies of these friendships and the light they shed on Elizabet, see Ethel Smyth, *The Memoirs of Ethel Smyth* (London, 1987), 118 ff.

[4] *SBB* ii. 387 ff. Johann Jakob's right to citizenship was non-hereditary. Johannes could have acquired the same right merely with the payment of a sum of money, but apparently did not.

As it is, you will just have to believe the simple words that would like to express the most heartfelt feelings to you. I also wanted to give expression to this feeling of great reverence and deep gratitude, and so I took the liberty of dedicating to you the *Fest- und Gedenksprüche* (performed at the Hamburg festival). According to its length, it is a miniscule work, certainly, but—aside from the fact that a larger work is not necessarily of greater value—it is the text and its meaning which suggests the idea of a dedication to me. If I had now not had the benefit of knowing you, I would be considering a name such as Bismarck or Moltke—but would probably keep silent about it.

Finally, to return again to the cheerful beginning: It was a really happy thought of yours to have my citizenship diploma transmitted to me by such a friendly and estimable emissary! Herr Duyffcke would also have taken great pleasure in his office, had he but given me more time. But Pesth and Prague tempted him even on the first day—and so did his wife at home, with all too swift a success! Nevertheless I hope he has been spurred to enjoy the old Imperial City at greater leisure sometime. I thank you also for your friendly greeting conveyed to me by the dear guest and trust that I may be permitted to commend myself most kindly to your family.

With high esteem and reverence,
your most devoted
Johs. Brahms.

Just before leaving for Hamburg Brahms received a thank you, in the form of a case of wine, from a friend who had visited Vienna in the spring, and who had left Brahms enough time to be an attentive host and guide.

485

Johannes Brahms to Felix Hecht

[Vienna, 5 September 1889]

Most esteemed friend,

For now, permit me to thank you most warmly with just a hasty word. Both the wine and I arrived here happily yesterday. *It* is well off and can stay here, but I must continue on to Hamburg this very day! After that, however, I'll be well off and its days will be numbered, and all the while I will be thinking cheerfully of you and will fervently hope to be your guide again very soon!

With affectionate greetings to you and especially to your wife,
your most devoted
J. Brahms.

The Citizenship ceremony took place on the occasion of an industrial fair in Hamburg, in conjunction with a music festival conducted by Hans von Bülow. Brahms's contribution, his *Fest- und Gedenksprüche*, was inspired by a different event, the 'Three Kaiser Year' (1888), during which two crowned heads of Germany died within a short time of each other. Brahms offered the pieces to Spengel when he learned of the honour he was to receive. As the next letters show, the work was virtually complete by the time he heard the news.[5] These three letters display the ease with which Brahms could now co-ordinate the printing and performance of new works.

486
Johnnes Brahms to Julius Spengel

[Ischl, 1 June 1889]

Dear Herr Spengel,

My very best thanks for your letter, which couldn't help but give me great pleasure. But this time you had it easy. All you had to do was simply tell a whole series of enjoyable and pretty stories! Well, by way of thanks I present you with something rather more dubious! For I have a few small choruses which, under certain circumstances, might be suitable for your music festival in September. They are three hymn-like epigrams for 8-part chorus a capella and intended expressly for national holidays.—You are now discovering what it's like to sing in your festival hall and how it sounds; furthermore, questions arise as to whether you'll have a strong chorus by September, whether it will be able to rehearse at that time, and whatever else may have to be considered. I have written to Bülow as well, and am now waiting to hear both of your qualms.

You don't need to economize on account of your jubilee this winter; more is at your disposal, if you so desire.[6]

Now I send heartfelt greetings to you and yours and may you be very merry on the 5th! Send a few Hamburg newspapers this time, if it's too much trouble for you to write an amusing letter!

All the best,

your

J. Br.

[5] The usual attribution of the composition of Op. 109 to his Honorary Citizenship is incorrect, and I can find no documentation for the related assertion that Brahms valued these pieces 'much less highly' than the Motets, Op. 110 (Michael Musgrave, *The Music of Brahms* (Oxford, 1994), 175). For the correct dating of the work see *BB* 444, and McC 438.

[6] A reference to the *Three Motets*, Op. 110. It seems clear that all of Brahms's later a capella music was written with Spengel and his well-trained chorus in mind.

487
Johannes Brahms to Fritz Simrock

[Ischl, 7 June 1889]

D[ear] S[imrock],

In case Herr Spengel sends you my 3 choruses for 8 voices, it is crucial to have the parts written out, engraved, and printed very quickly, and we ask you for it most kindly.

On the 9th of September there is a music festival in Hamburg (under Bülow and Spengel) where we might do the thing. Over the summer, choral rehearsals look problematical, however. If you could manage to have the parts for us by, say, the 25th of June, much would be gained, since there are still rehearsals, set for the 25th and then the 2nd and 3rd of July. After that, there are only the last ones from August 27th on. I am presenting the 3 choruses as a single work, but am still not decided about the title. Therefore leave the space at the head of the parts free and set aside for me: J.B., Op. (106?). The title will be something like: 'German Epigrams of Celebration and Commemoration', and in that case I am tempted to suggest you give a second title for other countries (Switzerland, England): 'National etc.'. Is that feasible? If Spengel does not write or send, you don't need to read this a second time; otherwise, however, I'd really like to be able to count on you and Keller.

The pictures have arrived and I thank you sincerely. I must have written very unclearly about Klinger, at least, none of your words apply to what I believe I wrote. Incidentally, with regard to the new title-page I am quite delighted, or what you will—except for the figure at the bottom—which may disappear in the printing, to the advantage of it and of comprehensibility. It is simply a different matter to look at a collection of sketches and fantasies—(there one can put up with many oddities)—from seeing the title-page of a widely used collection every day, etc.? Pointless, for you will respond to something entirely different! I deplore the latest punishment for your sins—but the latter more so, of course![7]

If Spengel sends, you'll tell me with a postcard!

All the best,

your

J. B.

---

[7] The 'sins' are his songs, Simrock's 'punishment' is to publish them in a new, multi-volume selection, for which Klinger designed the title-pages.

488
Johnnes Brahms to Julius Spengel

[Ischl, 8 June 1889]

Dear Herr Spengel,

I do not want to influence your decision. You now have the choruses and I request that you think it over—but particularly, that you also not be embarrassed, and to consider and decide candidly if you like them and if you can promise yourself the proper effect! Should you decide on a performance, I ask you to send the score to Simrock (171 Friedrichstr.) immediately. I have just written to him that he should, in that case, produce the parts as quickly as possible, by 25 May, if possible.—[8]

One other small matter: in choral things it is now the custom to indicate the bars with 5, 10, 15, etc., instead of letters (in order to start again anywhere at rehearsals). I don't like this custom. However, if it also seems good and practical to you, would you write to Simrock—or take the modest trouble yourself of deleting the letters and inserting the numbers.

(The *Triumphlied* would of course be omitted, if the three choruses are performed!)

I hope to hear a word very soon and to read a great deal about the happy concert on the 5th.

With best greeting,
your J. Br.

Clara Schumann had just performed the Third Violin Sonata for the first time, at a Museum concert. Now she hoped Brahms would conduct his Fourth Symphony there and bring his Trio, Op. 8, in its new version. He was not yet satisfied with the revision, but did, however, have news of an amazing new invention.

489
Johannes Brahms to Clara Schumann

Vienna, November 1889

Dear Clara,

That my D minor Sonata is strolling tenderly and dreamily beneath your fingers is a most agreeable and friendly thought to me. I have actually placed it on the music stand and accompanied you very thoughtfully and tenderly

---

[8] *Recte*: 25 June.

through the pedal-point shrubbery. Always with you at my side, and I simply know of no greater pleasure than to sit at your side or, as in this case, to stroll with you.

But first, before anything else, I must address a few words to the esteemed Museum administration which you may be good enough to pass on sometime. How dearly I would like to play my Trio there! For that, after all, would be a sign that it pleases me a little! But unfortunately that's not the case, not in the least, and since I can't have this pleasure, I must do without the other!

So I suppose we'd also better leave the 4th Symphony to the old man! He is certainly going to study it more zealously and lovingly than I, and that the musicians would be stimulated by an unfamiliar conductor is only a half-pleasure, the other half would be taken away by the thought of the old man, etc.

Have you heard that Wüllner recently performed the 4th symphony by Sch[umann] in the original instrumentation (before the Faust)? He enjoyed it greatly and is considering writing to Härtels about it. If they then plan an edition, would that suit you?

And in that case, would it also suit you if W[üllner] were to take care of this? He is a really splendid editor, as he has often proved (for example, in the big Bach edition, as well).

You really ought to listen to the change that's come over music-making in Cologne, sometime or other! W. could also have my Celebratory Epitaphs and other motets sung for you very soon, and wonderfully well, no doubt; I'm just in the process of providing them with everything here.

We live here now under the sign of the phonograph, and I had the opportunity to hear it often and in comfort. You will have read plenty about the new miracle or will have had it described for you; once again it's as though one were living a fairy-tale. Tomorrow night Dr Fellinger will have it at his home—how cosy if you could be there too—by any chance? But in the mean time, fare you very well, *bis bald* [till very soon], as they say on the Rhine; give greetings to the Fräuleins and one or two others besides.

With all love,

your Johannes.

❧ 1890 ❧

The revised version of the B major Trio appeared on one of Wüllner's concert programmes. Brahms couldn't resist inviting his old friend Grimm, who had known the
piece from the very start.

490
Johannes Brahms to Julius Otto Grimm

[Beginning of March 1890]

Dear old friend,

On March 13th I'm planning to take part in a choral concert in Cologne
and it would be quite exceptionally splendid and lovely if you and even Pine
Gur could be there. You'll hear all sorts of worthy choral music, a heap of
motets by me, and one piece that is bound to interest you.

Do you still remember something of a Trio in B major from the time of
our youth and wouldn't you be eager to hear it now that—I didn't put a wig
on it—but combed and tidied its hair a bit.

If you can make yourself free, I hope you'll come for a few days, so you
can attend rehearsals in the room and in comfort!

I look forward to it enormously, pleased as Punch.

With warm greetings to all of you,

your

J. Brahms.

Two letters provide some insight into Brahms's view of himself, at this time. The first
was written as Spengel was considering changing jobs, and asked Brahms for a reference.

491
Johannes Brahms to Julius Spengel

[January 1890]

Most esteemed Herr Spengel,

You have long been recognized, without contradiction, as the worthy
leader of a highly regarded, venerable, choral society, and by my participation [I] have often shown how highly I regard the accomplishments of you
and your Society—since I do actually take part on such occasions. I state this

here in accordance with your wish, although it seems to me neither necessary, appropriate, nor fitting that [I] should warrant and recommend in this manner.

Your sincerely devoted
J. Brahms.

Dear friend,

The enclosed scrap of paper, which, however, I request that you keep for similar occasions, provides me with a welcome opportunity for finally saying a few words in response to your letters. I wish you all sorts of good luck—but, as far as I can see, you have every reason to reflect very carefully before exchanging your present position for another. Your entire nature, your inclination and your talent seem to me well suited for this particular activity. On the other hand, I doubt that you, or I, too, would feel comfortable as proper municipal music directors, for example. We both lack the necessary qualities, and the fact that you have cause to complain about your external situation and that of your Society seems to me to constitute proof. Equally (please not to misunderstand me), the fact that for your festivals you turn to me instead of to Bülow, and [do so] instead of diligently planning how and to whatever you can attract him and the audience. If I am in Hamburg at that time, I would be happy to listen, possibly even participate—but I don't know how and what you think about this! However, I don't promise anything. Concerts never were my hobby, and I now dodge them with great energy. All kinds of things are more important to me than audiences and concerts; that I need hardly say—but as a man without a position I may say so unabashedly. And were I to continue in this vein, you would get to hear a lot that sounds good to you!

But now I just want to add that I consider myself to be a most impractical person and therefore can be readily and easily mistaken in my fantasies about you, now and later on. Do please forgive my writing so hastily about such a serious and important matter—but otherwise, there would be no end to it! I suppose you have received the 'Beneke'?[!][1]

With sincere greetings to you both,
your J. Br.

Spengel remained at his job.

The next letter was written in response to a very sombre letter and long poem by Billroth. The Swiss friend, of course, is J. V. Widmann.

---

[1] Benecke's *Geschichten und Sagen* ('Stories and Legends'), which Brahms had borrowed from Spengel to read on his trip home.

492
Johannes Brahms to Theodor Billroth

[dated March, 1890 by Billroth]

Best of friends!

Your dear and beautiful letter, so rich in content, stimulates in many ways and demands and invites quite a few responses.

It almost seduces me to let myself go and chat just as confidentially; but that might not sound as pleasant as your letter, in spite of everything.

Basically, however, you are so very nimble with word and pen and can say to others what I recite in monologue to myself.

And the manner in which I understand and perceive, also the things I take pleasure in, your letter says the same to me in spite of all its seriousness and agitation.

Too serious and agitated it may well be—but not gloomy; and gloomy contemplations are the ones we ought to guard against with care; others, and the most serious ones, we'll be able to cope with.

For today, please accept herewith the friendliest (and for me, the most convenient) response: enclosed are additional books by the Swiss friend with whom you too felt such immediate sympathy. You consider him (as I also would like to) a fortunate man—if only your (our) supposition is correct! We see and judge simply according to those particulars which our friend lets us see, neatly wrapped and sealed—by that measure, you may occasionally also consider very fortunate

your deeply devoted
J.B.

Brahms never ceased to be irritated by Simrock's practice of charging the highest prices for his music.

493
Johannes Brahms to Fritz Simrock

[Vienna, 11 December 1890]

D[ear] S[imrock],

The enclosed is the ending of the 1st movement *à 4 mains*. With that scrap of paper you can take your farewell from my music—because quite generally, it is time to stop, and also, honestly: the fact that you have the Quintet is a trick my modesty has played on me. I had planned to write really pretty things for Peters this summer. It seems that only the Quintet remains, and I didn't think I could offer that to Peters when compared to the first quintet. I had no thought of bettering myself or experiencing something wonderful, but I feel an obligation towards Peters, and my annoyance will [not] evaporate. You know that I don't complain about anything, also have every reason to be grateful—except that you don't grant me the one and only pleasure that I could derive from scribbling music. For no one can persuade me that I would not gain more enjoyment (and you more money) from my symphonies and my songs if buying them were anywhere near affordable, as are those of all my colleagues. Please do not reply—I would simply put the letter aside and wait for the next one that says—the opposite! But I wouldn't be a bit surprised if, in order to purchase the new Quintet and Trio, one had to present proof of possession of the previous one, and perhaps of 'my' latest Hungarian Trios, and possibly of the Hermione.[2]

In all other matters, however, as always utterly your

J.B.

The Second String Quintet, Op. 111 in G major, was written during the summer and performed in Vienna and Berlin that autumn. It was immediately clear that there were problems with the dynamics of the opening, the cello solo at the beginning difficult to hear, what with four upper strings playing undulating sixteenth-notes as loudly as they can, or so it seems to the cellist. The solution for the performance in Vienna was to allow the violins to play more softly all through the opening, but Brahms wrote into the part 'Only for the Rosé Quartet and at the wish of Herr Hummer! JB'. Next he wanted Joachim's advice.

494
Johannes Brahms to Joseph Joachim

[Vienna, 27 November 1890]

Dear Joachim,

As you see, I keep my word about G major better than you do—here is mine!—?—[3] Naturally, it's at your service for the 10th and any other time; but the mere performance of a 'novelty' won't by itself count as a 'Bravo' with me; that has to be stated expressly!

---

[2] An unsuccessful opera of Max Bruch (Op. 40) published by Simrock in the early 1870s, copies of which were evidently still in his warehouse.

[3] Joachim was still working on his G major Violin Concerto.

Much more important for me is every reservation you report, of whatever kind.

One thing I must specifically and urgently ask you to comment on clearly. We didn't settle the issue of the first seven measures of the piece, here. I had simply marked the four upper voices with an *f*. Now here, in my opinion, one is all too accustomed to accompanying every solo *p*.

The cellist Hummer also immediately expressed the opinion, just here, that he would have to have a *p* above him. I didn't give in, but the proper sound wasn't achieved either.

For next time (as you see), I am planning 2 experiments. A *fp—cresc— f* or the change in the figuration as is also pasted into your parts.

Would you be good enough to disregard these versions completely for the time being and hear how Hausmann fares with your *f* and your broad strokes. Then write to me if the *fp—cresc—f* will do, or if it can be otherwise improved.

Forgive me, but this trivial point was quite irksome to me.

I also ask you to take this first movement quite moderately, in the *f*, and in the *p* as though sustained (at least for the time being and until it goes very smoothly).

In case you only need the piece until the 10th I'd like to ask you to send it back to me right away, since I must be off to Pesth just then. If you want it for Hamburg or elsewhere, however, I just ask that you tell me in time, then I can plan accordingly since your parts are a 2nd copy.

And now my heartfelt wish that the piece may be somewhat to your liking; but don't be embarrassed to tell me the opposite. In that case I'll console myself with the first one, and find consolation for both of them with the Mozartian!

> Sincerely,
> your
> Johs. Br.

Joachim answered:

> ... and now for the information you requested about the beginning passage of the work. True, what one would really like is to have three cellists in one; but in the end, Hausmann could be heard very well. We tried it several different ways, but we finally came back to your original version except that from the end of the second measure on, we moderated the *forte* somewhat and made a crescendo again starting with the *fp* in parentheses. My humble suggestion is to indicate it thus:

Brahms sent Simrock his own suggestion, instructing the copyist to add a *diminuendo* at the beginning of the second measure in the four upper voices[4]—but when the work appeared in print it was with the original dynamics. Performers therefore still struggle to discover the means of keeping the cello from drowning while the upper strings play broadly—and a frequent solution is to follow Joachim's advice after all.

Three days after the Berlin performance the string parts were on their way to be printed, along with the revised Trio, Op. 8. Once again it had required trial performances to convince Brahms to publish.

495
Johannes Brahms to Fritz Simrock

[Vienna, 13 December 1890]

D[ear] S[imrock],

Today I am sending trio and quintet, parts and score, everything. To start with, would you very kindly have the quintet parts and the violin and cello parts of the trio engraved. My evening in Pest is not until the 8th or 10th of January; I can have the parts by then, can't I?

Herr Keller:[5]

Herr Keller should note carefully that in parts and score I quite often mark differently! ⌒ and ⌒ etc. With the abbreviation of the figure ♩♩ ♩· ♩· I mean that the quarter notes should have a double stem, *but not* the half-[notes]. I find that clear and correct! (If you don't abbreviate at all, you can raise the price by 10 Marks!) If the four-hand version is still there, you can mark the first movement 'Allegro energico', and the last, 'Vivace ma non troppo presto'.[6] I am a grateful recipient of critical reviews, particularly of nasty ones, that is Moszkowski, Tappert!

---

[4] *BW* xii. 37–8.

[5] Robert Keller, frequently the copyist for Brahms's music. In this instance the work was actually done by William Kupfer.

[6] In the complete edition (Breitkopf & Härtel, vol. vii) there are no examples of ⌒ , a marking which indicates an interrupted legato (as opposed to a series of short notes) played on one bow

N.B. With regard to the refurbished trio, I want to add expressly that while it's true that the old one is bad, I do not nevertheless claim that the new one is good! What you now do with the old one, whether you melt it down or print it anew is quite seriously all the same to me. Incidentally, it would also be useless to have a particular wish in that regard. I simply want to say that the old one will continue to sell poorly not because so much of it is ugly, but because so much of it is unnecessarily difficult.

Etc.

All the best, your

J. B.

Brahms's prediction was accurate. Although the first version of Op. 8 was reprinted and is still available, it is rarely played, a result at least in part of the many awkward passages in it.

The new tempo markings for the Quintet came from Joachim. Curiously, the designation *Allegro energico* was not given to the string parts in the old complete edition (B-H vol. vii), but only to the four-hand version for piano. Performers may want to consider that very suitable designation anyway.

stroke. Brahms's autograph was not used in preparing Breitkopf & Härtel's complete edition, however, and perhaps the new complete edition now under way will reveal additional textures in the music.

PART VIII

☙⚜❧

The Final Years

1891–1897

☙ Introduction ❧

Important works come from the last years of Brahms's life—the clarinet music, the late piano pieces, Op. 116–19, and the *Four Serious Songs* (*Vier ernste Gesänge*). None the less, one distinct impression left by letters of this period is that of a man managing an extensive and diverse network of friends and family. 'Outsider', lonely man, he who never laughed inwardly (as he once said to Alwin von Beckerath); if he was those things in his own mind and where it counts most, he was also a person with a very active social life who wrote a great many letters to maintain it.

But death severely diminished the circle closest to him: Hans von Bülow, Theodor Billroth, and Philipp Spitta died within the space of three months, Otto Dessoff a few years earlier. They were none of them old men. Death also took two women he especially cared for, Elizabet von Herzogenberg and Hermine Spies. And in his family, both his sister Elise, and his cousin and family mainstay in Hamburg, Christian Detmering, died in successive years (Christian succumbed to a cholera epidemic which swept Hamburg). Heaviest blow of all was the loss of Clara Schumann, even though her death was expected. Photographs of Brahms taken on the weekend of her funeral show him with a somewhat swarthy complexion, indication that the disease which killed him had already advanced far enough to cause the first sign of jaundice; but he was so overcome at her funeral that many understandably drew a connection between her death and his own, ten months later.

Brahms used the 1890s to complete a number of projects long sitting in his cupboard: a final collection of folk-songs, publication of his piano études, a collection of assorted canons for women's voices, and twelve chorale preludes, most of which had been written in previous decades. He kept up with events all over, and let his views be known to his friends when he felt justified in doing so.

⁂ 1891 ⁂

496
Johannes Brahms to Hans von Bülow

[end of January 1891]

My dear friend,

When one has done something good and right, or believes he has done so, he is surely permitted to wait serenely for what follows. You are definitely in that situation and should forbid your thoughts to fantasize quite pointlessly (about 'finding it not worth the trouble', etc.). Chr[ysander] is a curious saint, but you cannot know or imagine what's now going through his head. But whether it is for or against accepting this present—he can surely think of you and your offer only in the very best light. I see myself in both of you and could learn from you both. If I were in Chr[ysander]'s place, I'd be in dire need of the lesson that in a case like this, one should absolutely say a provisional word right away. But in your place, my fantasy would also be only too much inclined to wander about in a dusky minor chord! Finally, I must add that I'm quite delighted at the thought of Chrysander turning it down (with the most touching and cheerful thanks) because he has absolutely no further need of money! Well, that should really please you! And should that leave you without a ready plan—I already have one—then let me again join in with a discreet word.

Dear friend, I am appalled at my chit-chat and should confess instead that I had resolved not to allow myself to write really confidentially about Chr[ysander].

I find, by the way, that the first sentence of my letter really says everything necessary. Should you not be of that opinion—and still have heard nothing from Chrysander—let me have a word and I'll write to him. I can do that all the more easily and kindly since, as I said, I might well be capable of behaving the same way, after all.

Do give my warmest greetings to Kirchner. That would indeed be a good lesson for Frl. Mätzenbecherchen. Even though there are several other Hamburg ladies ready to adore him—quite exhaustively!

Be content [with this] for now, with my heartfelt greetings.

Utterly your
J. Brahms.

At issue here were 10,000 Marks von Bülow had offered Friedrich Chrysander. The money was a gift which Bülow's admirers had given him to honour his sixtieth birthday; the expectation was that Bülow would bestow it upon a worthy artistic cause. Brahms suggested that Chysander fitted the description, having just finished his edition of the complete works of Handel after a lifetime of work. Chrysander could not at first make up his mind to accept the money, and for a time did not even acknowledge Bülow's stylish presentation. Brahms's letter to Bülow was in answer to an amusing but disgusted letter from the latter.[1]

497

Johannes Brahms to Elise Grund née Brahms

[Ischl, 25 May 1891]

Dear Elise,

My best thanks for your dear letter. It tells me so very beautifully and explicitly how pleasantly you live and what comfort you enjoy; in my thoughts I was actually strolling around there, and I look forward, as I think and hope, to seeing it for myself in all its glory in the autumn.

You have finally also expressed something that has long been on my mind: that in your 'last will' you wish to exclude the children entirely and only remember a few lady friends. That's all very well and good, but it doesn't exactly please me. Does your late husband not come to mind, then, and that he would probably look upon it somewhat sadly? The relationship to a stepmother is rarely a tender one; but nevertheless I think you really ought to consider that they are his children and that he probably would have the quiet wish you might retain some sympathy for them.

Besides, we don't know whether they aren't entitled to an obligatory share. In that case, Christian and I might well encounter difficulties. I would therefore like to make a suggestion to you—but not until the next letter, and today I'll merely indicate generally what I have in mind.

It goes without saying that in the event of my death, I have taken care that your untroubled circumstances will not change. You therefore have no need of your small fortune (derived from Fritz) for your own use.

Now I think that you might just as well give as *presents* to your friends, while you are alive, whatever you had intended for them—or a part thereof—so that the children could *also* be remembered with what you eventually leave behind. I would like it very much if you would again write to me how many children there are, and where and what they may be and how much money you

---

[1] For more about this incident see *BB* vii. 289, 321–4, 327–31, and Geiringer, *Brahms*, 174–5.

have. (I don't recall these two things exactly.) I can then make my suggestion more explicit, and maybe you will also reconsider the business?

And now, continue to enjoy the summer so happily and be greeted warmly
by your
Johannes.

It is possible that Brahms intended the String Quintet in G major to be his last opus. He confided to Mandyczewski that recent attempts to write symphonies and other works had come to nought, and thought perhaps he was now too old. In this frame of mind, with Clara and Billroth ailing and with many other friends gone, he wrote his will shortly after arriving in Ischl for the summer. It was sent to Simrock, whom he asked to be his executor, and was then followed up by a laconic afterthought, later that day.

498
Johannes Brahms to Fritz Simrock

[Ischl, 20 May 1891]

D[ear] S[imrock],

When convenient, let me have a word about today's missive, and if the business is not agreeable to you, *quite simply* send it back to me.

Entirely at your convenience could you purchase *300 gulden* for me *there*, and send them here?

Yesterday I visited Billroth in St Gilgen, who is feeling better but who is returning to Vienna again this week and won't be able to thoroughly savour his Tusculum until later.[2] My best thanks for Bruch and Strauss. Don't suppose I was melancholy this morning!

All the best,
your
J. Br.

Simrock was astonished. '*He sent me his last will!*', he noted in pencil at the bottom of the letter, and replied: 'I thank you honestly and sincerely for having put this piece of paper in my hands: I don't need to say in *which* sense it is of inestimable value to me . . .'[3]

Wonderfully, the urge to create now returned.

---

[2] A Roman town near Frascati, Tusculum was a fashionable resort where Lucullus, Maecenas, and especially Cicero, had their villas. It was destroyed in medieval times. Brahms refers here to Billroth's villa in St Gilgen.

[3] Kurt Stephenson, *Johannes Brahms und Fritz Simrock: Weg einer Freundschaft* (Hamburg, 1961), 221, in a letter to Brahms dated 23 May. For the complete text of the will and the letter which accompanied it, see Kal, iv. 227 ff. The will was later altered without proper witnesses, causing almost a decade of litigation.

499
Johannes Brahms to Fritz Simrock

[Ischl, 10 August 1891]

D[ear] S[imrock],

That I found your balance sheet to be correct, I won't say; but since it is so teeming with mistakes that every day I find them somewhere else, I won't even begin to quarrel. Besides, I have other matters to write to you about and want to keep us both in a good mood. So then: the pill Peters must be swallowed sometime or other, and this summer is very favourable since Brüll, who otherwise snatches the best melodies away from me, is not here;[4] furthermore—but first I must briefly tell you about it: How often have I firmly resolved to let nothing further be printed, but never so surely, cheerfully, and energetically as when I wrote my 'last will' to you this spring. I was so happy, felt so free and secure—that the loveliest and most amusing things kept flying into my mind! I played around with a number of things during the summer and some of it will probably remain. And so I can give to Peters what I promised ages ago—and to you, as well. To begin with, I want to publish two things which I have certain thoughts about, regarding cheapness, etc. One is my famous Collection of Piano Exercises, with which you could leave me in the lurch. The other are canons, of which for the time being I will provide a collection for women's voices and which, when published in a practical and inexpensive edition by Peters may disappoint me. You don't need to enlighten me about this later on, for I have no right to expect any consideration from P. for my hobbies. What's more, P. merely has one volume of solo quartets with piano (which you have plenty of and also the best and most expensive, the *Wechsellied*[5]).

As for you, I hope to be able to stalk you with two really decent works—which, moreover, are completely new in our catalogue. But if you prefer the quartets instead of the two more substantial things, P. would probably agree to the swap.

Now I hope that basically you've always understood that I haven't behaved nicely towards P.—also all sorts of other things—furthermore, [you understand] what should be charged to both our accounts, etc. In short—

---

[4] It was at the Brüll family's suggestion that Brahms first came to Ischl. As he normally took his lunch with Brüll or his brother nearly every day, it was much to his dismay that Brüll now acquired a summer place about an hour away. See Hermine Schwarz [née Brüll], *Ignaz Brüll und sein Freundeskreis* (Vienna, 1922), 78, 90–4.

[5] Because Simrock had to buy it from Breitkopf.

etc. Are you really going to miss the Bern festival!? It tempted me greatly, only the trip, naturally, is just too far.

　　Now hike merrily up the mountain again and afterwards give my sincere greetings to yours and to the Widmanns

and don't be angry with

your

J.B.

Inspired by the silken sound of Richard Mühlfeld, the self-taught clarinettist of the Meiningen Court Orchestra, Brahms's used his new-found creativity to celebrate the instrument, honouring it with a magnificent expansion of its concert repertory. A trio and quintet came first, the 'two really decent works' mentioned here. The other works mentioned here are his 51 *Studies for Piano*, and, published that autumn by Peters, the 13 *Canons for Women's Voices*, Op. 113.[6]

　　First to know anything of his new work was Eusebius Mandyczewski, a great favourite with Brahms. Brahms sent him the Trio asking, as usual, for the opinion of a trusted friend.

500

Johannes Brahms to Eusebius Mandyczewski

[Ischl, 14 July 1891]

D[ear] fr[iend],

　　I am sending the Trio truly without any need or purpose, with the small request that you give it to Kupfer; to start with he should write out the score, then the parts, and finally the clarinet part also for viola (largely in treble clef on account of the high register). A larger request is actually the main point and my secret purpose. I should like to hear a word about it and would be delighted if you could be induced thereto—and it need not be a Hurrah! Kupfer will probably want money, would you give it to him for the time being? So then—in some anticipation

with sincere greetings,

your

J. Br.

---

[6] The other work for Peters was his Op. 112, *Six Vocal Quartets* with piano. Regarding the Canons, see his letters to Mandyczewski in *ZfM*, 4/7 (Apr. 1922), 345–8, esp. 1 July 1891, and his letter to Dr Abraham (*BW* xiv. 395), where he described them as 'innocent, small, lovable verses meant to be sung easily and happily by pretty girls'.

Mandyczewski fulfilled his commission promptly, turning the manuscript over to the copyist Kupfer, whose name means copper. 'The trio, dearest and most esteemed Doctor,' he replied, 'is being coppered. Simrock is going to silver it, but I should like to be the one to gild it.' And he proceeded to write rapturously about the music.[7]

In his usual self-deprecating way, Brahms brushed aside the enthusiastic comments and tantalized with the announcement of yet another new work.

501

Johannes Brahms to Eusebius Mandyczewski

[Ischl, 21 July 1891]

My best thanks for your kind letter. For the time being, I can all the more easily leave praise and Trio be since this one is the twin to a much greater folly, which I am now tempted to nurse into existence. And just so as not to shortchange your good nature: would you, for that purpose, buy 6 wide-format sheets with 12 systems for me and ask Kupfer to enclose them with his very next shipment. Please to send it *registered*! I was actually able to appreciate fully your splendid oddity only after looking at it for the third time![8]

With sincere greetings,
your
J. Br.

'Mandy', as his friends called him, now requested permission to arrange a private performance in Vienna, and was of course curious about the twin Brahms hinted at.

502

Johannes Brahms to Eusebius Mandyczewski

[Ischl, 24 July 1891]

I have no objections to your private concert—if afterwards, you nicely describe to me how the thing came off and how you liked it. Your letter, otherwise so sagacious, is mistaken if by chance it anticipates a 2nd trio! I am mightily tempted to go to Bern in mid-August for the celebration of the 700th anniversary of its founding! I am tremendously pleased that for it, as festive music in the cathedral, they are singing my *Fest- und Gedenksprüche*.

---

[7] Letter of 19 July 1891, *ZfM*, 4/7 (Apr. 1922), 354.

[8] Whatever the curiosity, it was no longer part of the correspondence by the time of first publication in 1933.

But then, a festive performance and parade with 1,200 participants! Those should be jolly days!

With sincere greetings from your
J. Br.

In the light of letters like this, it is difficult to understand the rationale for performing Brahms's large choral works with small forces.

Brahms announced the clarinet pieces to one more person. His letter, flirtatious and tongue-in-cheek, went to the mistress of Meiningen.

503
Johannes Brahms to Baroness Helene von Heldburg

[Ischl, 25 July 1891]

Most esteemed Baroness,

Your letter gave me uncommon pleasure. You wrote with as much lovely sincerity and warmth about Chronegk and your relationship to him as I could possibly have hoped and wished for. And so let Death come, one must take one's farewell sometime. We have a treasure for a lifetime, and a most precious possession—even though he may have disappeared from view. Perhaps he won't be replaced, but neither has he been lost.[9]

Now forgive me if I chat a bit about myself. For I wish to invite myself, most presumptuously, to Meiningen! But this time it isn't pure egoism. I take the liberty of telling you, quite confidentially, how much I have been thinking and even working for you.

It has not escaped me (just between us) how partial you are toward the Ducal K[ammermusiker] and M[usic] Dir[ector] Mühlfeld, and I have often wistfully observed how painstakingly and inadequately your eye sought him out in his orchestra seat.

Last winter, at least, I was able to place him out in front—but now—I am bringing him into My Lady's chamber,[10] he is to sit on your chair, you can turn pages for him and employ the rests I grant him for the most intimate conversation!

The rest will be of no interest to you, but for completeness sake I will add that for this purpose I have written a trio and a quintet in which he has to blow along, and which I place at your disposal—offer them for use. And by

---

[9] Ludwig Chronegk (1837–91) had just died. Under his guidance as the director, the Meiningen Theatre Company had become one of the leading companies of the time.

[10] Brahms writes *Kemenate*, the Lady's apartment in a medieval castle. The Baroness was nearsighted, hence her difficulty in spotting Mühlfeld.

the way, your M. is simply the best master of his instrument, and for these pieces I wish to consider absolutely no place other than Meiningen.

In that case I have one more wish; I should like to have a splendid cellist for it, perhaps Herr Hausmann from Berlin. Would his coming not be inconvenient for you? I believe he could easily be induced.

But now finally I commend myself to His Highness and to you with all my s[oul], with all my h[eart], with all my spirit, and beg that you forgive the chatter of

your most devoted

J. Brahms.

Clara published her cadenzas to those Mozart concertos which were in her repertory, and in preparing them was horrified to discover that she had forgotten how much of Brahms's music they contained. To atone, she planned to print his initials in the appropriate places and add 'with partial use of a Cadenza by Brahms' along with her name.

504
Johannes Brahms to Clara Schumann

Vienna, 2 October 1891

Dear Clara,

I beg you very sincerely simply to let the cadenzas go into the world with your name.

Even the smallest J.B. would only look peculiar; it really isn't worth the trouble, and I could show you many a more recent work in which there is more by me than an entire cadenza! What's more, by rights I would then have to add to my loveliest melodies: actually by Cl. Sch.!

For after all if I think of myself, nothing clever, let alone, beautiful, could occur to me! I owe more melodies to you than there are passages or suchlike that you could take from me.

And that reminds me again of how unfortunate it is that I can't hope that you might listen to your latest Adagios in Meiningen! I really do believe that the Trio and Quintet would not interfere with your usual pleasure in Meiningen, and playing the things for you merely on the piano might be a dubious pleasure.

But regarding the cadenzas, surely you'll ease your mind readily enough? With warm greetings to you and yours,

Johannes.

(In Vienna since yesterday!)

Four years after his interest was first aroused, Brahms finally had the satisfaction of seeing the original version of Schumann's Fourth Symphony in print. From out of the blue, and only five days after thanking him for his friendly encouragement with the cadenzas, Clara flew into a rage. She was unwell, and since July had been unable to enjoy music due to an ear ailment that prevented her from hearing pitches correctly; perhaps that will serve to explain her extreme irritation, for there is no other obvious reason. Brahms had expressly asked her permission to publish the symphony a few years previously, without receiving any discouragement, and her extreme reaction now took Brahms entirely by surprise. It required a letter from Joachim one month later, to smooth the way for a gentle letter from Brahms. The breech was healed for the time being, but the incident rankled for another year.[11]

505
Johannes Brahms to Clara Schumann

Vienna, 10 October 1891

Dear Clara,

I am truly distressed and sorry that the publication of the Symphony comes so unexpectedly for you, but I am reassured nevertheless that you are only speaking of the business side of the affair. And so I'll tell you first of all that it is hardly good business for anyone and cannot be good for you, either. You could have laid claim to only very, very little, if Härtels had agreed to the undertaking. Whether Wüllner is receiving an honorarium (definitely a puny one) for his very great efforts, I don't know. I have merely had rather significant expenses for copying and am particularly pleased with the beautiful double score (in which both versions can be seen side by side)—but will presumably have to purchase a copy if I wish to possess one.

It was always my express view that the work should appear in this form; you knew about it, and also—in any case, you didn't say No to it, of that I am certain. Only whether I can find proof for this, whether it occurred in writing or orally, that I don't know. If I didn't speak or write to you about it more often, and lately not at all, that is simply because, unfortunately, I absolutely cannot assume that you would be receptive to my recommendation and passion for it, or that you would be favourably disposed. That's simply the way it is. I don't want to cite evidence and names, above all, but—how dearly I should have liked to let you too thoroughly examine that beautiful double score, if you hadn't viewed it with such a doubtful expression from the start. Only after Müller's judgement were you reassured, only then were you satis-

---

[11] See commentary before Letter 474, and Letters 475 ff., Letter 489, and Litz, iii. 550 ff.

fied and considered the matter closed, as far as you were concerned. And so I don't wish to speak of it more explicitly even now, of how much I love and admire this first version and how necessary I consider its publication. But as I said, of your concurrence I am in no doubt, though it may only have been an unspoken, a non-negative one.

I hope your agitation concerns only the business side of the affair. Surely you will easily be able to forgive me for failing to consider your interests, since those interests cannot be of much weight!

Apart from that, I don't know what else to say for now and only send warmest greetings, hoping your condition will keep improving.

Utterly your

Johannes.

Unmollified, Clara answered even more disagreeably, attacking Wüllner's role in particular, and declaring herself now to be 'richer by one more sad experience'.

This was a sentence Brahms would not forget.

506

Johannes Brahms to Clara Schumann

Vienna, 16 October 1891

D[ear] Cl[ara],

The publisher of the Symphony am I, and am at the same time the only one who is responsible for it and caused it to be published.

I could not set my name to it, firstly because I don't have an orchestra at my disposal for trying out what is necessary and to provide proof for the ear itself; furthermore—because, unfortunately, I know from experience that I am not a good editor. I have tried it often enough and always with immense love and diligence but cannot award myself particularly good marks, and must concede that others are better suited for the business. That being the case, to this day I can't think of a better person than Wüllner, whom I consider one of our most competent, most learned musicians, who heads an excellent orchestra, who approached this task with the greatest of interest and, finally, who has proved himself a splendid editor (for example in some difficult volumes of the Bach edition, as well).—Actually this is all being expressed with too much consideration, for in your letter you treat me and W. not like two honest men and artists who may err in your eyes, but who, in their opinion, nevertheless pursued with seriousness and love an undertaking which is holy and dear to them, instead of—as the exact opposite of all that.

Well that is what I'd have to reply to what your letter says. What can be read between the lines, what virtually exudes from your letter, I have no wish to go into. I have suspected and sensed it for the longest time, but never feared I would have to hear it so explicitly.

It has been on my mind a great deal. But, just as today, I have always had to regard it as hopeless to try to fight against it.[12]

But your letter of today really is too sharp for a merely honest person and forbids me anything further.

In deference as ever,

your devoted

J.

❧ 1892 ❧

At the end of 1891, Elizabet von Herzogenberg died in Nice, of the heart ailment that had plagued her adult life.

507
Johannes Brahms to Heinrich von Herzogenberg

[Vienna, January 1892]

Dearest friend,

I am unable to write to you, however much my thoughts are with you. To try to express to you what possesses me so completely and deeply is a futile endeavour. And you will be sitting silently with your pain, having no words, nor requiring to hear any.

But I think of you with concern and the utmost sympathy, and know not how to refrain from enquiring.

You know how inexpressibly much I have lost in your dear wife, and can gauge accordingly with what emotion I think of you, you who were joined to her as only human beings can be.

When you are once again at all disposed to thinking of yourself and of other people, do let me know how you are, and how and where you plan to carry on with your life.

---

[12] Namely, that Clara was unfriendly to his editions of Schumann's music. See Letter 514 for his more blunt clarification of this remark.

What a comfort it would be for me if I could only sit with you in silence and press your hand and recall with you the dear, magnificent person!

Your friend

J. Brahms.

Six months later, Brahms's sister was gone.

508

Johannes Brahms to Christian Detmering

[6 June 1892]

Dear Christian,

Your telegram has just arrived. I wrote to you and to her only yesterday, and reflect involuntarily how gladly I would keep writing to her, how much I wish I had been twice as friendly to her and could keep on being so. Life is not as simple as it appears at the moment of death. With what emotions and wishes do I now think back even to my parents! Now—for the last time— you have some very disagreeable and sad chores because of us, and on my account. I have no particular wishes and anything you arrange and any way you arrange it suits me. I hope there are, as in Vienna, companies to whom one can simply turn the whole affair over. I don't really know what else might be necessary to say. You probably know that a watch was intended for you— perhaps also which one? Frl. Rostock is supposed to have another one. Furniture, clothing, and linens, as I have said before, I would like to have distributed among Fr. Rostock, the girl, and the woman attendant. I don't know how you get along with Fr. Rostock; but it would be very gratifying if you could arrange the whole thing truly with love and kindness?! Should anything at all seem desirable to you, naturally it is yours and I only ask that you let me know.

A small silver ink-well (writing set) is engraved with my name and I request that it be kept for me—likewise, as I have already asked, everything there is by way of letters, books, and pictures.

I have already asked you to be sure to deal with the maidservant and attendant very decently, and to take care of them well.

Fr. and Frl. Rostock are supposed to get money out of Fritz's estate! Where does that stand? I don't know what else remains for me to say, only that I owe you my greatest, most solemn thanks!

I send you heartfelt greetings.

Your Johannes.

Thus the silver ink-well presented to him by the Hamburg Frauenchor came back into Brahms's possession, where it was found at his death. His early letters home, which Elise had carefully kept for so many years, he burned. Who could have imagined, he remarked to a friend, that he could ever have had the patience to write such long and detailed letters!

His stepmother wrote to express sympathy that he was now the last of his immediate family.

509
Johannes Brahms to Karoline Brahms

[Ischl, 26 June 1892]

Dear Mother,

I thank you sincerely for your sympathy, now and during the long time Elise was ill. The final respite has been granted to her and was to be hoped for—life *like that* is no longer a life.

But Elise was not the last remnant of my parents and siblings! You two must take good care and pull yourselves together valiantly, so that I keep a cherished sample of each sort for a long time yet! So Fritz has to go to Wyk on [the Island of] Föhr—that's probably more and better than Flensburg. And he should feed and entertain his melancholy properly, I think that is very helpful.

That the quiet of Pinneberg is better for you, I also believe.

You write explicitly that you need no money—in that case I can depend with that much more confidence on you also writing *when* money would at sometime be agreeable to you!!?!!

Something else occurs to me: Is there this or that in Elise's estate that either of you would like to have? Do let me know; after all, everything is being given away and divided up.

Elise had noted a few wishes for me in this circumstance. I have the piece of paper in Vienna, however, and don't remember if there was something intended for you.

Don't forget to think about this.

Most of all, however, I ask that Fritz do everything possible for himself and his melancholy, remain on Föhr as long as possible and then continue to rest as much as possible.

Warmest greetings from your
Johannes.

That summer in Ischl produced the piano pieces in Opp. 116 and 117. Brahms said he wrote them because there were so many women pianists in Ischl—there were, indeed, a number of talented young women who summered in the musical and fashionable resort (Ilona Eibenschütz, among them), but he probably also had Clara in mind, whose musicianship was intact even if her pyrotechnical abilities were not. And, referring to them once as the 'Lullabies of my sorrows', the illness and death among so many of those close to him must have been very much on his mind.[1]

He offered the manuscript of the *Seven Fantasies*, Op. 116, to Hans von Bülow, who was to open the new Saal Bechstein in Berlin later in the year, with an ambitious programme including music by Brahms. In doing so he set off another touchy round between the two over-sensitive friends. Bülow was also ill, jealous that a rival pianist had already seen the manuscript during the summer, but occupied with an idea for the city of Hamburg which he was confident Brahms would contribute to: an album of pieces to coincide with the dedication of a new monument to honour the city's greatest poet, Heinrich Heine. Bülow accepted the new piano pieces enthusiastically 'with all ten fingers', and asked Brahms to dig up a few 'valses oubliées' for his album. Brahms declined, firm in his lifelong opposition to occasional music; Bülow acknowledged receipt of the manuscript with only a telegram and played no Brahms at all on his programme; and the composer fretted that his new work had been rejected. In reality, Bülow was simply too ill to learn new music, but made a copy of the pieces for himself. Although Brahms was present for the opening of the new hall (and performed in the second programme, the next day), Bülow was too sick to receive him. The pianist never recovered his health, and died in 1894 without meeting Brahms again. Contact was maintained, oddly, through third parties, especially through Bülow's wife, Marie, but no further letters passed between the two men.[2]

510

Johannes Brahms to Hans von Bülow

[Ischl, end of July 1892]

D[ear] fr[iend],

Of your composers on the 4th of October I am, unfortunately, the only one who can still write notes. And so in view of the nice things we can accomplish together, all I ask is: whether you wouldn't also like to play some new little pieces in the new hall?

---

[1] Ottilie Ebner must be added to the list of the seriously ill; and that summer, her sister and mother died. Each incident was marked by a sympathetic letter from Brahms.

[2] For a thorough account of this period see Hans-Joachim Hinrichsen, *Hans von Bülow: Die Briefe an Johannes Brahms* (Tutzing, 1994), 22 ff. See also *BB* vii. 395–404.

But perhaps you prefer to get started at a more comfortable pace and still savour September in peace. Should you be tempted, however, send word to Ischl and a trial volume will be dispatched 'for yr. kind consideration and selection', with his most sincere greetings,

by your

J. Brahms.

511

Johannes Brahms to Hans von Bülow

[Ischl, 8 August 1892]

You too, Brutus!

—I seize hold of you by one of your dagger-words: you will surely grant me that it is commendable to allow the 'valses oubliées' to remain truly forgotten.

I always hoped and believed that nothing could ever seduce me to do anything of the sort. Only this summer I have had to fight off a $^1/_2$ dozen exhibition and master albums, and how often with a more serious, better justification; and now—you too, Brutus!

Like everyone in such circumstances, you have only your own objective in view—I, on the other hand, always see only what emerges artistically, and consider only what concerns the artist; All kinds of things that you too are well aware of and have considered fully, when another interest hasn't prevented you, as now. And so I don't consider your poet the seducer even now, but only you and your wish to which, for now, I reply only with this sigh.

With regard to that poet, I must confess that at home he is very far in the rear of a cupboard and is rarely fetched out for pleasure.

The piano pieces, in a fit of panic, have fallen under the table. Since they have time, I will leave them there for now, while I send you heartfelt sighs and greetings from your

J. B.

512

Johannes Brahms to Fritz Simrock

[Vienna, 26 September 1892]

D[ear] S[imrock],

For the present, I plan to arrive there on the 3rd at 12 o'clock, and would gladly starve until 3 o'clock if I might then eat at your house. Now permit me hastily to bring up a small confidential matter. I don't know how I stand with Bülow. This summer he had the inspiration of organizing a Heine memorial on the Jungfernsteg in Hamburg! Bülow's inspirations don't lend themselves to serious discussion; NB. to start with, for that occasion, he naturally wanted to put out an album of songs. Apart from the fact that the idea is not to my liking, I have declined participation and contribution. I was therefore very pleased to be able to oblige him (as I thought) with new piano pieces. However, except for a telegram announcing their arrival, I have heard nothing from him since, neither about these pieces, nor about my refusal—which was, after all, only a provisional one.

I don't know whether you are on visiting terms with Bülow. In case you would or could pay him a visit (he is there already), you might discover what various fantasies are occupying him. I will definitely not play along; I am heartily fed up with dealing with acquaintances and friends other than in the most straightforward fashion.

With sincere greetings,

your

J. Br.

513

Johannes Brahms to Hans von Bülow

[October 1892]

D[ear] fr[iend],

The other day in Berlin, I put the piano pieces quietly into my suitcase, after considering that I couldn't very well send them to you once again, since I had no word to tell me whether they suited you and were to your liking.

Well, today I came across them and I see with astonishment and deep emotion that a copy by you was even included!

Had I only seen that in Berlin! My doubts would have become needless in the loveliest fashion; of course I would have kept your copy; but mine, which was written just for you, I would have brought back to you.

But rather: had I only been able to see you at all! I mustn't complain too much about that now, since I carried away with me as a most congenial souvenir the brief visit with your wife; and your brilliant victory on the 4th, precisely because it was so hard fought, allows you and us to look forward to the more extensive winter campaign with cheerful confidence. You won't mind, will you, if I have the piano pieces sent to you again with a detour by way of Simrock?

With my best greetings to you and your wife,
your sincerely devoted
J. Brahms.

514
Johannes Brahms to Clara Schumann

Vienna, 13 September 1892

Dear Clara,

Grant a poor outsider the pleasure of telling you today that he thinks of you with never changing veneration and that he wishes you, the person dearest to him, everything good, kind and beautiful, from the fullness of his heart. I am unfortunately an outsider to you more than any other. That I have sensed for long and painfully, only had not expected that it would be expressed so harshly. You know that I cannot accept the quite superficial reason (the printing of the Symphony). Years ago I had already sensed the very same thing, silently, but deeply—when the Schumann piano pieces, which I was the first to edit, were not included in the Complete Edition. On both occasions I could only surmise that you didn't care to see my name linked to them; with the best will, I can discover or acknowledge no other reason.

I am aware of just one fault *vis-à-vis* my friends: awkwardness in my relations. You have treated this with great forbearance for a long time. Had you only done so for a few years more.

It is hard, after 40 years of faithful service (or whatever you wish to call my relationship to you) to be nothing more than 'one more bad experience'. Well, that can be endured, I am used to loneliness and ought to be, at the thought of this great emptiness. But I can repeat to you today that you and your husband are for me the most beautiful experience of my life, and represent its greatest treasure and its noblest content.

I sense that—through my manner, not through anything else, I might have deserved the great pain of your turning away from me, but my loving and reverent contemplation of you and him will always shine brightly and warmly,

for your deeply devoted
J. B.

This bitterest of all his letters to Clara was written on her birthday. Brahms was deeply hurt that the Schumann pieces he had edited years before were not included in the Complete Schumann Edition, and still smarted from Clara's reaction to the publication of the early version of Schumann's Fourth Symphony. From his point of view, Clara was avoiding all Schumann works in which he had a special interest. Now it was Clara's turn to be taken by surprise and to reply in a conciliatory tone, expressing herself ready to do whatever Brahms advised for the Complete Edition. She ended her letter: 'So then, dear Johannes, let us strike up a more friendly tone towards each other, to which end your beautiful new piano pieces, which Ilona wrote to me about, offer the best opportunity if you want it!'

In this atmosphere of co-operation the idea for a Supplemental Volume to the Complete Schumann Edition was gradually born, the only volume for which Brahms was the named editor. In addition to the three works already under discussion,[3] he suggested several unpublished vocal pieces, as well as the *Andante and Variations for Two Pianos, Two Cellos and Horn*, Op. 46, in its original version; and it was his idea to end the entire Complete Edition with the last melody Schumann wrote, the *Theme in E flat*.[4]

515

Johannes Brahms to Clara Schumann

[Beginning of October 1892]

Dear Clara,

I thank you with all my heart for your friendly and soothing reply to my letter. I don't remember the topic of our conversation that had distressed you so deeply, but I greatly regret not having been more taciturn. Concerning the Schumann edition, I don't know whether you or I had written ambiguously.

I was talking of the G minor Presto, F minor Scherzo and possibly the subsequent Symphonic Etudes that had been published by Rieter. You 'don't recall; why *these pieces* did not appear *the way* I wanted'—what I mean is, they simply were not included at all in the Complete Edition?! To me, that's just incomprehensible, since the pieces are incontestably among the most beautiful ones (numerous, to be sure) by Schumann.

I was delighted that you enjoyed the summer so thoroughly, and with regard to future summers, that you have grown so fond of Interlaken. That

---

[3] The *Presto* and *Scherzo*, both Op. Posth., published by Rieter-Biedermann in 1866, and the five additional Symphonic Variations discovered by Brahms in Schumann's papers and published, with great reluctance on Clara's part, by Simrock in 1873.

[4] The complete Supplemental Volume includes nine works: *Andante and Variations for Two Pianos, Two Cellos and Horn*; the songs 'An Anna', 'Im Herbst', and 'Hirtenknabe' for one voice and piano; 'Sommerruh' for two voices and piano; 'Symphonic Études' for piano (addition to Op. 13); *Scherzo* for piano (addition to Op. 14); *Presto* for piano (addition to Op. 22); and Schumann's last musical utterance, *Theme in E flat major* for piano. Brahms bowed to Clara's wishes of long ago, omitting the variations Schumann composed for this theme.

being so, you're sure to be able to indulge yourself there many more times. A somewhat larger place like that does indeed have its distinct advantages.

Since you asked for them, I'm sending herewith a volume of piano pieces. I am going to Berlin on Monday, when I return (in about a week) I'll have a few more copied and will send them, so you can then send back the lot when convenient.

I don't need to ask you not to let them out of your hands,—unfortunately also, not to give them too often to your own for their enjoyment!![5]

In the little E minor piece, it's probably better if you always take the 6th eighth as indicated on the first beat, in parentheses.[6]

Of course, the peculiar appeal which is always connected with a difficulty is then lost, as here, the strong pliant curve of the hands—of *large* hands! But all the pieces put together aren't worth such a lot of words—put them aside and pick up the Rhapsodies, say, if you want to recall with pleasure the music

of your most affectionately
devoted
Johannes.

Henceforth and for the rest of their lives, the tone of their letters and their face-to-face relations were markedly smoother. It is as though a deep thorn was removed from Brahms's soul. And for the first time in years, a gentle letter from him reached Clara in time for Christmas Eve.

[5] He sent eleven pieces in all; Op. 116 and 117, and additional works either later rejected or included in Op. 118 or 119. Although Clara now suffered from a variety of ailments which affected her ability to play, the new piano pieces gave her great pleasure. See Litz, iii. 562–3.

[6] Op. 116 No. 5. Brahms was probably playing this work when Willi von Beckerath sketched the famous drawing of him at the piano. Errors in the published German text of two of Brahms's letters have caused confusion here. Litzmann's version of the passage just given has a 'C' and therefore reads: 'in the little C minor piece' ('In dem kleinen C Moll-Stück . . .'). In the published version of Op. 116, of course, there is no piece in C minor, leading to the conclusion that at least one of the original Op. 116 pieces is missing (see, e.g. McC 660). But a look at the autograph of the letter shows that Brahms wrote 'E', not 'C', and the passage should read as printed here. Furthermore, there never were more than seven pieces in Op. 116. The *manuscript* of Brahms's letter to Simrock of 20 October 1892 directs him to publish the pieces in two volumes, 'the first three and the last four together' ('die ersten drei und die letzten vier zusammen')—which is in fact the way they appeared, in November 1892. However, in *BW* xii, where the German text of this letter appears in print, another error of transcription has Brahms writing '. . . the first three and the last *two* together' [emphasis added]. Michael Struck has looked at the autographs of both letters and untangled the confusion. See his 'Revisionsbedürftig: Zur gedruckten Korrespondenz von Johannes Brahms und Clara Schumann' in *Die Musikforschung*, vol. 41, no. 3 (1988), 235–41.

516
Johannes Brahms to Clara Schumann

Vienna, 23 December 1892

It's a long time since I last celebrated Christmas with you—but never again was it as beautiful and pleasant for me as then; and this time too the best of it will be when I think back to how the tree glowed brightly, that evening, and all eyes, young and old, along with it. May this feast be—as then, a feast for you!

You will be surprised: the 'Final Volume' is still sitting here with me. I told myself for some time now, Härtels will have enough to do for the holidays, but actually and to be honest, they [*sic*] sit here only because I generally have such a hard time sending anything off to be engraved. With my things there is good reason. Here, however, I am thinking of you, whether it will truly give you pleasure, whether you may merely have acquiesced—I could wish other friends of yours had joined with you and coaxed me. The Variations are indeed a curious and irresistible work! The other day I returned home from a long dress rehearsal, and quite as a matter of course and without giving it any particular thought, I was sitting at the piano again and very intimately playing them to myself with my own two hands.

It's as if one were strolling on a beautiful soft spring day under alders, birches, and flowering trees, with a softly murmuring brook at one side. One doesn't tire of enjoying the calm air, neither warm nor cold, the gentle blue, the mild green; one doesn't consider that worry also exists, and has no wish for dark forests and steep rocks and waterfalls to intrude upon that lovely monotony.

Now, if one listened to the music with extra philistine ears, one might note with misgivings that the theme closes in the same key four times, one might call the sweet, soft harmonies all too sweetish, softish, would worry about hearing them repeated frequently in the variations. To no avail! One dives in and relishes the fair music as delicate refreshing spring air and scenery.

God Almighty, if every letter-writer today is going to detain you for so long, what about all the work on the Christmas tree! So go to it now with good cheer and once in a while think fondly of

the one sending you heartfelt greetings,
                    your
                         Johannes.

Brahms's fanciful comments about the Piano, Horn, and Cello Variations were much appreciated by Clara. As editor of the Supplemental Volume, Brahms gave further, succinct expression to his love for Schumann. Writing of the last melody, he ended his brief preface with a comment about the man himself:

> He appeals to us like a spirit bidding a friendly farewell as it wafts away, and we reflect with reverence and emotion on the splendid human being and artist.

and signed it 'Johannes Brahms, *Ischl*, July 1893'. It is his only published comment.

Another of his closest friends was ill, possessed of only a shadow of his former energy: Theodor Billroth. He was, consequently, less able to put up with Brahms's rough edges. In a letter to Hanslick, Billroth attributed Brahms's manners to deficiencies of up-bringing, and in an extraordinarily unfortunate train of events, Hanslick sent this very letter on to Brahms by mistake. Hanslick was quick to ask for it back, but the damage was done.

517
Johannes Brahms to Eduard Hanslick

[1892]

Dear friend,

You need not concern yourself in the least! I scarcely read Billroth's letter, returned it immediately to its envelope and merely shook my head softly. I should say nothing to him—ah, dear friend, with me, unfortunately, that happens automatically! That one is also taken by all friends and acquaintances for something other than what he is (or indeed, to their mind, what he pretends to be), that's an old experience for me. I know how formerly in such a case I fell silent, aghast and dejected, now for the longest time quite calmly and as a matter of course. To a good and kind soul like you that may seem hard or boorish—but I hope that so far I have not strayed too far from Goethe's words: Blest is he who, without hatred, shuts himself off from the world.—[7]

Very affectionately, your
J. Brahms.

In publishing this letter shortly after Brahms's death, Hanslick portrayed the incident as having bred no ill consequences. That was disingenuous of him. The attack on Brahms's family was deeply felt and contributed to the strains already apparent in the friendship between himself and Billroth. It was surely the underlying cause of

---

[7] From the last stanzas of *An den Mond*.

a most unpleasant evening at Billroth's house some weeks later, at which Brahms displayed his churlish side to the utmost. That sour evening was Billroth's last musical soirée, a wretched end to a long history of brilliant evenings. As pointed out elsewhere, Hanslick's failure of courage to tell Billroth what had transpired left his friend with no idea of the ill-feeling brewing in Brahms's heart—a feeling intensified by the fact that Billroth had always blamed Brahms senior for the difficult childhood of the son, and unswayed by Brahms's filial affection, had never had a kind word to say about Johann Jakob Brahms in all the years of their friendship.[8]

English musicians were still hoping to confer an honorary degree on Brahms. Although he had enjoyed reading Hanslick's 'Letters from London' (published in 1886), he refused once again to travel to Britain. Hanslick's view of English life probably explains why, and judging from Max Bruch's description of the investiture—he was honoured in Brahms's place—one can be quite certain that Brahms would have suffered through every moment of it.[9]

518
Johannes Brahms to John Peile,
Vice Chancellor and Master of Christ College, Cambridge

[23 November 1892]

Your Magnificence,
Highly esteemed Chancellor,
    Since I have taken the liberty of writing more explicitly to Herr Stanford, all that remains is for me to express to you my devoted and sincere thanks for this most highly prized distinction with which you are honouring me. Herr Stanford will doubtless inform you of my letter and you will not be delighted by its vagueness. It cannot get itself to say No, but also cannot be taken to mean Yes. Pardon this, to the extent that your kindness permits, in a person who has always been accustomed to withdraw and now naturally discovers that with the years such a habit is increasing. It is impossible to doubt my gratitude towards you, I need hardly ask for that expressly. How much, on the other hand, must I ask your indulgence for the rest!
                To Your Magnificence,
                    with great deference and esteem,
                        your most devoted
                            J. Brahms.

[8] See the thorough discussion by Otto Gottlieb-Billroth, editor of the Brahms–Billroth letters, 148 ff.

[9] Hanslick's essay is translated by Henry Pleasants in *Hanslick's Music Criticisms* (New York, 1988), 246–76. For Bruch's experience in England see Fifield, *Max Bruch*, 248 ff.

Despite feelings of melancholy and loneliness expressed in some of his letters, Brahms enjoyed his everyday life to the fullest. He relished food and friends, and his regular Sunday excursions to the Wienerwald were famous events greeted with pleasure by the men who belonged to his Viennese circle.

The Menzel mentioned here is the Berlin painter Adolf von Menzel.[10] A book of the artist's works was a present from Simrock.

519

Johannes Brahms to Fritz Simrock

[Vienna, 27 December 1892]

D[ear] S[imrock],

One could hardly make an entrance with greater effect than you with your Menzel at my house. Yesterday, in splendid winter weather, 8 of us made our customary Sunday excursion, this time to Weidling-am-Bach for lunch, to Klosterneuburg for afternoon coffee. When I came home in the evening, wonderfully refreshed but nevertheless looking forward to the peace and quiet, there was your Menzel. I discovered once again what a piano desk is good for: one covers up the keys, places the lovely picture book on the desk, and is off on a second wonderful walk. On top of that, the effect also of having just seen Kugler, hence being absolutely full of love for our hero. My very best thanks to you![11]

So you cannot even look at a picture of me without wishing a girl were in it with me! Well here you have it, you do recognize it don't you? In the background is the Hotel Imperial—from which, in this case, you would be looking out very enviously!

The English Dr[octorate] is getting to be more and more dubious! Bruch will get it in the company of Boito! Who knows how many more there will be before and between us; Rubinstein, Mascagni, Gounod, Massenet, for sure! For today then, I'll only add the warmest greetings and my especially sincere thanks!

Your

J. Br.

The composers listed here as candidates for the honorary degree were among those Brahms least respected.

---

[10] See Plate 44.

[11] Menzel provided 400 woodcut illustrations for Franz Theodor Kugler's *Geschichte Friedrichs des Grossen* (*History of Frederick the Great*). Among other attributes which gave life to his drawings was his expertise on the military uniforms of that period.

Enclosed in the letter was a snapshot of himself with the singer Alice Barbi, considered by many friends to be his last love. He sounds quite pleased with himself at having a beautiful woman on his arm once more. See Plate 39.

❧ 1893 ❧

Brahms celebrated his sixtieth birthday in Italy with Widmann and other Swiss friends, escaping from Vienna and the usual asparagus dinner served in his honour. Although he lost his money and Widmann nearly lost his life, the trip left good memories.

520
Johannes Brahms to Fritz Simrock

[Vienna, 14 May 1893]

D[ear] S[imrock],

Your last few weeks were not as enjoyable as mine. I could and would chitchat to you about them and tell of many lovely things, if not for a deluge of letters and telegrams lying here.

For Widmann, the danger of being utterly shattered was so terribly close that I feel greatly relieved he escaped with a broken leg—today as then, at the moment of the horror. My money, on the other hand, is thoroughly shattered, I have not one penny more and humbly beg for a friendly thousand!

Fortunately I had already given a goodly portion to the cashier Widmann, and so I now only owe *492 frcs.* to Hegar.

That being so, I'd like to enquire if you wouldn't let Hegar have that amount perhaps by bank draft or whatever? Let me know. If it's inconvenient for you, I'll take care of it from here. 492 Lire (I suppose that's exactly the same as Swiss francs, which he would naturally prefer!?!?)

That our journey was otherwise quite wonderful you could probably tell from my postcards. The weather was incomparable throughout. The crossing to and from Sicily so beautiful that nobody felt sick, etc. About Palermo, Girgenti, Taormina, etc., you can read elsewhere!

Finally, I hope that our wheel of fortune will turn once again! You, as usual, coming out on top, but under the wheel—as usual,

greeting you warmly, your

J. Br.

521
Johannes Brahms to Clara Schumann

[Vienna, after 10 May 1893]

Dear Clara,

Hearing good news about you was my greatest joy, when I came back home. I would gladly have written to you too of all the beauty and happiness, which I had more than enough to write about. But in Italy I don't get to writing and am actually also careful to avoid it; one can read Italian letters, so very beautifully printed![1] But now I have belatedly got into a dreadful turmoil here, and while I generally make short shrift of letters and telegrams—when Bürgermeister, City, and University send congratulations, one must doff one's hat and say thank you, you know. The Gesellschaft der Musikfreunde even had a beautiful gold medal struck which you would certainly like. I myself don't notice my 60 years, fortunately—I am, in any case, very bad at arithmetic. But on the trip I was definitely the sturdiest one and the one with the greatest perseverance, always the last to bed and the first one out. And my three companions were much younger: Widmann, Hegar, and Rob. Freund from Pesth, a most congenial and cultured young man and a piano teacher in Zurich.

Our journey could be deemed perfect in every respect. The weather consistently splendid, as were land and people. But one travels through the whole of Italy as if through a most beautiful garden which for me is very often elevated to a paradise. And then one gets off and looks a bit more closely. As we did, for example, in Naples, Girgenti, Syracuse, Taormina, Naples again, and finally, Venice (I with Freund).

But now, just to make it completely human: Right at the beginning of the journey I lost most of my money. I remarked cheerfully that it was a sacrifice to the gods and hoped it might satisfy them. Unfortunately they demanded more. On the way back from Messina to Naples, Widmann had a bad accident near the cargohold of the steamer. It was a terrible moment, he hung by just a hair (literally: by one foot in a chain loop)—else he would have been flung down and smashed to pieces, we would have had to bring his corpse back to his wife. And so we felt a sense of relief in spite of the broken leg.

6 weeks will get him through it, but naturally how fearful he will be regarding future travel, he and even more so, his wife!

But now I have to see to other letters and will only add: that the Final Volume has now been printed and is sitting here. As soon as I have done the

---

[1] Was he thinking of Felix Mendelssohn's? They were beautifully in print by mid-century.

corrections, I'll send the manuscripts back to you, I liked having them here still. I am tempted to send you the brief preamble. Will *not* do so, and therefore tell you now that it contains only what is factual and necessary, but that I restrained myself with great effort from saying all kinds of rapturous things in it (also to you). But I don't consider that appropriate there.[2]

The little Eibenschütz was here yesterday. Young Rottenberg is a pleasant, fine person, extremely musical and a very gifted conductor. Unfortunately not strong or healthy enough and of a somewhat sluggish or easy-going disposition.[3]

But now I'll just send the warmest possible greetings and beg you to be satisfied with this prattle,

as with all of your loving
Johannes.

In celebration of his birthday, a number of close friends gathered in Spitta's house on 7 May. Their greeting reached him in Vienna upon his return:

> The friends gathered at the home of the last undersigned send their dear Master, whose music has just now inspired them and whom they can reach today neither by letter or telegram, their most reverential greetings and best wishes.

It was signed among others by Joachim and the members of his quartet, by Moser (editor of the Brahms–Joachim letters), and by the Spitta family.

522

Johannes Brahms to Philipp Spitta

[June/July 1893]

D[ear] fr[iend],

Naturally, I'll gladly sign your petition. I wonder if I may as a German citizen? I think so. I have *become* a bit of a—not an Austrian, either. If my rights as the son of a citizen of Hamburg should by chance have become invalid I am, after all, still an Honorary Citizen—will that do?

And now I still want to thank you most warmly for the very kind and friendly greeting on May 7th. Every time I wanted to say so—so many others came to mind—forgive me that a coincidence had to come to my aid.

With warmest greetings to the entire assembled company from the 7th,

your
J. Brahms.

[2] See p. 700.

[3] Ilona Eibenschütz (see Biographical Sketches) and Ludwig Rottenberg (1864–1932).

The petition (for a cause unknown) came to naught, but it is interesting that Brahms was willing to put his name to something again, and notable that despite a deep affection for Austria and long residency there, he considered himself a German. Doubts about his 'German nationality' refer to the fact that he was born before the birth of the German nation, in 1871.

Soon after arriving in Ischl, Brahms sent Clara the first of the Op. 119 piano pieces, a work whose roving tonality shows Brahms to have been quite aware of contemporary musical developments.

523
Johannes Brahms to Clara Schumann [Fragment][4]

May 1893

. . . I'm tempted to copy out a small piano piece for you because I'd like to know how you get along with it. It is crawling with dissonnaces! These are deemed appropriate and can be explained—but maybe you don't like their taste, in which case I wish they were less appropriate but appetizing and to your taste. The little piece is exceptionally melancholy and to say 'to be played very slowly' isn't saying enough. Every measure and every note must sound ritard[ando], as though one wished to suck melancholy out of each and every one, with a wantonness and contentment derived from the aforementioned dissonnaces! God Almighty, this description will surely whet your appetite! . . .

To his delight and apparently genuine surprise, Clara was full of enthusiasm for the piece, encouraging Brahms to send the rest of Op. 119. They are the last piano pieces he wrote.

524
Johannes Brahms to Clara Schumann

Ischl, June 1893

Dear Clara,

It is so very tempting to be able to give you a little pleasure, and since I just happen to have a small piece here that is, if nothing else, a good fit for your fingers, I'll copy it for you most daintily. If this daintiness hampers your reading, at least you will see my good intentions. In the mean time, the empty room seduced me to write yet another piece to add to it! Don't

---

[4] The rest of the letter in *SBB* ii. 512.

torment yourself with the scrawl, which I just cannot manage to get any prettier. However: I hardly need say that this kind of thing comes absolutely for your fingers alone, and certainly mustn't get into anyone else's. And so I take my most courteous leave, with my warmest greetings to Marie as well, and walk away as

your

Johannes.[5]

Bülow's condition deteriorated steadily. According to Marie von Bülow, this letter to her moved her husband to tears.[6]

525

Johannes Brahms to Marie von Bülow

[Ischl, August 1893]

Highly esteemed and dear Baroness,

I feel a most powerful and earnest desire to hear about your dear husband. I feel it twice as strongly when I observe the warmth with which all his acquaintances and friends here think of him. And so in vain I tell myself that you have responsibilities towards many and are very much in demand. I must ask you to grant a word to me, too, and place my hope in your kindness. How much more agreeable it already is to know where one's thoughts might seek him out. And I firmly hope you may also be able to write of further agreeable prospects.

As I greet you and him right from the heart, I repeat my urgent request for news. You won't believe how gratefully each little word will be read

by your deeply and sincerely devoted

J. Brahms.

(Ischl, Upper Austria)

---

[5] Pasted to the letter is a small photo of Brahms walking, apparently stepping off the page.

[6] *BB* vii. 447.

526

Johannes Brahms to Philipp Spitta

[Vienna, 5 December 1893]

Dear, esteemed friend,

That's what I call a conservatory student, and That a professor and friend!

I cannot thank you both warmly enough and would immediately try to do so with many words if I didn't first have to use one for scolding and one for asking.

How can anyone mistreat such lovely paper so badly!

Beg and command Frl. Kätchen cordially to separate the precious sheets with care, then immediately place them in a bound book with a few others on top the way I used to, and only after that enjoyed the treasure.

But furthermore: Does Frl. K. have other letters to Hegel? And is what Schwab says in his 1846 Hölderlin edition (II, 285), still valid: 'These letters of Hölderlin (to Hegel) have not surfaced until now and may be lost.'

But you will know that better or can easily find out and act accordingly.

It will be a meagre repetition of my thanks if I have some piano pieces sent to you in the near future. But should they include 51 honest finger exercises, you should feel free to toss them into a corner or in the direction of a conservatory student.

But it is not only possible but even probable that at one time you too practised the piano fanatically. In that case, a few things about them may be of interest you. They are very ancient (compared to me) and many a time I have wanted to publish them or tear them up. It never came to the latter, only each year there were fewer of them—well, before they completely disappear in this way, I hasten to publish them all. I would really have said all kinds of things in a preface.

Now once again my very best thanks and warm greetings to the Misses at home and at the conservatory,

from your

devoted

J. Brahms.

The collector speaks! The 'precious leaves' were a letter from Hölderlin to Hegel; their donor was Käthe Schillbach, a young woman at the Berlin Academy. Brahms thanked Spitta with his newly published Op. 118 and 119, and the *51 Études* (WoO 7).

In his last years, Billroth was interested in trying to define what makes a melody beautiful or not, meaningful or bland, memorable or indifferent. He found the work absorbing: 'At the start I had all sorts of thoughts about all sorts of musical issues; now they have me,' he told Brahms. In the course of thinking through the thorny questions of physiology, perception, and culture, he came to the conclusion that the concept of melodic beauty could not be satisfactorily dealt with verbally. Brahms disagreed, and dissected a Goethe poem with great skill to show how it had been constructed and wherein lay its beauty. According to Billroth, Brahms held the view that technique and specific artistic beauty are indissolubly bound one to the other. The composer, on the other hand, was not particularly impressed with the surgeons's insights.[7]

527
Johannes Brahms to Theodor Billroth

[20 November, 1893]

'Feeling is everything.' Very good and fine for a religion exam—when spoken to a young girl! But of greater concern to us at the moment is what Goethe unrelentingly preached with word and deed, also with respect to art.

The 3 pieces you have in mind are from 1852 and 1853.[8] My best thanks for the book—Presumably I will be wanting in just too many things to enjoy it properly. But I'll have a go at it!

Affectionately, your
J. Br.

The connection between music and the visual arts interested Brahms from the beginning of his career; even during his first stay in Düsseldorf he had gone out of his way to meet painters. He made himself knowledgeable about the prints of several artists, and was something of a collector. The sculptor, painter, and engraver, Max Klinger, was in turn greatly inspired by Brahms's music, and based many of his works on it. Best known is a singular collection entitled *Brahms-Fantasy*, a cycle of forty-one drawings, etchings and lithographs based on various vocal pieces, for which the complete text and melody is included. That work appeared in 1894; Klinger was obviously in touch with Brahms before the work was published. Brahms's comments here are unusually explicit, spoken as one artist to another. They are also a reminder that *absolute music* did not necessarily mean absolute abstraction.

---

[7] See *Bil–B*, 473 ff. for this very interesting exchange of letters, excellent commentary, and excerpts from Billroth's notes.

[8] Billroth was looking for four-hand versions of Brahms's piano sonatas at this time.

528
Johannes Brahms to Max Klinger

[Vienna, 29 December 1893]

Dear, most honoured Sir,

You have given me a very singular and most profound pleasure, for which I cannot thank you sincerely enough. I also think I cannot express these my thanks without your help. Perhaps it has not occurred to you to imagine what I must feel as I contemplate your pictures. I see the music, along with the lovely words—and then quite imperceptibly your wonderful drawings carry me further; looking at them, it seems as if the music resounded into the infinite and expressed all I could have said, more clearly than the music can but nevertheless just as enigmatically and portentously. At times I could envy you, that you with your pencil can be clearer; at other times I feel pleased that I don't need to be so, but must conclude in the end that all art is the same and speaks the same language.

I experience today, in an astonishingly intensified fashion, what your first unforgettable folios allowed me to experience (for the *Feldeinsamkeit*, for the first cello sonata). I speak only of this quite particular delight and, being unqualified, am reluctant to speak of my admiration and pleasure in your creations themselves. Of the beauty of your line, the boldness, the wealth of your invention, of the noble and deeply stirring expressiveness of your figures and heads, which one cannot ponder enough. I don't wish to begin to cite particulars—but in the end request quite generally your indulgence for these scribblings, and that you simply infer from them that you have given me very happy hours through your work.

As a minor point, lastly, I make mention of your idea and your reservations regarding the 'Alte Liebe'. I believe it's better as it is now. The first word inadvertently has a very explicit ring, as here the title of the first song, which automatically resonates with the others. As a title for the whole, on the other hand, it seems too conspicuous, indeed, brazen to me.[9]

     With my heartfelt gratitude and devotion,
      J. Brahms.

---

[9] 'Alte Liebe', Op. 72 No. 1, is the first song depicted in the *Brahms-Fantasy*. For a thorough look at the *Brahms-Fantasy*, see Karin Mayer-Pasinski, *Max Klingers Brahmsphantasie* (Frankfurt am Main, 1981).

❧ 1894 ❧

Brahms was an inveterate theatre-goer. In the following letter he reviews the current scene at the Burgtheater in Vienna: an actress named Stella Hohenfels, seasonal Christmas plays, and productions of two plays by Gerhart Hauptmann, *Hannele's Journey to Heaven* and *The Thieves' Comedy*.

529
Johannes Brahms to Josef Viktor Widmann

[Vienna, 6 January 1894]

Dear friend,

You know that I have the unfortunate habit of wanting to read and see everything imaginable. As a result, my pleasure in our Hohenfels has now vanished. After having endured with difficulty her sugary-sweet smile in Hannele, it became utterly repugnant to me in a travesty of the old Christmas plays. After all, one would have to call it a travesty if your peasants were to perform Tasso, and equally so when those guileless folk plays are performed in our concert-hall with electric light effects.

If you want to recuperate from the beaver fur (which well and truly loses its head in the 5th act) and from Hannele (which would be better of without the ghastly illustrations),[1] then get yourself Max Klinger's Brahms-Fantasy. Don't you have art lovers there who would buy such a thing?

They are quite wonderful folios, and are made as if for forgetting every possible wretchedness and allowing oneself to be carried to the most sublime heights.

You wouldn't believe with what pleasure one delves into them with ever wider and deeper vision and thought.

I restrain myself from going on about it and look forward to you enthusing to me sometime soon!

Affectionate greetings to you and yours!

J. Br.

On 6 February 1894, Billroth died. Knowing of their close friendship, friends from all over wrote condolence letters to Brahms.

---

[1] *Hannele's Journey* first appeared in a special illustrated edition. The beaver is from *The Thieves' Comedy*.

530
Johannes Brahms to Josef Viktor Widmann

[Vienna, 9 February 1894]

Dear friend,

I would like to know whether your dear wife will agree to let the usual wanderlust stir within you as spring arrives? At least, whether she will allow the staunchly republican courtier perchance to think about Villa Carlotta and the Italian lakes?

As far as I know, you didn't know Billroth at all? He has actually been dying *since* his serious illness, '87. I have a letter from that year *addressed to Thun*, in which he describes his first, survived, averted death. You will have read the letter at the time.[2]

You are reading the *Rundschau* and Hanslick's memoirs, aren't you? I imagine they must be a particular joy for you; the chapter about Billroth was that man's last but assuredly wonderful pleasure. Billroth had all the qualities—great and small—for becoming popular. But I wish you could see, as I can, what it means to be loved around here. We don't know how and cannot, where we come from, you or I. We don't wear our heart on our sleeve as openly, love is not displayed as beautifully and warmly as here, particularly among the best segment of the people (but I mean: among the ordinary people, in the galleries!)

However: etc. and best greetings all around from
your
J. Br.

531
Johannes Brahms to Josef Viktor Widmann

[Vienna, 11 February 1894]

Dear friend,

Our letters have crossed, you and how many others expressing sympathy to me for the loss of my friend. But I have sensed that [loss] for years and will do so again in later years, and more forcefully. Just now, however, I felt, probably along with many of his acquaintances, a sense of deliverance.

In the last few years I was never together with Billroth without leaving quite gloomy and sad. His serious illness and his ailing heart had simply

---

[2] 12 June 1887, *Bil–B*, 416.

made an old man of him, whom he wished to conceal for days with ever larger doses of digitalis.

It's true that his extremely powerful drive for action stayed with him to the very end, but to me it was like a shadow of its former energy and joie de vivre, embarrassing and uncomfortable.

Once again I want to start up about the dear Viennese, for whom a 'handsome corpse' is usually a 'major merriment' as well. Among the entire countless mass of humanity there was not one [idly] curious, uncaring face to be seen, each one expressing only the deepest sympathy and love. In ambling through the narrow streets and in the cemetery I was quite uncommonly comforted by that.[3]

With affectionate greetings,

your

J. Br.

Billroth's last correspondence with Brahms revolved about folk-song, a relatively recent interest for the surgeon, stimulated by his study of the question of musicality, but an interest of long standing for Brahms, who had started collecting folk-songs in his teen years. While Brahms was not a field collector, nevertheless his was not a casual hobby. He compiled several large catalogues for his own use, facilitated by his personal contact with the group gathered around the folklorist Jacob Grimm. These were home-made reference works, with melody and text cross-indexed, sources noted, and variants indicated particularly if metrical. He owned most of the important published collections, including a favourite source, Christoph Friedrich Nicolai's *Ein feyner kleyner ALMANACH vol schönerr echterr liblicherr Volckslieder etc*; but above all, he had found in Schumann's library a collection he would often return to, Kretchmer-Zuccalmaglio's *German Folk-Songs With Their Original Melodies* (*Deutsche Volkslieder mit ihren Original-Weisen*).[4]

In 1894, he published his last settings of these beloved songs, *49 German Folk-Songs*, WoO 33, in seven volumes. He took enormous care over the details, guiding their publication with almost two dozen letters to Simrock. Although the age and authenticity of a song was of interest to him, the following letters—among his most caustic—demonstrate that his primary concern was the intrinsic value of the music and folk texts; in fact, he was spurred to publish this collection as a passionate

---

[3] 'A schöne Leich' (handsome corpse) and 'Haupthetz' (major merriment), typical Viennese idioms descriptive of the ceremony-rich funerals of prominent persons. Brahms walked from the funeral service to the burial (Kal, iv. 340 ff.).

[4] It is difficult to do justice to Nicolai's title in English—something like *A Fyne, Wee ALMANAC filled with Beautifull Genuine Charmingg Folcsongs etc.* It was published in 1777–8. Kretchmer-Zuccalmaglio was published in Berlin, 1838–40, in two volumes containing 699 songs. For the complete listing of Brahms's folk-song compilations and other activities, see McC 552–609, and 695–715.

protest against the Erk-Böhme *Deutscher Liederhort*, a collection of folk-songs which had just appeared.[5]

Brahms's quarrel was with the *artistic* value of the songs included in the *Liederhort*. Ludwig Erk called himself a 'collector of the folk-song in its present form (as it lives today in the voice of the People) . . .'. He preferred to include clear, unsophisticated melodies in the major mode, and generally avoided the unusual, the very old, and melodies which deviated from what he considered the norm. Böhme carried on in that tradition; Brahms apparently took great exception not only to the work, but to the man himself.

In contrast, Wilhelm Florentin von Zuccalmaglio sought out precisely the old and unusual tunes in out-of-the-way villages and backwaters. Brahms is not the only one who thought his collection contained songs of greater depth and beauty. But because in some cases Zuccalmaglio tidied up melodies, gave them a certain romantic colour and set new words to them, he has long been accused of slipping some of his own creations into his collection. Brahms was unconcerned with the charge; and ironically, modern research re-establishes the authenticity of all the famous melodies which were held to be Zuccalmaglio's own (among others the Brahms favourites, 'Verstohlen geht der Mond auf' and 'Schwesterlein').[6]

Brahms was so unusually inflamed by the Erk-Böhme publication that he not only exaggerated its failings, but went so far as to write a polemic. In the act of revising his words before sending them to Philipp Spitta, he thought better of the whole enterprise and, instead, arranged his own favourite songs for publication. Judging from the dates of the two letters to Spitta, most of the arrangements must have been ready and waiting.

532
Johannes Brahms to Philipp Spitta

[Vienna, 3 April 1894]

Dear and esteemed Sir!

Some time ago I was going to come to Berlin and would then have asked you and the Herzogenbergs for a quiet little hour in which I could recite my polemic against Böhme's *Liederhort* to you!

Motivated initially by that book, which has annoyed me outrageously, but then against him generally, even against Erk and all of these types who have a monopoly on folk-song. [*sic*]

I don't know if I cut you to the quick with this. But can you find one

---

[5] Collected by Ludwig C. Erk, enlarged and republished by Franz Magnus Böhme in 1893–4: not to be confused with another collection Böhme published in 1877, which Brahms owned.

[6] See Joseph Müller-Blattau, *Deutsche Volkslieder* (Königstein im Taunus, 1959), 188 ff.

measure of music in the whole of B[öhme] that interests you in the least, or simply affects you? With it, could you give even the slightest concept of our folk-song to anyone (let alone to one of another nationality)? Is it so necessary for science that someone (like F.) print every scrap of paper which a great man has graciously used on his worthy posterior, or that one step on and squash flat every bit of dung from the highway as Böhme does?[7]

Since I am now not coming to B[erlin], I want to ask whether I might perhaps be permitted to send you the above-mentioned 'polemic' and whether you would say a few words as to how it appears to you.

To ease your mind I'll say: that I would not put up with such a missive and such a request.

Nevertheless, you may perhaps feel differently about this. Perhaps, in the mean time, you have also put Böhme's books on your shelf, as surely being a useful reference.

That I would also have liked to do. But my copies have been read meticulously enough to demonstrate that they are certainly unsuitable for that, that not a word or note in them can be relied upon.

Well—looking forward amiably to your declining amiably, with warm greetings from your

J. Brahms.

533
Johannes Brahms to Philipp Spitta

[Vienna, 6 April 1894]

Dear fr[iend],

I was serious about the polemic. But you'll get it tomorrow, transformed into something more beautiful, I hope. For while I was busy writing furiously, these old, beloved songs of mine came to mind.

I believe that in my life I have changed my spots only rarely and but slightly; therefore I was eager to know if my old love had been all that unworthy. Joachim might remember how anno 52 in Göttingen, he couldn't help

---

[7] 'F' refers to Hoffmann von Fallersleben (1798–1874). See the next letter, as well. Brahms's scathing view (and Spitta's concurrence) contrasts sharply with that of the author of a very popular contemporary survey of German literature, who referred to Hoffmann as 'the only important modern poet to understand the old folk-song, and even to reproduce it in the most outstanding manner'. A. Vilmar, *Geschichte der deutschen National-Literatur*, 21st edn. (Marburg, 1883), 228. In the end, Brahms was anxious to stay away from a public row with Böhme. '. . . my work has nothing to do with quarrels and disputes,' he wrote to a journalist, the next summer. See Heuberger, *Erinnerungen*, 66 ff. (esp. 69–70).

but go into raptures with me over *Gunhilde* and the *Schwesterlein*. I behold them today with the selfsame eyes and feel the selfsame affection.[8]

I don't know to what extent the songs bring you something new. You definitely don't need to look for the sources. Except for a few which I brought with me from the Rhine, they are all in Nicolai and Zuccalmaglio.

In my polemic I mentioned that not a single one of the *old* songs that have been preserved appears in the *Liederhort*, and *furthermore*, not a one of the kind I present here.

(NB: The *Liederhort*, naturally, lacks an index.) Of the former [sort] I need not give an example, only to name them; regarding the *latter*, however, I feel impelled to do so—because they are definitely very little known, but particularly also because Erk, Hoffmann, but worst of all, Böhme, constantly denigrate the men to whom we owe the [songs'] preservation (or for all I care, the songs themselves).

Now, since in the naked state in which Nicolai displayed them they weren't really being seen, I decided upon the dubious attempt of dressing them up a little.

I myself never had nor have the need to enjoy them with piano! But I now feel inclined to let the quarrel be, and to present this kind of a collection as a *cheerful polemic*! I would like to ask you two things:

Do you find the words and the music to be anything like as beautiful as I do, and does my accompaniment strike you as being such that the songs might touch people's hearts? A third question: In the entire *Liederhort*, can you show me a single song that you wish to have appended to these!?

To you I don't need to say that I don't consider melodies of songs like 'Wach auf, mein Hort' to be of the same age, also absolutely unworthy of the lovely words; that I know the old melodies in Forster, etc. very well—but am nevertheless glad to be able to sing songs such as that with so healthy, lively a melody.[9] Not a folk tune? Fine, so then we have one more cherished composer and I need not be modest on his behalf as I am on mine—my own melodies to such texts I have (almost always) held back. May I ask you to be so good as to forward the songs to Frau Schumann, after kindly perusing them for the fewest possible days? I would be gladly and deeply grateful for any comment concerning the whole or any particulars—for or against—and am with warm greetings,

your

J. Brahms.

[8] No. 7 and 15 of the *49 Folk-Songs*. It was really the summer of 1853.

[9] No. 13. The song was an old favourite with him; see p. 207. Georg Forster (d. 1568) compiled a five-volume collection which Brahms owned.

Spitta was in full agreement with Brahms on the failings of the Erk-Böhme collection and had even unkinder things to say about the men who compiled them. Sadly, the great musicologist died suddenly while at his desk, the day after receiving Brahms's parcel.

Hans von Bülow had died in March, so that within three months Brahms lost three of the friends whose intellectual stimulation he most prized. Nevertheless, at least in his letters, he concentrated on his work and on the joys which were still left to him, a lifelong trait he never lost.

534
Johannes Brahms to Baroness Helene von Heldburg

[Vienna, 2 May 1894]

Most esteemed Baroness,

I must thank you for here and for there. For here, because you sent us Mühlfeld; along with his wife and clarinet, I believe he is feeling very comfortable here and, I hope, will have only kind things to tell you about us. For there—I'd like to owe you an even greater debt of gratitude than I do today. Today, because I have only your kind invitation to thank you for. If I could take a trip now, I would in fact be unable to resist. Indeed, I hardly need any special and specially beautiful opportunity for *dolce far niente*, for I engage in absolutely nothing else and my only wish is to be able to continue doing so contentedly for a good long time. There are so many wonderful things that are part of it or that I consider to be so—and that also includes the work which I should now complete and which is the first clever thing I'm publishing! (A little late, you are thinking!) But, if I were now sitting with you behind the glorious wall of spruces and roses, I would gladly tell you more about it. As it is, I'll only say that it's a collection of old and beautiful German songs and that I must remain sitting among my books to compare and tabulate texts and what not.

Mühlfeld will be most pleased when I'm be able to tell him at noon that I have commended not only myself, but also him, to His Highness and to you. Not too many hours have passed since I left him, after a very beautiful and beautifully musical gathering. The exceedingly great kindness of His Highness towards him has delighted not only him, but also very many and nice people here. But now, greet the azaleas, the fireflies, the nightingales for me—there is actually not that much difference between being there or contemplating it!? But that is what is done often and most affectionately

by your respectfully devoted

J. Brahms.

The fine and very musical company Mühlfeld joined took part in a two-week series of house concerts at the Fellingers, various Wittgensteins, and the Fabers.[10]

535
Johannes Brahms to Hermann Deiters

[Ischl, 29 June 1894]

Dear esteemed friend,

I feel the need to attach a warm greeting to what I'm sending you next. I'm afraid it's also the thanks for your last greeting, which pleased me greatly and more than you could have assumed from this. Your home in Bonn, your dear wife and everything that made it so agreeable and comfortable is as much with me as something that happened today.

Well, what I'm sending you now also concerns the Rhine, they are folk-songs that largely have their origin there.

What I'm sending is actually—what remains of an extensive polemic against Böhme, in whose books there is a remarkable amount I find fault with. These examples of mine say just one thing, however: that I am unable to take an interest in the all too philistine texts and melodies which have become customary since Erk; I present poems and melodies of a type I deem beautiful and fine and have loved and prized for the longest time.

The dispute 'genuine or not' I can easily overcome. Erk and Böhme collected in Pommeria, Mecklenburg, etc., Zuccalmaglio and others in the Rhine valleys, before the railway era. The reliance on faith—as well as trust in the arrangements, applies in equal measure to both parties. However,— etc. After all, I don't even know if this business is of any interest to you and how much sympathy you have for Erk, possibly also for Herr Böhme's diligence.

This is probably the first time that my eyes tenderly follow something that comes from me! Today this same friendly sensation definitely also applies to you and your home, and I am with best greetings,
your sincerely devoted
J. Brahms.

One of the people to receive the set of songs was Agathe von Siebold. She was still living in Göttingen, now as Frau Dr Sanitation Commissioner Schütte. Joachim, taking a water cure in the university town when the volumes reached him, looked through them with her and saw to it that she obtained the entire set. He himself seemed especially delighted by them.

[10] Kal, iii. 349 ff.

536
Johannes Brahms to Joseph Joachim

Vienna, 14 October [1894]

Cherished friend,

Your kind words about my folk-songs have given me the greatest pleasure and I thank you from my heart.

I have never before written up anything with so much love, indeed, a sense of being in love, and of course I could be in love without embarrassment—with something external to me. That is also the way I now feel about a work which bears my name: the Brahms-Fantasy of Max Klinger. I would like you to own one, in fact one coming from me; therfore permit me to have it sent to you.

In your quietest hours immerse yourself in its pages; no matter how high and wide Klinger's fantasy takes him, image, word, and sound will merge for you, and just as I, you will be delighted and touched by the beauty and the deep, serious expressiveness of the pictures.

With regard to the folk-songs, I wish you would let Frau Spitta show you my last letters to him, her treasured, unforgettable husband. It will interest you to read how I actually came to publish my old sweethearts—and what a loss the world has suffered as a consequence!

You and Göttingen also enter into it, and so I was doubly moved by your twofold reminiscence of G[öttingen]. The songs themselves arrived at Spitta's on the evening before his death!

Spitta was also surely involved in your very fine enterprise of cleansing our classics for schools—of ever so much rubbish! I was quite extraordinarily pleased about it and also hope for the badly needed effect, even though it will only become apparent softly and tentatively, at first.[11] Should you be coming to Frankfurt, particularly in the first half of the winter, do let me know. In that case I would come too, would either invite Mühlfeld along or bring a viola part with me—to two clarinet sonatas that I would like to let Frau Schumann hear. These undemanding pieces would not disturb our contentment—but it would be nice!

So then, with that lovely prospect and warm greetings,
                    your
                    Johannes.

---

[11] Urtext editions of the classics.

The piles of mail which Brahms had to deal with daily never ceased to be a burden. For a moment he thought he had the solution.

537
Johannes Brahms to Eusebius Mandyczewski

[Ischl, 27 May 1894]

D[ear] fr[iend],

You are sure to be well versed in this kind of thing through the *Tonkünstlerverein*: couldn't you have postcards made for me, as follows:

P.T. (is that sufficient?)[12]

It is impossible for me to answer all the letters which reach me. As gratefully as I receive some of them, as interesting as others may be for me—the demands on me are too many and I beg to be excused for expressing my thanks or acknowledging receipt merely in this way.

Most respectfully,   J. Br.

Does that seem at all possible or appropriate to you? If so, you could simply give it to your printer and send me about 2 dozen. (Very soon!) Unfortunately, I can only use it in the rarest instances and people will prefer to be annoyed by non-answers rather than by these! But you have no conception what a preposterous amount has already collected in these few, short days—I've let it lie there, as an experiment.

'Since the revisions will soon come to an end'[13] you might be kind enough to look up in the second part of the *Liederhort*: 'Es saß ein schneeweiß Vögelein'. I have the song long ago from Arnold,[14] and there the 5th verse goes: 'I'm *not* asleep, I'm *not* awake, I've been married for a year, now.' Böhme has, in Dutch and German, *still* asleep instead of the first *not* and I've let myself be enticed into correcting this—without considering that he is not reliable even in the simplest cases. After all, both amount to a play on words, and that being so I find mine neater and prettier. What it says is: 'I do not sleep and wake *for you*, but am married.' With *still* asleep, the joke escapes me and I bet that Böhme made the change!

It would be nice if you would agree with me once again. Now you

---

[12] *Pleno Titulo*, 'With all due titles': a courtly form of address common under the Austro-Hungarian Empire. A last remnant of its use was still observable in Vienna in the 1930s, where signs in the public toilets read: 'The P. T. Public are kindly requested to adjust their clothing before departing from the establishment' ['Das P.T. Publikum wird gebeten die Kleidung vor dem verlassen der Anstalt in Ordnung zu bringen'].

[13] Of the *49 Folk-Songs*. He is quoting his previous letter to Mandy.

[14] Friedrich Wilhelm Arnold, the publisher and folk-song collector.

too can get yourself cards made for people such as me, sending warm greeet-ings,

J. Br.

On the envelope underneath the address, in Brahms's hand, is the following musical quotation:

538
Johannes Brahms to Eusebius Mandyczewski

[Ischl, 29 May 1894]

D[ear] fr[iend],

What I had in mind is the whole business printed with full name at the bottom. Many thanks for taking care of it. I have another method against letter-writing: Candid photographs as temporary thanks. But for those I get the most rhapsodic thank-you letters!

With my best greetings, your
J. Br.

Another perpetual grumble was over the spate of arrangements of his works. In this case it was the Intermezzo, Op. 117 No. 1, arranged by Paul Klengel not only for violin and piano, viola and piano, or cello and piano, but also for full orchestra. Brahms was not generally fond of Klengel's work.[16]

---

[15] Nein, es ist nicht auszukommen mit den Leuten! ('No, there's just no getting along with those people!', the start of the *Liebeslieder Waltz*, Op. 52 No. 11).

[16] He is also the arranger of the cello and piano version of the First Violin Sonata.

539
Johannes Brahms to Fritz Simrock

[Ischl, 17 September 1894]

D[ear] S[imrock],

I plan to be in Vienna at the end of this week. Tomorrow I am going to Berchtesgaden for one day, where I may still get to see and hear Fr. Joachim.

But now tell me: Do your accursed orchestral arrangements bring in all that much money, and is this utterly inartistic lack of taste therefore so absolutely necessary?

Meanwhile I have considered assembling several piano pieces and making a kind of largish rhapsody for orchestra out of them. The bare piano piece just isn't an orchestral piece and will never become one. If it is an absolutely essential part of business, at least wait until somebody makes it of his own accord—and creates an impact with it! It's definitely not a job for a Leipzig conservatory student.

By the way, has it struck you that I have clearly said my farewell as a composer? The last of the folk-songs and the same one in my Op. 1 represents the snake that bites its tail—and thus states with pretty symbolism that the tale is finished. Even if I write something for my own amusement sometime— I'm renouncing absolutely nothing—I'll take very good care that publishers are not going to be seduced. And so I'm planning to play two sonatas with Mühlfeld in Berchtesgaden and am looking forward to it. Well, I don't suppose you want two clarinet sonatas, and should I forget my fine resolution, I am surely entitled to give them to Dr Abraham as a farewell present—after all, you have one in 7 volumes that could and will even be published in 77 arrangements!

For today my best greetings, and writing from Carlsgasse next time,

your

J. Br.

In your last letter, for which I thank you kindly, there is no address.

To Clara, too, Brahms pointed out that with his set of folk-song arrangements he had come full circle, that the very last of the series, 'Verstohlen geht der Mond auf', was quoted in the slow movement of his very first opus, the Piano Sonata in C major. But the circle wiggled open again. Two sonatas for clarinet, Op. 120, were written during the summer in Ischl. Brahms took them happily to Berchtesgaden, where he met Mühlfeld for a run-through of the new pieces.

540
Johannes Brahms to Gustav Wendt[17]

[Ischl, 17 September 1894]

Dear friend.

Your very fine essay came yesterday, and I thank you most warmly—but briefly—for I am truly hoping for a worthy, jolly ending to my summer. I leave tomorrow for a few days in Berchtesgaden, where Mühlfeld is to play splendidly for us. I shall then think of you, to whom I would gladly have granted this pleasure.

With best greetings,
your
J. Brahms

⚘ 1895 ⚘

As far as one knows and for the only time in his life, Brahms wrote no music for a year.

He was now on 'Du' terms with his publisher, having agreed to this intimacy during the few days Simrock spent in Vienna at the beginning of the year. Their change in relations came just in time for Simrock to lose a very substantial sum of Brahms's money, as, on his own initiative, he had invested 20,000 Marks for him in a venture which failed. Brahms's attitude towards money is nowhere more clearly expressed than in Letters 543–4.[1]

Far more important to Brahms, he had made contact again with his old friend Allgeyer, rejoicing in the splendid biography the photographer wrote of their mutual friend, the painter Anselm Feuerbach. While at Clara Schumann's house in Frankfurt to rehearse the clarinet sonatas, before going on to Meiningen, Brahms found Allgeyer's newly published biography in a local bookshop and promptly

---

[17] See Styra Avins, ' "A Jolly End to My Summer": Gustav Wendt and the Clarinet Sonatas', *Newsletter of the American Brahms Society*, 9/2 (Autumn 1991), 6.

[1] But he was not as utterly uninterested in how his money was banked as he sounds in some of his letters. Many of his letters to Clara from the 1860s and 1870s are evidence he paid attention to how much interest one investment or the other would pay; and his letters to Wilhelm Lindeck show that, at least for a time, he kept track of when interest payments were due. However, unlike Simrock, he made low-risk investments. By the time of this investment disaster, he had a large supply of money available at any time and was no doubt genuinely indifferent to the loss; although 20,000 Marks was a great deal of money, it was a fraction of his fortune, and its loss made no difference to his style of living. In fact, when a British admirer left him the equivalent of 30,000 Marks, a few months later, he gave the money away. See Letter 548.

bought it. Once home, he found an inscribed copy sent by the author waiting for him. That Christmas, he bought the book for many of his best friends.

541
Johannes Brahms to Julius Allgeyer

[Vienna, *c*.21 November 1894]

Dear Allgeyer,

I'm just back from a trip—above all, completely overcome by your book which I had brought with me in my suitcase; and now I find it at home, sent by you, and must thank you twice: for the splendid book itself and for the joy of owning it now from your hand.

I would have written to you in any case even without this kindness of yours, I needed to express to you with what pleasure and admiration I have read your book in quiet, beautiful hours, how I consider it worthy of the lofty name it bears in every respect, yes, how it seems to me to be so utterly infused with his quiet, beautiful, serious spirit—as if it were a part of him.[2] I cannot help thinking of his mother, and how I wish she had been granted the pleasure of holding the finished work in her hand, for I hope she was permitted to take part continuously and in detail during its creation and thus knew that your work was destined to live on with his.

But I cannot thank you warmly enough for the exceedingly rare, high artistic prize which *your Feuerbach* represents for me.

With grateful greetings,
your J. Brahms.

But writing the book was not at all as Brahms imagined. Henriette Feuerbach, no longer the appealing mother the friends admired and to whom *Nänie* was dedicated, ended her days a bitter and reclusive woman, admonishing Allgeyer to 'leave Anselm in peace in his grave', scornfully telling him to satisfy his writing urge elsewhere, and refusing him any help. Allgeyer described the shock, and what it had cost him to carry on with his biography.[3]

---

[2] '. . . als wär's ein Stück von ihm', paraphrasing the well-known German song ('als wär's ein Stück von mir'), in which a surviving soldier feels the loss of his comrade as though a part of himself were gone.

[3] In subsequent years, Allgeyer succeeded in obtaining the primary documents held by Frau Feuerbach; the second edition of the biography is in two volumes, and contains a large number of the letters the artist wrote to his mother.

542
Johannes Brahms to Julius Allgeyer

[April or May 1895]

D[ear] fr[iend],

Your friendly greeting provides me with an occasion finally to thank you for your older letter. I've often wanted to answer it with sympathy, but its content moved me too deeply so that the words got stuck and only my thoughts were with you and probably floated off elsewhere, as well.

I am used to taking relationships with friends very seriously and very simply and I know what it means and how difficult it is to maintain a relationship as close as yours with Frau Feuerbach at all, let alone unclouded. In that you did not succeed, you were not granted the great good fortune of seeing her eyes rest lovingly on your work.

However, it's simply impossible for us to reflect upon that splendid woman and her distinguished son without reminding ourselves how difficult life was for both, and how often sad for the mother. What you so gently intimate about her last years, how all too plausible and natural it seems. Time mitigates, death transfigures. When you think of her today, the cloud is no longer there. You must feel with quiet satisfaction how completely you are a part of them and now, with your work, doubly so and in the finest sense.

However—'turn ye back to life'! It was not only your card that reminded me of you and Feuerbach!

On the same day, a friend presented me with the oil sketch No. 69 in your catalogue, and from Mannheim, Dr Hecht sent a photograph of the portrait of F[euerbach] which he owns.

When I saw the precious picture in his home this winter, I couldn't help but recall how Gottfr[ied] Keller often spoke of the youthful F[euerbach], and how he had never again seen such an ideally beautiful youth.

Well, I consider that his mother, too, was an ideal woman, but that to both of them you were an ideal friend in the highest sense.

And so I close with a bright pure triad, sending my heartfelt greetings.

J. Brahms.

'That's a silly and not very pretty business, your [Berlin] Philharmonic giving three concerts here', Brahms wrote to Simrock, predicting that no good would come of their appearance in Vienna. Touring orchestras were virtually unknown then (Meiningen's was the exception), but Brahms quickly changed his opinion.

543
Johannes Brahms to Fritz Simrock

[Vienna, 5 April 1895]

D[ear] fr[iend],

I was very much mistaken. Your *Philharmoniker* did extraordinarily well here in every regard. They played superbly, and that was most enthusiastically and warmly acknowledged by the public and the critics. By far the most enjoyable and best was the second evening under Weingartner, whose healthy and fresh personality was uncommonly appealing. It began with my symphony which he conducted from memory and quite splendidly. Even after just the first movement, the whole orchestra finally had to rise in thanks. The third movement had to be repeated. The performance was quite wonderful. Yesterday, in Schönbrunn, Gutmann gave a breakfast for the gentlemen, which d'Albert, Wolff, Weingartner, and I attended as guests; it was most delightful, merry, and good.

But don't make a useless scene over the famous bankruptcy—that's what it would surely be if you were to—for my losses—ridiculous! You must know that for now I still have enough to live on, in spite of the bankruptcy. I have obviously not given the matter a moment's thought—except while writing to you! Only one thing about it could have annoyed me: if it had been my own fault, namely, if I myself had requested the purchase of those shares!

You won't misunderstand that, will you?! I would be ashamed and very annoyed if I had wanted to earn money in such a manner. If a good friend has erred, I am more sorry for him than for myself—no, only for him, for I really think about money only as long as it is under discussion.

A greeting from Hanslick has just come—from the Acropolis! I still have to thank you—for getting me the Klinger, the Kladderadatsch[4]—well, and probably also for several other things!—Best greetings all around

from your

J. Br.

Just now Hr. was here, the one who sent the variations on my *Wiegenlied*, etc. Do send them back to the poor chap thanking him kindly—unless you want to keep them, thanking him kindly! He has even enclosed the postage!

Weingartner had conducted the Second Symphony. The people entertained by the Viennese publisher Albert Gutmann, in addition to Brahms and the 'gentlemen' of

---

[4] *Kladderadatsch* was an illustrated satirical political weekly, published in Berlin. It was among Brahms's favourite reading, and he had long wanted the complete set.

the Philharmonic, were the pianist and composer Eugen d'Albert, and Hermann Wolff, who arranged the tour.

544
Johannes Brahms to Fritz Simrock

[Vienna, 13 April 1895]

D[ear] fr[iend],

I beg you urgently and order you earnestly to send nothing in wake of the bankruptcy, that would only be even more annoying. I think we can come to an arrangement. If you were to hand over the money now it would only benefit my heiress, and she can hardly be of interest to you? Acknowledge therefore in your next letter that you owe me 20 M[ill] and will pay them whenever I wish. I think that should satisfy both of us?!

This then reminds me that I have wanted to send you a new last will for the longest time (naturally!). For apart from a few legacies, I want to make the Gesellschaft der Musikfreunde here my heiress. Not for stipends and the like, but rather for absolutely unrestricted use, to free itself of debts and otherwise carry on more freely. What do you think of this generally? But you're not familiar enough with the circumstances.

Well, to enable me to write this business down, I would like to have a summary of what there is. Do you have one? Otherwise, one could simply request it from the *Reichsbank*, I suppose? In that case would you be good enough to arrange it.

That Dvořák is coming from America very soon and is not going back you will hear from the Bohemians—with whom you will then be having lots of fun there![5]

But poor Bruch! How sorry I am for him! The wife dying, what a difficult, sad episode; the sick woman, what great, serious worries! In any case, do keep me informed as to how it looks, I think with deepest compassion of him and of her, that dear woman.[6]—No package, no letter from you has come all morning long—sad but soothed, I can therefore close with best greetings to all, also to the quintet,

your

J. Br.

---

[5] Brahms had news of Dvořák through the Bohemian String Quartet, who spent time in Ischl. For his relationship to the Czech composer at this time, see Letter 546.

[6] Clara Bruch was suffering from severe asthma and migraine headaches, but although Bruch described the miserable condition of his wife in a letter to Simrock, there was no talk of her dying. I am grateful to Christopher Fifield for clearing up this point.

Brahms was at times painfully aware of Hanslick's limitations; the music critic who wrote so well and was so influential had little of the depth of the composer's musical understanding, and almost no feel for music before Mozart. But that was not the point.

545

Johannes Brahms to Clara Schumann

Ischl, 27 August 1895

Dear Clara,

I like your title-page best the way it is now.

That way, the list of individual pieces can also be omitted.

Both musical examples suit me. The E flat by itself, without the G flat ... must have been my writing error.

But that I'm taking part in the music festival, of which I enclose a flyer,—you probably find inconceivable?! I don't want to talk about it, nor am I able to. But I don't know what to do, opposing it is useless, and by staying away I hurt the feelings of a lot of good people.

On September 11th Hanslick is celebrating his 70th birthday at a friend's house in Gmunden. If you want to delight him with a greeting card, do let me have it a few days earlier.

I can't help it, I know few people to whom I feel as sincerely drawn as to him. I consider it very fine and very rare to be as simply good, well-meaning, honest, truly modest, and everything else I know him to be.

How many opportunities I've had to get to know him thus, with pleasure, indeed with emotion. That he is uncommonly competent in his field I am entitled to say, the more so since we have very different outlooks—however, I demand and expect of him nothing that's unjustifiable.

Well now, have them send you your English gold pieces and drink champagne cheerfully—every evening in Interlaken—I hope there's enough to last even longer!

Warm greetings to all three dear ones,

your

Johannes.

The gold pieces were for Clara's edition of Schumann's pieces for Pedal Piano, published by Novello in 1896 as *Studies for the Pedal Piano from Op. 56 and 58, Arranged for Pianoforte Solo by Clara Schumann*. As always, Brahms had a hand in correcting proofs and making revisions.[7] As is evident from this letter, he kept Clara well

---

[7] See *SBB*, letters 737–42.

informed of his activities. The music festival mentioned was a three-day Bach-Beethoven-Brahms orgy in Meiningen, which Brahms seems to have endured with pleasure.[8]

❧ 1896 ☙

Brahms composed very little now, but was assiduously interested in the works of other composers. His letters to Simrock often contain requests for volumes of recently published music, old and new. Of contemporary composers, he was particularly interested in the works of Dvořák, so much so that for most of Dvořák's American sojourn, Brahms corrected the proofs of the many works which flowed from him at that time. Dvořák was at a loss as to how to thank him.

> Highly honoured master and friend! How and where shall I begin, today? For five years I have not seen you—I have already been in America for two years—this summer I was in Bohemia—and did not see you! How much I would have to say to you!—But how and where to begin? I find it difficult.
>   I should have written long ago. Simrock told me that you had the great kindness to look through my things . . . and much much else tells me what an inestimable patron I have in you—and so today I can only say the simple words: thanks, sincerest thanks to you for all that you have done to me and for me![1]

Among the works Brahms proof-read was the *Te Deum*, Op. 103, and the Cello Concerto, Op. 104.

546
Johannes Brahms to Fritz Simrock

[Vienna, 27 January 1896]

D[ear] S[imrock],

The d . . . . with it!

Every time I sit down to thank you, or rather, your dear wife, very nicely and sincerely for all that kindness and loveliness in Berlin, along comes a fat Dvořák and insists on being corrected! Just pause for a moment to let me tell you that I felt so comfortable in your house that I was on the verge of going

---

[8] Delightfully described by Edward Speyer, *My Life and Friends* (London, 1937), 100–2 (partially included in Kal, iv. 406 ff.). The Brahms programme contained: The *Triumphlied*, First Symphony, Double Concerto, Clarinet Sonata in F, Clarinet Quintet, Handel Variations, and three Vocal Quartets with piano.

[1] 28 Dec. 1894. *Antonin Dvořák: Correspondence and Documents* (Prague, 1987–9), iii. 339 ff.

back there from Leipzig! Therefore, accept my 1,000 thanks and me again, very soon! Incidentally, it was very nice in Leipzig and the symphony quite exemplary, it's impossible to hear it any better.[2] But cellists can be grateful to your Dvořák for bestowing upon them such a great and skilful work. It seems to me better and also more practical than his piano and his violin concerto.

I suppose the *Te Deum* is intended for the 'Celebration of the Destruction of Vienna and Berlin by the Bohemians' and also seems to me very suitable for that.[3] Do those silly accents have to stay on the stressed syllables? One sees that often, these days. Since the music stresses the syllables, the markings obviously make no sense whatever.

Am I not getting the Bach works through you? I haven't received the last one yet (manuscripts), others I have had for a long time. I used to get them directly, but for some time now I think, by way of Berlin?

What better use can I put this empty page[4] to than to ask for a Mille, when convenient!

And so, finally, thank you for that, and so very very much for your exemplary hospitality, which did me a world of good. I hope that better news is coming from Zurich!

Herr Sommerhoff, Frau Schumann's son-in-law, had a stroke, and is very critical, it seems. Fate certainly grants the poor woman all too little peace!

Sincerely, your
Joh.

The date of this letter is important. Brahms is often 'quoted' as having commented, upon hearing Hausmann play Dvořák's cello concerto for him in his rooms in early 1897, when he was already very ill, that if only he had known that such a concerto could be composed for the cello he too would have written a concerto for it. There is no better evidence for the dubious nature of that story than this letter. He knew Dvořák's concerto intimately at a time when he was in perfect health and in full command of his faculties. Whatever prevented him, too, from bestowing a great concerto upon a flock of eager cellists, it was not for lack of knowing the instrument's capabilities.[5]

---

[2] Arthur Nikisch conducted the Fourth Symphony.

[3] *Groves*[3] calls the *Te Deum* 'joyous, uplifting', but apparently Brahms did not agree.

[4] Side four of folded writing paper.

[5] The origin of the 'quote' is Florence May (*Brahms*, ii. 663), apparently quoting Hausmann quoting Brahms. She interviewed the cellist in preparing her biography, which just goes to show how difficult it is even for the most conscientious biographer to arrive at the truth. Hausmann told a similar story to Donald Tovey.

In 1892, much to Brahms's pleasure, Simrock had finally been able to purchase the full score to Bizet's *Carmen* for him, providing 'a thoroughly special and unexpected pleasure'.[6] Now Brahms urged Simrock to publish other operas of Bizet in piano scores.

547
Johannes Brahms to Fritz Simrock

[Vienna, 4 February 1896]

D[ear] fr[iend],

I keep forgetting to ask whether you have engraved any piano reductions of Bizet other than Djamileh? Specifically, the Maid of Perth? The orchestral scores are so horrendous (typically French) that one wants to improve on them a bit with the aid of a piano reduction. And how goes it with Widmann's poem? I asked you to send one to Wendt in Carlsruhe.[7]

Excuse these pesterings of your

J. Br.

At the end of March, Clara Schumnnn had a slight stroke. She was 76. Joachim wrote to Brahms: 'The thought of losing her makes me reel, and yet one has to get used to it.' His letter included news of a bequest to Brahms by a wealthy British music lover.[8]

548
Johannes Brahms to Joseph Joachim

Vienna, 10 April 1896

Cherished friend,

Well, I don't suppose one can experience anything more beautiful or inspiring than what you now tell me.

That a man whom I don't even know, who, as far as I know, has never even addressed me by letter, should honour me in such a manner, that moves me most deeply and sincerely. I have had the inestimable good fortune of being allowed to experience and feel something similar before—how all external honours fade into insignificance by comparison!

---

[6] *BW* xii. 69.

[7] A poem celebrating the violin sonata written in Thun, Op. 100 ('Thunersonate von Johannes Brahms'). It is printed in Widmann's *Erinnerungen* (German edn. only, 175 ff.).

[8] Adolf Behrens. He left £1,000 each to Brahms, Joachim, and Bargiel, his teacher: the equivalent of 30,000 Marks for each.

Since I have no need to 'invest' the money, I'll enjoy it in the most agreeable fashion, by looking forward with pleasure to its distribution.

But the pleasure your letter gave me doesn't stop there! The canons of Haydn I possess only in my own copy; coming from you, the old edition is therefore doubly welcome.[9]

But now—I cannot consider sad what you then speak of in your letter. I have often thought that Frau Schumann might outlive all her children and me, to boot—but I never wished it for her. The thought of losing her can terrify us no longer, not even me, the lonely one, for whom there is all too little alive in the world.

And when she will have gone from us, will our faces not glow with pleasure whenever we recollect her? That wonderful woman, whom we were privileged to take delight in throughout a long life—to love and admire her, more and more.

Only thus do we mourn her.

Greetings straight from the heart.

Your
J. Br.

But Brahms was more concerned than he let on.

549
Johannes Brahms to Marie Schumann

Vienna, April 1896

Dear Fräulein Marie,

Your dear mother gave us a real fright. Fortunately, your news arrived together with other, more encouraging reports, so for the time being I ought to be reassured.

You can hardly doubt my most sincere compassion, but in that case I would also so like to show every possible consideration towards you. But it won't do, I must express to you this earnest, heartfelt plea: If you believe that the worst is to be expected, grant me a word so I can come and still see open those dear eyes which, when they close—will close so much for me!

Forgive me! I hope with all my soul that my concern may be unnecessary. However: consider how gladly I would also make the journey in vain and how joyously I would travel back if the person more precious to us than anything were preserved for us! I beg you as urgently as I can, and Ferdinand

---

[9] The *Holy Ten Commandments in Canonic Form*, in the old Härtel edition.

will surely be good enough to telegraph me briefly—I continue to hope: gentle and comforting news!

With all my heart,

your

J. Brahms.

550
Johannes Brahms to Fritz Simrock

[Vienna, 8 May 1896]

D[ear] fr[iend],

To celebrate my birthday I really must give you a little pleasure—as I did to myself on that day, by writing myself a few small songs. I am thinking of publishing them and dedicating them to—Max Klinger! From this you can see that they aren't exactly fun—on the contrary, they are damnedly serious and at the same time so impious that the police might prohibit them—if the words weren't all in the Bible! Nevertheless, they won't really be good fun for you, because there's nothing further to be done with them than to let them be sung by a basso with piano. It would be ridiculous to expect a girl or a tenor to sing them.[10] It occurs to me to send you a few poems. The one by Widmann is from '93, the others are by a woman (whose husband is a colonel in Alsace). The Fellingers made multiple copies for me.[11]

—Just now the tailor was here. You might be surprised that a man of my age is still having a new coat made for himself! I, however, was unable to pay him and I ask you to please let me have a Mille sometime!

Is the gleeful mood growing?[12]

Sincerely hoping such is the case,

your

J. Br.

The 'small songs' were the *Four Serious Songs*, Op. 121, which some consider to be Brahms's most profound and powerful, music stripped down to its essentials. Concern over the legal consequences of publicly performing such agnostic meditations was not frivolous in a society (Austria) where neglecting to raise one's hat to a

---

[10] But by the end of the year there was a version in print for alto or baritone, and another for tenor or soprano.

[11] Widmann's poem, 'Op. 118. Intermezzo E flat minor' is given in Kal, iv. 552. It deals with death, and life's strivings. The Fellingers continued to be Brahms's source for the latest in technological developments.

[12] Simrock was recovering from a bout of gout.

passing religious procession had been known to land a person in gaol. Brahms actually consulted a young solicitor, Gustav Ophüls, on this point.[13] He dedicated the songs to Max Klinger, whose father had recently died.

551
Johannes Brahms to Max Klinger

[Ischl, 28 June 1896]

Dear revered friend,

What will you say when sometime soon you receive a few little songs by me, dedicated expressly to you! But while working on them I often thought of you, and of how deeply the momentous words, heavy with meaning, might affect you. Even if you are a reader of the Bible you may well be unprepared for them, and surely so with music.

Well, in any case, with them I wanted to convey my sincere greetings to you, something I have often wanted to do since those days in Vienna—but writing paper comes to my hand with such difficulty! I think back very affectionately to your friendly family life and to your mother, for whom you are now the best comfort. Commend me to her most kindly, and be greeted most warmly

by

your

J. Brahms.

In no way was Brahms spending all of his time sunk in thoughts of death, however. Like Mozart and Beethoven, he loved puns and plays on words. The following little poem reached Mandyczewski on 15 May. Each couplet is a rhyming spoonerism, in which the initial stressed consonant of the last two words of one line are transposed in the next, and yet still produce recognizable words, if not entirely sensible doggerel; even without knowing German, one can enjoy the joke by reading the 'poem' aloud.[14]

---

[13] Gustav Ophüls, *Erinnerungen an Johannes Brahms* (Ebenhausen bei München, 1983), 26 ff. He was protected by the text's biblical provenance.

[14] 'You have hissed the mystery lessons', is the *Concise Oxford Dictionary*'s example of a spoonerism.

552
Johannes Brahms to Eusebius Mandyczewski

Am 15. Mai 1896	*On the 15th of May 1896*
Da sich am Freitag die Sonne gewendet,	Since the sun had turned on Friday,
Und so uns dreifach die Wonne gesendet	And sent us joy three times as great,
Die klar uns sehen läßt, was netter,	Which showed us clearly what is nicer,
Was schöner und besser, als naß Wetter,	Better and finer than weather wet,
Und wie sich des Glückes Blätter wenden—	And just as fortune's leaves keep turning—
So laß ich mich nimmer vom Wetter blenden!	I'll never let weather bedazzle me!
Natur beut mir am Tischl alle	Nature serves up at every table
Die Reize dar vom Ischlthale	The Ischl valley's many charms,
Und von der Wetterseite her	And wafting in from the windward side
Beruhigt sie mich heute sehr.	It greatly calms my soul today.

Five days later, Clara Schumann died. Despite Brahms's words to Joachim, he was overcome at her graveside, and was persuaded to spend the rest of that Whitsun weekend nearby in the company of his old friends, the von Beckeraths. They took him to an estate on the Rhine where a private music party was under way and the participants were all old friends and acquaintances.[15]

553
Johannes Brahms to Marie Fellinger

[Ischl, 4/5 June 1896]

Dear Frau D[okto]r,

Please forgive me that my thanks for all your kindness come so late. I sense very well how sincerely and earnestly your words are intended, and I thank you just as sincerely and earnestly. I brought the enclosed with me, with you in mind[16]—now, unfortunately, you can incorporate it in your chronicle! I never would have thought that a picture of the dear one would now be welcome to me, but that is the case and I thank you most warmly for yours.

I cannot help thinking a great deal about Marie and Eugenie and would like to stand by them in some way, advising and helping. Neither young nor healthy, the poor girls sit alone now in the big house where a full, long life has accumulated such a large and diverse collection of treasures and vanities. It is, in fact, with considerable concern that I think of them and of their

---

[15] Gustav Ophüls's *Erinnerungen* describes the weekend in detail.
[16] A cypress branch, symbol of mourning, from Clara Schumann's grave.

beautiful, but awkward, belongings, but wouldn't know at all what to say to them even if they should happen to ask.

I stayed on for a few days in the *Siebengebirge* where every year at Whitsuntide there is a gathering of a fair number of particularly precious friends at the large estate of a mutual friend. This time I was less inclined than usual to attend. Fortunately, I let myself to be taken along. How empty and desolate my mood would doubtless have been on the way home, and how beautifully did the earnest funeral solemnities now fade away in that glorious region, amid excellent company and the loveliest music! I am still ashamed and beg your husband's pardon 1,000 times for the silly business with the flowers in Hamburg. Spengel's very young daughters had committed this foolishness with their pocket money.[17]

But now do send good and ever better news soon,

to your

warmly greeting

J. Brahms.

554
Johannes Brahms to Marie and Eugenie Schumann

[Ischl], 12 June 1896

Dear Fräulein Marie and Eugenie,

I think I really ought sometime to tell you how often and with what earnest sympathy my thoughts are with you. You have true friends who are faithfully attached and wholly devoted to you—far more than you know or assume, because from the very best ones you will hear it said the least.

But I now think that the loss of your dear mother has not only brought you great sorrow, but also altered your situation, your circumstances, quite inordinately, and has possibly made them difficult in many regards. What a great, precious legacy was left to you by that rich, long life! Could it be that you are perplexed when faced with certain matters? Could it be that you are in a dilemma about this or that? (I don't really know what.)

Forgive me for saying a few muddled words to you. Their gist is simply that you have a good and serious friend in me, that I am quite independent in every respect, and that I can think of no greater pleasure than to be able to serve, advise, or help you in any way whatever—unfortunately I am

---

[17] They sent flowers from Hamburg. Dr Fellinger had to retrieve the wilted bouquets from Austrian customs.

unable to add here that I am a very practical person! Nevertheless: you know me, and I trust I'm not telling you anything unexpected with all this.

I hope Herr Sommerhoff is continuing to improve, so that your sister Elise can be your best support.

Greetings from the bottom of my heart to all three of you, your deeply and faithfully devoted

J. Brahms.

The women do not seem to have required his help to manage their affairs. Brahms's real concern was the great legacy of papers Clara had left behind, but he need not have worried. Marie was as circumspect about their private lives as Brahms himself; Clara's adult diaries, once her authorized biographer had made use of them, were destroyed, and the letters were carefully screened before being published twenty-five years later.

555
Johannes Brahms to Marie Schumann

7 July 1896

Dear Fräulein Marie,

To be sure, in regard to things which might embarrass you, I was mainly thinking of diaries, letters, and such.

Unfortunately, I know of just the one word for now: Caution! First of all, ensure that in any case (or in this one case!) these things pass with all rights from your possession to that of the next older sister, that is, Elise. I also ask that you not give anything to anyone without first having conferred with me or another friend in whom you can truly have complete trust. I can say more about this another time, I am definitely ready, however, to come to Frankfurt at any time should you have any questions or wishes.

I cannot get used to the idea that you are leaving and selling your house. But I ask you for no particulars about it, for I can imagine how carefully you have considered it. But while you still have it, do try to think about the matter very frankly and quickly. You could certainly find a good tenant for part of the house, and although you will be living more expensively than is exactly necessary, what amenities you have! On the other hand, the move, a twofold one if you change (!), as seems likely—how much trouble and expense that causes.

One more thing. When in the near future you receive a volume of 'Serious Songs', do not misunderstand that shipment. Apart from the old and cherished habit of writing your name first in such cases, the songs also concern you quite particularly.

I wrote them in the first week of May; similar texts often occupied me, I didn't think that I had to anticipate worse news of your mother—but deep inside a human being there is often something that speaks and germinates almost unbeknownst to us, and which occasionally may ring out as poetry or music. You cannot play through the songs, because the texts would affect you too deeply now. But I ask you to consider them quite literally a funeral offering to your beloved mother and to set them aside.

For your kind offer to let me have a memento, I must thank you most sincerely—but want nothing.

I suppose people do require and desire some sort of external token of their memories, the smallest would suffice for me—but I possess the most beautiful ones!

My truly heartfelt greetings to all of you.
Your wholly devoted
J. Brahms.

In addition to the Schumanns, a long list of people were designated to receive the Songs when they were published. Julius Otto Grimm was particularly shaken by them, having just lost his wife:

> My warmest thanks for sending me your Op. 121; you've given me much pleasure with it. The songs are splendid and stir powerfully—remorseless in word as in sound;—I admire in equal measure *how* and *that* you have set these texts to music.—[18]

For a long time, Hanslick had sought permission to publish the letters Schumann had written to his family while in Endenich. With Clara's death, he hoped that might now be possible.

556
Johannes Brahms to Eduard Hanslick

[Ischl, end of July 1896]

Dearest friend,

Everything you write is correct and true and concerns you, as well as me. So I'll just briefly say that an account of Robert Schumann in Endenich from your pen has always been my fondest wish. I had, as you, the consent of

---

[18] *BW* iv. 157–8.

Clara. Then N.N. came in between and her change of mind. It hurt me more deeply than you—but on your account, something to which I quietly tried to reconcile myself, as to many similar matters.

Confidential relationships with women are difficult, the more serious and confidential, the more difficult. In this case, one must definitely make allowances for the fact that Frau Schumann didn't see her husband at that time and it is understandable that she didn't like to hear about the patient. Now Maria is in possession of the entire written estate and free to decide what to do with it. Again I ask you to consider how difficult her position is, or that of the three sisters—with regard to such possessions!

I don't believe that they will do anything without first asking my advice; whether they will follow my advice, I don't know. In any case, I would like to present the matter to Marie and to ask her to let us have the remaining material (concerning Endenich), and first of all, kindly to agree that you may use everything you now have in hand.

Now, it is my earnest wish that you not rush the *publication* of your work. It is possible, after all, that we will obtain *everything* pertaining to it, but in any case: I am the only one who had frequent contact with Schumann at that time, and you are the only one to whom I would want to entrust my recollections rather than to my own pen. Nothing remarkable will come out anyway, but—shouldn't we devote a few quiet hours to it?

In true friendship,

your
J. Brahms.

By the end of the summer, Brahms's own fatal illness was apparent to all. No one gave him an honest prognosis about his disease; it seems quite clear that he did not want one. Widmann, among the last of his closest friends, was also ill.

557
Johannes Brahms to Josef Viktor Widmann

[Vienna, 28 October 1896]

Dear friend,

I only wish I had really nice and consoling things to tell you in response to your news, which occupies and saddens me quite inordinately.

The best consolation I read in your letter itself: and that is the wonderful, indestructible freshness of your spirit, your joy in all things beautiful and the delight in your own creativity.

What you are now announcing with such comforting satisfaction will be received and examined with utmost affection.[19] Since otherwise your letter contains much that is not pleasant, for today allow me to respond only to the pleasant, the engagement, by sending my warmest greetings and good wishes.

My indisposition need not worry you in the slightest. It is a quite commonplace jaundice, which unfortunately has taken a notion not to leave me. It has no significance beyond that, however, as is asserted following the most thorough examinations of every kind. Incidentally, I have not had one day of pain or anything—nor lost my appetite for even *one* meal—which, th[ank G[od], I may gratify particularly now just as I please.

But I like to think of how content you must be feeling at home in the evening; there I would happily join you for a chat sometime, and the very best greetings are being sent there by

your

J. Brahms.

Brahms was still in touch with the family of the teacher who had guided his earliest musical training. Cossel's daughter Marie sent Brahms a photo of her two young children, inscribed 'to their dear Uncle Johannes | for Christmas 1896 | Vincent and Marie | Otto Cossel's grandchildren'.

558
Johannes Brahms to Marie Janssen née Cossel [fragment[20]]

[Vienna, 28 December 1896]

Last time (after Freiburg) I missed following up on your letter, and so I want at least to send a small token of my thanks with the enclosed! The lovely picture of your children has given me great pleasure and shall be a fond memento for me of your dear, unforgettable father, whose memory is one of holiest and most precious of my life.

Regarding my health you may set your mind at rest, I only suffer from a commonplace jaundice, which, however, is positively reluctant to leave me, and has its very uncomfortable aspects.

---

[19] Probably the forthcoming publication of his latest poem, the *Maikäferkomödie* (The June-bug or May-bug Comedy, depending on which side of the Atlantic one inhabits) which Brahms liked so much he presented copies to his friends for Christmas. Resonating with the *Four Serious Songs*, it too finds common ground between animals and humans as they suffer in death. Widmann had a fine feeling for animals, and pioneered in working for their protection in Switzerland.
[20] The upper portion of the letter is missing.

With warmest greetings and best wishes for your well-being,
                           your devoted
                           Joh. Brahms.

Friends sent him gifts from all over: gelée from Clara Simrock in Berlin by express post; wine from his Rhineland friends; and from the Duke of Meiningen, a shipment of the best tobacco.

559
Johannes Brahms to Georg II

[Vienna, after Christmas 1896]

Your Highness,
Most Gracious Duke and Lord.

It is a fine, gentle, and powerful force that compels me to take pen in hand at last. I ought to be ashamed that this is necessary, but I am, in fact, delighted by it—so secure am I in my conviction of how gladly and often I would have written.[21]

I am writing this while enjoying the first cigarette and in doing so I can't help but think that for the serious person and smoker, tobacco is no ordinary present! Right up to the very last one, I shall take none of the precious, majestic cigarettes into my hand without at the same time remembering the kind hand which offers it to me and seeing a friendly pair of eyes smiling about it. And so I thank Your Highness with my whole heart for this exceedingly welcome proof of your continued kind sentiments.

Of Your Highness and the revered Baroness I hear, praise God, only good and welcome news. Of myself and my small affliction I have little wish to speak. I can report no better news. The physicians, on the other hand, who have examined everything in and on me repeatedly and thoroughly, reassure me absolutely: it is nothing but an commonplace middle-class jaundice. Unfortunately it does not want to leave me and so I need patience which, where my body is concerned, I am not accustomed to!

With a repetition of affectionately devoted thanks and the request that you commend me most kindly to the gracious Baroness, I am,
                           most devoted to Your Highness,
                           Joh. Brahms.

---

[21] i.e. he is sure he would have written eventually, even if the Duke had not sent him the tobacco.

৯১ 1897 ৯১

Although Brahms's appearance was now very altered and his illness very grave, at the beginning of the year he was still able to accept invitations to dine with his best friends, attend concerts (the last one on 13 March), and to interest himself in musical matters.

560
Johannes Brahms to Hermann Deiters

[Vienna, 5 January 1897]

Most esteemed, dear friend,

I had actually intended to ask you to allow me to keep my opinion of your Schubert score to myself. You and your Music Director have become so very used to the idea of a special Koblenz symphony by Schubert that it is really cruel to wish to awaken you from this dream. You view the score with such tender, worshipful love—as, say, a father the work of his son; under these circumstances I neither insist on nor expect a stern nor a merely just verdict, but my own I then prefer to keep to myself. But this time I will not, must not, be that delicate, and I say right out that according to my firm conviction, not one page, not one bar of the score can be by Schubert. No hint of the work's poetry has been retained in the arrangement, everything coarsened and misunderstood; nor could a musician of the last rank (of that time) write such a score—that honour you may leave to a Coblenz jurist!

Do I have to beg pardon for expressing my opinion so openly and tersely? I have never been so convinced that it is absolutely the correct one.—I have read through the score from the first to the last bar with the same impression, so indignant and repulsed that I am reluctant to cite particulars.

Finally, if you are not angry, put up with with my sincerest greetings,
with which I remain,
your most devoted
J. Brahms.

Under discussion was a version of the great C major Schubert String Quintet with two cellos, music which Brahms knew intimately. A jurist in Koblenz had found an orchestral score which both Deiters and a conductor friend believed to be the original version of the quintet, and the quintet therefore an arrangement of the 'symphony'.

Freifrau von Heldberg and Simrock were in close touch over Brahms's health, arranging how best to visit him in Vienna without arousing his suspicions as to the seriousness of his condition; to the friends, it was a foregone conclusion that death was near. The Baroness sent him slipper-socks knitted by children in the orphanage she sponsored, and with them a ready-to-mail postcard, so that without bothering to write a letter, he could tell her if more socks were wanted.

561
Johannes Brahms to Baroness Helene von Heldberg

[Vienna, 21 February 1897]

Most esteemed friend,

As with everything you do, the postcard enclosed with your package was a model of the most gracious kindness. But it is inadequate for expressing my admiration and my thanks. I also have to tell you how it all happened.

I was sitting comfortably at the supper table and, as usual, had slipped out of the endlessly annoying slippers, but, as usual, without being truly satisfied with what remained.[1] Just then came the last post [of the day]. With love I examined the work of your wards, and with gratitude I put them on. Eureka! That's exactly what I had always missed! Warmer than any shoe and yet one doesn't feel them; delightful, masterful, ideal! Have a thousand thanks, and I would be glad to thank again for a repeat. But I hope that by then the beginning of spring will put an end to it all!

I can report nothing better about myself, but [I] don't forget that compared to others, I have no reason to complain. Only patience is needed, and that is hard for one who is not used to paying attention to his body.

May everything go entirely according to your wishes, and do commend me to H[is] H[ighness] the Duke and to the esteemed Princess, entirely according to my wishes.

—The new pen is now ready but it merely says Addio and once more, the best thanks

of your deeply devoted
J. Brahms.

He must have cut a new quill for the last sentence. The appearance of the handwriting and the many corrections are an indication of the effort it cost Brahms to write this letter.[2]

[1] i.e. with the result.
[2] The autograph is described by Renata Hofmann, editor of the recent complete edition of this correspondence, *BW* xvii. 150.

In a letter written on the same day, Brahms responded to Joachim's request that he help put together the programme of an all-Brahms evening of chamber music at the forthcoming Beethoven Festival in Bonn. Joachim was Honorary President of the Beethoven House Society there (hence Brahms's quip in his reply, probably alluding to the many houses Beethoven inhabited in Vienna). The festival was held every three years, and this time, for the first time, would include music other than by Beethoven. Joachim wrote of the 'embarrassment of riches' Brahms had composed, and listed ten possible pieces for the concert.

562
Johannes Brahms to Joseph Joachim

[Vienna,] 21 February 1897

Esteemed, dear friend,

I wish I could participate in your festival with more than my thoughts and by making up programmes. But even the latter needs a greater appetite for life and writing than my present tired-and-listlessness permits. For you know how one might then suggest a different programme every day with equal fervour. The G major Quintet still rings most beautifully in my ear—add to that C minor Trio, Clarinet Quintet or one of your other suggestions—and the next time a couple of entirely different ones![3]

I am definitely not any better; that makes me irritable and despondent. But when I feel like complaining, I need merely look around in my closest circle and no longer have any grounds. And so I think with deepest sympathy of Bargiel and Radecke there, and beg you to give them my best greetings. What difficult times they and theirs have to go through—with a little patience, I at least can hope to make it.[4]

So it's not yet: Honorary President of the United Beethoven Houses?! But looking forward to it the next time,

with his best greetings,

is your

J. Br.

[3] On tour in Vienna, Joachim's quartet had performed the G major String Quintet. He told a friend, 'I have never heard him [Brahms] express his gratitude so from the heart as after hearing his G major Quintet: a sense of satisfaction with his creation, almost' (Moser, *Joseph Joachim*[1], 298).

[4] Robert Radecke (1830–1911), a well-known choral conductor, recovered, but Bargiel died a few days after this letter.

563
Johannes Brahms to Joseph Joachim

[Vienna, 24 March 1897]

Dear Joachim,

To you, to the revered Menzel, and to all who so amiably and kindly signed the greeting, far too flattering for me, my heartfelt thanks!

But I cannot reply; I am doing more and more miserably; each word, spoken or written, is torture for me.

Since we saw each other here I've not gone out one evening—not even taken one step on foot.

But believe my joy and my thanks and transmit to all the warmest thoughts

from your

J. Brahms

To Karoline Brahms he said nothing regarding the severity of his illness, but sent her 2,000 Marks at Christmas rather than the ususal 1,000. The last letter of his life is a postcard he wrote to her in pencil, a few days before his death.

564
Johannes Brahms to Karoline Brahms

[Vienna, 29 March 1897]

Dear Mother,

For the sake of a change I have lain down for a while and writing is therefore uncomfortable. Apart from that have no fear, nothing has changed and as usual, all I need is patience.

With all my heart, your Johannes.

Additional Notes

p. 10 Review of Brahms's concert of 14 April 1849, at a soirée presented at the Jenisches Haus, in Hamburg. It was the second of two concerts he gave at the age of 15. Quoted in Thalmann, *Untersuchungen zum Frühwerk von Johannes Brahms*, 100–1, n. 193.

Concert of the Pianist J. Brahms

It gave us the keenest pleasure, at the concert presented on Saturday the 14th by the 15-year-old J. Brahms, a native of Hamburg, to make the acquaintance of this youthful concert artist, a young pianist as modest in his demeanour as he is talented, and one who undoubtedly has a most promising future before him.

It goes without saying that in assessing the début of a budding Apostle of Art, one cannot use the same standards as for a seasoned artist. But that aside, the performance provided evidence not only of remarkable technical skill attained in the course of sound schooling, but especially of an unusual aesthetic conception not often found at this age, one which, while still lacking critical maturity, can be recognized irrefutably by its outstanding talent. This was particularly evident in the presentation of Beethoven's C major Sonata [Op. 53]. His execution is light and relaxed, his attack uncommonly clean, and even when wielding its greatest power, never lapsing into that intolerable hammering of the piano that has become the custom of so many of today's virtuosos. Thalberg's *Variations on a Theme by Mozart* was performed with all of its innate elegance, and Ch. Mayer's well-known *Air Italien*, which the soloist also performed, presumably in order to satisfy the demand for dazzling technique, was taken at a courageous tempo and, to good effect, a little faster than usual, in disregard of the continuous tremolo which in any case puts such demands on the player. The intricate passage of the left hand, which Ch. Mayer himself did not always like to perform, was brought off with conspicuous pluck.

The artist went on to play a *Pieçe* of his own composition. Should the young composer continue forth stoutly along the path which he has evidently entered upon, he will achieve something of significance. Nature appears to have endowed him in full measure with the glorious gifts of free creation, ideas, and expression, and it will only depend on him and on his diligence whether one day he will indeed put them on display in the radiant garb of beauty, and with absolute outward clarity.

We understand that to date, the young artist owes his musical development to the local music teacher, Mr E. Marxsen. The concert, which was very well attended, was most valiantly supported by several local musicians, in particular by Mad[ame] Cornet, who performed several songs with her usual verve, and by the tenor Mr Wachtel, whose excellent voice here too was fully accorded its due.

[*Note*: Charles Mayer, 1799–1862. 'His pieces reach the astonishing number of 900'. Groves[2]].

p. 33   Clara's tour of northern Germany, in February and March of 1840, had taken place under the most trying of circumstances. Her father had been actively circulating a 'Declaration' to musical circles in Leipzig, Berlin, Hamburg, and Bremen in an attempt to smear her reputation and doom her attempt to give successful concerts on her own. Among the musicians who had stood by her so that 'from this time forth she was bound to Hamburg by indissoluble ties' were Otten and Avé-Lallement. For details of this particularly bizarre episode in Clara's life and and to the many references to Hamburg's leading musicians, most of them still active thirteen years later, see Bertholt Litzmann, *Clara Schumann, ein Künstlerleben* (Leipzig, 1920), i. 393 ff. (henceforth Litz). In English translation, *Clara Schumann, an Artist's Life*, trans. and abridged Grace E. Hadow (London, 1913, repr. New York, 1972), i. 272–82. Further citations will be to the German original only.

p. 127   Schumann's collective symptoms were classic indications of tertiary cerebral neurosyphilis. Although the specific infectious agent was only identified in 1905, the disease has been recorded and observed since 1494, and accurate clinical accounts of its course have existed in the medical literature from the early sixteenth century onwards. In Schumann's case, according to the medical records Richarz kept during Schumann's stay in Endenich, his patient informed him *explicitly* that he had been treated for syphilis with mercury, in 1831, 'and had been cured' (Schumann's words).

In 1994, after having been intentionally kept in private hands and out of view until then, Schumann's medical records were finally placed in the public domain. Substantial portions are excerpted in Aribert Reimann and Franz Hermann Franken, MD, *Robert Schumanns letzte Lebensjahre: Protokoll einer Krankheit* (Archiv der Akademie der Künste, Berlin: 1994). The recorded symptoms are consistent with the degeneration of the brain one expects in stage III cerebral neurosyphilis: severe and fluctuating personality changes, loss of speech, violent behaviour (for the first time making sense of the apparently cruel injunction against Clara's visits), delusions, seizures, unequal pupillary enlargement (present in 90 per cent of late-stage patients); and failure of his pupils to dilate in the dark (Argyll Robinson pupil).

Richarz chose not to reveal the facts of Schumann's illness—he could do so because the clinical manifestation of the disease may mimic a very wide range of psychoses, and the full facts were recorded only in his hand—and he took his records with him when he retired from Endenich. In so doing he set off a century and a half of speculation while biographers and psychiatrists argue over whether Schumann's problems were psychiatric or organic.

From Brahms's letter to Joachim, it is obvious that he had no idea of the true nature of Schumann's final illness then, and nothing suggests that he ever learned.

p. 173 In 1989 and again in 1991, I interviewed Agathe von Siebold's great-grand-
daughter, who was brought up in the house of her great-aunt Antonie
Schütte in Göttingen (to whom Emil Michelmann's book about Agathe von
Siebold is dedicated). She remembers that there was a box with papers supposedly in Brahms's hand, primarily song manuscripts, she thought. The
papers have since disappeared, under circumstances not quite clear to anyone of the family to whom I spoke. Although Göttingen was spared serious
war damage during the Second World War, there was turmoil and house-
moving all the same. Add that her great-aunt's memory became somewhat
confused, and that some members of the family claim a musicologist or historian came after the war, 'borrowed' the papers to make copies, and then
disappeared, and the makings of a very murky story are in place. It seems
impossible by now to determine whether there ever were letters to Agathe
alone. The extant letters to Grimm would lead me to think not (but see Letter
103, in which Brahms encloses a separate letter to her in the envelope to the
Grimms). What does remain from this period is the engagement ring
Brahms gave to Agathe, which is still in the possession of her great-grand-
daughter. It is a modest little gold ring set with a small stone, just about right
for the amount of money Brahms would have had at his disposal for such an
item, and fitting Michelmann's description. (Emil Michelmann, *Agathe von
Siebold, Johannes Brahms' Jugendliebe* (Göttingen, 1930), 166–7).

p. 177 This letter undoubtedly falls between *BW* iv, letters 43 and 44, to judge
and from internal requests and replies. The correspondence between Brahms
178 and Julius Otto Grimm was attentively edited by Richard Barth, an outstanding violinist, protégé of Joachim, and concertmaster of Grimm's
orchestra in Münster while still only in his teens (much later, Music
Director of the Hamburg Philharmonic). But even though most of the
principal figures who appear in the letters were known to him personally,
it was not always easy to arrange the letters in sequence, because Brahms
rarely dated his letters. Not one of the letters to his 'Kleeblatt', during the
autumn of 1858, is dated, for example, and Grimm apparently caught the
disease. Barth did not gain access to documents which would have allowed
him to deduce the correct sequence. Other letters can be dated by external
events—Brahms's return to Detmold by 1 October (established by his letter to Ferdinand Hiller); the publication of his *Volks-Kinderlieder*, which
Brahms offered to the Grimms (Nov.); Joachim's letter informing Grimm
of the death of his violin student Friedemann Bach (28 Nov.); and deaths
in the Dirichlet family, discussed variously by Clara, Joachim, and Brahms
(Dec.). I date and order the letters Brahms and Grimm wrote each other
in the autumn of 1858 as follows (numbers refer to *BW* iv): 39 [early Oct.];
41 [early Oct.]; 42 [mid-Oct.]; 43 [late Oct. or early Nov.]; 40 [late Oct. or
early Nov.]; 44 [early Nov.]; 45 [mid–Nov.]; 46 [mid–late Nov.]; 47 [mid-
late Nov.]; 48 [after 28 Nov.]; 49 [second week in Dec.].

p. 207　The song 'Wach auf, mein Hort' (*Tageweis von einer schönen Frau*) is one
which Brahms particularly liked. It is very old, included in the Lochamer
Liederbuch of 1460, but Brahms's source was the collection made by
Kretchmer-Zuccalmaglio under the title *Deutsche Volkslieder mit ihren
Original-Weisen* [*German Folk-Songs with their Original Melodies*] (Berlin
1838–40), which Brahms first found in the Schumann library. Brahms played
with the song for many years. In the 1850s he arranged it for three women's
voices, performed it with his Frauenchor, and also sent a version of it to
Clara. He included the song when he published his *49 Deutsche Volkslieder* in
1895 (WoO 33, No. 13), and his earlier versions are included in two other collections of his folk-song arrangements published posthumously, WoO 32 and
WoO 37. 'O Strassburg' (*Der Geworbene*) is a song traditionally set to an old
dance tune. The title appears in the list of songs Brahms copied for his collection in the 1850s, but no arrangement for the Frauenchor has survived. See
McC 703, 705. Part of the romance with Strassburg was due to the belief, mistaken but prevalent at the time, that the great cathedral there was the high
point of German Gothic architecture.

p. 213　The premature appearance of the Declaration appeared in the Berlin paper
and　*Echo*. The full list of signatories and those who agreed to sign, as gathered from
221　a reading of his correspondence, included: *Carl, Freiherr von Perfall*, composer
of several operas, Intendant of the Court Opera in Munich; *Carl Reinecke*,
Professor of Piano and Counterpoint at the Cologne Conservatory, a
Mendelssohnian, and eventual conductor of the Gewandhaus Orchestra; *Emil
Naumann*, composer, writer about music, Director of Royal Court Church
music in Berlin; *Ludwig Meinardus*, composer, writer on music, later teacher at
the Dresden Conservatory and then music critic of the *Hamburger
Correspondent*; *Gustav Schumann*, at the time a highly regarded composer and
pianist; *Julius Hermann Krigar*, Royal Music Director in Berlin, and founder of
the *Allgemeiner deutscher Musiker-Kalender*; *Karl Lührsz*, a highly regarded composer in Berlin; *Selmar Bagge*, composer, music critic in Vienna (later in Berlin),
relatively sympathetic to the music of Brahms; *Moritz Hauptmann*, Cantor of
the Thomasschule, Leipzig, and the most celebrated theorist and teacher of his
day; *Julius Rietz*, cellist, conductor, head of the Gewandhaus Orchestra from
1848 to 1861, and teacher of composition at the Leipzig Conservatory; and names
which are more familiar—*Max Bruch*; *Woldemar Bargiel*, Clara's half-brother;
Albert Dietrich; *Carl Grädener*; *Theodor Kirchner*; *Franz Wüllner*; *Ferdinand
Hiller*, *Lachner* (*Franz* or *Vincenz*). Clara Schumann was also planning to sign.

　　Others contacted, but who did *not* agree to sign (most of them are mentioned in Brahms's letter to Joachim, 10 March 1860): *Niels Gade* (1817–90),
the Leipzig-trained Danish composer; *Robert Franz* (1815–92), a composer
primarily of songs and other vocal music, and one who was deeply interested
in Handel and Bach. He was highly regarded by Mendelssohn, Schumann,
Liszt; *Ferdinand Laub* (1832–75), violinist and composer, active in Berlin and

Vienna at about this time; *Robert Volkmann* (1815–83), a Schumann disciple but also an admirer of Liszt; *Julius Schäffer* (1823–1902), a composer particularly of piano and vocal music; *Ludwig Christian Bischoff*, founder of one of the most conservative journals of the time, the *Rheinische* (later *Niederrheinische*) *Musikzeitung*; *Debrois von Bruyk*, Viennese music critic, one of the first to write favourably of Brahms's music.

p. 250 In his memoir, Wendt refers discreetly to the circumstances under which Brahms made these confidences, but omits any particulars. In interviewing Wendt for his Brahms biography, Max Kalbeck elicited the details, and quoted Wendt quoting Brahms: 'Joachim had the unhealthy inclination to feel compelled to complain about his lot. Is it possibly a Semitic characteristic? Even much earlier, when we had a lot to do with each other, he came often, sat on my bed, and asked even then if I liked him, because he always doubted it. I specifically explained to him that we would always be the same to each other, but that that kind of question was utterly unbearable to me' (Kal, ii. 435).

There are further examples of Joachim's continuous, excessive doubts about the depth of their friendship, including a most remarkable paragraph to Clara Schumann, in a letter of 14 October 1862: '. . . in my imagination I had convinced myself quite firmly, and had coloured my fantasy in most lurid shades, that you and Johannes . . . had simply given me up! So as to make you understand this, I must tell you that I had written to Johannes from Hastings [19 September] that he should let me know as soon as possible (in a week, at the latest), whether he had the desire to try out and perform his symphony in Hanover; it was very important to me *before* I went back to Hanover. My intention, in the event of a 'Yes', was to go there and definitely resign my post only *after the concert*. But no answer came. *What was more natural than to think he had just then broken off with me and had no wish to make use of my friendly efforts to get his works heard*' (emphasis added).

In fact, there were other, more benign ways of interpreting Brahms's silence: Brahms had just then gone to Vienna and had no symphony ready to try out, and a less apprehensive person could just as easily have construed his silence to mean merely that he had other things on his mind at that moment. In fact, Brahms replied two weeks later to Hanover, thinking that Joachim was by now back home—but since Joachim remained in England long past his original intention, he didn't receive Brahms's letter—a detail lost to him, in his anxiety. The consequences of this mix-up are abundantly apparent in Letters 155–61.

p. 258 Ludwig Deppe surfaces occasionally in the Brahms literature. He is mentioned from time to time in connection with Brahms as a drinking companion; when he came to Vienna to visit, they spent Christmas Eve together in a tavern (Brahms to his father, 24–5 Dec. 1867). An unpublished letter from the early 1870s confirms that they were on 'Du' terms (Wiener Stadt-und

Landesbibliothek). Deppe founded a musical society in Hamburg in 1857, and remained its conductor until 1868. Readers of Amy Fay's *Music Study in Germany* (Chicago, 1880, repr. New York, 1965) are sure to recognize his name; he is the piano teacher she held in such high esteem, and to whom the young American musician felt she owed her transformation to an artist and successful pianist. Since Amy Fay's description of Deppe's teaching has many similarities to Florence May's account of Brahms's methods, it would be very instructive to know more about the connection between the two men. Deppe, who was primarily a violinist and conductor, nevertheless studied piano with Marxsen in the 1840s or perhaps early 1850s. It is not only Amy Fay who was impressed with his teaching method: his most distinguished students and advocates were Emil Saur and Donald Francis Tovey.

p. 280 For a study of Brahms's edition, see David Brodbeck, 'Dance Music as High
and Art: Schubert's Twelve Ländler, Op. 171 (D. 790)', in *Schubert: Critical and*
324 *Analytical Studies*, ed. Walter Frisch (Lincoln, Neb. Press, 1986). Brahms's activity as Schubert editor is also discussed by David Brodbeck in his article 'Brahms's Edition of Twenty Schubert Ländler', in George Bozarth (ed.), *Brahms Studies* (Oxford, 1990), 229–50. In addition, for those with the patience to read through all his correspondence with his publishers, Brahms makes many references to his interest in Schubert, well beyond what is reproduced in this volume.

p. 388 The material for the story of *Rinaldo* comes from *La Gierusalemme Liberate*
and (*The Deliverance of Jerusalem*), the epic poem by Torquato Tasso published in
389 1581, and subsequently used by many artists, Handel, Haydn, Gluck, Lully, and Goethe among them. In Tasso's story, Rinaldo is a resplendent knight in the service of Godfrey of Bouillon (Goffredo), who leads the mission to take Jerusalem from the Infidel. Just as the knights have reached their goal and are camped outside the city, the enchantress Armide appears at the gates, sent by the powers of Darkness to bewitch the men. Instead, she is herself dazzled by Rinaldo, and transports them both to an island paradise. A company of knights is sent to rescue Rinaldo. In Tasso's version, Rinaldo wounds Armide in a subsequent battle, but instead of killing her, converts her to Christianity and takes her back to Rome as his wife.

Goethe's version takes quite a different turn. He concentrates on the small portion of the action which takes place on the island, after the company of knights has arrived to rescue Rinaldo. In Goethe's rendering, Rinaldo falls under Armide's spell once on the island with her, and has to be shamed by his rescuers into leaving his new-found bliss. Once having left, however, he never turns back. What appealed to Goethe, and presumably to Brahms, is the inner struggle of Rinaldo during his transformation—during his re-education—away from the pleasures of the flesh and back to the call of duty; and Brahms went to unusual lengths, for him, to depict the inner and outer landscape of the knight. As Kalbeck noted, Brahms confused his listeners by printing both the text by Goethe and some of Tasso's verses in the programme and the parts, since the two versions conflict. (*BW* ix. 67 n. 1.)

It is both easy and, in my view, correct, to see in the cantata a metaphor for Brahms's own renunciation of passion and earthly love in the service of his strong creative calling, useful to recall that the work was all but complete by 1863, at a time when Brahms was still feeling the entanglements of his ties to a number of women. Brahms's sparse comment to Spitta, that he 'simply found himself on the island with the knights' tells it all.

p. 401   The list, probably incomplete:

1. Mathilde Wesendonck, with her five-act play *Gudrun*, 1867;

2. Josef Viktor Widmann, *Der geraubte Schleier* (The Purloined Veil), and *Iphigenia at Delphi*, 1869;

3. Anna Ettlinger, the fairy-tale *Melusine*, set to verse at Levi's urging, 1871;

4. Ivan Turgenev, whose operettas, written in collaboration with Pauline Garcia-Viardot Brahms enjoyed. Turgenev offered Brahms a libretto in 1869, which Brahms rejected as having too preposterous a plot. Brahms nevertheless kept the manuscript, which is presently in the Frederick Koch collection at the Pierpont Morgan Library in New York. (See also Patrick Waddington, 'Turgenev's scenario for Brahms', *New Zealand Slavonic Journal*, 1–16, for the complete scenario and a thorough discussion of the circumstances.)

5. Hermann Levi, whose tireless efforts included ransacking the archives of the Karlsruhe Theatre for forgotten libretti, encouraging Anna Ettlinger in her *Melusine*, and urging on the leading local Protestant minister, resulting in a libretto by

6. Emil Zittel, *Sulamith*, from the Song of Songs, 1871.

After moving to Munich, Levi also put Brahms in contact with Paul Heyse.

7. Paul Heyse (later Nobel Laureate for Literature) discussed the possibility of Calderon's *The Noisy Secret*, Gozzi's *Köning Hirsch* and *Love for Three Oranges*. In 1873 he sketched out a libretto of *Bayard the Knight* specifically for Brahms.

8. Julius Allgeyer made two attempts to create libretti, shaped Calderon's *The Noisy Secret* at Brahms's request, and then made his own version of *Norma*, which Bellini had already composed (1869, 1870).

9. Henriette Feuerbach, the mother of the artist and friend Anselm, was also asked for her advice. She suggested the poem *Parzival*.

10. Brahms asked Adolf Schubring to 'get me an opera libretto! I waste a lot of time looking over [the] unusable and dubious, and cannot get myself ready to make a scenario' (March 1870). Schubring's brother had written oratorio texts for Mendelssohn, so it was not a cry out of the blue.

A number of writers have dealt with Brahms's involvement with opera, including Kalbeck, and Josef Widmann, in his *Erinnerungen*. Frithjof Haas's remarks are concise and informative ('Johannes Brahms und Hermann Levi', in Draheim, *Brahms in Baden-Baden und Karlsruhe*, 73–4); and Alfred Orel's discussion deserves to be much better known (in *Johannes Brahms und Julius Allgeyer, Eine Künstlerfreundschaft in Briefen*, 54 ff.).

p. 469 From 1873 to 1876, Feuerbach was in Vienna, where he held the prestigious appointment as professor at the Imperial and Royal Academy of Art. He got in touch with Brahms as soon as the latter returned from his summer holiday, but their friendship did not prosper. Julius Allgeyer, his friend and biographer, explains that, while one of Feuerbach's strengths was his ability to disregard utterly the conditions he worked in, refusing to take into account any negative reactions to his work, it was also a weakness which led to continuous disappointment and misjudgement. Brahms, far more astute about Viennese conditions, tried to bring Feuerbach down to earth. According to Allgeyer, the artist took his friend's advice very much amiss. Allgeyer's biography (*Anselm Feuerbach* (Berlin, 1904), ii. 230–2) quotes from letters Feuerbach wrote to his mother: (2 Nov. 1873) 'I am painting Brahms in November'; (3 Nov. 1873) 'Brahms ruined another evening for me.'

The excerpt on p. 469, n. 20, is from this source. Brahms had his own way of explaining the decline of their friendship, in a letter to Allgeyer written two years later (Letter 320 in this volume).

p. 587 To Schubring, from Vienna, April 1873: 'I consider Streicher to be good and reliable. . . . I like them quite a lot in a room, and for myself, even now, cannot get used to the local grand pianos in the concert halls' [i.e. Bösendorfer?] (*BW* viii. 224–5).

To Julius Otto Grimm, 18 November 1881: 'Do be so good as to find out from Cologne or elsewhere, whether we can't have a Bechstein or Steinway sent. I'll gladly pay the transportation. But I'll no longer play on some dubious or questionable instrument' (*BW* iv. 144).

To Emil Paur in Mannheim, 31 December 1885, a request for a Bechstein rather than Blüthner, for a performance of the Second Piano Concerto. Unpublished, autograph in the Pierpont Morgan Library.

To Wüllner, 11 December 1883: '. . . be sure to see to it that I get a most beautiful Bechstein!'—this for a performance of his First Piano Concerto in Berlin. He repeated the request for his performance in Dresden (*BW* xv. 114).

And in 1886, as he was again arranging for his performance of Op. 15 with Wüllner, he wrote: '. . . do write to me which day the rehearsals are on! Is there a splendid Bechstein (or American Steinway) there?' (p. 128).

Two letters to Julius Spengel from 1883 and 1884 repeat the request, for his practice piano as well as for his concerts (Annemarie Spengel, *Johannes Brahms an Julius Spengel* (private printing: Hamburg, 1959), 16–17, 19).

Ottilie Ebner's daughter recounts that when she came down with scarlet fever as a young married woman living in Vienna [1892], Brahms came to keep her company and entertain her with his piano-playing.

It gave him pleasure not only because he knew how happy he made me, but also because he had never played on such a marvellous grand piano. It was a particularly successful Steinway [the name is written in English. Ed] '. . . When I met Professor Mandyczewski thirty-three years later and he heard my name, he was very pleased and said straight away, 'So you're the lucky owner of that most excellent Steinway. Many years ago Brahms came to me quite excited and told me he had played on a fabulous instrument at your house. It was superb, and in particular, didn't have the sound of an ordinary piano at all.' *Die Brahmsfreundin Ottilie Ebner und ihr Kreis*, 114.

From the memoir of Edward Speyer, *My Life and Friends* (London, 1937), 90:

In the course of the evening [11 January 1889] I asked Clara Schumann whether she would do us the great favour of playing to us. With an expression of deep melancholy she replied, 'Oh, what a pity it is that in your house of all others there should be a Steinway. I find the Steinway action too hard for me, is it not so, Johannes?' 'You are right, Clara, but, for myself, I must say this is about the finest pianoforte my fingers have ever touched.'

p. 618 Brahms had another view of Raff, best described by an amusing excerpt from George Henschel's diary. In the published versions of the Diary (*Personal Recollections*, 24–5) Raff's name is indicated only with an X; but in a version Henschel made for a radio address in 1933 Raff is explicitly named (manuscript privately owned).

In the afternoon we paid a visit to Joachim Raff. Raff was one of the most popular composers of the time, and lived at that time in Wiesbaden. Of his over 300 works, scarcely 3 are still known today. 'I really like Raff a lot,' said Brahms, 'and he likes to hear himself speak so much that it's as much fun as going to the theatre. . . . He isn't happy unless he composes a certain number of hours each day, and on top of that he writes out his orchestra parts himself.'

So off we went to Raff's house and found him and his wife at home. Brahms seemed somewhat tired and spoke little, Raff and his wife, on the contrary, that much the more. After a time Raff, who reminded me of Dr Bartolo, was called away; his barber had come and he asked us to excuse him for ten minutes. In his absence, the duty of entertaining us fell to his wife. 'You have no idea,' she said, 'how tireless a worker Raff is (she never said 'my husband,' but always 'Raff'). I am proud and happy that I was finally able to prevail upon him to go for a walk with our daughter now that she's grown up, every day for 2 hours, that keeps him from composing at least 2 hours a day. 'Ah, that's good, yes, that's very good,' cried out Brahms, with the most innocent face in the world.

p. 660 At issue was a huntsmen's phrase (the 'one word' Brahms referred to) used by the young Kaiser in describing his determination to hold on to the Alsace which, in the wake of the Franco-Prussian War, was once again German (as it had been, on and off, before the 17th century). Now an Imperial Territory, directly under control of the Emperor, it differed in that regard from the twenty-five other states of the German Empire, which had some degree of autonomy as well as their own constitutions. In response to anti-German sentiment in the territory and calls for its return to France, the new Kaiser expressed himself in harsh terms: every stone would remain German even if it took the slaughter of eighteen army corps and 42 million Germans laid out in a row 'like animals killed in the hunt' ('auf der Strecke'). Widmann was appalled that the new Kaiser had aligned himself so quickly with the military faction, and could think of his people in such brutal terms. He feared for the future. His essay in the Bernese *Bund* was the harshest of any to appear in the European press.

Brahms's nationalistic, not to say jingoistic, point of view on this issue is the one political stance to have been discussed *in print* by a contemporary, a situation which has led many to place Brahms in the conservative camp in general. Widmann himself, however, saw Brahms's position (correctly, I think) as coming simply from an intensely nationalistic desire to see Germany *publicly* portrayed in a positive light. It is too simple-minded to regard Brahms as politically authoritarian generally on the basis of this single incident. Brahms was very comfortable with Widmann over a long period of time, and Widmann was one of the strikingly humanitarian and liberal journalists of the nineteenth century: a public supporter of women's right to education and the vote, sympathetic to the underclass and the need for social reform, and one of the founders of the Swiss movement to protect the environment and animals. If not an open supporter of Socialism, he nevertheless understood and sympathized with the forces that created the Socialist movement. Quite possibly, Widmann's dismay and surprise at Brahms's reaction arose exactly because his friend was otherwise so at home with his political points of view.

For additional perspectives on Brahms's political thinking, see his letter to Hanslick regarding the Beethoven manuscript and Beethoven's own politics (Letter 435), and Margaret Notley's 'Brahms as Liberal', *19th Century Music*, vol. 17, no. 2 (1993), 107–23.

Appendices

❧❧❧

A. Johannes Brahms and Clara Schumann

Of all the intriguing aspects of Brahms's life, it is unquestionably his attachment to Clara Schumann that has aroused the most speculation. Protégé, lover, son, brother, adviser, potential son-in-law—Brahms has been cast in one or more of these roles in the course of his lifelong friendship with her.

There are surely many reasons to be interested in this attachment, so central to Brahms's life, but inevitably most attention is directed to the question of whether or not Brahms and Clara were lovers, something I was asked without fail by any person to whom I mentioned I was working on this book.

While the question is impossible to ignore, ultimately it is not the most interesting one to ask. Rather, that question is what, given their difference in background, character, and age, kept them bound to each other throughout their entire lives, in an alliance as close as any family tie.

Of the letters Brahms wrote to Clara, those included in this volume have been selected with the aim of suggesting an answer to the second question, and to record how their association evolved with time. In this space I should like to offer some perspective on the letters, to summarize what they document, and to take on the question of a possible love-affair. It has to be said for this last, that dealing with it in a completely convincing fashion is impossible for the simple reason that there is no hard evidence one way or the other. There is, however, a great deal of circumstantial material, which people will continue to look at from their own points of view. My own, set forth here, is based on extensive reading and what I hope is common sense, and coincides with the conclusion reached by virtually everyone who has spent considerable time studying the lives of Clara and of Brahms: namely, that this complex friendship, however extraordinary, however intense, was platonic, and that if it is difficult to reconcile that bland word with the ardour of Brahms's youthful feelings as he expressed them in his letters, it is even more difficult to imagine the circumstances under which a full-blown affair could have developed.

Consider first the character of Clara and Robert Schumann and the circle close around them, including Joachim, Julius Otto Grimm, and Brahms. The high idealism which moved them sets them apart from most people; but for their extraordinary musical abilities, they might not have seemed out of place somewhere in a nineteenth-century Utopian community. The words 'pure', 'finer nature', 'nobility of spirit', 'sacred', occur frequently in their letters to each other, and they used them naturally, without embarrassment or affectation. In this regard Joachim's letters to his friends Gisela von Arnim and Hermann Grimm are particularly striking, but not unique. Clara, writing to Brahms during her Russian journey, for example (Litz, i, Letter 212): 'I have not met a single artist who really is one, heart and soul . . . I cannot exempt Rubinstein . . . Above all, he lacks a sacred seriousness, and one feels that as he composes and conducts.' Or Clara writing to Brahms from Vienna (ibid., Letter 148): 'we, the little band of right-minded people, must maintain our self-respect before all else.'

Clara herself was nothing if not sacredly serious. She and everyone around her looked upon her marriage to Robert as something holy, perfect, rare. For the rest of his life, Brahms referred to that unique union in almost reverential terms, and given everything we know about Clara, as well as the highly moral stance Brahms took towards his friends and family throughout his life, it is very difficult to imagine them involved in a love-affair while her husband was still alive. Therefore it is important to remember that until perhaps ten months before his death, everyone involved actually had hopes for Schumann's recovery, and did not give up entirely until a few months before the end.[1] Yet Brahms's most ardent love letters cover exactly that period, 1854–6, and no one has reason to suggest that they were lovers at any later time. On the contrary, Brahms's letters cooled perceptibly very soon after Schumann's death in July 1856—a cooling off that took place not gradually, but abruptly, thereby leaving us with some really fascinating food for thought.[2]

Clara's idealism was matched by Joachim and Brahms. Rubinstein once referred to the pair as 'High Priests of Virtue'.[3] All three of them broke with Franz Liszt on matters essentially philosophical and aesthetic, with detrimental effects especially for Brahms.[4] It was not the only time their idealism triumphed over their self-

---

[1] J. O. Grimm to Brahms, Oct. 1855: 'I recently heard a grave rumour from a student; is there anything to it? The doctor from Endenich is said to have written to her that Schumann was incurable.—Is it true?—' (*BW* iv. 35). Brahms to Joachim, 25 Apr. 1856: '[The doctor] says that Schumann's brain is plainly affected . . . and therefore all medical help is useless . . . And from Frau Brahms to Johannes, 26 May 1856: 'We have heard the doctors have declared Schumann to be incurable. That is very sad' (*Familie*, 67).

[2] Brahms's letter from Hamburg of 22 Oct. (Letter 82) is striking in this regard.

[3] Litz, iii. 20.

[4] For Clara, this meant refusing to attend his concerts or listen to his music. Joachim took the trouble to write to Liszt, who at the time was a great admirer of his, telling him that henceforth they could have nothing to do with each other musically because their points of view were too far apart. Two years previously he had already written to Clara (10 Dec. 1855): 'I shall never be able to meet Liszt again, because I should want to tell him that instead of taking him for a mighty erring spirit striving to return to God, I have suddenly realized that he is a cunning contriver of effects, who has miscalculated' (*JJ* i. 298–9). For Brahms, the consequences were much more serious, as his career was not yet established when he signed the Manifesto, in 1860, declaring himself unalterably opposed to the 'Musicians of the Future' (see pp. 211–22). Although Liszt was too courteous a person to respond overtly, and he and Brahms remained on speaking terms, Liszt never once performed or conducted a work of Brahms throughout his influential career.

interest. Clara refused to attend or to participate in any concert in which Wagner's music was being played. She and Joachim consistently refused to play popular virtuoso pieces merely to please audiences, and Joachim gave up a lucrative concert tour in England so as not to prostitute his art, Brahms voicing his approval. And they all refused to co-operate in a festival of the music of Robert Schumann, because the wrong people were organizing it.

A purely practical consideration, one apparently neglected by the more romantically inclined among us but probably not by Clara, provides another reason to doubt the reality of a conventional love-affair in the years 1854–6: Clara's fertility, and her evident ignorance of contraception. Robert and Clara lived together for thirteen and a half years. During that time, she was pregnant nine times, and bore eight children. While the early births were welcomed joyously, succeeding pregnancies were greeted with dismay and alarm, referred to as 'her new fear', her 'frightening expectation'.[5] The view that Brahms's impetuous ardour would have been irresistible for her does not ring true for the mother of seven who was keenly aware of the proprieties, who had borne more children than she had wanted, and who prided herself above all on knowing her duty and fulfilling it conscientiously.

And what should one make of the extreme distress Brahms displayed at the news that Clara's daughter, Julie, was to be married? Of the four Schumann daughters, Julie was by far the most beautiful (see Plate 24); and as she had accompanied her mother to Hamburg for a month in 1861 and with her mother took dinner together with Brahms virtually every day, she was also the daughter he knew best. For some time thereafter, his letters to Clara included specific greetings to her, and he wrote to Clara that one could not think of Julie without being captivated. His own captivation is evidenced by his dedication of the Variations, Op. 23, to her—she is the only Schumann child so honoured—and it would seem that he eventually imagined himself to be in love. This revelation, in the summer of her engagement, came not from Brahms but from Hermann Levi, who was close to Brahms at that period. Clara expressed great surprise, but no antipathy or revulsion, remarking to her diary only that he had never given any hint of it, had in fact assured her he would never marry. Although love-affairs with mothers which then lead to hopes of marriage with their daughters are certainly not unheard of, it is very hard to imagine that such a strait-laced person as Clara could have accepted this sequence of events with equanimity.

The case for assuming that Brahms and Clara were lovers is built on a number of elements, in addition to his impassioned letters to her: for example, that the young Brahms received many tokens of Clara's affection—a generous assortment of books, a fine steel watch chain, a coffee set, a calf-skin leather pocket diary, even, eventually, Schumann's piano.

It is true, too, that Brahms was godfather to her last-born son, Felix, and there

---

[5] Reich, 153.

was a time when this was taken as a tacit sign that she and Brahms were lovers—a rather extraordinary notion when one realizes that Clara was most likely pregnant with Felix before they met. The notion, in any case, is based on a misconception. Brahms was only one of three people asked to stand godparent to the new baby. The second was the singer Mathilde Hartmann, the third, Joachim. It was a request the latter was ineligible to fulfil, because he was a Jew. He took his designation very seriously, though, and when the 6-year-old Felix began violin lessons, Joachim made plans to present him with his Guarneri violin, deeming the valuable instrument a fitting present for a godchild.[6]

Joachim was on Clara's gift list almost as frequently as Brahms. She presented him with a number of books, and, on tour once, bought identical presents for both young men.

'He is equally as dear a friend to me as Brahms,' she wrote of Joachim in her diary, 'and with him too, I feel deep trust in his nature; his sensibility is so tender that he immediately understands my slightest, most delicate feelings. These two friends, how exactly they are as though created for Robert—he does not yet know them as I do!'[7] By focusing only on Brahms, in considering their relationship during this appalling period of Schumann's illness, a faulty picture emerges. Brahms was by no means the only person to involve himself with her, and generally it is Joachim she toured with, not Brahms.

It is true that Brahms gradually took the more prominent place, as he remained in Düsseldorf, helped to raise her younger children, especially the boys Ludwig and Ferdinand, began to take part in some aspects of household affairs—and showed himself to be passionately devoted to her.

It is also true that Brahms and Clara took a number of trips together during the 1850s, and that to the casual eye, these periods look like perfect occasions for romance. They made several walking tours along the Rhine and in the Teutoburger Forest; in January 1855 Brahms followed her to Rotterdam and stayed with her for a week; they went to Ostend together in July 1856, shortly before Robert died, so that Brahms could get his first look at the sea; and after Robert's death, they went together to Switzerland for a month, to recuperate. Suggestive as this all appears at first glance, however, the reality was anything but conducive to romance; it would have been rather complicated for them to be lovers, for they were never alone. On every one of these journeys Clara was accompanied by travelling companions, and on the holidays her housekeeper and some of her children were with her, as well. Lest anyone doubt that they took appearances seriously, there are on record sufficient utterances of Brahms and Clara regarding malicious tongues to make it clear that they each wished to avoid compromising their reputations (see Brahms's comment about Bargiel in Letter 74).

---

[6] In the mean time Joachim had been baptized. See *JJ* ii, letter of 22 Dec. 1860.
[7] Litz, ii. 321.

With them in Switzerland after Schumann's death were the two elder Schumann boys and Brahms's sister Elise, who had been invited to come too as mother's helper. After reading the letter Brahms wrote to Julius Otto Grimm at the end of this trip, it would be difficult to escape the conclusion that the vacation was no tryst (Letter 80). Instead, one wonders whether the experience did not contribute significantly to Brahms's decision to chart his future course alone. Whatever the immediate cause for that decision (one of the questions one would like to have an answer to), the results are plain enough: that October, Brahms left Düsseldorf and went back to live with his parents in Hamburg. Clara told her diary that she returned from the railway station as if from a funeral. Brahms came back to spend Christmas with Clara and her children, and visited on other occasions, but their communal life in Düsseldorf was over.

The correspondence from this period is ambiguous. Brahms's feelings were set forth in dozens of suggestive letters, written during the time Robert was still alive and hospitalized in Endenich. Although most of these letters were addressed to Clara, the young Brahms broadcast his adoration of her to his friends, and even to Robert Schumann himself. He wrote to Grimm, Joachim, Robert Schumann, and to a distant father figure, as though they would understand (Letters 27, 31, 39). The emotional tone of the letters in the 1850s is not confined to those he wrote to Clara. And why should it be? With examples of highly charged outpourings from the men who populate the novels of Jean Paul and other German Romantics widely admired, it was far more acceptable then than now for a man to write in such a fashion, and it is all too easy for us now to mistake those outpourings as a sure sign of consummated love then.

The voluminous correspondence between Brahms and Clara presents other problems—it has great gaps, due to a mutual agreement to return each other's letters and Brahms's insistence that they then destroy them. Even as early as 1856, Brahms was concerned with shielding his correspondence from the eyes of others. The actual exchange took place in 1887 (Letters 462 and 469). Brahms disposed of his letters, and Clara did burn the first few years' worth of hers before her daughter Marie convinced her to stop. As a result, during the years that Brahms was passionately devoted to Clara we have *only* his letters, without Clara's response; and in later years, where we might have hoped to learn about the internal struggles concerning the direction of his life and his decision to go it alone, we have many more of Clara's letters than of his. Moreover, her daughters edited her letters and adult diaries before authorizing Berthold Litzmann to use them in preparing his important three-volume biography.[8]

---

[8] The deleted passages in the autographs of letters I have inspected were omitted out of a sense of decorum towards famous or living persons, or because they were uninteresting. Compare with *SBB* the restored passages in Letters 32–3, 35–7, and 47 in this volume. The diaries, unfortunately, were destroyed after Litzmann had made use of them.

Nevertheless we have those early letters of Brahms precisely because Clara managed to hold on to the ones which meant the most to her, and implicit in that rescue is another indication of the nature of their friendship in those early years. Would she have kept them back and let posterity have them if they were, indeed, the very letters that would point to indiscretion on their part? Or would her daughter Marie, who supervised their publication many years later albeit in slightly censored form, have allowed their publication in any form at all had she reason to believe that her mother had been Brahms's lover?[9]

In the memoir Eugenie Schumann wrote in the 1920s, the youngest Schumann daughter referred to Brahms's return to Hamburg in veiled language which nevertheless leaves no doubt that Clara was deeply hurt by Brahms's action.[10] Eugenie even wondered whether the erratic and sometimes irascible behaviour Brahms displayed in subsequent years wasn't brought on by feelings of guilt at the way he had abandoned their mother. But Eugenie herself was a little girl at the time, and can only have known of these events through her mother or older sisters. Can Clara have imagined that Brahms would stay on in Düsseldorf indefinitely, to babysit and look after the household accounts while she was away on concert tours? Did she think they might marry? These question marks will remain. Clara was fourteen years older, but not unattractive (Plate 14), and a uniquely interesting and remarkable woman; the possibility of marriage was not unthinkable, given the much odder one Brahms's own parents had made. On the other hand, it is just that marriage which must have given Brahms pause for thought. Although he could not then have foretold the dismal ending to his parents' marriage eight years later, he was not unaware of their difficulties. Frau Brahms was becoming an old woman, his father still a vigorous man. Brahms was deeply fond of his mother, a woman who also gained the warmest appreciation of Joachim, Grimm, and Clara, as they took turns being guests in the Brahms home. But when his father abandoned their home, unmoved by their thirty-five-year marriage and her failing eyesight and health, Brahms had some sympathy for his father, a realization which deeply shocked Clara. He seems quite to have understood his father's needs, separating them from the question of right or wrong, and must have had an appreciation of the difficulties caused by their difference in age. For whatever it is worth, seventy years later, Clara's granddaughter Julie, who spent four formative years in Clara's house, believed firmly that had Brahms asked, Clara would have married him.[11]

The real issue for Brahms is something else: whether these two and a half years

[9] See Part VII (1887), n. 14, for more on this question.

[10] *Erinnerungen* (Stuttgart, 1925), 156–7.

[11] Ferdinand's daughter Julie ('Julchen'). Along with her brothers Alfred, Walter, Erich, and Ferdinand, she was educated by Clara, and lived with her for a time in Frankfurt. She was, however, appalled at the parody later produced by her brother Alfred (using the pseudonym Titus Frazeni) claiming that the last of Clara's sons was Brahms's child. Dietz-Rüdiger Moser, *Mein liebes Julchen. Briefe* (Munich, 1990), 21–3.

of high-voltage entanglement with the Schumanns had spent his store of passion for life, forever preventing him from falling in love so deeply again, or whether his change of heart, when Schumann died and the object of his passion was now within reach, was part of a lifelong pattern in his dealings with women. The record can be read to support both points of view. On the one hand, Brahms never again allowed himself to be so drained by emotion or to become so enmeshed in the lives of others as he had been with Robert and Clara. No other woman drove him to compare himself to Prince Kamar-ez-zeman (Letter 42). His letter to Clara about passion, written from Detmold in 1858, is tremendously instructive on this point, and cannot be properly understood outside the events of 1854–6 (Letter 90).

On the other hand, Brahms did fall in love again, several times, and throughout his life was always involved with a woman at one level of intensity or other. His relationships fit the classic pattern of the loner, the man of few words who requires an unencumbered life, withdraws to a real or imaginary wilderness to create, emerges occasionally to seek the consolation and stimulation which love of a woman can provide, frequently imagines himself in love, needs, in fact, to feel himself in love, but always retreats before it is too late. However, unlike many loners, Brahms never wavered in his determination to remain single, even as he grew older, had a great deal of money, and had begun to feel the sting of loneliness. His brother Fritz also remained single, and there is good reason to believe that their parents' difficult marriage had more to do with this decision than any lifelong attachment to a woman, no matter how remarkable she might be.[12]

Shortly after Clara and Brahms went their respective ways, she wrote a letter to her children which she entrusted to her diary, carefully explaining to them what Brahms had meant to her in those difficult two and a half years of Schumann's hospitalization, asking them never to forget the debt they owed him or what he had done for them all. It is a curious document, not so much because of what it says, as because of Clara's need to say it.[13] Less well known is a passage from Eugenie's *Recollections* (p. 246):

> [Mother] once asked me whether I could begin to grasp what it means to
> have had a friend, from childhood on, who in the course of his daily, hourly
> relations with you had strewn your path, like precious pearls, with artistic

[12] Once again, the behaviour of E. T. A. Hoffman's character Johannes Kreisler seems to coincide remarkably with that of the real-life Johannes Brahms, as Kreisler speaks about love as 'true musicians' experience it: '[They] carry their chosen lady in their hearts and wish only to sing, to write poetry, and to paint for her, and are comparable to the gallant knights of old in matters of courtoisie' (p. 135 of the English translation of *Kater Murr*). Indeed, the entire portion of the novel which recounts Kreisler's encounter with the Abbot of a Benedictine monastery, and the views expressed there about women, marriage, and renunciation, ring very true with regard to Brahms's own life. Particularly pertinent is Hoffmann's restatement of the Romantic notion that the entire lure of love lies in the impossibility of its fulfilment. In this area too, it seems that in Johannes Kreisler, Brahms recognized a kindred spirit.

[13] Litz, ii. 336–8.

inspiration of the highest, noblest kind; whether I could grasp that without such inspiration, she couldn't have gone on living, that she clings to *those* persons who, like Brahms, could to some extent replace what she had lost as an artist; that without their loving efforts to snatch her from her pain through music, she could not have survived the terrible period of suffering.

In both cases, Clara was perhaps attempting to clarify for herself the meaning of Brahms's relationship to her during the two and a half years of Robert's hospitalization. If so, she did not entirely succeed. When Brahms fell in love again, in her very presence, she suffered acute pangs of jealousy and played the part of the jilted sweetheart.[14]

Some part of this early history is told in his music, the events from 1854 to 1856 and their aftermath inevitably leaving their mark. The Brahms who rushed to Düsseldorf to offer aid and comfort to Clara Schumann may have been a 20-year-old youth, voice still high, cheek still unshaven, head still filled with his favourite tales of knights and *courtoisie* and with music planned on a broad, bold, and enthusiastic scale; but once there, he was plunged into adulthood. It was an abrupt coming of age. The conflict which ensued as he determined to help the wife of his benefactor and then discovered he had fallen in love with her, resulted in compositions much darker and tumultuous, in which the inner anguish is audible to anyone who has even a small idea of his condition. We have just a hint of what he felt thanks to the words which accompanied the Piano Quartet, Op. 60, when he sent it to Simrock, twenty years later—two movements originate from this period—suggesting that the work be published with the picture of a suicidal, love-stricken youth on the cover (Letter 315). His recommendation is all the more instructive because the allusion, to Goethe's hero *Werther*, is one more indication that Brahms's passion for Clara was unrequited.

If Clara had not burned the first few years of her correspondence to Brahms, we might have learned the degree to which Brahms's love letters reflected his behaviour to Clara in person, how she interpreted his behaviour, and how she reacted. Clara's diary only reveals how much she came to depend on him: '*The hours when I am writing [to Johannes] are the most bearable*' (during her first English trip (p. 137)); '*But Johannes exercised an influence on me as he always does and speedily drew me out of my gloomy thoughts*' (in passing through Bonn on the way to a concert performance, 1855, p. 113); '*A sorrowful day . . . How hard I found it to say goodbye to Johannes. I cling to this friend with all my heart and . . . always feel it terribly when I have to part from him*' (Clara, preparing to go to Detmold, p. 111); '*How happy to see my dear friend again . . . He is my prop, my support, without him my courage dwindles more and more*' (returning from tour 22 March 1855, p. 105).[15] Letters to her oldest friend confirm what she wrote in her diary. To Emilie List, November 1855:

---

[14] See pp. 170–3.   [15] All quotes here are from the English language translation of Litz, ii.

... one consolation ... heaven has sent me, a friend who has borne all my sufferings with me, and truly does only what can cheer me; he is a young composer, Johannes Brahms, a great favourite of my Robert's, a person with God-given talents in every regard. He has so truly supported me, ever renewing my courage when it threatened to fail—in short he is a friend to me in the highest and finest sense of the word.[16]

Another diary entry of 1855 shows to what extent Brahms had become family, in her mind. When she performed in a concert with Jenny Lind and felt her talents had been used unworthily, she was *'glad my dear ones [were] not there, for Robert's heart, or Johannes's, would have bled to see me in so humiliating a position'* (p. 113). Her diary also informs us that she agreed to address Brahms in the familiar 'Du' form from November 1854 (a liberty he himself was not allowed until shortly before Schumann's death (Letters 74–5), so that for most of the early correspondence, the conflict between his highly charged and intimate words and the formality in which they are framed gives a flavour that cannot be translated into English).

For Brahms there were a host of other dimensions to their relationship, which the letters included in this volume are intended to illustrate. With Clara and her family he had his first opportunity to fill an important role, to be needed, indeed, to be a man. Not only did he become the adult male figure of the house, for a time, keep the household accounts, and teach the younger boys to read, he gave Clara theory lessons and advised her on repertory, performance style, and interpretation. He was soon conferring with her regarding her job offers, decisions on where to live, con-tracts with music publishers, and, not infrequently, on how to handle her sons. His comments about the boys are surprisingly loving and filled with common sense (one more indication of the kind of upbringing he himself had had). In later life he gave his time willingly and generously as she undertook to edit the complete works of Schumann for Breitkopf & Härtel (Letters 347–9). Even then, more than twenty years after his mad passion was over, his letters give one the feeling that it was a real joy for him still to be able to help Clara in a concrete manner. Over the course of their lives, with tact and charm, he also gave her substantial sums of money (Letter 475), the only direct financial aid that independent woman ever accepted apart from a loan in the early days of Schumann's illness.

Clara was not only the object of his first love, she also played a crucial role in the development of his career. He needed someone who would recognize his gifts as fully as Schumann had. Not only did she do so, she also understood the unlikely background he had come from, and the need to intervene with his parents when they worried he was not giving concerts and earning money. That may have been the most important help she ever gave Brahms, but it was only the beginning. His career

---

[16] Eugen Wendler (ed.), *'Das Band der ewigen Liebe': Clara Schumanns Briefwechsel mit Emilie und Elise List* (Stuttgart, 1996), 186. She wrote similarly to Emilie during the next few years: pp. 191, 194.

as pianist and composer was furthered by her formidable energies in every way she knew how; she gave Vienna, Paris, and England their first taste of his music, she premièred new works (Opp. 24 and 25), importuned publishers and conductors on his behalf (the publication of Op. 10 and Op. 17 was due to her efforts, and she went to great lengths to obtain a hearing for Op. 16 in Leipzig). When Brahms needed to restart his performing career, it was Clara's advice he took and her concerts he played in. His introduction to well-known artists and intellectuals (Otto Jahn, Julius Stockhausen, and Klaus Groth, for example), and to the publishing house of Simrock, came through her. She found pupils for him, and arranged the contacts which led to his post in Detmold. She taught him how to handle money, how to buy securities, and what to do with them. She even eventually suggested a wife for him, Ida Rieter-Biedermann, daughter of his Swiss publisher, having first ascertained that the young woman in question was well disposed to the idea.[17]

The hundred letters to Clara included in the present collection span the lifetime of both artists. It will be clear to any reader that Brahms's relationship to Clara changed substantially over time. What began in an atmosphere of intense excitement as the 20-year-old composer moved from obscurity to fame, and was heightened by an atmosphere of intense crisis as Schumann attempted suicide, matured through forty-three years while the artists themselves evolved and led their lives under very different circumstances from each other. Brahms became increasingly independent and successful, while Clara carried on her own immensely successful career but was weighted down by multiple personal tragedies. Brahms's early passion was soon replaced by a more temperate love, and Clara soon had cause to complain that she was no longer privy to Brahms's innermost thoughts. The chances are she never understood how much she was the focus of Brahms's emotional well-being throughout his life. There is no one to whom he wrote more letters (except to his publisher, Fritz Simrock), and she remained the only person to whom he could confide his pain, and who in turn felt the right to give him advice—sometimes remarkably sound and wise. 'My best friend', Brahms described her, when she died, the same term Clara used to describe him. She is one of the few people to whom he dedicated more than one work, and he gave her many more as gifts.

In the larger picture, the question of whether they were lovers seems less and less important. For Brahms she was and remained the epitome of a personal ideal which was crucially important to him, a living example of the highest artistic and ethical integrity in a world, where, just as now, such a person was painfully rare. She was his model of motherhood and womanhood, and something like his conscience. On an unexpected visit to her in Frankfurt towards the end of her life, he commanded her to perform for him, needing to reassure himself that she still played

---

[17] Clara to Brahms, 4 Sept. 1868 (*SBB* i. 594). Brahms subsequently congratulated Ida on her marriage to a nice young man, and remained on friendly terms with the couple for the rest of his life. Peter Sulzer, *Die fünfte Schweizerreise von Johannes Brahms* (Winterthur, 1971), 28 ff.

with her accustomed beauty. And to a friend he advised, 'If ever you are in doubt as to how to behave, think of what Frau Schumann would do.' If that was how he perceived Clara, his vision of Clara and Robert as a pair was equally exalted. In fact, his falling out of love with her may well have happened abruptly when the world of fantasy crumbled before his eyes, as he saw husband and wife united again even under the grisly circumstances of Robert's last hours (Letter 80).

Although they never again lived in the same city after Schumann's death, for a long time they continued to spend some part of their holidays together, even if not always with happy results. When Clara bought a house in Baden-Baden, enabling her entire family to be together for part of the year, Brahms took rooms in a cottage not far away and spent part of eight summers there (plate 25). With the exception of the summer of 1868, when relations between them were particularly strained, there was always a place set for him at Clara's dinner table, an open invitation he made use of frequently.[18] In later years, he knew that any time he came to Frankfurt for a visit, staying in Clara's house for a few days and throwing the establishment into turmoil for the duration, there would be no doubt of a welcome for him or his friends.

These two artists offered each other something irreplaceable. Clara's scrutiny of Brahms's work was a necessity for him. For many years she remained the first person, apart from Joachim, to see his work, as he sent every new piece to her in manuscript for her opinion. She never failed him by offering him anything but her honest judgement. Reading her comments today, one is still struck by their remarkable perspicacity.

As for Clara, Brahms offered her above all that most prized ingredient of her life: intimate contact with genuine creative genius, which life with Robert had provided her, and which was the only condition in which she felt fulfilled. He was for her the only great living composer, and in her diary she thanked heaven more than once for sending him into the world. 'I play some of Brahms's new works every day ... How grateful I am to him for the comfort which he gives me in the midst of my sorrow!' she wrote in her diary for 19 October 1893, and forgave him, while nevertheless noting it, the pain he caused her.

Withal, it is difficult to imagine two people whose fundamental style was more different one from the other. Brahms was witty, informal, intellectual, and tremendously well read, a practical joker, simple in his tastes but a *bon vivant* nevertheless, who enjoyed his schnapps, wine, beer, cigarettes, and cigars, and was unconcerned about aspects of decorum which Clara took seriously. Nothing in his life had required him to mellow, to smooth the rough edges, to yield to another's needs. He could be very funny and full of life, but also rough, sarcastic, moody, and deeply wounding. Clara was none of those things. She lived surrounded by loving and

---

[18] During the summer of 1871, the young English pianist Florence May studied the piano with him, and has detailed the setting in her Brahms biography, *Johannes Brahms*. See esp. pp. 3–4, but the whole chapter, 'Personal Recollections', is of outstanding interest.

dutiful daughters and grandchildren, and became quite autocratic as she grew older. She was ever aware of her position and obligations, and above all had very little sense of humour, a trial for Brahms, which he nevertheless did not allow to interfere with his plans for teasing her in elaborate ways.[19]

Despite their incompatabilities, they never ceased to regard each other's artistic achievements with the utmost of respect and admiration. Their love and friendship, tested to the limit by each through serious misunderstandings, anger, jealousy, or moodiness, held together to the very end for the same reasons it had blossomed in the very beginning: Brahms's reverence for Clara's artistry and purity of character; and Clara's appreciation of Brahms's genius, the incorruptible honesty of his heart, and the depth of his devotion to her.

[19] From Antonia Speyer Kufferath's memoir, published in Speyer, *My Life and Friends* (London, 1937), 114–15: 'In the winter of 1881, during a short stay at Frankfurt, I went to a large evening party . . . Clara Schumann and Brahms had agreed to play a four-hand pianoforte arrangement of Brahms's *Tragic Overture*, a work which had then just been published. Before sitting down Brahms took aside Marie Wurm, a pupil of Clara Schumann, who had asked her to turn the pages, and said to her: "When you come to page 4 you must be careful to turn two pages instead of one, because in this copy two have been printed twice by mistake." At the crucial moment, Clara Schumann, startled and angry, hastily turned back the page and thus just avoided a breakdown. At the end she turned on Marie Wurm and reproached her for what she took to be her carelessness, upon which the young girl burst into tears, explaining that she had acted under orders. Thereupon Clara Schumann scolded Brahms, saying, "Johannes, how could you do such a thing?" "Never mind, Clara," answered Brahms, "I only wanted to see whether you knew it all by heart already." '

B. List of Correspondents

(by Letter Number)

From Brahms

C. Biographical Sketches

Names in bold indicate letter recipient or writer.

Abraham, Max (1831–1900), partner, then owner of C. F. Peters Verlag, music publishers in Leipzig. He inaugurated the Edition Peters to make high-quality music available at low cost, a goal Brahms supported. Peters published Brahms's *Nänie* Op. 82, and vocal music, Opp. 112, 113.

Allgeyer, Julius (1828–1900), trained as a copper engraver, and founder of an art reproduction studio in Karlsruhe. He was also one of the earliest and most distinguished photographers in Germany. He and Brahms first met in Düsseldorf in 1854, then resumed contact in Karlsruhe in 1864. It is he who introduced Brahms to Anselm Feuerbach, a painter whose work both men admired. For a brief period and in the company of another mutual friend, the conductor Hermann Levi, Allgeyer, Brahms, and Feuerbach formed a close-knit group in Karlsruhe. Allgeyer's letters to Brahms are written in flowing language and proclaim a notion of friendship quintessentially Germanic-Romantic, one which Brahms outgrew, to some extent, living as he did in the much more cosmopolitan and cynical Vienna. There is a five-year hiatus in their friendship, broken by Allgeyer himself when he was desperate for money; Brahms came to his aid munificently. Allgeyer wrote the first full-scale biography of Feuerbach, and was later commissioned by Marie Schumann to write the biography of Clara Schumann, a project cut short by his death. The *Ballades and Romances*, Op. 75, are dedicated to him.

Arnim, Bettina von (1785–1859), something of a cult figure and central character in the latter phases of German Romantic literature. She was the sister of the writer Clemens Brentano (1778–1842), and the wife of Achim von Armin (Karl Joachim Friedrich Ludwig von, 1781–1831), whose collection of German folk poetry, *Des Knaben Wunderhorn* (1805–8), was a major contribution to German Romanticism and one of Brahms's favourite books. Bettina wrote poetry, painted, and sculpted. A quarrelsome, vocal opponent of Liszt and his 'Music of the Future', she was nevertheless a regular visitor to Liszt's home in Weimar, revered as someone who had known Beethoven and had been particularly close to Goethe. (This 'closeness' has now been shown to be something of a hoax, but the deception succeeded for well over a hundred years.) She met Brahms in Düsseldorf in the autumn of 1853, when she was 68 years old. Max Kalbeck (i. 136) claims that Bettina still turned men's heads. Brahms must have been one of them: his Op. 3 is dedicated to her. **Gisela von Arnim** was one of her seven children, the wife of Hermann Grimm, Joseph Joachim's successful rival for her affections. She died in Rome at an early age.

Arnold, Friedrich Wilhelm (1810–64), an important folk-song collector and music publisher in Elberfeld. Brahms was first in touch with him in 1854, concerning the publication of the third and fourth volumes of Schumann's Choral Romances and Ballades, Opp. 145 and 146. Brahms came to know him personally, and gathered material from him for his own folk-song collections.

Astor, Edmond, Melchior Rieter-Biedermann's son-in-law (married to Ida Rieter-Biedermann) and successor as director and proprietor of the Rieter-Biedermann Verlag.

Avé-Lallement, Theodor (1806–90), a leading Hamburg musician and piano teacher. Mentioned frequently in early letters between Clara and Brahms, he was also a friend of Joachim. A faithful supporter of the young Brahms and his Frauenchor, he and his daughter attended most rehearsals. He was a member of the Committee of the Hamburg Philharmonic for decades. Despite strained relations arising from Brahms's failure to be appointed as director of the organization, he remained helpful to the Brahms family long after the composer's departure for Vienna.

Bagge, Selmar (1823–96), composer, music critic, and from 1863 to 1866, editor of Breitkopf & Härtel's house journal, the *Allgemeine Musikalische Zeitung*. Generally sympathetic to Brahms's music, he was asked to sign the Brahms–Joachim Manifesto in 1860, but did not. From 1868 until his death he directed the Basle Music Conservatory.

Barbi, Alice (1862–1948), mezzo-soprano of international fame, she was the object of Brahms's last flirtation. At her farewell concert, given before her impending marriage to Baron Wolf-Stomersee, Brahms was her accompanist.

Bargheer, Karl (1831–1902), violinist, student of Joachim. He was concertmaster in Detmold in the 1850s and 1860s, where he was Brahms's closest friend and often made music with him. He was twice married, both times to members of Julius Otto Grimm's womens' chorus in Göttingen. After Detmold he served as concertmaster of the Hamburg Philharmonic.

Bargiel, Woldemar (1828–97), Clara Schumann's half-brother (not stepbrother, as is often claimed), a composer highly regarded by Joachim and others. He wrote much chamber music and several choral works, lived and worked in Berlin, and was appointed to the Prussian Senate.

Barth, Karl Heinrich (1840–1922), no relation of Richard, he was a pianist, teacher, and from 1871, professor of piano at Joachim's *Hochschule* in Berlin.

Barth, Richard (1850–1925), precocious violin student of Joachim (a left-handed violinist), and a conducting student and protégé of Grimm, in whose house he lived for several years while the teenage concertmaster of the Münster Orchestral Association concerts. He was later appointed Director of Philharmonic Concerts and the Choral Society in Hamburg at Brahms's suggestion, when he turned down the job for himself. During the breach between Brahms and Joachim, Barth was Brahms's favourite violinist. He is the editor of *BW* iv, the Grimm–Brahms correspondence.

Becker, Rupert, violinist in Düsseldorf, and friend of the Schumanns.

Beckerath, Alwin von (1849–1930), an influential leader of musical life in Krefeld. He was both uncle and brother-in-law of Rudolf von der Leyen, a fine amateur violinist and violist, and an admirer of Brahms. He kept a Brahms diary which his son used in writing a little memoir.

Beckerath, Laura von (1840–1921), wife of Rudolf von Beckerath. A charming and cordial woman, she maintained her friendship with Brahms by letter, after the death of her husband. Their son Willy made the widely reproduced sketches of Brahms conducting, and at the piano.

Beckerath, Rudolph von (1833–88), vintner and businessman in Wiesbaden, with vineyards and a country estate in Rüdesheim. He was part of a circle of well-to-do and musically active Mennonites centred in Krefeld, and was responsible for bringing Brahms and his music to that town four times. An accomplished amateur violinist, he played with von Bülow as well as Brahms. He was the uncle of Rudolf von der Leyen.

Bernays, Michael (1834–97), Hamburg-born, an enthusiast of Brahms's music from the time of their meeting in Göttingen, 1858. He was appointed to the University of Munich as Extraordinary Professor of Literature in 1873.

Bernuth, Julius (1830–1902), conductor in Leipzig before succeeding Julius Stockhausen as conductor of the Hamburg Philharmonic, a post he held from 1867 into the 1890s. He founded the Hamburg Conservatory.

Billroth, Theodor (1829–94), German-born surgeon, founder of modern abdominal surgery, he was Professor and Director of Surgery at Vienna University, and was so well known that his portrait appeared on an Austrian coin. He first met Brahms in Zurich, but the friendship, among Brahms closest, ripened in Vienna when Billroth moved there. He was an excellent pianist, a passable violist, and an early enthusiast of Brahms's music (in Zurich). Many of Brahms's chamber works premièred in his music room; he is the dedicatee of the string quartets, Op. 51.

Bischoff, Ludwig Friedrich Christian (1794–1867), founder and editor of the *Rheinische Musikzeitung* (1850) and *Niederrheinische Musikzeitung* (1853), two of the most conservative journals of the time.

Bismarck, Count Otto von (1815–98), German statesman, Chancellor of Prussia, founder of the modern political entity called Germany.

Bitter, Carl Hermann (1813–85), Regierungspräsident in Düsseldorf (the highest official in the city administration) at the time Brahms was considering a position there, and involved in making Brahms the offer. He was Prussian Finance minister from 1879 to 1882, and an early biographer of J. S. Bach, and of the Bach sons.

Blume, Herr Amtsvogt (Bailiff) (late eighteenth–mid-nineteenth century), administrator in northern Hanover, Beethoven enthusiast, and member of the musical circle in the village of Winsen-an-der-Luhe which encouraged the 14- and 15-year-old Brahms, he later helped send him on tour with Reményi.

Böhme, Franz Magnus (1827–98), writer on musical topics who taught at the Hoch Conservatory in Frankfurt from 1878 to 1885. He published his own collection of folk-songs in 1877, then collaborated on Erk's three-volume *Deutscher Liederhort*. See the comments to Letter 530 in Part VIII.

Böie, John (1822–1900), violinist and music director in Altona, one of Brahms's most reliable friends and supporters in Hamburg from 1853 on. For decades he led Hamburg's most distinguished string quartet. His wife was Marie Völkers, a member of the Frauenchor and of the more select Frauenquartet.

Brahms, Christiane Johanna née Nissen (1789–1865), mother of Johannes, Fritz, and Elise Brahms.

Brahms, Elise (Elisabeth) Wilhelmina Louise (1831–92), older sister of Johannes, married to clockmaker *Grund*.

Brahms, Fritz (Friederich) (1835–86), younger brother of Johannes, well-regarded music and piano teacher in Hamburg, where, however, he suffered in the shadow of his brother.

Brahms, Johann Jakob (1806–72), father of Elise, Fritz, and Johannes. Musician.

Brahms, Karoline Schnack née Paasch (1824–1902), second wife of Jakob Brahms, stepmother of Johannes, mother of Fritz Schnack.

Brandt, Auguste (1822–87), aunt of Bertha Porubsky, who lived with her during the year she spent in Hamburg. Aunt Auguste chaperoned the Hamburg Frauenchor, and served as the addressee for the letters Brahms sent to Bertha.

Breitkopf & Härtel, the most eminent German music publishing firm. It was founded in 1719 and located in Leipzig at that time. Breitkopf & Härtel published Brahms's Opp. 1–4, 7–11, and the *Variations on a Theme by Handel*, Op. 24, but turned down many other of his works. They published none after 1865, but obtained his editorial co-operation for several of their Complete Editions (Mozart, Schubert, Schumann, Chopin).

Brendel, Karl Franz (1811–68), music journalist, who succeeded Robert Schumann as editor of the *Neue Zeitschrift für Musik*.

Bronsart, Hans von Schellendorf (1830–1913), pianist and composer who was director of the theatre in Hanover.

Bruch, Max (1838–1920), primarily composer of oratorios and opera, but the works he is best known for are those for solo instrument and orchestra, a symphony, and some chamber music. For a while he was court conductor in Sondershausen, then Manchester, Breslau, and finally, Berlin. His First Symphony is dedicated to Brahms, with whom he had a relationship which oscillated between admiration and antagonism.

Brücke, Theodor von, the musical husband of Millie Wittgenstein, a good pianist, and one of the many Wittgenstein relations Brahms was in touch with. See also **Wittgenstein**.

Brüll, Ignaz (1846–1907), Moravian-born and Viennese-trained composer and brilliant pianist, gentle friend, and Brahms's preferred two-piano partner. Not merely a fine pianist, he was especially adept at score and sight-reading. Brahms was friendly with other members of his family both in Vienna and in Ischl, where they were neighbours. Brüll's son-in-law, Dr Robert Breuer, attended Brahms during his last illness.

Bruyck, Karl Debrois van (1828–1902), poet, and in the 1850s music critic for Vienna's *Wiener Zeitung*. An admirer of Schumann's music, he was the only Viennese critic to take note of Clara's performance of Brahms's Andante from the F minor Sonata, in 1856. Kalbeck called him a fine, perceptive, discerning, unprejudiced critic.

Bülow, Hans Guido, Freiherr von (1830–94), first great virtuoso conductor. A contemporary lexicon (by La Mara) described him thus: 'Presently the most perfect, exemplary pianist and greatest conductor and teacher: a "Missionary of purity and truth in Art", sensitive composer and spirited writer. Born in Dresden, he studied with Wieck and Hauptmann, then later with Wagner and Liszt.' An ardent Wagnerian, he came to treasure and promote Brahms's music only after the great trauma of his life, betrayal by his best friend (Wagner) with his wife, Cosima Liszt. Von Bülow's tours with the Meiningen Court Orchestra were not only a significant factor in spreading Brahms's fame, they were the first of their kind, and paved the way for other orchestra tours. Highly strung and prone to excruciating headaches, he suffered from a tumour pressing on nerves in his neck (discovered only during a post-mortem), and died while undergoing a 'cure' in Cairo. Brahms's Third Violin Sonata is dedicated to him. **Marie von B. née Schanzer** (1857–1941) was an actress before becoming his second wife. She edited and published her husband's writings after his death.

Chrysander, (Karl Franz) Friedrich (1826–1901), long-time friend of Brahms. An outstanding musicologist, he devoted his life to a biography of Handel (unfinished), and a complete edition of his works. Brahms collaborated with him on a complete edition of Couperin's keyboard music (Brahms edited the *Pieces de Clavecin*, Vol. iv of Chrysander's *Denkmäler der Tonkunst*). For a time Chrysander was editor-in-chief of the *Allgemeine Musikalische Zeitung*, Rieter's house journal.

Cornelius, Peter (1824–74), composer and poet, disciple of Wagner and Liszt, he first met Brahms in Düsseldorf. He was in Vienna when Brahms first arrived there, delicate, retiring, and barely eking out a living as music teacher. He enthusiastically introduced Brahms to his circle of friends, including Carl Tausig. The friendship cooled (Cornelius wrote a condescending review of a Singakademie concert) but survived until Cornelius moved to Munich and fell again under the sway of Wagner.

Cossel, Otto Friedrich Willibald (1813–65), Brahms's first piano teacher, and the first person to receive a letter from him. He was a student of **Eduard Marxsen**. One of Cossel's children was Brahms first godchild (there were at least a dozen more).

Cranz, August (1789–1870), owner of the Hamburg music-publishing firm of the same name. He gave the teenage Brahms work as piano teacher for his son, Alwin, and as arranger for piano of various popular pieces (published under a pseudonym).

Damrosch, Leopold (1832–85), conductor, composer, and violinist who, with his sons *Walter* and *Frank*, moved to New York City and played a central role in the development of musical life of that city in the latter half of the nineteenth, and first quarter of the twentieth centuries. Frank D. was founder and first director of the Institute of Musical Art in New York (now the Juilliard School).

Daumer, Georg Friedrich (1800–75), teacher and poet, hardly known now but for the music Brahms set to many of his verses. His eclectic taste in poetry resulted in the collection *Polydora*, supposedly drawn from many countries and translated by him. Brahms admired him personally, visiting him in Würtzburg shortly before his death only to discover that the old man, now with some fame as the poet of the *Liebeslieder Waltzes*, had never heard of him.

David, Ferdinand (1810–73), great early nineteenth-century violin virtuoso, and leading teacher (of Joachim, among others). Himself a student of Ludwig Spohr and a friend of Felix Mendelssohn, he also composed and is the author of a Violin School still in use. He was the concertmaster of the Leipzig Gewandhaus Orchestra from 1836 till his death. His was the only encouraging word at the Leipzig première of Brahms's Piano Concerto, Op. 15.

David, Paul, son of Ferdinand, he was concertmaster under Levi in Karlsruhe. He soon moved to England to conduct the boys' choir at a prominent school.

Deichmann family, well-to-do music-lovers, they lived in Melhem, just outside Bonn, and were partial to Schumann and his circle. Thanks to an introduction from Joachim, Brahms met them in 1853, and in their hospitable home he met many musicians with whom he stayed in contact for life.

Deiters, Hermann (1833–1907), early friend and enthusiast of Brahms, whom he met in 1855. Later organist at the Evangelical church in Vienna, he was a philologue, writer, music critic, publisher of the 4th edition of Jahn's Mozart Biography and the German edition of Thayer's *Life of Beethoven*, and was editor of the *Allgemeine Musikalische Zeitung* at the time Brahms wrote the *German Requiem*. He is Brahms's earliest biographer. Brahms was a frequent guest at his home in Bonn in 1868.

Deppe, Ludwig (1828–90), born near Detmold, music teacher, composer, and conductor. He belonged for a long time to Brahms's closest circle. He studied the piano with Marxsen, and became a distinguished piano teacher, settling in Hamburg in 1857 and founding a musical society which dissolved in 1868. From 1874 to 1886 he was court conductor in Berlin. Emil Sauer and Donald Tovey are among the most distinguished followers of the Deppe system of piano study, which Amy Fay has described in great detail in her *Music Study in Germany*.

Dessoff, Otto (1835–92), director of the Vienna Philharmonic Concerts from 1860 to 1875, whose fame and excellence was due to his 'energy and sense of purpose' (Kal, ii. 21). A North German, to Brahms he was the living example of the complete *Capellmeister*—despite a most unfavourable remark about him to Levi (Letter 241). Brahms was invited to dinner in his home after every Sunday concert—Frau Frederike was a good cook—until Dessoff moved to Karlsruhe to take over Levi's position as municipal director of music. Brahms entrusted him with the first performance of his First Symphony. Dessoff dedicated a string quartet to Brahms. His daughter Marguerite moved to New York, founded and directed the Dessoff Choir, and from 1925 on was professor at the Institute of Musical Art in New York (now the Juilliard School).

Detmering, Christian (1830–92), Brahms's cousin on his mother's side, the mainstay of the family in Hamburg. Trained as a musician by Brahms's father, he founded and ran a musical instrument shop. He died in the cholera epidemic which swept Hamburg in 1892.

Detmold: see Lippe-Detmold

Devrient, Edward (1801–77), began his career as a baritone in Berlin, and was director of the opera-house in Karslruhe. Member of a famous family of actors, he was the first middle-class director of a Royal Theatre, and author of the five-volume *History of the German Theatre* (*Geschichte der deutschen Schauspielkunst*). His son Otto was a prominent Shakespeare scholar.

Dietrich, Albert (1829–1908), Brahms met him in Düsseldorf, where he was Schumann's pupil (and where he collaborated with Schumann and Brahms in the F-A-E Sonata for Joachim). A lifelong friend, he was also an early adviser on some musical points—especially orchestration—when Brahms still felt very inadequately trained. After a short appointment as Municipal Music Director for Bonn, and a subsequent nervous breakdown, he spent the remainder of his career as music director at the Court in Oldenburg. Brahms was godfather to his first child.

Dömpke, Gustav, respected music critic in Vienna, flourishing in the latter decades of the century.

Door, Anton (1833–1919), pupil of Czerny, professor of piano at the Vienna Conservatory for thirty-two years, and one of the organizers and regulars of the walking and eating parties which gathered around Brahms. As President of the Tonkünstlerverein for many years he instituted the association's public concerts.

Dunkl, Johann Nepomuk (1832–1910), Hungarian-born, one of Liszt's earliest students, he met Brahms in Vienna in 1862 where he was studying with Anton Rubinstein. He ran Rósavölgyi's in Vienna, a branch of Budapest's leading music publisher and shop, owned then by his father-in-law and later by him.

Dustmann-Meyer, Louise née Meyer (1831–99), dramatic soprano, prima donna of the Viennese Court Opera from 1857 to 1875. She was a friend of Wagner, and the first Viennese *Isolde*. Married to a book dealer in 1858, she met Brahms at the Festival of the Lower Rhine in June 1862 and according to Kalbeck, captivated him 'by her voice and abilities'; she is the only person ever known to get away with calling him 'Hansi', and their association, of whatever kind it was, lasted for decades.

Dvořák, Antonin (1841–1904), with Smetana, the most important Czech composer of the nineteenth century. His career in German-speaking countries was aided immensely by the interest Brahms took in him from 1877 on.

Ebner, Ottilie née Hauer (1836–1920), daughter of one of Franz Schubert's comrades at the school of the Wiener Sängerknaben (Vienna Boys' Choir). On that score alone she would have interested Brahms; but in addition she caught his attention as a determined, gifted, and self-made young woman, who came alone to Vienna to make her career and supported herself by giving ten piano and voice lessons in a day and performing as a singer at every opportunity. She met Brahms in the Vienna Ladies' Choir, formed when he first came to Vienna. In 1864 Brahms 'almost committed a foolishness' with her at a Christmas party, as he told Clara: he was planning to propose to her when she arrived at the party having accepted another's offer of marriage that very morning.

Brahms's relationship to Ottilie seems to have been unique among his women friends. He wrote as easily to her as he would have to a favourite sister, at times even about personal matters close to his heart. He liked her company, invited her and her children to come to visit him on holiday, visited her daily to play for her when she was ill, and stayed in touch with her throughout his life even when she moved to Budapest. Forty of his letters to her survive in the memoir written by her daughter. For her part, Ottilie was utterly unabashed by him, wrote him spirited and lively letters which she signed 'Tilie', and allowed her admiration for him and his music to show unaffectedly. Some biographers have been less than kind to her (Schauffler, for example, and Kalbeck). Quite likely she was a forceful and independent woman, not quite the contemporary ideal of womanhood. But Brahms apparently liked her very much—perhaps they had in common a rough determination to succeed—and in later years he gave her an introduction to Joachim (which she hardly needed, as they knew each other) that anyone would be proud to have.

Ottilie grew up in the Oed, an isolated valley north-west of Vienna, frequently mentioned in the correspondence.

Eibenschütz, Ilona (1873–1967), Hungarian-born pianist, student of Clara Schumann, and highly regarded young piano talent. She spent several summers in Ischl during Brahms's sojourns there, then married and moved to England, virtually giving up her career in 1902. However, she made a few recordings of Brahms's late piano works, which have been reissued on CD.

Engelmann, Emma Brandes, such a spirited and fine pianist that Clara Schumann considered her a genuine threat. She gave up her career to marry Theodor W. Engelmann and raise a family. Nevertheless, her household was a centre of musical activity in Holland and she continued to play for her circle of friends well into old age. Although her letters were withheld from publication, Brahms's letters to her show he was on very easy terms with her.

Engelmann, Dr Theodor W. (1843–1909), distinguished scientist from Leipzig, who laid the groundwork for the study of bacterial photosynthesis, he was also a capable amateur cellist and married to Emma Brandes. He first met Brahms in 1874 at the Festival of the Lower Rhine. Professor at the University in Utrecht (later in Berlin), Engelmann was instrumental in arranging concerts for Brahms in Holland. He is the dedicatee of the Third String Quartet.

Ehlert, Louis (1825–84), pianist, author, and distinguished writer on music, his reviews were instrumental in gaining German acceptance for Dvořák. He retired to Wiesbaden, where he was a friend of the Beckeraths and where Brahms saw him frequently during the summer of 1883. He was a student of Jean Paul, Mendelssohn, Schumann, and taught for a while at Tausig's Piano School in Berlin.

Enderes, Hofrat Dr, Viennese, owner of many Schubert manuscripts.

Epstein, Julius (1832–1918), Croatian-born, he was an outstanding Viennese pianist, known as a Mozart and Beethoven specialist. He was introduced to Brahms's music and person by Bertha Porubsky in Vienna, 1862. Epstein gave him pupils, hired the hall for his first Viennese concert, and introduced him to the influential Joseph Hellmesberger. He was a leading piano teacher at the Conservatory (1867–1901), a founding member of Brahms's eating and walking group, and a lifelong friend. In 1875 he took another newcomer to Vienna under his protection, the 15-year-old Gustav Mahler, accepting him as his piano student at the Conservatory without fee.

Erk, Ludwig C. (1807–83), editor of several important collections of German folk-songs, the last of which was enlarged by Franz Böhme and published in three volumes as the Erk-Böhme *Deutscher Liederhort* in 1894. See the comments to Letter 532 in Part VIII.

Ettlinger, Anna (1841–1934), writer and poet in Karlsruhe, member of a prominent and musical family, she had four sisters, all of whom were singers. Together with Levi, Brahms was a frequent guest in her parents' home. Her five-act poem, *Melusine*, was written as an opera libretto for him. She sang in the first performance of the *Schicksalslied* and *Triumphlied*, and in one of the earliest performances of the Requiem. Her memoir of those events is of considerable interest.

Faber, Arthur, Viennese industrialist and husband of Bertha Porubsky. He acted for Brahms in Viennese financial matters.

Faber, Bertha, see Bertha Porubsky.

Fellinger, Maria (1849–1925) and her husband, *Richard* (1848–1903), among Brahms's closest Viennese friends from 1881 onwards. Along with the Fabers, they more and more took on the role of family in Brahms's later years. Maria was a sculptor and an ingenious photographer, to whom we owe many fine informal photographs of Brahms, and some curious montages ('showing' Brahms at home in his sitting-room, although he never sat for such photos). *Richard* was the General Director of the Siemens Corp. in Austria; thanks to that connection, Brahms was one of the first in Vienna to have electricity in his flat. Fellinger was the court-appointed executor of Brahms's estate.

Feuerbach, Anselm (1829–80), German painter and a mutual friend of Brahms and Allgeyer. Trained in Düsseldorf (1845) and in Rome, he was Professor at the Viennese Academy of Art (1873–6), but was never very successful. His letters to his stepmother Henriette show him to have had a very high opinion of himself and a vast disdain for his critics. In Vienna he was overshadowed by Makart, who was much more colourful, and much more successful. Although Brahms greatly admired his painting—they are almost all on Classical subjects, strangely static and subtly coloured—his refusal to learn how to get on in Vienna cooled Brahms's interest in him personally. Feuerbach left Vienna to live in Venice, where he died a few years later. *Nänie* was composed in his memory, but dedicated to his stepmother.

Feuerbach, Henriette (1812–92), second wife of Anselm the archaeologist and stepmother of Anselm the artist, to whom she was as attached as if he were her own. After his death, she devoted herself to finding homes for his paintings. She was educated, musical, and a writer, and Brahms admired her greatly.

Flatz, Franz, early Viennese enthusiast of Brahms. As a member of the Singakademie, he was one of the people who urged the selection of Brahms as its director.

Frank, Ernst (1847–89), one of Brahms's many *Kapellmeister* friends, he was choir director of the Court Opera in Vienna from 1869 and director of the Wiener Akademischer Gesangverein, before conducting opera in Mannheim. There he suffered at the hands of the Wagner clique, who accused him of being Brahms's puppet. He eventually lost his job, but took von Bülow's place in Hanover when the latter went to Meiningen. A mental collapse ended his career.

Franz, Robert (1815–92), during his lifetime, considered the third in Germany's trio of great Lieder composers, along with Schubert and Schumann. A composer in the conservative camp, he was highly regarded by Mendelssohn, Liszt, Schumann, Joachim, and, at the time of the Manifesto, by Brahms. He refused to put his name to the protest, however, and in September 1862, in a letter to Albert Dietrich, Brahms commented on how repugnant Franz was to him.

Frege, Livia (1818–91), singer and old Leipzig friend of Clara's. She retired from the concert platform early in life, but remained an important figure in Leipzig's music world for decades, arranging for performances of a great many works, old and new, in her home.

Fritzsch, Ernst Wilhelm (1840–1902), music publisher in Leipzig. Wagner enthusiast but also on good terms with Brahms, he was the editor of the *Musikalisches Wochenblatt* from 1870. In 1875 Brahms offered him his *Abendregen*, Op. 70, for publication in a journal devoted to music for the home, to further the availability of good music for popular consumption.

Fürstenau, Moritz (1824–89), Dresden-born and active there throughout his career, he was a child-prodigy flautist whose interest shifted early on to history. He became the Keeper of the Royal Private Collection in Dresden. He also founded the first Musicians' Association (Tonkünstlerverein) in Germany (1854), whose president he remained for life.

Gänsbacher, Josef (1829–1911), jurist, voice teacher, cellist, mountaineer, and son of a famous South Tyrolean Austrian patriot, he was one of the Viennese who quickly recognized Brahms's gifts and rose to the occasion to offer support right from the start of his career there. That Brahms was chosen as director of the Singakademie was due particularly to his efforts. Gänsbacher's friendship extended to helping Brahms in his quest for Schubert manuscripts. He was long a member of the voice faculty at the Vienna Conservatory and is the dedicatee of Op. 38.

Garcia-Viardot, Pauline (1821–1910), girlhood friend of Clara Schumann, one of the most distinguished singers in Europe, a good pianist, the student of Liszt, and the composer of several operettas. She was the daughter of Manual Garcia, perhaps the most influential voice teacher of the nineteenth century; the sister of Marie Malibran; the wife of a wealthy businessman, who built her a little theatre on the grounds of their villa in Baden-Baden; and the mistress of Ivan Turgenev. She sang the première of the Alto Rhapsody when she was nearly 50.

Georg II, Duke of Sachsen-Meiningen, see Meiningen.

Gernsheim, Friedrich (1839–1916), pianist, composer, and protégé of Hiller. He held increasingly important posts in Saarbrücken, Cologne, Rotterdam, and Berlin. He became well acquainted with Brahms in Bonn during the summer of 1868, where he had the chance to learn *Rinaldo* and the Requiem while they were still in proof. Letters begin in 1870. Brahms took him under his wing when he came to Vienna to perform in December and January of 1870/1.

Girzick, Rosa, impecunious Viennese singer (alto) who came to Hamburg to study with Stockhausen in 1863. The Brahms family looked after her there, and Brahms helped her when she was flat broke. It is possible that she was the impetus for the *Liebeslieder Waltzes*. She gave concerts with Brahms in Vienna, and was an important early interpreter of his songs.

Goldmark, Carl (1830–1915), Hungarian born, he settled in Vienna. His *Rustic Wedding Symphony* is still performed, his opera *The Queen of Saba* was a great success during his life. He also wrote chamber music, and was considered one of the outstanding Austrian composers. He and Brahms made a trip to Italy together, and spent several summers in the same area. They got on most of the time.

Gotthard[t], Johann Peter (1839–1919), Viennse music publisher and owner of a music shop, student of Simon Sechter (violin and viola). For years, Brahms used his shop as a postal address. An admirer of Brahms starting in Düsseldorf and Hamburg, he shared his enthusiasm with a group of like-minded friends which included Gänsbacher, Nottebohm, Julius Epstein, J. N. Dunkl, and Carl Goldmark. He arranged for Spina to publish Brahms's Opp. 27 and 28. Genuinely fond of music, he founded an amateur choral society, from which he resigned over their refusal to sing a Brahms work.

Grädener, Carl Georg Peter (1812–83), Hamburg musician, who befriended Brahms upon his return in 1853. Cellist, choral director, and composer, he was much older than Brahms, but a good friend and on 'Du' terms with him. Brahms described him to Clara as 'a highly gifted man'. He wrote on musical topics with power and integrity. Apart from Brahms, he was for many years Hamburg's only subscriber to the complete Bach edition then being published.

Grimm, Julius Otto (1827–1903), lifelong friend, with especially close ties in the early years. He met Brahms in Leipzig, where he was studying at the Conservatory at the time of Brahms's first visit to the city. He settled in Göttingen long enough to marry *Phillipine Ritmüller* (Pine Gur, 1835–96), the daughter of a well-known piano manufacturer, then spent the rest of his long career in Münster as Municipal Music

Director. He championed Brahms's music faithfully. Grimm composed songs in Platt-Deutsch, and wrote orchestral suites and chamber music which were popular in their day. Brahms dedicated his Ballades, Op. 10, to him, and was godfather to his first child.

Groth, Klaus (1819–99), widely read poet. He came from Brahms's ancestral village of Heide, in the Ditmarsch area of Schleswig-Holstein, and met Brahms in Düsseldorf in 1856, through Clara Schumann. Brahms felt a special affinity for him and his *Quickborn*, a collection of poetry in Platt-Deutsch. Brahms set many of his German poems, including the 'Regenlied', and the three 'Heimats'.

Grund, Friedrich Wilhelm (1791–1874), conductor of Singakademie and Philharmonic Concerts in Hamburg 1828–63, and the voice teacher of at least one member of the Frauenchor. In 1859 he called Brahms '. . . a pleasant little fellow'. Was he aware Brahms hoped to have the post he was just about to retire from?

Grünwald-Zerkowitz-Kolokotroni, Sidonie (1852–1907), Moravian-born writer. She settled in Vienna in 1880, where she caused a commotion with her naturalistic writings which deplored the double standard in morality, a husband's love-affairs before his 'sensible' marriage, and the lot of the wife. She worked to emancipate Viennese women from Parisian and noble fashions. Her books, *Lieder einer Mormonin* and *Gretchen von heute* ran to many editions. *Gretchen* was banned in Austria, even in 1959.

Hallier Family, cultured and well-to-do Hamburgers, very friendly to Brahms, especially after his return from Düsseldorf in 1857. Two of their daughters sang in the Frauenchor. Brahms spent many evenings in their home, participating in concerts and discussion groups, and expressing opinions on politics and religion; it is possible he made his ideas as a free-thinker *too* well known for conservative tastes. Brahms attended the father's lectures in art history, and was tutored in Latin by one of the sons. Clara stayed with the family when she came to Hamburg.

Hanslick, Eduard (1825–1904), born in Prague, Vienna's most powerful music critic, unyieldingly biased against Wagner and Bruckner, a man for whom music started with Mozart and ended with Brahms. Although uncomprehending of much of Brahms's music, he approved of its 'absolute' nature; and Brahms, cognizant of Hanslick's shortcomings, was nevertheless very fond of him personally. He was Professor of Aesthetics at the University of Vienna.

Härtel, Raimund (1810–88), one of the owners of the Leipzig music publishers, Breitkopf & Härtel.

Hartmann, Mathilde (1817–1907), young singer in Düsseldorf and friend of the Schumann family. She was godmother to Felix Schumann.

Hasenclever, Dr Richard (1813–76), Schumann family's physician and friend from 1851 to 1854, he arranged for Schumann's commitment to the asylum in Endenich; he was a member of the Düsseldorf Singverein committee, and the eventual director of music in Koblenz.

Hauptmann, Moritz (1792–1868), one of the great figures in Germany's musical life. Through his teaching he exercised a major infuence on many important musicians. Educated in French, Italian, classical languages, mathematics, and science, he was among other things an architect with acoustical interests. He was also a violin student of Spohr, and the teacher of Ferdinand David, among many others. He composed motets, masses, cantatas, songs, opera, carried on musicological work, and was appointed as Cantor of the Thomasschule (Bach's old position) and professor at the Leipzig Conservatory. He was awarded many decorations, knighthoods, and honorary doctorates.

Hausmann, Robert (1852–1909), cellist of the Joachim Quartet throughout its entire existence, groomed from the start by Joachim for that position. When he enrolled in the Berlin Hochschule, he was for a time the only cello student. He studied for a year in England with Piatti. With his return he joined the Hochschule faculty, where he remained until his death. Brahms was especially fond of his playing, and wrote the Second Cello Sonata and the Double Concerto with his playing in mind. Hausmann premièred both works, as well as a number of other chamber pieces. He is the dedicatee of Max Bruch's *Kol Nidrei*.

Hecht, Felix (1847–1909), one of Brahms's Mannheim friends, along with Ernst Franck, with whom Hecht once shared a bachelor flat. He was a Doctor of Law, later married to a skilled amateur pianist. Brahms usually stayed with them when in Mannheim.

Hegar, Friedrich (1841–1927), violinst and conductor. Under his direction, the orchestra in Zurich developed into a major organization. He was an important promoter of Brahms's music, having met him in 1865; it was a happy connection which lasted for their lives. His brother Emil (1843–1921) is the cellist who premièred Brahms's First Cello Sonata; his son Johannes was Brahms's godson (and also a cellist).

Heimsoeth, Friedrich (1814–77), member of the committee for the Schumann Festival in Bonn, 1873. He was Hermann Deiters's father-in-law.

Hellmesberger, Joseph, the Elder (1828–93), Director of the Conservatory in Vienna. In 1869 he was concertmaster of the Court Opera, later (1877) court conductor, and founder of the famous quartet bearing his name. He was the best-known member of a Viennese family long known for its musical ability. Kalbeck (ii. 21) notes that the family was a prime example of the Viennese genius for music, with lightness of character, sweet tone, and lyric performances of late Beethoven and Schubert which contrasted with Joachim's seriousness. He met Brahms through Julius Epstein in 1862, and soon after, programmed the first ever Viennese performance of a Brahms chamber work (Op. 25, in November 1862); not fond of Brahms, he later claimed to have agreed only because he drank too much Croatian wine at Epstein's house. But he must have had a change of heart, for he later programmed many other first performances of Brahms works.

Henschel, Sir George (1850–1934), first and foremost a singer, noted among other things for accompanying himself at the piano at his Lieder recitals. He was an important voice teacher, the first conductor of the Boston Symphony (1881–4), and after moving to England, founded the London Symphony Orchestra. Witty and cheerful, Brahms took to him immediately, and spent his holiday of 1876 with him on the island of Rügen. He became a British citizen, and was knighted in 1914. He gave a Schubert recital at the age of 78, and was still conducting when he was past 80. He wrote an important memoir of Brahms.

Herbeck, Johann von (1831–77), Viennese conductor, ambitious and politically astute. First associated with the Court Opera in 1863, he became its Director in 1870, giving up his position as Director of the Gesellschaft der Musikfreunde concerts to do so. In 1875, dismissed from the Opera, he wanted his old job back, held now by Brahms. Brahms resigned before the Board had to make a choice. Herbeck broadened an appreciation for the choral creations of Schubert, Liszt, Bruckner, and Schumann, and premièred Schubert's 'Unfinished' Symphony, the score of which he discovered.

Herzogenberg, Elizabet von, née Stockhausen (1847–92), daughter of a musical and high-ranking diplomat, she grew up in Paris and Vienna. She studied the piano with Brahms briefly before her marriage, and went on to become an exceptional pianist, musician, and letter-writer, with great charm and deep insight into Brahms's music. She later became one of Brahms's dearest friends; her letters to Brahms are particularly rewarding to read. The Rhapsodies, Op. 79, are dedicated to her.

Herzogenberg, Heinrich Picot de Peccaduc, Freiherr von (1843–1900), Viennese born, and husband of Elizabet, he was a serious but rather uninspired composer, a fact which complicated his relations with Brahms, whom he admired vastly. He devoted himself to the Bach Verein in Leipzig, and later in life taught at Joachim's Hochschule in Berlin. He wrote much choral, chamber, instrumental, and orchestral music.

Heyse, Paul (1830–1914), influential German poet and novelist, who won the Nobel Prize for Literature in 1910. Through their mothers, he and Felix Mendelssohn were second cousins. Greatly admired by Brahms as a poet and friend (but they saw each other only rarely), Brahms set some of his poems to music.

Hildebrand, Adolf (1847–1921), prominent sculptor. His commissions included gravestone memorials for Elizabet & Heinrich von Herzogenberg, the Brahms memorial in Meiningen, and Spitta's gravestone. He lived for many years in Florence.

Hiller, Ferdinand (1811–85), leading conductor, piano prodigy, student of Hummel, friend of Mendelssohn, conductor of the Gewandhaus Orchestra 1843–4, Municipal Music Director in Düsseldorf in 1847, he was named to the same post in Cologne in 1850, and spent the rest of his career there. He founded the Cologne Conservatory, and became conductor of the famed Gurzenich Concerts. He also wrote books and journalistic articles on musical matters. Brahms met him in Cologne, 1853, during his first visit to Schumann. Their friendship strengthened over the years so that Hiller was one of the few people who could speak his mind to Brahms plainly and scold when necessary. They were on 'Du' terms from 1874, when Brahms was elected honorary member of Kölnischer Tonkünstlerverein (Cologne Musician's Association).

Hummer, Reinhold, solo cellist of the Court Opera and Philharmonic in Vienna, and cellist first of the Hellmesberger, then of the Rosé Quartet, in which capacity he found himself competing with Robert Hausmann. As both had names which are also ordinary nouns, some Viennese wit remarked that 'Hausmannskost ist gut, aber wir sind an Hummer gewöhnt' (Home cooking is good, but we're used to Lobster). With Anton Door, he resurrected the Cello Sonata in E minor, Op. 38 from oblivion.

Jaëll, Alfred (1832–82), brilliant pianist from Trieste. By virtue of his flashy musical taste, he aroused the scorn of Brahms and Joachim, although they recognized his pianistic prowess and were in frequent contact when they were young. He was a child prodigy, and when Brahms and Joachim met him, had recently returned from America, where he fled after 1848, and where he left his mark as one of the first great pianists to set foot on that continent. His compositions ran to pot-pourris and other salon pieces; but he genuinely admired Brahms's works, and performed the Piano Concerto, Op. 15, in England when the work was quite unknown there.

Jahn, Otto (1813–69), Rector of the University of Bonn, Professor of Classical Philology and Archaeology, he was also an important early biographer of Mozart. He was a friend of Grimm, Joachim, and the Schumanns.

Janssen, Marie née Cossel, oldest daughter of Otto Cossel. Brahms remained in touch with her throughout his life.

Japha, Louise (1826–1910), pianist and composer from Hamburg, she knew Brahms from the time he was 11 or 12, and was one of the few musical friends of his youth; he would perform his compositions for her, and they sometimes played duets together. She studied with Schumann in Düsseldorf, where Brahms met her again. He dedicated his Op. 6 songs to her and to her sister Minna.

Jenner, Gustav Uwe (1865–1920), composer from Kiel. A protégé of Klaus Groth, he became Brahms's only composition student, the most lasting result of which is an interesting memoir of his experiences. He spent most of his career as Music Director for the University of Marburg.

Joachim, Amalie (1839–98), mezzo-soprano and one of the most important Lieder singers of her time, she was also the wife of Joseph, and bore him five children, one of whom was Brahms's godson. Her singing career was carried on despite frequent illness; she was particularly identified with Brahms's Alto Rhapsody. She is the dedicatee of the Duets, Op. 28. The songs with viola, Op. 91, were written with her and Joseph in mind, but not publicly dedicated as such, as their marriage had foundered by the time of publication.

Joachim, Joseph (1831–1907), Hungarian born but trained in Vienna and Leipzig, he was one of the leading violinists and musicians of his day on the Continent, and very influential in shaping musical life in Britain, where he visited every year. A child prodigy, he was a protégé of Mendelssohn, in whose home he lived while he studied in Leipzig. A later protégé of Liszt, he broke with the latter on ideological grounds. His friendship with Brahms, starting in 1853, was one of the central events of both of their lives. From its inception, Joachim was intimately identified with Brahms's music, even during their period of estrangement following his suit to divorce Amalie. A composer of note in his own right (his Hungarian Violin Concerto and pieces for viola are making a comeback, and he wrote the standard cadenza for Brahms's violin concerto), he was also noted during his lifetime as a conductor and as head of the Music Conservatory at the Royal Academy of Art in Berlin (the Hochschule), which he founded. Led by him, the Joachim String Quartet was instrumental in making the quartets of Josef Haydn part of the standard quartet repertory. The Bruch, Dvořák, and Brahms violin concertos are dedicated to him, as is Brahms's Op. 1.

Joachim, Fritz and Heinrich, brothers of Joseph. They lived in Vienna and London respectively.

Kalbeck, Max (1850–1921), born in Breslau, he spent the major part of his career in Vienna, writing about music. Very partisan regarding Brahms's music, his lasting contribution is an eight-volume biography of the composer which incorporates a large number of small, contemporary memoirs, and would be indispensable on that account alone. It also discusses all of Brahms's music, and if not always in a manner which stands up to modern methods and tastes, nevertheless it set the direction for future works about Brahms and is the essential reading for any serious study of the composer. Kalbeck was a faithful friend to Brahms, always available if the composer needed a concert, mealtime, or strolling companion. A few of Brahms's songs are set to Kalbeck's poems.

Keller, Gottfried (1819–90), one of Switzerland's most notable and prolific German-language novelists and poets, particularly known for his short stories and the novel *Der grüne Heinrich.* He was friendly with Brahms from 1866, who found in him a kindred spirit. Their association sheds indirect light on an aspect of Brahms which we otherwise know little about, namely his social and political philosophy.

Keller, Robert (1828–91), music editor for the Simrock Verlag, as well as Brahms's editor beginning in the early 1870s. He saw most of the mature masterpieces into print, and is the compiler of the Thematic Catalogue of Brahms's work for the 1887 edition. He also worked for Simrock as an arranger.

Kiel, Clemens August (1813–71), violin and composition student of Ludwig Spohr, he spent his entire career in Detmold. Starting as a member of the wind band, he was later named concertmaster, Director of the Court Theatre and Court Conductor. He wrote susbtantial concertos, primarily for wind instruments. At 49 he was ignominiously dismissed as a result of an argument with a young officer of the regiment, and died a broken man nine years later.

Kiel, Friedrich (1821–85), composer from the Rhineland, and professor of composition at the Berlin Hochschule until his death. Among other music, he wrote four violin sonatas.

Kirchner, Theodor (1823–1903), German-born, a disciple of Schumann, he composed over 1,000 opuses, almost all piano music. He met Brahms in the 1850s, and became an early enthusiast. Brahms found in his music 'the sweetest of the sweet'. Kirchner was Brahms's preferred arranger and made many piano reductions of Brahms's music, including the *German Requiem*, and an outstanding version of the string sextets for piano trio. Organist in Winterthur for a number of years, he was then director in Zurich (1862–72), and subsequently composition and piano teacher in various German cities. In later years he fell on hard times; Brahms helped him financially to a very considerable degree. He died in Hamburg.

Klinger, Max (1857–1920), painter, engraver, sculptor, capable pianist, and corresponding member of the Secession movement in Vienna, he was very taken with Brahms's music. His series of engravings, *Amor und Psyche,* was dedicated to Brahms in 1880. A decade later he created the *Brahms-Fantasy,* a series of forty-one engravings, etchings, and lithographs, semi-surrealist responses to Brahms's texts as well as his music. He is the dedicatee of the *Four Serious Songs,* Op. 121.

Knorr, Iwan (1853–1916), pianist, composer, and teacher, he was born in Germany, raised in Russia, and trained in Leipzig. In 1877 his visit to Brahms in Pörtschach led to an advantageous friendship; Brahms recommended him for a position at the Hoch Conservatory in Frankfurt, where he spent the rest of his life and of which he was the eventual director.

Königslow, Otto von (1824–85), leading violinist in Cologne. He was the concertmaster of the Gurzenich Concerts orchestra there, and leader of an important string quartet bearing his name.

Kupfer, William (1843–1914), copyist of the Fourth Symphony and other late Brahms works, he grew up in Hamburg, a few doors from Brahms's childhood home on the Dammtorwall. He came to Vienna as a cellist, then turned to copying music. Modest and quiet, Brahms was fond of him, and godfather to one of his children.

Lachner, Franz (1803–90), celebrated conductor and composer in Munich, he was one of the people who recommended Brahms for the Order of Maximilian for Science and Art in 1873. He was organist of the Protestant church in Vienna 1826–34, theatre conductor in Vienna and Mannheim, and from 1836, in Munich. By 1852 he was Generalmusikdirector in Munich, retiring in 1868 but still influential in musical matters. His younger brother Ignaz (1807–95) worked in Hamburg from 1853 to 1858, and was an early admirer of Brahms.

Lachner, Vincenz (1811–93), another younger brother of Franz, primarily a conductor. He was the court conductor in Mannheim for a while, until he was undermined by the Wagner faction.

La Mara: see Lipsius.

Laub, Ferdinand (1832–75), violinist, leader of prominent Viennese string quartet in the 1860s, a rival of Hellmesberger.

Laurens, Jean-Joseph-Bonaventure (1801–90), French writer, composer, artist, and Secretary of the University of Montpellier. In the autumn of 1853, while on a visit to the Schumanns, he made well-known sketches of the young Brahms, of Joachim, and of Schumann.

Leser, Rosalie (d. 1896), intimate friend of the Schumann family in Düsseldorf. Clara leaned upon her as a sister, after Schumann's breakdown, and could always be reached through her.

Lessing, Carl Friedrich (1808–80), director of the Portrait and Print Gallery of the Archduke Friedrich I of Baden-Württemberg (Karlsruhe). Brahms was acquainted with him from Düsseldorf days. His wife **Ida** (1817–80) was a painter of flowers with a great talent for entertaining. Together, and with the entire upper floor of one wing of the Art Gallery at their disposal, they reigned over Karlsruhe's leading salon, where Brahms was a frequent guest. See also *Schroedter.*

Levi, Hermann (1839–1900), one of the great conductors of the nineteenth century. Especially noted for his performances of Wagner, he was reluctantly chosen to première *Parsifal*, for lack of anyone else capable of conducting the work to Wagner's satisfaction. A student of Vincenz Lachner, his was an extremely precocious talent.

He was appointed Conductor of the Karlsruhe Court Opera in 1864, where he and Brahms became the closest of friends in a circle that included Julius Allgeyer, Paul David, Anselm Feuerbach, and in a wider circle, Gustav Wendt and Clara Schumann, the Lessings, the Schroedters, and the Ettlingers. In 1872 he accepted the appointment as co-conductor in Munich, which led to a very uncomfortable rivalry with another good friend of Brahms's, Franz Wüllner. His friendship with Brahms did not survive the ensuing strains of conflicting loyalties, musical and personal.

Leyen, Rudolf von der (1851–1910), banker and fine amateur pianist brought up on and devoted to the chamber music of Brahms, a nephew of Rudolf von Beckerath and brother-in-law of Alwin von Beckerath. Von der Leyen was host to Brahms during several visits to the musically enthusiastic town of Krefeld. He is the author of a small memoir of Brahms, very evocative of the world of well-to-do musical amateurs.

Limburger, Paul Bernhard (1826–91), Consul, businessman, member, and then chairman of the Board of Directors of the Gewandhaus in Leipzig, and one of the few Brahms enthusiasts there in a position of importance.

Lindeck, Wilhelm (1833–1911), brother of Hermann Levi. Himself a professionally trained and accomplished basso, he nevertheless gave up a promising operatic career to marry, converting to Catholicism in the process. He kept his stage name, and made his banking career in the prominent banking house of W. H. Ladenburg & Sons. He rose quickly in the firm to become a director, but was, even so, happy to take up his brother's suggestion that he help Brahms arrange his financial matters. He served as Brahms's financial adviser and personal banker for ten years, at which time Fritz Simrock took on that role.

Lippe-Detmold, small principality in Westphalia, near Kassel, at the foot of the Teutoburger Forest. From 1851 to 1876 the reigning prince of the small principality in Westphalia was Count (Fürst) Paul Friedrich Emil Leopold, who supported an active theatre and a full orchestra, took part in chamber music, and with his sisters, sang in the chorus he founded in 1848. His wife, the Princess Friederike, was an unusually talented pianist and musician who studied first with Clara, then with Brahms. With the Count's death, the court orchestra was disbanded abruptly, as his son and successor devoted himself to hunting; by the end of the First World War the considerable wild animal population of the Teutoburger Forest was gone.

Lipsius, Ida Marie (1837–1927), prolific writer on music and biographer of musicians, she wrote under the pseudonym La Mara. Her biographical comments about Brahms and his contemporaries are of interest now because they were written during their lifetimes.

Liszt, Franz (1811–86). The great pianist, composer, and teacher extended a welcoming hand to Brahms immediately upon recognizing his talent, and remained cordial even when Brahms did not join his 'Musicians of the Future'. After the Manifesto of 1860, published by Brahms and Joachim and directed specifically against him, they had little to do with each other. Brahms never lost his admiration and respect for Liszt as a pianist and as an exceptional human being, and the suave Liszt never lost his temper with Brahms; but he also never performed a note of his music in public.

Lobe, Johann Christian (1797–1881), German flautist, composer, and prolific writer on music. He wrote a *Textbook of Musical Composition* in four volumes which went into many editions, and edited the *Allgemeine Musikzeitung* (Leipzig) from 1846 until 1848.

Lübke, Wilhelm (1826–96), historian of art and architecture, and professor in Stuttgart for most of his career. Brahms admired his writings and referred to him frequently in letters. With Billroth and Wesendonck, Lübke hired an orchestra for a private performance of Brahms's Opp. 15 and 16, in Zurich, 1865.

Ludwig II, King of Bavaria (1845–86), reigned from 1864 until his suicide in Starnberg Lake. He is best known to musicians as the patron of Richard Wagner.

Maho, J., French publisher who owned his own publishing house in the Boulevarde Mal Herbe, 1851–77.

Mandyczewski, Eusebius (1857–1929), Viennese composer, choral conductor, and musicologist. For a number of years, he conducted a small women's choir presided over by Frau Bertha Faber. Mild-mannered, much liked by many people, he was esteemed by Brahms, at whose suggestion he was appointed archivist and librarian of the Gesellschaft der Musikfreunde after the death of Ferdinand Pohl. For the last decade of his life Brahms relied on Mandyczewski's judgement in musical matters, and for help in carrying out various errands. He is the principal editor of the Complete Brahms Edition published by Breitkopf & Härtel, for which he enlisted the aid of his student, Hans Gál.

Marpurg, Friedrich Wilhelm (1718–95), most important music teacher of his time, he lived in Hamburg. His *Abhandlung von der Fuge*, appeared in 1753–4.

Marxsen, Eduard (1806–87), composer and highly regarded piano teacher in Hamburg, who lived in the adjoining suburb of Altona, after returning from his studies in Vienna with Seyfried and Bocklet. He taught Johannes and Fritz Brahms without accepting any fee, and was a trusted adviser to the Brahms family. For many years, Brahms continued to consult with him about various compositional problems (but he destroyed their correspondence after Marxsen's death) and the Second Piano Concerto is dedicated to him. It is puzzling that despite his renown and Johannes's brilliant début at the age of 15, Marxsen was unable to help him develop a career in Hamburg. In his entry for 5 March 1842, Robert Schumann wrote in his marriage diary, 'E. Marxsen also visited us; his Jewish physiognomy disgusted me'. It is an intriguing idea, worth further study, that Marxsen's inability to help Brahms's career had to do with his own background. At this juncture, however, Schumann's suggestive remark only raises questions.

Mattheson, Johann (1681–1764), one of Hamburg's most renowned composers and writers on music.

Meiningen, Georg II, Duke of Sachsen-Meiningen (1826–1914), devoted to the arts and sciences, with a talent for drawing and painting. He made the small duchy of Sachsen-Meiningen a model of artistic patronage, supporting a theatre and symphony orchestra. As a student in Leipzig, he spent a year living in the home of Felix Mendelssohn, a fact probably not unrelated to his support for the arts.

Meiningen, Helene, Freifrau von Heldberg (1839–1923), the Morganatic second wife of **Georg** II. Before her marriage she was an actress in the Meiningen Theatre troupe, and was also a trained pianist, having studied with von Bülow. In the early 1860s, *Julius Stockhausen* was deeply in love with her, but failed to gain his parents' approval for the match.

Meiningen, Princess Marie, the daughter of Georg II by his first wife. She was an accomplished pianist, student of Kirchner and Bülow, and tutored by Louis Ehlert (1825–84), the composer and writer.

Menzel, Adolf Friedrich Erdmann von (1815–1905), celebrated artist, among the last of the great pre-photographic book illustrators, with particular expertise in the history and military details of the era of Frederick the Great. Like Brahms, he held the Prussian Order 'Pour le Mérite'. When he and Brahms first met in Berlin, he was a lively, wiry, energetic man of 76, and Brahms took to him immediately.

Meysenbug, Carl von, scion of the Meysenbug family (courtiers at the Court of Lippe-Detmold) and a teenager when Brahms came to Detmold and joined him in various adventures. After Brahms's death he wrote a delightful memoir for a Viennese newspaper, in which he admitted that he had had no idea of the genius he was dealing with.

Meysenbug, Hofmarschall von, Carl's father and Laura's brother. He was responsible for arranging the details of Brahms's sojourns at Court.

Meysenbug, Laura von, piano student of Clara in Düsseldorf, then of Brahms, in Düsseldorf and Detmold. She was Carl's aunt.

Mühlfeld, Richard (1856–1907), initially a violinist, who taught himself to play the clarinet and became the principal clarinettist in the orchestra at Meiningen, as well as at Bayreuth from 1884 to 1896. His particularly beautiful tone attracted Brahms, who wrote all of his clarinet chamber music for him.

Nottebohm, (Martin) Gustav (1817–82), born in Westphalia and trained by Mendelssohn, Schumann, and Sechter. Best known now for his groundbreaking works on Beethoven's sketchbooks, during his lifetime he eked out a living teaching composition, theory, and counterpoint. A confirmed bachelor and member of the group who met with Brahms's friends at Gauses's Pub, he had few good friends apart from Robert Volkmann and Brahms, who tended him in Graz in his last illness and made the funeral arrangements after his death.

Oser, Josefine, see Wittgenstein.

Otten, Georg Dietrich (1806–90), well-to-do Hamburg musician. In the 1850s he founded an orchestra to play contemporary music, in contrast with the more conservative Hamburg Philharmonic conducted by Grund. He was very helpful to the young Brahms, who described him to Clara Schumann as 'the best and most educated musician here'. Their relationship cooled very rapidly, virtually ceasing by 1860.

Otterer, Christian (*fl.* 1815–1900), violist in Hamburg, colleague of Jakob Brahms, and neighbour of the Brahms family. He assisted in Johannes's first concert at the age of 10.

Perfall, Baron Karl von (1824–1907), minor government official who studied music, and became director of the Court Opera in Munich. He composed a number of fairly successful operas.

Perger, Richard von (1854–1911), Viennese musician, one of the young composers in the circle around Brahms in the 1880s. In 1895 he was appointed director of the Gesellschaft der Musikfreunde Orchestra, then headed the Vienna Conservatory from 1899 to 1907. He published a biography of Brahms and a history of the Gesellschaft der Musikfreunde, in addition to a number of operas.

Petersen, Dr Carl Friedrich (1809–92), Mayor of Hamburg at the time Brahms was awarded the Honorary Citizenship of the city. Under the stimulus of his daughter Antonie (Toni), his home was a focus of musical activity, where all important musicians who came to the city were received. The *Fest- und Gedenksprüche*, Op. 109, are dedicated to him.

Pohl, (Karl) Ferdinand (1819–87), the very knowledgeable librarian and archivist of the Gesellschaft der Musikfreunde from 1866 until his death. He began work on an important two-volume biography of Haydn, but did not live to finish it. He was part of Brahms's closest circle of friends.

Porubsky, Bertha, a member of Brahms's Frauenchor in Hamburg, daughter of the Protestant minister in Vienna, sent to Hamburg for a year to finish her education. Brahms was probably romantically inclined towards her; she was undoubtedly fond of him, and was partially responsible for Brahms's decision to visit Vienna. Once arrived, she provided him with many contacts, social and musical, but by then she was engaged to marry a wealthy industrialist, Arthur Faber. Bertha organized the 'Faber Chorus' for Brahms, enabling him to hear trial performances of his a capella music. The Fabers essentially took the place of family for Brahms. He was a standing guest in their home, and when he was away from Vienna, they took care of his affairs and once even reorganized his apartment. Arthur Faber acted as Brahms's Viennese banker. The famous Lullaby was written for their second child, and Bertha was the recipient of many other song manuscripts.

Raff, Joseph Joachim (1822–1882): 'Important and prolific, composed in all genres, sought traditional forms with modern content' (La Mara). In all he wrote about 300 works. Swiss-born, he became the Director of the Hoch Conservatory in Frankfurt—i.e. Clara Schumann's employer.

Reimers, Christian, Hamburger, trained first as a pianist, then principal cellist of the Düsseldorf Orchestra under Schumann. Joachim, Brahms, and Clara played with him, and Schumann wrote his cello concerto for him.

Reinecke, Carl (1824–1910), first met Brahms in 1853. He was the conductor of the Gewandhaus Orchestra from 1860 until 1893, and a fine pianist in his own right. With the cellist Emil Heger, he gave the world première of Brahms's Cello Sonata in E minor, Op. 38, in 1871 (an event quite unnoticed), as well as the world première of the complete *German Requiem*. His willingness to perform Brahms's new works as they appeared was offset, unfortunately, by mediocre performances of excessively long programmes. Nevertheless, his efforts played some part in Leipzig's eventual acceptance of Brahms's music in a city where Mendelssohn was still king.

Reinthaler, Karl (1822–96), choral composer and music director of Bremen Cathedral, who arranged for the first major performance of the *German Requiem*, establishing a life long friendship with Brahms.

Reményi, Eduard (1828–98), noted violinist, and the person who provided Brahms with the chance to escape from Hamburg by taking him on tour in 1853. He was born in Miskolcz, Hungary, of German parents named Hoffmann who Hungarianized their name (Reményi is Hungarian for the German 'Hoffnung', hope). He studied at the Vienna Conservatory 1840–2 with Joseph Böhm, Joachim's principal teacher as well. Banished from Austria for participating in the Hungarian Revolution of 1848, he fled through Hamburg to America, and returned in 1853. Named solo violinist to Queen Victoria, he received the same appointment to the Emperor of Austria in 1860, after being amnestied. Neither Brahms nor Joachim nor Brahms scholars have paid much attention to his gifts, but he was a formidable violinist and aroused great enthusiasm for his virtuosity and transcriptions. He died on stage while on tour in San Fransisco.

Richarz, Franz, M.D. (1812–87) founder (in 1844) and director of an asylum for the mentally ill in Endenich, just outside of Bonn. His establishment was guided by the most modern and humane standards of the day; it made minimal use of physical restraint and avoided punitive measures, in accordance with the pioneering work of John Conolly. Richarz treated Robert Schumann from 4 March 1854 until his death, on 29 July 1856.

Rieter-Biedermann, Melchior (1811–76), eminent Swiss music publisher, based in Winterthur. He published the Piano Concerto, Op. 15, after Breitkopf & Härtel refused it, and took a chance on many other pieces as well, acting essentially as Brahms's patron during a particularly lean time for the composer. His relationship with Brahms developed into a friendship which extended to other members of the family; Brahms was a frequent guest in his home in the 1860s. The publishing house moved to Leipzig and eventually was bought by C. F. Peters in 1917.

Rietz, Julius (1812–77), conductor, a student of Romberg, and Mendelssohn's successor first in Düsseldorf (1834), then in Leipzig. He was on the podium for the première of the Piano Concerto, Op. 15, and no friend to Brahms's music. He taught at the Leipzig Conservatory from 1848 until moving to Dresden, where he served as general music director until his death.

Rosé, Carl (Carlo Rosa) (1842–89), violinist active in Hamburg, then concertmaster of the Philharmonic there from 1863 to 1865.

Rösing, Frau Dr Elizabeth, aunt of the Völkers sisters, who lived outside Hamburg in the suburb of Hamm, and rented a room to Brahms for a few years before his departure for Vienna. The *Variations on a Theme by Handel* and the piano quartets, Opp. 25 and 26 were written there; Op. 26 is dedicated to her.

Rubinstein, Anton (1829–94), 'Next to Bülow, the leading living pianist and one of the most important composers . . . studied in Moscow and Berlin as a youth . . . lived 1848–68 in Petersburg, founded and led the Conservatory and Music Society . . . since then lives exclusively for his compositions, year-long tours and pianistic activities' (La Mara). Rubinstein took a very jaundiced view of the young Brahms, but through the good offices of Clara Schumann and Pauline Garcia-Viardot in Baden-Baden, he was civil and even generous to him for a time. He was active as a conductor, and Brahms's predecessor at the Gesellschaft der Musikfreunde. In 1872 he came to a complete parting of the ways with Brahms over his performances of the *Schicksalslied* and *Triumphlied*.

Rudorff, Ernst (1840–1916), pianist, composer, and professor of piano in Cologne under Hiller, and then in Berlin, under Joachim. He dedicated his Piano Fantasy, Op. 14, to Brahms, and worked with him as co-editor of Breitkopf & Härtel's complete Chopin edition, as well as the complete Schumann and Mozart editions. He is recognized in Germany as the founder of the German environmental movement, for which he received an honorary doctorate in 1910, and in which capacity he is now better known than for his musical activities.

Sahr, Heinrich von, wealthy music student in Leipzig, and friend of Dietrich. During Brahms's first visits to Leipzig he took the young composer under his wing, introducing him to influential people and putting him up in his comfortable flat. He is mentioned occasionally in the correspondence with Grimm and Joachim over the next dozen years.

Schaeffer, Julius (1823–1902), composer of songs, but known primarily as the conductor of the Breslau Singakademie, which he led from 1860 until his death.

Schmitt, Aloys (1827–1902), pianist, and court conducter in Schwerin from 1857. He was the piano teacher of the very talented Emma Brandes.

Schnack, Fritz (1849–1919), son of Karoline Schnack Brahms, Jakob Brahms's second wife, he became a clock-maker and lived in Pinneburg. His devotion to his stepbrother Johannes was undoubtedly enhanced by the latter's generosity, which among other things, supplied the money for medical care which saved his life. Many of the items which form the core of the Brahms Archive in Hamburg's Stadt- und Universitätsbibliothek were collected by him.

Schnitzler, Robert (1825–97), government minister in Cologne, and Chairman of the Board of Directors of the concert association. Brahms's cordial feelings towards him were based on the minister's years of support for his music in Cologne, a city otherwise slow to show approval. During Wüllner's years as conductor of the Gurzenich Concerts, Brahms was a regular guest at Schnitzler's house, and was godfather to his granddaughter Olga Johanna.

Scholz, Bernhard (1835–1916), one of the four signatories of the Manifesto, while he was court conductor in Hanover. He taught at the Royal School of Music in Munich, and from 1871 to 1883, directed the Orchestra Society Concerts in Breslau, then succeeded Raff as director of the Hoch Conservatory in Frankfurt. Compositions include opera, orchestra, choral, and chamber works. His wife *Luise* was a sophisticated and charming host to Brahms.

Schradiek, Henry (1846–1918), violinist and concertmaster of the Hamburg Philharmonic for a time, he is the composer of violin études still in use today.

Schroedter, Adolf (1805–75), 'The King of Arabesques', a painter famous for his decorative work, and professor of decorative and water-colour painting in Karlsruhe. Brahms knew him from the time they both lived in Düsseldorf. With Clara's approval, Brahms commissioned him to design Robert Schumann's first gravestone. His wife **Alwine** (1820–92) was a painter especially well known for her floral borders in water-colour; Brahms sent a page with four canons for women's voices for her to decorate. She was the younger sister of **Ida Lessing**.

Schubring, Adolf (1817–93), jurist in Dessau by profession and music critic by avocation, he was an admirer of Schumann's music, and one of the earliest writers to pay serious attention to Brahms. He published comprehensive essays on Opp. 1–18 in the spring of 1862, the first full-scale assessment of Brahms to appear in print. Brahms became god-father to Schubring's second son in 1856, although the two men had not yet met in person; his friendship with Brahms was carried on mostly by letters and music. Their correspondence lasted until Schubring was no longer active as a critic, a circumstance which rather embittered him in his old age, and which caused Brahms a certain remorse when Schubring died.

Schumann, Clara (1819–96), the child of two musicians, Friedrich Wieck, a renowned piano teacher, and Marianne Tromlitz, a pianist, she became one of a handful of the most important pianists in Europe before she was 20. She braved her father's wrath to marry Robert Schumann (in 1840), a marriage filled with idealism and fraught with difficulty. The muse of Robert Schumann and Johannes Brahms, her life was also filled with personal tragedy. Although best known as the wife of Schumann and as a great pianist, she composed many fine vocal, choral, chamber, and piano works; in the wake of renewed interest in her life, they are beginning to attract attention.

Schumann, Robert (1810–56), one of the leading composers of the German Romantic era, as well as an influential writer and founder of the *Neue Zeitschrift für Musik*, a journal still in existence. He studied the piano with Friedrich Wieck, living in the Wieck household for a while. His immediate recognition of Brahms's genius, and the steps he took on behalf of the young composer, form the turning-point of Brahms's life. He died of cerebral neuro-syphillis in Endenich, near Bonn.

Schumann Children: Marie (1841–1929), as an adult, the mainstay in the running of the Schumann household. She also served as Clara's teaching assistant, and was her sole heir. She moved to Switzerland after her mother's death.

Elise (1843–1928), capable pianist and the most self-sufficient of the children, she made an independent life for herself by working as a governess and giving piano lessons. She eventually married a well-to-do German businessman, lived with him in America for a time, then settled in Frankfurt near her mother, where she raised a family.

Julie (1845–72), the most photogenic of the Schumann girls, she was sickly from childhood, and contracted tuberculosis. She married an Italian nobleman nevertheless, bore two children, and died shortly after the second birth. Brahms was particularly fond of her, dedicated the Variations, Op. 23, to her in 1861, and was deeply distressed at her marriage in 1869.

Ludwig (1848–99), showed signs of mental instability early in life, and was hospitalized from the age of 22 until his death, virtually abandoned by his family.

Ferdinand (1849–91), pursued a career in business, married the daughter of a German-American farmer against his mother's wishes, and had five children. Wounds suffered in the Franco-Prussian War led to morphine addiction, the impossibility of earning a living, and the collapse of his health.

Eugenie (1851–1938), the only Schumann offspring to study the piano with Brahms. She has written a memoir of the family, and included a valuable account of her lessons. For much of her life she remained at home along side Marie and her mother, then lived in England, Holland, and Switzerland.

Felix (1854–79), Brahms's godson, and the most gifted of the Schumann children. Like his father, his talent tended towards literature and music. He contracted tuberculosis in his early twenties and died a few years later. Three Brahms songs are set to his poems.

Brahms dedicated his *Children's Folk-Songs [Volks-Kinderlieder]*, WoO 31 to all 'the children of Robert and Clara Schumann'.

Senff, Bartolf (1815–1900), Leipzig publisher of Brahms's Opp. 5 and 6. Brahms wrote enthusiastically about him during his first visit to Leipzig, and judging from the very familiar and almost flippant tone of Brahms's early correspondence with him, so in contrast with descriptions of Brahms as a shy youth, their relationship must have been unusually congenial. Senff published the newsletter *Signale für die musikalische Welt*, one of the major music periodicals of the nineteenth century.

Siebold, Agathe von (1835–1909), daughter of a Professor of Medicine in Göttingen, with a fine alto voice. She and Brahms fell in love during the summer of 1858, and exchanged engagement rings. After withdrawing from the engagement which Brahms would not make public, she never saw him again. After Brahms's death she wrote 'In Memoriam J. B.', an autobiographical story meant for her children, which briefly describes their love-affair.

Simrock, August Fritz (1838–1901), son of P. J. Simrock, and next in line to head the Bonn music publishing firm of N. Simrock Verlag, Fritz went his own way for a while. After his father's death, he moved the firm to Berlin, and became Brahms's principal publisher, friend, and even his financial manager. He was a trained musician, able to make decisions based on his own understanding of the music at hand.

Simrock, Peter Joseph (1792–1868), father of Fritz, and the publisher of Opp. 17, 18, 36, and 38.

Spengel, Julius (1853–1936), primarily a choral conductor, and Director of Cäcilienverein in Hamburg from 1877. Brahms thought highly of his ability to teach his chorus, and considered his a capella performances the best in northern Germany. The later choral works were written with his singers in mind.

Spina, Karl Anton (1827–1906), proprietor of 'Diabelli am Graben', a music shop and publishing house in Vienna, as well as a treasure-trove of Schubert manuscripts. The firm later merged with August Cranz, of Hamburg. Brahms received his mail at the shop when he first came to Vienna.

Spies, Hermine (1857–93), contralto, student of Stockhausen in Frankfurt. Her career began to flourish in Wiesbaden, 1883, just as the von Beckeraths introduced her to Brahms, by whom she was highly regarded, and with whom she was romantically linked for several years. Her career took her to Denmark, Russia, and Austria. She married shortly before her untimely death.

Spitta, Philipp (1841–94), along with Nottebohm, the foremost musicologist of his time. He wrote an important biography of Bach based on his own discoveries of manuscripts, edited major editions of Schütz and Buxtehude, and participated in founding the Bach-Verein in Leipzig, devoted to the modern performances of Bach church cantatas. His admiration for Brahms's music went back to student days in Göttingen, and in 1892 he wrote a comprehensive essay about Brahms's music. For the last part of his career, he was Professor Extraordinarius in Musicology at Berlin University, and Professor of Music History at the Hochschule in Berlin. Brahms's Motets, Op. 74, are dedicated to him.

Stern, Julius (1820–83), as composer, eminent conductor, founder of the *Sternscher Gesangverein*, and the Stern Conservatory in Berlin, an active force in Berlin's musical life for many decades.

Stockhausen, Julius (1826–1906), Alsatian-born, the son of musicians, and trilingual by the age of 12, the leading German baritone of his time. He was also one of the most important teachers on the Continent, with an influence in the Lieder tradition which can still be traced today. He was the first person to perform complete song cycles of Schubert and Schumann (in one case with Brahms at the piano). Extremely successful by 1862, he advocated public concerts and low prices for 'the People', singing a Lieder recital in Cologne for an audience of more than 2,000 enthusiastic listeners. That year he was named as music director of the Hamburg Philharmonic, a job Brahms desperately wanted. Brahms's disappointment had only a temporary effect on their friendship and musical partnership, which endured for life. Stockhausen was the first baritone soloist in the *German Requiem*, is the dedicatee of the *Magelone Lieder*, Op. 33, and was extremely important in establishing a tradition for the performance of Brahms songs.

Streicher, Viennese piano builders of great repute. The family were very friendly to Clara, who introduced them to Brahms. **Emil** (1836–1916) was the head of the piano factory in partnership with his father, and very accommodating to Brahms, whose personal piano in Vienna was a gift from the firm.

Steinmetz, Dr, high government official (Regierungsrat) in Düsseldorf, he was involved in the attempt to bring Brahms there as Municipal Music Director.

Tausig, Carl (1841–71), perhaps Liszt's most outstanding pupil, technically the most extraordinary young pianist of the day. In 1862 he met Brahms in Vienna, where the two became good friends. Brahms learned many things from him, including a taste for old cognac, expensive cigars, and Schopenhauer. He and Brahms gave the first performance of Op. 34*b*; the Paganini Variations were written for him as a kind of dare. He died suddenly of typhoid fever, at the age of 31.

Verhulst, Johannes (1816–91), leading Dutch composer and conductor who held posts as music director in The Hague and Amsterdam. An early admirer and promoter of Schumann's music, he extended his admiration to Brahms.

Völkers, Betty and Marie, members of the Hamburg Frauenchor and of the Solo Quartet, and nieces of Frau Rösing. They stayed in touch with the Brahms family, particularly with sister Elise and mother Christiane, and included Elise in their circle of friends. Their father, *Karl Ludwig,* was equally a friend to the Brahms family, helping them in various ways after Brahms left Hamburg.

Volkmann, Robert (1815–83), 'one of the most outstanding of the newer composers (of the Schumann School), particularly in the instrumental area (symphonies, serenades, Concertstücke, trios, etc)' (La Mara). He was Professor of Harmony and Counterpoint at the Landes-Musikakademie in Budapest, casually friendly with Brahms, a close friend of Nottebohm's.

Wagemann, cousin of J. O. Grimm living in Hanover. He is mentioned occasionally in the early correspondence.

Wagner, Friedchen (1831–1917), cousin of Georg Otten, Brahms's best piano student in Hamburg, and the organizer of the Frauenchor, which first met at her house. She occasionally played duets with Clara and remained her friend for life, staying with her for several days as late as 1893, by then as Friedchen Sauermann. Her son Kurt provided many documents relating to the Frauenchor to Sophie Drinker for her book on Brahms's women's choruses.

Wasielewski, Josef Wilhelm von (1822–96), Music Director in Bonn while Schumann was in Düsseldorf. He was a student of David (violin), Mendelssohn, and Hauptman, then concertmaster in Düsseldorf under Schumann; Clara often played with him. He wrote on musical topics and was the first Schumann biographer (a work not approved by Clara). Brahms stayed with him on his Rhine journey in 1853, thanks to an introduction by Joachim.

Wehner, Arnold (1810–80), Music Director in Göttingen in 1853 and a friend of Joachim, he quickly took a fatherly interest in Brahms and is mentioned frequently in early letters to and from Joachim. He safeguarded Brahms's manuscripts as the youth went off on his walking tour of the Rhine in 1853, sending them to the Schumann house at Brahms's request. They had a falling out when Wehner intrigued to keep J. O. Grimm from getting his post, as he left it to go to Hanover.

Weitzmann, Karl Friedrich (1808–80), writer on musical subjects, including a volume of 1800 preludes and modulations and a book entitled *The Diminished Seventh Chord and History of Seventh Chords.*

Wendt, Gustav (1827–1912), distinguished linguist, educator, and classicist, and head of the Gymnasium in Karlsruhe from 1873 until his death. Brahms relished his active, rigorous mind, and for several years spent time with him on holiday. They first met in 1863, at Julius Otto Grimm's home in Münster, then again in Karlsruhe (1866) in the circle of friends which included Levi and Allgeyer. Wendt dedicated his important translation of the plays of Sophocles to Brahms (1884), whose music and character he prized.

Wenzel, Ernst Ferdinand (1808–80), celebrated pianist and teacher, friend of Schumann and Mendelssohn, active in Leipzig, Brahms met him there in 1853 and dedicated the Scherzo, Op. 4, to him.

Wesendonck, Mathilde (1828–1902), born in Dresden, poet and playwright, she married Otto Wesendonck, a cosmopolitan patron of the arts. In their sumptuous villa outside Zurich, she entertained most of the prominent or interesting artists who came to the city. She was Wagner's lover for the years spanning the creation of *Tristan*, and supplied the poems for his Wesendonck Songs. Her keen interest in Brahms, in evidence from 1864, was marginally reciprocated.

Widmann, Josef Viktor (1842–1911), born in Moravia of Viennese parents, but made his home in Switzerland from early childhood. Poet, pastor, librettist, editor, political columnist, one-time organist, his insight into Brahms's character is illuminating, and his memoir of the composer is particularly useful. Although they met casually in 1866, their friendship really dates from 1874 and the Zurich music festival. Brahms made three journeys to Italy with Widmann, and spent three summers near him in Hofstetten, on the Lake of Thun. Widmann was a supporter of women's rights and of other liberal social causes, and one of the founders of the Swiss environmental movement. His son-in-law, the anthropologist Professor Ferdinand Vetter, is occasionally mentioned in the correspondence.

Wittgenstein family, large Viennese family comprised of Hermann and his wife Fanny (née Figdor), their eleven children, and the families they founded in turn. The Wittgensteins were essentially Joachim's immediate family; when he was a child, Fanny, his first cousin, undertook to support his musical education and took Joachim to live with her and her growing family. Brahms was therefore introduced to them shortly after his first arrival in Vienna. Among the eight sisters, several were particularly musical or artistic: Frau Anna Franz, Frau Dr Bertha Kupelwieser, Fräulein Klara Wittgenstein (1850–1935), Frau Professor Millie Brücke (who was not musical, but had a husband who was), and Frau Dr Josefine Oser (1844–1933). As adults, they made him a welcome and regular guest in their homes. Most of the women sang in the Singakademie under Brahms's direction. Josefine was a good pianist, having studied in Berlin; Klara studied music with Carl Goldmark; Anna studied the piano with Brahms for a year (1866, and before then with Wieck), and Bertha sculpted the marble bust of Brahms in Pörtschach. There were also three sons: Paul (an artist), Louis (wealthy, active as a presbyter in the Protestant church, and patron of the arts), and Karl (d. 1913), a violinist, Austria's leading steel magnate, a great patron of the arts, and father of the philosopher Ludwig Wittgenstein and an otherwise remarkably talented and ill-fated family.

Wolff, Hermann (1845–1902), a prominent concert impresario in Berlin. Among his clients was von Bülow. Brahms was a guest in his Berlin home on several occasions.

Wüllner, Franz (1832–1902), first made his career as a highly regarded pianist, then turned to conducting. In his capacity as Court Conductor in Munich, he led the first performances of Wagner's *Rheingold* (1869), and *Walküre* (1870). Hermann Levi's arrival in 1871 made unwilling rivals of both men, and he eventually moved to Dresden. An early and faithful performer of Brahms's works (they first met in 1853 at the Deichmann home), Brahms entrusted him with early performances of the *Variations on a Theme by Haydn* and the First Symphony. At Brahms's suggestion, Wüllner was chosen to succeeded Ferdinand Hiller as director of the Cologne Conservatory and conductor of the Gurzenich Concerts. In that capacity he gave the première of Richard Strauss's *Till Eulenspiegel*.

Zuccalmaglio, Wilhelm Florentin von (1803–69), primarily known as the co-author of *Deutsche Volkslieder mit ihren Original-Weisen* (German Folk-Songs and Their Original Melodies), an important source of German folk-songs and texts. See the comments to Letter 532.

D. Sources of the Letters

List of Libraries and Archives

There are two striking omissions from the following list of libraries and archives consulted in the preparation of this work: the Archive of the Gesellschaft der Musikfreunde in Vienna was closed for reconstruction during the entire duration of work on this book; and the Brahms collection in the Kammerhof Museum in Gmunden was inaccessible, due to the uniquely unco-operative curator of the museum. These omissions were to a large degree offset by the collections of the Brahms-Haus Museum in Baden-Baden, by the willingness of the Gesellschaft to locate specifically identified materials, and above all by the remarkable collection at the Brahms-Institut in Lübeck and the private collection of its directors, Kurt and Renate Hofmann.

American Brahms Society Archive, Seattle
Bodleian Library, Oxford
Brahms-Institut, Lübeck
Brahms-Haus Museum, Baden-Baden
Breslau University Archive, Wroclaw
British Library, London
Burgerbibliothek, Bern
Cambridge University Library, Cambridge
Drew University Library, Madison, NJ
Dichtermuseum Liestal, Liestal, Switzerland
Fitzwilliam Museum, Cambridge
Glinka Library, Moscow
Harvard University, Loeb Music Library, Cambridge, Mass.
Leipzig Universitätsbibliothek, Leipzig
Library of Congress, Music Division, Washington, DC
Lippische Landesbibliothek, Detmold
Museum für Hamburgische Geschichte
Pierpont Morgan Library, New York
Music Library of the City College of New York, City University of New York
Musikbibliothek der Stadt Leipzig, Leipzig
New York Public Library at Lincoln Center, New York
Österreichische Nationalbibliothek, Vienna
Princeton University Library, Princeton
Sächsische Stadt- und Landesbibliothek, Dresden
Schumannhaus, Bonn

Robert-Schumann-Haus, Zwickau
Staatsbibliothek zu Berlin-Preussischer Kulturbesitz
Staats- und Universitätsbibliothek Hamburg, Carl von Ossietzky (Brahms-Archiv)
Wiener Stadt- und Landesbibliothek, Vienna
Washington State University, Holland Library, Pullman, Washington
Zentralbibliothek, Zürich

Brahms wrote thousands of letters. To judge from what remains, his friends and
associates did not lightly throw them out, and a very large number were published
in books and journals within the first fifty years of his death, edited and annotated
with more or less care depending on the editor.

By and large these published letters have been our sources. We have made some
effort to work from autographs, but did not have resources to attempt to track down
the whereabouts of most of the letters published long ago, before the chaos of two
world wars. There are numerous exceptions, however: these include unpublished
letters found in the course of research for this volume; the Brahms–Joachim,
Brahms–Levi, Brahms–Dietrich, and Brahms–Stockhausen letters, and some
Brahms–Grimm, Brahms–Henschel, and Brahms–Simrock letters. A comparison of
these with the published letters gives us the confidence that in general, the published
letters differ only in minor details from the autographs—i.e. details which do not
effect the essential meaning of the letters. In the main they consist in 'improving'
Brahms's punctuation or modernizing his spelling, and rearranging his paragraphs
and filling in abbreviations. Whenever possible, we have retained Brahms's original,
so that the reader who compares these details with the published German texts will
find some discrepancies.

Some omissions are more considerable, however, and have been rectified when
possible: the important deletions in the Joachim correspondence were addressed
some years ago, and recent scholarship has filled in other gaps. The complete
Stockhausen–Brahms correspondence is now in print, as well as von Bülow's letters
to Brahms; some of the deletions in the Schumann–Brahms correspondence reproduced in this volume were restored in consultation with the autographs located in
the Staatsbibliothek zu Berlin-Preussischer Kulturbesitz (Letters 32–3, 35–7, 47, 59,
65, 68, 82). One will have to await the reopening of the Archive of the Gesellschaft
der Musikfreunde in Vienna for access to Brahms's letters to von Bülow, and to some
of the correspondence within the Brahms family.

The largest single source of Brahms's letters is the sixteen-volume set of Brahms's
correspondence published by the Deutsche Brahms Gesellschaft in Berlin from 1912 to
1922, referred to in the text as *BW*. The Schneider Verlag in Tutzing, Germany, has
added to the series (*Neue Folge*) for a current total of eighteen. The present collection
relies heavily on the letters in volumes i–xvi. References to these letters in the text
include the volume number in roman numerals and page number in arabic numbers:
i.e. *BW* vii. 25. Correspondents included in *BW* are as follows:

Volumes i, ii: *Heinrich and Elizabet von Herzogenberg.*

Volume iii: *Karl Reinthaler, Max Bruch, Hermann Deiters, Friedrich Heimsoeth, Karl Reinecke, Ernst Rudorff, Bernhard and Luise Scholz.*

Volume iv: *Julius Otto Grimm.* Where noted, the autographs have been consulted.

Volume v, vi: *Joseph Joachim.* The letters up to July 1856 were graciously revised in consultation with the autographs held in the Staats- und Universitätsbibliothek Hamburg Carl von Ossietzky (Brahms-Archiv), with their generous permission, by Dr. Michael Struck of the Kiel Research Group of the *Johannes Brahms Gesamtausgabe.* Letters from 1856 to 1897 have been revised by the editor, from the same collection of autographs.

Volume vii: *Hermann Levi, Friedrich Gernsheim sowie die Familien Hecht und Fellinger.* The slight revisions of the Levi letters in the present volume were made in consultation with the autographs in Library of Congress, Whittall Collection, with generous permission.

Volume viii: *Joseph Victor Widmann, Ellen und Ferdinand Vetter, Adolf Schubring.*

Volume ix, x: *P. J. Simrock und Fritz Simrock.*

Volume xi, xii: *Fritz Simrock.*

Volume xiii: *Th. Wilhelm Engelmann.*

Volume xiv: *Breitkopf & Härtel, Bartholf Senff, J. Rieter-Biedermann, Max Abraham, E. W. Fritzsch und Robert Lienau.*

Volume xv: *Franz Wüllner.*

Volume xvi: *Philipp Spitta, Otto Dessoff.*

Volume xvii: *Herzog Georg II. von Sachsen-Meiningen und Helene Freifrau von Heldburg.*

Volume xviii: *Julius Stockhausen*

The other major sources of correspondence with individuals are:

JULIUS ALLGEYER: Alfred Orel, *Johannes Brahms and Julius Allgeyer* (Tutzing, 1964).

THEODOR BILLROTH: Otto Gottlieb-Billroth (ed.), *Billroth und Brahms in Briefwechsel* (Berlin, 1935; repr. 1991).

CHRISTIANE, KAROLINE, ELISE, JOHANN, and FRITZ BRAHMS: Stephenson, *Brahms und seine Familie* (Hamburg, 1973).

HANS VON BÜLOW: *Briefe und Schriften,* ed. Marie von Bülow, 7 vols. (Leipzig, 1895–1908). The letters reproduced here are from vols. vi and vii.

ALBERT DIETRICH: from Dietrich's *Erinnerungen an Johannes Brahms* (Leipzig, 1898). Where noted, letters have been corrected from autographs in the Staats- und Universitätsbibliothek Hamburg Carl von Ossietzky (Brahms-Archiv), with their kind permission, and in that form are published and translated here for the first time.

ANTONIN DVOŘÁK: *Correspondence and Documents*, ed. Milan Kuna *et al.* (Prague, 1987–9).

OTTILIE EBNER: Ottilie von Balassa, *Die Brahms Freundin Ottilie Ebner* (Vienna, 1933).

KLAUS GROTH: Volquart Pauls, *Briefe der Freundschaft* (Heide in Holstein, 1956).

FERDINAND HILLER: Reinhold Sietz, *Aus Ferdinand Hillers Briefwechsel* (Cologne, 1958–66).

MAX KLINGER: *Der Briefwechsel zwischen Johannes Brahms und Max Klinger* (Leipzig, 1924).

WILLIAM LINDECK: Michael Martin, *Johannes Brahms: Briefwechsel mit dem Mannheimer Bankprokuristen Wilhelm Lindeck 1872–1882* (Stadtarchiv Mannheim, 1983).

EUSEBIUS MANDYCZEWSKI: Karl Geiringer, 'Joh. Brahms in Briefwechsel mit Eusebius Mandyczewsky', *Zeitschrift für Musikwissenschaft*, 15/8 (May 1933), 339–70.

GEORG II, DUKE OF SACHSEN-MEININGEN AND HELENE FREIFRAU VON HELDBERG: *Beiträge zur Musikwissenschaft*, 2 (1978), 85–131. These letters are reprinted in *BW* xvii, which includes additional letters from Freifrau von Heldberg, and meticulous notes by Renate Hofmann.

CLARA, ROBERT, MARIE and EUGENIE SCHUMANN: Berthold Litzmann, *Clara Schumann–Johannes Brahms: Briefe aus den Jahren 1853–1896* (Leipzig, 1927).

FRITZ SIMROCK to Johannes Brahms: Kurt Stephenson, *Johannes Brahms und Fritz Simrock: Weg einer Freundschaft* (Hamburg, 1961).

HERMINE SPIES: *Hermine Spies: Ein Gedenkbuch* (Leipzig, 1905).

JULIUS STOCKHAUSEN: Julia Wirth geb. Stockhausen, *Julius Stockhausen, der Sänger des deutschen Liedes* (Frankfurt am Main, 1927); contains some but not all correspondence with Brahms, but many useful notes and other relevant letters. *BW* xviii contains the complete correspondence with Brahms, with some additions and corrections to Wirth's edition.

JULIUS SPENGEL: Annemari Spengel, *Johannes Brahms an Julius Spengel, Unpublished Letters from the year 1882–1897* (Hamburg, 1959).

MATHILDE WESENDONCK: Erich H. Müller von Asow, *Johannes Brahms und Mathilde Wesendonck, ein Briefwechsel* (Vienna, 1943).

Sources of letters not found above are listed here:

1. to Cossel: Pierpont Morgan Library MFC B8135.C836. The letter is reproduced [Plate 3] with kind permission.

2. to the parents of Johannes Brahms: Kalbeck² iv. 534. French portion from a copy of the autograph, provisionally at Linderman Library, Lehigh University, with kind permission.

3. to Joseph Joachim: from 'Although I cannot hope to repay', in Staats- und Universitätsbibliothek Hamburg Carl von Ossietzky (Brahms-Archiv); the remainder in *BW* v.

4. Joseph Joachim to Johann Jakob Brahms: England, private collection.

8. to Amtsvogt Blume: British Library Add MS 40730.

24. Julius Otto Grimm to Joseph Joachim: *BW* v.

31. to Amtsvogt Blume: British Library Add MS 40730.

48. to Julius Otto Grimm: from the autograph (excluding the pages devoted to Breitkopf), which differs in some details from the printed version. With kind permission of the Brahms-Institut, Lübeck, Sig. Hofmann. The date, in Brahms's hand, is incorrect. The letter was written after Clara returned from tour (10 Feb.). Brahms must have allowed the letter to sit on his desk until Clara left for her next tour (19 Feb.), since the enclosed letter from Breitkopf & Härtel is dated 20 Feb.

62. to Georg Dietrich Otten: Stephenson, *J. Brahms und G. D. Otten*, Brahms Gesellschaft Hamburg.

64. to Georg Dietrich Otten: Stephenson, *J. Brahms und G. D. Otten*.

67. to Clara Schumann: Litz, ii. 404–5.

79. Clara Schumann to Joseph Joachim: *BW* v, as for Letter 78.

88. to Carl Peter Grädener: with the kind permission of the Staats- und Universitätsbibliothek Hamburg Carl von Ossietzky (sig.: Brahms-Archiv G 1965). First complete publication.

98. Clara Schumann to Woldemar Bargiel: Litz, iii, 34–5.

101. J. O. Grimm to Joseph Joachim: Küntzel, *Brahms in Göttingen* (Göttingen, 1985), 54.

111. to Laura von Meysenbug: Reimann, *Johannes Brahms* (Berlin, 1903), 22a–d.

118. to Friedchen Wagner: Hubbe, *Brahms in Hamburg* (Hamburg, 1902), 22.

119. to Auguste Brandt and Bertha Porubsky: *Brahms-Studien*, vol. 8 (1990).

120. to Auguste Brandt and Bertha Porubsky: *Brahms-Studien*, vol. 8 (1990).

121. to Georg Dietrich Otten: Stephenson, *J. Brahms and G. D. Otten*, Brahms Gesellschaft Hamburg.

122. to Auguste Brandt and Bertha Porubsky: *Brahms-Studien*, vol. 8 (1990).

123. to Auguste Brandt and Bertha Porubsky: *Brahms-Studien*, vol. 8 (1990).

134. to Hofmarschall von Meysenbug: Carl v. Meysenbug, 'Aus Brahms' Jugendtagen', *Neues Wiener Tagblatt*, 4 Apr. 1902, 3.

139. to Melchior Rieter-Biedermann: with kind permission of the Staats- und Universitätsbibliothek Hamburg Carl von Ossietzky (sig.: Brahms-Archiv G1658). First publication.

147. to Albert Dietrich: with kind permission of the Staats- und Universitätsbibliothek Hamburg Carl von Ossietzky (sig.: Brahms-Archiv 25.6330). The text differs somewhat from the version published by Dietrich in his Memoir (Leipzig, 1898, pp. 37 ff.), and is the first complete publication.

148. to Albert Dietrich: with kind permission of the Staats- und Universitätsbibliothek Hamburg Carl von Ossietzky (sig.: Brahms-Archiv 25.6331). First complete publication. Dated with reference to a letter to Rieter-Biedermann.

152. to Albert Dietrich: with kind permission of the Staats- und Universitätsbibliothek Hamburg Carl von Ossietzky (sig.: Brahms-Archiv 25.6332). First complete publication. Misdated in the Memoir as January 1863.

172. to Committee of the Vienna *Singakademie*: Kal, ii. 73–5.

173. to Josef Gänsbacher: Kal, ii. 75. Although there was a lively correspondence between the two men, and Ehrmann refers to letters then in the Archive of the Gesellschaft der Musikfreunde (in 1933), the letters apparently disappeared subsequently; my enquiry to the current director of the Archive yielded only the information that no letters are presently there. It is possible that the correspondence as published in Kalbeck's biography is all that remains.

174. to Eduard Hanslick: Neue Freie Presse, July 1897.

191. autograph in the Archive of the Gesellschaft der Musikfreunde. First complete publication by Hofmann, *Johannes Brahms und Hamburg* (Reinbek, 1986). Our translation is based on that publication, and is the first one in English.

198. to Peter Cornelius: *Peter Cornelius, Literarische Werke*, ii. 251–2 . On dating the letter: on 6 September 1865, Cornelius wrote to Tausig about the affair, saying 'Brahms has graciously declined to answer'.

199. to Breitkopf & Härtel: omitted from *BW* xiv, published in 1933 by Alfred Ehrmann, *Johannes Brahms, Weg, Werke und Welt* (Leipzig, 1933), 186–90.

204. to Karl Bargheer: Karl Bargheer, 'Erinnerungen an Johannes Brahms in Detmold', 13–14. Unpublished typescript (Ex.2: 16 S), Detmold Landes-bibliothek. By kind permission.

209. to Eduard Hanslick: Hanslick, *Die Moderne Oper VIII*, Vienna (1889), and in *Neue Freie Presse*, July 1897. Hanslick's date 'August 1866' must be wrong, as Brahms was already in Switzerland by then.

215. to Johann Nepomuk Dunkl: first published in the *Neues Wiener Journal*, 12 Nov. 1932, repr. as 'Unbekannte Briefe von Brahms' in *Die Musik*, vol. 25, no. 8 (May 1933), 612–13. The date given by Norbert Dunkel (1868) is incorrect, as Joachim and Brahms did not play in Budapest in that year. The letter was recently republished in *Johannes Brahms, 22 Briefe nach Ungarn* (Gádor and Ebert: Mürzzuschlag, 1993), with a suggested date of October 1867. August or September is more likely.

222. to Arthur and Bertha Faber: New York City, private collection. First complete publication.

223. to a French publisher [probably J. Maho]: by kind permission of Albi Rosenthal, London and Oxford. First publication.

230. to Rosa Girzick: Kal³ ii. 273–4.

245. to Emil Streicher: MS in Oesterreichische Nationalbibliothek, published in *Brahms Studien*, vol. 3 (1979).

251. to Johann Nepomuk Dunkl: *Die Musik*, vol. 25, no. 8 (May 1933). Recently republished as in Letter 215.

266. to Joseph Joachim: by kind permission of the Robert-Schumann-Haus, Zwickau. 6137-A2. First publication.

268. Dr Franz Egger, President of the Board of the GdMf: Kal, iii. 49, with additions and corrections from the autograph, with kind permission of the Gesellschaft der Musikfreunde.

280. Anna Ettlinger *et al.* to Johannes Brahms: Whittall Collection, Library of Congress, Music Division, with kind permission. First publication.

283. to Friedrich Heimsoeth: *BW* iii.

294. to Ludwig II, King of Bavaria: *Brahms-Studien*, vol. 7, 63. Autograph in the Bayrische Staatsbibliothek, Munich.

303. to Robert Volkmann: *Die Musik*, vol. 11, no. 13 (1 Apr. 1912).

304. to the Directors of the Gesellschaft der Musikfreunde: Archive of the Gesellschaft der Musikfreunde, with kind permission. First complete publication.

307–10. to and from Richard Wagner: Gál, *Brahms Briefe*, 79–82; also Grasberger, *Johannes Brahms, Variationen um sein Wesen* (Vienna, 1952), 218–21. Our translation of Brahms's side of the correspondence was made from photocopies of the autographs at New York Public Library, Lincoln Center Library for the Performing Arts. Gal's transcription is closer to the originals than Grasberger's, but both differ only in small details.

337.   to Carl Hermann Bitter: *Hil*, vol. iv.

340.   to Emil Streicher: Oesterreichische Nationalbibliothek, published in *Brahms-Studien*, vol 3 (1979).

341.   to Wilhelm Lindeck: with kind permission of the British Library, Add MS 47841 H ff 52–3. First publication.

350.   to Theodor Kirchner: with kind permission of the Brahms-Institut Lübeck, Sig. Hofmann. First publication.

364.   to Antonin Dvořák: Geiringer, 'Brahms und Dvořák', *Der Auftakt*, vol. 17 (1937), 101.

366–7. to Eugenie and Marie Schumann: translation from the autographs with the kind permission of the Schumann-Haus, Zwickau. Published in Eugenie Schumann, *Erinnerungen*.

371.   to Eduard Hanslick: *Neue Freie Presse*, 1 July 1897.

382.   to Vincenz Lachner: with kind permission of the Library of Congress, Whittall Collection.

386.   to George Henschel: G. Henschel, *Personal Recollections of Johannes Brahms* (Boston, 1907). The section from 'I hardly know how I should answer such a question . . .' to 'I wish I had heard that once from her' is translated from the German-language version of the memoir which Henschel prepared by hand for a radio talk in the 1930s. Private collection.

389.   to Eduard Hanslick: *Neue Freie Presse*, 1 July 1897.

396.   to Elise Denninghoff née Giesemann: Wiener Stadt- und Landesbibliothek [MS 30419]. The letter was printed in essentially the same form in the *Allgemeine Musik-Zeitung*, nos. 32/3, (10 and 17 Aug. 1900), 473.

398.   to Amalie Joachim: from Geiringer, *Brahms* (Zurich, 1955), and the copy of the original (made by Amalie's brother) in the Archive of the GdMf.

399.   to the Directors of the Royal Philharmonic: with kind permission of The British Library, Loan 48/13/5. First publication.

406.   to Henriette Feuerbach: Kal, iii. 295. First printed in *Süddeutsche Monathefte* (Mar. 1907).

409.   to Julius Bernuth: with kind permission of the Staats- und Landesbibliothek Hamburg Carl von Ossietzky (sig.: Brahms-Archiv 1959.32). First publication.

410. to George Henschel: English text by Henschel, from his memoir, *Personal Recollections* (p. 84). Regrettably, a wide-ranging search for the German originals of the letters presented by Henschel turned up only a few examples sold at auction. Henschel's date (1882) must be incorrect, as Brahms went from Budapest to Stuttgart in November 1881, for the première and tour of the Second Piano Concerto.

411–12. to Josefine Oser née Wittgenstein: with kind permission of Marie Kuhn-Oser. First publication.

413. to Theodor v. Brücke: with kind permission of Marie Kuhn-Oser.

415. to Hans von Bülow: autograph in the Pierpont Morgan Library, MFC B8135.B939 (1), published in Kal, iii. 347–8 (with incorrect date). Dated from the autograph. Bülow's marriage took place on 29 July.

418. to [Dr Adolf Kaufmann, Chairman of the Orchestra Committee in Breslau]: Private collection. First publication.

419. to Gustav Nottebohm: with kind permission of the Staats- und Landesbibliothek Hamburg Carl von Ossietzky (sig.: Brahms-Archiv 1960.312). First publication?

420. to Robert Volkmann: *Die Musik*, vol. 43 (Apr. 1912), 12.

422. to Laura von Beckerath: Stephenson, *Johannes Brahms und die Familie von Beckerath* (Hamburg, 1979).

423. to Rudolf von Beckerath: Stephenson, *Johannes Brahms und die Familie von Beckerath*.

424. Antonin Dvořák to Fritz Simrock: *Antonin Dvořák, Correspondence and Documents*, ed. Milan Kuna *et al.* (Prague, 1987), 366–7. Original in Gesellschaft der Musikfreunde.

425. to Joseph Joachim: from the autograph, with the kind permission of the Staats- und Universitätsbibliothek Hamburg Carl von Ossietzky. First complete publication.

433. to Alwin von Beckerath: Rudolf von der Leyen, *Johannes Brahms als Mensch und Freund* (Düsseldorf, 1905), 93–4. The letter is undated, but on 9 February 1884, Brahms arrived in Cologne from Leipzig.

434. to Regierungsrat Robert Schnitzler: Kal, iii³. 419.

435. to Eduard Hanslick: Hanslick, *Am Ende des Jahrhunderts* (Berlin, 1899), 379–83.

436. to Rudolf von der Leyen: *Johannes Brahms als Mensch und Freund*, 51–2.

437. to Regierungsrat Robert Schnitzler: Kal, iii³. 427.

440. to Elizabet von Herzogenberg: passage omitted in *BW* ii ('Everything has its limits . . . one should not even discuss with you') is included in Kal iii. 408.

442. to Marie Lipsius (La Mara): *Musikerbriefe aus Fünf Jahrhunderten*, 348–9.

443. to Eduard Hanslick: *Neue Freie Presse*, 27 June 1897.

452. to Moritz Fürstenau: with kind permission of the *Sächsische Landesbibliothek Dresden*, Mscr. Dresd. s 721. First publication.

458. to Hermine Spies: *Gedenkbuch*, 308–9. Undated, but the date of the trip to Hamburg and Bremen, and publication date of Op. 94, is conclusive.

464. to Elizabet von Herzogenberg: by kind permission of the Manuscript Division, Universitätsbibliothek Leipzig (Sammlung Clodius). First publication.

468. to Hermine Spies: Minna Spies, *Hermine Spies: Ein Gedenkbuch* (Leipzig, 1905), 307–8, without date. Dated here from contents of Hermine's letter.

481. to Bürgermeister Carl Petersen: *BB* vii. 252.

482. to Hans von Bülow: Kal, iv. 183–4.

484. to Bürgermeister Carl Petersen: K. Hofmann, 'Brahmsiana der Familie Petersen', *Brahms-Studien*, vol. 3 (1979), 92.

496. to Hans von Bülow: Archive of the Gesellschaft der Musikfreunde, with kind permission.

497. to Elise Grund née Brahms: MS in Wiener Stadt- und Landesbibliothek [I. N. 74490] with kind permission.

498. to Fritz Simrock: autograph in the Library of Congress, Whittall Collection. Incorrectly dated in *BW* xii.

508. to Christian Detmering: MS in Wiener Stadt- und Landesbibliothek [I. N. 74489] with kind permission.

517. to Eduard Hanslick: Hanslick, *Am Ende des Jahrhunderts*, 403.

518. to John Peile, Vice Chancellor and Master of Christ College, Cambridge: Cambridge University, by kind permission of the Syndics of Cambridge University Library. First publication.

525. to Marie von Bülow: *BB* vii. 447.

528. to Max Klinger: *Der Briefwechsel zwischen Johannes Brahms und Max Klinger*, private printing, Leipzig, 1924.

540. to Gustav Wendt: by kind permission of Dorothy Reichenberger.

556. to Eduard Hanslick: *Am Ende des Jahrhunderts*, 404–5.

558. to Marie Janssen née Cossel: autograph of fragment. With the kind permission of the Brahms-Institut, Lübeck, Sig. Hofmann. First publication.

E. Brahms's Works Mentioned in the Letters

Numbers in parentheses refer to the year of publication (rarely the same as date of composition). Numbers following the work identify the letter in which the work is mentioned. Note that in the letters, pieces are not necessarily identified by name or opus number. Works not mentioned in letters, but only in the editorial commentary, footnotes, or additional notes are listed in the general index.

Works with Orchestra

Serenade No. 1 in D major Op. 11 (1860): 102–4, 106, 111–13, 116–17, 124–5, 127, 129–30, 132, 135, 147, 163, 200, 205, 276;   arr. for piano: 258

Serenade No. 2 in A major, Op. 16 (1860): 116, 124, 127–8, 132, 138, 141, 147?, 148, 163, 205, 317–18;   four-hand arr.: 177, 258

Symphony No. 1 in C minor, Op. 68 (1877): 152, 154, 226, 311, 324–32, 334, 338, 351–4, 360, 363

Symphony No. 2 in D major, Op. 73 (1878): 353, 355–7, 359, 362–3, 367, 371, 382, 543

Symphony No. 3 in F major, Op. 90 (1884): 424–31;   arr. for two pianos: 436–7

Symphony No. 4 in E minor, Op. 98 (1886): 446, 448–51, 459, 489, 546

Variations on a Theme by Haydn, Op. 56*a* (1874): 292;   arr. for piano four-hands: 351

Academic Fest. Ov., Op. 80 (1881): 393–4;   arr. for piano: 408

Tragic Overture, Op. 81 (1881): 394; arr. for piano: 408

Piano Concerto No. 1 in D minor, Op. 15 (1861): 24, 27–8, 34, 46, 83–7, 89, 92–4, 96–8, 106, 110–12, 117, 128–30, 133, 135–7, 139, 151, 157, 203, 205, 261, 357–8, 415; four-hand arr.: 151, 177–8, 180, 258

Piano Concerto No. 2 in B flat major, Op. 83 (1882): 403–5, 407–8, 416

Violin Concerto in D major, Op. 77 (1879): 368–9, 370, 374, 378–80, 383, 387, 393, 408, 429

Double Concerto for Violin and Cello in A minor, Op. 102 (1888): 465, 467, 469

Instrumental Chamber Music

With Piano

Piano Quintet in F minor, Op. 34*a* (1865);   as string quintet: 152, 154–60, 165, 167, 170;   as piano quintet: 201, 321, 373

Piano Quartet No. 1 in G minor, Op. 25 (1863): 144–7, 153, 155, 157, 163, 165, 168, 175?, 182–3, 297;   arr. for piano: 258

Piano Quarter No. 2 in A major, Op. 26 (1863): 144–7, 153, 157, 163, 165, 168, 175?, 182–3, 205

Piano Quartet No. 3 in C minor, Op. 60 (1875): 48, 83–4, 87, 315, 357 (Andante);   arr. for piano four hands: 351

Piano Trio in B major, Op. 8 (1854): 24–5, 27, 42, 191

Revised version Op. 8 bis (1891):
489–90, 493, 495

Horn Trio in E flat major, Op. 40
(1866): 203, 205

Clarinet Trio in A minor, Op. 114
(1892): 499–504

Piano Trio in C major, Op. 87 (1882):
391

Piano Trio in C minor, Op. 101 (1887):
461, 562

Violin Sonata No. 1 in G major, Op. 78
(1879): 380–1

Violin Sonata No. 2 in A major, Op. 100
(1887): 461

Violin Sonata No 3 in D minor, Op. 108
(1889): 479, 482, 489

Cello Sonata in E minor, Op. 38 (1887):
453, 528

Cello Sonata in F major, Op. 99 (1866):
461

Clarinet Sonata in F minor, Op. 120 No.
1 (1895): 536, 539–40

Clarinet Sonata in E flat major, Op. 120
No. 2 (1895): 536, 539–40
as Viola Sonatas Op. 120 Nos. 1 and 2
(1895): 536

Without Piano

String Sextet in B flat major, Op. 18 No.
1 (1862): 124, 142–5, 151, 157, 160, 180,
199; four-hand arr.: 142, 143, 177,
258, 354

String Sextet in G major, Op. 36 No. 2
(1866): 199, 354

String Quintet in F major, Op. 88 No. 1
(1882): 494

String Quintet No. 2 in G major, Op. 111
(1891): 493–5, 562; four-hand arr.:
493

Clarinet Quintet in B minor, Op. 115
(1892): 499, 501–2, 503–4, 562

String Quartet in C minor, Op. 51 No. 1
(1873): 289–91, 295; four-hand arr.:
290

String Quartet in A minor, Op. 51 No. 2
(1873): 289–91, 295, 433; four-hand
arr.: 290

String Quartet in B flat major, Op. 67
(1876): 322, 325, 327; four-hand
arr.: 351

Piano Music

Solo

Sonata in C major, Op. 1 (1853): 11, 14,
17–20, 40, 51, 60, 527, 539; four-
hand arr.: 527

Sonata in F sharp minor, Op. 2 (1854):
14–17, 23, 415; four-hand arr.:
527

Sonata in F minor, Op. 5 (1854): 14, 16,
18, 21–3, 34–5, 40; four-hand arr.:
527

Scherzo in E flat minor, Op. 4 (1854):
11?, 14, 16–17, 23, 41, 77, 383

Variations on a Theme by Schumann, Op.
9 (1854): 26, 27?, 33–5, 39–41, 45, 90

Four Ballades, Op. 10 (1856): 35, 40–2,
45, 48, 51, 59

Variations on an Original Theme, Op. 21
No. 1 (1862): 142–3, 153

Variations on a Hungarian Theme,
Op. 21 No. 2 (1862): 86, 142–3, 153,
236

Variations on a Theme by Handel, Op.
24 (1862): 146–7, 149, 150, 152, 336,
383?; four-hand arr.: 350

Variations on a Theme by Paganini, Op.
35 (1866): 197, 205

Waltzes, Op. 39 version for solo piano
(1867): 212

Eight Piano Pieces, Op. 76 (1879): 381, 415 (No. 3)

Two Rhapsodies, Op. 79 (1880): 381, 390, 515

Seven Fantasies, Op. 116 (1892): 510–13, 515

Three Intermezzi, Op. 117 (1892): 515, 539 (No. 1)

Six Piano Pieces, Op. 118 (1893): 515, 526

Four Piano Pieces, Op. 119 (1893): 515, 523 (No. 1), 524, 526

For Piano Four Hands

Variations on a Theme by Schumann, Op. 23 (1863): 153, 161, 170–1

Waltzes, Op. 39 (1866): 209, 212, 223

Hungarian Dances, WoO 1 (Four volumes 1869, 1880): 223, 235;   arr. for Piano Solo (No. 1–10) (1872): 235; arr. by Joachim for Violin and Piano: 391, 395;   arr. for Trio: 493

Liebeslieder Waltzes, Op. 65a (1877): 315; arr. for piano 4-hands: 351, 354?

For Two Pianos

Waltzes, Op. 39 (1897): 212

Sonata in F minor, Op. 34 bis (1871): 180, 182, 184, 258

Variations on a Theme by Haydn, Op. 56 bis (1873): 180, 351

Organ Music

See Works Without Opus [WoO]

Choral Music

Mixed Chorus and Orchestra

Begräbnisgesang, Op. 13 (1860): 117, 121, 136, 139, 141

A German Requiem, Op. 45 (1869): 194, 197, 216–21, 224, 227–9, 232–4, 236, 239, 261, 276, 283–7, 311, 313, 321, 385–6;   arr. for piano: 258

Schicksalslied, Op. 54 (1871): 267, 271, 276, 283, 306

Triumphlied, Op. 55 (1872): 261–2, 266, 267, 269, 270–1, 277–8, 281, 298, 438, 461, 488

Nänie, Op. 82 (1881): 406–8, 410

Gesang der Parzen, Op. 89 (1883): 417

Works with Men's Chorus

Rinaldo, Cantata for tenor, male chorus, and orchestra, Op. 50 (1869): 227, 234–6, 238–9, 244, 297

Alto Rhapsody for alto, male chorus, and orchestra, Op. 53 (1870): 243–4, 250, 266–7, 319

Mixed Voices A Capella

Marienlieder, Op. 22 (1862): 124, 145, 152–3, 170, 180

Two Motets, Op. 29 (1864): 142, 180, 183

Three Songs for six-voice chorus, Op. 42 (1869?): 142?, 180 (referred to as 'other choral songs')

Two Motets, Op. 74 (1878): 382 (*Warum ist das Licht gegeben dem Mühseligen*)

Six Songs and Romances, Op. 93a (1884): 438

Five Songs, Op. 104 (1888): 474

Fest- und Gedenksprüche, Op. 109 (1890): 482–4, 486–9, 490, 502

Three Motets, Op. 110 (1890): 486, 489–90

Women's Chorus with Accompaniment
Ave Maria with organ or orchestra, Op. 12 (1860): 116–17, 124, 136, 180
Psalm 13 with organ or piano, Op. 27 (1864): 116–17, 124, 178, 200

Four Songs with two French Horns and Harp, Op. 17 (1861): 130, 137

Women's Chorus A Capella
Twelve Songs and Romances, Op. 44 (1866): 143, 210
Thirteen Canons for womens' voices, Op. 113 (1891): 141, 499

Vocal Chamber Music

Geistlisches Lied with organ or piano, Op. 30 (1864): 142?, 180
Three Vocal Quartets with piano, Op. 31 (1864): 180, 182–3, 197 (No. 3), 199, 499 (No. 1)
Four Vocal Quartets with piano, Op. 92 (1884): 357 (No. 1)
Ziegeunerlieder, Op. 103 (1889): 474
Six Vocal Quartets with piano, Op. 112 (1891): 499
Liebeslieder Waltzes for vocal quartet with piano four hands, Op. 52 (1869): 242–4, 247–8, 250, 473, 536 (No. 11);   arr. for orchestra: 247

New Liebeslieder Waltzes for vocal quartet with piano four hands, Op. 65 (1875): 315, 317–18, 363
Two Songs for alto with viola and piano, Op. 91 (1884): 164 (No. 2) 'Resonet in Laudibus'

Duets with Piano Accompaniment
Three Duets for soprano and alto, Op. 20 (1862): 131, 142–3, 153, 354?
Four Duets for alto and baritone, Op. 28 (1863): 142?, 178, 197 (No. 1), 354?
Four Duets for soprano and alto, Op. 61 (1874): 354?
Five Duets for soprano and alto, Op. 66 (1875): 354?

Solo Songs with Piano

Six Songs, Op. 3 (1853): 11?, 14, 16–20, 33
Six Songs, Op. 6 (1853): 16, 17, 33?
Six Songs, Op. 7 (1854): 27, 33?, 35
Eight Lieder and Romances, Op. 14 (1860): 136, 139
Five Poems (Songs), Op. 19 (1862): 142–3, 153
Nine Lieder and Songs, Op. 32 (1865): 197 (No. 1, 2)

Magelone Lieder, Op. 33 (1865, 1869): 188, 197, 199, 203, 244, 258 (vol. III–V)
Four Songs, Op. 43 (1868): 102 (No. 4), 203?, 236–7
Four Songs, Op. 46 (1868): 236 (No. 3, 4), 237
Five Lieder, Op. 47 (1868): (No. 5), 'Die Liebende schreibt'), 102, 237

Seven Lieder, Op. 48 (1868): 237

Five Lieder, Op. 49 (1868): (No. 4, Lullaby), 222, 237, 271, 352, 543

Eight Lieder and Songs, Op. 58 (1871): 271 (Nos. 1, 3)

Nine Lieder and Songs, Op. 63 (1874): 301–2 (Nos. 7, 8, 9: 'Heimweh' 1, 2, 3)

Nine Songs, Op. 69 (1877): 338, 350, 353

Four Songs, Op. 70 (1877): 338, 350, 353

Five Songs, Op. 71 (1877): 338, 350, 353

Five Songs, Op. 72 (1877): 338, 350, 353, 528 (No. 1: 'Alte Liebe')

Five Romances and Lieder for one or two voices, Op. 84 (1882): 414–16

Six Lieder, Op. 85 (1882): 414–16

Six Lieder, Op. 86 (1882): 414–16; 453, 528 (No. 2, 'Feldeinsamkeit')

Five Lieder for low voice, Op. 94 (1884): 458 (No. 1)

Four Lieder, Op. 96 (1886): 453

Six Lieder, Op. 97 (1886): 453

Five Lieder for low voice, Op. 105 (1888): 474

Five Lieder, Op. 106 (1888): 474

Five Lieder, Op. 107 (1888): 474

Vier ernste Gesänge, Op. 121 (1896): 550, 551, 555

Other Works without Opus Number

For Orchestra

Three Hungarian Dances, orchestral arr. of Piano Duets No. 1, 3, 10, WoO 1 (1874): 297

For Piano

Two Sarabandes, WoO 5 (1917): possibly 27

51 Übungen für Klavier, WoO 6 (1893): 499, 526

Cadenzas to Mozart Concertos: 504

'Souvenir de la Russie' for Piano Four Hands (before 1852): 21

For Organ

Choral Prelude and Fugue in A minor 'O Traurigkeit', WoO 7 (1882): 76

Fugue for Organ in A flat minor, WoO 8 (1864): 76–7, 182–3

Fugue in A minor for Organ, WoO 9 (1927): 74, 76–7

For Solo Voice or Duet with Accompaniment

Volks-Kinderlieder (Children's Folk–Songs), WoO 31 (1858): 105, 197 (Dornröschen)

49 German Folk-Songs, WoO 33 (1894): 532–7, 539

For Mixed Voices A Capella

Kyrie in G minor, WoO 17 (1984): 76

Missa Canonica in C major, WoO 18 (1984): 76, 89, 133

14 German Folk-Songs for mixed choir, WoO 34 (1864): 178–80

16 German Folk-Songs for 3 and 4 part women's chorus, WoO 37 (1964): 127, 133, 137, 141

20 German Folk-Songs for 3 and 4 part women's chorus, WoO 38 (1968): 127, 133, 137, 141

Works Lost or Destroyed

Brautgesang (Bridal Song): 104–5
Choral arrangements for the men's
    choral society in Winsen-an-der-
    Luhe: 396
Violin Sonata in A minor: 11, 16, 17
Trios, (1852?): 14
Fantasy Trio in D minor for piano,
    violin, and cello (Largo and Allegro)
    (1852?): 11, 14
Trio Movement in E flat (1880): 391

Quartet in F sharp minor: 11
Piano Pieces, *Blätter aus dem Tagebuche
    eines Musikers* (Pages from the Diary
    of a Musician. Minuet, Scherzino, In
    Memory of M. B.): 27
Symphony/Sonata for Two Pianos (pre-
    cursor of Op. 15): 24, 27 (three
    movements), 28, 34, 46 (three move-
    ments)
Quartet in B minor: 11

Arrangements of Other Composers' Works

J. S. Bach, *Christ lag in Todesbanden,*
    BWV 4, continuo realization:
    316
Franz Schubert, Great Mass in E flat
    major D. 950, piano reduction
    (1865): 196
Robert Schumann, Piano Quintet, Op.
    44 for four-hands (1854, lost): 34, 37,
    48, 51
Robert Schumann, Scherzo from the
    Piano Quintet, Op. 44 for Piano
    (1983): 34

J. S. Bach, Presto from the Sonata for
    Solo Violin, BWV 1001, for Piano
    (1878): 338
J. S. Bach, D minor Chaconne from
    the Violin Partita BWV 1004, for
    Piano left hand alone (1878): 345,
    347
Rakoczy March, arr. for piano (unpub-
    lished): 179

Editions of Other Composers

C. P. E. Bach, Violin Sonatas Wq 76 and
    Wa 78 (1864): 114, 179
W. Fr. Bach, Sonata for Two Klaviers,
    Falck No. 10 (1864): 114, 179
Frederick Chopin, work on seven vol-
    umes of the *Complete Critical
    Edition* (1878 ff.): 355–6, 360
François Couperin, Livres I and II of
    Pieces de Clavecin (1871): 263

George Frederick Handel, piano real-
    ization for *Six Duets with Figured
    Bass* (1880, 1881): 400, 410
Franz Schubert, *12 German
    Dances/Ländler* (1864): 171, 197
Robert Schumann, *Complete Edition,*
    347–9;   Supplemental Volume
    (1893): 514–16, 521

Works not Precisely Identified

'Songs' from Opp. 14, 19, 20, 47: 101, 102, 103

'Choral Songs'. Possibly some of WoO 32, 35, Opp. 42, 63: 124

'Frauenchor Songs'. Probably similar to above: 117, 121, 133

'New Canons'. Possibly some of Op. 113, published decades later: 141

'Canons': 196

'New Songs' from Opp. 67–72: 354

Miscellaneous

Counterpoint exchange with Joseph Joachim: 69–72, 76, 81, 89, 91, 132, 144

Select Bibliography

❧

Books

ALLGEYER, JULIUS, *Anselm Feuerbach*, 2nd edn. with an introduction by Carl Neumann, with newly included letters and drawings by the artist, 2 vols. (W. Spemann Verlag: Berlin, 1904).

ANTONICEK, SUSAN, and OTTO BIBA (eds.), *Brahms-Kongress Wien 1983* (Hans Schneider: Tutzing, 1988).

ASOW, ERICH MÜLLER VON, *Johannes Brahms und Mathilde Wesendonck: ein Briefwechsel* (I. Luckmann Verlag: Vienna, 1943).

AVÉ-LALLEMENT, THEODOR, *Rückerinnerungen eines alten Musikanten* (Langhoff: Hamburg, 1878).

Baker's Biographical Dictionary of Musicians, 7th rev. edn. by N. Slonimsky (G. Schirmer: New York, 1984).

BACH, C. P. E., *Essay on the True Art of Playing Keyboard Instruments*, trans. and ed. William J. Mitchell (Norton: New York, 1949).

BALASSA, OTTILIE VON, *Die Brahmsfreundin Ottilie Ebner und ihr Kreis* (Komissionsverlag Franz Bondy: Vienna, 1933).

BECK, WALTER, *Robert Schumann und seine Geister-Variationen* (Hans Schneider: Tutzing, 1992).

BERGER, DOROTHEA, *Jean Paul Friedrich Richter* (Twaine Publishers: New York, 1972).

BERLIOZ, HECTOR, *Correspondance générale*, ed. Pierre Citron, 4 vols. (Flammarion: Paris, 1983).

BIBA, OTTO (ed.), *Mit den Gedanken in Wien*, Five Brahms Letters, facsimile, trans. Eugene Hartzell (Doblinger: Vienna, 1984).

—— *Johannes Brahms in Wien*, Catalogue of the Exhibition of the Archives of the Gesellschaft der Musikfreunde (GdMf: Vienna, 1983).

BLUM, KLAUS, *Hundert Jahre ein deutsches Requiem von Johannes Brahms: Entstehung, Uraufführung, Interpretation, Würdigung* (Hans Schneider: Tutzing, 1971).

Book of the Thousand and One Nights, vol. ii, English trans. from the French by Powys Mathers; 'The Tale of Kaman al-Zamen and the Princess Budur, Moon of Moons' (George Routledge: London, n.d. (post 1945); see also *The Arabian Nights' Entertainments*, trans. Edward William Lane: 'The 'Efreet's Beauty Contest, the Prince Kamar-ez-zemán and the Princess Budoor' (New York, 1927).

BOZARTH, GEORGE, (ed.), *Brahms Studies: Analytical and Historical Perspectives* (OUP: Oxford, 1990).

—— (ed.), with WILFRED MARTIN, *The Brahms–Keller Correspondence* (University of Nebraska Press: Lincoln, Nebr., 1996).

BRAHMS, JOHANNES, *Des jungen Kreislers Schatzkästlein: Aussprüche von Dichtern, Philosophen und Künstlern*, compiled by Johannes Brahms, ed. Carl Krebs (Deutsche Brahms Gesellschaft: Berlin, 1909).

—— *Briefwechsel*, 16 vols. (Deutsche Brahms Gesellschaft: Berlin, 1912–22; repr. Hans Schneider: Tutzing, 1974)
vols. i, ii: *Johannes Brahms im Briefwechsel mit Heinrich und Elizabet von Herzogenberg*, 1st edn., ed. Max Kalbeck (1907); English trans. (in 1 vol.) Hannah Bryant, *The Herzogenberg Correspondence*, repr., with new introduction by Walter Frisch (Da Capo Press: New York, 1987);
vol. iii: *Johannes Brahms im Briefwechsel mit Karl Reinthaler, Max Bruch, Hermann Deiters, Friedrich Heimsoeth, Karl Reinecke, Ernst Rudorff, Bernhard und Luise Scholz*, 2nd rev. edn., ed. Wilhelm Altmann (1912);
vol. iv: *Johannes Brahms im Briefwechsel mit Julius Otto Grimm*, ed. Richard Barth (1912);
vols. v, vi: *Johannes Brahms im Briefwechsel mit Joseph Joachim*, ed. Andreas Moser, 2 vols.; vol. v: 3rd rev. edn. (1921); vol. vi: 2nd rev. edn. (1912);
vol. vii: *Johannes Brahms im Briefwechsel mit Hermann Levi, Friedrich Gernsheim sowie den Familien Hecht und Fellinger*, ed. Leopold Schmidt (1910);
vol. viii: *Johannes Brahms an Joseph Victor Widmann, Ellen und Ferdinand Vetter, Adolf Schubring*, ed. Max Kalbeck (1915);
vols. ix, x: *Johannes Brahms Briefe an P. J. Simrock und Fritz Simrock*, ed. Max Kalbeck (1917);
vols. xi, xii: *Johanne Brahms Briefe an Fritz Simrock*, ed. Max Kalbeck (1919);
vol. xiii: *Johannes Brahms im Briefwechsel mit Th. Wilhelm Engelmann*, ed. Julius Roentgen (1918);
vol. xiv: *Johannes Brahms im Briefwechsel mit Breitkopf & Härtel, Bartholf Senff, J. Rieter-Biedermann, Max Abraham, E. W. Fritzsch und Robert Lienau*, ed. Wilhelm Altmann (1920);
vol. xv: *Johannes Brahms im Briefwechsel mit Franz Wüllner*, ed. Ernst Wolff (1922);
vol. xvi: *Johannes Brahms im Briefwechsel mit Philipp Spitta, Otto Dessoff*, ed. Carl Krebs (1920);
Briefwechsel, New Series, ed. Otto Biba and Kurt and Renate Hofmann (Hans Schneider: Tutzing (1991);
vol. xvii: *Johannes Brahms im Briefwechsel mit Herzog Georg II. von Sachsen-Meiningen und Helene Freifrau von Heldburg*, ed. Herta Müller and Renate Hofmann (1991);
vol. xviii: *Johannes Brahms im Briefwechsel mit Julius Stockhausen*, ed. Renate Hofmann (1993).

—— *Briefwechsel zwischen Johannes Brahms und Max Klinger* (private printing: Leipzig, 1924).

BRODBECK, DAVID (ed.), *Brahms Studies* (University of Nebraska Press: Lincoln, Nebr., 1994). In particular, Brodbeck, 'The Brahms-Joachim Counterpoint Exchange; or Robert, Clara, and the "Best Harmony between Joseph and Johannes" '.

—— *Brahms: Symphony No. 1* (CUP: Cambridge, 1997).

BUCK, F. GEORG, *Handbuch der Hamburgischen Verfassung und Verwaltung* (Holffmann und Campe: Hamburg, 1828).

BÜLOW, HANS VON, *Briefe und Schriften*, ed. Marie von Bülow, 8 vols. (Breitkopf & Härtel: Leipzig, 1895–1908).

CHARLTON, DAVID (ed.), trans. Martyn Clarke. *E. T. A. Hoffmann's Musical Writings: 'Kreisleriana', 'The Poet and the Composer', Music Criticism* (CUP: Cambridge, 1989).

CLAPHAM, JOHN, *Dvořák* (W. W. Norton: New York, 1979).

CORNELIUS, PETER, *Literarische Werke: Erste Gesamtausgabe im Auftrag seiner Familie* (vols. i, ii), ed. Carl Maria Cornelius (Breitkopf & Härtel: Leipzig, 1904–5).

DANEK, VICTOR, 'A Historical Study of the Kneisel Quartet', Doctoral Thesis, Indiana University Mus. Ed. D. 1962 (University Microfilms: Ann Arbor, Mich. 62–5556).

DEITERS, HERMANN, *Johannes Brahms*, rev. edn. (Paul Graf Waldersee: Leipzig, 1898); trans. Rosa Newmarch with additional notes, ed. Fuller-Maitland (T. Fisher Unwin: London, 1888).

DIETRICH, ALBERT, *Erinnerungen an Johannes Brahms in Briefen besonders aus seiner Jugendzeit* (Otto Wigand: Leipzig, 1898).

DIETRICH, ALBERT, and WIDMANN, JOSEF V., *Recollections of Johannes Brahms*, trans. Dora E. Hecht (Seeley & Co.: London, 1899) (see also previous entry).

DOERNBERG, ERWIN, *The Life and Symphonies of Anton Bruckner* (Barrie & Rockcliff: London, 1960; repr. Dover: New York, 1968).

DOLMETSCH, CARL, *'Our Famous Guest': Mark Twain in Vienna* (University of Georgia Press: Athens, Ga., 1992).

DRAHEIM, JOACHIM, et al., (eds.), *Johannes Brahms in Baden-Baden und Karlsruhe* (Badische Landesbibliothek: Karlsruhe, 1983).

DRINKER, SOPHIE, *Brahms and his Women's Choruses* (Private Printing [Musurgia Publishers]: Merion, Pa., 1952).

DÜRIEGL, GUNTER, *Wien auf alten Photographien* (Jugund und Volk Verlag: Vienna, 1981).

DVOŘÁK, ANTONIN, *Correspondence and Documents*, ed. Kuny et al., 3 vols. (Editio Supraphon: Prague 1987–9).

—— *Bibliographical Catalogue*, Dr Blanka Cervinkova et al. (eds.) (Mestska knihovna: Prague, 1991).

EDLER, ARNFRIED, *Robert Schumann und seine Zeit* ([no place]: Laaber-Verlag, 1982).

EVANS, EDWIN, *Historical, Descriptive & Analytical Account of the Entire Works of Johannes Brahms*, vol. i, *The Vocal Works* (Wm. Reeves: London, 1912).

FAHL, ANDREAS, *Das Hamburger Bürgermilitär, 1814–1868*, [Series title: *Lebensformen*] (Reimer: Berlin, 1987).

FAY, AMY, *Music Study in Germany*, (A. C. McClurg: Chicago, 1880; repr., with new introduction by Frances Dillon, Dover Publications: New York, 1965).

FIFIELD, CHRISTOPHER, *Max Bruch: His Life and Works* (Victor Gollancz: London, 1988).

FLOROS, CONSTANTIN, *et al.* (eds.), *Johannes Brahms* (Deutsche Bank: Hamburg, 1981).

FORNER, JOHANNES, *Brahms in Leipzig* (Peters: Leipzig, 1987).

FREUND, ROBERT, *Memoiren eines Pianisten* (Kommissionsverlag Hug & Co.: Zurich, 1951).

FRISCH, WALTER (ed.), *Brahms and his World* (Princeton University Press: Princeton, 1990).

FULLER-MAITLAND, J. A., *Brahms* (Methuen: London, 1911).

GÁDOR, ÁGNES, and EBERT, WOLFGANG, *Johannes Brahms: 22 Briefe nach Ungarn* (Österreichische Johannes Brahms-Gesellschaft: Mürzzuschlag, 1993).

GÁL, HANS (ed.), *Brahms Briefe* (Fischer Taschenbuch Verlag: Frankfurt am Main, 1979).

—— *Johannes Brahms: His Work and Personality*, trans. Joseph Stein (Alfred A. Knopf: New York, 1963).

GAY, PETER, *Freud, Jews and other Germans* (OUP: New York, 1978).

GEIRINGER, KARL, *Brahms: His Life and Work*, 3rd edn. (OUP: New York, 1982); in German, *Johannes Brahms: Sein Leben und Schaffen* [paperback reprint, 2nd edn., Zurich, 1955], (Bärenreiter: Basle, 1974).

GOLDMARK, KARL, *Erinnerungen aus meinem Leben* (Ricola Verlag: Vienna, 1922).

GOTTLIEB-BILLROTH, OTTO (ed.), *Billroth und Brahms in Briefwechsel* (Urban & Schwarzenberg: Berlin, 1935; repr. 1991).

GRASBERGER, FRANZ, *Johannes Brahms: Variationen um sein Wesen* (Paul Kaltschmid: Vienna, 1952).

Groves Dictionary of Music and Musicians, 2nd edn., ed. Fuller-Maitland, 5 vols. (Macmillan: London, 1904; repr. New York, 1911).

GUTMAN, ROBERT W., *Richard Wagner, the Man, his Mind, and his Music* (Harcourt Brace Jovanovich: New York, 1990).

HAAS, FRITJOF, *Zwischen Brahms und Wagner: Der Dirigent Hermann Levi* (Atlantis Musikbuch-Verlag: Zurich, 1995).

HAGEMANN, RUDOLF, *Henry Litolff*, 2nd edn. (R. Hagemann Herne: no place, 1981).

HANCOCK, VIRGINIA, *Brahms's Choral Compositions and his Library of Early Music* (UMI Research Press: Ann Arbor, 1983).

HANSLICK, EDUARD, *Am Ende des Jahrhunderts [1895–1899] (Die Moderne Oper, part 8)*, 2nd edn. (Allgemeiner Verein für deutsche Literatur: Berlin, 1899).

—— *Vienna's Golden Years of Music 1850–1900* (Simon & Schuster: New York, 1950) [enlarged and currently in print as *Hanslick's Music Criticism*, trans. and ed. Henry Pleasants (Dover: New York, 1988)].

HEISSMANN, AUGUST, *Robert Schumann: sein Leben und seine Werke*, 3rd edn. (Verlag J. Guttentag [D. Collin]: Berlin, 1879).

HENSCHEL, SIR GEORGE, *Personal Recollections of Johannes Brahms* (Gorham Press: Boston, 1907).

—— *Musings and Memories of a Musician* (Macmillan: New York, 1919: London, 1918).

HENSCHEL, HELEN, *When Soft Voices Die* (John Westhouse: London, 1944).

HERZIG, ARNO, *Arbeiter in Hamburg: Unterschichten, Arbeiter und Arbeiterbewegung seit dem ausgehenden 18. Jahrhundert* (Hamburg, 1983).

—— (ed.), *Das Alte Hamburg (1500–1848/49): Vergleiche, Beziehungen* (Reimer: Berlin, 1989).

HEUBERGER, RICHARD, *Erinnerungen an Johannes Brahms: Tagebuchnotizen aus den Jahren 1875 bis 1897*, first complete edn. by Kurt Hofmann, 2nd edn. (Hans Schneider: Tutzing, 1976).

HILLER, FERDINAND, *Mendelssohn: Letters and Recollections* (Cologne, 1874), trans. M. E. von Glehn (London, 1874), reissue, introduction by Joel Sachs (Vienna House: New York, 1972).

—— *Aus Ferdinand Hillers Briefwechsel*, ed. Reinhold Sietz, 7 vols. (Arno Volk-Verlag: Cologne, 1958–70).

HINRICHSEN, HANS-JOACHIM, *Hans von Bülow: Die Briefe an Johannes Brahms* (Hans Schneider: Tutzing, 1994).

HOFFMANN, E. T. A., *The Best Tales of Hoffmann*, ed. and trans. with an introduction by E. F. Bleiler (Dover: New York, 1967).

—— *Kreisleriana*, ed. and with an intoduction by Edgar Istel (Philipp Reclam jun: no date, *c*.1910). In English, listed under Charlton, David.

—— *Lebensansichten des Katers Murr* (Insel Taschenbuch: Frankfurt am Main, 1967); *The Life and Opinions of Kater Murr*, trans. Leonard Kent and Elizabeth Knight (University of Chicago Press: Chicago, 1969).

HOFMANN, KURT, *Die Bibliothek von Joh. Brahms: Bücher- und Musikalienverzeichnis* (Karl Dieter Wagner: Hamburg, 1974).

—— *Johannes Brahms in den Erinnerungen von Richard Barth: Barths Wirken in Hamburg* (J. Schuberth: Hamburg, 1979).

—— *Johannes Brahms und Hamburg* (Dialog Verlag: Reinbek, 1986).

—— and RENATE, *Johannes Brahms Zeittafel zu Leben und Werk* (Hans Schneider: Tutzing, 1983).

HOLMES, PAUL, *Brahms, His Life and Times* (Hippocrene Books: Southborough, Kent, 1984).

HÜBBE, WALTER, *Brahms in Hamburg* (Hamburgische Liebhaberbibliothek [Gesellschaft der Hamburger Kunstfreunde]: Hamburg, 1902).

JAMES, BURNETT, *Brahms: A Critical Study* (Praeger: New York, 1972).

JANIK, ALLAN, and STEPHEN TOULMIN, *Wittgenstein's Vienna* (Simon & Schuster [Touchstone]: New York, 1973).

JENNER, GUSTAV, *Brahms als Mensch, Lehrer und Künstler* (N. G. Elwert'sche Verlagsbuchhandlung: Marburg, 1905).

JOACHIM, JOSEPH, *Briefe von und an Joseph Joachim*, ed. Johannes Joachim and Andreas Moser, 3 vols. (Julius Bard: Berlin, 1911–13).

KAHNT, HELMUT, and BERNDT KNORR, *Alte Masse, Münzen und Gewichte* (Bibliographisches Institut: Zurich, 1987).

KALBECK, MAX, *Johannes Brahms*, 4th edn. [unless otherwise indicated in text], 4 vols. (Deutsche Brahms Gesellschaft: Berlin, 1908–21).

KEYS, IVOR, *Johannes Brahms* (Amadeus Press: Portland, Ore., 1989).

KOCH, CARL, *Der Rammelsberg* (Goslar, 1837), repr. [Historischer Harzer Bergbau], with an Afterword by Heinfried Spier (Hagenberg-Verlag: Hornburg, 1987).

KOCH, LUDWIG, *Brahms-Bibliografia* (Stadtbibliothek Budapest: Budapest, 1943).

KOLOMON, D. KERN (ed.), *The Nineteenth-Century Symphony* (Schirmer Books: New York, 1997). Especially the chapter 'Brahms', by David Brodbeck.

KRAUS, ANTJE, *Die Unterschichten Hamburgs in der ersten Hälfte des 19. Jahrhunderts* (Gustav Fischer Verlag: Stuttgart, 1965).

KÜNTZEL, HANS, *Brahms in Göttingen* (Edition Herodot: Göttingen, 1985).

LA GRANGE, HENRI-LOUIS DE, *Gustav Mahler*, vol. 1 (Doubleday: New York, 1973); vol. 2 (OUP: New York, 1995).

LA MARA (IDA LIPSIUS), *Musikerbriefe aus fünf Jahrhunderten* (Breitkopf & Härtel: Leipzig, 1886), 2 vols.

LANGNER, MARTIN-M., *Brahms und seine schleswig-holsteinischen Dichter*, (Westholsteinische Verlagsanstalt Boyens & Co.: Heide in Holstein, 1990).

LAURENTIUS [SAMUEL LA'MERT], *Der Persönliche Schutz: Aerztlicher Rathgeber*, 17th edn. (Hohe Strasse Nr. 26: Leipzig, 1855), trans. from *Self-Preservation, A Medical Treatise*, 20th edn. (9, Bedford Street, Bedford Square: London, 1846).

LEYEN, RUDOLF VON DER, *Johannes Brahms als Mensch und Freund* (Karl Robert Langewiesche: Düsseldorf, 1905).

LICHTENBERG, GEORG CHRISTIAN, *Commentaries to Hogarth's High Life, Marriage à la Mode*, with the complete plates and introductory essay by Arthur S. Wensiger and W. B. Coley (Wesleyan University Press: Middletown, Conn., 1970).

LIENAU, ROBERT, *Unvergesslishe Jahre mit Johannes Brahms* (Musikverlag Robert Lienau: Berlin-Lichterfeld, 1934, repr. 1990).

LITTERSCHEID, RICHARD, *Brahms in seinen Schriften und Briefen* (Bernhard Hahnfeld Verlag: Berlin, 1943).

LITZMANN, BERTHOLT, *Clara Schumann: ein Künstlerleben*, 4th edn., 3 vols. (Breitkopf & Härtel: Leipzig, 1920).

—— *Clara Schumann–Johannes Brahms: Briefe aus den Jahren 1853–1896*, 2 vols. (Breitkopf & Härtel: Leipzig, 1927).

McCORKLE, MARGIT L., *Johannes Brahms: Thematisch-Bibliographisches Werkverzeichnis* (Henle Verlag: Munich, 1984).

MACDONALD, MALCOLM, *Brahms* (Schirmer Books [Macmillan]: New York, 1990).

MAEHL, WILLIAM H., *Germany in Western Civilization* (University of Alabama Press: Tuscaloosa, Ala., 1979).

MARTIN, MICHAEL, *Johannes Brahms: Briefwechsel mit dem Mannheimer Bankprokuristen Wilhelm Lindeck 1872–1882* (Stadtarchiv Mannheim: 1983).

MASON, WILLIAM, *Memories of a Musical Life* (The Century Co.: New York, 1901).

MAY, FLORENCE, *The Life of Brahms*, 2 vols. (William Reeves: London, 1905; 2nd rev. edn. [1948]).

MAYER-PASINSKI, KARIN, *Max Klingers Brahmsphantasie* (R. G. Fischer Verlag: Frankfurt am Main, 1981).

Meisner, Heinrich (ed.), *Klaus Groth und die Musik: Erinnerungen an Johannes Brahms* (Westholsteinische Verlagsanstalt: Heide in Holstein, 1933).

Michelman, Emil, *Agathe von Siebold: Johannes Brahms' Jugendliebe* (Verlag Dr Ludwig Häntzschel: Göttingen, 1930).

—— *Johannes Brahms und die Kritik*, [pamphlet] (Buchdruckerei des Göttinger Tageblattes: 1938).

Moser, Andreas, *Joseph Joachim: ein Lebensbild* (B. Behr's Verlag [E. Bock]: Berlin, 1898).

Moser, Dietz-Rüdiger (ed.), *Clara Schumann: Mein liebes Julchen*, Letters from Clara Schumann to her Granddaughter Julie Schumann with Excerpts from Julie Schumann's Diary and an Account of her Meeting with Johannes Brahms (Nymphenburger: Munich, 1990).

Müller-Blattau, Joseph, *Deutsche Volkslieder, Worte und Weise, Wesen und Werden* (Karl Robert Langewiesche Nachfolger Hans Köster: Königstein im Taunus, 1959).

Musgrave, Michael (ed.), *Brahms 2: Biographical, Documentary and Analytical Studies* (CUP: Cambridge, 1986).

—— *The Music of Brahms* (Clarendon Press: Oxford, 1994).

Niemann, Walter, *Brahms*, trans. Catherine A. Phillips (Alfred A. Knopf: New York, 1946 [1920]).

Neunzig, Hans A., *Johannes Brahms* (Rowohlt: Reinbek bei Hamburg, 1973).

Ophüls, Gustav, *Erinnerungen an Johannes Brahms* (Deutsche Brahms Gesellschaft: Berlin, 1921; reissued Langewiesche-Brandt: Ebenhausen-bei-München, 1983).

Orel, Alfred, *Johannes Brahms & Julius Allgeyer. Eine Künstlerfreundschaft in Briefen* (Hans Schneider: Tutzing, 1964).

Osterreichisches Biographisches Lexikon 1815–1950, vol. ii, ed. Hermann Böhlaus (Graz-Köln: 1959).

Pascall, Robert (ed.), *Brahms: Biographical, Documentary and Analytical Studies* (CUP: Cambridge, 1983).

Pauls, Volquart, *Briefe der Freundschaft: Johannes Brahms–Klaus Groth* (Westholsteinische Verlagsanstalt Boyens & Co.: Heide in Holstein, 1956).

Quigley, Thomas, *Johannes Brahms: An Annotated Bibliography of the Literature through 1982* (Scarecrow Press: Metuchen, NJ, 1990).

Rehberg, Walter and Paula, *Johannes Brahms: sein Leben und Werk*, 2nd edn. (Büchergilde Gutenberg: Frankfurt am Main, 1963).

Reich, Nancy B. *Clara Schumann: the Artist and the Woman* (Victor Gollancz: London, 1985).

Reich, Willi, *Johannes Brahms in Dokumenten zu Leben und Werk* (Manesse Verlag: Zurich, 1975).

Reimann, Heinrich, *Johannes Brahms*, 3rd edn. (Harmonie: Berlin, 1903).

Reiners, Ludwig, *Der ewige Brunnen: ein Hausbuch deutscher Dichtung*, 2nd edn. (Verlag C. H. Beck: Munich, 1988).

Reinicke, Rolf, *Rügen: Innenansichten* (Konrad Reich Verlag: Rostock, 1992).

REISSMANN, AUGUST, *Illustrierte Geschichte der deutschen Musik*, 2nd edn. (Leipzig, 1892).

REIMANN, ARIBERT, and FRANZ HERMANN FRANKEN, M.D., *Robert Schumanns letzte Lebensjahre: Protokoll einer Krankheit* (Archiv Blätter 1, Stiftung Archiv der Akademie der Künste: Berlin, 1995).

RÖHRICH, LUTZ, *Lexikon der sprichwörtlichen Redensarten*, vol. i (Herder: Freiburg, 1973).

RÖPKE, GEORG-WILHELM, *Zwischen Alster und Wandsee* (Otto Heinevetter: Hamburg, 1985).

ROSTAND, CLAUDE, *Johannes Brahms*, preface Brigitte and Jean Massin (Fayard: [Paris], 1978).

SAN-GALLI, THOMAS, *Johannes Brahms*, 5th edn. (R. Piper Verlag: Munich, 1922).

SCHAUFFLER, ROBERT HAVEN, *The Unknown Brahms* (Dodd, Mead & Co.: New York, 1933).

SCHMIDT, LEOPOLD, *Aus dem Musikleben der Gegenwart* (Max Hesses Verlag: Berlin, 1922).

SCHMITT, BRÄUNSCHE and KOCH (eds.), *Juden in Karlsruhe: Veröffentlichung des Karlsruher Statsarchivs*, vol. viii (Badenea Verlag: Karlsruhe, 1988).

SCHNEIDER, HANS, *Johannes Brahms: Leben und Werk: seine Freunde und seine Zeit* [Catalog no. 100 of the Musikantiquarian Hans Schneider] (Schneider: Tutzing, 1964).

SCHORSKY, CARL E., *Fin de Siècle Vienna: Politics and Culture* (Random/Vintage: New York, 1981).

SCHRAMM, WILLI, *Johannes Brahms in Detmold* [Beiträge zur westfälischen Musikgeschichte, vol. 18], [reprint of 1st edn., 1933], newly ed. and annotated by Richard Müller-Dombois (Kommissionsverlag v. d. Linnepe: Hagen, 1983).

SCHUMANN, CLARA, *'Das Band der ewigen Liebe': Clara Schumanns Briefwechsel mit Emilie und Elise List*, ed. Eugen Wendler (Verlag J. B. Hetzler: Stuttgart, 1996).

SCHUMANN, EUGENIE, *Erinnerungen* (J. Engelhorns Nachfolger Adolf Spemann: Stuttgart, 1925); in English, *Memoirs*, trans. Marie Busch (Heinemann: London, 1927) [also appeared as *The Schumanns and Johannes Brahms: The Memoirs of Eugenie Schumann* (Dial Press: New York, 1927)].

SCHUMANN, FERDINAND, *Reminiscences of Clara Schumann as Found in the Diary of her Grandsons Ferdinand Schumann of Dresden*, 2nd edn., ed. June M. Dickinson (Musical Scope: New York, 1973).

SCHUMANN, ROBERT, *Gesammelte Schriften über Musik und Musiker*, 4th edn., ed. F. Gustav Jansen, 2 vols. (Breitkopf & Härtel: Leipzig, 1891).

—— *On Music and Musicians*, trans. Paul Rosenfeld (Pantheon: New York, 1946; paperback, University of California Press: Berkeley and Los Angeles, 1983).

—— and CLARA SCHUMANN, *The Marriage Diaries*, ed. Gerd Nauhaus, trans. Peter Ostwald (Northeastern University Press: Boston, 1993).

SCHWARZ, HERMINE BRÜLL, *Ignaz Brüll und sein Freundeskreis* (Rikola Verlag: Vienna, 1922).

SITTARD, JOSEF, *Geschichte des Musik- und Concertwesens in Hamburg vom 14. Jahrhundert bis auf die Gegenwart* (Leipzig, 1890).

SMYTH, ETHEL, *Impressions that Remained* (Alfred A. Knopf: New York, 1946).

—— *The Memoirs of Ethel Smyth*, ed. R. Creighton (Viking: London, 1987).

SOUREK, OTAKAR, *Antonín Dvořák: Letters and Reminiscences*, trans. Roberta Samsour (Artia: Prague, 1954).

SPECHT, RICHARD, *Johannes Brahms: Leben und Werk eines deutschen Meisters* (Avalon Verlag: Hellerau, 1928); trans. Eric Blom (E. P. Dutton: New York, 1930).

SPENGEL, ANNEMARI, *Johannes Brahms an Julius Spengel, Unveröffentliche Briefe aus den Jahren 1882–1897* [Private printing] (Gesellschaft der Bücherfreunde zu Hamburg: Hamburg, 1959).

SPEYER, EDWARD, *My Life and Friends* (Cobden-Sanderson: London, 1937).

SPIES, MINNA, *Hermine Spies: Ein Gedenkbuch für ihre Freunde von ihrer Schwester*, 3rd edn., with unpublished letters from Brahms and Klaus Groth (G. J. Göschen'sche Verlag: Leipzig, 1905).

SPITTA, PHILIPP, *Zur Musik* (Gebrüder Paetel: Berlin, 1892), esp. the chapter devoted to Brahms.

STARGARDT-WOLFF, EDITH, *Wegbereiter grosser Meister: unter Verwendung von Tagebuchblättern, Briefen und vielen persönlichen Erinnerungen von Hermann und Louise Wolff, den Gründern der ersten Konzertdirektion 1880–1935*, esp. ch. 8, 'Zusammensein mit Johannes Brahms' (Bote & G. Bock: Berlin, 1954).

STEPHENSON, KURT, *Johannes Brahms' Heimatbekenntnis: Lebensbild, Charakterstudie, Briefe* (Hoffmann und Campe Verlag: Hamburg, 1948).

—— *Johannes Brahms und Fritz Simrock: Weg einer Freundschaft* (J. J. Augustin: Hamburg, 1961).

—— *Johannes Brahms und Georg Dietrich Otten* (Brahms-Gesellschaft Hamburg E.V.: 1972), repr. from *Festschrift 1962 Karl Gustav Fellerer* (Bosse Verlag: Regensburg).

—— *Johannes Brahms in seiner Familie* (Dr Ernst Hauswedell & Co.: Hamburg, 1973).

—— *Johannes Brahms und die Familie von Beckerath* (Hans Christians Verlag: Hamburg, 1979).

STRUCK, MICHAEL, *Schumann Violinkonzert d-Moll* (Wilhelm Fink Verlag: Munich, 1988).

SULZER, PETER, *Die fünfte Schweizerreise von Johannes Brahms*, General-Programm 1971/72 (Musikkollegium Winterthur: Winterthur, 1971).

TAYLOR, RONALD, *Hoffmann* (Hillary House Publishers: New York, 1963).

THALMANN, JOACHIM, *Untersuchungen zum Frühwerk von Johannes Brahms* (Bärenreiter [Hochschulschriften]: Kassel, 1989).

Thematisch-Systematisches Verzeichnis der Musikalischen Werke von Johann Sebastian Bach, [Bach-Werke-Verzeichnis], ed. Wolfgang Schmieder (Breitkopf & Härtel: Leipzig, 1950).

TOVEY, DONALD FRANCIS, *Essays in Musical Analysis: Chamber Music* (OUP: London, 1944 [1949]).

UKA, WALTER (ed.), *Rund um die Gängeviertel Hamburg 1889–1930*, photos by Hamann, Wutcke, Höge, Dührkoop [Edition Photothek XIV] (Dirk Nishen Verlag in Kreuzberg: Berlin, 1986).

UNGER, WILLIAM, *Aus meinem Leben* (Gesellschaft für vervielfältigende Kunst: Vienna, 1929).

VILMAR, A. E. C., *Geschichte der deutschen National-Literatur*, 21st edn. (N. G. Elwert'sche Verlagsbuchhandlung: Marburg and Leipzig, 1883).

WAGNER, RICHARD, *Letters of Richard Wagner*, ed. John N. Burk, Burrell Collection (Macmillan: New York, 1950).

WALKER, ALAN, *Franz Liszt*, 2nd vol. (Knopf: New York, 1989).

—— (ed.), *Robert Schumann: The Man and his Music* (Barrie & Jenkins: London, 1972).

WASIELEWSKI, JOSEPH WILHELM VON, *Life of Robert Schumann*, trans. Al. L. Alger (Oliver Ditson Co.: Boston, 1871, repr. Detroit Reprints in Music, Information Coordinators, Inc.: Detroit, 1975).

WENDT, GUSTAV, *Lebenserinnerungen eines Schulmanns* (Grote'sche Verlag: Berlin, 1909).

WIDMANN, JOSEF VIKTOR, *Sizilien und andere Gegenden Italiens* (J. Huber: Frauenfeld, 1898).

—— *Erinnerungen an Johannes Brahms* (Gebrüder Paetel: Berlin, 1898); repr., introduction by Samuel Geiser (Rotapfel-Verlag: Zurich, 1980).

WIECK, MARIE, *Aus dem Kreise Wieck-Schumann* (Zahn & Jaensch: Dresden, 1912; 2nd enlarged edn. 1914).

WIRTH GEB. STOCKHAUSEN, JULIA, *Julius Stockhausen. Der Sänger des deutschen Liedes* (Schlosser & Englert: Frankfurt am Main, 1927).

WOLF, HUGO, *The Music Criticism of Hugo Wolf*, ed. Henry Pleasants (Holmes and Meier: New York, 1979).

ZIMMERMAN, WERNER G., *Brahms in der Schweiz* (Atlantis Musikbuch-Verlag: Zurich, 1983).

ZWEIG, STEFAN, *The World of Yesterday*, introduction by Harry Zohn (University of Nebraska Press: Lincoln, Nebr., 1964).

Unpublished Documents

BARGHEER, KARL, 'Erinnerungen an Johannes Brahms in Detmold 1857–1865', Lippische Landesbibliothek, Detmold.

FREUND, ROBERT, 'Memoirs', unpublished typescript.

WIDMANN, JOSEF VIKTOR, *Household Book*, Dichtermuseum, Liestal.

WITTGENSTEIN, HERMINE, 'Familienerinnerungen', Vienna (June 1944).

Journals and Anthologies

ADLER, GUIDO, 'Johannes Brahms: His Achievement, his Personality, and his Position', *Musical Quarterly*, vol. 19, no. 2 (Apr. 1933), 113–50.

Allgemeine Musik-Zeitung, 32/3, 10/17 (Aug. 1900), 'Ungedruckte Briefe von Johannes Brahms', to Elise Denninghof née Giesmann.

ALTMANN, WILHELM, 'Brahmssche Urteile über Tonsetzer', *Die Musik* [Berlin], 12/1 (Bd. 45) (Oct. 1912), 45–55.

AVINS, STYRA, 'Brahms the Cellist', *Newsletter of the Violoncello Society*, [New York], May and Nov. (1992), 1–4, 5–6.

BIBA, OTTO, 'Neuerwerbungen des Archivs der Gesellschaft der Musikfreunde', *Österreichische Musikzeitschrift*, vol. 36, no. 12 (Dec. 1981), 647–9.

BOZARTH, GEORGE, 'Brahms's Lieder Inventory of 1859–60 and other Documents of his Life and Work', *Fontes Artis Musicae* (1983), 98–117.

BRINKMANN, REINHOLD, 'Die "heitre Sinfonie" und der "schwer melancholische Mensch": Johannes Brahms antwortet Vincenz Lachner', *Archiv für Musikwissenschaft*, vol. 46, no. 4 (1989), 294–303.

Brahms-Studien, starting in 1975, published biennially by the International Brahms Gesellschaft, Hamburg. Particularly useful papers are referred to separately in this bibliography.

BRODBECK, DAVID, 'Brahms's Edition of *Twenty Schubert Ländler*: An Essay in Criticism', in George Bozarth (ed.), *Brahms Studies* (OUP: Oxford, 1990).

—— 'Dance Music as High Art: Schubert's Twelve Ländler, Op. 171 (D. 790)', in Walter Frisch (ed.), *Schubert: Critical and Analytical Studies* (Lincoln, Nebr., 1986), 31–47.

CAILLOT, R. and GÖPEL, E., 'Ein Brahmsfund in Südfrankreich', *Zeitschrift für Musikwissenschaft*, vol. 15, no. 8 (May 1933), 371–3.

CALLOMON, F., 'Some Unpublished Brahms Correspondence', *Musical Quarterly*, vol. 29, no. 1 (Jan. 1943), 32–44.

CLAPHAM, JOHN, 'Dvořák's Relations with Brahms and Hanslick', *Musical Quarterly*, vol. 57, no. 2 (Apr. 1971), 241–54.

CONRAT, HUGO, 'Joh. Brahms (Souvenirs Personnels)', *La Revue Musicale* [Paris], vol. 4 no. ?? (Jan. 1904), 514–20.

Dwight's Journal of Music, Boston (20 Nov. 1852), 51.

—— Frequent articles on the careers of Brahms and Schumann circle in other issues.

EINSTEIN, ALFRED, 'Briefe von Brahms an Ernst Frank', *Zeitschrift für Musikwissenschaft*, vol. 4, no. 7 (Apr. 1922) 385–416.

EHRMANN, ALFRED VON, 'The "Terrible" Brahms', *Musical Quarterly*, vol. 23, no. 1 (Jan. 1937), 64–76.

ELVERS, RUDOLF, 'Die Brahms Autographen in der Musikabteilung der Staatsbibliothek Preuss. Kulturbesitz, Berlin', *Brahms-Studien*, 2 (1977), 79–83.

ENGELMANN, THEODOR W., 'Neue Methode zur Untersuchung der Sauerstoffausscheidung pflanzlicher und thierischer Organismen' (New Methods for Detection of Oxygen Evolution in Plant and Animal Organisms), *Pflügers Archiv für die gesammte Physiologie*, 25 (1881), 285–92.

FEDERHOFER-KÖNIGS, RENATE (ed.), 'Wilhelm Joseph von Wasielewski (1822–1896) im Spiegel seiner Korrespondenz', in *Mainzer Studien zur Musikwissenschaft*, 7 (Hans Schneider: Tutzing, 1975), 163–78.

FELLINGER, IMOGEN, 'Brahms zur Edition Chopinscher Klavierwerke', *Musicae Scientiae Collectanea: Festschrift Karl Gustav Fellerer zum siebzigsten Geburtstag*, ed. H. Hüschen (Arno Volk-Verlag: Cologne, 1973), 110–16.

—— 'Johannes Brahms und Richard Mühlfeld', *Brahms-Studien*, 4 (1981), 77–93.

—— 'Zum Stand der Brahms-Forschung', *Acta Musicologica*, 55 (1983), 131–201.

—— 'Das Brahms-Jahr 1983', *Acta Musicologica*, 56 (1984), 145–210.

FLINDELL, E. FRED, 'Ursprung und Geschichte der Sammlung Wittgenstein im 19. Jahrhundert', *Die Musikforschung*, vol. 20, no. 3 (1969), 298–314.

FLOTZINGER, RUDOLF, 'Brahms als Briefschreiber', *Bruckner Symposion, Johannes Brahms und Anton Bruckner* (Anton Bruckner-Institut Linz 1985), 95–114.

FRISCH, WALTER, 'Brahms and Schubring: Musical Criticism and Politics at Mid-Century', *19th Century Music*, 7 (1983–4), 271–81.

GEIRINGER, KARL, 'Brahms as Reader and Collector', *Musical Quarterly*, vol. 19, no. 2 (Apr. 1933), 156–68.

—— 'Joh. Brahms in Briefwechsel mit Eusebius Mandyczewsky', *Zeitschrift fur Musikwissenschaft*, vol. 15, no. 8 (May 1933), 337–70.

—— 'Der Brahms-Freund C. F. Pohl', *Zeitschrift für Musik*, 4 (Apr. 1935), 397–9.

—— 'Brahms and Wagner with Unpublished Letters', *Musical Quarterly*, vol. 22, no. 2 (Apr. 1936), 178–89.

—— 'Brahms und Dvořák (mit ungedruckten Briefen Anton Dvořáks)', *Der Auftakt*, vol. 17, nos. 7–8 (1937), 100–2.

—— 'Brahms and Henschel: Some hitherto Unpublished Letters', *Musical Times*, vol. 79, no. 1141 (Mar. 1938), 173–7.

—— 'Brahms and Chrysander', [in four parts] *The Monthly Musical Record* 67/8 (June–Sept. 1937, Mar.–Apr. 1938).

—— 'The Brahms Library in the "Gesellschaft der Musikfreunde", Wien', *Notes, Quarterly Journal of the Music Library Association*, vol. 30, no. 1 (Sept. 1973), 7–14.

GROTH, KLAUS, 'Erinnerungen an J. Brahms', *Die Gegenwart*, 1897 [also in *Klaus Groth und die Musik*].

HANCOCK, VIRGINIA, 'Sources of Brahms's Manuscript Copies of Early Music in the Archiv der Gesellschaft der Musikfreunde in Wien', *Fontes Artis Musicae*, 24 (1977) 113 ff.

—— 'Brahms and Early Music: Evidence from his Library and his Choral Compositions', in George Bozarth (ed.), *Brahms Studies* (OUP: Oxford, 1990).

HAUSMANN, FRIEDRICH BERNHARD, 'Brahms und Hausmann', *Brahms-Studien*, 7 (1987), 21–39.

HEUBERGER, RICHARD, 'My Early Acquaintance with Brahms', *Musical World*, 3 (Boston, 1903).

HOFMANN, KURT, 'Brahmsiana der Familie Petersen: Erinnerungen und Briefe', *Brahms-Studien*, 3 (1979), 69–105.

—— 'Ein neu aufgefundener Brief von Johannes Brahms an seine Stiefmutter', *Brahms-Studien*, 4 (1981), 94–6.

HOFMANN, KURT, 'Die Beziehungen zwischen Johannes Brahms und Theodor Kirchner', in Rudolf Elvers and Ernst Vögel (eds.), *Festschrift Hans Schneider: zum 60. Geburtstag* (Verlag Ernst Vögel: Munich, 1981).

—— 'Marginalien zum Wirken des jungen Johannes Brahms', *Oesterreischische Musik-Zeitschrift*, 4–5 (1983), 235–44.

HOFMANN, RENATE, 'Johannes Brahms im Spiegel der Korrespondenz Clara Schumanns', in *Brahms u. seine Zeit, Symposium, Hamburg 1983. Hamburger Jahrbuch für Musikwissenschaft*, vol. 7.

HOLDE, ARTHUR, 'Unpublished Letters by Beethoven, Liszt, Brahms', *Musical Quarterly*, vol. 32, no. 2 (Apr. 1946), 278–88.

HOLDE, ARTHUR, 'Suppressed Passages in the Joachim-Brahms Correspondence Published for the First Time', *Musical Quarterly*, vol. 45, no. 3 (July 1959), 312–24.

KALBECK, MAX, 'Brahms in Wiesbaden' (From the Festbuch des 2. deutschen Brahmsfestes in Wiesbaden im Jahre 1912) *Signale für die musikalische Welt*, 79/22 (June 1921), 568–77.

KAMEN, MARTIN, 'On Creativity of Eye and Ear: A Commentary on the Career of T. W. Engelmann', *Proceedings of the American Philosophical Society*, vol. 130, no. 1 (1986), 232–47.

KOCH, FRIEDERIKE CHRISTIANE, 'Der 15-jährige Brahms gibt sein erstes Konzert', *Mitteilungen der Brahms-Gesellschaft Hamburg e. V.*, 4 (1973), 10.

KNIERBEIN, INGRID, 'Solche Medicin lobe ich mir', *Neue Zeitschrift für Musik*, 147 (Mar. 1986), 4–7.

KORMORN, MARIA, 'Brahms, Choral Conductor', *Musical Quarterly*, vol. 19, no. 2 (Apr. 1933), 151–7.

KROSS, SIEGFRIED, 'Brahmsiana: Der Nachlass der Schwestern Völkers', *Die Musikforschung*, vol. 17, no. 1 (1964), 110–36.

LACH, ROBERT, 'Aus dem Handschriftenschatz der Musikaliensammlung der Wiener Nationalbibliothek', *Festschrift der Nationalbibliothek in Wien* (Vienna, 1926), 553–74.

—— 'Die Musikaliensammlung der Nationalbibliothek', *Der Merkur* [Vienna], 11 (1920), 526–31.

LEDERER, JOSEF-HORST, 'Cornelius und Johannes Brahms', in Hellmut Federhofer and Kurt Oehl (eds.), *Peter Cornelius als Componist, Dichter, Kritiker und Essayist* (Gustav Bosse Verlag: Regensburg, 1977), 57–63.

Lippische Tag Zeitung, 'Johannes Brahms in Detmold', vol. 6, nos. 147–50 (26–9 June 1911).

Lippland Zeitung, 'Johannes Brahms†', no. 80 (5 Apr. 1897).

MAIER, ELISABETH, 'Die Brahms-Autographen der Oesterreichischen National-Bibliothek', *Brahms-Studien*, 3 (1979), 7–34.

McCORKLE, MARGIT L., 'The Role of Trial Performances for Brahms's Orchestral and Large Choral Works: Sources and Circumstances', in George Bozarth (ed.), *Brahms Studies* (OUP: Oxford, 1990).

MEISNER, ROBERT, 'Aus Brahms's Schulzeit', *Brahms-Studien*, 2 (Hamburg, 1977), 85–94.

MEYSENBUG, CARL VON, 'Aus Johannes Brahms' Jugendtagen', *Neues Wiener Tagblatt*, vol. 36, no. 91 (3 Apr. 1902) 1–3, no. 92 (4 Apr. 1902) 1–3.

MEYSENBUG, HERMANN VON, 'Aus Johannes Brahms' Jugendtagen', *Neues Wiener Tagblatt*, vol. 35, no. 126 (9 May 1901).

MILLER, HERTA, 'Brahms's Briefwechsel mit Meiningen', *Beiträge zur Musikwissenschaft*, 2 (1978), 85–131.

MÜNSTER, ROBERT, 'Brahms und Paul Heyse: Eine Künstlerfreundschaft', *Brahms-Studien*, 7 (1987), 51–76.

MUSGRAVE, MICHAEL, ' "Frei aber Froh": A Reconsideration', *19th Century Music*, vol. 3, no. 3 (1980), 251–8.

—— 'Brahms and Kalbeck: A Misunderstood Relationship?', in Susan Antonicek and Otto Biba (eds.), *Brahms-Kongress Wien* 1983 (Schneider Verlag: Tutzing, 1988), 397–404.

Musik, Die [Berlin], 'Brahms Number', vol. 7 (May 1903). Anniversary issue devoted to Brahms; articles by Gustav Jenner, R. Hohenemser, Anton Door, Arthur Egidi, Ludwig Karpath.

Musik, Die [Berlin], 'Brahms Number', vol. 25, no. 8 (May 1933). Anniversary issue; short memoirs by Norbert Dunkel [Dunkl], Richard Wintzer, Frederick Lamond, Paul Vogt, M. Mayer-Mahr, Karl Moser, Otto Roy, Hermann Fink, pp. 607–13.

Neue Zeitschrift fur Musik, 'Brahmsiana', vol. 93, nos. 16 and 17, 21 and 28 April (1897), 181–3, 193–5.

NOTLEY, MARGARET, 'Brahms as Liberal: Genre, Style, and Politics in Late Nineteenth-Century Vienna', *19th Century Music*, vol. 17, no. 2 (1993), 107–23.

PRILLINGER, ELFRIEDA, 'Johannes Brahms und Gmunden', *Brahms-Studien*, 5/6 (1983, 1985).

PULVER, JEFFREY, 'Personal Contacts with Brahms', *Monthly Musical Record* (Feb. 1935), 35–6, (Mar.–Apr. 1935), 57–8.

REMÉNYI, EDUARD, 'Johannes Brahms Dead', *Music* [Chicago], vol. 15, no. 1 (Nov. 1898), 43–6.

RICHTER, KURT, 'Drei unveröffentlichte Briefe Max Klingers an Johannes Brahms aus dem Brahms-Archiv', *Mitteilungen der Brahms-Gesellschaft Hamburg e.V.*, 4 (1973), 3–6.

ROESNER, LINDA CORRELL, 'Brahms's Editions of Schumann', in George Bozarth (ed.), *Brahms Studies* (OUP: Oxford, 1990).

RUDORFF, ERNST, 'Johannes Brahms. Erinnerungen und Betrachtungen', *Schweizerische Musikzeitung/Revue musicale suisse*, vol. 97, no. 3 (Mar. 1957), 81–6, 139–45, 182–7.

SAMS, ERIC, 'Brahms and his Clara Themes', *Musical Times*, 112 (1971), 432–44.

SCHUMANN, FERDINAND, 'Brahms and Clara Schumann', *Musical Quarterly*, 2 (1916), 507–15, trans. of 'Erinnerungen an Brahms', *Neue Zeitschrift für Musik*, 82

(1915), 225–8, 233–6, 241–3; and 'Erinnerungen an Clara Schumann', *NZfürM*, 84 (1917), 69–72, 77–80, 85–8, 93–6, 101–4.

SCHUMANN-REYE, IRMGARD, 'Johannes Brahms im Leben unserer Mutter und Grossmutter: berichtet von Gertrud Reye', *Brahms-Studien*, 8 (1990), 61–70.

SIEVERS, HEINRICH, 'Joseph Joachim', in *Leben und Schicksal: zur Einweihung der Synagoge in Hannover* (Press of the Provincial Capital of Hanover), 79–87.

SIETZ, REINHOLD, 'Johannes Brahms und Theodor Kirchner', *Die Musikforschung*, vol. 13, no. 4 (1960), 396–404.

SISMAN, ELAINE, 'Brahms and the Variation Canon', *19th Century Music*, vol. 14, no. 2 (Fall 1990), 132–53.

STEPHENSON, KURT, 'Die Wohnungen der Familie Brahms 1830 bis 1883', *Mitteilungen der Brahms-Gesellschaft Hamburg e.V.*, no. 3 (1972), 5–7.

STOJOWSKI, SIGISMOND, 'Recollections of Brahms', *Musical Quarterly*, vol. 19, no. 2 (Apr. 1933).

STRUCK, MICHAEL, 'Revisionsbedürftig: Zur gedruckten Korrespondenz von Johannes Brahms und Clara Schumann', *Die Musikforschung*, vol. 41, no. 3 (1988), 235–41.

SUK, JOSEF, 'Aus meiner Jugend', *Der Merkur* [Vienna], vol. 2, no. 4 (1910), 147–50.

SULZER, PETER, '13 neu aufgefundene Postkarten und ein Brief von Johannes Brahms an Jakob Melchior Rieter-Biedermann', *Brahms-Studien*, 6 (1985), 31–59.

WIEPKING, HENNY, 'Wo ging Brahms zur Schule?', *Mitteilungen der Brahms-Gesellschaft Hamburg e.V.*, no. 2 (1971), 9–10.

VOLKMANN, DR HANS, 'Johannes Brahms' Beziehungen zu Robert Volkmann', *Die Musik*, vol. 11, no. 13 (Apr. 1912), 3–13 and appendix.

WADDINGTON, PATRICK, 'Turgenev's Scenario for Brahms', *New Zealand Slavonic Journal* (1982), 1–16.

ZEILEIS, FRIEDERICH G., '2 Manuscript Sources of Brahms's German Requiem', *Music and Letters*, vol. 60, no. 2 (Apr. 1979), 149–55.

ZEMLINSKY, ALEXANDER VON, 'Brahms und die neuere Generation: Persönliche Erinnerungen', *Musikblätter des Anbruchs* (Mar. 1922), 69–70.

Music

BRAHMS, JOHANNES, *Sämtliche Werke; Ausgabe der Gesellschaft der Musikfreunde, Wien*, ed. Eusebius Mandyczewski *et al.*, 26 vols. (Breitkopf & Härtel: Leipzig, 1926–8, 17 vols. repr. Dover Press: New York, 1968–91).

—— *String Quartets arr. Piano Four Hands*, pub. anon. (Simrock: Berlin, 1874 and 1877), repub. as *The Brahms Arrangements for Piano Four Hands of His String Quartets*, Introduction and Note by Ellwood Derr (Dover: New York, 1985).

—— *Alto Rhapsody: A Facsimile Edition [. . .] with an introduction by Walter Frisch* (New York Public Library: New York, 1983).

Brahms und seine Freunde, ed. Joachim Draheim, (edn. Breitkopf 8303: Wiesbaden, 1983), piano music of Brahms, Bruch, Dessoff, Dietrich, Grädener, J. O. Grimm, the Herzogenbergs, Joachim, Kirchner, and Rudorff.

BUXTEHUDE, DIETRICH, *Orgelwerke: Freie Kompositionen Part I* (Breitkopf & Härtel: Wiesbaden, 1903–4), ed. Philipp Spitta, rev. Max Seiffert with introduction by Walter Kraft.

Recordings

Pupils of Clara Schumann, Gemm CDS 9904–9 (Pearl Records), Recordings of Ilona Eibenschütz.

Illustration Acknowledgements

❧

The Plates are reproduced by kind permission of the following:

PLATE 1: by courtesy of the Trustees of Kneisel Hall, Blue Hill, Maine.

PLATES 2, 4, 5, 6, 7, 17, 18: by courtesy of the Brahms-Institut Lübeck, Sig: Hofmann.

PLATE 3: by courtesy of the Mary Flagler Cary Collection in the Pierpont Morgan Library, New York, MFC B8135. C836.

PLATES 8, 19, 21, 23, 27, 29, 36: by courtesy of the Brahms-Haus Museum, Baden-Baden.

PLATE 9: by courtesy of the Robert Schumann-Haus, Zwickau.

PLATES 10, 11, 13: by courtesy of the Schumannhaus, Bonn.

PLATE 12: by courtesy of the Bodleian Library, Oxford, MS M.D.M.c.1, fos. 27r–27v, 28r.

PLATES 15, 16: by courtesy of the Lippische Landesbibliothek, Album Düstersieh, Alt Detmold Nr. 29 HSA6 (16); 1D45 (15).

PLATES 20, 30, 33, 34, 49, 45: by courtesy of the Bildarchiv der Österreichischen Nationalbibliothek, 79.417 (20); NB 533.956 (30); 422.371 BRF (33); NB 533.955 (34); NB 532.233 (39); K0330 (45).

PLATES 24, 28, 31, 35, 38, 40–3, 46: by courtesy of Marie Kuhn-Oser.

PLATES 25, 32, 50: private collection.

PLATE 26: by courtesy of the Historisches Museum der Stadt Wien.

PLATES 37, 46–8: by courtesy of the Dichtermuseum Liestal.

PLATE 44: by courtesy of the J. Paul Getty Museum, Malibu, California.

Index

✧

Correspondents appear in Appendix B, listed by letter number. Works by Brahms mentioned in letters are listed in Appendix E.

The general index lists subjects, places, and music other than by Johannes Brahms (JB), also music by JB discussed in the commentary, but not in adjoining letters. Years appear in **bold face** and a page number in brackets indicates an implied reference.